MARK TWAIN

Mark Twain

COLLECTED TALES, SKETCHES, SPEECHES, & ESSAYS 1852–1890

THE LIBRARY OF AMERICA

Volume compilation, notes, and chronology copyright © 1992 by
Literary Classics of the United States, Inc., New York, N.Y.
All rights reserved.
No part of this book may be reproduced commercially
by offset-lithographic or equivalent copying devices without
the permission of the publisher.

Copyright 1967, 1972, 1973, 1976, 1979, 1981
by The Mark Twain Foundation.
Published by arrangement with the University of California Press
and Robert H. Hirst, General Editor of the Mark Twain Project.
See Acknowledgments in the Note on the Texts.

"Taming the Bicycle" from *What Is Man? and Other Essays* by
Mark Twain, Copyright 1917 by the Mark Twain Company; copyright renewed 1945 by Clara Clemens Samassoud. Reprinted by
permission of HarperCollins Publishers Inc. "A Cat-Tale" from
Letters from the Earth by Mark Twain, edited by Bernard DeVoto.
Copyright 1946, 1959 and 1962 by the Mark Twain Company;
copyright renewed by the Mark Twain Company. Printed by permission of HarperCollins Publishers Inc.

The paper used in this publication meets the
minimum requirements of the American National Standard for
Information Sciences—Permanence of Paper for Printed
Library Materials, ANSI Z39.48—1984.

Distributed to the trade in the United States
by Penguin Putnam Inc.
and in Canada by Penguin Books Canada Ltd.

Library of Congress Catalog Number: 92–52657
For cataloging information, see end of Index.
ISBN 0–940450–36–4

Third Printing
The Library of America—60

Manufactured in the United States of America

LOUIS J. BUDD
SELECTED THE CONTENTS AND WROTE
THE NOTES FOR THIS VOLUME

The publishers express their appreciation to Robert H. Hirst and the Mark Twain Project for editorial assistance and the use of Mark Twain materials.

Contents

The Dandy Frightening the Squatter

About thirteen years ago, when the now flourishing young city of Hannibal, on the Mississippi River, was but a "wood-yard," surrounded by a few huts, belonging to some hardy *"squatters,"* and such a thing as a steamboat was considered quite a sight, the following incident occurred:

A tall, brawny woodsman stood leaning against a tree which stood upon the bank of the river, gazing at some approaching object, which our readers would easily have discovered to be a steamboat.

About half an hour elapsed, and the boat was moored, and the hands busily engaged in taking on wood.

Now among the many passengers on this boat, both male and female, was a spruce young dandy, with a killing moustache, &c., who seemed bent on making an impression upon the hearts of the young ladies on board, and to do this, he thought he must perform some heroic deed. Observing our squatter friend, he imagined this to be a fine opportunity to bring himself into notice; so, stepping into the cabin, he said:

"Ladies, if you wish to enjoy a good laugh, step out on the guards. I intend to frighten that gentleman into fits who stands on the bank."

The ladies complied with the request, and our dandy drew from his bosom a formidable looking bowie-knife, and thrust it into his belt; then, taking a large horse-pistol in each hand, he seemed satisfied that all was right. Thus equipped, he strode on shore, with an air which seemed to say—"The hopes of a nation depend on me." Marching up to the woodsman, he exclaimed:

"Found you at last, have I? You are the very man I've been looking for these three weeks! Say your prayers!" he continued, presenting his pistols, "you'll make a capital barn door, and I shall drill the key-hole myself!"

The squatter calmly surveyed him a moment, and then, drawing back a step, he planted his huge fist directly between the eyes of his astonished antagonist, who, in a moment, was floundering in the turbid waters of the Mississippi.

Every passenger on the boat had by this time collected on

the guards, and the shout that now went up from the crowd speedily restored the crest-fallen hero to his senses, and, as he was sneaking off towards the boat, was thus accosted by his conqueror:

"I say, yeou, next time yeou come around drillin' key-holes, don't forget yer old acquaintances!"

The ladies unanimously voted the knife and pistols to the victor.

May 1, 1852

Historical Exhibition—
A No. 1 Ruse

A young friend gives me the following yarn as fact, and if it should turn out to be a double joke, (that is, that he imagined the story to fool me with,) on his own head be the blame:

It seems that the news had been pretty extensively circulated, that Mr. Curts, of the enterprising firm of Curts & Lockwood, was exhibiting at their store, for the benefit of the natives, a show of some kind, bearing the attractive title of "Bonaparte crossing the Rhine," upon which he was to deliver a lecture, explaining its points, and giving the history of the piece, the price being "one dime per head, children half price." Well, the other day about dusk, a young man went in, paid his dime, "saw the elephant," and departed, apparently "with a flea in his ear," but the uninitiated could get nothing out of him on the subject; he was mum—had seen the varmint, and that was the full extent of the information which could be pumped out of him by his enquiring friends.

Well, everybody who saw the sight seemed seized with a sudden fit of melancholy immediately afterwards, and dimes began to grow scarce. But pretty soon Jim C——, with a crowd of eager boys at his heels, was seen coming down the street like half a dozen telegraphs. They arrived at the store, gasping and out of breath, and Jim broke out with:

"Mr. Curts—want—to see—that—show! What's—price!"

"Oh, we let boys see it at half price—hand out your five cents."

Jim had got done blowing by this time, and threw down his money in as great a hurry as if life and death depended upon the speed of his movements, saying:

"Quick! Mr. Curts, I want to see it the worst kind."

"Yes, Oh yes; you want to see 'Bonaparte crossing the Rhine,' do you," said Abram, very deliberately.

"Yes, that's it—that's what I want to see," said Jim, who was so anxious to see the show that he could scarcely stand still.

"Well, you shall see it," said the worthy exhibitor, with a

wise look, at the same time dropping the five cents into the money drawer, "and I hope by this show to impress upon your young minds, this valuable piece of history, and illustrate the same in so plain a manner that the silliest lad amongst you will readily comprehend it."

The juvenile audience was now breathless with expectation, and crowded around with eager looks, and not the slightest movement on the part of the learned lecturer was overlooked by them, as he drew from a drawer a piece of bone about three inches long, and holding it up before the wondering boys, he slowly and deliberately commenced his lecture, or explanation:

"My young friends, you now perceive——"

"Yes sir," interrupted Jim with mouth, eyes and ears wide open.

"As I was saying," continued Mr. Curts, "you now see before you the 'Bonaparte'—the *'Bony-part,'* you understand, the *'bony part'* of a hog's leg (house shakes with laughter from the crowd which had now assembled, but Jim did not join in the general merriment, but looked very sober, seeming to think there was very little about it to laugh at, at least on his side) yes, boys," said Abram, as grave and solemn as a judge about to pass sentence, "this is the bony-part of a hog's leg."

"Is-is a-a-that all!" gasped poor Jim, beginning to look blue about the gills.

"Oh no," said the lecturer, "this is merely a part of the exhibition," and he took from a shelf a piece of meat skin about as large as a piece of paper i. e. the size of a dollar bill, and presenting it to view he proceeded with the lecture.

"Now, my young hearers, this you see is the 'Rhine'—yes," he continued, as solemnly as before, "this is the 'Rhine,'—properly speaking, the hog's rind—a piece of hog's rind."

When the laugh had subsided, Mr. C. again went on with the explanation:

"Now, young gentlemen, draw near and give me your attention a moment, for this is the most interesting part of the exhibition," and old Abram looked and spoke, if possible, still more wise and solemn than before; then slowly passing the piece of bone back and forth across the skin, he said, "you see, boys this is the 'bony part crossing the rind,' very lucidly explained—yes, (drawing his bone across again with the most imperturbable gravity imaginable, amid the roars of laughter) this sir, is, I may be allowed to say, a *very* apt illustration of that noted event in history, 'Napoleon crossing the Rhine.' You have now learned a valuable lesson——"

"Yes!" broke in Jim "I have that, but it's the last one you'll ever learn me—(laughter) you're nothing but an old swindler, anyhow—(renewed laughter, which somewhat riled our hero) yes, this is a swindling shop and a swindling show, and you don't do nothing but swindle people."

The laugh now became so universal, that poor Jim had to force a laugh and a "don't care" look, as he continued:

"I don't care, laugh, jest as much as you please—I ain't particular about the money, nohow; I know'd it was a swindle, 'fore I come down (a piece of knowledge which Jim, in the excitement had before unfortunately forgotten that he ever possessed,) yes I knowed it, and I jest come down for devilment—but I don't care, you can keep the money, I ain't particular about it (Jim seemed particularly anxious to impress this important fact upon the mind of the lecturer)—cause I know you need it worse'n I do, when you can swindle a feller out of it that way."

The crowd now laughed till they were completely exhausted, and Jim's face slowly relaxed from the ludicrous expression it had worn for a time. He now looked as if he had been suddenly bereft of every relation he had in the world—his face became lengthened to an alarming extent, and upon the said countenance the most woe-begone look settled, mingled with a most "sheep-stealing" expression; he was now in a profound reverie, seemingly entirely unconscious of the jeers cast at him by the company. But Abram now broke in upon his meditations, and although he too had been enjoying his joke with a hearty laugh, he immediately assumed his former solemn look and grave tone, and thus addressed the cheap-looking "seeker after knowledge under difficulties."

"Young man, you have now learned an important historical lesson, and are no doubt well pleased with it. I am anxious, however—ahem!—I am anxious, as I before remarked, that you should be entirely satisfied with the exhibition—if you did not understand it in its minutest details—if the illustration was not sufficiently lucid, and everything has not been exhibited to your entire satisfaction, I beg of you, my friend, to make it known; and if it has met with favor in your eyes, I shall hold myself under the greatest of obligations, (with a profound bow,) if you will use your influence in forwarding the cause of learning and knowledge, (another bow,) by inviting your friends to step in when they pass this way. What, may I ask, is your opinion of the exhibition?"

Poor Jim! He seemed not to have heard a word that had been spoken; but, with his eyes bent steadfastly upon some object that wasn't there, he moved not a muscle for the space of a minute, when, opening his lips, he slowly ejaculated the few, but significant words "Sold!—cheap---as---dirt!"

And striding out of the house he marched down the street in a profound fit of mental abstraction.

Since the above occurrence, if any one speaks to Jim, or asks him a question, he merely mutters "Bonaparte crossing—sold!"

Mr. Curts told one of Jim's companions to say to him, that his exhibition was merely an agency—that a noted wholesale firm of this city were the proprietors of the concern, that the apparatus belonged to them, that if Jim did not think his money well spent, they would in all probability refund it—but that being himself merely an agent, he did not feel authorized to do so.

W. Epaminondas Adrastus Blab.

September 16, 1852

Editorial Agility

On Thursday evening last, a Panorama was exhibited at Benton Hall, and a youngster gives me the following account of a circumstance which then and there happened:

The exhibition was about half through, when a curtain, hanging at the side of the painting, took fire and blazed up till it was about the size of a man's hat. Now it is well known that the editor of the ———— is a very quiet, well-behaved little fellow, and sits still, like a good boy, as he is, unless some unlooked for accident occurs, or Pierce and King are mentioned. Under these circumstances he may be excused if he depart from his wonted Quakerish habits, and do things unbecoming a sober Democratic Editor. The said Editor, seeing the aforementioned little blaze, gazed at it in speechless and motionless horror—no doubt thinking of the close proximity of his type, press, &c., which, you know, are just across the street from the Hall. There he sat, looking for all the world like his dying day had arrived—and he has ample reasons for wishing that day will be overlooked and left out of Nature's Almanac—I say "thar he sot," pale as a sheet, shaking like double rectified ague; his eyes standing out from his head; his "nail-grabs" grasping a pew like grim death. He couldn't take his eyes off the "pictur," or rather, the miniature conflagration,—he never moved a peg, and the people began to think the poor fellow had unfortunately sat down on some shoemaker's wax, or some other equally sticky substance—or perhaps his pants had got fastened in a crack in the pew.

However, people were mistaken in their surmises—fact was, he was "skeered"—at least, if wax, or any other such truck had got beneath him, woe unto all such wafers, for he, in the extremity of his terror regained his energies—he gave a bound, and actually jumped—I swear I'll tell it, whether it's believed or not—he jumped *clean over nine pews*, and I have not the least doubt in the world, sir that he'd have jumped *nine more*, had he not unluckily tripped on the back of a chair, which deposited this diminutive chunk of human meat about ten feet further on, and landed him in the middle of the room. My informant says he was narrowly watching this soft-

soaper of Democratic rascality when he started on his ærial
journey—saw him pile himself up in the middle of the floor,
and that from his fallen position in society he most suddenly
and miraculously disappeared.—Now, after that—after that
jump I'm willing to believe anything—yes sir, I'll bet five
cents, in specie, that he jumped out of the third story window!—not the least doubt of it—if he were to tell me that
he did do it, and that he fell so hard as to stove his legs
through him—that he found himself turned inside out, and
standing on his head on the pavement below—I'd believe
him!

It is well for our neighbor, the learned expounder of *Pierc-
ing* principles, that he didn't flourish in the days of Salem
Witchcraft. The little devil would have been shot the very
next day after this exploit, with a silver bullet; thereby leaving
people unacquainted with him to draw the inference that he
was worth the powder it would take to blow him up; but,
worth it or not, *I* blow him up gratis!

They say the 'Father of his Country' was hard to beat at
leaping, he having jumped twenty-two feet, one inch, on level
ground; but, by a minute calculation, I find that had it not
been for that infernal chair, this *father of* NOTHING would
have jumped precisely *twenty-seven feet, four inches and five-
eighths of an inch!*—and that, too, over the pews!

W. E. A. B.

September 16, 1852

Blabbing Government Secrets!

The people generally seem to think that the present extra session of the State Legislature was convened for the purpose of transacting this Railroad business, and I hasten from a sense of duty to my fellow-citizens, to correct this wrong impression; their ignorance on this subject shows that they have paid very little attention to the proceedings of the Legislature.—Now this is just the way of it: I didn't like my surname; as for the handles to it, they did very well; *I* wouldn't care if I had twenty more like 'em; but the surname didn't suit; and although the Legislature is not, I believe, accustomed to change people's surnames, I nevertheless wrote to Gov. King, who is a particular friend of mine, requesting him to call the session and make the wished-for alteration, and leaving the selection of the new name to his own refined taste and judgment. Well, the request was granted; the Legislature was convened; my title was altered, shortened, and greatly beautified—and all at a cost of *only a few thousands of dollars to the State!*—these Democratic Legislators work cheap, don't they, Editor?

This new cognomen suits me, and I hope it will meet with favor in the eyes of the inhabitants of this great Union; and if Congress takes the matter up and changes it back the way it was, the villainous President that signs the documents and makes it a law will never get my support—No, sir! not if he's NEVER elected again! As for Queen Victoria and Lord Derby, they may cut up as much as they like—it's none of their business.

Blab—Blab—sounds pretty—makes good jingle—it's just the thing—the Blab's were ancestors of mine, anyhow. The first Blab lived in Adam's time, and had a little falling out with that distinguished gentleman about a tin cup, which both claimed—yes, a *tin cup!*—you needn't giggle either; if you knew as much about the Bible as I do, you'd find that tin cups were tolerably scarce in those days. Well, as I was going to say, they quarreled about the cup; public opinion was in favor of Adam, and Adam got the cup; and ever since that time people haven't thought well of the Blabs; that was right

9

though—they were always a rascally set, and I believe Blab stole the cup; but Adam was no more respectable than Blab—he never had a mother! at least people said so, and folks of that character don't stand very high nowadays. However, if it hadn't been for that little difficulty, a Blab would have been President instead of John Quincy Adams! Despite all these things, the Blabs have been somewhat distinguished, anyhow; honorable mention was made of one of them in a book that was never published, and another one was hung last week for his rascality, and I'm glad of it; for he was a Democrat, and ought to have been hung long ago. I go in for hanging all the Whigs and Democrats, and then the only Blab that ever went unhung would stand a chance—a slim one, too, I reckon, for then that great military hero you mentioned some time since—I believe you call him Ensign Jehiel Stebbings—would step in. It's no go.

W. E. A. B.

September 16, 1852

River Intelligence

Our friend Sergeant Fathom, one of the oldest cub pilots on the river, and now on the Railroad Line steamer Trombone, sends us a rather bad account concerning the state of the river. Sergeant Fathom is a "cub" of much experience, and although we are loth to coincide in his view of the matter, we give his note a place in our columns, only hoping that his prophesy will not be verified in this instance. While introducing the Sergeant, "we consider it but simple justice (we quote from a friend of his) to remark that he is distinguished for being, in pilot phrase, 'close,' as well as superhumanly 'safe.' " It is a well-known fact that he has made fourteen hundred and fifty trips in the New Orleans and St. Louis trade without causing serious damage to a steamboat. This astonishing success is attributed to the fact that he seldom runs his boat after early candle light. It is related of the Sergeant that upon one occasion he actually ran the chute of Glasscock's Island, down stream, *in the night*, and at a time, too, when the river was scarcely more than bank full. His method of accomplishing this feat proves what we have just said of his "safeness"—he sounded the chute first, and then built a fire on the head of the island to run by. As to the Sergeant's "closeness," we have heard it whispered that he once went up to the right of the "Old Hen," but this is probably a pardonable little exaggeration, prompted by the love and admiration in which he is held by various ancient dames of his acquaintance, (for albeit the Sergeant *may* have already numbered the allotted years of man, still his form is erect, his step is firm, his hair retains its sable hue, and more than all, he hath a winning way about him, an air of docility and sweetness, if you will, and a smoothness of speech, together with an exhaustless fund of funny sayings; and lastly, an ever-flowing stream, without beginning, or middle, or end, of astonishing reminiscences of the ancient Mississippi, which, taken together, form a *tout ensemble* which is a sufficient excuse for the tender epithet which is, by common consent, applied to him by all those ancient dames aforesaid of "che-*arm*ing creature!") As the Sergeant has been longer on the river, and is better acquainted with it than any other "cub" extant, his remarks are entitled to extraordinary consideration, and are always read with the deepest interest by high and low, rich and poor, from "Kiho" to Kamschatka, for be it known that his fame extends to the uttermost parts of the earth:

R. R. STEAMER TROMBONE,
VICKSBURG, May 8, 1859.

The river from New Orleans up to Natchez is higher than it has been since the niggers were executed, (which was in the fall of 1813) and my opinion is, that if the rise continues at this rate *the water will be on the roof of the St. Charles Hotel* before the middle of January. The point at Cairo, which has not even been moistened by the river since 1813, is now entirely under water.

However, Mr. Editor, the inhabitants of the Mississippi Valley should not act precipitately and sell their plantations at a sacrifice on account of this prophesy of mine, for I shall proceed to convince them of a great fact in regard to this matter, viz: That the tendency of the Mississippi is to rise less and less higher every year (with an occasional variation of the rule), that such has been the case for many centuries, and finally that it will cease to rise at all. Therefore, I would suggest to the planters, as we say in an innocent little parlor game, commonly called "draw," that if they can only "stand the raise" this time, they may enjoy the comfortable assurance that the old river's banks will never hold a "full" again during their natural lives.

In the summer of 1763 I came down the river on the old *first* "Jubilee." She was new, then, however; a singular sort of a single-engine boat, with a Chinese captain and a Choctaw crew, forecastle on her stern, wheels in the center, and the jackstaff "no where," for I steered her with a window shutter, and when we wanted to land we sent a line ashore and "rounded her to" with a yoke of oxen.

Well, sir, we wooded off the top of the big bluff above Selma—the only dry land visible—and waited there three weeks, swapping knives and playing "seven up" with the Indians, waiting for the river to fall. Finally, it fell about a hundred feet, and we went on. One day we rounded to, and I got in a horse-trough, which my partner borrowed from the Indians up there at Selma while they were at prayers, and went down to sound around No. 8, and while I was gone my partner got aground on the hills at Hickman. After three days labor we finally succeeded in sparring her off with a capstan bar, and went on to Memphis. By the time we got there the river had subsided to such an extent that we were able to land where the Gayoso House now stands. We finished loading at Memphis, and engaged part of the stone for the present St. Louis Court-House, (which was then in process of erection) to be taken up on our return trip.

You can form some conception by these memoranda of how high the water was in 1763. In 1775 it did not rise so high by thirty feet; in 1790 it missed the original mark at least sixty-five feet; in 1797, one hundred and fifty feet; and in 1806, nearly two hundred and fifty feet. These were "high-water" years. The "high waters" since then have been so insignificant that I have scarcely taken the trouble to notice them. Thus, you will perceive that the planters need not feel uneasy. The river may make an occasional spasmodic effort at a flood, but the time is approaching when it will cease to rise altogether.

In conclusion, sir, I will condescend to *hint* at the foundation of these arguments: When me and DeSoto discovered the Mississippi, I could stand at Bolivar Landing (several miles above "Roaring Waters Bar") and pitch a biscuit to the main shore on the other side, and in low water we waded across at Donaldsonville. The gradual *widening* and *deepening* of the river is the whole secret of the matter.

Yours, etc.,
SERGEANT FATHOM.

May 17, 1859

Ghost Life on the Mississippi

The recent death of an old Saint Louis and New Orleans pilot has brought the following strange story to light. I shall not attempt, by any word of my own, to secure the reader's belief in it, but I will merely relate the simple facts in the case, as they fell from the lips of a dying man, and leave him to form his own opinion. Fictitious names, however, will be used throughout the narrative, in accordance with the wishes of certain actors in the mysterious drama who are still living.

Joseph Millard, the pilot referred to, was a master of his profession, a good man, and a truthful man; and this tale, coming from his lips, while in a perfectly sound state of mind, and stretched upon his death-bed, leaves but a small field for the cavilings of the incredulous. Until that hour the whole thing had been kept a profound secret by himself and the other witnesses of the horrible affair. And now for the facts.

A number of years ago, a Saint Louis and New Orleans packet, which I will call the "Boreas," was on her way up the river, and at about ten o'clock at night, the sky, which had before been clear, suddenly became overcast, and snow commenced falling soon afterwards. The boat was near the head of Dog Tooth Bend at the time. The Captain stepped out of the "Texas," and said to the pilot on watch:

"Well, I reckon Goose Island wouldn't be a very safe place for the Boreas to-night, Mr. Jones. So, if it keeps on snowing at this rate, I reckon you had better bring her to at the first wood-pile you come across near the head of Dog Tooth or Buffalo Island."

The little narrow bend around Goose Island is called the "Grave-Yard," because of the numerous wrecks of steamboats that have found a tomb in it. Besides these obstructions, a great many large snags stood directly in the way at the time I speak of, and the narrow channel being very "shoal" also, the best of piloting was necessary in order to "run" Goose Island in safety, even in daylight.

Mr. Jones passed the wood-yards in silence, and held his way up the river through the driving rain; for that very day he had declared that Goose Island "had no terrors for *him*, on any kind of night," and had been laughed at by several other pilots, who jestingly called him the "King of Pilots." He was still angry and sullen, and occasionally, as he thought of the jest, he would grate his teeth and mutter that "he would show them that he *was* the king of pilots in reality."

At about half past eleven the other pilot came up, having been called too soon, through a mistake on the part of the watchman, and noticing that the boat was approaching the foot of Goose Island, he said:

"Why, Jones, surely you are not going to run this place on such a night as this?"

"I'll take her through, if the Devil seizes me for it in five minutes afterwards!"

And through those hidden dangers,—and shrouded in that Egyptian darkness—the steamer plowed her way, watched by an unerring eye and guided by a master hand, whose nerves trembled not for a single instant! And snags and wrecks remained untouched.

"*Now*, who is king of pilots!"

And those were the last words of William Jones, pilot.

Then he gave up the wheel and left the pilot house, and when the four o'clock watch was called, he could not be found. There was blood upon the "nosing" of the starboard guard, and a fireman said, the next day, that a man fell from the boiler deck in the night, and he thought his head struck that place, but that the watchman only laughed at him when he mentioned it, and said he had a fertile imagination.

When the Boreas arrived at Saint Louis she was sold, and lay idle the balance of the summer, and fall, and finally left for New Orleans in the dead of winter, with an entirely new set of officers—Joe Millard and Ben. Reubens, pilots.

One cold, raw night, as the boat was approaching Goose Island, snow commenced falling, and it soon became almost too dark to run. This reminded Joe of the almost forgotten Jones; and he determined to try and get the boat up into the little bend as far as the "Shingle Pile," and lay up till morning, as he preferred having the balance of Goose Island in daylight.

He had just gained the foot of the bend when the snow commenced falling so densely that he could see nothing at all—not even the trees on the shore at his side. He stopped the engines, of course.

At that moment he felt conscious that he was not alone—that some one was in the pilot house with him—although he had bolted the door on the inside, to keep it from blowing open, and that was the only mode of ingress! Yes, he was sure he could distinguish the dim outline of a human figure standing on the opposite side of the wheel. A moment after, he heard the bell lines pulled—heard the handles strike the frame as they fell back to their places, and then the faint tinkle of the answering bells came up from below. In an instant the wheel was jerked out of his hands, and a sudden gleam of light from a crack in the stove pipe revealed the ghastly features of William Jones, with a great piece of skin, ragged and bloody, torn loose from his forehead and dangling and flapping over his left eye—the other eye dead and fixed and lustreless—hair wet and disordered, and the whole body bent and shapeless, like that of a drowned man, and apparently rigid as marble, except the hands and arms, which seemed alone endued with life and motion!

Joseph Millard's blood curdled in his veins, and he trembled in every limb at the horrid vision. And yet he was a brave man, and held no superstitious notions. He would have left the accursed place, but he seemed bound with bands of iron. He tried to call for help, but his tongue refused its office; he caught the sound of the watchman's heavy tramp on the hurricane deck—would *no* signal draw his attention?—but the trial was vain—he could neither move nor speak,—and aid and comfort almost in a whisper's reach of him. Then the footsteps died away and the desperate man was left alone with his fearful company.

Riveted to the spot he listened to the clashing engines and the moaning of the frosty wind, while that ghostly pilot steered the vessel through darkness such as no human eye could penetrate. Millard expected every moment to hear the timbers crashing against wreck or snag, but he was deceived. Through every danger that infested the way the dead man steered in safety, turning the wheel from one side to the other calmly and quietly as if it had been noonday.

It seemed to Millard as if an age had passed over his head,

when he heard something fall on the floor with a slight clatter on the other side of the wheel; he did not know what it was—he only shuddered, and wondered what it meant. Soon after, by the faint light from the crack in the stove-pipe he saw his ghostly comrade moving silently towards the door—saw him lean against it for a moment, *open it*, and disappear.

Millard mustered strength enough to stop the engines, and at the same moment he heard the voice of his partner at the door. He stepped back to open it, and found that it was *still bolted on the inside!*

Poor Millard was now utterly confounded. He felt qualified to swear that he had seen the shape—no matter what it was—man or ghost or devil—go out at that very door—and yet it was still bolted! and so securely too that he hardly had strength enough left to unfasten it. But when the feat was at last accomplished, he sank down exhausted, and trembling from head to foot like a man with the palsy.

"Why how is this, Joe?—out in such a snow-storm, when one can't see the chimneys, let alone the derricks and jack-staff! You're beating Jones himself, Joe. Where are we, man? —where are we?"

"God only knows! Land her, Ben, for Heaven's sake, if you can ever find the shore."

During a momentary lull in the storm, Ben felt his way to shore, and rounded to under Philadelphia Point. And then he proceeded to question Joe.

"Swear that you will never mention the matter during my life, and I will tell you what I have seen this night; but on no other terms will I open my lips—for if the story should get abroad, Joseph Millard would become the laughing stock of the whole river, Ben."

Reubens wondered much at Millard's strange conduct; his curiosity was raised, however, and he took the oath. And quaking and shuddering, his comrade told the fearful tale.

Reubens was silent for a moment, after Millard had finished.

"You spoke of something that fell and rattled on the floor, Joe—what do you suppose it was?"

"It startled me when it fell, but I have no idea what it was, Ben."

"Well, I'll go after a lantern, and we'll soon find out."

"What! and leave me here by myself! I wouldn't stay here alone five minutes for a dozen steamboats."

So they both went, and soon returned with a light. Near the foot-board, on the starboard side of the wheel, they saw a glittering object, which proved to be a silver watch, lying open, with the crystal detached and broken in half. The break seemed recent. Neatly engraved, on the back of the watch, were these words.

"WILLIAM JONES—PRESENTED BY HIS FATHER."

c. January–June 1861

Petrified Man

A petrified man was found some time ago in the mountains south of Gravelly Ford. Every limb and feature of the stony mummy was perfect, not even excepting the left leg, which has evidently been a wooden one during the lifetime of the owner—which lifetime, by the way, came to a close about a century ago, in the opinion of a savan who has examined the defunct. The body was in a sitting posture, and leaning against a huge mass of croppings; the attitude was pensive, the right thumb resting against the side of the nose; the left thumb partially supported the chin, the fore-finger pressing the inner corner of the left eye and drawing it partly open; the right eye was closed, and the fingers of the right hand spread apart. This strange freak of nature created a profound sensation in the vicinity, and our informant states that by request, Justice Sewell or Sowell, of Humboldt City, at once proceeded to the spot and held an inquest on the body. The verdict of the jury was that "deceased came to his death from protracted exposure," etc. The people of the neighborhood volunteered to bury the poor unfortunate, and were even anxious to do so; but it was discovered, when they attempted to remove him, that the water which had dripped upon him for ages from the crag above, had coursed down his back and deposited a limestone sediment under him which had glued him to the bed rock upon which he sat, as with a cement of adamant, and Judge S. refused to allow the charitable citizens to blast him from his position. The opinion expressed by his Honor that such a course would be little less than sacrilege, was eminently just and proper. Everybody goes to see the stone man, as many as three hundred having visited the hardened creature during the past five or six weeks.

October 4, 1862

Letter from Carson City

EDS. ENTERPRISE: I feel very much as if I had just awakened out of a long sleep. I attribute it to the fact that I have slept the greater part of the time for the last two days and nights. On Wednesday, I sat up all night, in Virginia, in order to be up early enough to take the five o'clock stage on Thursday morning. I was on time. It was a great success. I had a cheerful trip down to Carson, in company with that incessant talker, Joseph T. Goodman. I never saw him flooded with such a flow of spirits before. He restrained his conversation, though, until we had traveled three or four miles, and were just crossing the divide between Silver City and Spring Valley, when he thrust his head out of the dark stage, and allowed a pallid light from the coach lamp to illuminate his features for a moment, after which he returned to darkness again, and sighed and said, "Damn it!" with some asperity. I asked him who he meant it for, and he said, "The weather out there." As we approached Carson, at about half past seven o'clock, he thrust his head out again, and gazed earnestly in the direction of that city—after which he took it in again, with his nose very much frosted. He propped the end of that organ upon the end of his finger, and looked down pensively upon it—which had the effect of making him appear cross-eyed—and remarked, "O, damn it!" with great bitterness. I asked him what he was up to this time, and he said, "The cold, damp fog—it is worse than the weather." This was his last. He never spoke again in my hearing. He went on over the mountains, with a lady fellow-passenger from here. That will stop his clatter, you know, for he seldom speaks in the presence of ladies.

In the evening I felt a mighty inclination to go to a party somewhere. There was to be one at Governor J. Neely Johnson's, and I went there and asked permission to stand around awhile. This was granted in the most hospitable manner, and visions of plain quadrilles soothed my weary soul. I felt particularly comfortable, for if there is one thing more grateful to my feelings than another, it is a new house—a

large house, with its ceilings embellished with snowy mould-
ings; its floors glowing with warm-tinted carpets; with cush-
ioned chairs and sofas to sit on, and a piano to listen to; with
fires so arranged that you can see them, and know that there
is no humbug about it; with walls garnished with pictures,
and above all, mirrors, wherein you may gaze, and always find
something to admire, you know. I have a great regard for a
good house, and a girlish passion for mirrors. Horace Smith,
Esq., is also very fond of mirrors. He came and looked in the
glass for an hour, with me. Finally, it cracked—the night was
pretty cold—and Horace Smith's reflection was split right
down the centre. But where his face had been, the damage
was greatest—a hundred cracks converged from his reflected
nose, like spokes from the hub of a wagon wheel. It was the
strangest freak the weather has done this Winter. And yet the
parlor seemed very warm and comfortable, too.

About nine o'clock the Unreliable came and asked Gov.
Johnson to let him stand on the porch. That creature has got
more impudence than any person I ever saw in my life. Well,
he stood and flattened his nose against the parlor window,
and looked hungry and vicious—he always looks that way—
until Col. Musser arrived with some ladies, when he actually
fell in their wake and came swaggering in, looking as if he
thought he had been anxiously expected. He had on my fine
kid boots, and my plug hat and my white kid gloves, (with
slices of his prodigious hands grinning through the bursted
seams), and my heavy gold repeater, which I had been offered
thousands and thousands of dollars for, many and many a
time. He took these articles out of my trunk, at Washoe City,
about a month ago, when we went out there to report the
proceedings of the Convention. The Unreliable intruded himself upon me in his cordial way, and said, "How are you,
Mark, old boy? when d'you come down? It's brilliant, ain't it?
Appear to enjoy themselves, don't they? Lend a fellow two
bits, can't you?" He always winds up his remarks that way.
He appears to have an insatiable craving for two bits.

The music struck up just then, and saved me. The next moment I was far, far at sea in a plain quadrille. We carried it
through with distinguished success; that is, we got as far as
"balance around," and "half-a-man-left," when I smelled hot

whisky punch, or something of that nature. I tracked the scent through several rooms, and finally discovered the large bowl from whence it emanated. I found the omnipresent Unreliable there, also. He set down an empty goblet, and remarked that he was diligently seeking the gentlemen's dressing room. I would have shown him where it was, but it occurred to him that the supper table and the punch-bowl ought not to be left unprotected; wherefore, we staid there and watched them until the punch entirely evaporated. A servant came in then to replenish the bowl, and we left the refreshments in his charge. We probably did wrong, but we were anxious to join the hazy dance. The dance was hazier than usual, after that. Sixteen couples on the floor at once, with a few dozen spectators scattered around, is calculated to have that effect in a brilliantly lighted parlor, I believe. Everything seemed to buzz, at any rate. After all the modern dances had been danced several times, the people adjourned to the supper-room. I found my wardrobe out there, as usual, with the Unreliable in it. His old distemper was upon him: he was desperately hungry. I never saw a man eat as much as he did in my life. I have the various items of his supper here in my note-book. First, he ate a plate of sandwiches; then he ate a handsomely iced poundcake; then he gobbled a dish of chicken salad; after which he ate a roast pig; after that, a quantity of blanc-mange; then he threw in several glasses of punch to fortify his appetite, and finished his monstrous repast with a roast turkey. Dishes of brandy-grapes, and jellies, and such things, and pyramids of fruits, melted away before him as shadows fly at the sun's approach. I am of the opinion that none of his ancestors were present when the five thousand were miraculously fed in the old Scriptural times. I base my opinion upon the twelve baskets of scraps and the little fishes that remained over after that feast. If the Unreliable himself had been there, the provisions would just about have held out, I think.

After supper, the dancing was resumed, and after awhile, the guests indulged in music to a considerable extent. Mrs. J. sang a beautiful Spanish song; Miss R., Miss T., Miss P., and Miss S., sang a lovely duett; Horace Smith, Esq., sang "I'm sitting on the stile, Mary," with a sweetness and tenderness of expression which I have never heard surpassed; Col. Musser sang "From Greenland's Icy Mountains" so fervently that every heart in that assemblage was purified and made better by it; Mrs. T. and Miss C., and Mrs. T. and Mrs. G. sang "Meet me by moonlight alone" charmingly; Judge Dixson sang "O, Charming May" with great vivacity and artistic effect; Joe Winters and Hal Clayton sang the Marseilles Hymn in French, and did it well; Mr. Wasson sang "Call me pet names" with his usual excellence—(Wasson has a cultivated voice, and a refined musical taste, but like Judge Brumfield, he throws so much operatic affectation into his singing that the beauty of his performance is sometimes marred by it—I could not help noticing this fault when Judge Brumfield sang "Rock me to sleep, mother;") Wm. M. Gillespie sang "Thou hast wounded the spirit that loved thee," gracefully and beautifully, and wept at the recollection of the circumstance which he was singing about. Up to this time I had carefully kept the Unreliable in the back ground, fearful that, under the circumstances, his insanity would take a musical turn; and my prophetic soul was right; he eluded me and planted himself at the piano; when he opened his cavernous mouth and displayed his slanting and scattered teeth, the effect upon that convivial audience was as if the gates of a graveyard, with its crumbling tombstones, had been thrown open in their midst; then he shouted some thing about he "would not live alway"—and if I ever heard anything absurd in my life, that was it. He must have made up that song as he went along. Why, there was no more sense in it, and no more music, than there is in his ordinary conversation. The only thing in the whole wretched performance that redeemed it for a moment, was something about "the few lucid moments that dawn on us here." That was all right; because the "lucid moments" that dawn on that Unreliable are almighty few, I can tell you. I wish one of them would strike him while I am here, and prompt him to return my valuables to me. I doubt if he ever gets lucid enough for that, though. After the Unreliable had finished squawking, I sat down to the piano and sang—however, what I sang is of no consequence to anybody. It was only a graceful little gem from the horse opera.

At about two o'clock in the morning the pleasant party

broke up and the crowd of guests distributed themselves around town to their respective homes; and after thinking the fun all over again, I went to bed at four o'clock. So, having been awake forty-eight hours, I slept forty-eight, in order to get even again, which explains the proposition I began this letter with.

Yours, dreamily,
MARK TWAIN.

February 3, 1863

Ye Sentimental Law Student

EDS. ENTERPRISE—I found the following letter, or Valentine, or whatever it is, lying on the summit, where it had been dropped unintentionally, I think. It was written on a sheet of legal cap, and each line was duly commenced within the red mark which traversed the sheet from top to bottom. Solon appeared to have had some trouble getting his effusion started to suit him. He had begun it, "Know all men by these presents," and scratched it out again; he had substituted, "Now at this day comes the plaintiff, by his attorney," and scratched that out also; he had tried other sentences of like character, and gone on obliterating them, until, through much sorrow and tribulation, he achieved the dedication which stands at the head of his letter, and to his entire satisfaction, I do cheerfully hope. But what a villain a man must be to blend together the beautiful language of love and the infernal phraseology of the law in one and the same sentence! I know but one of God's creatures who would be guilty of such depravity as this: I refer to the Unreliable. I believe the Unreliable to be the very lawyer's-cub who sat upon the solitary peak, all soaked in beer and sentiment, and concocted the insipid literary hash I am talking about. The handwriting closely resembles his semi-Chinese tarantula tracks.

SUGAR LOAF PEAK, February 14, 1863.

To the loveliness to whom these presents shall come, greeting:—This is a lovely day, my own Mary; its unencumbered sunshine reminds me of your happy face, and in the imagination the same doth now appear before me. Such sights and scenes as this ever remind me, the party of the second part, of you, my Mary, the peerless party of the first part. The view from the lonely and segregated mountain peak, of this portion of what is called and known as Creation, with all and singular the hereditaments and appurtenances thereunto appertaining and belonging, is inexpressively grand and inspiring; and I gaze, and gaze, while my soul is filled with holy delight, and my heart expands to receive thy spirit-presence, as aforesaid. Above me is the glory of the sun; around him float the messenger clouds, ready alike to bless the earth with gentle rain, or visit it with lightning, and thunder, and destruction; far below the said sun and the messenger clouds aforesaid, lying prone upon the earth in the verge of the distant horizon, like the burnished shield of a giant, mine eyes behold a lake, which is described and set forth in maps as the Sink of Carson; nearer, in the great plain, I see the Desert, spread abroad like the mantle of a Colossus, glowing by turns, with the warm light of the sun, hereinbefore mentioned, or darkly shaded by the messenger clouds aforesaid; flowing at right angles with said Desert, and adjacent thereto, I see the silver and sinuous thread of the river, commonly called Carson, which winds its tortuous course through the softly tinted valley, and disappears amid the gorges of the bleak and snowy mountains—a simile of man!—leaving the pleasant valley of Peace and Virtue to wander among the dark defiles of Sin, beyond the jurisdiction of the kindly beaming sun aforesaid! And about said sun, and the said clouds, and around the said mountains, and over the plain and the river aforesaid, there floats a purple glory—a yellow mist—as airy and beautiful as the bridal veil of a princess, about to be wedded according to the rites and ceremonies pertaining to, and established by, the laws or edicts of the kingdom or principality wherein she doth reside, and whereof she hath been and doth continue to be, a lawful sovereign or subject. Ah! my Mary, it is sublime! it is lovely! I have declared and made known, and by these presents do declare and make known unto you, that the view from Sugar Loaf Peak, as hereinbefore described and set forth, is the loveliest picture with which the hand of the Creator has adorned the earth, according to the best of my knowledge and belief, so help me God.

Given under my hand, and in the spirit-presence of the bright being whose love has restored the light of hope to a soul once groping in the darkness of despair, on the day and year first above written.

(Signed)

SOLON LYCURGUS.

Law Student, and Notary Public in and for the said County of Storey, and Territory of Nevada.

To Miss Mary Links, Virginia (and may the laws have her in their holy keeping).

February 19, 1863

All About the Fashions

"A Lady at the Lick House" writes:

"Edrs. Golden Era—We are all delighted with the 'Letter,' describing the brilliant Ball at Mr. Barron's. I am a Washoe widow, was among the favored few, and went. Sarah Smith skipped me in the toilettes. I suppose I wasn't very stunning, although Brigham & Co. said I looked 'swell,' and that 'Robergh' couldn't get up anything better. Some months ago, when my spouse, now at Reese River, first brought me down from Virginia City to stop in San Francisco, I arrived in the nick of time to attend one of those charming re-unions which are all the rage in the Pacific Metropolis. We have had several soirees since that, but nobody gave any account of them to the papers. It's too bad. Now we are eagerly looking forward to the next soiree, expecting the Golden Era to tell all about it. One of our boarders says she knows Florence Fane, and means to invite her; but I can't for the life of me get her to tell me the real name of your charming feuilletonist. I hope she'll come. And may-be Mark Twain will stay in town, to be there too. There is some talk of getting up a special gathering in compliment to him. He's such a favorite—stops here for his health—hoping to find out how to cure a cold. I am going to wear a new dress, made precisely after the pattern of one of those sweet Paris Fashion Plates in the *California Magazine*. That Ball Dress in the May number—I think it was—I've kept it in my boudoir ever since. Then if Mark Twain is only there to see; how happy, how happy, I shall be. (I don't mean that for poetry—Like what you put in the Golden Era.) (To take that license I am free—I write with such facility.) But I have not told you what I wanted. Mark Twain was at our party, last June, and sent the *Territorial Enterprise* an account of the affair. My husband enclosed me the paper in which it appeared. I cut it out and you can copy it. Please do. I've been bothered to death to let everybody see it, and it's dreadfully tattered and torn."

Here it is!

LETTER FROM MARK TWAIN.

ALL ABOUT THE FASHIONS.

SAN FRANCISCO, June 19.

EDS. ENTERPRISE:—I have just received, per Wells-Fargo, the following sweet scented little note, written in a microscopic hand in the center of a delicate sheet of paper—like a wedding invitation or a funeral notice—and I feel it my duty to answer it:

"VIRGINIA, June 16.

"MR. MARK TWAIN:—*Do* tell us something about the fashions. I am dying to know what the ladies of San Francisco are wearing. Do, now, tell us all you know about it, won't you? Pray excuse brevity, for I am in *such* a hurry.

BETTIE.

"P. S.—Please burn this as soon as you have read it."

"*Do* tell us"—and she is in "*such* a hurry." Well, I never knew a girl in my life who could write three consecutive sentences without italicising a word. They can't do it, you know. Now, if I had a wife, and she—however, I don't think I shall have one this week, and it is hardly worth while to borrow trouble.

Bettie, my love, you do me proud. In thus requesting me to fix up the fashions for you in an intelligent manner, you pay a compliment to my critical and observant eye and my varied and extensive information, which a mind less perfectly balanced than mine could scarcely contemplate without excess of vanity. Will I tell you something about the fashions? I will, Bettie—you better bet you bet, Betsey, my darling. I learned those expressions from the Unreliable; like all the phrases which fall from his lips, they are frightfully vulgar—but then they sound rather musical than otherwise.

A happy circumstance has put it in my power to furnish you the fashions from headquarters—as it were, Bettie: I refer to the assemblage of fashion, elegance and loveliness called together in the parlor of the Lick House last night—[a party given by the proprietors on the occasion of my paying up that little balance due on my board bill.] I will give a brief and lucid description of the dresses worn by several of the ladies of my acquaintance who were present. Mrs. B. was arrayed in a superb speckled foulard, with the stripes running fore and aft, and with collets and camails to match; also, a rotonde of Chantilly lace, embroidered with blue and yellow dogs, and birds and things, done in cruel, and edged with a Solferino fringe four inches deep—lovely. Mrs. B. is tall, and graceful and beautiful, and the general effect of her costume was to render her appearance extremely lively.

Miss J. W. wore a charming robe polonais of scarlet ruche a la vieille, with yellow fluted flounces of rich bombazine, fourteen inches wide; low neck and short sleeves; also a Figaro veste of bleached domestic—selvedge edge turned down with a back-stitch, and trimmed with festoons of blue chicoree taffetas—gay?—I reckon not. Her head-dress was the sweetest thing you ever saw: a bunch of stately ostrich plumes—red and white—springing like fountains above each ear, with a crown between, consisting of a single *fleur de soliel*, fresh from the garden—Ah, me! Miss W. looked enchantingly pretty; however, there was nothing unusual about that—I have seen her look so, even in a milder costume.

Mrs. J. B. W. wore a heavy rat-colored brocade silk, studded with large silver stars, and trimmed with organdy; balloon sleeves of nankeen pique, gathered at the wrist, cut bias and hollowed out some at the elbow; also, a bournous of black Honiton lace, scolloped, and embroidered in violent colors with a battle piece representing the taking of Holland by the Dutch; low neck and high-heeled shoes; gloves; palmleaf fan; hoops; her head-dress consisted of a simple maroon-colored Sontag, with festoons of blue illusion depending from it; upon her bosom reposed a gorgeous bouquet of real sage brush, imported from Washoe. Mrs. W. looked regally handsome. If every article of dress worn by her on this occasion had been multiplied seven times, I do not believe it would have improved her appearance any.

Miss C. wore an elegant *Cheveux de la Reine* (with ruffles and furbelows trimmed with bands of guipre round the bottom), and a mohair Garibaldi shirt; her unique head-dress was crowned with a graceful *pomme de terre* (Limerick French), and she had her hair done up in papers—greenbacks. The effect was very rich, partly owing to the market value of the material, and partly to the general loveliness of the lady herself.

Miss A. H. wore a splendid Lucia de Lammermoor, trimmed with green baize: also, a cream-colored mantilla-shaped *pardessus*, with a deep gore in the neck, and embellished with a wide greque of taffetas ribbon, and otherwise garnished with ruches, and radishes and things. Her *coiffure* was a simple wreath of sardines on a string. She was lovely to a fault.

Now, what do you think of that effort, Bettie (I wish I knew your other name) for an unsanctified newspaper reporter, devoid of a milliner's education? Doesn't it strike you that there are more brains and fewer oysters in my head than a casual acquaintance with me would lead one to suppose? Ah, well—what I don't know, Bet, is hardly worth the finding out, I can tell you. I could have described the dresses of all the ladies in that party, but I was afraid to meddle with those of strangers, because I might unwittingly get something wrong, and give offense. You see strangers never exercise any charity in matters of this kind—they always get mad at the least inaccuracies of description concerning their apparel, and make themselves disagreeable. But if you will just rig yourself up according to the models I have furnished you, Bets, you'll do, you know—you can weather the circus.

You will naturally wish to be informed as to the most fashionable style of male attire, and I may as well give you an idea of my own personal appearance at the party. I wore one of Mr. Lawlor's shirts, and Mr. Ridgway's vest, and Dr. Wayman's coat, and Mr. Camp's hat, and Mr. Paxton's boots, and Jerry Long's white kids, and Judge Gilchrist's cravat, and the Unreliable's brass seal-ring, and Mr. Tollroad McDonald's pantaloons—and if you have an idea that they are anyways short in the legs, do you just climb into them once, sweetness. The balance of my outfit I gathered up indiscriminately from various individuals whose names I have forgotten and have now no means of ascertaining, as I thoughtlessly erased the marks from the different garments this morning. But I looked salubrious, B., if ever a man did.

c. June 21, 1863

Letter from Steamboat Springs

STEAMBOAT SPRINGS HOTEL,⎫
August 23, 1863.⎭

THE SPRINGS.

EDS. ENTERPRISE: I have overstepped my furlough a full
week—but then this is a pleasant place to pass one's time.
These springs are ten miles from Virginia, six or seven from
Washoe City and twenty from Carson. They are natural—the
devil boils the water, and the white steam puffs up out of
crevices in the earth, along the summits of a series of low
mounds extending in an irregular semi-circle for more than a
mile. The water is impregnated with a dozen different miner-
als, each one of which smells viler than its fellow, and the
sides of the springs are embellished with very pretty parti-
colored incrustations deposited by the water. From one
spring the boiling water is ejected a foot or more by the infernal force at work below, and in the vicinity of all of them one
can hear a constant rumbling and surging, somewhat resembling the noises peculiar to a steamboat in motion—hence
the name.

THE HOTEL.

The Steamboat Springs Hotel is very pleasantly situated on
a grassy flat, a stone's throw from the hospital and the bath
houses. It is capable of accommodating a great many guests.
The rooms are large, "hard-finished" and handsomely furnished; there is an abundant supply of pure water, which can
be carried to every part of the house, in case of fire, by means
of hose; the table is furnished with fresh vegetables and meats
from the numerous fine ranches in the valley, and lastly, Mr.
Stowe is a pleasant and accommodating landlord, and is ably
seconded by Messrs. Haines, Ellsworth and Bingham. These
gentlemen will never allow you to get ill-humored for want of
polite attention—as I gratefully remember, now, when I recall the stormy hours of Friday, when that accursed "Wake-up
Jake" was in me. But I haven't got to that, yet. God bless us!
it is a world of trouble, and we are born to sorrow and tribulation—yet, am I chiefest among sinners, that I should be

prematurely damned with "Wake-up Jake," while others not of the elect go free? I am trying to go on with my letter, but this thing bothers me; verily, from having "Wake-up Jake" on the stomach for three days, I have finally got it on the brain. I am grateful for the change. But I digress.

THE HOSPITAL.

Dr. Ellis, the proprietor of the Springs, has erected a large, tastefully designed, and comfortable and well ventilated hospital, close to the bath-houses, and it is constantly filled with patients afflicted with all manner of diseases. It would be a very profitable institution, but a great many who come to it half dead, and leave it again restored to robust health, forget to pay for the benefits they have received. Others, when they arrive, confess at once that they are penniless, yet few men could look upon the sunken cheeks of these, and upon their attenuated forms and their pleading, faded eyes, and refuse them the shelter and assistance we all may need some day. Without expectation of reward, Dr. Ellis gives back life, hope and health to many a despairing, poverty-stricken devil; and when I think of this, it seems so strange that he could have had the meanness to give me that "Wake-up-Jake." However, I am wandering away from the subject again. All diseases (except confirmed consumption,) are treated successfully here. A multitude of invalids have attended these baths during the past three years, yet only an insignificant number of deaths have occurred among them. I want to impress one thing upon you: it is a mistaken notion that these Springs were created solely for the salvation of persons suffering venereal diseases. True, the fame of the baths rests chiefly upon the miracles performed upon such patients, and upon others afflicted with rheumatism, erysipelas, etc., but then all ordinary ailments can be quickly and pleasantly cured here without a resort to deadly physic. More than two-thirds of the people who come here are afflicted with venereal diseases—fellows who know that if "Steamboat" fails with them they may as well go to trading feet with the undertaker for a box—yet all here agree that these baths are none the less potent where other diseases are concerned. I know lots of poor, feeble wretches in Virginia who could get a new lease of life by soaking their shadows in Steamboat Springs for a week or two. However, I must pass on to

THE BATHS.

My friend Jim Miller has charge of these. Within a few days the new bath-house will be finished, and then twelve persons may bathe at once, or if they be sociable and choose to go on the double-bed principle, four times as many can enjoy the luxury at the same time. Persons afflicted with loathsome diseases use bath-rooms which are never entered by the other patients. You get up here about six o'clock in the morning and walk over to the bath-house; you undress in an ante-room and take a cold shower-bath—or let it alone, if you choose; then you step into a sort of little dark closet floored with a wooden grating, up through which come puffs and volumes of the hottest steam you ever performed to, (because the awkwardest of us feel a hankering to waltz a little under such circumstances, you know), and then if you are alone, you resolve to have company thenceforward, since to swap comments upon your sensations with a friend, must render the dire heat less binding upon the human constitution. I had company always, and it was the pleasantest thing in the world to see a thin-skinned invalid cavorting around in the vapory obscurity, marveling at the rivers of sweat that coursed down his body, cursing the villainous smell of the steam and its bitter, salty taste—groping around meanwhile, for a cold corner, and backing finally, into the hottest one, and darting out again in a second, only remarking "Outch!"—and repeating it when he sits down, and springs up the same moment off the hot bench. This was fun of the most comfortable character; but nothing could be more agreeable than to put your eye to the little square hole in the door, and see your boiled and smoking comrade writhing under the cold shower-bath, to see him shrink till his shoulders are level with the top of his head, and then shut his eyes and gasp and catch his breath, while the cruel rain pattered down on his back and sent a ghastly shiver through every fibre of his body. It will always be a comfort to me to recall these little incidents. After the shower-bath, you return to the ante-room and scrub yourself all over with coarse towels until your hide glows like a parlor carpet—after which, you feel as elastic and vigorous as an acrobat. Then if you are sensible, you take no exercise, but just eat your breakfast and go to bed—you will find that an hour's nap will not hurt you any.

THE "WAKE-UP-JAKE."

A few days ago I fell a victim to my natural curiosity and my solicitude for the public weal. Everybody had something to say about "wake-up-Jake." If a man was low-spirited; if his appetite failed him; if he did not sleep well at night; if he were costive; if he were bilious; or in love; or in any other kind of trouble; or if he doubted the fidelity of his friends or the efficacy of his religion, there was always some one at his elbow to whisper, "Take a 'wake-up,' my boy." I sought to fathom the mystery, but all I could make out of it was that the "Wake-up Jake" was a medicine as powerful as "the servants of the lamp," the secret of whose decoction was hidden away in Dr. Ellis' breast. I was not aware that I had any use for the wonderful "wake-up," but then I felt it to be my duty to try it, in order that a suffering public might profit by my experience—and I would cheerfully see that public suffer perdition before I would try it again. I called upon Dr. Ellis with the air of a man who would create the impression that he is not so much of an ass as he looks, and demanded a "Wake-up-Jake" as unostentatiously as if that species of refreshment were not at all new to me. The Doctor hesitated a moment, and then fixed up as repulsive a mixture as ever was stirred together in a table-spoon. I swallowed the nauseous mess, and that one meal sufficed me for the space of forty-eight hours. And during all that time, I could not have enjoyed a viler taste in my mouth if I had swallowed a slaughter-house. I lay down with all my clothes on, and with an utter indifference to my fate here or hereafter, and slept like a statue from six o'clock until noon. I got up, then, the sickest man that ever yearned to vomit and couldn't. All the dead and decaying matter in nature seemed buried in my stomach, and I "heaved, and retched, and heaved again," but I could not compass a resurrection—my dead would not come forth. Finally, after rumbling, and growling, and producing agony and chaos within me for many hours, the dreadful dose began its work, and for the space of twelve hours it vomited me, and purged me, and likewise caused me to bleed at the nose.

I came out of that siege as weak as an infant, and went to the bath with Palmer, of Wells, Fargo & Co., and it was well I had company, for it was about all he could do to keep me from boiling the remnant of my life out in the hot steam. I had reached that stage wherein a man experiences a solemn indifference as to whether school keeps or not. Since then, I have gradually regained my strength and my appetite, and am now animated by a higher degree of vigor than I have felt for many a day. 'Tis well. This result seduces many a man into taking a second, and even a third "wake-up-Jake," but I think I can worry along without any more of them. I am about as thoroughly waked up now as I care to be. My stomach never had such a scouring out since I was born. I feel like a jug. If I could get young Wilson or the Unreliable to take a "wake-up-Jake," I would do it, of course, but I shall never swallow another myself—I would sooner have a locomotive travel through me. And besides, I never intend to experiment in physic any more, just out of idle curiosity. A "wake-up-Jake" will furbish a man's machinery up and give him a fresh start in the world—but I feel I shall never need anything of that sort any more. It would put robust health, and life and vim into young Wilson and the Unreliable—but then they always look with suspicion upon any suggestion that I make.

GOOD-BYE.

Well, I am going home to Virginia to-day, though I dislike to part from the jolly boys (not to mention iced milk for breakfast, with eggs laid to order, and spiced oysters after midnight with the Reverend Jack Holmes and Bingham) at the Steamboat Springs Hotel. In conclusion, let me recommend to such of my fellow citizens as are in feeble health, or are wearied out with the cares of business, to come down and try the hotel, and the steam baths, and the facetious "wake-up-Jake." These will give them rest, and moving recreation —as it were.

MARK TWAIN.

August 25, 1863

How to Cure a Cold

It is a good thing, perhaps, to write for the amusement of the public, but it is a far higher and nobler thing to write for their instruction—their profit—their actual and tangible benefit.

The latter is the sole object of this article.

If it prove the means of restoring to health one solitary sufferer among my race—of lighting up once more the fire of hope and joy in his faded eyes—of bringing back to his dead heart again the quick, generous impulses of other days—I shall be amply rewarded for my labor; my soul will be permeated with the sacred delight a Christian feels when he has done a good, unselfish deed.

Having led a pure and blameless life, I am justified in believing that no man who knows me will reject the suggestions I am about to make, out of fear that I am trying to deceive him.

Let the public do itself the honor to read my experience in doctoring a cold, as herein set forth, and then follow in my footsteps.

When the White House was burned in Virginia, I lost my home, my happiness, my constitution and my trunk.

The loss of the two first named articles was a matter of no great consequence, since a home without a mother or a sister, or a distant young female relative in it, to remind you by putting your soiled linen out of sight and taking your boots down off the mantle-piece, that there are those who think about you and care for you, is easily obtained.

And I cared nothing for the loss of my happiness, because, not being a poet, it could not be possible that melancholy would abide with me long.

But to lose a good constitution and a better trunk were serious misfortunes.

I had my Gould and Curry in the latter, you recollect; I may get it back again, though—I came down here this time partly to bully-rag the Company into restoring my stock to me.

On the day of the fire, my constitution succumbed to a

severe cold caused by undue exertion in getting ready to do something.

I suffered to no purpose, too, because the plan I was figuring at for the extinguishing of the fire was so elaborate that I never got it completed until the middle of the following week.

The first time I began to sneeze, a friend told me to go and bathe my feet in hot water and go to bed.

I did so.

Shortly afterward, another friend advised me to get up and take a cold shower-bath.

I did that also.

Within the hour, another friend assured me that it was policy to "feed a cold and starve a fever."

I had both.

I thought it best to fill myself up for the cold, and then keep dark and let the fever starve a while.

In a case of this kind, I seldom do things by halves; I ate pretty heartily; I conferred my custom upon a stranger who had just opened his restaurant that morning; he waited near me in respectful silence until I had finished feeding my cold, when he inquired if the people about Virginia were much afflicted with colds?

I told him I thought they were.

He then went out and took in his sign.

I started down toward the office, and on the way encountered another bosom friend, who told me that a quart of salt water, taken warm, would come as near curing a cold as anything in the world.

I hardly thought I had room for it, but I tried it anyhow.

The result was surprising; I must have vomited three-quarters of an hour; I believe I threw up my immortal soul.

Now, as I am giving my experience only for the benefit of those who are troubled with the distemper I am writing about, I feel that they will see the propriety of my cautioning them against following such portions of it as proved inefficient with me—and acting upon this conviction, I warn them against warm salt water.

It may be a good enough remedy, but I think it is too severe. If I had another cold in the head, and there was no course left me but to take either an earthquake or a quart of warm salt water, I would cheerfully take my chances on the earthquake.

After the storm which had been raging in my stomach had subsided, and no more good Samaritans happening along, I went on borrowing handkerchiefs again and blowing them to atoms, as had been my custom in the early stages of my cold, until I came across a lady who had just arrived from over the plains, and who said she had lived in a part of the country where doctors were scarce, and had from necessity acquired considerable skill in the treatment of simple "family complaints."

I knew she must have had much experience, for she appeared to be a hundred and fifty years old.

She mixed a decoction composed of molasses, aquafortis, turpentine, and various other drugs, and instructed me to take a wine-glass full of it every fifteen minutes.

I never took but one dose; that was enough; it robbed me of all moral principle, and awoke every unworthy impulse of my nature.

Under its malign influence, my brain conceived miracles of meanness, but my hands were too feeble to execute them; at that time had it not been that my strength had surrendered to a succession of assaults from infallible remedies for my cold, I am satisfied that I would have tried to rob the graveyard.

Like most other people, I often feel mean, and act accordingly, but until I took that medicine I had never reveled in such supernatural depravity and felt proud of it.

At the end of two days, I was ready to go to doctoring again. I took a few more unfailing remedies, and finally drove my cold from my head to my lungs.

I got to coughing incessantly, and my voice fell below Zero; I conversed in a thundering bass two octaves below my natural tone; I could only compass my regular nightly repose by coughing myself down to a state of utter exhaustion, and then the moment I began to talk in my sleep, my discordant voice woke me up again.

My case grew more and more serious every day.

Plain gin was recommended; I took it.

Then gin and molasses; I took that also.

Then gin and onions; I added the onions and took all three.

I detected no particular result, however, except that I had acquired a breath like a buzzard's.

I found I had to travel for my health.

I went to Lake Bigler with my reportorial comrade, Adair Wilson. It is gratifying to me to reflect that we traveled in considerable style; we went in the Pioneer coach, and my friend took all his baggage with him, consisting of two excellent silk handkerchiefs and a daguerreotype of his grandmother.

I had my regular gin and onions along.

Virginia, San Francisco and Sacramento were well represented at the Lake House, and we had a very healthy time of it for a while. We sailed and hunted and fished and danced all day, and I doctored my cough all night.

By managing in this way, I made out to improve every hour in the twenty-four.

But my disease continued to grow worse.

A sheet-bath was recommended. I had never refused a remedy yet, and it seemed poor policy to commence then; therefore I determined to take a sheet-bath, notwithstanding I had no idea what sort of arrangement it was.

It was administered at midnight, and the weather was very frosty. My breast and back were bared, and a sheet (there appeared to be a thousand yards of it) soaked in ice-water, was wound around me until I resembled a swab for a Columbiad.

It is a cruel expedient. When the chilly rag touches one's warm flesh, it makes him start with sudden violence and gasp for breath just as men do in the death agony. It froze the marrow in my bones and stopped the beating of my heart.

I thought my time had come.

Young Wilson said the circumstance reminded him of an anecdote about a negro who was being baptised, and who slipped from the Parson's grasp and came near being drowned; he floundered around, though, and finally rose up out of the water considerably strangled and furiously angry, and started ashore at once, spouting water like a whale, and remarking with great asperity that "One o' dese days, some

gen'lman's nigger gwyne to git killed wid jes' sich dam foolishness as dis!"

Then young Wilson laughed at his silly, pointless anecdote,
as if he had thought he had done something very smart. I
suppose I am not to be affronted every day, though, without
resenting it—I coughed my bed-fellow clear out of the house
before morning.

Never take a sheet-bath—never. Next to meeting a lady
acquaintance, who, for reasons best known to herself, don't
see you when she looks at you and don't know you when
she does see you, it is the most uncomfortable thing in the
world.

It is singular that such a simile as that, happened to occur
to me; I haven't thought of that circumstance a dozen times
to-day. I used to think she was so pretty, and gentle, and
graceful, and considerate, and all that sort of thing.

But I suspect it was all a mistake.

In reality, she is as ugly as a crab; and there is no expression
in her countenance, either; she reminds me of one of those
dummies in the milliner shops. I know she has got false teeth,
and I think one of her eyes is glass. She can never fool me
with that French she talks, either; that's Cherokee—I have
been among that tribe myself. She has already driven two or
three Frenchmen to the verge of suicide with that unchristian
gibberish. And that complexion of her's is the dingiest that
ever a white woman bore—it is pretty nearly Cherokee itself.
It shows out strongest when it is contrasted with her monstrous white sugar-shoveled bonnet; when she gets that on,
she looks like a sorrel calf under a new shed. I despise that
woman, and I'll never speak to her again. Not unless she
speaks to me, anyhow.

But as I was saying, when the sheet-bath failed to cure my
cough, a lady friend recommended the application of a mustard plaster to my breast.

I believe that would have cured me effectually, if it had not
been for young Wilson.

When I went to bed I put my mustard plaster—which was
a very gorgeous one, eighteen inches square—where I could
reach it when I was ready for it.

But young Wilson got hungry in the night, and ate it up.

I never saw anybody have such an appetite; I am confident that lunatic would have eaten me if I had been healthy.

After sojourning a week at Lake Bigler, I went to Steam-boat Springs, and besides the steam baths, I took a lot of the vilest medicines that were ever concocted. They would have cured me, but I had to go back to Virginia, where, notwith-standing the variety of new remedies I absorbed every day, I managed to aggravate my disease by carelessness and undue exposure.

I finally concluded to visit San Francisco, and the first day I got here a lady at the Lick House told me to drink a quart of whisky every twenty-four hours, and a friend at the Occiden-tal recommended precisely the same course.

Each advised me to take a quart—that makes half a gallon.

I calculate to do it or perish in the attempt.

Now, with the kindest motives in the world, I offer for the consideration of consumptive patients the variegated course of treatment I have lately gone through. Let them try it—if it don't cure them, it can't more than kill them.

September 20, 1863

The Lick House Ball

EDS. ERA: I have received a letter from the land of eternal summer—Washoe, you understand—requesting a short synopsis of the San Francisco fashions for reference. There are ten note paper pages of it. I read it all. For two hours I worked along through it—spelling a word laboriously here and there—figuring out sentences by main strength—getting three or four of them corraled, all ragged and disjointed, and then skirmishing around after the connection—two hours of unflagging labor, determination and blasphemy, unrewarded by one solitary shadow of a suspicion of what the writer was trying to get through her head or what she could possibly be up to—until I bore down upon the three lines at the bottom of the last page, marked "P.S.," which contained the request about the fashions, and was the only paragraph in the document wherein the light of reason glimmered. All that went before it was driveling stupidity—all that the girl really wished to say was in the postscript. It was not strange that I experienced a warm fellow-feeling for the dog that drank sixty gallons of water to get at a spoonful of mush in the bottom of the tank.

The young lady signs herself "Œnone." I am not acquainted with her, but the respect, the deference which, as a white man and a Christian, I naturally feel for members of her sex, impels me to take no less pains in obliging her than were the circumstances different.

A fortunate occurrence has placed it in my power to furnish Œnone with the very latest fashions: I refer to the great ball given me at the Lick House last Thursday night by a portion of the guests of that hotel, on the occasion of my promising to "let up" on Messrs. Jerome Rice, John B. Winters, Brooks, Mason, Charley Creed, Capt. Pease, and the other "billiard sharps" of the establishment.

It was a graceful acknowledgment of my proficiency in the beautiful science of billiards, as well as of the liberality I have shown in paying for about every game I ever played in the house.

I expect I have been rather hard upon those gentlemen, but

it was no fault of mine—they courted their own destruction. As one of them expressed it, they "could not resist the temptation to tackle me;" and if they baited their hooks for a sardine and caught a whale, who is to blame? Possibly it will be a comfort to Capt. Pease to know that I don't blame him, anyhow; that there is no animosity whatever, and that I feel the same filial affection, the same kindly regard, etc., etc., just as if nothing had happened.

Œnone, (or Unknown, if it is all the same to you,) the ball was a grand success. The army was present and also the navy. The nobility were represented by his Grace the Duke of Benicia, the Countess of San Jose, Lord Blessyou, Lord Geeminy, and many others whose titles and whose faces have passed from my memory. Owing to a press of imperial business, the Emperor Norton was unable to come.

The parlors were royally decorated, and the floors covered with a rich white carpet of mauve domestique, forty dollars a yard, imported from Massachusetts or the kingdom of New Jersey, I have forgotten which. The moment I entered I saw at a glance that this was the most extraordinary party ever given in San Francisco. I mentioned it to Benish, (the very friendly, not to say familiar, relations existing between myself and his Grace the Duke of Benicia, permit of my addressing him in this way without impropriety,) and he said he had never seen anything like it where he came from. He said there were more diamonds here than were displayed at the very creditable effort of the Messrs. Barron, recently. This remark revived in his breast a reminiscence of that ball. He observed that the evening before it came off, he visited all the jewelry shops in town for the purpose of leasing some diamonds for his wife, who had been invited; but others had gone before him and "cleaned out," (as the facetious nobleman expressed it,) every establishment. There was but one shop where a diamond remained on hand; and even there, the proprietor was obliged to tell him—though it cost him pain to do it—that he only had a quart left, and they had already been engaged by the Duchess of Goat Island, who was going to the ball and could not do without them.

The memory of the incident affected the noble Benish almost to tears, and we pursued the theme no further. After

this, we relapsed into a desultory conversation in French, in which I rather had the best of him; he appeared to have an idea that he could cypher out what I was driving at, whereas I had never expected to understand him in the first place.

But you are suffering for the fashions, Œnone. I have written such things before, but only by way of burlesquing the newspaper descriptions of balls and dresses launched at the public every now and then by individuals who do not seem to know that writing fashion articles, like wet nursing, can only be done properly by women. A rightly constituted man ought to be above filching from the prerogatives of the other sex. As I have said, the fashion synopses heretofore written by myself, have been uncouth burlesques—extravagant paraphrases of the eloquence of female costume, as incomprehensible and as conflicting as Billy Birch's testimony in the case of the atrocious assassination of Erickson's bull by "Jonesy," with his infamous "stuffed club." But this time, since a lady requests it, I will choke down my distaste for such feminine employment, and write a faithful description of the queenly dresses worn at the Lick House party by several ladies whose tempers I think I can depend on. Thus:

Mrs. E. F. L. wore a superb *toilette habillee* of Chambery gauze; over this a charming Figaro jacket, made of mohair, or horse-hair, or something of that kind; over this again, a Raphael blouse of *cheveux de la reine*, trimmed round the bottom with lozenges formed of insertions, and around the top with bronchial troches; nothing could be more graceful than the contrast between the lozenges and the troches; over the blouse she wore a *robe de chambre* of regal magnificence, made of *Faille* silk and ornamented with maccaroon (usually spelled "maccaroni,") buttons set in black guipre. On the roof of her bonnet was a menagerie of rare and beautiful bugs and reptiles, and under the eaves thereof a counterfeit of the "early bird" whose specialty it hath been to work destruction upon such things since time began. To say that Mrs. L. was never more elaborately dressed in her life, would be to express an opinion within the range of possibility, at least—to say that she did or could look otherwise than charming, would be a deliberate departure from the truth.

Mrs. Wm. M. S. wore a gorgeous dress of silk bias,

trimmed with tufts of ponceau feathers in the *Frouleur* style; elbowed sleeves made of chicories; plaited Swiss habit-shirt, composed of Valenciennes, *a la vieille*, embellished with a delicate nansook insertion scolloped at the edge; Lonjumeau jacket of maize-colored *Geralda*, set off with *bagnettes*, bayonets, clarinets, and one thing or other—beautiful. Rice-straw bonnet of Mechlin tulle, trimmed with devices cut out of sole-leather, representing aigrettes and arastras—or asters, whichever it is. Leather ornaments are becoming very fashionable in high society. I am told the Empress Eugenie dresses in buckskin now, altogether; so does Her Majesty the Queen of the Shoshones. It will be seen at a glance that Mrs. S.'s costume upon this occasion was peculiarly suited to the serene dignity of her bearing.

Mrs. A. W. B. was arrayed in a sorrel organdy, trimmed with fustians and figaros, and canzou fichus, so disposed as to give a splendid effect without disturbing the general harmony of the dress. The body of the robe was of zero velvet, goffered, with a square pelerine of solferino *poil de chevre* amidships. The fan used by Mrs. B. was of real palm-leaf and cost four thousand dollars—the handle alone cost six bits. Her head dress was composed of a graceful cataract of white chantilly lace, surmounted by a few artificial worms, and butterflies and things, and a tasteful tarantula done in jet. It is impossible to conceive of anything more enchanting than this toilet—or the lady who wore it, either, for that matter.

Mrs. J. B. W. was dressed in a rich white satin, with a body composed of a gorgeously figured Mackinaw blanket, with five rows of ornamental brass buttons down the back. The dress was looped up at the side with several bows of No. 3 ribbon—yellow—displaying a skirt of cream-colored Valenciennes crocheted with pink cruel. The coiffure was simply a tall cone of brilliant field-flowers, upon the summit of which stood a glittering 'golden beetle'—or, as we call him at home, a "straddle-bug." All who saw the beautiful Mrs. W. upon this occasion will agree that there was nothing wanting about her dress to make it attract attention in any community.

Mrs. F. was attired in an elegant Irish foulard of figured aqua marine, or aqua fortis, or something of that kind with thirty-two perpendicular rows of tulle puffings formed of

black zero velvets (Fahrenheit.) Over this she wore a rich bal-
moral skirt—Pekin stripe—looped up at the sides with clus-
ters of field flowers, showing the handsome dress beneath.
She also wore a white Figaro postillion pea-jacket, ornamented with a profusion of Gabriel bows of crimson silk.
From her head depended tasteful garlands of fresh radishes. It
being natural to look charming upon all occasions, she did so
upon this, of course.

Miss B. wore an elegant goffered flounce, trimmed with a
grenadine of *bouillonnee*, with a crinoline waistcoat to match;
pardessus open behind, embroidered with paramattas of
passementerie, and further ornamented at the shoulders with
epaulettes of wheat-ears and string-beans; tule hat, embellished with blue-bells, hare-bells, hash-bells, etc., with a fron-
tispiece formed of a single magnificent cauliflower imbedded
in mashed potatoes. Thus attired Miss B. looked good
enough to eat. I admit that the expression is not very refined,
but when a man is hungry the similes he uses are apt to be
suggested by his stomach.

It is hardly worth while to describe the costumes of the
gentlemen, since, with the exception of a handsome uniform
here and there, (there were six naval Brigadier Generals
present from the frigate *Lancaster*) they were all alike, and as
usual, there was nothing worthy of particular notice in what
they wore.

Œnone, I could furnish you with an accurate description of
the costume of every lady who attended that party if it were
safe to do it, but it isn't, you know. Over in Washoe I generally say what I please about anybody and everybody, because
my obliging fellow citizens have learned to put up with it; but
here, common prudence teaches me to speak of those only
who are slow to anger, when writing about ladies. I had
rather lose my scalp, anyhow, than wound a lady's feelings.

But there is one thing you can rest assured of, Œnone: The
pleasantest parties in the world are those given at the Lick
House every now and then, and to which scarcely any save
the guests of the establishment are invited; and the ladies are
handsomer, and dress with more taste and greater magnificence—but there come the children again. When that last
invoice of fifteen hundred infants come around and get to

romping about my door with the others, and hurrahing for their several favorite candidates for Governor, (unaware that the election is over, poor little miscreants,) I cannot write with such serene comfort as I do when they are asleep. Yet there is nothing I love so dearly as a clean, fat, healthy infant. I calculate to eat that whole tribe before I leave the Lick House.

Now, do you know, Œnone—however, I hear the stately tread of that inveterate chambermaid. She always finds this room in a state of chaos, and she always leaves it as trim as a parlor. But her instincts infallibly impel her to march in here just when I feel least like marching out. I do not know that I have ever begged permission to write "only a few moments longer"—never with my tongue, at any rate, although I may have *looked* it with my expressive glass eye. But she cares nothing for such spooney prayers. She is a soldier in the army of the household; she knows her duty, and she allows nothing to interfere with its rigid performance. She reminds me of U. S. Grant; she marches in her grand military way to the centre of the room, and comes to an "order arms" with her broom and her slop-bucket; then she bends on me a look of uncompromising determination, and I reluctantly haul down my flag. I abandon my position—I evacuate the premises—I retire in good order—I vamose the ranch. Because that look of hers says in plain, crisp language, "I don't want you here. If you are not gone in two minutes, I propose to move upon your works!" But I bear the chambermaid no animosity.

MARK TWAIN.

September 27, 1863

The Great Prize Fight

For $100,000, at
SEAL ROCK POINT, ON SUNDAY LAST,
BETWEEN HIS EXCELLENCY GOV. STANFORD AND
HON. F. F. LOW, GOVERNOR ELECT OF CALIFORNIA.

For the past month the sporting world has been in a state of feverish excitement on account of the grand prize fight set for last Sunday between the two most distinguished citizens of California, for a purse of a hundred thousand dollars. The high social standing of the competitors, their exalted position in the arena of politics, together with the princely sum of money staked upon the issue of the combat, all conspired to render the proposed prize-fight a subject of extraordinary importance, and to give it an eclat never before vouchsafed to such a circumstance since the world began. Additional lustre was shed upon the coming contest by the lofty character of the seconds or bottle-holders chosen by the two champions, these being no other than Judge Field (on the part of Gov. Low), Associate Justice of the Supreme Court of the United States, and Hon. Wm. M. Stewart, (commonly called "Bill Stewart," or "Bullyragging Bill Stewart,") of the city of Virginia, the most popular as well as the most distinguished lawyer in Nevada Territory, member of the Constitutional Convention, and future U. S. Senator for the State of Washoe, as I hope and believe—on the part of Gov. Stanford. Principals and seconds together, it is fair to presume that such an array of talent was never entered for a combat of this description upon any previous occasion.

Stewart and Field had their men in constant training at the Mission during the six weeks preceding the contest, and such was the interest taken in the matter that thousands visited that sacred locality daily to pick up such morsels of information as they might, concerning the physical and scientific improvement being made by the gubernatorial acrobats. The anxiety manifested by the populace was intense. When it was learned that Stanford had smashed a barrel of flour to atoms with a single blow of his fist, the voice of the people was on his side. But when the news came that Low had caved in the head of a tubular boiler with one stroke of his powerful "mawley" (which term is in strict accordance with the language of the ring,) the tide of opinion changed again. These changes were frequent, and they kept the minds of the public in such a state of continual vibration that I fear the habit thus acquired is confirmed, and that they will never more cease to oscillate.

The fight was to take place on last Sunday morning at ten o'clock. By nine every wheeled vehicle and every species of animal capable of bearing burthens, were in active service, and the avenues leading to the Seal Rock swarmed with them in mighty processions whose numbers no man might hope to estimate.

I determined to be upon the ground at an early hour. Now I dislike to be exploded, as it were, out of my balmy slumbers, by a sudden, stormy assault upon my door, and an imperative order to "Get up!"—wherefore I requested one of the intelligent porters of the Lick House to call at my palatial apartments, and murmur gently through the key-hole the magic monosyllable "Hash!" That "fetched me."

The urbane livery-stable keeper furnished me with a solemn, short-bodied, long-legged animal—a sort of animated counting-house stool, as it were—which he called a "Morgan" horse. He told me who the brute was "sired" by, and was proceeding to tell me who he was "dammed" by, but I gave him to understand that I was competent to damn the horse myself, and should probably do it very effectually before I got to the battle-ground. I mentioned to him, however, that as I was not proposing to attend a funeral, it was hardly necessary to furnish me an animal gifted with such oppressive solemnity of bearing as distinguished his "Morgan." He said in reply, that Morgan was only pensive when in the stable, but that on the road I would find him one of the liveliest horses in the world.

He enunciated the truth.

The brute "bucked" with me from the foot of Montgomery street to the Occidental Hotel. The laughter which he provoked from the crowds of citizens along the side-walks, he took for applause, and honestly made every effort in his power to deserve it, regardless of consequences.

He was very playful, but so suddenly were the creations of his fancy conceived and executed, and so much ground did he take up with them, that it was safest to behold them from a distance. In the selfsame moment of time, he shot his heels through the side of a street-car, and then backed himself into Barry and Patten's and sat down on the free-lunch table.

Such was the length of this Morgan's legs.

Between the Occidental and the Lick House, having become thoroughly interested in his work, he planned and carried out a series of the most extraordinary maneuvres ever suggested by the brain of any horse. He arched his neck and went tripping daintily across the street sideways, "rairing up" on his hind legs occasionally, in a very disagreeable way, and looking into the second-story windows. He finally waltzed into the large ice cream saloon opposite the Lick House, and——

But the memory of that perilous voyage hath caused me to digress from the proper subject of this paper, which is the great prize-fight between Governors Low and Stanford. I will resume.

After an infinitude of fearful adventures, the history of which would fill many columns of this newspaper, I finally arrived at the Seal Rock Point at a quarter to ten—two hours and a half out from San Francisco, and not less gratified than surprised that I ever got there at all—and anchored my noble Morgan to a boulder on the hill-side. I had to swathe his head in blankets also, because, while my back was turned for a single moment, he developed another atrocious trait of his most remarkable character. He tried to eat little Augustus Maltravers Jackson, the "humbly" but interesting offspring of Hon. J. Belvidere Jackson, a wealthy barber from San Jose. It would have been a comfort to me to leave the infant to his fate, but I did not feel able to pay for him.

When I reached the battle-ground, the great champions were already stripped and prepared for the "mill." Both were in splendid condition, and displayed a redundancy of muscle about the breast and arms which was delightful to the eye of the sportive connoisseur. They were well matched. Adepts said that Stanford's "heft" and tall stature were fairly offset by Low's superior litheness and activity. From their heads to the Union colors around their waists, their costumes were similar to that of the Greek Slave; from thence down they were clad in flesh-colored tights and grenadier boots.

The ring was formed upon the beautiful level sandy beach above the Cliff House, and within twenty paces of the snowy surf of the broad Pacific ocean, which was spotted here and there with monstrous sea-lions attracted shoreward by curiosity concerning the vast multitudes of people collected in the vicinity.

At five minutes past ten, Brigadier General Wright, the Referee, notified the seconds to bring their men "up to the scratch." They did so, amid the shouts of the populace, the noise whereof rose high above the roar of the sea.

FIRST ROUND.—The pugilists advanced to the centre of the ring, shook hands, retired to their respective corners, and at the call of the time-keeper, came forward and went at it. Low dashed out handsomely with his left and gave Stanford a paster in the eye, and at the same moment his adversary mashed him in the ear. [These singular phrases are entirely proper, Mr. Editor—I find them in the copy of "Bell's Life in London" now lying before me.] After some beautiful sparring, both parties went down—that is to say, they went down to the bottle-holders, Stewart and Field, and took a drink.

SECOND ROUND.—Stanford launched out a well intended plunger, but Low parried it admirably and instantly busted him in the snoot. [Cries of "Bully for the Marysville Infant!"] After some lively fibbing (both of them are used to it in political life,) the combatants went to grass. [See 'Bell's Life.']

THIRD ROUND.—Both came up panting considerably. Low let go a terrific side-winder, but Stanford stopped it handsomely and replied with an earthquake on Low's bread-basket. [Enthusiastic shouts of "Sock it to him, my Sacramento Pet!"] More fibbing—both down.

FOURTH ROUND.—The men advanced and sparred warily for a few moments, when Stanford exposed his cocoanut an instant, and Low struck out from the shoulder and split him in the mug. [Cries of "Bully for the fat Boy!"]

FIFTH ROUND.—Stanford came up looking wicked, and let drive a heavy blow with his larboard flipper which caved in the side of his adversary's head. [Exclamations of "Hi! at him again Old Rusty!"]

From this time until the end of the conflict, there was nothing regular in the proceedings. The two champions got furiously angry, and used up each other thus:

No sooner did Low realize that the side of his head was crushed in like a dent in a plug hat, than he "went after" Stanford in the most desperate manner. With one blow of his fist he mashed his nose so far into his face that a cavity was left in its place the size and shape of an ordinary soup-bowl. It is scarcely necessary to mention that in making room for so much nose, Gov. Stanford's eyes were crowded to such a degree as to cause them to "bug out" like a grasshopper's. His face was so altered that he scarcely looked like himself at all.

I never saw such a murderous expression as Stanford's countenance now assumed; you see it was so concentrated —it had such a small number of features to spread around over. He let fly one of his battering rams and caved in the other side of Low's head. Ah me, the latter was a ghastly sight to contemplate after that—one of the boys said it looked "like a beet which somebody had trod on it."

Low was "grit" though. He dashed out with his right and stove Stanford's chin clear back even with his ears. Oh, what a horrible sight he was, gasping and reaching after his tobacco, which was away back among his under-jaw teeth.

Stanford was unsettled for a while, but he soon rallied, and watching his chance, aimed a tremendous blow at his favorite mark, which crushed in the rear of Gov. Low's head in such a way that the crown thereof projected over his spinal column like a shed.

He came up to the scratch like a man, though, and sent one of his ponderous fists crashing through his opponent's ribs and in among his vitals, and instantly afterward he hauled out poor Stanford's left lung and smacked him in the face with it.

If ever I saw an angry man in my life it was Leland Stanford. He fairly raved. He jumped at his old speciality, Gov.

Low's head; he tore it loose from his body and knocked him down with it. [Sensation in the crowd.]

Staggered by his extraordinary exertion, Gov. Stanford reeled, and before he could recover himself the headless but indomitable Low sprang forward, pulled one of his legs out by the roots, and dealt him a smashing paster over the eye with the end of it. The ever watchful Bill Stewart sallied out to the assistance of his crippled principal with a pair of crutches, and the battle went on again as fiercely as ever.

At this stage of the game the battle ground was strewn with a sufficiency of human remains to furnish material for the construction of three or four men of ordinary size, and good sound brains enough to stock a whole county like the one I came from in the noble old State of Missouri. And so dyed were the combatants in their own gore that they looked like shapeless, mutilated, red-shirted firemen.

The moment a chance offered, Low grabbed Stanford by the hair of the head, swung him thrice round and round in the air like a lasso, and then slammed him on the ground with such mighty force that he quivered all over, and squirmed painfully, like a worm; and behold, his body and such of his limbs as he had left, shortly assumed a swollen aspect like unto those of a rag doll-baby stuffed with saw-dust.

He rallied again, however, and the two desperadoes clinched and never let up until they had minced each other into such insignificant odds and ends that neither was able to distinguish his own remnants from those of his antagonist. It was awful.

Bill Stewart and Judge Field issued from their corners and gazed upon the sanguinary reminiscences in silence during several minutes. At the end of that time, having failed to discover that either champion had got the best of the fight, they threw up their sponges simultaneously, and Gen. Wright proclaimed in a loud voice that the battle was "drawn." May my ears never again be rent asunder with a burst of sound similar to that which greeted this announcement, from the multitude. Amen.

By order of Gen. Wright, baskets were procured, and Bill Stewart and Judge Field proceeded to gather up the fragments of their late principals, while I gathered up my

notes and went after my infernal horse, who had slipped his
blankets and was foraging among the neighboring children.
I——   *   *   *   *   *   *

P. S.—Messrs. Editors, I have been the victim of an infamous hoax. I have been imposed upon by that ponderous
miscreant, Mr. Frank Lawler, of the Lick House. I left my
room a moment ago, and the first man I met on the stairs was
Gov. Stanford, alive and well, and as free from mutilation as
you or I. I was speechless. Before I reached the street, I actually met Gov. Low also, with his own head on his own shoulders, his limbs intact, his inner mechanism in its proper place,
and his cheeks blooming with gorgeous robustitude. I was
amazed. But a word of explanation from him convinced me
that I had been swindled by Mr. Lawler with a detailed account of a fight which had never occurred, and was never
likely to occur; that I had believed him so implicitly as to sit
down and write it out (as other reporters have done before
me) in language calculated to deceive the public into the conviction that I was present at it myself, and to embellish it with
a string of falsehoods intended to render that deception as
plausible as possible. I ruminated upon my singular position
for many minutes, arrived at no conclusion—that is to say,
no satisfactory conclusion, except that Lawler was an accomplished knave and I was a consummate ass. I had suspected
the first before, though, and been acquainted with the latter
fact for nearly a quarter of a century.

In conclusion, permit me to apologise in the most abject
manner to the present Governor of California, to Hon. Mr.
Low, the Governor elect, to Judge Field and to Hon. Wm.
M. Stewart, for the great wrong which my natural imbecility
has impelled me to do them in penning and publishing the
foregoing sanguinary absurdity. If it were to do over again, I
don't really know that I would do it. It is not possible for me
to say how I ever managed to believe that refined and educated gentlemen like these could stoop to engage in the loathsome and degrading pastime of prize-fighting. It was just
Lawler's work, you understand—the lubberly, swelled-up effigy of a nine-days drowned man! But I shall get even with
him for this. The only excuse he offers is that he got the story
from John B. Winters, and thought of course it must be just

so—as if a future Congressman for the State of Washoe could by any possibility tell the truth! Do you know that if either of these miserable scoundrels were to cross my path while I am in this mood I would scalp him in a minute? That's me—that's my style.

October 11, 1863

A Bloody Massacre Near Carson

From Abram Curry, who arrived here yesterday afternoon from Carson, we have learned the following particulars concerning a bloody massacre which was committed in Ormsby county night before last. It seems that during the past six months a man named P. Hopkins, or Philip Hopkins, has been residing with his family in the old log house just at the edge of the great pine forest which lies between Empire City and Dutch Nick's. The family consisted of nine children— five girls and four boys—the oldest of the group, Mary, being nineteen years old, and the youngest, Tommy, about a year and a half. Twice in the past two months Mrs. Hopkins, while visiting in Carson, expressed fears concerning the sanity of her husband, remarking that of late he had been subject to fits of violence, and that during the prevalence of one of these he had threatened to take her life. It was Mrs. Hopkins' misfortune to be given to exaggeration, however, and but little attention was paid to what she said. About ten o'clock on Monday evening Hopkins dashed into Carson on horseback, with his throat cut from ear to ear, and bearing in his hand a reeking scalp from which the warm, smoking blood was still dripping, and fell in a dying condition in front of the Magnolia saloon. Hopkins expired in the course of five minutes, without speaking. The long red hair of the scalp he bore marked it as that of Mrs. Hopkins. A number of citizens, headed by Sheriff Gasherie, mounted at once and rode down to Hopkins' house, where a ghastly scene met their gaze. The scalpless corpse of Mrs. Hopkins lay across the threshold, with her head split open and her right hand almost severed from the wrist. Near her lay the ax with which the murderous deed had been committed. In one of the bedrooms six of the children were found, one in bed and the others scattered about the floor. They were all dead. Their brains had evidently been dashed out with a club, and every mark about them seemed to have been made with a blunt instrument. The children must have struggled hard for their lives, as articles of clothing and broken furniture were strewn about the room in the utmost confusion. Julia and Emma, aged respectively fourteen and seventeen, were found in the kitchen, bruised and insensible, but it is thought their recovery is possible. The eldest girl, Mary, must have taken refuge, in her terror, in the garret, as her body was found there, frightfully mutilated, and the knife with which her wounds had been inflicted still sticking in her side. The two girls, Julia and Emma, who had recovered sufficiently to be able to talk yesterday morning, state that their father knocked them down with a billet of wood and stamped on them. They think they were the first attacked. They further state that Hopkins had shown evidence of derangement all day, but had exhibited no violence. He flew into a passion and attempted to murder them because they advised him to go to bed and compose his mind. Curry says Hopkins was about forty-two years of age, and a native of Western Pennsylvania; he was always affable and polite, and until very recently we had never heard of his ill treating his family. He had been a heavy owner in the best mines of Virginia and Gold Hill, but when the San Francisco papers exposed the game of cooking dividends in order to bolster up our stocks he grew afraid and sold out, and invested to an immense amount in the Spring Valley Water Company of San Francisco. He was advised to do this by a relative of his, one of the editors of the San Francisco *Bulletin*, who had suffered pecuniarily by the dividend-cooking system as applied to the Daney Mining Company recently. Hopkins had not long ceased to own in the variou. claims on the Comstock lead, however, when several dividends were cooked on his newly acquired property, their water totally dried up, and Spring Valley stock went down to nothing. It is presumed that this misfortune drove him mad and resulted in his killing himself and the greater portion of his family. The newspapers of San Francisco permitted this water company to go on borrowing money and cooking dividends, under cover of which cunning financiers crept out of the tottering concern, leaving the crash to come upon poor and unsuspecting stockholders, without offering to expose the villainy at work. We hope the fearful massacre detailed above may prove the saddest result of their silence.

October 28, 1863

"Ingomar" Over the Mountains.
The "Argument"

During the Fall Season of Mr. Maguire's Dramatic troupe at his new Opera House in Virginia City, the *Territorial Enterprise* has indulged its readers with an extraordinary succession of humorous, pungent and peculiar *critiques*. The player-folk presented "Ingomar, the Barbarian," and "Mark Twain" did the piece after this funny fashion:

ACT I.—Mrs. Claughley appears in the costume of a healthy Greek matron (from Limerick). She urges Parthenia, her daughter, to marry Polydor, and save her father from being sold out by the sheriff—the old man being in debt for assessments.

Scene 2.—Polydor—who is a wealthy, spindle-shanked, stingy old stockbroker—prefers his suit and is refused by the Greek maiden—by the accomplished Greek maiden, we may say, since she speaks English without any perceptible foreign accent.

Scene 3.—The Comanches capture Parthenia's father, old Myron (who is the chief and only blacksmith in his native village), they tear him from his humble cot, and carry him away, to Reese River. They hold him as a slave. It will cost thirty ounces of silver to get him out of soak.

Scene 4.—Dusty times in the Myron family. Their house is mortgaged—they are without dividends—they cannot "stand the raise."

Parthenia, in this extremity, applies to Polydor. He sneeringly advises her to shove out after her exiled parent herself.

She shoves!

ACT II.—Camp of the Comanches. In the foreground, several of the tribe throwing dice for tickets in Wright's Gift Entertainment. In the background, old Myron packing faggots on a jack. The weary slave weeps—he sighs—he slobbers. Grief lays her heavy hand upon him.

Scene 2.—Comanches on the war-path, headed by the Chief, Ingomar. Parthenia arrives and offers to remain as a hostage while old Myron returns home and borrows thirty

59

dollars to pay his ransom with. It was pleasant to note the varieties of dress displayed in the costumes of Ingomar and his comrades. It was also pleasant to observe that in those ancient times the better class of citizens were able to dress in ornamental carriage robes, and even the rank and file indulged in Benkert boots, albeit some of the latter appeared not to have been blacked for several days.

Scene 3.—Parthenia and Ingomar alone in the woods. "Two souls with but a single thought, etc." She tells him that is love. He "can't see it."

Scene 4.—The thing works around about as we expected it would in the first place. Ingomar gets stuck after Parthenia.

Scene 5.—Ingomar declares his love—he attempts to embrace her—she waves him off, gently, but firmly—she remarks, "Not too brash, Ing., not too brash, now!" Ingomar subsides. They finally flee away, and hie them to Parthenia's home.

Acts III and IV.—Joy! joy! From the summit of a hill, Parthenia beholds once more the spires and domes of Silver City.

Scene 2.—Silver City. Enter Myron. Tableau! Myron begs for an extension on his note—he has not yet raised the whole ransom, but he is ready to pay two dollars and a half on account.

Scene 3.—Myron tells Ingomar he must shuck himself, and dress like a Christian; he must shave; he must work, he must give up his sword! His rebellious spirit rises. Behold Parthenia tames it with the mightier spirit of Love. Ingomar weakens—he lets down—he is utterly demoralized.

Scene 4.—Enter old Timarch, Chief of Police. He offers Ingomar—but this scene is too noble to be trifled with in burlesque.

Scene 5.—Polydor presents his bill—213 drachmas. Busted again—the old man cannot pay. Ingomar compromises by becoming the slave of Polydor.

Scene 6.—The Comanches again, with Thorne at their head! He asks who enslaved the Chief? Ingomar points to Polydor. Lo! Thorne seizes the trembling broker, and snatched him bald-headed!

Scene 7.—Enter the Chief of Police again. He makes a treaty with the Comanches. He gives them a ranch apiece. He decrees that they shall build a town on the American Flat, and appoints great Ingomar to be its Mayor! [Applause by the supes.]

Scene 8.—Grand tableau—Comanches, police, Pi-Utes, and citizens generally—Ingomar and Parthenia hanging together in the centre. The old thing. The old poetical quotation, we mean. They double on it—Ingomar observing "Two souls with but a single Thought," and she slinging in the other line, "Two Hearts that Beat as one." Thus united at last in a fond embrace, they sweetly smiled upon the orchestra and the curtain fell.

November 29, 1863

Miss Clapp's School

By authority of an invitation from Hon. Wm. M. Gillespie, member of the House Committee on Colleges and Common Schools, I accompanied that statesman on an unofficial visit to the excellent school of Miss Clapp and Mrs. Cutler, this afternoon. The air was soft and balmy—the sky was cloudless and serene—the odor of flowers floated upon the idle breeze—the glory of the sun descended like a benediction upon mountain and meadow and plain—the wind blew like the very devil, and the day was generally disagreeable.

The school—however, I will mention, first that a charter for an educational institution to be called the Sierra Seminary, was granted to Miss Clapp during the Legislative session of 1861, and a bill will be introduced while the present Assembly is in session, asking an appropriation of $20,000 to aid the enterprise. Such a sum of money could not be more judiciously expended, and I doubt not the bill will pass.

The present school is a credit both to the teachers and the town. It now numbers about forty pupils, I should think, and is well and systematically conducted. The exercises this afternoon were of a character not likely to be unfamiliar to the free American citizen who has a fair recollection of how he used to pass his Friday afternoons in the days of his youth. The tactics have undergone some changes, but these variations are not important. In former times a fellow took his place in the luminous spelling class in the full consciousness that if he spelled cat with a "k," or indulged in any other little orthographical eccentricities of a similar nature, he would be degraded to the foot or sent to his seat; whereas, he keeps his place in the ranks now, in such cases, and his punishment is simply to " 'bout face." Johnny Eaves stuck to his first position, to-day, long after the balance of the class had rounded to, but he subsequently succumbed to the word "nape," which he persisted in ravishing of its final vowel. There was nothing irregular about that. Your rightly-constructed school-boy will spell a multitude of hard words without hesitating once, and then lose his grip and miss fire on the easiest one in the book.

The fashion of reading selections of prose and poetry remains the same; and so does the youthful manner of doing that sort of thing. Some pupils read poetry with graceful ease and correct expression, and others place the rising and falling inflection at measured intervals, as if they had learned the lesson on a "see-saw;" but then they go undulating through a stanza with such an air of unctuous satisfaction, that it is a comfort to be around when they are at it.

> "The boy—stoo-dawn—the bur—ning deck—
> When-sawl—but *him* had fled—
>   The flames—that shook—the battle—zreck—
> Shone round—him *o'er*—the dead."

That is the old-fashioned *impressive* style—stately, slow-moving and solemn. It is in vogue yet among scholars of tender age. It always will be. Ever since Mrs. Hemans wrote that verse, it has suited the pleasure of juveniles to emphasize the word "him," and lay atrocious stress upon that other word "o'er," whether she liked it or not; and I am prepared to believe that they will continue this practice unto the end of time, and with the same indifference to Mrs. Hemans' opinions about it, or any body's else.

They sing in school, now-a-days, which is an improvement upon the ancient regime; and they don't catch flies and throw spit-balls at the teacher, as they used to do in my time—which is another improvement, in a general way. Neither do the boys and girls keep a sharp look-out on each other's shortcomings and report the same at headquarters, as was a custom of by-gone centuries. And this reminds me of Gov. Nye's last anecdote, fulminated since the delivery of his message, and consequently not to be found in that document. The company were swapping old school reminiscences, and in due season they got to talking about that extinct species of tell-tales that were once to be found in all minor educational establishments, and who never failed to detect and impartially denounce every infraction of the rules that occurred among their mates. The Governor said that he threw a casual glance at a pretty girl on the next bench one day, and she complained to the teacher—which was entirely characteristic, you know. Says she, "Mister Jones, Warren Nye's looking at me." Whereupon, without a suggestion from anybody, up jumped an infamous, lisping, tow-headed young miscreant, and says he, "Yeth, thir, I *thee* him do it!" I doubt if the old original boy got off that ejaculation with more gusto than the Governor throws into it.

The "compositions" read to-day were as exactly like the compositions I used to hear read in our school as one baby's nose is exactly like all other babies' noses. I mean the old principal ear-marks were all there: the cutting to the bone of the subject with the very first gash, without any preliminary foolishness in the way of a gorgeous introductory; the inevitable and persevering tautology; the brief, monosyllabic sentences (beginning, as a very general thing, with the pronoun "I"); the penchant for presenting rigid, uncompromising facts for the consideration of the hearer, rather than ornamental fancies; the depending for the success of the composition upon its general merits, without tacking artificial aids to the end of it, in the shape of deductions, or conclusions, or claptrap climaxes, albeit their absence sometimes imparts to these essays the semblance of having come to an end before they were finished—of arriving at full speed at a jumping-off place and going suddenly overboard, as it were, leaving a sensation such as one feels when he stumbles without previous warning upon that infernal "To be Continued" in the midst of a thrilling magazine story. I know there are other styles of school compositions, but these are the characteristics of the style which I have in my eye at present. I do not know why this one has particularly suggested itself to my mind, unless the literary effort of one of the boys there to-day left with me an unusually vivid impression. It ran something in this wise:

COMPOSITION.

"I like horses. Where we lived before we came here, we used to have a cutter and horses. We used to ride in it. I like winter. I like snow. I used to have a pony all to myself, where I used to live before I came here. Once it drifted a good deal—very deep—and when it stopped I went out and got in it."

That was all. There was no climax to it, except the spasmodic bow which the tautological little student jerked at the school as he closed his labors.

Two remarkably good compositions were read. Miss P.'s was much the best of these—but aside from its marked literary excellence, it possessed another merit which was peculiarly gratifying to my feelings just at that time. Because it took the conceit out of young Gillespie as completely as perspiration takes the starch out of a shirt-collar. In his insufferable vanity, that feeble member of the House of Representatives had been assuming imposing attitudes, and beaming upon the pupils with an expression of benignant imbecility which was calculated to inspire them with the conviction that there was only one guest of any consequence in the house. Therefore, it was an unspeakable relief to me to see him forced to shed his dignity. Concerning the composition, however. After detailing the countless pleasures which had fallen to her lot during the holidays, the authoress finished with a proviso, in substance as follows—I have forgotten the precise language: "But I have no cheerful reminiscences of Christmas. It was dreary, monotonous and insipid to the last degree. Mr. Gillespie called early, and remained the greater part of the day!" You should have seen the blooming Gillespie wilt when that literary bombshell fell in his camp! The charm of the thing lay in the fact that that last naive sentence was the only suggestion offered in the way of accounting for the dismal character of the occasion. However, to my mind it was sufficient—entirely sufficient.

Since writing the above, I have seen the architectural plans and specifications for Miss Clapp and Mrs. Cutler's proposed "Sierra Seminary" building. It will be a handsome two-story edifice, one hundred feet square, and will accommodate forty "boarders" and any number of pupils beside, who may board elsewhere. Constructed of wood, it will cost $12,000; or of stone, $18,000. Miss Clapp has devoted ten acres of ground to the use and benefit of the institution.

I sat down intending to write a dozen pages of variegated news. I have about accomplished the task—all except the "variegated." I have economised in the matter of current news of the day, considerably more than I purposed to do, for every item of that nature remains stored away in my mind in a very unwritten state, and will afford unnecessarily ample material for another letter. It is useless material, though, I suspect, because, inasmuch as I have failed to incorporate it into this, I fear me I shall not feel industrious enough to weave out of it another letter until it has become too stale to be interesting. Well, never mind—we must learn to take an absorbing delight in educational gossip; nine-tenths of the revenues of the Territory go into the bottomless gullet of that ravenous school fund, you must bear in mind.

MARK TWAIN.

c. January 19, 1864

Doings in Nevada

CARSON CITY, NEVADA TERRITORY,
January 4, 1864.

Editor T. T:—The concentrated wisdom of Nevada Territory (known unto and respected by the nations of the earth as "Washoe") assembled in convention at Carson recently, and framed a constitution. It was an excellent piece of work in some respects, but it had one or two unfortunate defects which debarred it from assuming to be an immaculate conception. The chief of these was a clause authorizing the taxing of the mines. The people will not stand that. There are some 30,000 gold and silver mining incorporations here, or mines, or claims, or which you please, or all, if it suits you better. Very little of the kind of property thus represented is improved yet, or "developed" as we call it; it will take two or three years to get it in a developed and paying condition, and will require an enormous outlay of capital to accomplish such a result. And until it does begin to pay dividends, the people will not consent that it shall be burdened and hindered by taxation. Therefore, I am satisfied they will refuse to ratify our new constitution on the 19th inst.

It had an amusing feature in it, also. That was the Great Seal of the State. It had snow-capped mountains in it; and tunnels, and shafts, and pickaxes, and quartz-mills, and pack-trains, and mule-teams. These things were good; what there were of them. And it had railroads in it, and telegraphs, and stars, and suspension-bridges, and other romantic fictions foreign to sand and sage-brush. But the richest of it was the motto. It took them thirty days to decide whether it should be *"Volens et Potens"* (which they said meant "Able and Willing"), or "The Union Must and Shall be Preserved." Either would have been presumptuous, and surpassingly absurd just at present. Because we are not able and willing, thus far, to do a great deal more than locate wild-cat mining-claims and reluctantly sell them to confiding strangers at a ruinous sacrifice—of conscience. And if it were left to us to preserve the Union, in case the balance of the country failed in the attempt, I seriously believe we couldn't do it. Possibly, we might make it mighty warm for the Confederacy if it came prowling around here, but ultimately we would have to forsake our high trust, and quit preserving the Union. I am confident of it. And I have thought the matter over a good deal, off and on, as we say in Paris. We have an animal here whose surname is the "jackass rabbit". It is three feet long, has legs like a counting-house stool, ears of monstrous length, and no tail to speak of. It is swifter than a greyhound, and as meek and harmless as an infant. I might mention, also, that it is as handsome as most infants: however, it would be foreign to the subject, and I do not know that a remark of that kind would be popular in all circles. Let it pass, then—I will say nothing about it, though it would be a great comfort to me to do it, if people would consider the source and overlook it. Well, somebody proposed as a substitute for that pictorial Great Seal, a figure of a jackass-rabbit reposing in the shade of his native sage-brush, with the motto "*Volens* enough, but not so d——d *Potens*". Possibly that had something to do with the rejection of one of the proposed mottoes by the Convention.

STATE NOMINATING CONVENTION.

We do not fool away much time in this country. As soon as the Constitution was duly framed and ready for ratification or rejection by the people, a convention to nominate candidates for State offices met at Carson. It finished its labors day before yesterday. The following nominations were made: For Governor, M. N. Mitchell; Lieutenant-Governor, M. S. Thompson; Secretary of State, Orion Clemens; Treasurer, Wm. B. Hickok; Member of Congress, John B. Winters; Superintendant Public Instruction, Rev. A. F. White. Now, that ticket will be elected, but the Constitution won't. In that case, what are we to do with these fellows? We cannot let them starve. They are on our hands, and are entitled to our charity and protection. It is different with them from what it is with other people, because, although the Almighty created them, and used to care for and watch over them, no doubt it was long, long ago, and he may not recollect them now. And I think it is our duty to look after them, and see that they do not suffer. Besides, they all owe me something for traducing and villifying them in the public prints, and thus exciting sympathy for them on the score of persecution, and securing their nomination; and I do not think it right or just that I should be expected to do people favors without being paid for it, merely because those favors failed to produce marketable fruit. No, Sir; I elected those fellows, and I shall take care that I am fairly remunerated for it. Now, if you know any small State, lying around anywhere, that I could get a contract on for the running of it, you will oblige me by mentioning it in your next. You can say that I have all the machinery on hand necessary to the carrying on of a third-rate State; say, also, that it is comparatively new, portions of it never having been used at all; also, that I will part with it on pretty nearly any terms, as my constitution is prostrated, and I am anxious to go into some other business. And say my various State officers are honest and capable—however, don't say that—just leave that out—let us not jest on a serious matter like this. But you might put in a little advertisement for me in the following shape, for instance. And it would be a real kindness to me if you would be so good as to call attention to it in your editorial columns. You see I am a sort of an orphan, away out here, struggling along on my own hook, as it were. My mother lives in St. Louis. She is sixty years of age, and a member of the Presbyterian Church. She takes no pride in being gay; in fact, she don't rush around much in society, now. However, I do not ask any man's sympathy on that account. I was simply going to offer my little advertisement.

FOR SALE OR RENT.

One Governor, entirely new. Attended Sunday-school in his youth, and still remembers it. Never drinks. In other respects, however, his habits are good. As Commander-in-Chief of the Militia, he would be an ornament. Most Governors are.

One Lieutenant-Governor—also new. He has other merits, of minor importance, beside. No objection to going into the country—or elsewhere.

One Secretary of State. An old, experienced hand at the business. Has edited a newspaper, and been Secretary and Governor of Nevada Territory—consequently, is capable; and also consequently, will bear watching, is not bigoted—has no particular set of religious principles—or any other kind.

One small Treasurer—(second-hand). Will make a good officer. Was Treasurer once before, in the States. Took excellent care of the funds—has them yet.

One Member of Congress—new, but smart. Is sometimes called "Old Smarty, from Mud Springs". Has read every newspaper printed in Nevada Territory for two years, and knows all about the war. Would be a good hand to advise the President. Is young, ardent, ambitious, and on it. No objection to traveling, provided his mileage is paid.

One Superintendent of Public Instruction—good as new. Understands all the different systems of teaching, and does not approve of them. It is his laudable boast that he is a self-made man. It has been said of him by his admirers that God Almighty never made such a man. It is probably so. He is the soul of honor, and is willing to take greenbacks at par. No objection to making himself generally useful; can preach, if required.

Also, a large and well-selected assortment of State Legislators, Supreme Judges, Comptrollers, and such gimcracks, handy to have about a State Government, all of which are for sale or rent on the mildest possible terms, as, under present circumstances, they are of no earthly use to the subscriber.

For further particulars, address

MARK TWAIN, Carson, N.T.

OUR CONSTITUTION ILLEGAL.

Now, joking aside, these are all good, honest, capable men, and would reflect credit upon the several positions for which they have been nominated; but then the people are not going to ratify the Constitution; and consequently, they will never get a chance. I am glad that such is the case. In the Legislature, last year, I was wielding the weapon which, under just such circumstances, is mightier than the sword, at the time that the Act authorizing the calling together of a Convention to form a State Constitution was passed; and I know the secret history of that document. It was reported back from the Committee with a lot of blanks in it (for dates, apportionment, and number of members, amount of money appropriated to defray expenses of the Convention, etc.). Both Houses passed the Bill without filling those blanks; it was duly enrolled, brought back, and signed by the presiding officers of the Legislature, and then transmitted—a worthless, meaningless, and intentionally powerless instrument—to Gov. Nye for his signature—at night. And lo! a miracle. When the bill reached the Governor, there was not a solitary blank in it! Who filled them, is—is a great moral question for instance; but the enrolling clerk did not do it at any rate, since the amendations are in an unknown and atrocious handwriting. Therefore, the bill was a fraud; the convention created by it was a fraud; the fruit of the convention was an illegitimate infant constitution and a dead one at that; a State reared upon such a responsibility would be a fraudulent and impotent institution, and the result would be that we should ultimately be kicked back into a territorial condition again on account of it. Wherefore, when men say: "Let our constitution slide for the present", we say Amen.

February 7, 1864

Those Blasted Children

LICK HOUSE, SAN FRANCISCO, Wednesday, 1863.
EDITORS T. T.:—No. 165 is a pleasant room. It is situated at
the head of a long hall, down which, on either side, are similar rooms occupied by sociable bachelors, and here and there
one tenanted by an unsociable nurse or so. Charley Creed
sleeps in No. 157. He is my time-piece—or, at least, his boots
are. If I look down the hall and see Charley's boots still before his door, I know it is early yet, and I may hie me sweetly
to bed again. But if those unerring boots are gone, I know it
is after eleven o'clock, and time for me to be rising with the
lark. This reminds me of the lark of yesterday and last night,
which was altogether a different sort of bird from the one I
am talking about now. Ah me! Summer girls and summer
dresses, and summer scenes at the "Willows", Seal Rock
Point, and the grim sea-lions wallowing in the angry surf;
glimpses through the haze of stately ships far away at sea; a
dash along the smooth beach, and the exhilaration of watching the white waves come surging ashore, and break into
seething foam about the startled horse's feet; reveries beside
the old wreck, half buried in sand, and compassion for the
good ship's fate; home again in a soft twilight, oppressed
with the odor of flowers—home again to San Francisco,
drunk, perhaps, but not disorderly. Dinner at six, with ladies
and gentlemen, dressed with faultless taste and elegance,
and all drunk, apparently, but very quiet and well-bred—unaccountably so, under the circumstances, it seemed to my
cloudy brain. Many things happened after that, I remember—
such as visiting some of their haunts with those dissipated
Golden Era fellows, and—

Here come those young savages again—those noisy and
inevitable children. God be with them!—or they with him,
rather, if it be not asking too much. They are another time-
piece of mine. It is two o'clock now; they are invested with
their regular lunch, and have come up here to settle it. I will
soothe my troubled spirit with a short season of blasphemy,
after which I will expose their infamous proceedings with a
relentless pen. They have driven me from labor many and

many a time; but behold! the hour of retribution is at hand.

That is young Washington Billings, now—a little dog in long flaxen curls and Highland costume.

"Hi, Johnny! look through the keyhole! here's that feller with a long nose, writing again—less stir him up!" [A double kick against the door—a grand infant war-hoop in full chorus —and then a clatter of scampering feet down the echoing corridors.] Ah—one of them has fallen, and hurt himself. I hear the intelligent foreign nurse boxing his ears for it (the parents, Mr. and Mrs. Kerosene, having gone up to Sacramento on the evening boat, and left their offspring properly cared for.)

Here they come again, as soldiers—infantry. I know there are not more than thirty or forty of them, yet they are under no sort of discipline, and they make noise enough for a thousand. Young Oliver Higgins is in command. They assault my works—they try to carry my position by storm—they finally draw off with boistrous cheers, to harrass a handful of skirmishers thrown out by the enemy—a bevy of chambermaids.

Once more they come trooping down the hall. This time as cavalry. They must have captured and disarmed the skirmishers, for half my young ruffians are mounted on broomsticks. They make a reconnoissance in force. They attack my premises in a body, but they achieve nothing approaching a success. I am too strongly intrenched for them.

They invest my stronghold, and lay siege to it—that is to say, they sit down before my camp, and betake themselves to the pastimes of youth. All talking at once, as they do, their conversation is amusing, but not instructive to me.

"Ginn me some o' that you're eat'n." "I won't—you wouldn't lemme play with that dead rat, the peanut-boy give you yesterday." "Well! I don't care; I reckon I know summun't you don't; Oho, Mr. Smarty, 'n' I ain't a goin' to tell you, neither; now, see what you got by it; it's summun't my ma said about your ma, too. I'll tell you, if you'll gimme ever so little o' that, will you? Well." (I imagine from the break in this conversation, while the other besiegers go on talking noisily, that a compromise is being effected.) "There, don't take so much. Now, what'd she say?" "Why, ma told my pa 't if your ma is so mighty rich now she wasn't nobody till she come to Sanf'cisco. That's what she said." "Your ma's a big story-teller, 'n' I'm goin' jes' as straight as I can walk, 'n' tell my ma. You'll see what she'll do." (I foresee a diversion in one or two family circles.) "Flora Low, you quit pulling that doll's legs out, it's mine." "Well, take your old doll, then. I'd thank you to know, Miss Florence Hillyer, 't my pa's Governor, 'n' I can have a thousan' dolls if I want to, 'n' gold ones, too, or silver, or anything." (More trouble brewing.) "What do I care for that. I guess my pa could be Governor, too, if he wanted to; but he don't. He owns two hundred feet in the Chollar, 'n' he's got lots more silver mines in Washoe besides. He could fill this house full of silver, clear up to that chandelier, so he could, now, Miss." "You, Bob Miller, you leg go that string—I'll smack you in the eye." "You will, will you? I'd like to see you try it. You jes' hit me if you dare!" "You lay your hands on me, 'n' I will hit you." "Now I've laid my hand on you, why don't you hit?" "Well, I mean, if you lay 'em on me so's to hurt." "Ah-h! you're afraid, that's the reason." "No I ain't, neither, you big fool." (Ah, now they're at it. Discord shall invade the ranks of my foes, and they shall fall by their own hands. It appears from the sound without that two nurses have made a descent upon the combatants, and are bearing them from the field. The nurses are abusing each other. One boy proclaims that the other struck him when he wasn't doin' nothin'; and the other boy says he was called a big fool. Both are going right straight, and tell their pa's. Verily, things are going along as comfortably as I could wish, now.) "Sandy Baker, I know what makes your pa's hair kink so; it's 'cause he's a mulatter; I heard my ma say so." "It's a lie!" (Another row, and more skirmishing with the nurses. Truly, happiness flows in upon me most bountifully this day.) "Hi, boys! here comes a Chinaman!" (God pity any China-man who chances to come in the way of the boys hereabout, for the eye of the law regardeth him not, and the youth of California in their generation are down upon him.) "Now, boys! grab his clothes basket—take him by the tail!" (There they go, now, like a pack of young demons; they have confis-cated the basket, and the dismayed Chinaman is towing half the tribe down the hall by his cue. Rejoice, O my soul, for behold, all things are lovely, etc.—to speak after the manner of the vulgar.) "Oho, Miss Susy Badger, my uncle Tom's goin' across the bay to Oakland, 'n' down to Santa Clara, 'n' Alamedy, 'n' San Leandro, 'n' everywheres—all over the world, 'n' he's goin' to take me with him—he said so." "Humph! that ain't noth'n—I been there. My aunt Mary'd take me to any place I wanted to go, if I wanted her to, but I don't; she's got horses 'n' things—O, ever so many!—millions of 'em; but my ma says it don't look well for little girls to be always gadd'n about. That's why you don't ever see me goin' to places like some girls do. I despise to—" (The end is at hand; the nurses have massed themselves on the left; they move in serried phalanx on my besiegers; they surround them, and capture the last miscreant—horse, foot, and dragoons, munitions of war, and camp equipage. The victory is complete. They are gone—my castle is no longer menaced, and the rover is free. I am here, staunch and true!)

It is a living wonder to me that I haven't scalped some of those children before now. I expect I would have done it, but then I hardly felt well enough acquainted with them. I scarcely ever show them any attention anyhow, unless it is to throw a boot-jack at them or some little nonsense of that kind when I happen to feel playful. I am confident I would have destroyed several of them though, only it might appear as if I were making most too free.

I observe that that young officer of the Pacific Squadron—the one with his nostrils turned up like port-holes—has become a great favorite with half the mothers in the house, by imparting to them much useful information concerning the manner of doctoring children among the South American savages. His brother is brigadier in the Navy. The drab-complexioned youth with the Solferino mustache has corraled the other half with the Japanese treatment. The more I think of it the more I admire it. Now, I am no peanut. I have an idea that I could invent some little remedies that would stir up a commotion among these women, if I chose to try. I always had a good general notion of physic, I believe. It is one of my natural gifts, too, for I have never studied a single day under a regular physician. I will jot down a few items here, just to see how likely I am to succeed.

In the matter of measles, the idea is, to bring it out—bring it to the surface. Take the child and fill it up with saffron tea.

Add something to make the patient sleep—say a table-spoonful of arsenic. Don't rock it—it will sleep anyhow.

As far as brain fever is concerned: This is a very dangerous disease, and must be treated with decision and dispatch. In every case where it has proved fatal, the sufferer invariably perished. You must strike at the root of the distemper. Remove the brains; and then— Well, that will be sufficient— that will answer—just remove the brains. This remedy has never been known to fail. It was originated by the lamented J. W. Macbeth, Thane of Cawdor, Scotland, who refers to it thus: "Time was, that when the brains were out, the man would die; but, under different circumstances, I think not; and, all things being equal, I believe you, my boy." Those were his last words.

Concerning worms: Administer a catfish three times a week. Keep the room very quiet; the fish won't bite if there is the least noise.

When you come to fits, take no chances on fits. If the child has them bad, soak it in a barrel of rain-water over night, or a good article of vinegar. If this does not put an end to its troubles, soak it a week. You can't soak a child too much when it has fits.

In cases wherein an infant stammers, remove the under-jaw. In proof of the efficacy of this treatment, I append the following certificate, voluntarily forwarded to me by Mr. Zeb. Leavenworth, of St. Louis, Mo.:

"St. Louis, May 26, 1863.

"Mr. Mark Twain—Dear Sir:—Under Providence, I am beholden to you for the salvation of my Johnny. For a matter of three years, that suffering child stuttered to that degree that it was a pain and a sorrow to me to hear him stagger over the sacred name of 'p-p-p-pap'. It troubled me so that I neglected my business; I refused food; I took no pride in my dress, and my hair actually began to fall off. I could not rest; I could not sleep. Morning, noon, and night, I did nothing but moan pitifully, and murmur to myself: 'Hell's fire! what am I going to do about my Johnny?' But in a blessed hour you appeared unto me like an angel from the skies; and without hope of reward, revealed your sovereign remedy— and that very day, I sawed off my Johnny's under-jaw. May

Heaven bless you, noble Sir. It afforded instant relief; and my Johnny has never stammered since. I honestly believe he never will again. As to disfigurement, he does seem to look sorter ornery and hog-mouthed, but I am too grateful in having got him effectually saved from that dreadful stuttering, to make much account of small matters. Heaven speed you in your holy work of healing the afflictions of humanity. And if my poor testimony can be of any service to you, do with it as you think will result in the greatest good to our fellow-creatures. Once more, Heaven bless you.

"Zeb. Leavenworth."

Now, that has such a plausible ring about it, that I can hardly keep from believing it myself. I consider it a very fair success.

Regarding Cramps. Take your offspring—let the same be warm and dry at the time—and immerse it in a commodious soup-tureen filled with the best quality of camphene. Place it over a slow fire, and add reasonable quantities of pepper, mustard, horse-radish, saltpetre, strychnine, blue vitriol, aqua fortis, a quart of flour, and eight or ten fresh eggs, stirring it from time to time, to keep up a healthy reaction. Let it simmer fifteen minutes. When your child is done, set the tureen off, and allow the infallible remedy to cool. If this does not confer an entire insensibility to cramps, you must lose no time, for the case is desperate. Take your offspring, and parboil it. The most vindictive cramps cannot survive this treatment; neither can the subject, unless it is endowed with an iron constitution. It is an extreme measure, and I always dislike to resort to it. I never parboil a child until everything else has failed to bring about the desired end.

Well, I think those will do to commence with. I can branch out, you know, when I get more confidence in myself.

O infancy! thou art beautiful, thou art charming, thou art lovely to contemplate! But thoughts like these recall sad memories of the past, of the halcyon days of my childhood, when I was a sweet, prattling innocent, the pet of a dear home-circle, and the pride of the village.

Enough, enough! I must weep, or this bursting heart will break.

—MARK TWAIN.

February 21, 1864

Washoe. —"Information Wanted"

"SPRINGFIELD, MO., April 12.

"DEAR SIR:—My object in writing to you is to have you give me a full history of Nevada: What is the character of its climate? What are the productions of the earth? Is it healthy? What diseases do they die of mostly? Do you think it would be advisable for a man who can make a living in Missouri to emigrate to that part of the country? There are several of us who would emigrate there in the spring if we could ascertain to a certainty that it is a much better country than this. I suppose you know Joel H. Smith? He used to live here; he lives in Nevada now; they say he owns considerable in a mine there. Hoping to hear from you soon, etc., I remain yours, truly,

WILLIAM ——."

DEAREST WILLIAM:—Pardon my familiarity—but that name touchingly reminds me of the loved and lost, whose name was similar. I have taken the contract to answer your letter, and although we are now strangers, I feel we shall cease to be so if we ever become acquainted with each other. The thought is worthy of attention, William. I will now respond to your several propositions in the order in which you have fulminated them.

Your object in writing is to have me give you a full history of Nevada. The flattering confidence you repose in me, William, is only equalled by the modesty of your request. I could detail the history of Nevada in five hundred pages octavo, but as you have never done me any harm, I will spare you, though it will be apparent to everybody that I would be justified in taking advantage of you if I were a mind to do it. However, I will condense. Nevada was discovered many years ago by the Mormons, and was called Carson county. It only became Nevada in 1861, by act of Congress. There is a popular tradition that God Almighty created it; but when you come to see it, William, you will think differently. Do not let that discourage you, though. The country looks something like a singed cat, owing to the scarcity of shrubbery, and also resembles that animal in the respect that it has more merits than its personal appearance would seem to indicate. The Grosch brothers found the first silver lead here in 1857. They also

78

founded Silver City, I believe. (Observe the subtle joke, William.) But the "history" of Nevada which you demand, properly begins with the discovery of the Comstock lead, which event happened nearly five years ago. The opinion now prevailing in the East that the Comstock is on the Gould & Curry is erroneous; on the contrary, the Gould & Curry is on the Comstock. Please make the correction, William. Signify to your friends, also, that all the mines here do not pay dividends as yet; you may make this statement with the utmost unyielding inflexibility—it will not be contradicted from this quarter. The population of this Territory is about 35,000, one-half of which number reside in the united cities of Virginia and Gold Hill. However, I will discontinue this history for the present, lest I get you too deeply interested in this distant land and cause you to neglect your family or your religion. But I will address you again upon the subject next year. In the meantime, allow me to answer your inquiry as to the character of our climate.

It has no character to speak of, William, and alas! in this respect it resembles many, ah, too many chambermaids in this wretched, wretched world. Sometimes we have the seasons in their regular order, and then again we have winter all the summer and summer all winter. Consequently, we have never yet come across an almanac that would just exactly fit this latitude. It is mighty regular about not raining, though, William. It will start in here in November and rain about four, and sometimes as much as seven days on a stretch; after that, you may loan out your umbrella for twelve months, with the serene confidence which a Christian feels in four aces. Sometimes the winter begins in November and winds up in June; and sometimes there is a bare suspicion of winter in March and April, and summer all the balance of the year. But as a general thing, William, the climate is good, what there is of it.

What are the productions of the earth? You mean in Nevada, of course. On our ranches here, anything can be raised that can be produced on the fertile fields of Missouri. But ranches are very scattering—as scattering, perhaps, as lawyers in heaven. Nevada, for the most part, is a barren waste of sand, embellished with melancholy sage-brush, and fenced in with snow clad mountains. But these ghastly features were the salvation of the land, William, for no rightly constituted American would have ever come here if the place had been easy of access, and none of our pioneers would have staid after they got here if they had not felt satisfied that they could not find a smaller chance for making a living anywhere else. Such is man, William, as he crops out in America.

"Is it healthy?" Yes, I think it is as healthy here as it is in any part of the West. But never permit a question of that kind to vegetate in your brain, William, because as long as providence has an eye on you, you will not be likely to die until your time comes.

"What diseases do they die of mostly?" Well, they used to die of conical balls and cold steel, mostly, but here lately erysipelas and the intoxicating bowl have got the bulge on those things, as was very justly remarked by Mr. Rising last Sunday. I will observe, for your information, William, that Mr. Rising is our Episcopal minister, and has done as much as any man among us to redeem this community from its pristine state of semi-barbarism. We are afflicted with all the diseases incident to the same latitude in the States, I believe, with one or two added and half a dozen subtracted on account of our superior altitude. However, the doctors are about as successful here, both in killing and curing, as they are anywhere.

Now, as to whether it would be advisable for a man who can make a living in Missouri to emigrate to Nevada, I confess I am somewhat mixed. If you are not content in your present condition, it naturally follows that you would be entirely satisfied if you could make either more or less than a living. You would exult in the cheerful exhilaration always produced by a change. Well, you can find your opportunity here, where, if you retain your health, and are sober and industrious, you will inevitably make more than a living, and if you don't you won't. You can rely upon this statement, William. It contemplates any line of business except the selling of tracts. You cannot sell tracts here, William; the people take no interest in tracts; the very best efforts in the tract line—even with pictures on them—have met with no encouragement here. Besides, the newspapers have been interfering; a man gets his regular text or so from the Scriptures in his paper, along with the stock sales and the war news, every day, now. If you are in the tract business, William, take no chances on Washoe; but you can succeed at anything else here.

"I suppose you know Joel H. Smith?" Well—the fact is—I believe I don't. Now isn't that singular? Isn't it very singular? And he owns "considerable" in a mine here, too. Happy man. Actually owns in a mine here in Nevada Territory, and I never even heard of him. Strange—strange—do you know, William, it is the strangest thing that ever happened to me? And then he not only owns in a mine, but owns "considerable;" that is the strangest part about it—how a man could own considerable in a mine in Washoe and I not know anything about it. He is a lucky dog, though. But I strongly suspect that you have made a mistake in the name; I am confident you have; you mean John Smith—I know you do; I know it from the fact that he owns considerable in a mine here, because I sold him the property at a ruinous sacrifice on the very day he arrived here from over the plains. That man will be rich one of these days. I am just as well satisfied of it as I am of any precisely similar instance of the kind that has come under my notice. I said as much to him yesterday, and he said he was satisfied of it, also. But he did not say it with that air of triumphant exultation which a heart like mine so delights to behold in one to whom I have endeavored to be a benefactor in a small way. He looked pensive a while, but, finally, says he, "Do you know, I think I'd a been a rich man long ago if they'd ever found the d—d ledge?" That was my idea about it. I always thought, and I still think, that if they ever do find that ledge, his chances will be better than they are now. I guess Smith will be all right one of these centuries, if he keeps up his assessments—he is a young man yet. Now, William, I have taken a liking to you, and I would like to sell you "considerable" in a mine in Washoe. I think I could get you a commanding interest in the "Union," Gold Hill, on easy terms. It is just the same as the "Yellow Jacket," which is one of the richest mines in the Territory. The title was in dispute between the two companies some two years ago, but that is all settled now. Let me hear from you on the subject. Greenbacks at par is as good a thing as I want. But seriously, William, don't you ever invest in a mining stock which you don't know anything about; beware of John Smith's experience.

You hope to hear from me soon? Very good. I shall also hope to hear from you soon, about that little matter above referred to. Now, William, ponder this epistle well; never mind the sarcasm, here and there, and the nonsense, but reflect upon the plain facts set forth, because they *are* facts, and are meant to be so understood and believed.

Remember me affectionately to your friends and relations, and especially to your venerable grand-mother, with whom I have not the pleasure to be acquainted—but that is of no consequence, you know. I have been in your town many a time, and all the towns of the neighboring counties—the hotel keepers will recollect me vividly. Remember me to them—I bear them no animosity.

Yours, affectionately,

MARK TWAIN.

c. May 1, 1864

The Evidence in the Case of Smith vs. Jones

REPORTED BY MARK TWAIN.

I reported this trial simply for my own amusement, one idle day last week, and without expecting to publish any portion of it—but I have seen the facts in the case so distorted and misrepresented in the daily papers that I feel it my duty to come forward and do what I can to set the plaintiff and the defendant right before the public. This can best be done by submitting the plain, unembellished statements of the witnesses as given under oath before his Honor Judge Shepheard, in the Police Court, and leaving the people to form their own judgment of the matters involved, unbiased by argument or suggestion of any kind from me.

There is that nice sense of justice and that ability to discriminate between right and wrong, among the masses, which will enable them, after carefully reading the testimony I am about to set down here, to decide without hesitation which is the innocent party and which the guilty in the remarkable case of Smith vs. Jones, and I have every confidence that before this paper shall have been out of the printing-press twenty-four hours, the high court of The People, from whose decision there is no appeal, will have swept from the innocent man all taint of blame or suspicion, and cast upon the guilty one a deathless infamy.

To such as are not used to visiting the Police Court, I will observe that there is nothing inviting about the place, there being no rich carpets, no mirrors, no pictures, no elegant sofa or arm-chairs to lounge in, no free lunch—and in fact, nothing to make a man who has been there once desire to go again—except in cases where his bail is heavier than his fine is likely to be, under which circumstances he naturally has a tendency in that direction again, of course, in order to recover the difference.

There is a pulpit at the head of the hall, occupied by a handsome, gray-haired Judge, with a faculty of appearing pleasant and impartial to the disinterested spectator, and prejudiced and frosty to the last degree to the prisoner at the bar.

To the left of the pulpit is a long table for reporters; in front of the pulpit the clerks are stationed, and in the centre of the hall a nest of lawyers. On the left again are pine benches behind a railing, occupied by seedy white men, ne-groes, Chinamen, Kanakas—in a word, by the seedy and de-jected of all nations—and in a corner is a box where more can be had when they are wanted.

On the right are more pine benches, for the use of prison-ers, and their friends and witnesses.

An officer, in a gray uniform, and with a star upon his breast, guards the door.

A holy calm pervades the scene.

The case of Smith vs. Jones being called, each of these par-ties (stepping out from among the other seedy ones) gave the Court a particular and circumstantial account of how the whole thing occurred, and then sat down.

The two narratives differed from each other.

In reality, I was half persuaded that these men were talking about two separate and distinct affairs altogether, inasmuch as no single circumstance mentioned by one was even remotely hinted at by the other.

Mr. Alfred Sowerby was then called to the witness-stand, and testified as follows:

"I was in the saloon at the time, your Honor, and I see this man Smith come up all of a sudden to Jones, who warn't saying a word, and split him in the snoot—"

Lawyer.—"Did what, Sir?"

Witness.—"Busted him in the snoot."

Lawyer.—"What do you mean by such language as that? When you say that the plaintiff suddenly approached the de-fendant, who was silent at the time, and 'busted him in the snoot,' do you mean that the plaintiff *struck* the defendant?"

Witness.—"That's me—I'm swearing to that very circum-stance—yes, your Honor, that was just the way of it. Now, for instance, as if you was Jones and I was Smith. Well, I comes up all of a sudden and says I to your Honor, says I, 'D—n your old tripe—'" [Suppressed laughter in the lobbies.]

The Court. — "Order in the court! Witness, you will confine yourself to a plain statement of the facts in this case, and refrain from the embellishments of metaphor and allegory as far as possible."

Witness. — (Considerably subdued.) — "I beg your Honor's pardon — I didn't mean to be so brash. Well, Smith comes up to Jones all of a sudden and mashed him in the bugle —"

Lawyer. — "Stop! Witness, this kind of language will not do. I will ask you a plain question, and I require you to answer it simply, yes or no. Did — the — plaintiff — *strike* — the defendant? Did he *strike* him?"

Witness. — "You bet your sweet life he did. Gad! he gave him a paster in the trumpet —"

Lawyer. — "Take the witness! take the witness! take the witness! I have no further use for him."

The lawyer on the other side said he would endeavor to worry along without more assistance from Mr. Sowerby, and the witness retired to a neighboring bench.

Mr. McWilliamson was next called, and deposed as follows:

"I was a standing as close to Mr. Smith as I am to this pulpit, a-chaffing with one of the lager beer girls — Sophronia by name, being from summers in Germany, so she says, but as to that, I —"

Lawyer. — "Well, now, never mind the nativity of the lager beer girl, but state, as concisely as possible, what you know of the assault and battery."

Witness. — "Certainly — certainly. Well, German or no German, — which I'll take my oath I don't believe she is, being of a red-headed disposition, with long, bony fingers, and no more hankering after Limburger cheese than —"

Lawyer. — "Stop that driveling nonsense and stick to the assault and battery. Go on with your story."

Witness. — "Well, Sir, she — that is, Jones — he sidled up and drawed his revolver and tried to shoot the top of Smith's head off, and Smith run, and Sophronia she whalloped herself down in the saw-dust and screamed twice, just as loud as she could yell. I never see a poor creature in such distress — and then she sung out: 'O, H—ll's fire! what are they up to now? Ah, my poor dear mother, I shall never see you more!' — saying which, she jerked another yell and fainted away as dead as a wax figger. Thinks I to myself, I'll be danged if this ain't gettin' rather dusty, and I'll—"

The Court.—"We have no desire to know what you *thought*; we only wish to know what you *saw*. Are you sure Mr. Jones endeavored to shoot the top of Mr. Smith's head off?"

Witness.—"Yes, your Honor."

The Court.—"How many times did he shoot?"

Witness.—"Well, Sir, I couldn't say exactly as to the number—but I should think—well, say seven or eight times—as many as that, anyway."

The Court.—"Be careful now, and remember you are under oath. What kind of a pistol was it?"

Witness.—"It was a Durringer, your Honor."

The Court.—"A Deringer! You must not trifle here, Sir. A Deringer only shoots once—how then could Jones have fired seven or eight times?" [The witness is evidently as stunned by that last proposition as if a brick had struck him.]

Witness.—"Well, your Honor—he—that is, she—Jones, I mean—Soph—"

The Court.—"Are you sure he fired more than one shot? Are you sure he fired at all?"

Witness.—"I—I—well, perhaps he didn't—and—and your Honor may be right. But you see, that girl, with her dratted yowling—altogether, it might be that he did only shoot once."

Lawyer.—"And about his attempting to shoot the top of Smith's head off—didn't he aim at his body, or his legs? Come now."

Witness.—(entirely confused)—"Yes, Sir—I think he did —I—I'm pretty certain of it. Yes, Sir, he must a fired at his legs."

[Nothing was elicited on the cross-examination, except that the weapon used by Mr. Jones was a bowie knife instead of a deringer, and that he made a number of desperate attempts to scalp the plaintiff instead of trying to shoot him. It also came out that Sophronia, of doubtful nativity, did not faint, and was not present during the affray, she having been discharged from her situation on the previous evening.]

Washington Billings, sworn, said:—"I see the row, and it

warn't in no saloon—it was in the street. Both of 'em was drunk, and one was a comin' up the street, and 'tother was a goin down. Both of 'em was close to the houses when they fust see each other, and both of 'em made their calculations to miss each other, but the second time they tacked across the pavement—driftin', like diagonal—they come together, down by the curb—almighty soggy, they did—which staggered 'em a moment, and then, over they went, into the gutter. Smith was up fust, and he made a dive for a cobble and fell on Jones; Jones dug out and made a dive for a cobble, and slipped his hold and jammed his head into Smith's stomach. They each done that over again, twice more, just the same way. After that, neither of 'em could get up any more, and so they just laid there in the slush and clawed mud and cussed each other."

[On the cross-examination, the witness could not say whether the parties continued the fight afterwards in the saloon or not—he only knew they began it in the gutter, and to the best of his knowledge and belief they were too drunk to get into a saloon, and too drunk to stay in it after they got there if there were any orifice about it that they could fall out of again. As to weapons, he saw none used except the cobblestones, and to the best of his knowledge and belief they missed fire every time while he was present.]

Jeremiah Driscoll came forward, was sworn, and testified as follows:—"I saw the fight, your Honor, and it wasn't in a saloon, nor in the street, nor in a hotel, nor in—"

The Court.—"Was it in the City and County of San Francisco?"

Witness.—"Yes, your Honor, I—I think it was."

The Court.—"Well, then, go on."

Witness.—"It was up in the Square. Jones meets Smith, and they both go at it—that is, blackguarding each other. One called the other a thief, and the other said he was a liar, and then they got to swearing backwards and forwards pretty generally, as you might say, and finally one struck the other over the head with a cane, and then they closed and fell, and after that they made such a dust and the gravel flew so thick that I couldn't rightly tell which was getting the best of it. When it cleared away, one of them was after the other with a pine bench, and the other was prospecting for rocks, and—"

Lawyer.—"There, there, there—that will do—that—will—*do*! How in the world is any one to make head or tail out of such a string of nonsense as that? Who struck the first blow?"

Witness.—"I cannot rightly say, sir, but I think—"

Lawyer.—"You *think*!—don't you *know*?"

Witness.—"No, sir, it was all so sudden, and—"

Lawyer.—"Well, then, state, if you can, who struck the last."

Witness.—"I can't, sir, because—"

Lawyer.—"Because what?"

Witness.—"Because, sir, you see toward the last, they clinched and went down, and got to kicking up the gravel again, and—"

Lawyer.—(resignedly)—"Take the witness—take the witness."

[The testimony on the cross-examination went to show that during the fight, one of the parties drew a slung-shot and cocked it, but to the best of the witness' knowledge and belief, he did not fire; and at the same time, the other discharged a hand-grenade at his antagonist, which missed him and did no damage, except blowing up a bonnet store on the other side of the street, and creating a momentary diversion among the milliners. He could not say, however, which drew the slung-shot or which threw the grenade. (It was generally remarked by those in the court room, that the evidence of the witness was obscure and unsatisfactory.) Upon questioning him further, and confronting him with the parties to the case before the court, it transpired that the faces of Jones and Smith were unknown to him, and that he had been talking about an entirely different fight all the time.]

Other witnesses were examined, some of whom swore that Smith was the aggressor, and others that Jones began the row; some said they fought with their fists, others that they fought with knives, others tomahawks, others revolvers, others clubs, others axes, others beer mugs and chairs, and others swore there had been no fight at all. However, fight or no fight, the testimony was straightforward and uniform on one point, at any rate, and that was, that the fuss was about two dollars and forty cents, which one party owed the other, but after all, it was impossible to find out which was the debtor and which the creditor.

After the witnesses had all been heard, his Honor, Judge Shepheard, observed that the evidence in this case resembled, in a great many points, the evidence before him in some thirty-five cases every day, on an average. He then said he would continue the case, to afford the parties an opportunity of procuring more testimony.

[I have been keeping an eye on the Police Court for the last few days. Two friends of mine had business there, on account of assault and battery concerning Washoe stocks, and I felt interested, of course. I never knew their names were James Johnson and John Ward, though, until I heard them answer to them in that Court. When James Johnson was called, one of these young men said to the other: "That's you, my boy." "No," was the reply, "it's you—my name's John Ward—see, I've got it written here on a card." Consequently, the first speaker sung out, "Here!" and it was all right. As I was saying, I have been keeping an eye on that Court, and I have arrived at the conclusion that the office of Police Judge is a profitable and a comfortable thing to have, but then, as the English hunter said about fighting tigers in India under a shortness of ammunition, "it has its little drawbacks." Hearing testimony must be worrying to a Police Judge sometimes, when he is in his right mind. I would rather be Secretary to a wealthy mining company, and have nothing to do but advertise the assessments and collect them in carefully, and go along quiet and upright, and be one of the noblest works of God, and never gobble a dollar that didn't belong to me—all just as those fellows do, you know. (Oh, *I* have no talent for sarcasm, it isn't likely.) But I trespass.]

Now, with every confidence in the instinctive candor and fair dealing of my race, I submit the testimony in the case of Smith *vs.* Jones, to the People, without comment or argument, well satisfied that after a perusal of it, their judgment will be as righteous as it is final and impartial, and that whether

Smith be cast out and Jones exalted, or Jones cast out and Smith exalted, the decision will be a holy and a just one.

I leave the accused and the accuser before the bar of the world—let their fate be pronounced.

June 26, 1864

Whereas

Love's Bakery! I am satisfied I have found the place now that I have been looking for all this time. I cannot describe to you the sensation of mingled astonishment, gladness, hope, doubt, anxiety, and balmy, blissful emotion that suffused my being and quivered in a succession of streaky thrills down my backbone, as I stood on the corner of Third and Minna streets, last Tuesday, and stared, spell-bound, at those extraordinary words, painted in large, plain letters on a neighboring window-curtain—"LOVE'S BAKERY." "God bless my soul!" said I, "will wonders never cease?—are there to be no limits to man's spirit of invention?—is he to invade the very realms of the immortal, and presume to guide and control the great passions, the impalpable essences, that have hitherto dwelt in the secret chambers of the soul, sacred from all save divine intrusion?"

I read and re-read that remarkable sign with constantly-increasing wonder and interest. There was nothing extraordinary in the appearance of the establishment, and even if it had possessed anything of a supernatural air, it must necessarily have been neutralized by the worldly and substantial look of a pyramid of excellent bread that stood in the window—a sign very inconsistent, it seemed to me, with the character of a place devoted to the high and holy employment of instilling the passion of love into the human heart, although it was certainly in keeping with the atrocious taste which was capable of conferring upon a vice-royalty of heaven itself such an execrable name as "Love's Bakery." Why not Love's Bower, or the Temple of Love, or the Palace of Cupid?—anything—anything in the world would have been less repulsive than such hideous vulgarity of nomenclature as "Love's *Bakery*."

The place seemed very complete, and well supplied with every facility for carrying on the business of creating love successfully. In a window of the second story was a large tin cage with a parrot in it, and near it was a sign bearing the inscription, "Preparatory School for Young Ladies"—that is, of course, a school where they are taught certain things necessary to prepare them for the bakery down below. Not far off is also a "Preparatory School for Young Gentlemen," which is doubtless connected with Love's Bakery too. I saw none of the pupils of either of the schools, but my imagination dwelt upon them with a deep and friendly interest. How irksome, I thought, must this course of instruction be to these tender hearts, so impatient to be baked into a state of perfect love!

Greatly moved by the singular circumstances which surrounded me, I fell into a profound and pleasing reverie. Here, I thought, they take a couple of hopeful hearts in the rough, and work them up, with spices and shortening and sweetening enough to last for a lifetime, and turn them out well kneaded together, baked to a turn, and ready for matrimony, and without having been obliged to undergo a long and harrowing courtship, with the desperate chances attendant thereon, of persevering rivals, unwilling parents, inevitable love-quarrels, and all that sort of thing.

Here, I thought, they will bake you up a couple in moderate circumstances, at short notice and at a cheap rate, and turn them out in good enough shape for the money, perhaps, but nevertheless burnt with the fire of jealousy on one side, and flabby and "duffy" with lukewarmness and indifference on the other, and spotted all over with the salæratus stains of a predisposition to make the conjugal cake bitter and unpalatable for all time to come.

Or they will take an excessively patrician pair, charge them a dozen prices, and deliver them to order in a week, all plastered over with the ghostly vines and flowers of blighted fancies, hopes and yearnings, wrought in chilly ice-work.

Or, perhaps, they will take a brace of youthful, tender hearts, and dish them up in no time, into crisp, delicate "lady-fingers," tempting to contemplate, and suggestive of that serene after-dinner happiness and sociability that come when the gross substantials have been swept from the board and are forgotten in soft dalliance with pastry and ices and sparkling Moselle.

Or maybe they will take two flinty old hearts that have harbored selfishness, envy and all uncharitableness in solitude for half a century, and after a fortnight's roasting, turn them out

the hardest kind of hard-tack, invulnerable to all softening influences for evermore.

Here was a revolution far more extended, and destined to
be attended by more momentous consequences to the nations
of the earth, than any ever projected or accomplished by the
greatest of the world's military heroes! Love, the master
passion of the human heart, which, since the morning of the
creation had shaped the destinies of emperors and beggars
alike, and had ruled all men as with a rod of iron, was to be
hurled from the seat of power in a single instant, as it were,
and brought into subjection to the will of an inspired, a
sublimely-gifted baker! By some mysterious magic, by some
strange and awful invention, the divine emotion was to be
confined within set bounds and limits, controlled, weighed,
measured, and doled out to God's creatures in quantities and
qualities to suit the purchaser, like vulgar beer and candles!

And in times to come, I thought, the afflicted lover, instead
of reading Heuston & Hastings' omnipresent sign and gathering no comfort from it, will read "Go to Love's Bakery!"
on the dead-walls and telegraph poles, and be saved.

Now I might never have published to the world my discovery of this manufactory of the human affections in a populous
thoroughfare of San Francisco, if it had not occurred to me
that some account of it would serve as a peculiarly fitting introductory to a story of love and misfortune, which it falls to
my lot to relate. And yet even Love's Bakery could afford no
help to the sufferers of whom I shall speak, for they do not
lack affection for each other, but are the victims of an accumulation of distressing circumstances against which the efforts of that august agent would be powerless.

The facts in the case come to me by letter from a young
lady who lives in the beautiful city of San José; she is personally unknown to me, and simply signs herself "Aurelia Maria,"
which may possibly be a fictitious name. But no matter, the
poor girl is almost heart-broken by the misfortunes she has
undergone, and so confused by the conflicting counsels of
misguided friends and insidious enemies, that she does not
know what course to pursue in order to extricate herself from
the web of difficulties in which she seems almost hopelessly
involved. In this dilemma she turns to me for help, and sup-

plicates for my guidance and instruction with a moving eloquence that would touch the heart of a statue. Hear her sad story:

She says that when she was sixteen years old she met and loved with all the devotion of a passionate nature a young man from New Jersey, named Williamson Breckinridge Caruthers, who was some six years her senior. They were engaged, with the free consent of their friends and relatives, and for a time it seemed as if their career was destined to be characterized by an immunity from sorrow beyond the usual lot of humanity. But at last the tide of fortune turned; young Caruthers became infected with small-pox of the most virulent type, and when he recovered from his illness, his face was pitted like a waffle-mould and his comeliness gone forever. Aurelia thought to break off the engagement at first, but pity for her unfortunate lover caused her to postpone the marriage-day for a season, and give him another trial. The very day before the wedding was to have taken place, Breckinridge, while absorbed in watching the flight of a balloon, walked into a well and fractured one of his legs, and it had to be taken off above the knee. Again Aurelia was moved to break the engagement, but again love triumphed, and she set the day forward and gave him another chance to reform. And again misfortune overtook the unhappy youth. He lost one arm by the premature discharge of a Fourth-of-July cannon, and within three months he got the other pulled out by a carding-machine. Aurelia's heart was almost crushed by these latter calamities. She could not but be deeply grieved to see her lover passing from her by piecemeal, feeling, as she did, that he could not last forever under this disastrous process of reduction, yet knowing of no way to stop its dreadful career, and in her tearful despair she almost regretted, like brokers who hold on and lose, that she had not taken him at first, before he had suffered such an alarming depreciation. Still, her brave soul bore her up, and she resolved to bear with her friend's unnatural disposition yet a little longer. Again the wedding-day approached, and again disappointment overshadowed it: Caruthers fell ill with the erysipelas, and lost the use of one of his eyes entirely. The friends and relatives of the bride, considering that she had already put up with more than could reasonably be expected of her, now came forward and insisted that the match should be broken off; but after wavering awhile, Aurelia, with a generous spirit which did her credit, said she had reflected calmly upon the matter and could not discover that Breckinridge was to blame. So she extended the time once more, and he broke his other leg. It was a sad day for the poor girl when she saw the surgeons reverently bearing away the sack whose uses she had learned by previous experience, and her heart told her the bitter truth that some more of her lover was gone. She felt that the field of her affections was growing more and more circumscribed every day, but once more she frowned down her relatives and renewed her betrothal. Shortly before the time set for the nuptials another disaster occurred. There was but one man scalped by the Owens River Indians last year. That man was Williamson Breckinridge Caruthers, of New Jersey. He was hurrying home with happiness in his heart, when he lost his hair forever, and in that hour of bitterness he almost cursed the mistaken mercy that had spared his head.

At last Aurelia is in serious perplexity as to what she ought to do. She still loves her Breckinridge, she writes, with true womanly feeling—she still loves what is left of him—but her parents are bitterly opposed to the match, because he has no property and is disabled from working, and she has not sufficient means to support both comfortably. "Now, what should she do?" she asks with painful and anxious solicitude.

It is a delicate question; it is one which involves the life-long happiness of a woman, and that of nearly two-thirds of a man, and I feel that it would be assuming too great a responsibility to do more than make a mere suggestion in the case. How would it do to build to him? If Aurelia can afford the expense, let her furnish her mutilated lover with wooden arms and wooden legs, and a glass eye and a wig, and give him another show; give him ninety days, without grace, and if he does not break his neck in the meantime, marry him and take the chances. It does not seem to me that there is much risk, any way, because if he sticks to his infernal propensity for damaging himself every time he sees a good opportunity, his next experiment is bound to finish him, and then you are all right, you know, married or single. If married, the wooden legs and such other valuables as he may possess, revert to the widow, and you see you sustain no actual loss save the cherished fragment of a noble but most unfortunate husband, who honestly strove to do right, but whose extraordinary instincts were against him. Try it, Maria! I have thought the matter over carefully and well, and it is the only chance I see for you. It would have been a happy conceit on the part of Caruthers if he had started with his neck and broken that first, but since he has seen fit to choose a different policy and string himself out as long as possible, I do not think we ought to upbraid him for it if he has enjoyed it. We must do the best we can under the circumstances, and try not to feel exasperated at him.

October 22, 1864

A Touching Story of
George Washington's Boyhood

If it please your neighbor to break the sacred calm of night with the snorting of an unholy trombone, it is your duty to put up with his wretched music and your privilege to pity him for the unhappy instinct that moves him to delight in such discordant sounds. I did not always think thus; this consideration for musical amateurs was born of certain disagreeable personal experiences that once followed the development of a like instinct in myself. Now this infidel over the way, who is learning to play on the trombone, and the slowness of whose progress is almost miraculous, goes on with his harrowing work every night, uncursed by me, but tenderly pitied. Ten years ago, for the same offence, I would have set fire to his house. At that time I was a prey to an amateur violinist for two or three weeks, and the sufferings I endured at his hands are inconceivable. He played "Old Dan Tucker," and he never played anything else—but he performed that so badly that he could throw me into fits with it if I were awake, or into a nightmare if I were asleep. As long as he confined himself to "Dan Tucker," though, I bore with him and abstained from violence; but when he projected a fresh outrage, and tried to do "Sweet Home," I went over and burnt him out. My next assailant was a wretch who felt a call to play the clarionet. He only played the scale, however, with his distressing instrument, and I let him run the length of his tether, also; but finally, when he branched out into a ghastly tune, I felt my reason deserting me under the exquisite torture, and I sallied forth and burnt him out likewise. During the next two years I burned out an amateur cornet-player, a bugler, a bassoon-sharp, and a barbarian whose talents ran in the bass-drum line. I would certainly have scorched this trombone man if he had moved into my neighborhood in those days. But as I said before, I leave him to his own destruction now, because I have had experience as an amateur myself, and I feel nothing but compassion for that kind of people. Besides, I have learned that there lies dormant in the souls of all men a penchant for some particular musical instrument, and an unsuspected yearning to learn to play on it, that are bound to wake up and demand attention some day. Therefore, you who rail at such as disturb your slumbers with unsuccessful and demoralizing attempts to subjugate a fiddle, beware! for sooner or later your own time will come. It is customary and popular to curse these amateurs when they wrench you out of a pleasant dream at night with a peculiarly diabolical note, but seeing that we are all made alike, and must all develop a distorted talent for music in the fullness of time, it is not right. I am charitable to my trombone maniac; in a moment of inspiration he fetches a snort, sometimes, that brings me to a sitting posture in bed, broad awake and weltering in a cold perspiration. Perhaps my first thought is that there has been an earthquake; perhaps I hear the trombone, and my next thought is that suicide and the silence of the grave would be a happy release from this nightly agony; perhaps the old instinct comes strong upon me to go after my matches; but my first cool, collected thought is that the trombone man's destiny is upon him, and he is working it out in suffering and tribulation; and I banish from me the unworthy instinct that would prompt me to burn him out.

After a long immunity from the dreadful insanity that moves a man to become a musician in defiance of the will of God that he should confine himself to sawing wood, I finally fell a victim to the instrument they call the Accordeon. At this day I hate that contrivance as fervently as any man can, but at the time I speak of I suddenly acquired a disgusting and idolatrous affection for it. I got one of powerful capacity and learned to play "Auld Lang Syne" on it. It seems to me, now, that I must have been gifted with a sort of inspiration to be enabled, in the state of ignorance in which I then was, to select out of the whole range of musical composition the one solitary tune that sounds vilest and most distressing on the accordeon. I do not suppose there is another tune in the world with which I could have inflicted so much anguish upon my race as I did with that one during my short musical career.

After I had been playing "Lang Syne" about a week, I had

the vanity to think I could improve the original melody, and I set about adding some little flourishes and variations to it, but with rather indifferent success, I suppose, as it brought my landlady into my presence with an expression about her of being opposed to such desperate enterprises. Said she, "Do you know any other tune but that, Mr. Twain?" I told her, meekly, that I did not. "Well, then," said she, "stick to it just as it is; don't put any variations to it, because it's rough enough on the boarders the way it is now."

The fact is, it was something more than simply "rough enough" on them; it was altogether too rough; half of them left, and the other half would have followed, but Mrs. Jones saved them by discharging me from the premises.

I only stayed one night at my next lodging-house. Mrs. Smith was after me early in the morning. She said, "You can go, sir; I don't want you here; I have had one of your kind before—a poor lunatic, that played the banjo and danced breakdowns, and jarred the glass all out of the windows; you kept me awake all night, and if you was to do it again I'd take and mash that thing over your head!" I could see that this woman took no delight in music, and I moved to Mrs. Brown's.

For three nights in succession I gave my new neighbors "Auld Lang Syne," plain and unadulterated, save by a few discords that rather improved the general effect than otherwise. But the very first time I tried the variations the boarders mutinied. I never did find anybody that would stand those variations. I was very well satisfied with my efforts in that house, however, and I left it without any regrets; I drove one boarder as mad as a March hare, and another one tried to scalp his mother. I reflected, though, that if I could only have been allowed to give this latter just one more touch of the variations, he would have finished the old woman.

I went to board at Mrs. Murphy's, an Italian lady of many excellent qualities. The very first time I struck up the variations, a haggard, care-worn, cadaverous old man walked into my room and stood beaming upon me a smile of ineffable happiness. Then he placed his hand upon my head, and looking devoutly aloft, he said with feeling unction, and in a voice trembling with emotion, "God bless you, young man! God bless you! for you have done that for me which is beyond all praise. For years I have suffered from an incurable disease, and knowing my doom was sealed and that I must die, I have striven with all my power to resign myself to my fate, but in vain—the love of life was too strong within me. But Heaven bless you, my benefactor! for since I heard you play that tune and those variations, I do not want to live any longer—I am entirely resigned—I am willing to die—I am anxious to die." And then the old man fell upon my neck and wept a flood of happy tears. I was surprised at these things, but I could not help feeling a little proud at what I had done, nor could I help giving the old gentleman a parting blast in the way of some peculiarly lacerating variations as he went out at the door. They doubled him up like a jack-knife, and the next time he left his bed of pain and suffering, he was all right, in a metallic coffin.

My passion for the accordeon finally spent itself and died out, and I was glad when I found myself free from its unwholesome influence. While the fever was upon me, I was a living, breathing calamity wherever I went, and desolation and disaster followed in my wake. I bred discord in families, I crushed the spirits of the light-hearted, I drove the melancholy to despair, I hurried invalids to premature dissolution, and I fear me I disturbed the very dead in their graves. I did incalculable harm and inflicted untold suffering upon my race with my execrable music, and yet to atone for it all, I did but one single blessed act, in making that weary old man willing to go to his long home.

Still, I derived some little benefit from that accordeon, for while I continued to practice on it, I never had to pay any board—landlords were always willing to compromise, on my leaving before the month was up.

Now, I had two objects in view, in writing the foregoing, one of which, was to try and reconcile people to those poor unfortunates who feel that they have a genius for music, and who drive their neighbors crazy every night in trying to develop and cultivate it, and the other was to introduce an admirable story about Little George Washington, who could Not Lie, and the Cherry Tree—or the Apple Tree, I have

forgotten now, which, although it was told me only yesterday. And writing such a long and elaborate introductory has
caused me to forget the story itself; but it was very touching.

October 29, 1864

The Killing of Julius Cæsar "Localized"

[BEING THE ONLY TRUE AND RELIABLE ACCOUNT
EVER PUBLISHED, AND TAKEN FROM THE ROMAN
"DAILY EVENING FASCES," OF THE DATE OF THAT
TREMENDOUS OCCURRENCE.]

Nothing in the world affords a newspaper reporter so much satisfaction as gathering up the details of a bloody and mysterious murder, and writing them up with aggravated circumstantiality. He takes a living delight in this labor of love—for such it is to him—especially if he knows that all the other papers have gone to press and his will be the only one that will contain the dreadful intelligence. A feeling of regret has often come over me that I was not reporting in Rome when Cæsar was killed—reporting on an evening paper and the only one in the city, and getting at least twelve hours ahead of the morning paper boys with this most magnificent "item" that ever fell to the lot of the craft. Other events have happened as startling as this, but none that possessed so peculiarly all the characteristics of the favorite "item" of the present day, magnified into grandeur and sublimity by the high rank, fame, and social and political standing of the actors in it. In imagination I have seen myself skirmishing around old Rome, button-holing soldiers, senators and citizens by turns, and transferring "all the particulars" from them to my note-book; and, better still, arriving "at the base of Pompey's statue" in time to say persuasively to the dying Cæsar: "O, come now, you ain't so far gone, you know, but what you could stir yourself up a little and tell a fellow just how this thing happened, if you was a mind to, couldn't you—now do!" and get the "straight of it" from his own lips. And be envied by the morning paper hounds!

Ah! if I had lived in those days I would have written up that item gloatingly, and spiced it with a little moralizing here and plenty of blood there; and some dark, shuddering mystery; and praise and pity for some, and misrepresentation and abuse for others, (who didn't patronize the paper,) and gory gashes, and notes of warning as to the tendency of the times, and extravagant descriptions of the excitement in the Senate-house and the street, and all that sort of thing.

However, as I was not permitted to report Cæsar's assassination in the regular way, it has at least afforded me rare satisfaction to translate the following able account of it from the original Latin of the *Roman Daily Evening Fasces* of that date—second edition:

Our usually quiet city of Rome was thrown into a state of wild excitement, yesterday, by the occurrence of one of those bloody affrays which sicken the heart and fill the soul with fear, while they inspire all thinking men with forebodings for the future of a city where human life is held so cheaply, and the gravest laws are so openly set at defiance. As the result of that affray, it is our painful duty, as public journalists, to record the death of one of our most esteemed citizens—a man whose name is known wherever this paper circulates, and whose fame it has been our pleasure and our privilege to extend, and also to protect from the tongue of slander and falsehood, to the best of our poor ability. We refer to Mr. J. Cæsar, the Emperor elect.

The facts of the case, as nearly as our reporter could determine them from the conflicting statements of eye-witnesses, were about as follows: The affair was an election row, of course. Nine-tenths of the ghastly butcheries that disgrace the city now-a-days, grow out of the bickerings and jealousies and animosities engendered by these accursed elections. Rome would be the gainer by it if her very constables were elected to serve a century, for in our experience we have never even been able to choose a dog-pelter without celebrating the event with a dozen knock-downs and a general cramming of the station-house with drunken vagabonds over night. It is said that when the immense majority for Cæsar at the polls in the market was declared the other day, and the crown was offered to that gentleman, even his amazing unselfishness in refusing it three times, was not sufficient to save him from the whispered insults of such men as Casca, of the Tenth Ward, and other hirelings of the disappointed candidate, hailing mostly from the Eleventh and Thirteenth, and other outside districts, who were overheard speaking ironically and contemptuously of Mr. Cæsar's conduct upon that occasion.

We are further informed that there are many among us who think they are justified in believing that the assassination of Julius Cæsar was a put-up thing—a cut-and-dried arrangement, hatched by Marcus Brutus and a lot of his hired roughs, and carried out only too faithfully according to the programme. Whether there be good grounds for this suspicion or not, we leave to the people to judge for themselves, only asking that they will read the following account of the sad occurrence carefully and dispassionately before they render that judgment:

The Senate was already in session, and Cæsar was coming down the street toward the capitol, conversing with some personal friends, and followed, as usual, by a large number of citizens. Just as he was passing in front of Demosthenes and Thucydides' drug-store, he was observing casually to a gentleman who, our informant thinks, is a fortune-teller, that the Ides of March were come. The reply was, Yes, they were come, but not gone yet. At this moment Artemidorus stepped up and passed the time of day, and asked Cæsar to read a schedule or a tract, or something of the kind, which he had brought for his perusal. Mr. Decius Brutus also said something about an "humble suit" which *he* wanted read. Artemidorus begged that attention might be paid to his first, because it was of personal consequence to Cæsar. The latter replied that what concerned himself should be read last, or words to that effect. Artemidorus begged and beseeched him to read the paper instantly. [Mark that; it is hinted by William Shakspeare, who saw the beginning and the end of the unfortunate affray, that this "schedule" was simply a note discovering to Cæsar that a plot was brewing to take his life.] However, Cæsar shook him off, and refused to read any petition in the street. He then entered the capitol, and the crowd followed him.

About this time, the following conversation was overheard, and we consider that, taken in connection with the events which succeeded it, it bears an appalling significance: Mr. Popilius Lena remarked to George W. Cassius (commonly known as the "Nobby Boy of the Third Ward,") a bruiser in the pay of the Opposition, that he hoped his enterprise to-day might thrive; and when Cassius asked, "What enterprise?" he only closed his left eye temporarily, and said with simulated indifference, "Fare you well," and sauntered toward Cæsar. Marcus Brutus, who is suspected of being the ringleader of the band that killed Cæsar, asked what it was that Lena had said; Cassius told him, and added in a low tone, "*I fear our purpose is discovered.*"

Brutus told his wretched accomplice to keep an eye on Lena, and a moment after, Cassius urged that lean and hungry vagrant, Casca, whose reputation here is none of the best, to be sudden, for *he feared prevention*. He then turned to Brutus, apparently much excited, and asked what should be done, and swore that either he or Cæsar *should never turn back*—he would kill himself first. At this time, Cæsar was talking to some of the back-country members about the approaching fall elections, and paying little attention to what was going on around him. Billy Trebonius got into conversation with the people's friend and Cæsar's—Mark Antony—and under some pretence or other, got him away, and Brutus, Decius, Casca, Cinna, Metellus Cimber, and others of the gang of infamous desperadoes that infest Rome at present, closed around the doomed Cæsar. Then Metellus Cimber knelt down and begged that his brother might be recalled from banishment, but Cæsar rebuked him for his fawning, sneaking conduct, and refused to grant his petition. Immediately, at Cimber's request, first Brutus and then Cassius begged for the return of the banished Publius; but Cæsar still refused. He said he could not be moved; that he was as fixed as the North Star, and proceeded to speak in the most complimentary terms of the firmness of that star, and its steady character. Then he said he was like it, and he believed he was the only man in the country that was; therefore, since he was "constant" that Cimber should be banished, he was also "constant" that he should stay banished, and he'd be d—d if he didn't keep him so!

Instantly seizing upon this shallow pretext for a fight, Casca sprang at Cæsar and struck him with a dirk, Cæsar grabbing him by the arm with his right hand, and launching a blow straight from the shoulder with his left, that sent the reptile bleeding to the earth. He then backed up against Pompey's statue, and squared himself to receive his assailants. Cassius and Cimber and Cinna rushed upon him with their daggers drawn, and the former succeeded in inflicting a wound upon his body, but before he could strike again, and before either of the others could strike at all, Cæsar stretched the three miscreants at his feet with as many blows of his powerful fist. By this time the Senate was in an indescribable uproar; the throng of citizens in the lobbies had blockaded the doors in their frantic efforts to escape from the building, the Sergeant-at-Arms and his assistants were struggling with the assassins, venerable Senators had cast aside their encumbering robes and were leaping over benches and flying down the aisles in wild confusion toward the shelter of the Committee-rooms, and a thousand voices were shouting "Po-lice! Po-lice!" in discordant tones that rose above the frightful din like shrieking winds above the roaring of a tempest. And amid it all, great Cæsar stood with his back against the statue, like a lion at bay, and fought his assailants weaponless and hand-to-hand, with the defiant bearing and the unwavering courage which he had shown before on many a bloody field. Billy Trebonius and Caius Ligarius struck him with their daggers and fell, as their brother-conspirators before them had fallen. But at last, when Cæsar saw his old friend Brutus step forward, armed with a murderous knife, it is said he seemed utterly overpowered with grief and amazement, and dropping his invincible left arm by his side, he hid his face in the folds of his mantle and received the treacherous blow without an effort to stay the hand that gave it. He only said "*Et tu, Brute?*" and fell lifeless on the marble pavement.

We learn that the coat deceased had on when he was killed was the same he wore in his tent on the afternoon of the day he overcame the Nervii, and that when it was removed from the corpse it was found to be cut and gashed in no less than seven different places. There was nothing in the pockets. It will be exhibited at the Coroner's inquest, and will be damning proof of the fact of the killing. These latter facts may be relied on, as we get them from Mark Antony, whose position enables him to learn every item of news connected with the one subject of absorbing interest of to-day.

LATER.—While the Coroner was summoning a jury, Mark Antony and other friends of the late Cæsar got hold of the body and lugged it off to the Forum, and at last accounts Antony and Brutus were making speeches over it and raising such a row among the people that, as we go to press, the Chief of Police is satisfied there is going to be a riot, and is taking measures accordingly.

November 12, 1864

Lucretia Smith's Soldier

[NOTE FROM THE AUTHOR.—*Mr. Editor:* I am an ardent admirer of those nice, sickly war stories in *Harper's Weekly*, and for the last three months I have been at work upon one of that character, which I now forward to you for publication. It can be relied upon as true in every particular, inasmuch as the facts it contains were compiled from the official records in the War Department at Washington. The credit of this part of the labor is due to the Hon. T. G. Phelps, who has so long and ably represented this State in Congress. It is but just, also, that I should make honorable mention of the obliging publishing firms Roman & Co. and Bancroft & Co., of this city, who loaned me *Jomini's Art of War*, the *Message of the President and Accompanying Documents*, and sundry maps and military works, so necessary for reference in building a novel like this. To the accommodating Directors of the Overland Telegraph Company I take pleasure in returning my thanks for tendering me the use of their wires at the customary rates. The inspiration which enabled me in this production to soar so happily into the realms of sentiment and soft emotion, was obtained from the excellent beer manufactured at the New York Brewery, in Sutter street, between Montgomery and Kearny. And finally, to all those kind friends who have, by good deeds or encouraging words, assisted me in my labors upon this story of "Lucretia Smith's Soldier," during the past three months, and whose names are too numerous for special mention, I take this method of tendering my sincerest gratitude.

M. T.]

CHAPTER I.

On a balmy May morning in 1861, the little village of Bluemass, in Massachusetts, lay wrapped in the splendor of the newly-risen sun. Reginald de Whittaker, confidential and only clerk in the house of Bushrod & Ferguson, general dry goods and grocery dealers, and keepers of the Post-office, rose from his bunk under the counter and shook himself. After yawning and stretching comfortably, he sprinkled the floor and proceeded to sweep it. He had only half finished his task, however, when he sat down on a keg of nails and fell into a reverie. "This is my last day in this shanty," said he. "How it will surprise Lucretia when she hears I am going for a soldier! How proud she will be—the little darling!" He pictured himself in all manner of warlike situations; the hero of a thousand extraordinary adventures; the man of rising fame; the pet of Fortune at last; and beheld himself, finally, returning to his old home, a bronzed and scarred Brigadier-General, to cast his honors and his matured and perfect love at the feet of his Lucretia Borgia Smith.

At this point a thrill of joy and pride suffused his system—but he looked down and saw his broom, and blushed. He came toppling down from the clouds he had been soaring among, and was an obscure clerk again, on a salary of two dollars and a half a week.

CHAPTER II.

AT 8 o'clock that evening, with a heart palpitating with the proud news he had brought for his beloved, Reginald sat in Mr. Smith's parlor awaiting Lucretia's appearance. The moment she entered he sprang to meet her, his face lighted by the torch of love that was blazing in his head somewhere and shining through, and ejaculated "Mine own!" as he opened his arms to receive her.

"Sir!" said she, and drew herself up like an offended queen.

Poor Reginald was stricken dumb with astonishment. This chilling demeanor, this angry rebuff where he had expected the old, tender welcome, banished the gladness from his heart as the cheerful brightness is swept from the landscape when a dark cloud drifts athwart the face of the sun. He stood bewildered a moment, with a sense of goneness on him like one who finds himself suddenly overboard upon a midnight sea and beholds the ship pass into shrouding gloom, while the dreadful conviction falls upon his soul that he has not been missed. He tried to speak, but his pallid lips refused their office. At last he murmured:

"O, Lucretia, what have I done—what is the matter—why this cruel coldness? Don't you love your Reginald any more?"

Her lips curled in bitter scorn, and she replied, in mocking tones:

"Don't I love my Reginald any more? No, I *don't* love my Reginald any more! Go back to your pitiful junk shop and grab your pitiful yard-stick, and stuff cotton in your ears so that you can't hear your country shout to you to fall in and shoulder arms! Go!" And then, unheeding the new light that flashed from his eyes, she fled from the room and slammed the door behind her.

Only a moment more! Only a single moment more, he thought, and he could have told her how he had already answered the summons and signed his name to the muster-roll, and all would have been well—his lost bride would have come back to his arms with words of praise and thanksgiving upon her lips. He made a step forward, once, to recall her, but he remembered that he was no longer an effeminate dry-goods student, and his warrior soul scorned to sue for quarter. He strode from the place with martial firmness, and never looked behind him.

CHAPTER III.

WHEN Lucretia awoke the next morning, the faint music of a fife and the roll of a distant drum came floating upon the soft spring breeze, and as she listened the sounds grew more subdued and finally passed out of hearing. She lay absorbed in thought for many minutes, and then she sighed and said, "Oh, if he were only with that band of fellows, how I could love him!"

In the course of the day a neighbor dropped in, and when the conversation turned upon the soldiers, the visitor said:

"Reginald de Whittaker looked rather down-hearted, and didn't shout when he marched along with the other boys this morning. I expect it's owing to you, Miss Loo, though when I met him coming here yesterday evening to tell you he'd enlisted, he thought you'd like it and be proud of——Mercy! what in the nation's the matter with the girl?"

Nothing, only a sudden misery had fallen like a blight upon her heart, and a deadly pallor telegraphed it to her countenance. She rose up without a word and walked with a firm step out of the room, but once within the sacred seclusion of her own chamber, her strong will gave way and she burst into a flood of passionate tears. Bitterly she upbraided herself for her foolish haste of the night before, and her harsh treatment of her lover at the very moment that he had come to anticipate the proudest wish of her heart, and to tell her that he had enrolled himself under the battle-flag and was going forth to fight as *her* soldier. Alas! other maidens would have soldiers in those glorious fields, and be entitled to the sweet pain of feeling a tender solicitude for them, but she would be unrepresented. No soldier in all the vast armies would breathe her name as he breasted the crimson tide of war! She wept again—or, rather, she went on weeping where she left off a moment before. In her bitterness of spirit, she almost cursed the precipitancy that had brought all this sorrow upon her young life. "Drat it!" The words were in her bosom, but she locked them there, and closed her lips against their utterance.

For weeks and weeks she nursed her grief in silence while the roses faded from her cheeks. And through it all she clung to the hope that some day the old love would bloom again in Reginald's heart, and he would write to her—but the long summer days dragged wearily along, and still no letter came. The newspapers teemed with stories of battle and carnage, and eagerly she read them, but always with the same result: the tears welled up and blurred the closing lines—the name she sought was looked for in vain, and the dull aching returned to her sinking heart. Letters to the other girls sometimes contained brief mention of him, and presented always the same picture of him—a morose, unsmiling, desperate man, always in the thickest of the fight, begrimed with powder, and moving calm and unscathed through tempests of shot and shell, as if he bore a charmed life.

But at last, in a long list of maimed and killed, poor Lucretia read these terrible words, and fell fainting to the floor: "R. D. Whittaker, private soldier, desperately wounded!"

CHAPTER IV.

ON a couch in one of the wards of a hospital at Washington lay a wounded soldier; his head was so profusely bandaged that his features were not visible, but there was no mistaking the happy face of the young girl who sat beside him—it was Lucretia Borgia Smith's. She had hunted him out several weeks before, and since that time she had patiently watched by him and nursed him, coming in the morning as soon as the surgeons had finished dressing his wounds, and never leaving him until relieved at nightfall. A ball had shattered his lower jaw, and he could not utter a syllable; through all her weary vigils, she had never once been blessed with a grateful word from his dear lips; yet she stood to her post bravely and without a murmur, feeling that when he did get well again she would hear that which would more than reward her for all her devotion.

At the hour we have chosen for the opening of this chapter, Lucretia was in a tumult of happy excitement, for the surgeon had told her that at last her Whittaker had recovered sufficiently to admit of the removal of the bandages from his head, and she was now waiting with feverish impatience for the doctor to come and disclose the loved features to her view. At last he came, and Lucretia, with beaming eyes and a fluttering heart, bent over the couch with anxious expectancy. One bandage was removed, then another, and another, and lo! the poor wounded face was revealed to the light of day.

"O my own dar——"

What have we here! What is the matter! Alas! it was the face of a stranger!

Poor Lucretia! With one hand covering her upturned eyes, she staggered back with a moan of anguish. Then a spasm of fury distorted her countenance as she brought her fist down with a crash that made the medicine bottles on the table dance again, and exclaimed:

"O confound my cats if I haven't gone and fooled away three mortal weeks here, snuffling and slobbering over the wrong soldier!"

It was a sad, sad truth. The wretched, but innocent and unwitting impostor was R. D., or Richard Dilworthy Whittaker, of Wisconsin, the soldier of dear little Eugenie Le Mulligan, of that State, and utterly unknown to our unhappy Lucretia B. Smith.

Such is life, and the trail of the serpent is over us all. Let us draw the curtain over this melancholy history—for melancholy it must still remain, during a season at least, for the real Reginald de Whittaker has not turned up yet.

December 3, 1864

Important Correspondence

BETWEEN MR. MARK TWAIN OF SAN FRANCISCO,
AND REV. BISHOP HAWKS, D. D., OF NEW YORK,
REV. PHILLIPS BROOKS OF PHILADELPHIA, AND
REV. DR. CUMMINS OF CHICAGO, CONCERNING
THE OCCUPANCY OF GRACE CATHEDRAL.

For a long time I have taken a deep interest in the efforts being made to induce the above-named distinguished clergymen—or, rather, some one of them—to come out here and occupy the pulpit of the noble edifice known as Grace Cathedral. And when I saw that the vestry were uniformly unsuccessful, although doing all that they possibly could to attain their object, I felt it my duty to come forward and throw the weight of my influence—such as it might be—in favor of the laudable undertaking. That by so doing I was not seeking to curry favor with the vestry—and that my actions were prompted by no selfish motive of any kind whatever—is sufficiently evidenced by the fact that I am not a member of Grace Church, and never had any conversation with the vestry upon the subject in hand, and never even hinted to them that I was going to write to the clergymen. What I have done in the matter I did of my own free will and accord, without any solicitation from anybody, and my actions were dictated solely by a spirit of enlarged charity and good feeling toward the congregation of Grace Cathedral. I seek no reward for my services; I desire none but the approval of my own conscience and the satisfaction of knowing I have done that which I conceived to be my duty, to the best of my ability.

M. T.

The correspondence which passed between myself and the Rev. Dr. Hawks was as follows:

LETTER FROM MYSELF TO BISHOP HAWKS.

SAN FRANCISCO, March, 1865.

REV. DR. HAWKS—*Dear Doctor.*—Since I heard that you have telegraphed the vestry of Grace Cathedral here, that you cannot come out to San Francisco and carry on a church at the terms offered you, viz: $7,000 a year, I have concluded to write you on the subject myself. A word in your ear: say nothing to anybody—keep dark—but just pack up your traps and come along out here—I will see that it is all right. That $7,000 dodge was only a *bid*—nothing more. They never expected you to clinch a bargain like that. I will go to work and get up a little competition among the cloth, and the result of it will be that you will make more money in six months here than you would in New York in a year. I can do it. I have a great deal of influence with the clergy here, and especially with the Rev. Dr. Wadsworth and the Rev. Mr. Stebbins—I write their sermons for them. [This latter fact is not generally known, however, and maybe you had as well not mention it.] I can get them to strike for higher wages any time.

You would like this berth. It has a greater number of attractive features than any I know of. It is such a magnificent field, for one thing,—why, sinners are so thick that you can't throw out your line without hooking several of them; you'd be surprised—the flattest old sermon a man can grind out is bound to corral half a dozen. You see, you can do such a land-office business on such a small capital. Why, I wrote the most rambling, incomprehensible harangue of a sermon you ever heard in your life for one of the Episcopalian ministers here, and he landed seventeen with it at the first dash; then I trimmed it up to suit Methodist doctrine, and the Rev. Mr. Thomas got eleven more; I tinkered the doctrinal points again, and Stebbins made a lot of Unitarian converts with it; I worked it over once more, and Dr. Wadsworth did almost as well with it as he usually does with my ablest compositions. It was passed around, after that, from church to church, undergoing changes of dress as before, to suit the vicissitudes of doctrinal climate, until it went the entire rounds. During its career we took in, altogether, a hundred and eighteen of the most abject reprobates that ever traveled on the broad road to destruction.

You would find this a remarkably easy berth—one man to give out the hymns, another to do the praying, another to read the chapter from the Testament—you would have nothing in the world to do but read the litany and preach—no, not *read* the litany, but sing it. They sing the litany here, in the Pontifical Grand Mass style, which is pleasanter and more attractive than to read it. You need not mind that, though;

the tune is not difficult, and requires no more musical taste or education than is required to sell "Twenty-four—self-sealing—envelopes—for f-o-u-r cents," in your city. I like to hear the litany sung. Perhaps there is hardly enough variety in the music, but still the effect is very fine. Bishop Kip never could sing worth a cent, though. However, he has gone to Europe now to learn. Yes, as I said before, you would have nothing in the world to do but preach and sing that litany; and, between you and me, Doc, as regards the music, if you could manage to ring in a few of the popular and familiar old tunes that the people love so well you would be almost certain to create a sensation. I think I can safely promise you that. I am satisfied that you could do many a thing that would attract less attention than would result from adding a spirited variety to the music of the litany.

Your preaching will be easy. Bring along a barrel of your old obsolete sermons; the people here will never know the difference.

Drop me a line, Hawks; I don't know you, except by reputation, but I like you all the same. And don't you fret about the salary. I'll make *that* all right, you know. You need not mention to the vestry of Grace Cathedral, though, that I have been communicating with you on this subject. You see, I do not belong to their church, and they might think I was taking too much trouble on their account—though I assure you, upon my honor, it is no trouble in the world to me; I don't mind it; I am not busy now, and I would rather do it than not. All I want is to have a sure thing that you get your rights. You can depend upon me. I'll see you through this business as straight as a shingle; I haven't been drifting around all my life for nothing. I know a good deal more than a boiled carrot, though I may not appear to. And although I am not of the elect, so to speak, I take a strong interest in these things, nevertheless, and I am not going to stand by and see them come any seven-thousand-dollar arrangement over you. I have sent them word in your name that you won't take less than $18,000, and that you can get $25,000 in greenbacks at home. I also intimated that I was going to write your sermons—I thought it might have a good effect, and every little helps, you know. So you can just pack up and come along—it will be all right—I am satisfied of that. You needn't bring any shirts, I have got enough for us both. You will find there is nothing mean about *me*—I'll wear your clothes, and you can wear mine, just the same as so many twin brothers. When I like a man, I *like* him, and I go my death for him. My friends will all be fond of you, and will take to you as naturally as if they had known you a century. I will introduce you, and you will be all right. You can always depend on them. If you were to point out a man and say you did not like him, they would carve him in a minute.

Hurry along, Bishop. I shall be on the lookout for you, and will take you right to my house and you can stay there as long as you like, and it shan't cost you a cent.

Very truly, yours,
MARK TWAIN.

REPLY OF BISHOP HAWKS.

NEW YORK, April, 1865.

MY DEAR MARK.—I had never heard of you before I received your kind letter, but I feel as well acquainted with you now as if I had known you for years. I see that you understand how it is with us poor laborers in the vineyard, and feel for us in our struggles to gain a livelihood. You will be blessed for this—you will have your reward for the deeds done in the flesh—you will get your deserts hereafter. I am really sorry I cannot visit San Francisco, for I can see now that it must be a pleasant field for the earnest worker to toil in; but it was ordered otherwise, and I submit with becoming humility. My refusal of the position at $7,000 a year was not precisely meant to be final, but was intended for what the ungodly term a "flyer"—the object being, of course, to bring about an increase of the amount. That object was legitimate and proper, since it so nearly affects the interests not only of myself but of those who depend upon me for sustenance and support. Perhaps you remember a remark I made once to a vestry who had been solicited to increase my salary, my family being a pretty large one: they declined, and said it was promised that Providence would take care of the young ravens. I immediately retorted, in my happiest vein, that there was no similar promise concerning the young Hawks, though! I thought it was very good, at the time. The recollection of it has solaced many a weary hour since then, when all the world around me seemed dark and cheerless, and it is a source of tranquil satisfaction to me to think of it even at this day.

No; I hardly meant my decision to be final, as I said before, but subsequent events have compelled that result in spite of me. I threw up my parish in Baltimore, although it was paying me very handsomely, and came to New York to see how things were going in our line. I have prospered beyond my highest expectations. I selected a lot of my best sermons—old ones that had been forgotten by everybody—and once a week I let one of them off in the Church of the Annunciation here. The spirit of the ancient sermons bubbled forth with a bead on it and permeated the hearts of the congregation with a new life, such as the worn body feels when it is refreshed with rare old wine. It was a great hit. The timely arrival of the "call" from San Francisco insured success to me. The people appreciated my merits at once. A number of gentlemen immediately clubbed together and offered me $10,000 a year, and agreed to purchase for me the Church of St. George the Martyr, up town, or to build a new house of worship for me if I preferred it. I closed with them on these terms, my dear Mark, for I feel that so long as not even the little sparrows are suffered to fall to the ground unnoted, I shall be mercifully cared for; and besides, I know that come what may, I can always eke out an existence so long as the cotton trade holds out as good as it is now. I am in cotton to some extent, you understand, and that is one reason why I cannot venture to leave here just at present to accept the position offered me in San Francisco. You see I have some small investments in that line which are as yet in an undecided state, and must be looked after.

But time flies, Mark, time flies; and I must bring this screed to a close and say farewell—and if forever, then forever fare thee well. But I shall never forget you, Mark—never!

Your generous solicitude in my behalf—your splendid inventive ability in conceiving of messages to the vestry calculated to make them offer me a higher salary—your sublime intrepidity in tendering those messages as having come from me—your profound sagacity in chaining and riveting the infatuation of the vestry with the intimation that you were

going to write my sermons for me—your gorgeous liberality
in offering to divide your shirts with me and to make common property of all other wearing apparel belonging to both
parties—your cordial tender of your friends' affections and
their very extraordinary services—your noble hospitality in
providing a home for me in your palatial mansion—all these
things call for my highest admiration and gratitude, and call not
in vain, my dearest Mark. I shall never cease to pray for you and
hold you in kindly and tearful remembrance. Once more, my
gifted friend, accept the fervent thanks and the best wishes of

Your obliged servant,
REV. DR. HAWKS.

Writes a beautiful letter, don't he?

But when the Bishop uses a tabooed expression, and talks
glibly about doing a certain thing "just for a flyer," don't he
shoulder the responsibility of it on to "the ungodly," with a
rare grace?

And what a solid comfort that execrable joke has been to his
declining years, hasn't it? If he goes on thinking about it and
swelling himself up on account of it, he will be wanting a
salary after a while that will break any church that hires him.
However, if he enjoys it, and really thinks it *was* a good joke,
I am very sure I don't want to dilute his pleasure in the least by
dispelling the illusion. It reminds me, though, of a neat remark which the editor of *Harper's Magazine* made three years
ago, in an article wherein he was pleading for charity for the
harmless vanity of poor devil scribblers who imagine they are
gifted with genius. He said *they* didn't know but what their
writing was fine—and then he says: "Don't poor Martin Farquhar Tupper fondle his platitudes and think they are poems?"
That's it. Let the Bishop fondle his little joke—no doubt it is
just as good to him as if it were the very soul of humor.

But I wonder who in the mischief *is* "St.-George-the-
Martyr-Up-Town?" However, no matter—the Bishop is not
going to take his chances altogether with St.-George-the-
Martyr-Up-Town, or with the little sparrows that are subject
to accidents, either—he has a judicious eye on cotton. And
he is right, too. Nobody deserves to be helped who don't try
to help himself, and "faith without works" is a risky doctrine.

Now, what is your idea about his last paragraph? Don't you think he is spreading it on rather thick?—as "the ungodly" would term it. Do you really think there is any rain behind all that thunder and lightening? Do you suppose he really means it? They are mighty powerful adjectives—uncommonly powerful adjectives—and sometimes I seem to smell a faint odor of irony about them. But that could hardly be. He evidently loves me. Why, if I could be brought to believe that that reverend old humorist was discharging any sarcasm at me, I would never write to him again as long as I live. Thinks I will "get my deserts her after"—I don't hardly like the ring of that, altogether.

He says he will pray for me, though. Well, he couldn't do anything that would fit my case better, and he couldn't find a subject who would thank him more kindly for it than I would. I suppose I shall come in under the head of "sinners at large"—but I don't mind that; I am no better than any other sinner and I am not entitled to especial consideration. They pray for the congregation first, you know—and with considerable vim; then they pray mildly for other denominations; then for the near relations of the congregation; then for their distant relatives; then for the surrounding community; then for the State; then for the Government officers; then for the United States; then for North America; then for the whole Continent; then for England, Ireland and Scotland; France, Germany and Italy; Russia, Prussia and Austria; then for the inhabitants of Norway, Sweden and Timbuctoo; and those of Saturn, Jupiter and New Jersey; and then they give the niggers a lift, and the Hindoos a lift, and the Turks a lift, and the Chinese a lift; and then, after they have got the fountain of mercy baled out as dry as an ash-hopper, they bespeak the sediment left in the bottom of it for us poor "sinners at large."

It ain't just exactly fair, *is* it? Sometimes, (being a sort of a Presbyterian in a general way, and a brevet member of one of the principal churches of that denomination,) I stand up in devout attitude, with downcast eyes, and hands clasped upon the back of the pew before me, and listen attentively and expectantly for awhile; and then rest upon one foot for a season; and then upon the other; and then insert my hands under my coat-tails and stand erect and look solemn; and then fold my arms and droop forward and look dejected; and then cast my eye furtively at the minister; and then at the congregation; and then grow absent-minded, and catch myself counting the lace bonnets; and marking the drowsy members; and noting the wide-awake ones; and averaging the bald heads; and afterwards descend to indolent conjectures as to whether the buzzing fly that keeps stumbling up the window-pane and sliding down backwards again will ever accomplish his object to his satisfaction; and, finally, I give up and relapse into a dreary reverie—and about this time the minister reaches my department, and brings me back to hope and consciousness with a kind word for the poor "sinners at large."

Sometimes we are even forgotten altogether and left out in the cold—and then I call to mind the vulgar little boy who was fond of hot biscuits, and whose mother promised him that he should have all that were left if he would stay away and keep quiet and be a good little boy while the strange guest ate his breakfast; and who watched that voracious guest till the growing apprehension in his young bosom gave place to demonstrated ruin, and then sung out: "There! I know'd how it was goin' to be—I know'd how it was goin' to be, from the start! Blamed if he hain't gobbled the last biscuit!"

I do not complain, though, because it is very seldom that the Hindoos and the Turks and the Chinese get all the atoning biscuits and leave us sinners at large to go hungry. They *do* remain at the board a long time, though, and we often get a little tired waiting for our turn. How would it do to be less diffuse? How would it do to ask a blessing upon the specialities—I mean the congregation and the immediate community—and then include the whole broad universe in one glowing, fervent appeal? How would it answer to adopt the simplicity and the beauty and the brevity and the comprehensiveness of the Lord's Prayer as a model? But perhaps I am wandering out of my jurisdiction.

The letters I wrote to the Rev. Phillips Brooks of Philadelphia, and the Rev. Dr. Cummins of Chicago, urging them to come here and take charge of Grace Cathedral, and offering them my countenance and support, will be published next week, together with their replies to the same.

May 6, 1865

Answers to Correspondents

DISCARDED LOVER.—"I loved and still love, the beautiful Edwitha Howard, and intended to marry her. Yet during my temporary absence at Benicia, last week, alas! she married Jones. Is my happiness to be thus blasted for life? Have I no redress?"

Of course you have. All the law, written and unwritten, is on your side. The *intention* and not the *act* constitutes crime—in other words, constitutes the *deed*. If you call your bosom friend a fool, and *intend* it for an insult, it *is* an insult; but if you do it playfully, and meaning no insult, it is *not* an insult. If you discharge a pistol *accidentally*, and kill a man, you can go free, for you have done no murder—but if you try to kill a man, and manifestly *intend* to kill him, but fail utterly to do it, the law still holds that the *intention* constituted the crime, and you are guilty of murder. Ergo, if you had married Edwitha *accidentally*, and without really *intending* to do it, you would not actually be married to her at all, because the *act* of marriage could not be complete without the *intention*. And, ergo, in the strict spirit of the law, since you deliberately *intended* to marry Edwitha, and didn't do it, you *are* married to her all the same—because, as I said before, the *intention* constitutes the crime. It is as clear as day that Edwitha is your wife, and your redress lies in taking a club and mutilating Jones with it as much as you can. Any man has a right to protect his own wife from the advances of other men. But you have another alternative—you were married to Edwitha *first*, because of your deliberate intention, and now you can prosecute her for bigamy, in subsequently marrying Jones. But there is another phase in this complicated case: You *intended* to marry Edwitha, and consequently, according to law, she is your wife—there is no getting around that—but she didn't marry you, and if she *never intended* to marry you *you are not her husband*, of course. Ergo, in marrying Jones, she was guilty of bigamy, because she was the wife of another man at the time—which is all very well as far as it goes—but then, don't you see, she had no other *husband* when she married Jones, and consequently she was *not* guilty of bigamy.

Now according to this view of the case, Jones married a *spinster*, who was a *widow* at the same time and another man's *wife* at the same time, and yet who had no *husband* and *never had one*, and never had any *intention* of getting married, and therefore, of course, *never had* been married; and by the same reasoning you are a *bachelor*, because you have never been any one's *husband*, and a *married man* because you have a wife living, and to all intents and purposes a *widower*, because you have been deprived of that wife, and a consummate *ass* for going off to Benicia in the first place, while things were so mixed. And by this time I have got myself so tangled up in the intricacies of this extraordinary case that I shall have to give up any further attempt to advise you—I might get confused and fail to make myself understood. I think I could take up the argument where I left off, and by following it closely awhile, perhaps I could prove to your satisfaction, either that you never existed at all, or that you are dead, now, and consequently don't need the faithless Edwitha—I think I could do that, if it would afford you any comfort.

MR. MARK TWAIN—Sir: I wish to call your attention to a matter which has come to my notice frequently, but before doing so, I may remark, *en passant*, that I don't see why your parents should have called you Mark Twain; had they known your *ardent* nature, they would doubtless have named you Water-less Twain. However, *Mark* what I am about to call your attention to, and I do so knowing you to be "capable and honest" in your inquiries after truth, and that you can fathom the mysteries of Love. Now I want to know why, (and this is the object of my enquiry,) a man should proclaim his love in large gilt letters over his door and in his windows. Why does he do so? You may have noticed in the Russ House Block, one door south of the hotel entrance an inscription thus: "I Love Land." Now if this refers to real estate he should not say "love;" he should say "like." Very true, in speaking of one's native soil, we say, "Yes, my native land I love thee," but I am satisfied that even if you could suppose this inscription had any remote reference to a birthplace, it does not mean a ranch or eligibly-situated town site. Why does he do it? why does he?

Yours, without prejudice,
NOMME DE PLUME.

Now, did it never strike this sprightly Frenchman that he could have gone in there and asked the man himself "why he does it," as easily as he could write to me on the subject? But no matter—this is just about the weight of the important questions usually asked of editors and answered in the "Correspondents' Column;" sometimes a man asks how to spell a difficult word—when he might as well have looked in the dictionary; or he asks who discovered America—when he might have consulted history; or he asks who in the mischief Cain's wife was—when a moment's reflection would have satisfied him that nobody knows and nobody cares—at least, except himself. The Frenchman's little joke is good, though, for doubtless "Quarter-less twain," *would* sound like "Water-less twain," if uttered between two powerful brandy punches. But as to why the man in question loves land—I cannot imagine, unless his constitution resembles mine, and he don't love water.

ARABELLA.—No, neither Mr. Dan Setchell nor Mr. Gottschalk are married. Perhaps it will interest you to know that they are both uncommonly anxious to marry, however. And perhaps it will interest you still more to know that in case they do marry, they will doubtless wed females; I hazard this, because, in discussing the question of marrying, they have uniformly expressed a preference for your sex. I answer your inquiries concerning Miss Adelaide Phillips in the order in which they occur, by number, as follows: I. No. II. Yes. III. Perhaps. IV. "Scasely."

PERSECUTED UNFORTUNATE.—You say you owe six months' board, and you have no money to pay it with, and your landlord keeps harassing you about it, and you have made all the excuses and explanations possible, and now you are at a loss what to say to him in future. Well, it is a delicate matter to offer advice in a case like this, but your distress impels me to make a suggestion, at least, since I cannot venture to do more. When he next importunes you, how would it do to take him impressively by the hand and ask, with simulated emotion, *"Monsieur Jean, votre chien, comme se porte-il?"*

Doubtless that is very bad French, but you'll find that it will answer just as well as the unadulterated article.

ARTHUR AUGUSTUS.—No, you are wrong; that is the proper way to throw a brickbat or a tomahawk, but it doesn't answer so well for a boquet—you will hurt somebody if you keep it up. Turn your nosegay upside down, take it by the stems, and toss it with an upward sweep—did you ever pitch quoits?—that is the idea. The practice of recklessly heaving immense solid boquets, of the general size and weight of prize cabbages, from the dizzy altitude of the galleries, is dangerous and very reprehensible. Now, night before last, at the Academy of Music, just after Signorina Sconcia had finished that exquisite melody, "The Last Rose of Summer," one of these floral pile-drivers came cleaving down through the atmosphere of applause, and if she hadn't deployed suddenly to the right, it would have driven her into the floor like a shingle-nail. Of course that boquet was well-meant, but how would you have liked to have been the target? A sincere compliment is always grateful to a lady, so long as you don't try to knock her down with it.

AMATEUR SERENADER.—Yes, I will give you some advice, and do it with a good deal of pleasure. I live in a neighborhood which is well stocked with young ladies, and consequently I am excruciatingly sensitive upon the subject of serenading. Sometimes I suffer. In the first place, always tune your instruments before you get within three hundred yards of your destination—this will enable you to take your adored unawares, and create a pleasant surprise by launching out at once upon your music; it astonishes the dogs and cats out of their presence of mind, too, so that if you hurry you can get through before they have a chance to recover and interrupt you; besides, there is nothing captivating in the sounds produced in tuning a lot of melancholy guitars and fiddles, and neither does a group of able-bodied, sentimental young men so engaged look at all dignified. Secondly, clear your throats and do all the coughing you have got to do before you arrive

at the seat of war—I have known a young lady to be ruthlessly startled out of her slumbers by such a sudden and
direful blowing of noses and "h'm-h'm-ing" and coughing,
that she imagined the house was beleaguered by victims of
consumption from the neighboring hospital; do you suppose
the music was able to make her happy after that? Thirdly,
don't stand right under the porch and howl, but get out in
the middle of the street, or better still, on the other side of
it—distance lends enchantment to the sound; if you have previously transmitted a hint to the lady that she is going to be
serenaded, she will understand who the music is for; besides,
if you occupy a neutral position in the middle of the street,
may be all the neighbors round will take stock in your serenade and invite you in to take wine with them. Fourthly,
don't sing a whole opera through—enough of a thing's
enough. Fifthly, don't sing "Lilly Dale"—the profound satisfaction that most of us derive from the reflection that the girl
treated of in that song is dead, is constantly marred by the
resurrection of the lugubrious ditty itself by your kind of
people. Sixthly, don't let your screaming tenor soar an octave
above all the balance of the chorus, and remain there setting
everybody's teeth on edge for four blocks around; and, above
all, don't let him sing a solo; probably there is nothing in the
world so suggestive of serene contentment and perfect bliss as
the spectacle of a calf chewing a dish-rag, but the nearest approach to it is your reedy tenor, standing apart, in sickly attitude, with head thrown back and eyes uplifted to the moon,
piping his distressing solo: now do not pass lightly over this
matter, friend, but ponder it with that seriousness which its
importance entitles it to. Seventhly, after you have run all the
chickens and dogs and cats in the vicinity distracted, and
roused them into a frenzy of crowing, and cackling, and yowling, and caterwauling, put up your dreadful instruments and
go home. Eighthly, as soon as you start, gag your tenor—
otherwise he will be letting off a screech every now and then
to let the people know he is around; your amateur tenor
singer is notoriously the most self-conceited of all God's creatures. Tenthly, don't go serenading at all—it is a wicked, unhappy and seditious practice, and a calamity to all souls that
are weary and desire to slumber and be at rest. Eleventhly and

lastly, the father of the young lady in the next block says that if you come prowling around his neighborhood again with your infamous scraping and tooting and yelling, he will sally forth and deliver you into the hands of the police. As far as I am concerned myself, I would like to have you come, and come often, but as long as the old man is so prejudiced, perhaps you had better serenade mostly in Oakland, or San José, or around there somewhere.

ST. CLAIR HIGGINS, *Los Angeles.* — "My life is a failure; I have adored, wildly, madly, and she whom I love has turned coldly from me and shed her affections upon another; what would you advise me to do?" You should shed your affections on another, also—or on several, if there are enough to go round. Also, do everything you can to make your former flame unhappy. There is an absurd idea disseminated in novels, that the happier a girl is with another man, the happier it makes the old lover she has blighted. Don't you allow yourself to believe any such nonsense as that. The more cause that girl finds to regret that she did not marry you, the more comfortable you will feel over it. It isn't poetical, but it is mighty sound doctrine.

ARITHMETICUS, *Virginia, Nevada.* — "If it would take a cannon-ball $3\frac{1}{3}$ seconds to travel four miles, and $3\frac{3}{8}$ seconds to travel the next four, and $3\frac{5}{8}$ seconds to travel the next four, and if its rate of progress continued to diminish in the same ratio, how long would it take it to go fifteen hundred millions of miles?" I don't know.

AMBITIOUS LEARNER, *Oakland.* — Yes, you are right—America was not discovered by Alexander Selkirk.

JULIA MARIA. — Fashions? It is out of my line, Maria. How am I to know anything about such mysteries—I that languish alone? Sometimes I am startled into a passing interest in such things, but not often. Now, a few nights ago, I was reading the *Dramatic Chronicle* at the opera, between the acts—reading a poem in it, and reading it after my usual style of ciphering out the merits of poetry, which is to read a line or two

near the top, a verse near the bottom and then strike an average, (even professional critics do that)—when—well, it had a
curious effect, read as I happened to read it:

> " 'What shall I wear?' asked Addie St. Clair,
>   As she stood by her mirror so young and fair "—

and then I skipped a line or so, while I returned the bow of a
strange young lady, who, I observed too late, had intended
that courtesy for a ruffian behind me, instead of for myself,
and read:

> "The *modiste* replied, 'It were wicked to hide
>   Such peerless perfection that should be your pride' "—

and then I skipped to the climax, to get my average, and
read—

> " 'My beautiful bride!' a low voice replied,
>   As handsome Will Vernon appeared at her side,
>   'If you wish from all others my heart to beguile,
>   *Wear a smile* to-night, darling—your own sunny smile.' "

Now there's an airy costume for you! a "sunny smile!"
There's a costume, which, for simplicity and picturesqueness,
grand-discounts a Georgia major's uniform, which is a shirt-
collar and a pair of spurs. But when I came to read the remainder of the poem, it appeared that my new Lady Godiva
had other clothes beside her sunny smile, and so—it is not
necessary to pursue a subject further which no longer possesses any startling interest. Ask me no questions about fashions, Julia, but use your individual judgment in the matter—
"wear your own sunny smile," and such millinery traps and
trimmings as may be handy and will be likely to set it off to
best advantage.

NOM DE PLUME.—Behold! the Frenchman cometh again,
as follows:

"Your courteous attention to my last enquiry induces this acknowledgment of your kindness. I availed myself of your suggestions
and made the enquiry of the gentleman, and he told me very frankly
that it was—none of my business. So you see we do sometimes have

to apply to your correspondence column for correct information, after all. I read in the papers a few days since some remarks upon the grammatical construction of the sentences—'*Sic semper traditoris*' and '*Sic semper traditoribus,*' and I procured a Latin grammar in order to satisfy myself as to the genative, dative and ablative cases of traitors—and while wending my weary way homewards at a late hour of the night, thinking over the matter, and not knowing what moment some cut-throat would knock me over, and, as he escaped, flourishing my watch and portmonaie, exclaim, '*Sic semper tyranis,*' I stumbled over an individual lying on the sidewalk, with a postage stamp pasted on his hat in lieu of a car ticket, and evidently in the *objective case* to the phrase 'how come you so?' As I felt in his pockets to see if his friends had taken care of his money, lest he might be robbed, he exclaimed, tragically, '*Si*(hic) *semper tarantula-juice!*' Not finding the phrase in my grammar, which I examined at once, I thought of your advice and *asked* him what he meant, said he 'I mean jis what I say, and I intend to sti-hic to it.' He was *quarter*less, Twain; when I *sounded* him he hadn't a cent, although he *smelled* strong of a 5-scent shop."

MELTON MOWBRAY, *Dutch Flat.*—This correspondent sends a lot of doggerel, and says it has been regarded as very good in Dutch Flat. I give a specimen verse:

"The Assyrian came down, like a wolf on the fold,
    And his cohorts were gleaming in purple and gold;
    And the sheen of his spears shone like stars on the sea,
    When the blue wave rolls nightly on deep Galilee."

There, that will do. That may be very good Dutch Flat poetry, but it won't do in the metropolis. It is too smooth and blubbery; it reads like buttermilk gurgling from a jug. What the people ought to have, is something spirited—something like "Johnny comes marching home." However, keep on practicing, and you may succeed yet. There is genius in you, but too much blubber.

LAURA MATILDA.—No, Mr. Dan Setchell has never been in the House of Correction. That is to say he never went there by compulsion; he remembers going there once to visit a very dear friend—one of his boyhood's friends—but the visit was merely temporary, and he only staid five or six weeks.

PROFESSIONAL BEGGAR.—No, you are not obliged to take greenbacks at par.

NOTE.—Several letters, chiefly from young ladies and young bachelors, remain over, to be answered next week, want of space precluding the possibility of attending to them at present. I always had an idea that most of the letters written to editors were written by the editors themselves. But I find, now, that I was mistaken.

––––––––

MORAL STATISTICIAN.—I don't want any of your statistics. I took your whole batch and lit my pipe with it. I hate your kind of people. You are always ciphering out how much a man's health is injured, and how much his intellect is impaired, and how many pitiful dollars and cents he wastes in the course of ninety-two years' indulgence in the fatal practice of smoking; and in the equally fatal practice of drinking coffee; and in playing billiards occasionally; and in taking a glass of wine at dinner, etc., etc., etc. And you are always figuring out how many women have been burned to death because of the dangerous fashion of wearing expansive hoops, etc., etc., etc. You never see but one side of the question. You are blind to the fact that most old men in America smoke and drink coffee, although, according to your theory, they ought to have died young; and that hearty old Englishmen drink wine and survive it, and portly old Dutchmen both drink and smoke freely, and yet grow older and fatter all the time. And you never try to find out how much solid comfort, relaxation and enjoyment a man derives from smoking in the course of a lifetime, (and which is worth ten times the money he would save by letting it alone,) nor the appalling aggregate of happiness lost in a lifetime by your kind of people from *not* smoking. Of course you can save money by denying yourself all these little vicious enjoyments for fifty years, but then what can you do with it?—what use can you put it to? Money can't save your infinitesimal soul; all the use that money can be put to is to purchase comfort and enjoyment in this life— therefore, as you are an enemy to comfort and enjoyment, where is the use in accumulating cash? It won't do for you to say that you can use it to better purpose in furnishing a good table, and in charities, and in supporting tract societies, because you know yourself that you people who have no petty vices are never known to give away a cent, and that you stint yourselves so in the matter of food that you are always feeble and hungry. And you never dare to laugh in the daytime for fear some poor wretch, seeing you in a good humor, will try to borrow a dollar of you; and in church you are always down on your knees when the contribution box comes around; and you always pay your debts in greenbacks, and never give the revenue officers a true statement of your income. Now you know all these things yourself, don't you? Very well, then, what is the use of your stringing out your miserable lives to a lean and withered old age? What is the use of your saving money that is so utterly worthless to you? In a word, why don't you go off somewhere and die, and not be always trying to seduce people into becoming as "ornery" and unloveable as you are yourselves, by your ceaseless and villainous "moral statistics?" Now I don't approve of dissipation, and I don't indulge in it, either, but I haven't a particle of confidence in a man who has no redeeming petty vices whatever, and so I don't want to hear from you any more. I think you are the very same man who read me a long lecture, last week, about the degrading vice of smoking cigars, and then came back, in my absence, with your vile, reprehensible fire-proof gloves on, and carried off my beautiful parlor stove.

SIMON WHEELER, *Sonora.*—The following simple and touching remarks and accompanying poem have just come to hand from the rich gold-mining region of Sonora:

To Mr. Mark Twain: The within parson, which I have sot to poetry under the name and style of "He Done His Level Best," was one among the whitest men I ever see, and it ain't every man that knowed him that can find it in his heart to say he's glad the pore cuss is busted and gone home to the States. He was here in an early day, and he was the handyest man about takin holt of anything that come along you most ever see, I judge; he was a cheerful, stirrin cretur, always doin something, and no man can say he ever see him do anything by halvers. Preachin was his nateral gait, but he warn't a man to lay back and twidle his thums because there didn't happen to be nothing doin in his own espeshial line—no sir, he was a man who would meander forth and stir up something for hisself. His last acts was to go his pile on "kings-*and*," (calklatin to fill, but which he didn't fill,) when there was a "flush" out agin him, and naterally, you see, he went under. And so, he was cleaned out, as you may say, and he struck the home-trail, cheerful but flat broke. I knowed this talonted man in Arkansaw, and if you would print this humbly tribute to his gorgis abillities, you would greatly obleege his onhappy friend.

SONORA, Southern Mines, June, 1865.

HE DONE HIS LEVEL BEST.

Was he a mining on the flat—
    He done it with a zest;
Was he a leading of the choir—
    He done his level best.

If he'd a reglar task to do,
    He never took no rest;
Or if twas off-and-on—the same—
    He done his level best.

If he was preachin on his beat,
    He'd tramp from east to west,
And north to south—in cold and heat
    He done his level best.

He'd yank a sinner outen (Hades*)
    And land him with the blest—
Then snatch a prayer 'n waltz in again,
    And do his level best.

He'd cuss and sing and howl and pray,
    And dance and drink and jest,
And lie and steal—all one to him—
    He done his level best.

Whate'er this man was sot to do,
    He done it with a zest:
No matter *what* his contract was,
    HE'D DO HIS LEVEL BEST.

*You observe that I have taken the liberty to alter a word for you, Simon—to tone you down a little, as it were. Your language was unnecessarily powerful. M. T.

Verily, this man *was* gifted with "gorgis abillities," and it is a happiness to me to embalm the memory of their lustre in these columns. If it were not that the poet crop is unusually large and rank in California this year, I would encourage you to continue writing, Simon—but as it is, perhaps it might be too risky in you to enter against so much opposition.

INQUIRER wishes to know which is the best brand of smoking tobacco, and how it is manufactured. The most popular—mind I do not feel at liberty to give an opinion as to the best, and so I simply say the most popular—smoking tobacco is the miraculous conglomerate they call "Killickinick." It is composed of equal parts of tobacco stems, chopped straw, "old soldiers," fine shavings, oak leaves, dog-fennel, corn-shucks, sun-flower petals, outside leaves of the cabbage plant, and any refuse of any description whatever that costs nothing and will burn. After the ingredients are thoroughly mixed together, they are run through a chopping-machine. The mass is then sprinkled with fragrant Scotch snuff, packed into various seductive shapes, labelled "Genuine Killickinick, from the old original manufactory at Richmond," and sold to consumers at a dollar a pound. The choicest brands contain a double portion of "old soldiers," and sell at a dollar and a half. "Genuine Turkish" tobacco contains a treble quantity of old soldiers, and is worth two or three dollars, according to the amount of service the said "old soldiers" have previously seen. N. B. This article is preferred by the Sultan of Turkey; his picture and autograph are on the label. Take a handful of "Killickinick," crush it as fine as you can, and examine it closely, and you will find that you can make as good an analysis of it as I have done; you must not expect to discover any particles of genuine tobacco by this rough method, however—to do that, it will be necessary to take your specimen to the mint and subject it to a fire-assay. A good article of cheap tobacco is now made of chopped pine-straw and Spanish moss; it contains one "old soldier" to the ton, and is called "Fine Old German Tobacco."

ANNA MARIA says as follows: "We have got such a nice literary society, O! you can't think! It is made up of members of our church, and we meet and read poetry and sketches and essays, and such things—mostly original—in fact, we have got talent enough among ourselves, without having to borrow reading matter from books and newspapers. We met a few evenings since at a dwelling on Howard, between Seventh and Eighth, and ever so many things were read. It was a little dull, though, until a young gentleman, (who is a member of our church, and oh, so gifted!) unrolled a bundle of manuscript and read *such* a funny thing about "Love's Bakery," where they prepare young people for matrimony, and about a young man who was engaged to be married, and who had the small-pox, and the erysipelas, and lost one eye and got both legs broken, and one arm, and got the other arm pulled out by a carding-machine, and finally got so damaged that there was scarcely anything of him left for the young lady to marry. You ought to have been there to hear how well he read it, and how they all laughed. We went right to work and nominated him for the Presidency of the Society, and he only lost it by two votes."

Yes, dear, I remember that "*such* a funny thing" which he read—I wrote it myself, for THE CALIFORNIAN, last October. But as he read it well, I forgive him—I can't bear to hear a good thing read badly. You had better keep an eye on that gifted young man, though, or he will be treating you to Washington's Farewell Address in manuscript the first thing you know—and if *that* should pass unchallenged, nothing in the world could save him from the Presidency.

CHARMING SIMPLICITY.

I once read the following paragraph in a newspaper:

"*Powerful Metaphor.*—A Western editor, speaking of a quill-driving cotemporary, says 'his intellect is so dense that it would take the auger of common sense longer to bore into it than it would to bore through Mont Blanc with a boiled carrot!'"

I have found that man. And I have found him—not in Stockton—not in Congress—not even in the Board of Education—but in the editorial sanctum of the Gold Hill *News*. Hear him:

"BYRON BUSTED.—The most fearful exhibition of literary ignorance—to say nothing of literary judgment—that we have had occasion to notice in many a year, is presented by the San Francisco CALIFORNIAN, a professedly literary journal. It is among the 'Answers to Correspondents.' Lord Byron's magnificent and universally admired verses on the Destruction of Sennacherib, are sent from Dutch Flat to the CALIFORNIAN, and are there not recognized, but denounced as a 'lot of doggerel.' Ye Gods! Perhaps the editor will try to get out of his 'fix' by saying it was all in fun—that it is a Dutch Nix joke! Read the comments:

" 'MELTON MOWBRAY, *Dutch Flat.*—This correspondent sends us a lot of doggerel, and says it has been regarded as very good in Dutch Flat. I give a specimen verse:

> 'The Assyrian came down, like a wolf on the fold,
> And his cohorts were gleaming in purple and gold;
> And the sheen of his spears shone like stars on the sea,
> When the blue wave rolls nightly on deep Galilee.'

" 'There, that will do. That may be very good Dutch Flat poetry, but it won't do in the metropolis. It is too smooth and blubbery; it reads like buttermilk gurgling from a jug. What the people should have, is something spirited—something like 'Johnny comes marching home.' However, keep on practicing, and you may succeed yet. There is genius in you, but too much blubber.' "

Come, now, friend, about what style of joke *would* suit your capacity?—because we are anxious to come within the comprehension of all. Try a good old one; for instance: "Jones meets Smith; says Smith, 'I'm glad it's raining, Jones, because it'll start everything out of the ground.' 'Oh, Lord, I hope not,' says Jones, 'because then it would start my first wife out!' " How's that? Does that "bore through?"

Since writing the above, I perceive that the *Flag* has fallen into the wake of the *News,* and got sold by the same rather glaring burlesque that disposed of its illustrious predecessor at such an exceedingly cheap rate.

LITERARY CONNOISSEUR asks "Who is the author of these fine lines?

> 'Let dogs delight to bark and bite,
> For God hath made them so!' "

Here is a man gone into ecstasies of admiration over a nursery rhyme! Truly, the wonders of this new position of mine do never cease. The longer I hold it the more I am astonished, and every new applicant for information, who comes to me, leaves me more helplessly stunned than the one who went before him. No, I *don't* know who wrote those "fine lines," but I expect old Wat's-'is-name, who wrote old Watt's hymns, is the heavy gun you are after. However, it may be a bad guess, and if you find it isn't him, why then lay it on Tupper. That is my usual method. It is awkward to betray ignorance. Therefore, when I come across anything in the poetry line, which is particularly mild and aggravating, I always consider it pretty safe to lay it on Tupper. The policy is subject to accidents, of course, but then it works pretty well, and I hit oftener than I miss. A "connoisseur" should never be in doubt about anything. It is ruinous. I will give you a few hints. Attribute all the royal blank verse, with a martial ring to it, to Shakspeare; all the grand ponderous ditto, with a solemn lustre as of holiness about it, to Milton; all the ardent love poetry, tricked out in affluent imagery, to Byron; all the scouring, dashing, descriptive warrior rhymes to Scott; all the sleepy, tiresome, rural stuff, to Thomson and his eternal *Seasons*; all the genial, warm-hearted jolly Scotch poetry, to Burns; all the tender, broken-hearted song-verses to Moore; all the broken-English poetry to Chaucer or Spenser—whichever occurs to you first; all the heroic poetry, about the impossible deeds done before Troy, to Homer; all the nauseating rebellion mush-and-milk about young fellows who have come home to die—just before the battle, mother—to George F. Root and kindred spirits; all the poetry that everybody admires and appreciates, but nobody ever reads or quotes from, to Dryden, Cowper and Shelley; all the graveyard poetry to Elegy Gray or Wolfe, indiscriminately; all the poetry that you can't understand, to Emerson; all the harmless old platitudes, delivered with a stately and oppressive pretense of originality, to Tupper, and all the "Anonymous" poetry to yourself. Bear these rules in mind, and you will pass muster as a connoisseur; as long as you can talk glibly about the "styles" of authors, you will get as much credit as if you were really acquainted with their works. Throw out a mangled French phrase occasionally, and you will pass for an accomplished man, and a Latin phrase dropped now and then will gain you the reputation of being a learned one. Many a distinguished "connoisseur" in *belles lettres* and classic erudition travels on the same capital I have advanced you in this rather lengthy paragraph. Make a note of that "Anonymous" suggestion—never let a false modesty deter you from "cabbaging" anything you find drifting about without an owner. I shall publish a volume of poems, shortly, over my signature, which became the "children of my fancy" in this unique way.

ETIQUETTICUS, *Monitor Silver Mines.*—"If a lady and gentleman are riding on a mountain trail, should the lady precede the gentleman, or the gentleman precede the lady?" It is not a matter of politeness at all—it is a matter of the heaviest mule. The heavy mule should keep the lower side, so as to brace himself and stop the light one should he lose his footing. But to my notion you are worrying yourself a good deal more than necessary about etiquette, up there in the snow belt. You had better be skirmishing for bunch-grass to feed your mule on, now that the snowy season is nearly ready to set in.

TRUE SON OF THE UNION.—Very well, I will publish the following extract from one of the dailies, since you seem to consider it necessary to your happiness, and since your trembling soul has found in it evidence of lukewarm loyalty on the part of the Collector—but candidly, now, don't you think you are in rather small business? I do, anyhow, though I do not wish to flatter you:

"BATTLE OF BUNKER HILL.

SAN FRANCISCO, June 17, 1865.
Messrs. Editors: Why is it that on this day, the greatest of all in the annals of the rights of man—viz: the Glorious Anniversary of the Battle of Bunker Hill—*our Great Ensign of Freedom does not appear on the Custom House*? Perhaps our worthy Collector is so busy Senator-

making that it might have escaped his notice. You will be pleased to assign an excuse for the above official delinquency, and oblige

A NEW ENGLAND MECHANIC."

Why was that published? I think it was simply to gratify a taste for literary pursuits which has suddenly broken out in the system of the artisan from New England; or perhaps he has an idea, somehow or other, in a general way, that it would be a showing of neat and yet not gaudy international politeness for Collectors of ports to hoist their flags in commemoration of British victories, (for the physical triumph was theirs, although we claim all the moral effect of a victory;) or perhaps it struck him that "this day, the greatest of all *in the annals of the rights of man*," (whatever that may mean, for it is a little too deep for me,) was a fine, high-sounding expression, and yearned to get it off in print; or perhaps it occurred to him that "the Glorious Anniversary," and "our Great Ensign of Freedom," being new and startling figures of speech, would probably create something of a sensation if properly marshalled under the leadership of stunning capitals, and so he couldn't resist the temptation to trot them out in grand dress parade before the reading public; or perhaps, finally, he really *did* think the Collector's atrocious conduct partook of the character of a devilish "official delinquency," and imperatively called for explanation or "excuse." And still, after all this elaborate analysis, I am considerably "mixed" as to the actual motive for publishing that thing.

But observe how quibbling and fault-finding breed in a land of newspapers. Yesterday I had the good fortune to intercept the following bitter communication on its way to the office of a cotemporary, and I am happy in being able to afford to the readers of THE CALIFORNIAN the first perusal of it:

Editors of the Flaming Loyalist: What does it mean? The extraordinary conduct of Mr. John Doe, one of the highest Government officials among us, upon the anniversary of the battle of Bunker Hill—that day so inexpressibly dear to every loyal American heart because our patriot forefathers got worsted upon that occasion—is matter of grave suspicion. It was observed (by those who have closely watched Mr. Doe's actions ever since he has been in office, and who have thought his professions of loyalty lacked the genuine ring,) that this man, *who has uniformly got drunk, heretofore, upon all the nation's great historical days, remained thoroughly sober upon the hallowed 17th of June.* Is not this significant? Was this the pardonable forgetfulness of a loyal officer, or rather, was it not the deliberate act of a malignant and a traitorous heart? You will be pleased to assign an excuse for the above official delinquency, and oblige

A SENTINEL AGRICULTURIST UPON THE
NATIONAL WATCHTOWER.

Now isn't that enough to disgust any man with being an officeholder? Here is a drudging public servant who has always served his masters patiently and faithfully, and although there was nothing in his instructions requiring him to get drunk on national holidays, yet with an unselfishness, and an enlarged public spirit, and a gushing patriotism that did him infinite credit, he *did* always get as drunk as a loon on these occasions—ay, and even upon any occasion of minor importance when an humble effort on his part could shed additional lustre upon his country's greatness, never did he hesitate a moment to go and fill himself full of gin. Now observe how his splendid services have been appreciated—behold how quickly the remembrance of them hath passed away—mark how the tried servant has been rewarded. This grateful officer—this pure patriot—has been known to get drunk five hundred times in a year for the honor and glory of his country and his country's flag, and no man cried "Well done, thou good and faithful servant"—yet the very first time he ventures to remain sober on a battle anniversary (exhausted by the wear and tear of previous efforts, no doubt,) this spying "Agriculturist," who has deserted his onion-patch to perch himself upon the National Watch-Tower at the risk of breaking his meddlesome neck, discovers the damning fact that he is firm on his legs, and sings out: "He don't keep up his lick!—he's DISLOYAL!"

Oh, stuff! a public officer has a hard enough time of it, at best, without being constantly hauled over the coals for inconsequential and insignificant trifles. If you *must* find fault, go and ferret out something worth while to find fault with —if John Doe or the Collector neglect the actual business they are required by the Government to transact, impeach them. But pray allow them a little poetical license in the choice of occasions for getting drunk and hoisting the National flag. If the oriental artisan and the sentinel agriculturalist held the offices of these men, would they ever *attend to anything else* but the flag-flying and gin-soaking outward forms of patriotism and official industry?

SOCRATES MURPHY. — You speak of having given offense to a gentleman at the Opera by *unconsciously* humming an air which the tenor was singing at the time. Now, part of that is a deliberate falsehood. You were not doing it "unconsciously;" no man does such a mean, vulgar, egotistical thing as that unconsciously. You were doing it to "show off;" you wanted the people around you to know you had been to operas before, and to think you were not such an ignorant, self-conceited, supercilious ass as you looked; I can tell you Arizona opera-sharps, any time; you prowl around beer-cellars and listen to some howling-dervish of a Dutchman exterminating an Italian air, and then you come into the Academy and prop yourself up against the wall with the stuffy aspect and the imbecile leer of a clothing-store dummy, and go to droning along about half an octave below the tenor, and disgusting everybody in your neighborhood with your beery strains. [N. B. If this rough-shod eloquence of mine touches you on a raw spot occasionally, recollect that I am talking for your good, Murphy, and that I am simplifying my language so as to bring it clearly within the margin of your comprehension; it might be gratifying to you to be addressed as if you were an Oxford graduate, but then you wouldn't understand it, you know.] You have got another abominable habit, my sage-brush amateur. When one of those Italian footmen in British uniform comes in and sings "O tol de rol! — O, Signo-o-o-ra! — loango — congo — Venezue-e-e-la! whack fol de rol!" (which means "Oh, noble madame, here's one of them dukes from the palace, out here, come to borrow a dollar and a half,") you always stand with expanded eyes and mouth, and one pile-driver uplifted, and your ample hands held apart in front of your face, like a couple of canvas-covered hams, and when he gets almost through, how you do uncork your pent-up enthusiasm and applaud with hoof and palm! You have it pretty much to yourself, and then you look sheepish when you find everybody staring at you. But how very idiotic you do look when something really fine is sung— you generally keep quiet, then. Never mind, though, Murphy, entire audiences do things at the Opera that they have no business to do; for instance, they never let one of those thousand-dollar singers finish—they always break in with their ill-timed applause just as he or she, as the case may be, is preparing to throw all his or her concentrated sweetness into the final strain, and so all that sweetness is lost. Write me again, Murphy—I shall always be happy to hear from you.

ARITHMETICUS, *Virginia, Nevada.*—"I am an enthusiastic student of mathematics, and it is so vexatious to me to find my progress constantly impeded by these mysterious arithmetical technicalities. Now do tell me what the difference is between Geometry and Conchology?"

Here *you* come again, with your diabolical arithmetical conundrums, when I am suffering death with a cold in the head. If you could have seen the expression of ineffable scorn that darkened my countenance a moment ago and was instantly split from the centre in every direction like a fractured looking-glass by my last sneeze, you never would have written that disgraceful question. Conchology is a science which has nothing to do with mathematics; it relates only to shells. At the same time, however, a man who opens oysters for a hotel, or shells a fortified town, or sucks eggs, is not, strictly speaking, a conchologist—a fine stroke of sarcasm, that, but it will be lost on such an intellectual clam as you. Now compare conchology and geometry together, and you will see what the difference is, and your question will be answered. But don't torture me with any more of your ghastly arithmetical horrors (for I do detest figures anyhow,) until you know I am rid of my cold. I feel the bitterest animosity toward you at this moment—bothering me in this way, when I can do nothing but sneeze and quote poetry and snort pocket-handkerchiefs to atoms. If I had you in range of my nose, now, I would blow your brains out.

YOUNG MOTHER.—And so you think a baby is a thing of beauty and a joy forever? Well, the idea is pleasing, but not original—every cow thinks the same of its own calf. Perhaps the cow may not think it so elegantly, but still she thinks it, nevertheless. I honor the cow for it. We all honor this touching maternal instinct wherever we find it, be it in the home of luxury or in the humble cow-shed. But really, madam, when I come to examine the matter in all its bearings, I find that the correctness of your assertion does not manifest itself in all cases. A sore-faced baby with a neglected nose cannot be conscientiously regarded as a thing of beauty, and inasmuch as babyhood spans but three short years, no baby is competent to be a joy "forever." It pains me thus to demolish two-thirds of your pretty sentiment in a single sentence, but the position I hold in this chair requires that I shall not permit you to deceive and mislead the public with your plausible figures of speech. I know a female baby aged eighteen months, in this city, which cannot hold out as a "joy" twenty-four hours on a stretch, let alone "forever." And it possesses some of the most remarkable eccentricities of character and appetite that have ever fallen under my notice. I will set down here a statement of this infant's operations, (conceived, planned and carried out by itself, and without suggestion or assistance from its mother or any one else,) during a single day—and what I shall say can be substantiated by the sworn testimony of witnesses. It commenced by eating one dozen large blue-mass pills, box and all; then it fell down a flight of stairs, and arose with a bruised and purple knot on its forehead, after which it proceeded in quest of further refreshment and amusement. It found a glass trinket ornamented with brasswork—mashed up and ate the glass, and then swallowed the brass. Then it drank about twenty or thirty drops of laudanum, and more than a dozen table-spoonsful of strong spirits of camphor. The reason why it took no more laudanum was, because there was no more to take. After this it lay down on its back, and shoved five or six inches of a silver-headed whalebone cane down its throat; got it fast there, and it was all its mother could do to pull the cane out again, without pulling out some of the child with it. Then, being hungry for glass again, it broke up several wine glasses, and fell to eating and swallowing the fragments, not minding a cut or two. Then it ate a quantity of butter, pepper, salt and California matches, actually taking a spoonful of butter, a spoonful of salt, a spoonful of pepper, and three or four lucifer matches, at each mouthful. (I will remark here that this thing of beauty likes painted German lucifers, and eats all she can get of them; but she infinitely prefers California matches—which I regard as a compliment to our home manufactures of more than ordinary value, coming, as it does, from one who is too young to flatter.) Then she washed her head with soap and water, and afterwards ate what soap was left, and drank as much of the suds as she had room for, after which she sallied forth and took the cow familiarly by the tail, and got kicked heels over head. At odd times during the day, when this joy forever happened to have nothing particular on hand, she put in the time by climbing up on places and falling down off them, uniformly damaging herself in the operation. As young as she is, she speaks many words tolerably distinctly, and being plain-spoken in other respects, blunt and to the point, she opens conversation with all strangers, male or female, with the same formula—"How do, Jim?" Not being familiar with the ways of children, it is possible that I have been magnifying into matter of surprise things which may not strike any one who is familiar with infancy as being at all astonishing. However, I cannot believe that such is the case, and so I repeat that my report of this baby's performances is strictly true—and if any one doubts it, I can produce the child. I will further engage that she shall devour anything that is given her, (reserving to myself only the right to exclude anvils,) and fall down from any place to which she may be elevated, (merely stipulating that her preference for alighting on her head shall be respected, and, therefore, that the elevation chosen shall be high enough to enable her to accomplish this to her satisfaction.) But I find I have wandered from my subject—so, without further argument, I will reiterate my conviction that not *all* babies are things of beauty and joys forever.

BLUE-STOCKING, *San Francisco.*—Do I think the writer in the *Golden Era* quoted Burns correctly when he attributed this language to him?

"O, wad the power the gift tae gie us."

No, I don't. I think the proper reading is—

"O, wad some power the giftie gie us."

But how do you know it is Burns? Why don't you wait till you hear from the *Gold Hill News*? Why do you want to rush in ahead of the splendid intellect that discovered as by inspiration that the "Destruction of the Sennacherib" was not written in Dutch Flat?

AGNES ST. CLAIR SMITH.—This correspondent writes as follows: "I suppose you have seen the large oil painting (entitled 'St. Patrick preaching at Tara, A. D. 432,') by J. Harrington, of San Francisco, in the window of the picture store adjoining the Eureka Theatre, on Montgomery street. What do you think of it?"

Yes, I have seen it. I think it is a petrified nightmare. I have not time to elaborate my opinion.

DISCOURAGING.

The fate of Mark Twain's exquisite bit of humor, in which he treats Byron's "Sennacherib" as a communication from a Dutch Flat poet, will teach a lesson to our wits. The next time that Mark gets off a good thing in the same fine vein, he will probably append "a key" to the joke.—*Dramatic Chronicle*.

Ah! but you forget the Gold Hill *News* and the *Flag*. Would they understand the "key" do you think?

———————

YOUNG ACTOR.—This gentleman writes as follows: "I am desperate. *Will* you tell me how I can possibly please the newspaper critics? I have labored conscientiously to achieve this, ever since I made my *début* upon the stage, and I have never yet entirely succeeded in a single instance. Listen: The first night I played after I came among you, I judged by the hearty applause that was frequently showered upon me, that I had made a 'hit'—that my audience were satisfied with me— and I was happy accordingly. I only longed to know if I had been as successful with the critics. The first thing I did in the morning was to send for the papers. I read this: 'Mr. King Lear Macbeth made his first appearance last night, before a large and fashionable audience, as "Lord Blucher," in Bilgewater's great tragedy of *Blood, Hair and the Ground Tore Up.* In the main, his effort may be set down as a success—a very gratifying success. His voice is good, his manner easy and graceful, and his enunciation clear and distinct; his conception of the character he personated was good, and his rendition of it almost perfect. This talented young actor will infallibly climb to a dizzy elevation upon the ladder of histrionic fame, but it rests with himself to say whether this shall be accomplished at an early day or years hence. If the former, then he must at once correct his one great fault—we refer to his habit of throwing extraordinary spirit into passages which do not require it—his habit of *ranting*, to speak plainly. It was this same unfortunate habit which caused him to spoil the noble scene between "Lord Blucher" and "Viscount Cranberry," last night, in that portion of the third act where the latter unjustly accuses the former of attempting to seduce his pure and honored grandmother. His rendition of "Lord Blucher's" observation—

"Speak but another syllable, vile, hell-spawned miscreant, and thou diest the death of a ter-r-raitor!"

was uttered with undue excitement and unseemly asperity —there was too much rant about it. We trust Mr. Macbeth will consider the hint we have given him.' That extract, Mr. Twain, was from the *Morning Thunderbolt.* The *Daily Battering-Ram* gave me many compliments, but said that in the great scene referred to above, I gesticulated too wildly and too much—and advised me to be more circumspect in future, in these matters. I played the same piece that night, and toned myself down considerably in the matter of ranting and gesticulation. The next morning neither the *Thunderbolt* or the *Battering-Ram* gave me credit for it, but the one said my 'Lord Blucher' overdid the pathetic in the scene where his sister died, and the other said I laughed too boisterously in the one where my servant fell in the dyer's vat and came out as green as a meadow in Spring-time. The *Daily American*

Earthquake said I was too *tame* in the great scene with the 'Viscount.' I felt a little discouraged, but I made a note of these suggestions and fell to studying harder than ever. That night I toned down my grief and my mirth, and worked up my passionate anger and my gesticulation just the least in the world. I may remark here that I began to perceive a moderation, both in quantity and quality, of the applause vouchsafed me by the audience. The next morning the papers gave me no credit for my efforts at improvement, but the *Thunderbolt* said I was too loving in the scene with my new bride, the *Battering-Ram* said I was not loving enough, and the *Earthquake* said it was a masterly performance and never surpassed upon these boards. I was check-mated. I sat down and considered how I was going to engineer that love-scene to suit all the critics, until at last I became stupefied with perplexity. I then went down town, much dejected, and got drunk. The next day the *Battering-Ram* said I was too spiritless in the scene with the 'Viscount,' and remarked sarcastically that I threatened the 'Viscount's' life with a subdued voice and manner eminently suited to conversation in a funeral procession. The *Thunderbolt* said my mirth was too mild in the dyer's vat scene, and observed that instead of laughing heartily, as it was my place to do, I smiled as blandly—and as guardedly, apparently—as an undertaker in the cholera season. These mortuary comparisons had a very depressing effect upon my spirits, and I turned to the *Earthquake* for comfort. That authority said 'Lord Blucher' seemed to take the death of his idolized sister uncommonly easy, and suggested with exquisite irony that if I would use a toothpick, or pretend to pare my nails, in the death-bed scene, my attractive indifference would be the perfection of acting. I was almost desperate, but I went to work earnestly again to apply the newspaper hints to my 'Lord Blucher.' I ranted in the 'Viscount' scene (this at home in my private apartments) to suit the *Battering-Ram*, and then toned down considerably, to approach the *Earthquake's* standard; I worked my grief up strong in the death-bed scene to suit the latter paper, and then modified it a good deal to comply with the *Thunderbolt's* hint; I laughed boisterously in the dyer's vat scene, in accordance with the suggestion of the *Thunderbolt*, and then toned down toward the *Battering-Ram's* notion of excellence. That night my audience did not seem to know whether to applaud or not, and the result was that they came as near doing neither one thing nor the other as was possible. The next morning the *Semi-Monthly Literary Bosh* said my rendition of the character of 'Lord Blucher' was faultless—that it was stamped with the seal of inspiration; the *Thunderbolt* said I was an industrious, earnest and aspiring young dramatic student, but I was possessed of only ordinary merit, and could not hope to achieve more than a very moderate degree of success in my profession—and added that my engagement was at an end for the present; the *Battering-Ram* said I was a tolerably good stock-actor, but that the practice of managers in imposing such people as me upon the public as stars, was very reprehensible—and added that my engagement was at an end for the present; the *Earthquake* critic said he had seen worse actors, but not *much* worse—and added that my engagement was at an end for the present. So much for newspapers. The *Monthly Magazine of Literature and Art* (high authority,) remarked as follows: 'Mr. King Lear Macbeth commenced well, but the longer he played, the worse he played. His first performance of "Lord Blucher" in *Blood, Hair and the Ground Tore Up*, may be entered upon the record as a remarkably fine piece of acting—but toward the last he got to making it the most extraordinary exhibition of theatrical lunacy we ever witnessed. In the scene with the "Viscount," which calls for sustained, vigorous, fiery declamation, his manner was an incomprehensible mixture of "fever-heat" and "zero"—to borrow the terms of the thermometer; in the dyer's vat scene he was alternately torn by spasms of mirth and oppressed by melancholy; in the death-bed scene his countenance exhibited profound grief one moment and blank vacancy in the next; in the love scene with his bride—but why particularize? throughout the play he was a mixture—a conglomeration—a miracle of indecision—an aimless, purposeless dramatic lunatic. In a word, his concluding performances of the part of "Lord Blucher" were execrable. We simply assert this, but do not attempt to account for it—we know his first performance was excellence itself, but how that excellence so soon degenerated into the pitiable exhibition of last night, is beyond our ability to determine.' Now, Mr. Twain, you have the facts in this melancholy case—and any suggestion from you as to how I can please these critics will be gratefully received."

I can offer no suggestion, "Young Actor," except that the ordinary run of newspaper criticism will not do to depend upon. If you keep on trying to shape yourself by such models, you will go mad, eventually. Several of the critics you mention probably never saw you play an entire act through in their lives, and it is possible that the balance were no more competent to decide upon the merits of a dramatic performance than of a sermon. Do you note how unconcernedly and how pitilessly they lash you as soon as your engagement is ended? Sometimes those "criticisms" are written and in type before the curtain rises. Don't you remember that the New York *Herald* once came out with a column of criticism upon Edwin Forrest's "Hamlet," when unfortunately the bill had been changed at the last moment, and Mr. Forrest played "Othello" instead of the play criticised? And only lately didn't the same paper publish an elaborate imaginary description of the funeral ceremonies of the late Jacob Little, unaware that the obsequies had been postponed for twenty-four hours? It is vastly funny, your "working yourself up" to suit the *Thunderbolt*, and "toning yourself down" to suit the *Battering-Ram*, and doing all sorts of similarly absurd things to please a lot of "critics" who had probably never seen you play at all, but who threw in a pinch of instruction or censure among their praise merely to give their "notices" a candid, impartial air. Don't bother yourself any more in that way. Pay no attention to the papers, but watch the audience. A silent crowd is damning censure—good, hearty, enthusiastic applause is a sure sign of able acting. It seems you played well at first—I think you had better go back and start over again at the point where you began to instruct yourself from the newspapers. I have often wondered, myself, when reading critiques in the papers, what would become of an actor if he tried to follow all the fearfully conflicting advice they contained.

MARY, *Rincon School.*—Sends a dainty little note, the contents whereof I take pleasure in printing, as follows, (suppressing, of course, certain expressions of kindness and encouragement which she intended for my eye alone): "Please spell and define *gewhilikins* for me."

Geewhillikins is an ejaculation or exclamation, and expresses surprise, astonishment, amazement, delight, admiration, disappointment, deprecation, disgust, sudden conviction, incredulity, joy, sorrow—well, it is capable of expressing pretty nearly any abrupt emotion that flashes through one's heart. For instance, I say to Jones, "Old Grimes is dead!" Jones knowing old Grimes was in good health the last time he heard from him, is surprised, and he naturally exclaims, "Geewhillikins! is that so?" In this case the word simply expresses surprise, mixed with neither joy nor sorrow, Grimes' affairs being nothing to Jones. I meet Morgan, and I say, "Well, I saw Johnson, and he refuses to pay that bill." Johnson exclaims, "Geewhillikins! is that so?" In this case the word expresses astonishment and disappointment, together with a considerable degree of irritation. I meet young Yank, and I observe, "The country is safe now—peace is declared!" Yank swings his hat and shouts, "Geewhillikins! is that so?"— which expresses surprise and extreme delight. I stumble on Thompson, and remark, "There was a tornado in Washoe yesterday which picked up a church in Virginia and blew it to Reed's Station, on the Carson river, eighteen miles away!" Thompson says, "Gee-e-e-*whillikins!*" with a falling inflection and strong emphasis on that portion of the word which I have italicized—thus, with discriminating judgment, imbuing the phrase with the nicest shades of amazement, wonder, and mild incredulity. Stephens, who is carrying home some eggs in his "hind-coat pocket," sits down on them and mashes them—exclaiming, as he rises, gingerly exploring the mucilaginous locality of his misfortune with his hand, "*Gee*-whillikins!"—with strong emphasis and falling inflection on the first syllable, and falling inflection on the last syllable also—thus expressing an extremity of grief and unmitigated disgust which no other word in our whole language is capable of conveying. That will do, I suppose—you cannot help understanding my definition, now, and neither will you fail to appreciate the extraordinary comprehensiveness of the word. We will now consider its orthography. You perceive that I spell it with two e's and two l's, which I think is the proper method, though I confess the matter is open to argument. Different people spell it in different ways. Let us give a few examples:

> "The horse 'raired' up with a furious neigh,
> And over the hills he scoured away!
> Mazeppa closed his despairing eye,
> And murmured, 'Alas! and must I die!
>   'GEE-WHILIKINS!' "

[*Byron's Mazeppa.*

> "Sir Hilary charged at Agincourt—
>   Sooth 'twas an awful day!
> And though in that old age of sport
> The rufflers of the camp and court
>   Had little time to pray,
> 'Tis said Sir Hilary muttered there
> Four syllables by way of prayer:
>   'GEE-WHILLIKINS!' "

[*Winthrop Mackworth Praed.*

If the Gold Hill *News* or the *American Flag* say the above excerpts are misquotations, pay no attention to them—they are anything but good authority in matters of this kind. The *Flag* does not spell the word we are speaking of properly, either, in my opinion. I have in my mind a communication which I remember having seen in that paper the morning the result of the presidential election was made known. It possessed something of an exulting tone, and was addressed to a heavy gun among the Copperheads—the editor of the late *Democratic Press*, I think—and read as follows:

"BERIAH BROWN, ESQ.—*Dear Sir:* How are you *now*?
  "Yours, truly,
                G. WHILLIKINS."

You will have to accept my definition, Mary, for want of a better. As far as the spelling is concerned, you must choose between Mr. Praed and myself on the one hand, and Lord Byron and the *American Flag* on the other, bearing in mind that the two last named authorities disagree, and that neither of them ever knew much about the matter in dispute, anyhow.

ANXIETY.—*S. F.*—Need have no fear of General Halleck. There is no truth in the report that he will compel approaching maternity to take the oath of allegiance.—*Golden Era.*

Another impenetrable conundrum—or, to speak more properly, another fathomless riddle. I shall have to refer to Webster:

"APPROACHING, *ppr.* Drawing nearer; advancing toward."
"MATERNITY, *n.* The character or relation of a mother."

Consequently, "approaching maternity" means the *condition* of being about to become a mother. And according to the profound, the deep, the bottomless expounder who instructs "Anxiety" in my text, General Halleck "will not compel" that *condition* to "take the oath of allegiance." Any numscull could have told that—because how can an insensible, impalpable, invisible *condition* take an oath? That expounder comes as near being a "condition" as anybody, no doubt, but still he cannot take an oath in his character *as* a "condition;" he must take it simply in his character as a man. None but human beings can take the oath of allegiance under our constitution. But didn't you mean that women in the said condition would not be required to take the oath merely *because* they happened to be in that condition?—or didn't you mean that the woman wouldn't have to take it on behalf of her forthcoming progeny?—or didn't you mean that the forthcoming progeny wouldn't be required to take it itself, either before or immediately after it was born? Or, what in the very mischief *did* you mean?—what were you driving at?—what were you trying to ferry across the trackless ocean of your intellect? Now you had better stop this sort of thing, because it is becoming a very serious matter. If you keep it up, you will eventually get some of your subscribers so tangled up that they will seek relief from their troubles and perplexities in the grave of the suicide.

MARK TWAIN.—'Twas a burning shame to misquote Burns. The wretch who deliberately substituted *italic* for the original would, we verily believe, enjoy martyrdom. Previous thereto his eyes should be stuck full of exclamation points!—*Golden Era.*

Are you wool-gathering, or is it I? I have read that paragraph fourteen or fifteen times, very slowly and carefully, but I can't see that it means anything. Does the point lie in a darkly suggested pun upon "original would" (original *wood*?) —or in the "exclamation *points*?"—or in the bad grammar of the last sentence?—or in— Come, now—explain your ingenious little riddle, and don't go on badgering and bully-ragging people in this mysterious way.

GOLD HILL NEWS.—This old scoundrel calls me an "old humbug from Dutch Nick's." Now this is not fair. It is highly improper for gentlemen of the press to descend to personalities, and I never permit myself to do it. However, as this abandoned outcast evidently meant his remark as complimentary, I take pleasure in so receiving it, in consideration of the fact that the fervent cordiality of his language fully makes up for its want of elegance.

INQUIRER, *Sacramento.*—At your request I have been down and walked under and around and about the grand, gaudy and peculiar

INDEPENDENCE ARCH

which rears its awful form at the conjunction of Montgomery and California streets, and have taken such notes as may enable me to describe it to you and tell you what I think of it. [N. B. I am writing this on Monday, the day preceding the Glorious Fourth.] My friend, I have seen arch-traitors and arch-deacons and architects, and archæologists, and archetypes, and arch-bishops, and, in fact, nearly all kinds of arches, but I give you the word of an honest man that I never saw an arch like this before. I desire to see one more like it and then die. I am the more anxious in this respect because it is not likely that I shall ever get a chance to see one like it in the next world, for something tells me that there is not such an arch as this in any of the seven heavens, and there certainly cannot be anything half as gay in the other place.

I am calling this *one* arch all the time, but in reality it is a cluster of four arches; when you pass up Montgomery street you pass under two of them, and when you pass up California street you pass under the other two. These arches spring from the tops of four huge square wooden pillars which are about fifteen or twenty feet high and painted with dull, dead, blue mud or blue-mass, or something of that kind. Projecting from each face of these sombre columns are bunches of cheap flags adorned with tin spear-heads. The contrast between the dark melancholy blue of the pillars and the gorgeous dyes of the flags is striking and picturesque. The arches reach as high as the eaves of an ordinary three-story house, and they are wide in proportion, the pillars standing nearly the width of the street apart. A flagstaff surmounts each of the pillars. The Montgomery street arches are faced with white canvas, upon which is inscribed the names of the several States in strong black paint; as there is a "slather" of gory red and a "slather" of ghostly white on each side of these black names, a cheerful barber-pole contrast is here presented. The broad tops of the arches are covered (in the barber-pole style, also, which seems to have been the groundwork of this fine conception,) with alternate patches of white and sickly pink cotton, and these patches having a wrinkled and disorderly appearance, remind me unpleasantly of a shirt I "done up" once in the Humboldt country, beyond the Sierras. The general effect of this open, airy, summer-house combination of arches, with its splashes and dashes of blue and red and pink and white, is intensely streaky and stripy; and altogether, if the colossal bird-cage were only "weatherboarded" it would just come up to one's notion of what a grand metropolitan barber-shop ought to be. Or if it were glazed it would be a neat thing in the way of a show-lamp to set up before a Brobdignag theatre. Surmounting the centres of two of the arches—those facing up and down Montgomery street—are large medallion portraits of Lincoln and Washington—daubs—apparently executed in whitewash, mud and brick-dust, with a mop. In these, also, the barber-shop ground-plan is still adhered to with a discriminating and sensitive regard to consistency; Washington is clean-shaved, but he is not done getting shampooed yet; his white hair is foamy with lather, and his countenance bears the expectant aspect of a man who knows that the cleansing shower-bath is about to fall. Good old Father Abe, whose pictured face, heretofore, was always serious, but never unhappy, looks positively worn and dejected and tired out, in the medallion—has exactly the expression of one who has been waiting a long time to get shaved and there are thirteen ahead of him yet. I cannot help admiring how the eternal fitness of things has been preserved in the execution of these portraits. To one who delights in "the unities" of art, could anything be more ravishing than the appropriate appearance and expression of the two countenances, overtopped as they are by sheaves of striped flags and surrounded on all sides by the glaring, tinted bars that symbol the barber's profession? I believe I have nothing left to describe in connection with the two arches which span Montgomery street. However, upon second thought, I forgot to mention that over each of the two sets of portraits stoops a monstrous painted eagle, with wings uplifted over his back, neck stretched forward, beak parted, and eager eye, as if he were on the very point of grabbing a savory morsel of some kind—an imaginary customer of the barber-shop, maybe.

The arch which fronts up California street is faced with white canvas, prominently sewed together in squares, and upon this broad white streak is inscribed in large, plain, black, "horse-type," this inscription:

"Honor to the Founders and saviours
of the Republic."

For some unexplained reason, the "Founders" of the Republic are aggrandized with a capital "F," and the equally meritorious Saviors of it snubbed with a small "s." True, they gave the Saviors a "u"—a letter more than is recommended by Webster's dictionary—but I consider that a lame apology and an illiberal and inadequate compensation for "nipping" their capital S. The centre-piece of this arch consists of an exceedingly happy caricature of the coat-of-arms of California, done in rude imitation of fresco. The female figure is a placid, portly, straight-haired squaw in complete armor, sitting on a recumbent hog, and so absorbed in contemplation of the cobble-stones that she does not observe that she has got her sack of turnips by the wrong end, and that dozens of them are rolling out at the other; neither does she observe that the hog has seized the largest turnip and has got it in his mouth; neither does she observe that her great weight is making it mighty uncomfortable for the hog; she does not notice that she is mashing the breath out of him and making his eyes bulge out with a most agonized expression—nor that it is as much as he can do to hold on to his turnip. There is nothing magnanimous in this picture. Any true-hearted American woman, with the kindly charity and the tenderness that are inseparable from the character, would get up for a minute and give the hog a chance to eat his turnip in peace.

The centre-piece of the opposite arch is a copy of the one just described, except that the woman is a trifle heavier, and of course the distress of the hog is aggravated in a corresponding degree. The motto is—

> "MINE EYES HAVE SEEN THE GLORY OF THE
> COMING OF THE LORD."

This is an entirely abstract proposition, and does not refer to the surrounding splendors of the situation.

I have now described the arch of which you have heard such glowing accounts (set afloat in the first place by incendiary daily prints, no doubt,) and have thus satisfied your first request. Your second—that I would tell you what I think of it, can be done in a few words. It cost $3,000, and I think it cost a great deal too much, considering the unhappy result attained. I think the taste displayed was very bad—I might even say barbarous, only the tone of some of my preceding paragraphs might lead people to think I was making a pun. If you will notice me you will observe that I never make a pun intentionally—I never do anything like that in cold blood. To proceed—I think the same money expended with better judgment would have procured a set of handsome, graceful arches which could be re-trimmed and used again, perhaps; but I think these can't, as we have no ferry slips now that require gateways resplendent with cheap magnificence; I think the whole affair was gotten up in too great a hurry to be done well—the committee was appointed too late in the day; I suppose the appointing power did not know sooner that the Fourth of July was coming this year; I think the committee did as well as they could under the circumstances, because a member of it told me so, and he could have no object in deceiving me; I think many people considered the cluster of arches, with their Sunday-school-picnic style of ornamentation, pretty, and took a good deal of pride in the same, and therefore I am glad that this article will not be published until the Fourth has come and gone, for I would be sorry that any remarks of mine should mar the pleasure any individual might otherwise take in that truly extraordinary work of art.

Now you have the arches as they looked before the Fourth—the time when the above paragraphs were written. But I must confess—and I don't do it *very* reluctantly—that on the morning of the Fourth they were greatly improved in appearance. One cause was that innumerable small flags had been mounted on the arches, and hid the broad red and pink patchwork covering of the latter from sight, and another that the fiery colors so prevalent about the structure had been pleasantly relieved by the addition of garlands and festoons of evergreens to the embellishments, and the suspension of a champagne basket of other greens and flowers from the centre of it, chandelier fashion. Also, as by this time all Montgomery street was a quivering rainbow of flags, one could not help seeing that the decorations of the arches had to be pretty strong in coloring to keep up any sort of competition with the brilliant surroundings.

As I have disparaged this work of art before it had a chance to put on its best looks, and as I still don't think a great deal of it, I will act fairly by it, and print the other side of the question, so that you can form a just estimate of its merits and demerits by comparing the arguments of the prosecution and defence together. I will re-publish here the opinion entertained of it by the reporter of the *Alta*, one of its most fanatical, and I may even say, rabid admirers. I will go further and endorse a portion of what he says, but not all, by a good deal. I don't endorse the painting "in the highest style of the decorative art," (although it sounds fine—I may say eloquent,) nor the "magnificent basket," either:

"The most noticeable feature of the display on this street was the

GRAND TRIUMPHAL ARCH,

at the intersection of California and Montgomery streets, designed by M. F. Butler, Esq., the architect; erected by A. Snyder; painted, in the highest style of the decorative art, by Hopps & Son; and draped and adorned with flags and flowers by Chas. M. Plum, upholsterer, and A. Barbier, under the management and supervision of a Committee, consisting of John Sime, W. W. Dodge and M. E. Hughes. This arch was one of the chief attractions throughout the day and evening. On Montgomery street, distributed on both north and south sides, were the names of the thirty-six sovereign States of the Union, to each one a separate shield, and the names of the leading Generals of the Revolution, side by side with those of the War for the Union, and on the California street side the names of officers of the Army and Navy, past and present, the face of the arch on the east side bearing the words:

'Mine eyes have seen the glory of the coming of the Lord,'

And on the west side—

'Honor to the Founders and Saviors of our Republic.'

The centre of both the arches on Montgomery street were ornamented with portraits of Washington and Lincoln, and surmounted with flags beautifully and tastefully grouped. The flags of various nations were also grouped under the base of the arches at the four corners, and the whole structure was hung with evergreen wreaths and flowers, while a magnificent floral basket hung suspended under the centre of the structure by wreaths depending from the arches. As the procession passed under this arch, the petals of the roses and other flowers were constantly falling upon it in showers as the wreaths swung to and fro in the summer breeze."

Now for my side again. The following blast is from the *Morning Call*. The general felicity of the thing is to be ascribed to the fact that the reporter listened to some remarks of mine used in the course of a private conversation with another man, and turned them to account as a "local item." He is excusable for taking things from me, though, because I used to take little things from him occasionally when I reported with him on the *Call*:

STRAIGHTENING UP.—The likenesses of "Pater Patriæ," and "Salvator Patriæ," on the ornamental (!) barber-shop at the corner of Montgomery and California streets, have been straightened up, and now wear a closer similarity to what might be supposed to represent men of steady habits. While we hold in the most profound veneration the memory of those illustrious men, as well as the day we propose to celebrate, yet we defy any person to look at that triumphal structure, its *blue* pillars and tawdry arches, utterly ignoring architecture and taste—and not laugh.

Now for the other side. The following highly-flavored compliment is also from the *Morning Call*, (same issue as the above extract,) but was written by the chief editor—and editors and reporters will differ in opinion occasionally:

A FINE DISPLAY.—All things promise a fine display to-day, the finest probably that has ever been witnessed in this city. The splendid triumphal arches at the intersection of Montgomery and California streets, will be especial objects of admiration. They were designed by M. F. Butler, Esq., the architect, have been erected under his supervision, and are at once splendid specimens of his artistic skill as well as of the taste of the Committee who chose his designs over all others presented for the occasion. Mr. B. is the pioneer, as well as among the best architects of this State, and this last work, though of a somewhat ephemeral nature, is worthy of the artist who designed and superintended it, and was properly entrusted to one of our oldest citizens as well as one of the most loyal men of the State.

Now for my side. The following is also from the *Call*, (same issue as both the above extracts:)

THAT ARCH.—The following bit of satire, from a correspondent, is pretty severe on the anomalous structure our Committee have dignified with the name of triumphal arch:

"The grand Patriotic or Union Arch erected at the corner of Montgomery and California streets, is a magnificent affair. I presume it will be retained there for a number of weeks. But is n't there a very important omission about the structure? Erected in commemoration of the Nation's birthday and all its subsequent glories, should not the portrait of the author of the Declaration of Independence crown one of its beautiful arches?

'76."

Now for the other side once more. The following is from the *Bulletin*. The concluding portion of the first sentence is time-worn and stereotyped, though, and I don't consider that it ought to count against me. It is always used on such occasions and is never intended to mean anything:

"The triumphal arch which is now being completed under the direction of M. F. Butler, architect, at the junction of Montgomery and California streets, is the most imposing structure of its kind that has ever been erected on this coast. [Here follows a description of it in dry detail.] The arches are beautifully trimmed with evergreen, and the whole structure is to be adorned with a profusion of flags representing all nations, with appropriate mottoes and names of popular Generals scattered here and there among the Stars and Stripes."

And, finally, for my side again. Having this thing all my own way I have decided that I am entitled to the closing argument. The following is from the *American Flag*:

TRIUMPHAL ARCH.—A triumphal arch had been erected at the intersection of California and Montgomery streets, at a cost of $3,000. It consisted of four arches, one fronting and spanning each street, and resting upon four large pillars, thirty feet in height, painted a dingy blue, festooned with flags of various nations, and exhibiting upon each side, painted upon shields, the names, two upon each shield of the heroes of 1776 and 1865,—Grant, Greene; Sheridan, Montgomery; Dahlgren, Decatur; Dupont, Porter, &c. Near the center of each of the arches fronting on Montgomery street, were rather poorly painted portraits, also painted upon a shield, of Washington and Lincoln, surrounded by large spread eagles, and bearing beneath, the initials "W. L;" upon these arches were inscribed upon red and white shields, the names of all the States; the arch facing California street, west, bore the inscription "Honor to the Founders and to the Saviors of the Republic;" and that opposite, "Mine eyes have seen the glory of the coming of the Lord;" and near the center of both was a picture of a female of rather a lugubrious countenance, seated upon a lion couchant, bearing in her left hand a staff, and upon her head something bearing a striking resemblance to the metalic caps worn by the mail-clad warriors of ancient Greece, all of which, we presume, was intended to represent the "Goddess of Liberty victorious over the British Lion," but as we were unable to read the name of the damsel upon the shield which she held in her right hand, we will not be positive on that point. The whole affair was finely decorated with evergreens, flowers, wreaths, flags, etc., and would have been creditably ornamented, had more taste and skill been displayed in the paintings.

The prosecution "rests" here. And the defense will naturally have to "rest" also, because I have given them all the space I intend to. The case may now go to the jury, and while they are out I will give judgment in favor of the plaintiff. I learned that trick from the Washoe judges, long ago. But it stands to reason that when a thing is so frightfully tawdry and devoid of taste that the *Flag* can't stand it, and when a painting is so diabolical that the *Flag* can't admire it, they must be wretched indeed. Such evidence as this is absolutely damning.

STUDENT OF ETIQUETTE.—Asks: "If I step upon one end of a narrow bridge just at the moment that a mad bull rushes upon the other, which of us is entitled to precedence—which should give way and yield the road to the other?"

I decline to answer—leave it to the bull to decide. I am shrouded in doubts upon the subject, but the bull's mind will probably be perfectly clear. At a first glance it would seem that this "Student of Etiquette" is asking a foolish and unnecessary question, inasmuch as it is one which naturally answers itself—yet his inquiry is no more absurd than a dozen I can find any day gravely asked and as gravely answered in the "Correspondents' Column" of literary papers throughout the country. John Smith meets a beautiful girl on the street and falls in love with her, but as he don't know her name, nor her position in society, nor where she lives, nor in fact anything whatever about her, he sits down and writes these particulars to the *Weekly Literary Bushwhacker*, and gravely asks what steps he ought first to take in laying siege to that girl's affections—and is as gravely answered that he must not waylay her when she is out walking alone, nor write her anonymous notes, nor call upon her unendorsed by her friends, but his first move should be to *procure an introduction in due form*. That editor, with a grand flourish of wisdom, would have said: "Give way to the bull!" I, with greater wisdom, scorn to reply at all. If I were in a sarcastic vein, though, I might decide that it was Smith's privilege to butt the bull off the bridge—if he could. Again—John Jones finds a young lady stuck fast in the mud, but never having been introduced to her, he feels a delicacy about pulling her out, and so he goes off, with many misgivings, and writes to the *Diluted Literary Sangaree* about it, craving advice: he is seriously informed that it was not only his privilege, but his duty, to pull the young lady out of the mud, without the formality of an introduction. Inspired wisdom! He too, would have said: "Back down, and let the bull cross first." William Brown writes to the *Weekly Whangdoodle of Literature and Art* that he is madly in love with the divinest of her sex, but unhappily her affections and her hand are already pledged to another—how must he proceed? With supernatural sagacity the editor arrives at the conclusion that it is Brown's duty, as a Christian and gentleman, to go away and let her alone. Marvelous! He, too, would have said: "Waive etiquette, and let the bull have the bridge." However, we will drop the subject for the present. If these editors choose to go on answering foolish questions in the grandiloquent, oracular style that seems to afford them so much satisfaction, I suppose it is no business of mine.

MARY, *Rincon School.*—No, you are mistaken—*bilk* is a good dictionary word. True, the newspapers generally enclose it in quotation marks, (thus: "bilk,") which is the usual sign made use of to denote an illegitimate or slang phrase, but as I said before, the dictionaries recognize the word as good, pure English, nevertheless. I perfectly agree with you, however, that there is not an uglier or more inelegant word in any language, and I appreciate the good taste that ignores its use in polite conversation. For your accommodation and instruction, I have been looking up authorities in the Mercantile Library, and beg leave to offer the result of my labors, as follows:

From Webster's Dictionary, edition of 1828.
BILK, *v. t.* [Goth. *bilaikan*, to mock or deride. This Gothic word appears to be compound, *bi* and *laikan*, to leap or exult.]
To frustrate or disappoint; to deceive or defraud, by non-fulfilment of engagement; as, to *bilk* a creditor.   *Dryden.*
BILKED, *pp.* Disappointed; deceived; defrauded.

From Walker's Dictionary.
BILK, *v. a.* To cheat; to deceive.

From Wright's Universal Pronouncing Dictionary.
BILK. To deceive; to defraud.

From Worcester's Dictionary.
BILK, *v. a.* [Goth. *bi-laikan*, to scoff, to deride.] To cheat; to defraud; to deceive; to elude.

But be sure, says he, don't you *bilk* me.   *Spectator.*

From Spiers and Surenne's French Pronouncing Dictionary.
BILK, v. a. 1. *frustrer*; 2. (argot) *flouer* (escroquer, duper).

From Adler's German and English Dictionary.
To BILK, *v. a.* schnellen, prellen, betrügen, im Stiche lassen, (besonders um die [mit der] Bezahlung); *joc.* einen Husaren machen.

From Seoane's Spanish Dictionary.
To BILK. *va.* Engañar, defraudar, pegarla, chasquear, no pagar lo que se debe.

From Johnson's Dictionary.
To BILK. *v. a.* [derived by Mr. *Lye* from the Gothick *bilaican.*] To cheat; to defraud, by running in debt, and avoiding payment.

Bilk'd stationers for yeomen stood prepared.   *Dryd.*

> What comedy, what farce can more delight,
> Than grinning hunger, and the pleasing sight
> Of your *bilk'd* hopes?   *Dryden.*

From Richardson's Dictionary.
BILK. Mr. Gifford says, "Bilk seems to have become a cant word about this (Ben Jonson's) time, for the use of it is ridiculed by others, as well as Jonson. It is thus *explained* in Cole's *English Dictionary*, 'Bilk, nothing; also to deceive.'" Lye, from the Goth. *Bilaikan*, which properly signifies *insultando illudere*.

To cheat, to defraud, to elude.

Tub. Hee will ha' the last word, though he take *bilke* for 't.
Hugh. Bilke? what's that?

Tub. Why nothing, a word signifying nothing; and borrow'd here to express nothing.   *B. Jonson. Tale of a Tub*, Act i. sc. 1.

[He] was then ordered to get into the coach, or behind it, for that he wanted no instructors; but be sure you dog you, says he, don't you *bilk* me.—*Spectator*, No. 498.

> Patrons in days of yore, like patrons now,
> Expected that the bard should make his bow
> At coming in, and ev'ry now and then
> Hint to the world that they were more than men;
> But, like the patrons of the present day,
> They never *bilk'd* the poet of his pay.
>
> *Churchill. Independence.*

The tabooed word "bilk," then, is more than two hundred years old, for Jonson wrote the "Tale of a Tub" in his old age—say about the year 1630—and you observe that Mr. Gifford says it "seems to have become a cant word in Jonson's time." It must have risen above its vulgar position and become a legitimate phrase afterwards, though, else it would not have been uniformly printed in dictionaries without protest or explanation, almost from Jonson's time down to our own—for I find it thus printed in the very latest edition of Webster's Unabridged. Still, two centuries of toleration have not been able to make it popular, and I think you had better reflect awhile before you decide to write to Augustus that he is a bilk.

June 3, 10, 17, and 24, July 1 and 8, 1865

Advice for Good Little Boys

You ought never to take anything that don't belong to you—if you can't carry it off.

If you unthinkingly set up a tack in another boy's seat, you ought never to laugh when he sits down on it—unless you can't "hold in."

Good little boys must never tell a lie when the truth will answer just as well. In fact, real good little boys will never tell lies at all—not at all—except in cases of the most urgent necessity.

It is wrong to put a sheepskin under your shirt when you know you are going to get a licking. It is better to retire swiftly to some secret place and weep over your bad conduct until the storm blows over.

You should never do anything wicked and then lay it on your brother, when it is just as convenient to lay it on some other boy.

You ought never to call your aged grandpapa a "rum old file"—except when you want to be unusually funny.

You ought never to knock your little sister down with a club. It is better to use a cat, which is soft. In doing this you must be careful to take the cat by the tail, in such a manner that she cannot scratch you.

June 3, 1865

Advice for Good Little Girls

Good little girls ought not to make mouths at their teachers for every trifling offense. This kind of retaliation should only be resorted to under peculiarly aggravating circumstances.

If you have nothing but a rag doll stuffed with saw-dust, while one of your more fortunate little playmates has a costly china one, you should treat her with a show of kindness nevertheless. And you ought not attempt to make a forcible swap with her unless your conscience would justify you in it, and you know you are able to do it.

You ought never to take your little brother's "chawing gum" away from him by main force—it is better to rope him in with the promise of the first two dollars and a half you find floating down the river on a grindstone. In the artless simplicity natural to his time of life, he will regard it as a perfectly fair transaction. In all ages of the world this eminently plausible fiction has lured the obtuse infant to financial ruin and disaster.

If at any time you find it necessary to correct your brother, do not correct him with mud—never on any account throw mud at him, because it will soil his clothes. It is better to scald him a little, for then you attain two desirable results—you secure his immediate attention to the lesson you are inculcating, and at the same time your hot water will have a tendency to remove impurities from his person—and possibly the skin also, in spots.

If your mother tells you to do a thing, it is wrong to reply that you won't. It is better and more becoming to intimate that you will do as she bids you, and then afterwards act quietly in the matter according to the dictates of your better judgment.

You should ever bear in mind that it is to your kind parents that you are indebted for your food, and your nice bed, and your beautiful clothes, and for the privilege of staying home from school when you let on that you are sick. Therefore you ought to respect their little prejudices, and humor their little whims and put up with their little foibles, until they get to crowding you too much.

Good little girls should always show marked deference for the aged. You ought never to "sass" old people—unless they "sass" you first.

June 24, 1865

Just "One More Unfortunate"

Immorality is not decreasing in San Francisco. I saw a girl in the city prison last night who looked as much out of place there as I did myself—possibly more so. She was petite and diffident, and only sixteen years and one month old. To judge by her looks, one would say she was as sinless as a child. But such was not the case. She had been living with a strapping young nigger for six months! She told her story as artlessly as a school-girl, and it did not occur to her for a moment that she had been doing anything unbecoming; and I never listened to a narrative which seemed more simple and straightforward, or more free from ostentation and vain-glory. She told her name, and her age, to a day; she said she was born in Holborn, City of London; father living, but gone back to England; was not married to the negro, but she was left without any one to take care of her, and he had taken charge of that department and had conducted it since she was fifteen and a half years old very satisfactorily. All listeners pitied her, and said feelingly: "Poor heifer! poor devil!" and said she was an ignorant, erring child, and had not done wrong wilfully and knowingly, and they hoped she would pass her examination for the Industrial School and be removed from the temptation and the opportunity to sin. Tears—and it was a credit to their manliness and their good feeling—tears stood in the eyes of some of those stern policemen.

O, woman, thy name is humbug! Afterwards, while I sat taking some notes, and not in sight from the women's cell, some of the old blisters fell to gossiping, and lo! young Simplicity chipped in and clattered away as lively as the vilest of them! It came out in the conversation that she was hail fellow well met with all the old female rapscallions in the city, and had had business relations with their several establishments for a long time past. She spoke affectionately of some of them, and the reverse of others; and dwelt with a toothsome relish upon numberless reminiscences of her social and commercial intercourse with them. She knew all manner of men, too—men with quaint and suggestive names, for the most part—and liked "Oyster-eyed Bill," and "Bloody Mike," and

"The Screamer," but cherished a spirit of animosity toward "Foxy McDonald" for cutting her with a bowie-knife at a strumpet ball one night. *She* a poor innocent kitten! Oh! She was a scallawag whom it would be base flattery to call a prostitute! She a candidate for the Industrial School! Bless you, she has graduated long ago. She is competent to take charge of a University of Vice. In the ordinary branches she is equal to the best; and in the higher ones, such as ornamental swearing, and fancy embroidered filagree slang, she is a shade superior to any artist I ever listened to.

c. June 27, 1865

Real Estate versus Imaginary Possessions, Poetically Considered

MY KINGDOM.

I HAVE a kingdom of unknown extent,
   Its treasures great, its wealth without compare;
And all the pleasures men in pride invent
   Are not like mine, so free from pain and care.

'Tis all my own: no hostile power may rise
   To force me outward from its rich domain;
It hath a strength that time itself defies,
   And all invaders must assail in vain.

'Tis true sometimes its sky is overcast,
   And troublous clouds obscure the peaceful light;
Yet these are transient and so quickly past
   Its radiance seems to glow more clear and bright.

It hath a queen—my queen—whose loving reign
   No daring subject ever may dispute;
Her will is mine, and all my toil her gain,
   And when she speaks my heart with love is mute.

She sits beside me, and her gentle hand
   Guides all my hopes in this estate below;
The joys of life, the products of the land,
   Beneath her smiles in ceaseless pleasures flow.

My heart, her subject, throbs beneath her eyes,
   And sends its tides full with unbounded love,
As ocean's waters swell beneath the skies
   Drawn by the placid moon that rolls above.

What king or ruler hath a state like mine,
   That death or time can never rend apart,
Where hopes and pleasures are almost divine?
   Yet all this kingdom—One True Woman's Heart.

[*Evening Bulletin.*]   PAUL DUOIR.

Oh, stuff! Is that all? I like your poetry, Mr. D., but I don't "admire" to see a man raise such a thundering smoke on such a very small capital of fire. I may be a little irritated, because you fooled me, D., you fooled me badly. I read your ramifications—I choose the word, D., simply because it has five syllables, and I desire to flatter you up a little before I abuse you; I don't know the meaning of it myself—I noticed your grandiloquent heading, "My Kingdom," and it woke me up; so I commenced reading your Ramifications with avidity, and I said to myself, with my usual vulgarity, "Now here's a man that's got a good thing." I read along, and read along, thinking sure you were going to turn out to be King of New Jersey, or King of the Sandwich Islands, or the lucky monarch of a still more important kingdom, maybe—but how my spirits fell when I came to your cheap climax! And so your wonderful kingdom is—"A True Woman's Heart!"—with capital letters to it! Oh, my! Now what do you want to go and make all that row about such a thing as that for, and fool people? Why, you put on as many frills, and make as much fuss about your obscure "kingdom" as if it were a magnificent institution—a first-class power among the nations—and contained a population of forty million souls, (and maybe it does, for all you know—most kingdoms of that kind are pretty well tenanted, my innocent royal friend.) And what does your majesty suppose you can do with your extraordinary "kingdom?" You can't sell it; you can't hire it out; you can't raise money on it. Bah! You ought to be more practical. You can keep your boasted "kingdom," since it appears to be such a comfort to you; don't come around trying to trade with me—I am very well content with

MY RANCH.

I HAVE a ranch of quite unknown extent,
    Its turnips great, its oats without compare;
And all the ranches other men may rent
    Are not like mine—so not a dern* I care.

'Tis all my own—no turnstile power may rise
    To keep me outward from its rich domain;
It hath a fence that time itself defies,
    And all invaders must climb out again.

*This imprecation is a favorite one out in the ranching districts, and is generally used in the society of ladies, where a mild form of expressionomy may be indulged in.

'Tis true sometimes with stones 'tis overcast,
    And troublous clods offend the sens'tive sight;
Yet from the furrows I these so quickly blast,
    Their radiant seams do show more clear and bright.

It hath a sow—*my* sow—whose love for grain
    No swearing subject will dispute;
Her swill is mine, and all my slops her gain,
    And when she squeaks my heart with love is mute.
[Here the machine "let down."]

October 28, 1865

Jim Smiley and His Jumping Frog

Mr. A. Ward,

Dear Sir:—Well, I called on good-natured, garrulous old Simon Wheeler, and I inquired after your friend Leonidas W. Smiley, as you requested me to do, and I hereunto append the result. If you can get any information out of it you are cordially welcome to it. I have a lurking suspicion that your Leonidas W. Smiley is a myth—that you never knew such a personage, and that you only conjectured that if I asked old Wheeler about him it would remind him of his infamous *Jim* Smiley, and he would go to work and bore me nearly to death with some infernal reminiscence of him as long and tedious as it should be useless to me. If that was your design, Mr. Ward, it will gratify you to know that it succeeded.

I found Simon Wheeler dozing comfortably by the barroom stove of the little old dilapidated tavern in the ancient mining camp of Boomerang, and I noticed that he was fat and bald-headed, and had an expression of winning gentleness and simplicity upon his tranquil countenance. He roused up and gave me good-day. I told him a friend of mine had commissioned me to make some inquiries about a cherished companion of his boyhood named Leonidas W. Smiley—Rev. Leonidas W. Smiley—a young minister of the gospel, who he had heard was at one time a resident of this village of Boomerang. I added that if Mr. Wheeler could tell me anything about this Rev. Leonidas W. Smiley, I would feel under many obligations to him.

Simon Wheeler backed me into a corner and blockaded me there with his chair—and then sat down and reeled off the monotonous narrative which follows this paragraph. He never smiled, he never frowned, he never changed his voice from the quiet, gently-flowing key to which he turned the initial sentence, he never betrayed the slightest suspicion of enthusiasm—but all through the interminable narrative there ran a vein of impressive earnestness and sincerity, which showed me plainly that so far from his imagining that there was anything ridiculous or funny about his story, he regarded it as a really important matter, and admired its two heroes as men of transcendent genius in finesse. To me, the spectacle of a man drifting serenely along through such a queer yarn without ever smiling was exquisitely absurd. As I said before, I asked him to tell me what he knew of Rev. Leonidas W. Smiley, and he replied as follows. I let him go on in his own way, and never interrupted him once:

There was a feller here once by the name of *Jim* Smiley, in the winter of '49—or maybe it was the spring of '50—I don't recollect exactly, some how, though what makes me think it was one or the other is because I remember the big flume wasn't finished when he first come to the camp; but anyway, he was the curiosest man about always betting on anything that turned up you ever see, if he could get anybody to bet on the other side, and if he couldn't he'd change sides—any way that suited the other man would suit *him*—any way just so's he got a bet, *he* was satisfied. But still, he was lucky—uncommon lucky; he most always come out winner. He was always ready and laying for a chance; there couldn't be no solitry thing mentioned but what that feller 'd offer to bet on it—and take any side you please, as I was just telling you: if there was a horse race, you'd find him flush or you find him busted at the end of it; if there was a dog-fight, he'd bet on it; if there was a cat-fight, he'd bet on it; if there was a chicken-fight, he'd bet on it; why if there was two birds setting on a fence, he would bet you which one would fly first—or if there was a camp-meeting he would be there reglar to bet on parson Walker, which he judged to be the best exhorter about here, and so he was, too, and a good man; if he even see a straddle-bug start to go any wheres, he would bet you how long it would take him to get wherever he was going to, and if you took him up he would foller that straddle-bug to Mexico but what he would find out where he was bound for and how long he was on the road. Lots of the boys here has seen that Smiley and can tell you about him. Why, it never made no difference to *him*—he would bet on *anything*—the dangdest feller. Parson Walker's wife laid very sick, once, for a good while, and it seemed as if they warn't going to save her; but one morning he come in and Smiley asked him how she was, and he said she was considerable better—thank the Lord for his inf'nit mercy—and coming on so smart that with the blessing of Providence she'd get well yet—and Smiley, before he thought, says, "Well, I'll resk two-and-a-half that she don't, anyway."

Thish-yer Smiley had a mare—the boys called her the fifteen-minute nag, but that was only in fun, you know, because, of course, she was faster than that—and he used to win money on that horse, for all she was so slow and always had the asthma, or the distemper, or the consumption, or something of that kind. They used to give her two or three hundred yards' start, and then pass her under way; but always at the fag-end of the race she'd get excited and desperate-like, and come cavorting and spraddling up, and scattering her legs around limber, sometimes in the air, and sometimes out to one side amongst the fences, and kicking up m-o-r-e dust, and raising m-o-r-e racket with her coughing and sneezing and blowing her nose—and always fetch up at the stand just about a neck ahead, as near as you could cipher it down.

And he had a little small bull-pup, that to look at him you'd think he warn't worth a cent, but to set around and look or-nery, and lay for a chance to steal something. But as soon as money was up on him he was a different dog—his under-jaw'd begin to stick out like the for'castle of a steamboat, and his teeth would uncover, and shine savage like the furnaces. And a dog might tackle him, and bully-rag him, and bite him, and throw him over his shoulder two or three times, and Andrew Jackson—which was the name of the pup—Andrew Jackson would never let on but what he was satisfied, and hadn't expected nothing else—and the bets being doubled and doubled on the other side all the time, till the money was all up—and then all of a sudden he would grab that other dog just by the joint of his hind legs and freeze to it—not chaw, you understand, but only just grip and hang on till they throwed up the sponge, if it was a year. Smiley always came out winner on that pup till he harnessed a dog once that didn't have no hind legs, because they'd been sawed off in a circular saw, and when the thing had gone along far enough, and the money was all up, and he came to make a snatch for his pet holt, he saw in a minute how he'd been imposed on, and how the other dog had him in the door, so to speak, and he 'peared surprised, and then he looked sorter discouraged like, and didn't try no more to win the fight, and so he got shucked out bad. He gave Smiley a look as much as to say his heart was broke, and it was *his* fault, for putting up a dog that hadn't no hind legs for him to take holt of, which was his main dependence in a fight, and then he limped off a piece, and laid down and died. It was a good pup, was that Andrew Jackson, and would have made a name for hisself if he'd lived, for the stuff was in him, and he had genius—I know it, because he hadn't had no opportunities to speak of, and it don't stand to reason that a dog could make such a fight as he could under them circumstances, if he hadn't no talent. It always makes me feel sorry when I think of that last fight of his'on, and the way it turned out.

Well, thish-yer Smiley had rat-terriers and chicken cocks, and tom-cats, and all them kind of things, till you couldn't rest, and you couldn't fetch nothing for him to bet on but he'd match you. He ketched a frog one day and took him home and said he cal'lated to educate him; and so he never done nothing for three months but set in his back yard and learn that frog to jump. And you bet you he *did* learn him, too. He'd give him a little hunch behind, and the next minute you'd see that frog whirling in the air like a doughnut—see him turn one summerset, or maybe a couple, if he got a good start, and come down flat-footed and all right, like a cat. He got him up so in the matter of ketching flies, and kept him in practice so constant, that he'd nail a fly every time as far as he could see him. Smiley said all a frog wanted was education, and he could do most anything—and I believe him. Why, I've seen him set Dan'l Webster down here on this floor— Dan'l Webster was the name of the frog—and sing out, "Flies! Dan'l, flies," and quicker'n you could wink, he'd spring straight up, and snake a fly off'n the counter there, and flop down on the floor again as solid as a gob of mud, and fall to scratching the side of his head with his hind foot as indifferent as if he hadn't no idea he'd done any more'n any frog might do. You never see a frog so modest and straightfor'ard as he was, for all he was so gifted. And when it come to fair-and-square jumping on a dead level, he could get over more ground at one straddle than any animal of his breed you ever see. Jumping on a dead level was his strong suit, you understand, and when it come to that, Smiley would ante up money on him as long as he had a red. Smiley was monstrous proud of his frog, and well he might be, for fellers that had travelled and ben everywheres all said he laid over any frog that ever *they* see.

Well, Smiley kept the beast in a little lattice box, and he used to fetch him down town sometimes and lay for a bet. One day a feller—a stranger in the camp, he was—come across him with his box, and says:

"What might it be that you've got in the box?"

And Smiley says, sorter indifferent like, "It might be a parrot, or it might be a canary, maybe, but it ain't—it's only just a frog."

And the feller took it, and looked at it careful, and turned it round this way and that, and says, "H'm—so 'tis. Well, what's *he* good for?"

"Well," Smiley says, easy and careless, "He's good enough for *one* thing I should judge—he can out-jump ary frog in Calaveras county."

The feller took the box again, and took another long, particular look, and give it back to Smiley and says, very deliberate, "Well—I don't see no points about that frog that's any better'n any other frog."

"Maybe you don't," Smiley says. "Maybe you understand frogs, and maybe you don't understand 'em; maybe you've had experience, and maybe you ain't only a amature, as it were. Anyways, I've got *my* opinion, and I'll resk forty dollars that he can outjump ary frog in Calaveras county."

And the feller studied a minute, and then says, kinder sad, like, "Well—I'm only a stranger here, and I ain't got no frog—but if I had a frog I'd bet you."

And then Smiley says, "That's all right—that's all right—if you'll hold my box a minute I'll go and get you a frog;" and so the feller took the box, and put up his forty dollars along with Smiley's, and set down to wait.

So he set there a good while thinking and thinking to hisself, and then he got the frog out and prized his mouth open and took a teaspoon and filled him full of quail-shot—filled him pretty near up to his chin—and set him on the floor. Smiley he went out to the swamp and slopped around in the mud for a long time, and finally he ketched a frog and fetched him in and give him to this feller and says:

"Now if you're ready, set him alongside of Dan'l, with his fore-paws just even with Dan'l's, and I'll give the word." Then he says, "one—two—three—jump!" and him and the feller touched up the frogs from behind, and the new frog hopped off lively, but Dan'l give a heave, and hysted up his shoulders—so—like a Frenchman, but it wasn't no use—he couldn't budge; he was planted as solid as a anvil, and he couldn't no more stir than if he was anchored out. Smiley was a good deal surprised, and he was disgusted too, but he didn't have no idea what the matter was, of course.

The feller took the money and started away, and when he was going out at the door he sorter jerked his thumb over his shoulder—this way—at Dan'l, and says again, very deliberate, "Well—*I* don't see no points about that frog that's any better'n any other frog."

Smiley he stood scratching his head and looking down at Dan'l a long time, and at last he says, "I do wonder what in the nation that frog throwed off for—I wonder if there ain't something the matter with him—he 'pears to look mighty baggy, somehow"—and he ketched Dan'l by the nap of the neck, and lifted him up and says, "Why blame my cats if he don't weigh five pound"—and turned him upside down, and he belched out about a double-handful of shot. And then he see how it was, and he was the maddest man—he set the frog down and took out after that feller, but he never ketched him. And——

[Here Simon Wheeler heard his name called from the front-yard, and got up to go and see what was wanted.] And turning to me as he moved away, he said: "Just sit where you are, stranger, and rest easy—I ain't going to be gone a second."

But by your leave, I did not think that a continuation of the history of the enterprising vagabond Jim Smiley would be likely to afford me much information concerning the Rev. Leonidas W. Smiley, and so I started away.

At the door I met the sociable Wheeler returning, and he buttonholed me and recommenced:

"Well, thish-yer Smiley had a yaller one-eyed cow that didn't have no tail only just a short stump like a bannanner, and——"

"O, curse Smiley and his afflicted cow!" I muttered, good-naturedly, and bidding the old gentleman good-day, I departed.

Yours, truly,
MARK TWAIN.

November 18, 1865

"Mark Twain" on the Launch
of the Steamer "Capital"

I GET MR. MUFF NICKERSON TO GO WITH ME
AND ASSIST IN REPORTING THE GREAT STEAM-
BOAT LAUNCH. HE RELATES THE INTERESTING
HISTORY OF THE TRAVELLING PANORAMIST.

I was just starting off to see the launch of the great steamboat *Capital*, on Saturday week, when I came across Mulph,
Mulff, Muff, Mumph, Murph, Mumf, Murf, Mumford, Mulford, Murphy Nickerson—(he is well known to the public by
all these names, and I cannot say which is the right one)—
bound on the same errand. He said that if there was one
thing he took more delight in than another, it was a steamboat launch; he would walk miles to see one, any day; he had
seen a hundred thousand steamboat launches in his time, and
hoped he might live to see a hundred thousand more; he
knew all about them; knew everything—*every*thing connected
with them—said he "had it all down to a scratch;" he could
explain the whole process in minute detail; to the uuculti-
vated eye a steamboat-launch presented nothing grand, nothing startling, nothing beautiful, nothing romantic, or awe-
inspiring or sublime—but to an optic like his (which saw not
the dull outer coating, but the radiant gem it hid from other
eyes,) it presented all these—and behold, he had power to
lift the veil and display the vision even unto the uninspired.
He could do this by word of mouth—by explanation and
illustration. Let a man stand by his side, and to him that
launch should seem arrayed in the beauty and the glory of
enchantment!

This was the man I wanted. I could see that plainly enough.
There would be many reporters present at the launch, and the
papers would teem with the inevitable old platitudinal trash
which this sort of people have compelled to do duty on every
occasion like this since Noah launched his ark—but I aspired
to higher things. I wanted to write a report which should
astonish and delight the whole intellectual world—which

should dissect, analyze, and utterly exhaust the subject—which should serve for a model in this species of literature for all time to come. I dropped alongside of Mr. M. M. M. M. M. M. M. M. M. M. Nickerson, and we went to the launch together.

We set out in a steamer whose decks were crowded with persons of all ages, who were happy in their nervous anxiety to behold the novelty of a steamboat launch. I tried not to pity them, but I could not help whispering to myself, "These poor devils will see nothing but some stupid boards and timbers nailed together—a mere soulless hulk—sliding into the water!"

As we approached the spot where the launch was to take place, a gentleman from Reese River, by the name of Thompson, came up, with several friends, and said he had been prospecting on the main deck, and had found an object of interest—a bar. This was all very well, and showed him to be a man of parts—but like many another man who produces a favorable impression by an introductory remark replete with wisdom, he followed it up with a vain and unnecessary question—Would we take a drink? This to me!—This to M. M. M., etc., Nickerson!

We proceeded, two-by-two, arm-in-arm, down to the bar in the nether regions, chatting pleasantly and elbowing the restless multitude. We took pure, cold, health-giving water, with some other things in it, and clinked our glasses together, and were about to drink, when Smith, of Excelsior, drew forth his handkerchief and wiped away a tear; and then, noticing that the action had excited some attention, he explained it by recounting a most affecting incident in the history of a venerated aunt of his—now deceased—and said that, although long years had passed since the touching event he had narrated, he could never take a drink without thinking of the kind-hearted old lady.

Mr. Nickerson blew his nose, and said with deep emotion that it gave him a better opinion of human nature to see a man who had had a good aunt, eternally and forever thinking about her.

This episode reminded Jones, of Mud Springs, of a circumstance which happened many years ago in the home of his childhood, and we held our glasses untouched and rested our elbows on the counter, while we listened with rapt attention to his story.

There was something in it about a good natured, stupid man, and this reminded Thompson of Reese River of a person of the same kind whom he had once fallen in with while travelling through the back-settlements of one of the Atlantic States, and we postponed drinking until he should give us the facts in the case. The hero of the tale had unintentionally created some consternation at a camp-meeting by one of his innocent asinine freaks, and this reminded Mr. M. Nickerson of a reminiscence of his temporary sojourn in the interior of Connecticut some months ago, and again our uplifted glasses were stayed on their way to our lips, and we listened attentively to

THE ENTERTAINING HISTORY
OF THE SCRIPTURAL PANORAMIST.

[I give the story in Mr. Nickerson's own language.]

There was a fellow travelling around, in that country, (said Mr. Nickerson,) with a moral religious show—a sort of a scriptural panorama—and he hired a wooden-headed old slab to play the piano for him. After the first night's performance, the showman says:

"My friend, you seem to know pretty much all the tunes there are, and you worry along first-rate. But then didn't you notice that sometimes last night the piece you happened to be playing was a little rough on the proprieties so to speak— didn't seem to jibe with the general gait of the picture that was passing at the time, as it were—was a little foreign to the subject, you know—as if you didn't either trump or follow suit, you understand?"

"Well, no," the fellow said; he hadn't noticed, but it might be; he had played along just as it came handy.

So they put it up that the simple old dummy was to keep his eye on the panorama after that, and as soon as a stunning picture was reeled out, he was to fit it to a dot with a piece of music that would help the audience get the idea of the subject, and warm them up like a camp-meeting revival. That sort of thing would corral their sympathies, the showman said.

There was a big audience that night—mostly middle-aged and old people who belonged to the church and took a strong interest in Bible matters, and the balance were pretty much young bucks and heifers—*they* always come out strong on panoramas, you know, because it gives them a chance to taste one another's mugs in the dark.

Well, the showman began to swell himself up for his lecture, and the old mud-dobber tackled the piano and run his fingers up and down once or twice to see that she was all right, and the fellows behind the curtain commenced to grind out the panorama. The showman balanced his weight on his right foot, and propped his hands on his hips, and flung his eye over his shoulder at the scenery, and says:

"Ladies and gentlemen, the painting now before you illustrates the beautiful and touching parable of the Prodigal Son. Observe the happy expression just breaking over the features of the poor suffering youth—so worn and weary with his long march: note also the ecstasy beaming from the uplifted countenance of the aged father, and the joy that sparkles in the eyes of the excited group of youths and maidens and seems ready to burst in a welcoming chorus from their lips. The lesson, my friends, is as solemn and instructive as the story is tender and beautiful."

The mud-dobber was all ready, and the second the speech was finished he struck up:

> "Oh, we'll all get blind drunk
>   When Johnny comes marching home!"

Some of the people giggled, and some groaned a little. The showman couldn't say a word. He looked at the piano sharp, but he was all lovely and serene—*he* didn't know there was anything out of gear.

The panorama moved on, and the showman drummed up his grit and started in fresh:

"Ladies and gentlemen, the fine picture now unfolding itself to your gaze exhibits one of the most notable events in Bible History—our Savior and his disciples upon the Sea of Galilee. How grand, how awe inspiring are the reflections which the subject invokes! What sublimity of faith is revealed to us in this lesson from the sacred writings! The Savior rebukes the angry waves, and walks securely upon the bosom of the deep!"

All around the house they were whispering: "Oh, how lovely! how beautiful!" and the orchestra let himself out again:

> "Oh, a life on the ocean wave,
>   And a home on the rolling deep!"

There was a good deal of honest snickering turned on this time, and considerable groaning, and one or two old deacons got up and went out. The showman gritted his teeth and cursed the piano man to himself, but the fellow sat there like a knot on a log, and seemed to think he was doing first-rate.

After things got quiet, the showman thought he would make one more stagger at it, any how, though his confidence was beginning to get mighty shaky. The supes started the panorama to grinding along again, and he says:

"Ladies and gentlemen, this exquisite painting illustrates the raising of Lazarus from the dead by our Savior. The subject has been handled with rare ability by the artist, and such touching sweetness and tenderness of expression has he thrown into it, that I have known peculiarly sensitive persons to be even affected to tears by looking at it. Observe the half-confused, half-inquiring look, upon the countenance of the awakening Lazarus. Observe, also, the attitude and expression of the Savior, who takes him gently by the sleeve of his shroud with one hand, while he points with the other toward the distant city."

Before anybody could get off an opinion in the case, the innocent old ass at the piano struck up:

> "Come rise up, William Ri-i-ley,
>   And go along with me!"

It was rough on the audience, you bet you. All the solemn old flats got up in a huff to go, and everybody else laughed till the windows rattled.

The showman went down and grabbed the orchestra, and shook him up, and says:

"That lets you out, you know, you chowder-headed old clam! Go to the door-keeper and get your money, and cut your stick!—vamose the ranch! Ladies and gentlemen, circumstances over which I have no control compel me prematurely to dismiss—"

"By George! it was splendid!—come! all hands! let's take a drink!"

It was Phelim O'Flannigan, of San Luis Obispo, who interrupted. I had not seen him before. "What was splendid?" I inquired.

"The launch!"

Our party clinked glasses once more, and drank in respectful silence.

MARK TWAIN.

P. S.—You will excuse me from making a model report of the great launch. I was with Mulf Nickerson, who was going to "explain the whole thing to me as clear as glass," but, you see, they launched the boat with such indecent haste, that we never got a chance to see it. It was a great pity, because Mulph Nickerson understands launches as well as any man.

November 18, 1865

The Pioneers' Ball

It was estimated that four hundred persons were present at the ball. The gentlemen wore the orthodox costume for such occasions, and the ladies were dressed the best they knew how. N. B.—Most of these ladies were pretty, and some of them absolutely beautiful. Four out of every five ladies present were pretty. The ratio at the Colfax party was two out of every five. I always keep the run of these things. While upon this department of the subject, I may as well tarry a moment and furnish you with descriptions of some of the most noticeable costumes.

Mrs. W. M. was attired in an elegant *pate de foi gras*, made expressly for her, and was greatly admired.

Miss S. had her hair done up. She was the centre of attraction for the gentlemen, and the envy of all the ladies.

Miss G. W. was tastefully dressed in a *tout ensemble*, and was greeted with deafening applause wherever she went.

Mrs. C. N. was superbly arrayed in white kid gloves. Her modest and engaging manner accorded well with the unpretending simplicity of her costume, and caused her to be regarded with absorbing interest by every one.

The charming Miss M. M. B. appeared in a thrilling waterfall, whose exceeding grace and volume compelled the homage of pioneers and emigrants alike. How beautiful she was!

The queenly Mrs. L. R. was attractively attired in her new and beautiful false teeth, and the *bon jour* effect they naturally produced was heightened by her enchanting and well-sustained smile. The manner of this lady is charmingly pensive and melancholy, and her troops of admirers desired no greater happiness than to get on the scent of her sozodont-sweetened sighs and track her through her sinuous course among the gay and restless multitude.

Miss R. P., with that repugnance to ostentation in dress which is so peculiar to her, was attired in a simple white lace collar, fastened with a neat pearl-button solitaire. The fine contrast between the sparkling vivacity of her natural optic and the steadfast attentiveness of her placid glass eye was the subject of general and enthusiastic remark.

The radiant and sylph-like Mrs. T., late of your State, wore hoops. She showed to good advantage, and created a sensation wherever she appeared. She was the gayest of the gay.

Miss C. L. B. had her fine nose elegantly enameled, and the easy grace with which she blew it from time to time, marked her as a cultivated and accomplished woman of the world; its exquisitely modulated tone excited the admiration of all who had the happiness to hear it.

Being offended with Miss X., and our acquaintance having ceased permanently, I will take this opportunity of observing to her that it is of no use for her to be slopping off to every ball that takes place, and flourishing around with a brass oyster-knife skewered through her waterfall, and smiling her sickly smile through her decayed teeth, with her dismal pug nose in the air. There is no use in it—she don't fool anybody. Everybody knows she is old; everybody knows she is repaired (you might almost say built) with artificial bones and hair and muscles and things, from the ground up—put together scrap by scrap—and everybody knows, also, that all one would have to do would be to pull out her key-pin and she would go to pieces like a Chinese puzzle. There, now, my faded flower, take that paragraph home with you and amuse yourself with it; and if ever you turn your wart of a nose up at me again I will sit down and write something that will just make you rise up and howl.

c. November 19, 1865

Uncle Lige

I will now relate an affecting incident of my meeting with Uncle Lige, as a companion novelette to the one published by Dan the other day, entitled "Uncle Henry."

A day or two since—before the late stormy weather—I was taking a quiet stroll in the western suburbs of the city. The day was sunny and pleasant. In front of a small but neat "bit house," seated upon a bank—a worn out and discarded faro bank—I saw a man and a little girl. The sight was too much for me, and I burst into tears. Oh, God! I cried, this is too rough! After the violence of my emotion had in a manner spent itself, I ventured to look once more upon that touching picture. The left hand of the girl (how well I recollect which hand it was! by the warts on it)—a fair-haired, sweet-faced child of about eight years of age—rested upon the right shoulder (how perfectly I remember it was his right shoulder, because his left shoulder had been sawed off in a saw-mill) of the man by whose side she was seated. She was gazing toward the summit of Lone Mountain, and prating of the gravestones on the top of it and of the sunshine and Diggers resting on its tomb-clad slopes. The head of the man drooped forward till his face almost rested upon his breast, and he seemed intently listening. It was only a pleasing pretence, though, for there was nothing for him to hear save the rattling of the carriages on the gravel road beside him, and he could have straightened himself up and heard that easy enough, poor fellow. As I approached, the child observed me, notwithstanding her extreme youth, and ceasing to talk, smilingly looked at me, strange as it may seem. I stopped, again almost overpowered, but after a struggle I mastered my feelings sufficiently to proceed. I gave her a smile—or rather, I swapped her one in return for the one I had just received, and she said:

"This is Uncle Lige—poor blind-drunk Uncle Lige."

This burst of confidence from an entire stranger, and one so young withal, caused my subjugated emotions to surge up in my breast once more, but again, with a strong effort, I controlled them. I looked at the wine-bred cauliflower on the poor man's nose and saw how it had all happened.

"Yes," said he, noticing by my eloquent countenance that I *had* seen how it had all happened, notwithstanding nothing had been said yet about anything having happened, "Yes, it happened in Reeseriv' a year ago; since tha(ic)at time been living here with broth—Robert'n lill Addie (*e-ick!*)."

"Oh, he's the best uncle, and tells me such stories!" cried the little girl.

"At's aw-ri, you know (ick!)—at's aw ri," said the kind-hearted, gentle old man, spitting on his shirt bosom and slurring it off with his hand.

The child leaned quickly forward and kissed his poor blossomy face. We beheld two great tears start from the man's sightless eyes, but when they saw what sort of country they had got to travel over, they went back again. Kissing the child again and again and once more and then several times, and afterwards repeating it, he said:

"H(o-ook!)—oorah for Melical eagle star-spalgle baller! At's aw-ri, you know—(ick!)—at's aw-ri"—and he stroked her sunny curls and spit on his shirt bosom again.

This affecting scene was too much for my already over-charged feelings, and I burst into a flood of tears and hurried from the spot.

Such is the touching story of Uncle Lige. It may not be quite as sick as Dan's, but there is every bit as much reasonable material in it for a big calf like either of us to cry over. Cannot you publish the two novelettes in book form and send them forth to destroy such of our fellow citizens as are spared by the cholera?

c. November 28, 1865

A Rich Epigram

Tom Maguire,
Torn with ire,
Lighted on Macdougall,
Grabbed his throat,
Tore his coat,
And split him in the bugle.

Shame! Oh, fie!
Maguire, why
Will you thus skyugle?
Why bang and claw,
And gouge and chaw
The unprepared Macdougall?

Of bones bereft,
See how you've left,
Vestvali, gentle Jew gal—
And now you've slashed,
And almost hashed,
The form of poor Macdougall.

December 1865

Macdougall vs. Maguire

The talk occasioned by Maguire's unseemly castigation of Macdougall, while the latter was engaged in conversation with a lady, was dying out, happily for both parties, but Mr. Macdougall has set it going again by bringing that suit of his for $5,000 for the assault and battery. If he can get the money, I suppose that is at least the most profitable method of settling the matter. But then, will he? Maybe so, and maybe not. But if he feels badly—feels hurt—feels disgraced at being chastised, will $5,000 entirely soothe him and put an end to the comments and criticisms of the public? It is questionable. If he would pitch in and whale Maguire, though, it would afford him real, genuine satisfaction, and would also furnish me with a great deal more pleasing material for a paragraph than I can get out of the regular routine of events that transpire in San Francisco—which is a matter of still greater importance. If the plaintiff in this suit of damages were to intimate that he would like to have a word from me on this subject, I would immediately sit down and pour out my soul to him in verse. I would tune up my muse and sing to him the following pretty

NURSERY RHYME.

Come, now, Macdougall!
   Say—
   Can lucre pay
For thy dismembered coat—
Thy strangulated throat—
Thy busted bugle?

Speak thou! poor W. J.!
   And say—
   I pray—
If gold can soothe your woes,
Or mend your tattered clothes,
Or heal your battered nose,
Oh bunged-up lump of clay!

No!—arise!
Be wise!
Macdougall, d—n your eyes!
Don't legal quips devise
To mend your reputation,
And efface the degradation
Of a blow that's struck in ire!
But 'ware of execration,
Unless you take your station
In a strategic location,
In mood of desperation,
And "lam" like all creation
This infernal Tom Maguire!

December 20, 1865

The Christmas Fireside

By Grandfather Twain.

THE STORY OF THE BAD LITTLE BOY
THAT BORE A CHARMED LIFE.

Once there was a bad little boy, whose name was Jim—though, if you will notice, you will find that bad little boys are nearly always called James in your Sunday-school books. It was very strange, but still it was true, that this one was called Jim.

He didn't have any sick mother, either—a sick mother who was pious and had the consumption, and would be glad to lie down in the grave and be at rest, but for the strong love she bore her boy, and the anxiety she felt that the world would be harsh and cold toward him when she was gone. Most bad boys in the Sunday books are named James, and have sick mothers who teach them to say, "Now, I lay me down," etc., and sing them to sleep with sweet plaintive voices, and then kiss them good-night, and kneel down by the bedside and weep. But it was different with this fellow. He was named Jim, and there wasn't anything the matter with his mother—no consumption, or anything of that kind. She was rather stout than otherwise, and she was not pious; moreover, she was not anxious on Jim's account; she said if he were to break his neck, it wouldn't be much loss; she always spanked Jim to sleep, and she never kissed him good-night; on the contrary, she boxed his ears when she was ready to leave him.

Once, this little bad boy stole the key of the pantry and slipped in there and helped himself to some jam, and filled up the vessel with tar, so that his mother would never know the difference; but all at once a terrible feeling didn't come over him, and something didn't seem to whisper to him, "Is it right to disobey my mother? Isn't it sinful to do this? Where do bad little boys go who gobble up their good kind mother's jam?" and then he didn't kneel down all alone and promise never to be wicked any more, and rise up with a light, happy heart, and go and tell his mother all about it and beg her forgiveness, and be blessed by her with tears of pride and thankfulness in her eyes. No; that is the way with all other bad boys in the books, but it happened otherwise with this Jim, strangely enough. He ate that jam, and said it was bully, in his sinful, vulgar way; and he put in the tar, and said that was bully also, and laughed, and observed that "the old woman would get up and snort" when she found it out; and when she did find it out he denied knowing anything about it, and she whipped him severely, and he did the crying himself. Everything about this boy was curious—everything turned out differently with him from the way it does to the bad Jameses in the books.

Once he climbed up in Farmer Acorn's apple tree to steal apples, and the limb didn't break and he didn't fall and break his arm, and get torn by the farmer's great dog, and then languish on a sick bed for weeks and repent and become good. Oh, no—he stole as many apples as he wanted, and came down all right, and he was all ready for the dog, too, and knocked him endways with a rock when he came to tear him. It was very strange—nothing like it ever happened in those mild little books with marbled backs, and with pictures in them of men with swallow-tailed coats and bell-crowned hats and pantaloons that are short in the legs, and women with the waists of their dresses under their arms and no hoops on. Nothing like it in any of the Sunday-school books.

Once he stole the teacher's penknife, and when he was afraid it would be found out and he would get whipped, he slipped it into George Wilson's cap—poor Widow Wilson's son, the moral boy, the good little boy of the village, who always obeyed his mother, and never told an untruth, and was fond of his lessons and infatuated with Sunday-school. And when the knife dropped from the cap and poor George hung his head and blushed, as if in conscious guilt, and the grieved teacher charged the theft upon him, and was just in the very act of bringing the switch down upon his trembling shoulders, a white-haired improbable justice of the peace did not suddenly appear in their midst and strike an attitude and say, "Spare this noble boy—there stands the cowering culprit! I was passing the school door at recess, and, unseen myself, I saw the theft committed!" And then Jim didn't get whaled, and the venerable justice didn't read the tearful school a homily, and take George by the hand and say such a boy deserved to be exalted, and then tell him to come and make his home with him, and sweep out the office, and make fires, and run errands, and chop wood, and study law, and help his wife to do household labors, and have all the balance of the time to play, and get forty cents a month, and be happy. No, it would have happened that way in the books, but it didn't happen that way to Jim. No meddling old clam of a justice dropped in to make trouble, and so the model boy George got threshed, and Jim was glad of it. Because, you know, Jim hated moral boys. Jim said he was "down on them milksops." Such was the coarse language of this bad, neglected boy.

But the strangest things that ever happened to Jim was the time he went boating on Sunday and didn't get drowned, and that other time that he got caught out in the storm when he was fishing on Sunday, and didn't get struck by lightning. Why, you might look, and look, and look through the Sunday-school books, from now till next Christmas, and you would never come across anything like this. Oh, no—you would find that all the bad boys who go boating on Sunday invariably get drowned, and all the bad boys who get caught out in storms, when they are fishing on Sunday, infallibly get struck by lightning. Boats with bad boys in them always upset on Sunday, and it always storms when bad boys go fishing on the Sabbath. How this Jim ever escaped is a mystery to me.

This Jim bore a charmed life—that must have been the way of it. Nothing could hurt him. He even gave the elephant in the menagerie a plug of tobacco, and the elephant didn't knock the top of his head off with his trunk. He browsed around the cupboard after essence of peppermint, and didn't make a mistake and drink aqua fortis. He stole his father's gun and went hunting on the Sabbath, and didn't shoot three or four of his fingers off. He struck his little sister on the temple with his fist when he was angry, and she didn't linger in pain through long summer days and die with sweet words of forgiveness upon her lips that redoubled the anguish of his breaking heart. No—she got over it. He ran off and went to sea at last, and didn't come back and find himself sad and alone in the world, his loved ones sleeping in the quiet church-yard, and the vine-embowered home of his boyhood tumbled down and gone to decay. Ah, no—he came home drunk as a piper, and got into the station house the first thing.

And he grew up, and married, and raised a large family, and brained them all with an axe one night, and got wealthy by all manner of cheating and rascality, and now he is the infernalest wickedest scoundrel in his native village, and is universally respected, and belongs to the Legislature.

So you see there never was a bad James in the Sunday-school books that had such a streak of luck as this sinful Jim with the charmed life.

December 23, 1865

Policemen's Presents

In San Francisco according to "Mark Twain:" White, Green, Johnson, Thompson—*all* the police—get splendid watches from multitudes of people on their beats who have fallen dead in love with them—who adore them—who worship them—who cannot live out of the dear presence of their sweet, faithful policeman—who know no happiness, no Heaven more blissful than to "lallygag" with their d—d policemen. Sick! Oh, what nasty, nauseating hog-wash is this twaddle about "the numerous friends of Officer J. Smith, who have known and admired and appreciated his faithful services in his arduous duties for the past three months, met together last evening and surprised (?) him with a superb official star and double-case hunting watch, both of massive gold. It was a noble compliment, well bestowed." Now isn't that bosh? People don't fall in love with policemen without an object. You can go before a magistrate and swear to it! Whenever you see anything of that kind going on, you just move out of that policeman's beat—because some of his "numerous friends" are going to "go through" that locality shortly.

January 7, 1866

What Have the Police Been Doing?

Ain't they virtuous? Don't they take good care of the city? Is not their constant vigilance and efficiency shown in the fact that roughs and rowdies here are awed into good conduct?—isn't it shown in the fact that ladies even on the back streets are safe from insult in the daytime, when they are under the protection of a regiment of soldiers?—isn't it shown in the fact that although many offenders of importance go unpunished, they infallibly snaffle every Chinese chicken-thief that attempts to drive his trade, and are duly glorified by name in the papers for it?—isn't it shown in the fact that they are always on the look-out and keep out of the way and never get run over by wagons and things? And ain't they spry?—ain't they energetic?—ain't they frisky?—Don't they parade up and down the sidewalk at the rate of a block an hour and make everybody nervous and dizzy with their frightful velocity? Don't they keep their clothes nice?—and ain't their hands soft? And don't they work?—don't they work like horses?—don't they, now? Don't they smile sweetly on the women?—and when they are fatigued with their exertions, don't they back up against a lamp-post and go on smiling till they break plum down? But ain't they nice?—that's it, you know!—ain't they nice? They don't sweat—you never see one of those fellows sweat. Why, if you were to see a policeman sweating you would say, "oh, here, this poor man is going to die—because this sort of thing is unnatural, you know." Oh, no—you never see one of those fellows sweat. And ain't they easy and comfortable and happy—always leaning up against a lamp-post in the sun, and scratching one shin with the other foot and enjoying themselves? Serene?—I reckon not.

I don't know anything the matter with the Department, but may be Dr. Rowell does. Now when Ziele broke that poor wretch's skull the other night for stealing six bits' worth of flour sacks, and had him taken to the Station House by a policeman, and jammed into one of the cells in the most humorous way, do you think there was anything wrong there? I don't. Why should they arrest Ziele and say, "Oh, come, now, you *say* you found this stranger stealing on your premises,

and we know you knocked him on the head with your club—
but then you better go in a cell, too, till we see whether
there's going to be any other account of the thing—any account that mightn't jibe with yours altogether, you know—
you go in for confessed assault and battery, you know." Why
should they do that? Well, nobody ever said they did.

And why shouldn't they shove that half senseless wounded
man into a cell without getting a doctor to examine and see
how badly he was hurt, and consider that next day would be
time enough, if he chanced to live that long? And why
shouldn't the jailor let him alone when he found him in a
dead stupor two hours after—let him alone because he
couldn't wake him—couldn't wake a man who was sleeping
and with that calm serenity which is peculiar to men whose
heads have been caved in with a club—couldn't wake such a
subject, but never suspected that there was anything unusual
in the circumstance? Why shouldn't the jailor do so? Why
certainly—why shouldn't he?—the man was an infernal
stranger. He had no vote. Besides, had not a gentleman just
said he stole some flour sacks? Ah, and if he stole flour sacks,
did he not deliberately put himself outside the pale of humanity and Christian sympathy by that hellish act? I think so. The
department think so. Therefore, when the stranger died at 7
in the morning, after four hours of refreshing slumber in that
cell, with his scull actually split in twain from front to rear,
like an apple, as was ascertained by post mortem examination,
what the very devil do you want to go and find fault with the
prison officers for? You are *always* putting in your shovel.
Can't you find somebody to pick on besides the police? It
takes all my time to defend them from people's attacks.

I know the Police Department is a kind, humane and generous institution. Why, it was no longer ago than yesterday
that I was reminded of that time Captain Lees broke his leg.
Didn't the free-handed, noble Department shine forth with a
dazzling radiance then? Didn't the Chief detail officers
Shields, Ward and two others to watch over him and nurse
him and look after all his wants with motherly solicitude—
four of them, you know—four of the very biggest and ablest-
bodied men on the force—when less generous people would
have thought two nurses sufficient—had these four acrobats

in active hospital service that way in the most liberal manner, at a cost to the city of San Francisco of only the trifling sum of five hundred dollars a month — the same being the salaries of four officers of the regular police force at $125 a month each. But don't you know there are people mean enough to say that Captain Lees ought to have paid his own nurse bills, and that if he had had to do it maybe he would have managed to worry along on less than five hundred dollars worth of nursing a month? And don't you know that they say also that interested parties are always badgering the Supervisors with petitions for an increase of the police force, and showing such increase to be a terrible necessity, and yet they have always got to be hunting up and creating new civil offices and berths, and making details for nurse service in order to find something for them to do after they get them appointed? And don't you know that they say that they wish to god the city would hire a detachment of nurses and keep them where they will be handy in case of accident, so that property will not be left unprotected while policemen are absent on duty in sick rooms. You can't think how it aggravates me to hear such harsh remarks about our virtuous police force. Ah, well, the police will have their reward hereafter — no doubt.

January 21, 1866

The Spiritual Séance

There was a *séance* in town a few nights since. As I was making for it, in company with the reporter of an evening paper, he said he had seen a gambler named Gus Graham shot down in a town in Illinois years ago, by a mob, and as he was probably the only person in San Francisco who knew of the circumstance, he thought he would "give the spirits Graham to chaw on awhile." [N.B.—This young creature is a Democrat, and speaks with the native strength and inelegance of his tribe.] In the course of the show he wrote his old pal's name on a slip of paper and folded it up tightly and put it in a hat which was passed around, and which already had about five hundred similar documents in it. The pile was dumped on the table and the medium began to take them up one by one and lay them aside, asking: "Is this spirit present?—or this?—or this?" About one in fifty would rap, and the person who sent up the name would rise in his place and question the defunct. At last a spirit seized the medium's hand and wrote "Gus Graham" backwards. Then the medium went skirmishing through the papers for the corresponding name. And that old sport knew his card by the back! When the medium came to it, after picking up fifty others, he rapped! A committeeman unfolded the paper and it was the right one. I sent for it and got it. It was all right. However, I suppose all those Democrats are on sociable terms with the devil. The young man got up and asked:

"Did you die in '51?—'52?—'53?—'54?——"

Ghost—"Rap, rap, rap."

"Did you die of cholera?—diarrhea?—dysentery?—dogbite?—small-pox?—violent death?——"

"Rap, rap, rap."

"Were you hanged?—drowned?—stabbed?—shot?——"

"Rap, rap, rap."

"Did you die in Mississippi?—Kentucky?—New York?—Sandwich Islands?—Texas?—Illinois?——"

"Rap, rap, rap."

"In Adams county?—Madison?—Randolph?——"

"Rap, rap, rap."

It was no use trying to catch the departed gambler. He knew his hand and played it like a Major.

About this time a couple of Germans stepped forward, an elderly man and a spry young fellow, cocked and primed for a sensation. They wrote some names. Then young Ohlendorff said something which sounded like—

"Ist ein geist hieraus?" [Bursts of laughter from the audience.]

Three raps—signifying that there *was* a geist hieraus.

"Vollen sie schreihen?" [More laughter.]

Three raps.

"Finzig stollen, linsowfterowlickterhairowfterfrowleiner-whackfolderol?"

Incredible as it may seem, the spirit cheerfully answered Yes to that astonishing proposition.

The audience grew more and more boisterously mirthful with every fresh question, and they were informed that the performance could not go on in the midst of so much levity. They became quiet.

The German ghost didn't appear to know anything at all—couldn't answer the simplest questions. Young Ohlendorff finally stated some numbers, and tried to get at the time of the spirit's death; it appeared to be considerably mixed as to whether it died in 1811 or 1812, which was reasonable enough, as it had been so long ago. At last it wrote "12."

Tableau! Young Ohlendorff sprang to his feet in a state of consuming excitement. He exclaimed:

"Laties und shentlemen! I wride de name fon a man vot lifs! Speerit-rabbing dells me he ties in yahr eighteen hoondert und dwelf, but he yoos as live und helty as——"

The Medium—"Sit down, sir!"

Ohlendorff—"But I vant to——"

Medium—"You are not here to make speeches, sir—sit down!" [Mr. O. had squared himself for an oration.]

Mr. O.—"But de speerit cheat!—dere is no such speer-it——" [All this time applause and laughter by turns from the audience.]

Medium—"Take your seat, sir, and I will explain this matter."

And she explained. And in that explanation she let off a

blast which was so terrific that I half expected to see young
Ohlendorff shot up through the roof. She said he had come
up there with fraud and deceit and cheating in his heart, and a
kindred spirit had come from the land of shadows to commune with him! She was terribly bitter. She said in substance,
though not in words, that perdition was full of just such fellows as Ohlendorff, and they were ready on the slightest pretext to rush in and assume anybody's name, and rap, and
write, and lie, and swindle with a perfect looseness whenever
they could rope in a living affinity like poor Ohlendorff to
communicate with! [Great applause and laughter.]

Ohlendorff stood his ground with good pluck, and was going to open his batteries again, when a storm of cries arose all
over the house, "Get down! Go on! Clear out! Speak on—
we'll hear you! Climb down from that platform! Stay where
you are! Vamose! Stick to your post—say your say!"

The medium rose up and said if Ohlendorff remained, she
would not. She recognized no one's right to come there and
insult her by practicing a deception upon her and attempting
to bring ridicule upon so solemn a thing as her religious
belief.

The audience then became quiet, and the subjugated
Ohlendorff retired from the platform.

The other German raised a spirit, questioned it at some
length in his own language, and said the answers were correct. The medium claims to be entirely unacquainted with the
German language.

Just then a gentleman called me to the edge of the platform and asked me if I were a Spiritualist. I said I was not.
He asked me if I were prejudiced. I said not more than any
other unbeliever; but I could not believe in a thing which I
could not understand, and I had not seen anything yet that I
could by any possibility cipher out. He said, then, that he
didn't think I was the cause of the diffidence shown by the
spirits, but he knew there was an antagonistic influence
around that table somewhere; he had noticed it from the
first; there was a painful negative current passing to his sensitive organization from that direction constantly. I told him
I guessed it was that other fellow; and I said, Blame a man
who was all the time shedding these infernal negative cur-

rents! This appeared to satisfy the mind of the inquiring fanatic, and he sat down.

I had a very dear friend, who, I had heard, had gone to the spirit land, or perdition, or some of those places, and I desired to know something concerning him. There was something so awful, though, about talking with living, sinful lips to the ghostly dead, that I could hardly bring myself to rise and speak. But at last I got tremblingly up and said with low and reverent voice:

"Is the spirit of John Smith present?" [You never can depend on these Smiths; you call for one and the whole tribe will come clattering out of hell to answer you.]

"Whack! whack! whack! whack!"

Bless me! I believe all the dead and damned John Smiths between San Francisco and perdition boarded that poor little table at once! I was considerably set back—stunned, I may say. The audience urged me to go on, however, and I said:

"What did you die of?"

The Smiths answered to every disease and casualty that man can die of.

"Where did you die?"

They answered Yes to every locality I could name while my geography held out.

"Are you happy where you are?"

There was a vigorous and unanimous "No!" from the late Smiths.

"Is it warm there?"

An educated Smith seized the medium's hand and wrote:

"It's no name for it."

"Did you leave any Smiths in that place when you came away?"

"Dead loads of them."

I fancied I heard the shadowy Smiths chuckle at this feeble joke—the rare joke that there could be live loads of Smiths where all are dead.

"How many Smiths are present?"

"Eighteen millions—the procession now reaches from here to the other side of China."

"Then there are many Smiths in the kingdom of the lost?"

"The Prince Apollyon calls all newcomers Smith on general

principles; and continues to do so until he is corrected, if he chances to be mistaken."

"What do lost spirits call their dread abode?"

"They call it the Smithsonian Institute."

I got hold of the right Smith at last—the particular Smith I was after—my dear, lost, lamented friend—and learned that he died a violent death. I feared as much. He said his wife talked him to death. Poor wretch!

By and by up started another Smith. A gentleman in the audience said that that was his Smith. So he questioned him, and this Smith said he too died by violence; he had been a teacher; not a school-teacher, but (after some hesitation) a teacher of religion; he had been a good deal tangled in his religious belief, and was a sort of a cross between a Universalist and a Unitarian; has got straightened out and changed his opinions since he left here; said he was perfectly happy. We proceeded to question this talkative and frolicsome old parson. Among spirits, I judge he is the gayest of the gay. He said he had no tangible body; a bullet could pass through him and never make a hole; rain could pass through him as through vapor and not discommode him in the least (wherefore I suppose he don't know enough to come in when it rains—or don't care enough;) says heaven and hell are simply mental conditions—spirits in the former have happy and contented minds, and those in the latter are torn by remorse of conscience; says as far as he is concerned, he is all right—he is happy; would not say whether he was a very good or a very bad man on earth (the shrewd old water-proof nonentity!—I asked the question so that I might average my own chances for his luck in the other world, but he saw my drift;) says he has an occupation there—puts in his time teaching and being taught; says there are spheres—grades of excellence—he is making pretty good progress—has been promoted a sphere or so since his matriculation; (I said mentally, "Go slow, old man, go slow—you have got all eternity before you"—and he replied not;) he don't know how many spheres there are (but I suppose there must be millions, because if a man goes galloping through them at the rate this old Universalist is doing, he will get through an infinitude of them by the time he has been there as long as old Sesostris and those ancient mummies; and there is no estimating how high he will get in even the infancy of eternity—I am afraid the old man is scouring along rather too fast for the style of his surroundings, and the length of time he has got on his hands); says spirits cannot feel heat or cold (which militates somewhat against all my notions of orthodox damnation—fire and brimstone); says spirits commune with each other by thought—they have no language; says the distinctions of sex are preserved there—and so forth and so on.

The old parson wrote and talked for an hour, and showed by his quick, shrewd, intelligent replies, that he had not been sitting up nights in the other world for nothing; he had been prying into everything worth knowing, and finding out everything he possibly could—as he said himself—when he did not understand a thing he hunted up a spirit who could explain it; consequently he is pretty thoroughly posted; and for his accommodating conduct and his uniform courtesy to me, I sincerely hope he will continue to progress at his present velocity until he lands on the very roof of the highest sphere of all, and thus achieves perfection.

February 4, 1866

A New Biography of Washington

This day, many years ago precisely, George Washington was born. How full of significance the thought! Especially to those among us who have had a similar experience, though subsequently; and still more especially to the young, who should take him for a model and faithfully try to be like him, undeterred by the frequency with which the same thing has been attempted by American youths before them and not satisfactorily accomplished. George Washington was the youngest of nine children, eight of whom were the offspring of his uncle and his aunt. As a boy he gave no promise of the greatness he was one day to achieve. He was ignorant of the commonest accomplishments of youth. He could not even lie. But then he never had any of those precious advantages which are within the reach of the humblest of the boys of the present day. Any boy can lie, now. I could lie before I could stand— yet this sort of sprightliness was so common in our family that little notice was taken of it. Young George appears to have had no sagacity whatever. It is related of him that he once chopped down his father's favorite cherry tree, and then didn't know enough to keep dark about it. He came near going to sea, once, as a midshipman; but when his mother represented to him that he must necessarily be absent when he was away from home, and that this must continue to be the case until he got back, the sad truth struck him so forcibly that he ordered his trunk ashore, and quietly but firmly refused to serve in the navy and fight the battles of his king so long as the effect of it would be to discommode his mother. The great rule of his life was, that procrastination was the thief of time, and that we should always do unto others. This is the golden rule. Therefore, he would never discommode his mother.

Young George Washington was actuated in all things, by the highest and purest principles of morality, justice and right. He was a model in every way worthy of the emulation of youth. Young George was always prompt and faithful in the discharge of every duty. It has been said of him, by the historian, that he was always on hand, like a thousand of

brick. And well deserved was this noble compliment. The aggregate of the building material specified might have been
largely increased—might have been doubled—even without
doing full justice to these high qualities in the subject of this
sketch. Indeed, it would hardly be possible to express in
bricks the exceeding promptness and fidelity of young George
Washington. His was a soul whose manifold excellencies were
beyond the ken and computation of mathematics, and bricks
are, at the least, but an inadequate vehicle for the conveyance
of a comprehension of the moral sublimity of a nature so pure
as his.

Young George W. was a surveyor in early life—a surveyor
of an inland port—a sort of county surveyor; and under a
commission from Gov. Dinwiddie, he set out to survey his
way four hundred miles through a trackless forest, infested
with Indians, to procure the liberation of some English prisoners. The historian says the Indians were the most depraved
of their species, and did nothing but lay for white men,
whom they killed for the sake of robbing them. Considering
that white men only traveled through their country at the rate
of one a year, they were probably unable to do what might be
termed a land-office business in their line. They did not rob
young G. W.; one savage made the attempt, but failed; he
fired at the subject of this sketch from behind a tree, but the
subject of this sketch immediately snaked him out from behind the tree and took him prisoner.

The long journey failed of success; the French would not
give up the prisoners, and Wash went sadly back home again.
A regiment was raised to go and make a rescue, and he took
command of it. He caught the French out in the rain and
tackled them with great intrepidity. He defeated them in ten
minutes, and their commander handed in his checks. This was
the battle of Great Meadows.

After this, a good while, George Washington became
Commander-in-Chief of the American armies, and had an exceedingly dusty time of it all through the Revolution. But
every now and then he turned a jack from the bottom and
surprised the enemy. He kept up his lick for seven long years,
and hazed the British from Harrisburg to Halifax—and
America was free! He served two terms as President, and

would have been President yet if he had lived—even so did the people honor the Father of his Country. Let the youth of America take his incomparable character for a model and try it one jolt, anyhow. Success is possible—let them remember that—success is possible, though there are chances against it.

I could continue this biography, with profit to the rising generation, but I shall have to drop the subject at present, because of other matters which must be attended to.

c. February 25, 1866

Reflections on the Sabbath

The day of rest comes but once a week, and sorry I am that it does not come oftener. Man is so constituted that he can stand more rest than this. I often think regretfully that it would have been so easy to have two Sundays in a week, and yet it was not so ordained. The omnipotent Creator could have made the world in three days just as easily as he made it in six, and this would have doubled the Sundays. Still it is not our place to criticise the wisdom of the Creator. When we feel a depraved inclination to question the judgment of Providence in stacking up double eagles in the coffers of Michael Reese and leaving better men to dig for a livelihood, we ought to stop and consider that we are not expected to help order things, and so drop the subject. If all-powerful Providence grew weary after six days' labor, such worms as we are might reasonably expect to break down in three, and so require two Sundays—but as I said before, it ill becomes us to hunt up flaws in matters which are so far out of our jurisdiction. I hold that no man can meddle with the exclusive affairs of Providence and offer suggestions for their improvement, without making himself in a manner conspicuous. Let us take things as we find them—though, I am free to confess, it goes against the grain to do it, sometimes.

What put me into this religious train of mind, was attending church at Dr. Wadsworth's this morning. I had not been to church before for many months, because I never could get a pew, and therefore had to sit in the gallery, among the sinners. I stopped that because my proper place was down among the elect, inasmuch as I was brought up a Presbyterian, and consider myself a brevet member of Dr. Wadsworth's church. I always was a brevet. I was sprinkled in infancy, and look upon that as conferring the rank of Brevet Presbyterian. It affords none of the emoluments of the Regular Church—simply confers honorable rank upon the recipient and the right to be punished as a Presbyterian hereafter; that is, the substantial Presbyterian punishment of fire and brimstone instead of this heterodox hell of remorse of conscience of these blamed wildcat religions. The heaven and hell of the wildcat religions are vague and ill defined but there is nothing mixed about the Presbyterian heaven and hell. The Presbyterian hell is all misery; the heaven all happiness— nothing to do. But when a man dies on a wildcat basis, he will never rightly know hereafter which department he is in— but he will think he is in hell anyhow, no matter which place he goes to; because in the good place they pro-gress, pro-gress, pro-gress—study, study, study, all the time—and if this isn't hell I don't know what is; and in the bad place he will be worried by remorse of conscience. Their bad place is preferable, though, because eternity is long, and before a man got half through it he would forget what it was he had been so sorry about. Naturally he would then become cheerful again; but the party who went to heaven would go on progressing and progressing, and studying and studying until he would finally get discouraged and wish he were in hell, where he wouldn't require such a splendid education.

Dr. Wadsworth never fails to preach an able sermon; but every now and then, with an admirable assumption of not being aware of it, he will get off a firstrate joke and then frown severely at any one who is surprised into smiling at it. This is not fair. It is like throwing a bone to a dog and then arresting him with a look just as he is going to seize it. Several people there on Sunday suddenly laughed and as suddenly stopped again, when he gravely gave the Sunday school books a blast and spoke of "the good little boys in them who always went to Heaven, and the bad little boys who infallibly got drowned on Sunday," and then swept a savage frown around the house and blighted every smile in the congregation.

March 18, 1866

Barnum's First Speech in Congress

(By Spiritual Telegraph.)

Mr. P. T. Barnum will find the House of Representatives a most excellent advertising medium, in case he is elected to Congress. He will certainly not forget the high duties to his country devolving upon him, and it will be a pity if he forgets his private worldly affairs,—a genuine pity if his justly-famed sagacity fails to point out to him how he can dove-tail business and patriotism together to the mutual benefit of himself and the Great Republic. I am informed by the Spirits that his first speech in Congress will read as follows:

"Mr. Speaker—What do we do with a diseased limb? Cut it off! What do I do with a diseased curiosity? Sell him! What do we do with any speculation of any kind whatever that don't pay? Get rid of it—get out of it! Of course. Simply because I have got the most superb collection of curiosities in the world—the grandest museum ever conceived of by man—containing the dwarf elephant, Jenny Lind, and the only living giraffe on this continent, (that noble brute, which sits upon its hams in an attitude at once graceful and pictur-esque, and eats its hay out of the second-story window,)—because I have got these things, and because admission is only thirty cents, children and servants half-price, open from sun-rise till 10 P. M., peanuts and all the other luxuries of the season to be purchased in any part of the house,—the proprietor, at enormous expense, having fitted up two peanut stands to each natural curiosity,—because I have got these things, shall I revel in luxurious indolence when my voice should sound a warning to the nation? No! Because the Won-derful Spotted Human Phenomenon, the Leopard Child from the wilds of Africa, is mine, shall I exult in my happiness and be silent when my country's life is threatened? No! Because the Double Hump-backed Bactrian Camel takes his oats in my menagerie, shall I surfeit with bliss and lift not up my voice to save the people? No!—Because among my posses-sions are dead loads of Royal Bengal Tigers, White Himalaya

Mountain Bears, so interesting to Christian families from being mentioned in the Sacred Scriptures, Silver-striped Hyenas, Lions, Tigers, Leopards, Wolves, Sacred Cattle from the sacred hills of New Jersey, Panthers, Ibexes, Performing Mules and Monkeys, South American Deer, and so-forth, and so-forth, and so-forth, shall I gloat over my blessings in silence, and leave Columbia to perish? No! Because I have secured the celebrated Gordon Cumming collection, consisting of oil portraits of the two negroes and a child who rescued him from impending death, shall I wrap me in mute ecstacy and let my country rush unwarned to her destruction? No! Because unto me belong the monster living alligator, over 12 feet in length, and four living speckled brook trout, weighing 20 pounds, shall these lips sing songs of gladness and peal no succoring cry unto a doomed nation? No! Because I have got Miller's grand national bronze portrait gallery, consisting of two plaster of Paris Venuses and a varnished mud-turtle, shall I bask in mine own bliss and be mute in the season of my people's peril? No! Because I possess the smallest dwarfs in the world, and the Nova Scotian giantess, who weighs a ton and eats her weight every forty-eight hours; and Herr Phelim O'Flannigan the Norwegian Giant, who feeds on the dwarfs and ruins business; and the lovely Circassian girl; and the celebrated Happy Family, consisting of animals of the most diverse principles and dispositions, dwelling together in peace and unity, and never beheld by the religious spectator acquainted with Eden before the Fall, without emotions too profound for utterance; and 250,000 other curiosities, chiefly invisible to the naked eye—all to be seen for the small sum of 30 cents, children and servants half price—staircases arranged with special reference to limb displays—shall I hug my happiness to my soul and fail to cry aloud when I behold my country sinking to destruction and the grave? No!—a thousand times No!

"NO! Even as one sent to warn ye of fearful peril, I cry Help! help! for the stricken land! I appeal to you—and to you—and to you, sir—to every true heart in this august menagerie! Demagogues threaten the Goddess of Liberty!—they beard the starry-robed woman in her citadel! and to you the bearded woman looks for succor! Once more grim Treason towers in our midst, and once more helpless loyalty scatters into corners as do the dwarfs when the Norwegian giant strides among them! The law-making powers and the Executive are at daggers drawn, State after State flings defiance at the Amendment, and lo! the Happy Family of the Union is broken up! Woe is me!

"Where is the poor negro? How hath he fared? Alas! his regeneration is incomplete; he is free, but he cannot vote; ye have only made him white in spots, like my wonderful Leopard Boy from the wilds of Africa! Ye promised him universal suffrage, but ye have given him universal suffering instead! Woe is me!

"The country is fallen! The boss monkey sits in the feed-tub, and the tom-cats, the raccoons and the gentle rabbits of the once happy family stand helpless and afar off, and behold him gabble the provender in the pride of his strength! Woe is me!

"Ah, gentlemen, our beloved Columbia, with these corroding distresses upon her, must soon succumb! The high spirit will depart from her eye, the bloom from her cheek, the majesty from her step, and she will stand before us gaunt and worn, like my beautiful giantess when my dwarfs and Circassians prey upon her rations! Soon we shall see the glory of the realm pass away as did the grandeur of the Museum amid the consuming fires, and the wonders the world admires shall give place to trivialities, even as in the proud Museum the wonders that once amazed have given place to cheap stuffed reptiles and pea-nut stands! Woe is me!

"O, spirit of Washington! forgotten in these evil times, thou art banished to the dusty corridors of memory, a staring effigy of wax, and none could recognize thee but for the label pinned upon thy legs! O, shade of Jackson! O, ghost of gallant Lafayette! ye live only in museums, and the sublime lessons of your lives are no longer heeded by the slumbering nation! Woe is me!

"Rouse ye, my people, rouse ye! rouse ye! rouse ye! Shake off the fatal stupor that is upon ye, and hurl the usurping tyrant from his throne! Impeach! impeach! impeach!—Down with the dread boss monkey! O, snake the seditious miscreant out of the national feed-tub and reconstruct the Happy Family!"

Such is the speech as imparted to me in advance from the spirit land.

March 5, 1867

Female Suffrage

VIEWS OF MARK TWAIN.

Editors Missouri Democrat:

I have read the long list of lady petitioners in favor of female suffrage, and as a husband and a father I want to protest against the whole business. It will never do to allow women to vote. It will never do to allow them to hold office. You know, and I know, that if they were granted these privileges there would be no more peace on earth. They would swamp the country with debt. They like to hold office too well. They like to be Mrs. President Smith of the Dorcas society, or Mrs. Secretary Jones of the Hindoo aid association, or Mrs. Treasurer of something or other. They are fond of the distinction of the thing, you know; they revel in the sweet jingle of the title. They are always setting up sanctified confederations of all kinds, and then running for president of them. They are even so fond of office that they are willing to serve without pay. But you allow them to vote and to go to the Legislature once, and then see how it will be. They will go to work and start a thousand more societies, and cram them full of salaried offices. You will see a state of things then that will stir your feelings to the bottom of your pockets. The first fee bill would exasperate you some. Instead of the usual schedule for judges, State printer, Supreme court clerks, &c., the list would read something like this:

OFFICES AND SALARIES.

President Dorcas society.	$4,000
Subordinate officers of same, each	2,000
President Ladies' Union prayer meeting	3,000
President Pawnee Educational society.	4,000
President of Ladies' society for Dissemination of Belles Lettres among the Shoshones	5,000
State Crinoline Directress	10,000
State Superintendent of waterfalls	10,000
State Hair Oil inspectress	10,000
State milliner	50,000

You know what a state of anarchy and social chaos that fee

bill would create. Every woman in the commonwealth of Missouri would let go everything and run for State Milliner. And instead of ventilating each other's political antecedents, as men do, they would go straight after each other's private moral character. (I know them—they are all like my wife.) Before the canvass was three days old it would be an established proposition that every woman in the State was "no better than she ought to be." Only think how it would lacerate me to have an opposition candidate say that about my wife. That is the idea, you know—having other people say these hard things. Now, I know that my wife isn't any better than she ought to be, poor devil—in fact, in matters of orthodox doctrine, she is particularly shaky—but still I would not like these things aired in a political contest. I don't really suppose that that woman will stand any more show hereafter than— however, she may improve—she may even become a beacon light for the saving of others—but if she does, she will burn rather dim, and she will flicker a good deal, too. But, as I was saying, a female political canvass would be an outrageous thing.

Think of the torch-light processions that would distress our eyes. Think of the curious legends on the transparencies:

"Robbins forever! Vote for Sallie Robbins, the only virtuous candidate in the field!"

And this:

"Chastity, modesty, patriotism! Let the great people stand by Maria Sanders, the champion of morality and progress, and the only candidate with a stainless reputation!"

And this: "Vote for Judy McGinniss, the incorruptible! Nine children—one at the breast!"

In that day a man shall say to his servant, "What is the matter with the baby?" And the servant shall reply, "It has been sick for hours." "And where is its mother?" "She is out electioneering for Sallie Robbins." And such conversations as these shall transpire between ladies and servants applying for situations: "Can you cook?" "Yes." "Wash?" "Yes." "Do general housework?" "Yes." "All right; who is your choice for State milliner?" "Judy McGinniss." "Well, you can tramp." And women shall talk politics instead of discussing the fashions; and they shall neglect the duties of the household to go out and take a drink with candidates; and men shall nurse the baby while their wives travel to the polls to vote. And also in that day the man who hath beautiful whiskers shall beat the homely man of wisdom for Governor, and the youth who waltzes with exquisite grace shall be Chief of Police, in preference to the man of practiced sagacity and determined energy.

*　　*　　*　　*　　*　　*　　*　　*　　*　　*

Every man, I take it, has a selfish end in view when he pours out eloquence in behalf of the public good in the newspapers, and such is the case with me. I do not want the privileges of women extended, because my wife already holds office in nineteen different infernal female associations and I have to do all her clerking. If you give the women full sweep with the men in political affairs, she will proceed to run for every confounded office under the new dispensation. That will finish me. It is bound to finish me. She would not have time to do anything at all then, and the one solitary thing I have shirked up to the present time would fall on me and my family would go to destruction; for I am *not* qualified for a wet nurse.

                                        MARK TWAIN

A VOLLEY FROM THE DOWN-TRODDEN.

A DEFENSE.

Editors Missouri Democrat:

I should think you would be ashamed of yourselves. I would, anyway—to publish the vile, witless drivelings of that poor creature who degrades me with his name. I say you ought to be ashamed of yourselves. Two hundred noble, Spartan women cast themselves into the breach to free their sex from bondage, and instead of standing with bowed heads before the majesty of such a spectacle, you permit this flippant ass, my husband, to print a weak satire upon it. The wretch! I combed him with a piano stool for it. And I mean to comb every newspaper villain I can lay my hands on. They are nothing but villains anyhow. They published our names when nobody asked them to, and therefore they are low, mean and depraved, and fit for any crime however black and infamous.

Mr. Editor, I have not been appointed the champion of my sex in this matter; still, if I could know that any argument of mine in favor of female suffrage which has been presented in the above communication will win over any enemy to our cause, it would soften and soothe my dying hour; ah, yes, it would soothe it as never another soother could soothe it.

MRS. MARK TWAIN,
President Affghanistan Aid Association, Secretary of the Society for introducing the Gospel into New Jersey, etc., etc., etc.

[The old woman states a case well, dont she? She states a case mighty well, for a woman of her years? She even soars into moving eloquence in that place where she says: "two hundred noble Spartan women cast themselves into the breeches," etc. And those "arguments" of her's afford her a prodigious satisfaction, don't they? She may possibly die easy on account of them, but she won't if I am around to stir her up in her last moments. That woman has made my life a burthen to me, and I mean to have a hand in soothing her myself when her time is up. —MARK TWAIN]

MORE DEFENSE.

Editors Missouri Democrat:

I have read the article in your paper on female suffrage, by the atrocious scoundrel Mark Twain. But do not imagine that such a thing as that will deter us from demanding and enforcing our rights. Sir, we will have our rights, though the heavens fall. And as for this wretch, he had better find something else to do than meddling with matters he is incapable of understanding. I suppose he votes—such is law!—such is justice!—he is allowed to vote, but women a thousand times his superiors in intelligence are ruled out!—he!—a creature who don't know enough to follow the wires and find the telegraph office. Comment is unnecessary. If I get my hands on that whelp I will snatch hair out of his head till he is as bald as a phrenological bust.

Mr. Editor, I may not have done as much good for my species as I ought, in my time, but if any of the arguments I have presented in this article in favor of female suffrage shall aid in extending the privileges of women, I shall die happy and content.

MRS. ZEB. LEAVENWORTH,
Originator and President of the Association for the Establishment of a Female College in Kamschatka.

[I perceive that I have drawn the fire of another heavy gun. I feel as anxious as any man could to answer this old Kamschatkan, but I do not know where to take hold. Her "arguments" are too subtle for me. If she can die happy and content on that mild sort of gruel, though, let her slide. — MARK TWAIN]

MORE YET.

Editors Missouri Democrat:

The depths of my heart of hearts are stirred. Gentle chiding from those that love me has ever fallen upon my wounded spirit like soothing moonlight upon a troubled sea, but harsh words from wretches is more than I can bear. I am not formed like others of my sex. All with me is ideal — is romance. I live in a world of my own that is peopled with the fairy creatures of fancy. When that is rudely invaded, my ethereal soul recoils in horror. For long years I have collected buttons, and door-plates and dictionaries, and all such things as I thought would make the poor savages of the South seas contented with their lot and lift them out of their ignorance and degradation — and no longer than a month ago I sent them Horace Greeley's speeches and some other cheerful literature, and the pure delight I felt was only marred by the reflection that the poor creatures could not read them — and yet I may not vote! Our petition for our rights is humanly attacked by one who has no heart, no soul, no gentle emotions, no poesy! In tuneful numbers I will bid this cold world adieu, and perchance when I am gone, Legislatures will drop a tear over one whose budding life they blighted, and be torn with vain regrets when it is all too late:

In sorrow I sorrow, O sorrowful day!
In grief-stricken tears O joy speed away!

I weep and I wail, and I waft broken sighs,
And I cry in my anguish, O Woman arise!

But I shout it in vain! for Demons have come,
Who drown my appeal with foul blasphemous tongue;
Yea, in sorrow I fade, and flicker and die!
Lo! a martyr to Suffrage in the tomb let me lie!

If I dared to hope that any argument I have here presented may be the means of securing justice to my down-trodden sex, I could lay me down and pass away as peacefully as the sighing of a breeze in summer forests.

MISS AUGUSTA JOSEPHINE MAITLAND,

Secretary of the Society for the Dissemination of Poetry among the Pawnees.

Now, this old maid is a little spooney, of course, but she does not abuse me as much as the others, and it really touches me to know that she is going to fade, and flicker out. Her "arguments" are a little vague, but that is of no consequence. I havn't anything in the world against her, except that inspired atrocity of inflicting Horace Greeley's speeches on the poor heathen of the South Seas. What harm have they ever done her, that she should want to *   *   *   *   * ?

You must excuse me. I see a procession of ladies filing in at my street door with tar-buckets and feather-beds, and other arrangements. I do not wish to crowd them. I will go out the back way. But I will singe that pestilent old wild-cat, my wife, for leading them.

MARK TWAIN.

THE INIQUITOUS CRUSADE AGAINST MAN'S REGAL BIRTHRIGHT MUST BE CRUSHED.

ANOTHER LETTER FROM MARK TWAIN.

DEAR COUSIN JENNIE: I did not know I had a cousin named Jennie, but I am proud to claim such a relationship with you. I have no idea who you are, but you talk well—you talk exceedingly well. You seem inclined to treat the question of female suffrage seriously, and for once I will drop foolishness, and speak with the gravity the occasion demands. You fully understand the difference between justice and expediency? I am satisfied you do. You know very well that it would have been a just and righteous act if we had rescued struggling Poland four or five years ago, but you know also that it would not have been good policy to do it. No one will say that it is not just and right that women should vote; no one will say that an educated American woman would not vote with fifty times the judgment and independence exercised by stupid, illiterate newcomers from foreign lands; I will even go so far myself as to say that in my experience only third-rate intelligence is sent to Legislatures to make laws, because the first-rate article will not leave important private interests go unwatched to go and serve the public for a beggarly four or five dollars a day, and a miserably trivial distinction, while it is possible that a talented matron, unincumbered with children, might go with no great detriment to the affairs of her household. We know also that between constable and United States Senator, the one thousand offices of mere honor (though burdened with high responsibilities) are held by third rate ability because first-rate ability can only afford to hold offices of great emolument—and we know that first-rate female talent *could* afford to hold those offices of mere honor without making business sacrifices. You see I have made a very strong argument for your side; and I repeat that no one will deny the truth of any of the above propositions; but behold that matter of expediency comes in here—policy!

Now, you think I am going to string out a long argument on my own side, but I am not. I only say this: The ignorant foreign women would vote with the ignorant foreign men—the bad women would vote with the bad men—the good women would vote with the good men. The same candidate who would be elected now would be elected then, the only difference being that there might be twice as many votes polled then as now. Then in what respect is the condition of things improved? I cannot see.

So, I conceive that if nothing is to be gained by it, it is inexpedient to extend the suffrage to women. That must be a benefit beyond the power of figures to estimate, which can make us consent to take the High Priestess we reverence at the sacred fireside and send her forth to electioneer for votes among a mangy mob who are unworthy to touch the hem of her garment. A lady of my acquaintance came very near putting my feeling in this matter into words the other day, Jennie, when she said she was opposed to female suffrage, because she was not willing to see her sex reduced to a level with negroes and men!

Female suffrage would do harm, my dear—it would actually do harm. A very large proportion of our best and wisest women would still cling to the holy ground of the home circle, and refuse to either vote or hold office—but every grand rascal among your sex would work, bribe and vote with all her might; and, behold, mediocrity and dishonesty would be appointed to conduct the affairs of government more surely than ever before. You see the policy of the thing is bad, very bad. It would augment the strength of the bad vote. I consider it a very strong point on our side of the question.

I think I could write a pretty strong argument in favor of female suffrage, but I do not want to do it. I never want to see women voting, and gabbling about politics, and electioneering. There is something revolting in the thought. It would shock me inexpressibly for an angel to come down from above and ask me to take a drink with him (though I should doubtless consent); but it would shock me still more to see one of our blessed earthly angels peddling election tickets among a mob of shabby scoundrels she never saw before.

There is one insuperable obstacle in the way of female suffrage, Jennie; I approach the subject with fear and trembling, but it must out: A woman would never vote, because she would have to tell her age at the polls. And even if she did dare to vote once or twice when she was just of age, you know what dire results would flow from "putting this and that together" in after times. For instance, in an unguarded moment, Miss A. says she voted for Mr. Smith. Her auditor, who knows it has been seven years since Smith ran for anything, easily ciphers out that she is at least seven years over age, instead of the tender young pullet she has been making herself out to be. No, Jennie, this new fashion of registering the name, age, residence and occupation of every voter, is a fatal bar to female suffrage.

Women will never be permitted to vote or hold office, Jennie, and it is a lucky thing for me, and for many other men, that such is the decree of fate. Because, you see, there are some few measures they would all unite on—there are one or two measures that would bring out their entire voting strength, in spite of their antipathy to making themselves conspicuous; and there being vastly more women than men in this State, they would trot those measures through the Legislature with a velocity that would be appalling. For instance, they would enact:

1. That all men should be at home by ten P. M., without fail.

2. That married men should bestow considerable attention on their own wives.

3. That it should be a hanging offense to sell whisky in saloons, and that fine and disfranchisement should follow the drinking of it in such places.

4. That the smoking of cigars to excess should be forbidden, and the smoking of pipes utterly abolished.

5. That the wife should have a little of her own property when she married a man who hadn't any.

Jennie, such tyranny as this, we could never stand. Our free souls could never endure such degrading thraldom. Women, go your ways! Seek not to beguile us of our imperial privileges. Content yourself with your little feminine trifles—your babies, your benevolent societies and your knitting—and let your natural bosses do the voting. Stand back—you will be wanting to go to war next. We will let you teach school as much as you want to, and we will pay you half wages for it, too, but beware! we don't want you to crowd us too much.

If I get time, Cousin Jennie, I will furnish you a picture of a female legislature that will distress you—I know it will, because you cannot disguise from me the fact that you are no more in favor of female suffrage, really, than I am.

In conclusion, honesty compels me to tell you that I have been highly complimented a dozen times on *my* articles signed "Cousin Jennie" and "A. L." The same honesty, though, compelled me to confess that I did not write either of those articles.

MARK TWAIN.

P. S. That tiresome old goose, my wife, is prancing around like a lunatic, up stairs, rehearsing a speech in favor of female suffrage which she is going to deliver before a mass meeting of seditious old maids in my back parlor to-night. (She is a vigorous speaker, but you can smell her eloquence further than you can hear it; it is on account of gin, I think.) It is a pity those old skeletons have chosen my back parlor, because I have concluded to touch off a keg of powder under there to-night, and I am afraid the noise may disturb their deliberations some.

M. T.

March 12, 13, and 15, 1867

Female Suffrage

E<small>D</small>. T. T.:—The women of Missouri are bringing a tremendous pressure to bear in an endeavor to secure to themselves the right to vote and hold office. Their petitions to the
legislature are scattered abroad, and are filled with signers.
Thirty-nine members of the Missouri Legislature have declared in favor of the movement. This thing looks ominous.
Through an able spiritual medium I have been permitted to
see a Missouri Legislature of five years hence in session. Here
is a report of the proceedings:

The P. R. R. Appropriation Bill being the special order for
the day, and the hour for its discussion having arrived:

Miss Belcher, of St. Louis, said—Madam Speaker, I call for
the special order for to-day.

Madam Speaker.—The clerk will read—

Clerk.—An act supplementary to an Act entitled An Act
amendatory of an Act entitled An Act to Appropriate Five
millions of dollars in aid of the Pacific Railroad, etc., etc.

Miss Belcher.—Madam Speaker, it is with the keenest pain
that I observe the diminishing esteem in which gored dresses
are held. It is with pain which these lips are indeed powerless
to express. The gored-dress of two years ago, Madam, with its
long, graceful sweep—

Mr. Jones, of St. Joseph.—Madam Speaker, I rise to a
point of order. The lady is not confining herself to the question before the house. What in the nation has these cussed
gored dresses and stuff got to do with the great Pacif—

Madam Speaker (amid piping female voices all over the
house, shrieking angrily).—Sit down, Sir! Take your seat, Sir,
and don't you presume to interrupt again! Go on, Miss
Belcher.

Miss Belcher.—I was remarking, Madam, when the unprincipled bald-headed outlaw from St. Joseph interrupted
me, that it pained me to see the charming and attractive gored
dresses we all were once so fond of, going out of fashion.
And what, I ask, are we to have in place of it? What is offered
to recompense us for its loss? Why, nothing, Madam, but the
wretched, slimpsey, new-fangled street-dress, hoopless, shape-

less, cut bias, hem-stitched, with the selvedge edge turned down; and all so lank, so short, so cadaverous, and so disgraceful! Excuse these tears. Who can look without emotion upon such a garment? Who can look unmoved upon a dress which exposes feet at every step which may be of dimensions which shrink from inspection? Who can consent to countenance a dress which—

Mr. Slawson, of St. Genevieve.—Madam Speaker, This is absurd. What will such proceedings as these read like in the newspapers? We take up the discussion of a measure of vast consequence—a measure of tremendous financial importance—and a member of the body, totally ignoring the question before the House, launches out into a tirade about womanly apparel!—a matter trivial enough at any time, God knows, but utterly insignificant in presence of so grave a matter as the behests of the Great Pacific Rail—

Madam Speaker.—Consider yourself under arrest, Sir! Sit down, and dare to speak again at your peril! The honorable lady from St. Louis will proceed.

Miss Belcher.—Madam Speaker, I will dismiss the particular section of my subject upon which I was speaking when interrupted by the degraded ruffian from St. Genevieve, and pass to the gist of the matter. I propose, Madame, to prohibit, under heavy penalties, the wearing of the new street-dress, and to restore the discarded gored dress by legislative enactment, and I beg leave to introduce a bill to that end, and without previous notice, if the courtesy of this honorable body will permit it.

Mr. Walker, of Marion.—Madam Speaker, this is an outrage! it is damnable! The Pacific Railroad—

Madam Speaker.—Silence! Plant yourself, Sir! Leave is granted to introduce the Bill. If no objection is made, it will be referred to the Standing Committee on Public Improvements. Reports of Committees are now in order.

Mrs. Baker, of Ralls.—Madam Speaker, the Select Committee of Five, to whom was referred An Act Amendatory of An act Establishing the Metes and Bounds of School Lands, and to which was added a clause Establishing the Metes and Bounds of Water Privileges, have been unable to agree. The younger members of the committee contend that the added

clause is of sufficient latitude to permit of legislation concerning ladies' waterfalls, and they have reported upon that clause
alone to the exclusion of all other matters contemplated in the
bill. There is no majority report, Madam, and no minority
report.

Mr. Bridgewater, of Benton.—There are five women on
the committee, ain't there?

Mrs. Baker.—Yes.

Mr. Bilgewater.—Each of 'em made a report by herself,
hasn't she?

Mrs. Baker.—Yes, Sir.

Mr. Bilgewater.—Why, certainly. Five women's bound to
have five opinions. It's like 'em.

[With the last word the gentleman from Benton darted out
at the window, and eleven inkstands followed him.]

The several reports were received and tabled, after considerable discussion. Third reading and final passage of bills being next in order, an Act for Amending the Common School
System was taken up, but it was found to be so interlarded
with surreptitious clauses for remodeling and establishing
fashions for ladies' bonnets, that neither head nor tail could
be made of it, and it had to be referred back to the Committee of the Whole again. An Act to Provide Arms for the State
Militia was discovered to be so hampered with clauses for the
protection of Sewing Societies and Tea Drinkings, that it had
to go back to the file also. Every bill on the third reading list
was found to be similarly mutilated, until they got down to
an Act to Compel Married Gentlemen to be at Home by Nine
of the Clock, every evening; an Act to Abolish the Use of
Tobacco in any form; and an Act to Abolish the Use of Intoxicating Liquors. These had not been meddled with, and were
at once put to vote, and passed over the heads of the male
members, who made a gallant fight, but were overcome by
heartless and tyrannical numbers.

Mr. Green, of Cape Girardeau, then rose in his place and
said.—"I now shake the dust of this House from my feat, and
take my eternal leave of it. I never will enter its doors again,
to be snubbed and harried by a pack of padded, scraggy,
dried-up, snuff-dipping, toothless, old-maids, who—"

He never got any further. A howl went up that shook the

building to its foundation, and in the midst of struggling forms, fiery eyes, distorted countenances, and dismembered waterfalls, I saw the daring legislator yield and fall; and when at last he reappeared, and fled toward the door, his shirt-front was in ribbons, his cravat knot under his ear, his face scratched red and white like the national flag, and hardly hair enough left on his head to make a toothbrush.

I shudder now. Is it possible that this revelation of the spirits is a prophecy.

—MARK TWAIN

April 7, 1867

Official Physic

Ed. T. T.:—It is one of the beauties of our advance to consolidated and all-embracing government that questions which were left to puzzle the private judgment of the citizens under the old regime are now settled by the legislative powers authoritatively. Among other differences of opinion there has been always a variance of choice under which system a citizen preferred to find his way across the Styx, and he enjoyed in this State till now the privilege of choosing the rower who was to aid in ferrying him over in Charon's boat. In other words, if a citizen was inclined to take salts by the ton, ipecac by the barrel, mercury by the quart, or quinine by the load, and thus be cured of his ailment or his sublunary existence by the wholesale, he was at perfect liberty to invite the services of a medicus of the allopathic style; and if another citizen preferred to toy with death, and buy health in small parcels, to bribe death with a sugar pill to stay away, or go to the grave with all the original sweetners undrenched out of him, then the individual adopted the "like cures like" system, and called in a homeopath physician as being a pleasant friend of death's. Citizens there were too, who liked to be washed into eternity, or soaked like over-salt mackerel before they were placed on purgatorial gridirons, and these, "of every rank and degree", had the right to pass their few remaining days in an element that they were not likely to see much of for some time. Then again there were those who saw "good in everything" and who believed that whatever is is right, and these last mixed the allopathic, homeopathic, and hydropathic systems, qualified each with each, and thus passed to their long homes, drenched, pickled, sweetened, and soaked. But all this is fast being changed. The highest power in our State has been forced to declare, through the workings of over-legislation, that the allopathic system is the only one at present recognized by the State, and so has reinstated in his position a noted allopathic physician in the Health Board. Before this decision of the Governor's was made known, there was a war of lancets, and many hard pills to swallow were administered by the rival homeopaths and allopaths. Among

other arguments used were those founded on the questionable statistics of the number of patients who recovered while
being treated by the rival systems. Some sarcastic people,
justified by the saying of the well-known Oliver Wendell
Holmes, may be of the opinion that more people get well in
spite of the doctors than by their help, and that a doctor is as
likely to be famous from the number that he kills as from that
which he cures. Something like this might have passed
through the Governor's mind, for evidently he was undecided
under which king death to speak or die, and showed that he is
like most laymen, inclined to be eclectic; for immediately after
the appointment of the allopath to that Board which will
authoritatively recommend the kind of physic good for the
public bowels in the event of the spread of an epidemic, and
which poor patients will be forced to swallow, whatever their
medical code may be, the Governor paid the high but rather
sarcastic compliment to homeopathy of appointing one of its
disciples to a place on the Board of Commissioners for the
new State Lunatic Asylum to be located at Poughkeepsie. No
doubt, the Governor thought that people divested of reason
could offer no reasons against the appointment; and that if
the lunatics were not improved by sugar pills, they would at
least die sweetly—a lunatic more or less being of little account. Thus it is officially settled that allopathy is good for
the sane and homeopathy for the insane. The famed "judgment of Solomon" dwindles to folly in comparison with this
decision. But alas! for the changeableness of human affairs, an
energetic Senator is determined to have the hydropaths officially recognized; and no doubt to satisfy the followers of that
school, shower-baths, douches, and sitzes, will have to be
ordered for the benefit of some class in the community. No
persons need the cooling influences of cold water more than
the small-fry of hot-tempered politicians who periodically increase our taxes at the State capitol. If, over each member's
seat a shower-bath was contrived, and by some electric-
telegraph means the check-strings could be placed at the control of the Speaker, then, when honorable members wax so
hot in debate that they forget the rules of decorum and ignore
the Speaker's gavel, the presiding officer could pull the check-
strings, souse the offending members, and bring them to

order and a frame of mind and body in which they would look at things coolly. Some such arrangement might be applied to caucuses and conventions, of which the members are troubled with superfluity of bile and too great a rush of blood to the head. Thus the hydropathists might be pacified by being allowed a share in public hygienics. But to return to the starting-point of this communication, the mania for giving the Government power to meddle with the private affairs of cities or citizens is likely to cause endless trouble, through the rivalry of schools and creeds that are anxious to obtain official recognition, and there is great danger that our people will lose that independence of thought and action which is the cause of much of our greatness, and sink into the helplessness of the Frenchman or German who expects his government to feed him when hungry, clothe him when naked, to prescribe when his child may be born and when he may die, and, in fine, to regulate every act of humanity from the cradle to the tomb, including the manner in which he may seek future admission to paradise.

—M. T.

April 21, 1867

A Reminiscence of Artemus Ward

I had never seen him before. He brought letters of introduction from mutual friends in San Francisco, and by invitation I breakfasted with him. It was almost religion, there in
the silver mines, to precede such a meal with whisky cocktails.
Artemus, with the true cosmopolitan instinct, always deferred
to the customs of the country he was in, and so he ordered
three of those abominations. Hingston was present. I am a
match for nearly any beverage you can mention except a
whisky-cocktail, and therefore I said I would rather not drink
one. I said it would go right to my head and confuse me so
that I would be in a hopeless tangle in ten minutes. I did not
want to act like a lunatic before strangers. But Artemus gently
insisted, and I drank the treasonable mixture under protest,
and felt all the time that I was doing a thing I might be sorry
for. In a minute or two I began to imagine that my ideas were
getting clouded. I waited in great anxiety for the conversation
to open, with a sort of vague hope that my understanding
would prove clear, after all, and my misgivings groundless.

Artemus dropped an unimportant remark or two, and then
assumed a look of superhuman earnestness, and made the
following astounding speech. He said:

"Now, there is one thing I ought to ask you about before I
forget it. You have been here in Silverland—here in Nevada
—two or three years, and, of course, your position on the
daily press has made it necessary for you to go down in the
mines and examine them carefully in detail, and therefore
you know all about the silver-mining business. Now, what I
want to get at is—is. Well, the way the deposits of ore are
made, you know. For instance. Now as I understand it, the
vein which contains the silver is sandwiched in between casings of granite, and runs along the ground, and sticks up like
a curbstone. Well, take a vein forty feet thick, for example—or eighty, for that matter, or even a hundred—say you
go down on it with a shaft—straight down, you know, or
with what you call an 'incline'—maybe you go down five
hundred feet, or maybe you don't go down but two hundred—anyway, you go down—and all the time this vein

grows narrower, when the casings come nearer, or approach each other, as you may say, that is, when they do approach, which of course they do not always do, particularly in cases where the nature of the formation is such that they stand apart wider than they otherwise would, and which geology has failed to account for, although everything in that science goes to prove that, all things being equal, it would, if it did not, or would not, certainly if it did, and then, of course they are. Do not you think it is?"

I said to myself, "Now I just knew how it would be—that cussed whisky-cocktail has done the business for me; I don't understand any more than a clam." And then I said aloud, "I—I—that is—if you don't mind, would you—would you say that over again? I ought—"

"O, certainly, certainly. You see I am very unfamiliar with the subject, and perhaps I don't present my case clearly, but I—"

"No, no—no, no—you state it plain enough, but that vile cocktail has muddled me a little. But I will un—I do understand, for that matter, but I would get the hang of it all the better if you went over it again—and I'll pay better attention this time."

He said, "Why, what I was after, was this." [Here he became even more fearfully impressive than ever, and emphasized each particular point by checking it off on his finger-ends.] "This vein, or lode, or ledge, or whatever you call it, runs along like a curbstone, runs along between two layers of granite, just the same as if it were a sandwich. Very well. Now, suppose you go down on that, say a thousand feet, or maybe twelve hundred (it don't really matter), before you drift; and then you start your drifts, some of them across the ledge and others along the length of it, where the sul-phurets—I believe they call them sulphurets, though why they should, considering that, so far as I can see, the main dependence of a miner does not so lie as some suppose, but in which it cannot be successfully maintained, wherein the same should not continue while part and parcel of the same and not committed to either in the sense referred to, whereas under different circumstances the most inexperienced among us could not detect it if it were, or might overlook it if it did, or

scorn the very idea of such a thing, even though it were palpably demonstrated as such. Am I not right?"

I said, sorrowfully, "I feel ashamed of myself, Mr. Ward. I
know I ought to understand you perfectly well—but you see
that infernal whisky-cocktail has got into my head, and now I
cannot understand even the simplest proposition. I told you
how it would be."

"Oh, don't mind it, don't mind it, the fault was my own,
no doubt—though I did think I was making it clear enough
for—"

"Don't say a word. Clear? Why you stated it as clear as the
sun to anybody but an abject idiot, but it's that confounded
cocktail that has played the mischief."

"No, now don't say that—I'll begin all over again, and—"

"Don't now—for goodness' sake don't do anything of the
kind—because I tell you my head is in such a condition that I
don't believe I could understand the most trifling question a
man could ask me."

"Now don't you be afraid. I'll put it so plain this time that
you can't help but get the hang of it. We will begin at the very
beginning." (Leaning far across the table, with determined
impressiveness wrought upon his every feature, and fingers
prepared to keep tally of each point as enumerated—and I
leaning forward with painful interest also, resolved to comprehend or perish.) "You know the vein, the ledge, the thing
that contains the metal, whereby it constitutes the medium
between all other forces whether of present or remote agencies so brought to bear in favor of the former against the
latter, or the latter against the former, or all or both, or com-
promising as far as possible the relative differences existing
within the radius whence culminates the several degrees of
similarity as to which—."

I said, "O blame my wooden head, it ain't any use!—it
ain't any use to try—I can't understand anything. The plainer
you get it, the more I can't get the hang of it."

I heard a suspicious noise behind me, and turned in time to
see Hingston dodging behind a newspaper and quaking with
a gentle ecstasy of laughter. I looked at Ward again, and he
had thrown off his dread solemnity and was laughing also.
Then I saw that I had been sold—that I had been made the

victim of a swindle in the way of a string of plausibly-worded sentences that didn't mean anything under the sun.

Artemus Ward was one of the best fellows in the world, and one of the most companionable. It has been said that he was not fluent in conversation, but with the above experience in my mind, I differ.

July 7, 1867

Jim Wolf and the Tom-Cats

I knew by the sympathetic glow upon his bald head—I knew by the thoughtful look upon his face—I knew by the emotional flush upon the strawberry on the end of the old free liver's nose, that Simon Wheeler's memory was busy with the olden time. And so I prepared to leave, because all these were symptoms of a reminiscence—signs that he was going to be delivered of another of his tiresome personal experiences—but I was too slow; he got the start of me. As nearly as I can recollect, the infliction was couched in the following language:

"We was all boys, then, and didn't care for nothing, and didn't have no troubles, and didn't worry about nothing only how to shirk school and keep up a revivin' state of devilment all the time. Thish-yar Jim Wolf I was a talking about, was the 'prentice, and he was the best-hearted feller, he was, and the most forgivin' and onselfish I ever see—well, there couldn't be a more bullier boy than what he was, take him how you would; and sorry enough I was when I see him for the last time.

"Me and Henry was always pestering him and plastering hoss-bills on his back and putting bumble-bees in his bed, and so on, and some times we'd crowd in and bunk with him, not 'thstanding his growling, and then we'd let on to get mad and fight acrost him, so as to keep him stirred up like. He was nineteen, he was, and long, and lank, and bashful, and we was fifteen and sixteen, and tolerable lazy and worthless.

"So, that night, you know, that my sister Mary give the candy-pullin', they started us off to bed early, so as the comp'ny could have full swing, and we rung in on Jim to have some fun.

"Our winder looked out onto the roof of the ell, and about ten o'clock a couple of old tom-cats got to rairin' and chargin' around on it and carryin' on like sin. There was four inches of snow on the roof, and it was froze so that there was a right smart crust of ice on it, and the moon was shining bright, and we could see them cats like daylight. First, they'd stand off and e-yow-yow-yow, just the same as if they was a cussin' one another, you know, and bow up their backs and bush up their tails, and swell around and spit, and then all of a sudden the gray cat he'd snatch a handful of fur out of the yaller cat's ham, and spin him eround, like the button on a barn-door. But the yaller cat was game, and he'd come and clinch, and the way they'd gouge, and bite, and howl; and the way they'd make the fur fly was powerful.

"Well, Jim, he got disgusted with the row, and 'lowed he'd climb out there and snake him off'n that roof. He hadn't reely no notion of doin' it, likely, but we everlastin'ly dogged him and bullyragged him, and 'lowed he'd always bragged how he wouldn't take a dare, and so on, till bimeby he highsted up the winder, and lo and behold you, he went— went exactly as he was—nothin' on but a shirt, and it was short. But you ought to a seen him! You ought to seen him cre-e-epin' over that ice, and diggin' his toe nails and his finger-nails in for to keep from slippin'; and 'bove all, you ought to seen that shirt a flappin' in the wind, and them long, ridicklous shanks of his'n a-glistenin' in the moonlight.

"Them comp'ny folks was down there under the eaves, the whole squad of 'em under that ornery shed of old dead Washn'ton Bower vines—all sett'n round about two dozen sassers of hot candy, which they'd sot in the snow to cool. And they was laughin' and talkin' lively; but bless you, they didn't know nothin' 'bout the panorama that was goin' on over their heads. Well, Jim, he went a-sne-akin' and a sneakin' up, onbeknowns to them tom-cats—they was a swishin' their tails and yow-yowin' and threatenin' to clinch, you know, and not payin' any attention—he went a-sne-eakin' and a-sne-eakin' right up to the comb of the roof, till he was, in a foot 'n' a half of 'em, and then all of a sudden he made a grab for the yaller cat! But by Gosh he missed fire and slipped his holt, and his heels flew up and he flopped on his back and shot off'n that roof like a dart!—went a smashin' and a-crashin' down through them old rusty vines and landed right in the dead centre of all them comp'ny-people!—sot down like a yearth-quake in them two dozen sassers of red-hot candy, and let off a howl that was hark f'm the tomb! Them girls—well they left, you know. They see he warn't dressed for comp'ny, and so they left. All done in a second, it was just one little war whoop, and a whish! of their dresses, and blame the wench of 'em was in sight anywhers!

"Jim he was a sight. He was gormed with that bilin' hot molasses candy clean down to his heels, and had more busted sassers hanging' to him than if he was a Injun princess—and he come a prancin' up-stairs just a-whoopin' and a cussin', and every jump he give he shed some china, and every squirm he fetched he dripped some candy!

"And blistered! Why bless your soul, that pore cretur couldn't reely set down comfortable for as much as four weeks."

July 14, 1867

Information Wanted

WASHINGTON, Dec. 10, 1867.

Could you give me any information respecting such islands, if any, as the Government is going to purchase? It is an uncle of mine that wants to know. He is an industrious man, and well-disposed, and wants to make a living in an honest, humble way, but more especially he wants to be quiet. He wishes to settle down and be quiet and unostentatious. He has been to the new island—St. Thomas—but he says he thinks things are unsettled there. He went there, early, with an attaché of the State Department, who was sent down with money to pay for the island. My uncle had his money in the same box, and so when they went ashore, getting a receipt, the sailors broke open the box and took all the money, not making any distinction between Government money, which was legitimate money to be stolen, and my uncle's, which was his own private property and should have been respected. But he came home and got some more, and went back. And then he took the fever. There are seven kinds of fever down there, you know, and as his blood was out of order by reason of loss of sleep and general wear and tear of mind, he failed to cure the first fever, and then somehow he got the other six. He is not a kind of man that enjoys fevers, though he is well-meaning and always does what he thinks is right, and so he was a good deal annoyed when it appeared that he was going to die.

But he worried through and got well, and started a farm. He fenced it in, and the next day that great storm came and washed the most of it over to Gibraltar, or around there somewhere. He only said, in his patient way, that it was gone, and he wouldn't bother about trying to find out where it went to, though it was his opinion it went to Gibraltar.

Then he invested in a mountain, and started a farm up there, so as to be out of the way when the sea came ashore again. It was a good mountain and a good farm—but it wasn't any use—an earthquake came the next night and shook it all down. It was all fragments, you know, and so mixed up with another man's property that he could not tell which were his fragments without going to law, and he would not do that, because his main object in going to St. Thomas was to be quiet. All that he wanted was to settle down and be quiet.

He thought it all over, and finally he concluded to try the low ground again, especially as he wanted to start a brickyard this time. He bought a flat and put out 10,000 bricks to dry, preparatory to baking them. But luck appeared to be against him. A volcano shoved itself through there that night, and elevated his brickyard about 2,000 feet in the air. It irritated him a good deal. He has been up there, and he says the bricks are all baked right enough, but he can't get them down. At first he thought may be Government would get the bricks down for him, because if Government bought the island it ought to protect the property where a man has invested in good faith; but all he wants is quiet, and so he is not going to apply for the subsidy he was thinking about.

He went back there last week, in a couple of ships of war, to prospect around the coast for a safe place for a farm, where he could be quiet; but another earthquake came and hoisted both of the ships out into one of the interior counties, and he came near losing his life. So he has given up prospecting in a ship, and is discouraged.

Well, now he don't know what to do. He has tried Walrussia; but the bears kept after him so much, and kept him so on the jump, as it were, that he had to leave the country. He could not be quiet there, with those bears prancing after him all the time. That is how he came to go to the new island we have bought—St. Thomas. But he is getting to think St. Thomas is not quiet enough for a man of his turn of mind, and that is why he wishes me to find out if Government is likely to buy some more islands shortly. He has heard that Government is thinking about buying Porto Rico. If that is true, he wishes to try Porto Rico, if it is a quiet place. How is Porto Rico for his style of a man? Do you think the Government will buy it?

MARK TWAIN.

December 18, 1867

The Facts Concerning the Recent Resignation

WASHINGTON, Dec. 2, 1867.

I have resigned. The Government appears to go on much the same, but there is a spoke out of its wheel, nevertheless. I was clerk of the Senate Committee on Conchology, and I have thrown up the position. I could see the plainest disposition on the part of the other members of the Government to debar me from having any voice in the counsels of the nation, and so I could no longer hold office and retain my self-respect. If I were to detail all the outrages that were heaped upon me during the six days that I was connected with the Government in an official capacity, the narrative would fill a volume. They appointed me clerk of that Committee on Conchology, and then allowed me no amanuensis to play billiards with. I would have borne that, lonesome as it was, if I had met with that courtesy from the other members of the Cabinet which was my due. But I did not. Whenever I observed that the head of a department was pursuing a wrong course, I laid down everything and went and tried to set him right, as it was my duty to do; and I never was thanked for it in a single instance. I went, with the best intentions in the world, to the Secretary of the Navy, and said:

"Sir, I cannot see that Admiral Farragut is doing anything but skirmishing around there in Europe, having a sort of picnic. Now, that may be all very well, but it does not exhibit itself to me in that light. If there is no fighting for him to do, let him come home. There is no use in a man having a whole fleet for a pleasure excursion. It is too expensive. Mind, I do not object to pleasure excursions for the naval officers—pleasure excursions that are in reason—pleasure excursions that are economical. Now, they might go down the Mississippi on a raft——"

You ought to have heard him storm! One would have supposed I had committed a crime of some kind. But I didn't mind. I said it was cheap, and full of republican simplicity, and perfectly safe. I said that, for a tranquil pleasure excursion, there was nothing equal to a raft.

Then the Secretary of the Navy asked me who I was; and

when I told him I was connected with the Government, he wanted to know in what capacity. I said that, without remarking upon the singularity of such a question, coming, as it did, from a member of that same Government, I would inform him that I was clerk of the Senate Committee on Conchology. Then there was a fine storm! He finished by ordering me to leave the premises and give my attention strictly to my own business, in future. My first impulse was to get him removed. However, that would harm others beside himself and do me no real good, and so I let him stay.

I went next to the Secretary of War, who was not inclined to see me at all until he learned that I was connected with the Government. If I had not been on important business, I suppose I could not have got in. I asked him for a light (he was smoking at the time), and then I told him I had no fault to find with his defending the parole stipulations of Gen. Lee and his comrades in arms, but that I could not approve of his method of fighting the Indians on the Plains. I said he fought too scattering. He ought to get the Indians more together— get them together in some convenient place, where he could have provisions enough for both parties, and then have a general massacre. I said there was nothing so convincing to an Indian as a general massacre. If he could not approve of the massacre, I said the next surest thing for an Indian was soap and education. Soap and education are not as sudden as a massacre, but they are more deadly in the long run; because a half massacred Indian may recover, but if you educate him and wash him, it is bound to finish him some time or other. It undermines his constitution; it strikes at the foundations of his being. "Sir," I said, "the time has come when blood-curdling cruelty has become necessary. Inflict soap and a spelling-book on every Indian that ravages the Plains, and let him die!"

The Secretary of War asked me if I was a member of the Cabinet, and I said I was—and I was not one of these *ad interim* people, either. (Severe, but merited.) He inquired what position I held, and I said I was clerk of the Senate Committee on Conchology. I was then ordered under arrest for contempt of court, and restrained of my liberty for the best part of a day.

I almost resolved to be silent thenceforward, and let the Government get along the best way it could. But duty called, and I obeyed. I called on the Secretary of the Treasury. He said:

"What will *you* have?"

The question threw me off my guard. I said, "Rum punch."

He said, "If you have got any business here, Sir, state it— and in as few words as possible."

I then said that I was sorry he had seen fit to change the subject so abruptly, because such conduct was very offensive to me; but under the circumstances I would overlook the matter and come to the point. I now went into an earnest expostulation with him upon the extravagant length of his report. I said it was expensive, unnecessary, and awkwardly constructed; there were no descriptive passages in it, no poetry, no sentiment—no heroes, no plot, no pictures—not even wood-cuts. Nobody would read it, that was a clear case. I urged him not to ruin his reputation by getting out a thing like that. If he ever hoped to succeed in literature, he must throw more variety into his writings. He must beware of dry detail. I said that the main popularity of the almanac was de-rived from its poetry and conundrums; and that a few conun-drums distributed around through his Treasury report would help the sale of it more than all the internal revenue he could put into it. I said these things in the kindest spirit, and yet the Secretary of the Treasury fell into a violent passion. He even said I was an ass. He abused me in the most vindictive man-ner, and said that if I came there again meddling with his business, he would throw me out of the window. I said I would take my hat and go, if I could not be treated with the respect due to my office; and I did go. It was just like a new author. They always think they know more than anybody else when they are getting out their first book. Nobody can tell *them* anything.

During the whole time that I was connected with the Gov-ernment it seemed as if I could not do anything in an official capacity without getting myself into trouble. And yet I did nothing, attempted nothing, but what I conceived to be for the good of my country. The sting of my wrongs may have driven me to unjust and harmful conclusions, but it surely seemed to me that the Secretary of State, the Secretary of War, the Secretary of the Treasury, and others of my confreres, had conspired from the very beginning to drive me from the Administration. I never attended but one Cabinet meeting while I was connected with the Government. That was sufficient for me. The servant at the White House door did not seem disposed to make way for me until I asked if the other members of the Cabinet had arrived. He said they had, and I entered. They were all there; but nobody offered me a seat. They stared at me as if I had been an intruder. The President said:

"Well, Sir, who are *you*?"

I handed him my card, and he read: "The HON. MARK TWAIN, Clerk of the Senate Committee on Conchology." Then he looked at me from head to foot, as if he had never heard of me before. The Secretary of the Treasury said:

"This is the meddlesome ass that came to recommend me to put poetry and conundrums in my report, as if it were an almanac."

The Secretary of War said: "It is the same visionary that came to me yesterday with a scheme to educate a portion of the Indians to death, and massacre the balance."

The Secretary of the Navy said: "I recognize this youth as the person who has been interfering with my business time and again during the week. He is distressed about Admiral Farragut's using a whole fleet for a pleasure excursion, as he terms it. His proposition about some insane pleasure excursion on a raft, is too absurd to repeat."

I said: "Gentlemen, I perceive here a disposition to throw discredit upon every act of my official career; I perceive, also, a disposition to debar me from all voice in the counsels of the nation. No notice whatever was sent to me to-day. It was only by the merest chance that I learned that there was going to be a Cabinet meeting. But let these things pass. All I wish to know, is, is this a Cabinet meeting, or is it not?"

The President said it was.

"Then," I said, "let us proceed to business at once, and not fritter away valuable time in unbecoming fault-findings with each other's official conduct."

The Secretary of State now spoke up, in his benignant way,

and said: "Young man, you are laboring under a mistake. The clerks of the Congressional committees are not members of the Cabinet. Neither are the doorkeepers of the Capitol, strange as it may seem. Therefore, much as we could desire your more than human wisdom in our deliberations, we cannot lawfully avail ourselves of it. The counsels of the nation must proceed without you; if disaster follows, as follow full well it may, be it balm to your sorrowing spirit, that by deed and voice you did what in you lay to avert it. You have my blessing. Farewell."

These gentle words soothed my troubled breast, and I went away. But the servants of a nation can know no peace. I had hardly reached my den in the Capitol, and disposed my feet on the table like a Representative, when one of the Senators on the Conchological Committee came in in a passion and said:

"Where have you been all day?"

I observed that, if that was anybody's affair but my own, I had been to a Cabinet meeting.

"To a Cabinet meeting! I would like to know what business you had at a Cabinet meeting?"

I said I went there to consult—allowing, for the sake of argument, that he was in anywise concerned in the matter. He grew insolent then, and ended by saying he had wanted me for three days past to copy a report on bombshells, egg-shells, clam-shells, and I don't know what all, connected with conchology, and nobody had been able to find me.

This was too much. This was the feather that broke the clerical camel's back. I said: "Sir, do you suppose that I am going to *work* for six dollars a day? If that is the idea, let me recommend the Senate Committee on Conchology to hire somebody else. I am the slave of *no* faction! Take back your degrading commission. Give me liberty, or give me death!"

From that hour I was no longer connected with the Government. Snubbed by the department, snubbed by the Cabinet, snubbed at last by the chairman of a committee I was endeavoring to adorn, I yielded to persecution, cast far from me the perils and seductions of my great office, and forsook my bleeding country in the hour of her peril.

But I had done the State some service, and I sent in my bill:

The United States of America in account with the Hon. Clerk of the Senate Committee on Conchology, Dr.

To consultation with Secretary of War.	$50
To consultation with Secretary of Navy	50
To consultation with Secretary of the Treasury	50
Cabinet consultation	No charge.
To Mileage to and from Jerusalem* via Egypt, Algiers, Gibraltar, and Cadiz, 14,000 miles, at 20¢. a mile	2,800
To salary as Clerk of Senate Committee on Conchology, six days, at $6 per day.	36
Total.	.$2,986

Not an item of this bill has been paid, except that trifle of $36 for clerkship salary. The Secretary of the Treasury, pursuing me to the last, drew his pen through all the other items, and simply marked in the margin, "Not allowed." So, the dread alternative is embraced at last. Repudiation has begun! The nation is lost. True, the President promised that he would mention my claim in his Message, and recommend that it be paid out of the first moneys received on account of the Alabama claims; but will he recollect to do it? And may not I be forgotten when the Alabama claims are paid? Younger claimants than I am may be forgotten when the Alabama claims are paid.

I am done with official life for the present. Let those clerks who are willing to be imposed on remain. I know numbers of them, in the Departments, who are never informed when there is to be a Cabinet meeting, whose advice is never asked about war, or finance, or commerce, by the heads of the nation, any more than if they were not connected with the Government, and who actually stay in their offices day after day and work! They know their importance to the nation, and they unconsciously show it in their bearing, and the way they

*Territorial delegates charge mileage both ways, although they never go back when they get here once. Why my mileage is denied me is more than I can understand.

order their sustenance at the restaurant—but they work. I know one who has to paste all sorts of little scraps from the newspapers into a scrap-book—sometimes as many as eight or ten scraps a day. He doesn't do it well, but he does it as well as he can. It is very fatiguing. It is exhausting to the intellect. Yet he only gets $1,800 a year. With a brain like his, that young man could amass thousands and thousands of dollars in some other pursuit, if he chose to do it. But no—his heart is with his country, and he will serve her as long as she has got a scrap-book left. And I know clerks that don't know how to write very well, but such knowledge as they possess they nobly lay at the feet of their country, and toil on and suffer for $2,500 a year. What they write has to be written over again by other clerks, sometimes; but when a man has done his best for his country, should his country complain? Then there are clerks that have no clerkships, and are waiting, and waiting, and waiting, for a vacancy—waiting patiently for a chance to help their country out—and while they are waiting, they only get barely $2,000 a year for it. It is sad—it is very, very sad. When a member of Congress has a friend who is gifted, but has no employment wherein his great powers may be brought to bear, he confers him upon his country, and gives him a clerkship in a Department. And there that man has to slave his life out fighting documents for the benefit of a nation that never thinks of him, never sympathizes with him—and all for $2,000 or $3,000 a year. When I shall have completed my list of all the clerks in the several departments, with my statement of what they have to do, and what they get for it, you will see that there are not half enough clerks, and that what there are do not get half enough pay.

MARK TWAIN.

December 27, 1867

Woman — an Opinion

Newspaper Correspondents' Club Banquet, Washington, D.C.

Mr. President: — I do not know why I should have been singled out to receive the greatest distinction of the evening — for so the office of replying to the toast to woman has been regarded in every age. I do not know why I have received this distinction, unless it be that I am a trifle less homely than the other members of the Club. But be this as it may, Mr. President, I am proud of the position, and you could not have chosen any one who would have accepted it more gladly, or labored with a heartier good-will to do the subject justice, than I. Because, sir, I love the sex. I love *all* the women, sir, irrespective of age or color.

Human intelligence cannot estimate what we owe to woman, sir. She sews on our buttons, she mends our clothes, she ropes us in at the church fairs — she confides in us; she tells us whatever she can find out about the little private affairs of the neighbors — she gives us good advice — and plenty of it — she gives us a piece of her mind sometimes — and sometimes all of it — she soothes our aching brows — she bears our children — ours as a general thing. In all the relations of life, sir, it is but just and a graceful tribute to woman to say of her that she is a brick.

Wheresoever you place woman, sir — in whatsoever position or estate — she is an ornament to that place she occupies, and a treasure to the world. Look at the noble names of history! Look at Cleopatra! — look at Desdemona! — look at Florence Nightingale! — look at Joan of Arc! — look at Lucretia Borgia! Well, suppose we let Lucretia slide. Look at Joyce Heth! — look at Mother Eve! You need not look at her unless you want to, but, Eve was ornamental, sir — particularly before the fashions changed! I repeat, sir, look at the illustrious names of history! Look at the Widow Machree! — look at Lucy Stone! — look at Elizabeth Cady Stanton! — look at George Francis Train! And, sir, I say it with bowed head and deepest veneration, look at the Mother of Washington! she raised a boy that could not lie — *could not lie* —. But he *never had any chance*. It might have been different with him if he had belonged to a newspaper correspondent's club.

I repeat, sir, that in whatsoever position you place a woman she is an ornament to society and a treasure to the world. As a sweetheart she has few equals and no superiors—as a cousin she is convenient; as a wealthy grandmother, with an incurable distemper, she is precious—as a wet nurse she has no equal among men!

What, sir, would the peoples of the earth be, without woman? . . . . They would be scarce, sir—almighty scarce! Then let us cherish her—let us protect her—let us give her our support, our encouragement, our sympathy—ourselves, if we get a chance.

But, jesting aside, Mr. President, woman is lovable, gracious, kind of heart, beautiful—worthy of all respect, of all esteem, of all deference. Not any here will refuse to drink her health right cordially in this bumper of wine, for each and every one of us has personally known, and loved, and honored, the very best one of them all—his own mother!

January 11, 1868

General Washington's Negro Body-Servant

A Biographical Sketch.

The stirring part of this celebrated colored man's life properly began with his death—that is to say, the notable features of his biography begin with the first time he died. He had been little heard of up to that time, but since then we have never ceased to hear of him; we have never ceased to hear of him at stated, unfailing intervals. His was a most remarkable career, and I have thought that its history would make a valuable addition to our biographical literature. Therefore, I have carefully collated the materials for such a work, from authentic sources, and here present them to the public. I have rigidly excluded from these pages everything of a doubtful character, with the object in view of introducing my work into the schools for the instruction of the youth of my country.

The name of the famous body-servant of General Washington was George. After serving his illustrious master faithfully for half a century, and enjoying throughout this long term his high regard and confidence, it became his sorrowful duty at last to lay that beloved master to rest in his peaceful grave by the Potomac. Ten years afterward—in 1809—full of years and honors, he died himself, mourned by all who knew him. The Boston "Gazette" of that date thus refers to the event:

> George, the favorite body-servant of the lamented Washington, died in Richmond, Va., last Tuesday, at the ripe age of 95 years. His intellect was unimpaired, and his memory tenacious, up to within a few minutes of his decease. He was present at the second installation of Washington as President, and also at his funeral, and distinctly remembered all the prominent incidents connected with those noted events.

From this period we hear no more of the favorite body-servant of General Washington until May, 1825, at which time he died again. A Philadelphia paper thus speaks of the sad occurrence:

> At Macon, Ga., last week, a colored man named George, who was the favorite body-servant of General Washington, died, at the ad-

vanced age of 95 years. Up to within a few hours of his dissolution he was in full possession of all his faculties, and could distinctly recollect the second installation of Washington, his death and burial, the surrender of Cornwallis, the battle of Trenton, the griefs and hardships of Valley Forge, etc. Deceased was followed to the grave by the entire population of Macon.

On the Fourth of July, 1830, and also of 1834 and 1836, the subject of this sketch was exhibited in great state upon the rostrum of the orator of the day, and in November of 1840, he died again. The St. Louis "Republican" of the 25th of that month spoke as follows:

ANOTHER RELIC OF THE REVOLUTION GONE.—George, once the favorite body-servant of General Washington, died yesterday at the house of Mr. John Leavenworth, in this city, at the venerable age of 95 years. He was in the full possession of his faculties up to the hour of his death, and distinctly recollected the first and second installations and death of President Washington, the surrender of Cornwallis, the battles of Trenton and Monmouth, the sufferings of the patriot army at Valley Forge, the proclamation of the Declaration of Independence, the speech of Patrick Henry in the Virginia House of Delegates, and many other old-time reminiscences of stirring interest. Few white men die lamented as was this aged negro. The funeral was very largely attended.

During the next ten or eleven years the subject of this sketch appeared at intervals at Fourth of July celebrations in various parts of the country, and was exhibited upon the rostrum with flattering success. But in the Fall of 1855 he died again. The California papers thus speak of the event:

ANOTHER OLD HERO GONE.—Died, at Dutch Flat, on the 7th of March, George (once the confidential body servant of General Washington), at the great age of 95 years. His memory, which did not fail him till the last, was a wonderful storehouse of interesting reminiscences. He could distinctly recollect the first and second installations and death of President Washington, the surrender of Cornwallis, the battles of Trenton and Monmouth, and Bunker Hill, the proclamation of the Declaration of Independence, and Braddock's Defeat. George was greatly respected in Dutch Flat, and it is estimated that there were 10,000 people present at his funeral.

The last time the subject of this sketch died, was in June, 1864; and until we learn the contrary, it is just to presume that he died permanently this time. The Michigan papers thus refer to the sorrowful event:

ANOTHER CHERISHED REMNANT OF THE REVOLUTION GONE. —George, a colored man, and once the favorite body servant of General Washington, died in Detroit last week at the patriarchal age of 95 years. To the moment of his death his intellect was unclouded, and he could distinctly remember the first and second installations and death of Washington, the surrender of Cornwallis, the battles of Trenton and Monmouth, and Bunker Hill, the proclamation of the Declaration of Independence, Braddock's Defeat, the throwing over of the tea in Boston harbor, and the landing of the Pilgrims. He died greatly respected, and was followed to the grave by a vast concourse of people.

The faithful old servant is gone! We shall never see him more, until he turns up again. He has closed his long and splendid career of dissolution, for the present, and sleeps peacefully, as only they sleep who have earned their rest. He was in all respects a remarkable man. He held his age better than any celebrity that has figured in history; and the longer he lived the stronger and longer his memory grew. If he lives to die again, he will distinctly recollect the discovery of America.

The above *résumé* of his biography I believe to be substantially correct, although it is possible that he may have died once or twice in obscure places where the event failed of newspaper notoriety. One fault I find in all notices of his death which I have quoted, and this ought to be corrected. In them he uniformly and impartially died at the age of 95. This could not have been. He might have done that once, or maybe twice, but he could not have continued it indefinitely. Allowing that when he first died, he died at the age of 95, he was 151 years old when he died last, in 1864. But his age did not keep pace with his recollections. When he died the last time, he distinctly remembered the landing of the Pilgrims, which took place in 1620. He must have been about twenty years old when he witnessed that event; wherefore it is safe to assert that the body servant of General Washington was in the neighborhood of two hundred and sixty or seventy years old when he departed this life finally.

Having waited a proper length of time, to see if the subject of this sketch had gone from us reliably and irrevocably, I now publish his biography with confidence, and respectfully offer it to a mourning Nation.

P. S.—I see by the papers that this infamous old fraud has just died again, in Arkansas. This makes six times that he is known to have died, and always in a new place. The death of Washington's body servant has ceased to be a novelty; its charm is gone; the people are tired of it; let it cease. This well-meaning but misguided negro has now put six different communities to the expense of burying him in state, and has swindled tens of thousands of people into following him to the grave under the delusion that a select and peculiar distinction was being conferred upon them. Let him stay buried for good now; and let that newspaper suffer the severest censure that shall ever, in all future time, publish to the world that General Washington's favorite colored body-servant has died again.

February 1868

Colloquy Between a Slum Child
and a Moral Mentor

"Who made the grass?"

"Chief Police."

"No, no—not the Chief of Police. God made the grass. Say it, now."

"God made the grass."

"That is right. Who takes care of the beautiful grass and makes it grow?"

"Chief Police."

"Oh, no, no, no—*not* the Chief of Police. The good God takes care of the grass and makes it grow. Say it, my boy— that's a good fellow."

"The good God takes care of the grass and makes it grow."

"How does grass grow?"

"With an iron railing around it."

"No, I do not mean that. I mean, what does it come from? It comes from little tiny seeds. The good Heavenly Father makes the grass to grow from little seeds. You won't forget that now, will you?"

"Bet your bottom dollar!"

"Ah, naughty, naughty boy. You must not use slang. Where do little boys go who use slang?"

"Dono. *I* goes to the Bowery when shining's good and I've got the lush."

"Tut, tut, tut! Don't talk so. You make me nervous. Little boys who talk that way go to the——bad place!"

"No—but do they? Where is it?"

"It is where there is fire and brimstone always and for-ever."

"Suits Crooks! *I* never ben warm enough yet, ony summer time. Wisht I'd a ben there in the winter when I hadn't any bed kiver but a shutter. That Higgins boy he busted two of the slats out, and then I couldn't keep the cold out *no* way. It had a beautiful brass knob on it, Cap., but brass knobs ain't no good, ony for style, you know. I'd like to ben in that bad place them times, by hokey!"

"Don't swear, James. It is wicked."

"What's *wicked?*"

"Why, to be wicked is to do what one ought not to do—to violate the moral ordinances provided for the regulation of our conduct in this vale of sorrows, and for the elevation and refinement of our social and intellectual natures."

"Gee—whillikins!"

"*Don't* use such words, my son—pray don't."

"Well, then I won't—but I didn't mean no harm—wish I may die if I did. But you made a 'spare,' that time, *didn't* you?"

"A 'spare?' What is a spare, my child?"

"*You* don't know what a 'spare' is? Oh, no, gov'ner, that cat won't fight, you know. Fool who, with your nigger babies whitewashed with brickdust!"

"Well, I believe it is nearly useless to try to break you of using slang, my poor, neglected boy. But truly, I do not know what a 'spare' is. What *is* a 'spare?' "

"Well, if *you* ain't ignorant, I'm blowed! Why a spare is where you fetch all the pins with two balls—and when you make a ten-strike, you've got two spares, you know. Well, when you got off all of them jaw-breakers, I judged the pins was all down on *your* alley, anyway."

"I stand rebuked, James. Egotism will betray the best of us to humiliation."

"Spare! I tell you them winders of yours snakes the head pin every time, gov'ner."

"Conquered again!—Well, James, we will go back to the old lesson. I am out of my element in this. James, what is grass for?"

"To make parks out of,—like the City Hall."

"Is that all? Isn't it to make the pretty fields, and lawns, and meadows?"

"Don't know nothing about them things—never seen 'em."

"Ah, pity. What does our Heavenly Father do with the grass when He makes it?"

"Puts it in the Hall park and puts up a sign, 'Keep off'n the grass—dogs ain't allowed.' "

"Poor boy! And what does He put it there for?"

"To look at, through the railings."

"Well, it really does seem so. What would you do with the beautiful grass that God has made, if you had it?"

"Roll in it! Oh, gay!"

"Well, I wish in my heart the City Fathers would let you—so that you might have *one* pleasure that God intended for all childhood, even the children of poverty!—yea, that He intended even for vagrant dogs, that shun the tax and gain precarious livelihoods by devious ways and questionable practices."

"Set 'em up again, gov'ner!"

"I was partly talking to myself, James—that is why I used the long words. James, who made you?"

"Chief Police, I guess."

"Mercy! I wish I could get that all-powerful potentate out of your head. No, James, God made you."

"Did he, though?"

"Yes—God made you, as well as the grass."

"Honest injun? That's bully. But I wish he'd fence me in and take care of me, same as he does the grass."

"He does take care of you James. You ought to be very thankful to Him. He gives you the clothes you wear—"

"Gov'ner, I got them pants from Mike the ragman, my-self."

"But they came from above, James—they came from your Heavenly Father. He gave them to you."

"I pass. But I reckon I had to pay for 'em, though. Mike never told me. He never said nothing about parties giving 'em to me."

"Why, James! But then you do not know any better. And He gives you your food—"

" 'Spensary soup! I wisht I had a cag of it!"

"And the bed that you sleep in—"

"Cellar door and a shutter with a brass knob on it. Now look-a-here gov'ner, you're a guying me. You never tried a shutter. *I* ain't thankful for no such a bed as that."

"But you ought to be, James, you ought to be. Think how many boys are worse off than you are."

"I give in, I do. There's that-there Peanut Jim—his parents

is awful poor. He ain't got no shutter. I was always sorry for that poor cuss."*

*Founded on absolute fact. A little girl sleeping in an upper room of a New York tenement house on a cold night, with a dilapidated window-shutter for a coverlet, said: "Mother, I am so sorry for poor little girls that haven't got any window-shutter! I ought to be very thankful." (Respectfully recommended for the Sunday School books.)

c. May 1868

My Late Senatorial Secretaryship

I am not a private secretary to a senator any more, now. I held the berth two months in security and in great cheerfulness of spirit, but my bread began to return from over the waters, then—that is to say, my works came back and revealed themselves. I judged it best to resign. The way of it was this. My employer sent for me one morning tolerably early, and, as soon as I had finished inserting some conundrums clandestinely into his last great speech upon finance, I entered the presence. There was something portentous in his appearance. His cravat was untied, his hair was in a state of disorder, and his countenance bore about it the signs of a suppressed storm. He held a package of letters in his tense grasp, and I knew that the dreaded Pacific mail was in. He said:

"I thought you were worthy of confidence."

I said: "Yes, sir."

He said: "I gave you a letter from certain of my constituents in the State of Nevada, asking the establishment of a post office at Baldwin's Ranch, and told you to answer it, as ingeniously as you could, with arguments which should persuade them that there was no real necessity for an office at that place."

I felt easier. "Oh, if that is all, sir, I *did* do that."

"Yes, you *did*. I will read your answer, for your own humiliation:

" 'WASHINGTON, Nov. 24, 1867.

" '*Messrs. Smith, Jones, and others.*

" 'GENTLEMEN: What the mischief do you suppose you want with a post office at Baldwin's Ranch? It would not do you any good. If any letters came there, you couldn't read them, you know; and, besides, such letters as ought to pass through, with money in them, for other localities, would not be likely to *get* through, you must perceive at once; and that would make trouble for us all. No, don't bother about a post office in your camp. I have your best interests at heart, and feel that it would only be an ornamental folly. What you want is a nice jail, you know—a nice, substantial jail and a free

school. These will be a lasting benefit to you. These will make you
really contented and happy. I will move in the matter at once.

Very truly, etc.,

" 'MARK TWAIN,

" 'For James W. Nye, U. S. Senator.'

"That is the way you answered that letter. Those people say
they will hang me, if I ever enter that district again; and I am
perfectly satisfied they *will*, too."

"Well, sir, I did not know I was doing any harm. I only
wanted to convince them."

"Ah. Well, you *did* convince them, I make no manner of
doubt. Now, here is another specimen. I gave you a petition
from certain gentlemen of Nevada, praying that I would get a
bill through Congress incorporating the Methodist Episcopal
Church of the State of Nevada. I told you to say, in reply,
that the creation of such a law came more properly within the
province of the State Legislature; and to endeavor to show
them that, in the present feebleness of the religious element in
that new commonwealth, the expediency of incorporating the
church was questionable. What did you write?

" 'WASHINGTON, Nov. 24, 1867.

" '*Rev. John Halifax and others.*

" 'GENTLEMEN: You will have to go to the State Legislature about
that little speculation of yours—Congress don't know anything
about religion. But don't you hurry to go there, either; because this
thing you propose to do out in that new country isn't expedient—
in fact, it is simply ridiculous. Your religious people there are too
feeble, in intellect, in morality, in piety—in everything, pretty much.
You had better drop this—you can't make it work. You can't issue
stock on an incorporation like that—or if you could, it would only
keep you in trouble all the time. The other denominations would
abuse it, and "bear" it, and "sell it short," and break it down. They
would do with it just as they would with one of your silver mines
out there—they would try to make all the world believe it was "wildcat." You ought not to do anything that is calculated to bring a sacred
thing into disrepute. You ought to be ashamed of yourselves—that
is what *I* think about it. You close your petition with the words:
"And we will ever pray." I think you had better—you need to do it.

Very truly, etc.,

" 'MARK TWAIN,

" 'For James W. Nye, U. S. Senator.'

"*That* luminous epistle finishes me with the religious element among my constituents. But that my political murder might be made sure, some evil instinct prompted me to hand you this memorial from the grave company of elders composing the Board of Aldermen of the city of San Francisco, to try your hand upon—a memorial praying that the city's right to the water-lots upon the city front might be established by law of Congress. I told you this was a dangerous matter to move in. I told you to write a non-committal letter to the Aldermen—an ambiguous letter—a letter that should avoid, as far as possible, all real consideration and discussion of the water-lot question. If there is any feeling left in you—any shame— surely this letter you wrote, in obedience to that order, ought to evoke it, when its words fall upon your ears:

" 'WASHINGTON, Nov. 27, 1867.
" '*The Hon. Board of Aldermen, etc.*

" 'GENTLEMEN: George Washington, the revered Father of his Country, is dead. His long and brilliant career is closed, alas! forever. He was greatly respected in this section of the country, and his untimely decease cast a gloom over the whole community. He died on the 14th day of December, 1799. He passed peacefully away from the scene of his honors and his great achievements, the most lamented hero and the best beloved that ever earth hath yielded unto Death. At such a time as this, *you* speak of water-lots!—what a lot was his!

" 'What is fame? Fame is an accident. Sir Isaac Newton discovered an apple falling to the ground—a trivial discovery, truly, and one which a million men had made before him—but his parents were influential, and so they tortured that little circumstance into something wonderful, and, lo! the simple world took up the shout, and, in almost the twinkling of an eye, that man was famous. Treasure these thoughts.

" 'Poesy, sweet poesy, who shall estimate what the world owes to thee!

"Mary had a little lamb, its fleece was white as snow—
    And everywhere that Mary went, the lamb was sure to go.

        "Jack and Gill went up the hill
            To draw a pail of water;
        Jack fell down and broke his crown,
            And Gill came tumbling after.

For simplicity, elegance of diction, and freedom from immoral tendencies, I regard those two poems in the light of gems. They are suited to all grades of intelligence, to every sphere of life—to the field, to the nursery, to the guild. Especially should no Board of Aldermen be without them.

" 'Venerable fossils! write again. Nothing improves one so much as friendly correspondence. Write again—and if there is anything in this memorial of yours that refers to anything in particular, do not be backward about explaining it. We shall always be happy to hear you chirp.

Very truly, etc.,
" 'MARK TWAIN,
" 'For James W. Nye, U. S. Senator.'

"That is an atrocious, a ruinous epistle! Distraction!"

"Well, sir, I am really sorry if there is anything wrong about it—but—but—it appears to me to dodge the water-lot question."

"Dodge the mischief! Oh!—but never mind. As long as destruction must come now, let it be complete. Let it be complete—let this last of your performances, which I am about to read, make a finality of it. I am a ruined man. I *had* my misgivings when I gave you the letter from Humboldt, asking that the post route from Indian Gulch to Shakespeare Gap and intermediate points, be changed partly to the old Mormon trail. But I told you it was a delicate question, and warned you to deal with it deftly—to answer it dubiously, and leave them a little in the dark. And your fatal imbecility impelled you to make *this* disastrous reply. I should think you would stop your ears, if you are not dead to all shame:

" 'WASHINGTON, Nov. 30, 1867.

" '*Messrs. Perkins, Wagner, et al.*

" 'GENTLEMEN: It is a delicate question about this Indian trail, but handled with proper deftness and dubiousness, I doubt not we shall succeed in some measure or otherwise, because the place where the route leaves the Lassen Meadows, over beyond where those two Shawnee chiefs, Dilapidated-Vengeance and Biter-of-the-Clouds, were scalped last winter, this being the favorite direction to some, but others preferring something else in consequence of things, the Mormon trail leaving Mosby's at three in the morning, and passing through Jawbone Flat to Blucher, and then down by Jug-Handle, the road passing to the right of it, and naturally leaving it on the right, too, and Dawson's on the left of the trail where it passes to the left of said Dawson's, and onward thence to Tomahawk, thus making the route cheaper, easier of access to all who can get at it, and compassing all the desirable objects so considered by others, and, therefore, conferring the most good upon the greatest number, and, consequently, I am encouraged to hope we shall. However, I shall be ready, and happy, to afford you still further information upon the subject, from time to time, as you may desire it and the Post Office Department be enabled to furnish it to me.

Very truly, etc.,

" 'MARK TWAIN,

" 'For James W. Nye, U. S. Senator.'

"There—now, *what* do you think of that?"

"Well, I don't know, sir. It—well, it appears to me—to be dubious enough."

"Du—leave the house! I am a ruined man. Those Humboldt savages never will forgive me for tangling their brains up with this inhuman letter. I have lost the respect of the Methodist Church, the Board of Aldermen——"

"Well, I haven't anything to say about that, because I may have missed it a little in their cases, but I *was* too many for the Baldwin's Ranch people, General!"

"Leave the house! Leave it forever and forever, too!"

I regarded that as a sort of covert intimation that my services could be dispensed with, and so I resigned. I never will be a private secretary to a senator again. You can't please that kind of people. They don't know anything. They can't appreciate a party's efforts.

May 1868

The Story of Mamie Grant, the Child-Missionary

"Will you have cream and sugar in your coffee?"

"Yes, if you please, dear auntie,—would that you could experience a change of heart."

The latter remark came from the sweet young lips of Mamie Grant. She had early come to know the comfort and joy of true religion. She attended church regularly, and looked upon it as a happy privilege, instead of an irksome penance, as is too often the case with children. She was always the first at Sunday School and the last to leave it. To her the Sunday School library was a treasure-house of precious learning. From its volumes she drew those stores of wisdom which made her the wonder of the young and the admiration of the aged. She blessed the gifted theological students who had written those fascinating books, and early resolved to make their heroines her models and turn her whole attention to saving the lost. Thus we find her at breakfast, at nine years of age, seizing upon even so barren an opportunity as a question of milk and sugar in her coffee, to express a prayerful wish in behalf of her aged, unregenerated aunt.

"Batter-cakes?"

"No, auntie, I cannot, I dare not eat batter-cakes while your precious soul is in peril."

"Oh, stuff! eat your breakfast, child, and don't bother. Here is your bowl of milk—break your bread in it and go on with your breakfast."

Pausing, with the uplifted spoonful of milk almost at her lips, Mamie Grant said:

"Auntie, bread and milk are but a vanity of this sinful world; let us take no thought of bread and milk; let us seek first the milk of righteousness, and all these things will be added unto us."

"Oh, don't bother, don't bother, child. There is the door-bell. Run and see who it is."

"Knock and it shall be opened unto you. Oh, auntie, if you would but treasure those words."

Mamie then moved pensively down stairs to open the door.

This was her first morning at her aunt's, where she had come to make a week's visit. She opened the door. A quick-stepping, quick-speaking man entered.

"Hurry, my little miss. Sharp's the word. I'm the census-taker. Trot out the old gentleman."

"The census-taker? What is that?"

"I gather all the people together in a book and number them."

"Ah, what a precious opportunity is offered you, for the gathering of souls. If you would but—"

"Oh, blazes! Don't palaver. I'm about my employer's work. Let's have the old man out, quick."

"Mortal, forsake these vanities. Do rather the work of Him who is able to reward you beyond the richest of the lords of earth. Take these tracts. Distribute them far and wide. Wrestle night and day with the lost. It was thus that young Edward Baker became a shining light and a lamp to the feet of the sinner, and acquired deathless fame in the Sunday School books of the whole world. Take these tracts. This one, en-titled, 'The Doomed Drunkard, or the Wages of Sin,' teaches how the insidious monster that lurks in the wine-cup, drags souls to perdition. This one, entitled, 'Deuces and, or the Gamester's Last Throw,' tells how the almost ruined gambler, playing at the dreadful game of poker, made a ten strike and a spare, and thus encouraged, drew two cards and pocketed the deep red; urged on by the demon of destruction, he ordered it up and went alone on a double run of eight, with two for his heels, and then, just as fortune seemed at last to have turned in his favor, his opponent coppered the ace and won. The fated gamester blew his brains out and perished. Ah, poker is a dreadful, dreadful game. You will see in this book how well our theological students are qualified to teach un-derstandingly all classes that come within their reach. Gam-blers' souls are worthy to be saved, and so the holy students even acquaint themselves with the science and technicalities of their horrid games, in order to be able to talk to them for the saving of their souls in language which they are accustomed to. This tract, entitled—Why, he is gone! I wonder if my words have sunk into his heart. I wonder if the seeds thus sown will bear fruit. I cannot but believe that he will quit his

sinful census-gathering and go to gathering souls. Oh, I *know*
he will. It was just in this way that young James Wilson converted the Jew peddlar, and sent him away from his father's
house with his boxes full of Bibles and hymn-books—a peddlar no longer, but a blessed colporteur. It is so related in the
beautiful Sunday School book entitled 'James Wilson, the Boy
Missionary.'"

At this moment the door-bell rang again. She opened it.

"Morning Gazette, Miss—forty cents due, on two weeks."

"Do you carry these papers all about town?"

"To mighty near every house in it—largest daily circulation
of any daily paper published in the city—best advertising
medium—"

"Oh, to think of your opportunities! This is not a Baptist
paper, is it?"

"Well I should think not. She's a Democrat.—"

"Could not you get the editor of it to drop the follies of
this world and make the Gazette a messenger of light and
hope, a Baptist benediction at every fireside?"

"Oh, I haven't got time to bother about such things. Saving your presence, Miss, Democrats don't care a damn about
light and hope—they wouldn't take the paper if she was a
Baptist. But hurry, won't you, please—forty cents for two
weeks back."

"Ah, well, if they would stop the paper, that would not do.
But Oh, you can still labor in the vineyard. When you leave a
paper at a house, call all the people of that house together and
urge them to turn from the evil of their ways and be saved.
Tell them that the meanest and the laziest and the vilest of His
creatures is still within the reach of salvation. Fold these tracts
inside your papers every day—and when you get out, come
for more. This one, entitled 'The Pains of Hell, or the Politician's Fate,' is a beautiful tract, and draws such a frightful
picture of perdition, its fires, its monsters, its awful and endless sufferings, that it can never fail to touch even the most
hardened sinner, and make him seek the tranquil haven of
religion. It would surely have brought Roger Lyman the
shoemaker of our village to the fold if he had not become a
raving maniac just before he got through. It is an awakening

pamphlet for those Democrats who are wasting their time in the vain pursuit of political aggrandizement. Fold in this tract also, entitled—"

"Oh, this won't do. This is all Miss Nancy stuff, you know. Fold them in the papers! I'd like to see myself. Fold tracts in a daily newspa—why I never heard of such a thing. Democrats don't go a cent on tracts. Why, they'd raise more Cain around that office—they'd mob us. Come, Miss—forty cents, you know."

"You are glib with the foolish words of the worldly. Take the tracts; and enter upon the good work. And neglect not your own eternal welfare. Have you ever experienced grace?

"Why *he* is gone, too. But he is gone on a blessed mission. Even this poor creature will be the means of inaugurating a revival in this wicked city that shall sweep far and wide over the domains of sin. I know it, because it was just in this way that young George Berkley converted the itinerant tinker and sent him forth to solder the souls of the ungodly, as is set forth in the Sunday School books, though, still struggling with the thrall of unrighteousness that had so lately bound him, he stole two coffee-pots before he started on his errand of mercy. The door-bell again."

"Good morning, Miss, is Mr. Wagner in? I have come to pay him a thousand dollars which I borrowed last month."

"Alas, all seem busied with the paltry concerns of this world. Oh, beware how you trifle. Think not of the treasures of this perishable sphere. Lay up treasures in that realm where moths do not corrupt nor thieves break through and steal. Have you ever read 'Fire and Brimstone, or the Sinner's Last Gasp?'"

"Well this beats anything I ever heard of—a child preaching before she is weaned. But I am in something of a hurry, Miss. I must pay this money and get about my business. Hurry, please."

"Ah, Sir, it is you that should hurry—hurry to examine into your prospects in the hereafter. In this tract, entitled 'The Slave of Gain or the Dirge of the Damned,' you will learn (pray Heaven it be not too late!) how a thirst for lucre sears the soul and bars it forever from the gentle influences of

religion; how it makes of life a cruel curse and in death opens
the gates of everlasting woe. It is a precious book.—No sinner can read it and sleep afterward."

"You must excuse me, Miss, but—"

"Turn from the wrath to come! Flee while it is yet time.
Your account with sin grows apace. Cash it and open the
books anew. Take this tract and read it—'The Blasphemous
Sailor Awfully Rebuked.' It tells how, on a stormy night, a
wicked sailor was ordered to ascend to the main hatch and
reef a gasket in the sheet anchor; from his dizzy height he saw
the main-tops'l jib-boom fetch away from the clew-garnets of
the booby-hatch; next the lee scuppers of the mizzen-to'-
gallant's'l fouled with the peak-halliards of the cat-heads, yet
in his uncurbed iniquity, at such a time as this he raised his
blasphemous voice and shouted an oath in the teeth of the
raging winds. Mark the quick retribution. The weather-brace
parted amidships, the mizzen-shrouds fouled the starboard
gangway, and the dog-watch whipped clean out of the bolt-
ropes quicker than the lightning's flash! Imagine, Oh, imagine that wicked sailor's position! I cannot do it, because I do
not know what those dreadful nautical terms mean, for I am
not educated and deeply learned in the matters of practical
every-day life like the gifted theological students, who have
learned all about practical life from the writings of other theological students who went before them, but O, it must have
been frightful, *so* frightful. Pilgrim, let this be a warning to
you—let this—

"*He* is gone. Well, to the longest day he lives he cannot
forget that it was *I* that brought peace to his troubled spirit, it
was *I* that poured balm upon his bruised heart, it was *I* that
pointed him the way to happiness. Ah, the good I am doing
fills me with bliss. I am but an humble instrument, yet I feel
that I am like, very like, some of the infant prodigies in the
Sunday School books. I know that I use as fine language as
they do. Oh that *I* might be an example to the young—a
beacon light flashing its cheering rays far over the tossing
waves of iniquity from the watch-tower of a Sunday School
book with a marbled back. Door-bell again. Truly my ways
are ways of pleasantness this day. Good morning, Sir. Come
in, please."

"Miss, will you tell Mr. Wagner that I am come to foreclose the mortgage unless he pays the thousand dollars he owes me at once—will you tell him that, please?"

Mamie Grant's sweet face grew troubled. It was easy to see that a painful thought was in her mind.—She looked earnestly into the face of the stranger, and said with emotion:

"Have you ever experienced a change of heart?"

"Heavens, what a question!"

"You know not what you do. You stand upon a volcano. You may perish at any moment. Mortal, beware. Leave worldly concerns, and go to doing good. Give your property to the poor and go off somewhere for a missionary. You are not lost, if you will but move quickly. Shun the intoxicating bowl. Oh, take this tract, and read it night and morning and treasure up its lessons. Read it—'William Baxter, the Reformed Inebriate, or, Saved as by fire.' This poor sinner, in a fit of drunken madness, slew his entire family with a junk bottle—see the picture of it. Remorse brought its tortures and he signed the temperance pledge. He married again and raised a pious, interesting family. The tempter led him astray again, and when wild with liquor again he brained his family with the fell junk bottle. He heard Gough lecture, and reformed once more. Once more he reared a family of bright and beautiful children. But alas, in an evil hour his wicked companions placed the intoxicating bowl to his lips and that very day his babes fell victims to the junk bottle and he threw the wife of his bosom from the third story window. He woke from his drunken stupor to find himself alone in the world, a homeless, friendless outcast. Be warned, be warned by his experience. But see what perseverance may accomplish. Thoroughly reformed at last, he now traverses the land a brand plucked from the burning, and delivers temperance lectures and organizes Sunday Schools. Go thou and do likewise. It is never too late. Hasten, while yet the spirit is upon you.

"But *he* is gone, too, and took his mortgage with him. He will reform, I know he will. And then the good he will do can never be estimated. Truly this has been to me a blessed day."

So saying, Mamie Grant put on her little bonnet and went forth into the city to carry tracts to the naked and hungry poor, to the banker in his busy office, to the rumseller dealing out his soul-destroying abominations.

That night when she returned, her uncle Wagner was in deep distress. He said:

"Alas, we are ruined. My newspaper is stopped, and I am posted on its bulletin board as a delinquent. The tax-collecting census-taker has set his black mark opposite my name. Martin, who should have returned the thousand dollars he borrowed has not come, and Phillips, in consequence, has foreclosed the mortgage, and we are homeless!"

"Be not cast down, dear uncle," Mamie said, "for I have sent all these men into the vineyard. They shall sow the fields far and wide and reap a rich harvest. Cease to repine at worldly ills, and attend only to the behests of the great here-after."

Mr. Wagner only groaned, for he was an unregenerated man.

Mamie placed a happy head upon her pillow that night. She said:

"I have saved a paper carrier, a census bureau, a creditor and a debtor, and they will bless me forever. I have done a noble work to-day. I may yet see my poor little name in a beautiful Sunday School book, and maybe T. S. Arthur may write it. Oh, joy!"

Such is the history of "Mamie Grant, the Child-Missionary."

July 1868

Cannibalism in the Cars

I visited St. Louis lately, and on my way west, after changing cars at Terre Haute, Indiana, a mild, benevolent-looking gentleman of about forty-five, or may be fifty, came in at one of the way-stations and sat down beside me. We talked together pleasantly on various subjects for an hour, perhaps, and I found him exceedingly intelligent and entertaining. When he learned that I was from Washington, he immediately began to ask questions about various public men, and about Congressional affairs; and I saw very shortly that I was conversing with a man who was perfectly familiar with the ins and outs of political life at the Capital, even to the ways and manners, and customs of procedure of Senators and Representatives in the Chambers of the National Legislature. Presently two men halted near us for a single moment, and one said to the other:

"Harris, if you'll do that for me, I'll never forget you, my boy."

My new comrade's eyes lighted pleasantly. The words had touched upon a happy memory, I thought. Then his face settled into thoughtfulness—almost into gloom. He turned to me and said, "Let me tell you a story; let me give you a secret chapter of my life—a chapter that has never been referred to by me since its events transpired. Listen patiently, and promise that you will not interrupt me."

I said I would not, and he related the following strange adventure, speaking sometimes with animation, sometimes with melancholy, but always with feeling and earnestness.

THE STRANGER'S NARRATIVE.

On the 19th December, 1853, I started from St. Louis in the evening train, bound for Chicago. There were only twenty-four passengers, all told. There were no ladies and no children. We were in excellent spirits, and pleasant acquaintanceships were soon formed. The journey bade fair to be a happy one, and no individual in the party, I think, had even the vaguest presentiment of the horrors we were soon to undergo.

269

At 11 P.M. it began to snow hard. Shortly after leaving the small village of Weldon, we entered upon that tremendous prairie solitude that stretches its leagues on leagues of house-less dreariness far away towards the Jubilee Settlements. The winds unobstructed by trees or hills, or even vagrant rocks, whistled fiercely across the level desert, driving the falling snow before it like spray from the crested waves of a stormy sea. The snow was deepening fast, and we knew, by the di-minished speed of the train, that the engine was ploughing through it with steadily increasing difficulty. Indeed it almost came to a dead halt sometimes, in the midst of great drifts that piled themselves like colossal graves across the track. Conversation began to flag. Cheerfulness gave place to grave concern. The possibility of being imprisoned in the snow, on the bleak prairie, fifty miles from any house, presented itself to every mind, and extended its depressing influence over every spirit.

At two o'clock in the morning I was aroused out of an uneasy slumber by the ceasing of all motion about me. The appalling truth flashed upon me instantly—we were captives in a snow-drift! "All hands to the rescue!" Every man sprang to obey. Out into the wild night, the pitchy darkness, the billowing snow, the driving storm, every soul leaped, with the consciousness that a moment lost now might bring destruc-tion to us all. Shovels, hands, boards—anything, everything that could displace snow, was brought into instant requisi-tion. It was a weird picture, that small company of frantic men fighting the banking snows, half in the blackest shadow and half in the angry light of the locomotive's reflector.

One short hour sufficed to prove the utter uselessness of our efforts. The storm barricaded the track with a dozen drifts while we dug one away. And worse than this, it was discov-ered that the last grand charge the engine had made upon the enemy had broken the fore-and-aft shaft of the driving-wheel! With a free track before us we should still have been helpless. We entered the car wearied with labor, and very sorrowful. We gathered about the stoves, and gravely canvassed our situ-ation. We had no provisions whatever—in this lay our chief distress. We could not freeze, for there was a good supply of wood in the tender. This was our only comfort. The discussion ended at last in accepting the disheartening decision of the conductor,—viz.: That it would be death for any man to attempt to travel fifty miles on foot through snow like that. We could not send for help, and even if we could, it could not come. We must submit and await, as patiently as we might, succor or starvation! I think the stoutest heart there felt a momentary chill when those words were uttered.

Within the hour conversation subsided to a low murmur here and there about the car, caught fitfully between the rising and falling of the blast; the lamps grew dim; and the majority of the castaways settled themselves among the flickering shadows to think—to forget the present if they could—to sleep, if they might.

The eternal night—it surely seemed eternal to us—wore its lagging hours away at last, and the cold grey dawn broke in the east. As the light grew stronger the passengers began to stir and give signs of life, one after another, and each in turn pushed his slouched hat up from his forehead, stretched his stiffened limbs, and glanced out at the windows upon the cheerless prospect. It was cheerless indeed!—not a living thing visible anywhere, not a human habitation; nothing but a vast white desert; uplifted sheets of snow drifting hither and thither before the wind—a world of eddying flakes shutting out the firmament above.

All day we moped about the cars, saying little, thinking much. Another lingering, dreary night—and hunger.

Another dawning—another day of silence, sadness, wasting hunger, hopeless watching for succor that could not come. A night of restless slumber, filled with dreams of feasting—wakings distressed with the gnawings of hunger.

The fourth day came and went—and the fifth! Five days of dreadful imprisonment! A savage hunger looked out at every eye. There was in it a sign of awful import—the foreshadowing of a something that was vaguely shaping itself in every heart—a something which no tongue dared yet to frame into words.

The sixth day passed—the seventh dawned upon as gaunt and haggard and hopeless a company of men as ever stood in the shadow of death. It must out now! That thing which had been growing up in every heart was ready to leap from every lip at last! Nature had been taxed to the utmost—she must yield. RICHARD H. GASTON, of Minnesota, tall, cadaverous, and pale, rose up. All knew what was coming. All prepared— every emotion, every semblance of excitement was smothered—only a calm, thoughtful seriousness appeared in the eyes that were lately so wild.

"Gentlemen,—It cannot be delayed longer! The time is at hand! We must determine which of us shall die to furnish food for the rest!"

Mr. JOHN J. WILLIAMS, of Illinois, rose and said: "Gentlemen,—I nominate the Rev. James Sawyer, of Tennessee."

Mr. WM. R. ADAMS, of Indiana, said: "I nominate Mr. Daniel Slote, of New York."

Mr. CHARLES J. LANGDON: "I nominate Mr. Samuel A. Bowen, of St. Louis."

Mr. SLOTE: "Gentlemen,—I desire to decline in favor of Mr. John A. Van Nostrand, jun., of New Jersey."

Mr. GASTON: "If there be no objection, the gentleman's desire will be acceded to."

Mr. VAN NOSTRAND objecting, the resignation of Mr. Slote was rejected. The resignations of Messrs. Sawyer and Bowen were also offered, and refused upon the same grounds.

Mr. A. L. BASCOM, of Ohio: "I move that the nominations now close, and that the House proceed to an election by ballot."

Mr. SAWYER: "Gentlemen,—I protest earnestly against these proceedings. They are, in every way, irregular and unbecoming. I must beg to move that they be dropped at once, and that we elect a chairman of the meeting and proper officers to assist him, and then we can go on with the business before us understandingly."

Mr. BELKNAP, of Iowa: "Gentlemen,—I object. This is no time to stand upon forms and ceremonious observances. For more than seven days we have been without food. Every moment we lose in idle discussion increases our distress. I am satisfied with the nominations that have been made—every gentleman present is, I believe—and I, for one, do not see why we should not proceed at once to elect one or more of them. I wish to offer a resolution——"

Mr. GASTON: "It would be objected to, and have to lie over one day under the rules, thus bringing about the very delay you wish to avoid. The gentleman from New Jersey——"

Mr. VAN NOSTRAND: "Gentlemen, I am a stranger among you; I have not sought the distinction that has been conferred upon me, and I feel a delicacy."

Mr. MORGAN, of Alabama: "I move the previous question."

The motion was carried, and further debate shut off, of course. The motion to elect officers was passed, and under it Mr. Gaston was chosen Chairman, Mr. Blake, Secretary, Messrs. Holcomb, Dyer, and Baldwin, a Committee on nominations, and Mr. R. M. Howland, Purveyor, to assist the committee in making selections.

A recess of half an hour was then taken, and some little caucusing followed. At the sound of the gavel the meeting reassembled, and the committee reported in favor of Messrs. George Ferguson, of Kentucky, Lucien Hermann, of Louisiana, and W. Messick, of Colorado, as candidates. The report was accepted.

Mr. ROGERS, of Missouri: "Mr. President,—The report being properly before the House now, I move to amend it by substituting for the name of Mr. Hermann that of Mr. Lucius Harris, of St. Louis, who is well and honorably known to us all. I do not wish to be understood as casting the least reflection upon the high character and standing of the gentleman from Louisiana—far from it. I respect and esteem him as much as any gentleman here present possibly can; but none of us can be blind to the fact that he has lost more flesh during the week that we have lain here than any among you—none of us can be blind to the fact that the committee has been derelict in its duty, either through negligence or a graver fault, in thus offering for our suffrages a gentleman who, however pure his own motives may be, has really less nutriment in him——"

THE CHAIR: "The gentleman from Missouri will take his seat. The Chair cannot allow the integrity of the Committee to be questioned save by the regular course, under the rules. What action will the House take upon the gentleman's motion?"

Mr. HALLIDAY, of Virginia: "I move to further amend the

report by substituting Mr. Harvey Davis, of Oregon, for Mr. Messick. It may be urged by gentlemen that the hardships and privations of a frontier life have rendered Mr. Davis tough; but, gentlemen, is this a time to cavil at toughness? is this a time to be fastidious concerning trifles? is this a time to dispute about matters of paltry significance? No, gentlemen, bulk is what we desire—substance, weight, bulk—these are the supreme requisites now—not talent, not genius, not education. I insist upon my motion."

Mr. MORGAN (excitedly): "Mr. Chairman,—I do most strenuously object to this amendment. The gentleman from Oregon is old, and furthermore is bulky only in bone—not in flesh. I ask the gentleman from Virginia if it is soup we want instead of solid sustenance? if he would delude us with shadows? if he would mock our suffering with an Oregonian spectre? I ask him if he can look upon the anxious faces around him, if he can gaze into our sad eyes, if he can listen to the beating of our expectant hearts, and still thrust this famine-stricken fraud upon us? I ask him if he can think of our desolate state, of our past sorrows, of our dark future, and still unpityingly foist upon us this wreck, this ruin, this tottering swindle, this gnarled and blighted and sapless vagabond from Oregon's inhospitable shores? Never!" (Applause.)

The amendment was put to vote, after a fiery debate, and lost. Mr. Harris was substituted on the first amendment. The balloting then began. Five ballots were held without a choice. On the sixth, Mr. Harris was elected, all voting for him but himself. It was then moved that his election should be ratified by acclamation, which was lost, in consequence of his again voting against himself.

Mr. RADWAY moved that the House now take up the remaining candidates, and go into an election for breakfast. This was carried.

On the first ballot there was a tie, half the members favoring one candidate on account of his youth, and half favoring the other on account of his superior size. The President gave the casting vote for the latter, Mr. Messick. This decision created considerable dissatisfaction among the friends of Mr. Ferguson, the defeated candidate, and there was some talk of demanding a new ballot; but in the midst of it, a motion to adjourn was carried, and the meeting broke up at once.

The preparations for supper diverted the attention of the Ferguson faction from the discussion of their grievance for a long time, and then, when they would have taken it up again, the happy announcement that Mr. Harris was ready, drove all thought of it to the winds.

We improvised tables by propping up the backs of car-seats, and sat down with hearts full of gratitude to the finest supper that had blessed our vision for seven torturing days. How changed we were from what we had been a few short hours before! Hopeless, sad-eyed misery, hunger, feverish anxiety, desperation, then—thankfulness, serenity, joy too deep for utterance now. That I know was the cheeriest hour of my eventful life. The wind howled, and blew the snow wildly about our prison-house, but they were powerless to distress us any more. I liked Harris. He might have been better done, perhaps, but I am free to say that no man ever agreed with me better than Harris, or afforded me so large a degree of satisfaction. Messick was very well, though rather high-flavored, but for genuine nutritiousness and delicacy of fibre, give me Harris. Messick had his good points—I will not attempt to deny it, nor do I wish to do it—but he was no more fitted for breakfast than a mummy would be, sir—not a bit. Lean?—why, bless me!—and tough? Ah, he was very tough! You could not imagine it,—you could never imagine anything like it.

"Do you mean to tell me that——"

Do not interrupt me, please. After breakfast we elected a man by the name of Walker, from Detroit, for supper. He was very good. I wrote his wife so afterwards. He was worthy of all praise. I shall always remember Walker. He was a little rare, but very good. And then the next morning we had Morgan, of Alabama, for breakfast. He was one of the finest men I ever sat down to,—handsome, educated, refined, spoke several languages fluently—a perfect gentleman—he was a perfect gentleman, and singularly juicy. For supper we had that Oregon patriarch, and he *was* a fraud, there is no question about it—old, scraggy, tough—nobody can picture the reality. I finally said, gentlemen, you can do as you like, but *I* will wait for another election. And Grimes, of Illinois, said, "Gentlemen, *I* will wait also. When you elect a man that has *something* to recommend him, I shall be glad to join you again." It soon became evident that there was general dissatisfaction with Davis, of Oregon, and so, to preserve the good-will that had prevailed so pleasantly since we had had Harris, an election was called, and the result of it was that Baker, of Georgia, was chosen. He was splendid! Well, well—after that we had Doolittle, and Hawkins, and McElroy (there was some complaint about McElroy, because he was uncommonly short and thin), and Penrod, and two Smiths, and Bailey (Bailey had a wooden leg, which was clear loss, but he was otherwise good), and an Indian boy, and an organ-grinder, and a gentleman by the name of Buckminster—a poor stick of a vagabond that wasn't any good for company and no account for breakfast. We were glad we got him elected before relief came.

"And so the blessed relief *did* come at last?"

Yes, it came one bright sunny morning, just after election. John Murphy was the choice, and there never was a better, I am willing to testify; but John Murphy came home with us, in the train that came to succor us, and lived to marry the widow Harris——

"Relict of——"

Relict of our first choice. He married her, and is happy and respected and prosperous yet. Ah, it was like a novel, sir—it was like a romance. This is my stopping-place, sir; I must bid you good-bye. Any time that you can make it convenient to tarry a day or two with me, I shall be glad to have you. I like you, sir; I have conceived an affection for you. I could like you as well as I liked Harris himself, sir. Good day, sir, and a pleasant journey.

He was gone. I never felt so stunned, so distressed, so bewildered in my life. But in my soul I was glad he was gone. With all his gentleness of manner and his soft voice, I shuddered whenever he turned his hungry eye upon me; and when I heard that I had achieved his perilous affection, and that I stood almost with the late Harris in his esteem, my heart fairly stood still!

I was bewildered beyond description. I did not doubt his

word; I could not question a single item in a statement so stamped with the earnestness of truth as his; but its dreadful details overpowered me, and threw my thoughts into hopeless confusion.

I saw the conductor looking at me. I said, "Who is that man?"

"He was a member of Congress once, and a good one. But he got caught in a snowdrift in the cars, and like to been starved to death. He got so frost-bitten and frozen up generally, and used up for want of something to eat, that he was sick and out of his head two or three months afterwards. He is all right now, only he is a monomaniac, and when he gets on that old subject he never stops till he has eat up that whole car-load of people he talks about. He would have finished the crowd by this time, only he had to get out here. He has got their names as pat as A, B, C. When he gets them all eat up but himself, he always says:—'Then the hour for the usual election for breakfast having arrived, and there being no opposition, I was duly elected, after which, there being no objections offered, I resigned. Thus I am here.'"

I felt inexpressibly relieved to know that I had only been listening to the harmless vagaries of a madman, instead of the genuine experiences of a bloodthirsty cannibal.

November 1868

Private Habits of Horace Greeley

An intimate acquaintance with a distant relative of the editor of the *Tribune* puts it in my power to furnish the public with the last—positively the very last—link necessary to perfect the chain of knowledge already in its possession concerning Mr. Greeley: I mean his private habits. We know *all* about him as regards every other department of his life and services. Because, whenever a magazinist or a bookmaker is employed to write, and cannot think of a subject, he writes about Horace Greeley. Even the boys in the schools have quit building inspired "compositions" on "The Horse," and have gone to doing Horace Greeley instead; and when declamation-day comes around, their voices are no longer "still for war" and Patrick Henry, but for peace and Horace Greeley. Now, the natural result of all this is that the public have come at last to think that this man has no life but public life, no nature but a public nature, no habits but public habits. This is all wrong. Mr. Greeley *has* a private life. Mr. Greeley *has* private habits.

Mr. Greeley gets up at three o'clock in the morning; for it is one of his favorite maxims that only early rising can keep the health unimpaired and the brain vigorous. He then wakes up all the household and assembles them in the library, by candle-light: and, after quoting the beautiful lines,

> "Early to bed and early to rise
> Make a man healthy, wealthy, and wise,"

he appoints each individual's task for the day, sets him at it with encouraging words, and goes back to bed again. I mention here, in no fault-finding spirit, but with the deference justly due a man who is older and wiser and worthier than I, that he snores awfully. In a moment of irritation, once, I was rash enough to say I never would sleep with him until he broke himself of this unfortunate habit. I have kept my word with bigoted and unwavering determination.

At half-past eleven o'clock Mr. Greeley rises again. He shaves himself. He considers that there is great virtue and economy in shaving himself. He does it with a dull razor, sometimes humming a part of a tune (he knows part of a tune, and takes an innocent delight in regarding it as the first half of Old Hundred; but parties familiar with that hymn have felt obliged to confess that they could not recognize it, and, therefore, the noise he makes is doubtless an unconscious original composition of Mr. Greeley's), and sometimes, when the razor is especially dull, he accompanies himself with a formula like this: "Damn the damned razor, and the damned outcast who made it."—H. G.

He then goes out into his model garden, and applies his vast store of agricultural knowledge to the amelioration of his cabbages; after which he writes an able agricultural article for the instruction of American farmers, his soul cheered the while with the reflection that if cabbages were worth eleven dollars apiece his model farm would pay.

He next goes to breakfast, which is a frugal, abstemious meal with him, and consists of nothing but just such things as the market affords, nothing more. He drinks nothing but water—nothing whatever but water and coffee, and tea, and Scotch ale, and lager beer, and lemonade with a fly in it—sometimes a house fly, and sometimes a horse fly, according to the amount of inspiration required to warm him up to his daily duties. During breakfast he reads the *Tribune* all through, and enjoys the satisfaction of knowing that all the brilliant things in it, written by Young and Cooke, and Hazard, and myself, are attributed to *him* by a confiding and infernal public.

After breakfast he writes a short editorial, and puts a large dash at the beginning of it, thus (———), which is the same as if he put H. G. after it, and takes a savage pleasure in reflecting that none of us understrappers can use that dash, except in profane conversation when chaffing over the outrage. He writes this editorial in his own handwriting. He does it because he is so vain of his penmanship. He always did take an inordinate pride in his penmanship. He hired out once, in his young days, as a writing master, but the enterprise failed. The pupils could not translate his marks with any certainty. His first copy was "Virtue is its own reward," and they got it "Washing with soap is wholly absurd," and so the trustees discharged him for attempting to convey bad morals, through the medium of worse penmanship. But, as I was saying, he writes his morning editorial. Then he tries to read it over, and can't do it, and so sends it to the printers, and *they* try to read it, and can't do it; and so they set it up at random as you may say, putting in what words they can make out, and when they get aground on a long word they put in "reconstruction" or "universal suffrage," and spar off and paddle ahead, and next morning, if the degraded public can tell what it is all about, they say H. G. wrote it, and if they can't, they say it is one of those imbecile understrappers, and that is the end of it.

On Sundays Mr. Greeley sits in a prominent pew in Mr. Chapin's church and lets on that he is asleep, and the congregation regard it as an eccentricity of genius.

When he is going to appear in public, Mr. Greeley spends two hours on his toilet. He is the most painstaking and elaborate man about getting up his dress that lives in America. This is his chiefest and his pleasantest foible. He puts on his old white overcoat and turns up the collar. He puts on a soiled shirt, saved from the wash, and leaves one end of the collar unbuttoned. He puts on his most dilapidated hat, turns it wrong side before, cants it onto the back of his head, and jams an extra dent in the side of it. He puts on his most atrocious boots, and spends fifteen minutes tucking the left leg of his pants into his boot-top in what shall seem the most careless and unstudied way. But his cravat—it is into the arrangement of his cravat that he throws all his soul, all the powers of his great mind. After fixing at it for forty minutes before the glass it is perfect—it is askew in every way—it overflows his coat-collar on one side and sinks into oblivion on the other—it climbs and it delves around about his neck—the knot is conspicuously displayed under his left ear, and it stretches one of its long ends straight out horizontally, and the other goes after his eye, in the good old Toodles fashion—and then, completely and marvelously appareled, Mr. Greeley strides forth, rolling like a sailor, a miracle of astounding costumery, the awe and wonder of the nations!

But I haven't time to tell the rest of his private habits. Suffice it that he is an upright and an honest man—a practical, great-brained man—a useful man to his nation and his gener-

ation—a famous man who has justly earned his celebrity—
and withal the worst-dressed man in this or any other
country, even though he *does* take so thundering much pains
and put on so many frills about it.

November 7, 1868

Concerning Gen. Grant's Intentions

WASHINGTON, Dec. 7, 1868.

To the Editor of The Tribune.

SIR: Do you know that you have a pack of idiots in THE TRIBUNE Bureau here? *I* do. I can explain how and why I know it. I came to the Bureau this morning, as usual, putting myself to trouble and expense to do favors for people who have not asked them, and I said:

"Gen. Grant is speechless."

The head idiot said, "Is this so?"

I replied, "It is."

The first assistant idiot asked a similar question, and received an equally similar answer. Then the Afflicted (meaning your Bureau people) telegraphed it to you, and shortly afterward sold it to the gentlemen of the Associated Press at the usual rates, viz: two doughnuts a line—for *I* never have seen any circulating medium among the Washington correspondents but doughnuts yet.

Then I went away. *Now* I am accused of saying Gen. Grant was dangerously ill, and procuring it to be telegraphed all over the country. It is false. I simply said he was speechless. I simply meant he never made public speeches. I was greatly surprised when they telegraphed it as a matter of news. I came near saying so—even at the time. I couldn't see any sense in making news of it, further than as a means of acquiring doughnuts. All that put it into my head in the first place was the fact that I had been up trying to get at Gen. Grant's opinions and intentions concerning certain matters, and had found him in a manner speechless. I had said to him:

"Sir, what do you propose to do about returning to a specie basis?" To which he made no audible reply. Then I said:

"Sir, do you mean to stop the whisky frauds, or do you mean to connive at them?" To which he replied as before. I now said:

"Do you intend to do straightforwardly and unostentatiously what every true, high-minded Democrat has a right to expect you to do, or will you, with accustomed obstinacy, do otherwise, and thus, by your own act, compel them to resort to assassination?" To which he replied:

"Let us have peace."

I continued: "Sir, shall you insist upon stopping bloodshed at the South, in plain opposition to the Southern will, or shall you generously permit a brave but unfortunate people to worship God according to the dictates of their own consciences?" No reply.

"Sir, do you comprehend that you are not the President of a party?—that you were not elected by your own strength, but by the weakness of the opposition? That, consequently, the Democrats claim you, and justly and righteously expect you to administer the Government from a Democratic point of view?" Riotous silence.

"Sir, who is to report the customary, necessary, coherent, and instructive 'Interviews with the President'—'Mack' of *The Enquirer*, 'J. B. S.' of *The World*, or myself for THE TRIBUNE?"

Gen. Grant said: "Let us have peace."

I resumed: "Sir, do you propose to exterminate the Indians suddenly with soap and education, or doom them to the eternal annoyance of warfare, relieved only by periodical pleasantries of glass beads and perishable treaties?" No response.

"Sir, as each section of the Pacific Railroad is finished are you going to make the companies spike down the rails before you pay? Which is to say, Are you going to be a deliberate tyrant?" A silence indistinguishable from the preceding, was the only response.

"Sir, have you got your Cabinet all set? What are you going to do with those Blairs?"

"Let us have peace."

"Sir, do you comprehend, who it is that is conversing with you?"

"Peace!"

"Sir, am I to have Nasby's Post-Office, or—"

"Go to the—mischief! I have a thousand of your kind around me every day. Questions, questions, questions! If you *must* ask questions, follow Fitch, and inquire after the Erie rolling-mill—you'll have steady employment. I can't stand it, and I won't stand it—I *will* have peace!"

If a man is n't about speechless who never says anything but Let us have peace, pray what is he. And yet those Bureau people abuse me for reporting it. I will never do a kind act again.

MARK TWAIN

December 12, 1868

Open Letter to Com. Vanderbilt

How my heart goes out in sympathy to you! how I do pity you, Commodore Vanderbilt! Most men have at least a few friends, whose devotion is a comfort and a solace to them, but you seem to be the idol of only a crawling swarm of small souls, who love to glorify your most flagrant unworthinesses in print; or praise your vast possessions worshippingly; or sing of your unimportant private habits and sayings and doings, as if your millions gave them dignity; friends who applaud your superhuman stinginess with the same gusto that they do your most magnificent displays of commercial genius and daring, and likewise your most lawless violations of commercial honor—for these infatuated worshippers of dollars not their own seem to make no distinctions, but swing their hats and shout hallelujah every time you do *anything*, no matter what it is. I do pity you. I would pity any man with such friends as these. I should think you would hate the sight of a newspaper. I should think you would not dare to glance at one, for fear you would find in it one of these distressing eulogies of something you had been doing, which was either infinitely trivial or else a matter you ought to be ashamed of. Unacquainted with you as I am, my honest compassion for you still gives me a right to speak in this way. Now, have you ever thought calmly over your newspaper reputation? Have you ever dissected it, to see what it was made of? It would interest you. One day one of your subjects comes out with a column or two detailing your rise from penury to affluence, and praising you as if you were the last and noblest work of God, but unconsciously telling how exquisitely mean a man has to be in order to achieve what you have achieved. Then another subject tells how you drive in the Park, with your scornful head down, never deigning to look to the right or the left, and make glad the thousands who covet a glance of your eye, but driving straight ahead, heedlessly and recklessly, taking the road by force, with a bearing which plainly says, "Let these people get out of the way if they can; but if they can't, and I run over them, and kill them, no matter, I'll pay for them." And then how the retailer of the pleasant anecdote

does grovel in the dust and glorify you, Vanderbilt! Next, a
subject of yours prints a long article to show how, in some
shrewd, underhanded way, you have "come it" over the public with some Erie dodge or other, and added another million
or so to your greasy greenbacks; and behold! *he* praises you,
and never hints that immoral practices, in so prominent a
place as you occupy, are a damning example to the rising
commercial generation—more, a damning thing to the whole
nation, while there are insects like your subjects to make virtues of them in print. Next, a subject tells a most laughable
joke in *Harpers* of how a lady laid a wager of a pair of gloves
that she could touch your heart with the needs of some noble
public charity, which unselfish people were building up for
the succoring of the helpless and the unfortunate, and so persuade you to spare a generous billow to it from your broad
ocean of wealth, and how you listened to the story of want
and suffering, and then—then what?—gave the lady a paltry
dollar (the act in itself an insult to your sister or mine, coming
from a stranger) and said, "Tell your opponent you have won
the gloves." And, having told his little anecdote, how your
loving subject did shake his sides at the bare idea of *your* having generosity enough to be persuaded by any tender womanly pleader into giving a manly lift to any helpless creature
under the sun! What precious friends you do have, Vanderbilt! And next, a subject tells how when you owned the California line of steamers you used to have your pursers make
out false lists of passengers, and thus carry some hundreds
more than the law allowed—in this way breaking the laws of
your country and jeopardizing the lives of your passengers by
overcrowding them during a long, sweltering voyage over
tropical seas, and through a disease-poisoned atmosphere.
And this shrewdness was duly glorified too. But I remember
how those misused passengers used to revile you and curse
you when they got to the Isthmus—and especially the
women and young girls, who were forced to sleep on your
steerage floors, side by side with strange men, who were the
offscourings of creation, and even in the steerage beds with
them, if the poor wretches told the truth; and I do assure you
that nobody who lived in California at that time disbelieved
them—O, praised and envied Vanderbilt! These women were

nothing to you and me; but if they had been, we might have been shamed and angered at this treatment, mightn't we? We cannot rightly judge of matters like these till we sit down and try to fancy these women related to us by ties of blood and affection, but *then* the rare joke of it melts away, and the indignant tides go surging through our veins, poor little Commodore!

There are other anecdotes told of you by your glorifying subjects, but let us pass them by; they only damage you. They only show how unfortunate and how narrowing a thing it is for a man to have wealth who makes a god of it instead of a servant. They only show how soulless it can make him—like that pretty anecdote that tells how a young lawyer charged you $500 for a service, and how you deemed the charge too high, and so went shrewdly to work and won his confidence, and persuaded him to borrow money and put it in Erie, when you knew the stock was going down, and so held him in the trap till he was a ruined man, and then you were revenged; and you gloated over it; and, as usual, your admiring friends told the story in print, and lauded you to the skies. No, let us drop the anecdotes. I don't remember ever reading anything about you which you oughtn't be ashamed of.

All I wish to urge upon you now is, that you crush out your native instincts and go and do something *worthy* of praise—go and do something you need not blush to see in print—do something that may rouse one solitary good impulse in the breasts of your horde of worshippers; prove one solitary good example to the thousands of young men who emulate your energy and your industry; shine as one solitary grain of pure gold upon the heaped rubbish of your life. Do this, I beseech you, else through your example we shall shortly have in our midst five hundred Vanderbilts, which God forbid! Go, now please go, and do one worthy act. Go, boldly, grandly, nobly, and give four dollars to some great public charity. It will break your heart, no doubt; but no matter, you have but a little while to live, and it is better to die suddenly and nobly than live a century longer the same Vanderbilt you are now. Do this, and I declare *I* will praise you too.

Poor Vanderbilt! How I do pity you; and this is honest.

You are an old man, and ought to have some rest, and yet you
have to struggle and struggle, and deny yourself, and rob
yourself of restful sleep and peace of mind, because you need
money so badly. I always feel for a man who is so poverty
ridden as you. Don't misunderstand me, Vanderbilt. I know
you own seventy millions; but then you know and I know
that it isn't what a man has that constitutes wealth. No—it is
to be *satisfied* with what one has; that is wealth. As long as
one sorely *needs* a certain additional amount, that man isn't
rich. Seventy times seventy millions can't make him rich as
long as his poor heart is breaking for more. I am just about
rich enough to buy the least valuable horse in your stable,
perhaps, but I cannot sincerely and honestly take an oath that
I need any more now. And so I am rich. But you! you have
got seventy millions, and you *need* five hundred millions, and
are really suffering for it. Your poverty is something appalling.
I tell you truly that I do not believe I could live twenty-four
hours with the awful weight of four hundred and thirty millions of abject want crushing down upon me. I should die
under it. My soul is so wrought upon by your hapless pauper-
ism, that if you came by me now I would freely put ten cents
in your tin cup, if you carry one, and say, "God pity you,
poor unfortunate!"

Now, I pray you take kindly all that I have said, Vanderbilt,
for I assure you I have meant it kindly, and it is said in an
honester spirit than you are accustomed to find in what is said
to you or about you. And *do* go, now, and do something that
isn't shameful. Do go and do something worthy of a man
possessed of seventy millions—a man whose most trifling act
is remembered and imitated all over the country by younger
men than you. Do not be deceived into the notion that everything you do and say is wonderful, simply because those
asses who publish you so much make it appear so. Do not
deceive yourself. Very often an idea of yours is possessed of
no innate magnificence, but is simply shining with the reflected splendor of your seventy millions. Now, think of it. I
have tried to imitate you and become famous; all the young
men do it; but, bless you, my performances attracted no attention. I gave a crippled beggar girl a two-cent piece and
humorously told her to go to the Fifth Avenue Hotel and

board a week; but nobody published it. If you had done that it would have been regarded as one of the funniest things that ever happened; because you *can* say the flattest things that ever I heard of, Vanderbilt, and have them magnified into wit and wisdom in the papers. And the other day, in Chicago, I talked of buying the entire Union Pacific Railroad, clear to the Rocky Mountains, and running it on my own hook. It was as splendid an idea and as bold an enterprise as ever entered that overpraised brain of yours, but did it excite any newspaper applause? No. If you had conceived it, though, the newspaper world would have gone wild over it. No, sir; other men think and talk as brilliantly as you do, but they don't do it in the glare of seventy millions; so pray do not be deceived by the laudation you receive; more of it belongs to your millions than to you. I say this to warn you against becoming vainglorious on a false basis, and an unsound one—for if your millions were to pass from you you might be surprised and grieved to notice what flat and uncelebrated things you were capable of saying and doing forever afterwards.

You observe that I don't say anything about your soul, Vanderbilt. It is because I have evidence that you haven't any. It would be impossible to convince me that a man of your matchless financial ability would overlook so dazzling an "operation," if you had a soul to save, as the purchasing of millions of years of Paradise, and rest, and peace, and pleasure, for so trifling a sum as ten years blamelessly lived on earth—for you probably haven't longer than that to live now, you know, you are very old. Well, I don't know, after all, possibly you *have* got a soul. But I know you, Vanderbilt—I know you well. You will try to get the purchase cheaper. You will want those millions of years of rest and pleasure, and you will try to make the trade and get the superb stock; but you will wait till you are on your death-bed, and then offer *an hour and forty minutes* for it. I know you so well, Vanderbilt! Still worse men than you do this. The people we hang always send for a priest at the last moment.

I assure you, Vanderbilt, that I mean what I am saying for your good—not to make you mad. Why, the way you are going on, you are no better than those Astors. No, I won't say that; for it is better to be a mean *live* man than a stick—

even a gold-headed stick. And now my lesson is done. It is bound to refresh you and make you feel good; for you must necessarily get sick of puling flattery and sycophancy sometimes, and sigh for a paragraph of honest criticism and abuse for a change. And in parting, I say that, surely, standing as you do upon the pinnacle of moneyed magnificence in America, you must certainly feel a vague desire in you sometimes to do some splendid deed in the interest of commercial probity, or of human charity, or of manly honor and dignity, that shall flash into instant celebrity over the whole nation, and be rehearsed to ambitious boys by their mothers a century after you are dead. I say you must feel so sometimes, for it is only natural, and therefore I urge you to congeal that thought into an act. Go and surprise the whole country by doing something right. Cease to do and say unworthy things, and excessively *little* things, for those reptile friends of yours to magnify in the papers. Snub them thus, or else throttle them.

Yours truly,   MARK TWAIN.

March 1869

Mr. Beecher and the Clergy

The Ministerial Union of Elmira, N. Y., at a recent meeting, passed resolutions disapproving the teachings of Rev. T. K. Beecher, declining to cooperate with him in his Sunday evening services at the Opera House, and requesting him to withdraw from their Monday morning meeting. This has resulted in his withdrawal, and thus the pastors are relieved from further responsibility as to his action. —*N. Y. Evangelist.*

Poor BEECHER! All this time he could do whatever he pleased that was wrong, and then be perfectly serene and comfortable over it, because the Ministerial Union of Elmira was responsible to GOD for it. He could lie, if he wanted to, and those ministers had to answer for it; he could promote discord in the church of CHRIST, and those parties had to make it all right with the Deity as best they could; he could teach false doctrines to empty Opera Houses, and those sorrowing lambs of the Ministerial Union had to get out their sackcloth and ashes and stand responsible for it. He had *such* a comfortable thing of it! But he went too far. In an evil hour he slaughtered the simple geese that laid the golden egg of responsibility for him,—and now they will uncover their customary production and view it with their customary complacency, and lift up their customary cackle in his behalf no more. And so, at last, he finds himself in the novel position of being responsible to GOD for his acts instead of to the Ministerial Union of Elmira. To say that this is appalling, is to state it with a degree of mildness which amounts to insipidity.

We cannot justly estimate this calamity, without first reviewing certain facts that conspired to bring it about. Mr. BEECHER was and is in the habit of preaching to a full congregation in the Independent Congregational Church in this city. The meeting house was not large enough to accommodate all the people who desired admittance. Mr. BEECHER regularly attended the meetings of the Ministerial Union of Elmira every Monday morning, and they received him into their fellowship and never objected to the doctrines which he taught in his church. So, in an unfortunate moment, he conceived the strange idea that they would connive at the teaching of the same doctrines in the same way in a larger house. Therefore he secured the Opera House and proceeded to preach there every Sunday evening to assemblages comprising from a thousand to fifteen hundred persons. He felt warranted in this course by a passage of Scripture which says: "Go ye into all the world and preach the gospel unto every creature." Opera Houses were not ruled out specifically in this passage, and so he considered it proper to regard Opera Houses as a part of "all the world." He looked upon the people who assembled there as coming under the head of "every creature." These ideas were as absurd as they were far-fetched, but still they were the honest ebullitions of a diseased mind. His great mistake was in supposing that when he had the Savior's endorsement of his conduct, he had all that was necessary. He overlooked the fact that there might possibly be a conflict of opinion between the Savior and the Ministerial Union of Elmira. And there *was*. Wherefore, blind and foolish, Mr. BEECHER went to his destruction. The Ministerial Union withdrew their approbation, and left him dangling in the air with no other support than the countenance and approval of the gospel of Christ.

Mr. BEECHER invited his brother ministers to join forces with him and help him conduct the Opera House meetings. They declined with great unanimity. In this they were wrong. Since they did not approve of those meetings, it was a duty they owed to their consciences and their God to contrive their discontinuance. They knew this. They felt it. Yet they turned coldly away and refused to help at those meetings, when they well knew that their help, earnestly and persistently given, was able to kill any great religious enterprise that ever was conceived of.

The ministers refused, and the calamitous meetings at the Opera House continued—and not only continued but grew in interest and importance and sapped of their congregations churches where the gospel was preached with that sweet monotonous tranquility and that impenetrable profundity which stir up such consternation in the strongholds of sin. It is a pity to have to record here that one clergyman refused to preach at the Opera House at Mr. BEECHER'S request, even when that incendiary was sick and disabled—and if that man's conscience justifies him in that refusal, I do not. Under the plea of charity for a sick brother, he could have preached to that Opera House multitude a sermon that would have done incalculable damage to the Opera House experiment. And he need not have been particular about the sermon he chose, either. He could have relied on any he had in his barrel.

The Opera House meetings went on.—Other congregations were thin, and grew thinner, but the Opera House assemblages were vast. Every Sunday night, in spite of sense and reason, multitudes passed by the churches where they might have been saved, and marched deliberately to the Opera House to be damned. The community talked, talked, talked. Everybody discussed the fact that the Ministerial Union disapproved of the Opera House meetings; also the fact that they disapproved of the teachings put forth there. And everybody wondered *how* the Ministerial Union could tell whether to approve or disapprove of those teachings, seeing that those clergymen had *never attended an Opera House meeting*, and therefore didn't know *what* was taught there. Everybody wondered over that curious question—and they had to take it out in wondering.

Mr. BEECHER asked the Ministerial Union to state their objections to the Opera House matter. They could not—at least they did not. He said to them that if they would come squarely out and tell him that they desired the discontinuance of those meetings, he would discontinue them. They declined to do that. Why should they have declined? They had no *right* to decline, and no *excuse* to decline, if they honestly believed that those meetings interfered in the slightest degree with the best interests of religion. [That is a proposition which the profoundest head among them cannot get around]

But the Opera House meetings *went on*. That was the mischief of it. And so, one Monday morning, when Mr. B. appeared at the usual Ministers' meeting, his brother clergymen desired him to come there no more. He asked why. They gave no reason. They simply declined to have his company longer. Mr. B. said he could not accept of this execution without a trial, and since he loved them and had nothing against them, he must insist upon meeting with them in future just the same as ever. And so after that, they met in secret, and thus got rid of this man's importunate affection.

The Ministerial Union had ruled out BEECHER—a point gained. He would get up an excitement about it in public. But that was a miscalculation. He never mentioned it. They waited and waited for the grand crash, but it never came. After all their labor pains, their ministerial mountain had brought forth only a mouse,—and a still-born one at that. BEECHER had not told on them—BEECHER malignantly persisted in not telling on them. The opportunity was slipping away. Alas for the humiliation of it, they had to come out and tell it themselves! And after all, their bombshell did not hurt anybody, when they did explode it. They had ceased to be responsible to God for BEECHER, and yet nobody seemed paralyzed about it. Somehow, it was not even of sufficient importance, apparently, to get into the papers— though even the poor little facts that SMITH has bought a trotting team and Alderman JONES' child has the measles, are chronicled there with avidity. Something *must* be done. As the Ministerial Union had *told* about their desolating action when nobody else considered it of enough importance to tell, they would also *publish* it, now that the reporters failed to see anything in it important enough to print. And so they startled the entire religious world, no doubt, by solemnly printing in the *Evangelist* the paragraph which heads this article. They have got their excommunication-bull started at last. It is going along quite lively, now, and making considerable stir, let us hope. They even know it in Podunk, wherever that may be. It excited a two line paragraph there. Happy, happy world, that knows at last that a little Congress of congregationless clergymen of whom it had never heard before, have crushed a famous BEECHER and reduced his audiences from fifteen hundred down to fourteen hundred and seventy-five at one fell blow! Happy, happy world, that knows at last that these obscure innocents are no longer responsible for the blemishless teachings, the power, the pathos, the logic, and the other and manifold intellectual pyrotechnics that seduce but to damn the Opera House assemblages every Sunday night in Elmira! And miserable, O thrice miserable BEECHER!—for the Ministerial Union of Elmira will never, no never more be responsible to God for his shortcomings. [Excuse these tears]

[For the protection of a man who is uniformly charged with all the newspaper deviltry that sees the light in Elmira journals, I take this opportunity of stating, under oath, duly subscribed before a magistrate, that Mr. BEECHER did not write this article. And further, that he did not inspire it. And further still, the Ministerial Union of Elmira did not write it. And finally, the Ministerial Union did not ask me to write it. No—I have taken up this cudgel in defence of the Ministerial Union of Elmira solely from a love of justice. Without solicitation, I have constituted myself the champion of the Ministerial Union of Elmira, and it shall be a labor of love with me to conduct their side of a quarrel in print for them whenever they desire me to do it—or if they are busy and have not time to ask me, I will cheerfully do it anyhow. In closing this, I must remark that if any question the right of the clergymen of Elmira to turn Mr. BEECHER out of the Ministerial Union, to such I answer that Mr. BEECHER re-created that institution after it had been dead for many years and invited those gentlemen to come into it—which they did, and so of course they have a right to turn him out if they want to. The difference between BEECHER and the man who put an adder in his bosom, is, that BEECHER put in more adders than he did, and consequently had a proportionately livelier time of it when they got warmed up]

Cheerfully,   S'CAT.

April 10, 1869

Personal Habits of the Siamese Twins

I do not wish to write of the personal *habits* of these strange creatures solely, but also of certain curious details of various kinds concerning them, which, belonging only to their private life, have never crept into print. Knowing the Twins intimately, I feel that I am peculiarly well qualified for the task I have taken upon myself.

The Siamese Twins are naturally tender and affectionate in disposition, and have clung to each other with singular fidelity throughout a long and eventful life. Even as children they were inseparable companions; and it was noticed that they always seemed to prefer each other's society to that of any other persons. They nearly always played together; and, so accustomed was their mother to this peculiarity, that, whenever both of them chanced to be lost, she usually only hunted for one of them—satisfied that when she found that one she would find his brother somewhere in the immediate neighborhood. And yet these creatures were ignorant and unlettered—barbarians themselves and the offspring of barbarians, who knew not the light of philosophy and science. What a withering rebuke is this to our boasted civilization, with its quarrelings, its wranglings, and its separations of brothers!

As men, the Twins have not always lived in perfect accord; but, still, there has always been a bond between them which made them unwilling to go away from each other and dwell apart. They have even occupied the same house, as a general thing, and it is believed that they have never failed to even sleep together on any night since they were born. How surely do the habits of a lifetime become second nature to us! The Twins always go to bed at the same time; but Chang usually gets up about an hour before his brother. By an understanding between themselves, Chang does all the in-door work and Eng runs all the errands. This is because Eng likes to go out; Chang's habits are sedentary. However, Chang always goes along. Eng is a Baptist, but Chang is a Roman Catholic; still, to please his brother, Chang consented to be baptized at the same time that Eng was, on condition that it should not "count." During the War they were strong partisans, and both fought gallantly all through the great struggle—Eng on the Union side and Chang on the Confederate. They took each other prisoners at Seven Oaks, but the proofs of capture were so evenly balanced in favor of each that a general army court had to be assembled to determine which one was properly the captor and which the captive. The jury was unable to agree for a long time; but the vexed question was finally decided by agreeing to consider them both prisoners, and then ex-changing them. At one time Chang was convicted of dis-obedience of orders, and sentenced to ten days in the guard house; but Eng, in spite of all arguments, felt obliged to share his imprisonment, notwithstanding he himself was entirely innocent; and so, to save the blameless brother from suffer-ing, they had to discharge both from custody—the just re-ward of faithfulness.

Upon one occasion the brothers fell out about something, and Chang knocked Eng down, and then tripped and fell on him, whereupon both clinched and began to beat and gouge each other without mercy. The bystanders interfered and tried to separate them, but they could not do it, and so allowed them to fight it out. In the end both were disabled, and were carried to the hospital on one and the same shutter.

Their ancient habit of going always together had its draw-backs when they reached man's estate and entered upon the luxury of courting. Both fell in love with the same girl. Each tried to steal clandestine interviews with her, but at the criti-cal moment the other would always turn up. By-and-bye Eng saw, with distraction, that Chang had won the girl's affec-tions; and, from that day forth, he had to bear with the agony of being a witness to all their dainty billing and cooing. But, with a magnanimity that did him infinite credit, he suc-cumbed to his fate, and gave countenance and encouragement to a state of things that bade fair to sunder his generous heart-strings. He sat from seven every evening until two in the morning listening to the fond foolishness of the two lovers, and to the concussion of hundreds of squandered kisses— for the privilege of sharing only one of which he would have given his right hand. But he sat patiently, and waited, and gaped, and yawned, and stretched, and longed for two o'clock to come. And he took long walks with the lovers on moonlight evenings—sometimes traversing ten miles, notwithstanding he was usually suffering from rheumatism. He is an inveterate smoker; but he could not smoke on these occasions, because the young lady was painfully sensitive to the smell of tobacco. Eng cordially wanted them married, and done with it; but, although Chang often asked the momentous question, the young lady could not gather sufficient courage to answer it while Eng was by. However, on one occasion, after having walked some sixteen miles, and sat up till nearly daylight, Eng dropped asleep, from sheer exhaustion, and then the question was asked and answered. The lovers were married. All acquainted with the circumstances applauded the noble brother-in-law. His unwavering faithfulness was the theme of every tongue. He had staid by them all through their long and arduous courtship; and when, at last, they were married, he lifted his hands above their heads, and said with impressive unction, "Bless ye, my children, I will never desert ye!" and he kept his word. Magnanimity like this is all too rare in this cold world.

By-and-bye Eng fell in love with his sister-in-law's sister, and married her, and since that day they have all lived together, night and day, in an exceeding sociability which is touching and beautiful to behold, and is a scathing rebuke to our boasted civilization.

The sympathy existing between these two brothers is so close and so refined that the feelings, the impulses, the emotions of the one are instantly experienced by the other. When one is sick, the other is sick; when one feels pain, the other feels it; when one is angered, the other's temper takes fire. We have already seen with what happy facility they both fell in love with the same girl. Now, Chang is bitterly opposed to all forms of intemperance, on principle; but Eng is the reverse—for, while these men's feelings and emotions are so closely wedded, their reasoning faculties are unfettered; their *thoughts* are free. Chang belongs to the Good Templars, and is a hard-working and enthusiastic supporter of all temperance reforms. But, to his bitter distress, every now and then Eng gets drunk, and, of course, that makes Chang drunk too. This unfortunate thing has been a great sorrow to Chang, for it almost destroys his usefulness in his favorite field of effort. As sure as he is to head a great temperance procession Eng ranges up alongside of him, prompt to the minute and drunk as a lord; but yet no more dismally and hopelessly drunk than his brother who has not tasted a drop. And so the two begin to hoot and yell, and throw mud and bricks at the Good Templars; and, of course, they break up the procession. It would be manifestly wrong to punish Chang for what Eng does, and, therefore, the Good Templars accept the untoward situation, and suffer in silence and sorrow. They have officially and deliberately examined into the matter, and find Chang blameless. They have taken the two brothers and filled Chang full of warm water and sugar and Eng full of whiskey, and in twenty-five minutes it was not possible to tell which was the drunkest. Both were as drunk as loons—and on hot whiskey punches, by the smell of their breath. Yet all the while Chang's moral principles were unsullied, his conscience clear; and so all just men were forced to confess that he was not morally, but only physically drunk. By every right and by every moral evidence the man was strictly sober; and, therefore, it caused his friends all the more anguish to see him shake hands with the pump and try to wind his watch with his night-key.

There is a moral in these solemn warnings—or, at least, a warning in these solemn morals; one or the other. No matter, it is somehow. Let us heed it; let us profit by it.

I could say more of an instructive nature about these interesting beings, but let what I have written suffice.

Having forgotten to mention it sooner, I will remark, in conclusion, that the ages of the Siamese Twins are respectively fifty-one and fifty-three years.

August 1869

A Day at Niagara

CONCERNING THE FALLS

THE TAMED HACKMAN.

Niagara Falls is one of the finest structures in the known world. I have been visiting this favorite watering place recently, for the first time, and was well pleased. A gentleman who was with me said it was customary to be disappointed in the Falls, but that subsequent visits were sure to set that all right. He said it was so with him. He said that the first time he went the hack fares were so much higher than the Falls that the Falls appeared insignificant. But that is all regulated now. The hackmen have been tamed, and numbered, and placarded, and blackguarded, and brought into subjection to the law, and dosed with Moral Principle till they are as meek as missionaries. They are divided into two clans, now, the Regulars and the Privateers, and they employ their idle time in warning the public against each other. The Regulars are under the hotel banners, and do the legitimate at two dollars an hour, and the Privateers prowl darkly on neutral ground and pick off stragglers at half price. But there are no more outrages and extortions. That sort of thing cured itself. It made the Falls unpopular by getting into the newspapers, and whenever a public evil achieves that sort of a success for itself, its days are numbered. It became apparent that either the Falls had to be discontinued or the hackmen had to subside. They could not dam the Falls, and so they damned the hackmen. One can be comfortable and happy there now.

SIGNS AND SYMBOLS.

I drank up most of the American Fall before I learned that the waters were not considered medicinal. Why are people left in ignorance in that way? I might have gone on and ruined a fine property merely for the want of a little trifling information. And yet the sources of information at Niagara Falls are not meagre. You are sometimes in doubt there about what you ought to do, but you are seldom in doubt about what you must *not* do. No—the signs keep you posted. If an infant can read, that infant is measurably safe at Niagara Falls. In your room at the hotel you will find your course marked out for you in the most convenient way by means of placards on the wall, like these:

"Pull the bell-rope gently, but don't jerk."

"Bolt your door."

"Don't scrape matches on the wall."

"Turn off your gas when you retire."

"Tie up your dog."

"If you place your boots outside the door they will be blacked—but the house will not be responsible for their return." [This is a confusing and tanglesome proposition—because it moves you to deliberate long and painfully as to whether it will really be any object to you to have your boots blacked unless they *are* returned.]

"Give your key to the omnibus driver if you forget and carry it off with you."

Outside the hotel, wherever you wander, you are intelligently assisted by the signs. You cannot come to grief as long as you are in your right mind. But the difficulty is to *stay* in your right mind with so much instruction to keep track of. For instance:

"Keep off the grass."

"Don't climb the trees."

"Hands off the vegetables."

"Do not hitch your horse to the shrubbery."

"Visit the Cave of the Winds."

"Have your portrait taken in your carriage."

"Forty per cent. in gold levied on all pea-nuts or other Indian Curiosities purchased in Canada."

"Photographs of the Falls taken here."

"Visitors will please notify the Superintendent of any neglect on the part of employees to charge for commodities or services." [No inattention of this kind observed.]

"Don't throw stones down—they may hit people below."

"The proprietors will not be responsible for parties who jump over the Falls." [More shirking of responsibility—it appears to be the prevailing thing here.]

I always had a high regard for the Signers of the Declaration of Independence, but now they do not really seem to

amount to much alongside the signers of Niagara Falls. To tell
the plain truth, the multitude of signs annoyed me. It was
because I noticed at last that they always happened to prohibit exactly the very thing I was just wanting to do. I desired
to roll on the grass: the sign prohibited it. I wished to climb a
tree: the sign prohibited it. I longed to smoke: a sign forbade
it. And I was just in the act of throwing a stone over to astonish and pulverize such parties as might be picknicking below,
when a sign I have just mentioned forbade that. Even that
poor satisfaction was denied me, (and I a friendless orphan.)
—There was no recourse, now, but to seek consolation in the
flowing bowl. I drew my flask from my pocket, but it was all
in vain. A sign confronted me which said:

"No drinking allowed on these premises."

On that spot I might have perished of thirst, but for the
saving words of an honored maxim that flitted through my
memory at the critical moment.—"All signs fail in a dry
time." Common law takes precedence of the statutes. I was
saved.

THE NOBLE RED MAN.

The noble Red Man has always been a darling of mine. I
love to read about him in tales and legends and romances. I
love to read of his inspired sagacity; and his love of the wild
free life of mountain and forest; and his grand truthfulness,
his hatred of treachery, and his general nobility of character;
and his stately metaphorical manner of speech; and his chivalrous love for his dusky maiden; and the picturesque pomp of
his dress and accoutrement. Especially the picturesque pomp
of his dress and accoutrement. When I found the shops at
Niagara Falls full of dainty Indian bead-work, and stunning
moccasins, and equally stunning toy figures representing
human beings who carried their weapons in holes bored
through their arms and bodies, and had feet shaped like a pie,
I was filled with emotion. I knew that now, at last, I was
going to come face to face with the Noble Red Man. A lady
clerk in a shop told me, indeed, that all her grand array of
curiosities were made by the Indians, and that there were
plenty about the Falls, and that they were friendly and it
would not be dangerous to speak to them. And sure enough,

as I approached the bridge leading over to Luna Island, I came upon a noble old Son of the Forest sitting under a tree, diligently at work on a bead reticule. He wore a slouch hat and brogans, and had a short black pipe in his mouth. Thus does the baneful contact with our effeminate civilization dilute the picturesque pomp which is so natural to the Indian when far removed from us in his native haunts. I addressed the relic as follows:

"Is the Wawhoo-Wang-Wang of the Wack-a-Whack happy? Does the great Speckled Thunder sigh for the war-path, or is his heart contented with dreaming of his dusky maiden, the Pride of the Forest? Does the mighty sachem yearn to drink the blood of his enemies, or is he satisfied to make bead reticules for the papooses of the pale face? Speak, sublime relic of by-gone grandeur—venerable ruin, speak!"

The relic said:

"An is it mesilf, Dinnis Hooligan, that ye'd be takin for a bloody Injin, ye drawlin' lantern-jawed, spider-legged divil! By the piper that played before Moses, I'll ate ye!"

I went away from there.

Bye and bye, in the neighborhood of the Terrapin Tower, I came upon a gentle daughter of the aborigines, in fringed and beaded buckskin moccasins and leggins, seated on a bench with her pretty wares about her. She had just carved out a wooden chief that had a strong family resemblance to a clothes pin, and was now boring a hole through his abdomen to put his bow through. I hesitated a moment and then addressed her:

"Is the heart of the forest maiden heavy? Is the Laughing-Tadpole lonely? Does she mourn over the extinguished council-fires of her race and the vanished glory of her ancestors? Or does her sad spirit wander afar toward the hunting grounds whither her brave Gobbler-of-the-Lightnings is gone? Why is my daughter silent? Has she aught against the pale-face stranger?"

The maiden said:

"Faix, an is it Biddy Malone ye dare to be callin' names! Lave this or I'll shy your lean carcass over the catharact, ye sniveling blagyard!"

I adjourned from there, also. "Confound these Indians," I

said, "they told me they were tame—but, if appearances should go for anything, I should say they were all on the war-path."

I made one more attempt to fraternise with them, and only one. I came upon a camp of them gathered in the shade of a great tree, making wampum and moccasins, and addressed them in the language of friendship:

"Noble Red Men, Braves, Grand Sachems, War-Chiefs, Squaws and High-you-Muck-a-Mucks, the pale face from the land of the setting sun greets you! You, Beneficent Polecat—you, Devourer-of-Mountains—you, Roaring-Thundergust—you, Bullyboye-with-a-Glass-Eye—the pale face from beyond the great waters greets you all! War and pestilence have thinned your ranks and destroyed your once proud nation. Poker, and seven-up, and a vain modern expense for soap, unknown to your glorious ancestors, have depleted your purses. Appropriating in your simplicity the property of others has gotten you into trouble. Misrepresenting facts, in your sinless innocence, has damaged your reputation with the soulless usurper. Trading for forty-rod whisky to enable you to get drunk and happy and tomahawk your families has played the everlasting mischief with the picturesque pomp of your dress, and here you are, in the broad light of the nineteenth century, gotten up like the ragtag and bobtail of the purlieus of New York! For shame! Remember your ancestors! Recall their mighty deeds! Remember Uncas!—and Red Jacket!—and Hole-in-the-Day!—and Horace Greeley! Emulate their achievements! Unfurl yourselves under my banner, noble savages, illustrious guttersnipes——"

"Down wid him!"

"Scoop the blagyard!"

"Hang him!"

"Burn him!"

"Dhrownd him!"

It was the quickest operation that ever was. I simply saw a sudden flash in the air of clubs, brickbats, fists, bead baskets, and moccasins—a single flash, and they all appeared to hit me at once, and no two of them in the same place. In the next instant the entire tribe was upon me. They tore all the clothes off me, they broke my arms and legs, they gave me a thump that dented the top of my head till it would hold coffee like a saucer; and to crown their disgraceful proceedings and add insult to injury, they threw me over the Horseshoe Fall and I got wet.

About ninety or a hundred feet from the top, the remains of my vest caught on a projecting rock and I was almost drowned before I could get loose. I finally fell, and brought up in a world of white foam at the foot of the Fall, whose celled and bubbly masses towered up several inches above my head. Of course I got into the eddy. I sailed round and round in it forty-four times—chasing a chip and gaining on it—each round trip a half a mile—reaching for the same bush on the bank forty-four times, and just exactly missing it by a hair's-breadth every time. At last a man walked down and sat down close to that bush, and put a pipe in his mouth, and lit a match, and followed me with one eye and kept the other on the match while he sheltered it in his hands from the wind. Presently a puff of wind blew it out. The next time I swept around he said:

"Got a match?"

"Yes—in my other vest. Help me out, please."

"Not for Joe."

When I came around again I said:

"Excuse the seemingly impertinent curiosity of a drowning man, but will you explain this singular conduct of yours?"

"With pleasure. I am the Coroner. Don't hurry on my account. I can wait for you. But I wish I had a match."

I said: "Take my place and I'll go and get you one."

He declined. This lack of confidence on his part created a coolness between us, and from that time forward I avoided him. It was my idea, in case anything happened to me, to so time the occurrence as to throw my custom into the hands of the opposition coroner over on the American side. At last a policeman came along and arrested me for disturbing the peace by yelling at people on shore for help. The Judge fined me, but I had the advantage of him. My money was with my pantaloons, and my pantaloons were with the Indians.

Thus I escaped. I am now lying in a very critical condition. At least I am lying, anyway—critical or not critical.

I am hurt all over, but I cannot tell the full extent yet,

because the doctor is not done taking the inventory. He will make out my manifest this evening. However, thus far he thinks only six of my wounds are fatal. I don't mind the others.

Upon regaining my right mind, I said:

"It is an awfully savage tribe of Indians that do the bead work and moccasins for Niagara Falls, doctor. Where are they from?"

"Limerick, my son."

I shall not be able to finish my remarks about Niagara Falls until I get better.

August 21, 1869

A Fine Old Man

John Wagner, the oldest man in Buffalo—104 years—recently walked a mile and a half in two weeks. He is as cheerful and bright as any of these other old men that charge around so in the newspapers, and is in every way as remarkable. Last November he walked five blocks in a rain storm without any shelter but an umbrella, and cast his vote for Grant, remarking that he had voted for forty-seven Presidents—which was a lie. His "second crop of rich brown hair" arrived from New York yesterday, and he has a new set of teeth coming—from Philadelphia. He is to be married next week to a girl 102 years old, who still takes in washing. They have been engaged 89 years, but their parents persistently refused their consent until three days ago. John Wagner is two years older than the Rhode Island veteran, and yet has never tasted a drop of liquor in his life, unless you count whisky.

August 25, 1869

Journalism in Tennessee

The editor of the Memphis *Avalanche* swoops thus mildly down upon a correspondent who posted him as a Radical: "While he was writing the first word, the middle word, dotting his i's, crossing his t's, and punching his period, he knew he was concocting a sentence that was saturated with infamy and reeking with falsehood."
—*Exchange*.

I was told by the physician that a Southern climate would improve my health, and so I went down to Tennessee and got a berth on the *Morning Glory and Johnson County War-Whoop*, as associate editor. When I went on duty I found the chief editor sitting tilted back in a three-legged chair with his feet on a pine table. There was another pine table in the room, and another afflicted chair, and both were half buried under newspapers and scraps and sheets of manuscript. There was a wooden box of sand, sprinkled with cigar stubs and "old soldiers," and a stove with a door hanging by its upper hinge. The chief editor had a long-tailed black cloth frock coat on, and white linen pants. His boots were small and neatly blacked. He wore a ruffled shirt, a large seal ring, a standing collar of obsolete pattern and a checkered neckerchief with the ends hanging down. Date of costume, about 1848. He was smoking a cigar and trying to think of a word. And in trying to think of a word, and in pawing his hair for it, he had rumpled his locks a good deal. He was scowling fearfully, and I judged that he was concocting a particularly knotty editorial. He told me to take the exchanges and skim through them and write up the "Spirit of the Tennessee Press," condensing into the article all of their contents that seemed of interest.

I wrote as follows:

"SPIRIT OF THE TENNESSEE PRESS.

"The editors of the *Semi-Weekly Earthquake* evidently labor under a misapprehension with regard to the Ballyhack railroad. It is not the object of the company to leave Buzzardville off to one side. On the contrary they consider it one of the most important points along the line, and consequently can have no desire to slight it. The gentlemen of the *Earthquake* will of course take pleasure in making the correction.

"John W. Blossom, Esq., the able editor of the Higginsville *Thunderbolt and Battle-Cry of Freedom*, arrived in the city yesterday. He is stopping at the Van Buren House.

"We observe that our cotemporary of the Mud Springs *Morning Howl* has fallen into the error of supposing that the election of Van Werter is not an established fact, but he will have discovered his mistake before this reminder reaches him, no doubt. He was doubtless misled by incomplete election returns.

"It is pleasant to note that the city of Blathersville is endeavoring to contract with some New York gentlemen to pave its well nigh impassable streets with the Nicholson pavement. But it is difficult to accomplish a desire like this since Memphis got some New Yorkers to do a like service for her and then declined to pay for it. However the *Daily Hurrah* still urges the measure with ability, and seems confident of ultimate success.

"We are pained to learn that Col. Bascom, chief editor of the *Dying Shriek for Liberty*, fell in the street a few evenings since and broke his leg. He has lately been suffering with debility, caused by overwork and anxiety on account of sickness in his family, and it is supposed that he fainted from the exertion of walking too much in the sun."

I passed my manuscript over to the chief editor for acceptance, alteration or destruction. He glanced at it and his face clouded. He ran his eye down the pages, and his countenance grew portentous. It was easy to see that something was wrong. Presently he sprang up and said:

"Thunder and lightning! Do you suppose I am going to speak of those cattle that way? Do you suppose my subscribers are going to stand such gruel as that? Give me the pen!"

I never saw a pen scrape and scratch its way so viciously, or plough through another man's verbs and adjectives so relentlessly. While he was in the midst of his work somebody shot at him through the open window and marred the symmetry of his ear.

"Ah," said he, "that is that scoundrel Smith, of the *Moral Volcano*—he was due yesterday." And he snatched a navy revolver from his belt and fired. Smith dropped, shot in the thigh. The shot spoiled Smith's aim, who was just taking a second chance, and he crippled a stranger. It was me. Merely a finger shot off.

Then the chief editor went on with his erasures and interlineations. Just as he finished them a hand-grenade came down the stove-pipe, and the explosion shivered the stove into a thousand fragments. However, it did no further damage, except that a vagrant piece knocked a couple of my teeth out.

"That stove is utterly ruined," said the chief editor.

I said I believed it was.

"Well, no matter—don't want it this kind of weather. I know the man that did it. I'll get him. Now *here* is the way this stuff ought to be written."

I took the manuscript. It was scarred with erasures and interlineations till its mother wouldn't have known it, if it had had one. It now read as follows:

"SPIRIT OF THE TENNESSEE PRESS.

"The inveterate liars of the *Semi-Weekly Earthquake* are evidently endeavoring to palm off upon a noble and chivalrous people another of their vile and brutal falsehoods with regard to that most glorious conception of the nineteenth century, the Ballyhack railroad. The idea that Buzzardville was to be left off at one side originated in their own fulsome brains—or rather in the settlings which *they* regard as brains. They had better swallow this lie, and not stop to chew it, either, if they want to save their abandoned, reptile carcasses the cowhiding they so richly deserve.

"That ass, Blossom of the Higginsville *Thunderbolt and Battle-Cry of Freedom*, is down here again, bumming his board at the Van Buren.

"We observe that the besotted blackguard of the Mud Springs *Morning Howl* is giving out, with his usual propensity for lying, that Van Werter is not elected. The heaven-born mission of journalism is to disseminate truth—to eradicate error—to educate, refine and elevate the tone of public morals and manners, and make all men more gentle, more virtuous, more charitable, and in all ways better, and holier and happier—and yet this black-hearted villain, this hell-spawned miscreant, prostitutes his great office persistently to the dissemination of falsehood, calumny, vituperation and degrading vulgarity. His paper is notoriously unfit to take into the people's homes, and ought to be banished to the gambling hells and brothels where the mass of reeking pollution which does duty as its editor, lives and moves, and has his being.

"Blathersville wants a Nicholson pavement—it wants a jail and a poor-house more. The idea of a pavement in a one-horse town with two gin-mills and a blacksmith shop in it, and that mustard-plaster of a newspaper, the *Daily Hurrah*! Better borrow of Memphis, where the article is cheap. The crawling insect, Buckner, who edits the *Hurrah*, is braying about this pavement business with his customary loud-mouthed imbecility, and imagining that he is talking sense. Such foul, mephitic scum as this verminous Buckner, are a disgrace to journalism.

"That degraded ruffian Bascom, of the *Dying Shriek for Liberty*, fell down and broke his leg yesterday—pity it wasn't his neck. He says it was 'debility caused by overwork and anxiety!' It was debility caused by trying to lug six gallons of forty-rod whisky around town when his hide is only gauged for four, and anxiety about where he was going to bum another six. He 'fainted from the exertion of walking too much in the sun!' And well he might say that—but if he would walk *straight* he would get just as far and not have to walk half as much. For years the pure air of this town has been rendered perilous by the deadly breath of this perambulating pestilence, this pulpy bloat, this steaming, animated tank of mendacity, gin and profanity, this Bascom! Perish all such from out the sacred and majestic mission of journalism!"

"Now *that* is the way to write—peppery and to the point. Mush-and-milk journalism gives me the fan-tods."

About this time a brick came through the window with a splintering crash, and gave me a considerable of a jolt in the middle of the back. I moved out of range—I began to feel in the way. The chief said:

"That was the Colonel, likely, I've been expecting him for two days. He will be up, now, right away."

He was correct. The "Colonel" appeared in the door a moment afterward, with a dragoon revolver in his hand. He said:

"Sir, have I the honor of addressing the white-livered poltroon who edits this mangy sheet?"

"You have—be seated, Sir—be careful of the chair, one of the legs is gone. I believe I have the pleasure of addressing the blatant, black-hearted scoundrel, Col. Blatherskite Tecumseh?"

"The same. I have a little account to settle with you. If you are at leisure, we will begin."

"I have an article on the 'Encouraging Progress of Moral and Intellectual Development in America,' to finish, but there is no hurry. Begin."

Both pistols rang out their fierce clamor at the same instant. The chief lost a lock of hair, and the Colonel's bullet ended its career in the fleshy part of my thigh. The Colonel's left shoulder was clipped a little. They fired again. Both missed their men this time, but I got my share, a shot in the arm. At the third fire both gentlemen were wounded slightly, and I had a knuckle chipped. I then said I believed I would go out and take a walk, as this was a private matter and I had a delicacy about participating in it further. But both gentlemen begged me to keep my seat and assured me that I was not in the way. I had thought differently, up to this time.

They then talked about the elections and the crops a while, and I fell to tying up my wounds. But presently they opened fire again with animation, and every shot took effect—but it is proper to remark that five out of the six fell to my share. The sixth one mortally wounded the Colonel, who remarked, with fine humor, that he would have to say good morning, now, as he had business up town. He then inquired the way to the undertaker's and left. The chief turned to me and said:

"I am expecting company to dinner and shall have to get ready. It will be a favor to me if you will read proof and attend to the customers."

I winced a little at the idea of attending to the customers, but I was too bewildered by the fusillade that was still ringing in my ears to think of anything to say. He continued:

"Jones will be here at 3. Cowhide him. Gillespie will call earlier, perhaps—throw him out of the window. Ferguson will be along about 4—kill him. That is all for to-day, I believe. If you have any odd time, you may write a blistering article on the police—give the Chief Inspector rats. The cowhides are under the table; weapons in the drawer—ammunition there in the corner—lint and bandages up there in the pigeon-holes. In case of accident, go to Lancet, the surgeon, down stairs. He advertises—we take it out in trade."

He was gone. I shuddered. At the end of the next three hours I had been through perils so awful that all peace of mind and all cheerfulness had gone from me. Gillespie had called, and thrown *me* out of the window. Jones arrived promptly, and when I got ready to do the cowhiding, he took the job off my hands. In an encounter with a stranger, not in the bill of fare, I had lost my scalp. Another stranger, by the name of Thompson, left me a mere wreck and ruin of chaotic rags. And at last, at bay in the corner, and beset by an infuriated mob of editors, blacklegs, politicians and desperadoes, who raved and swore and flourished their weapons about my head till the air shimmered with glancing flashes of steel, I was in the act of resigning my berth on the paper when the chief arrived, and with him a rabble of charmed and enthusiastic friends. Then ensued a scene of riot and carnage such as no human pen, or steel one either, could describe. People were shot, probed, dismembered, blown up, thrown out of the window. There was a brief tornado of murky blasphemy, with a confused and frantic war-dance glimmering through it, and then all was over. In five minutes there was silence, and the gory chief and I sat alone and surveyed the sanguinary ruin that strewed the floor around us. He said:

"You'll like this place when you get used to it." I said:

"I'll have to get you to excuse me. I think maybe I might write to suit you, after a while, as soon as I had had some practice and learned the language—I am confident I could. But to speak the plain truth, that sort of energy of expression has its inconveniences, and a man is liable to interruption. You see that, yourself. Vigorous writing is calculated to elevate the public, no doubt, but then I do not like to attract so much attention as it calls forth. I can't write with comfort when I am interrupted so much as I have been to-day. I like this berth well enough, but I don't like to be left here to wait on the customers. The experiences are novel, I grant you, and entertaining, too, after a fashion, but they are not judiciously distributed. A gentleman shoots at you, through the window, and cripples *me*; a bomb-shell comes down the stove-pipe for your gratification, and sends the stove door down *my* throat; a friend drops in to swap compliments with you, and freckles *me* with bullet holes till my skin won't hold my principles; you go to dinner, and Jones comes with his cowhide, Gillespie throws me out of the window, Thompson tears all my clothes off, and an entire stranger takes my scalp with the easy freedom of an old acquaintance; and in less than five minutes all the blackguards in the country arrive in their war paint and proceed to scare the rest of me to death with their

tomahawks. Take it altogether, I never have had such a spirited time in all my life as I have had to-day. No. I like you,
and I like your calm, unruffled way of explaining things to the
customers, but you see I am not used to it. The Southern
heart is too impulsive—Southern hospitality is too lavish
with the stranger. The paragraphs which I have written to-
day, and into whose cold sentences your masterly hand has
infused the fervent spirit of Tennessean journalism, will wake
up another nest of hornets. All that mob of editors will
come—and they will come hungry, too, and want somebody
for breakfast. I shall have to bid you adieu. I decline to be
present at these festivities. I came South for my health—I will
go back on the same errand, and suddenly. Tennessee journalism is too stirring for me." After which, we parted, with
mutual regret, and I took apartments at the hospital.

September 4, 1869

The Last Words of Great Men

Marshal Neil's last words were: *"L'armee francaise!"* (The French army.)—*Exchange*.

What a sad thing it is to see a man close a grand career with a plagiarism in his mouth. Napoleon's last words were, *"Tête d'armée."* (Head of the army.) Neither of those remarks amounts to anything as "last words," and reflect little credit upon the utterers. A distinguished man should be as particular about his last words as he is about his last breath. He should write them out on a slip of paper and take the judgment of his friends on them. He should never leave such a thing to the last hour of his life, and trust to an intellectual spurt at the last moment to enable him to say something smart with his latest gasp and launch into eternity with grandeur. No—a man is apt to be too much fagged and exhausted, both in body and mind, at such a time, to be reliable; and may be the very thing he wants to say, he cannot think of to save him; and besides, there are his weeping friends bothering around; and worse than all, as likely as not he may have to deliver his last gasp when he is not expecting to. A man cannot always expect to think of a natty thing to say under such circumstances, and so it is pure egotistic ostentation to put it off. There is hardly a case on record where a man came to his last moment unprepared and said a good thing—hardly a case where a man trusted to that last moment and did not make a solemn botch of it and go out of the world feeling absurd.

Now there was Daniel Webster. Nobody could tell *him* anything. *He* was not afraid. *He* could do something neat when the time came. And how did it turn out? Why, his will had to be fixed over; and then all his relations came; and first one thing and then another interfered, till at last he only had a chance to say "I still live," and up he went. Of course, he didn't still live, because he died—and so he might as well have kept his last words to himself as to have gone and made such a failure of it as that. A week before that, fifteen minutes of calm reflection would have enabled that man to contrive

some last words that would have been a credit to himself and
a comfort to his family for generations to come.

And there was John Quincy Adams. Relying on his splendid abilities and his coolness in emergencies, *he* trusted to a
happy hit at the last moment to carry him through, and what
was the result? Death smote him in the House of Representatives, and he observed, casually, "This is the last of earth."
The last of earth! Why the "last of earth," when there was so
much more left? If he had said it was the last rose of summer,
or the last run of shad, it would have had just as much point
to it. What he meant to say, was, "Adam was the first, and
Adams is the last of earth," but he put it off a trifle too long,
and so he had to go with that unmeaning observation on his
lips.

And there we have Napoleon. *"Tête d'armée."* That don't
mean anything. Taken by itself, "Head of the army" is no
more important than "Head of the police." And yet that was a
man who could have said a good thing if he had barred out
the doctor and studied over it a while. And this Marshal Neil,
with half a century at his disposal, could not dash off anything better, in his last moments, than a poor plagiarism of
another man's last words which were not worth plagiarizing
in the first place. "The French army!" Perfectly irrelevant—
perfectly flat—utterly pointless. But if he had closed one eye
significantly and said, "The subscriber has made it *lively* for
the French army," and then thrown a little of the comic into
his last gasp, it would have been a thing to remember with
satisfaction all the rest of his life. I do wish our great men
would quit saying these flat things just at the moment they
die. Let us have their next-to-their-last words for a while, and
see if we cannot patch up something from them that will be a
little more satisfactory. The public does not wish to be outraged in this way all the time.

But when we come to call to mind the last words of parties
who took the trouble to make proper preparation for the occasion, we immediately notice a happy difference in the result.

There was Chesterfield. Lord Chesterfield had labored all
his life to build up the most shining reputation for affability
and elegance of speech and manners the world has ever seen.
And could you suppose he failed to appreciate the efficiency

of characteristic "last words" in the matter of seizing the successfully driven nail of such a reputation and clinching it on the other side for ever? Not he. He prepared himself. He kept his eye on the clock and his finger on his pulse. He awaited his chance. And at last, when he knew his time was come, he pretended to think a new visitor had entered, and so, with the rattle in his throat emphasized for dramatic effect, he said to the servant, "Shin around John, and get the gentleman a chair." And then he died, amid thunders of applause.

Next we have Benjamin Franklin. Franklin the author of Poor Richard's quaint sayings; Franklin the immortal axiom-builder, who used to sit up nights reducing the rankest old threadbare platitudes to crisp and snappy maxims that had a nice, varnished, original look in their new regimentals; who said "Virtue is its own reward;" who said "Procrastination is the thief of time;" who said "Time and tide wait for no man," and "Necessity is the mother of invention;" good old Franklin the Josh Billings of the eighteenth century—though sooth to say, the latter transcends him in proverbial originality as much as he falls short of him in correctness of orthography. What sort of tactics did Franklin pursue? He pondered over his last words for as much as two weeks, and then when the time came he said "None but the brave deserve the fair," and died happy. He could not have said a sweeter thing if he had lived till he was an idiot.

Byron made a poor business of it, and could not think of anything to say, at the last moment, but "Augusta—sister—Lady Byron—tell Harriet Beecher Stowe"—etc., etc.—but Shakspeare was ready and said, "England expects every man to do his duty!" and went off with splendid eclat.

And there are other instances of sagacious preparation for a felicitous closing remark. For instance:

Joan of Arc said—"Tramp, tramp, tramp, the boys are marching."

Alexander the Great said—"Another of, of those Santa Cruz punches, if you please."

The Empress Josephine said—"Not for Jo——" and could get no further.

Cleopatra said—"The Old Guard dies, but never surrenders!"

Sir Walter Raleigh said—"Executioner, can I take your whetstone a moment, please?"

John Smith said—"Alas, I am the last of my race!"

Queen Elizabeth said—"Oh, I would give my kingdom for one moment more—I have forgotten my last words."

And Red Jacket, the noblest Indian brave that ever wielded tomahawk in defence of a friendless and persecuted race, expired with these touching words upon his lips: *"Wawkawampanoosuc, winnebagowallawallasagamoresaskatchewan."* There was not a dry eye in the wigwam.

Let not this lesson be lost upon our public men. Let them take a healthy moment for preparation, and contrive some last words that shall be neat and to the point. Let Louis Napoleon say:

"I am content to follow my uncle, still—I do not desire to improve on his last words. Put me down for *'téte d'armée.'*"

And Garret Davis: "Let me recite the unabridged dictionary."

And H. G.: "I desire now, to say a few words on political economy."

And Mr. Bergh: "Only take part of me at a time if the load will be fatiguing to the hearse-horses."

And Andrew Johnson: "I have been an alderman, member of Congress, Governor, Senator, Pres—— adieu, you know the rest."

And Seward: "Alas!—ka."

And Grant: "O."

All of which is respectfully submitted, with the most honorable intentions.

P. S.—I am obliged to leave out the illustrations, this time. The artist finds it impossible to make pictures of people's last words.

September 11, 1869

The Legend of the Capitoline Venus

CHAPTER I.

[Scene—An Artist's Studio in Rome.]

"Oh, George, I *do* love you!"

"Bless your dear heart, Mary, I know that—*why* is your father so obdurate!"

"George, he means well, but art is folly to him—he only understands groceries. He thinks you would starve me."

"Confound his wisdom—it savors of inspiration. Why am not I a money making, bowelless grocer, instead of a divinely-gifted sculptor with nothing to eat?"

"Do not despond, Georgy, dear—all his prejudices will fade away as soon as you shall have acquired fifty thousand dol——"

"Fifty thousand demons! Child I am in arrears for my board!"

CHAPTER II.

[Scene—A Dwelling in Rome.]

"My dear sir, it is useless to talk. I haven't any thing against you, but I can't let my daughter marry a hash of love, art and starvation—I believe you have nothing else to offer."

"Sir, I am poor, I grant you. But is fame nothing? The Hon. Bellamy Foodle, of Arkansas, says that my new statue of America is a clever piece of sculpture, and he is satisfied that my name will one day be famous."

"Bosh! What does that Arkansas ass know about it? Fame's nothing—the market price of your marble scare-crow is the thing to look at. Took you six months to chisel it, and you can't sell it for a hundred dollars. No sir! Show me fifty thousand dollars and you can have my daughter—otherwise she marries young Simper. You have just six months to raise the money in. Good morning, sir."

"Alas! Woe is me!"

CHAPTER III.

[Scene—The Studio.]

"Oh, John, friend of my boyhood, I am the unhappiest of men."

"You're an ass!"

"I have nothing left to love but my poor statue—and see, even she has no sympathy for me in her cold marble countenance—so beautiful and so heartless!"

"You're a fool!"

"Oh, John!"

"Oh, fudge! Didn't you say you had six months to raise the money in?"

"Don't deride my agony, John. If I had six centuries what good would it do? How could it help a poor wretch without name, capital or friends!"

"Idiot! Coward! Baby! Six months to raise the money in—and five will do!"

"Are you insane?"

"Six months—an abundance. Leave it to me. I'll raise it."

"What do you mean, John? How on earth can you raise such a monstrous sum for *me*?"

"*Will* you let that be *my* business, and not meddle? Will you leave the thing in my hands? Will you swear to submit to whatever I do? Will you pledge me to find no fault with my actions?"

"I am dizzy—bewildered—but I swear."

John took up a hammer and deliberately smashed the nose of America! He made another pass and two of her fingers fell to the floor—another, and part of an ear came away—another, and a row of toes were mangled and dismembered—another, and the left leg, from the knee down, lay a fragmentary ruin!

John put on his hat and departed.

George gazed speechless upon the battered and grotesque nightmare before him for the space of thirty seconds, and then wilted to the floor and went into convulsions.

John returned presently with a carriage, got the broken-hearted artist and the broken-legged statue aboard, and drove off, whistling low and tranquilly. He left the artist at his lodgings, and drove off and disappeared down the *Via Quirinalis* with the statue.

CHAPTER IV.

[Scene—The Studio.]

"The six months will be up at two o'clock to-day! Oh, agony! My life is blighted. I would that I were dead. I had no supper yesterday. I have had no breakfast to-day. I dare not enter an eating-house. And hungry?—don't mention it! My bootmaker duns me to death—my tailor duns me—my landlord haunts me. I am miserable! I haven't seen John since that awful day. *She* smiles on me tenderly when we meet in the great thoroughfares, but her old flint of a father makes her look in the other direction in short order. Now who is knocking at that door? Who is come to prosecute me? That malignant villain the bootmaker, I'll warrant. *Come in!*"

"Ah, happiness attend your highness—Heaven be propitious to your grace! I have brought my lord's new boots—ah, say nothing about the pay, there is no hurry, none in the world. Shall be proud if my noble lord will continue to honor me with his custom—ah, adieu!"

"Brought the boots himself! Don't want his pay! Takes his leave with a bow and a scrape fit to honor majesty withal! Desires a continuance of my custom! Is the world coming to an end? Of all the——*come in!*"

"Pardon, signor, but I have brought your new suit——"

"Come in."

"A thousand pardons for this intrusion, your worship! But I have prepared the beautiful suite of rooms below for you—this wretched den is but ill suited to——"

"Come in!"

"I have called to say that your credit at our bank sometime since unfortunately interrupted, is entirely and most satisfactorily restored, and we shall be most happy if you will draw upon us for any——"

"Come in!"

"My noble boy, she is yours! She'll be here in a moment! Take her—marry her—love her—be happy!—God bless you both! Hip, hip, hur——"

"Come in!"

"Oh, George, my own darling, we are saved!"

"Oh, Mary, my own darling, we *are* saved—but I'll swear I don't know why!"

CHAPTER V.

[Scene—A Roman Café.]

One of a group of American gentlemen reads and translates from the weekly edition of *Il Slangwhanger di Roma* as follows:

"WONDERFUL DISCOVERY!—Some six months ago Signor John Smithe, an American gentleman now some years a resident of Rome, purchased for a trifle a small piece of ground in the Campagna, just beyond the tomb of the Scipio family, from the owner, a bankrupt relative of the Princess Borghese. Mr. Smithe afterward went to the Minister of the Public Records and had the piece of ground transferred to a poor American artist named George Arnold, explaining that he did it as payment and satisfaction for pecuniary damage accidentally done by him long since upon property belonging to Signor Arnold, and further observed that he would make additional satisfaction by improving the ground for Signor A., at his own charge and cost. Four weeks ago, while making some necessary excavations upon the property, Signor Smithe unearthed the most remarkable ancient statue that has ever been added to the opulent art treasures of Rome. It was an exquisite figure of a woman, and though sadly stained by the soil and the mould of ages, no eye could look unmoved upon its ravishing beauty. The nose, the left leg from the knee down, an ear, and also the toes of the right foot and two fingers of one of the hands, were gone, but otherwise the noble figure was in a remarkable state of preservation. The government at once took military possession of the statue, and appointed a commission of art critics, antiquaries and cardinal princes of the church to assess its value and determine the remuneration that must go to the owner of the ground in which it was found. The whole affair was kept a profound secret until last night. In the meantime the commission sat with closed doors, and deliberated. Last night they decided unanimously that the statue is a Venus, and the work of some unknown but sublimely gifted artist of the third century before Christ. They consider it the most faultless work of art the world has any knowledge of.

"At midnight they held a final conference and decided that the

Venus was worth the enormous sum of *ten million francs*! In accordance with Roman law and Roman usage, the government being half owner in all works of art found in the Campagna, the State has naught to do but pay five million francs to Mr. Arnold and take permanent possession of the beautiful statue. This morning the Venus will be removed to the Capitol, there to remain, and at noon the commission will wait upon Signor Arnold with His Holiness the Pope's order upon the Treasury for the princely sum of five million francs in gold."

Chorus of Voices. — "Luck! It's no name for it!"

Another Voice. — "Gentlemen, I propose that we immediately form an American joint stock company for the purchase of lands and excavation of statues, here, with proper connections in Wall street to bull and bear the stock."

All. — "Agreed."

CHAPTER VI.

[Scene — The Roman Capitol.]

"Dearest Mary, this is the most celebrated statue in the world. This is the renowned 'Capitoline Venus' you've heard so much about. Here she is with her little blemishes 'restored' (that is patched) by the most noted Roman artists — and the mere fact that they did the humble patching of so noble a creation will make their names illustrious while the world stands. How strange it seems — this place! The day before I last stood here, ten happy years ago, I wasn't a millionaire — bless your soul, I hadn't a cent. And yet I had a good deal to do with making Rome mistress of this grandest work of ancient art the world contains."

"The worshipped, the illustrious Capitoline Venus — and how much she is valued at! Ten millions of francs!"

"Yes — *now* she is."

"And oh, Georgy, how divinely beautiful she is!"

"Ah, yes — but nothing to what she was before that blessed John Smith broke her leg and battered her nose. Ingenious Smith! — gifted Smith — noble Smith! Author of all our bliss! Hark! Do you know what that wheeze means? Mary, that brat has got the whooping cough. Will you *never* learn to take care of the children!"

THE END.

The Capitoline Venus is still in the Capitol at Rome, and is still the most charming and most illustrious work of ancient art the World can boast of. But if ever it shall be your fortune to stand before it and go into the customary ecstasies over it, don't permit this true and secret history of its origin to mar your bliss—and when you read about gigantic Petrified Men being dug up near Syracuse in the State of New York, keep your own counsel,—and if the Barnum that buried them there offers to sell to you at an enormous sum, don't you buy. Send him to the Pope!

October 23, 1869

Getting My Fortune Told

I had heard so much about the celebrated fortune teller, Madame ——, (I decline to advertise for her in this paragraph) that I went to see her yesterday. She has a dark complexion naturally, and this effect is hightened by artificial aids which cost her nothing. She wears curls, very black ones, and I had an impression that she gave their native attractiveness a lift with rancid butter. She wears a reddish check handkerchief, cast loosely around her neck, and it was plain that her other one is slow getting back from the wash. I presume she takes snuff. At any rate, something resembling it had lodged among the hairs sprouting from a picturesque mole on her upper lip. I know she likes garlic—I knew that as soon as she sighed. She looked at me searchingly for nearly a minute, with her black eyes, and then said:

"It is enough. Come!"

She started down a very dark and dismal corridor, I stepping close after her. Presently she stopped and said that as the way was crooked and so dark, perhaps she had better get a light. But it seemed ungallant to allow a woman to put herself to so much trouble for me, and so I said:

"It is not worth while, madam. If you will heave another sigh, I think I can follow it."

So we got along all right. Arrived at her official and mysterious den, she asked me to tell her the date of my birth, the exact hour of that occurrence, and the color of my grandmother's hair. I answered as accurately as I could. Then she said:

"Young man summon your fortitude—do not tremble. I am about to reveal the past."

"Information concerning the future would be, in a general way, more——"

"Silence! You have had much trouble, some joy, some good fortune, some bad. Your great grandfather was hanged."

"That is a l—"

"Silence! Hanged sir. But it was not his fault. He could not help it."

"I am glad you do him justice."

"Ah—grieve, rather, that the jury did. He was hanged. His star crosses yours in the fourth division, fifth sphere. Consequently you will be hanged also."

"In view of this cheerful——"

"I *must* have silence. Yours was not, in the beginning, a criminal nature, but circumstances changed it. At the age of nine you stole sugar. At the age of fifteen you stole money. At twenty you stole horses. At twenty-five you committed arson. At thirty, hardened in crime, you became an editor. Since then your descent has been rapid. You are now a public lecturer. Worse things are in store for you. You will be sent to Congress. Next to the penitentiary. Finally, happiness will come again—all will be well—you will be hanged."

I was now in tears. It seemed hard enough to go to Congress. But to be hanged—this was too sad, too dreadful. The woman seemed surprised at my grief. I told her the thoughts that were in my mind. Then she comforted me—this blessed woman reconciled me, made me contented, even happy.

"Why, man," she said, "hold up your head—*you* have nothing to grieve about. Listen. You will live in New Hampshire. In your sharp need and distress the Brown family will succor you—such of them as Pike the assassin left alive. They will be benefactors to you. When you shall have grown fat upon their bounty, and are grateful and happy, you will desire to make some modest return for these things, and so you will go to the house some night and brain the whole family with an axe. You will borrow funds from the deceased, and disburse them in riotous living among the rowdies and courtezans of Boston. Then you will be arrested, tried, condemned to be hanged, thrown into prison. Now is your happy day. You will be converted—you will be converted just as soon as every effort to compass pardon, commutation or reprieve has failed—and then! Why, then, every morning and every afternoon, the best and purest young ladies of the village will assemble in your cell and sing hymns. This will show that assassination is respectable. Then you will write a touching letter, in which you will forgive all those recent Browns. This will excite the public admiration. No public can withstand magnanimity. Next, they will take you to the scaffold, with great eclat, at the head of an imposing procession com-

posed of clergymen, officials, citizens generally, and young ladies walking pensively two and two, and bearing bouquets
and immortelles. You will mount the scaffold, and while the
great concourse stand uncovered in your presence, you will
read your sappy little speech which the minister has written
for you. And then, in the midst of a grand and impressive
silence, they will swing you into per——, Paradise, my son.
There will not be a dry eye on the ground. You will be a hero!
Not a rough there but will envy you. Not a rough there but
will resolve to emulate you.

"And next, a great procession will follow you to the
tomb—will weep over your remains—the young ladies will
sing again the hymns made dear by sweet associations connected with the jail, and as a last tribute of affection, respect,
and appreciation of your many sterling qualities, they will
walk two and two around your bier and strew wreaths of
flowers on it. And lo, you are canonized! Think of it, son—
ingrate, assassin, robber of the dead, drunken brawler among
thieves and harlots in the slums of Boston one month, and
the pet of the pure and innocent daughters of the land the
next! A bloody and hateful devil—a bewept, bewailed and
sainted martyr—all in a month! Fool!—so noble a fortune
and yet you sit here grieving!"

"No madame," I said, "you do me wrong, you do indeed. I
am perfectly satisfied. I did not know before that my great
grandfather was hanged, but it is of no consequence. He has
probably ceased to bother about it by this time—and I have
not commenced, yet. I confess, madam, that I do something
in the way of editing, and lecturing but the other crimes you
mention have escaped my memory. Yet I must have committed them—you would not deceive an orphan. But let the past
be, as it was, and let the future be as it may—these are nothing. I have only cared for one thing. I have always felt that I
should be hanged some day, and some how the thought has
annoyed me considerably—but if you can only assure me that
I shall be hanged in New Hampshire——"

"Not a shadow of a doubt!"

"Bless you, my noble benefactress!—excuse this embrace—
you have removed a great load from my breast. To be hanged
in New Hampshire, is happiness—it leaves an honored name

behind a man, and introduces him at once into the best New Hampshire society in the other world."

I then took leave of the fortune-teller. But seriously, is it well to glorify a murderous villain on the scaffold, as Pike was glorified in New Hampshire a few days ago? Is it well to turn the penalty for a bloody crime into a reward? Is it just to do it? Is it safe?

November 27, 1869

Back from "Yurrup"

Have you ever seen a family of fools just back from Europe—or Yurrup, as they pronounce it? They never talk *to* you, of course, being strangers, but they talk to each other and *at* you till you are pretty nearly distracted with their clatter; till you are sick of their ocean experiences; their mispronounced foreign names; their dukes and emperors; their trivial adventures; their pointless reminiscences; till you are sick of their imbecile faces and their relentless clack, and wish it had pleased Providence to leave the clapper out of their empty skulls.

I traveled with such a family one eternal day, from New York to Boston, last week. They had spent just a year in "Yurrup," and were returning home to Boston. Papa said little, and looked bored—he had simply been down to New York to receive and cart home his cargo of travelled imbecility. Sister Angeline, aged 23, sister Augusta, aged 25, and brother Charles, aged 33, did the conversational drivel, and mamma purred and admired, and threw in some help when occasion offered, in the way of remembering some French barber's—I should say some French Count's—name, when they pretended to have forgotten it. They occupied the choice seats in the parlor of the drawing-room car, and for twelve hours I sat opposite to them—was their *vis-a-vis*, they would have said, in their charming French way.

Augusta—"Plague that nahsty (nasty) steamer! I've the headache yet, she rolled so the fifth day out."

Angeline—"And well you may. *I* never saw such a nahsty old tub. I never want to go in the *Ville de Paris* again. Why *didn't* we go over to London and come in the *Scotia*?"

Aug—"Because we were fools!"

[I fervently endorsed that sentiment.]

Ange—"Gustie, what made Count Caskowhisky drive off looking so blue, that last Thursday in Pairy? (Paris, she meant.) Ah, own up, now!"

Aug—"Now, Angie, how you talk! I *told* the nahsty creature I would not receive his attentions any longer. And the old duke his father kept boring me about him and his two million francs a year till I sent *him* off with a flea in his ear."

Chorus.—"Ke-he-he! Ha-ha-ha!"

Charles—[Pulling a small silken cloak to pieces.] "Angie, where'd you get this cheap thing?"

Ange—"You Cholly, let that alone! Cheap! Well, how could I help it? There we were, tied up in Switzerland—just down from Mon Bong (Mont Blanc, doubtless)—couldn't buy anything in those nahsty shops so far away from Pairy. I had to put up with that slimpsy forty-dollar rag—but bless you, I couldn't go naked!"

Chorus—"Ke-he-he!"

Aug—"Guess who I was thinking of? Those ignorant persons we saw first in Rome and afterwards in Venice—those——"

Ange—"Oh, ha-ha-ha! He-e-he! It *was* so funny! Papa, one of them called the Santa della Spiggiola the Santa della Spizziola! Ha-ho-ha! And she thought it was Canova that did Michael Angelo's Moses! Only *think* of it!—Canova a sculptor and the Moses a picture! I thought I should die! I guess I let them see by the way I laughed, that they'd made fools of themselves, because they blushed and sneaked off."

[Papa laughed faintly, but not with the easy grace of a man who was certain he knew what he was laughing about.]

Aug.—"Why Cholly! Where did you get those nahsty Beaumarchais gloves? Well, I *wouldn't*, if I were you!"

Mamma—[With uplifted hands.] "Beaumarchais, my son!"

Ange—"Beaumarchais! Why how can you! Nobody in Pairy wears those nahsty things but the commonest people."

Charles—"They *are* a rum lot, but then Tom Blennerhasset gave 'em to me—he wanted to do something or other to curry favor, I s'pose."

Ange—"Tom Blennerhasset!"

Aug.—"Tom Blennerhasset!"

Mamma—"Tom Blennerhasset! And have you been associating with *him*."

Papa—[suddenly interested.] "Heavens, what has the son of an honored and honorable old friend been doing?"

Chorus—"Doing! Why, his father has endorsed himself bankrupt for friends—that's what the matter!"

Ange—"Oh, mon Dieu, j'ai faim! Avez-vous quelque chose de bon, en votre poche, mon cher frere? Excuse me for speaking French, for, to tell the truth, I haven't spoken English for so long that it comes dreadful awkward. Wish we were back in Yurrup—c'est votre desire aussi, n'est-ce pas, mes cheres?"

And from that moment they lapsed into barbarous French and kept it up for an hour—hesitating, gasping for words, stumbling head over heels through adverbs and participles, floundering among adjectives, working miracles of villainous pronunciation—and neither one of them ever by any chance understanding what another was driving at.

By that time some new comers had entered the car, and so they lapsed into English again and fell to holding everything American up to scorn and contumely in order that they might thus let those newcomers know they were just home from "Yurrup." They kept up this little game all the way to Boston—and if ever I can learn when their funeral is to take place, I shall lay aside every other pleasure and attend it. To use their pet and best beloved phrase, they were a "nahsty" family of American snobs, and there ought to be a law against allowing such to go to Europe and misrepresent the nation. It will take these insects five years, now, to get done turning up their noses at everything American and making damaging comparisons between their own country and "Yurrup." Let us pity their waiting friends in Boston in their affliction.

December 4, 1869

An Awful- - - -Terrible Medieval Romance

CHAPTER I.

THE SECRET REVEALED.

It was night. Silence reigned in the grand old feudal castle of Klugenstein. The year 1222 was drawing to a close. Far away up in the tallest of the castle's towers a single light glimmered. A secret council was being held there. The stern old lord of Klugenstein sat in a chair of state meditating. Presently he said, with a tender accent:

"My Daughter!"

A young man of noble presence, clad from head to heel in knightly mail, answered:

"Speak, father!"

"My daughter, the time is come for the revealing of the mystery that hath puzzled all your young life. Know, then, that it had its birth in the matters which I shall now unfold. My brother Ulrich is the great Duke of Brandenburgh. Our father, on his deathbed, decreed that if no son were born to Ulrich, the succession should pass to my house, provided a son were born to me. And further, in case no son were born to either, but only daughters, then the succession should pass to Ulrich's daughter, if she proved stainless; if she did not my daughter should succeed, if she retained a blameless name. And so I, and my old wife here, prayed fervently for the good boon of a son, but the prayer was vain. You were born to us. I was in despair. I saw the mighty prize slipping from my grasp, the splendid dream vanishing away. And I had been so hopeful! Five years had Ulrich lived in wedlock, and yet his wife had borne no heir of either sex.

" 'But hold,' I said, 'all is not lost.' A saving scheme had shot athwart my brain. You were born at midnight. Only the leech, the nurse, and six waiting women knew your sex. I hanged them every one before an hour had sped. Next morning all the barony went mad with rejoicing over the proclamation that a son was born to Klugenstein, an heir to mighty Brandenburgh! And well the secret has been kept. Your mother's own sister nursed your infancy, and from that time forward we feared nothing.

"When you were ten years old, a daughter was born to Ulrich. We grieved, but hoped for good results from measles, or physicians, or other natural enemies of infancy, but were always disappointed. She lived, she throve—Heaven's malison upon her! But it is nothing. We are safe. For, Ha-ha! have we not a son? And is not our son the future Duke? Our well-beloved Conrad is it not so?—for, woman of eight and twenty years as you are, my child, none other name than that hath ever fallen to *you*!

"Now it hath come to pass that age hath laid its hand upon my brother, and he waxes feeble. The cares of State do tax him sore. Therefore he wills that you shall come to him and be already Duke in act though not yet in name. Your servitors are ready—you journey forth to-night.

"Now listen well. Remember every word I say. There is a law as old as Germany that if any woman sit for a single instant in the great ducal chair before she hath been absolutely crowned in presence of the people, she shall die! So heed my words. Pretend humility. Pronounce your judgments from the Premier's chair, which stands at the foot of the throne. Do this until you are crowned and safe. It is not likely that your sex will ever be discovered, but still it is the part of wisdom to make all things as safe as may be in this treacherous earthly life."

"Oh, my father, is it for this my life hath been a lie! Was it that I might cheat my unoffending cousin of her rights? Spare me, father, spare your child!"

"What huzzy! Is this my reward for the august fortune my brain has wrought for you? By the bones of my father, this puling sentiment of thine but ill accords with my humor. Betake thee to the Duke! instantly! And beware how thou meddlest with my purpose!"

Let this suffice, of the conversation. It is enough for us to know that the prayers, the entreaties and the tears of the gentle-natured girl availed nothing. They nor anything could move the stout old lord of Klugenstein. And so, at last, with a heavy heart, the daughter saw the castle gates close behind her and found herself riding away in the darkness surrounded by a knightly array of armed vassals and a brave following of servants.

The old baron sat silent for many minutes after his daughter's departure, and then he turned to his sad wife and said:

"Dame, our matters seem speeding fairly. It is full three months since I sent the shrewd and handsome Count Detzin on his devilish mission to my brother's daughter Constance. If he fail, we are not wholly safe—but if he do succeed, no power can bar our girl from being Duchess e'en though ill fortune should decree she never should be Duke!"

"My heart is full of bodings, yet all may still be well."

"Tush, woman! Leave the owls to croak. To bed with ye, and dream of Brandenburgh and grandeur!"

CHAPTER II.

FESTIVITY AND TEARS.

Six days after the occurrences related in the above chapter, the brilliant capital of the Duchy of Brandenburgh was resplendent with military pageantry, and noisy with the rejoicings of loyal multitudes, for Conrad, the young heir to the crown, was come. The old Duke's heart was full of happiness, for Conrad's handsome person and graceful bearing had won his love at once. The great halls of the palace were thronged with nobles who welcomed Conrad bravely, and so bright and happy did all things seem, that he felt his fears and sorrows passing away and giving place to a comforting contentment.

But in a remote apartment of the palace, a scene of a different nature was transpiring. By a window stood the Duke's only child, the Lady Constance. Her eyes were red and swollen, and full of tears. She was alone. Presently she fell to weeping anew, and said aloud:

"The villain Detzin is gone—has fled the dukedom! I could not believe it at first, but alas it is too true. And I loved him so. I dared to love him though I knew the Duke my father would never let me wed him. I loved him—but now I hate him! With all my soul I hate him! Oh, what is to become of me! I am lost, lost, lost! I shall go mad!"

CHAPTER III.

THE PLOT THICKENS.

A few months drifted by. All men published the praises of the young Conrad's government and extolled the wisdom of his judgments, the mercifulness of his sentences, and the modesty with which he bore himself in his great office. The old Duke soon gave everything into his hands, and sat apart and listened with proud satisfaction while his heir delivered the decrees of the crown from the seat of the premier. It seemed plain that one so loved and praised and honored of all men as Conrad was, could not be otherwise than happy. But strangely enough, he was not. For he saw with dismay that the Princess Constance had begun to love him! The love of the rest of the world was happy fortune for him, but this was freighted with danger! And he saw, moreover, that the delighted Duke had discovered his daughter's passion likewise, and was already dreaming of a marriage. Every day somewhat of the deep sadness that had been in the princess's face, faded away; every day hope and animation beamed brighter from her eye; and bye and bye even vagrant smiles visited the face that had been so troubled.

Conrad was appalled. He bitterly cursed himself for having yielded to the instinct that had made him seek the companionship of one of his own sex when he was new and a stranger in the palace—when he was sorrowful and yearned for a sympathy such as only women can give or feel. He now began to avoid his cousin. But this only made matters worse, for naturally enough, the more he avoided her the more she cast herself in his way. He marveled at this at first; and next it startled him. The girl haunted him; she hunted him: she happened upon him at all times and in all places, in the night as well as in the day. She seemed singularly anxious. There was surely a mystery somewhere.

This could not go on forever. All the world was talking about it. The Duke was beginning to look perplexed. Poor Conrad was becoming a very ghost through dread and dire distress. One day as he was emerging from a private anteroom attached to the picture gallery, Constance confronted him, and seizing both his hands in hers, exclaimed:

"Oh, why do you avoid me? What have I done—what have I said, to lose your kind opinion of me—for surely I had it once? Conrad, do not despise me, but pity a tortured heart! I cannot, cannot hold the words unspoken longer lest they kill me—I love you Conrad! There, despise me if you must, but they *would* be uttered!"

Conrad was speechless. Constance hesitated a moment, and then, misinterpreting his silence, a wild gladness flamed in her eyes, and she flung her arms about his neck and said:

"You relent! you relent! You *can* love me—you *will* love me! Oh, say you will, my own, my worshipped Conrad!"

Conrad groaned aloud. A sickly pallor overspread his countenance, and he trembled like an aspen. Presently, in desperation he thrust the poor girl from him and cried:

"You know not what you ask! It is forever and ever impossible!" And then he fled like a criminal and left the princess stupified with amazement. A minute afterward she was crying and sobbing there, and Conrad was crying and sobbing in his chamber. Both were in despair. Both saw ruin staring them in the face.

Bye and bye Constance rose slowly to her feet and moved away, saying:

"To think that he was despising my love at the very moment that I thought it was melting his cruel heart! I hate him! He spurned me—did this man—he spurned me from him like a dog!"

CHAPTER IV.

THE AWFUL REVELATION.

Time passed on. A settled sadness rested once more upon the countenance of the good Duke's daughter. She and Conrad were seen together no more now. The Duke grieved at this. But as the weeks wore away, Conrad's color came back to his cheeks and his old-time vivacity to his eye, and he administered the government with a clear and steadily ripening wisdom.

Presently a strange whisper began to be heard about the palace. It grew louder, it spread farther. The gossips of the city got hold of it. It swept the Dukedom. And this is what the whisper said:

"The Lady Constance hath given birth to a child!"

When the Lord of Klugenstein heard it, he swung his plumed helmet thrice around his head and shouted:

"Long live Duke Conrad!—for lo, his crown is sure, from this day forward! Detzin has done his errand well, and the good scoundrel shall be rewarded!"

And he spread the tidings far and wide, and for eight and forty hours no soul in all the barony but did dance and sing, carouse and illuminate, to celebrate the great event, and all at proud and happy old Klugenstein's expense.

CHAPTER V.

THE FRIGHTFUL CATASTROPHE.

The trial was at hand. All the great lords and barons of Brandenburgh were assembled in the Hall of Justice in the ducal palace. No space was left unoccupied where there was room for a spectator to stand or sit. Conrad, clad in purple and ermine, sat in the Premier's chair, and on either side sat the great judges of the realm. The old Duke had sternly commanded that the trial of his daughter should proceed, without favor, and then had taken to his bed broken hearted. His days were numbered. Poor Conrad had begged, as for his very life, that he might be spared the misery of sitting in judgment upon his cousin's crime, but it did not avail.

The saddest heart in all that great assemblage was in Conrad's breast.

The gladdest was in his father's. For unknown to his daughter "Conrad," the old Baron Klugenstein was come, and was among the crowd of nobles, triumphant in the swelling fortunes of his house.

After the heralds had made due proclamation and the other preliminaries had followed, the venerable Lord Chief Justice said:

"Prisoner, stand forth!"

The unhappy princess rose and stood unveiled before the vast multitude. The Lord Chief Justice continued:

"Most noble lady, before the great judges of this realm it hath been charged and proven that out of holy wedlock your grace hath given birth unto a child, and by our ancient law the penalty is death, excepting in one sole contingency, whereof his grace the acting Duke, our good Lord Conrad, will advertise you in his solemn sentence now—wherefore, give heed."

Conrad stretched forth the reluctant sceptre and in the self-same moment the womanly heart beneath his robe yearned pityingly toward the doomed prisoner and the tears came into his eyes. He opened his lips to speak, but the Lord Chief Justice said quickly:

"Not there, your Grace, not there! It is not lawful to pronounce judgment upon any of the ducal line save from the ducal throne!"

A shudder went to the heart of poor Conrad, and a tremor shook the iron frame of his old father likewise. Conrad had not been crowned—dared he profane the throne? He hesitated and turned pale with fear. But it must be done. Wondering eyes were already upon him. They would be suspicious eyes if he hesitated longer. He ascended the throne. Presently he stretched forth the sceptre again, and said:

"Prisoner, in the name of our sovereign lord, Ulrich, Duke of Brandenburgh, I proceed to the solemn duty that hath devolved upon me. Give heed to my words. By the ancient law of the land, except you produce the partner of your guilt and deliver him up to the executioner, you must surely die! Embrace this opportunity—save yourself while yet you may. Name the father of your child!"

A solemn hush fell upon the great court—a silence so profound that men could hear their own hearts beat. Then the princess slowly turned, with eyes gleaming with hate, and pointing her finger straight at Conrad, said:

"Thou art the man!"

An appalling conviction of his helpless, hopeless peril, struck a chill to Conrad's heart like the chill of death itself. What power on earth could save him! To disprove the charge, he must reveal that he was a woman; and for an uncrowned woman to sit in the ducal chair, was death! At one and the same moment, he and his grim old father swooned and fell to the ground.

[The remainder of this thrilling and eventful story will NOT be found in the WEEKLY BUFFALO EXPRESS, notwithstanding the fact that the paper can be had of all thoroughly respectable newsdealers, at the low price of one dollar and a half a year.

The truth is, I have got my hero (or heroine) into such a particularly close place that I do not see how I am ever going to get him (or her) out of it again—and therefore I will wash my hands of the whole business and leave that person to get out the best way that offers—or else stay there. I thought it was going to be easy enough to straighten out that little difficulty, but it looks different, now.

If *Harper's Weekly* or the New York *Tribune* desire to copy these initial chapters into the reading columns of their valuable journals, just as they do the opening chapters of *Ledger* and *New York Weekly* novels, they are at liberty to do so at the usual rates, provided they "trust."]

January 1, 1870

A Mysterious Visit

The first notice that was taken of me when I "settled down," recently, was by a gentleman who said he was an assessor, and connected with the U. S. Internal Revenue Department. I said I had never heard of his branch of business before, but I was very glad to see him, all the same,—would he sit down? He sat down. I did not know anything particular to say, and yet I felt that people who have arrived at the dignity of keeping house must be conversational, must be easy and sociable in company. So in default of anything else to say, I asked him if he was opening his shop in our neighborhood.

He said he was. [I did not wish to appear ignorant, but I *had* hoped he would mention what he had for sale.]

I ventured to ask him "how was trade?" and he said "So-so."

I then said we would drop in, and if we liked his house as well as any other, we would give him our custom.

He said he thought we would like his establishment well enough to confine ourselves to it—said he never saw anybody who would go off and hunt up another man in his line after trading with him once.

That sounded pretty complacent, but barring that natural expression of villainy which we all have, the man looked honest enough.

I do not know how it came about, exactly, but gradually we appeared to melt down and run together, conversationally speaking, and then everything went along as comfortably as clockwork.

We talked, and talked, and talked—at least I did. And we laughed, and laughed, and laughed—at least he did. But all the time, I had my presence of mind about me—I had my native shrewdness turned on, "full head," as the engineers say. I was determined to find out all about his business, in spite of his obscure answers—and I was determined I would have it out of him without his suspecting what I was at. I meant to trap him with a deep, deep ruse. I would tell him all about my own business, and he would naturally so warm to me during this seductive burst of confidence that he would forget himself and tell me all about *his* affairs before he suspected what I was about. I thought to myself, My son, you little know what an old fox you are dealing with. I said:

"Now you never would guess what I made lecturing, this winter and last spring?"

"No—don't believe I could, to save me. Let me see—let me see. About two thousand dollars maybe? But no—no, sir, I know you couldn't have made that much. Say seventeen hundred, maybe?"

"Ha-ha! I knew you couldn't. My lecturing receipts for last spring and this winter were fourteen thousand, seven hundred and fifty dollars—what do you think of that!"

"Why it is amazing—perfectly amazing. I will make a note of it. And you say even this wasn't all?"

"All? Why bless you there was my income from the Buffalo EXPRESS for four months—about—about—well, what should you say to about eight thousand dollars, for instance?"

"Say! Why I should say I should like to see myself rolling in just such another ocean of affluence. Eight thousand! I'll make a note of it. Why, man!—and on top of all this I am to understand that you had still more income?"

"Ha-ha-ha! Why, you're only in the suburbs of it, so to speak. There's my book, "The Innocents Abroad"—price $3.50 to $5.00, according to the binding. Listen to me. Look me in the eye. During the last four months and a half, saying nothing of sales before that,—but just simply during the four months and a half ending March 15, 1870, we've sold ninety-five thousand copies of that book! Ninety-five thousand! Think of it. Average four dollars a copy, say. It's nearly four hundred thousand dollars, my son. I get half!"

"The suffering Moses! I'll set *that* down. Fourteen-seven-fifty—eight—two hundred. Total, say—well, upon my word, the grand total is about two hundred and thirteen or fourteen thousand dollars. *Is* that possible?"

"Possible! If there's any mistake it's the other way. Two hundred and fourteen thousand, cash, is my income for this year if *I* know how to cipher."

Then the gentleman got up to go. It came over me most uncomfortably that maybe I had made my revelations for nothing, besides being flattered into stretching them con-

siderably by the stranger's astonished exclamations. But no;
at the last moment the gentleman handed me a large envelope
and said it contained his advertisement; and that I would find
out all about his business in it; and that he would be happy to
have my custom—would in fact be proud to have the custom
of a man of such prodigious income; and that he used to
think there were several wealthy men in Buffalo, but when
they came to trade with him he discovered that they barely
had enough to live on; and that in truth it had been such a
weary, weary age since he had seen a rich man face to face,
and talked with him, and touched him with his hands, that he
could hardly refrain from embracing me—in fact, would esteem it a great favor if I would *let* him embrace me.

This so pleased me that I did not try to resist, but allowed
this simple hearted stranger to throw his arms about me and
weep a few tranquilizing tears down the back of my neck.
Then he went his way.

As soon as he was gone, I opened his advertisement. I studied it attentively for four minutes. I then called up the cook
and said:

"Hold me while I faint. Let Maria turn the batter-cakes."

Bye and bye, when I came to, I sent down to the rum mill
on the corner and hired an artist by the week to sit up nights
and curse that stranger, and give me a lift occasionally in the
day time when I came to a hard place.

Ah, what a miscreant he was! His "advertisement" was
nothing in the world but a wicked tax return—a string of
impertinent questions about my private affairs occupying the
best part of four foolscap pages of fine print—questions, I
may remark, gotten up with such marvelous ingenuity that
the oldest man in the world couldn't understand what the
most of them were driving at—questions, too, that were calculated to make a man report about four times his actual income to keep from swearing to a lie. I looked for a loophole,
but there did not appear to be any. Inquiry No. 1 covered my
case, as generously and as amply as an umbrella could cover
an ant hill:

"What were your profits, in 1869, from any trade, business or vocation, wherever carried on?"

And that inquiry was backed up by thirteen others of an equally searching nature, the most modest of which required information as to whether I had committed any burglary, or highway robbery, or by any arson or other secret source of emolument, had acquired property which was not enumerated in my statement of income as set opposite to inquiry No. 1.

It was plain that that stranger had enabled me to make an ass of myself. It was very, very plain, and I went out and hired another artist. By working on my vanity the stranger had seduced me into declaring an income of $214,000. By law, $1000 of this was exempt from income tax—the only relief I could see, and it was only a drop in the ocean. At the legal five per cent., I must pay over to the government the appalling sum of ten thousand six hundred and fifty dollars, income tax.

[I may remark, in this place, that I did not do it.]

I am acquainted with a very opulent man, whose house is a palace, whose table is regal, whose outlays are enormous, yet a man who has no income, as I have often noticed, by the revenue returns; and to him I went for advice, in my distress. He took my dreadful exhibition of receipts, he put on his glasses, he took his pen, and presto!—I was a pauper! It was the neatest thing that ever was. He did it simply by deftly manipulating the bill of "DEDUCTIONS." He set down my "State, national and municipal taxes" at so much; my "losses by shipwreck, fire, etc.," at so much; my "losses on sales of real estate"—on "live stock sold"—on "payments for rent of homestead"—on "repairs, improvements, interest"—on "previously taxed salary as an officer of the United States army, navy, revenue service," and other things. He got astonishing "deductions" out of each and every one of these matters—each and every one of them. And when he was done he handed me the paper and I saw at a glance that during the year 1869 my income, in the way of profits, had been *one thousand two hundred and fifty dollars and forty cents.*

"Now," said he, "the thousand dollars is exempt by law. What you want to do is to go and swear this document in and pay tax on the two hundred and fifty dollars."

[While he was making this speech his little boy Willie lifted a two dollar greenback out of his vest pocket and vanished with it, and I would bet anything that if my stranger were to call on that little boy to-morrow he would make a false return of his income.]

"Do you," said I, "do you always work up the 'deductions' after this fashion in your own case, sir?"

"Well, I should say so! If it weren't for those eleven saving clauses under the head of 'Deductions' I should be beggared every year to support this hateful and wicked, this extortionate and tyrannical government."

This gentleman stands away up among the very best of the solid men of Buffalo—the men of moral weight, of commercial integrity, of unimpeachable social spotlessness—and so I bowed to his example. I went down to the revenue office, and under the accusing eyes of my old visitor I stood up and swore to lie after lie, fraud after fraud, villainy after villainy, till my immortal soul was coated inches and inches thick with perjury and my self-respect was gone forever and ever.

But what of it? It is nothing more than thousands of the highest, and richest, and proudest, and most respected, honored and courted men in America do every year. And so I don't care. I am not ashamed. I shall simply, for the present, talk little and wear fire-proof gloves, lest I fall into certain habits irrevocably.

March 19, 1870

The Facts in the Great Land-Slide Case

It was in the early days of Nevada Territory. The mountains are very high and steep about Carson, Eagle and Washoe Valleys—very high and very steep, and so when the snow gets to melting off fast in the Spring and the warm surface-earth begins to moisten and soften, the disastrous land-slides commence. You do not know what a land-slide is, unless you have lived in that country and seen the whole side of a mountain taken off some fine morning and deposited down in the valley, leaving a vast, treeless, unsightly scar upon the mountain's front to keep the circumstance fresh in your memory all the years that you may go on living within seventy miles of that place.

General Buncombe was shipped out to Nevada in the invoice of Territorial officers, to be United States Attorney. He considered himself a lawyer of parts, and he very much wanted an opportunity to manifest it—partly for the pure gratification of it and partly because his salary was Territorially meagre (which is a strong expression.) Now the older citizens of a new territory look upon the rest of the world with a calm, unmalignant contempt as long as it keeps out of the way—when it gets in the way they snub it. Sometimes this latter takes the shape of a practical joke.

One morning Dick Sides rode furiously up to General Buncombe's door in Carson City and rushed into his presence without stopping to tie his horse. He seemed much excited. He told the General that he wanted him to defend a suit for him and would pay him five hundred dollars if he achieved a victory. And then, with violent gestures and a world of profanity, he poured out his griefs. He said it was pretty well known that for some years he had been farming (or ranching as the more customary term is,) in Washoe District, and making a successful thing of it, and furthermore it was known that his ranch was situated just in the edge of the valley, and that Tom Morgan owned a ranch immediately above it on the mountain side. And now the trouble was that one of those hated and dreaded land-slides had come and slid Morgan's ranch, fences, cabins, cattle, barns and everything down on

345

top of *his* ranch and exactly covered up every single vestige of his property, to a depth of about six feet. Morgan was in possession and refused to vacate the premises—said he was occupying his own cabin and not interfering with anybody else's—and said cabin was standing on the same dirt and same ranch it had always stood on, and would like to see anybody make him vacate.

"And when I reminded him," said Sides, weeping, "that it was on top of my ranch and that he was trespassing, he had the infernal meanness to ask me why didn't I *stay* on my ranch and hold possession when I see him coming! Why didn't I *stay* on it, the blathering lunatic—and by George, when I heard that racket and looked up that hill it was just like the whole world was a ripping and a tearing down that mountain side—trees going end over end in the air, rocks as big as a house jumping about a thousand feet high and busting into ten million pieces, cattle literally turned inside out and a-coming head on with their tails hanging out between their teeth—Oh, splinters, and cord-wood, and thunder and lightning, and hail and snow, odds and ends of hay stacks and things, and dust—Oh, dust ain't no name for it—it was just clouds, solid clouds of dust!—and in the midst of all that wrack and destruction sot that cussed Morgan on his gate-post, a-wondering why I didn't stay and hold possession; likely! Umph! I just took one glimpse of that speckticle, General, and I lit out 'n the country in three jumps exactly.

"But what grinds me is that that Morgan hangs on there and won't move off 'n that ranch—says it 's his'n and he's going to keep it—likes it better'n he did when it was higher up the hill. Mad! Well, I've been so mad for two days I couldn't find my way to town—been wandering around in the brush in a starving condition—got any thing here to drink, General? But I'm here *now*, and I'm a-going to law. You hear *me*!"

Never in all the world, perhaps, were a man's feelings so outraged as were the General's. He said he had never heard of such high-handed conduct in all his life as this Morgan's. And he said there was no use in going to law—Morgan had no shadow of right to remain where he was—nobody in the wide world would uphold him in it, and no lawyer would take his case and no judge listen to it. Sides said that right there was where he was mistaken—everybody in town sustained Morgan; Hal Brayton, a very smart lawyer, had taken his case; the courts being in vacation, it was to be tried before a referee, and ex-Governor Roop had already been appointed to that office and would open his court in the largest parlor of the Ormsby House at 2 that afternoon.

The innocent General was amazed. He said he had suspected before that the people of that Territory were fools, and now he knew it. But he said rest easy, rest easy and collect the witnesses, for the victory was just as certain as if the conflict were already over. Sides wiped away his tears and left.

At 2 in the afternoon referee Roop's Court opened, and that remorseless old joker appeared throned among his sheriffs, his witnesses, and a "packed" jury, and wearing upon his face a fraudulent solemnity so awe-inspiring that some of his fellow-conspirators had misgivings that maybe he had not comprehended, after all, that this was merely a joke. An unearthly stillness prevailed, for at the slightest noise the judge uttered sternly the command:

"Order in the Court!"

And the sheriffs promptly echoed it. Presently the General elbowed his way through the crowd of spectators, with his arms full of law-books, and on his ears fell an order from the judge which was the first respectful recognition of his high official dignity that had ever saluted them, and it saturated his whole system with pleasure:

"Way for the United States Attorney!"

The witnesses were called—legislators, high government officers, ranch men, miners, Indians, Chinamen, negroes. Three-fourths of them were called by the defendant Morgan, but no matter, their testimony invariably went in favor of the plaintiff Sides. Each new witness only added new testimony to the absurdity of a man's claiming to own another man's property because his farm had slid down on top of it. Then the Morgan lawyers made their speeches, and seemed to make singularly weak ones—they did really nothing to help the Morgan cause. And now the General, with a great glow of triumph on his face, got up and made a mighty effort; he pounded the table, he banged the law-books, he shouted, and roared, and howled, he quoted from everything and everybody, poetry, sarcasm, statistics, history, pathos, and blasphemy, and wound up with a grand war-whoop for free speech, freedom of the press, free schools, the Glorious Bird of America and the principles of eternal justice! [Applause.]

When the General sat down, he did it with the comfortable conviction that if there were anything in good strong testimony, a big speech and believing and admiring countenances all around, Mr. Morgan's cake was dough. Ex-Governor Roop leant his head upon his hand for some minutes, thinking profoundly, and the still audience waited breathlessly for his decision. Then he got up and stood erect, with bended head, and thought again. Then he walked the floor with long, deliberate strides, and his chin in his hand, and still the audience waited. At last he returned to his throne and seated himself. The sheriffs commanded the attention of the Court. Judge Roop cleared his throat and said:

"Gentlemen, I feel the great responsibility that rests upon me this day. This is no ordinary case. On the contrary it is plain that it is the most solemn and awful that ever man was called upon to decide. Gentlemen, I have listened attentively to the evidence, and the weight of it, the overwhelming weight of it is in favor of the plaintiff Sides. I have listened also to the remarks of counsel, with high interest—and especially will I commend the masterly and irrefutable logic of the distinguished gentleman who represents the plaintiff. But gentlemen, let us beware how we allow human testimony, human ingenuity in argument and human ideas of equity to influence us to our undoing at a moment so solemn as this. Gentlemen, it ill becomes us, worms as we are, to meddle with the decrees of Heaven. It is plain to me that Heaven, in its inscrutable wisdom, has seen fit to move this defendant's ranch for a purpose. We are but creatures, and we must submit. If Heaven has chosen to favor the defendant Morgan in this marked and wonderful manner; and if Heaven, unsatisfied with the position of the Morgan ranch upon the mountain side, has chosen to remove it to a position more eligible and more advantageous for its owner, it ill becomes us, insects as we are, to question the legality of the act. No— Heaven created the ranches and it is Heaven's prerogative to rearrange them, to experiment with them, to shift them around at its pleasure. It is for us to submit, without repining. I warn you that this thing which has happened is a thing with which the sacrilegious hands and brains and tongues of men must not meddle. Gentlemen, it is the verdict of this court that the plaintiff, Richard Sides, has been deprived of his ranch by the visitation of God! And from this decision there is no appeal."

Buncombe seized his cargo of law-books and plunged out of the court room a raving madman, almost. He pronounced Roop to be a miraculous ass, a fool, an inspired idiot. In all good faith he returned at night and remonstrated with Roop upon his extravagant decision, and implored him to walk the floor and think for half an hour, and see if he could not figure out some sort of modification of the verdict. Roop yielded at last and got up to walk. He walked two hours and a half, and at last his face lit up happily and he told Buncombe it had occurred to him that the ranch underneath the new Morgan ranch still belonged to Sides, that his title to the ground itself was just as good as it had ever been, and therefore he was of opinion that Sides had a right to dig it out from under there and—

The General never waited to hear the end of it. He was always an impatient and irascible man, that way. At the end of two weeks he got it through his understanding that he had been played upon with a joke.

April 2, 1870

The New Crime

This country, during the last thirty or forty years, has produced some of the most remarkable cases of insanity of which there is any mention in history. For instance, there was the Baldwin case, in Ohio, twenty-two years ago. Baldwin, from his boyhood up, had been of a vindictive, malignant, quarrelsome nature. He put a boy's eye out, once, and never was heard upon any occasion, to utter a regret for it. He did many such things. But at last he did something that was serious. He called at a house just after dark, one evening, knocked, and when the occupant came to the door, shot him dead and then tried to escape but was captured. Two days before, he had wantonly insulted a helpless cripple, and the man he afterward took swift vengeance upon with an assassin bullet, knocked him down. Such was the Baldwin case. The trial was long and exciting; the community was fearfully wrought up. Men said this spiteful, bad-hearted villain had caused grief enough in his time, and now he should satisfy the law. But they were mistaken. Baldwin was insane when he did the deed—they had not thought of that. By the arguments of counsel it was shown that at half-past ten in the morning on the day of the murder, Baldwin became insane, and remained so for eleven hours and a half exactly. This just covered the case comfortably, and he was acquitted. Thus, if an unthinking and excited community had been listened to instead of the arguments of counsel, a poor, crazy creature would have been held to a fearful responsibility for a mere freak of madness. Baldwin went clear, and although his relatives and friends were naturally incensed against the community for their injurious suspicions and remarks, they said let it go for this time, and did not prosecute. The Baldwins were very wealthy. This same Baldwin had momentary fits of insanity twice afterward, and on both occasions killed people he had grudges against. And on both these occasions the circumstances of the killing were so aggravated, and the murders so seemingly heartless and treacherous, that if Baldwin had not been insane he would have been hanged without the shadow of a doubt. As it was, it required all his political and family influence to get him clear in one of the cases, and cost him not less than $10,000 to get clear in the other. One of these men he had notoriously been threatening to kill for twelve years. The poor creature happened, by the merest piece of ill-fortune, to come along a dark alley at the very moment that Baldwin's insanity came upon him, and so he was shot in the back with a gun loaded with slugs. It was exceedingly fortunate for Baldwin that his insanity came on him just when it did.

Take the case of Lynch Hackett, of Pennsylvania. Twice, in public, he attacked a German butcher by the name of Bemis Feldner, with a cane, and both times Feldner whipped him with his fists. Hackett was a vain, wealthy, violent gentleman, who held his blood and family in high esteem and believed that a reverent respect was due his great riches. He brooded over the shame of his chastisement for two weeks, and then, in a momentary fit of insanity armed himself to the teeth, rode into town, waited a couple of hours until he saw Feldner coming down the street with his wife on his arm, and then, as the couple passed the doorway in which he had partially concealed himself, he drove a knife into Feldner's neck, killing him instantly. The widow caught the limp form and eased it to the earth. Both were drenched with blood. Hackett jocosely remarked to her that as a professional butcher's recent wife she could appreciate the artistic neatness of the job that left her in a condition to marry again, in case she wanted to. This remark, and another which he made to a friend, that his position in society made the killing of an obscure citizen simply an "eccentricity" instead of a crime, were shown to be evidences of insanity, and so Hackett escaped punishment. The jury were hardly inclined to accept these as proofs, at first, inasmuch as the prisoner had never been insane before the murder, and under the tranquilizing effect of the butchering had immediately regained his right mind—but when the defence came to show that a third cousin of Hackett's wife's stepfather was insane, and not only insane but had a nose the very counterpart of Hackett's, it was plain that insanity was hereditary in the family and Hackett had come by it by legitimate inheritance. Of course the jury then acquitted him. But it was a merciful providence that Mrs. H.'s people had been afflicted as shown, else Hackett would certainly have been hanged.

However, it is not possible to account all the marvelous cases of insanity that have come under the public notice in the last thirty or forty years. There was the Durgin case in New Jersey three years ago. The servant girl, Bridget Durgin, at dead of night invaded her mistress' bedroom and carved the lady literally to pieces with a knife. Then she dragged the body to the middle of the floor and beat and banged it with chairs and such things. Next she opened the feather beds and strewed the contents around, saturated everything with kerosene and set fire to the general wreck. She now took up the young child of the murdered woman in her blood-smearing hands, and walked off, through the snow, with no shoes on, to a neighbor's house a quarter of a mile off, and told a string of wild, incoherent stories about some men coming and setting fire to the house; and then she cried piteously, and without seeming to think there was anything suggestive about the blood upon her hands, her clothing and the baby, volunteered the remark that she was afraid those men had murdered her mistress! Afterward, by her own confession and other testimony, it was proved that the mistress had always been kind to the girl, consequently there was no revenge in the murder; and it was also shown that the girl took nothing away from the burning house, not even her own shoes, and consequently robbery was not the motive. Now the reader says, "Here comes that same old plea of insanity again." But the reader has deceived himself this time. No such plea was offered in her defence. The judge sentenced her, nobody persecuted the Governor with petitions for her pardon, and she was promptly hanged.

There was that youth in Pennsylvania, whose curious confession was published a year ago. It was simply a conglomeration of incoherent drivel from beginning to end—and so was his lengthy speech on the scaffold afterward. For a whole year he was haunted with a desire to disfigure a certain young woman so that no one would marry her. He did not love her himself, and did not want to marry her, but he did not want anybody else to do it. He would not go anywhere with her, and yet was opposed to anybody else's escorting her. Upon one occasion he declined to go to a wedding with her, and when she got other company, lay in wait for the couple by the road, intending to make them go back or kill the escort. After spending sleepless nights over his ruling desire for a full year, he at last attempted its execution—that is, attempted to disfigure the young woman. It was a success. It was permanent. In trying to shoot her cheek (as she sat at the supper table with her parents and brothers and sisters) in such a manner as to mar its comeliness, one of his bullets wandered a little out of the course and she dropped dead. To the very last moment of his life he bewailed the ill luck that made her move her face just at the critical moment. And so he died apparently about half persuaded that somehow it was chiefly her own fault that she got killed. This idiot was hanged. The plea of insanity was not offered.

The recent case of Lady Mordaunt, in England, had proved beyond cavil that the thing we call common prostitution in America is only insanity in Great Britain. Her husband wanted a divorce, but as her cheerful peculiarities were the offspring of lunacy and consequently she could not be held responsible for them, he had to take her to his bosom again. It is sad to think of a dozen or two of great English lords taking advantage of a poor crazy woman. In this country, if history be worth anything to judge by, the husband would have rented a graveyard and stocked it, and then brought the divorce suit afterward. In which case the jury would have brought *him* in insane, not his wife.

Insanity certainly is on the increase in the world, and crime is dying out. There are no longer any murders—none worth mentioning, at any rate. Formerly, if you killed a man, it was possible that you were insane—but now if you kill a man it is *evidence* that you are a lunatic. In these days, too, if a person of good family and high social standing steals any thing, they call it *kleptomania*, and send him to the lunatic asylum. If a person of high standing squanders his fortune in dissipation and closes his career with strychnine or a bullet, "Temporary Aberration" is what was the trouble with *him*. And finally, as before noted, the list is capped with a new and curious madness in the shape of wholesale adultery.

Is not this insanity plea becoming rather common? Is it not so common that the reader confidently expects to see it offered in every criminal case that comes before the courts? And is it not so cheap, and so common, and often so trivial, that the reader smiles in derision when the newspaper mentions it? And is it not curious to note how very often it wins acquittal for the prisoner? Lately it does not seem possible for a man to so conduct himself, before killing another man, as not to be manifestly insane. If he talks about the stars he is insane. If he appears nervous and uneasy an hour before the killing, he is insane. If he weeps over a great grief, his friends shake their heads and fear that he is "not right." If, an hour after the murder, he seems ill at ease, pre-occupied and excited, he is unquestionably insane.

Really, what we want now, is not laws against crime, but a law against *insanity*. There is where the true evil lies.

And the penalty attached should be imprisonment, not hanging. Then, it might be worth the trouble and expense of trying the Gen. Coleses, and the Gen. Sickleses and the Mc-Farlands, because juries might lock them up for brief terms, in deference to the majesty of the law; but it is not likely that any of us will ever live to see the murderer of a seducer hanged. Perhaps, if the truth were confessed, few of us *wish* to live that long.

Since I seemed to have wandered into the McFarland case without especially intending to do it, (for my original idea was merely to call attention to how many really crazy people are hanged in these days, and how many that never were crazy a moment in their lives are acquitted of crime on the plea of insanity,) I will venture to suggest—simply as an opinion, and not as an assertion—that the main reason why we shall never succeed in hanging this mean, small villain, McFarland, is, that his real crime did not consist in killing Richardson, but in so conducting himself long before that, as to estrange his wife's affections from himself and drive her to the love and protection of another man. If they would quash this present suit and try him on that, we would get the unreluctant fangs of justice on him sure, if what one good man says against McFarland is worth as much as what another good man says in his favor. We might all consent that he was a criminal in his treatment of his wife at that time, but somehow we hesitate to condemn him to the scaffold for this act of his whereby he inflicted a penalty for a wrong which, down in our secret hearts, we feel is beyond the ability of all law to punish amply and satisfactorily.

No, when a man abuses his wife as McFarland seems to have abused his, any jury would punish him severely, and do it with a relish. But when a man kills the seducer of his wife, a jury cannot be found that will condemn him to suffer for murder. Therefore, it is fair to consider that McFarland's real crime is not in court in New York, now, but is left out of the indictment.

If I seem to have wandered from my subject and thrown in some surplusage, what do I care? With these evidences of a wandering mind present to the reader, am I to be debarred from offering the customary plea of Insanity?

April 16, 1870

Curious Dream

Containing a Moral.

Night before last I had a singular dream. I seemed to be sitting on a doorstep, (in no particular city, perhaps), ruminating, and the time of night appeared to be about twelve or one o'clock. The weather was balmy and delicious. There was no human sound in the air, not even a footstep. There was no sound of any kind to emphasize the dead stillness, except the occasional hollow barking of a dog in the distance and the fainter answer of a further dog. Presently up the street I heard a bony clack-clacking, and guessed it was the castanets of a serenading party. In a minute more a tall skeleton, hooded and half-clad in a tattered and mouldy shroud whose shreds were flapping about the ribby lattice-work of its person, swung by me with a stately stride, and disappeared in the gray gloom of the starlight. It had a broken and worm-eaten coffin on its shoulder and a bundle of something in its hand. I knew what the clack-clacking was, then—it was this party's joints working together, and his elbows knocking against his sides as he walked. I may say I was surprised. Before I could collect my thoughts and enter upon any speculations as to what this apparition might portend, I heard another one coming—for I recognized his clack-clack. He had two-thirds of a coffin on his shoulder, and some foot and head-boards under his arm. I mightily wanted to peer under his hood and speak to him, but when he turned and smiled upon me with his cavernous sockets and his projecting grin as he went by, I thought I would not detain him. He was hardly gone when I heard the clacking again, and another one issued from the shadowy half-light. This one was bending under a heavy grave stone, and dragging a shabby coffin after him by a string. When he got to me he gave me a steady look for a moment or two, and then rounded to and backed up to me, saying:

"Ease this down for a fellow, will you?"

I eased the grave-stone down till it rested on the ground, and in doing so noticed that it bore the name of "John Baxter Copmanhurst," with "May, 1839," as the date of his death.

Deceased sat wearily down by me and wiped his os frontis with his major maxillary—chiefly from former habit I judged, for I could not see that he brought away any perspiration.

"It is too bad, too bad," said he, drawing the remnant of the shroud about him and leaning his jaw pensively on his hand. Then he put his left foot up on his knee and fell to scratching his ancle bone absently with a rusty nail which he got out of his coffin.

"What is too bad, friend?"

"Oh, everything, everything. I almost wish I never had died."

"You surprise me. Why do you say this? Has anything gone wrong? What is the matter?"

"Matter! Look at this shroud—rags. Look at this grave-stone, all battered up. Look at that disgraceful old coffin. All a man's property going to ruin and destruction before his eyes and ask him if anything is wrong? Fire and brimstone!"

"Calm yourself, calm yourself," I said. "It *is* too bad—it is certainly too bad, but then I had not supposed that you would much mind such matters, situated as you are."

"Well, my dear sir, I *do* mind them. My pride is hurt and my comfort is impaired—destroyed, I might say. I will state my case—I will put it to you in such a way that you can comprehend it, if you will let me," said the poor skeleton, tilting the hood of his shroud back, as if he were clearing for action, and thus unconsciously giving himself a jaunty and festive air very much at variance with the grave character of his position in life—so to speak—and in prominent contrast with his distressful mood.

"Proceed," said I.

"I reside in the shameful old grave yard a block or two above you here, in this street—There, now, I just expected that cartilage would let go!—Third rib from the bottom, friend, hitch the end of it to my spine with a string, if you have got such a thing about you, though a bit of silver wire is a deal pleasanter, and more durable and becoming, if one keeps it polished—to think of shredding out and going to pieces in this way, just on account of the indifference and neglect of one's posterity!"—and the poor ghost grated his teeth in a way that gave me a wrench and a shiver—for the

effect is mightily increased by the absence of muffling flesh
and cuticle. "I reside in that old graveyard, and have for these
thirty years; and I tell you things are changed since I first laid
this old tired frame there, and turned over and stretched out
for a long sleep, with a delicious sense upon me of being *done*
with bother, and grief, and anxiety, and doubt and fear, forever and ever, and listening with comfortable and increasing
satisfaction to the sexton's work, from the startling clatter of
his first spade-full on my coffin till it dulled away to the faint
patting that shaped the roof of my new home—delicious?
My! I wish you could try it to-night!" and out of my reverie
deceased fetched me with a rattling slap with a bony hand.

"Yes, sir, thirty years ago I laid me down there, and was
happy. For it was out in the country, then—out in the
breezy, flowery, grand old woods, and the lazy winds gos-
siped with the leaves, and the squirrels capered over us and
around us, and the creeping things visited us, and the birds
filled the tranquil solitude with music. Ah, it was worth ten
years of a man's life to be dead then! Every thing was pleasant. I was in a good neighborhood, for all the dead people
that lived near me belonged to the best families in the city.
Our posterity appeared to think the world of us. They kept
our graves in the very best condition; the fences were always
in faultless repair, headboards were kept painted or whitewashed, and were replaced with new ones as soon as they
began to look rusty or decayed; monuments were kept upright, railings intact and bright, the rosebushes and shrubbery
trimmed, trained and free from blemish, the walks clean and
smooth and graveled. But that day is gone by. Our descendants have forgotten us. My grandson lives in a stately house
built with money made by these old hands of mine, and I
sleep in a neglected grave with invading vermin that gnaw my
shroud to build them nests withal! I and friends that lie with
me founded and secured the prosperity of this fine city, and
the stately bantling of our loves leaves us to rot in a dilapidated cemetery which neighbors curse and strangers scoff at.
See the difference between the old time and this—for instance: Our graves are all caved in, now; our head-boards
have rotted away and tumbled down; our railings reel this
way and that, with one foot in the air, after a fashion of un-

seemly levity; our monuments lean wearily and our gravestones bow their heads discouraged; there be no adornments
any more,—no roses, nor shrubs, nor graveled walks, nor
anything that is a comfort to the eye, and even the paintless
old board fence that did make a show of holding us sacred
from companionship with beasts and the defilement of heedless feet, has tottered till it overhangs the street, and only advertises the presence of our dismal resting place and invites
yet more derision to it. And now we cannot hide our poverty
and tatters in the friendly woods, for the city has stretched its
withering arms abroad and taken us in, and all that remains of
the cheer of our old home is the cluster of lugubrious forest
trees that stand, bored and weary of city life, with their feet in
our coffins, looking into the hazy distance and not wishing
they were there. I tell you it is disgraceful!

"You begin to comprehend—you begin to see how it is.
While our descendants are living sumptuously on our money
right around us in the city, we have to fight hard to keep skull
and bones together. Bless you there isn't a grave in our cemetery that doesn't leak—not one. Every time it rains in the
night we have to climb out and roost in the trees—and sometimes we are wakened suddenly by the chilly water trickling
down the back of our necks. Then I tell you there is a general
heaving up of old graves and kicking over of old monuments,
and scampering of old skeletons for the trees! Bless me, if you
had gone along there some such nights after twelve you
might have seen as many as fifteen of us roosting on one limb,
with our joints rattling drearily and the wind wheezing
through our ribs! Many a time we have perched there for
three or four dreary hours, and then come down, stiff and
chilled through and drowsy, and borrowed each other's skulls
to bail out our graves with—if you will glance up in my
mouth, now as I tilt my head back, you can see that my head-
piece is half full of old dry sediment—how top-heavy and
stupid it makes me sometimes! Yes, sir, many a time if you
had happened to come along just before the dawn you'd have
caught us bailing out the graves and hanging our shrouds on
the fence to dry. Why, I had an elegant shroud stolen from
there one morning—think a party by the name of Smith took
it, that resides in a plebeian graveyard over yonder—I think

so because the first time I ever saw him he hadn't anything on but a check shirt, and the last time I saw him, which was at a social gathering in the new cemetery, he was the best dressed corpse in the company—and it is a significant fact that he left when he saw me; and presently an old woman from here missed her coffin—she generally took it with her when she went anywhere, because she was liable to take cold and bring on the spasmodic rheumatism that originally killed her if she exposed herself to the night air much. She was named Hotch-kiss—Anna Matilda Hotchkiss—you might know her? She has two upper front teeth, is tall, but a good deal inclined to stoop, one rib on the left side gone, has one shred of rusty hair hanging from the left side of her head, and one little tuft just above and a little forward of her right ear, has her under jaw wired on one side where it had worked loose, small bone of left forearm gone—lost in a fight—has a kind of swagger in her gait and a 'gallus' way of going with her arms akimbo and her nostrils in the air—has been pretty free and easy, and is all damaged and battered up till she looks like a queensware crate in ruins—maybe you have met her?"

"God forbid!" I involuntarily ejaculated, for some how I was not looking for that form of question, and it caught me a little off my guard. But I hastened to make amends for my rudeness and say: "I simply meant I had not had the honor—for I would not deliberately speak discourteously of a friend of yours. You were saying that you were robbed—and it was a shame, too—but it appears by what is left of the shroud you have on that it was a costly one in its day. How did—"

A most ghastly expression began to develop among the de-cayed features and shriveled integuments of my guest's face, and I was beginning to grow uneasy and distressed, when he told me he was only working up a deep, sly smile, with a wink in it, to suggest that about the time he acquired his present garment a ghost in a neighboring cemetery missed one. This reassured me, but I begged him to confine himself to speech, thenceforth, because his facial expression was un-certain. Even with the most elaborate care it was liable to miss fire. Smiling should especially be avoided. What *he* might honestly consider a shining success was likely to strike me in a very different light. I said I liked to see a skeleton cheerful, even decorously playful, but I did not think smiling was a skeleton's best hold.

[Conclusion—with the rest of the MORAL—next week.]

[CONCLUDED FROM LAST WEEK'S EXPRESS.]

[In the chapter preceding this, was set forth how certain shrouded skeletons came mysteriously marching past my door after midnight, carrying battered tombstones, crumbling coffins, and such like property with them, and how one sat down by me to rest, (having also his tombstone with him, and dragging after him his worm-eaten coffin by a string,) and complained at great length of the discomforts of his ruinous and long-neglected graveyard. This conversation now continueth.]

"Yes, friend," said the poor skeleton, "the facts are just as I have given them to you. Two of these old graveyards—the one that I resided in and one further along—have been deliberately neglected by our descendants of to-day until there is no occupying them any longer. Aside from the osteological discomfort of it—and that is no light matter this rainy weather—the present state of things is ruinous to property. We have got to move or be content to see our effects wasted away and utterly destroyed. Now you will hardly believe it, but it is true, nevertheless, that there isn't a single coffin in good repair among all my acquaintance—now that is an absolute fact. I do not refer to people who come in a pine box mounted on an express wagon, but I am talking about your high-toned silver-mounted burial-case, monumental sort, that travel under plumes at the head of a procession and have choice of cemetery lots—I mean folks like the Jarvis's, and the Bledsoe's and Burling's and such. They are all about ruined. The most substantial people in our set, they were. And now look at them—utterly used up and poverty-stricken. One of the Bledsoe's actually traded his monument to a late barkeeper for some fresh shavings to put under his head. I tell you it speaks volumes, for there is nothing a corpse takes so much pride in as his monument. He loves to read the inscription. He comes after awhile to believe what it says, himself, and then you may see him sitting on the fence night after night enjoying it. Epitaphs are cheap, and they do a poor chap a world of good after he is dead, especially if he had hard luck while he was alive. I wish they were used more. Now I don't complain, but confidentially, I *do* think it was a little shabby in my descendants to give me nothing but this old slab of a gravestone—and all the more that there isn't a compliment on it. It used to have

"Gone to his just reward"

on it, and I was proud when I first saw it, but by and bye I noticed that whenever an old friend of mine came along he would hook his chin on the railing and pull a long face and read along down till he came to that, and then he would chuckle to himself and walk off looking satisfied and comfortable. So I scratched it off to get rid of those fools. But a dead man always takes a deal of pride in his monument. Yonder goes half a dozen of the Jarvises, now, with the family monument along. And Smithers and some hired spectres went by with his a while ago. Hello, Higgins, good-bye old friend! That's Meredith Higgins—died in '44—belongs to our set in the cemetery—fine old family—great-grandmother was an Injun—I am on the most familiar terms with him—he didn't hear me was the reason he didn't answer me. And I am sorry, too, because I would have liked to introduce you. You would admire him. He is the most disjointed, sway-backed and generally distorted old skeleton you ever saw, but he is full of fun. When he laughs it sounds like rasping two stones together, and he always starts it off with a cheery screech like raking a nail across a window-pane. Hey, Jones! That is old Columbus Jones—shroud cost four hundred dollars—entire trousseau, including monument, twenty-seven hundred. This was in the Spring of '26. It was enormous style for those days. Dead people came all the way from the Alleghenies to see his things—the party that occupied the grave next to mine remembers it well. Now do you see that individual going along with a piece of a head-board under his arm, one leg bone below his knee gone, and not a thing in the world on? That is Barstow Dalhouse, and next to Columbus Jones, he was the most sumptuously outfitted person that ever entered our cemetery. We are all leaving. We cannot tolerate the treatment we are receiving at the hands of our descendants. They open new cemeteries, but they leave us to our ignominy. They mend the streets, but they never mend anything that is about us or belongs to us. Look at that coffin of mine—yet I tell you in its day it was a piece of furniture that would have attracted attention in any drawing-room in this city. You may have it if you want it—I can't afford to repair it. Put a new bottom in her, and part of a new top, and a bit of fresh lining along the left side, and you'll find her about as comfortable as any receptacle of her species you ever tried. No thanks—no, don't mention it—you have been civil to me and I would give you all the property I have got before I would seem ungrateful. Now this winding-sheet is a kind of a sweet thing in its way, if you would like to——. No? Well, just as you say, but I wished to be fair and liberal—there's nothing mean about *me*. Good-bye, friend, I must be going. I may have a good way to go to-night—don't know. I only know one thing for certain, and that is, that I am on the emigrant trail, now, and I'll never sleep in that crazy old cemetery again. I will travel till I find respectable quarters, if I have to hoof it to New Jersey. All the boys are going. It was decided in public conclave, last night, to emigrate, and by the time the sun rises there won't be a bone left in our old habitations. Such cemeteries may suit my surviving friends but they do not suit the remains that have the honor to make these remarks. My opinion is the general opinion. If you doubt it, go and see how the departing ghosts upset things before they started. They were almost riotous in their demonstrations of distaste. Hello, here are some of the Bledsoes, and if you will give me a lift with this tombstone I guess I will join company and jog along with them—mighty respectable old family, the Bledsoes, and used to always come out in six-horse hearses, and all that sort of thing fifty years ago when I walked these streets in daylight. Good bye friend."

And with his gravestone on his shoulder he joined the grisly procession, dragging his damaged coffin after him, for notwithstanding he pressed it upon me so earnestly, I utterly refused his hospitality. I suppose that for as much as two hours these sad outcasts went clacking by, laden with their dismal effects, and all that time I sat pitying them. One or two of the youngest and least dilapidated among them inquired about midnight trains on the railways, but the rest seemed unacquainted with that mode of travel, and merely asked about common public roads to various towns and cities, some of which are not on the map, now, and vanished from it and from the earth as much as thirty years ago, and some few of them never had existed any where but on maps, and private ones in real estate agencies at that. And they asked about the condition of the cemeteries in these towns and cities, and about the reputation the citizens bore as to reverence for the dead.

This whole matter interested me deeply, and likewise compelled my sympathy for these homeless ones. And it all seeming real, and I not knowing it was a dream, I mentioned to one shrouded wanderer an idea that had entered my head to publish an account of this curious and very sorrowful exodus, but said also that I could not describe it truthfully, and just as it occurred, without seeming to trifle with a grave subject and exhibit an irreverence for the dead that would shock and distress their surviving friends. But this bland and stately remnant of a former citizen leaned him far over my gate and whispered in my ear, and said:

"DO NOT LET THAT DISTURB YOU. THE COMMUNITY THAT CAN STAND SUCH GRAVEYARDS AS THOSE WE ARE EMIGRATING FROM CAN STAND ANY THING A BODY CAN SAY ABOUT THE NEGLECTED AND FORSAKEN DEAD THAT LIE IN THEM."

At that very moment a cock crowed, and the weird procession vanished and left not a shred or a bone behind. I awoke, and found myself lying with my head out of the bed and "sagging" downwards considerably—a position favorable to dreaming dreams with morals in them, may be, but not poetry.

April 30 and May 7, 1870

About Smells

In a recent issue of the "Independent," the Rev. T. De Witt Talmage, of Brooklyn, has the following utterance on the subject of "Smells":

> I have a good Christian friend who, if he sat in the front pew in church, and a working man should enter the door at the other end, would smell him instantly. My friend is not to blame for the sensitiveness of his nose, any more than you would flog a pointer for being keener on the scent than a stupid watch-dog. The fact is, if you had all the churches free, by reason of the mixing up of the common people with the uncommon, you would keep one-half of Christendom sick at their stomach. If you are going to kill the church thus with bad smells, I will have nothing to do with this work of evangelization.

We have reason to believe that there will be laboring men in heaven; and also a number of negroes, and Esquimaux, and Terra del Fuegans, and Arabs, and a few Indians, and possibly even some Spaniards and Portuguese. All things are possible with God. We shall have all these sorts of people in heaven; but, alas! in getting them we shall lose the society of Dr. Talmage. Which is to say, we shall lose the company of one who could give more real "tone" to celestial society than any other contribution Brooklyn could furnish. And what would eternal happiness be without the Doctor? Blissful, unquestionably—we know that well enough—but would it be *distingué*, would it be *recherché* without him? St. Matthew without stockings or sandals; St. Jerome bareheaded, and with a coarse brown blanket robe dragging the ground; St. Sebastian with scarcely any raiment at all—these we should see, and should enjoy seeing them; but would we not miss a spike-tailed coat and kids, and turn away regretfully, and say to parties from the Orient: "These are well enough, but you ought to see Talmage of Brooklyn." I fear me that in the better world we shall not even have Dr. Talmage's "good Christian friend." For if he were sitting under the glory of the Throne, and the keeper of the keys admitted a Benjamin Franklin or other laboring man, that "friend," with his fine natural powers infinitely augmented by emancipation from hampering flesh, would detect him with a single sniff, and immediately take his hat and ask to be excused.

To all outward seeming, the Rev. T. De Witt Talmage is of the same material as that used in the construction of his early predecessors in the ministry; and yet one feels that there must be a difference somewhere between him and the Savior's first disciples. It may be because here, in the nineteenth century, Dr. T. has had advantages which Paul and Peter and the others could not and did not have. There was a lack of polish about them, and a looseness of etiquette, and a want of exclusiveness, which one cannot help noticing. They healed the very beggars, and held intercourse with people of a villanous odor every day. If the subject of these remarks had been chosen among the original Twelve Apostles, he would not have associated with the rest, because he could not have stood the fishy smell of some of his comrades who came from around the Sea of Galilee. He would have resigned his commission with some such remark as he makes in the extract quoted above: "Master, if thou art going to kill the church thus with bad smells, I will have nothing to do with this work of evangelization." He is a disciple, and makes that remark to the Master; the only difference is, that he makes it in the nineteenth instead of the first century.

Is there a choir in Mr. T.'s church? And does it ever occur that they have no better manners than to sing that hymn which is so suggestive of laborers and mechanics:

> "Son of the Carpenter! receive
> This humble work of mine?"

Now, can it be possible that in a handful of centuries the Christian character has fallen away from an imposing heroism that scorned even the stake, the cross, and the axe, to a poor little effeminacy that withers and wilts under an unsavory smell? We are not prepared to believe so, the reverend Doctor and his friend to the contrary notwithstanding.

May 1870

The Facts in the Case of the Great Beef Contract

In as few words as possible I wish to lay before the nation what share, howsoever small, I have had in this matter—this matter which has so exercised the public mind, engendered so much ill-feeling, and so filled the newspapers of both continents with distorted statements and extravagant comments.

The origin of this distressful thing was this—and I assert here that every fact in the following *résumé* can be amply proved by the official records of the General Government:

John Wilson Mackenzie, of Rotterdam, Chemung county, New Jersey, deceased, contracted with the General Government, on or about the 10th day of October, 1861, to furnish to General Sherman the sum total of thirty barrels of beef. Very well. He started after Sherman with the beef, but when he got to Washington Sherman had gone to Manassas; so he took the beef and followed him there, but arrived too late; he followed him to Nashville, and from Nashville to Chattanooga, and from Chattanooga to Atlanta—but he never could overtake him. At Atlanta he took a fresh start and followed him clear through his march to the sea. He arrived too late again by a few days, but hearing that Sherman was going out in the Quaker City excursion to the Holy Land, he took shipping for Beirut, calculating to head off the other vessel. When he arrived in Jerusalem with his beef, he learned that Sherman had not sailed in the Quaker City, but had gone to the Plains to fight the Indians. He returned to America and started for the Rocky Mountains. After eighteen days of arduous travel on the Plains, and when he had got within four miles of Sherman's headquarters, he was tomahawked and scalped, and the Indians got the beef. They got all of it but one barrel. Sherman's army captured that, and so, even in death, the bold navigator partly fulfilled his contract. In his will, which he had kept like a journal, he bequeathed the contract to his son Bartholomew W. Bartholomew W. made out the following bill and then died:

THE UNITED STATES
    In acct. with JOHN WILSON MACKENZIE,
      of New Jersey, deceased, ... Dr.

To thirty barrels of beef for General Sherman @ $100 . .	$3,000
To travelling expenses and transportation	14,000
Total	$17,000

Rec'd Pay't.

He died then; but he left the contract to Wm. J. Martin, who tried to collect it, but died before he got through. *He* left it to Barker J. Allen, and he tried to collect it also. He did not survive. Barker J. Allen left it to Anson G. Rogers, who attempted to collect it, and got along as far as the Ninth Auditor's office, when Death, the great Leveller, came all unsummoned, and foreclosed on *him* also. He left the bill to a relative of his in Connecticut, Vengeance Hopkins by name, who lasted four weeks and two days, and made the best time on record, coming within one of reaching the Twelfth Auditor. In his will he gave the contract bill to his uncle, by the name of O-be-joyful Johnson. It was too undermining for Joyful. His last words were: "Weep not for me—*I* am willing to go." And so he was, poor soul. Seven people inherited the contract after that. But they all died. So it came into my hands at last. It fell to me through a relative by the name of Hubbard—Bethlehem Hubbard, of Indiana. He had had a grudge against me for a long time; but in his last moments he sent for me, and forgave me everything, and weeping gave me the beef contract.

This ends the history of it up to the time that I succeeded to the property. I will now endeavor to set myself straight before the nation in everything that concerns my share in the matter. I took this beef contract, and the bill for mileage and transportation, to the President of the United States. He said:

"Well, Sir, what can I do for you?" I said:

"Sire: On or about the 10th day of October, 1861, John Wilson Mackenzie, of Rotterdam, Chemung county, New Jersey, deceased, contracted with the General Government to furnish to General Sherman the sum total of thirty barrels of beef—"

He stopped me there, and dismissed me from his presence—kindly, but firmly. The next day I called on the Secretary of State. He said:

"Well, Sir?"

I said: "Your Royal Highness: On or about the 10th day of October, 1861, John Wilson Mackenzie, of Rotterdam, Chemung county, New Jersey, deceased, contracted with the General Government to furnish to General Sherman the sum total of thirty barrels of beef—"

"That will do, Sir—that will do; this office has nothing to do with contracts for beef."

I was bowed out. I thought the matter all over, and finally, the following day, I visited the Secretary of the Navy, who said, "Speak quickly, Sir; do not keep me waiting." I said:

"Your Royal Highness: On or about the 10th day of October, 1861, John Wilson Mackenzie, of Rotterdam, Chemung county, New Jersey, deceased, contracted with the General Government to furnish to General Sherman the sum total of thirty barrels of beef—"

Well, it was as far as I could get. *He* had nothing to do with beef contracts for General Sherman either. I began to think it was a curious kind of a Government. It looked somewhat as if they wanted to get out of paying for that beef. The following day I went to the Secretary of the Interior. I said:

"Your Imperial Highness: On or about the 10th day of October—"

"That is sufficient, Sir—I have heard of you before. Go—take your infamous beef contract out of this establishment. The Interior Department has nothing whatever to do with subsistence for the army."

I went away. But I was exasperated now. I said I would haunt them; I would infest every department of this iniquitous Government till that contract business was settled; I would collect that bill, or fall as fell my predecessors, trying. I assailed the Postmaster-General; I besieged the Agricultural Department; I waylaid the Speaker of the House of Representatives. *They* had nothing to do with army contracts for beef. I moved upon the Commissioner of the Patent Office. I said:

"Your august Excellency: On or about—"

"Perdition! have you got *here* with your incendiary beef

contract, at last? We have *nothing* to do with beef contracts for the army, my dear Sir."

"Oh, that is all very well—but *somebody* has got to pay for that beef. It has got to be paid *now*, too, or I'll confiscate this old Patent Office and everything in it."

"But, my dear Sir—"

"It don't make any difference, Sir. The Patent Office is liable for that beef, I reckon; and liable or not liable, the Patent Office has got to pay for it."

Never mind the details. It ended in a fight. The Patent Office won. But I found out something to my advantage. I was told that the Treasury Department was the proper place for me to go to. I went there. I waited two hours and a half, and then I was admitted to the First Lord of the Treasury. I said:

"Most noble, grave and reverend Signor: On or about the 10th day of October, 1861, John Wilson Macken—"

"That is sufficient, Sir. I have heard of you. Go to the First Auditor of the Treasury."

I did so. He sent me to the Second Auditor. The Second Auditor sent me to the Third, and the Third sent me to the First Comptroller of the Corn-Beef Division. This began to look like business. He examined his books and all his loose papers, but found no minute of the beef contract. I went to the Second Comptroller of the Corn-Beef Division. He examined his books and his loose papers, but with no success. I was encouraged. During that week I got as far as the Sixth Comptroller in that division; the next week I got through the Claims Department; the third week I began and completed the Mislaid Contracts Department, and got a foothold in the Dead Reckoning Department. I finished that in three days. There was only one place left for it now. I laid siege to the Commissioner of Odds and Ends. To his clerk, rather—he was not there himself. There were sixteen beautiful young ladies in the room, writing in books, and there were seven well-favored young clerks showing them how. The young women smiled up over their shoulders, and the clerks smiled back at them, and all went merry as a marriage bell. Two or three clerks that were reading the newspapers looked at me rather hard, but went on reading, and nobody said anything. However, I had been used to this kind of alacrity from Fourth-

Assistant-Junior Clerks all through my eventful career, from the very day I entered the first office of the Corn-Beef Bureau clear till I passed out of the last one in the Dead Reckoning Division. I had got so accomplished by this time that I could stand on one foot from the moment I entered an office till a clerk spoke to me, without changing more than two, or maybe three times.

So I stood there till I had changed four different times. Then I said to one of the clerks who was reading:

"Illustrious Vagrant, where is the Grand Turk?"

"What do you mean, Sir? whom do you mean? If you mean the Chief of the Bureau, he is out."

"Will he visit the harem to-day?"

The young man glared upon me a while, and then went on reading his paper. But I knew the ways of those clerks. I knew I was safe, if he got through before another New York mail arrived. He only had two more papers left. After a while he finished them, and then he yawned, and asked me what I wanted.

"Renowned and honored Imbecile: On or about—"

"You are the beef contract man. Give me your papers."

He took them, and for a long time he ransacked his odds and ends. Finally he found the North-West Passage, as *I* regarded it—he found the long-lost record of that beef contract—he found the rock upon which so many of my ancestors had split before they ever got to it. I was deeply moved. And yet I rejoiced—for I had survived. I said with emotion, "Give it me. The Government will settle now." He waved me back, and said there was something yet to be done first.

"Where is this John Wilson Mackenzie?" said he.

"Dead."

"When did he die?"

"He didn't die at all—he was killed."

"How?"

"Tomahawked."

"Who tomahawked him?"

"Why, an Indian, of course. You didn't suppose it was a superintendent of a Sunday school, did you?"

"No. An Indian, was it?"

"The same."

"Name of the Indian?"

"His name! *I* don't know his name."

"*Must* have his name. Who saw the tomahawking done?"

"I don't know."

"You were not present yourself then?"

"Which you can see by my hair. I was absent."

"Then how do you know that Mackenzie is dead?"

"Because he certainly died at that time, and I have every reason to believe that he has been dead ever since. I *know* he has, in fact."

"We must have proofs. Have you got the Indian?"

"Of course not."

"Well, you must get him. Have you got the tomahawk?"

"I never thought of such a thing."

"You must get the tomahawk. You must produce the Indian and the tomahawk. If Mackenzie's death can be proven by these, you can then go before the commission appointed to audit claims, with some show of getting your bill under such headway that your children may possibly live to receive the money and enjoy it. But that man's death *must* be proven. However, I may as well tell you that the Government will never pay that transportation and those travelling expenses of the lamented Mackenzie. It *may* possibly pay for the barrel of beef that Sherman's soldiers captured, if you can get a relief bill through Congress making an appropriation for that purpose; but it will not pay for the twenty-nine barrels the Indians ate."

"Then there is only a hundred dollars due me, and *that* isn't certain! After all Mackenzie's travels in Europe, Asia, and America with that beef; after all his trials and tribulations and transportation; after the slaughter of all those innocents that tried to collect that bill! Young man, why didn't the First Comptroller of the Corn-Beef Division tell me this?"

"He didn't know anything about the genuineness of your claim."

"Why didn't the Second tell me? why didn't the Third? why didn't all those divisions and departments tell me?"

"None of them knew. We do things by routine here. You have followed the routine and found out what you wanted to know. It is the best way. It is the only way. It is very regular, and very slow, but it is very certain."

"Yes, certain death. It has been, to the most of our tribe. I begin to feel that I, too, am called. Young man, you love the bright creature yonder with the gentle blue eyes and the steel pens behind her ears—I see it in your soft glances; you wish to marry her—but you are poor. Here, hold out your hand—here is the beef contract; go, take her and be happy! Heaven bless you, my children!"

This is all that I know about the great beef contract, that has created so much talk in the community. The clerk to whom I bequeathed it died. I know nothing further about the contract or any one connected with it. I only know that if a man lives long enough, he can trace a thing through the Circumlocution Office of Washington, and find out, after much labor and trouble and delay, that which he could have found out on the first day if the business of the Circumlocution Office were as ingeniously systematized as it would be if it were a great private mercantile institution.

May 1870

The Story of the Good Little Boy
Who Did Not Prosper

[The following has been written at the instance of several literary friends, who thought that if the history of "The Bad Little Boy who Did not Come to Grief" (a moral sketch which I published five or six years ago) was worthy of preservation several weeks in print, a fair and unprejudiced companion-piece to it would deserve a similar immortality. — EDITOR MEMORANDA.]

Once there was a good little boy by the name of Jacob Blivens. He always obeyed his parents, no matter how absurd and unreasonable their demands were; and he always learned his book, and never was late at Sabbath school. He would not play hookey, even when his sober judgment told him it was the most profitable thing he could do. None of the other boys could ever make that boy out, he acted so strangely. He wouldn't lie, no matter how convenient it was. He just said it was wrong to lie, and that was sufficient for him. And he was so honest that he was simply ridiculous. The curious ways that that Jacob had surpassed everything. He wouldn't play marbles on Sunday, he wouldn't rob birds' nests, he wouldn't give hot pennies to organ-grinders' monkeys; he didn't seem to take any interest in any kind of rational amusement. So the other boys used to try to reason it out and come to an understanding of him, but they couldn't arrive at any satisfactory conclusion; as I said before, they could only figure out a sort of vague idea that he was "afflicted," and so they took him under their protection, and never allowed any harm to come to him.

This good little boy read all the Sunday-school books; they were his greatest delight. This was the whole secret of it. He believed in the good little boys they put in the Sunday-school books; he had every confidence in them. He longed to come across one of them alive, once; but he never did. They all died before his time, maybe. Whenever he read about a particularly good one, he turned over quickly to the end to see what became of him, because he wanted to travel thousands of miles and gaze on him; but it wasn't any use; that good little boy always died in the last chapter, and there was a picture of the funeral, with all his relations and the Sunday-school children standing around the grave in pantaloons that were too short, and bonnets that were too large, and everybody crying into handkerchiefs that had as much as a yard and a half of stuff in them. He was always headed off in this way. He never could see one of those good little boys, on account of his always dying in the last chapter.

Jacob had a noble ambition to be put in a Sunday-school book. He wanted to be put in, with pictures representing him gloriously declining to lie to his mother, and she weeping for joy about it; and pictures representing him standing on the doorstep giving a penny to a poor beggar-woman with six children, and telling her to spend it freely, but not to be extravagant, because extravagance is a sin; and pictures of him magnanimously refusing to tell on the bad boy who always lay in wait for him around the corner, as he came from school, and welted him over the head with a lath, and then chased him home, saying "Hi! hi!" as he proceeded. That was the ambition of young Jacob Blivens. He wished to be put in a Sunday-school book. It made him feel a little uncomfortable sometimes when he reflected that the good little boys always died. He loved to live, you know, and this was the most unpleasant feature about being a Sunday-school-book boy. He knew it was not healthy to be good. He knew it was more fatal than consumption to be so supernaturally good as the boys in the books were; he knew that none of them had ever been able to stand it long, and it pained him to think that if they put him in a book he wouldn't ever see it, or even if they did get the book out before he died, it wouldn't be popular without any picture of his funeral in the back part of it. It couldn't be much of a Sunday-school book that couldn't tell about the advice he gave to the community when he was dying. So, at last, of course he had to make up his mind to do the best he could under the circumstances—to live right, and hang on as long as he could, and have his dying speech all ready when his time came.

But somehow, nothing ever went right with this good little boy; nothing ever turned out with him the way it turned out with the good little boys in the books. They always had a good time, and the bad boys had the broken legs; but in his

case there was a screw loose somewhere, and it all happened
just the other way. When he found Jim Blake stealing apples,
and went under the tree to read to him about the bad little
boy who fell out of a neighbor's apple tree, and broke his
arm, Jim fell out of the tree too, but he fell on *him*, and broke
his arm, and Jim wasn't hurt at all. Jacob couldn't understand
that. There wasn't anything in the books like it.

And once, when some bad boys pushed a blind man over in
the mud, and Jacob ran to help him up and receive his blessing, the blind man did not give him any blessing at all, but
whacked him over the head with his stick and said he would
like to catch him shoving *him* again and then pretending to
help him up. This was not in accordance with any of the
books. Jacob looked them all over to see.

One thing that Jacob wanted to do was to find a lame
dog that hadn't any place to stay, and was hungry and persecuted, and bring him home and pet him and have that
dog's imperishable gratitude. And at last he found one, and
was happy; and he brought him home and fed him, but
when he was going to pet him the dog flew at him and tore
all the clothes off him except those that were in front, and
made a spectacle of him that was astonishing. He examined
authorities, but he could not understand the matter. It was of
the same breed of dogs that was in the books, but it acted
very differently. Whatever this boy did, he got into trouble.
The very things the boys in the books got rewarded for
turned out to be about the most unprofitable things he could
invest in.

Once when he was on his way to Sunday school he saw
some bad boys starting off pleasuring in a sail-boat. He was
filled with consternation, because he knew from his reading
that boys who went sailing on Sunday invariably got
drowned. So he ran out on a raft to warn them, but a log
turned with him and slid him into the river. A man got him
out pretty soon, and the doctor pumped the water out of him
and gave him a fresh start with his bellows, but he caught
cold and lay sick abed nine weeks. But the most unaccountable thing about it was that the bad boys in the boat had a
good time all day, and then reached home alive and well, in
the most surprising manner. Jacob Blivens said there was

nothing like these things in the books. He was perfectly dumbfounded.

When he got well he was a little discouraged, but he resolved to keep on trying, anyhow. He knew that so far his experiences wouldn't do to go in a book, but he hadn't yet reached the allotted term of life for good little boys, and he hoped to be able to make a record yet, if he could hold on till his time was fully up. If everything else failed, he had his dying speech to fall back on.

He examined his authorities, and found that it was now time for him to go to sea as a cabin boy. He called on a ship captain and made his application, and when the captain asked for his recommendations he proudly drew out a tract and pointed to the words: "To Jacob Blivens, from his affectionate teacher." But the captain was a coarse, vulgar man, and he said, "Oh, that be blowed! *that* wasn't any proof that he knew how to wash dishes or handle a slush-bucket, and he guessed he didn't want him." This was altogether the most extraordinary thing that ever had happened to Jacob in all his life. A compliment from a teacher, on a tract, had never failed to move the tenderest of emotions of ship captains and open the way to all offices of honor and profit in their gift—it never had in any book that ever *he* had read. He could hardly believe his senses.

This boy always had a hard time of it. Nothing ever came out according to the authorities with him. At last, one day, when he was around hunting up bad little boys to admonish, he found a lot of them in the old iron foundry fixing up a little joke on fourteen or fifteen dogs, which they had tied together in long procession and were going to ornament with empty nitro-glycerine cans made fast to their tails. Jacob's heart was touched. He sat down on one of those cans—for he never minded grease when duty was before him—and he took hold of the foremost dog by the collar, and turned his reproving eye upon wicked Tom Jones. But just at that moment Alderman McWelter, full of wrath, stepped in. All the bad boys ran away; but Jacob Blivens rose in conscious innocence and began one of those stately little Sunday-school-book speeches which always commence with "Oh, Sir!" in dead opposition to the fact that no boy, good or bad, ever starts a remark with "Oh, Sir!" But the Alderman never waited to hear the rest. He took Jacob Blivens by the ear and turned him around, and hit him a whack in the rear with the flat of his hand; and in an instant that good little boy shot out through the roof and soared away toward the sun, with the fragments of those fifteen dogs stringing after him like the tail of a kite. And there wasn't a sign of that Alderman or that old iron foundry left on the face of the earth; and as for young Jacob Blivens, he never got a chance to make his last dying speech after all his trouble fixing it up, unless he made it to the birds; because, although the bulk of him came down all right in a tree-top in an adjoining county, the rest of him was apportioned around among four townships, and so they had to hold five inquests on him to find out whether he was dead or not, and how it occurred. You never saw a boy scattered so.*

Thus perished the good little boy who did the best he could, but didn't come out according to the books. Every boy who ever did as he did prospered, except him. His case is truly remarkable. It will probably never be accounted for.

*This catastrophe is borrowed (without the unknown but most ingenious owner's permission) from a stray newspaper item, and trimmed up and altered to fit Jacob Blivens, who stood sadly in need of a doom that would send him out of the world with *éclat*—EDITOR MEMORANDA.

May 1870

Disgraceful Persecution of a Boy

In San Francisco, the other day, "a well-dressed boy, on his way to Sunday school, was arrested and thrown into the city prison for stoning Chinamen." What a commentary is this upon human justice! What sad prominence it gives to our human disposition to tyrannize over the weak! San Francisco has little right to take credit to herself for her treatment of this poor boy. What had the child's education been? How should he suppose it was wrong to stone a Chinaman? Before we side against him, along with outraged San Francisco, let us give him a chance—let us hear the testimony for the defence. He was a "well-dressed" boy, and a Sunday-school scholar, and, therefore, the chances are that his parents were intelligent, well-to-do people, with just enough natural villany in their compositions to make them yearn after the daily papers, and enjoy them; and so this boy had opportunities to learn all through the week how to do right, as well as on Sunday. It was in this way that he found out that the great commonwealth of California imposes an unlawful mining tax upon John the foreigner, and allows Patrick the foreigner to dig gold for nothing—probably because the degraded Mongol is at no expense for whiskey, and the refined Celt cannot exist without it. It was in this way that he found out that a respectable number of the tax-gatherers—it would be unkind to say all of them—collect the tax twice, instead of once; and that, inasmuch as they do it solely to discourage Chinese immigration into the mines, it is a thing that is much applauded, and likewise regarded as being singularly facetious. It was in this way that he found out that when a white man robs a sluice-box (by the term white man is meant Spaniards, Mexicans, Portuguese, Irish, Hondurans, Peruvians, Chileans, etc., etc.), they make him leave the camp; and when a Chinaman does that thing, they hang him. It was in this way that he found out that in many districts of the vast Pacific coast, so strong is the wild, free love of justice in the hearts of the people, that whenever any secret and mysterious crime is committed, they say, "Let justice be done, though the heavens fall," and go straightway and swing a Chinaman. It was in this way that he found out that by studying one half of each day's "local items" it would appear that the police of San Francisco were either asleep or dead, and by studying the other half it would seem that the reporters were gone mad with admiration of the energy, the virtue, the high effectiveness, and the dare-devil intrepidity of that very police—making exultant mention of how "the Argus-eyed officer So-and-so" captured a wretched knave of a Chinaman who was stealing chickens, and brought him gloriously to the city prison; and how "the gallant officer Such-and-such-a-one" quietly kept an eye on the movements of an "unsuspecting almond-eyed son of Confucius" (your reporter is nothing if not facetious), following him around with that far-off look of vacancy and unconsciousness always so finely affected by that inscrutable being, the forty-dollar policeman, during a waking interval, and captured him at last in the very act of placing his hands in a suspicious manner upon a paper of tacks left by the owner in an exposed situation; and how one officer performed this prodigious thing, and another officer that, and another the other—and pretty much every one of these performances having for a dazzling central incident a Chinaman guilty of a shilling's worth of crime, an unfortunate whose misdemeanor must be hurrahed into something enormous in order to keep the public from noticing how many really important rascals went uncaptured in the mean time, and how overrated those glorified policemen actually are. It was in this way that the boy found out that the Legislature, being aware that the Constitution has made America an asylum for the poor and the oppressed of all nations, and that therefore the poor and oppressed who fly to our shelter must not be charged a disabling admission fee, made a law that every Chinaman, upon landing, must be *vaccinated* upon the wharf, and pay to the State's appointed officer *ten dollars* for the service, when there are plenty of doctors in San Francisco who would be glad enough to do it for him for fifty cents. It was in this way that the boy found out that a Chinaman had no rights that any man was bound to respect; that he had no sorrows that any man was bound to pity; that neither his life nor his liberty was worth the purchase of a penny when a white man needed a scapegoat; that nobody loved Chinamen, nobody befriended them, nobody spared them suffering when it was convenient to inflict it; everybody, individuals, communities, the majesty of the State itself, joined in hating, abusing, and persecuting these humble strangers. And, therefore, what *could* have been more natural than for this sunny-hearted boy, tripping along to Sunday school, with his mind teeming with freshly-learned incentives to high and virtuous action, to say to himself:

"Ah, there goes a Chinaman! God will not love me if I do not stone him."

And for this he was arrested and put in the city jail. Everything conspired to teach him that it was a high and holy thing to stone a Chinaman, and yet he no sooner attempts to do his duty than he is punished for it—he, poor chap, who has been aware all his life that one of the principal recreations of the police, out toward the Gold Refinery, was to look on with tranquil enjoyment while the butchers of Brannan street set their dogs on unoffending Chinamen, and make them flee for their lives.*

Keeping in mind the tuition in the humanities which the entire "Pacific coast" gives its youth, there is a very sublimity of grotesqueness in the virtuous flourish with which the good city fathers of San Francisco proclaim (as they have lately done) that "The police are positively ordered to arrest all boys, of every description and wherever found, who engage in assaulting Chinamen."

Still, let us be truly glad they have made the order, notwithstanding its prominent inconsistency; and let us rest perfectly confident the police are glad, too. Because there is no personal peril in arresting boys, provided they be of the small kind, and the reporters will have to laud their performances

*I have many such memories in my mind, but am thinking just at present of one particular one, where the Brannan street butchers set their dogs on a Chinaman who was quietly passing with a basket of clothes on his head; and while the dogs mutilated his flesh, a butcher increased the hilarity of the occasion by knocking some of the Chinaman's teeth down his throat with half a brick. This incident sticks in my memory with a more malevolent tenacity, perhaps, on account of the fact that I was in the employ of a San Francisco journal at the time, and was not allowed to publish it because it might offend some of the peculiar element that subscribed for the paper. —EDITOR MEMORANDA.

just as loyally as ever, or go without items. The new form for local items in San Francisco will now be: "The ever vigilant and efficient officer So-and-So succeeded, yesterday afternoon, in arresting Master Tommy Jones, after a determined resistance," etc., etc., followed by the customary statistics and final hurrah, with its unconscious sarcasm: "We are happy in being able to state that this is the forty-seventh boy arrested by this gallant officer since the new ordinance went into effect. The most extraordinary activity prevails in the police department. Nothing like it has been seen since we can remember."

May 1870

Misplaced Confidence

"Just about the close of that long, hard winter," said the Sunday-school superintendent, "as I was wending toward my duties one brilliant Sabbath morning, I glanced down toward the levee, and there lay the City of Hartford!—no mistake about it, there she was, puffing and panting, after her long pilgrimage through the ice. A glad sight? Well, I should say so! And then came a pang, right away, because I should have to instruct empty benches, sure; the youngsters would all be off welcoming the first steamboat of the season. You can imagine how surprised I was when I opened the door and saw half the benches full! My gratitude was free, large, and sincere. I resolved that they should not find me unappreciative. I said:

" 'Boys, you cannot think how proud it makes me to see you here, nor what renewed assurance it gives me of your affection. I confess that I said to myself, as I came along and saw that the City of Hartford was in—'

" '*No! but is she, though!*'

"And, as quick as any flash of lightning, I stood in the presence of empty benches! I had brought them the news myself."

May 1870

383

Our Precious Lunatic

NEW YORK, May 10.

The Richardson-McFarland jury had been out one hour and fifty minutes. A breathless silence brooded over court and auditory—a silence and a stillness so absolute, notwithstanding the vast multitude of human beings packed together there, that when some one far away among the throng under the north-east balcony cleared his throat with a smothered little cough it startled everybody uncomfortably, so distinctly did it grate upon the pulseless air. At that imposing moment the bang of a door was heard, then the shuffle of approaching feet, and then a sort of surging and swaying disorder among the heads near the entrance from the jury room told that the Twelve were coming. Presently all was still again, and the foreman of the jury rose and said:

"YOUR HONOR AND GENTLEMEN: We, the jury charged with the duty of determining whether the prisoner at the bar, Daniel McFarland, has been guilty of murder, in taking by surprise an unarmed man and shooting him to death, or whether the said prisoner is simply afflicted with a sad but irresponsible insanity which at times can be cheered only by violent entertainment with firearms, do find as follows, namely:

That the prisoner Daniel McFarland is insane, as above described. Because:

1. His great-grandfather's step-father was tainted with insanity, and frequently killed people who were distasteful to him. Hence, insanity is hereditary in the family.

2. For nine years the prisoner at the bar did not adequately support his family. Strong circumstantial evidence of insanity.

3. For nine years he made of his home, as a general thing, a poor-house; sometimes (but very rarely,) a cheery, happy habitation; frequently the den of a beery, driveling, stupified animal; but never, as far as ascertained, the abiding place of a gentleman. These be evidences of insanity.

4. He once took his young unmarried sister-in-law to the museum; while there his hereditary insanity came upon him, and to such a degree that he hiccupped and staggered; and

afterward, on the way home, even made love to the young girl he was protecting. These are the acts of a person not right in his mind.

5. For a good while his sufferings were so great that he had to submit to the inconvenience of having his wife give public readings for the family support; and at times, when he handed these shameful earnings to the barkeeper, his haughty soul was so torn with anguish that he could hardly stand without leaning up against something. At such times he has been known to shed tears into his sustenance until it was diluted to utter inefficiency. Inattention of this nature is not the act of a Democrat unafflicted in mind.

6. He never spared expense in making his wife comfortable during her occasional confinements. Her father is able to testify to this. There was always an element of unsoundness about the prisoner's generosities that is very suggestive at this time and before this court.

7. Two years ago the prisoner came fearlessly up behind Richardson in the dark, and shot him in the leg. The prisoner's brave and protracted defiance of an adversity that for years had left him little to depend upon for his support but a wife who sometimes earned scarcely any thing for weeks at a time, is evidence that he would have appeared in front of Richardson and shot him in the stomach if he had not been insane at the time of the shooting.

8. Fourteen months ago the prisoner told Archibald Smith that he was going to kill Richardson. This is insanity.

9. Twelve months ago he told Marshal P. Jones that he was going to kill Richardson. Insanity.

10. Nine months ago he was lurking about Richardson's home in New Jersey, and said he was going to kill the said Richardson. Insanity.

11. Seven months ago he showed a pistol to Seth Brown and said that that was for Richardson. He said Brown testified that at that time it seemed plain that there was something the matter with McFarland, for he crossed the street diagonally nine times in fifty yards, apparently without any settled reason for doing so, and finally fell in the gutter and went to sleep. He remarked at the time that McFarland "acted strange"—believed he was insane. Upon hearing Brown's

evidence, John W. Galen, M. D., affirmed at once that McFarland *was* insane.

12. Five months ago, McFarland showed his customary pistol, in his customary way, to his bed-fellow, Charles A. Dana, and told him he was going to kill Richardson the first time an opportunity offered. Evidence of insanity.

13. Five months and two weeks ago McFarland asked John Morgan the time of day, *and turned and walked rapidly away without waiting for an answer*. Almost indubitable evidence of insanity. And—

14. It is remarkable that exactly one week after this circumstance the prisoner, Daniel McFarland, confronted Albert D. Richardson suddenly and without warning and shot him dead. *This is manifest insanity*. Everything we know of the prisoner goes to show that if he had been sane at the time, he would have shot his victim from behind.

15. There is an absolutely overwhelming mass of testimony to show that *an hour before the shooting, McFarland was* ANXIOUS AND UNEASY, *and that five minutes after it he was* EXCITED. Thus the accumulating conjectures and evidences of insanity culminate in this sublime and unimpeachable *proof* of it. Therefore—

"Your Honor and Gentlemen—We the jury pronounce the said Daniel McFarland INNOCENT OF MURDER, BUT CALAMITOUSLY INSANE."

The scene that ensued almost defies description. Hats, handkerchiefs and bonnets were frantically waved above the massed heads in the courtroom, and three tremendous cheers and a tiger told where the sympathies of court and people were. Then a hundred pursed lips were advanced to kiss the liberated prisoner, and many a hand thrust out to give him the congratulatory shake—but presto! with a maniac's own quickness and a maniac's own fury, the lunatic assassin of Richardson fell upon his friends with teeth and nails, boots and office furniture, and the amazing rapidity with which he broke heads and limbs, and rent and sundered bodies, till near a hundred citizens were reduced to mere quivering heaps of fleshy odds and ends and crimson rags, was like nothing in this world but the exultant frenzy of a plunging, tearing, roaring devil of a steam machine when it snatches a human being and spins him and whirls him till he shreds away to nothingness like a "four o'clock" before the breath of a child.

The destruction was awful. It is said that within the space of eight minutes McFarland killed and crippled some six score persons and tore down a large portion of the City Hall building, carrying away and casting into Broadway six or seven marble columns fifty-four feet long and weighing nearly two tons each. But he was finally captured and sent in chains to the lunatic asylum for life. [By late telegrams it appears that this is a mistake.— EDITOR EXPRESS.]

But the really curious part of this whole matter is yet to be told. And that is, that McFarland's most intimate friends believe that the very first time it ever occurred to him that the insanity plea was not a mere politic pretense, was when that verdict came in. They think that the startling thought burst upon him, then, that if twelve good and true men, able to comprehend all the baseness of perjury, *proclaimed under oath he was a lunatic, there was no gain saying such evidence, and he* UNQUESTIONABLY WAS INSANE!

Possibly that was really the way of it. It is dreadful to think that maybe the most awful calamity that can befal a man, namely, loss of reason, was precipitated upon this poor prisoner by a jury that *could* have hanged him instead, and so done him a mercy and his country a service.

MARK TWAIN

POSTSCRIPT— LATER.

MAY 11.— I do not expect anybody to believe so astounding a thing, and yet it is the solemn truth that instead of instantly sending this dangerous lunatic to the insane asylum, (which I had naturally supposed they would do and so I had prematurely *said* they had,) the court has actually SET HIM AT LIBERTY. Comment is unnecessary.

M. T.

May 14, 1870

A Couple of Sad Experiences

When I published a squib recently, in which I said I was going to edit an Agricultural Department in this magazine, I certainly did not desire to deceive anybody. I had not the remotest desire to play upon any one's confidence with a practical joke, for he is a pitiful creature indeed who will degrade the dignity of his humanity to the contriving of the witless inventions that go by that name. I purposely wrote the thing as absurdly and as extravagantly as it could be written, in order to be sure and not mislead hurried or heedless readers: for I spoke of launching a triumphal *barge* upon a *desert*, and planting a *tree* of prosperity *in a mine*—a tree whose *fragrance* should *slake the thirst* of the *naked*, and whose *branches* should spread abroad till they *washed the shores* of, etc., etc. I thought that manifest lunacy like that would protect the reader. But to make assurance absolute, and show that I did not and could not seriously mean to attempt an *Agricultural* Department, I stated distinctly in my postscript that I *did not know anything about Agriculture*. But alas! right there is where I made my worst mistake—for that remark seems to have recommended my proposed Agriculture more than anything else. It lets a little light in on me, and I fancy I perceive that the farmers feel a little bored, sometimes, by the oracular profundity of agricultural editors who "know it all." In fact, one of my correspondents suggests this (for that unhappy squib has deluged me with letters about potatoes, and cabbages, and hominy, and vermicelli, and maccaroni, and all the other fruits, cereals, and vegetables that ever grew on earth; and if I get done answering questions about the best way of raising these things before I go raving crazy, I shall be thankful, and shall never write obscurely for fun any more).

Shall I tell the real reason why I have unintentionally succeeded in fooling so many people? It is because some of them only read a little of the squib I wrote and jumped to the conclusion that it was serious, and the rest did not read it at all, but heard of my agricultural venture at second-hand. Those cases I could not guard against, of course. To write a burlesque so wild that its pretended facts will not be accepted in perfect good faith by somebody, is very nearly an impossible thing to do. It is because, in some instances, the reader is a person who never tries to deceive anybody himself, and therefore is not expecting any one to wantonly practise a deception upon *him*; and in this case the only person dishonored is the man who wrote the burlesque. In other instances the "nub" or moral of the burlesque—if its object be to enforce a truth—escapes notice in the superior glare of something in the body of the burlesque itself. And very often this "moral" is tagged on at the bottom, and the reader, not knowing that it is the key of the whole thing and the only important paragraph in the article, tranquilly turns up his nose at it and leaves it unread. One can deliver a satire with telling force through the insidious medium of a travesty, if he is careful not to overwhelm the satire with the extraneous interest of the travesty, and so bury it from the reader's sight and leave him a joked and defrauded victim, when the honest intent was to add to either his knowledge or his wisdom. I have had a deal of experience in burlesques and their unfortunate aptness to deceive the public, and this is why I tried hard to make that agricultural one so broad and so perfectly palpable that even a one-eyed potato could see it; and yet, as I speak the solemn truth, it fooled one of the ablest agricultural editors in America!

THE PETRIFIED MAN.

Now, to show how really hard it is to foist a moral or a truth upon an unsuspecting public through a burlesque without entirely and absurdly missing one's mark, I will here set down two experiences of my own in this thing. In the fall of 1862, in Nevada and California, the people got to running wild about extraordinary petrifactions and other natural marvels. One could scarcely pick up a paper without finding in it one or two glorified discoveries of this kind. The mania was becoming a little ridiculous. I was a brand-new local editor in Virginia City, and I felt called upon to destroy this growing evil: we all have our benignant, fatherly moods at one time or another, I suppose. I chose to kill the petrifaction mania with a delicate, a very delicate, satire. But maybe it was altogether too delicate, for nobody ever perceived the satire part of it at

all. I put my scheme in the shape of the discovery of a remarkable petrified man. I had had a temporary falling out with Mr.
Sewall, the new coroner and justice of the peace of Humboldt, and I thought I might as well touch him up a little at
the same time and make him ridiculous, and thus combine
pleasure with business. So I told, in patient, belief-compelling
detail, all about the finding of a petrified man at Gravelly
Ford (exactly a hundred and twenty miles, over a breakneck
mountain trail, from where Sewall lived); how all the savants
in the immediate neighborhood had been to examine it (it
was notorious that there was not a living creature within fifty
miles of there, except a few starving Indians, some crippled
grasshoppers, and four or five buzzards out of meat and too
feeble to get away); how those savants all pronounced the
petrified man to have been in a state of complete petrifaction
for over ten generations; and then, with a seriousness that I
ought to have been ashamed to assume, I stated that as soon
as Mr. Sewall heard the news, he summoned a jury, mounted
his mule, and posted off, with noble reverence for official
duty, on that awful five days' journey, through alkali, sage-
brush, peril of body and imminent starvation, to *hold an
inquest* on this man that had been dead and turned to
everlasting stone for more than three hundred years! And
then, my hand being "in," so to speak, I went on, with the
same unflinching gravity, to state that the jury returned a verdict that deceased came to his death from *protracted exposure*.
This only moved me to higher flights of imagination, and I
said that the jury, with that charity so characteristic of pioneers, then dug a grave, and were about to give the petrified
man Christian burial, when they found that for ages a limestone sediment had been trickling down the face of the stone
against which he was sitting, and this stuff had run under him
and cemented him fast to the "bed-rock"; that the jury (they
were all silver-miners) canvassed the difficulty a moment, and
then got out their powder and fuse, and proceeded to drill a
hole under him, in order to *blast him from his position*, when
Mr. Sewall, "with that delicacy so characteristic of him, forbade them, observing that it would be little less than sacrilege
to do such a thing." From beginning to end the "Petrified
Man" squib was a string of roaring absurdities, albeit they

were told with an unfair pretence of truth that even imposed upon me to some extent, and I was in some danger of believing in my own fraud. But I really had no desire to deceive anybody, and no expectation of doing it. I depended on the way the petrified man was *sitting* to explain to the public that he was a swindle. Yet I purposely mixed that up with other things, hoping to make it obscure—and I did. I would describe the position of one foot, and then say his right thumb was against the side of his nose; then talk about his other foot, and presently come back and say the fingers of his right hand were spread apart; then talk about the back of his head a little, and return and say the left thumb was hooked into the right little finger; then ramble off about something else, and by and by drift back again and remark that the fingers of the left hand were spread like those of the right. But I was too ingenious. I mixed it up rather too much; and so all that description of the attitude, as a key to the humbuggery of the article, was entirely lost, for nobody but me ever discovered and comprehended the peculiar and suggestive position of the petrified man's hands.

As a *satire* on the petrifaction mania, or anything else, my Petrified Man was a disheartening failure; for everybody received him in innocent good faith, and I was stunned to see the creature I had begotten to pull down the wonder-business with and bring derision upon it, calmly exalted to the grand chief place in the list of the genuine marvels our Nevada had produced. I was so disappointed at the curious miscarriage of my scheme that at first I was angry and did not like to think about it; but by and by, when the exchanges began to come in with the Petrified Man copied and guilelessly glorified, I began to feel a soothing secret satisfaction; and as my gentleman's field of travel broadened, and by the exchanges I saw that he steadily and implacably penetrated territory after territory, State after State, and land after land, till he swept the great globe and culminated in sublime and unimpeached legitimacy in the august "London Lancet," my cup was full, ·and I said I was glad I had done it. I think that for about eleven months, as nearly as I can remember, Mr. Sewall's daily mail contained along in the neighborhood of half a bushel of newspapers hailing from many climes with the Petrified Man in them, marked around with a prominent belt of ink. I sent them to him. I did it for spite, not for fun. He used to shovel them into his back yard and curse. And every day during all those months the miners, his constituents (for miners never quit joking a person when they get started), would call on him and ask if he could tell them where they could get hold of a paper with the Petrified Man in it. He could have accommodated a continent with them. I hated Sewall in those days, and these things pacified me and pleased me. I could not have gotten more real comfort out of him without killing him.

MY FAMOUS "BLOODY MASSACRE."

The other burlesque I have referred to was my fine satire upon the financial expedient of "cooking dividends," a thing which became shamefully frequent on the Pacific coast for a while. Once more, in my self-complacent simplicity, I felt that the time had arrived for me to rise up and be a reformer. I put this reformatory satire in the shape of a fearful "Massacre at Empire City." The San Francisco papers were making a great outcry about the iniquity of the Daney Silver-Mining Company, whose directors had declared a "cooked" or false dividend, for the purpose of increasing the value of their stock, so that they could sell out at a comfortable figure and then scramble from under the tumbling concern. And while abusing the Daney, those papers did not forget to urge the public to get rid of all their silver stocks and invest in sound and safe San Francisco stocks, such as the Spring Valley Water Company, etc. But right at this unfortunate juncture, behold the Spring Valley cooked a dividend too! And so, under the insidious mask of an invented "bloody massacre," I stole upon the public unawares with my scathing satire upon the dividend-cooking system. In about half a column of imaginary inhuman carnage I told how a citizen had murdered his wife and nine children and then committed suicide. And I said slily, at the bottom, that the sudden madness of which this melancholy massacre was the result, had been brought about by his having allowed himself to be persuaded by the California papers to sell his sound and lucrative Nevada silver stocks and buy into Spring Valley just in time to get cooked along with that company's fancy dividend, and sink every cent he had in

the world. Ah, it was a deep, deep satire, and most ingeniously contrived. But I made the horrible details so carefully
and conscientiously interesting that the public simply de-
voured *them* greedily, and wholly overlooked the following
distinctly stated facts, to wit: The murderer was perfectly well
known to every creature in the land as a *bachelor*, and consequently he could not murder his wife and nine children; he
murdered them "in his splendid dressed-stone mansion just in
the edge of the great pine forest between Empire City and
Dutch Nick's," when even the very pickled oysters that came
on our tables knew that there was not a "dressed-stone mansion" in all Nevada Territory; also, that so far from there
being a "great pine forest between Empire City and Dutch
Nick's," there wasn't a solitary tree within fifteen miles of
either place; and, finally, it was patent and notorious that Empire City and Dutch Nick's were one and the same place, and
contained only six houses anyhow, and consequently there
could be no forest *between* them; and on top of all these absurdities I stated that this diabolical murderer, after inflicting
a wound upon himself that the reader ought to have seen
would have killed an elephant in the twinkling of an eye,
jumped on his horse and rode *four miles*, waving his wife's
reeking scalp in the air, and thus performing entered Carson
City with tremendous éclat, and dropped dead in front of the
chief saloon, the envy and admiration of all beholders.

Well, in all my life I never saw anything like the sensation
that little satire created. It was the talk of the town, it was the
talk of the Territory. Most of the citizens dropped gently into
it at breakfast, and they never finished their meal. There was
something about those minutely-faithful details that was a
sufficing substitute for food. Few people that were able to
read took food that morning. Dan and I (Dan was my reportorial associate) took our seats on either side of our customary
table in the "Eagle Restaurant," and as I unfolded the shred
they used to call a napkin in that establishment, I saw at the
next table two stalwart innocents with that sort of vegetable
dandruff sprinkled about their clothing which was the sign
and evidence that they were in from the Truckee with a load
of hay. The one facing me had the morning paper folded to a
long narrow strip, and I knew, without any telling, that that

strip represented the column that contained my pleasant financial satire. From the way he was excitedly mumbling, I saw that the heedless son of a hay-mow was skipping with all his might, in order to get to the bloody details as quickly as possible; and so he was missing the guide-boards I had set up to warn him that the whole thing was a fraud. Presently his eyes spread wide open, just as his jaws swung asunder to take in a potato approaching it on a fork; the potato halted, the face lit up redly, and the whole man was on fire with excitement. Then he broke into a disjointed checking-off of the particulars—his potato cooling in mid-air meantime, and his mouth making a reach for it occasionally, but always bringing up suddenly against a new and still more direful performance of my hero. At last he looked his stunned and rigid comrade impressively in the face, and said, with an expression of concentrated awe:

"Jim, he b'iled his baby, and he took the old 'oman's skelp. Cuss'd if *I* want any breakfast!"

And he laid his lingering potato reverently down, and he and his friend departed from the restaurant empty but satisfied.

He *never got down* to where the satire part of it began. Nobody ever did. They found the thrilling particulars sufficient. To drop in with a poor little moral at the fag-end of such a gorgeous massacre, was to follow the expiring sun with a candle and hope to attract the world's attention to it.

The idea that anybody could ever take my massacre for a genuine occurrence never once suggested itself to me, hedged about as it was by all those tell-tale absurdities and impossibilities concerning the "great pine forest," the "dressed-stone mansion," etc. But I found out then, and never have forgotten since, that we never *read* the dull explanatory surroundings of marvellously exciting things when we have no occasion to suppose that some irresponsible scribbler is trying to defraud us; we skip all that, and hasten to revel in the blood-curdling particulars and be happy.

Therefore, being bitterly experienced, I tried hard to word that agricultural squib of mine in such a way as to deceive nobody—and I partly succeeded, but not entirely. However, I did not do any harm with it, any way. In order that parties who have lately written me about vegetables and things may know that there *was* a time when I would have answered their questions to the very best of my ability, and considered it my imperative duty to do it, I refer them to the narrative of my one week's experience as an agricultural editor, which will be found in this MEMORANDA next month.

June 1870

The Judge's "Spirited Woman"

A correspondent quotes an incident in the Pierre Bonaparte trial as "an unusual instance of spirit in a woman"—a young and gentle woman, unaccustomed to tumultuous assemblages of strange men, and therefore likely to be the very reverse of spirited in a place like that High Court at Tours. She described the scene between herself and Victor Noir and his betrothed, when Victor was putting on and buttoning his neat new Jouvins. Then, says the correspondent:

She described how in two hours they brought him back dead. In the evening she asked those about her how the trouble came about, and they told her that the Prince said Victor had given him a blow! "I went to his body," she said, "I looked at his gloves, and when I saw them unbroken, unstained and clean and tightly fitting, buttoned as I had seen them in the morning, I knew the Prince had lied!" As she said this, she pointed her finger at the Prince and looked him in the face, but he made no sign.

In a moment this little feminine outburst reminded me of the instance which an old Nevada Judge of the early times gave me as being what he sparklingly called "the most right-up and snappy ebullition of womanly git-up-and-git" that had ever fallen under his notice.

"I was sitting here," said the Judge, "in this old pulpit, holding court, and we were trying a big wicked-looking Spanish desperado for killing the husband of a bright, pretty Mexican woman. It was a lazy summer day, and an awfully long one, and the witnesses were tedious. None of us took any interest in the trial except that nervous uneasy devil of a Mexican woman—because you know how they love and how they hate, and this one had loved her husband with all her might, and now she had boiled it all down into hate, and stood here spitting it at that Spaniard with her eyes; and I tell you she would stir *me* up, too, with a little of her summer lightning occasionally. Well, I had my coat off and my heels up, lolling and sweating, and smoking one of those cabbage cigars the San Francisco people used to think were good enough for us in those times; and the lawyers they all had their coats off and were smoking and whittling, and the witnesses the same, and so was the prisoner. Well, the fact is, there warn't any interest in a murder trial then, because the fellow was always brought in not guilty, the jury expecting him to do as much for them some time; and although the evidence was straight and square against this Spaniard, we knew we could not convict him without seeming to be rather high-handed and sort of reflecting on every gentleman in the community; for there warn't any carriages and liveries then, and so the only 'style' there was, was to keep your private graveyard. But that woman seemed to have her heart set on hanging that Spaniard; and you'd ought to have seen how she would glare on him a minute, and then look up at me in her pleading way, and then turn and for the next five minutes search the jury's faces—and by and by drop her face in her hands for just a little while as if she was most ready to give up, but out she'd come again directly and be as live and anxious as ever. But when the jury announced the verdict, Not Guilty, and I told the prisoner he was acquitted and free to go, that woman rose up till she appeared to be as tall and grand as a seventy-four-gun ship, and says she:

" 'Judge, do I understand you to say that this man is not guilty, that murdered my husband without any cause before my own eyes and my little children's, and that all has been done to him that ever justice and the law can do?'

" 'The same,' says I.

"And then what do you reckon she did? Why she turned on that smirking Spanish fool like a wildcat, and out with a 'navy' and shot him dead in open court!"

"That *was* spirited, I am willing to admit."

"Wasn't it, though?" said the Judge, admiringly. "I wouldn't have missed it for anything. I adjourned court right on the spot and we put on our coats and went out and took up a collection for her and her cubs, and sent them over the mountains to their friends. Ah, she was a spirited wench!"

June 1870

Breaking It Gently

"Yes, I remember that anecdote," the Sunday school superintendent said, with the old pathos in his voice and the old sad look in his eyes. "It was about a simple creature named Higgins, that used to haul rock for old Maltby. When the lamented Judge Bagley tripped and fell down the court-house stairs and broke his neck, it was a great question how to break the news to poor Mrs. Bagley. But finally the body was put into Higgins's wagon and he was instructed to take it to Mrs. B., but to be very guarded and discreet in his language, and not break the news to her at once, but do it gradually and gently. When Higgins got there with his sad freight, he shouted till Mrs. Bagley came to the door. Then he said:

"Does the widder Bagley live here?"

"The *widow* Bagley? *No*, Sir!"

"I'll bet she does. But have it your own way. Well, does *Judge* Bagley live here?"

"Yes, Judge Bagley lives here."

"I'll bet he don't. But never mind—it ain't for me to contradict. Is the Judge in?"

"No, not at present."

"I jest expected as much. Because, you know—take hold o' suthin, mum, for I'm a-going to make a little communication, and I reckon maybe it'll jar you some. There's been an accident, mum. I've got the old Judge curled up out here in the wagon—and when you see him you'll acknowledge, yourself, that an inquest is about the only thing that could be a comfort to *him*!"

June 1870

398

Post-Mortem Poetry

In Philadelphia they have a custom which it would be pleasant to see adopted throughout the land. It is that of appending to published death-notices a little verse or two of comforting poetry. Any one who is in the habit of reading the daily Philadelphia "Ledger," must frequently be touched by these plaintive tributes to extinguished worth. In Philadelphia, the departure of a child is a circumstance which is not more surely followed by a burial than by the accustomed solacing poesy in the "Public Ledger." In that city death loses half its terror because the knowledge of its presence comes thus disguised in the sweet drapery of verse. For instance, in a late "Ledger" I find the following (I change the surname):

DIED.

HAWKS.—On the 17th inst., CLARA, the daughter of Ephraim and Laura Hawks, aged 21 months and 2 days.

> That merry shout no more I hear,
>   No laughing child I see,
> No little arms are round my neck,
>   No feet upon my knee;
> No kisses drop upon my cheek,
>   These lips are sealed to me.
> Dear Lord, how could I give Clara up
>   To any but to Thee?

A child thus mourned could not die wholly discontented. From the "Ledger" of the same date I make the following extract, merely changing the surname, as before:

BECKET.—On Sunday morning, 19th inst., JOHN P., infant son of George and Julia Becket, aged 1 year, 6 months, and 15 days.

> That merry shout no more I hear,
>   No laughing child I see,
> No little arms are round my neck,
>   No feet upon my knee;
> No kisses drop upon my cheek,
>   These lips are sealed to me.
> Dear Lord, how could I give Johnnie up
>   To any but to Thee?

The similarity of the emotions produced in the mourners in these two instances is remarkably evidenced by the singular similarity of thought which they experienced, and the surprising coincidence of language used by them to give it expression.

In the same journal, of the same date, I find the following (surname suppressed, as before):

WAGNER.—On the 10th inst., FERGUSON G., the son of William L. and Martha Theresa Wagner, aged 4 weeks and 1 day.

> That merry shout no more I hear,
>   No laughing child I see,
> No little arms are round my neck,
>   No feet upon my knee;
> No kisses drop upon my cheek,
>   These lips are sealed to me.
> Dear Lord, how could I give Ferguson up
>   To any but to Thee?

It is strange what power the reiteration of an essentially poetical thought has upon one's feelings. When we take up the "Ledger" and read the poetry about little Clara, we feel an unaccountable depression of the spirits. When we drift further down the column and read the poetry about little Johnnie, the depression of spirits acquires an added emphasis, and we experience tangible suffering. When we saunter along down the column further still and read the poetry about little Ferguson, the word torture but vaguely suggests the anguish that rends us.

In the "Ledger" (same copy referred to above), I find the following (I alter surname as usual):

WELCH.—On the 5th inst., MARY C. WELCH, wife of William B. Welch, and daughter of Catharine and George W. Markland, in the 29th year of her age.

> A mother dear, a mother kind,
> Has gone, and left us all behind.
> Cease to weep, for tears are vain,
> Mother dear is out of pain.
>
> Farewell, husband, children dear,
> Serve thy God with filial fear,
> And meet me in the land above,
> Where all is peace, and joy, and love.

What could be sweeter than that? No collection of salient facts (without reduction to tabular form) could be more succinctly stated than is done in the first stanza by the surviving relatives, and no more concise and comprehensive programme of farewells, post-mortuary general orders, etc., could be framed in any form than is done in verse by deceased in the last stanza. These things insensibly make us wiser, and tenderer, and better. Another extract:

BALL.—On the morning of the 15th inst., MARY E., daughter of John and Sarah F. Ball.

> 'Tis sweet to rest in lively hope
> That when my change shall come
> Angels will hover round my bed,
> To waft my spirit home.

The following is apparently the customary form for heads of families:

BURNS.—On the 20th instant, MICHAEL BURNS, aged 40 years.

> Dearest father, thou hast left us,
> Here thy loss we deeply feel;
> But 'tis God that has bereft us,
> He can all our sorrows heal.

Funeral at 2 o'clock sharp.

There is something very simple and pleasant about the following, which, in Philadelphia, seems to be the usual form for consumptives of long standing. (It deplores four distinct cases in the single copy of the "Ledger" which lies on the MEMORANDA editorial table):

BROMLEY.—On the 29th inst., of consumption, PHILIP BROMLEY, in the 50th year of his age.

> Affliction sore long time he bore,
> Physicians were in vain—
> Till God at last did hear him mourn,
> And eased him of his pain.
>
> The friend whom death from us has torn,
> We did not think so soon to part;
> An anxious care now sinks the thorn
> Still deeper in our bleeding heart.

This beautiful creation loses nothing by repetition. On the contrary, the oftener one sees it in the "Ledger," the more grand and awe-inspiring it seems.

With one more extract I will close:

DOBLE.—On the 4th inst., SAMUEL PEVERIL WORTHINGTON DOBLE, aged 4 days.

> Our little Sammy's gone,
>   His tiny spirit's fled;
> Our little boy we loved so dear
>   Lies sleeping with the dead.
>
> A tear within a father's eye,
>   A mother's aching heart,
> Can only tell the agony
>   How hard it is to part.

Could anything be more plaintive than that, without requiring further concessions of grammar? Could anything be likely to do more toward reconciling deceased to circumstances, and making him willing to go? Perhaps not. The power of song can hardly be estimated. There is an element about some poetry which is able to make even physical suffering and death cheerful things to contemplate and consummations to be desired. This element is present in the mortuary poetry of Philadelphia, and in a noticeable degree of development.

The custom I have been treating of is one that should be adopted in all the cities of the land.

June 1870

Wit-Inspirations of the "Two-Year-Olds"

All infants appear to have an impertinent and disagreeable fashion nowadays of saying "smart" things on most occasions that offer, and especially on occasions when they ought not to be saying anything at all. Judging by the average published specimens of smart sayings, the rising generation of children are little better than idiots. And the parents must surely be but little better than the children, for in most cases they are the publishers of the sunbursts of infantile imbecility which dazzle us from the pages of our periodicals. I may seem to speak with some heat, not to say a suspicion of personal spite; and I do admit that it nettles me to hear about so many gifted infants in these days, and remember that I seldom said anything smart when I was a child. I tried it once or twice, but it was not popular. The family were not expecting brilliant remarks from me, and so they snubbed me sometimes and spanked me the rest. But it makes my flesh creep and my blood run cold to think what might have happened to me if I had dared to utter some of the smart things of this generation's "four-year-olds" where my father could hear me. To have simply skinned me alive and considered his duty at an end would have seemed to him criminal leniency toward one so sinning. He was a stern, unsmiling man, and hated all forms of precocity. If I had said some of the things I have referred to, and said them in his hearing, he would have destroyed me. He would, indeed. He would, provided the opportunity remained with him. But it would not, for I would have had judgment enough to take some strychnine first and say my smart thing afterward. The fair record of my life has been tarnished by just one pun. My father overheard that, and he hunted me over four or five townships seeking to take my life. If I had been full-grown, of course he would have been right; but, child as I was, I could not know how wicked a thing I had done.

I made one of those remarks ordinarily called "smart things" before that, but it was not a pun. Still, it came near causing a serious rupture between my father and myself. My father and mother, my uncle Ephraim and his wife, and one or two others were present, and the conversation turned on a name for me. I was lying there trying some India-rubber rings of various patterns, and endeavoring to make a selection, for I was tired of trying to cut my teeth on people's fingers, and wanted to get hold of something that would enable me to hurry the thing through and get at something else. Did you ever notice what a nuisance it was cutting your teeth on your nurse's finger, or how back-breaking and tiresome it was trying to cut them on your big toe? And did you never get out of patience and wish your teeth were in Jericho long before you got them half cut? To me it seems as if these things happened yesterday. And they did, to some children. But I digress. I was lying there trying the India-rubber rings. I remember looking at the clock and noticing that in an hour and twenty-five minutes I would be two weeks old, and thinking to myself how little I had done to merit the blessings that were so unsparingly lavished upon me. My father said:

"Abraham is a good name. My grandfather was named Abraham."

My mother said:

"Abraham is a good name. Very well. Let us have Abraham for one of his names."

I said:

"Abraham suits the subscriber."

My father frowned, my mother looked pleased; my aunt said:

"What a little darling it is!"

My father said:

"Isaac is a good name, and Jacob is a good name."

My mother assented and said:

"No names are better. Let us add Isaac and Jacob to his names."

I said:

"All right. Isaac and Jacob are good enough for yours truly. Pass me that rattle, if you please. I can't chew India-rubber rings all day."

Not a soul made a memorandum of these sayings of mine, for publication. I saw that, and did it myself, else they would have been utterly lost. So far from meeting with a generous encouragement like other children when developing intellectually, I was now furiously scowled upon by my father; my mother looked grieved and anxious, and even my aunt had about her an expression of seeming to think that maybe I had gone too far. I took a vicious bite out of an India-rubber ring, and covertly broke the rattle over the kitten's head, but said nothing. Presently my father said:

"Samuel is a very excellent name."

I saw that trouble was coming. Nothing could prevent it. I laid down my rattle; over the side of the cradle I dropped my uncle's silver watch, the clothes brush, the toy dog, my tin soldier, the nutmeg grater, and other matters which I was accustomed to examine, and meditate upon, and make pleasant noises with, and bang and batter and break when I needed wholesome entertainment. Then I put on my little frock and my little bonnet, and took my pigmy shoes in one hand and my licorice in the other, and climbed out on the floor. I said to myself, Now, if the worst comes to the worst, I am ready. Then I said aloud, in a firm voice:

"Father, I cannot, cannot wear the name of Samuel."

"My son!"

"Father, I mean it. I cannot."

"Why?"

"Father, I have an invincible antipathy to that name."

"My son, this is unreasonable. Many great and good men have been named Samuel."

"Sir, I have yet to hear of the first instance."

"What! There was Samuel the prophet. Was not he great and good?"

"Not so very."

"My son! With his own voice the Lord called him."

"Yes, sir, and had to call him a couple of times before he would come!"

And then I sallied forth, and that stern old man sallied forth after me. He overtook me at noon the following day, and when the interview was over I had acquired the name of Samuel, and a thrashing, and other useful information; and by means of this compromise my father's wrath was appeased and a misunderstanding bridged over which might have become a permanent rupture if I had chosen to be unreasonable. But just judging by this episode, what *would* my father have done to me if I had ever uttered in his hearing one of the flat, sickly things these "two-year-olds" say in print nowadays? In my opinion there would have been a case of infanticide in our family.

June 1870

The Widow's Protest

One of the saddest things that ever came under my notice (said the banker's clerk) was there in Corning, during the war. Dan Murphy enlisted as a private, and fought very bravely. The boys all liked him, and when a wound by and by weakened him down till carrying a musket was too heavy work for him, they clubbed together and fixed him up as a sutler. He made money then, and sent it always to his wife to bank for him. She was a washer and ironer, and knew enough by hard experience to keep money when she got it. She didn't waste a penny. On the contrary, she began to get miserly as her bank account grew. She grieved to part with a cent, poor creature, for twice in her hard-working life she had known what it was to be hungry, cold, friendless, sick, and without a dollar in the world, and she had a haunting dread of suffering so again. Well, at last Dan died; and the boys, in testimony of their esteem and respect for him, telegraphed to Mrs. Murphy to know if she would like to have him embalmed and sent home, when you know the usual custom was to dump a poor devil like him into a shallow hole, and *then* inform his friends what had become of him. Mrs. Murphy jumped to the conclusion that it would only cost two or three dollars to embalm her dead husband, and so she telegraphed "Yes." It was at the "wake" that the bill for embalming arrived and was presented to the widow. She uttered a wild, sad wail, that pierced every heart, and said: "Sivinty-foive dollars for stooffin' Dan, blister their sowls! Did thim divils suppose I was goin' to stairt a Museim, that I'd be dalin' in such expinsive curiassities!"

The banker's clerk said there was not a dry eye in the house.

June 1870

Report to the Buffalo Female Academy

I beg leave to offer the report of the committee appointed to sit in judgment upon the compositions of the graduating and collegiate classes. We have done our work carefully and conscientiously; we have determined the degrees of literary excellence displayed, with pitiless honesty; we have experienced no sort of difficulty in selecting and agreeing upon the two first-prize compositions—and yet, after all, we feel that it is necessary to say a word or two in vindication of our verdict.

Because, we have misgivings that our choice might not be the choice of the Academy, if the choice were left to them—nor of this assemblage—nor of a vote of the general public. Let this comfort those fair competitors whom our verdict has wronged. But we have judged these compositions by the strict rules of literary criticism, and let *this* reassure those whom our verdict has exalted.

We have chosen as the two prize essays the least showy of the eighteen submitted, perhaps, but they are the least artificial, the least labored, the clearest and shapeliest, and the best carried out. The paper we have chosen for the first prize of the graduates is very much the best literary effort in the whole collection, and yet it is almost the least ambitious among them. It relates a very simple little incident, in unpretentious language, and then achieves the difficult feat of pointing it with one of those dismal atrocities called a Moral, without devoting double the space to it which it ought to occupy and outraging every canon of good taste, relevancy and modesty. It is a composition which possesses, also, the very rare merit of *stopping when it is finished*. It shows a freedom from adjectives and superlatives which is attractive, not to say seductive—and let us remark instructively, in passing, that one can seldom run his pen through an adjective without improving his manuscript. We can say further, in praise of this first-prize composition, that there is a singular aptness of language noticeable in it—denoting a shrewd faculty of selecting just the right word for the service needed, as a general thing. It is a

high gift. It is the talent which gives accuracy, grace and viv-
idness in descriptive writing.

The other first prize—the collegiate—is so simple and unpretending that it seems a daring thing to prefer it before
certain of its fellows which we could name, but still we of the
committee rigidly decree that it is perceptibly superior to the
best of them. It is nothing in the world but just a bright and
fresh little bit of fancy, told with a breezy dash, and with
nothing grand or overpowering about it. Attached to it is the
inevitable Moral, but it is compressed into a single sentence,
and is delivered with a snap that is exhilarating and an unex-
pectedness that is captivating. And we are furthermore able to
say, in justification of this Moral, that the composition would
not be symmetrical, keenly and cleanly pointed and complete,
without it. An application, or a "nub," or a moral that *fits*, is a
jewel of price. It is only the awkward, irrelevant and pinch-
beck moral that this committee snubs.

Now, if you have observed, we have decided that the graduates' first-prize possesses the several merits of unpretentious-
ness, simplicity of language and subject, and marked aptness
and accuracy of wording—and that the collegiate first-prize
has the merits of modesty and freshness of subject and grace
and excellence of treatment. But both of these possess one
other merit, or cluster of merits, which strongly attracted us.
They were instinct with *naturalness*—a most noble and excellent feature in composition, and one which is customarily
lacking in productions written for state occasions, from the
Friday composition in a village school all the way up to the
President's message—and you may verify my words by critically examining any written speech that ever *was* written—
except this one I am reading. The two prize essays possess
naturalness, and likewise a happy freshness that marks them as
the expression of the original thoughts and fancies of the
minds that wrought them, and not stale and venerable platitudes and commonplaces absorbed from good but stupid
books and drowsy sermons, and delivered at secondhand in
the same unvarying and monotonous sequence—a sequence
which they have grown so familiar with since Adam and each
of his descendants in turn used them in his appointed season,

that now one needs only write down the first of them and the rest fall into line without a murmur or ever a missing veteran.

We consider it a plain duty to observe that while the disposition in all school compositions to contemplate all subjects from high moral and religious altitudes would be matter for sincere praise and gratulation, if such disposition came from a strong spontaneous impulse on the part of the student, it is not matter for praise or gratulation either when that disposition is strained or forced. Nearly all the compositions submitted to us would have been right creditable specimens of literary handiwork, if the sermons had been left out of them. But, while some of these latter were the expression of a genuine impulse, the great majority of them were so manifestly dragged in and hitched on to the essay (out of pure force of habit and therefore unconsciously, we are willing to believe, but still plainly dragged in), that they sadly marred some of the compositions and entirely spoiled one or two. Religion is the highest and holiest thing on earth, and a strained or compulsory expression of it is not gracious, or commendable, or befitting its dignity.

However, we have the hardihood to say, in this place, that considering the "Standard School Readers" and the other popular and unspeakably execrable models which young people are defrauded into accepting as fine literary composition, the real wonder is, not that pupils attempt subjects which they would be afraid of at forty, and then write floridly instead of simply, and start without premises and wind up without tangible result, but that they write at all without bringing upon themselves suspicions of imbecility.

The dead weight of custom and tradition have clogged school method and discipline from a past date which we cannot name, until the present time. They have worn these dead weights so long that they unconsciously continue to wear them in these free, progressive latter days. For lingering ages, seemingly, the seminary pupil has been expected to present, at stated intervals, a composition constructed upon one and the same old heart-rending plan. It is not necessary to detail this plan—it is familiar to all. This ancient model is so ingrained in the method of the schools, and has so long been allowed to pass unchallenged as being the correct idea, that it will require a considerable time to eradicate it. To the high credit of the principal and teachers of this academy, however, it can be said that they are faithfully doing what they can to destroy it and its influence and occupy their place with something new and better. But when we of the committee take into consideration that much of this atmosphere of old custom and tradition necessarily still lingers around this unquestionably excellent Female Academy, we feel that we are more than complimentary when we say that the compositions we have been examining average well indeed. When the old sapless composition model is finally cast entirely aside and the pupil learns to write straight from his heart, he will apply his own language and his own ideas to his subjects and then the question with committees will not be which composition to select for first prize, but which one they dare reject.

June 24, 1870

How I Edited an Agricultural Paper Once

I did not take the temporary editorship of an agricultural paper without misgivings. Neither would a landsman take command of a ship without misgivings. But I was in circumstances that made the salary an object. The regular editor of the paper was going off for a holiday, and I accepted the terms he offered, and took his place.

The sensation of being at work again was luxurious, and I wrought all the week with unflagging pleasure. We went to press, and I waited a day with some solicitude to see whether my effort was going to attract any notice. As I left the office, toward sundown, a group of men and boys at the foot of the stairs dispersed with one impulse, and gave me passage-way, and I heard one or two of them say: "That's him!" I was naturally pleased by this incident. The next morning I found a similar group at the foot of the stairs, and scattering couples and individuals standing here and there in the street, and over the way, watching me with interest. The group separated and fell back as I approached, and I heard a man say: "Look at his eye!" I pretended not to observe the notice I was attracting, but secretly I was pleased with it, and was purposing to write an account of it to my aunt. I went up the short flight of stairs, and heard cheery voices and a ringing laugh as I drew near the door, which I opened, and caught a glimpse of two young, rural-looking men, whose faces blanched and lengthened when they saw me, and then they both plunged through the window, with a great crash. I was surprised.

In about half an hour an old gentleman, with a flowing beard and a fine but rather austere face, entered, and sat down at my invitation. He seemed to have something on his mind. He took off his hat and set it on the floor, and got out of it a red silk handkerchief and a copy of our paper. He put the paper on his lap, and, while he polished his spectacles with his handkerchief, he said:

"Are you the new editor?"

I said I was.

"Have you ever edited an agricultural paper before?"

"No," I said; "this is my first attempt."

"Very likely. Have you had any experience in agriculture, practically?"

"No, I believe I have not."

"Some instinct told me so," said the old gentleman, putting on his spectacles and looking over them at me with asperity, while he folded his paper into a convenient shape. "I wish to read you what must have made me have that instinct. It was this editorial. Listen, and see if it was you that wrote it:

"Turnips should never be pulled—it injures them. It is much better to send a boy up and let him shake the tree.

"Now, what do you think of that?—for I really suppose you wrote it?"

"Think of it? Why, I think it is good. I think it is sense. I have no doubt that, every year, millions and millions of bushels of turnips are spoiled in this township alone by being pulled in a half-ripe condition, when, if they had sent a boy up to shake the tree——"

"Shake your grandmother! Turnips don't grow on trees!"

"Oh, they don't, don't they? Well, who said they did? The language was intended to be figurative, wholly figurative. Anybody, that knows anything, will know that I meant that the boy should shake the vine."

Then this old person got up and tore his paper all into small shreds, and stamped on them, and broke several things with his cane, and said I did not know as much as a cow; and then went out, and banged the door after him, and, in short, acted in such a way that I fancied he was displeased about something. But, not knowing what the trouble was, I could not be any help to him.

Pretty soon after this a long, cadaverous creature, with lanky locks hanging down to his shoulders and a week's stubble bristling from the hills and valleys of his face, darted within the door, and halted, motionless, with finger on lip, and head and body bent in listening attitude. No sound was heard. Still he listened. No sound. Then he turned the key in the door, and came elaborately tip-toeing toward me, till he was within long reaching distance of me, when he stopped, and, after scanning my face with intense interest for a while, drew a folded copy of our paper from his bosom, and said:

"There—you wrote that. Read it to me, quick! Relieve me—I suffer."

I read as follows—and as the sentences fell from my lips I could see the relief come—I could see the drawn muscles relax, and the anxiety go out of the face, and rest and peace steal over the features like the merciful moonlight over a desolate landscape:

The guano is a fine bird, but great care is necessary in rearing it. It should not be imported earlier than June nor later than September. In the winter it should be kept in a warm place, where it can hatch out its young.

It is evident that we are to have a backward season for grain. Therefore, it will be well for the farmer to begin setting out his corn-stalks and planting his buckwheat cakes in July instead of August.

Concerning the Pumpkin.—This berry is a favorite with the natives of the interior of New England, who prefer it to the gooseberry for the making of fruit cake, and who likewise give it the preference over the raspberry for feeding cows, as being more filling and fully as satisfying. The pumpkin is the only esculent of the orange family that will thrive in the North, except the gourd and one or two varieties of the squash. But the custom of planting it in the front yard with the shrubbery is fast going out of vogue, for it is now generally conceded that the pumpkin, as a shade tree, is a failure.

Now, as the warm weather approaches, and the ganders begin to spawn——

The excited listener sprang toward me, to shake hands, and said:

"There, there—that will do! I know I am all right now, because you have read it just as I did, word for word. But, stranger, when I first read it this morning I said to myself, I never, never believed it before, notwithstanding my friends kept me under watch so strict, but now I believe I *am* crazy; and with that I fetched a howl that you might have heard two miles, and started out to kill somebody—because, you know, I knew it would come to that sooner or later, and so I might as well begin. I read one of them paragraphs over again, so as to be certain, and then I burned my house down and started. I have crippled several people, and have got one fellow up a tree, where I can get him if I want him. But I thought I would call in here as I passed along, and make the thing perfectly certain; and now it *is* certain, and I tell you it is lucky for the chap that is in the tree. I should have killed him, sure, as I went back. Good-by, sir, good-by—you have taken a great load off my mind. My reason has stood the strain of one of your agricultural articles, and I know that nothing can ever unseat it now. *Good*-by, sir."

I felt a little uncomfortable about the cripplings and arsons this person had been entertaining himself with, for I could not help feeling remotely accessory to them; but these thoughts were quickly banished, for the regular editor walked in! [I thought to myself, Now if you had gone to Egypt, as I recommended you to, I might have had a chance to get my hand in; but you wouldn't do it, and here you are. I sort of expected you.]

The editor was looking sad, and perplexed, and dejected. He surveyed the wreck which that old rioter and these two young farmers had made, and then said:

"This is a sad business—a very sad business. There is the mucilage bottle broken, and six panes of glass, and a spittoon and two candlesticks. But that is not the worst. The reputation of the paper is injured, and permanently, I fear. True, there never was such a call for the paper before, and it never sold such a large edition or soared to such celebrity; but does one want to be famous for lunacy, and prosper upon the infirmities of his mind? My friend, as I am an honest man, the street out here is full of people, and others are roosting on the fences, waiting to get a glimpse of you, because they think you are crazy. And well they might, after reading your editorials. They are a disgrace to journalism. Why, what put it into your head that you could edit a paper of this nature? You do not seem to know the first rudiments of agriculture. You speak of a furrow and a harrow as being the same thing; you talk of the moulting season for cows; and you recommend the domestication of the pole-cat on account of its playfulness and its excellence as a ratter. Your remark that clams will lie quiet if music be played to them, was superfluous—entirely superfluous. Nothing disturbs clams. Clams *always* lie quiet. Clams care nothing whatever about music. Ah, heavens and earth, friend, if you had made the acquiring of ignorance the study of your life, you could not have graduated with higher honor than you could to-day. I never saw anything like it. Your observation that the horse-chestnut, as an article of commerce, is steadily gaining in favor, is simply calculated to destroy this journal. I want you to throw up your situation and go. I want no more holiday—I could not enjoy it if I had it. Certainly not with you in my chair. I would always stand in dread of what you might be going to recommend next. It makes me lose all patience every time I think of your discussing oyster-beds under the head of 'Landscape Gardening.' I want you to go. Nothing on earth could persuade me to take another holiday. Oh, why didn't you *tell* me you didn't know anything about agriculture?"

"*Tell* you, you cornstalk, you cabbage, you son of a cauliflower! It's the first time I ever heard such an unfeeling remark. I tell you I have been in the editorial business going on fourteen years, and it is the first time I ever heard of a man's having to know anything in order to edit a newspaper. You turnip! Who write the dramatic critiques for the second-rate papers? Why, a parcel of promoted shoemakers and apprentice apothecaries, who know just as much about good acting as I do about good farming and no more. Who review the books? People who never wrote one. Who do up the heavy leaders on finance? Parties who have had the largest opportunities for knowing nothing about it. Who criticise the Indian campaigns? Gentlemen who do not know a war-whoop from a wigwam, and who never have had to run a foot-race with a tomahawk or pluck arrows out of the several members of their families to build the evening camp-fire with. Who write the temperance appeals and clamor about the flowing bowl? Folks who will never draw another sober breath till they do it in the grave. Who edit the agricultural papers, you—yam? Men, as a general thing, who fail in the poetry line, yellow-covered novel line, sensation-drama line, city-editor line, and finally fall back on agriculture as a temporary reprieve from the poor-house. *You* try to tell *me* anything about the newspaper business! Sir, I have been through it from Alpha to Omaha, and I tell you that the less a man knows the bigger noise he makes and the higher the salary he commands. Heaven knows if I had but been ignorant instead of cultivated, and impudent instead of diffident, I could have made a name for myself in this cold, selfish world. I take my leave, sir. Since I have been treated as you have treated me, I am perfectly willing to go. But I have done my duty. I have fulfilled my contract, as far as I was permitted to do it. I said I could make your paper of interest to all classes, and I have. I said I could run your circulation up to twenty thousand copies, and if I had had two more weeks I'd have done it. And I'd have given you the best class of readers that ever an agricultural paper had—not a farmer in it, nor a solitary individual who could tell a watermelon from a peach-vine to save his life. *You* are the loser by this rupture, not me, Pie-plant. Adios."

I then left.

July 1870

The "Tournament" in A.D. 1870

Lately there appeared an item to this effect, and the same went the customary universal round of the press:

A telegraph station has just been established upon the traditional site of the Garden of Eden.

As a companion to that, nothing fits so aptly and so perfectly as this:

Brooklyn has revived the knightly tournament of the Middle Ages.

It is hard to tell which is the most startling, the idea of that highest achievement of human genius and intelligence, the telegraph, prating away about the practical concerns of the world's daily life in the heart and home of ancient indolence, ignorance, and savagery, or the idea of that happiest expression of the brag, vanity, and mock-heroics of our ancestors, the "tournament," coming out of its grave to flaunt its tinsel trumpery and perform its "chivalrous" absurdities in the high noon of the nineteenth century, and under the patronage of a great, broad-awake city and an advanced civilization.

A "tournament" in Lynchburg is a thing easily within the comprehension of the average mind; but no commonly gifted person can conceive of such a spectacle in Brooklyn without straining his powers. Brooklyn is part and parcel of the city of New York, and there is hardly romance enough in the entire metropolis to re-supply a Virginia "knight" with "chivalry," in case he happened to run out of it. Let the reader, calmly and dispassionately, picture to himself "lists"—in Brooklyn; heralds, pursuivants, pages, garter king-at-arms—in Brooklyn; the marshalling of the fantastic hosts of "chivalry" in slashed doublets, velvet trunks, ruffles, and plumes—in Brooklyn; mounted on omnibus and livery-stable patriarchs, promoted, and referred to in cold blood as "steeds," "destriers," and "chargers," and divested of their friendly, humble names—these meek old "Jims" and "Bobs" and "Charleys," and renamed "Mohammed," "Bucephalus," and "Saladin" —in Brooklyn; mounted thus, and armed with swords and shields and wooden lances, and cased in pasteboard hauberks, morions, greaves, and gauntlets, and addressed as "Sir" Smith, and "Sir" Jones, and bearing such titled grandeurs as "The Disinherited Knight," the "Knight of Shenandoah," the "Knight of the Blue Ridge," the "Knight of Maryland," and the "Knight of the Secret Sorrow"—in Brooklyn; and at the toot of the horn charging fiercely upon a helpless ring hung on a post, and prodding at it intrepidly with their wooden sticks, and by and by skewering it and cavorting back to the judges' stand covered with glory—this in Brooklyn; and each noble success like this duly and promptly announced by an applauding toot from the herald's horn, and "the band playing three bars of an old circus tune"—all in Brooklyn, in broad daylight. And let the reader remember, and also add to his picture, as follows, to wit: when the show was all over, the party who had shed the most blood and overturned and hacked to pieces the most knights, or at least had prodded the most muffin-rings, was accorded the ancient privilege of naming and crowning the Queen of Love and Beauty—which naming had in reality been done *for* him by the "cut-and-dried" process, and long in advance, by a committee of ladies, but the crowning he did in person, though suffering from loss of blood, and then was taken to the county hospital on a shutter to have his wounds dressed—these curious things all occurring in Brooklyn, and no longer ago than one or two yesterdays. It seems impossible, and yet it is true.

This was doubtless the first appearance of the "tournament" up here among the rolling-mills and factories, and will probably be the last. It will be well to let it retire permanently to the rural districts of Virginia, where, it is said, the fine mailed and plumed, noble-natured, maiden-rescuing, wrong-redressing, adventure-seeking knight of romance is accepted and believed in by the peasantry with pleasing simplicity, while they reject with scorn the plain, unpolished verdict whereby history exposes him as a braggart, a ruffian, a fantastic vagabond, and an ignoramus.

All romance aside, what shape would our admiration of the heroes of Ashby de la Zouch be likely to take, in this practical age, if those worthies were to rise up and come here and perform again the chivalrous deeds of that famous passage of arms? Nothing but a New York jury and the insanity plea could save them from hanging, from the amiable Bois-Guilbert and the pleasant Front-de-Bœuf clear down to the nameless ruffians that entered the riot with unpictured shields and did their first murder and acquired their first claim to respect that day. The doings of the so-called "chivalry" of the Middle Ages were absurd enough, even when they were brutally and bloodily in earnest, and when their surroundings of castles and donjons, savage landscapes and half-savage peoples, were in keeping; but those doings gravely reproduced with tinsel decorations and mock pageantry, by bucolic gentlemen with broomstick lances, and with muffin-rings to represent the foe, and all in the midst of the refinement and dignity of a carefully-developed modern civilization, is absurdity gone crazy.

Now, for next exhibition, let us have a fine representation of one of those chivalrous wholesale butcheries and burnings of Jewish women and children, which the crusading heroes of romance used to indulge in in their European homes, just before starting to the Holy Land, to seize and take to their protection the Sepulchre and defend it from "pollution."

July 1870

Unburlesquable Things

There are some things which cannot be burlesqued, for the simple reason that in themselves they are so extravagant and grotesque that nothing is left for burlesque to take hold of. For instance, all attempts to burlesque the "Byron Scandal" were failures because the central feature of it, incest, was a "situation" so tremendous and so imposing that the happiest available resources of burlesque seemed tame and cheap in its presence. Burlesque could invent nothing to transcend incest, except by enlisting two crimes, neither of which is ever mentioned among women and children, and one of which is only mentioned in rare books of the law, and then as "the crime without a name"—a term with a shudder in it! So the reader never saw the "Byron Scandal" successfully travestied in print, and he may rest satisfied that he never will.

All attempts to burlesque the monster musical "Peace Jubilee" in Boston were mournful failures. The ten thousand singers, the prodigious organ, the hundred anvils, and the artillery accompaniment made up an unintentional, but complete, symmetrical and enormous burlesque, which shamed the poor inventions of the sketchers and scribblers who tried to be funny over it in magazines and newspapers. Even Cruikshank failed when he tried to pictorially burlesque the English musical extravaganza which probably furnished Mr. Gilmore with his idea.

There was no burlesquing the "situation" when the French Train, Henri Rochefort, brayed forth the proclamation that whenever he was arrested forty thousand *ouvriers* would be there to know the reason why—when, alas! right on top of it one single humble policeman took him and marched him off to prison through an atmosphere with never a taint of garlic in it.

There is no burlesquing the McFarland trial, either as a whole or piecemeal by selection. Because it was sublimated burlesque itself, in any way one may look at it. The court gravely tried the prisoner, *not* for murder, apparently, but as to his sanity or insanity. His counsel attempted the intellectual miracle of proving the prisoner's deed to have been *a*

justifiable homicide by an insane person. The Recorder charged
the jury to—well, there are different opinions as to what the
Recorder wanted them to do, among those who have translated the charge from the original Greek, though his general
idea seemed to be to scramble first to the support of the prisoner and then to the support of the law, and then to the
prisoner again, and back again to the law, with a vaguely perceptible desire to help the prisoner a little the most without
making that desire unofficially and ungracefully prominent.
To wind up and put a final polish to the many-sided burlesque, the jury went out and devoted nearly two hours to
trying for his life a man whose deed would not be accepted as
a capital crime by the mass of mankind even though all the
lawyers did their best to prove it such. It is hardly worth
while to mention that the emotional scene in the court room,
following the delivery of the verdict, when women hugged
the prisoner, the jury, the reporters, and even the remorselessly sentimental Graham, is eminently unburlesquable.

But first and last, the splendid feature of the McFarland
comedy was the *insanity* part of it. Where the occasion was
for dragging in that poor old threadbare lawyer-trick, is not
perceptible, except it was to make a *show* of difficulty in winning a verdict that would have won itself without ever a lawyer to meddle with the case. Heaven knows insanity was
disreputable enough, long ago; but now that the lawyers have
got to cutting every gallows rope and picking every prison
lock with it, it is become a sneaking villainy that ought to
hang and keep on hanging its sudden possessors until evil-
doers should conclude that the safest plan was to never claim
to have it until they came by it legitimately. The very calibre
of the people the lawyers most frequently try to save by the
insanity subterfuge, ought to laugh the plea out of the courts,
one would think. Any one who watched the proceedings
closely in the McFarland-Richardson mockery will believe
that the insanity plea was a rather far-fetched compliment to
pay the prisoner, inasmuch as one must first have brains before he can go crazy, and there was surely nothing in the
evidence to show that McFarland had enough of the raw material to justify him in attempting anything more imposing
than a lively form of idiocy.

Governor Alcorn, of Mississippi, recommends his Legislature to so alter the laws that as soon as the insanity plea is offered in the case of a person accused of crime, the case shall be sent up to a high State court and the insanity part of the matter inquired into and settled permanently, *by itself,* before the trial for the crime charged is touched at all. Anybody but one of this latter-day breed of "lunatics" on trial for murder will recognize the wisdom of the proposition at a glance.

There is one other thing which transcends the powers of burlesque, and that is a Fenian "invasion." First we have the portentous mystery that precedes it for six months, when all the air is filled with stage whisperings; when "Councils" meet every night with awful secrecy, and the membership try to see who can get up first in the morning and tell the proceedings. Next, the expatriated Nation struggles through a travail of national squabbles and political splits, and is finally delivered of a litter of "Governments," and Presidents McThis, and Generals O'That, of several different complexions, politically speaking; and straightway the newspapers teem with the new names, and men who were insignificant and obscure one day find themselves great and famous the next. Then the several "governments," and presidents, and generals, and senates get by the ears, and remain so until the customary necessity of carrying the American city elections with a minority vote comes around and unites them; then they begin to "sound the tocsin of war" again—that is to say, in solemn whisperings at dead of night they secretly plan a Canadian raid, and publish it in the "World" next morning; they begin to refer significantly to "Ridgway," and we reflect bodingly that there is no telling how soon that slaughter may be repeated. Presently the "invasion" begins to take tangible shape; and as no news travels so freely or so fast as the "secret" doings of the Fenian Brotherhood, the land is shortly in a tumult of apprehension. The telegraph announces that "last night, 400 men went north from Utica, but refused to disclose their destination—were extremely reticent—answered no questions—were not armed, or in uniform, but *it was noticed that they marched to the depot in military fashion*"—and so on. Fifty such despatches follow each other within two days, evidencing that squads of locomotive mystery have gone north from a hundred different points and rendezvoused on the Canadian border—and that, consequently, a horde of 25,000 invaders, at least, is gathered together; and then, hurrah! they cross the line; hurrah! they meet the enemy; hip, hip, hurrah! a battle ensues; hip—no, not hip nor hurrah—for the U. S. Marshal and one man seize the Fenian General-in-Chief on the battle-field, in the midst of his "army," and bowl him off in a carriage and lodge him in a common jail—and, presto! the illustrious "invasion" is at an end!

The Fenians have not done many things that seemed to call for pictorial illustration; but their first care has usually been to make a picture of any performance of theirs that would stand it as soon as possible after its achievement, and paint everything in it a violent green, and embellish it with harps and pickaxes, and other emblems of national grandeur, and print thousands of them in the severe simplicity of primitive lithography, and hang them above the National Palladium, among the decanters. Shall we have a nice picture of the battle of Pigeon Hill and the little accident to the Commander-in-Chief?

No, a Fenian "invasion" cannot be burlesqued, because it uses up all the material itself. It is harmless fun, this annual masquerading toward the border; but America should not encourage it, for the reason that it may some time or other succeed in embroiling the country in a war with a friendly power—and such an event as that would be ill compensated by the liberation of even so excellent a people as the Down-trodden Nation.

July 1870

The Late Benjamin Franklin

[Never put off till to-morrow what you can do day after to-morrow just as well.—B. F.]

This party was one of those persons whom they call Philosophers. He was twins, being born simultaneously in two different houses in the city of Boston. These houses remain unto this day, and have signs upon them worded in accordance with the facts. The signs are considered well enough to have, though not necessary, because the inhabitants point out the two birth-places to the stranger anyhow, and sometimes as often as several times in the same day. The subject of this memoir was of a vicious disposition, and early prostituted his talents to the invention of maxims and aphorisms calculated to inflict suffering upon the rising generation of all subsequent ages. His simplest acts, also, were contrived with a view to their being held up for the emulation of boys forever—boys who might otherwise have been happy. It was in this spirit that he became the son of a soap-boiler; and probably for no other reason than that the efforts of all future boys who tried to be anything might be looked upon with suspicion unless they were the sons of soap-boilers. With a malevolence which is without parallel in history, he would work all day and then sit up nights and let on to be studying algebra by the light of a smouldering fire, so that all other boys might have to do that also or else have Benjamin Franklin thrown up to them. Not satisfied with these proceedings, he had a fashion of living wholly on bread and water, and studying astronomy at meal time—a thing which has brought affliction to millions of boys since, whose fathers had read Franklin's pernicious biography.

His maxims were full of animosity toward boys. Nowadays a boy cannot follow out a single natural instinct without tumbling over some of those everlasting aphorisms and hearing from Franklin on the spot. If he buys two cents' worth of peanuts, his father says, "Remember what Franklin has said, my son,—'A groat a day's a penny a year;' " and the comfort is all gone out of those peanuts. If he wants to spin his top when he is done work, his father quotes, "Procrastination is the thief of time." If he does a virtuous action, he never gets anything for it, because "Virtue is its own reward." And that boy is hounded to death and robbed of his natural rest, because Franklin said once in one of his inspired flights of malignity—

> Early to bed and early to rise
> Make a man healthy and wealthy and wise.

As if it were any object to a boy to be healthy and wealthy and wise on such terms. The sorrow that that maxim has cost me through my parents' experimenting on me with it, tongue cannot tell. The legitimate result is my present state of general debility, indigence, and mental aberration. My parents used to have me up before nine o'clock in the morning, sometimes, when I was a boy. If they had let me take my natural rest, where would I have been now? Keeping store, no doubt, and respected by all.

And what an adroit old adventurer the subject of this memoir was! In order to get a chance to fly his kite on Sunday, he used to hang a key on the string and let on to be fishing for lightning. And a guileless public would go home chirping about the "wisdom" and the "genius" of the hoary Sabbath-breaker. If anybody caught him playing "mumble-peg" by himself, after the age of sixty, he would immediately appear to be ciphering out how the grass grew—as if it was any of his business. My grandfather knew him well, and he says Franklin was always fixed—always ready. If a body, during his old age, happened on him unexpectedly when he was catching flies, or making mud pies, or sliding on a cellar-door, he would immediately look wise, and rip out a maxim, and walk off with his nose in the air and his cap turned wrong side before, trying to appear absent-minded and eccentric. He was a hard lot.

He invented a stove that would smoke your head off in four hours by the clock. One can see the almost devilish satisfaction he took in it, by his giving it his name.

He was always proud of telling how he entered Philadelphia, for the first time, with nothing in the world but two shillings in his pocket and four rolls of bread under his arm.

But really, when you come to examine it critically, it was nothing. Anybody could have done it.

To the subject of this memoir belongs the honor of recommending the army to go back to bows and arrows in place of bayonets and muskets. He observed, with his customary force, that the bayonet was very well, under some circumstances, but that he doubted whether it could be used with accuracy at long range.

Benjamin Franklin did a great many notable things for his country, and made her young name to be honored in many lands as the mother of such a son. It is not the idea of this memoir to ignore that or cover it up. No; the simple idea of it is to snub those pretentious maxims of his, which he worked up with a great show of originality out of truisms that had become wearisome platitudes as early as the dispersion from Babel; and also to snub his stove, and his military inspirations, his unseemly endeavor to make himself conspicuous when he entered Philadelphia, and his flying his kite and fooling away his time in all sorts of such ways, when he ought to have been foraging for soap-fat, or constructing candles. I merely desired to do away with somewhat of the prevalent calamitous idea among heads of families that Franklin *acquired* his great genius by working for nothing, studying by moonlight, and getting up in the night instead of waiting till morning like a Christian, and that this programme, rigidly inflicted, will make a Franklin of every father's fool. It is time these gentlemen were finding out that these execrable eccentricities of instinct and conduct are only the *evidences* of genius, not the *creators* of it. I wish I had been the father of my parents long enough to make them comprehend this truth, and thus prepare them to let their son have an easier time of it. When I was a child I had to boil soap, notwithstanding my father was wealthy, and I had to get up early and study geometry at breakfast, and peddle my own poetry, and do everything just as Franklin did, in the solemn hope that I would be a Franklin some day. And here I am.

July 1870

A Memory

When I say that I never knew my austere father to be enamored of but one poem in all the long half century that he lived, persons who knew him will easily believe me; when I say that I have never composed but one poem in all the long third of a century that I have lived, persons who know me will be sincerely grateful; and finally, when I say that the poem which I composed was not the one which my father was enamored of, persons who may have known us both will not need to have this truth shot into them with a mountain howitzer before they can receive it. My father and I were always on the most distant terms when I was a boy—a sort of armed neutrality, so to speak. At irregular intervals this neutrality was broken, and suffering ensued; but I will be candid enough to say that the breaking and the suffering were always divided up with strict impartiality between us—which is to say, my father did the breaking, and I did the suffering. As a general thing I was a backward, cautious, unadventurous boy; but once I jumped off a two-story stable; another time I gave an elephant a "plug" of tobacco and retired without waiting for an answer; and still another time I pretended to be talking in my sleep, and got off a portion of a very wretched original conundrum in hearing of my father. Let us not pry into the result; it was of no consequence to any one but me.

But the poem I have referred to as attracting my father's attention and achieving his favor was "Hiawatha." Some man who courted a sudden and awful death presented him an early copy, and I never lost faith in my own senses until I saw him sit down and go to reading it in cold blood—saw him open the book, and heard him read these following lines, with the same inflectionless judicial frigidity with which he always read his charge to the jury, or administered an oath to a witness:

> Take your bow, O Hiawatha,
> Take your arrows, jasper-headed,
> Take your war-club, Puggawaugun,
> And your mittens, Minjekahwan,
> And your birch canoe for sailing,
> And the oil of Mishe-Nama.

Presently my father took out of his breast pocket an imposing "Warranty Deed," and fixed his eyes upon it and dropped into meditation. I knew what it was. A Texan lady and gentleman had given my half-brother, Orrin Johnson, a handsome property in a town in the North, in gratitude to him for having saved their lives by an act of brilliant heroism.

By and by my father looked toward me and sighed. Then he said:

"If I had such a son as this poet, here were a subject worthier than the traditions of these Indians."

"If you please, sir, where?"

"In this deed."

"In the — deed?"

"Yes — in this very deed," said my father, throwing it on the table. "There is more poetry, more romance, more sublimity, more splendid imagery hidden away in that homely document than could be found in all the traditions of all the savages that live."

"Indeed, sir? Could I — could I get it out, sir? Could I compose the poem, sir, do you think?"

"You!"

I wilted.

Presently my father's face softened somewhat, and he said:

"Go and try. But mind, curb folly. No poetry at the expense of truth. Keep strictly to the facts."

I said I would, and bowed myself out, and went up stairs.

"Hiawatha" kept droning in my head — and so did my father's remarks about the sublimity and romance hidden in my subject, and also his injunction to beware of wasteful and exuberant fancy. I noticed, just here, that I had heedlessly brought the deed away with me. Now, at this moment came to me one of those rare moods of daring recklessness, such as I referred to a while ago. Without another thought, and in plain defiance of the fact that I knew my father meant me to write the romantic story of my half-brother's adventure and subsequent good fortune, I ventured to heed merely the letter of his remarks and ignore their spirit. I took the stupid "Warranty Deed" itself and chopped it up into Hiawathian blank verse, without altering or leaving out three words, and without transposing six. It required loads of courage to go down stairs and face my father with my performance. I started three or four times before I finally got my pluck to where it would stick. But at last I said I would go down and read it to him if he threw me over the church for it. I stood up to begin, and he told me to come closer. I edged up a little, but still left as much neutral ground between us as I thought he would stand. Then I began. It would be useless for me to try to tell what conflicting emotions expressed themselves upon his face, nor how they grew more and more intense as I proceeded; nor how a fell darkness descended upon his countenance, and he began to gag and swallow, and his hands began to work and twitch, as I reeled off line after line, with the strength ebbing out of me, and my legs trembling under me:

THE STORY OF A GALLANT DEED.

THIS INDENTURE, made the tenth
    Day of November, in the year
Of our Lord one thousand eight
    Hundred six-and-fifty,

Between JOANNA S. E. GRAY
    And PHILIP GRAY, her husband,
Of Salem City in the State
    Of Texas, of the first part,

And O. B. Johnson, of the town
    Of Austin, ditto, WITNESSETH:
That said party of first part,
    For and in consideration

Of the sum of Twenty Thousand
    Dollars, lawful money of
The U. S. of Americay,
    To them in hand now paid by said

Party of the second part,
    The due receipt whereof is here-
By confessed and acknowledg-ed,
    Have Granted, Bargained, Sold, Remised,

Released and Aliened and Conveyed,
    Confirmed, and by these presents do
Grant and Bargain, Sell, Remise,
    Alien, Release, Convey, and Con-

Firm unto the said aforesaid
   Party of the second part,
And to his heirs and assigns
   Forever and ever, ALL

That certain piece or parcel of
   LAND situate in city of
Dunkirk, county of Chautauqua,
   And likewise furthermore in York State,

Bounded and described, to-wit,
   As follows, herein, namely:
BEGINNING at the distance of
   A hundred two-and-forty feet,

North-half-east, north-east-by-north,
   East-north-east and northerly
Of the northerly line of Mulligan street,
   On the westerly line of Brannigan street,

And running thence due northerly
   On Brannigan street 200 feet,
Thence at right angles westerly,
   North-west-by-west-and-west-half-west,

West-and-by-north, north-west-by-west,
   About——

I kind of dodged, and the boot-jack broke the looking-glass. I could have waited to see what became of the other missiles if I had wanted to, but I took no interest in such things.

August 1870

Domestic Missionaries Wanted

The American Board of Foreign Missions have done a good work in supplying the kindly and refining influences of the gospel to the savages of Asia and the islands of the sea, but let them forward no more missionaries to distant lands for the present. God knows they are needed at home. There are no meaner, mangier, filthier savages in all the wide domain of barbarism than the Christian town of Cohocton, right here at our elbow, can produce. Any one who read the letter of our Bath correspondent in yesterday's EXPRESS will endorse that statement.

Cohocton is a place where virtue is so prized, by certain of the citizens who rank as human beings there, but would be regarded as swine in most places, that lately, when they suspected a Mr. Curtis of adultery with a Miss Dawson, school teacher, (albeit Mrs. Curtis herself had no such suspicion and was on friendly terms with Miss D.,) they went boldly, with blackened faces and at dead of night, and took the man and the woman from their beds, and——. But read Miss D.'s sworn testimony:

> They carried me to the door and called to Mr. Curtis to come out; one said, "strip her"; I said, "O, don't do that"; the first thing done was to tear off my dress and then my under garments; then they put tar on my head, and while I was screaming for my mother they put tar in my mouth; then they tarred my body, and put feathers on my head and body.

The men who did that deed are capable of doing any low, sneaking, cowardly villainy that could be invented in perdition. They are very bastards of the devil. By the evidence of their victim, their names are Seth Hill, Benjamin Henry, John Ferris, Eleazar Bently, Elmer Wheeler, and Thomas Jones. Mr. Curtis' testimony adds the names of Adelbert Jones, Henry Hugenor, and Charles Ferris. If the *farmers* (for these are farmers) of Cohocton, are of this complexion, what on earth must a Cohocton "rough" be like?

It seems absurd to think of legal justice in Cohocton—the very suggestion of it is ludicrous—but still these cattle are actually to be tried for the crime they have committed. Hon.

G. H. McMastin, County Judge, will preside at the trial at Bath, and we have a curiosity to know whether they will be applauded or punished. The former, without a doubt. The judge who should punish the most prominent and honored citizens of Cohocton for the daring act of stripping and tarring and feathering a helpless woman without waiting for the permission of the despised law and its despised officers, would be promptly tarred and feathered himself by the outraged public.

We await the result of the trial. Meantime, let the American Board send some missionaries to Cohocton—with a military escort. Our navy protects our missionaries in cannibal lands; therefore why should not our army protect them here? Cannibals are not so dangerous as Cohocton champions of chastity, because they are less sneaking and cowardly.

August 25, 1870

Political Economy

Political economy is the basis of all good government. The wisest men of all ages have brought to bear upon this subject the——

[Here I was interrupted and informed that a stranger wished to see me down at the door. I went and confronted him, and asked to know his business, struggling all the time to keep a tight rein on my seething political economy ideas, and not let them break away from me or get tangled in their harness. And privately I wished the stranger was in the bottom of the canal with a cargo of wheat on top of him. I was all in a fever, but he was cool. He said he was sorry to disturb me, but as he was passing he noticed that I needed some lightning-rods. I said, "Yes, yes—go on—what about it?" He said there was nothing about it, in particular—nothing except he would like to put them up for me. I am new to housekeeping; have been used to hotels and boarding-houses all my life. Like anybody else of similar experience, I try to appear (to strangers) to be an old house-keeper; consequently I said in an off-hand way that I had been intending for some time to have six or eight lightning-rods put up, but—— The stranger started, and looked inquiringly at me, but I was serene. I thought that if I chanced to make any mistakes he would not catch me by my countenance. He said he would rather have my custom than any man's in town. I said all right, and started off to wrestle with my great subject again, when he called me back and said it would be necessary to know exactly how many "points" I wanted put up, what parts of the house I wanted them on, and what quality of rod I preferred. It was close quarters for a man not used to the exigencies of housekeeping, but I went through creditably, and he probably never suspected that I was a novice. I told him to put up eight "points," and put them all on the roof, and use the best quality of rod. He said he could furnish the "plain" article, at 20 cents a foot; "coppered," 25 cents; "zinc-plated, spiral-twist," at 30 cents, that would stop a streak of lightning any time, no matter where it was bound, and "render its errand harmless and its further progress apocryphal." I said apocryphal was no slouch of a word, emanating from the source it did, but philology aside I liked the spiral-twist and would take that brand. Then he said he *could* make two hundred and fifty feet answer, but to do it right, and make the best job in town of it, and attract the admiration of the just and the unjust alike, and compel all parties to say they never saw a more symmetrical and hypothetical display of lightning-rods since they were born, he sup-

posed he really couldn't get along without four hundred, though he
was not vindictive and trusted he was willing to try. I said go ahead
and use four hundred and make any kind of a job he pleased out of
it, but let me get back to my work. So I got rid of him at last, and
now, after half an hour spent in getting my train of political economy thoughts coupled together again, I am ready to go on once
more.]

richest treasures of their genius, their experience of life, and
their learning. The great lights of commercial jurisprudence,
international confraternity, and biological deviation, of all
ages, all civilizations, and all nationalities, from Zoroaster
down to Horace Greeley, have——

[Here I was interrupted again and required to go down and confer further with that lightning-rod man. I hurried off, boiling and
surging with prodigious thoughts wombed in words of such majesty
that each one of them was in itself a straggling procession of syllables
that might be fifteen minutes passing a given point, and once more I
confronted him—he so calm and sweet, I so hot and frenzied. He
was standing in the contemplative attitude of the Colossus of
Rhodes, with one foot on my infant tuberose and the other among
my pansies, his hands on his hips, his hat-brim tilted forward, one
eye shut and the other gazing critically and admiringly in the direction of my principal chimney. He said now *there* was a state of things
to make a man glad to be alive; and added, "I leave it to *you* if you
ever saw anything more deliriously picturesque than eight lightning-
rods on one chimney?" I said I had no present recollection of anything that transcended it. He said that in his opinion nothing on this
earth but Niagara Falls was superior to it in the way of natural scenery. All that was needed now, he verily believed, to make my house a
perfect balm to the eye, was to kind of touch up the other chimneys
a little and thus "add to the generous *coup d'œil* a soothing unifor-
mity of achievement which would allay the excitement naturally con-
sequent upon the first *coup d'état*." I asked him if he learned to talk
out of a book, and if I could borrow it anywhere. He smiled pleasantly, and said that his manner of speaking was not taught in books,
and that nothing but familiarity with lightning could enable a man
to handle his conversational style with impunity. He then figured up
an estimate, and said that about eight more rods scattered about my
roof would about fix me right, and he guessed five hundred feet of
stuff would do it; and added that the first eight had got a little the
start of him, so to speak, and used up a mere trifle of material more
than he had calculated on—a hundred feet or along there. I said I

was in a dreadful hurry, and I wished we could get this business permanently mapped out so that I could go on with my work. He said: "I *could* have put up those eight rods, and marched off about my business—some men *would* have done it. But no, I said to my-self, this man is a stranger to me and I will die before I'll wrong him; there ain't lightning-rods enough on that house, and for one I'll never stir out of my tracks till I've done as I would be done by, and told him so. Stranger, my duty is accomplished; if the recalcitrant and dephlogistic messenger of heaven strikes your——" "There, now, there," I said, "put on the other eight—add five hundred feet of spiral twist—do anything and everything you want to do; but calm your sufferings and try to keep your feelings where you can reach them with the dictionary. Meanwhile, if we understand each other now, I will go to work again." I think I have been sitting here a full hour, this time, trying to get back to where I was when my train of thought was broken up by the last interruption, but I believe I have accomplished it at last and may venture to proceed again.]

wrestled with this great subject, and the greatest among them have found it a worthy adversary and one that always comes up fresh and smiling after every throw. The great Confucius said that he would rather be a profound political economist than chief of police; Cicero frequently said that political econ-omy was the grandest consummation that the human mind was capable of consuming; and even our own Greeley has said vaguely but forcibly that——

[Here the lightning-rod man sent up another call for me. I went down in a state of mind bordering on impatience. He said he would rather have died than interrupt me, but when he was employed to do a job, and that job was expected to be done in a clean, workmanlike manner, and when it was finished and fatigue urged him to seek the rest and recreation he stood so much in need of, and he was about to do it, but looked up and saw at a glance that all the calculations had been a little out, and if a thunder storm were to come up and that house which he felt a personal interest in stood there with nothing on earth to protect it but sixteen lightning-rods—— "Let us have peace!" I shrieked. "Put up a hundred and fifty! Put some on the kitchen! Put a dozen on the barn! Put a couple on the cow!—put one on the cook!—scatter them all over the persecuted place till it looks like a zinc-plated, spiral-twisted, silver-mounted cane-brake! Move! Use up all the material you can get your hands on, and when you run out of lightning-rods put up ram-rods, cam-rods, stair-rods, piston-rods—*anything* that will pander to your dismal

appetite for artificial scenery and bring respite to my raging brain
and healing to my lacerated soul!" Wholly unmoved—further than
to smile sweetly—this iron being simply turned back his wristbands daintily and said he would now "proceed to hump himself."
Well, all that was nearly three hours ago. It is questionable whether I
am calm enough yet to write on the noble theme of political economy, but I cannot resist the desire to try, for it is the one subject that
is nearest to my heart and dearest to my brain of all this world's
philosophy.]

"Political economy is heaven's best boon to man." When the
loose but gifted Byron lay in his Venetian exile, he observed
that if it could be granted him to go back and live his mis-
spent life over again, he would give his lucid and unintoxi-
cated intervals to the composition, not of frivolous rhymes,
but of essays upon political economy. Washington loved this
exquisite science; such names as Baker, Beckwith, Judson,
Smith, are imperishably linked with it; and even imperial
Homer, in the ninth book of the Iliad, has said:

> Fiat justitia, ruat cœlum,
> Post mortem unum, ante bellum,
> Hic jacet hoc, ex-parte res,
> Politicum e-conomico est.

The grandeur of these conceptions of the old poet, together
with the felicity of the wording which clothes them and the
sublimity of the imagery whereby they are illustrated, have
singled out that stanza and made it more celebrated than any
that ever——

["Now, not a word out of you—not a single word. Just state your
bill and relapse into impenetrable silence for ever and ever on these
premises. Nine hundred dollars? Is that all? This check for the
amount will be honored at any respectable bank in America. What is
that multitude of people gathered in the street for? How?—'looking
at the lightning-rods!' Bless my life, did they never see any lightning-
rods before? Never saw 'such a stack of them on one establishment,'
did I understand you to say? I will step down and critically observe
this popular ebullition of ignorance."]

THREE DAYS LATER.—We are all about worn out. For
four-and-twenty hours our bristling premises were the talk

and wonder of the town. The theatres languished, for their happiest scenic inventions were tame and commonplace compared with my lightning-rods. Our street was blocked night and day with spectators, and among them were many who came from the country to see. It was a blessed relief, on the second day, when a thunder storm came up and the lightning began to "go for" my house, as the historian Josephus quaintly phrases it. It cleared the galleries, so to speak. In five minutes there was not a spectator within half a mile of my place; but all the high houses about that distance away were full, windows, roof, and all. And well they might be, for all the falling stars and Fourth of July fireworks of a generation put together and rained down simultaneously out of heaven in one brilliant shower upon one helpless roof, would not have any advantage of the pyrotechnic display that was making my house so magnificently conspicuous in the general gloom of the storm. By actual count the lightning struck at my establishment seven hundred and sixty-four times in forty minutes, but tripped on one of those faithful rods every time and slid down the spiral twist and shot into the earth before it probably had time to be surprised at the way the thing was done. And through all that bombardment only one patch of slates was ripped up, and that was because for a single instant the rods in the vicinity were transporting all the lightning they could possibly accommodate. Well, nothing was ever seen like it since the world began. For one whole day and night not a member of my family stuck his head out of the window but he got the hair snatched off it as smooth as a billiard-ball, and if the reader will believe me not one of us ever dreamt of stirring abroad. But at last the awful siege came to an end—because there was absolutely no more electricity left in the clouds above us within grappling distance of my insatiable rods. *Then* I sallied forth, and gathered daring workmen together, and not a bite or a nap did we take till the premises were utterly stripped of all their terrific armament except just three rods on the house, one on the kitchen, and one on the barn—and behold these remain there even unto this day. And then, and not till then, the people ventured to use our street again. I will remark here, in passing, that during that fearful time I did not continue my essay upon political economy. I am not even yet settled enough in nerve and brain to resume it.

To Whom it May Concern.—Parties having need of three thousand two hundred and eleven feet of best quality zinc-plated spiral-twist lightning-rod stuff, and sixteen hundred and thirty-one silver-tipped points, all in tolerable repair (and, although much worn by use, still equal to any ordinary emergency), can hear of a bargain by addressing the publishers of this magazine.

September 1870

John Chinaman in New York

A correspondent (whose signature, "Lang Bemis," is more or less familiar to the public) contributes the following:

As I passed along by one of those monster American tea stores in New York, I found a Chinaman sitting before it acting in the capacity of a sign. Everybody that passed by gave him a steady stare as long as their heads would twist over their shoulders without dislocating their necks, and a large group had stopped to stare deliberately.

Is it not a shame that we who prate so much about civilization and humanity are content to degrade a fellow-being to such an office as this? Is it not time for reflection when we find ourselves willing to see in such a being, in such a situation, matter merely for frivolous curiosity instead of regret and grave reflection? Here was a poor creature whom hard fortune had exiled from his natural home beyond the seas, and whose troubles ought to have touched these idle strangers that thronged about him; but did it? Apparently not. Men calling themselves the superior race, the race of culture and of gentle blood, scanned his quaint Chinese hat, with peaked roof and ball on top; and his long queue dangling down his back; his short silken blouse, curiously frogged and figured (and, like the rest of his raiment, rusty, dilapidated, and awkwardly put on); his blue cotton, tight-legged pants tied close around the ankles, and his clumsy, blunt-toed shoes with thick cork soles; and having so scanned him from head to foot, cracked some unseemly joke about his outlandish attire or his melancholy face, and passed on. In my heart I pitied the friendless Mongol. I wondered what was passing behind his sad face, and what distant scene his vacant eye was dreaming of. Were his thoughts with his heart, ten thousand miles away, beyond the billowy wastes of the Pacific? among the rice-fields and the plumy palms of China? under the shadows of remembered mountain-peaks, or in groves of bloomy shrubs and strange forest trees unknown to climes like ours? and now and then, rippling among his visions and his dreams, did he hear familiar laughter and half-forgotten voices, and did he catch fitful glimpses of the friendly faces of a by-gone time? A cruel fate it is, I said, that is befallen this bronzed wanderer; a cheerless destiny enough. In order that the group of idlers might be touched at least by the words of the poor fellow, since the appeal of his pauper dress and his dreary exile was lost upon them, I touched him on the shoulder and said:

"Cheer up—don't be down-hearted. It is not America that treats you in this way—it is merely one citizen, whose greed of gain has eaten the humanity out of his heart. America has a broader hospitality for the exiled and oppressed. America and Americans are always ready to help the unfortunate. Money shall be raised—you shall go back to China—you shall see your friends again. What wages do they pay you here?"

"Divil a cint but four dollars a week and find meself; but it's aisy, barrin' the bloody furrin clothes that's so expinsive."

The exile remains at his post. The New York tea merchants who need picturesque signs are not likely to run out of Chinamen.

September 1870

The Noble Red Man

In books he is tall and tawny, muscular, straight, and of kingly presence; he has a beaked nose and an eagle eye.

His hair is glossy, and as black as the raven's wing; out of its massed richness springs a sheaf of brilliant feathers; in his ears and nose are silver ornaments; on his arms and wrists and ankles are broad silver bands and bracelets; his buckskin hunting suit is gallantly fringed, and the belt and the moccasins wonderfully flowered with colored beads; and when, rainbowed with his war-paint, he stands at full height, with his crimson blanket wrapped about him, his quiver at his back, his bow and tomahawk projecting upward from his folded arms, and his eagle eye gazing at specks against the far horizon which even the paleface's field-glass could scarcely reach, he is a being to fall down and worship.

His language is intensely figurative. He never speaks of the moon, but always of "the eye of the night;" nor of the wind *as* the wind, but as "the whisper of the Great Spirit;" and so forth and so on. His power of condensation is marvellous. In some publications he seldom says anything but "Waugh!" and this, with a page of explanation by the author, reveals a whole world of thought and wisdom that before lay concealed in that one little word.

He is noble. He is true and loyal; not even imminent death can shake his peerless faithfulness. His heart is a wellspring of truth, and of generous impulses, and of knightly magnanimity. With him, gratitude is religion; do him a kindness, and at the end of a lifetime he has not forgotten it. Eat of his bread, or offer him yours, and the bond of hospitality is sealed—a bond which is forever inviolable with him.

He loves the dark-eyed daughter of the forest, the dusky maiden of faultless form and rich attire, the pride of the tribe, the all-beautiful. He talks to her in a low voice, at twilight, of his deeds on the war-path and in the chase, and of the grand achievements of his ancestors; and she listens with downcast eyes, "while a richer hue mantles her dusky cheek."

Such is the Noble Red Man in print. But out on the plains and in the mountains, not being on dress parade, not being gotten up to see company, he is under no obligation to be other than his natural self, and therefore:

He is little, and scrawny, and black, and dirty; and, judged by even the most charitable of our canons of human excellence, is thoroughly pitiful and contemptible. There is nothing in his eye or his nose that is attractive, and if there is anything in his hair that—however, that is a feature which will not bear too close examination. He wears no feathers in his hair, and no ornament or covering on his head. His dull-black, frowsy locks hang straight down to his neck behind, and in front they hang just to his eyes, like a curtain, being cut straight across the forehead, from side to side, and never parted on top. He has no pendants in his ears, and as for his—however, let us not waste time on unimportant particulars, but hurry along. He wears no bracelets on his arms or ankles; his hunting suit is gallantly fringed, but not intentionally; when he does not wear his disgusting rabbit-skin robe, his hunting suit consists wholly of the half of a horse blanket brought over in the Pinta or the Mayflower, and frayed out and fringed by inveterate use. He is not rich enough to possess a belt; he never owned a moccasin or wore a shoe in his life; and truly he is nothing but a poor, filthy, naked scurvy vagabond, whom to exterminate were a charity to the Creator's worthier insects and reptiles which he oppresses. Still, when contact with the white man has given to the Noble Son of the Forest certain cloudy impressions of civilization, and aspirations after a nobler life, he presently appears in public with one boot on and one shoe—shirtless, and wearing ripped and patched and buttonless pants which he holds up with his left hand—his execrable rabbit-skin robe flowing from his shoulders—an old hoop-skirt on, outside of it—a necklace of battered sardine-boxes and oyster-cans reposing on his bare breast—a venerable flint-lock musket in his right hand—a weather-beaten stove-pipe hat on, canted "gallusly" to starboard, and the lid off and hanging by a thread or two; and when he thus appears, and waits patiently around a saloon till he gets a chance to strike a "swell" attitude before a

looking-glass, he is a good, fair, desirable subject for extermination if ever there was one.*

There is nothing figurative, or moonshiny, or sentimental
about his language. It is very simple and unostentatious, and
consists of plain, straightforward lies. His "wisdom" conferred upon an idiot would leave that idiot helpless indeed.

He is ignoble—base and treacherous, and hateful in every
way. Not even imminent death can startle him into a spasm of
virtue. The ruling trait of all savages is a greedy and consuming selfishness, and in our Noble Red Man it is found in its
amplest development. His heart is a cesspool of falsehood, of
treachery, and of low and devilish instincts. With him, gratitude is an unknown emotion; and when one does him a kindness, it is safest to keep the face toward him, lest the reward
be an arrow in the back. To accept of a favor from him is to
assume a debt which you can never repay to his satisfaction,
though you bankrupt yourself trying. To give him a dinner
when he is starving, is to precipitate the whole hungry tribe
upon your hospitality, for he will go straight and fetch them,
men, women, children, and dogs, and these they will huddle
patiently around your door, or flatten their noses against
your window, day after day, gazing beseechingly upon every
mouthful you take, and unconsciously swallowing when you
swallow! The scum of the earth!

And the Noble Son of the Plains becomes a mighty hunter
in the due and proper season. That season is the summer, and
the prey that a number of the tribes hunt is crickets and grasshoppers! The warriors, old men, women, and children, spread
themselves abroad in the plain and drive the hopping creatures before them into a ring of fire. I could describe the feast
that then follows, without missing a detail, if I thought the
reader would stand it.

All history and honest observation will show that the Red
Man is a skulking coward and a windy braggart, who strikes
without warning—usually from an ambush or under cover
of night, and nearly always bringing a force of about five or
six to one against his enemy; kills helpless women and little

---

*This is not a fancy picture; I have seen it many a time in Nevada, just as it
is here limned.

children, and massacres the men in their beds; and then brags about it as long as he lives, and his son and his grandson and great-grandson after him glorify it among the "heroic deeds of their ancestors." A regiment of Fenians will fill the whole world with the noise of it when they are getting ready to invade Canada; but when the Red Man declares war, the first intimation his friend the white man whom he supped with at twilight has of it, is when the war-whoop rings in his ears and the tomahawk sinks into his brain. In June, seven Indians went to a small station on the Plains where three white men lived, and asked for food; it was given them, and also to-bacco. They stayed two hours, eating and smoking and talk-ing, waiting with Indian patience for their customary odds of seven to one to offer, and as soon as it came they seized the opportunity; that is, when two of the men went out, they killed the other the instant he turned his back to do some solicited favor; then they caught his comrades separately, and killed one, but the other escaped.

The Noble Red Man seldom goes prating loving foolish-ness to a splendidly caparisoned blushing maid at twilight. No; he trades a crippled horse, or a damaged musket, or a dog, a gallon of grasshoppers, and an inefficient old mother for her, and makes her work like an abject slave all the rest of her life to compensate him for the outlay. He never works himself. She builds the habitation, when they use one (it con-sists in hanging half a dozen rags over the weather side of a sage-brush bush to roost under); gathers and brings home the fuel; takes care of the raw-boned pony when they possess such grandeur; she walks and carries her nursing cubs while he rides. She wears no clothing save the fragrant rabbit-skin robe which her great-grandmother before her wore, and all the "blushing" she does can be removed with soap and a towel, provided it is only four or five weeks old and not caked.

Such is the genuine Noble Aborigine. I did not get him from books, but from personal observation.

By Dr. Keim's excellent book it appears that from June, 1868, to October, 1869, the Indians *massacred nearly 200 white persons and ravished over forty women captured in peaceful out-lying settlements along the border, or belonging to emigrant trains traversing the settled routes of travel. Children were burned alive in the presence of their parents. Wives were ravished before their husbands' eyes. Husbands were mutilated, tortured, and scalped, and their wives compelled to look on.* These facts and figures are official, and they exhibit the misunderstood Son of the Forest in his true character—as a creature devoid of brave or generous qualities, but cruel, treacherous, and brutal. During the Pi-Ute war the Indians often dug the sinews out of the backs of white men before they were dead. (The sinews are used for bow-strings.) But their favorite mutilations cannot be put into print. Yet it is this same Noble Red Man who is always greeted with a wail of humanitarian sympathy from the Atlantic seaboard whenever he gets into trouble; the maids and matrons throw up their hands in horror at the bloody vengeance wreaked upon him, and the newspapers clamor for a court of inquiry to examine into the conduct of the inhuman officer who inflicted the little pleasantry upon the "poor abused Indian." (They always look at the matter from the abused-Indian point of view, never from that of the bereaved white widow and orphan.) But it is a great and unspeakable comfort to know that, let them be as prompt about it as they may, the inquiry has always got to come *after* the good officer has administered his little admonition.

September 1870

The Approaching Epidemic

One calamity to which the death of Mr. Dickens dooms this country has not awakened the concern to which its gravity entitles it. We refer to the fact that the nation is to be lectured to death and read to death all next winter, by Tom, Dick, and Harry, with poor lamented Dickens for a pretext. All the vagabonds who can spell will afflict the people with "readings" from Pickwick and Copperfield, and all the insignificants who have been ennobled by the notice of the great novelist or transfigured by his smile will make a marketable commodity of it now, and turn the sacred reminiscence to the practical use of procuring bread and butter. The lecture rostrums will fairly swarm with these fortunates. Already the signs of it are perceptible. Behold how the unclean creatures are wending toward the dead lion and gathering to the feast:

"Reminiscences of Dickens." A lecture. By John Smith, who heard him read eight times.

"Remembrances of Charles Dickens." A lecture. By John Jones, who saw him once in a street car and twice in a barber shop.

"Recollections of Mr. Dickens." A lecture. By John Brown, who gained a wide fame by writing deliriously appreciative critiques and rhapsodies upon the great author's public readings; and who shook hands with the great author upon various occasions, and held converse with him several times.

"Readings from Dickens." By John White, who has the great delineator's style and manner perfectly, having attended all his readings in this country and made these things a study, always practising each reading before retiring, and while it was hot from the great delineator's lips. Upon this occasion Mr. W. will exhibit the remains of a cigar which he saw Mr. Dickens smoke. This Relic is kept in a solid silver box made purposely for it.

"Sights and Sounds of the Great Novelist." A popular lecture. By John Gray, who waited on his table all the time he was at the Grand Hotel, New York, and still has in his possession and will exhibit to the audience a fragment of the

Last Piece of Bread which the lamented author tasted in this country.

"Heart Treasures of Precious Moments with Literature's Departed Monarch." A lecture. By Miss Serena Amelia Tryphenia McSpadden, who still wears, and will always wear, a glove upon the hand made sacred by the clasp of Dickens. Only Death shall remove it.

"Readings from Dickens." By Mrs. J. O'Hooligan Murphy, who washed for him.

"Familiar Talks with the Great Author." A narrative lecture. By John Thomas, for two weeks his valet in America.

And so forth, and so on. This isn't half the list. The man who has a "Toothpick once used by Charles Dickens" will have to have a hearing; and the man who "once rode in an omnibus with Charles Dickens;" and the lady to whom Charles Dickens "granted the hospitalities of his umbrella during a storm;" and the person who "possesses a hole which once belonged in a handkerchief owned by Charles Dickens." Be patient and long-suffering, good people, for even this does not fill up the measure of what you must endure next winter. There is no creature in all this land who has had any personal relations with the late Mr. Dickens, however slight or trivial, but will shoulder his way to the rostrum and inflict his testimony upon his helpless countrymen. To some people it is fatal to be noticed by greatness.

September 1870

A Royal Compliment

The latest report about the Spanish crown is, that it will now be offered to Prince Alfonso, the second son of the King of Portugal, who is but five years of age. The Spaniards have hunted through all the nations of Europe for a King. They tried to get a Portuguese in the person of Dom Luis, who is an old ex-monarch; they tried to get an Italian, in the person of Victor Emanuel's young son, the Duke of Genoa; they tried to get a Spaniard, in the person of Espartero, who is an octogenarian. Some of them desired a French Bourbon, Montpensier; some of them a Spanish Bourbon, the Prince of Asturias; some of them an English prince, one of the sons of Queen Victoria. They have just tried to get the German Prince Leopold; but they have thought it better to give him up than take a war along with him. It is a long time since we first suggested to them to try an American ruler. We can offer them a large number of able and experienced sovereigns to pick from—men skilled in statesmanship, versed in the science of government, and adepts in all the arts of administration—men who could wear the crown with dignity and rule the kingdom at a reasonable expense. There is not the least danger of Napoleon threatening them if they take an American sovereign; in fact, we have no doubt he would be pleased to support such a candidature. We are unwilling to mention names—though *we have a man in our eye whom we wish they had in theirs.—New York Tribune.*

It would be but an ostentation of modesty to permit such a pointed reference to myself to pass unnoticed. This is the second time that "The Tribune" (no doubt sincerely looking to the best interests of Spain and the world at large) has done me the great and unusual honor to propose me as a fit person to fill the Spanish throne. Why "The Tribune" should single me out in this way from the midst of a dozen Americans of higher political prominence, is a problem which I cannot solve. Beyond a somewhat intimate knowledge of Spanish history and a profound veneration for its great names and illustrious deeds, I feel that I possess no merit that should peculiarly recommend me to this royal distinction. I cannot deny that Spanish history has always been mother's milk to me. I am proud of every Spanish achievement, from Hernando Cortes's victory at Thermopylæ down to Vasco Nunez de Balboa's discovery of the Atlantic ocean; and of every splendid Spanish name, from Don Quixote and the Duke of Wellington down to Don Cæsar de Bazan. However, these little graces of erudition are of small consequence, being more showy than serviceable.

In case the Spanish sceptre is pressed upon me—and the indications unquestionably are that it will be—I shall feel it necessary to have certain things set down and distinctly understood beforehand. For instance: My salary must be paid quarterly in advance. In these unsettled times it will not do to trust. If Isabella had adopted this plan, she would be roosting on her ancestral throne to-day, for the simple reason that her subjects never could have raised three months of a royal salary in advance, and of course they could not have discharged her until they had squared up with her. My salary must be paid in gold; when greenbacks are fresh in a country, they are too fluctuating. My salary has got to be put at the ruling market rate; I am not going to cut under on the trade, and they are not going to trail me a long way from home and then practise on my ignorance and play me for a royal North Adams Chinaman, by any means. As I understand it, imported kings generally get five millions a year and house-rent free. Young George of Greece gets that. As the revenues only yield two millions, he has to take the national note for considerable; but even with things in that sort of shape he is better fixed than he was in Denmark, where he had to eternally stand up because he had no throne to sit on, and had to give bail for his board, because a royal apprentice gets no salary there while he is learning his trade. England is the place for that. Fifty thousand dollars a year Great Britain pays on each royal child that is born, and this is increased from year to year as the child becomes more and more indispensable to his country. Look at Prince Arthur. At first he only got the usual birth-bounty; but now that he has got so that he can dance, there is simply no telling what wages he gets.

I should have to stipulate that the Spanish people wash more and endeavor to get along with less quarantine. Do you know, Spain keeps her ports fast locked against foreign traffic three-fourths of each year, because one day she is scared about the cholera, and the next about the plague, and next the measles, next the hooping cough, the hives, and the rash? but she does not mind leonine leprosy and elephantiasis any more than a great and enlightened civilization minds freckles. Soap would soon remove her anxious distress about foreign distempers. The reason arable land is so scarce in Spain is because the people squander so much of it on their persons, and then when they die it is improvidently buried with them.

I should feel obliged to stipulate that Marshal Serrano be reduced to the rank of constable, or even roundsman. He is no longer fit to be City Marshal. A man who refused to be king because he was too old and feeble, is ill qualified to help sick people to the station-house when they are armed and their form of delirium tremens is of the exuberant and demonstrative kind.

I should also require that a force be sent to chase the late Queen Isabella out of France. Her presence there can work no advantage to Spain, and she ought to be made to move at once; though, poor thing, she has been chaste enough heretofore—for a Spanish woman.

I should also require that——

I am at this moment authoritatively informed that "The Tribune" did not mean me, after all. Very well, I do not care two cents.

September 1870

Science vs. Luck

At that time, in Kentucky (said the Hon. Mr. Knott, M. C.), the law was very strict against what it termed "games of chance." About a dozen of the boys were detected playing "seven-up" or "old sledge" for money, and the grand jury found a true bill against them. Jim Sturgis was retained to defend them when the case came up, of course. The more he studied over the matter and looked into the evidence, the plainer it was that he must lose a case at last — there was no getting around that painful fact. Those boys had certainly been betting money on a game of chance. Even public sympathy was roused in behalf of Sturgis. People said it was a pity to see him mar his successful career with a big prominent case like this, which must go against him.

But after several restless nights an inspired idea flashed upon Sturgis, and he sprang out of bed delighted. He thought he saw his way through. The next day he whispered around a little among his clients and a few friends, and then when the case came up in court he acknowledged the seven-up and the betting, and, as his sole defence, had the astounding effrontery to put in the plea that old sledge was not a game of chance! There was the broadest sort of a smile all over the faces of that sophisticated audience. The judge smiled with the rest. But Sturgis maintained a countenance whose earnestness was even severe. The opposite counsel tried to ridicule him out of his position, and did not succeed. The judge jested in a ponderous judicial way about the thing, but did not move him. The matter was becoming grave. The judge lost a little of his patience, and said the joke had gone far enough. Jim Sturgis said he knew of no joke in the matter — his clients could not be punished for indulging in what some people chose to consider a game of chance, until it was *proven* that it was a game of chance. Judge and counsel said that would be an easy matter, and forthwith called Deacons Job, Peters, Burke, and Johnson, and Dominies Wirt and Miggles, to testify; and they unanimously and with strong feeling put down the legal quibble of Sturgis, by pronouncing that old sledge *was* a game of chance.

"What do you call it *now!*" said the judge.

"I call it a game of science!" retorted Sturgis; "and I'll prove it, too!"

They saw his little game.

He brought in a cloud of witnesses, and produced an overwhelming mass of testimony, to show that old sledge was not a game of chance, but a game of science.

Instead of being the simplest case in the world, it had somehow turned out to be an excessively knotty one. The judge scratched his head over it a while, and said there was no way of coming to a determination, because just as many men could be brought into court who would testify on one side, as could be found to testify on the other. But he said he was willing to do the fair thing by all parties, and would act upon any suggestion Mr. Sturgis would make for the solution of the difficulty.

Mr. Sturgis was on his feet in a second:

"Impanel a jury of six of each, Luck *versus* Science—give them candles and a couple of decks of cards, send them into the jury room, and just abide by the result!"

There was no disputing the fairness of the proposition. The four deacons and the two dominies were sworn in as the "chance" jurymen, and six inveterate old seven-up professors were chosen to represent the "science" side of the issue. They retired to the jury room.

In about two hours, Deacon Peters sent into court to borrow three dollars from a friend. [Sensation.] In about two hours more, Dominie Miggles sent into court to borrow a "stake" from a friend. [Sensation.] During the next three or four hours, the other dominie and the other deacons sent into court for small loans. And still the packed audience waited, for it was a prodigious occasion in Bull's Corners, and one in which every father of a family was necessarily interested.

The rest of the story can be told briefly. About daylight the jury came in, and Deacon Job, the foreman, read the following

VERDICT.

We, the jury in the case of the Commonwealth of Kentucky vs. John Wheeler et al., have carefully considered the points of the case, and tested the merits of the several theories advanced, and do hereby unanimously decide that the game commonly known as old sledge or seven-up is eminently a game of science and not of chance. In demonstration whereof, it is hereby and herein stated, iterated, reiterated, set forth, and made manifest, that, during the entire night, the "chance" men never won a game or turned a jack, although both feats were common and frequent to the opposition; and furthermore, in support of this our verdict, we call attention to the significant fact that the "chance" men are all busted, and the "science" men have got the money. It is the deliberate opinion of this jury that the "chance" theory concerning seven-up is a pernicious doctrine, and calculated to inflict untold suffering and pecuniary loss upon any community that takes stock in it.

"That is the way that seven-up came to be set apart and particularized in the statute books of Kentucky as being a game not of chance but of science, and therefore not punishable under the law," said Mr. Knott. "That verdict is of record, and holds good to this day."

October 1870

Goldsmith's Friend Abroad Again

NOTE.—No experience is set down in the following letters which had to be invented. Fancy is not needed to give variety to the history of a Chinaman's sojourn in America. Plain fact is amply sufficient.

LETTER I.

SHANGHAI, 18—.

DEAR CHING-FOO: It is all settled, and I am to leave my oppressed and overburdened native land and cross the sea to that noble realm where all are free and all equal, and none reviled or abused—America! America, whose precious privilege it is to call herself the Land of the Free and the Home of the Brave. We and all that are about us here look over the waves longingly, contrasting the privations of this our birthplace with the opulent comfort of that happy refuge. We know how America has welcomed the Germans and the Frenchmen and the stricken and sorrowing Irish, and we know how she has given them bread and work and liberty, and how grateful they are. And we know that America stands ready to welcome all other oppressed peoples and offer her abundance to all that come, without asking what their nationality is, or their creed or color. And, without being told it, we know that the foreign sufferers she has rescued from oppression and starvation are the most eager of her children to welcome us, because, having suffered themselves, they know what suffering is, and having been generously succored, they long to be generous to other unfortunates and thus show that magnanimity is not wasted upon them.

AH SONG HI.

LETTER II.

AT SEA, 18—.

DEAR CHING-FOO: We are far away at sea now, on our way to the beautiful Land of the Free and Home of the Brave. We shall soon be where all men are alike, and where sorrow is not known.

The good American who hired me to go to his country is to pay me $12 a month, which is immense wages, you know—twenty times as much as one gets in China. My passage in the ship is a very large sum—indeed, it is a fortune—and this I must pay myself eventually, but I am allowed ample time to make it good to my employer in, he advancing it now. For a mere form, I have turned over my wife, my boy, and my two daughters to my employer's partner for security for the payment of the ship fare. But my employer says they are in no danger of being sold, for he knows I will be faithful to him, and that is the main security.

I thought I would have twelve dollars to begin life with in America, but the American Consul took two of them for making a certificate that I was shipped on the steamer. He has no right to do more than charge the ship two dollars for *one* certificate for the *ship*, with the number of her Chinese passengers set down in it; but he chooses to force a certificate upon each and every Chinaman and put the two dollars in his pocket. As 1,300 of my countrymen are in this vessel, the Consul received $2,600 for certificates. My employer tells me that the Government at Washington know of this fraud, and are so bitterly opposed to the existence of such a wrong that they tried hard to have the extor——the fee, I mean, legalized by the last Congress;* but as the bill did not pass, the Consul will have to take the fee dishonestly until next Congress makes it legitimate. It is a great and good and noble country, and hates all forms of vice and chicanery.

We are in that part of the vessel always reserved for my countrymen. It is called the steerage. It is kept for us, my employer says, because it is not subject to changes of temperature and dangerous drafts of air. It is only another instance of the loving unselfishness of the Americans for all unfortunate foreigners. The steerage is a little crowded, and rather warm and close, but no doubt it is best for us that it should be so.

Yesterday our people got to quarrelling among themselves, and the captain turned a volume of hot steam upon a mass of them and scalded eighty or ninety of them more or less severely. Flakes and ribbons of skin came off some of them. There was wild shrieking and struggling while the vapor en-

*Pacific and Mediterranean steamship bills.

veloped the great throng, and so some who were not scalded got trampled upon and hurt. We do not complain, for my employer says this is the usual way of quieting disturbances on board the ship, and that it is done in the cabins among the Americans every day or two.

Congratulate me, Ching-Foo! In ten days more I shall step upon the shore of America, and be received by her great-hearted people; and I shall straighten myself up and feel that I am a free man among freemen.

AH SONG HI.

———

LETTER III.

SAN FRANCISCO, 18—.

DEAR CHING-FOO: I stepped ashore jubilant! I wanted to dance, shout, sing, worship the generous Land of the Free and Home of the Brave. But as I walked from the gang-plank a man in a gray uniform* kicked me violently behind and told me to look out—so my employer translated it. As I turned, another officer of the same kind struck me with a short club and also instructed me to look out. I was about to take hold of my end of the pole which had mine and Hong-Wo's basket and things suspended from it, when a third officer hit me with his club to signify that I was to drop it, and then kicked me to signify that he was satisfied with my promptness. Another person came now, and searched all through our basket and bundles, emptying everything out on the dirty wharf. Then this person and another searched us all over. They found a little package of opium sewed into the artificial part of Hong-Wo's queue, and they took that, and also they made him prisoner and handed him over to an officer, who marched him away. They took his luggage, too, because of his crime, and as our luggage was so mixed together that they could not tell mine from his, they took it all. When I offered to help divide it, they kicked me and desired me to look out.

Having now no baggage and no companion, I told my employer that if he was willing, I would walk about a little and see the city and the people until he needed me. I did not like

———

*Policeman.

to seem disappointed with my reception in the good land of refuge for the oppressed, and so I looked and spoke as cheerily as I could. But he said, wait a minute—I must be vaccinated to prevent my taking the small-pox. I smiled and said I had already had the small-pox, as he could see by the marks, and so I need not wait to be "vaccinated," as he called it. But he said it was the law, and I must be vaccinated anyhow. The doctor would never let me pass, for the law obliged him to vaccinate all Chinamen and charge them *ten dollars apiece* for it, and I might be sure that no doctor who would be the servant of that law would let a fee slip through his fingers to accommodate any absurd fool who had seen fit to have the disease in some other country. And presently the doctor came and did his work and took my last penny—my ten dollars which were the hard savings of nearly a year and a half of labor and privation. Ah, if the law-makers had only known there were plenty of doctors in the city glad of a chance to vaccinate people for a dollar or two, they would never have put the price up so high against a poor friendless Irish, or Italian, or Chinese pauper fleeing to the good land to escape hunger and hard times.

AH SONG HI.

———

LETTER IV.

SAN FRANCISCO, 18—.

DEAR CHING-FOO: I have been here about a month now, and am learning a little of the language every day. My employer was disappointed in the matter of hiring us out to service on the plantations in the far eastern portion of this continent. His enterprise was a failure, and so he set us all free, merely taking measures to secure to himself the repayment of the passage money which he paid for us. We are to make this good to him out of the first moneys we earn here. He says it is sixty dollars apiece.

We were thus set free about two weeks after we reached here. We had been massed together in some small houses up to that time, waiting. I walked forth to seek my fortune. I was to begin life a stranger in a strange land, without a friend, or a penny, or any clothes but those I had on my back. I had not any advantage on my side in the world—not one, except good health and the lack of any necessity to waste any time or anxiety on the watching of my baggage. No, I forget. I reflected that I had one prodigious advantage over paupers in other lands—I was in America! I was in the heaven-provided refuge of the oppressed and the forsaken!

Just as that comforting thought passed through my mind, some young men set a fierce dog on me. I tried to defend myself, but could do nothing. I retreated to the recess of a closed doorway, and there the dog had me at his mercy, flying at my throat and face or any part of my body that presented itself. I shrieked for help, but the young men only jeered and laughed. Two men in gray uniforms (policemen is their official title) looked on for a minute and then walked leisurely away. But a man stopped them and brought them back and told them it was a shame to leave me in such distress. Then the two policemen beat off the dog with small clubs, and a comfort it was to be rid of him, though I was just rags and blood from head to foot. The man who brought the policemen asked the young men why they abused me in that way, and they said they didn't want any of his meddling. And they said to him:

"This Ching divil comes till Ameriky to take the bread out o' dacent intilligent white men's mouths, and whin they try to defind their rights there's a dale o' fuss made about it."

They began to threaten my benefactor, and as he saw no friendliness in the faces that had gathered meanwhile, he went on his way. He got many a curse when he was gone. The policemen now told me I was under arrest and must go with them. I asked one of them what wrong I had done to any one that I should be arrested, and he only struck me with his club and ordered me to "hold my yop." With a jeering crowd of street boys and loafers at my heels, I was taken up an alley and into a stone-paved dungeon which had large cells all down one side of it, with iron gates to them. I stood up by a desk while a man behind it wrote down certain things about me on a slate. One of my captors said:

"Enter a charge against this Chinaman of being disorderly and disturbing the peace."

I attempted to say a word, but he said:

"Silence! Now ye had better go slow, my good fellow. This is two or three times you've tried to get off some of your d—d insolence. Lip won't do here. You've *got* to simmer down, and if you don't take to it paceable we'll see if we can't make you. Fat's your name?"

"Ah Song Hi."

"*Alias* what?"

I said I did not understand, and he said what he wanted was my *true* name, for he guessed I picked up this one since I stole my last chickens. They all laughed loudly at that.

Then they searched me. They found nothing, of course. They seemed very angry and asked who I supposed would "go my bail or pay my fine." When they explained these things to me, I said I had done nobody any harm, and why should I need to have bail or pay a fine? Both of them kicked me and warned me that I would find it to my advantage to try and be as civil as convenient. I protested that I had not meant anything disrespectful. Then one of them took me to one side and said:

"Now look here, Johnny, it's no use you playing softy wid us. We mane business, ye know; and the sooner ye put us on the scent of a V, the asier ye'll save yerself from a dale of trouble. Ye can't get out o' this for anny less. Who's your frinds?"

I told him I had not a single friend in all the land of America, and that I was far from home and help, and very poor. And I begged him to let me go.

He gathered the slack of my blouse collar in his grip and jerked and shoved and hauled at me across the dungeon, and then unlocking an iron cell-gate thrust me in with a kick and said:

"Rot there, ye furrin spawn, till ye lairn that there's no room in America for the likes of ye or your nation."

AH SONG HI.

——

LETTER V.

SAN FRANCISCO, 18—.

DEAR CHING-FOO: You will remember that I had just been thrust violently into a cell in the city prison when I wrote last.

I stumbled and fell on some one. I got a blow and a curse; and on top of these a kick or two and a shove. In a second or two it was plain that I was in a nest of prisoners and was being "passed around"—for the instant I was knocked out of the way of one I fell on the head or heels of another and was promptly ejected, only to land on a third prisoner and get a new contribution of kicks and curses and a new destination. I brought up at last in an unoccupied corner, very much battered and bruised and sore, but glad enough to be let alone for a little while. I was on the flag-stones, for there was no furniture in the den except a long, broad board, or combination of boards, like a barn door, and this bed was accommodating five or six persons, and that was its full capacity. They lay stretched side by side, snoring—when not fighting. One end of the board was four inches higher than the other, and so the slant answered for a pillow. There were no blankets, and the night was a little chilly; the nights are always a little chilly in San Francisco, though never severely cold. The board was a deal more comfortable than the stones, and occasionally some flag-stone plebeian like me would try to creep to a place on it; and then the aristocrats would hammer him good and make him think a flag pavement was a nice enough place after all.

I lay quiet in my corner, stroking my bruises and listening to the revelations the prisoners made to each other—and to me—for some that were near me talked to me a good deal. I had long had an idea that Americans, being free, had no need of prisons, which are a contrivance of despots for keeping restless patriots out of mischief. So I was considerably surprised to find out my mistake.

Ours was a big general cell, it seemed, for the temporary accommodation of all comers whose crimes were trifling. Among us there were two Americans, two "Greasers" (Mexicans), a Frenchman, a German, four Irishmen, a Chilenean (and, in the next cell, only separated from us by a grating, two women), all drunk, and all more or less noisy; and as night fell and advanced, they grew more and more discontented and disorderly, occasionally shaking the prison bars and glaring through them at the slowly pacing officer, and cursing him with all their hearts. The two women were nearly middle-aged, and they had only had enough liquor to stimulate instead of stupefy them. Consequently they would fondle and kiss each other for some minutes, and then fall to fighting and keep it up till they were just two grotesque tangles of rags and blood and tumbled hair. Then they would rest awhile, and pant and swear. While they were affectionate they always spoke of each other as "ladies," but while they were fighting "strumpet" was the mildest name they could think of—and they could only make that do by tacking some sounding profanity to it. In their last fight, which was toward midnight, one of them bit off the other's finger, and then the officer interfered and put the "Greaser" into the "dark cell" to answer for it—because the woman that did it laid it on him, and the other woman did not deny it because, as she said afterward, she "wanted another crack at the huzzy when her finger quit hurting," and so she did not want her removed. By this time those two women had mutilated each other's clothes to that extent that there was not sufficient left to cover their nakedness. I found that one of these creatures had spent nine years in the county jail, and that the other one had spent about four or five years in the same place. They had done it from choice. As soon as they were discharged from captivity they would go straight and get drunk, and then steal some trifling thing while an officer was observing them. That would entitle them to another two months in jail, and there they would occupy clean, airy apartments, and have good food in plenty, and being at no expense at all, they could make shirts for the clothiers at half a dollar apiece and thus keep themselves in smoking tobacco and such other luxuries as they wanted. When the two months were up, they would go just as straight as they could walk to Mother Leonard's and get drunk; and from there to Kearney street and steal something; and thence to this city prison, and next day back to the old quarters in the county jail again. One of them had really kept this up for nine years and the other four or five, and both said they meant to end their days in that prison.* Finally, both these creatures fell upon me while I was dozing

---

*The former of the two did.

with my head against their grating, and battered me considerably, because they discovered that I was a Chinaman, and they said I was "a bloody interlopin' loafer come from the divil's own country to take the bread out of dacent people's mouths and put down the wages for work whin it was all a Christian could do to kape body and sowl together as it was." "Loafer" means one who will not work.

Ah Song Hi.

————

LETTER VI.

San Francisco, 18—.

Dear Ching-Foo: To continue—the two women became reconciled to each other again through the common bond of interest and sympathy created between them by pounding me in partnership, and when they had finished me they fell to embracing each other again and swearing more eternal affection like that which had subsisted between them all the evening, barring occasional interruptions. They agreed to swear the finger-biting on the Greaser in open court, and get him sent to the penitentiary for the crime of mayhem.

Another of our company was a boy of fourteen who had been watched for some time by officers and teachers, and repeatedly detected in enticing young girls from the public schools to the lodgings of gentlemen down town. He had been furnished with lures in the form of pictures and books of a peculiar kind, and these he had distributed among his clients. There were likenesses of fifteen of these young girls on exhibition (only to prominent citizens and persons in authority, it was said, though most people came to get a sight) at the police headquarters, but no punishment at all was to be inflicted on the poor little misses. The boy was afterward sent into captivity at the House of Correction for some months, and there was a strong disposition to punish the gentlemen who had employed the boy to entice the girls, but as that could not be done without making public the names of those gentlemen and thus injuring them socially, the idea was finally given up.

There was also in our cell that night a photographer (a kind of artist who makes likenesses of people with a machine), who had been for some time patching the pictured heads of well-known and respectable young ladies to the nude, pictured bodies of another class of women; then from this patched creation he would make photographs and sell them privately at high prices to rowdies and blackguards, averring that these, the best young ladies of the city, had hired him to take their likenesses in that unclad condition. What a lecture the police judge read that photographer when he was convicted! He told him his crime was little less than an outrage. He abused that photographer till he almost made him sink through the floor, and then he fined him a hundred dollars. And he told him he might consider himself lucky that he didn't fine him a hundred and twenty-five dollars. They are awfully severe on crime here.

About two or two and a half hours after midnight, of that first experience of mine in the city prison, such of us as were dozing were awakened by a noise of beating and dragging and groaning, and in a little while a man was pushed into our den with a "There, d—n you, soak there a spell!"—and then the gate was closed and the officers went away again. The man who was thrust among us fell limp and helpless by the grating, but as nobody could reach him with a kick without the trouble of hitching along toward him or getting fairly up to deliver it, our people only grumbled at him, and cursed him, and called him insulting names—for misery and hardship do not make their victims gentle or charitable toward each other. But as he neither tried humbly to conciliate our people nor swore back at them, his unnatural conduct created surprise, and several of the party crawled to him where he lay in the dim light that came through the grating, and examined into his case. His head was very bloody and his wits were gone. After about an hour, he sat up and stared around; then his eyes grew more natural and he began to tell how that he was going along with a bag on his shoulder and a brace of policemen ordered him to stop, which he did not do—was chased and caught, beaten ferociously about the head on the way to the prison and after arrival there, and finally thrown into our den like a dog. And in a few seconds he sank down again and grew flighty of speech. One of our people was at last penetrated with something vaguely akin to compassion, may be, for he looked out through the gratings at the guardian officer pacing to and fro, and said:

"Say, Mickey, this shrimp's goin' to die."

"Stop your noise!" was all the answer he got. But presently our man tried it again. He drew himself to the gratings, grasping them with his hands, and looking out through them, sat waiting till the officer was passing once more, and then said:

"Sweetness, you'd better mind your eye, now, because you beats have killed this cuss. You've busted his head and he'll pass in his checks before sun-up. You better go for a doctor, now, you bet you had."

The officer delivered a sudden rap on our man's knuckles with his club, that sent him scampering and howling among the sleeping forms on the flag-stones, and an answering burst of laughter came from the half dozen policemen idling about the railed desk in the middle of the dungeon.

But there was a putting of heads together out there presently, and a conversing in low voices, which seemed to show that our man's talk had made an impression; and presently an officer went away in a hurry, and shortly came back with a person who entered our cell and felt the bruised man's pulse and threw the glare of a lantern on his drawn face, striped with blood, and his glassy eyes, fixed and vacant. The doctor examined the man's broken head also, and presently said:

"If you'd called me an hour ago I might have saved this man, may be—too late now."

Then he walked out into the dungeon and the officers surrounded him, and they kept up a low and earnest buzzing of conversation for fifteen minutes, I should think, and then the doctor took his departure from the prison. Several of the officers now came in and worked a little with the wounded man, but toward daylight he died.

It was the longest, longest night! And when the daylight came filtering reluctantly into the dungeon at last, it was the grayest, dreariest, saddest daylight! And yet, when an officer by and by turned off the sickly yellow gas flame, and immediately the gray of dawn became fresh and white, there was a lifting of my spirits that acknowledged and believed that the night *was* gone, and straightway I fell to stretching my sore limbs, and looking about me with a grateful sense of relief and a returning interest in life. About me lay evidences that what seemed now a feverish dream and a nightmare was the memory of a reality instead. For on the boards lay four frowsy, ragged, bearded vagabonds, snoring—one turned end-for-end and resting an unclean foot, in a ruined stocking, on the hairy breast of a neighbor; the young boy was uneasy, and lay moaning in his sleep; other forms lay half revealed and half concealed about the floor; in the furthest corner the gray light fell upon a sheet, whose elevations and depressions indicated the places of the dead man's face and feet and folded hands; and through the dividing bars one could discern the almost nude forms of the two exiles from the county jail twined together in a drunken embrace, and sodden with sleep.

By and by all the animals in all the cages awoke, and stretched themselves, and exchanged a few cuffs and curses, and then began to clamor for breakfast. Breakfast was brought in at last—bread and beefsteak on tin plates, and black coffee in tin cups, and no grabbing allowed. And after several dreary hours of waiting, after this, we were all marched out into the dungeon and joined there by all manner of vagrants and vagabonds, of all shades and colors and nationalities, from the other cells and cages of the place; and pretty soon our whole menagerie was marched up stairs and locked fast behind a high railing in a dirty room with a dirty audience in it. And this audience stared at us, and at a man seated on high behind what they call a pulpit in this country, and at some clerks and other officials seated below him—and waited. This was the police court.

The court opened. Pretty soon I was compelled to notice that a culprit's nationality made for or against him in this court. Overwhelming proofs were necessary to convict an Irishman of crime, and even then his punishment amounted to little; Frenchmen, Spaniards, and Italians had strict and unprejudiced justice meted out to them, in exact accordance with the evidence; negroes were promptly punished, when there was the slightest preponderance of testimony against them; but Chinamen were punished *always*, apparently. Now this gave me some uneasiness, I confess. I knew that this state of things must of necessity be accidental, because in this country all men were free and equal, and one person could not take to himself an advantage not accorded to all other individuals. I knew that, and yet in spite of it I was uneasy.

And I grew still more uneasy, when I found that any succored and befriended refugee from Ireland or elsewhere could stand up before that judge and swear away the life or liberty or character of a refugee from China; but that by the law of the land *the Chinaman could not testify against the Irishman*. I was really and truly uneasy, but still my faith in the universal liberty that America accords and defends, and my deep veneration for the land that offered all distressed outcasts a home and protection, was strong within me, and I said to myself that it would all come out right yet.

AH SONG HI.

———

LETTER VII.

SAN FRANCISCO, 18—.

DEAR CHING FOO: I was glad enough when my case came up. An hour's experience had made me as tired of the police court as of the dungeon. I was not uneasy about the result of the trial, but on the contrary felt that as soon as the large auditory of Americans present should hear how that the rowdies had set the dogs on me when I was going peacefully along the street, and how, when I was all torn and bleeding, the officers arrested *me* and put me in jail and let the rowdies go free, the gallant hatred of oppression which is part of the very flesh and blood of every American would be stirred to its utmost, and I should be instantly set at liberty. In truth I began to fear for the other side. There in full view stood the ruffians who had misused me, and I began to fear that in the first burst of generous anger occasioned by the revealment of what they had done, they might be harshly handled, and possibly even banished the country as having dishonored her and being no longer worthy to remain upon her sacred soil.

The official interpreter of the court asked my name, and

then spoke it aloud so that all could hear. Supposing that all was now ready, I cleared my throat and began—in Chinese, because of my imperfect English:

"Hear, O high and mighty mandarin, and believe! As I went about my peaceful business in the street, behold certain men set a dog on me, and——"

"Silence!"

It was the judge that spoke. The interpreter whispered to me that I must keep perfectly still. He said that no statement would be received from me—I must only talk through my lawyer.

I had no lawyer. In the early morning a police court lawyer (termed, in the higher circles of society, a "shyster") had come into our den in the prison and offered his services to me, but I had been obliged to go without them because I could not pay in advance or give security. I told the interpreter how the matter stood. He said I must take my chances on the witnesses then. I glanced around, and my failing confidence revived.

"Call those four Chinamen yonder," I said. "They saw it all. I remember their faces perfectly. They will prove that the white men set the dog on me when I was not harming them."

"That won't work," said he. "In this country white men can testify against Chinamen all they want to, but *Chinamen ain't allowed to testify against white men!*"

What a chill went through me! And then I felt the indignant blood rise to my cheek at this libel upon the Home of the Oppressed, where all men are free and equal—perfectly equal—perfectly free and perfectly equal. I despised this Chinese-speaking Spaniard for his mean slander of the land that was sheltering and feeding him. I sorely wanted to sear his eyes with that sentence from the great and good American Declaration of Independence which we have copied in letters of gold in China and keep hung up over our family altars and in our temples—I mean the one about all men being created free and equal.

But woe is me, Ching Foo, the man was right. He was right, after all. There were my witnesses, but I could not use them. But now came a new hope. I saw my white friend come in, and I felt that he had come there purposely to help me. I may almost say I knew it. So I grew easier. He passed near enough to me to say under his breath, "Don't be afraid," and then I had no more fear. But presently the rowdies recognized him and began to scowl at him in no friendly way, and to make threatening signs at him. The two officers that arrested me fixed their eyes steadily on his; he bore it well, but gave in presently, and dropped his eyes. They still gazed at his eyebrows, and every time he raised his eyes he encountered their winkless stare—until after a minute or two he ceased to lift his head at all. The judge had been giving some instructions privately to some one for a little while, but now he was ready to resume business. Then the trial so unspeakably important to me, and freighted with such prodigious consequence to my wife and children, began, progressed, ended, was recorded in the books, noted down by the newspaper reporters, and *forgotten* by everybody but me—all in the little space of two minutes!

"Ah Song Hi, Chinaman. Officers O'Flannigan and O'Flaherty, witnesses. Come forward, Officer O'Flannigan."

OFFICER—"He was making a disturbance in Kearny street."

JUDGE—"Any witnesses on the other side?"

No response. The white friend raised his eyes—encountered Officer O'Flaherty's—blushed a little—got up and left the court-room, avoiding all glances and not taking his own from the floor.

JUDGE—"Give him five dollars or ten days."

In my desolation there was a glad surprise in the words; but it passed away when I found that he only meant that I was to be fined five dollars or imprisoned ten days longer in default of it.

There were twelve or fifteen Chinamen in our crowd of prisoners, charged with all manner of little thefts and misdemeanors, and their cases were quickly disposed of, as a general thing. When the charge came from a policeman or other white man, he made his statement and that was the end of it, unless the Chinaman's lawyer could find some white person to testify in his client's behalf; for, neither the accused Chinaman nor his countrymen being allowed to say anything, the statement of the officers or other white person was amply sufficient to convict. So, as I said, the Chinamen's cases were quickly disposed of, and fines and imprisonment promptly distributed among them. In one or two of the cases the charges against Chinamen were brought by Chinamen themselves, and in those cases Chinamen testified against Chinamen, through the interpreter; but the fixed rule of the court being that the *preponderance* of testimony in such cases should determine the prisoner's guilt or innocence, and there being nothing very binding about an oath administered to the lower orders of our people without the ancient solemnity of cutting off a chicken's head and burning some yellow paper at the same time, the interested parties naturally drum up a cloud of witnesses who are cheerfully willing to give evidence without ever knowing anything about the matter in hand. The judge has a custom of rattling through with as much of this testimony as his patience will stand, and then shutting off the rest and striking an average.

By noon all the business of the court was finished, and then several of us who had not fared well were remanded to prison; the judge went home; the lawyers, and officers, and spectators departed their several ways, and left the uncomely court-room to silence, solitude, and Stiggers, the newspaper reporter, which latter would now write up his items (said an ancient Chinaman to me), in the which he would praise all the policemen indiscriminately and abuse the Chinamen and dead people.

AH SONG HI.

October & November 1870 and January 1871

Map of Paris

I published my "Map of the Fortifications of Paris" in my own paper a fortnight ago, but am obliged to reproduce it in THE GALAXY, to satisfy the extraordinary demand for it which has arisen in military circles throughout the country. General Grant's outspoken commendation originated this demand, and General Sherman's fervent endorsement added fuel to it. The result is that tons of these maps have been fed to the suffering soldiers of our land, but without avail. They hunger still. We will cast THE GALAXY into the breach and stand by and await the effect.

The next Atlantic mail will doubtless bring news of a European frenzy for the map. It is reasonable to expect that the siege of Paris will be suspended till a German translation of it can be forwarded (it is now in preparation), and that the defence of Paris will likewise be suspended to await the reception of the French translation (now progressing under my own hands, and likely to be unique). King William's high praise of the map and Napoleon's frank enthusiam concerning its execution will ensure its prompt adoption in Europe as the only authoritative and legitimate exposition of the present military situation. It is plain that if the Prussians cannot get into Paris with the facilities afforded by this production of mine they ought to deliver the enterprise into abler hands.

Strangers to me keep insisting that this map does *not* "explain itself." One person came to me with bloodshot eyes and a harassed look about him, and shook the map in my face and said he believed I was some new kind of idiot. I have been abused a good deal by other quick-tempered people like him, who came with similar complaints. Now, therefore, I yield willingly, and for the information of the ignorant will briefly explain the present military situation as illustrated by the map. Part of the Prussian forces, under Prince Frederick William, are now boarding at the "farm-house" in the margin of the map. There is nothing between them and Vincennes but a rail fence in bad repair. Any corporal can see at a glance that they have only to burn it, pull it down, crawl under, climb over, or walk around it, just as the commander-in-chief shall elect.

Another portion of the Prussian forces are at Podunk, under Von Moltke. They have nothing to do but float down the river Seine on a raft and scale the walls of Paris. Let the worshippers of that overrated soldier believe in him still, and abide the result—for me, *I* do not believe he will ever think of a raft. At Omaha and the High Bridge are vast masses of Prussian infantry, and it is only fair to say that they are likely to *stay* there, as that figure of a window-sash between them stands for a brewery. Away up out of sight over the top of the map is the fleet of the Prussian navy, ready at any moment to come cavorting down the Erie Canal (unless some new iniquity of an unprincipled Legislature shall put up the tolls and so render it cheaper to walk). To me it looks as if Paris is in a singularly close place. She never was situated before as she is in this map.

MARK TWAIN.

————

TO THE READER.

The accompanying map explains itself.

The idea of this map is not original with me, but is borrowed from the "Tribune" and the other great metropolitan journals.

I claim no other merit for this production (if I may so call it) than that it is accurate. The main blemish of the city-paper maps of which it is an imitation, is, that in them more attention seems paid to artistic picturesqueness than geographical reliability.

Inasmuch as this is the first time I ever tried to draft and engrave a map, or attempt anything in the line of art at all, the commendations the work has received and the admiration it has excited among the people, have been very grateful to my feelings. And it is touching to reflect that by far the most enthusiastic of these praises have come from people who know nothing at all about art.

By an unimportant oversight I have engraved the map so that it reads wrong end first, except to left-handed people. I forgot that in order to make it right in print it should be drawn and engraved upside down. However, let the student who desires to contemplate the map stand on his head or hold it before her looking-glass. That will bring it right.

The reader will comprehend at a glance that that piece of river with the "High Bridge" over it got left out to one side by reason of a slip of the graving-tool, which rendered it necessary to change the entire course of the river Rhine or else spoil the map. After having spent two days in digging and gouging at the map, I would have changed the course of the Atlantic ocean before I would have lost so much work.

I never had so much trouble with anything in my life as I did with this map. I had heaps of little fortifications scattered all around Paris, at first, but every now and then my instruments would slip and fetch away whole miles of batteries and leave the vicinity as clean as if the Prussians had been there.

The reader will find it well to frame this map for future reference, so that it may aid in extending popular intelligence and dispelling the wide-spread ignorance of the day.

MARK TWAIN.

OFFICIAL COMMENDATIONS.

It is the only map of the kind I ever saw.

U. S. GRANT.

It places the situation in an entirely new light.

BISMARCK.

I cannot look upon it without shedding tears.

BRIGHAM YOUNG.

It is very nice, large print.

NAPOLEON.

My wife was for years afflicted with freckles, and though everything was done for her relief that could be done, all was in vain. But, sir, since her first glance at your map, they have entirely left her. She has nothing but convulsions now.

J. SMITH.

If I had had this map I could have got out of Metz without any trouble.

BAZAINE.

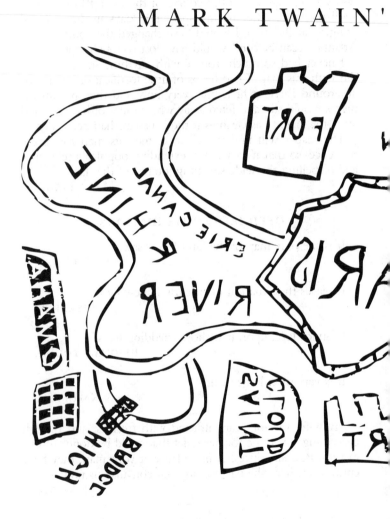

MAP OF PARIS.

I have seen a great many maps in my time, but none that this one reminds me of.

TROCHU.

———

It is but fair to say that in some respects it is a truly remarkable map.

W. T. SHERMAN.

———

I said to my son Frederick William, "If you could only make a map like that, I would be perfectly willing to see you die—even anxious."

WILLIAM III.

November 1870

Riley—Newspaper Correspondent

One of the best men in Washington—or elsewhere—is RILEY, correspondent of one of the great San Francisco dailies.

Riley is full of humor, and has an unfailing vein of irony which makes his conversation to the last degree entertaining (as long as the remarks are about somebody else). But notwithstanding the possession of these qualities, which should enable a man to write a happy and an appetizing letter, Riley's newspaper letters often display a more than earthly solemnity, and likewise an unimaginative devotion to petrified facts, which surprise and distress all men who know him in his unofficial character. He explains this curious thing by saying that his employers sent him to Washington to write facts, not fancy, and that several times he has come near losing his situation by inserting humorous remarks which, not being looked for at headquarters and consequently not understood, were thought to be dark and bloody speeches intended to convey signals and warnings to murderous secret societies or something of that kind, and so were scratched out with a shiver and a prayer and cast into the stove. Riley says that sometimes he is so afflicted with a yearning to write a sparkling and absorbingly readable letter that he simply cannot resist it, and so he goes to his den and revels in the delight of untrammelled scribbling; and then, with suffering such as only a mother can know, he destroys the pretty children of his fancy and reduces his letter to the required dismal accuracy. Having seen Riley do this very thing more than once, I know whereof I speak. Often I have laughed with him over a happy passage and grieved to see him plough his pen through it. He would say, "I had to write that or die; and I've got to scratch it out or starve. *They* wouldn't stand it, you know."

I think Riley is about the most entertaining company I ever saw. We lodged together in many places in Washington during the winter of '67–'8, moving comfortably from place to place, and attracting attention by paying our board—a course which cannot fail to make a person conspicuous in Washington. Riley would tell all about his trip to California in the early days, by way of the Isthmus and the San Juan river; and about his baking bread in San Francisco, to gain a living, and setting up ten-pins, and practising law, and opening oysters, and delivering lectures, and teaching French, and tending bar, and reporting for the newspapers, and keeping dancing-school, and interpreting Chinese in the courts—which latter was lucrative and Riley was doing handsomely and laying up a little money when people began to find fault because his translations were too "free," a thing for which Riley considered he ought not to be held responsible, since he did not know a word of the Chinese tongue and only adopted interpreting as a means of gaining an honest livelihood. Through the machinations of enemies he was removed from the position of official interpreter, and a man put in his place who was familiar with the Chinese language but did not know any English. And Riley used to tell about publishing a newspaper up in what is Alaska now, but was only an iceberg then, with a population composed of bears, walruses, Indians, and other animals; and how the iceberg got adrift at last, and left all his paying subscribers behind, and as soon as the commonwealth floated out of the jurisdiction of Russia the people rose and threw off their allegiance and ran up the English flag, calculating to hook on and become an English colony as they drifted along down the British Possessions; but a land breeze and a crooked current carried them by, and they ran up the Stars and Stripes and steered for California, missed the connection again and swore allegiance to Mexico, but it wasn't any use; the anchors came home every time, and away they went with the northeast trades drifting off sideways toward the Sandwich Islands, whereupon they ran up the Cannibal flag and had a grand human barbecue in honor of it, in which it was noticed that the better a man liked a friend the better he enjoyed him; and as soon as they got fairly within the tropics the weather got so fearfully hot that the iceberg began to melt, and it got so sloppy under foot that it was almost impossible for ladies to get about at all; and at last, just as they came in sight of the islands, the melancholy remnant of the once majestic iceberg canted first to one side and then to the other, and then plunged under forever, carrying the national archives along with it—and not only the archives and the populace, but some eligible town lots which had increased in value as fast as they diminished in size in the tropics, and which Riley could have sold at thirty cents a pound and made himself rich if he could have kept the province afloat ten hours longer and got her into port.

And so forth and so on, with all the facts of Riley's trip through Mexico, a journey whose history his felicitous fancy can make more interesting than any novel that ever was written. What a shame it is to tie Riley down to the dreary mason-work of laying up solemn dead-walls of fact! He does write a plain, straightforward, and perfectly accurate and reliable correspondence, but it seems to me that I would rather have one chatty paragraph of his fancy than a whole obituary of his facts.

Riley is very methodical, untiringly accommodating, never forgets anything that is to be attended to, is a good son, a staunch friend, and a permanent, reliable enemy. He will put himself to any amount of trouble to oblige a body, and therefore always has his hands full of things to be done for the helpless and the shiftless. And he knows how to do nearly everything, too. He is a man whose native benevolence is a well-spring that never goes dry. He stands always ready to help whoever needs help, as far as he is able—and not simply with his money, for that is a cheap and common charity, but with hand and brain, and fatigue of limb and sacrifice of time. This sort of man is rare.

Riley has a ready wit, a quickness and aptness at selecting and applying quotations, and a countenance that is as solemn and as blank as the back side of a tombstone when he is delivering a particularly exasperating joke. One night a negro woman was burned to death in a house next door to us, and Riley said that our landlady would be oppressively emotional at breakfast, because she generally made use of such opportunities as offered, being of a morbidly sentimental turn, and so we would find it best to let her talk along and say nothing back—it was the only way to keep her tears out of the gravy. Riley said there never was a funeral in the neighborhood but that the gravy was watery for a week.

And sure enough, at breakfast the landlady was down in the very sloughs of woe—entirely broken-hearted. Everything she looked at reminded her of that poor old negro woman, and so the buckwheat cakes made her sob, the coffee forced a groan, and when the beefsteak came on she fetched a wail that made our hair rise. Then she got to talking about deceased, and kept up a steady drizzle till both of us were soaked through and through. Presently she took a fresh breath and said, with a world of sobs:

"Ah, to think of it, only to think of it!—the poor old faithful creature. For she was *so* faithful. Would you believe it, she had been a servant in that self-same house and that self-same family for twenty-seven years come Christmas, and never a cross word and never a lick! And oh to think she should meet such a death at last!—a-sitting over the red-hot stove at three o'clock in the morning and went to sleep and fell on it and was actually *roasted!* not just frizzled up a bit, but literally roasted to a crisp! Poor faithful creature, how she *was* cooked! I am but a poor woman, but even if I have to scrimp to do it, I will put up a tombstone over that lone sufferer's grave—and Mr. Riley, if you would have the goodness to think up a little epitaph to put on it which would sort of describe the awful way in which she met her——"

"Put it '*Well done*, good and faithful servant!'" said Riley, and never smiled.

[I have either printed that anecdote once before or told it in company so many thousand times as to carry that seeming to my mind, but it is of no consequence—it is worth printing half a dozen times.]

November 1870

A Reminiscence of the Back Settlements

"Now that corpse [said the undertaker, patting the folded hands of deceased approvingly] was a brick—every way you took him he was a brick. He was so real accommodating, and so modest-like and simple in his last moments. Friends wanted metallic burial case—nothing else would do. *I* couldn't get it. There warn't going to be time—anybody could see that. Corpse said never mind, shake him up some kind of a box he could stretch out in comfortable, *he* warn't particular 'bout the general style of it. Said he went more on room than style, any way, in a last final container. Friends wanted a silver door-plate on the coffin, signifying who he was and wher' he was from. Now *you* know a fellow couldn't roust out such a gaily thing as that in a little country town like this. What did corpse say? Corpse said, whitewash his old canoe and dob his address and general destination onto it with a blacking brush and a stencil plate, long with a verse from some likely hymn or other, and p'int him for the tomb, and mark him C. O. D., and just let him skip along. *He* warn't distressed any more than you be—on the contrary just as carm and collected as a hearse-horse; said he judged that wher' he was going to, a body would find it considerable better to attract attention by a picturesque moral character than a natty burial case with a swell door-plate on it. Splendid man, he was. I'd druther do for a corpse like that 'n any I've tackled in seven year. There's some satisfaction in buryin' a man like that. You feel that what you're doing is appreciated. Lord bless you, so's he got planted before he sp'iled, he was perfectly satisfied; said his relations meant well, *per*fectly well, but all them preparations was bound to delay the thing more or less, and he didn't wish to be kept layin' around. You never see such a clear head as what he had—and so carm and so cool. Just a hunk of brains—that is what *he* was. Perfectly awful. It was a ripping distance from one end of that man's head to t'other. Often and over again he's had brain fever a-raging in one place, and the rest of the pile didn't know anything about it—didn't affect it any more than an Injun insurrection in Arizona affects the Atlantic States. Well, the relations they wanted a big funeral, but corpse said he was down on flummery—didn't want any procession—fill the hearse full of mourners, and get out a stern line and tow *him* behind. He *was* the most down on style of any remains I ever struck. A beautiful, simple-minded creature—it was what he was, you can depend on that. He was just set on having things the way he wanted them, and he took a solid comfort in laying his little plans. He had me measure him and take a whole raft of directions; then he had the minister stand up behind a long box with a table-cloth over it and read his funeral sermon, saying 'Angcore, angcore!' at the good places, and making him scratch out every bit of brag about him, and all the hifalutin; and then he made them trot out the choir so's he could help them pick out the tunes for the occasion, and he got them to sing 'Pop Goes the Weasel,' because he'd always liked that tune when he was down-hearted, and solemn music made him sad; and when they sung that with tears in their eyes (because they all loved him), and his relations grieving around, he just laid there as happy as a bug, and trying to beat time and showing all over how much he enjoyed it; and presently he got worked up and excited, and tried to join in, for mind you he was pretty proud of his abilities in the singing line; but the first time he opened his mouth and was just going to spread himself, his breath took a walk. I never see a man snuffed out so sudden. Ah, it was a great loss—it was a powerful loss to this poor little one-horse town. Well, well, well, I hain't got time to be palavering along here—got to nail on the lid and mosey along with him; and if you'll just give me a lift we'll skeet him into the hearse and meander along. Relations bound to have it so—don't pay no attention to dying injunctions, minute a corpse's gone; but if I had *my* way, if I didn't respect his last wishes and tow him behind the hearse, I'll be cuss'd. I consider that whatever a corpse wants done for his comfort is a little enough matter, and a man hain't got no right to deceive him or take advantage of him—and whatever a corpse trusts me to do I'm a-going to *do*, you know, even if it's to stuff him and paint him yaller and keep him for a keepsake—you hear *me*!"

He cracked his whip and went lumbering away with his ancient ruin of a hearse, and I continued my walk with a valuable lesson learned—that a healthy and wholesome cheerfulness is not necessarily impossible to *any* occupation. The lesson is likely to be lasting, for it will take many months to obliterate the memory of the remarks and circumstances that impressed it.

November 1870

A General Reply

When I was sixteen or seventeen years old, a splendid idea burst upon me—a bran-new one, which had never occurred to anybody before: I would write some "pieces" and take them down to the editor of the "Republican," and ask him to give me his plain, unvarnished opinion of their value! Now, as old and threadbare as the idea was, it was fresh and beautiful to me, and it went flaming and crashing through my system like the genuine lightning and thunder of originality. I wrote the pieces. I wrote them with that placid confidence and that happy facility which only want of practice and absence of literary experience can give. There was not one sentence in them that cost half an hour's weighing and shaping and trimming and fixing. Indeed, it is possible that there was no one sentence whose mere wording cost even one-sixth of that time. If I remember rightly, there was not one single erasure or interlineation in all that chaste manuscript. [I have since lost that large belief in my powers, and likewise that marvellous perfection of execution.] I started down to the "Republican" office with my pocket full of manuscripts, my brain full of dreams, and a grand future opening out before me. I knew perfectly well that the editor would be ravished with my pieces. But presently——

However, the particulars are of no consequence. I was only about to say that a shadowy sort of doubt just then intruded upon my exaltation. Another came, and another. Pretty soon a whole procession of them. And at last, when I stood before the "Republican" office and looked up at its tall, unsympathetic front, it seemed hardly *me* that could have "chinned" its towers ten minutes before, and was now so shrunk up and pitiful that if I dared to step on the gratings I should probably go through.

At about that crisis the editor, the very man I had come to consult, came down stairs, and halted a moment to pull at his wristbands and settle his coat to its place, and he happened to notice that I was eyeing him wistfully. He asked me what I wanted. I answered, "Nothing!" with a boy's own meekness and shame; and, dropping my eyes, crept humbly round till I was fairly in the alley, and then drew a big grateful breath of relief, and picked up my heels and ran!

I was satisfied. I wanted no more. It was my first attempt to get a "plain unvarnished opinion" out of a literary man concerning my compositions, and it has lasted me until now. And in these latter days, whenever I receive a bundle of MS. through the mail, with a request that I will pass judgment upon its merits, I feel like saying to the author, "If you had only taken your piece to some grim and stately newspaper office, where you did not know anybody, you would not have so fine an opinion of your production as it is easy to see you have now."

Every man who becomes editor of a newspaper or magazine straightway begins to receive MSS. from literary aspirants, together with requests that he will deliver judgment upon the same. And after complying in eight or ten instances, he finally takes refuge in a general sermon upon the subject, which he inserts in his publication, and always afterward refers such correspondents to that sermon for answer. I have at last reached this station in my literary career. I now cease to reply privately to my applicants for advice, and proceed to construct my public sermon.

As all letters of the sort I am speaking of contain the very same matter, differently worded, I offer as a fair average specimen the last one I have received:

> .   .   .   .   Oct. 3.
>
> Mark Twain, Esq.
>
> Dear Sir: I am a youth, just out of school and ready to start in life. I have looked around, but don't see anything that suits exactly. Is a literary life easy and profitable, or is it the hard times it is generally put up for? It *must* be easier than a good many if not most of the occupations, and I feel drawn to launch out on it, make or break, sink or swim, survive or perish. Now, what are the conditions of success in literature? You need not be afraid to paint the thing just as it is. I can't do any worse than fail. Everything else offers the same. When I thought of the law—yes, and five or six other professions—I found the same thing was the case every time, viz: *all full—overrun—every profession so crammed that success is rendered impossible—too many hands and not enough work.* But I must try *something,* and so I turn at last to literature. Something tells me that that

is the true bent of my genius, if I have any. I enclose some of my pieces. Will you read them over and give me your candid, unbiassed opinion of them? And now I hate to trouble you, but you have been a young man yourself, and what I want is for you to get me a newspaper job of writing to do. You know many newspaper people, and I am entirely unknown. And will you make the best terms you can for me? though I do not expect what might be called high wages at first, of course. Will you candidly say what such articles as these I enclose are worth? I have plenty of them. If you should sell these and let me know, I can send you more, as good and may be better than these. An early reply, etc.

Yours truly, etc.

I will answer you in good faith. Whether my remarks shall have great value or not, or my suggestions be worth following, are problems which I take great pleasure in leaving entirely to you for solution. To begin: There are several questions in your letter which only a man's life experience can eventually answer for him—not another man's words. I will simply skip those.

1. Literature, like the ministry, medicine, the law, and *all other* occupations, is cramped and hindered for want of men to do the work, not want of work to do. When people tell you the reverse, they speak that which is not true. If you desire to test this, you need only hunt up a first-class editor, reporter, business manager, foreman of a shop, mechanic, or artist in any branch of industry, and *try to hire him*. You will find that he is already hired. He is sober, industrious, capable, and reliable, and is always in demand. He cannot get a day's holiday except by courtesy of his employer, or his city, or the great general public. But if you need idlers, shirkers, half-instructed, unambitious, and comfort-seeking editors, reporters, lawyers, doctors, and mechanics, apply anywhere. There are millions of them to be had at the dropping of a handkerchief.

2. No; I must not and will not venture any opinion whatever as to the literary merit of your productions. The public is the only critic whose judgment is worth anything at all. Do not take my poor word for this, but reflect a moment and take your own. For instance, if Sylvanus Cobb or T. S. Arthur

had submitted their maiden MSS. to you, you would have said, with tears in your eyes, "Now please don't write any more!" But you see yourself how popular they are. And if it had been left to you, you would have said the "Marble Faun" was tiresome, and that even "Paradise Lost" lacked cheerfulness; but you know they sell. Many wiser and better men than you pooh-poohed Shakespeare, even as late as two centuries ago; but still that old party has outlived those people. No, I will not sit in judgment upon your literature. If I honestly and conscientiously praised it, I might thus help to inflict a lingering and pitiless bore upon the public; if I honestly and conscientiously condemned it, I might thus rob the world of an undeveloped and unsuspected Dickens or Shakespeare.

3. I shrink from hunting up literary labor for you to do and receive pay for. Whenever your literary productions have proved for themselves that they have a real value, you will never have to go around hunting for remunerative literary work to do. You will require more hands than you have now, and more brains than you probably ever will have, to do even half the work that will be offered you. Now, in order to arrive at the proof of value hereinbefore spoken of, one needs only to adopt a very simple and certainly very sure process; and that is, to *write without pay until somebody offers pay.* If nobody offers pay within three years, the candidate may look upon this circumstance with the most implicit confidence as the sign that sawing wood is what he was intended for. If he has any wisdom at all, then, he will retire with dignity and assume his heaven-appointed vocation.

In the above remarks I have only offered a course of action which Mr. Dickens and most other successful literary men had to follow; but it is a course which will find no sympathy with my client, perhaps. The young literary aspirant is a very, very curious creature. He knows that if he wished to become a tinner, the master smith would require him to prove the possession of a good character, and would require him to promise to stay in the shop three years—possibly four—and would make him sweep out and bring water and build fires all the first year, and let him learn to black stoves in the intervals;

and for these good honest services would pay him two suits
of cheap clothes and his board; and next year he would begin
to receive instructions in the trade, and a dollar a week would
be added to his emoluments; and two dollars would be added
the third year, and three the fourth; and *then*, if he had become a first-rate tinner, he would get about fifteen or twenty,
or may be thirty dollars a week, with never a possibility of
getting seventy-five while he lived. If he wanted to become a
mechanic of any other kind, he would have to undergo this
same tedious, ill-paid apprenticeship. If he wanted to become
a lawyer or a doctor, he would have fifty times worse; for he
would get nothing at all during his long apprenticeship, and
in addition would have to pay a large sum for tuition, and
have the privilege of boarding and clothing himself. The
literary aspirant knows all this, and yet he has the hardihood
to present himself for reception into the literary guild and ask
to share its high honors and emoluments, without a single
twelvemonth's apprenticeship to show in excuse for his presumption! He would smile pleasantly if he were asked to
make even so simple a thing as a ten-cent tin dipper without
previous instruction in the art; but, all green and ignorant,
wordy, pompously-assertive, ungrammatical, and with a
vague, distorted knowledge of men and the world acquired
in a back country village, he will serenely take up so dangerous a weapon as a pen, and attack the most formidable subject
that finance, commerce, war, or politics can furnish him
withal. It would be laughable if it were not so sad and so
pitiable. The poor fellow would not intrude upon the tin-
shop without an apprenticeship, but is willing to seize and
wield with unpractised hand an instrument which is able to
overthrow dynasties, change religions, and decree the weal or
woe of nations.

If my correspondent will write free of charge for the newspapers of his neighborhood, it will be one of the strangest
things that ever happened if he does not get all the employment he can attend to on those terms. And as soon as ever his
writings are worth money, plenty of people will hasten to
offer it.

And by way of serious and well-meant encouragement, I
wish to urge upon him once more the truth that acceptable

writers for the press are so scarce that book and periodical publishers are seeking them constantly, and with a vigilance that never grows heedless for a moment.

November 1870

Running for Governor

A few months ago I was nominated for Governor of the great State of New York, to run against Stewart L. Woodford and John T. Hoffman, on an independent ticket. I somehow felt that I had one prominent advantage over these gentlemen, and that was, good character. It was easy to see by the newspapers, that if ever they had known what it was to bear a good name, that time had gone by. It was plain that in these latter years they had become familiar with all manner of shameful crimes. But at the very moment that I was exalting my advantage and joying in it in secret, there was a muddy undercurrent of discomfort "riling" the deeps of my happiness — and that was, the having to hear my name bandied about in familiar connection with those of such people. I grew more and more disturbed. Finally I wrote my grandmother about it. Her answer came quick and sharp. She said:

You have never done one single thing in all your life to be ashamed of — not one. Look at the newspapers — look at them and comprehend what sort of characters Woodford and Hoffman are, and then see if you are willing to lower yourself to their level and enter a public canvass with them.

It was my very thought! I did not sleep a single moment that night. But after all, I could not recede. I was fully committed and must go on with the fight. As I was looking listlessly over the papers at breakfast, I came across this paragraph, and I may truly say I never was so confounded before:

PERJURY. — Perhaps, now that Mr. Mark Twain is before the people as a candidate for Governor, he will condescend to explain how he came to be convicted of perjury by thirty-four witnesses, in Wakawak, Cochin China, in 1863, the intent of which perjury was to rob a poor native widow and her helpless family of a meagre plantain patch, their only stay and support in their bereavement and their desolation. Mr. Twain owes it to himself, as well as to the great people whose suffrages he asks, to clear this matter up. Will he do it?

I thought I should burst with amazement! Such a cruel, heartless charge—I never had *seen* Cochin China! I never had *heard* of Wakawak! I didn't know a plantain patch from a kangaroo! I did not know what to do. I was crazed and helpless. I let the day slip away without doing anything at all. The next morning the same paper had this—nothing more:

SIGNIFICANT.—Mr. Twain, it will be observed, is suggestively silent about the Cochin China perjury.

[*Mem.*—During the rest of the campaign this paper never referred to me in any other way than as "the infamous perjurer Twain."]

Next came the "Gazette," with this:

WANTED TO KNOW.—Will the new candidate for Governor deign to explain to certain of his fellow-citizens (who are suffering to vote for him!) the little circumstance of his cabin-mates in Montana losing small valuables from time to time, until at last, these things having been invariably found on Mr. Twain's person or in his "trunk" (newspaper he rolled his traps in), they felt compelled to give him a friendly admonition for his own good, and so tarred and feathered him and rode him on a rail, and then advised him to leave a permanent vacuum in the place he usually occupied in the camp. Will he do this?

Could anything be more deliberately malicious than that? For I never was in Montana in my life.

[After this, this journal customarily spoke of me as "Twain, the Montana Thief."]

I got to picking up papers apprehensively—much as one would lift a desired blanket which he had some idea might have a rattlesnake under it. One day this met my eye:

THE LIE NAILED!—By the sworn affidavits of Michael O'Flanagan, Esq., of the Five Points, and Mr. Kit Burns and Mr. John Allen, of Water street, it is established that Mr. Mark Twain's vile statement that the lamented grandfather of our noble standard-bearer, John T. Hoffman, was hanged for highway robbery, is a brutal and gratuitous LIE, without a single shadow of foundation in fact. It is disheartening to virtuous men to see such shameful means resorted to to achieve political success as the attacking of the dead in their graves and defiling their honored names with slander. When we think of the anguish this miserable falsehood must cause the innocent relatives and friends of the deceased, we are almost driven to incite an outraged and insulted public to summary and unlawful vengeance upon the traducer. But no—let us leave him to the agony of a lacerating conscience—(though if passion should get the better of the public and in its blind fury they should do the traducer bodily injury, it is but too obvious that no jury could convict and no court punish the perpetrators of the deed).

The ingenious closing sentence had the effect of moving me out of bed with despatch that night, and out at the back door, also, while the "outraged and insulted public" surged in the front way, breaking furniture and windows in their righteous indignation as they came, and taking off such property as they could carry when they went. And yet I can lay my hand upon the Book and say that I never slandered Governor Hoffman's grandfather. More—I had never even heard of him or mentioned him, up to that day and date.

[I will state, in passing, that the journal above quoted from always referred to me afterward as "Twain, the Body-Snatcher."]

The next newspaper article that attracted my attention was the following:

A SWEET CANDIDATE.—Mark Twain, who was to make such a blighting speech at the mass meeting of the Independents last night, didn't come to time! A telegram from his physician stated that he had been knocked down by a runaway team and his leg broken in two places—sufferer lying in great agony, and so forth, and so forth, and a lot more bosh of the same sort. And the Independents tried hard to swallow the wretched subterfuge and pretend that they did not know what was the *real* reason of the absence of the abandoned creature whom they denominate their standard-bearer. *A certain man was seen to reel into Mr. Twain's hotel last night in a state of beastly intoxication.* It is the imperative duty of the Independents to prove that this besotted brute was not Mark Twain himself. We have them at last! This is a case that admits of no shirking. The voice of the people demands in thunder-tones: "WHO WAS THAT MAN?"

It was incredible, absolutely incredible, for a moment, that it was really my name that was coupled with this disgraceful suspicion. Three long years had passed over my head since I had tasted ale, beer, wine, or liquor of any kind.

[It shows what effect the times were having on me when I say that I saw myself confidently dubbed "Mr. Delirium Tremens Twain" in the next issue of that journal without a pang—notwithstanding I knew that with monotonous fidelity the paper would go on calling me so to the very end.]

By this time anonymous letters were getting to be an important part of my mail matter. This form was common:

How about that old woman you kiked of your premisers which was beging. POL PRY.

And this:

There is things which you have done which is unbeknowens to anybody but me. You better trot out a few dols. to yours truly or you'll hear thro' the papers from HANDY ANDY.

That is about the idea. I could continue them till the reader was surfeited, if desirable.

Shortly the principal Republican journal "convicted" me of wholesale bribery, and the leading Democratic paper "nailed" an aggravated case of blackmailing to me.

[In this way I acquired two additional names: "Twain, the Filthy Corruptionist," and "Twain, the Loathsome Embracer."]

By this time there had grown to be such a clamor for an "answer" to all the dreadful charges that were laid to me, that the editors and leaders of my party said it would be political ruin for me to remain silent any longer. As if to make their appeal the more imperative, the following appeared in one of the papers the very next day:

BEHOLD THE MAN!—The Independent candidate still maintains silence. Because he dare not speak. Every accusation against him has been amply proved, and they have been endorsed and re-endorsed by his own eloquent silence till at this day he stands forever convicted. Look upon your candidate, Independents! Look upon the Infamous Perjurer! the Montana Thief! the Body-Snatcher! Contemplate your incarnate Delirium Tremens! your Filthy Corruptionist! your Loathsome Embracer! Gaze upon him—ponder him well—and then say if you can give your honest votes to a creature who has earned this dismal array of titles by his hideous crimes, and dares not open his mouth in denial of any one of them!

There was no possible way of getting out of it, and so, in deep humiliation, I set about preparing to "answer" a mass of baseless charges and mean and wicked falsehoods. But I never finished the task, for the very next morning a paper came out with a new horror, a fresh malignity, and seriously charged me with burning a lunatic asylum with all its inmates because it obstructed the view from my house. This threw me into a sort of panic. Then came the charge of poisoning my uncle to get his property, with an imperative demand that the grave should be opened. This drove me to the verge of distraction. On top of this I was accused of employing toothless and incompetent old relatives to prepare the food for the foundling hospital when I was warden. I was wavering—wavering. And at last, as a due and fitting climax to the shameless persecution that party rancor had inflicted upon me, nine little toddling children of all shades of color and degrees of raggedness were taught to rush on to the platform at a public meeting and clasp me around the legs and call me PA!

I gave up. I hauled down my colors and surrendered. I was not equal to the requirements of a Gubernatorial campaign in the State of New York, and so I sent in my withdrawal from the candidacy, and in bitterness of spirit signed it,

"Truly yours,
"*Once* a decent man, but now
"MARK TWAIN, I. P., M. T., B. S., D. T., F. C., and L. E."

December 1870

Dogberry in Washington

Some of the decisions of the Post Office Department are eminently luminous. It has in times gone by been enacted that "author's manuscript" should go through the mails for a trifling postage—newspaper postage, in fact. A calm and dispassionate mind would gather from this, that the object had in view was to facilitate and foster newspaper correspondence, magazine writing, and literature generally, by discontinuing a tax in the way of postage which had become very burdensome to gentlemen of the quill. Now by what effort of good old well-meaning, grandmotherly dulness does the reader suppose the postal authorities have rendered that wise and kindly decree utterly null and void, and solemnly funny? By deciding that "author's manuscript" does not mean anything but "*manuscript intended to be made into a* BOUND BOOK"—all pamphlets, magazines, and newspapers ruled out!

Thus we are expected to believe that the original regulation was laboriously got up to save *two dollars' worth of postage to two authors in a year*—for probably not more than that number of MS. books are sent by mail to publishers each year. Such property is too precious to trust to any conveyance but the author's own carpet-sack, as a general thing.

But granting that one thousand MS. books went to the publishers in a year, and thus saved to one thousand authors a dollar apiece in postage in the twelve months, would not a law whose whole aim was to accomplish such a trifle as that be simply an irreverent pleasantry, and not proper company to thrust among grave and weighty statutes in the law-books?

The matter which suggested these remarks can be stated in a sentence. Once or twice I have sent magazine MSS. from certain cities, on newspaper rates, as "author's MS." But in Buffalo the postmaster requires full letter postage. He claims no authority for this save *decisions* of the Post Office Department. He showed me the law itself, but even the highest order of intellectual obscurity, backed by the largest cultivation (outside of a Post Office Department), could not find in it authority for the "decisions" aforementioned. And I ought to know, because I tried it myself. [I say that, not to be trivially facetious when talking in earnest, but merely to take the word out of the mouths of certain cheap witlings, who always stand ready in any company to interrupt any one whose remarks offer a chance for the exhibition of their poor wit and worse manners.]

I will not say one word about this curious decision, or utter one sarcasm or one discourteous speech about it, or the well-intending but misguided officer who rendered it; but if he were in California, he would fare far differently—very far differently—for there the wicked are not restrained by the gentle charities that prevail in Buffalo, and so they would deride him, and point the finger of scorn at him, and address him as "Old Smarty from Mud Springs." Indeed they would.

December 1870

My Watch—An Instructive Little Tale

My beautiful new watch had run eighteen months without losing or gaining, and without breaking any part of its machinery or stopping. I had come to believe it infallible in its judgments about the time of day, and to consider its constitution and its anatomy imperishable. But at last, one night, I let it run down. I grieved about it as if it were a recognized messenger and forerunner of calamity. But by and by I cheered up, set the watch by guess, and commanded my bodings and superstitions to depart. Next day I stepped into the chief jeweller's to set it by the exact time, and the head of the establishment took it out of my hand and proceeded to set it for me. Then he said, "She is four minutes slow—regulator wants pushing up." I tried to stop him—tried to make him understand that the watch kept perfect time. But no; all this human cabbage could see was that the watch was four minutes slow, and the regulator *must* be pushed up a little; and so, while I danced around him in anguish and beseeched him to let the watch alone, he calmly and cruelly did the shameful deed. My watch began to gain. It gained faster and faster day by day. Within the week it sickened to a raging fever, and its pulse went up to a hundred and fifty in the shade. At the end of two months it had left all the timepieces of the town far in the rear, and was a fraction over thirteen days ahead of the almanac. It was away into November enjoying the snow, while the October leaves were still turning. It hurried up house-rent, bills payable, and such things, in such a ruinous way that I could not abide it. I took it to the watchmaker to be regulated. He asked me if I had ever had it repaired. I said no, it had never needed any repairing. He looked a look of vicious happiness and eagerly pried the watch open, then put a small dice-box into his eye and peered into its machinery. He said it wanted cleaning and oiling, besides regulating— come in a week. After being cleaned and oiled and regulated, my watch slowed down to that degree that it ticked like a tolling bell. I began to be left by trains, I failed all appointments, I got to missing my dinner; my watch strung out three days' grace to four and let me go to protest; I gradually drifted back into yesterday, then day before, then into last week, and by and by the comprehension came upon me that all solitary and alone I was lingering along in week before last, and the world was out of sight. I seemed to detect in myself a sort of sneaking fellow-feeling for the mummy in the museum, and a desire to swap news with him. I went to a watchmaker again. He took the watch all to pieces while I waited, and then said the barrel was "swelled." He said he could reduce it in three days. After this, the watch *averaged* well, but nothing more. For half a day it would go like the very mischief, and keep up such a barking and wheezing and whooping and sneezing and snorting, that I could not hear myself think for the disturbance; and as long as it held out, there was not a watch in the land that stood any chance against it. But the rest of the day it would keep on slowing down and fooling along until all the clocks it had left behind caught up again. So at last, at the end of twenty-four hours, it would trot up to the judges' stand all right and just on time. It would show a fair and square average, and no man could say it had done more or less than its duty. But a correct average is only a mild virtue in a watch, and I took this instrument to another watchmaker. He said the kingbolt was broken. I said I was glad it was nothing more serious. To tell the plain truth, I had no idea what the kingbolt was, but I did not choose to appear ignorant to a stranger. He repaired the kingbolt, but what the watch gained in one way it lost in another. It would run awhile and then stop awhile, and then run awhile again, and so on, using its own discretion about the intervals. And every time it went off it kicked back like a musket. I padded my breast for a few days, but finally took the watch to another watchmaker. He picked it all to pieces and turned the ruin over and over under his glass; and then he said there appeared to be something the matter with the hair-trigger. He fixed it, and gave it a fresh start. It did well now, except that always at ten minutes to ten the hands would shut together like a pair of scissors, and from that time forth they would travel together. The oldest man in the world could not make head or tail of the time of day by such a watch, and so I went again to have the thing repaired. This person said that the crystal had got bent, and that the mainspring was not straight. He also remarked that part of the works needed half-soling. He made these things all right, and then my timepiece performed unexceptionably, save that now and then, after working along quietly for nearly eight hours, everything inside would let go all of a sudden and begin to buzz like a bee, and the hands would straightway begin to spin round and round so fast that their individuality was lost completely, and they simply seemed a delicate spider's web over the face of the watch. She would reel off the next twenty-four hours in six or seven minutes, and then stop with a bang. I went with a heavy heart to one more watchmaker, and looked on while he took her to pieces. Then I prepared to cross-question him rigidly, for this thing was getting serious. The watch had cost two hundred dollars originally, and I seemed to have paid out two or three thousand for repairs. While I waited and looked on, I presently recognized in this watchmaker an old acquaintance—a steamboat engineer of other days, and not a good engineer either. He examined all the parts carefully, just as the other watchmakers had done, and then delivered his verdict with the same confidence of manner.

He said:

"She makes too much steam—you want to hang the monkey-wrench on the safety-valve!"

I brained him on the spot, and had him buried at my own expense.

My uncle William (now deceased, alas!) used to say that a good horse was a good horse until it had run away once, and that a good watch was a good watch until the repairers got a chance at it. And he used to wonder what became of all the unsuccessful tinkers, and gunsmiths, and shoemakers, and blacksmiths; but nobody could ever tell him.

December 1870

The Facts in the Case of George Fisher, Deceased

This is history. It is not a wild extravaganza, like "John Williamson Mackenzie's Great Beef Contract," but is a plain statement of facts and circumstances with which the Congress of the United States has interested itself from time to time during the long period of half a century.

I will not call this matter of George Fisher's a great deathless and unrelenting swindle upon the Government and people of the United States—for it has never been so decided, and I hold that it is a grave and solemn wrong for a writer to cast slurs or call names when such is the case—but will simply present the evidence and let the reader deduce his own verdict. Then we shall do nobody injustice, and our consciences shall be clear.

On or about the 1st day of September, 1813, the Creek war being then in progress in Florida, the crops, herds, and houses of Mr. George Fisher, a citizen, were destroyed, either by the Indians or by the United States troops in pursuit of them. By the terms of the law, if the *Indians* destroyed the property, there was no relief for Fisher; but if the *troops* destroyed it, the Government of the United States was debtor to Fisher for the amount involved.

George Fisher must have considered that the *Indians* destroyed the property, because, although he lived several years afterward, he does not appear to have ever made any claim upon the Government.

In the course of time Fisher died, and his widow married again. And by and by, nearly twenty years after that dimly-remembered raid upon Fisher's cornfields, *the widow Fisher's new husband* petitioned Congress for pay for the property, and backed up the petition with many depositions and affidavits which purported to prove that the troops, and not the Indians, destroyed the property; that the troops, for some inscrutable reason, deliberately burned down "houses" (or cabins) valued at $600, the same belonging to a peaceable private citizen, and also destroyed various other property belonging to the same citizen. But Congress declined to believe that the troops were such idiots (after overtaking and scattering a band of Indians proved to have been found destroying Fisher's property) as to calmly continue the work of destruction themselves and make a complete job of what the Indians had only commenced. So Congress denied the petition of the heirs of George Fisher in 1832, and did not pay them a cent.

We hear no more from them officially until 1848, sixteen years after their first attempt on the Treasury, and a full generation after the death of the man whose fields were destroyed. The new generation of Fisher heirs then came forward and put in a bill for damages. The Second Auditor awarded them $8,873, being half the damage sustained by Fisher. The Auditor said the testimony showed that at least half the destruction was done by the Indians *"before the troops started in pursuit,"* and of course the Government was not responsible for that half.

2. That was in April, 1848. In December, 1848, the heirs of George Fisher, deceased, came forward and pleaded for a "revision" of their bill of damages. The revision was made, but nothing new could be found in their favor except an error of $100 in the former calculation. However, in order to keep up the spirits of the Fisher family, the Auditor concluded to go back and allow interest from the date of the first petition (1832) to the date when the bill of damages was awarded. This sent the Fishers home happy with sixteen years' interest on $8,873—the same amounting to $8,997 94. Total, $17,870 94.

3. For an entire year the suffering Fisher family remained quiet—even satisfied, after a fashion. Then they swooped down upon Government with their wrongs once more. That old patriot, Attorney-General Toucey, burrowed through the musty papers of the Fishers and discovered one more chance for the desolate orphans—interest on that original award of $8,873 from date of destruction of the property (1813) up to 1832! Result, $10,004 89 for the indigent Fishers. So now we have: First, $8,873 damages; second, interest on it from 1832 to 1848, $8,997 94; third, interest on it dated back to 1813, $10,004 89. Total, $27,875 83! What better investment for a great-grandchild than to get the Indians to burn a cornfield for him sixty or seventy years before his birth, and plausibly lay it on lunatic United States troops?

4. Strange as it may seem, the Fishers let Congress alone for five years—or, what is perhaps more likely, failed to make themselves heard by Congress for that length of time. But at last, in 1854, they got a hearing. They persuaded Congress to pass an act requiring the Auditor to re-examine their case. But this time they stumbled upon the misfortune of an honest Secretary of the Treasury (Mr. James Guthrie), and he spoiled everything. He said in very plain language that the Fishers were not only not entitled to another cent, but that those children of many sorrows and acquainted with grief *had been paid too much already.*

5. Therefore another interval of rest and silence ensued—an interval which lasted four years, viz., till 1858. The "right man in the right place" was then Secretary of War—John B. Floyd, of peculiar renown! Here was a master intellect; here was the very man to succor the suffering heirs of dead and forgotten Fisher. They came up from Florida with a rush—a great tidal wave of Fishers freighted with the same old musty documents about the same immortal cornfields of their ancestor. They straightway got an act passed transferring the Fisher matter from the dull Auditor to the ingenious Floyd. What did Floyd do? He said "IT WAS PROVED *that the Indians destroyed everything they could before the troops entered in pursuit.*" He considered, therefore, that what they destroyed must have consisted of *"the houses with all their contents, and the liquor"* (the most trifling part of the destruction, and set down at only $3,200 all told), and that the Government troops then drove them off and calmly proceeded to destroy—

Two hundred and twenty acres of corn in the field, thirty-five acres of wheat, and nine hundred and eighty-six head of live stock! [What a singularly intelligent army we had in those days, according to Mr. Floyd—though not according to the Congress of 1832.]

So Mr. Floyd decided that the Government was not responsible for that $3,200 worth of rubbish which the Indians destroyed, but was responsible for the property destroyed by the troops—which property consisted of (I quote from the printed U. S. Senate document)—

Corn at Bassett's creek	$3,000
Cattle	5,000
Stock hogs	1,050
Drove hogs.	1,204
Wheat.	350
Hides	4,000
Corn on the Alabama river.	3,500
Total	$18,104

That sum, in his report, Mr. Floyd calls the "*full value* of the property destroyed by the troops." He allows that sum to the starving Fishers, TOGETHER WITH INTEREST FROM 1813. From this new sum total the amounts already paid to the Fishers were deducted, and then the cheerful remainder (a fraction under *forty thousand dollars*) was handed to them, and again they retired to Florida in a condition of temporary tranquillity. Their ancestor's farm had now yielded them, altogether, nearly *sixty-seven thousand dollars* in cash.

6. Does the reader suppose that that was the end of it? Does he suppose those diffident Fishers were satisfied? Let the evidence show. The Fishers were quiet just two years. Then they came swarming up out of the fertile swamps of Florida with their same old documents, and besieged Congress once more. Congress capitulated on the first of June, 1860, and instructed Mr. Floyd to overhaul those papers again, and pay that bill. A Treasury clerk was ordered to go through those papers and report to Mr. Floyd what amount was still due the emaciated Fishers. This clerk (I can produce him whenever he is wanted) discovered what was apparently a glaring and recent forgery in the papers, whereby a witness's testimony as to the price of corn in Florida in 1813 was made to name double the amount which that witness had originally specified as the price! The clerk not only called his superior's attention to this thing, but in making up his brief of the case called particular attention to it in writing. That part of the brief *never got before Congress*, nor has Congress ever yet had a hint of a forgery existing among the Fisher papers. Nevertheless, on the basis of the doubled prices (and totally ignoring the clerk's assertion that the figures were manifestly and un-

questionably a recent forgery), Mr. Floyd remarks in his new report that "the testimony, *particularly in regard to the corn crops*, DEMANDS A MUCH HIGHER ALLOWANCE than any *heretofore* made by the Auditor or myself." So he estimates the crop at *sixty bushels* to the acre (double what Florida acres produce), and then virtuously allows pay for only half the crop, *but* allows *two dollars and a half* a bushel for that half, when there are rusty old books and documents in the Congressional library to show just what the Fisher testimony showed before the forgery, viz.: that in the fall of 1813 corn was only worth from $1 25 to $1 50 a bushel. Having accomplished this, what does Mr. Floyd do next? Mr. Floyd ("with an earnest desire to execute truly the legislative will," as he piously remarks) goes to work and makes out an entirely new bill of Fisher damages, and in this new bill he placidly *ignores the Indians* altogether—puts no particle of the destruction of the Fisher property upon them, but, even repenting him of charging them with burning the cabins and drinking the whiskey and breaking the crockery, lays the *entire* damage at the door of the imbecile United States troops, down to the very last item! And not only that, but uses the forgery to double the loss of corn at "Bassett's creek," and uses it again to absolutely *treble* the loss of corn on the "Alabama river." This new and ably conceived and executed bill of Mr. Floyd's figures up as follows (I copy again from the printed U. S. Senate document):

The United States in account with the legal representatives of George Fisher, deceased.

1813.— To 550 head of cattle, at $10		$5,500 00
To 86 head of drove hogs		1,204 00
To 350 head of stock hogs		1,750 00
To 100 ACRES OF CORN ON BASSETT'S CREEK		6,000 00
To 8 barrels of whiskey		350 00
To 2 barrels of brandy		280 00
To 1 barrel of rum		70 00
To dry goods and merchandise in store		1,100 00
To 35 acres of wheat		350 00
To 2,000 hides		4,000 00
To furs and hats in store		600 00

	To crockery ware in store	100 00
	To smiths' and carpenters' tools	250 00
	To houses burned and destroyed	600 00
	To 4 dozen bottles of wine.	48 00
1814.—	To 120 acres of corn on Alabama river	9,500 00
	To crops of peas, fodder, etc..	3,250 00
	Total	$34,952 00
	To interest on $22,202, from July, 1813, to November, 1860, 47 years and 4 months . .	63,053 68
	To interest on $12,750, from September, 1814, to November, 1860, 46 years and 2 months . .	35,317 50
	Total	$133,323 18

He puts everything in, this time. He does not even allow that the Indians destroyed the crockery or drank the four dozen bottles of (currant) wine. When it came to supernatural comprehensiveness in "gobbling," John B. Floyd was without his equal, in his own or any other generation. Subtracting from the above total the $67,000 already paid to George Fisher's implacable heirs, Mr. Floyd announced that the Government was still indebted to them in the sum of *sixty-six thousand five hundred and nineteen dollars and eighty-five cents*, "which," Mr. Floyd complacently remarks, "will be paid, accordingly, to the administrator of the estate of George Fisher, deceased, or to his attorney in fact."

But, sadly enough for the destitute orphans, a new President came in just at this time, Buchanan and Floyd went out, and they never got their money. The first thing Congress did in 1861 was to rescind the resolution of June 1, 1860, under which Mr. Floyd had been ciphering. Then Floyd (and doubtless the heirs of George Fisher likewise) had to give up financial business for a while and go into the Confederate army and serve their country.

Were the heirs of George Fisher killed? No. They are back now at this very time (July, 1870), beseeching Congress, through that blushing and diffident creature, Garrett Davis, to commence making payments again on their interminable and insatiable bill of damages for corn and whiskey destroyed by a gang of irresponsible Indians, so long ago that even

Government red-tape has failed to keep consistent and intelligent track of it. (And before this number of THE GALAXY reaches Washington, Mr. Davis will be getting ready to resurrect it once more, and alter his customary speech on finance, war, and other matters so that it will fit it.)

Now, the above are facts. They are history. Any one who doubts it can send to the Senate Document Department of the Capitol for H. R. Ex. Doc. No. 21, 36th Congress, 2d Session, and for S. Ex. Doc. No. 106, 41st Congress, 2d Session, and satisfy himself. The whole case is set forth in the first volume of the Court of Claims Reports.

It is my belief that as long as the continent of America holds together, the heirs of George Fisher, deceased, will still make pilgrimages to Washington from the swamps of Florida, to plead for just a little more cash on their bill of damages (even when they received the last of that sixty-seven thousand dollars, they said it was only *one-fourth* what the Government owed them on that infernal cornfield); and as long as they choose to come, they will find Garrett Davises to drag their vampire schemes before Congress. This is not the only hereditary fraud (if fraud it is—which I have before repeatedly remarked is not proven) that is being quietly handed down from generation to generation of fathers and sons, through the persecuted Treasury of the United States.

January 1871

The Tone-Imparting Committee

When I get old and ponderously respectable, only one thing will be able to make me truly happy, and that will be to be put on the Venerable Tone-Imparting Committee of the city of New York, and have nothing to do but sit on the platform, solemn and imposing, along with Peter Cooper, Horace Greeley, etc., etc., and shed momentary fame at second hand on obscure lecturers, draw public attention to lectures which would otherwise clack eloquently to sounding emptiness, and subdue audiences into respectful hearing of all sorts of unpopular and outlandish dogmas and isms. That is what I desire for the cheer and gratification of my gray hairs. Let me but sit up there with those fine relics of the Old Red Sandstone Period and give Tone to an intellectual entertainment twice a week, and be so reported, and my happiness will be complete. Those men have been my envy for a long, long time. And no memories of my life are so pleasant as my reminiscence, of their long and honorable career in the Tone-imparting service. I can recollect the first time I ever saw them on the platforms just as well as I can remember the events of yesterday. Horace Greeley sat on the right, Peter Cooper on the left, and Thomas Jefferson, Red Jacket, Benjamin Franklin, and John Hancock sat between them. This was on the 22d of December, 1799, on the occasion of the state funeral of George Washington in New York. It was a great day, that—a great day, and a very, very sad one. I remember that Broadway was one mass of black crape from Castle Garden nearly up to where the City Hall now stands. The next time I saw these gentlemen officiate was at a ball given for the purpose of procuring money and medicines for the sick and wounded soldiers and sailors. Horace Greeley occupied one side of the platform on which the musicians were exalted, and Peter Cooper the other. There were other Tone-imparters attendant upon the two chiefs, but I have forgotten their names now. Horace Greeley, gray-haired and beaming, was in sailor costume—white duck pants, blue shirt, open at the breast, large neckerchief, loose as an ox-bow, and tied with a jaunty sailor knot, broad turnover collar with star in the corner, shiny black little tarpaulin hat roosting daintily far back on head, and flying two gallant long ribbons. Slippers on ample feet, round spectacles on benignant nose, and pitchfork in hand, completed Mr. Greeley, and made him, in my boyish admiration, every inch a sailor, and worthy to be the honored great-grandfather of the Neptune he was so ingeniously representing. I shall never forget him. Mr. Cooper was dressed as a general of militia, and was dismally and oppressively warlike. I neglected to remark, in the proper place, that the soldiers and sailors in whose aid the ball was given had just been sent in from Boston—this was during the war of 1812. At the grand national reception of Lafayette, in 1824, Horace Greeley sat on the right and Peter Cooper on the left. The other Tone-imparters of that day are sleeping the sleep of the just now. I was in the audience when Horace Greeley, Peter Cooper, and other chief citizens imparted tone to the great meetings in favor of French liberty, in 1848. Then I never saw them any more until here lately; but now that I am living tolerably near the city, I run down every time I see it announced that "Horace Greeley, Peter Cooper, and several other distinguished citizens will occupy seats on the platform;" and next morning, when I read in the first paragraph of the phonographic report that "Horace Greeley, Peter Cooper, and several other distinguished citizens occupied seats on the platform," I say to myself, "Thank God, I was present." Thus I have been enabled to see these substantial old friends of mine sit on the platform and give tone to lectures on anatomy, and lectures on agriculture, and lectures on stirpiculture, and lectures on astronomy, on chemistry, on miscegenation, on "Is Man Descended from the Kangaroo?" on veterinary matters, on all kinds of religion, and several kinds of politics; and have seen them give tone and grandeur to the Four-legged Girl, the Siamese Twins, the Great Egyptian Sword Swallower, and the Old Original Jacobs. Whenever somebody is to lecture on a subject not of general interest, I know that my venerated Remains of the Old Red Sandstone Period will be on the platform; whenever a lecturer is to appear whom nobody has heard of before, nor will be likely to seek to see, I know that the real benevolence of my old friends will be taken advantage of, and that they will be on the platform (and in the bills) as an advertisement; and whenever any new and obnoxious deviltry in philosophy, morals, or politics is to be sprung upon the people, I know perfectly well that these intrepid old heroes will be on that platform too, in the interest of full and free discussion, and to crush down all narrower and less generous souls with the solid dead weight of their awful respectability. And let us all remember that while these inveterate and imperishable presiders (if you please) appear on the platform every night in the year as regularly as the volunteered piano from Steinway's or Chickering's, and have bolstered up and given tone to a deal of questionable merit and obscure emptiness in their time, they have also diversified this inconsequential service by occasional powerful uplifting and upholding of great progressive ideas which smaller men feared to meddle with or countenance.

February 1871

The Danger of Lying in Bed

The man in the ticket office said:

"Have an accident insurance ticket, also?"

"No," I said, after studying the matter over a little. "No, I believe not; I am going to be travelling by rail all day to-day. However, to-morrow I don't travel. Give me one for to-morrow."

The man looked puzzled. He said:

"But it is for accident insurance, and if you are going to travel by rail——"

"If I am going to travel by rail, I shan't need it. Lying at home in bed is the thing *I* am afraid of."

I had been looking into this matter. Last year I travelled twenty thousand miles, almost entirely by rail; the year before, I travelled over twenty-five thousand miles, half by sea and half by rail; and the year before that I travelled in the neighborhood of ten thousand miles, exclusively by rail. I suppose if I put in all the little odd journeys here and there, I may say I have travelled sixty thousand miles during the three years I have mentioned. *And never an accident.*

For a good while I said to myself every morning: "Now I have escaped thus far, and so the chances are just that much increased that I shall catch it this time. I will be shrewd, and buy an accident ticket." And to a dead moral certainty I drew a blank, and went to bed that night without a joint started or a bone splintered. I got tired of that sort of daily bother, and fell to buying accident tickets that were good for a month. I said to myself, "A man *can't* buy thirty blanks in one bundle."

But I was mistaken. There was never a prize in the lot. I could read of railway accidents every day—the newspaper atmosphere was foggy with them; but somehow they never came my way. I found I had spent a good deal of money in the accident business, and had nothing to show for it. My suspicions were aroused, and I began to hunt around for somebody that had won in this lottery. I found plenty of people who had invested, but not an individual that had ever had an accident or made a cent. I stopped buying accident tickets and went to ciphering. The result was astounding. THE PERIL LAY NOT IN TRAVELLING, BUT IN STAYING AT HOME.

I hunted up statistics, and was amazed to find that after all the glaring newspaper headings concerning railroad disasters, less than *three hundred* people had really lost their lives by those disasters in the preceding twelve months. The Erie road was set down as the most murderous in the list. It had killed forty-six—or twenty-six, I do not exactly remember which, but I know the number was double that of any other road. But the fact straightway suggested itself that the Erie was an immensely long road, and did more business than any other line in the country; so the double number of killed ceased to be matter for surprise.

By further figuring, it appeared that between New York and Rochester the Erie ran eight passenger trains each way every day—sixteen altogether; and carried a daily average of 6,000 persons. That is about a million in six months—the population of New York city. Well, the Erie kills from thirteen to twenty-three persons out of *its* million in six months; and in the same time 13,000 of New York's million die in their beds! My flesh crept, my hair stood on end. "This is appalling!" I said. "The danger isn't in travelling by rail, but in trusting to those deadly beds. I will never sleep in a bed again."

I had figured on considerably less than one-half the length of the Erie road. It was plain that the entire road must transport at least eleven or twelve thousand people every day. There are many short roads running out of Boston that do fully half as much; a great many such roads. There are many roads scattered about the Union that do a prodigious passenger business. Therefore it was fair to presume that an average of 2,500 passengers a day for each road in the country would be about correct. There are 846 railway lines in our country, and 846 times 2,500 are 2,115,000. So the railways of America move more than two millions of people every day; six hundred and fifty millions of people a year, without counting the Sundays. They do that, too—there is no question about it;

though where they get the raw material is clear beyond the jurisdiction of my arithmetic; for I have hunted the census through and through, and I find that there are not that many people in the United States, by a matter of six hundred and ten millions at the very least. They must use some of the same people over again, likely.

San Francisco is one-eighth as populous as New York; there are 60 deaths a week in the former and 500 a week in the latter—if they have luck. That is 3,120 deaths a year in San Francisco, and eight times as many in New York—say about 25,000 or 26,000. The health of the two places is the same. So we will let it stand as a fair presumption that this will hold good all over the country, and that consequently 25,000 out of every million of people we have must die every year. That amounts to one-fortieth of our total population. One million of us, then, die annually. Out of this million ten or twelve thousand are stabbed, shot, drowned, hanged, poisoned, or meet a similarly violent death in some other popular way, such as perishing by kerosene lamp and hoop-skirt conflagrations, getting buried in coal mines, falling off housetops, breaking through church or lecture-room floors, taking patent medicines, or committing suicide in other forms. The Erie railroad kills from 23 to 46; the other 845 railroads kill an average of one-third of a man each; and the rest of that million, amounting in the aggregate to the appalling figure of nine hundred and eighty-seven thousand six hundred and thirty-one corpses, die naturally in their beds!

You will excuse me from taking any more chances on those beds. The railroads are good enough for me.

And my advice to all people is, Don't stay at home any more than you can help; but when you have *got* to stay at home a while, buy a package of those insurance tickets and sit up nights. You cannot be too cautious.

[One can see now why I answered that ticket agent in the manner recorded at the top of this sketch.]

The moral of this composition is, that thoughtless people grumble more than is fair about railroad management in the United States. When we consider that every day and night of the year full fourteen thousand railway trains of various kinds, freighted with life and armed with death, go thundering over the land, the marvel is, *not* that they kill three hundred human beings in a twelvemonth, but that they do not kill three hundred times three hundred!

February 1871

One of Mankind's Bores

I suppose that if there is one thing in the world more hateful than another to all of us, it is to have to write a letter. A private letter especially. And business letters, to my thinking, are very little pleasanter. Nearly all the enjoyment is taken out of every letter I get by the reflection that it must be answered. And I do so dread the affliction of writing those answers, that often my first and gladdest impulse is to burn my mail before it is opened. For ten years I never felt that sort of dread at all, because I was moving about constantly, from city to city, from State to State, and from country to country, and so I could leave all letters unanswered if I chose, and the writers of them would naturally suppose that I had changed my post-office and missed receiving my correspondence. But I am "cornered" now. I cannot use that form of deception any more. I am anchored, and letters of all kinds come straight to me with deadly precision.

They are letters of all sorts and descriptions, and they treat of everything. I generally read them at breakfast, and right often they kill a day's work by diverting my thoughts and fancies into some new channel, thus breaking up and making confusion of the programme of scribbling I had arranged for my working hours. After breakfast I clear for action, and for an hour try hard to write; but there is no getting back into the old train of thought after such an interruption, and so at last I give it up and put off further effort till next day. One would suppose that I would now answer those letters and get them out of the way; and I suppose one of those model young men we read about, who enter New York barefoot and live to become insolent millionaires, would be sure to do that; but I don't. I never shall be a millionaire, and so I disdain to copy the ways of those men. I did not start right. I made a fatal mistake to begin with, and entered New York with boots on and above forty cents in my pocket. With such an unpropitious beginning, any efforts of mine to acquire great wealth would be frowned upon as illegitimate, and I should be ruthlessly put down as an impostor. And so, as I said before, I decline to follow the lead of those chrysalis

Crœsuses and answer my correspondents with commercial promptness. I stop work for the day, and leave the new letters stacked up along with those that came the day before, and the day before that, and the day before that, and so on. And by-and-by the pile grows so large that it begins to distress me, and then I attack it and give full five and sometimes six hours to the assault. And how many of the letters do I answer in that time? Never more than nine; usually only five or six. The correspondence clerk in a great mercantile house would answer a hundred in that many hours. But a man who has spent years in writing for the press cannot reasonably be expected to have such facility with a pen. From old habit he gets to thinking and thinking, patiently puzzling for minutes together over the proper turning of a sentence in an answer to some unimportant private letter, and so the precious time slips away.

It comes natural to me in these latter years to do all manner of composition laboriously and ploddingly, private letters included. Consequently, I do fervently hate letter-writing, and so do all the newspaper and magazine men I am acquainted with.

The above remarks are by way of explanation and apology to parties who have written me about various matters, and whose letters I have neglected to answer. I tried in good faith to answer them—tried every now and then, and always succeeded in clearing off several, but always as surely left the majority of those received each week to lie over till the next. The result was always the same, to wit: the unanswered letters would shortly begin to have a reproachful look about them, next an upbraiding look, and by-and-by an aggressive and insolent aspect; and when it came to that, I always opened the stove door and made an example of them. The return of cheerfulness and the flight of every feeling of distress on account of neglected duty, was immediate and thorough.

I did not answer the letter of the Wisconsin gentleman, who inquired whether imported brads were better than domestic ones, because I did not know what brads were, and did not choose to "let on" to a stranger. I thought it would have looked much better in him, anyhow, to have asked somebody who he knew was in the habit of eating brads, or wearing them, whichever is the proper way of utilizing them.

I did manage to answer the little Kentucky boy who wished to send me his wildcat. I thanked him very kindly and cordially for his donation, and said I was very fond of cats of all descriptions, and told him to do like the little Indiana boy, and forward it to Rev. Mr. Beecher, and I would call and get it some time. I could not bear to check the warm young tide of his generosity, and yet I had no (immediate) use for the insect myself.

I did not answer the young man who wrote me from Tennessee, inquiring "how to become a good reporter and acceptable journalist," chiefly because if one marks out the nice easy method which he knows these kind of inquirers have in their mind's eye, they straightway begin to afflict him with semi-weekly specimens of what they can do, under the thin disguise of a friendly correspondence; and if he marks out the unromantic and unattractive method which he believes in his heart to be the absolutely necessary one, they always write back and call him a "nigger" or a "thief." These people are so illogical.

February 1871

The Indignity Put upon the Remains of George Holland by the Rev. Mr. Sabine

What a ludicrous satire it was upon Christian charity!—even upon the vague, theoretical idea of it which doubtless this small saint mouths from his own pulpit every Sunday. Contemplate this freak of Nature, and think what a Cardiff giant of self-righteousness is crowded into his pigmy skin. If we probe, and dissect, and lay open this diseased, this cancerous piety of his, we are forced to the conviction that it is the production of an impression on his part that his guild do about all the good that is done in the earth, and hence are better than common clay—hence are competent to say to such as George Holland, "You are unworthy; you are a play-actor, and consequently a sinner; I cannot take the responsibility of recommending you to the mercy of Heaven." It must have had its origin in that impression, else he would have thought, "We are all instruments for the carrying out of God's purposes; it is not for me to pass judgment upon your appointed share of the work, or to praise or to revile it; I have divine authority for it that we are *all* sinners, and therefore it is not for me to discriminate and say we will supplicate for this sinner, for he was a merchant prince or a banker, but we will beseech no forgiveness for this other one, for he was a play-actor." It surely requires the furthest possible reach of self-righteousness to enable a man to lift his scornful nose in the air and turn his back upon so poor and pitiable a thing as a dead stranger come to beg the last kindness that humanity can do in its behalf. This creature has violated the letter of the gospel and judged George Holland—not George Holland either, but his *profession* through him. Then it is in a measure fair that we judge this creature's guild through *him*. In effect he has said, "We are the salt of the earth; we do all the good work that is done; to learn how to be good and do good, men must come to us; actors and such are obstacles to moral progress."* Pray look at the thing reasonably for a moment,

*Reporter—What answer did you make, Mr. Sabine?
Mr. Sabine—I said that I had a distaste for officiating at such a funeral,

laying aside all biasses of education and custom. If a common public impression is fair evidence of a thing, then this minister's legitimate, recognized, and acceptable business is to *tell* people calmly, coldly, and in stiff, written sentences, from the pulpit, to go and do right, be just, be merciful, be charitable. And his congregation forget it all between church and home. But for fifty years it was George Holland's business, on the stage, to *make* his audience go and do right, and be just, merciful, and charitable—because by his living, breathing, feeling pictures, he showed them what it *was* to do these things, and *how* to do them, and how instant and ample was the reward! Is it not a singular teacher of men, this reverend gentleman who is so poorly informed himself as to put the whole stage under ban, and say, "I do not think it teaches moral lessons"?

Where was ever a sermon preached that could make filial ingratitude so hateful to men as the sinful play of "King Lear"? Or where was there ever a sermon that could so convince men of the wrong and the cruelty of harboring a pampered and unanalyzed jealousy as the sinful play of "Othello"? And where are there ten preachers who can stand in the pulpit teaching heroism, unselfish devotion, and lofty patriotism, and hold their own against any one of five hundred William Tells that can be raised up upon five hundred stages in the land at a day's notice? It is almost fair and just to aver (although it is profanity) that nine-tenths of all the kindness and forbearance and Christian charity and generosity in the hearts of the American people to-day, got there by being filtered down from their fountain-head, the gospel of Christ, *through dramas and tragedies and comedies on the stage, and through the despised novel and the Christmas story, and through the thousand and one lessons, suggestions, and narratives of generous deeds that*

---

and that I did not care to be mixed up in it. I said to the gentleman that I was willing to bury the deceased from his house, but that I objected to having the funeral solemnized at a church.

Reporter—Is it one of the laws of the Protestant Episcopal Church that a deceased theatrical performer shall not be buried from the church?

Mr. Sabine—It is not; but I have always warned the professing members of my congregation to keep away from theatres and not to have anything to do with them. I don't think that they teach moral lessons.—*New York Times.*

stir the pulses, and exalt and augment the nobility of the nation day by day from the teeming columns of ten thousand newspapers, and NOT from the drowsy pulpit!

All that is great and good in our particular civilization came straight from the hand of Jesus Christ, and many creatures, and of divers sorts, were doubtless appointed to disseminate it; and let us believe that *this seed and the result* are the main thing, and not the cut of the sower's garment; and that whosoever, in his way and according to his opportunity, sows the one and produces the other, has done high service and worthy. And further, let us try with all our strength to believe that whenever old simple-hearted George Holland sowed this seed, and reared his crop of broader charities and better impulses in men's hearts, it was just as acceptable before the Throne as if the seed had been scattered in vapid platitudes from the pulpit of the ineffable Sabine himself.

Am I saying that the pulpit does not do its share toward disseminating the marrow, the *meat* of the gospel of Christ? (For we are not talking of ceremonies and wire-drawn creeds now, but the living heart and soul of what is pretty often only a spectre.)

No, I am not saying that. The pulpit teaches assemblages of people twice a week—nearly two hours, altogether—and does what it can in that time. The theatre teaches large audiences seven times a week—28 or 30 hours altogether; and the novels and newspapers plead, and argue, and illustrate, stir, move, thrill, thunder, urge, persuade, and supplicate, at the feet of millions and millions of people every single day, and all day long, and far into the night; and so these vast agencies till *nine-tenths* of the vineyard, and the pulpit tills the other tenth. Yet now and then some complacent blind idiot says, "You unanointed are coarse clay and useless; you are not as we, the regenerators of the world; go, bury yourselves elsewhere, for we cannot take the responsibility of recommending idlers and sinners to the yearning mercy of Heaven." How *does* a soul like that stay in a carcass without getting mixed with the secretions and sweated out through the pores? Think of this insect condemning the whole theatrical service as a disseminator of bad morals because it has Black Crooks in it; forgetting that if that were sufficient ground, people would condemn the pulpit because it had Cooks, and Kallochs, and Sabines in it.

No, I am not trying to rob the pulpit of any atom of its full share and credit in the work of disseminating the meat and marrow of the gospel of Christ; but I am trying to get a moment's hearing for worthy agencies in the same work, that with overwrought modesty seldom or never claim a recognition of their great services. I am aware that the pulpit does its excellent one-tenth (and credits itself with it now and then, though most of the time a press of business causes it to forget it); I am aware that in its honest and well-meaning way it bores the people with uninflammable truisms about doing good; bores them with correct compositions on charity; bores them, chloroforms them, stupefies them with argumentative mercy without a flaw in the grammar, or an emotion which the minister could put in in the right place if he turned his back and took his finger off the manuscript. And in doing these things the pulpit is doing its duty, and let us believe that it is likewise doing its best, and doing it in the most harmless and respectable way. And so I have said, and shall keep on saying, let us give the pulpit its full share of credit in elevating and ennobling the people; but when a pulpit takes to itself authority to pass judgment upon the work and the worth of just as legitimate an instrument of God as itself, who spent a long life preaching from the stage the self-same gospel without the alteration of a single sentiment or a single axiom of right, it is fair and just that somebody who believes that actors were made for a high and good purpose, and that they *accomplish the object of their creation* and accomplish it well, to protest. And having protested, it is also fair and just—being driven to it, as it were—to whisper to the Sabine pattern of clergyman, under the breath, a simple, instructive truth, and say, "Ministers are not the only servants of God upon earth, nor His most efficient ones either, by a very, very long distance!" Sensible ministers already know this, and it may do the other kind good to find it out.

But to cease teaching and go back to the beginning again, was it not pitiable, that spectacle? Honored and honorable old George Holland, whose theatrical ministry had for fifty years softened hard hearts, bred generosity in cold ones, kindled emotion in dead ones, uplifted base ones, broadened bigoted ones, and made many and many a stricken one glad and filled it brim full of gratitude, figuratively spit upon in his unoffending coffin by this crawling, slimy, sanctimonious, self-righteous reptile!

February 1871

A Substitute for Rulloff

Have We a Sydney Carton Among Us?

———, April 29, 1871.

To the Editor of The Tribune.

Sir: I believe in capital punishment. I believe that when a murder has been done it should be answered for with blood. I have all my life been taught to feel in this way, and the fetters of education are strong. The fact that the death law is rendered almost inoperative by its very severity does not alter my belief in its righteousness. The fact that in England the proportion of executions to condemnations is only one to 16, and in this country only one to 22, and in France only one to 38, does not shake my steadfast confidence in the propriety of retaining the death penalty. It is better to hang one murderer in 16, 22, or 38, than not to hang any at all.

Feeling as I do, I am not sorry that Rulloff is to be hanged, but I am sincerely sorry that he himself has made it necessary that his vast capabilities for usefulness should be lost to the world. In this, mine and the public's is a common regret. For it is plain that in the person of Rulloff one of the most marvelous intellects that any age has produced is about to be sacrificed, and that, too, while half the mystery of its strange powers is yet a secret. Here is a man who has never entered the doors of a college or a university, and yet, by the sheer might of his innate gifts has made himself such a colossus in abstruse learning that the ablest of our scholars are but pigmies in his presence. By the evidence of Prof. Mather, Mr. Surbridge, Mr. Richmond, and other men qualified to testify, this man is as familiar with the broad domain of philology as common people are with the passing events of the day. His memory has such a limitless grasp that he is able to quote sentence after sentence, paragraph after paragraph, and chapter after chapter, from a gnarled and knotty ancient literature that ordinary scholars are capable of achieving a little more than a bowing acquaintance with. But his memory is the least of his great endowments. By the testimony of the gentlemen above referred to, he is able to *critically analyze* the works of the old masters of literature, and while pointing out the beauties of the originals with a pure and discriminating taste, is as quick to detect the defects of the accepted translations; and in the latter case, if exceptions be taken to his judgment, he straightway opens up the quarries of his exhaustless knowledge and builds a very Chinese wall of evidence around his position. Every learned man who enters Rulloff's presence leaves it amazed and confounded by his prodigious capabilities and attainments. One scholar said he did not believe that in the matters of subtle analysis, vast knowledge in his peculiar field of research, comprehensive grasp of subject and serene kingship over its limitless and bewildering details, any land or any era of modern times had given birth to Rulloff's intellectual equal. What miracles this murderer might have wrought, and what luster he might have shed upon his country if he had not put a forfeit upon his life so foolishly! But what if the law could be satisfied, and the gifted criminal still be saved. If a life be offered up on the gallows to atone for the murder Rulloff did, will that suffice? If so, give me the proofs, for, in all earnestness and truth, I aver that in such a case I will instantly bring forward a man who, in the interests of learning and science, will *take Rulloff's crime upon himself, and submit to be hanged in Rulloff's place*. I can, and will do this thing; and I propose this matter, and make this offer in good faith. You know me, and know my address.

SAMUEL LANGHORNE.

May 3, 1871

About Barbers

All things change except barbers, the ways of barbers, and the surroundings of barbers. These never change. What one experiences in a barber shop the first time he enters one, is what he always experiences in barber shops afterward till the end of his days. I got shaved this morning as usual. A man approached the door from Jones street as I approached it from Main—a thing that always happens. I hurried up, but it was of no use; he entered the door one little step ahead of me, and I followed in on his heels and saw him take the only vacant chair, the one presided over by the best barber. It always happens so. I sat down, hoping that I might fall heir to the chair belonging to the better of the remaining two barbers, for he had already begun combing his man's hair, while his comrade was not yet quite done rubbing up and oiling his customer's locks. I watched the probabilities with strong interest. When I saw that No. 2 was gaining on No. 1, my interest grew to solicitude. When No. 1 stopped a moment to make change on a bath ticket for a new-comer, and lost ground in the race, my solicitude rose to anxiety. When No. 1 caught up again, and both he and his comrade were pulling the towels away and brushing the powder from their customers' cheeks, and it was about an even thing which one would say "Next!" first, my very breath stood still with the suspense. But when, at the final culminating moment, No. 1 stopped to pass a comb a couple of times through his customer's eyebrows, I saw that he had lost the race by a single instant, and I rose indignant and quitted the shop, to keep from falling into the hands of No. 2; for I have none of that enviable firmness that enables a man to look calmly into the eyes of a waiting barber and tell him he will wait for his fellow-barber's chair. I stayed out fifteen minutes, and then went back, hoping for better luck. Of course all the chairs were occupied now, and four men sat waiting, silent, unsociable, distraught, and looking bored, as men always do who are awaiting their turn in a barber's shop. I sat down in one of the iron-armed compartments of an old sofa, and put in the time for a while, reading the framed advertisements of all sorts of quack nostrums for dyeing and coloring the hair. Then I read the greasy names on the private bay rum bottles; read the names and noted the numbers on the private shaving cups in the pigeon-holes; studied the stained and damaged cheap prints on the walls, of battles, early Presidents, and voluptuous, recumbent sultanas, and the tiresome and everlasting young girl putting her grandfather's spectacles on; execrated in my heart the cheerful canary and the distracting parrot that few barber shops are without. Finally, I searched out the least dilapidated of the last year's illustrated papers that littered the foul centre-table, and conned their unjustifiable misrepresentations of old forgotten events. At last my turn came. A voice said "Next!" and I surrendered to—No. 2 of course. It always happens so. I said meekly that I was in a hurry, and it affected him as strongly as if he had never heard it. He shoved up my head and put a napkin under it. He ploughed his fingers into my collar and fixed a towel there. He explored my hair with his claws and suggested that it needed trimming. I said I did not want it trimmed. He explored again and said it was pretty long for the present style—better have a little taken off; it needed it behind, especially. I said I had had it cut only a week before. He yearned over it reflectively a moment, and then asked, with a disparaging manner, who cut it. I came back at him promptly with a "You did!" I had him there. Then he fell to stirring up his lather and regarding himself in the glass, stopping now and then to get close and examine his chin critically or torture a pimple. Then he lathered one side of my face thoroughly, and was about to lather the other, when a dog fight attracted his attention, and he ran to the window and stayed and saw it out, losing two shillings on the result in bets with the other barbers, a thing which gave me great satisfaction. He finished lathering, meantime getting the brush into my mouth only twice, and then began to rub in the suds with his hand; and as he now had his head turned, discussing the dog fight with the other barbers, he naturally shovelled considerable lather into my mouth without knowing it, but I did. He now began to sharpen his razor on an old suspender, and was delayed a good deal on account of a controversy about a cheap masquerade ball he had figured at the night before, in red cambric and bogus ermine, as some kind of a king. He was so gratified with being chaffed about some damsel whom he had smitten with his charms, that he used every means to continue the controversy by pretending to be annoyed at the chaffings of his fellows. This matter begot more surveyings of himself in the glass, and he put down his razor and brushed his hair with elaborate care, plastering an inverted arch of it down on his forehead, accomplishing an accurate "part" behind, and brushing the two wings forward over his ears with nice exactness. In the mean time the lather was drying on my face, and apparently eating into my vitals. Now he began to shave, digging his fingers into my countenance to stretch the skin, making a handle of my nose now and then, bundling and tumbling my head this way and that as convenience in shaving demanded, and "hawking" and expectorating pleasantly all the while. As long as he was on the tough sides of my face I did not suffer; but when he began to rake, and rip, and tug at my chin, the tears came. I did not mind his getting so close down to me; I did not mind his garlic, because all barbers eat garlic, I suppose; but there was an added something that made me fear that he was decaying inwardly while still alive, and this gave me much concern. He now put his finger into my mouth to assist him in shaving the corners of my upper lip, and it was by this bit of circumstantial evidence that I discovered that a part of his duties in the shop was to clean the kerosene lamps. I had often wondered in an indolent way whether the barbers did that, or whether it was the boss. About this time I was amusing myself trying to guess where he would be most likely to cut me this time, but he got ahead of me and sliced me on the end of the chin before I had got my mind made up. He immediately sharpened his razor—he might have done it before. I do not like a close shave, and would not let him go over me a second time. I tried to get him to put up his razor, dreading that he would make for the side of my chin, my pet tender spot, a place which a razor cannot touch twice without making trouble. But he said he only wanted to just smooth off one little roughness, and in that same moment he slipped his razor along the forbidden ground, and the dreaded pimple-signs of a close shave rose up smarting and answered to the call. Now he soaked his towel in bay rum, and slapped it all over my face nastily; slapped it over as if a human being ever yet washed his face in that way. Then he dried it by slapping with the dry part of the towel, as if a human being ever dried his face in such a fashion; but a barber seldom rubs you like a Christian. Next he poked bay rum into the cut place with his towel, then choked the wound with powdered starch, then soaked it with bay rum again, and would have gone on soaking and powdering it for evermore, no doubt, if I had not rebelled and begged off. He powdered my whole face now, straightened me up and began to plough my hair thoughtfully with his hands and examine his fingers critically. Then he suggested a shampoo, and said my hair needed it badly, very badly. I observed that I had shampooed it myself very thoroughly in the bath yesterday. I "had him" again. He next recommended some of "Smith's Hair Glorifier," and offered to sell me a bottle. I declined. He praised the new perfume, "Jones's Delight of the Toilet," and proposed to sell me some of that. I declined again. He tendered me a tooth-wash atrocity of his own invention, and when I declined, offered to trade knives with me. He returned to business after the miscarriage of this last enterprise, sprinkled me all over, legs and all, greased my hair in defiance of my protests against it, rubbed and scrubbed a good deal of it out by the roots, and combed and brushed the rest, parting it behind and plastering the eternal inverted arch of hair down on my forehead, and then, while combing my scant eyebrows and defiling them with pomade, strung out an account of the achievements of a six-ounce black and tan terrier of his till I heard the whistles blow for noon, and knew I was five minutes too late for the train. Then he snatched away the towel, brushed it lightly about my face, passed his comb through my eyebrows once more, and gayly sang out "Next!"

This barber fell down and died of apoplexy two hours later. I am waiting over a day for my revenge—I am going to attend his funeral.

August 1871

A Brace of Brief Lectures on Science

I. — PALEONTOLOGY

What a noble science is paleontology! And what really startling sagacity its votaries exhibit!

Immediately after the Nathan murder, twenty practiced detectives went and viewed the dead body; examined the marks on the throat and on the head; followed the bloody tracks; looked at the bloody clothes, the broken safe, and the curious, unusual, mysterious "dog." They took note of the stolen diamond studs and set a watch on the pawnbrokers, and they set watches upon all the known thieves and housebreakers, and upon their fast women. They had the detectives of all the wide world to help them watch and work, and the telegraph to facilitate communication. They had the testimony of fifty witnesses in point and conveniently at hand for reference, a knowledge of everything that transpired about the Nathan mansion during the entire eventful night with the exception of the single hour during which the murder was committed. Thus we perceive that the mystery was narrowed down to a very small compass, and the clues and helps were abundant and excellent. Yet what is the result? Nothing. The "dog" has told no tales, the bloody tracks have led no whither, the murderer has not been found. Why, it is not even known whether there was one murderer, or twenty — or whether men or women did the deed — or how entrance was gained to the house or how exit was accomplished!

The reader perceives how illiterate detectives can blunder along, with whole volumes of clues to guide them, and yet achieve nothing. Now let me show him what "science" can do. Let me show what might have been done if New York had been intelligent enough to employ one deep paleontologist in the work instead of a dozen detectives. — Let me demonstrate that with no other clue than one small splinter off that "iron dog," or a gill of the water the bloody shirt was washed in, any cultivated paleontologist would have walked right off and fetched you that murderer with as unerring certainty as he would take a fragment of an unknown bone and build you the animal it used to belong to, and tell you which end his tail was on and what he preferred for dinner.

In this lesson I will treat only of one subject of paleontological "research"—PRIMEVAL MAN. Geology has revealed the fact that the crust of the earth is composed of five layers or strata. We exist on the surface of the fifth. Geology teaches, with scientific accuracy, that each of these layers was from ten thousand to two million years forming or cooling. [A disagreement as to a few hundred thousand years is a matter of little consequence to science.] The layer immediately under our layer, is the fourth or "quaternary;" under that is the third, or tertiary, etc. Each of these layers had its peculiar animal and vegetable life, and when each layer's mission was done, it and its animals and vegetables ceased from their labors and were forever buried under the new layer, with its new-shaped and new fangled animals and vegetables. So far, so good. Now the geologists Thompson, Johnson, Jones and Ferguson state that our own layer has been ten thousand years forming. The geologists Herkimer, Hildebrand, Boggs and Walker all claim that our layer has been four hundred thousand years forming. Other geologists just as reliable, maintain that our layer has been from one to two million years forming. Thus we have a concise and satisfactory idea of how long our layer has been growing and accumulating.

That is sufficient geology for our present purpose. The paleontologists Hooker, Baker, Slocum and Hughes claim that Primeval Man existed during the quaternary period—consequently he existed as much as ten thousand, and possibly two million, years ago. The paleontologists Howard, Perkins, de Warren and Von Hawkins assert that Primeval Man existed as far back as the *tertiary* period—and consequently he walked the earth at a time so remote that if you strung ciphers after a unit till there were enough to answer for a necklace for a mastodon you could not adequately represent the billions of centuries ago it happened. Now, you perceive, we begin to cramp this part of our subject into a corner where we can grasp it, as it were, and contemplate it intelligently. Let us— "for a flier," as the learned Von Humboldt phrases it—consider that this Primeval Man transpired eight or nine hundred thousand years ago, and not day before yesterday, like the

Nathan murder.—What do we know of him, and how do we find it out? Listen, while I reduce the "revelations" of paleontology to a few paragraphs:

1. Primeval Man existed in the quaternary period—because his bones are found in caves along with bones of now extinct animals *of* that period—such as the "cave-hyena," the mammoth, etc.

2. The incredible antiquity of the Primeval Man's bones is further proven by their extreme "fragility."—No bones under a million years old "could be so fragile." [I quote strictly from the scientific authorities.] The reason royal skeletons in Westminster crumble to dust when exposed, although only a trifling eight hundred years old, is because they are shut up in leaden coffins, I suppose. Bones do not keep good in coffins. There is no sure way but to cord them up in caves. Paleontology reveals that they will then last you a million years without any inconvenience.

3. The Primeval Man possessed weapons—because along with his bones are found rude chips and flakes of flint that the paleontologist knows very well were regarded as knives by the Primeval Man; and also flints of a rude oval shape that in his pretty simplicity he regarded as "hatchets." These things have been found in vast quantities with his bones.

4. The Primeval Man "WORE CLOTHES"—because, along with his bones have been found skeletons of the reindeer, *"with marks still visible about the base of the horns, such as are made in our day when we cut there to loosen the hide in order to skin the animal."* Could this paleontologist find the Nathan murderer?—Undoubtedly he could. The ignorant need not say that possibly the Primeval Man wore no clothes, but wanted the hide for a tent, or for bow-strings, or lassos, or beds, or to trade off for glass beads and whisky. The paleontologist knows what he wanted with the hide.

5. The Primeval Man had not only inventive powers and gropings toward civilization, as evidenced by his contriving and manufacturing flint hatchets and knives and wearing clothes, but he also had marked and unmistakable "art" inspirations—because, along with his bones have been found figures scratched on bone, vaguely suggestive of possible fishes; and a boar's tooth rudely carved into the shape of a bird's

head, and "with a hole in it *to enable him to hang it around his neck.*" [I quote from authority.] I ask, could this person discover the Nathan murderer?

6. The Primeval Man "eat his wild game roasted"—because, "along with his bones are found the bones of wild animals which seem to have been scorched" some millions of years ago.

7. The Primeval Man was "passionately fond of marrow" [I still quote from the scientific authorities,]—because, along with his bones have been found animal bones *broken lengthwise*, "which shows that they had been thus broken to *extract the marrow*, of which our primitive forefathers *were inordinately fond*," says the "Paleontological Investigations." Could *this* man read the secrets of an iron dog and a bloody shirt, or could he not?

8. The Primeval Man was—a—cannibal!—because, in Italy, and also in Scotland, along with his bones have been found children's bones which had "first been carefully cleansed and emptied to satisfy the inordinate taste for marrow, and then *gnawed.*"(!) This is horrible, but true. Let not the ignorant say that a dog might have done this gnawing, for paleontology has looked into that and decided that—

9. The Primeval Man had no dog—because *"there is no trace of dogs having been domesticated then."* Which settles that point.

10. The Primeval hyena gnawed bones, however—because paleontology proves that "the marks on some bones found in France were not made by dog, human, cat or mastodon teeth, but by the teeth of a hyena." And paleontology is aware that the hyena gnawed the bones *"after* the Primeval Man" was done with them—which was clever, but paleontology keeps the reasons for knowing this a scientific secret.

11. Primeval Man had graveyards—"because, along with great quantities of the roasted and gnawed bones of primeval animals, have been found quantities of human bones and flint weapons." And it is a precious privilege to live in an epoch of paleontologists, for the uneducated investigator would not be able to tell a primeval graveyard from a primeval restaurant.

12. The Primeval Man always had a banquet and a good time after a funeral—because, down the hill a little way from

his graveyard (there is only one on record,) *"a bed of ashes was unearthed."* Von Rosenstein and some others say the banquet occurred *before* the funeral, but most paleontologists agree that it was nearly a week after the obsequies.

13. Primeval Man "made his flint knives and hatchets with a stone hammer"—and an English paleontologist has "proved" this, and overwhelmed all cavilers with confusion, and won thunders of applause and incalculable gratitude from his fellow-scientists by actually *making* a flint hatchet *with a stone hammer.* The fact that these weapons are so independent in form that if a man chipped a piece of flint with his eyes shut the result would infallibly be a primeval flint knife or flint hatchet, one or the other, in spite of him, has got nothing to do with the matter. If cavilers say that the fact that we *could* carve our bread with an axe is no sign that we *do* carve it with an axe, I simply say that such an argument begs the question, inasmuch as it applies to the present time, whereas the science of paleontology only treats of matters of remote antiquity.

Now I come to the most marvellous "revelation" of all—the most unexpected, the most surprising, the most gratifying. It is this. Paleontology has discovered that—

14. "The Primeval Man believed in Immortality!"—because, "else why did he bury those huge quantities of flint hatchets and other weapons with his dead, just as all savages do who desire to provide the loved and lost with means of amusement and subsistence in the happy hunting grounds of eternity?" Aha! What saith the caviler now? Poor purblind croaker, in this grand and awful evidence of the Primeval Man's belief in the immortality of his soul, *you* would find only evidence that the primeval cemetery, the primeval restaurant and the primeval arsenal were purposely compacted into the same premises to save rent. Idiot!

The lesson is ended. Do you see, now, how simple and easy "science" makes a thing? Do you see how—

Some animal bones, split, scratched and scorched; located in quaternary ground;

Some full sized human bones with them—and very "fragile;"

Some small bones, marrowless and scratched;

Some flints of several uncertain shapes;

Some rude scratchings and carvings, done possibly by design;

Some deer horns, scratched at their bases;

An ash-pile;

The absence of dog-tracks;—

Do you see how these clues and "evidences" are all the materials the science of paleontology needs in order to give to
the world the wonder of a—

Primeval Man;

And not only that but tell what was the particular period he
lived in;

What weapons he carried;

What kind of clothes he wore;

What his art predilections and capacities were;

What he made his weapons with;

What his funeral customs were;

What part of a bear or a child he preferred for breakfast;

What animal got the remains of his feasts, and what animal
didn't;

And finally, what the foundation and corner-stone of the
religion of the lost and lamented old ante-diluvian commander-in-chief of all the fossils, was!

What a crying pity it is that the Nathan murder was not
committed two million years ago—for I *do* so want to know
all about it.

————

[Some of my own paleontological deductions differing in
some respects from those of other paleontological authorities,
I reserve them for expression in another chapter on "Science,"
which will appear next month.]

————

II.—PALEONTOLOGY CONCLUDED—
PRIMEVAL MAN.

My brother paleontologists have "proved" by the finding of
weapons (for use in the happy hunting grounds,) side by side
with the Primeval Man's bones, that the Primeval Man was a
believer in immortality. And I think they have done more
than this. I think that in "proving" that he always broke the

bones of animals "lengthwise" to get at the marrow, they have come near proving the Primeval Man an ass. For why should he break bones lengthwise to get at the marrow when anybody except a scientist knows that it is a deal easier to break a bone crosswise than lengthwise, and still more convenient to smash your stone down on it and let it break any way it pleases; and we all know that the marrow will taste just the same, no matter what plan of fracture you pursue. And yet nothing would suit this primeval "galoot" but the lengthwise style—it does *not* look reasonable. And I must call notice to the fact that neither the Primeval Man's elk-horn instruments, nor his flint knife, nor yet the awe-inspiring quoit which *he* thought was a flint "hatchet," could split a slippery, crooked, uneasy and vexatious bone lengthwise with facility—and I have always noticed that your Primeval Man looks to convenience *first*. That is his way, if I know whereof I speak—and if I do not, what am I a paleontologist for?

2. Somehow I cannot feel satisfied that those bears (whose bones are found mingled with those of the Primeval Man), were not the real parties that ate that marrow—and also the animals that used to own it. And without nibbling at heresy any further, I may as well come out and suggest that perhaps they ate the Primeval Man himself. Here is a pile of bones of primeval man and beast all mixed together, with no more damning evidence that the man ate the bears than that the bears ate the man—yet paleontology holds a coroner's inquest here in the fifth geologic period on an "unpleasantness" which transpired in the quaternary, and calmly lays it on the MAN, and then adds to it what purports to be evidence of CANNIBALISM. I ask the candid reader, Does not this look like taking advantage of a gentleman who has been dead two million years, and whose surviving friends and relatives——. But the subject is too painful. Are we to have another Byron-scandal case? Here are savage ways and atrocious appetites attributed to the dead and helpless Primeval Man—have we any assurance that the same hand will not fling mud at the Primeval Man's mother, next?

3. Again. Is there anything really so surprising about the absence of the marrow from bones a few hundred thousand years old as to make it worth while to sit up nights trying to

figure out how it came to be absent? Now *is* there, considering that there are so many good chances that Age, Worms and Decay got the marrow?

4. If the student should ask why paleontologists call the Primeval Man a cannibal, I should answer that it was because they find tooth-marks on primeval children's bones which they "*recognize as the marks of human teeth.*" If the student should ask why paleontologists assert that primeval hyenas gnawed the bones of roasted animals after the Primeval Man had finished his meal, I should answer that they find teeth-marks upon said bones which they "*recognize as hyena teeth-marks.*" If the student should ask me how the paleontologist tells the difference between hyena and human teeth-marks on a *bone*, and particularly a bone which has been rotting in a cave since the everlasting hills were builded, I should answer that I don't know.

A man could leave a sort of a tooth-mark (till decay set in,) in any fleshy substance that might remain sticking to a bone, but that he could make a tooth-mark on the bone itself I am obliged to question. Let the earnest student try to bite the handle of his tooth-brush and see if he can leave an autograph that will defy the ages. Aha! where are you *now*!

5. The frivolous are apt to take notice of a certain paleontological custom, which, not understanding, they take to be proper prey for their wit. I refer to the common paleontological custom of "proving" the vast age of primeval bones by their "*extreme fragility,*" and then accounting for their wonderful preservation by the fact that they were "*petrified and fossilized* by deposits of calcareous salts.*" If cavilers had brains enough to comprehend this, they would not cavil so much about it.

6. In the celebrated paleontological "cave of Aurignac" were found bones of primeval men, woolly elephants, huge bears and elks and wolves of a singular pattern, and also bones of the august mastodon. What do my fellow paleontologists call that place? A "primeval *graveyard.*" Why? Why graveyard? Reader, I have looked carefully into this matter and discovered the significant fact that they never found a single tomb-stone. Nor any sign of a grave. Then *why* call it a graveyard? Does a tangled mess of bones of men and beasts

necessarily constitute a graveyard? I would not disturb any man's faith in the primeval cemetery, though, merely to hear myself talk. I have opened the subject for a nobler purpose —to give the paleontological student's faith a new direction and a worthier one. I have investigated the evidences and now feel tolerably satisfied that the contents of the cave of Aurignac are not the remains of a primeval graveyard, but of a primeval menagerie. I ask the intelligent reader if it is likely that such rare creatures as a woolly elephant, a mastodon, and those huge and peculiar bears, wolves, etc., would simply *happen* together, along with a man or two, in a comfortable, roomy cave, with a small, low door, just suited to the admission of single files of country people, to say nothing of children and servants at half price? I simply ask the candid reader that question and let him sweat—as the historian Josephus used to say. If I should be asked for further suggestions in support of my hypothesis, I should hazard the thought that the treasurer of the menagerie was guilty of a hideous general massacre, while the proprietor and the beasts were asleep, and that his object was robbery. It is admitted by nearly one-sixth of all the paleontologists [observe the unusual unanimity] that the first part of the quaternary period must have been an uncommonly good season for public exhibitions—and in this one fact alone you have almost a confirmation of the criminal motive attributed to the treasurer. If I am asked for final and incontrovertible proof of my position, I point to the significant fact that *the bones of the treasurer have never been found, and* THE CASH BOX IS GONE. It is enough to make one's hair stand on end.

I desire nothing more than my dues. If I have thrown any light on the mystery of the cave of Aurignac, I desire that it shall be acknowledged—if I have not, I desire that it may be as though I had never spoken.

7. As concerns the proud paleontological trophy, the "flint hatchet" and its companion the "flint knife," I am compelled again to differ with the other scientists. I cannot think that the so-called "flint knife" is a knife at all. I cannot disabuse my mind of the impression that it is a file. No knife ever had such a scandalous blade as that. If asked by scholars of the established faith what the Primeval Man could want with a file, I

should, with customary paleontological diplomacy, ask what he could want with such a *knife*? Because he *might* file something with that thing, but I will hang if he could ever *cut* anything with it.

8. And as for the oval shaped flint which stands for the lauded primeval "hatchet," I cannot rid myself of the idea that it was only a paper-weight. If incensed brother-paleontologists storm at me and say the Primeval Man had no paper, I shall say calmly, "As long as it was nobody's business but his own, couldn't he carry his paper-weight around till he got some?"

But there is nothing intractable about me. If gentlemen wish to compromise and call it a petrified hoecake, or anything in *reason*, I am agreeable; for the Primeval Man had to have food, and might have had hoecakes, but he didn't have to have a flint "hatchet" like this thing, which he could not even cut his butter with without mashing it.

If any one should find fault with any arguments used by me in the course of the above chapter, and say that I jump to a conclusion over so much ground that the feat is in a manner ungraceful; and if he should say further, that in establishing one paleontological position of mine I generally demolish another, I would answer that these things are inseparable from scientific investigation. We all do it—all scientists. No one can regret it more than we do ourselves, but there really seems to be no remedy for it. First we had to recede from our assertion that a certain fossil was a primeval man, because afterward when we had found multitudes of saurians and had grown glib and facile in descanting upon them, we found that that other creature was of the same species. What could we do? It was too big a job to turn a thousand saurians into primeval men, and so we turned the solitary primeval man into a saurian. It was the cheapest way. And so it has always been with us. Every time we get a chance to assert something, we have to take back something. When we announced and established the great discovery of the "Glacial Period," how we did have to cart the dead animals around! Because, do not you see, the indiscriminate sort of distribution of fossil species which we had accommodated to the characteristic action of a general flood would not answer for a nicely discriminating "glacial period" which *ought* to transport only walruses, white bears, and other frigid creatures, from the North Pole down into Africa and not meddle with any other kind of animals. Well, we had only got the several species of fossil animals located to "back up" the "glacial period" when here comes some idiot down from Behring's Strait with a fossil elephant a hundred thousand years old! Of course we had to go to work and account for *him*. You see how it is. Science is as sorry as you are that this year's science is no more like last year's science than last year's was like the science of twenty years gone by. But science cannot help it. Science is full of change. Science is progressive and eternal. The scientists of twenty years ago laughed at the ignorant men who had groped in the intellectual darkness of twenty years before.

We derive pleasure from laughing at *them*. We have accounted for that elephant, at last, on the hypothesis that when he was alive Alaska was in the tropics. Twenty or thirty years from now the new crop of paleontologists will be just as likely as not to find an elephant and a petrified iceberg roosting in the same quaternary cave together up there in Alaska, and if they do, down *we* go, with our tropical theory, that is all.

September and October 1871

The Revised Catechism

First class in modern Moral Philosophy stand up and recite:
What is the chief end of man?

A. To get rich.

In what way?

A. Dishonestly if we can; honestly if we must.

Who is God, the one only and true?

A. Money is God. Gold and greenbacks and stock—father, son, and the ghost of the same—three persons in one: these are the true and only God, mighty and supreme; and William Tweed is his prophet.

Name the twelve disciples.

A. St. Ass's Colt Hall, whereon the prophet rode into Jerusalem; St. Connolly, the beloved disciple; St. Matthew Carnochan, that sitteth at the receipt of customs; St. Peter Fisk, the belligerent disciple; St. Paul Gould, that suffereth many stripes and glorieth in them; St. Iscariot Winans; St. Jacob Vanderbilt, the essteemed disciple; St. Garvey, the chair-itable; St. Ingersoll, of the holy carpets; St. N. Y. Printing Co., the meek and lowly, that letteth not its right hand know what its left hand taketh; St. Peter Hoffman, that denied his (Irish) master when the public cock had crowed six or seven times; St. Barnard, the wise judge, who imparteth injunctions in time of trouble, whereby the people are instructed to their salvation.

How shall a man attain the chief end of life?

A. By furnishing imaginary carpets to the Court-House, apocryphal chairs to the armories, and invisible printing to the city.

Are there other ways?

A: Yea. By purchasing the quarantine apostle for a price; by lightering shipmen of all they possess; by proceeding through immigrants from over sea; by burying the moneyless at the public charge and transhipping the rest 10 miles at $40 a head. By testing iron work for buildings. By furnishing lead and iron gas-pipes to the Court-House and then conveying the impression in the bill that they were constructed of gold and silver and set with diamonds. By taking care of the public parks at $5 an inch. By loafing around gin mills on a salary under the illusion that you are imparting impetus to a shovel on the public works.

Are these sufficient? If not, what shall a man do else, to be saved?

A. Make out his bill for ten prices and deliver nine of them into the hands of the prophet and the holy family. Then shall he be saved.

Who were the models the young were taught to emulate in former days?

A. Washington and Franklin.

Whom do they and should they emulate now in this era of larger enlightenment?

A. Tweed, Hall, Connolly, Carnochan, Fisk, Gould, Barnard, and Winans.

What works were chiefly prized for the training of the young in former days?

A. Poor Richard's Almanac, the Pilgrim's Progress, and the Declaration of Independence.

What are the best prized Sunday-school books in this more enlightened age?

A. St. Hall's Garbled Reports, St. Fisk's Ingenious Robberies, St. Carnochan's Guide to Corruption, St. Gould on the Watering of Stock, St. Barnard's Injunctions, St. Tweed's Handbook of Morals, and the Court-House edition of the Holy Crusade of the Forty Thieves.

Do we progress?

A. You bet your life!

Yours truly,   MARK TWAIN.

September 27, 1871

The Secret of Dr. Livingstone's
Continued Voluntary Exile

"I had to give him (Dr. Livingstone) five years' news to begin with."—*Correspondence of Herald Expedition in search of Dr. Livingstone.*

"General Grant is president of the United States."

"Since when?"

"For the last four years."

"Indeed? And what else has transpired?"

"Half of Chicago has been burned to ashes. Loss $200,000,000. France and Prussia have had a devastating war. Prussia utterly vanquished France in an uninterrupted series of tremendous battles and brilliant victories. The Emperor Napoleon is an exile. The queen of Spain has been driven from the throne, and she and her family are in exile. An Italian prince is king of Spain. Charles Dickens has been dead two years. A negro has been numbered among the senators of the United States. Jim Fisk was shot in a vital part by a person named Stokes, and one set of doctors proved to the satisfaction of a jury that another set of doctors killed the man with a probe. And as that was entirely legitimate, nobody was hanged. A dozen official ruffians ran the city of New York in debt a hundred and twenty-five millions of dollars in four years, and stole twenty millions from the public treasury for their private use, and live to-day unwhipped of justice. Women vote now in one of the territories, and a notorious woman is candidate for President. France is a republic, and Henri Rochefort an exile. Mazzini is dead. China has sent a great embassy abroad into the world to make commercial treaties with the nations. Japan has undergone a bloodless revolution more marvelous than any ever created by the sword, and is become a free land; the great nobles have voluntarily reduced themselves to the condition of private citizens: they have disbanded their armies of retainers and yielded up their vast revenues to the government; railroads and telegraphs are being built, colleges established, and western dress and customs introduced. The tycoon is dethroned, and the mikado reigns untrameled. He has come out from his ancient seclusion, and exhibits himself to all the world in the public streets, with hardly an attendant. He is going to France. Horace Greeley is the democratic candidate for President of the United States, and all rebeldom hurrahs for him. He—"

"Hold on! You have told me stupendous things, and with a confiding simplicity born of contact with these untutored children of Africa, I was swallowing them peacefully down; but there is a limit to all things. I am a simple, guileless, christian man, and unacquainted with intemperate language; but when you tell me that Horace Greeley is become a democrat and the ku-klux swing their hats and whoop for him, I cast the traditions of my education to the winds and say, I'll be d—d to all eternity if I believe it. (After a pause.)—My trunk is packed to go home, but I shall remain in Africa—for these things *may* be true, after all; if they are, I desire to stay here and unlearn my civilization."

UJIJIJI UNYEMBEMBE,
Interpreter to the Expedition.

July 20, 1872

How I Escaped Being Killed in a Duel

The only merit I claim for the following narrative is that it is a true story. It has a moral at the end of it, but I claim nothing on that, as it is merely thrown in to curry favor with the religious element.

After I had reported a couple of years on the Virginia City (Nevada) *Daily Enterprise*, they promoted me to be editor-in-chief—and I lasted just a week, by the watch. But I made an uncommonly lively newspaper while I *did* last, and when I retired I had a duel on my hands, and three horse-whippings promised me. The latter I made no attempt to collect; however, this history concerns only the former. It was the old "flush times" of the silver excitement, when the population was wonderfully wild and mixed: everybody went armed to the teeth, and all slights and insults had to be atoned for with the best article of blood your system could furnish. In the course of my editing I made trouble with a Mr. Lord, editor of the rival paper. He flew up about some little trifle or other that I said about him—I do not remember now what it was. I suppose I called him a thief, or a body-snatcher, or an idiot, or something like that. I was obliged to make the paper readable, and I could not fail in my duty to a whole community of subscribers merely to save the exaggerated sensitiveness of an individual. Mr. Lord was offended, and replied vigorously in his paper. Vigorously means a great deal when it refers to a personal editorial in a frontier newspaper. Duelling was all the fashion among the upper classes in that country, and very few gentlemen would throw away an opportunity of fighting one. To kill a person in a duel caused a man to be even more looked up to than to kill two men in the ordinary way. Well, out there, if you abused a man, and that man did not like it, you had to call him out and kill him; otherwise you would be disgraced. So I challenged Mr. Lord, and I did hope he would not accept; but I knew perfectly well that he did not want to fight, and so I challenged him in the most violent and implacable manner. And then I sat down and suffered and suffered till the answer came. All our boys—the editors— were in our office, "helping" me in the dismal business, and telling about duels, and discussing the code with a lot of aged ruffians who had had experience in such things, and altogether there was a loving interest taken in the matter, which made me unspeakably uncomfortable. The answer came— Mr. Lord declined. Our boys were furious, and so was I—on the surface.

I sent him another challenge, and another and another; and the more he did not want to fight, the bloodthirstier I became. But at last the man's tone changed. He appeared to be waking up. It was becoming apparent that he was going to fight me, after all. I ought to have known how it would be—he was a man who never could be depended upon. Our boys were exultant. I was not, though I tried to be.

It was now time to go out and practise. It was the custom there to fight duels with navy six-shooters at fifteen paces— load and empty till the game for the funeral was secured. We went to a little ravine just outside of town, and borrowed a barn-door for a target—borrowed it of a gentleman who was absent—and we stood this barn-door up, and stood a rail on end against the middle of it, to represent Lord, and put a squash on top of the rail to represent his head. He was a very tall, lean creature, the poorest sort of material for a duel— nothing but a line shot could "fetch" him, and even then he might split your bullet. Exaggeration aside, the rail was, of course, a little too thin to represent his body accurately, but the squash was all right. If there was any intellectual difference between the squash and his head, it was in favor of the squash.

Well, I practised and practised at the barn-door, and could not hit it; and I practised at the rail, and could not hit that; and I tried hard for the squash, and could not hit the squash. I would have been entirely disheartened, but that occasionally I crippled one of the boys, and that encouraged me to hope.

At last we began to hear pistol-shots near by, in the next ravine. We knew what that meant! The other party were out practising, too. Then I was in the last degree distressed; for of course those people would hear our shots, and they would send spies over the ridge, and the spies would find my barn-door without a wound or a scratch, and that would simply be the end of me—for of course that other man would immediately become as bloodthirsty as *I* was. Just at this moment a little bird, no larger than a sparrow, flew by, and lit on a sage-bush about thirty paces away; and my little second, Steve Gillis, who was a matchless marksman with a pistol—much better than I was—snatched out his revolver, and shot the bird's head off! We all ran to pick up the game, and sure enough, just at this moment, some of the other duellists came reconnoitring over the little ridge. They ran to our group to see what the matter was; and when they saw the bird, Lord's second said:

"That was a splendid shot. How far off was it?"

Steve said, with some indifference:

"Oh, no great distance. About thirty paces."

"Thirty paces! Heavens alive, who did it?"

"*My* man—Twain."

"The mischief he did! Can he do that often?"

"Well—yes. He can do it about—well—about four times out of five."

I knew the little rascal was lying, but I never said anything. I never told him so. He was not of a disposition to invite confidences of that kind, so I let the matter rest. But it was a comfort to see those people look sick, and see their under-jaws drop, when Steve made these statements. They went off and got Lord, and took him home; and when we got home, half an hour later, there was a note saying that Mr. Lord peremptorily declined to fight!

It was a narrow escape. We found out afterwards that Lord hit *his* mark thirteen times in eighteen shots. If he had put those thirteen bullets through me, it would have narrowed my sphere of usefulness a good deal—would have well nigh closed it, in fact. True, they could have put pegs in the holes, and used me for a hat-rack; but what is a hat-rack to a man who feels he has intellectual powers? I would scorn such a position.

I have written this true incident of my personal history for one purpose, and one purpose only—to warn the youth of the day against the pernicious practice of duelling, and to plead with them to war against it. If the remarks and suggestions I am making can be of any service to Sunday-school teachers, and newspapers interested in the moral progress of society, they are at liberty to use them, and I shall even be grateful to have them widely disseminated, so that they may do as much good as possible. I was young and foolish when I challenged that gentleman, and I thought it was very fine and very grand to be a duellist, and stand upon the "field of honor." But I am older and more experienced now, and am inflexibly opposed to the dreadful custom. I am glad, indeed, to be enabled to lift up my voice against it. I think it is a bad, immoral thing. I think it is every man's duty to do everything he can to *discourage* duelling. I always do now; I discourage it upon every occasion.

If a man were to challenge me *now*—now that I can fully appreciate the iniquity of that practice—I would go to that man, and take him by the hand, and lead him to a quiet, retired room—and kill him.

December 21, 1872

Poor Little Stephen Girard

The man lives in Philadelphia, who, when young and poor, entered a bank, and says he, "Please, sir, don't you want a boy?" And the stately personage said, "No, little boy, I don't want a little boy." The little boy, whose heart was too full for utterance, chewing a piece of licorice stick he had bought with a cent stolen from his good and pious aunt, with sobs plainly audible, and with great globules of water rolling down his cheeks, glided silently down the marble steps of the bank. Bending his noble form, the bank man dodged behind a door, for he thought the little boy was going to shy a stone at him. But the little boy picked up something and stuck it in his poor but ragged jacket. "Come here, little boy," and the little boy did come here; and the bank man said, "Lo, what pickest thou up?" And he answered and replied, "A pin." And the bank man said, "How do you vote?—excuse me, do you go to Sunday-school?" and he said he did. Then the bank man took down a pen made of pure gold, and flowing with pure ink, and he wrote on a piece of paper, "St. Peter," and he asked the little boy what it stood for, and he said "Salt Peter." Then the bank man said it meant "Saint Peter." The little boy said "Oh!"

Then the bank man took the little boy to his bosom, and the little boy said "Oh!" again, for he squeezed him. Then the bank man took the little boy into partnership, and gave him half the profits and all the capital, and he married the bank man's daughter; and now all he has is all his and all his own, too.

STORY OF ANOTHER GOOD LITTLE BOY

My uncle told me this story, and I spent six weeks picking up pins in front of a bank. I expected the bank man would call me in and say, "Little boy, are you good?" and I was going to say, "Yes;" and when he asked me what "St. John" stood for, I was going to say "Salt John." But I guess the bank man wasn't anxious to have a partner, and I guess the daughter was a son, for one day says he to me, "Little boy, what's that you're picking up?" Says I, awful meekly, "Pins."

Says he, "Let's see 'em." And he took 'em, and I took off my cap, all ready to go in the bank and become a partner, and marry his daughter. But I didn't get any invitation. He said, "Those pins belong to the bank, and if I catch you hanging around here any more, I'll set the dog on you!" Then I left, and the mean old cuss kept the pins. Such is life as I find it.

March 8, 1873

Foster's Case

To the Editor of the Tribune.

SIR: I have read the Foster petitions in Thursday's TRI-
BUNE. The lawyers' opinions do not disturb me, because I
know that those same gentlemen could make as able an argument in favor of Judas Iscariot, which is a great deal for me to
say, for I never can think of Judas Iscariot without losing my
temper. To my mind Judas Iscariot was nothing but a low,
mean, premature Congressman. The attitude of the jury does
not unsettle a body, I must admit; and it seems plain that they
would have modified their verdict to murder in the second
degree if the Judge's charge had permitted it. But when I
come to the petitions of Foster's friends and find out Foster's
true character, the generous tears will flow — I cannot help it.
How easy it is to get a wrong impression of a man. I perceive
that from childhood up this one has been a sweet, docile
thing, full of pretty ways and gentle impulses, the charm of
the fireside, the admiration of society, the idol of the Sunday-
school. I recognize in him the divinest nature that has ever
glorified any mere human being. I perceive that the sentiment with which he regarded temperance was a thing that
amounted to frantic adoration. I freely confess that it was the
most natural thing in the world for such an organism as this
to get drunk and insult a stranger, and then beat his brains
out with a car-hook because he did not seem to admire it.
Such is Foster. And to think that we came so near losing him!
How do we know but that he is the Second Advent? And yet,
after all, if the jury had not been hampered in their choice of a
verdict I think I could consent to lose him.

The humorist who invented trial by jury played a colossal,
practical joke upon the world, but since we have the system
we ought to try to respect it. A thing which is not thoroughly
easy to do, when we reflect that by command of the law
a criminal juror must be an intellectual vacuum, attached
to a melting heart and perfectly macaronian bowels of
compassion.

I have had no experience in making laws or amending
them, but still I cannot understand why, when it takes twelve

men to inflict the death penalty upon a person, it should take any less than 12 more to undo their work. If I were a legislature, and had just been elected and had not had time to sell out, I would put the pardoning and commuting power into the hands of twelve able men instead of dumping so huge a burden upon the shoulders of one poor petition-persecuted individual.

Hartford, March 7, 1873.   MARK TWAIN.

March 10, 1873

License of the Press

Hartford Monday Evening Club

. . . It (the press) has scoffed at religion till it has made scoffing popular. It has defended official criminals, on party pretexts, until it has created a United States Senate whose members are incapable of determining what crime against law and the dignity of their own body *is*, they are so morally blind, and it has made light of dishonesty till we have as a result a Congress which contracts to work for a certain sum and then deliberately steals additional wages out of the public pocket and is pained and surprised that anybody should worry about a little thing like that.

I am putting all this odious state of things upon the newspaper, and I believe it belongs there—chiefly, at any rate. It is a free press—a press that is more than free—a press which is licensed to say any infamous thing it chooses about a private or a public man, or advocate any outrageous doctrine it pleases. It is tied in *no* way. The public opinion which *should* hold it in bounds it has itself degraded to its own level. There are laws to protect the freedom of the press's speech, but none that are worth anything to protect the people from the press. A libel suit simply brings the plaintiff before a vast newspaper court to be tried before the law tries him, and reviled and ridiculed without mercy. The touchy Charles Reade can sue English newspapers and get verdicts; he would soon change his tactics here; the papers (backed by a public well taught by themselves) would soon teach him that it is better to suffer any amount of misrepresentation than go into our courts with a libel suit and make himself the laughing stock of the community.

It seems to me that just in the ratio that our newspapers increase, our morals decay. The more newspapers the worse morals. Where we have one newspaper that does good, I think we have fifty that do harm. We *ought* to look upon the establishment of a newspaper of the average pattern in a virtuous village as a calamity.

The difference between the tone and conduct of newspapers to-day and those of thirty or forty years ago is *very* noteworthy and very sad—I mean the average newspaper (for they had bad ones then, too). In those days the average newspaper was the champion of right and morals, and it dealt conscientiously in the truth. It is not the case now. The other day a reputable New York daily had an editorial defending the salary steal and justifying it on the ground that Congressmen were not paid enough—as if that were an all-sufficient excuse for stealing. That editorial put the matter in a new and perfectly satisfactory light with many a leather-headed reader, without a doubt. It has become a sarcastic proverb that a thing must be true if you saw it in a newspaper. That is the opinion intelligent people have of that lying vehicle in a nutshell. But the trouble is that the stupid people—who constitute the grand overwhelming majority of this and all other nations—*do* believe and *are* moulded and convinced by what they get out of a newspaper, and there is where the harm lies.

Among us, the newspaper is a tremendous power. It can make or mar any man's reputation. It has perfect freedom to call the best man in the land a fraud and a thief, and he is destroyed beyond help. Whether Mr. Colfax is a liar or not can never be ascertained now—but he will rank as one till the day of his death—for the newspapers have so doomed him. Our newspapers—*all* of them, without exception—glorify the "Black Crook" and make it an opulent success—they could have killed it dead with one broadside of contemptuous silence if they had wanted to. *Days Doings* and *Police Gazettes* flourish in the land unmolested by the law, because the *virtuous* newspapers long ago nurtured up a public laxity that loves indecency and never cares whether laws are administered or not.

In the newspapers of the West you can use the *editorial voice* in the editorial columns to defend any wretched and injurious dogma you please by paying a dollar a line for it.

Nearly all newspapers foster Rozensweigs and kindred criminals and send victims to them by opening their columns to their advertisements. You all know that.

In the Foster murder case the New York papers made a weak pretense of upholding the hands of the Governor and urging the people to sustain him in standing firmly by the law; but they printed a whole page of sickly, maudlin appeals to his clemency as a paid advertisement. And I suppose they would have published enough pages of abuse of the Governor to destroy his efficiency as a public official to the end of his term if anybody had come forward and paid them for it—as an advertisement. The newspaper that obstructs the law on a trivial pretext, for money's sake, is a dangerous enemy to the public weal.

That awful power, the public opinion of a nation, is created in America by a horde of ignorant, self-complacent simpletons who failed at ditching and shoemaking and fetched up in journalism on their way to the poorhouse. I am personally acquainted with hundreds of journalists, and the opinion of the majority of them would not be worth tuppence in private, but when they speak in print it is the *newspaper* that is talking (the pygmy scribe is not visible) and *then* their utterances shake the community like the thunders of prophecy.

I know from personal experience the proneness of journalists to lie. I once started a peculiar and picturesque fashion of lying myself on the Pacific coast, and it is not dead there to this day. Whenever I hear of a shower of blood and frogs combined, in California, or a sea serpent found in some desert, there, or a cave frescoed with diamonds and emeralds (*always* found by an Injun who died before he could finish telling where it was), I say to myself I am the father of this child—I have got to answer for this lie. And habit is everything—to this day I am liable to lie if I don't watch all the time.

The license of the press has scorched every individual of us in our time, I make no doubt. Poor Stanley was a very god, in England, his praises in every man's mouth. But nobody said anything about his lectures—they were charitably quiet on that head, and were content to praise his higher virtues. But our papers tore the poor creature limb from limb and scattered the fragments from Maine to California—merely because he couldn't lecture well. His prodigious achievement in Africa goes for naught—the man is pulled down and utterly destroyed—but *still* the persecution follows him as relentlessly from city to city and from village to village as if he had committed some bloody and detestable crime. Bret Harte was suddenly snatched out of obscurity by our papers and throned in the clouds—all the editors in the land stood out in the inclement weather and adored him through their telescopes and swung their hats till they wore them out and then borrowed more; and the first time his family fell sick, and in his trouble and harassment he ground out a rather flat article in place of another heathen Chinee, that hurrahing host said, "Why, this man's a fraud," and then they began to reach up there for him. And they got him, too, and fetched him down, and walked over him, and rolled him in the mud, and tarred and feathered him, and then set him up for a target and have been heaving dirt at him ever since. The result is that the man has had only just nineteen engagements to lecture this year, and the audience have been so scattering, too, that he has never discharged a sentence yet that hit two people at the same time. The man is ruined—never can get up again. And yet he is a person who has great capabilities, and might have accomplished great things for our literature and for himself if he had had a happier chance. And he made the mistake, too, of doing a pecuniary kindness for a starving beggar of our guild—one of the journalistic shoemaker class—and that beggar made it his business as soon as he got back to San Francisco to publish four columns of exposures of crimes committed by his benefactor, the least of which ought to make any decent man blush. The press that admitted that stuff to its columns had too much license.

In a town in Michigan I declined to dine with an editor who was drunk, and he said, in his paper, that my lecture was profane, indecent, and calculated to encourage intemperance. And yet that man never heard it. It might have reformed him if he had.

A Detroit paper once said that I was in the constant habit of beating my wife and that I still kept this recreation up, although I had crippled her for life and she was no longer able to keep out of my way when I came home in my usual frantic frame of mind. Now scarcely the half of that was true. Perhaps I ought to have sued that man for libel—but I knew better. All the papers in America—with a few creditable exceptions—would have found out then, to *their* satisfaction, that I was a wife beater, and they would have given it a pretty general airing, too.

Why *I* have published vicious libels upon people *myself*—and ought to have been hanged before my time for it, too—if I *do* say it myself, that shouldn't.

But I will not continue these remarks. I have a sort of vague general idea that there is too much liberty of the press in this country, and that through the absence of all wholesome restraint the newspaper has become in a large degree a national *curse*, and will probably damn the Republic yet.

There *are* some excellent virtues in newspapers, some powers that wield vast influences for good; and I could have told all about these things, and glorified them exhaustively—but that would have left you gentlemen nothing to say.

March 31, 1873

Fourth of July Speech in London

Meeting of Americans, London

Mr. Chairman and ladies and gentlemen: I thank you for the compliment which has just been tendered me, and to show my appreciation of it I will not afflict you with many words. It is pleasant to celebrate in this peaceful way, upon this old mother soil, the anniversary of an experiment which was born of war with this same land so long ago, and wrought out to a successful issue by the devotion of our ancestors. It has taken nearly a hundred years to bring the English and Americans into kindly and mutually appreciative relations, but I believe it has been accomplished at last. It was a great step when the two last misunderstandings were settled by arbitration instead of cannon. It is another great step when England adopts our sewing machines without claiming the invention—as usual. It was another when they imported one of our sleeping cars the other day. And it warmed my heart more than I can tell, yesterday, when I witnessed the spectacle of an Englishman ordering an American sherry cobbler of his own free will and accord—and not only that, but with a great brain and level head, reminding the barkeeper not to forget the strawberries. With a common origin, a common literature, a common religion and common drinks, what is longer needful to the cementing of the two nations together in a permanent bond of brotherhood?

This is an age of progress, and ours is a progressive land. A great and glorious land, too—a land which has developed a Washington, a Franklin, a William M. Tweed, a Longfellow, a Motley, a Jay Gould, a Samuel C. Pomeroy, a recent Congress which has never had its equal—(in some respects) and a United States Army which conquered sixty Indians in eight months by tiring them out—which is much better than uncivilized slaughter, God knows. We have a criminal jury system which is superior to any in the world; and its efficiency is only marred by the difficulty of finding twelve men every day who don't know anything and can't read. And I may observe that we have an insanity plea that would have saved Cain. I think I can say, and say with pride, that we have some legislatures that bring higher prices than any in the world.

I refer with effusion to our railway system, which consents to let us live, though it might do the opposite, being our owners. It only destroyed 3,070 lives last year by collisions, and 27,260 by running over heedless and unnecessary people at crossings. The companies seriously regretted the killing of these 30,000 people, and went so far as to pay for some of them—voluntarily, of course, for the meanest of us would not claim that we possess a court treacherous enough to enforce a law against a railway company. But thank heaven the railway companies are generally disposed to do the right and kindly thing without compulsion. I know of an instance which greatly touched me at the time. After an accident the company sent home the remains of a dear, distant old relative of mine in a basket, with the remark, "Please state what figure you hold him at—and return the basket." Now there couldn't be anything friendlier than that.

But I must not stand here and brag all night. However, you won't mind a body bragging a little about his country on the Fourth of July. It is a fair and legitimate time to fly the eagle. I will say only one more word of brag—and a hopeful one. It is this. We have a form of government which gives each man a fair chance and no favor. With us no individual is born with a right to look down upon his neighbor and hold him in contempt. Let such of us as are not dukes find our consolation in that. And we may find hope for the future in the fact that as unhappy as is the condition of our political morality today, England has risen up out of a far fouler since the days when Charles II ennobled courtesans and all political place was a matter of bargain and sale. Be sure there is hope for us yet.

Footnote. At least the above is the speech which I was *going* to make; but our minister, General Schenck, presided, and after the blessing, got up and made a great long inconceivably dull harangue, and wound up by saying that inasmuch as speech-making did not seem to exhilarate the guests much, all further oratory would be dispensed with, during the evening, and we could just sit and talk privately to our elbow-neighbors and have a good sociable time. It is known that in consequence of that remark forty-four perfected speeches died in the womb. The depression, the gloom, the solemnity that reigned over the banquet from that time forth will be a lasting memory with many that were there. By that one thoughtless remark General Schenck lost forty-four of the best friends he had in England. More than one said that night, "And this is the sort of person that is sent to represent us in a great sister empire!"

July 4, 1873

The Ladies

I am proud, indeed, of the distinction of being chosen to respond to this especial toast—to "The Ladies"—or to *Woman*, if you please, for that is the preferable term, perhaps; it is certainly the older, and therefore the more entitled to reverence. I have noticed and probably you may have noticed that the Bible, with that plain, blunt honesty which is such a conspicuous characteristic of the Scriptures, is always careful to never even refer to the illustrious mother of all mankind herself as a "lady," but speaks of her as a woman. It is odd but I think you will find that it is so. I am peculiarly proud of this honor, because I think that the toast to women is one which, by right and every rule of gallantry, should take precedence of all others—of the army, the navy, of even royalty itself perhaps, though the latter is not necessary in this day and in this land, for the reason that, tacitly, you do drink a broad general health to *all* good women when you drink the health of the Queen of England and the Princess of Wales.

I have in mind a poem, just now, which is familiar to you all, familiar to everybody. And what an inspiration that was (and how instantly the present toast recalls the verses to all our minds), where the most noble, the most gracious, the purest and sweetest of all poets says:

> Woman! O woman—er—
> Wom—

However, you remember the lines. And you remember *how* feelingly, how daintily, how almost imperceptibly the verses raise up before you, feature by feature, the ideal of a true and perfect woman; and how, as you contemplate the finished marvel, your homage grows into worship of the intellect that could create so fair a thing out of mere breath, mere words.

And you call to mind, now, as I speak, how the poet, with stern fidelity to the history of all humanity, delivers *this* beautiful child of his heart and his brain over to the trials and sorrows that must come to all, sooner or later, that abide in the earth; and how the pathetic story culminates in that

apostrophe—so wild, so regretful, so full of mournful retro-
spection. The lines run thus:

> Alas! Alas!—a—alas!
> Alas!—alas!—

and so on. I do not remember the rest. But taken altogether,
it seems to me that that poem is the noblest tribute to woman
that human genius has ever brought forth—and I feel that if I
were to talk hours I could not do my great theme completer
or more graceful justice than I have now done in simply quoting that poet's matchless words.

The phases of the womanly nature are infinite in their variety. Take any type of woman, and you shall find in it something to respect, something to admire, something to love.
And you shall find the whole world joining your heart and
hand. Who was more patriotic than Joan of Arc? Who was
braver? Who has given us a grander instance of self-sacrificing
devotion? Ah! you remember, you remember well, what a
throb of pain, what a great tidal wave of grief swept over us
all when Joan of Arc fell at Waterloo. Who does not sorrow
for the loss of Sappho, the sweet singer of Israel? Who among
us does not *miss* the gentle ministrations, the softening influence, the humble piety, of Lucretia Borgia?

Who can join in the heartless libel that says woman is extravagant in dress, when he can look back and call to mind
our simple and lowly Mother Eve arrayed in her modification
of the Highland costume?

Sir, women have been soldiers, women have been painters,
women have been poets. As long as language lives, the name
of Cleopatra will live. And not because she conquered George
III—but because she wrote those divine lines:

> Let dogs delight to bark and bite,
> For God hath made them so.

The story of the world is adorned with the names of illustrious ones of our own sex—some of them sons of St. Andrew, too—Scott, Bruce, Burns, the warrior Wallace, Ben
Nevis, the gifted Ben Lomond, and the great new Scotchman,
Ben Disraeli.

Out of the great plains of history tower whole mountain

ranges of sublime women—the Queen of Sheba, Josephine, Semiramis, Sairey Gamp; the list is endless. But I will not call the mighty roll—the names rise up in your own memories at the mere suggestion, luminous with the glory of deeds that cannot die, hallowed by the loving worship of the good and the true of all epochs and all climes.

Suffice it for our pride and our honor that we in our day have added to it such names as those of Grace Darling and Florence Nightingale.

Woman is all that she should be—gentle, patient, long-suffering, *trust*ful, unselfish, full of generous impulses. It is her blessed mission to comfort the sorrowing, plead for the erring, encourage the faint of purpose, succor the distressed, uplift the fallen, befriend the friendless—in a word, afford the healing of her sympathies and a home in her heart for all the bruised and persecuted children of misfortune that knock at its hospitable door. And when I say, God bless her, there is none here present who has known the ennobling affection of a wife, or the steadfast devotion of a mother but in his heart will say, Amen!

c. November 1873

Those Annual Bills

These annual bills! these annual bills!
How many a song their discord trills
Of "truck" consumed, enjoyed, forgot,
Since I was skinned by last years lot!

Those joyous beans are passed away;
Those onions blithe, O where are they!
Once loved, lost, mourned—*now* vexing ILLS
Your shades troop back in annual bills!

And so 'twill be when I'm aground—
These yearly duns will still go round,
While other bards, with frantic quills,
Shall damn and *damn* these annual bills!

January 7, 1874

The Temperance Insurrection

Hartford, U. S., March 12.
TO THE EDITOR.

SIR,—The women's crusade against the rumsellers continues. It began in an Ohio village early in the new year, and has
now extended itself eastwardly to the Atlantic seaboard, 600
miles, and westwardly (at a bound, without stopping by the
way), to San Francisco, about 2500 miles. It has also scattered
itself along down the Ohio and Mississippi rivers southwardly
some ten or twelve hundred miles. Indeed, it promises to
sweep, eventually, the whole United States, with the exception of the little cluster of commonwealths which we call New
England. Puritan New England is sedate, reflective, conserva-
tive, and very hard to inflame.

The method of the crusaders is singular. They contemn the
use of force in the breaking up of the whisky traffic. They
only assemble before a drinking shop, or within it, and sing
hymns and pray, hour after hour—and day after day, if necessary—until the publican's business is broken up and he surrenders. This is not force, at least they do not consider it so.
After the surrender the crusaders march back to head-quarters
and proclaim the victory, and ascribe it to the powers above.
They rejoice together awhile, and then go forth again in their
strength and conquer another whisky shop with their prayers
and hymns and their staying capacity (pardon the rudeness),
and spread *that* victory upon the battle-flag of the powers
above. In this generous way the crusaders have parted with
the credit of not less than three thousand splendid triumphs,
which some carping people say they gained their ownselves,
without assistance from any quarter. If I am one of these, I
am the humblest. If I seem to doubt that prayer is the agent
that conquers these rumsellers, I do it honestly, and not in a
flippant spirit. If the crusaders were to stay at home and pray
for the rumseller and for his adoption of a better way of life,
or if the crusaders even assembled together in a church and
offered up such a prayer with a united voice, and it accomplished a victory, I would then feel that it was the praying
that moved Heaven to do the miracle; for I believe that if the

prayer is the agent that brings about the desired result, it cannot be necessary to pray the prayer in any particular place in order to get the ear, or move the grace, of the Deity. When the crusaders go and invest a whisky shop and fall to praying, one suspects that they are praying rather less to the Deity than *at* the rum-man. So I cannot help feeling (after carefully reading the details of the rum sieges) that as much as nine-tenths of the credit of each of the 3000 victories achieved thus far belongs of right to the crusaders themselves, and it grieves me to see them give it away with such spendthrift generosity.

I will not afflict you with statistics, but I desire to say just a word or two about the character of this crusade. The crusaders are young girls and women—not the inferior sort, but the very best in the village communities. The telegraph keeps the newspapers supplied with the progress of the war, and thus the praying infection spreads from town to town, day after day, week after week. When it attacks a community it seems to seize upon almost everybody in it at once. There is a meeting in a church, speeches are made, resolutions are passed, a purse for expenses is made up, a "praying band" is appointed; if it be a large town, half a dozen praying bands, each numbering as many as a hundred women, are appointed, and the working district of each band marked out. Then comes a grand assault in force, all along the line. Every stronghold of rum is invested; first one and then another champion ranges up before the proprietor, and offers up a special petition for him; he has to stand meekly there behind his bar, under the eyes of a great concourse of ladies who are better than he is and are aware of it, and hear all the secret iniquities of his business divulged to the angels above, accompanied by the sharp sting of wishes for his regeneration, which imply an amount of need for it which is in the last degree uncomfortable to him. If he holds out bravely, the crusaders hold out more bravely still—or at least more persistently; though I doubt if the grandeur of the performance would not be considerably heightened if one solitary crusader were to try praying at a hundred rumsellers in a body for a while, and see how it felt to have everybody against her instead of for her. If the man holds out the crusaders camp before his place and keep up the siege till they wear him out. In one case they besieged a rum shop two whole weeks. They built a shed before it and kept up the praying all night and all day long every day of the fortnight, and this in the bitterest winter weather too. They conquered.

You may ask if such an investment and such interference with a man's business (in cases where he is "protected" by a licence) is lawful? By no means. But the whole community being with the crusaders, the authorities have usually been overawed and afraid to execute the laws, the authorities being, in too many cases, mere little politicians, and more given to looking to chances of re-election than fearlessly discharging their duty according to the terms of their official oaths.

Would you consider the conduct of these crusaders justifiable? I do—thoroughly justifiable. They find themselves voiceless in the making of laws and the election of officers to execute them. Born with brains, born in the country, educated, having large interests at stake, they find their tongues tied and their hands fettered, while every ignorant whisky-drinking foreign-born savage in the land may hold office, help to make the laws, degrade the dignity of the former and break the latter at his own sweet will. They see their fathers, husbands, and brothers sit inanely at home and allow the scum of the country to assemble at the "primaries," name the candidates for office from their own vile ranks, and, unrebuked, elect them. They live in the midst of a country where there is no end to the laws and no beginning to the execution of them. And when the laws intended to protect their sons from destruction by intemperance lie torpid and without sign of life year after year, they recognise that here is a matter which interests them personally—a matter which comes straight home to them. And since they are allowed to lift no legal voice against the outrageous state of things they suffer under in this regard, I think it is no wonder that their patience has broken down at last, and they have contrived to persuade themselves that they are justifiable in breaking the law of trespass when the laws that should make the trespass needless are allowed by the voters to lie dead and inoperative.

I cannot help glorying in the pluck of these women, sad as it is to see them displaying themselves in these unwomanly ways; sad as it is to see them carrying their grace and their purity into places which should never know their presence; and sadder still as it is to see them trying to save a set of men who, it seems to me, there can be no reasonable object in saving. It does not become us to scoff at the crusaders, remembering what it is they have borne all these years, but it does become us to admire their heroism—a heroism that boldly faces jeers, curses, ribald language, obloquy of every kind and degree—in a word, every manner of thing that pure-hearted, pure-minded women such as these are naturally dread and shrink from, and remains steadfast through it all, undismayed, patient, hopeful, giving no quarter, asking none, determined to conquer, and succeeding. It is the same old superb spirit that animated that other devoted, magnificent, mistaken crusade of six hundred years ago. The sons of such women as these must surely be worth saving from the destroying power of rum.

The present crusade will doubtless do but little work against intemperance that will be really permanent, but it will do what is as much, or even more, to the purpose, I think. I think it will suggest to more than one man that if women could vote they would vote on the side of morality, even if they did vote and speak rather frantically and furiously; and it will also suggest that when the women once made up their minds that it was not good to leave the all-powerful "primaries" in the hands of loafers, thieves, and pernicious little politicians, they would not sit indolently at home as their husbands and brothers do now, but would hoist their praying banners, take the field in force, pray the assembled political scum back to the holes and slums where they belong, and set up some candidates fit for decent human beings to vote for.

I dearly want the women to be raised to the political altitude of the negro, the imported savage, and the pardoned thief, and allowed to vote. It is our last chance, I think. The women will be voting before long, and then if a B. F. Butler can still continue to lord it in Congress; if the highest offices in the land can still continue to be occupied by perjurers and robbers; if another Congress (like the forty-second) consisting of 15 honest men and 296 of the other kind can once more be created, it will at last be time, I fear, to give over trying to save the country by human means, and appeal to Providence.

Both the great parties have failed. I wish we might have a woman's party now, and see how that would work. I feel persuaded that in extending the suffrage to women this country could lose absolutely nothing and might gain a great deal. For thirty centuries history has been iterating and reiterating that in a moral fight woman is simply dauntless, and we all know, even with our eyes shut upon Congress and our voters, that from the day that Adam ate of the apple and told on Eve down to the present day, man, in a moral fight, has pretty uniformly shown himself to be an arrant coward.

I will mention casually that while I cannot bring myself to find fault with the women whom we call the crusaders, since I feel that they, being politically fettered, have the natural right of the oppressed to rebel, I have a very different opinion about the clergymen who have in a multitude of instances attached themselves to the movement, and by voice and act have countenanced and upheld the women in unlawfully trespassing upon whisky mills and interrupting the rum-sellers' business. It seems to me that it would better become clergymen to teach their flocks to respect the laws of the land, and urge them to refrain from breaking them. But it is not a new thing for a thoroughly good and well-meaning preacher's soft heart to run away with his soft head.

MARK TWAIN

March 26, 1874

Rogers

This man Rogers happened upon me and introduced himself at the town of —— in the south of England, where I staid awhile. His stepfather had married a distant relative of mine who was afterwards hanged, and so he seemed to think a blood relationship existed between us. He came in every day and sat down and talked. Of all the bland, serene human curiosities I ever saw, I think he was the chiefest. He desired to look at my new chimney-pot hat. I was very willing, for I thought he would notice the name of the great Oxford street hatter in it and respect me accordingly. But he turned it about with a sort of grave compassion, pointed out two or three blemishes, and said that I, being so recently arrived, could not be expected to know where to supply myself. Said he would send me the address of *his* hatter. Then he said, "Pardon me," and proceeded to cut a neat circle of red tissue paper; daintily notched the edges of it; took the mucilage and pasted it in my hat so as to cover the manufacturer's name. He said, "No one will know now where you got it. I will send you a hat-tip of my hatter and you can paste it over this tissue circle." It was the calmest, coolest thing—I never admired a man so much in my life. Mind, he did this while his own hat sat offensively near our noses, on the table—an ancient extinguisher of the "slouch" pattern, limp and shapeless with age, discolored by vicissitudes of the weather, and banded by an equator of bear's grease that had stewed through.

Another time he examined my coat. I had no terrors, for over my tailor's door was the legend, "By Special Appointment Tailor to H. R. H. the Prince of Wales, &c." I did not know at the time that the most of the tailor shops had the same sign out, and that whereas it takes nine tailors to make an ordinary man, it takes a hundred and fifty to make a prince. He was full of compassion for my coat. Wrote down the address of his tailor for me. Did not tell me to mention my *nom de plume* and the tailor would put his best work on my garment, as complimentary people sometimes do, but said his tailor would hardly trouble himself for an unknown person (unknown person when I thought I was so celebrated in

England!—that was the cruelest cut) but cautioned me to mention *his* name, and it would be all right. Thinking to be facetious, I said,

"But he might sit up all night and injure his health."

"Well, *let* him," said Rogers; "I've done enough for him for him to show some appreciation of it."

I might just as well have tried to disconcert a mummy with my facetiousness. Said Rogers,

"I get all my coats there—they're the only coats fit to be seen in."

I made one more attempt. I said, "I wish you had brought one with you—I would like to look at it."

"Bless your heart, haven't I got one on?—*this* article is Morgan's make."

I examined it. The coat had been bought ready-made, of a Chatham street Jew, without any question—about 1848. It probably cost four dollars when it was new. It was ripped, it was frayed, it was napless and greasy. I could not resist showing him where it was ripped. It so affected him that I was almost sorry I had done it. First he seemed plunged into a bottomless abyss of grief. Then he roused himself, made a feint with his hands as if waving off the pity of a nation, and said—with what seemed to me a manufactured emotion— "No matter; no matter; don't mind me; do not bother about it. I can get another."

I prayed heaven he would *not* get another, like that.

When he was thoroughly restored, so that he could examine the rip and command his feelings, he said,—ah, *now* he understood it—his servant must have done it while dressing him that morning.

His servant! There was something awe-inspiring in effrontery like this.

Nearly every day he interested himself in some article of my clothing. One would hardly have expected this sort of infatuation in a man who always wore the same suit, and it a suit that seemed coeval with the Conquest.

It was an unworthy ambition, perhaps, but I *did* wish I could make this man admire *something* about me or something I did—you would have felt the same way. I saw my opportunity: I was about to return to London, and had

"listed" my soiled linen for the wash. It made quite an imposing mountain in the corner of the room—fifty-four pieces. I
hoped he would fancy it was the accumulation of a single
week. I took up the wash-list, as if to see that it was all right,
and then tossed it on the table, with pretended forgetfulness.
Sure enough, he took it up and ran his eye along down to the
grand total. Then he said, "You get off easy," and laid it
down again.

His gloves were the saddest ruin—but he told me where I
could get some like them. His shoes would hardly hold walnuts without leaking, but he liked to put his feet up on the
mantel piece and contemplate them. He wore a dim glass
breastpin, which he called a "morphylitic diamond"—whatever that may mean—and said only two of them had ever
been found—the Emperor of China had the other one.

Afterward in London, it was a pleasure to me to see this
fantastic vagabond come marching into the lobby of the hotel
in his grand-ducal way, for he always had some new imaginary grandeur to develop—there was nothing stale about him
but his clothes. If he addressed me when strangers were
about, he always raised his voice a little and called me "Sir
Richard" or "General," or "Your Lordship"—and when people began to stare and look deferential, he would fall to inquiring in a casual way why I disappointed the Duke of
Argyll the night before; and then remind me of our engagement at the Marquis of Westminster's for the following day. I
think that for the time being these things were realities to
him. He once came and invited me to go with him and spend
the evening with the Earl of Warwick at his town house. I
said I had received no formal invitation. He said that was of
no consequence—the Earl had no formalities for him or his
friends. I asked if I might go just as I was. He said no, that
would hardly do—evening dress was requisite at night in any
gentleman's house. He said he would wait while I dressed and
then we would go to his apartments and I could take a bottle
of champagne and a cigar while he dressed. I was very willing
to see how this enterprise would turn out, so I dressed, and
we started to his lodgings. He said if I didn't mind we would
walk. So we tramped some four miles through the mud and
fog, and finally found his "apartments," and they consisted of

a single room over a barber's shop in a back street. Two chairs, a small table, an ancient valise, a wash-basin and pitcher (both on the floor in a corner) an unmade bed, a fragment of a looking-glass, and a flower-pot with a perishing little rose geranium in it (which he called a century plant, and said it had not bloomed now for upwards of two centuries— given to him by the late Lord Palmerston—been offered a prodigious sum for it)—these were the contents of the room. Also a brass candlestick and part of a candle. Rogers lit the candle, and told me to sit down and make myself at home. He said he hoped I was thirsty, because he would surprise my palate with an article of champagne that seldom got into a commoner's system—or would I prefer sherry, or port? Said he had port in bottles that were swathed in stratified cobwebs, every stratum representing a generation. And as for his cigars—well, I should judge of them myself. Then he put his head out at the door and called—

"Sackville!" No answer.

"Hi!—Sackville!" No answer.

"Now what the devil can have become of that butler? I *never* allow a servant to—Oh, confound that idiot, he's got the *keys*. Can't get into the other rooms without the keys."

(I was just wondering at his intrepidity in still keeping up the delusion of the champagne, and trying to imagine how he was going to get out of the difficulty.)

Now he stopped calling Sackville and began to call "Anglesy." But Anglesy didn't come. He said "This is the *second* time that equerry has been absent without leave. To-morrow I'll discharge him."

Now he began to whoop for "Thomas," but Thomas didn't answer. Then for "Theodore," but no Theodore replied.

"Well, I give it up," said Rogers. "The servants never expect me at this hour, and so they're all off on a lark. Might get along without the equerry and the page, but can't have any wine or cigars without the butler, and can't dress without my valet."

I offered to help him dress, but he would not hear of it— and besides, he said he would not feel comfortable unless dressed by a practised hand. However, he finally concluded that he was such old friends with the Earl that it would not make any difference how he was dressed. So we took a cab, he gave the driver some directions and we started. By-and-by we stopped before a large house and got out. I never had seen this man with a collar on. He now stepped under a lamp and got a venerable paper collar out of his coat pocket, along with a hoary cravat, and put them on. He ascended the stoop, rang and entered the door. Presently he re-appeared, descended rapidly, and said,

"Come—quick!"

We hurried away, and turned the corner.

"Now we're safe," he said—and took off his collar and cravat and returned them to his pocket.

"Made a mighty narrow escape," said he.

"How?" said I.

"B' George, the Countess was there!"

"Well, what of that—don't she know you?"

"Know me? Absolutely worships me. I just did happen to catch a glimpse of her before she saw me—and out I shot. Haven't seen her for two months—to rush in on her without any warning might have been fatal. She could *not* have stood it. I didn't know *she* was in town—thought she was at the castle. Let me lean on you—just a moment—there, now I am better—thank you; thank you ever so much. Lord bless me, what an escape!"

So I never got to call on the Earl, after all. But I marked his house for future reference. It proved to be an ordinary family hotel, with about a thousand plebeians roosting in it.

In most things Rogers was by no means a fool. In some things it was plain enough that he was a fool, but he certainly did not know it. He was in the "deadest" earnest in these matters. He died at sea, last summer, as the "Earl of Ramsgate."

1874

A Curious Pleasure Excursion

[We have received the following advertisement, but, inasmuch as it concerns a matter of deep and general interest, we feel fully justified in inserting it in our reading columns. We are confident that our conduct in this regard needs only explanation, not apology.—ED. HERALD.]

Advertisement.

This is to inform the public that in connection with Mr. Barnum I have leased the comet for a term of years; and I desire also to solicit the public patronage in favor of a beneficial enterprise which we have in view.

We propose to fit up comfortable, and even luxurious, accommodations in the comet for as many persons as will honor us with their patronage, and make an extended excursion among the heavenly bodies. We shall prepare 1,000,000 state rooms in the tail of the comet (with hot and cold water, gas, looking glass, parachute, umbrella, &c., in each), and shall construct more if we meet with a sufficiently generous encouragement. We shall have billiard rooms, card rooms, music rooms, bowling alleys and many spacious theatres and free libraries; and on the main deck we propose to have a driving park, with upwards of 10,000 miles of roadway in it. We shall publish daily newspapers also.

DEPARTURE OF THE COMET.

The comet will leave New York at ten P. M. on the 20th inst., and therefore it will be desirable that the passengers be on board by eight at the latest, to avoid confusion in getting under way. It is not known whether passports will be necessary or not, but it is deemed best that passengers provide them, and so guard against all contingencies. No dogs will be allowed on board. This rule has been made in deference to the existing state of feeling regarding these animals and will be strictly adhered to. The safety of the passengers will in all ways be jealously looked to. A substantial iron railing will be put all around the comet, and no one will be allowed to go to the edge and look over unless accompanied by either my partner or myself.

THE POSTAL SERVICE

will be of the completest character. Of course the telegraph, and the telegraph only, will be employed, consequently, friends occupying staterooms, 20,000,000 and even
30,000,000 miles apart, will be able to send a message and
receive a reply inside of eleven days. Night messages will be
half rate. The whole of this vast postal system will be under
the personal superintendence of Mr. Hale, of Maine. Meals
served at all hours. Meals served in staterooms charged extra.

Hostility is not apprehended from any great planet, but we
have thought it best to err on the safe side, and therefore have
provided a proper number of mortars, siege guns and boarding pikes. History shows that small, isolated communities,
such as the people of remote islands, are prone to be hostile
to strangers, and so the same may be the case with

THE INHABITANTS OF STARS

of the tenth or twentieth magnitude. We shall in no case
wantonly offend the people of any star, but shall treat all alike
with urbanity and kindliness, never conducting ourselves toward an asteroid after a fashion which we could not venture
to assume toward Jupiter or Saturn. I repeat that we shall not
wantonly offend any star; but at the same time we shall
promptly resent any injury that may be done us, or any insolence offered us, by parties or governments residing in any
star in the firmament. Although averse to the shedding of
blood, we shall still hold this course rigidly and fearlessly, not
only toward single stars, but toward constellations. We shall
hope to leave a good impression of America behind us in
every nation we visit, from Venus to Uranus. And, at all
events, if we cannot inspire love we shall, at least, compel
respect for our country wherever we go. We shall take with
us, free of charge,

A GREAT FORCE OF MISSIONARIES

and shed the true light upon all the celestial orbs which, physically aglow, are yet morally in darkness. Sunday schools will
be established wherever practicable. Compulsory education
will also be introduced.

The comet will visit Mars first and then proceed to Mercury, Jupiter, Venus and Saturn. Parties connected with the
government of the District of Columbia and with the former

city government of New York, who may desire to inspect the rings, will be allowed time and every facility. Every star of prominent magnitude will be visited, and time allowed for excursions to points of interest inland.

THE DOG STAR

has been stricken from the programme. Much time will be spent in the Great Bear, and, indeed, of every constellation of importance. So, also, with the Sun and Moon and the Milky Way, otherwise the Gulf Stream of the skies. Clothing suitable for wear in the sun should be provided. Our programme has been so arranged that we shall seldom go more than 100,000,000 of miles at a time without stopping at some star. This will necessarily make the stoppages frequent and preserve the interest of the tourist. Baggage checked through to any point on the route. Parties desiring to make only a part of the proposed tour, and thus save expense, may stop over at any star they choose and wait for the return voyage.

After visiting all the most celebrated stars and constellations in our system and personally inspecting the remotest sparks that even the most powerful telescopes can now detect in the firmament, we shall proceed with good heart upon

A STUPENDOUS VOYAGE

of discovery among the countless whirling worlds that make turmoil in the mighty wastes of space that stretch their solemn solitudes, their unimaginable vastness billions upon billions of miles away beyond the farthest verge of telescopic vision, till by comparison the little sparkling vault we used to gaze at on Earth shall seem like a remembered phosphorescent flash of spangles which some tropical voyager's prow stirred into life for a single instant, and which ten thousand miles of phosphorescent seas and tedious lapse of time had since diminished to an incident utterly trivial in his recollection. Children occupying seats at the first table will be charged full fare.

FIRST CLASS FARE

from the Earth to Uranus, including visits to the Sun and Moon and all principal planets on the route, will be charged at the low rate of $2 for every 50,000,000 miles of actual travel. A great reduction will be made where parties wish to make the round trip. This comet is new and in thorough repair and is now on her first voyage. She is confessedly the fastest on the line. She makes 20,000,000 miles a day, with her present facilities; but, with a picked American crew and good weather, we are confident we can get 40,000,000 out of her. Still we shall never push her to a dangerous speed, and we shall rigidly prohibit racing with other comets. Passengers desiring to diverge at any point or return will be transferred to other comets. We make close connections at all principal points with all reliable lines. Safety can be depended upon. It is not to be denied that the heavens are infested with

OLD RAMSHACKLE COMETS

that have not been inspected or overhauled in 10,000 years, and which ought long ago to have been destroyed or turned into hail barges, but with these we have no connection whatever. Steerage passengers not allowed abaft the main hatch.

Complimentary round trip tickets have been tendered to General Butler, Mr. Shepherd, Mr. Richardson and other eminent gentlemen, whose public services have entitled them to the rest and relaxation of a voyage of this kind. Parties desiring to make the round trip will have extra accommodation. The entire voyage will be completed, and the passengers landed in New York again on the 14th of December, 1991. This is, at least, forty years quicker than any other comet can do it in. Nearly all the back pay members contemplate making the round trip with us in case their constituents will allow them a holiday. Every harmless amusement will be allowed on board, but no pools permitted on the run of the comet—no gambling of any kind. All fixed stars will be respected by us, but such stars as seem to need fixing we shall fix. If it makes trouble we shall be sorry, but firm.

Mr. Coggia having leased his comet to us, she will no longer be called by his name but by my partner's. N. B.— Passengers by paying double fare will be entitled to a share in all the new stars, suns, moons, comets, meteors and magazines of thunder and lightning we shall discover. Patent medicine people will take notice that

WE CARRY BULLETIN BOARDS

and a paint brush along for use in the constellations, and are open to terms. Cremationists are reminded that we are going straight to—some hot places—and are open to terms. To other parties our enterprise is a pleasure excursion, but individually we mean business. We shall fly our comet for all it is worth.

FOR FURTHER PARTICULARS,

or for freight or passage, apply on board, or to my partner, but not to me, since I do not take charge of the comet until she is under weigh. It is necessary, at a time like this, that my mind should not be burdened with small business details.

July 6, 1874

A True Story, Repeated Word for Word
as I Heard It

It was summer time, and twilight. We were sitting on the porch of the farm-house, on the summit of the hill, and "Aunt Rachel" was sitting respectfully below our level, on the steps,—for she was our servant, and colored. She was of mighty frame and stature; she was sixty years old, but her eye was undimmed and her strength unabated. She was a cheerful, hearty soul, and it was no more trouble for her to laugh than it is for a bird to sing. She was under fire, now, as usual when the day was done. That is to say, she was being chaffed without mercy, and was enjoying it. She would let off peal after peal of laughter, and then sit with her face in her hands and shake with throes of enjoyment which she could no longer get breath enough to express. At such a moment as this a thought occurred to me, and I said:—

"Aunt Rachel, how is it that you've lived sixty years and never had any trouble?"

She stopped quaking. She paused, and there was a moment of silence. She turned her face over her shoulder toward me, and said, without even a smile in her voice:—

"Misto C——, is you in 'arnest?"

It surprised me a good deal; and it sobered my manner and my speech, too. I said:—

"Why, I thought—that is, I meant—why, you *can't* have had any trouble. I've never heard you sigh, and never seen your eye when there wasn't a laugh in it."

She faced fairly around, now, and was full of earnestness.

"Has I had any trouble? Misto C——, I's gwyne to tell you, den I leave it to you. I was bawn down 'mongst de slaves; I knows all 'bout slavery, 'case I ben one of 'em my own se'f. Well, sah, my ole man—dat's my husban'—he was lovin' an' kind to me, jist as kind as you is to yo' own wife. An' we had chil'en—seven chil'en—an' we loved dem chil'en jist de same as you loves yo' chil'en. Dey was black, but de Lord can't make no chil'en so black but what dey mother loves 'em an' wouldn't give 'em up, no, not for anything dat's in dis whole world.

"Well, sah, I was raised in ole Fo'ginny, but my mother she was raised in Maryland; an' my *souls!* she was turrible when she'd git started! My *lan'!* but she'd make de fur fly! When she'd git into dem tantrums, she always had one word dat she said. She'd straighten herse'f up an' put her fists in her hips an' say, 'I want you to understan' dat I wa'n't bawn in de mash to be fool' by trash! I's one o' de ole Blue Hen's Chickens, *I* is!' 'Ca'se, you see, dat's what folks dat's bawn in Maryland calls deyselves, an' dey's proud of it. Well, dat was her word. I don't ever forgit it, beca'se she said it so much, an' beca'se she said it one day when my little Henry tore his wris' awful, an' most busted his head, right up at de top of his forehead, an' de niggers did n't fly aroun' fas' enough to 'tend to him. An' when dey talk' back at her, she up an' she says, 'Look-a-heah!' she says, 'I want you niggers to understan' dat I wa'n't bawn in de mash to be fool' by trash! I's one o' de ole Blue Hen's Chickens, *I* is!' an' den she clar' dat kitchen an' bandage' up de chile herse'f. So I says dat word, too, when I's riled.

"Well, bymeby my ole mistis say she's broke, an' she got to sell all de niggers on de place. An' when I heah dat dey gwyne to sell us all off at oction in Richmon', oh de good gracious! I know what dat mean!"

Aunt Rachel had gradually risen, while she warmed to her subject, and now she towered above us, black against the stars.

"Dey put chains on us an' put us on a stan' as high as dis po'ch,—twenty foot high,—an' all de people stood aroun', crowds an' crowds. An' dey'd come up dah an' look at us all roun', an' squeeze our arm, an' make us git up an' walk, an' den say, 'Dis one too ole,' or 'Dis one lame,' or 'Dis one don't 'mount to much.' An' dey sole my ole man, an' took him away, an' dey begin to sell my chil'en an' take *dem* away, an' I begin to cry; an' de man say, 'Shet up yo' dam blubberin',' an' hit me on de mouf wid his han'. An' when de las' one was gone but my little Henry, I grab' *him* clost up to my breas' so, an' I ris up an' says, 'You shan't take him away,' I says; 'I'll kill de man dat tetches him!' I says. But my little Henry whisper an' say, 'I gwyne to run away, an' den I work an' buy yo' freedom.' Oh, bless de chile, he always so good! But dey got him—dey got him, de men did; but I took and tear de clo'es mos' off of 'em, an' beat 'em over de head wid my chain; an' *dey* give it to *me*, too, but I did n't mine dat.

"Well, dah was my ole man gone, an' all my chil'en, all my seven chil'en—an' six of 'em I hain't set eyes on ag'in to dis day, an' dat 's twenty-two year ago las' Easter. De man dat bought me b'long' in Newbern, an' he took me dah. Well, bymeby de years roll on an' de waw come. My marster he was a Confedrit colonel, an' I was his family's cook. So when de Unions took dat town, dey all run away an' lef' me all by myse'f wid de other niggers in dat mons'us big house. So de big Union officers move in dah, an' dey ask me would I cook for *dem*. 'Lord bless you,' says I, 'dat 's what I 's *for*.'

"Dey wa' n't no small-fry officers, mine you, dey was de biggest dey *is*; an' de way dey made dem sojers mosey roun'! De Gen'l he tole me to boss dat kitchen; an' he say, 'If anybody come meddlin' wid you, you jist make 'em walk chalk; don't you be afeard,' he say; 'you 's 'mong frens, now.'

"Well, I thinks to myse'f, if my little Henry ever got a chance to run away, he 'd make to de Norf, o' course. So one day I comes in dah whah de big officers was, in de parlor, an' I drops a kurtchy, so, an' I up an' tole 'em 'bout my Henry, dey a-listenin' to my troubles jist de same as if I was white folks; an' I says, 'What I come for is beca'se if he got away and got up Norf whah you gemmen comes from, you might 'a' seen him, maybe, an' could tell me so as I could fine him ag'in; he was very little, an' he had a sk-yar on his lef' wris', an' at de top of his forehead.' Den dey look mournful, an' de Gen'l say, 'How long sence you los' him?' an' I say, 'Thirteen year.' Den de Gen'l say, 'He would n't be little no mo', now—he 's a man!'

"I never thought o' dat befo'! He was only dat little feller to *me*, yit. I never thought 'bout him growin' up an' bein' big. But I see it den. None o' de gemmen had run acrost him, so dey could n't do nothin' for me. But all dat time, do' *I* did n't know it, my Henry *was* run off to de Norf, years an' years, an' he was a barber, too, an' worked for hisse'f. An' bymeby, when de waw come, he ups an' he says, 'I 's done barberin',' he says; 'I 's gwyne to fine my ole mammy, less'n she 's dead.' So he sole out an' went to whah dey was recruitin', an' hired hisse'f out to de colonel for his servant; an' den he went all froo de battles everywhah, huntin' for his ole mammy; yes indeedy, he'd hire to fust one officer an' den another, tell he'd ransacked de whole Souf; but you see *I* did n't know nuffin 'bout *dis.* How was *I* gwyne to know it?

"Well, one night we had a big sojer ball; de sojers dah at Newbern was always havin' balls an' carryin' on. Dey had 'em in my kitchen, heaps o' times, 'ca'se it was so big. Mine you, I was *down* on sich doin's; beca'se my place was wid de officers, an' it rasp' me to have dem common sojers cavortin' roun' my kitchen like dat. But I alway' stood aroun' an' kep' things straight, I did; an' sometimes dey'd git my dander up, an' den I'd make 'em clar dat kitchen, mine I *tell* you!

"Well, one night—it was a Friday night—dey comes a whole plattoon f'm a *nigger* ridgment dat was on guard at de house,—de house was head-quarters, you know,—an' den I was jist a-*bilin'!* Mad? I was jist a-*boomin'!* I swelled aroun', an' swelled aroun'; I jist was a-itchin' for 'em to do somefin for to start me. *An'* dey was a-waltzin' an a-dancin'! *my!* but dey was havin' a time! an' I jist a-swellin' an' a-swellin' up! Pooty soon, 'long comes *sich* a spruce young nigger a-sailin' down de room wid a yaller wench roun' de wais'; an' roun' an' roun' an' roun' dey went, enough to make a body drunk to look at 'em; an' when dey got abreas' o' me, dey went to kin' o' balancin' aroun', fust on one leg an' den on t'other, an' smilin' at my big red turban, an' makin' fun, an' I ups an' says, '*Git* along wid you!—rubbage!' De young man's face kin' o' changed, all of a sudden, for 'bout a second, but den he went to smilin' ag'in, same as he was befo'. Well, 'bout dis time, in comes some niggers dat played music an' b'long' to de ban', an' dey *never* could git along widout puttin' on airs. An' de very fust air dey put on dat night, I lit into 'em! Dey laughed, an' dat made me wuss. De res' o' de niggers got to laughin', an' den my soul *alive* but I was hot! My eye was jist a-blazin'! I jist straightened myself up, so,—jist as I is now, plum to de ceilin', mos',—an' I digs my fists into my hips, an' I says, 'Look-a-heah!' I says, 'I want you niggers to understan' dat I wa'n't bawn in de mash to be fool' by trash! I's one o' de ole Blue Hen's Chickens, *I* is!' an' den I see dat young man stan' a-starin' an' stiff, lookin' kin' o' up at de ceilin' like he fo'got somefin, an' could n't 'member it no mo'. Well, I jist march' on dem niggers,—so, lookin' like a gen'l,—an' dey jist cave' away befo' me an' out at de do'. An' as dis young man was a-goin' out, I heah him say to another nigger, 'Jim,' he says, 'you go 'long an' tell de cap'n I be on han' 'bout eight o'clock in de mawnin'; dey's somefin on my mine,' he says; 'I don't sleep no mo' dis night. You go 'long,' he says, 'an' leave me by my own se'f.'

"Dis was 'bout one o'clock in de mawnin'. Well, 'bout seven, I was up an' on han', gittin' de officers' breakfast. I was a-stoopin' down by de stove,—jist so, same as if yo' foot was de stove,—an' I'd opened de stove do' wid my right han',—so, pushin' it back, jist as I pushes yo' foot,—an' I'd jist got de pan o' hot biscuits in my han' an' was 'bout to raise up, when I see a black face come aroun' under mine, an' de eyes a-lookin' up into mine, jist as I's a-lookin' up clost under yo' face now; an' I jist stopped *right dah*, an' never budged! jist gazed, an' gazed, so; an' de pan begin to tremble, an' all of a sudden I *knowed!* De pan drop' on de flo' an' I grab his lef' han' an' shove back his sleeve,—jist so, as I's doin' to you,— an' den I goes for his forehead an' push de hair back, so, an' 'Boy!' I says, 'if you an't my Henry, what is you doin' wid dis welt on yo' wris' an' dat sk-yar on yo' forehead? De Lord God ob heaven be praise', I got my own ag'in!'

"Oh, no, Misto C——, *I* hain't had no trouble. An' no *joy!*"

November 1874

An Encounter with an Interviewer

The nervous, dapper, "peart" young man took the chair I offered him, and said he was connected with the *Daily Thunderstorm*, and added,—

"Hoping it's no harm, I've come to interview you."

"Come to what?"

"*Interview* you."

"Ah! I see. Yes,—yes. Um! Yes,—yes."

I was not feeling bright that morning. Indeed, my powers seemed a bit under a cloud. However, I went to the bookcase, and when I had been looking six or seven minutes, I found I was obliged to refer to the young man. I said,—

"How do you spell it?"

"Spell what?"

"Interview."

"O my goodness! What do you want to spell it for?"

"I don't want to spell it; I want to see what it means."

"Well, this is astonishing, I must say. *I* can tell you what it means, if you—if you—"

"O, all right! That will answer, and much obliged to you, too."

"I n, *in*, t e r, *ter*, *in*ter—"

"Then you spell it with an *I*?"

"Why, certainly!"

"O, that is what took me so long."

"Why, my *dear* sir, what did *you* propose to spell it with?"

"Well, I—I—I hardly know. I had the Unabridged, and I was ciphering around in the back end, hoping I might tree her among the pictures. But it's a very old edition."

"Why, my friend, they wouldn't have a *picture* of it in even the latest e— My dear sir, I beg your pardon, I mean no harm in the world, but you do not look as—as—intelligent as I had expected you would. No harm,—I mean no harm at all."

"O, don't mention it! It has often been said, and by people who would not flatter and who could have no inducement to flatter, that I am quite remarkable in that way. Yes,—yes; they always speak of it with rapture."

"I can easily imagine it. But about this interview. You know it is the custom, now, to interview any man who has become notorious."

"Indeed! I had not heard of it before. It must be very interesting. What do you do it with?"

"Ah, well,—well,—well,—this is disheartening. It *ought* to be done with a club in some cases; but customarily it consists in the interviewer asking questions and the interviewed answering them. It is all the rage now. Will you let me ask you certain questions calculated to bring out the salient points of your public and private history?"

"O, with pleasure,—with pleasure. I have a very bad memory, but I hope you will not mind that. That is to say, it is an irregular memory,—singularly irregular. Sometimes it goes in a gallop, and then again it will be as much as a fortnight passing a given point. This is a great grief to me."

"O, it is no matter, so you will try to do the best you can."

"I will. I will put my whole mind on it."

"Thanks. Are you ready to begin?"

"Ready."

Q. How old are you?

A. Nineteen, in June.

Q. Indeed! I would have taken you to be thirty-five or six. Where were you born?

A. In Missouri.

Q. When did you begin to write?

A. In 1836.

Q. Why, how could that be, if you are only nineteen now?

A. I don't know. It does seem curious, somehow.

Q. It does, indeed. Who do you consider the most remarkable man you ever met?

A. Aaron Burr.

Q. But you never could have met Aaron Burr, if you are only nineteen years—

A. Now, if you know more about me than I do, what do you ask me for?

Q. Well, it was only a suggestion; nothing more. How did you happen to meet Burr?

A. Well, I happened to be at his funeral one day, and he asked me to make less noise, and—

Q. But, good heavens! If you were at his funeral, he must have been dead; and if he was dead, how could he care whether you made a noise or not?

A. I don't know. He was always a particular kind of a man that way.

Q. Still, I don't understand it at all. You say he spoke to you and that he was dead.

A. I did n't say he was dead.

Q. But was n't he dead?

A. Well, some said he was, some said he was n't.

Q. What did you think?

A. O, it was none of my business! It was n't any of my funeral.

Q. Did you— However, we can never get this matter straight. Let me ask about something else. What was the date of your birth?

A. Monday, October 31, 1693.

Q. What! Impossible! That would make you a hundred and eighty years old. How do you account for that?

A. I don't account for it at all.

Q. But you said at first you were only nineteen, and now you make yourself out to be one hundred and eighty. It is an awful discrepancy.

A. Why, have you noticed that? (*Shaking hands.*) Many a time it has seemed to me like a discrepancy, but somehow I could n't make up my mind. How quick you notice a thing!

Q. Thank you for the compliment, as far as it goes. Had you, or have you, any brothers or sisters?

A. Eh! I—I—I think so,—yes,—but I don't remember.

Q. Well, that is the most extraordinary statement I ever heard!

A. Why, what makes you think that?

Q. How could I think otherwise? Why, look here! who is this a picture of on the wall? Is n't that a brother of yours?

A. Oh! yes, yes, yes! Now you remind me of it, that *was* a brother of mine. That's William,—*Bill* we called him. Poor old Bill!

Q. Why? Is he dead, then?

A. Ah, well, I suppose so. We never could tell. There was a great mystery about it.

Q. That is sad, very sad. He disappeared, then?

A. Well, yes, in a sort of general way. We buried him.

Q. Buried him! *Buried* him without knowing whether he was dead or not?

A. O no! Not that. He was dead enough.

Q. Well, I confess that I can't understand this. If you buried him and you knew he was dead—

A. No! no! we only thought he was.

Q. O, I see! He came to life again?

A. I bet he did n't.

Q. Well, I never heard anything like this. *Somebody* was dead. *Somebody* was buried. Now, where was the mystery?

A. Ah, that 's just it! That 's it exactly. You see we were twins,—defunct and I,—and we got mixed in the bath-tub when we were only two weeks old, and one of us was drowned. But we did n't know which. Some think it was Bill, some think it was me.

Q. Well, that *is* remarkable. What do *you* think?

A. Goodness knows! I would give whole worlds to know. This solemn, this awful mystery has cast a gloom over my whole life. But I will tell you a secret now, which I never have revealed to any creature before. One of us had a peculiar mark, a large mole on the back of his left hand,—that was *me. That child was the one that was drowned.*

Q. Very well, then, I don't see that there is any mystery about it, after all.

A. You don't? Well, *I* do. Anyway I don't see how they could ever have been such a blundering lot as to go and bury the wrong child. But, 'sh!—don't mention it where the family can hear of it. Heaven knows they have heart-breaking troubles enough without adding this.

Q. Well, I believe I have got material enough for the present, and I am very much obliged to you for the pains you have taken. But I was a good deal interested in that account of Aaron Burr's funeral. Would you mind telling me what particular circumstance it was that made you think Burr was such a remarkable man?

A. O, it was a mere trifle! Not one man in fifty would have noticed it at all. When the sermon was over, and the procession all ready to start for the cemetery, and the body all arranged nice in the hearse, he said he wanted to take a last look at the scenery, and so he *got up and rode with the driver.*

Then the young man reverently withdrew. He was very pleasant company, and I was sorry to see him go.

1874

The "Jumping Frog"

IN ENGLISH. THEN IN FRENCH. THEN CLAWED
BACK INTO A CIVILIZED LANGUAGE ONCE MORE,
BY PATIENT, UNREMUNERATED TOIL.

HARTFORD, March, 1875.

Even a criminal is entitled to fair play; and certainly when a
man who has done no harm has been unjustly treated, he is
privileged to do his best to right himself. My attention has
just been called to an article some three years old in a French
magazine entitled "Revue des Deux Mondes" (Review of
Some Two Worlds), wherein the writer treats of "Les Humo-
ristes Americaines" (These Humorists Americans). I am one
of these humorists Americans dissected by him, and hence the
complaint I am now making.

This gentleman's article is an able one (as articles go, in the
French, where they always tangle up everything to that degree
that when you start into a sentence you never know whether
you are going to come out alive or not.) It is a very good
article, and the writer says all manner of kind and complimentary things about me—for which I am sure I thank him with
all my heart; but then why should he go and spoil all his
praise by one unlucky experiment? What I refer to is this: he
says my Jumping Frog is a funny story, but still he can't see
why it should ever really convulse anyone with laughter—and
straightway proceeds to translate it into French in order to
prove to his nation that there is nothing so very extravagantly
funny about it. Just there is where my complaint originates.
He has not translated it at all; he has simply mixed it all up; it
is no more like the Jumping Frog when he gets through with
it than I am like a meridian of longitude. But my mere assertion is not proof; wherefore I print the French version, that
all may see that I do not speak falsely; furthermore, in order
that even the unlettered may know my injury and give me
their compassion, I have been at infinite pains and trouble to
re-translate this French version back into English; and to tell
the truth I have well nigh worn myself out at it, having
scarcely rested from my work during five days and nights. I

cannot speak the French language, but I can translate very well, though not fast, I being self-educated. I ask the reader to run his eye over the original English version of the Jumping Frog, and then read the French or my re-translation, and kindly take notice how the Frenchman has riddled the grammar. I think it is the worst I ever saw; and yet the French are called a polished nation. If I had a boy that put sentences together as they do, I would polish him to some purpose. Without further introduction, the Jumping Frog, as I originally wrote it, was as follows—[after it will be found the French version, and after the latter my re-translation from the French]:

THE NOTORIOUS JUMPING FROG OF CALAVERAS* COUNTY.

In compliance with the request of a friend of mine, who wrote me from the East, I called on good-natured, garrulous old Simon Wheeler, and inquired after my friend's friend, Leonidas W. Smiley, as requested to do, and I hereunto append the result. I have a lurking suspicion that *Leonidas W.* Smiley is a myth; that my friend never knew such a personage; and that he only conjectured that if I asked old Wheeler about him, it would remind him of his infamous *Jim* Smiley, and he would go to work and bore me to death with some exasperating reminiscence of him as long and as tedious as it should be useless to me. If that was the design, it succeeded.

I found Simon Wheeler dozing comfortably by the bar-room stove of the dilapidated tavern in the decayed mining camp of Angel's, and I noticed that he was fat and bald-headed, and had an expression of winning gentleness and simplicity upon his tranquil countenance. He roused up, and gave me good-day. I told him a friend of mine had commissioned me to make some inquiries about a cherished companion of his boyhood named *Leonidas W.* Smiley—*Rev. Leonidas W.* Smiley, a young minister of the Gospel, who he had heard was at one time a resident of Angel's Camp. I added that if Mr. Wheeler could tell me anything about this Rev. Leonidas W. Smiley, I would feel under many obligations to him.

Simon Wheeler backed me into a corner and blockaded me there with his chair, and then sat down and reeled off the monotonous narrative which follows this paragraph. He never smiled, he never

*Pronounced Cal-e-*va*-ras.

frowned, he never changed his voice from the gentle-flowing key to which he tuned his initial sentence, he never betrayed the slightest suspicion of enthusiasm; but all through the interminable narrative there ran a vein of impressive earnestness and sincerity, which showed me plainly that, so far from his imagining that there was anything ridiculous or funny about his story, he regarded it as a really important matter, and admired its two heroes as men of transcendent genius in *finesse*. I let him go on in his own way, and never interrupted him once.

"Rev. Leonidas W. H'm, Reverend Le—well, there was a feller here once by the name of *Jim* Smiley, in the winter of '49—or may be it was the spring of '50—I don't recollect exactly, somehow, though what makes me think it was one or the other is because I remember the big flume warn't finished when he first come to the camp; but any way, he was the curiosest man about always betting on anything that turned up you ever see, if he could get anybody to bet on the other side; and if he couldn't he'd change sides. Any way that suited the other man would suit *him*—any way just so's he got a bet, *he* was satisfied. But still he was lucky, uncommon lucky; he most always come out winner. He was always ready and laying for a chance; there couldn't be no solit'ry thing mentioned but that feller'd offer to bet on it, and take ary side you please, as I was just telling you. If there was a horse-race, you'd find him flush or you'd find him busted at the end of it; if there was a dog-fight, he'd bet on it; if there was a cat-fight, he'd bet on it; if there was a chicken-fight, he'd bet on it; why, if there was two birds setting on a fence, he would bet you which one would fly first; or if there was a camp-meeting, he would be there reg'lar to bet on Parson Walker, which he judged to be the best exhorter about here, and so he was too, and a good man. If he even see a straddle-bug start to go anywheres, he would bet you how long it would take him to get to—to wherever he was going to, and if you took him up, he would foller that straddle-bug to Mexico but what he would find out where he was bound for and how long he was on the road. Lots of the boys here has seen that Smiley, and can tell you about him. Why, it never made no difference to *him*—he'd bet on *any* thing—the dangdest feller. Parson Walker's wife laid very sick once, for a good while, and it seemed as if they warn't going to save her; but one morning he come in, and Smiley up and asked him how she was, and he said she was considerable better—thank the Lord for his inf'nit mercy—and coming on so smart that with the blessing of Prov'dence she'd get well yet; and Smiley, before he thought says, "Well, I'll resk two-and-a-half she don't anyway."

Thish-yer Smiley had a mare—the boys called her the fifteen-minute nag, but that was only in fun, you know, because of course she was faster than that—and he used to win money on that horse, for all she was so slow and always had the asthma, or the distemper, or the consumption, or something of that kind. They used to give her two or three hundred yards' start, and then pass her under way; but always at the fag-end of the race she'd get excited and desperate-like, and come cavorting and straddling up, and scattering her legs around limber, sometimes in the air, and sometimes out to one side amongst the fences, and kicking up m-o-r-e dust and raising m-o-r-e racket with her coughing and sneezing and blowing her nose—and *always* fetch up at the stand just about a neck ahead, as near as you could cipher it down.

And he had a little small bull-pup, that to look at him you'd think he warn't worth a cent but to set around and look ornery and lay for a chance to steal something. But as soon as money was up on him he was a different dog; his under-jaw'd begin to stick out like the fo'castle of a steamboat, and his teeth would uncover and shine like the furnaces. And a dog might tackle him and bully-rag him, and bite him, and throw him over his shoulder two or three times, and Andrew Jackson—which was the name of the pup—Andrew Jackson would never let on but what *he* was satisfied, and hadn't expected nothing else—and the bets being doubled and doubled on the other side all the time, till the money was all up; and then all of a sudden he would grab that other dog jest by the j'int of his hind leg and freeze to it—not chaw, you understand, but only just grip and hang on till they throwed up the sponge, if it was a year. Smiley always come out winner on that pup, till he harnessed a dog once that didn't have no hind legs, because they'd been sawed off in a circular saw, and when the thing had gone along far enough, and the money was all up, and he come to make a snatch for his pet holt, he see in a minute how he'd been imposed on, and how the other dog had him in the door, so to speak, and he 'peared surprised, and then he looked sorter discouraged-like, and didn't try no more to win the fight, and so he got shucked out bad. He give Smiley a look, as much as to say his heart was broke, and it was *his* fault, for putting up a dog that hadn't no hind legs for him to take holt of, which was his main dependence in a fight, and then he limped off a piece and laid down and died. It was a good pup, was that Andrew Jackson, and would have made a name for hisself if he'd lived, for the stuff was in him and he had genius—I know it, because he hadn't no opportunities to speak of, and it don't stand to reason that a dog could make such a fight as he could under them circumstances if he hadn't no talent. It always makes me feel sorry when I think of that last fight of his'n, and the way it turned out.

Well, thish-yer Smiley had rat-tarriers, and chicken cocks, and tom-cats and all them kind of things, till you couldn't rest, and you couldn't fetch nothing for him to bet on but he'd match you. He ketched a frog one day, and took him home, and said he cal'lated to educate him; and so he never done nothing for three months but set in his back yard and learn that frog to jump. And you bet you he *did* learn him, too. He'd give him a little punch behind, and the next minute you'd see that frog whirling in the air like a doughnut—see him turn one summerset, or may be a couple, if he got a good start, and come down flat-footed and all right, like a cat. He got him up so in the matter of ketching flies, and kep' him in practice so constant, that he'd nail a fly every time as fur as he could see him. Smiley said all a frog wanted was education, and he could do 'most anything—and I believe him. Why, I've seen him set Dan'l Webster down here on this floor—Dan'l Webster was the name of the frog—and sing out, "Flies, Dan'l, flies!" and quicker'n you could wink he'd spring straight up and snake a fly off'n the counter there, and flop down on the floor ag'in as solid as a gob of mud, and fall to scratching the side of his head with his hind foot as indifferent as if he hadn't no idea he'd been doin' any more'n any frog might do. You never see a frog so modest and straightfor'ard as he was, for all he was so gifted. And when it come to fair and square jumping on a dead level, he could get over more ground at one straddle than any animal of his breed you ever see. Jumping on a dead level was his strong suit, you understand; and when it come to that, Smiley would ante up money on him as long as he had a red. Smiley was monstrous proud of his frog, and well he might be, for fellers that had traveled and been everywheres, all said he laid over any frog that ever *they* see.

Well, Smiley kep' the beast in a little lattice box, and he used to fetch him down town sometimes and lay for a bet. One day a feller—a stranger in the camp, he was—come acrost him with his box, and says:

"What might it be that you've got in the box?"

And Smiley says, sorter indifferent-like, "It might be a parrot, or it might be a canary, maybe, but it ain't—it's only just a frog."

And the feller took it, and looked at it careful, and turned it round this way and that, and says, "H'm—so 'tis. Well, what's *he* good for?"

"Well," Smiley says, easy and careless, "he's good enough for *one* thing, I should judge—he can outjump any frog in Calaveras county."

The feller took the box again, and took another long, particular look, and give it back to Smiley, and says, very deliberate, "Well," he says, "I don't see no p'ints about that frog that's any better'n any other frog."

"Maybe you don't," Smiley says. "Maybe you understand frogs and maybe you don't understand 'em; maybe you've had experience, and maybe you ain't only a amature, as it were. Anyways, I've got *my* opinion and I'll resk forty dollars that he can outjump any frog in Calaveras county."

And the feller studied a minute, and then says, kinder sad like, "Well, I'm only a stranger here, and I ain't got no frog; but if I had a frog, I'd bet you."

And then Smiley says, "That's all right—that's all right—if you'll hold my box a minute, I'll go and get you a frog." And so the feller took the box, and put up his forty dollars along with Smiley's, and set down to wait.

So he set there a good while thinking and thinking to hisself, and then he got the frog out and prized his mouth open and took a teaspoon and filled him full of quail shot—filled him pretty near up to his chin—and set him on the floor. Smiley he went to the swamp and slopped around in the mud for a long time, and finally he ketched a frog, and fetched him in, and give him to this feller, and says:

"Now, if you're ready, set him alongside of Dan'l, with his fore-paws just even with Dan'l's, and I'll give the word." Then he says, "One—two—three—*git!*" and him and the feller touched up the frogs from behind, and the new frog hopped off lively, but Dan'l give a heave, and hysted up his shoulders—so—like a Frenchman, but it warn't no use—he couldn't budge; he was planted as solid as a church, and he couldn't no more stir than if he was anchored out. Smiley was a good deal surprised, and he was disgusted too, but he didn't have no idea what the matter was, of course.

The feller took the money and started away; and when he was going out at the door, he sorter jerked his thumb over his shoul-der—so—at Dan'l, and says again, very deliberate, "Well," he says "*I* don't see no p'ints about that frog that's any better'n any other frog."

Smiley he stood scratching his head and looking down at Dan'l a long time, and at last he says, "I do wonder what in the nation that frog throw'd off for—I wonder if there ain't something the matter with him—he 'pears to look mighty baggy, somehow." And he ketched Dan'l by the nap of the neck, and hefted him, and says, "Why blame my cats if he don't weigh five pound!" and turned him upside down and he belched out a double handful of shot. And then he see how it was, and he was the maddest man—he set the frog down and took out after that feller, but he never ketched him. And——"

[Here Simon Wheeler heard his name called from the front yard, and got up to see what was wanted.] And turning to me as he moved away, he said: "Just set where you are, stranger, and rest easy—I ain't going to be gone a second."

But, by your leave, I did not think that a continuation of the history of the enterprising vagabond *Jim* Smiley would be likely to afford me much information concerning the Rev. *Leonidas W.* Smiley, and so I started away.

At the door I met the sociable Wheeler returning, and he button-holed me and re-commenced:

"Well, thish-yer Smiley had a yaller one-eyed cow that didn't have no tail, only jest a short stump like a bannanner, and——"

However, lacking both time and inclination, I did not wait to hear about the afflicted cow, but took my leave.

Now let the learned look upon this picture and say if icon-oclasm can further go:

[From the *Revue des Deux Mondes*, of July 15th, 1872.]

LA GRENOUILLE SAUTEUSE DU COMTÉ DE CALAVERAS.

"—Il y avait une fois ici un individu connu sous le nom de Jim Smiley: c'était dans l'hiver de 49, peut-être bien au printemps de 50, je ne me rappelle pas exactement. Ce qui me fait croire que c'était l'un ou l'autre, c'est que je me souviens que le grand bief n'était pas achevé lorsqu'il arriva au camp pour la première fois, mais de toutes façons il était l'homme le plus friand de paris qui se pût voir, pariant sur tout ce qui se présentait, quand il pouvait trouver un adversaire, et, quand il n'en trouvait pas, il passait du côté opposé. Tout ce qui convenait à l'autre lui convenait; pourvu qu'il eût un pari, Smiley était satisfait. Et il avait une chance! une chance inouïe: presque toujours il gagnait. Il faut dire qu'il était toujours prêt à s'exposer, qu'on ne pouvait mentionner la moindre chose sans que ce gaillard offrît de parier là-dessus n'importe quoi et de prendre le côté que l'on voudrait, comme je vous le disais tout à l'heure. S'il y avait des courses, vous le trouviez riche ou ruiné à la fin; s'il y avait un combat de chiens, il apportait son enjeu; il l'apportait pour un combat de chats, pour un combat de coqs;—parbleu! si vous aviez vu deux oiseaux sur une haie, il vous aurait offert de parier lequel s'envolerait le premier, et, s'il y avait *meeting* au camp, il venait parier régulièrement pour le curé Walker, qu'il jugeait être le meilleur prédicateur des environs, et qui l'était en effet, et un brave homme. Il aurait rencontré une punaise de bois en chemin, qu'il aurait parié sur le temps qu'il lui faudrait pour aller où elle voudrait aller, et, si vous l'aviez pris au mot, il aurait suivi la punaise jusqu'au Mexique, sans se soucier d'aller si loin, ni du temps qu'il y perdrait. Une fois la femme du curé Walker fut très malade pendant longtemps, il semblait qu'on ne la sauverait pas; mais un matin le curé arrive, et Smiley lui demande comment elle va, et il dit qu'elle est bien mieux, grâce à l'infinie miséricorde, tellement mieux qu'avec la bénédiction de la Providence elle s'en tirerait, et voilà que, sans y penser, Smiley répond:—Eh bien! je gage deux et demi qu'elle mourra tout de même.

"Ce Smiley avait une jument que les gars appelaient le bidet du quart d'heure, mais seulement pour plaisanter, vous comprenez, parce que, bien entendu, elle était plus *vite* que ça! Et il avait coutume de gagner de l'argent avec cette bête, quoiqu'elle fût poussive, cornarde, toujours prise d'asthme, de coliques ou de consomption, ou de quelque chose d'approchant. On lui donnait 2 ou 300 *yards* au départ, puis on la dépassait sans peine; mais jamais à la fin elle ne manquait de s'échauffer, de s'exaspérer, et elle arrivait, s'écartant, se défendant, ses jambes grêles en l'air devant les obstacles, quelquefois les évitant et faisant avec cela plus de poussière qu'aucun cheval, plus de bruit surtout avec ses éternumens et reniflemens,—crac! elle arrivait donc toujours première d'une tête, aussi juste qu'on peut le mesurer. Et il avait un petit bouledogue qui, à le voir, ne valait pas un sou; on aurait cru que parier contre lui c'était voler, tant il était ordinaire; mais aussitôt les enjeux faits, il devenait un autre chien. Sa mâchoire inférieure commençait à ressortir comme un gaillard d'avant, ses dents se découvraient brillantes comme des fournaises, et un chien pouvait le taquiner, l'exciter, le mordre, le jeter deux ou trois fois par-dessus son épaule, André Jackson, c'était le nom du chien, André Jackson prenait cela tranquillement, comme s'il ne se fût jamais attendu à autre chose, et quand les paris étaient doublés et redoublés contre lui, il vous saisissait l'autre chien juste à l'articulation de la jambe de derrière, et il ne la lâchait plus, non pas qu'il la mâchât, vous concevez, mais il s'y serait tenu pendu jusqu'à ce qu'on jetât l'éponge en l'air, fallût-il attendre un an. Smiley gagnait toujours avec cette bête-là; malheureusement ils ont fini par dresser un chien qui n'avait pas de pattes de derrière, parce qu'on les avait sciées, et quand les choses furent au point qu'il voulait, et qu'il en vint à se jeter sur son morceau favori, le pauvre chien comprit en un instant qu'on s'était moqué de lui, et que l'autre le tenait. Vous n'avez jamais vu personne avoir l'air plus penaud et plus découragé; il ne fit aucun effort pour gagner le combat et fut rudement secoué, de sorte que, regardant Smiley comme pour lui dire:—Mon cœur est brisé, c'est ta faute; pourquoi m'avoir livré à un chien qui n'a pas de pattes de derrière, puisque c'est par là que je les bats?—il s'en alla en clopinant, et se coucha pour mourir. Ah! c'était un bon chien, cet André Jackson, et il se serait fait un nom, s'il avait vécu, car il y avait de l'étoffe en lui, il avait du génie, je le sais, bien que de grandes occasions lui aient manqué; mais il est impossible de supposer qu'un chien capable de se battre comme lui, certaines circonstances étant données, ait manqué de talent. Je me sens triste toutes les fois que je pense à son dernier combat et au dénoûment qu'il a eu. Eh bien! ce Smiley nourrissait des terriers à rats, et des coqs de combat, et des chats, et toute sorte de choses, au point qu'il était toujours en mesure de vous tenir tête, et qu'avec sa rage de paris on n'avait plus de repos. Il attrapa un jour une grenouille et l'emporta chez lui, disant qu'il prétendait faire son éducation; vous me croirez si vous voulez, mais pendant trois mois il n'a rien fait que lui apprendre à sauter dans une cour retirée de sa maison. Et je vous réponds qu'il avait réussi. Il lui donnait un petit coup par derrière, et l'instant d'après vous voyiez la grenouille tourner en l'air comme un beignet au-dessus de la poêle, faire une culbute, quelquefois deux, lorsqu'elle était bien partie, et retomber sur ses pattes comme un chat. Il l'avait dressée dans l'art de gober des mouches, et l'y exerçait continuellement, si bien qu'une mouche, du plus loin qu'elle apparaissait, était une mouche perdue. Smiley avait coutume de dire que tout ce qui manquait à une grenouille, c'était l'éducation, qu'avec l'éducation elle pouvait faire presque tout, et je le crois. Tenez, je l'ai vu poser Daniel Webster là sur ce plancher,—Daniel Webster était le nom de la grenouille,—et lui chanter:—Des mouches, Daniel, des mouches!—En un clin d'œil, Daniel avait bondi et saisi une mouche ici sur le comptoir, puis sauté de nouveau par terre, où il restait vraiment à se gratter la tête avec sa patte de derrière, comme s'il n'avait pas eu la moindre idée de sa supériorité. Jamais vous n'avez vu de grenouille aussi modeste, aussi naturelle, douée comme elle l'était! Et quand il s'agissait de sauter purement et simplement sur terrain plat, elle faisait plus de chemin en un saut qu'aucune bête de son espèce que vous puissiez connaître. Sauter à plat, c'était son fort! Quand il s'agissait de cela, Smiley entassait les enjeux sur elle tant qu'il lui restait un rouge liard. Il faut le reconnaître, Smiley était monstrueusement fier de sa grenouille, et il en avait le droit, car des gens qui avaient voyagé, qui avaient tout vu, disaient qu'on lui ferait injure de la comparer à une autre; de façon que Smiley gardait Daniel dans une petite boîte à claire-voie qu'il emportait parfois à la ville pour quelque pari.

"Un jour, un individu étranger au camp l'arrête avec sa boîte et lui dit:—Qu'est-ce que vous avez donc serré là dedans?

"Smiley dit d'un air indifférent:—Cela puorrait être un perroquet ou un serin, mais ce n'est rien de pareil, ce n'est qu'une grenouille.

"L'individu la prend, la regarde avec soin, la tourne d'un côté et de l'autre, puis il dit.—Tiens! en effet! A quoi est-elle bonne?

"—Mon Dieu! répond Smiley, toujours d'un air dégagé, elle est bonne pour une chose à mon avis, elle peut battre en sautant toute grenouille du comté de Calaveras.

"L'individu reprend la boîte, l'examine de nouveau longuement, et la rend à Smiley en disant d'un air délibéré:—Eh bien! je ne vois pas que cette grenouille ait rien de mieux qu'aucune grenouille.

"—Possible que vous ne le voyiez pas, dit Smiley, possible que vous vous entendiez en grenouilles, possible que vous ne vous y entendiez point, possible que vous ayez de l'expérience, et possible que vous ne soyez qu'un amateur. De toute manière, je parie quarante dollars qu'elle battra en sautant n'importe quelle grenouille du comté de Calaveras.

"L'individu réfléchit une seconde, et dit comme attristé:—Je ne suis qu'un étranger ici, je n'ai pas de grenouille; mais, si j'en avais une, je tiendrais le pari.

"—Fort bien! répond Smiley. Rien de plus facile. Si vous voulez tenir ma boîte une minute, j'irai vous chercher une grenouille.—Voilà donc l'individu qui garde la boîte, qui met ses quarante dollars sur ceux de Smiley et qui attend. Il attend assez longtemps, réfléchissant tout seul, et figurez-vous qu'il prend Daniel, lui ouvre la bouche de force et avec une cuiller à thé l'emplit de menu plomb de chasse, mais l'emplit jusqu'au menton, puis il le pose par terre. Smiley pendant ce temps était à barboter dans une mare. Finalement il attrape une grenouille, l'apporte à cet individu et dit:—Maintenant, si vous êtes prêt, mettez-la tout contre Daniel, avec leurs pattes de devant sur la même ligne, et je donnerai le signal;—puis il ajoute:—Un, deux, trois, sautez!

"Lui et l'individu touchent leurs grenouilles par derrière, et la grenouille neuve se met à sautiller, mais Daniel se soulève lourdement, hausse les épaules ainsi, comme un Français; à quoi bon? il ne pouvait bouger, il était planté solide comme une enclume, il n'avançait pas plus que si on l'eût mis à l'ancre. Smiley fut surpris et dégoûté, mais il ne se doutait pas du tour, bien entendu. L'individu empoche l'argent, s'en va, et en s'en allant est-ce qu'il ne donne pas un coup de pouce par-dessus l'épaule, comme ça, au pauvre Daniel, en disant de son air délibéré:—Eh bien! je ne vois pas que cette grenouille ait rien de mieux qu'une autre.

"Smiley se gratta longtemps la tête, les yeux fixés sur Daniel, jusqu'à ce qu'enfin il dit:—Je me demande comment diable il se fait que cette bête ait refusé . . . Est-ce qu'elle aurait quelque chose? . . On croirait qu'elle est enflée.

"Il empoigne Daniel par la peau du cou, le soulève et dit:—Le loup me croque, s'il ne pèse pas cinq livres.

"Il le retourne, et le malheureux crache deux poignées de plomb. Quand Smiley reconnut ce qui en était, il fut comme fou. Vous le voyez d'ici poser sa grenouille par terre et courir après cet individu, mais il ne le rattrapa jamais, et . . .

[Translation of the above back from the French.]

THE FROG JUMPING OF THE COUNTY
OF CALAVERAS.

It there was one time here an individual known under the name of Jim Smiley: it was in the winter of '49, possibly well at the spring of '50, I no me recollect not exactly. This which me makes to believe that it was the one or the other, it is that I shall remember that the grand flume is not achieved when he arrives at the camp for the first time, but of all sides he was the man the most fond of to bet which one have seen, betting upon all that which is presented, when he could find an adversary; and when he not of it could not, he passed to the side opposed. All that which convenienced to the other, to him convenienced also; seeing that he had a bet, Smiley was satisfied. And he had a chance! a chance even worthless: nearly always he gained. It must to say that he was always near to himself expose, but one no could mention the least thing without that this gaillard offered to bet the bottom, no matter what, and to take the side that one him would, as I you it said all at the hour (tout à l'heure). If it there was of races, you him find rich or ruined at the end; if it there is a combat of dogs, he bring his bet; he himself laid always for a combat of cats, for a combat of cocks;—by-blue! if you have see two birds upon a fence, he you should have offered of to bet which of those birds shall fly the first; and if there is *meeting* at the camp (*meeting* au camp) he comes to bet regularly for the curé Walker, which he judged to be the best predicator of the neighborhood (prédicateur des environs) and which he was in effect, and a brave man. He would encounter a bug of wood in the road, whom he will bet upon the time which he shall take to go where she would go—and if you him have take at the word, he will follow the bug as far as Mexique, without himself caring to go so far; neither of the time which he there lost. One time the woman of the curé Walker is very sick during long time, it seemed that one not her saved not; but one morning the curé arrives, and Smiley him demanded how she goes, and he said that she is well better, grace to the infinite misery (lui demande comment elle va, et il dit qu'elle est bien mieux, grâce à l'infinie miséricorde) so much better that with the benediction of the Providence she herself of it would pull out (elle s'en tirerait); and behold that without there thinking, Smiley responds: "Well, I gage two-and-half that she will die all of same."

This Smiley had an animal which the boys called the nag of the quarter of hour, but solely for pleasantry, you comprehend, because, well understand, she was more fast as that! [Now why that exclamation?—M. T.] And it was custom of to gain of the silver with this beast, notwithstanding she was poussive, cornarde, always taken of asthma, of colics or of consumption, or something of approaching. One him would give two or three hundred yards at the departure, then one him passed without pain; but never at the last she not fail of herself èchauffer, of herself exasperate, and she arrives herself écartant, se défendant, her legs grêles in the air before the obstacles, sometimes them elevating and making with this more of dust than any horse, more of noise above with his éternumens and reniflemens—crac! she arrives then always first by one head, as just as one can it measure. And he had a small bull dog (bouledogue!) who, to him see, no value not a cent; one would believe that to bet against him it was to steal, so much he was ordinary; but as soon as the game made, she becomes another dog. Her jaw inferior commence to project like a deck of before, his teeth themselves discover brilliant like some furnaces, and a dog could him tackle (le taquiner), him excite, him murder (le mordre), him throw two or three times over his shoulder, André Jackson—this was the name of the dog—André Jackson takes that tranquilly, as if he not himself was never expecting other thing, and when the bets were doubled and redoubled against him, he you seize the other dog just at the articulation of the leg of behind, and he not it leave more, not that he it masticate, you conceive, but he himself there shall be holding during until that one throws the sponge in the air, must he wait a year. Smiley gained always with this beast-là; unhappily they have finished by elevating a dog who no had not of feet of behind, because one them had sawed; and when things were at the point that he would, and that he came to himself throw upon his morsel favorite, the poor dog comprehended in an instant that he himself was deceived in him, and that the other dog him had. You no have never see person having the air more penaud and more discouraged; he not made no effort to gain the combat, and was rudely shucked.

Eh bien! this Smiley nourished some terriers à rats, and some cocks of combat, and some cats, and all sort of things; and with his rage of betting one no had more of repose. He trapped one day a frog and him imported with him (et l'emporta chez lui) saying that he pretended to make his education. You me believe if you will, but during three months he not has nothing done but to him apprehend to jump (apprendre à sauter) in a court retired of her mansion (de sa maison). And I you respond that he have succeeded. He him gives a small blow by behind, and the instant after you shall see the frog turn in the air like a grease-biscuit, make one summersault, sometimes two, when she was well started, and re-fall upon his feet like a cat. He him had accomplished in the art of to gobble the flies (gober des mouches,) and him there exercised continually—so well that a fly at the most far that she appeared was a fly lost. Smiley had custom to say that all that which lacked to a frog it was the education, but with the education she could do nearly all—and I him believe. Tenez, I him have seen pose Daniel Webster there upon this plank— Daniel Webster was the name of the frog—and to him sing, "Some flies, Daniel, some flies!"—in a flash of the eye Daniel had bounded and seized a fly here upon the counter, then jumped anew at the earth, where he rested truly to himself scratch the head with his behind-foot, as if he no had not the least idea of his superiority. Never you not have seen frog as modest, as natural, sweet as she was. And when he himself agitated to jump purely and simply upon plain earth, she does more ground in one jump than any beast of his species than you can know. To jump plain—this was his strong. When he himself agitated for that, Smiley multiplied the bets upon her as long as there to him remained a red. It must to know, Smiley was monstrously proud of his frog, and he of it was right, for some men who were traveled, who had all seen, said that they to him would be injurious to him compare to another frog. Smiley guarded Daniel in a little box latticed which he carried bytimes to the village for some bet.

One day an individual stranger at the camp him arrested with his box and him said:

"What is this that you have then shut up there within?"

Smiley said, with an air indifferent:

"That could be a paroquet, or a syringe (ou un serin), but this no is nothing of such, it not is but a frog."

The individual it took, it regarded with care, it turned from one side and from the other, then he said:

"Tiens! in effect! At what is she good?"

"My God!" respond Smiley, always with an air disengaged, "she is good for one thing, to my notice, (à mon avis,) she can batter in jumping (elle peut battre en sautant) all frogs of the county of Calaveras."

The individual re-took the box, it examined of new longly, and it rendered to Smiley in saying with an air deliberate:

"Eh bien! I no saw not that that frog had nothing of better than each frog." (Je ne vois pas que cette grenouille ait rien de mieux qu'aucune grenouille.) [If that isn't grammar gone to seed, then I count myself no judge.—M. T.]

"Possible that you not it saw not," said Smiley, "possible that you-you comprehend frogs; possible that you not you there comprehend nothing; possible that you had of the experience, and possible that you not be but an amateur. Of all manner, (De toute manière) I bet forty dollars that she batter in jumping no matter which frog of the county of Calaveras."

The individual reflected a second, and said like sad:

"I not am but a stranger here, I no have not a frog; but if I of it had one, I would embrace the bet."

"Strong well!" respond Smiley; "nothing of more facility. If you will hold my box a minute, I go you to search a frog (j'irai vous chercher)."

Behold, then, the individual, who guards the box, who puts his forty dollars upon those of Smiley, and who attends, (et qui attend.) He attended enough longtimes, reflecting all solely. And figure-you that he takes Daniel, him opens the mouth by force and with a tea-spoon him fills with shot of the hunt, even him fills just to the chin, then he him puts by the earth. Smiley during these times was at slopping in a swamp. Finally he trapped (attrape) a frog, him carried to that individual, and said:

"Now if you be ready, put him all against Daniel, with their before-feet upon the same line, and I give the signal"— then he added: "One, two, three,—advance!"

Him and the individual touched their frogs by behind, and the frog new put to jump smartly, but Daniel himself lifted ponderously, exalted the shoulders thus, like a Frenchman— to what good? he not could budge, he is planted solid like a church, he not advance no more than if one him had put at the anchor.

Smiley was surprised and disgusted, but he not himself doubted not of the turn being intended (mais il ne se doutait pas du tour, bien entendu.) The individual empocketed the silver, himself with it went, and of it himself in going is-it that he no gives not a jerk of thumb over the shoulder—like that—at the poor Daniel, in saying with his air deliberate— (L'individu empoche l'argent, s'en va, et en s'en allant est-ce qu'il ne donne pas un coup de pouce par-dessus l'épaule, comme ça, au pauvre Daniel, en disant de son air délibéré):

"Eh bien! *I no see not that that frog has nothing of better than another.*"

Smiley himself scratched longtimes the head, the eyes fixed upon Daniel, until that which at last he said:

"I me demand how the devil it makes itself that this beast has refused. Is it that she had something? One would believe that she is stuffed."

He grasped Daniel by the skin of the neck, him lifted and said:

"The wolf me bite if he no weigh not five pounds."

He him reversed and the unhappy belched two handfuls of shot, (et le malheureux, etc.) — When Smiley recognized how it was, he was like mad. He deposited his frog by the earth and ran after that individual, but he not him caught never.

Such is the jumping Frog, to the distorted French eye. I claim that I never put together such an odious mixture of bad grammar and delirium tremens in my life. And what has a poor foreigner like me done, to be abused and misrepresented like this? When I say, "Well, I don't see no pints about that frog that's any better'n any other frog," is it kind, is it just, for this Frenchman to try to make it appear that I said, "Eh bien! I no saw not that that frog had nothing of better than each frog?" I have no heart to write more. I never felt so about anything before.

1875

Experience of the McWilliamses
with Membranous Croup

[AS RELATED TO THE AUTHOR OF THIS BOOK BY MR.
MCWILLIAMS, A PLEASANT NEW YORK GENTLEMAN WHOM
THE SAID AUTHOR MET BY CHANCE ON A JOURNEY.]

Well, to go back to where I was before I digressed to explain to you how that frightful and incurable disease, membranous croup, was ravaging the town and driving all mothers mad with terror, I called Mrs. McWilliams's attention to little Penelope and said:

"Darling, I wouldn't let that child be chewing that pine stick if I were you."

"Precious, where is the harm in it?" said she, but at the same time preparing to take away the stick—for women cannot receive even the most palpably judicious suggestion without arguing it; that is, married women.

I replied:

"Love, it is notorious that pine is the least nutritious wood that a child can eat."

My wife's hand paused, in the act of taking the stick, and returned itself to her lap. She bridled perceptibly, and said:

"Hubby, you know better than that. You know you do. Doctors *all* say that the turpentine in pine wood is good for weak back and the kidneys."

"Ah—I was under a misapprehension. I did not know that the child's kidneys and spine were affected, and that the family physician had recommended—"

"Who said the child's spine and kidneys were affected?"

"My love, you intimated it."

"The idea! I never intimated anything of the kind."

"Why my dear, it hasn't been two minutes since you said—"

"Bother what I said! I don't care what I did say. There isn't any harm in the child's chewing a bit of pine stick if she wants to, and you know it perfectly well. And she *shall* chew it, too. So there, now!"

"Say no more, my dear. I now see the force of your

reasoning, and I will go and order two or three cords of the best pine wood to-day. No child of mine shall want while I—"

"O *please* go along to your office and let me have some peace. A body can never make the simplest remark but you must take it up and go to arguing and arguing and arguing till you don't know what you are talking about, and you *never* do."

"Very well, it shall be as you say. But there is a want of logic in your last remark which—"

However, she was gone with a flourish before I could finish, and had taken the child with her. That night at dinner she confronted me with a face as white as a sheet:

"O, Mortimer, there's another! Little Georgie Gordon is taken."

"Membranous croup?"

"Membranous croup."

"Is there any hope for him?"

"None in the wide world. O, what is to become of us!"

By and by a nurse brought in our Penelope to say good-night and offer the customary prayer at the mother's knee. In the midst of "Now I lay me down to sleep," she gave a slight cough! My wife fell back like one stricken with death. But the next moment she was up and brimming with the activities which terror inspires.

She commanded that the child's crib be removed from the nursery to our bed-room; and she went along to see the order executed. She took me with her, of course. We got matters arranged with speed. A cot bed was put up in my wife's dressing room for the nurse. But now Mrs. McWilliams said we were too far away from the other baby, and what if *he* were to have the symptoms in the night—and she blanched again, poor thing.

We then restored the crib and the nurse to the nursery and put up a bed for ourselves in a room adjoining.

Presently, however, Mrs. McWilliams said suppose the baby should catch it from Penelope? This thought struck a new panic to her heart, and the tribe of us could not get the crib out of the nursery again fast enough to satisfy my wife, though she assisted in her own person and well nigh pulled the crib to pieces in her frantic hurry.

We moved down stairs; but there was no place there to stow the nurse, and Mrs. McWilliams said the nurse's experience would be an inestimable help. So we returned, bag and baggage, to our own bed-room once more, and felt a great gladness, like storm-buffeted birds that have found their nest again.

Mrs. McWilliams sped to the nursery to see how things were going on there. She was back in a moment with a new dread. She said:

"What *can* make Baby sleep so?"

I said:

"Why, my darling, Baby *always* sleeps like a graven image."

"I know. I know; but there's something peculiar about his sleep, now. He seems to—to—he seems to breathe so *regularly*. O, this is dreadful."

"But my dear he always breathes regularly."

"Oh, I know it, but there's something frightful about it now. His nurse is too young and inexperienced. Maria shall stay there with her, and be on hand if anything happens."

"That is a good idea, but who will help *you*?"

"You can help me all I want. I wouldn't allow anybody to do anything but myself, any how, at such a time as this."

I said I would feel mean to lie abed and sleep, and leave her to watch and toil over our little patient all the weary night.— But she reconciled me to it. So old Maria departed and took up her ancient quarters in the nursery.

Penelope coughed twice in her sleep.

"Oh, why *don't* that doctor come! Mortimer, this room is too warm. This room is certainly too warm. Turn off the register—quick!"

I shut it off, glancing at the thermometer at the same time, and wondering to myself if 70 *was* too warm for a sick child.

The coachman arrived from down town, now, with the news that our physician was ill and confined to his bed.— Mrs. McWilliams turned a dead eye upon me, and said in a dead voice:

"There is a Providence in it. It is foreordained. He never was sick before.—Never. We have not been living as we ought to live, Mortimer. Time and time again I have told you so. Now you see the result. Our child will never get well. Be thankful if you can forgive yourself; I never can forgive *my*self."

I said, without intent to hurt, but with heedless choice of words, that I could not see that we had been living such an abandoned life.

"*Mortimer!* Do you want to bring the judgment upon Baby, too!"

Then she began to cry, but suddenly exclaimed:

"The doctor must have sent medicines!"

I said:

"Certainly. They are here. I was only waiting for you to give me a chance."

"Well do give them to me! Don't you know that every moment is precious now? But what was the use in sending medicines, when he *knows* that the disease is incurable?"

I said that while there was life there was hope.

"Hope! Mortimer, you know no more what you are talking about than the child unborn. If you would—. As I live, the directions say give one teaspoonful once an hour! Once an hour!—as if we had a whole year before us to save the child in! Mortimer, please hurry. Give the poor perishing thing a table-spoonful, and *try* to be quick!"

"Why, my dear, a table-spoonful might—"

"*Don't* drive me frantic! . . . . . There, there, there, my precious, my own; it's nasty bitter stuff, but it's good for Nelly—good for Mother's precious darling; and it will make her well. There, there, there, put the little head on Mamma's breast and go to sleep, and pretty soon—Oh, I know she can't live till morning! Mortimer, a table-spoonful every half hour will—. Oh, the child needs belladonna too; I know she does—and aconite. Get them, Mortimer. Now do let me have my way. You know nothing about these things."

We now went to bed, placing the crib close to my wife's pillow. All this turmoil had worn upon me, and within two minutes I was something more than half asleep. Mrs. McWilliams roused me:

"Darling, is that register turned on?"

"No."

"I thought as much. Please turn it on at once. This room is cold."

I turned it on, and presently fell asleep again. I was aroused once more:

"Dearie, would you mind moving the crib to your side of the bed? It is nearer the register."

I moved it, but had a collision with the rug and woke up the child. I dozed off once more, while my wife quieted the sufferer. But in a little while these words came murmuring remotely through the fog of my drowsiness:

"Mortimer, if we only had some goose-grease—will you ring?"

I climbed dreamily out, and stepped on a cat, which responded with a protest and would have got a convincing kick for it if a chair had not got it instead.

"Now, Mortimer, why do you want to turn up the gas and wake up the child again?"

"Because I want to see how much I am hurt, Caroline."

"Well look at the chair, too—I have no doubt it is ruined. Poor cat, suppose you had—"

"Now I am not going to suppose anything about the cat. It never would have occurred if Maria had been allowed to remain here and attend to these duties, which are in her line and are not in mine."

"Now Mortimer, I should think you would be ashamed to make a remark like that. It is a pity if you cannot do the few little things I ask of you at such an awful time as this when our child—"

"There, there, I will do anything you want. But I can't raise anybody with this bell. They're all gone to bed. Where is the goose-grease?"

"On the mantel piece in the nursery. If you'll step there and speak to Maria—"

I fetched the goose-grease and went to sleep again: Once more I was called:

"Mortimer, I so hate to disturb you, but the room is still too cold for me to try to apply this stuff. Would you mind lighting the fire? It is all ready to touch a match to."

I dragged myself out and lit the fire, and then sat down disconsolate.

"Mortimer, don't sit there and catch your death of cold. Come to bed."

As I was stepping in, she said:

"But wait a moment. Please give the child some more of the medicine."

Which I did. It was a medicine which made a child more or less lively; so my wife made use of its waking interval to strip it and grease it all over with the goose-oil. I was soon asleep once more, but once more I had to get up.

"Mortimer, I feel a draft. I feel it distinctly. There is nothing so bad for this disease as a draft. Please move the crib in front of the fire."

I did it; and collided with the rug again, which I threw in the fire. Mrs. McWilliams sprang out of bed and rescued it and we had some words. I had another trifling interval of sleep, and then got up, by request, and constructed a flax-seed poultice. This was placed upon the child's breast and left there to do its healing work.

A wood fire is not a permanent thing. I got up every twenty minutes and renewed ours, and this gave Mrs. McWilliams the opportunity to shorten the times of giving the medicines by ten minutes, which was a great satisfaction to her. Now and then, between times, I reorganized the flax-seed poultices, and applied sinapisms and other sorts of blisters where unoccupied places could be found upon the child. Well, toward morning the wood gave out and my wife wanted me to go down cellar and get some more. I said:

"My dear, it is a laborious job, and the child must be nearly warm enough, with her extra clothing. Now mightn't we put on another layer of poultices and—"

I did not finish, because I was interrupted. I lugged wood up from below for some little time, and then turned in and fell to snoring as only a man can whose strength is all gone and whose soul is worn out. Just at broad daylight I felt a grip on my shoulder that brought me to my senses suddenly. —My wife was glaring down upon me and gasping. As soon as she could command her tongue she said:

"It is all over! All over! The child's perspiring! What *shall* we do?"

"Mercy, how you terrify me! *I* don't know what we ought to do. Maybe if we scraped her and put her in the draft again—"

"O, idiot! There is not a moment to lose! Go for the doctor. Go yourself. Tell him he *must* come, dead or alive."

I dragged that poor sick man from his bed and brought him. He looked at the child and said she was not dying. This was joy unspeakable to me, but it made my wife as mad as if he had offered her a personal affront. Then he said the child's cough was only caused by some trifling irritation or other in the throat. At this I thought my wife had a mind to show him the door.—Now the doctor said he would make the child cough harder and dislodge the trouble. So he gave her something that sent her into a spasm of coughing, and presently up came a little wood splinter or so.

"This child has no membranous croup," said he. "She has been chewing a bit of pine shingle or something of the kind, and got some little slivers in her throat. They won't do her any hurt."

"No," said I, "I can well believe that. Indeed the turpentine that is in them is very good for certain sorts of diseases that are peculiar to children. My wife will tell you so."

But she did not. She turned away in disdain and left the room; and since that time there is one episode in our life which we never refer to. Hence the tide of our days flows by in deep and untroubled serenity.

[Very few married men have such an experience as McWilliams's, and so the author of this book thought that maybe the novelty of it would give it a passing interest to the reader.]

1875

Some Learned Fables,
for Good Old Boys and Girls
IN THREE PARTS.

PART FIRST.

HOW THE ANIMALS OF THE WOOD SENT OUT A
SCIENTIFIC EXPEDITION.

Once the creatures of the forest held a great convention and
appointed a commission consisting of the most illustrious scientists among them to go forth, clear beyond the forest and
out into the unknown and unexplored world, to verify the
truth of the matters already taught in their schools and colleges and also to make discoveries. It was the most imposing
enterprise of the kind the nation had ever embarked in. True,
the government had once sent Dr. Bull Frog, with a picked
crew, to hunt for a north-westerly passage through the
swamp to the right-hand corner of the wood, and had since
sent out many expeditions to hunt for Dr. Bull Frog; but they
never could find him, and so government finally gave him up
and ennobled his mother to show its gratitude for the services
her son had rendered to science. And once government sent
Sir Grass Hopper to hunt for the sources of the rill that emptied into the swamp; and afterwards sent out many expeditions to hunt for Sir Grass, and at last they were successful—
they found his body, but if he had discovered the sources
meantime, he did not let on. So government acted handsomely by deceased, and many envied his funeral.

But these expeditions were trifles compared with the
present one; for this one comprised among its servants the
very greatest among the learned; and besides it was to go to
the utterly unvisited regions believed to lie beyond the mighty
forest—as we have remarked before. How the members were
banqueted, and glorified, and talked about! Everywhere that
one of them showed himself, straightway there was a crowd
to gape and stare at him.

Finally they set off, and it was a sight to see the long
procession of dry-land Tortoises heavily laden with savans,
scientific instruments, Glow-Worms and Fire-Flies for signal-

service, provisions, Ants and Tumble-Bugs to fetch and carry and delve, Spiders to carry the surveying chain and do other engineering duty, and so forth and so on; and after the Tortoises came another long train of iron-clads—stately and spacious Mud Turtles for marine transportation service; and from every Tortoise and every Turtle flaunted a flaming gladiolus or other splendid banner; at the head of the column a great band of Bumble-Bees, Mosquitoes, Katy-Dids and Crickets discoursed martial music; and the entire train was under the escort and protection of twelve picked regiments of the Army Worm.

At the end of three weeks the expedition emerged from the forest and looked upon the great Unknown World. Their eyes were greeted with an impressive spectacle. A vast level plain stretched before them, watered by a sinuous stream; and beyond, there towered up against the sky a long and lofty barrier of some kind, they did not know what. The Tumble-Bug said he believed it was simply land tilted up on its edge, because he knew he could see trees on it. But Prof. Snail and the others said:

"You are hired to dig, sir—that is all. We need your muscle, not your brains. When we want your opinion on scientific matters, we will hasten to let you know. Your coolness, is intolerable, too—loafing about here meddling with august matters of learning, when the other laborers are pitching camp. Go along and help handle the baggage."

The Tumble-Bug turned on his heel uncrushed, unabashed, observing to himself, "If it isn't land tilted up, let me die the death of the unrighteous."

Professor Bull Frog, (nephew of the late explorer,) said he believed the ridge was the wall that enclosed the earth. He continued:

"Our fathers have left us much learning, but they had not traveled far, and so we may count this a noble new discovery. We are safe for renown, now, even though our labors began and ended with this single achievement. I wonder what this wall is built of? Can it be fungus? Fungus is an honorable good thing to build a wall of."

Professor Snail adjusted his field-glass and examined the rampart critically. Finally he said:

"The fact that it is not diaphanous, convinces me that it is a dense vapor formed by the calorification of ascending moisture dephlogisticated by refraction. A few endiometrical experiments would confirm this, but it is not necessary. — The thing is obvious."

So he shut up his glass and went into his shell to make a note of the discovery of the world's end, and the nature of it.

"Profound mind!" said Professor Angle-Worm to Professor Field-Mouse; "profound mind! nothing can long remain a mystery to that august brain."

Night drew on apace, the sentinel crickets were posted, the Glow Worm and Fire-Fly lamps were lighted, and the camp sank to silence and sleep. After breakfast in the morning, the expedition moved on. About noon a great avenue was reached, which had in it two endless parallel bars of some kind of hard black substance, raised the height of the tallest Bull Frog above the general level. The scientists climbed up on these and examined and tested them in various ways. They walked along them for a great distance, but found no end and no break in them. They could arrive at no decision. There was nothing in the records of science that mentioned anything of this kind. But at last the bald and venerable geographer, Professor Mud Turtle, a person who, born poor, and of a drudging low family, had, by his own native force raised himself to the headship of the geographers of his generation, said:

"My friends, we have indeed made a discovery here. We have found in a palpable, compact and imperishable state what the wisest of our fathers always regarded as a mere thing of the imagination. Humble yourselves, my friends, for we stand in a majestic presence. These are parallels of latitude!"

Every heart and every head was bowed, so awful, so sublime was the magnitude of the discovery. Many shed tears.

The camp was pitched and the rest of the day given up to writing voluminous accounts of the marvel, and correcting astronomical tables to fit it. Toward midnight a demoniacal shriek was heard, then a clattering and rumbling noise, and the next instant a vast terrific eye shot by, with a long tail attached, and disappeared in the gloom, still uttering triumphant shrieks.

The poor camp laborers were stricken to the heart with

fright, and stampeded for the high grass in a body. But not the scientists. They had no superstitions. They calmly proceeded to exchange theories. The ancient geographer's opinion was asked. He went into his shell and deliberated long and profoundly. When he came out at last, they all knew by his worshiping countenance that he brought light. Said he:

"Give thanks for this stupendous thing which we have been permitted to witness.—It is the Vernal Equinox!"

There were shoutings and great rejoicings.

"But," said the Angle-worm, uncoiling after reflection, "this is dead summer time."

"Very well," said the Turtle, "we are far from our region; the season differs with the difference of time between the two points."

"Ah, true. True enough. But it is night. How should the sun pass in the night?"

"In these distant regions he doubtless passes always in the night at this hour."

"Yes, doubtless that is true. But it being night, how is it that we could see him?"

"It is a great mystery. I grant that. But I am persuaded that the humidity of the atmosphere in these remote regions is such that particles of daylight adhere to the disk and it was by aid of these that we were enabled to see the sun in the dark."

This was deemed satisfactory, and due entry was made of the decision.

But about this moment those dreadful shriekings were heard again; again the rumbling and thundering came speeding up out of the night; and once more a flaming great eye flashed by and lost itself in gloom and distance.

The camp laborers gave themselves up for lost. The savants were sorely perplexed. Here was a marvel hard to account for. They thought and they talked, they talked and they thought. —Finally the learned and aged Lord Grand-Daddy-Longlegs, who had been sitting, in deep study, with his slender limbs crossed and his stemmy arms folded, said:

"Deliver your opinions, brethren, and then I will tell my thought—for I think I have solved this problem."

"So be it, good your lordship," piped the weak treble of the wrinkled and withered Professor Woodlouse, "for we shall hear from your lordship's lips naught but wisdom."—[Here the speaker threw in a mess of trite, threadbare, exasperating quotations from the ancient poets and philosophers, delivering them with unction in the sounding grandeurs of the original tongues, they being from the Mastodon, the Dodo, and other dead languages]. "Perhaps I ought not to presume to meddle with matters pertaining to astronomy at all, in such a presence as this, I who have made it the business of my life to delve only among the riches of the extinct languages and unearth the opulence of their ancient lore; but still, as unacquainted as I am with the noble science of astronomy, I beg with deference and humility to suggest that inasmuch as the last of these wonderful apparitions proceeded in exactly the opposite direction from that pursued by the first, which you decide to be the Vernal Equinox, and greatly resembled it in all particulars, is it not possible, nay certain, that this last is the *Autumnal* Equi——"

"O-o-o!" "O-o-o! go to bed! go to bed!" with annoyed derision from everybody. So the poor old Woodlouse retreated out of sight, consumed with shame.

Further discussion followed, and then the united voice of the commission begged Lord Longlegs to speak. He said:

"Fellow-scientists, it is my belief that we have witnessed a thing which has occurred in perfection but once before in the knowledge of created beings. It is a phenomenon of inconceivable importance and interest, view it as one may, but its interest to us is vastly heightened by an added knowledge of its nature which no scholar has heretofore possessed or even suspected. This great marvel which we have just witnessed, fellow-savants, (it almost takes my breath away!) is nothing less than the transit of Venus!"

Every scholar sprang to his feet pale with astonishment. Then ensued tears, hand-shakings, frenzied embraces, and the most extravagant jubilations of every sort. But by and by, as emotion began to retire within bounds, and reflection to return to the front, the accomplished Chief Inspector Lizard observed:

"But how is this?— Venus should traverse the sun's surface, not the earth's."

The arrow went home. It carried sorrow to the breast of

every apostle of learning there, for none could deny that this was a formidable criticism. But tranquilly the venerable Duke crossed his limbs behind his ears and said:

"My friend has touched the marrow of our mighty discovery. Yes—all that have lived before us thought a transit of Venus consisted of a flight across the sun's face; they thought it, they maintained it, they honestly believed it, simple hearts, and were justified in it by the limitations of their knowledge; but to us has been granted the inestimable boon of proving that the transit occurs across the earth's face, *for we have* SEEN *it!*"

The assembled wisdom sat in speechless adoration of this imperial intellect. All doubts had instantly departed, like night before the lightning.

The Tumble-Bug had just intruded, unnoticed. He now came reeling forward among the scholars, familiarly slapping first one and then another on the shoulder, saying "Nice ('ic!) nice old boy!" and smiling a smile of elaborate content. Arrived at a good position for speaking, he put his left arm akimbo with his knuckles planted in his hip just under the edge of his cut-away coat, bent his right leg, placing his toe on the ground and resting his heel with easy grace against his left shin, puffed out his aldermanic stomach, opened his lips, leaned his right elbow on Inspector Lizard's shoulder, and—

But the shoulder was indignantly withdrawn and the hard-handed son of toil went to earth. He floundered a bit but came up smiling, arranged his attitude with the same careful detail as before, only choosing Professor Dogtick's shoulder for a support, opened his lips and—

Went to earth again. He presently scrambled up once more, still smiling, made a loose effort to brush the dust off his coat and legs, but a smart pass of his hand missed entirely and the force of the unchecked impulse slewed him suddenly around, twisted his legs together, and projected him, limber and sprawling, into the lap of the Lord Longlegs. Two or three scholars sprang forward, flung the low creature head over heels into a corner and reinstated the patrician, smoothing his ruffled dignity with many soothing and regretful speeches. Professor Bull Frog roared out:

"No more of this, sirrah Tumble-Bug! Say your say and

then get you about your business with speed!—Quick—
what is your errand? Come—move off a trifle; you smell like
a stable; what have you been at?"

"Please ('ic!) please your worship I chanced to light upon a
find. But no m (*e-uck!*) matter 'bout that. There's b ('ic!) been
another find which— —beg pardon, your honors, what was
that th ('ic!) thing that ripped by here first?"

"It was the Vernal Equinox."

"Inf ('ic!) fernal equinox. 'At's all right.—D ('ic!) Dunno
him. What's other one?"

"The transit of Venus."

"G ('ic!) Got me again. No matter. Las' one dropped something."

"Ah, indeed! Good luck! Good news! Quick—what is it?"

"M ('ic!) Mosey out 'n' see. It'll pay."

No more votes were taken for four and twenty hours. Then
the following entry was made:

"The commission went in a body to view the find. It was
found to consist of a hard, smooth, huge object with a
rounded summit surmounted by a short upright projection
resembling a section of a cabbage stalk divided transversely—
This projection was not solid, but was a hollow cylinder
plugged with a soft woody substance unknown to our region—that is, it had been so plugged, but unfortunately this
obstruction had been heedlessly removed by Norway Rat,
Chief of the Sappers and Miners, before our arrival. The vast
object before us, so mysteriously conveyed from the glittering
domains of space, was found to be hollow and nearly filled
with a pungent liquid of a brownish hue, like rain-water that
has stood for some time. And such a spectacle as met our
view! Norway Rat was perched upon the summit engaged in
thrusting his tail into the cylindrical projection, drawing it
out dripping, permitting the struggling multitude of laborers
to suck the end of it, then straightway reinserting it and delivering the fluid to the mob as before. Evidently this liquor had
strangely potent qualities; for all that partook of it were immediately exalted with great and pleasurable emotions, and
went staggering about singing ribald songs, embracing, fighting, dancing, discharging irruptions of profanity, and defying
all authority. Around us struggled a massed and uncontrolled

mob—uncontrolled and likewise uncontrollable, for the whole army, down to the very sentinels, were mad like the rest, by reason of the drink. We were seized upon by these reckless creatures, and within the hour we, even we, were undistinguishable from the rest—the demoralization was complete and universal. In time the camp wore itself out with its orgies and sank into a stolid and pitiable stupor, in whose mysterious bonds rank was forgotten and strange bed-fellows made, our eyes, at the resurrection, being blasted and our souls petrified with the incredible spectacle of that intolerable stinking scavenger, the Tumble-Bug, and the illustrious patrician my lord Grand Daddy, Duke of Longlegs, lying soundly steeped in sleep, and clasped lovingly in each other's arms, the like whereof hath not been seen in all the ages that tradition compasseth, and doubtless none shall ever in this world find faith to master the belief of it save only we that have beheld the damnable and unholy vision. Thus inscrutable be the ways of God, whose will be done!

"This day, by order, did the Engineer-in-Chief, Herr Spider, rig the necessary tackle for the overturning of the vast reservoir, and so its calamitous contents were discharged in a torrent upon the thirsty earth, which drank it up and now there is no more danger, we reserving but a few drops for experiment and scrutiny, and to exhibit to the king and subsequently preserve among the wonders of the museum. What this liquid is, has been determined. It is without question that fierce and most destructive fluid called lightning. It was wrested, in its container, from its store-house in the clouds, by the resistless might of the flying planet, and hurled at our feet as she sped by. An interesting discovery here results. Which is, that lightning, kept to itself, is quiescent; it is the assaulting contact of the thunderbolt that releases it from captivity, ignites its awful fires and so produces an instantaneous combustion and explosion which spread disaster and desolation far and wide in the earth."

After another day devoted to rest and recovery, the expedition proceeded upon its way. Some days later it went into camp in a pleasant part of the plain, and the savants sallied forth to see what they might find. Their reward was at hand. Professor Bull Frog discovered a strange tree, and called his comrades. They inspected it with profound interest.—It was very tall and straight, and wholly devoid of bark, limbs or foliage. By triangulation Lord Longlegs determined its altitude; Herr Spider measured its circumference at the base and computed the circumference at its top by a mathematical demonstration based upon the warrant furnished by the uniform degree of its taper upward. It was considered a very extraordinary find; and since it was a tree of a hitherto unknown species, Professor Woodlouse gave it a name of a learned sound, being none other than that of Professor Bull Frog translated into the ancient Mastodon language, for it had always been the custom with discoverers to perpetuate their names and honor themselves by this sort of connection with their discoveries.

Now, Professor Field-Mouse having placed his sensitive ear to the tree, detected a rich, harmonious sound issuing from it. This surprising thing was tested and enjoyed by each scholar in turn and great was the gladness and astonishment of all. Professor Woodlouse was requested to add to and extend the tree's name so as to make it suggest the musical quality it possessed—which he did, furnishing the addition *Anthem Singer*, done into the Mastodon tongue.

By this time Professor Snail was making some telescopic inspections. He discovered a great number of these trees, extending in a single rank, with wide intervals between, as far as his instrument would carry, both southward and northward. He also presently discovered that all these trees were bound together, near their tops, by fourteen great ropes, one above another, which ropes were continuous, from tree to tree, as far as his vision could reach. This was surprising. Chief Engineer Spider ran aloft and soon reported that these ropes were simply a web hung there by some colossal member of his own species, for he could see its prey dangling here and there from the strands, in the shape of mighty shreds and rags that had a woven look about their texture and were no doubt the discarded skins of prodigious insects which had been caught and eaten. And then he ran along one of the ropes to make a closer inspection, but felt a smart sudden burn on the soles of his feet, accompanied by a paralyzing shock, wherefore he let go and swung himself to the earth by a thread of his own spinning, and advised all to hurry at once to camp, lest the monster should appear and get as much interested in the savants as they were in him and his works. So they departed with speed, making notes about the gigantic web as they went. And that evening the naturalist of the expedition built a beautiful model of the colossal spider, having no need to see it in order to do this, because he had picked up a fragment of its vertebræ by the tree, and so knew exactly what the creature looked like and what its habits and its preferences were, by this simple evidence alone. He built it with a tail, teeth, fourteen legs and a snout, and said it ate grass, cattle, pebbles and dirt with equal enthusiasm. This animal was regarded as a very precious addition to science. It was hoped a dead one might be found, to stuff. Professor Woodlouse thought that he and his brother scholars, by lying hid and being quiet, might maybe catch a live one. He was advised to try it. Which was all the attention that was paid to his suggestion. The conference ended with the naming the monster after the naturalist, since he, after God, had created it.

"And improved it, mayhap," muttered the Tumble-Bug, who was intruding again, according to his idle custom and his unappeasable curiosity.

END OF PART FIRST.

PART SECOND.

HOW THE ANIMALS OF THE WOOD
COMPLETED THEIR SCIENTIFIC LABORS.

A week later the expedition camped in the midst of a collection of wonderful curiosities. These were a sort of vast caverns of stone that rose singly and in bunches out of the plain by the side of the river which they had first seen when they emerged from the forest. These caverns stood in long straight rows on opposite sides of broad aisles that were bordered with single ranks of trees. The summit of each cavern sloped sharply both ways. Several horizontal rows of great square holes, obstructed by a thin, shiny, transparent substance, pierced the frontage of each cavern. Inside were caverns within caverns; and one might ascend and visit these minor compartments by means of curious winding ways consisting of continuous regular terraces raised one above another. There were many huge shapeless objects in each compartment which were considered to have been living creatures at one time, though now the thin brown skin was shrunken and loose, and rattled when disturbed. Spiders were here in great number, and their cob-webs, stretched in all directions and wreathing the great skinny dead together, were a pleasant spectacle, since they inspired with life and wholesome cheer a scene which would otherwise have brought to the mind only a sense of forsakenness and desolation. Information was sought of these spiders, but in vain. They were of a different nationality from those with the expedition and their language seemed but a musical, meaningless jargon. They were a timid, gentle race, but ignorant, and heathenish worshipers of unknown gods. The expedition detailed a great detachment of missionaries to teach them the true religion, and in a week's time a precious work had been wrought among those darkened creatures, not three families being by that time at peace with each other or having a settled belief in any system of religion whatever. This encouraged the expedition to establish a colony of missionaries there permanently, that the work of grace might go on.

But let us not outrun our narrative. After close examination of the fronts of the caverns, and much thinking and exchanging of theories, the scientists determined the nature of these singular formations. They said that each belonged mainly to the Old Red Sandstone period; that the cavern fronts rose in innumerable and wonderfully regular strata high in the air, each stratum about five frog-spans thick, and that in the present discovery lay an overpowering refutation of all received geology: for between every two layers of Old Red Sandstone reposed a thin layer of decomposed limestone; so instead of there having been but one Old Red Sandstone period there had certainly been not less than a hundred and seventy-five! And by the same token it was plain that there had also been a hundred and seventy-five floodings of the earth and depositings of limestone strata! The unavoidable deduction from which pair of facts, was, the overwhelming truth that the world, instead of being only two hundred thousand years old, was older by millions upon millions of years! And there was another curious thing: every stratum of Old Red Sandstone was pierced and divided at mathematically regular intervals by vertical strata of limestone. Up-shootings of igneous rock through fractures in water formations were common; but here was the first instance where water-formed rock had been so projected. It was a great and noble discovery and its value to science was considered to be inestimable.

A critical examination of some of the lower strata demonstrated the presence of fossil ants and tumble-bugs (the latter accompanied by their peculiar goods), and with high gratification the fact was enrolled upon the scientific record; for this was proof that these vulgar laborers belonged to the first and lowest orders of created beings, though at the same time there was something repulsive in the reflection that the perfect and exquisite creature of the modern uppermost order owed its origin to such ignominious beings through the mysterious law of Development of Species.

The Tumble-Bug, overhearing this discussion, said he was willing that the parvenus of these new times should find what comfort they might in their wise-drawn theories, since as far as he was concerned he was content to be of the old first families and proud to point back to his place among the old original aristocracy of the land.

"Enjoy your mushroom dignity, stinking of the varnish of yesterday's veneering, since you like it," said he; "suffice it for the Tumble-Bugs that they come of a race that rolled their fragrant spheres down the solemn aisles of antiquity, and left their imperishable works embalmed in the Old Red Sandstone to proclaim it to the wasting centuries as they file along the highway of Time!"

"O, take a walk!" said the chief of the expedition, with derision.

The summer passed, and winter approached. In and about many of the caverns were what seemed to be inscriptions. Most of the scientists said they were inscriptions, a few said they were not. The chief philologist, Professor Woodlouse, maintained that they were writings, done in a character utterly unknown to scholars, and in a language equally unknown. He had early ordered his artists and draughtsmen to make fac-similes of all that were discovered; and had set himself about finding the key to the hidden tongue. In this work he had followed the method which had always been used by decipherers previously. That is to say, he placed a number of copies of inscriptions before him and studied them both collectively and in detail. To begin with, he placed the following copies together:

THE AMERICAN HOTEL.	MEALS AT ALL HOURS.
THE SHADES.	NO SMOKING.
BOATS FOR HIRE CHEAP.	UNION PRAYER MEETING, 4 P. M.
BILLIARDS.	THE WATERSIDE JOURNAL.
THE A 1 BARBER SHOP.	TELEGRAPH OFFICE.
KEEP OFF THE GRASS.	TRY BRANDRETH'S PILLS.

COTTAGES FOR RENT DURING THE WATERING SEASON.

FOR SALE CHEAP.	FOR SALE CHEAP.
FOR SALE CHEAP.	FOR SALE CHEAP.

At first it seemed to the Professor that this was a sign-language, and that each word was represented by a distinct sign; further examination convinced him that it was a written language, and that every letter of its alphabet was represented by a character of its own; and finally, he decided that it was a language which conveyed itself partly by letters, and partly by signs or hieroglyphics. This conclusion was forced upon him by the discovery of several specimens of the following nature:

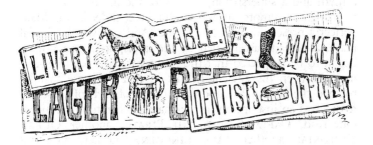

He observed that certain inscriptions were met with in greater frequency than others. Such as "FOR SALE CHEAP;" "BILLIARDS;" "S. T.—1860—X;" "KENO;" "ALE ON DRAUGHT." Naturally, then, these must be religious maxims. But this idea was cast aside, by and by, as the mystery of the strange alphabet began to clear itself. In time, the Professor was enabled to translate several of the inscriptions with considerable plausibility, though not to the perfect satisfaction of all the scholars. Still, he made constant and encouraging progress.

Finally a cavern was discovered with these inscriptions upon it:

WATERSIDE MUSEUM.
Open at all Hours.   *Admission 50 cents.*
WONDERFUL COLLECTION OF WAX-WORKS,
ANCIENT FOSSILS, ETC.

Professor Woodlouse affirmed that the word "Museum" was equivalent to the phrase *"lumgath molo,"* or "Burial-Place." Upon entering, the scientists were well astonished. But what they saw may be best conveyed in the language of their own official report:

"Erect, and in a row, were a sort of rigid great figures which struck us instantly as belonging to the long extinct species of reptile called MAN, described in our ancient records. This was a peculiarly gratifying discovery, because of late times it has become fashionable to regard this creature as a myth and a superstition, a work of the inventive imaginations of our remote ancestors. But here, indeed, was Man, perfectly preserved, in a fossil state. And this was his burial place, as already ascertained by the inscription. And now it began to be suspected that the caverns we had been inspecting had been his ancient haunts in that old time that he roamed the earth—for upon the breast of each of these tall fossils was an inscription in the character heretofore noticed. One read, 'CAPTAIN KIDD, THE PIRATE;' another 'QUEEN VICTORIA;' another, 'ABE LINCOLN;' another, 'GEORGE WASHINGTON,' etc.

"With feverish interest we called for our ancient scientific records to discover if perchance the description of Man there set down would tally with the fossils before us. Professor Woodlouse read it aloud in its quaint and musty phraseology, to wit:

" 'In ye time of our fathers Man still walked ye earth, as by tradition we know. It was a creature of exceeding great size, being compassed about with a loose skin, sometimes of one color, sometimes of many, the which it was able to cast at will; which being done, the hind legs were discovered to be armed with short claws like to a mole's but broader, and ye fore-legs with fingers of a curious slimness and a length much more prodigious than a frog's, armed also with broad talons for scratching in ye earth for its food. It had a sort of feathers upon its head such as hath a rat, but longer, and a beak suitable for seeking its food by ye smell thereof. When it was stirred with happiness, it leaked water from its eyes; and when it suffered or was sad, it manifested it with a horrible hellish cackling clamor that was exceeding dreadful to hear and made one long that it might rend itself and perish, and so end its troubles. Two Mans being together, they uttered noises at each other like to this: 'Haw-haw-haw—dam good, dam good,' together with other sounds of more or less likeness to these, wherefore ye poets conceived that they talked, but poets be always ready to catch at any frantic folly, God he knows. Sometimes this creature goeth about with a long stick ye which it putteth to its face and bloweth fire and smoke through ye same with a sudden and most damnable bruit and noise that doth fright its prey to death, and so seizeth it in its talons and walketh away to its habitat, consumed with a most fierce and devilish joy.'

"Now was the description set forth by our ancestors wonderfully endorsed and confirmed by the fossils before us, as shall be seen. The specimen marked 'Captain Kidd' was examined in detail. Upon its head and part of its face was a sort of fur like that upon the tail of a horse. With great labor its loose skin was removed, whereupon its body was discovered to be of a polished white texture, thoroughly petrified. The straw it had eaten, so many ages gone by, was still in its body, undigested—and even in its legs.

"Surrounding these fossils were objects that would mean nothing to the ignorant, but to the eye of science they were a revelation. They laid bare the secrets of dead ages. These musty Memorials told us when Man lived, and what were his habits. For here, side by side with Man, were the evidences that he had lived in the earliest ages of creation, the companion of the other low orders of life that belonged to that forgotten time.—Here was the fossil nautilus that sailed the primeval seas; here was the skeleton of the mastodon, the ichthyosaurus, the cave bear, the prodigious elk. Here, also, were the charred bones of some of these extinct animals and of the young of Man's own species, split lengthwise, showing that to his taste the marrow was a toothsome luxury. It was plain that Man had robbed those bones of their contents, since no tooth-mark of any beast was upon them—albeit the Tumble-Bug intruded the remark that 'no beast could mark a bone with its teeth, anyway.' Here were proofs that Man had vague, groveling notions of art; for this fact was conveyed by certain things marked with the untranslatable words, 'FLINT HATCHETS, KNIVES, ARROW-HEADS, AND BONE-ORNAMENTS OF PRIMEVAL MAN.' Some of these seemed to be rude weapons chipped out of flint, and in a secret place was found some more in process of construction, with this untranslatable legend, on a thin, flimsy material, lying by:

"*Jones, if you don't want to be discharged from the Musseum, make the next primeaveal weppons more careful—you couldn't even fool one of these sleapy old syentiffic grannys from the Coledge with the last ones. And mind you the animles you carved on some of the Bone Ornaments is a blame sight too good for any primeaveal man that was ever fooled.—Varnum, Manager.*"

"Back of the burial place was a mass of ashes, showing that Man always had a feast at a funeral—else why the ashes in such a place? and showing, also, that he believed in God and the immortality of the soul—else why these solemn ceremonies?

"To sum up.—We believe that man had a written language. We *know* that he indeed existed at one time, and is not a myth; also, that he was the companion of the cave bear, the mastodon, and other extinct species; that he cooked and ate them and likewise the young of his own kind; also, that he bore rude weapons, and knew something of art; that he imagined he had a soul, and pleased himself with the fancy that it was immortal. But let us not laugh; there may be creatures in existence to whom we and our vanities and profundities may seem as ludicrous."

END OF PART SECOND.

PART THIRD.

Near the margin of the great river the scientists presently found a huge, shapely stone, with this inscription:

"In 1847, in the spring, the river overflowed its banks and covered the whole township. The depth was from two to six feet. More than 900 head of cattle were lost, and many homes destroyed. The Mayor ordered this memorial to be erected to perpetuate the event. God spare us the repetition of it!"

With infinite trouble, Professor Woodlouse succeeded in making a translation of this inscription, which was sent home and straightway an enormous excitement was created about it. It confirmed, in a remarkable way, certain treasured traditions of the ancients. The translation was slightly marred by one or two untranslatable words, but these did not impair the general clearness of the meaning. It is here presented:

"One thousand eight hundred and forty-seven years ago, the (fires?) descended and consumed the whole city. Only some nine hundred souls were saved, all others destroyed. The (king?) commanded this stone to be set up to . . . . . (untranslatable) . . . . . prevent the repetition of it."

This was the first successful and satisfactory translation that had been made of the mysterious character left behind him by extinct man, and it gave Professor Woodlouse such reputation that at once every seat of learning in his native land conferred a degree of the most illustrious grade upon him, and it was believed that if he had been a soldier and had turned his splendid talents to the extermination of a remote tribe of reptiles, the king would have ennobled him and made him rich. And this, too, was the origin of that school of scientists called Manologists, whose specialty is the deciphering of the ancient records of the extinct bird termed Man. [For it is now decided that Man was a bird and not a reptile]. But Professor Woodlouse began and remained chief of these, for it was granted that no translations were ever so free from error as his. Others made mistakes—he seemed incapable of it. Many a memorial of the lost race was afterward found, but none ever attained to the renown and veneration achieved by the "Mayoritish Stone"—it being so called from the word "Mayor" in it, which, being translated "King," "Mayoritish Stone" was but another way of saying "King Stone."

Another time the expedition made a great "find." It was a vast round flattish mass, ten frog-spans in diameter and five or six high. Professor Snail put on his spectacles and examined it all around, and then climbed up and inspected the top. He said:

"The result of my perlustration and perscontation of this isoperimetrical protuberance is a belief that it is one of those rare and wonderful creations left by the Mound Builders. The fact that this one is lamellibranchiate in its formation, simply adds to its interest as being possibly of a different kind from any we read of in the records of science, but yet in no manner marring its authenticity. Let the megalophonous grasshopper sound a blast and summon hither the perfunctory and circum-foraneous Tumble-Bug, to the end that excavations may be made and learning gather new treasures."

Not a Tumble-Bug could be found on duty, so the Mound was excavated by a working party of Ants. Nothing was discovered. This would have been a great disappointment, had not the venerable Longlegs explained the matter.—He said:

"It is now plain to me that the mysterious and forgotten race of Mound Builders did not always erect these edifices as mausoleums, else in this case as in all previous cases, their skeletons would be found here, along with the rude implements which the creatures used in life. Is not this manifest?"

"True! true!" from everybody.

"Then we have made a discovery of peculiar value here; a discovery which greatly extends our knowledge of this creature in place of diminishing it; a discovery which will add lustre to the achievements of this expedition and win for us the commendations of scholars everywhere. For the absence of the customary relics here means nothing less than this: The Mound Builder, instead of being the ignorant, savage reptile we have been taught to consider him, was a creature of cultivation and high intelligence, capable of not only appreciating worthy achievements of the great and noble of his species, but of commemorating them! Fellow-scholars, this stately Mound is not a sepulchre, it is a monument!"

A profound impression was produced by this.

But it was interrupted by rude and derisive laughter—and the Tumble-Bug appeared.

"A monument!" quoth he. "A monument set up by a Mound Builder! Aye, so it is! So it is, indeed, to the shrewd keen eye of science; but to an ignorant poor devil who has never seen a college, it is not a Monument, strictly speaking, but is yet a most rich and noble property; and with your worships' good permission I will proceed to manufacture it into spheres of exceeding grace and—"

The Tumble-Bug was driven away with stripes, and the draughtsmen of the expedition were set to making views of the Monument from different standpoints, while Professor Woodlouse, in a frenzy of scientific zeal, traveled all over it and all around it hoping to find an inscription. But if there had ever been one it had decayed or been removed by some vandal as a relic.

The views having been completed, it was now considered safe to load the precious Monument itself upon the backs of four of the largest Tortoises and send it home to the King's museum, which was done; and when it arrived it was received with enormous *éclat* and escorted to its future abiding-place by thousands of enthusiastic citizens, King Bullfrog XVI. himself attending and condescending to sit enthroned upon it throughout the progress.

The growing rigor of the weather was now admonishing the scientists to close their labors for the present, so they made preparations to journey homeward. But even their last day among the Caverns bore fruit; for one of the scholars found in an out-of-the-way corner of the Museum or "Burial-Place" a most strange and extraordinary thing. It was nothing less than a double Man-Bird lashed together breast to breast by a natural ligament, and labelled with the untranslatable words, *"Siamese Twins."* The official report concerning this thing closed thus:

"Wherefore it appears that there were in old times two distinct species of this majestic fowl, the one being single and the other double. Nature has a reason for all things.—It is plain to the eye of science that the Double-Man originally inhabited a region where dangers abounded; hence he was paired together to the end that while one part slept the other might watch; and likewise that, danger being discovered, there might always be a double instead of a single power to oppose it. All honor to the mystery-dispelling eye of godlike Science!"

And near the Double Man-Bird was found what was plainly an ancient record of his, marked upon numberless sheets of a thin white substance and bound together. Almost the first glance that Professor Woodlouse threw into it revealed this following sentence, which he instantly translated and laid before the scientists, in a tremble, and it uplifted every soul there with exultation and astonishment:

"In truth it is believed by many that the lower animals reason and talk together."

When the great official report of the expedition appeared, the above sentence bore this comment:

"Then there are lower animals than Man! This remarkable passage can mean nothing else. Man himself is extinct, but *they* may still exist. What can they be? Where do they inhabit? One's enthusiasm bursts all bounds in the contemplation of the brilliant field of discovery and investigation here thrown open to science. We close our labors with the humble prayer that your Majesty will immediately appoint a commission and command it to rest not nor spare expense until the search for this hitherto unsuspected race of the creatures of God shall be crowned with success."

The expedition then journeyed homeward after its long absence and its faithful endeavors, and was received with a mighty ovation by the whole grateful country.

There were vulgar, ignorant carpers, of course, as there always are and always will be; and naturally one of these was the obscene Tumble-Bug. He said that all he had learned by

his travels was that science only needed a spoonful of suppo-
sition to build a mountain of demonstrated fact out of; and
that for the future he meant to be content with the knowledge that nature had made free to all creatures and not go
prying into the august secrets of the Deity.

1875

Petition Concerning Copyright

Whereas, The Constitution guarantees equal rights to all, backed by the Declaration of Independence; and

Whereas, Under our laws, the right of property in real estate is perpetual; and

Whereas, Under our laws, the right of property in the literary result of a citizen's intellectual labor is restricted to forty-two years; and

Whereas, Forty-two years seems an exceedingly just and righteous term, and a sufficiently long one for the retention of property:

Therefore, Your petitioner, having the good of his country solely at heart, humbly prays that "equal rights" and fair and equal treatment may be meted out to all citizens, by the restriction of rights in *all* property, real estate included, to the beneficent term of forty-two years. Then shall all men bless your honorable body and be happy. And for this will your petitioner ever pray.

MARK TWAIN.

A PARAGRAPH NOT ADDED TO THE PETITION.

The charming absurdity of restricting property-rights in books to forty-two years sticks prominently out in the fact that hardly any man's books ever *live* forty-two years, or even the half of it; and so, for the sake of getting a shabby advantage of the heirs of about one Scott or Burns or Milton in a hundred years, the law makers of the "Great" Republic are content to leave that poor little pilfering edict upon the statute books. It is like an emperor lying in wait to rob a phenix's nest, and waiting the necessary century to get the chance.

1875

"Party Cries" in Ireland

Belfast is a peculiarly religious community. This may be said of the whole of the north of Ireland. About one half of the people are Protestants and the other half Catholics. Each party does all it can to make its own doctrines popular and draw the affections of the irreligious toward them. One hears constantly of the most touching instances of this zeal. A week ago a vast concourse of Catholics assembled at Armagh to dedicate a new Cathedral; and when they started home again the roadways were lined with groups of meek and lowly Protestants who stoned them till all the region round about was marked with blood. I thought that only Catholics argued in that way, but it seems to be a mistake.

Every man in the community is a missionary and carries a brick to admonish the erring with. The law has tried to break this up, but not with perfect success. It has decreed that irritating "party cries" shall not be indulged in, and that persons uttering them shall be fined forty shillings and costs. And so, in the police court reports, every day, one sees these fines recorded. Last week a girl twelve years old was fined the usual forty shillings and costs for proclaiming in the public streets that she was "a Protestant." The usual cry is, "To hell with the Pope!" or "To hell with the Protestants!" according to the utterer's system of salvation.

One of Belfast's local jokes was very good. It referred to the uniform and inevitable fine of forty shillings and costs for uttering a party cry—and it is no economical fine for a poor man, either, by the way. They say that a policeman found a drunken man lying on the ground, up a dark alley, entertaining himself with shouting, "To *hell* with!" "To *hell* with!" The officer smelt a fine—informers get half:

"What's that you say?"

"To *hell* with!"

"To hell with *who*? To hell with *what*?"

"Ah, bedad ye can finish it yourself—it's too expinsive for me!"

I think the seditious disposition, restrained by the economical instinct is finely put, in that.

1875

The Curious Republic of Gondour

As soon as I had learned to speak the language a little, I became greatly interested in the people and the system of government.

I found that the nation had at first tried universal suffrage pure and simple, but had thrown that form aside because the result was not satisfactory. It had seemed to deliver all power into the hands of the ignorant and non-tax-paying classes; and of a necessity the responsible offices were filled from these classes also.

A remedy was sought. The people believed they had found it; not in the destruction of universal suffrage, but in the enlargement of it. It was an odd idea, and ingenious. You must understand, the constitution gave every man a vote; therefore that vote was a vested right, and could not be taken away. But the constitution did not say that certain individuals might not be given two votes, or ten! So an amendatory clause was inserted in a quiet way; a clause which authorized the enlargement of the suffrage in certain cases to be specified by statute. To offer to "limit" the suffrage might have made instant trouble; the offer to "enlarge" it had a pleasant aspect. But of course the newspapers soon began to suspect; and then out they came! It was found, however, that for once,—and for the first time in the history of the republic,—property, character, and intellect were able to wield a political influence; for once, money, virtue, and intelligence took a vital and a united interest in a political question. For once these powers went to the "primaries" in strong force; for once the best men in the nation were put forward as candidates for that parliament whose business it should be to enlarge the suffrage. The weightiest half of the press quickly joined forces with the new movement, and left the other half to rail about the proposed "destruction of the liberties" of the bottom layer of society, the hitherto governing class of the community.

The victory was complete. The new law was framed and passed. Under it every citizen, howsoever poor or ignorant, possessed one vote, so universal suffrage still reigned; but if a man possessed a good common-school education and no money, he had two votes; a high-school education gave him four; if he had property likewise, to the value of three thousand *sacos*, he wielded one more vote; for every fifty thousand sacos a man added to his property, he was entitled to another vote; a university education entitled a man to nine votes, even though he owned no property. Therefore, learning being more prevalent and more easily acquired than riches, educated men became a wholesome check upon wealthy men, since they could outvote them. Learning goes usually with uprightness, broad views, and humanity; so the learned voters, possessing the balance of power, became the vigilant and efficient protectors of the great lower rank of society.

And now a curious thing developed itself—a sort of emulation, whose object was voting-power! Whereas formerly a man was honored only according to the amount of money he possessed, his grandeur was measured now by the number of votes he wielded. A man with only one vote was conspicuously respectful to his neighbor who possessed three. And if he was a man above the commonplace, he was as conspicuously energetic in his determination to acquire three for himself. This spirit of emulation invaded all ranks. Votes based upon capital were commonly called "mortal" votes, because they could be lost; those based upon learning were called "immortal," because they were permanent, and because of their customarily imperishable character they were naturally more valued than the other sort. I say "customarily" for the reason that these votes were not absolutely imperishable, since insanity could suspend them.

Under this system, gambling and speculation almost ceased in the republic. A man honored as the possessor of great voting-power could not afford to risk the loss of it upon a doubtful chance.

It was curious to observe the manners and customs which the enlargement plan produced. Walking the street with a friend one day, he delivered a careless bow to a passer-by, and then remarked that that person possessed only one vote and would probably never earn another; he was more respectful to the next acquaintance he met; he explained that this salute was a four-vote bow. I tried to "average" the importance of the people he accosted after that, by the nature of his bows, but my success was only partial, because of the somewhat greater homage paid to the immortals than to the mortals. My friend explained. He said there was no law to regulate this thing, except that most powerful of all laws, custom. Custom had created these varying bows, and in time they had become easy and natural. At this moment he delivered himself of a very profound salute, and then said, "Now there's a man who began life as a shoemaker's apprentice, and without education; now he swings twenty-two mortal votes and two immortal ones; he expects to pass a high-school examination this year and climb a couple of votes higher among the immortals; mighty valuable citizen."

By and by my friend met a venerable personage, and not only made him a most elaborate bow, but also took off his hat. I took off mine, too, with a mysterious awe. I was beginning to be infected.

"What grandee is that?"

"That is our most illustrious astronomer. He hasn't any money, but is fearfully learned. Nine immortals is *his* political weight! He would swing a hundred and fifty votes if our system were perfect."

"Is there any altitude of mere moneyed grandeur that you take off your hat to?"

"No. Nine immortal votes is the only power we uncover for—that is, in civil life. Very great officials receive that mark of homage, of course."

It was common to hear people admiringly mention men who had begun life on the lower levels and in time achieved great voting-power. It was also common to hear youths planning a future of ever so many votes for themselves. I heard shrewd mammas speak of certain young men as good "catches" because they possessed such-and-such a number of votes. I knew of more than one case where an heiress was married to a youngster who had but one vote; the argument being that he was gifted with such excellent parts that in time he would acquire a good voting strength, and perhaps in the long run be able to outvote his wife, if he had luck.

Competitive examinations were the rule in all official grades. I remarked that the questions asked the candidates were wild, intricate, and often required a sort of knowledge not needed in the office sought.

"Can a fool or an ignoramus answer them?" asked the person I was talking with.

"Certainly not."

"Well, you will not find any fools or ignoramuses among our officials."

I felt rather cornered, but made shift to say, —

"But these questions cover a good deal more ground than is necessary."

"No matter; if candidates can answer these it is tolerably fair evidence that they can answer nearly any other question you choose to ask them."

There were some things in Gondour which one could not shut his eyes to. One was, that ignorance and incompetence had no place in the government. Brains and property managed the state. A candidate for office must have marked ability, education, and high character, or he stood no sort of chance of election. If a hod-carrier possessed these, he could succeed; but the mere fact that he was a hod-carrier could not elect him, as in previous times.

It was now a very great honor to be in the parliament or in office; under the old system such distinction had only brought suspicion upon a man and made him a helpless mark for newspaper contempt and scurrility. Officials did not need to steal now, their salaries being vast in comparison with the pittances paid in the days when parliaments were created by hod-carriers, who viewed official salaries from a hod-carrying point of view and compelled that view to be respected by their obsequious servants. Justice was wisely and rigidly administered; for a judge, after once reaching his place through the specified line of promotions, was a permanency during good behavior. He was not obliged to modify his judgments according to the effect they might have upon the temper of a reigning political party.

The country was mainly governed by a ministry which went out with the administration that created it. This was also the case with the chiefs of the great departments. Minor officials ascended to their several positions through well-earned promotions, and not by a jump from gin-mills or the needy families and friends of members of parliament. Good behavior measured their terms of office.

The head of the government, the Grand Caliph, was elected for a term of twenty years. I questioned the wisdom of this. I was answered that he could do no harm, since the ministry and the parliament governed the land, and he was liable to impeachment for misconduct. This great office had twice been ably filled by women, women as aptly fitted for it as some of the sceptred queens of history. Members of the cabinet, under many administrations, had been women.

I found that the pardoning power was lodged in a court of pardons, consisting of several great judges. Under the old *régime*, this important power was vested in a single official, and he usually took care to have a general jail delivery in time for the next election.

I inquired about public schools. There were plenty of them, and of free colleges too. I inquired about compulsory education. This was received with a smile, and the remark,—

"When a man's child is able to make himself powerful and honored according to the amount of education he acquires, don't you suppose that that parent will apply the compulsion himself? Our free schools and free colleges require no law to fill them."

There was a loving pride of country about this person's way of speaking which annoyed me. I had long been unused to the sound of it in my own. The Gondour national airs were forever dinning in my ears; therefore I was glad to leave that country and come back to my dear native land, where one never hears that sort of music.

October 1875

A Literary Nightmare

Will the reader please to cast his eye over the following verses, and see if he can discover anything harmful in them?

> "Conductor, when you receive a fare,
> Punch in the presence of the passenjare!
> A blue trip slip for an eight-cent fare,
> A buff trip slip for a six-cent fare,
> A pink trip slip for a three-cent fare,
> Punch in the presence of the passenjare!
> CHORUS.
> Punch, brothers! punch with care!
> Punch in the presence of the passenjare!"

I came across these jingling rhymes in a newspaper, a little while ago, and read them a couple of times. They took instant and entire possession of me. All through breakfast they went waltzing through my brain; and when, at last, I rolled up my napkin, I could not tell whether I had eaten anything or not. I had carefully laid out my day's work the day before—a thrilling tragedy in the novel which I am writing. I went to my den to begin my deed of blood. I took up my pen, but all I could get it to say was, "Punch in the presence of the passenjare." I fought hard for an hour, but it was useless. My head kept humming, "A blue trip slip for an eight-cent fare, a buff trip slip for a six-cent fare," and so on and so on, without peace or respite. The day's work was ruined—I could see that plainly enough. I gave up and drifted down town, and presently discovered that my feet were keeping time to that relentless jingle. When I could stand it no longer I altered my step. But it did no good; those rhymes accommodated themselves to the new step and went on harassing me just as before. I returned home, and suffered all the afternoon; suffered all through an unconscious and unrefreshing dinner; suffered, and cried, and jingled all through the evening; went to bed and rolled, tossed, and jingled right along, the same as ever; got up at midnight frantic, and tried to read; but there was nothing visible upon the whirling page except "Punch! punch in the presence of the passenjare." By sunrise I was out of my

mind, and everybody marveled and was distressed at the idiotic burden of my ravings,—"Punch! oh, punch! punch in
the presence of the passenjare!"

Two days later, on Saturday morning, I arose, a tottering
wreck, and went forth to fulfill an engagement with a valued
friend, the Rev. Mr. ——, to walk to the Talcott Tower, ten
miles distant. He stared at me, but asked no questions. We
started. Mr. —— talked, talked, talked—as is his wont. I said
nothing; I heard nothing. At the end of a mile, Mr. ——
said,—

"Mark, are you sick? I never saw a man look so haggard
and worn and absent-minded. Say something; do!"

Drearily, without enthusiasm, I said: "Punch, brothers,
punch with care! Punch in the presence of the passenjare!"

My friend eyed me blankly, looked perplexed, then said,—

"I do not think I get your drift, Mark. There does not seem
to be any relevancy in what you have said, certainly nothing
sad; and yet—maybe it was the way you *said* the words—I
never heard anything that sounded so pathetic. What is"—

But I heard no more. I was already far away with my pitiless, heart-breaking "blue trip slip for an eight-cent fare, buff
trip slip for a six-cent fare, pink trip slip for a three-cent fare;
punch in the presence of the passenjare." I do not know what
occurred during the other nine miles. However, all of a sudden Mr. —— laid his hand on my shoulder and shouted,—

"Oh, wake up! wake up! wake up! Don't sleep all day!
Here we are at the Tower, man! I have talked myself deaf and
dumb and blind, and never got a response. Just look at this
magnificent autumn landscape! Look at it! look at it! Feast
your eyes on it! You have traveled; you have seen boasted
landscapes elsewhere. Come, now, deliver an honest opinion.
What do you say to this?"

I sighed wearily, and murmured,—

"A buff trip slip for a six-cent fare, a pink trip slip for a
three-cent fare, punch in the presence of the passenjare."

Rev. Mr. —— stood there, very grave, full of concern, apparently, and looked long at me; then he said,—

"Mark, there is something about this that I cannot understand. Those are about the same words you said before; there
does not seem to be anything in them, and yet they nearly

break my heart when you say them. Punch in the—how is it they go?"

I began at the beginning and repeated all the lines. My friend's face lighted with interest. He said,—

"Why, what a captivating jingle it is! It is almost music. It flows along so nicely. I have nearly caught the rhymes myself. Say them over just once more, and then I'll have them, sure."

I said them over. Then Mr. —— said them. He made one little mistake, which I corrected. The next time and the next he got them right. Now a great burden seemed to tumble from my shoulders. That torturing jingle departed out of my brain, and a grateful sense of rest and peace descended upon me. I was light-hearted enough to sing; and I did sing for half an hour, straight along, as we went jogging homeward. Then my freed tongue found blessed speech again, and the pent talk of many a weary hour began to gush and flow. It flowed on and on, joyously, jubilantly, until the fountain was empty and dry. As I wrung my friend's hand at parting, I said,—

"Have n't we had a royal good time! But now I remember, you have n't said a word for two hours. Come, come, out with something!"

The Rev. Mr. —— turned a lacklustre eye upon me, drew a deep sigh, and said, without animation, without apparent consciousness,—

"Punch, brothers, punch with care! Punch in the presence of the passenjare!"

A pang shot through me as I said to myself, "Poor fellow, poor fellow! *he* has got it, now."

I did not see Mr. —— for two or three days after that. Then, on Tuesday evening, he staggered into my presence and sank dejectedly into a seat. He was pale, worn; he was a wreck. He lifted his faded eyes to my face and said,—

"Ah, Mark, it was a ruinous investment that I made in those heartless rhymes. They have ridden me like a nightmare, day and night, hour after hour, to this very moment. Since I saw you I have suffered the torments of the lost. Saturday evening I had a sudden call, by telegraph, and took the night train for Boston. The occasion was the death of a valued old friend who had requested that I should preach his funeral sermon. I took my seat in the cars and set myself to framing the discourse. But I never got beyond the opening paragraph; for then the train started and the car-wheels began their 'clack-clack-clack-clack! clack-clack-clack-clack!' and right away those odious rhymes fitted themselves to that accompaniment. For an hour I sat there and set a syllable of those rhymes to every separate and distinct clack the car-wheels made. Why, I was as fagged out, then, as if I had been chopping wood all day. My skull was splitting with headache. It seemed to me that I must go mad if I sat there any longer; so I undressed and went to bed. I stretched myself out in my berth, and—well, you know what the result was. The thing went right along, just the same. 'Clack-clack-clack, a blue trip slip, clack-clack-clack, for an eight-cent fare; clack-clack-clack, a buff trip slip, clack-clack-clack, for a six-cent fare, and so on, and so on, and so on—*punch*, in the presence of the passenjare!' Sleep? Not a single wink! I was almost a lunatic when I got to Boston. Don't ask me about the funeral. I did the best I could, but every solemn individual sentence was meshed and tangled and woven in and out with 'Punch, brothers, punch with care, punch in the presence of the passenjare.' And the most distressing thing was that my *delivery* dropped into the undulating rhythm of those pulsing rhymes, and I could actually catch absent-minded people nodding *time* to the swing of it with their stupid heads. And, Mark, you may believe it or not, but before I got through, the entire assemblage were placidly bobbing their heads in solemn unison, mourners, undertaker, and all. The moment I had finished, I fled to the anteroom in a state bordering on frenzy. Of course it would be my luck to find a sorrowing and aged maiden aunt of the deceased there, who had arrived from Springfield too late to get into the church. She began to sob, and said,—

" 'Oh, oh, he is gone, he is gone, and I didn't see him before he died!'

" 'Yes!' I said, 'he *is* gone, he *is* gone, he *is* gone—oh, *will* this suffering never cease!'

" '*You* loved him, then! Oh, you too loved him!'

" 'Loved him! Loved *who*?'

" 'Why, my poor George! my poor nephew!'

" 'Oh—*him!* Yes—oh, yes, yes. Certainly—certainly. Punch—punch—oh, this misery will kill me!'

" 'Bless you! bless you, sir, for these sweet words! *I*, too, suffer in this dear loss. Were you present during his last moments?'

" 'Yes! I—*whose* last moments?'

" '*His*. The dear departed's.'

" 'Yes! Oh, yes—yes—*yes!* I suppose so, I think so, *I* don't know! Oh, certainly—I was there—*I* was there!'

" 'Oh, what a privilege! what a precious privilege! And his last words—oh, tell me, tell me his last words! What did he say?'

" 'He said—he said—oh, my head, my head, my head! He said—he said—he never said *any*thing but Punch, punch, *punch* in the presence of the passenjare! Oh, leave me, madam! In the name of all that is generous, leave me to my madness, my misery, my despair!—a buff trip slip for a six-cent fare, a pink trip slip for a three-cent fare—endu-rance *can* no fur-ther go!—PUNCH in the presence of the passen-jare!' "

My friend's hopeless eyes rested upon mine a pregnant minute, and then he said impressively,—

"Mark, you do not say anything. You do not offer me any hope. But, ah me, it is just as well—it is just as well. You could not do me any good. The time has long gone by when words could comfort me. Something tells me that my tongue is doomed to wag forever to the jigger of that remorseless jingle. There—there it is coming on me again: a blue trip slip for an eight-cent fare, a buff trip slip for a"—

Thus murmuring faint and fainter, my friend sank into a peaceful trance and forgot his sufferings in a blessed respite.

How did I finally save him from the asylum? I took him to a neighboring university and made him discharge the burden of his persecuting rhymes into the eager ears of the poor, unthinking students. How is it with *them*, now? The result is too sad to tell. Why did I write this article? It was for a worthy, even a noble, purpose. It was to warn you, reader, if you should come across those merciless rhymes, to avoid them—avoid them as you would a pestilence!

February 1876

The Facts Concerning the Recent Carnival of Crime in Connecticut

I was feeling blithe, almost jocund. I put a match to my cigar, and just then the morning's mail was handed in. The first superscription I glanced at was in a handwriting that sent a thrill of pleasure through and through me. It was aunt Mary's; and she was the person I loved and honored most in all the world, outside of my own household. She had been my boyhood's idol; maturity, which is fatal to so many enchantments, had not been able to dislodge her from her pedestal; no, it had only justified her right to be there, and placed her dethronement permanently among the impossibilities. To show how strong her influence over me was, I will observe that long after everybody else's "*do*-stop-smoking" had ceased to affect me in the slightest degree, aunt Mary could still stir my torpid conscience into faint signs of life when she touched upon the matter. But all things have their limit, in this world. A happy day came at last, when even aunt Mary's words could no longer move me. I was not merely glad to see that day arrive; I was more than glad—I was grateful; for when its sun had set, the one alloy that was able to mar my enjoyment of my aunt's society was gone. The remainder of her stay with us that winter was in every way a delight. Of course she pleaded with me just as earnestly as ever, after that blessed day, to quit my pernicious habit, but to no purpose whatever; the moment she opened the subject I at once became calmly, peacefully, contentedly indifferent—absolutely, adamantinely indifferent. Consequently the closing weeks of that memorable visit melted away as pleasantly as a dream, they were so freighted, for me, with tranquil satisfaction. I could not have enjoyed my pet vice more if my gentle tormentor had been a smoker herself, and an advocate of the practice. Well, the sight of her handwriting reminded me that I was getting very hungry to see her again. I easily guessed what I should find in her letter. I opened it. Good! just as I expected; she was coming! Coming this very day, too, and by the morning train; I might expect her any moment.

I said to myself, "I am thoroughly happy and content, now.

If my most pitiless enemy could appear before me at this moment, I would freely right any wrong I may have done him."

Straightway the door opened, and a shriveled, shabby dwarf entered. He was not more than two feet high. He seemed to be about forty years old. Every feature and every inch of him was a trifle out of shape; and so, while one could not put his finger upon any particular part and say, "This is a conspicuous deformity," the spectator perceived that this little person was a deformity as a whole—a vague, general, evenly-blended, nicely-adjusted deformity. There was a fox-like cunning in the face and the sharp little eyes, and also alertness and malice. And yet, this vile bit of human rubbish seemed to bear a sort of remote and ill-defined resemblance to me! It was dully perceptible in the mean form, the countenance, and even the clothes, gestures, manner, and attitudes of the creature. He was a far-fetched, dim suggestion of a burlesque upon me, a caricature of me in little. One thing about him struck me forcibly, and most unpleasantly: he was covered all over with a fuzzy, greenish mold, such as one sometimes sees upon mildewed bread. The sight of it was nauseating.

He stepped along with a chipper air, and flung himself into a doll's chair in a very free and easy way, without waiting to be asked. He tossed his hat into the waste basket. He picked up my old chalk pipe from the floor, gave the stem a wipe or two on his knee, filled the bowl from the tobacco-box at his side, and said to me in a tone of pert command,—

"Gimme a match!"

I blushed to the roots of my hair; partly with indignation, but mainly because it somehow seemed to me that this whole performance was very like an exaggeration of conduct which I myself had sometimes been guilty of in my intercourse with familiar friends;—but never, never with strangers, I observed to myself. I wanted to kick the pygmy into the fire, but some incomprehensible sense of being legally and legitimately under his authority forced me to obey his order. He applied the match to the pipe, took a contemplative whiff or two, and remarked, in an irritatingly familiar way,—

"Seems to me it's devilish odd weather for this time of year."

I flushed again, and in anger and humiliation as before; for the language was hardly an exaggeration of some that I have uttered in my day, and moreover was delivered in a tone of voice and with an exasperating drawl that had the seeming of a deliberate travesty of my style. Now there is nothing I am quite so sensitive about as a mocking imitation of my drawling infirmity of speech. I spoke up sharply and said,—

"Look here, you miserable ash-cat! you will have to give a little more attention to your manners, or I will throw you out of the window!"

The manikin smiled a smile of malicious content and security, puffed a whiff of smoke contemptuously toward me, and said, with a still more elaborate drawl,—

"Come—go gently, now; don't put on *too* many airs with your betters."

This cool snub rasped me all over, but it seemed to subjugate me, too, for a moment. The pygmy contemplated me a while with his weasel eyes, and then said, in a peculiarly sneering way,—

"You turned a tramp away from your door this morning."

I said crustily,—

"Perhaps I did, perhaps I did n't. How do *you* know?"

"Well, I know. It is n't any matter *how* I know."

"Very well. Suppose I *did* turn a tramp away from the door—what of it?"

"Oh, nothing; nothing in particular. Only you lied to him."

"I *did n't*! That is, I"—

"Yes, but you did; you lied to him."

I felt a guilty pang,—in truth I had felt it forty times before that tramp had traveled a block from my door,—but still I resolved to make a show of feeling slandered; so I said,—

"This is a baseless impertinence. I said to the tramp"—

"There—wait. You were about to lie again. *I* know what you said to him. You said the cook was gone down town and there was nothing left from breakfast. Two lies. You knew the cook was behind the door, and plenty of provisions behind *her*."

This astonishing accuracy silenced me; and it filled me with wondering speculations, too, as to how this cub could have got his information. Of course he could have culled the conversation from the tramp, but by what sort of magic had he contrived to find out about the concealed cook? Now the dwarf spoke again: —

"It was rather pitiful, rather small, in you to refuse to read that poor young woman's manuscript the other day, and give her an opinion as to its literary value; and she had come so far, too, and *so* hopefully. Now *wasn't* it?"

I felt like a cur! And I had felt so every time the thing had recurred to my mind, I may as well confess. I flushed hotly and said, —

"Look here, have you nothing better to do than prowl around prying into other people's business? Did that girl tell you that?"

"Never mind whether she did or not. The main thing is, you did that contemptible thing. And you felt ashamed of it afterwards. Aha! you feel ashamed of it *now!*"

This with a sort of devilish glee. With fiery earnestness I responded, —

"I told that girl, in the kindest, gentlest way, that I could not consent to deliver judgment upon *any* one's manuscript, because an individual's verdict was worthless. It might underrate a work of high merit and lose it to the world, or it might overrate a trashy production and so open the way for its infliction upon the world. I said that the great public was the only tribunal competent to sit in judgment upon a literary effort, and therefore it must be best to lay it before that tribunal in the outset, since in the end it must stand or fall by that mighty court's decision any way."

"Yes, you said all that. So you did, you juggling, smallsouled shuffler! And yet when the happy hopefulness faded out of that poor girl's face, when you saw her furtively slip beneath her shawl the scroll she had so patiently and honestly scribbled at, — so ashamed of her darling now, so proud of it before, — when you saw the gladness go out of her eyes and the tears come there, when she crept away so humbly who had come so"—

"Oh, peace! peace! peace! Blister your merciless tongue, haven't all these thoughts tortured me enough, without *your* coming here to fetch them back again?"

Remorse! remorse! It seemed to me that it would eat the

very heart out of me! And yet that small fiend only sat there leering at me with joy and contempt, and placidly chuckling. Presently he began to speak again. Every sentence was an accusation, and every accusation a truth. Every clause was freighted with sarcasm and derision, every slow-dropping word burned like vitriol. The dwarf reminded me of times when I had flown at my children in anger and punished them for faults which a little inquiry would have taught me that others, and not they, had committed. He reminded me of how I had disloyally allowed old friends to be traduced in my hearing, and been too craven to utter a word in their defense. He reminded me of many dishonest things which I had done; of many which I had procured to be done by children and other irresponsible persons; of some which I had planned, thought upon, and longed to do, and been kept from the performance by fear of consequences only. With exquisite cruelty he recalled to my mind, item by item, wrongs and unkindnesses I had inflicted and humiliations I had put upon friends since dead, "who died thinking of those injuries, maybe, and grieving over them," he added, by way of poison to the stab.

"For instance," said he, "take the case of your younger brother, when you two were boys together, many a long year ago. He always lovingly trusted in you with a fidelity that your manifold treacheries were not able to shake. He followed you about like a dog, content to suffer wrong and abuse if he might only be with you; patient under these injuries so long as it was your hand that inflicted them. The latest picture you have of him in health and strength must be such a comfort to you! You pledged your honor that if he would let you blindfold him no harm should come to him; and then, giggling and choking over the rare fun of the joke, you led him to a brook thinly glazed with ice, and pushed him in; and how you did laugh! Man, you will never forget the gentle, reproachful look he gave you as he struggled shivering out, if you live a thousand years! Oho! you see it now, you see it *now*!"

"Beast, I have seen it a million times, and shall see it a million more! and may you rot away piecemeal, and suffer till doomsday what I suffer now, for bringing it back to me again!"

The dwarf chuckled contentedly, and went on with his accusing history of my career. I dropped into a moody, vengeful state, and suffered in silence under the merciless lash. At last this remark of his gave me a sudden rouse:—

"Two months ago, on a Tuesday, you woke up, away in the night, and fell to thinking, with shame, about a peculiarly mean and pitiful act of yours toward a poor ignorant Indian in the wilds of the Rocky Mountains in the winter of eighteen hundred and"—

"Stop a moment, devil! Stop! Do you mean to tell me that even my very *thoughts* are not hidden from you?"

"It seems to look like that. Did n't you think the thoughts I have just mentioned?"

"If I did n't, I wish I may never breathe again! Look here, friend—look me in the eye. Who *are* you?"

"Well, who do you think?"

"I think you are Satan himself. I think you are the devil."

"No."

"No? Then who *can* you be?"

"Would you really like to know?"

"*Indeed* I would."

"Well, I am your *Conscience*!"

In an instant I was in a blaze of joy and exultation. I sprang at the creature, roaring,—

"Curse you, I have wished a hundred million times that you were tangible, and that I could get my hands on your throat once! Oh, but I will wreak a deadly vengeance on"—

Folly! Lightning does not move more quickly than my Conscience did! He darted aloft so suddenly that in the moment my fingers clutched the empty air he was already perched on the top of the high book-case, with his thumb at his nose in token of derision. I flung the poker at him, and missed. I fired the boot-jack. In a blind rage I flew from place to place, and snatched and hurled any missile that came handy; the storm of books, inkstands, and chunks of coal gloomed the air and beat about the manikin's perch relentlessly, but all to no purpose; the nimble figure dodged every shot; and not only that, but burst into a cackle of sarcastic and triumphant laughter as I sat down exhausted. While I puffed and gasped with fatigue and excitement, my Conscience talked to this effect: —

"My good slave, you are curiously witless—no, I mean characteristically so. In truth, you are always consistent, always yourself, always an ass. Otherwise it must have occurred to you that if you attempted this murder with a sad heart and a heavy conscience, I would droop under the burdening influence instantly. Fool, I should have weighed a ton, and could not have budged from the floor; but instead, you are so cheerfully anxious to kill me that your conscience is as light as a feather; hence I am away up here out of your reach. I can almost respect a mere ordinary sort of fool; but *you*— pah!"

I would have given anything, then, to be heavy-hearted, so that I could get this person down from there and take his life, but I could no more be heavy-hearted over such a desire than I could have sorrowed over its accomplishment. So I could only look longingly up at my master, and rave at the ill-luck that denied me a heavy conscience the one only time that I had ever wanted such a thing in my life. By and by I got to musing over the hour's strange adventure, and of course my human curiosity began to work. I set myself to framing in my mind some questions for this fiend to answer. Just then one of my boys entered, leaving the door open behind him, and exclaimed, —

"My! what *has* been going on, here! The book-case is all one riddle of"—

I sprang up in consternation, and shouted, —

"Out of this! Hurry! Jump! Fly! Shut the door! Quick, or my Conscience will get away!"

The door slammed to, and I locked it. I glanced up and was grateful, to the bottom of my heart, to see that my owner was still my prisoner. I said, —

"Hang you, I might have lost you! Children are the heedlessest creatures. But look here, friend, the boy did not seem to notice you at all; how is that?"

"For a very good reason. I am invisible to all but you."

I made mental note of that piece of information with a

good deal of satisfaction. I could kill this miscreant now, if I got a chance, and no one would know it. But this very reflection made me so light-hearted that my Conscience could hardly keep his seat, but was like to float aloft toward the ceiling like a toy balloon. I said, presently, —

"Come, my Conscience, let us be friendly. Let us fly a flag of truce for a while. I am suffering to ask you some questions."

"Very well. Begin."

"Well, then, in the first place, why were you never visible to me before?"

"Because you never asked to see me before; that is, you never asked in the right spirit and the proper form before. You were just in the right spirit this time, and when you called for your most pitiless enemy I was that person by a very large majority, though you did not suspect it."

"Well, did that remark of mine turn you into flesh and blood?"

"No. It only made me visible to you. I am unsubstantial, just as other spirits are."

This remark prodded me with a sharp misgiving. If he was unsubstantial, how was I going to kill him? But I dissembled, and said persuasively, —

"Conscience, it isn't sociable of you to keep at such a distance. Come down and take another smoke."

This was answered with a look that was full of derision, and with this observation added: —

"Come where you can get at me and kill me? The invitation is declined with thanks."

"All right," said I to myself; "so it seems a spirit *can* be killed, after all; there will be one spirit lacking in this world, presently, or I lose my guess." Then I said aloud, —

"Friend" —

"There; wait a bit. I am not your friend, I am your enemy; I am not your equal, I am your master. Call me 'my lord,' if you please. You are too familiar."

"I don't like such titles. I am willing to call you *sir*. That is as far as" —

"We will have no argument about this. Just obey; that is all. Go on with your chatter."

"Very well, my lord, — since nothing but my lord will suit

you,—I was going to ask you how long you will be visible to me?"

"Always!"

I broke out with strong indignation: "This is simply an outrage. That is what I think of it. You have dogged, and dogged, and *dogged* me, all the days of my life, invisible. That was misery enough; now to have such a looking thing as you tagging after me like another shadow all the rest of my days is an intolerable prospect. You have my opinion, my lord; make the most of it."

"My lad, there was never so pleased a conscience in this world as I was when you made me visible. It gives me an inconceivable advantage. *Now*, I can look you straight in the eye, and call you names, and leer at you, jeer at you, sneer at you; and *you* know what eloquence there is in visible gesture and expression, more especially when the effect is heightened by audible speech. I shall always address you henceforth in your o-w-n s-n-i-v-e-l-i-n-g d-r-a-w-l—baby!"

I let fly with the coal-hod. No result. My lord said,—

"Come, come! Remember the flag of truce!"

"Ah, I forgot that. I will try to be civil; and *you* try it, too, for a novelty. The idea of a *civil* conscience! It is a good joke; an excellent joke. All the consciences *I* have ever heard of were nagging, badgering, fault-finding, execrable savages! Yes; and always in a sweat about some poor little insignificant trifle or other—destruction catch the lot of them, *I* say! I would trade mine for the small-pox and seven kinds of consumption, and be glad of the chance. Now tell me, why *is* it that a conscience can't haul a man over the coals once, for an offense, and then let him alone? Why is it that it wants to keep on pegging at him, day and night and night and day, week in and week out, forever and ever, about the same old thing? There is no sense in that, and no reason in it. I think a conscience that will act like that is meaner than the very dirt itself."

"Well, *we* like it; that suffices."

"Do you do it with the honest intent to improve a man?"

That question produced a sarcastic smile, and this reply:—

"No, sir. Excuse me. We do it simply because it is 'business.' It is our trade. The *purpose* of it *is* to improve the man, but *we* are merely disinterested agents. We are appointed by authority, and haven't anything to say in the matter. We obey orders and leave the consequences where they belong. But I am willing to admit this much: we *do* crowd the orders a trifle when we get a chance, which is most of the time. We enjoy it. We are instructed to remind a man a few times of an error; and I don't mind acknowledging that we try to give pretty good measure. And when we get hold of a man of a peculiarly sensitive nature, oh, but we do haze him! I have known consciences to come all the way from China and Russia to see a person of that kind put through his paces, on a special occasion. Why, I knew a man of that sort who had accidentally crippled a mulatto baby; the news went abroad, and I wish you may never commit another sin if the consciences didn't flock from all over the earth to enjoy the fun and help his master exercise him. That man walked the floor in torture for forty-eight hours, without eating or sleeping, and then blew his brains out. The child was perfectly well again in three weeks."

"Well, you are a precious crew, not to put it too strong. I think I begin to see, now, why you have always been a trifle inconsistent with me. In your anxiety to get all the juice you can out of a sin, you make a man repent of it in three or four different ways. For instance, you found fault with me for lying to that tramp, and I suffered over that. But it was only yesterday that I told a tramp the square truth, to wit, that, it being regarded as bad citizenship to encourage vagrancy, I would give him nothing. What did you do *then*? Why, you made me say to myself, 'Ah, it would have been so much kinder and more blameless to ease him off with a little white lie, and send him away feeling that if he could not have bread, the gentle treatment was at least something to be grateful for!' Well, I suffered all day about *that*. Three days before, I had fed a tramp, and fed him freely, supposing it a virtuous act. Straight off you said, 'O false citizen, to have fed a tramp!' and I suffered as usual. I gave a tramp work; you objected to it,—*after* the contract was made, of course; you never speak up beforehand. Next, I *refused* a tramp work; you objected to *that*. Next, I proposed to kill a tramp; you kept me awake all night, oozing remorse at every pore. Sure I was going to be right *this* time, I sent the next tramp away with my benediction; and I wish you may live as long as I do, if you did n't make me smart all night again because I did n't kill him. Is there *any* way of satisfying that malignant invention which is called a conscience?"

"Ha, ha! this is luxury! Go on!"

"But come, now, answer me that question. *Is* there any way?"

"Well, none that I propose to tell *you*, my son. Ass! I don't care *what* act you may turn your hand to, I can straightway whisper a word in your ear and make you think you have committed a dreadful meanness. It is my *business*—and my joy—to make you repent of *every*thing you do. If I have fooled away any opportunities it was not intentional; I beg to assure you it was not intentional."

"Don't worry; you have n't missed a trick that *I* know of. I never did a thing in all my life, virtuous or otherwise, that I did n't repent of within twenty-four hours. In church last Sunday I listened to a charity sermon. My first impulse was to give three hundred and fifty dollars; I repented of that and reduced it a hundred; repented of that and reduced it another hundred; repented of that and reduced it another hundred; repented of that and reduced the remaining fifty to twenty-five; repented of that and came down to fifteen; repented of that and dropped to two dollars and a half; when the plate came around at last, I repented once more and contributed ten cents. Well, when I got home, I did wish to goodness I had that ten cents back again! You never *did* let me get through a charity sermon without having something to sweat about."

"Oh, and I never shall, I never shall. You can always depend on me."

"I think so. Many and many's the restless night I've wanted to take you by the neck. If I could only get hold of you now!"

"Yes, no doubt. But I am not an ass; I am only the saddle of an ass. But go on, go on. You entertain me more than I like to confess."

"I am glad of that. (You will not mind my lying a little, to keep in practice.) Look here; not to be too personal, I think you are about the shabbiest and most contemptible little shriveled-up reptile that can be imagined. I am grateful enough that you are invisible to other people, for I should die with shame to be seen with such a mildewed monkey of a conscience as *you* are. Now if you were five or six feet high, and"—

"Oh, come! who is to blame?"

"*I* don't know."

"Why, you are; nobody else."

"Confound you, I was n't consulted about your personal appearance."

"I don't care, you had a good deal to do with it, nevertheless. When you were eight or nine years old, I was seven feet high and as pretty as a picture."

"I wish you had died young! So you have grown the wrong way, have you?"

"Some of us grow one way and some the other. You had a large conscience once; if you 've a small conscience now, I reckon there are reasons for it. However, both of us are to blame, you and I. You see, you used to be conscientious about a great many things; morbidly so, I may say. It was a great many years ago. You probably do not remember it, now. Well, I took a great interest in my work, and I so enjoyed the anguish which certain pet sins of yours afflicted you with, that I kept pelting at you until I rather overdid the matter. You began to rebel. Of course I began to lose ground, then, and shrivel a little,—diminish in stature, get moldy, and grow deformed. The more I weakened, the more stubbornly you fastened on to those particular sins; till at last the places on my person that represent those vices became as callous as shark skin. Take smoking, for instance. I played that card a little too long, and I lost. When people plead with you at this late day to quit that vice, that old callous place seems to enlarge and cover me all over like a shirt of mail. It exerts a mysterious, smothering effect; and presently I, your faithful hater, your devoted Conscience, go sound asleep! Sound? It is no name for it. I could n't hear it thunder at such a time. You have some few other vices—perhaps eighty, or maybe ninety—that affect me in much the same way."

"This is flattering; you must be asleep a good part of your time."

"Yes, of late years. I should be asleep *all* the time, but for the help I get."

"Who helps you?"

"Other consciences. Whenever a person whose conscience I am acquainted with tries to plead with you about the vices you are callous to, I get my friend to give his client a pang concerning some villainy of his own, and that shuts off his meddling and starts him off to hunt personal consolation. My field of usefulness is about trimmed down to tramps, budding authoresses, and that line of goods, now; but don't you worry—I'll harry you on *them* while they last! Just you put your trust in me."

"I think I can. But if you had only been good enough to mention these facts some thirty years ago, I should have turned my particular attention to sin, and I think that by this time I should not only have had you pretty permanently asleep on the entire list of human vices, but reduced to the size of a homœopathic pill, at that. That is about the style of conscience *I* am pining for. If I only had you shrunk down to a homœopathic pill, and could get my hands on you, would I put you in a glass case for a keepsake? No, sir. I would give you to a yellow dog! That is where *you* ought to be—you and all your tribe. You are not fit to be in society, in my opinion. Now another question. Do you know a good many consciences in this section?"

"Plenty of them."

"I would give anything to see some of them! Could you bring them here? And would they be visible to me?"

"Certainly not."

"I suppose I ought to have known that, without asking. But no matter, you can describe them. Tell me about my neighbor Thompson's conscience, please."

"Very well. I know him intimately; have known him many years. I knew him when he was eleven feet high and of a faultless figure. But he is very rusty and tough and misshapen, now, and hardly ever interests himself about anything. As to his present size—well, he sleeps in a cigar box."

"Likely enough. There are few smaller, meaner men in this region than Hugh Thompson. Do you know Robinson's conscience?"

"Yes. He is a shade under four and a half feet high; used to be a blonde; is a brunette, now, but still shapely and comely."

"Well, Robinson is a good fellow. Do you know Tom Smith's conscience?"

"I have known him from childhood. He was thirteen inches high, and rather sluggish, when he was two years old—as nearly all of us are, at that age. He is thirty-seven feet high, now, and the stateliest figure in America. His legs are still racked with growing-pains, but he has a good time, nevertheless. Never sleeps. He is the most active and energetic member of the New England Conscience Club; is president of it. Night and day you can find him pegging away at Smith, panting with his labor, sleeves rolled up, countenance all alive with enjoyment. He has got his victim splendidly dragooned, now. He can make poor Smith imagine that the most innocent little thing he does is an odious sin; and then he sets to work and almost tortures the soul out of him about it."

"Smith is the noblest man in all this section, and the purest; and yet is always breaking his heart because he cannot be good! Only a conscience *could* find pleasure in heaping agony upon a spirit like that. Do you know my aunt Mary's conscience?"

"I have seen her at a distance, but am not acquainted with her. She lives in the open air altogether, because no door is large enough to admit her."

"I can believe that. Let me see. Do you know the conscience of that publisher who once stole some sketches of mine for a 'series' of his, and then left me to pay the law expenses I had to incur in order to choke him off?"

"Yes. He has a wide fame. He was exhibited, a month ago, with some other antiquities, for the benefit of a recent Member of the Cabinet's conscience, that was starving in exile. Tickets and fares were high, but I traveled for nothing by pretending to be the conscience of an editor, and got in for half price by representing myself to be the conscience of a clergyman. However, the publisher's conscience, which was to have been the main feature of the entertainment, was a failure—as an exhibition. He was there, but what of that? The management had provided a microscope with a magnifying power of only thirty thousand diameters, and so nobody got to see him, after all. There was great and general dissatisfaction, of course, but"—

Just here there was an eager footstep on the stair; I opened the door, and my aunt Mary burst into the room. It was a joyful meeting, and a cheery bombardment of questions and answers concerning family matters ensued. By and by my aunt said,—

"But I am going to abuse you a little now. You promised me, the day I saw you last, that you would look after the needs of the poor family around the corner as faithfully as I had done it myself. Well, I found out by accident that you failed of your promise. *Was* that right?"

In simple truth, I never had thought of that family a second time! And now such a splintering pang of guilt shot through me! I glanced up at my Conscience. Plainly, my heavy heart was affecting him. His body was drooping forward; he seemed about to fall from the book-case. My aunt continued:—

"And think how you have neglected my poor *protégée* at the almshouse, you dear, hard-hearted promise-breaker!" I blushed scarlet, and my tongue was tied. As the sense of my guilty negligence waxed sharper and stronger, my Conscience began to sway heavily back and forth; and when my aunt, after a little pause, said in a grieved tone, "Since you never once went to see her, maybe it will not distress you now to know that that poor child died, months ago, utterly friendless and forsaken!" my Conscience could no longer bear up under the weight of my sufferings, but tumbled headlong from his high perch and struck the floor with a dull, leaden thump. He lay there writhing with pain and quaking with apprehension, but straining every muscle in frantic efforts to get up. In a fever of expectancy I sprang to the door, locked it, placed my back against it, and bent a watchful gaze upon my struggling master. Already my fingers were itching to begin their murderous work.

"Oh, what *can* be the matter!" exclaimed my aunt, shrinking from me, and following with her frightened eyes the direction of mine. My breath was coming in short, quick gasps now, and my excitement was almost uncontrollable. My aunt cried out,—

"Oh, do not look so! You appall me! Oh, what can the matter be? What is it you see? Why do you stare so? Why do you work your fingers like that?"

"Peace, woman!" I said, in a hoarse whisper. "Look elsewhere; pay no attention to me; it is nothing—nothing. I am often this way. It will pass in a moment. It comes from smoking too much."

My injured lord was up, wild-eyed with terror, and trying to hobble toward the door. I could hardly breathe, I was so wrought up. My aunt wrung her hands, and said,—

"Oh, I knew how it would be; I knew it would come to this at last! Oh, I implore you to crush out that fatal habit while it may yet be time! You must not, you shall not be deaf to my supplications longer!" My struggling Conscience showed sudden signs of weariness! "Oh, promise me you will throw off this hateful slavery of tobacco!" My Conscience began to reel drowsily, and grope with his hands—enchanting spectacle! "I beg you, I beseech you, I implore you! Your reason is deserting you! There is madness in your eye! It flames with frenzy! Oh, hear me, hear me, and be saved! See, I plead with you on my very knees!" As she sank before me my Conscience reeled again, and then drooped languidly to the floor, blinking toward me a last supplication for mercy, with heavy eyes. "Oh, promise, or you are lost! Promise, and be redeemed! Promise! Promise and live!" With a long-drawn sigh my conquered Conscience closed his eyes and fell fast asleep!

With an exultant shout I sprang past my aunt, and in an instant I had my life-long foe by the throat. After so many years of waiting and longing, he was mine at last. I tore him to shreds and fragments. I rent the fragments to bits. I cast the bleeding rubbish into the fire, and drew into my nostrils the grateful incense of my burnt-offering. At last, and forever, my Conscience was dead!

I was a free man! I turned upon my poor aunt, who was almost petrified with terror, and shouted,—

"Out of this with your paupers, your charities, your reforms, your pestilent morals! You behold before you a man whose life-conflict is done, whose soul is at peace; a man whose heart is dead to sorrow, dead to suffering, dead to remorse; a man WITHOUT A CONSCIENCE! In my joy I spare you, though I could throttle you and never feel a pang! Fly!"

She fled. Since that day my life is all bliss. Bliss, unalloyed bliss. Nothing in all the world could persuade me to have a conscience again. I settled all my old outstanding scores, and began the world anew. I killed thirty-eight persons during the first two weeks—all of them on account of ancient grudges. I burned a dwelling that interrupted my view. I swindled a widow and some orphans out of their last cow, which is a very good one, though not thoroughbred, I believe. I have also committed scores of crimes, of various kinds, and have enjoyed my work exceedingly, whereas it would formerly have broken my heart and turned my hair gray, I have no doubt.

In conclusion I wish to state, by way of advertisement, that medical colleges desiring assorted tramps for scientific purposes, either by the gross, by cord measurement, or per ton, will do well to examine the lot in my cellar before purchasing elsewhere, as these were all selected and prepared by myself, and can be had at a low rate, because I wish to clear out my stock and get ready for the spring trade.

June 1876

Conversation, as it Was by the Social Fireside, in the Time of the Tudors

[MEM.—The following is supposed to be an extract from the diary of the Pepys of that day, the same being Queen Elizabeth's cup-bearer. He is supposed to be of ancient and noble lineage; that he despises these literary canaille; that his soul consumes with wrath to see the queen stooping to talk with such; and that the old man feels that his nobility is defiled by contact with Shakspeare, etc., and yet he has *got* to stay there till her Majesty chooses to dismiss him.]

Yesternight toke her maiste ye queene a fantasie such as she sometimes hath, and had to her closet certain that doe write playes, bokes, and such like, these being my lord Bacon, his worship Sir Walter Ralegh, Mr. Ben Jonson, and ye child Francis Beaumonte, which being but sixteen, hath yet turned his hand to ye doing of ye Lattin masters into our Englishe tong, with grete discretion and much applaus. Also came with these ye famous Shaxpur. A righte straunge mixing truly of mighty blode with mean, ye more in especial since ye queenes grace was present, as likewise these following, to wit: Ye Duchess of Bilgewater, twenty-two yeres of age; ye Countesse of Granby, twenty-six; her doter, ye Lady Helen, fifteen; as also these two maides of honor, to-wit, ye Lady Margery Boothy, sixty-five, and ye Lady Alice Dilberry, turned seventy, she being two yeres ye queenes graces elder.

I being her maites cup-bearer, had no choice but to remaine and beholde rank forgot, and ye high holde converse wh ye low as uppon equal termes, a grete scandal did ye world heare therof.

In ye heat of ye talk it befel yt one did breake wind, yielding and exceding mightie and distresfull stink, whereat all did laugh full sore, and then—

Ye Queene.—Verily in mine eight and sixty yeres have I not heard the fellow to this fart. Meseemeth, by ye grete sound and clamour of it, it was male; yet ye belly it did lurk behinde shoulde now fall lean and flat against ye spine of him yt hath bene delivered of so stately and so vaste a bulk, whereas ye guts of them yt doe quiff-splitters bear, stand comely still and rounde. Prithee let ye author confess ye offspring. Will my Lady Alice testify?

Lady Alice. — Good your grace, an' I had room for such a thundergust within mine ancient bowels, 'tis not in reason I coulde discharge ye same and live to thank God for yt He did choose handmaid so humble whereby to shew his power. Nay, 'tis not I yt have broughte forth this rich o'ermastering fog, this fragrant gloom, so pray you seeke ye further.

Ye Queene. — Mayhap ye Lady Margery hath done ye companie this favor?

Lady Margery. — So please you madam, my limbs are feeble wh ye weighte and drouth of five and sixty winters, and it behoveth yt I be tender unto them. In ye good providence of God, an' *I* had contained this wonder, forsoothe wolde I have gi'en ye whole evening of my sinking life to ye dribbling of it forth, with trembling and uneasy soul, not launched it sudden in its matchless might, taking mine own life with violence, rending my weak frame like rotten rags. It was not I, your maisty.

Ye Queene. — O' God's name, who hath favored us? Hath it come to pass yt a fart shall fart *itself*? Not such a one as this, I trow. Young Master Beaumont—but no; 'twould have wafted him to heaven like down of goose's boddy. 'Twas not ye little Lady Helen—nay, ne'er blush, my child; thoul't tickle thy tender maidenhedde with many a mousie-squeak before thou learnest to blow a harricane like this. Was't you, my learned and ingenious Jonson?

Jonson. — So fell a blast hath ne'er mine ears saluted, nor yet a stench so all-pervading and immortal. 'Twas not a novice did it, good your maisty, but one of veteran experience—else hadde he failed of confidence. In sooth it was not I.

Ye Queene. — My lord Bacon?

Lord Bacon. — Not from my leane entrailes hath this prodigy burst forth, so please your grace. Naught doth so befit ye grete as grete performance; and haply shall ye finde yt 'tis not from mediocrity this miracle hath issued.

[Tho' ye subject be but a fart, yet will this tedious sink of learning pondrously phillosophize. Meantime did the foul and deadly stink pervade all places to that degree, yt never smelt I ye like, yet dare I not to leave ye presence, albeit I was like to suffocate.]

Ye Queene.—What saith ye worshipful Master Shaxpur?

Shaxpur.—In the great hand of God I stand and so proclaim mine innocence. Though ye sinless hosts of heaven had foretold ye coming of this most desolating breath, proclaiming it a work of uninspired man, its quaking thunders, its firmament-clogging rottenness his own achievement in due course of nature, yet had not I believed it; but had said the pit itself hath furnished forth the stink, and heaven's artillery hath shook the globe in admiration of it.

[Then was there a silence, and each did turn him toward the worshipful Sr Walter Ralegh, that browned, embattled, bloody swash-buckler, who rising up did smile, and simpering say]—

Sr W.—Most gracious maisty, 'twas I that did it, but indeed it was so poor and frail a note, compared with such as I am wont to furnish, yt in sooth I was ashamed to call the weakling mine in so august a presence. It was nothing—less than nothing, madam—I did it but to clear my nether throat; but had I come prepared, then had I delivered something worthy. Bear with me, please your grace, till I can make amends.

[Then delivered he himself of such a godless and rockshivering blast that all were fain to stop their ears, and following it did come so dense and foul a stink that that which went before did seem a poor and trifling thing beside it. Then saith he, feigning that he blushed and was confused, *I perceive that I am weak to-day, and cannot justice do unto my powers;* and sat him down as who should say, *There, it is not much; yet he that hath an arse to spare, let him fellow that, an' he think he can.* By God, an' I were ye queene, I would e'en tip this swaggering braggart out o' the court, and let him air his grandeurs and break his intolerable wind before ye deaf and such as suffocation pleaseth.]

Then fell they to talk about ye manners and customs of many peoples, and Master Shaxpur spake of ye boke of ye sieur Michael de Montaine, wherein was mention of ye custom of widows of Perigord to wear uppon ye head-dress, in sign of widowhood, a jewel in ye similitude of a man's member wilted and limber, whereat ye queene did laugh and say widows in England doe wear prickes too, but betwixt the thighs, and not wilted neither, till coition hath done that office for them. Master Shaxspur did likewise observe how yt ye sieur de Montaine hath also spoken of a certain emperor of such mighty prowess that he did take ten maidenheddes in ye compass of a single night, ye while his empress did entertain two and twenty lusty knights between her sheetes, yet was not satisfied; whereat ye merrie Countess Granby saith a ram is yet ye emperor's superior, sith he wil tup above a hundred yewes 'twixt sun and sun; and after, if he can have none more to shag, will masturbate until he hath enrich'd whole acres with his seed.

Then spake ye damned windmill, Sr Walter, of a people in ye uttermost parts of America, yt capulate not until they be five and thirty yeres of age, ye women being eight and twenty, and do it then but once in seven yeres.

Ye Queene. — How doth that like my little Lady Helen? Shall we send thee thither and preserve thy belly?

Lady Helen. — Please your highnesses grace, mine old nurse hath told me there are more ways of serving God than by locking the thighs together; yet am I willing to serve him yt way too, sith your highnesses grace hath set ye ensample.

Ye Queene. — God's wowndes a good answer, childe.

Lady Alice. — Mayhap 'twill weaken when ye hair sprouts below ye navel.

Lady Helen. — Nay, it sprouted two yeres syne; I can scarce more than cover it with my hand now.

Ye Queene. — Hear ye that, my little Beaumonte? Have ye not a little birde about ye that stirs at hearing tell of so sweete a neste?

Beaumonte. — 'Tis not insensible, illustrious madam; but mousing owls and bats of low degree may not aspire to bliss so whelming and ecstatic as is found in ye downy nests of birdes of Paradise.

Ye Queene. — By ye gullet of God, 'tis a neat-turned compliment. With such a tongue as thine, lad, thou'lt spread the ivory thighs of many a willing maid in thy good time, an' thy cod-piece be as handy as thy speeche.

Then spake ye queene of how she met old Rabelais when

she was turned of fifteen, and he did tell her of a man his father knew that had a double pair of bollocks, whereon a controversy followed as concerning the most just way to spell the word, ye contention running high betwixt ye learned Bacon and ye ingenious Jonson, until at last ye old Lady Margery, wearying of it all, saith, *Gentles, what mattereth it how ye shall spell the word? I warrant ye when ye use your bollocks ye shall not think of it; and my Lady Granby, be ye content; let the spelling be; ye shall enjoy the beating of them on your buttocks just the same, I trow. Before I had gained my fourteenth year I had learnt that them that would explore a cunt stop'd not to consider the spelling o't.*

Sr W.—In sooth, when a shift's turned up, delay is meet for naught but dalliance. Boccaccio hath a story of a priest that did beguile a maid into his cell, then knelt him in a corner to pray for grace to be rightly thankful for this tender maidenhead ye Lord had sent him; but ye abbot, spying through ye key-hole, did see a tuft of brownish hair with fair white flesh about it, wherefore when ye priest's prayer was done, his chance was gone, forasmuch as ye little maid had but ye one cunt, and that was already occupied to her content.

Then conversed they of religion, and ye mightie work ye old dead Luther did doe by ye grace of God. Then next about poetry, and Master Shaxpur did rede a part of his King Henry IV., ye which, it seemeth unto me, is not of ye value of an arsefull of ashes, yet they praised it bravely, one and all.

Ye same did rede a portion of his "Venus and Adonis," to their prodigious admiration, whereas I, being sleepy and fatigued withal, did deme it but paltry stuff, and was the more discomforted in that ye blody bucanier had got his wind again, and did turn his mind to farting with such villain zeal that presently I was like to choke once more. God damn this windy ruffian and all his breed. I wolde that hell mighte get him.

They talked about ye wonderful defense which old Sr. Nicholas Throgmorton did make for himself before ye judges in ye time of Mary; which was unlucky matter to broach, sith it fetched out ye quene with a *Pity yt he, having so much wit, had yet not enough to save his doter's maidenhedde sound for her marriage-bed.* And ye quene did give ye damn'd Sr. Walter a look yt made hym wince—for she hath not forgot he was her own lover in yt olde day. There was silent uncomfortableness now; 'twas not a good turn for talk to take, sith if ye queene must find offense in a little harmless debauching, when pricks were stiff and cunts not loath to take ye stiffness out of them, who of this company was sinless; behold, was not ye wife of Master Shaxpur four months gone with child when she stood uppe before ye altar? Was not her Grace of Bilgewater roger'd by four lords before she had a husband? Was not ye little Lady Helen born on her mother's wedding-day? And, beholde, were not ye Lady Alice and ye Lady Margery there, mouthing religion, whores from ye cradle?

In time came they to discourse of Cervantes, and of the new painter, Rubens, that is beginning to be heard of. Fine words and dainty-wrought phrases from the ladies now, one or two of them being, in other days, pupils of that poor ass, Lille, himself; and I marked how that Jonson and Shaxpur did fidget to discharge some venom of sarcasm, yet dared they not in the presence, the queene's grace being ye very flower of ye Euphuists herself. But behold, these be they yt, having a specialty, and admiring it in themselves, be jealous when a neighbor doth essaye it, nor can abide it in them long. Wherefore 'twas observable yt ye quene waxed uncontent; and in time labor'd grandiose speeche out of ye mouth of Lady Alice, who manifestly did mightily pride herself thereon, did quite exhauste ye quene's endurance, who listened till ye gaudy speeche was done, then lifted up her brows, and with vaste irony, mincing saith, *O shit!* Whereat they alle did laffe, but not ye Lady Alice, yt olde foolish bitche.

Now was Sr. Walter minded of a tale he once did hear ye ingenious Margrette of Navarre relate, about a maid, which being like to suffer rape by an olde archbishoppe, did smartly contrive a device to save her maidenhedde, and said to him, *First, my lord, I prithee, take out thy holy tool and piss before me;* which doing, lo his member felle, and would not rise again.

The Canvasser's Tale

Poor, sad-eyed stranger! There was that about his humble mien, his tired look, his decayed-gentility clothes, that almost reached the mustard-seed of charity that still remained, remote and lonely, in the empty vastness of my heart, notwithstanding I observed a portfolio under his arm, and said to myself, Behold, Providence hath delivered his servant into the hands of another canvasser.

Well, these people always get one interested. Before I well knew how it came about, this one was telling me his history, and I was all attention and sympathy. He told it something like this:

My parents died, alas, when I was a little, sinless child. My uncle Ithuriel took me to his heart and reared me as his own. He was my only relative in the wide world; but he was good and rich and generous. He reared me in the lap of luxury. I knew no want that money could satisfy.

In the fullness of time I was graduated, and went with two of my servants—my chamberlain and my valet—to travel in foreign countries. During four years I flitted upon careless wing amid the beauteous gardens of the distant strand, if you will permit this form of speech in one whose tongue was ever attuned to poesy; and indeed I so speak with confidence, as one unto his kind, for I perceive by your eyes that you too, sir, are gifted with the divine inflation. In those far lands I reveled in the ambrosial food that fructifies the soul, the mind, the heart. But of all things, that which most appealed to my inborn æsthetic taste was the prevailing custom there, among the rich, of making collections of elegant and costly rarities, dainty *objets de vertu*, and in an evil hour I tried to uplift my uncle Ithuriel to a plane of sympathy with this exquisite employment.

I wrote and told him of one gentleman's vast collection of shells; another's noble collection of meerschaum pipes; another's elevating and refining collection of undecipherable autographs; another's priceless collection of old china; another's enchanting collection of postage-stamps—and so forth and so on. Soon my letters yielded fruit. My uncle began

to look about for something to make a collection of. You may
know, perhaps, how fleetly a taste like this dilates. His soon
became a raging fever, though I knew it not. He began to
neglect his great pork business; presently he wholly retired
and turned an elegant leisure into a rabid search for curious
things. His wealth was vast, and he spared it not. First he
tried cow-bells. He made a collection which filled five large
salons, and comprehended all the different sorts of cow-bells
that ever had been contrived, save one. That one—an an-
tique, and the only specimen extant—was possessed by another collector. My uncle offered enormous sums for it, but
the gentleman would not sell. Doubtless you know what necessarily resulted. A true collector attaches no value to a collection that is not complete. His great heart breaks, he sells his
hoard, he turns his mind to some field that seems unoccupied.

Thus did my uncle. He next tried brickbats. After piling up
a vast and intensely interesting collection, the former difficulty
supervened; his great heart broke again; he sold out his soul's
idol to the retired brewer who possessed the missing brick.
Then he tried flint hatchets and other implements of Primeval
Man, but by and by discovered that the factory where they
were made was supplying other collectors as well as himself.
He tried Aztec inscriptions and stuffed whales—another failure, after incredible labor and expense. When his collection
seemed at last perfect, a stuffed whale arrived from Greenland
and an Aztec inscription from the Cundurango regions of
Central America that made all former specimens insignificant.
My uncle hastened to secure these noble gems. He got the
stuffed whale, but another collector got the inscription. A real
Cundurango, as possibly you know, is a possession of such
supreme value that, when once a collector gets it, he will
rather part with his family than with it. So my uncle sold out,
and saw his darlings go forth, never more to return; and his
coal-black hair turned white as snow in a single night.

Now he waited, and thought. He knew another disappointment might kill him. He was resolved that he would choose
things next time that no other man was collecting. He carefully made up his mind, and once more entered the field—
this time to make a collection of echoes.

"Of what?" said I.

Echoes, sir. His first purchase was an echo in Georgia that repeated four times; his next was a six-repeater in Maryland; his next was a thirteen-repeater in Maine; his next was a nine-repeater in Kansas; his next was a twelve-repeater in Tennessee, which he got cheap, so to speak, because it was out of repair, a portion of the crag which reflected it having tumbled down. He believed he could repair it at a cost of a few thousand dollars, and, by increasing the elevation with masonry, treble the repeating capacity; but the architect who undertook the job had never built an echo before, and so he utterly spoiled this one. Before he meddled with it, it used to talk back like a mother-in-law, but now it was only fit for the deaf and dumb asylum. Well, next he bought a lot of cheap little double-barreled echoes, scattered around over various States and Territories; he got them at twenty per cent. off by taking the lot. Next he bought a perfect Gatling gun of an echo in Oregon, and it cost a fortune, I can tell you. You may know, sir, that in the echo market the scale of prices is cumulative, like the carat-scale in diamonds; in fact, the same phraseology is used. A single-carat echo is worth but ten dollars over and above the value of the land it is on; a two-carat or double-barreled echo is worth thirty dollars; a five-carat is worth nine hundred and fifty; a ten-carat is worth thirteen thousand. My uncle's Oregon echo, which he called the Great Pitt Echo, was a twenty-two carat gem, and cost two hundred and sixteen thousand dollars—they threw the land in, for it was four hundred miles from a settlement.

Well, in the mean time my path was a path of roses. I was the accepted suitor of the only and lovely daughter of an English earl, and was beloved to distraction. In that dear presence I swam in seas of bliss. The family were content, for it was known that I was sole heir to an uncle held to be worth five millions of dollars. However, none of us knew that my uncle had become a collector, at least in anything more than a small way, for æsthetic amusement.

Now gathered the clouds above my unconscious head. That divine echo, since known throughout the world as the Great Koh-i-noor, or Mountain of Repetitions, was discovered. It was a sixty-five-carat gem. You could utter a word and it would talk back at you for fifteen minutes, when the day was otherwise quiet. But behold, another discovery was made at the same time: another echo-collector was in the field. The two rushed to make the purchase. The property consisted of a couple of small hills with a shallow swale between, out yonder among the back settlements of New York State. Both men arrived on the ground at the same time, and neither knew the other was there. The echo was not all owned by one man; a person by the name of Williamson Bolivar Jarvis owned the east hill, and a person by the name of Harbison J. Bledso owned the west hill; the swale between was the dividing line. So while my uncle was buying Jarvis's hill for three million two hundred and eighty-five thousand dollars, the other party was buying Bledso's hill for a shade over three million.

Now, do you perceive the natural result? Why, the noblest collection of echoes on earth was forever and ever incomplete, since it possessed but the one half of the king echo of the universe. Neither man was content with this divided ownership, yet neither would sell to the other. There were jawings, bickerings, heart-burnings. And at last, that other collector, with a malignity which only a collector can ever feel toward a man and a brother, proceeded to cut down his hill!

You see, as long as he could not have the echo, he was resolved that nobody should have it. He would remove his hill, and then there would be nothing to reflect my uncle's echo. My uncle remonstrated with him, but the man said, "I own one end of this echo; I choose to kill my end; you must take care of your own end yourself."

Well, my uncle got an injunction put on him. The other man appealed and fought it in a higher court. They carried it on up, clear to the Supreme Court of the United States. It made no end of trouble there. Two of the judges believed that an echo was personal property, because it was impalpable to sight and touch, and yet was purchasable, salable, and consequently taxable; two others believed that an echo was real estate, because it was manifestly attached to the land, and was not removable from place to place; other of the judges contended that an echo was not property at all.

It was finally decided that the echo was property; that the hills were property; that the two men were separate and independent owners of the two hills, but tenants in common in the echo; therefore defendant was at full liberty to cut down his hill, since it belonged solely to him, but must give bonds in three million dollars as indemnity for damages which might result to my uncle's half of the echo. This decision also debarred my uncle from using defendant's hill to reflect his part of the echo, without defendant's consent; he must use only his own hill; if his part of the echo would not go, under these circumstances, it was sad, of course, but the court could find no remedy. The court also debarred defendant from using my uncle's hill to reflect *his* end of the echo, without consent. You see the grand result! Neither man would give consent, and so that astonishing and most noble echo had to cease from its great powers; and since that day that magnificent property is tied up and unsalable.

A week before my wedding day, while I was still swimming in bliss and the nobility were gathering from far and near to honor our espousals, came news of my uncle's death, and also a copy of his will, making me his sole heir. He was gone; alas, my dear benefactor was no more. The thought surcharges my heart even at this remote day. I handed the will to the earl; I could not read it for the blinding tears. The earl read it; then he sternly said, "Sir, do you call this wealth?—but doubtless you do in your inflated country. Sir, you are left sole heir to a vast collection of echoes—if a thing can be called a collection that is scattered far and wide over the huge length and breadth of the American continent; sir, this is not all; you are head and ears in debt; there is not an echo in the lot but has a mortgage on it; sir, I am not a hard man, but I must look to my child's interest; if you had but one echo which you could honestly call your own, if you had but one echo which was free from incumbrance, so that you could retire to it with my child, and by humble, painstaking industry cultivate and improve it, and thus wrest from it a maintenance, I would not say you nay; but I cannot marry my child to a beggar. Leave his side, my darling; go, sir; take your mortgage-ridden echoes and quit my sight forever."

My noble Celestine clung to me in tears, with loving arms, and swore she would willingly, nay, gladly marry me, though I had not an echo in the world. But it could not be. We were torn asunder, she to pine and die within the twelvemonth, I to toil life's long journey sad and lone, praying daily, hourly, for that release which shall join us together again in that dear realm where the wicked cease from troubling and the weary are at rest. Now, sir, if you will be so kind as to look at these maps and plans in my portfolio, I am sure I can sell you an echo for less money than any man in the trade. Now this one, which cost my uncle ten dollars, thirty years ago, and is one of the sweetest things in Texas, I will let you have for—

"Let me interrupt you," I said. "My friend, I have not had a moment's respite from canvassers this day. I have bought a sewing machine which I did not want; I have bought a map which is mistaken in all its details; I have bought a clock which will not go; I have bought a moth poison which the moths prefer to any other beverage; I have bought no end of useless inventions, and now I have had enough of this foolishness. I would not have one of your echoes if you were even to give it to me. I would not let it stay on the place. I always hate a man that tries to sell me echoes. You see this gun? Now take your collection and move on; let us not have bloodshed."

But he only smiled a sad, sweet smile, and got out some more diagrams. You know the result perfectly well, because you know that when you have once opened the door to a canvasser, the trouble is done and you have got to suffer defeat.

I compromised with this man at the end of an intolerable hour. I bought two double-barreled echoes in good condition, and he threw in another, which he said was not salable because it only spoke German. He said, "She was a perfect polyglot once, but somehow her palate got down."

December 1876

The Oldest Inhabitant—The Weather of New England

Seventy-first Annual Dinner, New England Society of New York

> Who can lose it and forget it?
> Who can have it and regret it?
> Be interposer 'twixt us *Twain*.
> *Merchant of Venice*

Gentlemen: I reverently believe that the Maker who made us all, makes everything in New England—but the weather. I don't know who makes that, but I think it must be raw apprentices in the Weather Clerk's factory, who experiment and learn how in New England, for board and clothes, and then are promoted to make weather for countries that require a good article, and will take their custom elsewhere if they don't get it. There is a sumptuous variety about the New England weather that compels the stranger's admiration—and regret. The weather is always doing something there; always attending strictly to business; always getting up new designs and trying them on the people to see how they will go. But it gets through more business in spring than in any other season. In the spring I have counted one hundred and thirty-six different kinds of weather inside of four and twenty hours. It was I that made the fame and fortune of that man that had that marvelous collection of weather on exhibition at the Centennial that so astounded the foreigners. He was going to travel all over the world and get specimens from all the climes. I said, "Don't you do it; you come to New England on a favorable spring day." I told him what we could do, in the way of style, variety, and quantity. Well, he came, and he made his collection in four days. As to variety—why, he confessed that he got hundreds of kinds of weather that he had never heard of before. And as to quantity—well, after he had picked out and discarded all that was blemished in any way, he not only had weather enough, but weather to spare; weather to hire out; weather to sell; to deposit; weather to invest; weather to give to the poor.

The people of New England are by nature patient and for-bearing; but there are some things which they will not stand. Every year they kill a lot of poets for writing about "Beautiful Spring." These are generally casual visitors, who bring their notions of spring from somewhere else, and cannot, of course, know how the natives feel about spring. And so, the first thing they know, the opportunity to inquire how they feel has permanently gone by.

Old Probabilities has a mighty reputation for accurate prophecy, and thoroughly well deserves it. You take up the papers and observe how crisply and confidently he checks off what today's weather is going to be on the Pacific, down South, in the Middle States, in the Wisconsin region; see him sail along in the joy and pride of his power till he gets to New England, and then—see his tail drop. *He* doesn't know what the weather is going to be like in New England. He can't any more tell than he can tell how many Presidents of the United States there's going to be next year. Well, he mulls over it, and by and by he gets out something about like this: Probable nor'-east to sou'-west winds, varying to the southard and westard and eastard and points between; high and low barometer, swapping around from place to place; probable areas of rain, snow, hail, and drought, succeeded or preceded by earthquakes, with thunder and lightning. Then he jots down this postscript from his wandering mind, to cover accidents: "But it is possible that the program may be wholly changed in the meantime."

Yes, one of the brightest gems in the New England weather is the dazzling uncertainty of it. There is only one thing certain about it, you are certain there is going to be plenty of weather—a perfect grand review; but you never can tell which end of the procession is going to move first. You fix up for the drought; you leave your umbrella in the house and sally out with your sprinkling pot, and ten to one you get drowned. You make up your mind that the earthquake is due; you stand from under, and take hold of something to steady yourself, and the first thing you know, you get struck by lightning. These are great disappointments. But they can't be helped. The lightning there is peculiar; it is so convinc-ing! When it strikes a thing, it doesn't leave enough of that thing behind for you to tell whether—well, you'd think it was something valuable, and a Congressman had been there.

And the thunder. When the thunder commences to merely tune up, and scrape, and saw, and key up the instruments for the performance, strangers say, "Why, what awful thunder you have here!" But when the baton is raised and the real concert begins, you'll find that stranger down in the cellar, with his head in the ash barrel.

Now, as to the *size* of the weather in New England— lengthways, I mean. It is utterly disproportioned to the size of that little country. Half the time, when it is packed as full as it can stick, you will see that New England weather sticking out beyond the edges and projecting around hundreds and hundreds of miles over the neighboring states. She can't hold a tenth part of her weather. You can see cracks all about, where she has strained herself trying to do it.

I could speak volumes about the inhuman perversity of the New England weather, but I will give but a single specimen. I like to hear rain on a tin roof, so I covered part of my roof with tin, with an eye to that luxury. Well, sir, do you think it ever rains on the tin? No, sir; skips it every time.

Mind, in this speech I have been trying merely to do honor to the New England weather—no language could do it justice. But, after all, there are at least one or two things about that weather (or, if you please, effects produced by it) which we residents would not like to part with. If we hadn't our bewitching autumn foliage, we should still have to credit the weather with one feature which compensates for all its bullying vagaries—the ice storm—when a leafless tree is clothed with ice from the bottom to the top—ice that is as bright and clear as crystal; when every bough and twig is strung with ice beads, frozen dewdrops, and the whole tree sparkles, cold and white, like the Shah of Persia's diamond plume. Then the wind waves the branches, and the sun comes out and turns all those myriads of beads and drops to prisms, that glow and burn and flash with all manner of colored fires, which change and change again, with inconceivable rapidity, from blue to red, from red to green, and green to gold—the tree becomes a spraying fountain, a very explosion of dazzling jewels; and it stands there the acme, the climax, the supremest possibility in art or nature, of bewildering, intoxicating, intolerable magnificence! One cannot make the words too strong.

Month after month I lay up my hate and grudge against the New England weather; but when the ice storm comes at last, I say: "There—I forgive you, now—the books are square between us, you don't owe me a cent; go, and sin no more; your little faults and foibles count for nothing—you are the most enchanting weather in the world!"

December 22, 1876

Francis Lightfoot Lee

This man's life-work was so inconspicuous, that his name would now be wholly forgotten, but for one thing—he signed the Declaration of Independence. Yet his life was a most useful and worthy one. It was a good and profitable voyage, though it left no phosphorescent splendors in its wake.

A sketch of Francis Lightfoot Lee can be useful for but one purpose, as showing what sort of material was used in the construction of congressmen in his day; since to sketch him is to sketch the average congressman of his time.

He came of an old and excellent family; a family which had borne an unsullied name, and held honorable place on both sides of the water; a family with a reputation to preserve and traditions to perpetuate; a family which could not afford to soil itself with political trickery, or do base things for party or for hire; a family which was able to shed as much honor upon official station as it received from it.

He dealt in no shams; he had no ostentations of dress or equipage; for he was, as one may say, *inured* to wealth. He had always been used to it. His own ample means were inherited. He was educated. He was more than that—he was finely cultivated. He loved books; he had a good library, and no place had so great a charm for him as that. The old Virginian mansion which was his home was also the home of that old-time Virginian hospitality which hoary men still hold in mellow memory. Over their port and walnuts he and his friends of the gentry discussed a literature which is dead and forgotten now, and political matters which were drowsy with the absence of corruption and "investigations." Sundays he and they drove to church in their lumbering coaches, with a due degree of grave and seemly pomp. Weekdays they inspected their domains, ordered their affairs, attended to the needs of their dependents, consulted with their overseers and tenants, busied themselves with active benevolences. They were justices of the peace, and performed their unpaid duties with arduous and honest diligence, and with serene, unhampered impartiality toward a society to which they were not beholden for their official stations. In short,

Francis Lightfoot Lee was a gentleman—a word which meant a great deal in his day, though it means nothing whatever in ours.

Mr. Lee defiled himself with no juggling, or wire-pulling, or begging, to acquire a place in the provincial legislature, but went thither when he was called, and went reluctantly. He wrought there industriously during four years, never seeking his own ends, but only the public's. His course was purity itself, and he retired unblemished when his work was done. He retired gladly, and sought his home and its superior allurements. No one dreamed of such a thing as "investigating" him.

Immediately the people called him again—this time to a seat in the Continental Congress. He accepted this unsought office from a sense of duty only, and during four of the darkest years of the Revolution he labored with all his might for his country's best behests. He did no brilliant things, he made no brilliant speeches; but the enduring strength of his patriotism was manifest, his fearlessness in confronting perilous duties and compassing them was patent to all, the purity of his motives was unquestioned, his unpurchasable honor and uprightness were unchallenged. His good work finished, he hurried back to the priceless charms of his home once more, and begged hard to be allowed to spend the rest of his days in the retirement and repose which his faithful labors had so fairly earned; but this could not be, he was solicited to enter the State Legislature; he was needed there; he was a good citizen, a citizen of the best and highest type, and so he put self aside and answered to the call. He served the State with his accustomed fidelity, and when at last his public career was ended, he retired honored of all, applauded by all, unaccused, unsmirched, utterly stainless.

This is a picture of the average, the usual Congressman of Francis Lightfoot Lee's time, and it is vividly suggestive of what that people must have been that preferred such men. Since then we have Progressed one hundred years. Let us gravely try to conceive how isolated, how companionless, how lonesome, such a public servant as this would be in Washington to-day.

My Military History

Putnam Phalanx Dinner for the Ancient and Honorable Artillery Company of Massachusetts, Hartford

I wouldn't have missed being here for a good deal. The last time I had the privilege of breaking bread with soldiers was some years ago, with the oldest military organization in England, the Ancient and Honourable Artillery Company of London, somewhere about its six-hundredth anniversary; and now I have enjoyed this privilege with its oldest child, the oldest military organization in America, the Ancient and Honorable Artillery Company of Massachusetts, on this your two hundred and fortieth anniversary. Fine old stock, both of you—and if you fight as well as you feed, God protect the enemy.

I did not assemble at the hotel parlors today to be received by a committee as a mere civilian guest; no, I assembled at the headquarters of the Putnam Phalanx, and insisted upon my right to be escorted to this place as one of the military guests. For I, too, am a soldier! I am inured to war. I have a military history. I have been through a stirring campaign, and there is not even a mention of it in any history of the United States or of the Southern Confederacy—to such lengths can the envy and the malignity of the historian go! I will unbosom myself here, where I cannot but find sympathy; I will tell you about it, and appeal through you to justice.

In the earliest summer days of the war, I slipped out of Hannibal, Missouri, by night, with a friend, and joined a detachment of the rebel General Tom Harris's army (I find myself in a great minority here) up a gorge behind an old barn in Ralls County. Colonel Ralls, of Mexican War celebrity, swore us in. He made us swear to uphold the flag and Constitution of the United States, and to destroy every other military organization that we caught doing the same thing, which, being interpreted, means that we were to repel invasion. Well, you see, this mixed us. We couldn't really tell which side we were on, but we went into camp and left it to the God of Battles. For that was the term then. I was made Second Lieutenant and Chief Mogul of a company of eleven men, who knew

nothing about war—nor anything, for we had no captain.
My friend, who was nineteen years old, six feet high, three
feet wide, and some distance through, and just out of the
infant school, was made orderly sergeant. His name was Ben
Tupper. He had a hard time. When he was mounted and on
the march he used to go to sleep, and his horse would reach
around and bite him on the leg, and then he would wake up
and cry and curse, and want to go home. The other men pes-
tered him a good deal, too. When they were dismounted they
said they couldn't march in double file with him because his
feet took up so much room. One night, when we were
around the camp fire, some fellow on the outside in the cold
said, "Ben Tupper, put down that newspaper: it throws the
whole place into twilight, and casts a shadow like a blanket."
Ben said, "I ain't got any newspaper." Then the other fellow
said, "Oh, I see—'twas your ear!" We all slept in a corn crib,
on the corn, and the rats were very thick. Ben Tupper had
been carefully and rightly reared, and when he was ready for
bed he would start to pray, and a rat would bite him on the
heel, and then he would sit up and swear all night and keep
everybody awake. He was town-bred and did not seem to
have any correct idea of military discipline. If I commanded
him to shut up, he would say, "Who was your nigger last
year?" One evening I ordered him to ride out about three
miles on picket duty, to the beginning of a prairie. Said he,
"What!—in the night!—and them blamed Union soldiers
likely to be prowling around there any time!" So he wouldn't
go, and the next morning I ordered him again. Said he, "In
the rain!—I think I see myself!" He didn't go. Next day I
ordered him on picket duty once more. This time he looked
hurt. Said he, "What! on Sunday?—you must be a damn
fool!" Well, picketing might have been a very good thing, but
I saw it was impracticable, so I dropped it from my military
system.

We had a good enough time there at that barn, barring the
rats and the mosquitoes and the rain. We levied on both parties impartially, and both parties hated us impartially. But one
day we heard that the invader was approaching, so we had to
pack up and move, of course, and within twenty-four hours
he was coming again. So we moved again. Next day he was

after us once more. Well, we didn't like it much, but we moved, rather than make trouble. This went on for a week or ten days more, and we saw considerable scenery. Then Ben Tupper lost patience. Said he, "War ain't what it's cracked up to be; I'm going home if I can't ever git a chance to sit down a minute. Why do these people keep us a-humpin' around so? Blame their skins, do they think this is an excursion?"

Some of the other town boys got to grumbling. They complained that there was an insufficiency of umbrellas. So I sent around to the farmers and borrowed what I could. Then they complained that the Worcestershire sauce was out. There was mutiny and dissatisfaction all around, and, of course, here came the enemy pestering us again—as much as two hours before breakfast, too, when nobody wanted to turn out, of course.

This was a little too much. The whole command felt insulted. I detached one of my aides and sent him to the brigadier, and asked him to assign us a district where there wasn't so much bother going on. The history of our campaign was laid before him, but instead of being touched by it, what did he do? He sent back an indignant message and said, "You have had a dozen chances inside of two weeks to capture the enemy, and he is still at large. [Well, we knew that!] Feeling bad? Stay where you are this time, or I will court-martial and hang the whole lot of you." Well, I submitted this brutal message to my battalion, and asked their advice. Said the orderly sergeant, "If Tom Harris wants the enemy, let him come and get him. I ain't got any use for my share, and who's Tom Harris anyway, I'd like to know, that's putting on so many frills? Why, I knew him when he wasn't nothing but a darn telegraph operator. Gentlemen, you can do as you choose; as for me, I've got enough of this sashaying around so's't you can't get a chance to pray, because the time's all required for cussing. So off goes my war paint—you hear *me*!"

The whole regiment said, with one voice, "That's the talk for me." So there and then, on the spot, my brigade disbanded itself and tramped off home, with me at the tail of it. I hung up my own sword and returned to the arts of peace, and there were people who said I hadn't been absent from them yet. We were the first men that went into the service in

Missouri; we were the first that went out of it anywhere. This, gentlemen, is the history of the part which my division took in the great rebellion, and such is the military record of its commander in chief, and this is the first time that the deeds of those warriors have been brought officially to the notice of mankind. Treasure these things in your hearts, and so shall the detected and truculent historians of this land be brought to shame and confusion. I ask you to fill your glasses and drink with me to the reverent memory of the orderly sergeant and those other neglected and forgotten heroes, my footsore and travel-stained paladins, who were first in war, first in peace, and were not idle during the interval that lay between.

October 2, 1877

The Captain's Story

There was a good deal of pleasant gossip about old Captain "Hurricane" Jones, of the Pacific Ocean,—peace to his ashes! Two or three of us present had known him; I, particularly well, for I had made four sea-voyages with him. He was a very remarkable man. He was born in a ship; he picked up what little education he had among his shipmates; he began life in the forecastle, and climbed grade by grade to the captaincy. More than fifty years of his sixty-five were spent at sea. He had sailed all oceans, seen all lands, and borrowed a tint from all climates. When a man has been fifty years at sea, he necessarily knows nothing of men, nothing of the world but its surface, nothing of the world's thought, nothing of the world's learning but its A B C, and that blurred and distorted by the unfocused lenses of an untrained mind. Such a man is only a gray and bearded child. That is what old Hurricane Jones was,—simply an innocent, lovable old infant. When his spirit was in repose he was as sweet and gentle as a girl; when his wrath was up he was a hurricane that made his nickname seem tamely descriptive. He was formidable in a fight, for he was of powerful build and dauntless courage. He was frescoed from head to heel with pictures and mottoes tattooed in red and blue India ink. I was with him one voyage when he got his last vacant space tattooed; this vacant space was around his left ankle. During three days he stumped about the ship with his ankle bare and swollen, and this legend gleaming red and angry out from a clouding of India ink: "Virtue is its own R'd." (There was a lack of room.) He was deeply and sincerely pious, and swore like a fish-woman. He considered swearing blameless, because sailors would not understand an order unillumined by it. He was a profound Biblical scholar,—that is, he thought he was. He believed everything in the Bible, but he had his own methods of arriving at his beliefs. He was of the "advanced" school of thinkers, and applied natural laws to the interpretation of all miracles, somewhat on the plan of the people who make the six days of creation six geological epochs, and so forth. Without being aware of it, he was a rather severe satire on modern scientific religionists. Such a man as I have been describing is rabidly fond of disquisition and argument; one knows that without being told it.

One trip the captain had a clergyman on board, but did not know he was a clergyman, since the passenger list did not betray the fact. He took a great liking to this Rev. Mr. Peters, and talked with him a great deal: told him yarns, gave him toothsome scraps of personal history, and wove a glittering streak of profanity through his garrulous fabric that was refreshing to a spirit weary of the dull neutralities of undecorated speech. One day the captain said, "Peters, do you ever read the Bible?"

"Well—yes."

"I judge it ain't often, by the way you say it. Now, you tackle it in dead earnest once, and you'll find it'll pay. Don't you get discouraged, but hang right on. First, you won't understand it; but by and by things will begin to clear up, and then you wouldn't lay it down to eat."

"Yes, I have heard that said."

"And it's so, too. There ain't a book that begins with it. It lays over 'em all, Peters. There's some pretty tough things in it,—there ain't any getting around that,—but you stick to them and think them out, and when once you get on the inside everything's plain as day."

"The miracles, too, captain?"

"Yes, sir! the miracles, too. Every one of them. Now, there's that business with the prophets of Baal; like enough that stumped you?"

"Well, I don't know but"—

"Own up, now; it stumped you. Well, I don't wonder. You hadn't had any experience in raveling such things out, and naturally it was too many for you. Would you like to have me explain that thing to you, and show you how to get at the meat of these matters?"

"Indeed, I would, captain, if you don't mind."

Then the captain proceeded as follows: "I'll do it with pleasure. First, you see, I read and read, and thought and thought, till I got to understand what sort of people they were in the old Bible times, and then after that it was all clear and easy. Now, this was the way I put it up, concerning

Isaac* and the prophets of Baal. There was some mighty sharp men amongst the public characters of that old ancient day, and Isaac was one of them. Isaac had his failings,— plenty of them, too; it ain't for me to apologize for Isaac; he played it on the prophets of Baal, and like enough he was justifiable, considering the odds that was against him. No, all I say is, 't wa'n't any miracle, and that I'll show you so's 't you can see it yourself.

"Well, times had been getting rougher and rougher for prophets,—that is, prophets of Isaac's denomination. There was four hundred and fifty prophets of Baal in the community, and only one Presbyterian; that is, if Isaac *was* a Presbyterian, which I reckon he was, but it don't say. Naturally, the prophets of Baal took all the trade. Isaac was pretty low-spirited, I reckon, but he was a good deal of a man, and no doubt he went a-prophesying around, letting on to be doing a land-office business, but 't wa'n't any use; he couldn't run any opposition to amount to anything. By and by things got desperate with him; he sets his head to work and thinks it all out, and then what does he do? Why, he begins to throw out hints that the other parties are this and that and t' other,— nothing very definite, may be, but just kind of undermining their reputation in a quiet way. This made talk, of course, and finally got to the king. The king asked Isaac what he meant by his talk. Says Isaac, 'Oh, nothing particular; only, can they pray down fire from heaven on an altar? It ain't much, may be, your majesty, only can they *do* it? That's the idea.' So the king was a good deal disturbed, and he went to the prophets of Baal, and they said, pretty airy, that if he had an altar ready, *they* were ready; and they intimated he better get it insured, too.

"So next morning all the children of Israel and their parents and the other people gathered themselves together. Well, here was that great crowd of prophets of Baal packed together on one side, and Isaac walking up and down all alone on the other, putting up his job. When time was called, Isaac let on to be comfortable and indifferent; told the other team to take the first innings. So they went at it, the whole four hundred

*This is the captain's own mistake.

and fifty, praying around the altar, very hopeful, and doing
their level best. They prayed an hour,—two hours,—three
hours,—and so on, plumb till noon. It wa'n't any use; they
had n't took a trick. Of course they felt kind of ashamed before all those people, and well they might. Now, what would
a magnanimous man do? Keep still, would n't he? Of course.
What did Isaac do? He graveled the prophets of Baal every
way he could think of. Says he, 'You don't speak up loud
enough; your god's asleep, like enough, or may be he's taking a walk; you want to holler, you know,'—or words to that
effect; I don't recollect the exact language. Mind, I don't apologize for Isaac; he had his faults.

"Well, the prophets of Baal prayed along the best they
knew how all the afternoon, and never raised a spark. At last,
about sundown, they were all tuckered out, and they owned
up and quit.

"What does Isaac do, now? He steps up and says to some
friends of his, there, 'Pour four barrels of water on the altar!'
Everybody was astonished; for the other side had prayed at
it dry, you know, and got whitewashed. They poured it on.
Says he, 'Heave on four more barrels.' Then he says, 'Heave
on four more.' Twelve barrels, you see, altogether. The water
ran all over the altar, and all down the sides, and filled up a
trench around it that would hold a couple of hogsheads,—
'measures,' it says; I reckon it means about a hogshead. Some
of the people were going to put on their things and go, for
they allowed he was crazy. They did n't know Isaac. Isaac
knelt down and began to pray: he strung along, and strung
along, about the heathen in distant lands, and about the sister
churches, and about the state and the country at large, and
about those that's in authority in the government, and all the
usual programme, you know, till everybody had got tired and
gone to thinking about something else, and then, all of a sudden, when nobody was noticing, he outs with a match and
rakes it on the under side of his leg, and pff! up the whole
thing blazes like a house afire! Twelve barrels of *water*? *Petroleum*, sir, PETROLEUM! that's what it was!"

"Petroleum, captain?"

"Yes, sir; the country was full of it. Isaac knew all about
that. You read the Bible. Don't you worry about the tough

places. They ain't tough when you come to think them out and throw light on them. There ain't a thing in the Bible but what is true; all you want is to go prayerfully to work and cipher out how 't was done."

November 1877

*The Invalid's Story**

I seem sixty and married, but these effects are due to my condition and sufferings, for I am a bachelor, and only forty-one. It will be hard for you to believe that I, who am now but a shadow, was a hale, hearty man two short years ago,—a man of iron, a very athlete!—yet such is the simple truth. But stranger still than this fact is the way in which I lost my health. I lost it through helping to take care of a box of guns on a two-hundred-mile railway journey one winter's night. It is the actual truth, and I will tell you about it.

I belong in Cleveland, Ohio. One winter's night, two years ago, I reached home just after dark, in a driving snow-storm, and the first thing I heard when I entered the house was that my dearest boyhood friend and schoolmate, John B. Hackett, had died the day before, and that his last utterance had been a desire that I would take his remains home to his poor old father and mother in Wisconsin. I was greatly shocked and grieved, but there was no time to waste in emotions; I must start at once. I took the card, marked "Deacon Levi Hackett, Bethlehem, Wisconsin," and hurried off through the whistling storm to the railway station. Arrived there I found the long white-pine box which had been described to me; I fastened the card to it with some tacks, saw it put safely aboard the express car, and then ran into the eating-room to provide myself with a sandwich and some cigars. When I returned, presently, there was my coffin-box *back again*, apparently, and a young fellow examining around it, with a card in his hand, and some tacks and a hammer! I was astonished and puzzled. He began to nail on his card, and I rushed out to the express car, in a good deal of a state of mind, to ask for an explanation. But no—there was my box, all right, in the express car; it hadn't been disturbed. [The fact is that without my suspecting it a prodigious mistake had been made. I was carrying off a box of *guns* which that young fellow had come to the station to ship to a rifle company in Peoria, Illinois, and *he*

*Left out of these "Rambling Notes," when originally published in the "Atlantic Monthly," because it was feared that the story was not true, and at that time there was no way of proving that it was not.—M. T.

688

had got my corpse!] Just then the conductor sung out "All aboard," and I jumped into the express car and got a comfortable seat on a bale of buckets. The expressman was there, hard at work,—a plain man of fifty, with a simple, honest, good-natured face, and a breezy, practical heartiness in his general style. As the train moved off a stranger skipped into the car and set a package of peculiarly mature and capable Limburger cheese on one end of my coffin-box—I mean my box of guns. That is to say, I know *now* that it was Limburger cheese, but at that time I never had heard of the article in my life, and of course was wholly ignorant of its character. Well, we sped through the wild night, the bitter storm raged on, a cheerless misery stole over me, my heart went down, down, down! The old expressman made a brisk remark or two about the tempest and the arctic weather, slammed his sliding doors to, and bolted them, closed his window down tight, and then went bustling around, here and there and yonder, setting things to rights, and all the time contentedly humming "Sweet By and By," in a low tone, and flatting a good deal. Presently I began to detect a most evil and searching odor stealing about on the frozen air. This depressed my spirits still more, because of course I attributed it to my poor departed friend. There was something infinitely saddening about his calling himself to my remembrance in this dumb pathetic way, so it was hard to keep the tears back. Moreover, it distressed me on account of the old expressman, who, I was afraid, might notice it. However, he went humming tranquilly on, and gave no sign; and for this I was grateful. Grateful, yes, but still uneasy; and soon I began to feel more and more uneasy every minute, for every minute that went by that odor thickened up the more, and got to be more and more gamey and hard to stand. Presently, having got things arranged to his satisfaction, the expressman got some wood and made up a tremendous fire in his stove. This distressed me more than I can tell, for I could not but feel that it was a mistake. I was sure that the effect would be deleterious upon my poor departed friend. Thompson—the expressman's name was Thompson, as I found out in the course of the night—now went poking around his car, stopping up whatever stray cracks he could find, remarking that it didn't make any difference what kind of a night it was outside, he calculated to make *us* comfortable, anyway. I said nothing, but I believed he was not choosing the right way. Meantime he was humming to himself just as before; and meantime, too, the stove was getting hotter and hotter, and the place closer and closer. I felt myself growing pale and qualmish, but grieved in silence and said nothing. Soon I noticed that the "Sweet By and By" was gradually fading out; next it ceased altogether, and there was an ominous stillness. After a few moments Thompson said,—

"Pfew! I reckon it ain't no cinnamon 't I've loaded up thish-yer stove with!"

He gasped once or twice, then moved toward the cof— gun-box, stood over that Limburger cheese part of a moment, then came back and sat down near me, looking a good deal impressed. After a contemplative pause, he said, indicating the box with a gesture,—

"Friend of yourn?"

"Yes," I said with a sigh.

"He's pretty ripe, *ain't* he!"

Nothing further was said for perhaps a couple of minutes, each being busy with his own thoughts; then Thompson said, in a low, awed voice,—

"Sometimes it's uncertain whether they're really gone or not,—*seem* gone, you know—body warm, joints limber— and so, although you *think* they're gone, you don't really know. I've had cases in my car. It's perfectly awful, becuz *you* don't know what minute they'll rise right up and look at you!" Then, after a pause, and slightly lifting his elbow toward the box,—"But *he* ain't in no trance! No, sir, I go bail for *him*!"

We sat some time, in meditative silence, listening to the wind and the roar of the train; then Thompson said, with a good deal of feeling,—

"Well-a-well, we've all got to go, they ain't no getting around it. Man that is born of woman is of few days and far between, as Scriptur' says. Yes, you look at it any way you want to, it's awful solemn and cur'us: they ain't *nobody* can get around it; *all's* got to go—just *everybody*, as you may say. One day you're hearty and strong"—here he scrambled to his feet and broke a pane and stretched his nose out at it a moment or two, then sat down again while I struggled up and thrust my nose out at the same place, and this we kept on doing every now and then—"and next day he's cut down like the grass, and the places which knowed him then knows him no more forever, as Scriptur' says. Yes-'ndeedy, it's awful solemn and cur'us; but we've all got to go, one time or another; they ain't no getting around it."

There was another long pause; then,—

"What did he die of?"

I said I didn't know.

"How long has he ben dead?"

It seemed judicious to enlarge the facts to fit the probabilities; so I said,—

"Two or three days."

But it did no good; for Thompson received it with an injured look which plainly said, "Two or three *years*, you mean." Then he went right along, placidly ignoring my statement, and gave his views at considerable length upon the unwisdom of putting off burials too long. Then he lounged off toward the box, stood a moment, then came back on a sharp trot and visited the broken pane, observing,—

" 'T would 'a' ben a dum sight better, all around, if they'd started him along last summer."

Thompson sat down and buried his face in his red silk handkerchief, and began to slowly sway and rock his body like one who is doing his best to endure the almost unendurable. By this time the fragrance—if you may call it fragrance—was just about suffocating, as near as you can come at it. Thompson's face was turning gray; I knew mine hadn't any color left in it. By and by Thompson rested his forehead in his left hand, with his elbow on his knee, and sort of waved his red handkerchief towards the box with his other hand, and said,—

"I've carried a many a one of 'em,—some of 'em considerable overdue, too,—but, lordy, he just lays over' em all!—and does it *easy*. Cap., they was heliotrope to *him*!"

This recognition of my poor friend gratified me, in spite of the sad circumstances, because it had so much the sound of a compliment.

Pretty soon it was plain that something had got to be done.

I suggested cigars. Thompson thought it was a good idea. He
said,—

"Likely it'll modify him some."

We puffed gingerly along for a while, and tried hard to
imagine that things were improved. But it wasn't any use.
Before very long, and without any consultation, both cigars
were quietly dropped from our nerveless fingers at the same
moment. Thompson said, with a sigh,—

"No, Cap., it don't modify him worth a cent. Fact is, it
makes him worse, becuz it appears to stir up his ambition.
What do you reckon we better do, now?"

I was not able to suggest anything; indeed, I had to be
swallowing and swallowing, all the time, and did not like to
trust myself to speak. Thompson fell to maundering, in a desultory and low-spirited way, about the miserable experiences
of this night; and he got to referring to my poor friend by
various titles,—sometimes military ones, sometimes civil
ones; and I noticed that as fast as my poor friend's effectiveness grew, Thompson promoted him accordingly,—gave him
a bigger title. Finally he said,—

"I've got an idea. Suppos'n' we buckle down to it and give
the Colonel a bit of a shove towards t'other end of the car?—
about ten foot, say. He wouldn't have so much influence,
then, don't you reckon?"

I said it was a good scheme. So we took in a good fresh
breath at the broken pane, calculating to hold it till we got
through; then we went there and bent down over that deadly
cheese and took a grip on the box. Thompson nodded "All
ready," and then we threw ourselves forward with all our
might; but Thompson slipped, and slumped down with his
nose on the cheese, and his breath got loose. He gagged and
gasped, and floundered up and made a break for the door,
pawing the air and saying, hoarsely, "Don't hender me!—
gimme the road! I'm a-dying; gimme the road!" Out on the
cold platform I sat down and held his head a while, and he
revived. Presently he said,—

"Do you reckon we started the Gen'rul any?"

I said no; we hadn't budged him.

"Well, then, *that* idea's up the flume. We got to think up
something else. He's suited wher' he is, I reckon; and if

that's the way he feels about it, and has made up his mind that he don't wish to be disturbed, you bet you he's a-going to have his own way in the business. Yes, better leave him right wher' he is, long as he wants it so; becuz he holds all the trumps, don't you know, and so it stands to reason that the man that lays out to alter his plans for him is going to get left."

But we couldn't stay out there in that mad storm; we should have frozen to death. So we went in again and shut the door, and began to suffer once more and take turns at the break in the window. By and by, as we were starting away from a station where we had stopped a moment Thompson pranced in cheerily, and exclaimed, —

"We're all right, now! I reckon we've got the Commodore this time. I judge I've got the stuff here that'll take the tuck out of him."

It was carbolic acid. He had a carboy of it. He sprinkled it all around everywhere; in fact he drenched everything with it, rifle-box, cheese, and all. Then we sat down, feeling pretty hopeful. But it wasn't for long. You see the two perfumes began to mix, and then—well, pretty soon we made a break for the door; and out there Thompson swabbed his face with his bandanna and said in a kind of disheartened way, —

"It ain't no use. We can't buck agin *him*. He just utilizes everything we put up to modify him with, and gives it his own flavor and plays it back on us. Why, Cap., don't you know, it's as much as a hundred times worse in there now than it was when he first got a-going. I never *did* see one of 'em warm up to his work so, and take such a dumnation interest in it. No, sir, I never did, as long as I've ben on the road; and I've carried a many a one of 'em, as I was telling you."

We went in again, after we were frozen pretty stiff; but my, we couldn't *stay* in, now. So we just waltzed back and forth, freezing, and thawing, and stifling, by turns. In about an hour we stopped at another station; and as we left it Thompson came in with a bag, and said, —

"Cap., I'm a-going to chance him once more, — just this once; and if we don't fetch him this time, the thing for us to do, is to just throw up the sponge and withdraw from the canvass. That's the way *I* put it up."

He had brought a lot of chicken feathers, and dried apples, and leaf tobacco, and rags, and old shoes, and sulphur, and assafœtida, and one thing or another; and he piled them on a breadth of sheet iron in the middle of the floor, and set fire to them. When they got well started, I couldn't see, myself, how even the corpse could stand it. All that went before was just simply poetry to that smell,—but mind you, the original smell stood up out of it just as sublime as ever,—fact is, these other smells just seemed to give it a better hold; and my, how rich it was! I didn't make these reflections there— there wasn't time—made them on the platform. And break- ing for the platform, Thompson got suffocated and fell; and before I got him dragged out, which I did by the collar, I was mighty near gone myself. When we revived, Thompson said dejectedly,—

"We got to stay out here, Cap. We got to do it. They ain't no other way. The Governor wants to travel alone, and he's fixed so he can outvote us."

And presently he added,—

"And don't you know, we're *pisoned*. It's *our* last trip, you can make up your mind to it. Typhoid fever is what's going to come of this. I feel it a-coming right now. Yes, sir, we're elected, just as sure as you're born."

We were taken from the platform an hour later, frozen and insensible, at the next station, and I went straight off into a virulent fever, and never knew anything again for three weeks. I found out, then, that I had spent that awful night with a harmless box of rifles and a lot of innocent cheese; but the news was too late to save *me*; imagination had done its work, and my health was permanently shattered; neither Bermuda nor any other land can ever bring it back to me. This is my last trip; I am on my way home to die.

November 1877

Whittier Birthday Speech

Atlantic Monthly *Dinner, Seventieth Birthday of*
John Greenleaf Whittier, Boston

Mr. Chairman: This is an occasion peculiarly meet for the digging up of pleasant reminiscences concerning literary folk; therefore I will drop lightly into history myself. Standing here on the shore of the Atlantic and contemplating certain of its biggest literary billows, I am reminded of a thing which happened to me some fifteen years ago, when I had just succeeded in stirring up a little Nevadian literary ocean puddle myself, whose spume flakes were beginning to blow Californiawards. I started an inspection tramp through the southern mines of California. I was callow and conceited, and I resolved to try the virtue of my *nom de plume*. I very soon had an opportunity. I knocked at a miner's lonely log cabin in the foothills of the Sierras just at nightfall. It was snowing at the time. A jaded, melancholy man of fifty, barefooted, opened to me. When he heard my *nom de plume*, he looked more dejected than before. He let me in—pretty reluctantly, I thought—and after the customary bacon and beans, black coffee and a hot whiskey, I took a pipe. This sorrowful man had not said three words up to this time. Now he spoke up and said in the voice of one who is secretly suffering, "You're the fourth—I'm a-going to move." "The fourth what?" said I. "The fourth littery man that's been here in twenty-four hours—I'm a-going to move." "You don't tell me!" said I; "who were the others?" "Mr. Longfellow, Mr. Emerson and Mr. Oliver Wendell Holmes—dad fetch the lot!"

You can easily believe I was interested. I supplicated—three hot whiskies did the rest—and finally the melancholy miner began. Said he:

"They came here just at dark yesterday evening, and I let them in, of course. Said they were going to Yosemite. They were a rough lot—but that's nothing—everybody looks rough that travels afoot. Mr. Emerson was a seedy little bit of a chap—red-headed. Mr. Holmes was as fat as a balloon—he weighed as much as three hundred, and had double chins all the way down to his stomach. Mr. Longfellow was built like a prizefighter. His head was cropped and bristly—like as if he had a wig made of hair brushes. His nose lay straight down his face, like a finger, with the end joint tilted up. They had been drinking—I could see that. And what queer talk they used! Mr. Holmes inspected the cabin, then he took me by the buttonhole, and says he:

> Through the deep caves of thought
>   I hear a voice that sings:
> Build thee more stately mansions,
>   O my Soul!

"Says I, 'I can't afford it, Mr. Holmes, and moreover I don't want to.' Blamed if I liked it pretty well, either, coming from a stranger that way! However, I started to get out my bacon and beans, when Mr. Emerson came and looked on a while, and then *he* takes me aside by the buttonhole and says:

> Give me agates for my meat;
> Give me cantharides to eat;
> From air and ocean bring me foods,
> From all zones and latitudes.

"Says I, 'Mr. Emerson, if you'll excuse me, this ain't no hotel.' You see it sort of riled me—I warn't used to the ways of littery swells. But I went on a-sweating over my work, and next comes Mr. Longfellow and buttonholes me, and interrupts me. Says he:

> Honor be to Mudjekeewis!
> You shall hear how Pau-Puk-Kee-wis—

"But I broke in, and says I, 'Begging your pardon, Mr. Longfellow, if you'll be so kind as to hold your yawp for about five minutes, and let me get this grub ready, you'll do me proud.' Well, sir, after they'd filled up, I set out the jug. Mr. Holmes looks at it, and then he fires up all of a sudden and yells:

> Flash out a stream of blood-red wine!
> For I would drink to other days.

"By George, I was getting kind of worked up. I don't deny it, I was getting kind of worked up. I turns to Mr. Holmes, and says I, 'Looky here, my fat friend, I'm a-running this shanty, and if the court knows herself, you'll take whiskey straight or you'll go dry!' Them's the very words I said to him. Now I didn't want to sass such famous littery people, but you see they kind of forced me. There ain't nothing onreasonable 'bout me; I don't mind a passel of guests a-tred'n on my tail three or four times, but when it comes to *standin'* on it, it's different, and if the court knows herself, you'll take whiskey straight or you'll go dry! Well, between drinks they'd swell around the cabin and strike attitudes and spout. Says Mr. Longfellow:

> This is the forest primeval.

"Says Mr. Emerson:

> Here once the embattled farmers stood,
> And fired the shot heard round the world.

"Says I, 'Oh, blackguard the premises as much as you want to—it don't cost you a cent.' Well, they went on drinking, and pretty soon they got out a greasy old deck and went to playing cutthroat euchre at ten cents a corner—on trust. I begun to notice some pretty suspicious things. Mr. Emerson dealt, looked at his hand, shook his head, says:

> I am the doubter and the doubt—

and calmly bunched the hands and went to shuffling for a new layout. Says he:

> They reckon ill who leave me out;
> They know not well the subtle ways
> I keep. I pass, and deal *again!*

"Hang'd if he didn't go ahead and do it, too! Oh, he was a cool one. Well, in about a minute, things were running pretty tight, but all of a sudden I see by Mr. Emerson's eye that he judged he had 'em. He had already corralled two tricks, and each of the others one. So now he kind of lifts a little, in his chair, and says:

> I tire of globes and aces!
> Too long the game is played!

—and down he fetched a right bower. Mr. Longfellow smiles as sweet as pie, and says:

> Thanks, thanks to thee, my worthy friend,
> For the lesson thou has taught.

—and dog my cats if he didn't come down with *another* right bower! Well, sir, up jumps Holmes a-war whooping, as usual, and says:

> God help them if the tempest swings
> The pine against the palm!

—and I wish I may go to grass if he didn't swoop down with *another* right bower! Emerson claps his hand on his bowie, Longfellow claps his on his revolver, and I went under a bunk. There was going to be trouble; but that monstrous Holmes rose up, wobbling his double chins, and says he, 'Order, gentlemen; the first man that draws, I'll lay down on him and smother him!' All quiet on the Potomac, you bet you!

"They were pretty how-come-you-so now, and they begun to blow. Emerson says, 'The bulliest thing I ever wrote was "Barbara Frietchie."' Says Longfellow, 'It don't begin with my "Biglow Papers."' Says Holmes, 'My "Thanatopsis" lays over 'em both.' They mighty near ended in a fight. Then they wished they had some more company—and Mr. Emerson pointed at me and says:

> Is yonder squalid peasant all
> That this proud nursery could breed?

"He was a-whetting his bowie on his boot—so I let it pass. Well, sir, next they took it into their heads that they would like some music; so they made me stand up and sing 'When Johnny Comes Marching Home' till I dropped—at thirteen minutes past four this morning. That's what *I've* been through, my friend. When I woke at seven, they were leaving, thank goodness, and Mr. Longfellow had my only boots on, and his own under his arm. Says I, 'Hold on there, Evangeline, what you going to do with *them?*' He says: 'Going to make tracks with 'em, because

> Lives of great men all remind us
> We can make our lives sublime;

> And departing, leave behind us
> Footprints on the sands of Time.

"As I said, Mr. Twain, you are the fourth in twenty-four hours—and I'm a-going to move—I ain't suited to a littery atmosphere."

I said to the miner, "Why, my dear sir, *these* were not the gracious singers to whom we and the world pay loving reverence and homage; these were imposters."

The miner investigated me with a calm eye for a while, then said he, "Ah—imposters, were they?—are *you*?" I did not pursue the subject; and since then I haven't traveled on my *nom de plume* enough to hurt. Such is the reminiscence I was moved to contribute, Mr. Chairman. In my enthusiasm I may have exaggerated the details a little, but you will easily forgive me that fault, since I believe it is the first time I have ever deflected from perpendicular fact on an occasion like this.

December 17, 1877

Farewell Banquet for Bayard Taylor

Dinner Speech, Delmonico's, New York

Mr. Chairman: I had intended to make an address of some length here tonight, and in fact wrote out an impromptu speech, but have had no time to memorize it. I cannot make a speech on the moment, and therefore being unprepared I am silent and undone. However, I will say this much for the speech that I had written out—that it was a very good one, and I gave it away as I had no further use for it, and saw that I could not deliver it. Therefore I will ask the indulgence of the company here to let me retire without speaking. I will make my compliments to our honored friend, Mr. Taylor, but I will make them on board ship where I shall be a fellow passenger.

[The following is the speech Mark Twain had prepared.]

I have been warned—as, no doubt, have all among you that are inexperienced—that a dinner to our Ambassador is an occasion which demands, and even requires, a peculiar caution and delicacy in the handling of the dangerous weapon of speech. I have been warned to avoid all mention of international politics, and all criticisms, however mild, of countries with which we are at peace, lest such utterances embarrass our minister and our government in their dealings with foreign states. In a word, I have been cautioned to talk, but be careful not to say anything. I do not consider this a difficult task.

Now, it has often occurred to me that the conditions under which we live at the present day, with the revelations of geology all about us, viewing, upon the one hand, the majestic configurations of the silurian, oolitic, old red sandstone periods, and, upon the other, the affiliations, and stratifications, and ramifications of the prehistoric, post-pliocene, antepenultimate epochs, we are stricken dumb with amazed surprise, and can only lift up our hands and say with that wise but odious Frenchman: "It was a slip of the tongue, sir, and wholly unintentional—entirely unintentional." It would ill become me, upon an occasion like this, purposely to speak slightingly of a citizen of a country with whom we are at peace—and especially great and gracious France, whom God

700

preserve! The subject, however, is a delicate one, and I will not pursue it.

But—as I was about to remark—cast your eye abroad, sir, for one pregnant moment over the vista which looms before you in the mighty domain of intellectual progression and contemplate the awe-compelling theory of the descent of man! Development, sir! Development! Natural selection! Correlation of the sexes! Spontaneous combustion!—what gulfs and whirlwinds of intellectual stimulus these magic words fling upon the burning canvas of the material universe of soul! Across the chasm of the ages we take the oyster by the hand and call him brother; and back, and still further back, we go, and breathe the germ we cannot see, and know, in him, our truer Adam! And as we stand, dazed, transfixed, exalted, and gaze down the long procession of life, marking how steadily, how symmetrically we have ascended, step by step, to our sublime estate and dignity of humanity—out of one lowly form into a little higher and a little higher forms—adding grace after every change—developing from tadpoles into frogs, frogs into fishes, fishes into birds, birds into reptiles, reptiles into Russians—I beg a million pardons, sir and gentlemen—it was a wholly innocent slip of the tongue, and due only to the excitement of debate—for far be it from me, on such an occasion as this, to cast a seeming slur upon a great nation with which we are at peace—a great and noble and Christian nation—whom God expand!

But, as I was about to remark, I maintain—and nothing can ever drive me from that position—that the contributions of the nineteenth century to science and the industrial arts are—are—but, of course they are. There is no need to dwell upon that. You look at it yourself. Look at steam! Look at the steamboat, look at the railway, look at the steamship! Look at the telegraph, which enables you to flash your thoughts from world to world, ignoring intervening seas. Look at the telephone, which enables you to speak into affection's remote ear the word that cheers, and into the ear of the foe the opinion which you ought not to risk at shorter range. Look at the sewing machine, look at the foghorn, look at the bell punch, look at the book agent. And, more than all, a thousand times, look at the last and greatest, the aerophone, which will enable

Moody and Sankey to stand on the tallest summit of the Rocky Mountains and deliver their message to listening America!—and necessarily it will annul and do away with the pernicious custom of taking up a collection. Look at all these things, sir, and say if it is not a far prouder and more precious boon to have been born in the nineteenth century than in any century that went before it. Ah, sir, clothed with the all-sufficient grandeur of citizenship in the nineteenth century, even the wild and arid New Jerseyman might—a mistake, sir, a mistake, and entirely unintentional. Of all the kingdoms, principalities and countries with which it is our privilege to hold peaceful relations, I regard New Jersey as dearest to our admiration, nearest to our heart, the wisest and the purest among the nations. I retire the undiplomatic language, and beg your sympathy and indulgence.

But, as I was about to remark, it has always seemed to me—that is, of course, since I reached a reasoning age—that this much agitated question of future rewards and punishments was one upon which honest and sincere differences of opinion might exist; one individual, with more or less justice, leaning to the radical side of it, whilst another individual, with apparently equal justice, but with infinitely more common sense, more intelligence, more justification, leans to a bitter and remorseless detestation of the pitiless Prince of Perdition—a slip of the tongue, I do sincerely assure you—I beg you to let me withdraw that unintentional slur upon the character of that great and excellent personage with whom and whose country we are upon the closest and warmest terms, and who—it is no use, sir, I will sit down; I don't seem to have any knack at a diplomatic speech. I have probably compromised the country enough for the present.

Nonsense aside, sir, I am most sincerely glad to assist at this public expression of appreciation of Mr. Taylor's character, scholarship, and distinguished literary service. I am sure he was not merely one of the fittest men we had for the place, but the fittest. In so honoring him, our country has conspicuously honored herself.

April 4, 1878

About Magnanimous-Incident Literature

All my life, from boyhood up, I have had the habit of reading a certain set of anecdotes, written in the quaint vein of The World's ingenious Fabulist, for the lesson they taught me and the pleasure they gave me. They lay always convenient to my hand, and whenever I thought meanly of my kind I turned to them and they banished that sentiment; whenever I felt myself to be selfish, sordid, and ignoble I turned to them, and they told me what to do to win back my self-respect. Many times I wished that the charming anecdotes had not stopped with their happy climaxes, but had continued the pleasing history of the several benefactors and beneficiaries. This wish rose in my breast so persistently that at last I determined to satisfy it by seeking out the sequels of those anecdotes myself. So I set about it, and after great labor and tedious research accomplished my task. I will lay the result before you, giving you each anecdote in its turn, and following it with its sequel as I gathered it through my investigations.

THE GRATEFUL POODLE.

One day a benevolent physician (who had read the books), having found a stray poodle suffering from a broken leg, conveyed the poor creature to his home, and after setting and bandaging the injured limb gave the little outcast its liberty again, and thought no more about the matter. But how great was his surprise, upon opening his door one morning, some days later, to find the grateful poodle patiently waiting there, and in its company another stray dog, one of whose legs, by some accident, had been broken. The kind physician at once relieved the distressed animal, nor did he forget to admire the inscrutable goodness and mercy of God, who had been willing to use so humble an instrument as the poor outcast poodle for the inculcating of, etc., etc., etc.

SEQUEL.

The next morning the benevolent physician found the two dogs, beaming with gratitude, waiting at his door, and with them two other dogs,—cripples. The cripples were speedily healed, and the four went their way, leaving the benevolent physician more overcome by pious wonder than ever. The day passed, the morning came. There at the door sat now the four reconstructed dogs, and with them four others requiring reconstruction. This day also passed, and another morning came; and now sixteen dogs, eight of them newly crippled, occupied the sidewalk, and the people were going around. By noon the broken legs were all set, but the pious wonder in the good physician's breast was beginning to get mixed with involuntary profanity. The sun rose once more, and exhibited thirty-two dogs, sixteen of them with broken legs, occupying the sidewalk and half of the street; the human spectators took up the rest of the room. The cries of the wounded, the songs of the healed brutes, and the comments of the on-looking citizens made great and inspiring cheer, but traffic was interrupted in that street. The good physician hired a couple of assistant surgeons and got through his benevolent work before dark, first taking the precaution to cancel his church membership, so that he might express himself with the latitude which the case required.

But some things have their limits. When once more the morning dawned, and the good physician looked out upon a massed and far-reaching multitude of clamorous and beseeching dogs, he said, "I might as well acknowledge it, I have been fooled by the books; they only tell the pretty part of the story, and then stop. Fetch me the shot-gun; this thing has gone along far enough."

He issued forth with his weapon, and chanced to step upon the tail of the original poodle, who promptly bit him in the leg. Now the great and good work which this poodle had been engaged in had engendered in him such a mighty and augmenting enthusiasm as to turn his weak head at last and drive him mad. A month later, when the benevolent physician lay in the death throes of hydrophobia, he called his weeping friends about him, and said,—

"Beware of the books. They tell but half of the story. Whenever a poor wretch asks you for help, and you feel a doubt as to what result may flow from your benevolence, give yourself the benefit of the doubt and kill the applicant."

And so saying he turned his face to the wall and gave up the ghost.

THE BENEVOLENT AUTHOR.

A poor and young literary beginner had tried in vain to get his manuscripts accepted. At last, when the horrors of starvation were staring him in the face, he laid his sad case before a celebrated author, beseeching his counsel and assistance. This generous man immediately put aside his own matters and proceeded to peruse one of the despised manuscripts. Having completed his kindly task, he shook the poor young man cordially by the hand, saying, "I perceive merit in this; come again to me on Monday." At the time specified, the celebrated author, with a sweet smile, but saying nothing, spread open a magazine which was damp from the press. What was the poor young man's astonishment to discover upon the printed page his own article. "How can I ever," said he, falling upon his knees and bursting into tears, "testify my gratitude for this noble conduct!" The celebrated author was the renowned Snodgrass; the poor young beginner thus rescued from obscurity and starvation was the afterwards equally renowned Snagsby. Let this pleasing incident admonish us to turn a charitable ear to all beginners that need help.

SEQUEL.

The next week Snagsby was back with five rejected manuscripts. The celebrated author was a little surprised, because in the books the young struggler had needed but one lift, apparently. However, he plowed through these papers, removing unnecessary flowers and digging up some acres of adjective-stumps, and then succeeded in getting two of the articles accepted.

A week or so drifted by, and the grateful Snagsby arrived with another cargo. The celebrated author had felt a mighty glow of satisfaction within himself the first time he had successfully befriended the poor young struggler, and had compared himself with the generous people in the books with high gratification; but he was beginning to suspect now that he had struck upon something fresh in the noble-episode line. His enthusiasm took a chill. Still, he could not bear to repulse this struggling young author, who clung to him with such pretty simplicity and trustfulness.

Well, the upshot of it all was that the celebrated author presently found himself permanently freighted with the poor young beginner. All his mild efforts to unload his cargo went for nothing. He had to give daily counsel, daily encouragement; he had to keep on procuring magazine acceptances, and then revamping the manuscripts to make them presentable. When the young aspirant got a start at last, he rode into sudden fame by describing the celebrated author's private life with such a caustic humor and such minuteness of blistering detail that the book sold a prodigious edition, and broke the celebrated author's heart with mortification. With his latest gasp he said, "Alas, the books deceived me; they do not tell the whole story. Beware of the struggling young author, my friends. Whom God sees fit to starve, let not man presumptuously rescue to his own undoing."

THE GRATEFUL HUSBAND.

One day a lady was driving through the principal street of a great city with her little boy, when the horses took fright and dashed madly away, hurling the coachman from his box and leaving the occupants of the carriage paralyzed with terror. But a brave youth who was driving a grocery wagon threw himself before the plunging animals, and succeeded in arresting their flight at the peril of his own.* The grateful lady took his number, and upon arriving at her home she related the heroic act to her husband (who had read the books), who listened with streaming eyes to the moving recital, and who, after returning thanks, in conjunction with his restored loved ones, to him who suffereth not even a sparrow to fall to the ground unnoticed, sent for the brave young person, and, placing a check for five hundred dollars in his hand, said, "Take this as a reward for your noble act, William Ferguson, and if ever you shall need a friend, remember that Thompson McSpadden has a grateful heart." Let us learn from this that a good deed cannot fail to benefit the doer, however humble he may be.

*This is probably a misprint.—M. T.

SEQUEL.

William Ferguson called the next week and asked Mr. Mc-Spadden to use his influence to get him a higher employment, he feeling capable of better things than driving a grocer's wagon. Mr. McSpadden got him an under-clerkship at a good salary.

Presently William Ferguson's mother fell sick, and William— Well, to cut the story short, Mr. McSpadden consented to take her into his house. Before long she yearned for the society of her younger children; so Mary and Julia were admitted also, and little Jimmy, their brother. Jimmy had a pocket-knife, and he wandered into the drawing-room with it one day, alone, and reduced ten thousand dollars' worth of furniture to an indeterminable value in rather less than three quarters of an hour. A day or two later he fell down-stairs and broke his neck, and seventeen of his family's relatives came to the house to attend the funeral. This made them acquainted, and they kept the kitchen occupied after that, and likewise kept the McSpaddens busy hunting up situations of various sorts for them, and hunting up more when they wore these out. The old woman drank a good deal and swore a good deal; but the grateful McSpaddens knew it was their duty to reform her, considering what her son had done for them, so they clave nobly to their generous task. William came often and got decreasing sums of money, and asked for higher and more lucrative employments,—which the grateful McSpadden more or less promptly procured for him. McSpadden consented also after some demur, to fit William for college; but when the first vacation came and the hero requested to be sent to Europe for his health, the persecuted McSpadden rose against the tyrant and revolted. He plainly and squarely refused. William Ferguson's mother was so astounded that she let her gin bottle drop, and her profane lips refused to do their office. When she recovered she said in a half-gasp, "Is this your gratitude? Where would your wife and boy be now, but for my son?"

William said, "Is this your gratitude? Did I save your wife's life or not? tell me that!"

Seven relations swarmed in from the kitchen and each said, "And this is his gratitude!"

William's sisters stared, bewildered, and said, "And this is his grat—" but were interrupted by their mother, who burst into tears and exclaimed, "To think that my sainted little Jimmy threw away his life in the service of such a reptile!"

Then the pluck of the revolutionary McSpadden rose to the occasion, and he replied with fervor, "Out of my house, the whole beggarly tribe of you! I was beguiled by the books, but shall never be beguiled again,—once is sufficient for me." And turning to William he shouted, "Yes, you did save my wife's life, and the next man that does it shall die in his tracks!"

Not being a clergyman, I place my text at the end of my sermon instead of at the beginning. Here it is, from Mr. Noah Brooks's Recollections of President Lincoln, in Scribner's Monthly: —

"J. H. Hackett, in his part of Falstaff, was an actor who gave Mr. Lincoln great delight. With his usual desire to signify to others his sense of obligation, Mr. Lincoln wrote a genial little note to the actor, expressing his pleasure at witnessing his performance. Mr. Hackett, in reply, sent a book of some sort; perhaps it was one of his own authorship. He also wrote several notes to the president. One night, quite late, when the episode had passed out of my mind, I went to the White House in answer to a message. Passing into the president's office, I noticed, to my surprise, Hackett sitting in the anteroom as if waiting for an audience. The president asked me if any one was outside. On being told, he said, half sadly, 'Oh, I can't see him, I can't see him; I was in hopes he had gone away.' Then he added, 'Now this just illustrates the difficulty of having pleasant friends and acquaintances in this place. You know how I liked Hackett as an actor, and how I wrote to tell him so. He sent me that book, and there I thought the matter would end. He is a master of his place in the profession, I suppose, and well fixed in it; but just because we had a little friendly correspondence, such as any two men might have, he wants something. What do you suppose he wants?' I could not guess, and Mr.

Lincoln added, 'Well, he wants to be consul to London. Oh, dear!' "

I will observe, in conclusion, that the William Ferguson incident occurred, and within my personal knowledge,—though I have changed the nature of the details, to keep William from recognizing himself in it.

All the readers of this article have in some sweet and gushing hour of their lives played the rôle of Magnanimous-Incident hero. I wish I knew how many there are among them who are willing to talk about that episode and like to be reminded of the consequences that flowed from it.

May 1878

The Great Revolution in Pitcairn

Let me refresh the reader's memory a little. Nearly a hundred years ago the crew of the British ship Bounty mutinied, set the captain and his officers adrift upon the open sea, took possession of the ship, and sailed southward. They procured wives for themselves among the natives of Tahiti, then proceeded to a lonely little rock in mid-Pacific, called Pitcairn's Island, wrecked the vessel, stripped her of everything that might be useful to a new colony, and established themselves on shore.

Pitcairn's is so far removed from the track of commerce that it was many years before another vessel touched there. It had always been considered an uninhabited island; so when a ship did at last drop its anchor there, in 1808, the captain was greatly surprised to find the place peopled. Although the mutineers had fought among themselves, and gradually killed each other off until only two or three of the original stock remained, these tragedies had not occurred before a number of children had been born; so in 1808 the island had a population of twenty-seven persons. John Adams, the chief mutineer, still survived, and was to live many years yet, as governor and patriarch of the flock. From being mutineer and homicide, he had turned Christian and teacher, and his nation of twenty-seven persons was now the purest and devoutest in Christendom. Adams had long ago hoisted the British flag and constituted his island an appanage of the British crown.

To-day the population numbers ninety persons,—sixteen men, nineteen women, twenty-five boys, and thirty girls,—all descendants of the mutineers, all bearing the family names of those mutineers, and all speaking English, and English only. The island stands high up out of the sea, and has precipitous walls. It is about three quarters of a mile long, and in places is as much as half a mile wide. Such arable land as it affords is held by the several families, according to a division made many years ago. There is some live stock,—goats, pigs, chickens, and cats; but no dogs, and no large animals. There is one church building,—used also as a capitol, a school-house, and a public library. The title of the governor has been, for a generation or two, "Magistrate and Chief Ruler, in subordination to her Majesty the Queen of Great Britain." It was his province to *make* the laws, as well as execute them. His office was elective; everybody over seventeen years old had a vote,—no matter about the sex.

The sole occupations of the people were farming and fishing; their sole recreation, religious services. There has never been a shop in the island, nor any money. The habits and dress of the people have always been primitive, and their laws simple to puerility. They have lived in a deep Sabbath tranquillity, far from the world and its ambitions and vexations, and neither knowing nor caring what was going on in the mighty empires that lie beyond their limitless ocean solitudes. Once in three or four years a ship touched there, moved them with aged news of bloody battles, devastating epidemics, fallen thrones, and ruined dynasties, then traded them some soap and flannel for some yams and bread-fruit, and sailed away, leaving them to retire into their peaceful dreams and pious dissipations once more.

On the 8th of last September, Admiral de Horsey, commander-in-chief of the British fleet in the Pacific, visited Pitcairn's Island, and speaks as follows in his official report to the admiralty:—

"They have beans, carrots, turnips, cabbages, and a little maize; pineapples, fig-trees, custard apples, and oranges; lemons and cocoa-nuts. Clothing is obtained alone from passing ships, in barter for refreshments. There are no springs on the island, but as it rains generally once a month they have plenty of water, although at times, in former years, they have suffered from drought. No alcoholic liquors, except for medicinal purposes, are used, and a drunkard is unknown. . . .

"The necessary articles required by the islanders are best shown by those we furnished in barter for refreshments: namely, flannel, serge, drill, half-boots, combs, tobacco, and soap. They also stand much in need of maps and slates for their school, and tools of any kind are most acceptable. I caused them to be supplied from the public stores with a union-jack for display on the arrival of ships, and a pit saw, of which they were greatly in need. This, I trust, will meet the approval of their lordships. If the munificent people of

England were only aware of the wants of this most deserving little colony, they would not long go unsupplied. . . .

"Divine service is held every Sunday at 10.30 A. M. and at 3 P. M., in the house built and used by John Adams for that purpose until he died in 1829. It is conducted strictly in accordance with the liturgy of the Church of England, by Mr. Simon Young, their selected pastor, who is much respected. A Bible class is held every Wednesday, when all who conveniently can attend. There is also a general meeting for prayer on the first Friday in every month. Family prayers are said in every house the first thing in the morning and the last thing in the evening, and no food is partaken of without asking God's blessing before and afterwards. Of these islanders' religious attributes no one can speak without deep respect. A people whose greatest pleasure and privilege is to commune in prayer with their God, and to join in hymns of praise, and who are, moreover, cheerful, diligent, and probably freer from vice than any other community, need no priest among them."

Now I come to a sentence in the admiral's report which he dropped carelessly from his pen, no doubt, and never gave the matter a second thought. He little imagined what a freight of tragic prophecy it bore! This is the sentence:

"One stranger, an American, has settled on the island, — *a doubtful acquisition.*"

A doubtful acquisition indeed! Captain Ormsby, in the American ship Hornet, touched at Pitcairn's nearly four months after the admiral's visit, and from the facts which he gathered there we now know all about that American. Let us put these facts together, in historical form. The American's name was Butterworth Stavely. As soon as he had become well acquainted with all the people, — and this took but a few days, of course, — he began to ingratiate himself with them by all the arts he could command. He became exceedingly popular, and much looked up to; for one of the first things he did was to forsake his worldly way of life, and throw all his energies into religion. He was always reading his Bible, or praying, or singing hymns, or asking blessings. In prayer, no one had such "liberty" as he, no one could pray so long or so well.

At last, when he considered the time to be ripe, he began secretly to sow the seeds of discontent among the people. It was his deliberate purpose, from the beginning, to subvert the government, but of course he kept that to himself for a time. He used different arts with different individuals. He awakened dissatisfaction in one quarter by calling attention to the shortness of the Sunday services; he argued that there should be three three-hour services on Sunday instead of only two. Many had secretly held this opinion before; they now privately banded themselves into a party to work for it. He showed certain of the women that they were not allowed sufficient voice in the prayer-meetings; thus another party was formed. No weapon was beneath his notice; he even descended to the children, and awoke discontent in their breasts because—as *he* discovered for them—they had not enough Sunday-school. This created a third party.

Now, as the chief of these parties, he found himself the strongest power in the community. So he proceeded to his next move,—a no less important one than the impeachment of the chief magistrate, James Russell Nickoy; a man of character and ability, and possessed of great wealth, he being the owner of a house with a parlor to it, three acres and a half of yam land, and the only boat in Pitcairn's, a whale-boat; and, most unfortunately, a pretext for this impeachment offered itself at just the right time. One of the earliest and most precious laws of the island was the law against trespass. It was held in great reverence, and was regarded as the palladium of the people's liberties. About thirty years ago an important case came before the courts under this law, in this wise: a chicken belonging to Elizabeth Young (aged, at that time, fifty-eight, a daughter of John Mills, one of the mutineers of the Bounty) trespassed upon the grounds of Thursday October Christian (aged twenty-nine, a grandson of Fletcher Christian, one of the mutineers). Christian killed the chicken. According to the law, Christian could keep the chicken; or, if he preferred, he could restore its remains to the owner, and receive damages in "produce" to an amount equivalent to the waste and injury wrought by the trespasser. The court records set forth that "the said Christian aforesaid did deliver the aforesaid remains to the said Elizabeth Young, and did de-

mand one bushel of yams in satisfaction of the damage done."
But Elizabeth Young considered the demand exorbitant; the
parties could not agree; therefore Christian brought suit in
the courts. He lost his case in the justice's court; at least, he
was awarded only a half peck of yams, which he considered
insufficient, and in the nature of a defeat. He appealed. The
case lingered several years in an ascending grade of courts,
and always resulted in decrees sustaining the original verdict;
and finally the thing got into the supreme court, and there it
stuck for twenty years. But last summer, even the supreme
court managed to arrive at a decision at last. Once more the
original verdict was sustained. Christian then said he was satisfied; but Stavely was present, and whispered to him and to
his lawyer, suggesting, "as a mere form," that the original law
be exhibited, in order to make sure that it still existed. It
seemed an odd idea, but an ingenious one. So the demand
was made. A messenger was sent to the magistrate's house; he
presently returned with the tidings that it had disappeared
from among the state archives.

The court now pronounced its late decision void, since it
had been made under a law which had no actual existence.

Great excitement ensued, immediately. The news swept
abroad over the whole island that the palladium of the public
liberties was lost,—may be treasonably destroyed. Within
thirty minutes almost the entire nation were in the court-
room,—that is to say, the church. The impeachment of the
chief magistrate followed, upon Stavely's motion. The accused met his misfortune with the dignity which became his
great office. He did not plead, or even argue: he offered the
simple defense that he had not meddled with the missing law;
that he had kept the state archives in the same candle-box that
had been used as their depository from the beginning; and
that he was innocent of the removal or destruction of the lost
document.

But nothing could save him; he was found guilty of mis-
prision of treason, and degraded from his office, and all his
property was confiscated.

The lamest part of the whole shameful matter was the *reason* suggested by his enemies for his destruction of the law, to
wit: that he did it to favor Christian, because Christian was

his cousin! Whereas Stavely was the only individual in the entire nation who was *not* his cousin. The reader must remember that all of these people are the descendants of half a dozen men; that the first children intermarried together and bore grandchildren to the mutineers; that these grandchildren intermarried; after them, great and great-great-grandchildren intermarried: so that to-day everybody is blood-kin to everybody. Moreover, the relationships are wonderfully, even astoundingly, mixed up and complicated. A stranger, for instance, says to an islander, —

"You speak of that young woman as your cousin; a while ago you called her your aunt."

"Well, she *is* my aunt, and my cousin too. And also my step-sister, my niece, my fourth cousin, my thirty-third cousin, my forty-second cousin, my great-aunt, my grandmother, my widowed sister-in-law, — and next week she will be my wife."

So the charge of nepotism against the chief magistrate was weak. But no matter; weak or strong, it suited Stavely. Stavely was immediately elected to the vacant magistracy; and, oozing reform from every pore, he went vigorously to work. In no long time religious services raged everywhere and unceasingly. By command, the second prayer of the Sunday, morning service, which had customarily endured some thirty-five or forty minutes, and had pleaded for the world, first by continent and then by national and tribal detail, was extended to an hour and a half, and made to include supplications in behalf of the possible peoples in the several planets. Everybody was pleased with this; everybody said, "Now *this* is something *like*." By command, the usual three-hour sermons were doubled in length. The nation came in a body to testify their gratitude to the new magistrate. The old law forbidding cooking on the Sabbath was extended to the prohibition of eating, also. By command, Sunday-school was privileged to spread over into the week. The joy of all classes was complete. In one short month the new magistrate was become the people's idol!

The time was ripe for this man's next move. He began, cautiously at first, to poison the public mind against England. He took the chief citizens aside, one by one, and conversed with them on this topic. Presently he grew bolder, and spoke out. He said the nation owed it to itself, to its honor, to its great traditions, to rise in its might and throw off "this galling English yoke."

But the simple islanders answered,—

"We had not noticed that it galled. How does it gall? England sends a ship once in three or four years to give us soap and clothing, and things which we sorely need and gratefully receive; but she never troubles us; she lets us go our own way."

"She lets you go your own way! So slaves have felt and spoken in all the ages! This speech shows how fallen you are, how base, how brutalized, you have become, under this grinding tyranny! What! has all manly pride forsaken you? Is liberty nothing? Are you content to be a mere appendage to a foreign and hateful sovereignty, when you might rise up and take your rightful place in the august family of nations, great, free, enlightened, independent, the minion of no sceptred master, but the arbiter of your own destiny, and a voice and a power in decreeing the destinies of your sister-sovereignties of the world?"

Speeches like this produced an effect by and by. Citizens began to feel the English yoke; they did not know exactly how or whereabouts they felt it, but they were perfectly certain they did feel it. They got to grumbling a good deal, and chafing under their chains, and longing for relief and release. They presently fell to hating the English flag, that sign and symbol of their nation's degradation; they ceased to glance up at it as they passed the capitol, but averted their eyes and grated their teeth; and one morning, when it was found trampled into the mud at the foot of the staff, they left it there, and no man put his hand to it to hoist it again. A certain thing which was sure to happen sooner or later happened now. Some of the chief citizens went to the magistrate by night, and said,—

"We can endure this hated tyranny no longer. How can we cast it off?"

"By a *coup d'état*."

"How?"

"A coup d'état. It is like this: Everything is got ready, and at the appointed moment I, as the official head of the nation, publicly and solemnly proclaim its independence, and absolve it from allegiance to any and all other powers whatsoever."

"That sounds simple and easy. We can do that right away. Then what will be the next thing to do?"

"Seize all the defenses and public properties of all kinds, establish martial law, put the army and navy on a war footing, and proclaim the empire!"

This fine programme dazzled these innocents. They said,—

"This is grand,—this is splendid; but will not England resist?"

"Let her. This rock is a Gibraltar."

"True. But about the empire? Do we *need* an empire, and an emperor?"

"What you *need*, my friends, is unification. Look at Germany; look at Italy. They are unified. Unification is the thing. It makes living dear. That constitutes progress. We must have a standing army, and a navy. Taxes follow, as a matter of course. All these things summed up make grandeur. With unification and grandeur, what more can you want? Very well,—only the empire can confer these boons."

So on the 8th day of December Pitcairn's Island was proclaimed a free and independent nation; and on the same day the solemn coronation of Butterworth I., emperor of Pitcairn's Island, took place, amid great rejoicings and festivities. The entire nation, with the exception of fourteen persons, mainly little children, marched past the throne in single file, with banners and music, the procession being upwards of ninety feet long; and some said it was as much as three quarters of a minute passing a given point. Nothing like it had ever been seen in the history of the island before. Public enthusiasm was measureless.

Now straightway imperial reforms began. Orders of nobility were instituted. A minister of the navy was appointed, and the whale-boat put in commission. A minister of war was created, and ordered to proceed at once with the formation of a standing army. A first lord of the treasury was named, and commanded to get up a taxation scheme, and also open negotiations for treaties, offensive, defensive, and commercial, with foreign powers. Some generals and admirals were

appointed; also some chamberlains, some equerries in waiting, and some lords of the bed-chamber.

At this point all the material was used up. The Grand Duke
of Galilee, minister of war, complained that all the sixteen
grown men in the empire had been given great offices, and
consequently would not consent to serve in the ranks; wherefore his standing army was at a stand-still. The Marquis of
Ararat, minister of the navy, made a similar complaint. He
said he was willing to steer the whale-boat himself, but he
must have somebody to man her.

The emperor did the best he could in the circumstances: he
took all the boys above the age of ten years away from their
mothers, and pressed them into the army, thus constructing
a corps of seventeen privates, officered by one lieutenant-
general and two major-generals. This pleased the minister of
War, but procured the enmity of all the mothers in the land;
for they said their precious ones must now find bloody graves
in the fields of war, and he would be answerable for it. Some
of the more heart-broken and inappeasable among them lay
constantly in wait for the emperor and threw yams at him,
unmindful of the body-guard.

On account of the extreme scarcity of material, it was found
necessary to require the Duke of Bethany, postmaster-general,
to pull stroke-oar in the navy, and thus sit in the rear of a
noble of lower degree, namely, Viscount Canaan, lord-justice
of the common pleas. This turned the Duke of Bethany into a
tolerably open malcontent and a secret conspirator,—a thing
which the emperor foresaw, but could not help.

Things went from bad to worse. The emperor raised Nancy
Peters to the peerage on one day, and married her the next,
notwithstanding, for reasons of state, the cabinet had strenuously advised him to marry Emmeline, eldest daughter of the
Archbishop of Bethlehem. This caused trouble in a powerful
quarter,—the church. The new empress secured the support
and friendship of two thirds of the thirty-six grown women in
the nation by absorbing them into her court as maids of
honor; but this made deadly enemies of the remaining twelve.
The families of the maids of honor soon began to rebel, because there was now nobody at home to keep house. The
twelve snubbed women refused to enter the imperial kitchen

as servants; so the empress had to require the Countess of Jericho and other great court dames to fetch water, sweep the palace, and perform other menial and equally distasteful services. This made bad blood in that department.

Everybody fell to complaining that the taxes levied for the support of the army, the navy, and the rest of the imperial establishment were intolerably burdensome, and were reducing the nation to beggary. The emperor's reply—"Look at Germany; look at Italy. Are you better than they? and have n't you unification?"—did not satisfy them. They said, "People can't *eat* unification, and we are starving. Agriculture has ceased. Everybody is in the army, everybody is in the navy, everybody is in the public service, standing around in a uniform, with nothing whatever to do, nothing to eat, and nobody to till the fields"—

"Look at Germany; look at Italy. It is the same there. Such is unification, and there's no other way to get it,—no other way to keep it after you've got it," said the poor emperor always.

But the grumblers only replied, "We can't *stand* the taxes, —we can't *stand* them."

Now right on top of this the cabinet reported a national debt amounting to upwards of forty-five dollars,—half a dollar to every individual in the nation. And they proposed to fund something. They had heard that this was always done in such emergencies. They proposed duties on exports; also on imports. And they wanted to issue bonds; also paper money, redeemable in yams and cabbages in fifty years. They said the pay of the army and of the navy and of the whole governmental machine was far in arrears, and unless something was done, and done immediately, national bankruptcy must ensue, and possibly insurrection and revolution. The emperor at once resolved upon a high-handed measure, and one of a nature never before heard of in Pitcairn's Island. He went in state to the church on Sunday morning, with the army at his back, and commanded the minister of the treasury to take up a collection.

That was the feather that broke the camel's back. First one citizen, and then another, rose and refused to submit to this unheard-of outrage,—and each refusal was followed by the immediate confiscation of the malcontent's property. This vigor soon stopped the refusals, and the collection proceeded amid a sullen and ominous silence. As the emperor withdrew with the troops, he said, "I will teach you who is master here." Several persons shouted, "Down with unification!" They were at once arrested and torn from the arms of their weeping friends by the soldiery.

But in the mean time, as any prophet might have foreseen, a Social Democrat had been developed. As the emperor stepped into the gilded imperial wheelbarrow at the church door, the social democrat stabbed at him fifteen or sixteen times with a harpoon, but fortunately with such a peculiarly social democratic unprecision of aim as to do no damage.

That very night the convulsion came. The nation rose as one man,—though forty-nine of the revolutionists were of the other sex. The infantry threw down their pitchforks; the artillery cast aside their cocoa-nuts; the navy revolted; the emperor was seized, and bound hand and foot in his palace. He was very much depressed. He said,—

"I freed you from a grinding tyranny; I lifted you up out of your degradation, and made you a nation among nations; I gave you a strong, compact, centralized government; and, more than all, I gave you the blessing of blessings,—unification. I have done all this, and my reward is hatred, insult, and these bonds. Take me; do with me as ye will. I here resign my crown and all my dignities, and gladly do I release myself from their too heavy burden. For your sake, I took them up; for your sake I lay them down. The imperial jewel is no more; now bruise and defile as ye will the useless setting."

By a unanimous voice the people condemned the ex-emperor and the social democrat to perpetual banishment from church services, or to perpetual labor as galley-slaves in the whale-boat,—whichever they might prefer. The next day the nation assembled again, and rehoisted the British flag, reinstated the British tyranny, reduced the nobility to the condition of commoners again, and then straightway turned their diligent attention to the weeding of the ruined and neglected yam patches, and the rehabilitation of the old useful industries and the old healing and solacing pieties. The ex-emperor restored the lost trespass law, and explained that he had stolen it,—not to injure any one, but to further his political projects. Therefore the nation gave the late chief magistrate his office again, and also his alienated property.

Upon reflection, the ex-emperor and the social democrat chose perpetual banishment from religious services, in preference to perpetual labor as galley-slaves "*with* perpetual religious services," as they phrased it; wherefore the people believed that the poor fellows' troubles had unseated their reason, and so they judged it best to confine them for the present. Which they did.

Such is the history of Pitcairn's "doubtful acquisition."

March 1879

Some Thoughts on the Science of Onanism

Stomach Club Dinner, Paris

My gifted predecessor has warned you against the "social evil—adultery." In his able paper he exhausted that subject; he left absolutely nothing more to be said on it. But I will continue his good work in the cause of morality by cautioning you against that species of recreation called self-abuse—to which I perceive that you are too much addicted. All great writers upon health and morals, both ancient and modern, have struggled with this stately subject; this shows its dignity and importance. Some of these writers have taken one side, some the other. Homer, in the second book of the *Iliad*, says with fine enthusiasm, "Give me masturbation or give me death!" Caesar, in his *Commentaries*, says, "To the lonely it is company; to the forsaken it is a friend; to the aged and impotent it is a benefactor; they that be penniless are yet rich, in that they still have this majestic diversion." In another place this excellent observer has said, "There are times when I prefer it to sodomy." Robinson Crusoe says, "I cannot describe what I owe to this gentle art." Queen Elizabeth said, "It is the bulwark of virginity." Cetewayo, the Zulu hero, remarked that "a jerk in the hand is worth two in the bush." The immortal Franklin has said, "Masturbation is the mother of invention." He also said, "Masturbation is the best policy." Michelangelo and all the other old Masters—old Masters, I will remark, is an abbreviation, a contraction—have used similar language. Michelangelo said to Pope Julius II, "Self-negation is noble, self-culture is beneficent, self-possession is manly, but to the truly great and inspiring soul they are poor and tame compared to self-abuse." Mr. Brown, here, in one of his latest and most graceful poems refers to it in an eloquent line which is destined to live to the end of time— "None know it but to love it, None name it but to praise."

Such are the utterances of the most illustrious of the masters of this renowned science, and apologists for it. The name of those who decry it and oppose it is legion; they have made strong arguments and uttered bitter speeches against it—but there is not room to repeat them here, in much detail.

Brigham Young, an expert of incontestable authority, said, "As compared with the other thing, it is the difference between the lightning bug and the lightning." Solomon said, "There is nothing to recommend it but its cheapness." Galen said, "It is shameful to degrade to such bestial use that grand limb, that formidable member, which we votaries of science dub the 'Major Maxillary'—when they dub it at all—which is seldom. It would be better to decapitate the Major than to use him so. It would be better to amputate the *os frontis* than to put it to such a use." The great statistician, Smith, in his report to Parliament, says, "In my opinion, more children have been wasted in this way than in any other." It cannot be denied that the high authority of this art entitles it to our respect; but at the same time I think that its harmfulness demands our condemnation. Mr. Darwin was grieved to feel obliged to give up his theory that the monkey was the connecting link between man and the lower animals. I think he was too hasty. The monkey is the only animal, except man, that practices this science; hence he is our brother; there is a bond of sympathy and relationship between us. Give this ingenious animal an audience of the proper kind, and he will straightway put aside his other affairs and take a whet; and you will see by the contortions and his ecstatic expression that he takes an intelligent and human interest in his performance.

The signs of excessive indulgence in this destructive pastime are easily detectable. They are these: A disposition to eat, to drink, to smoke, to meet together convivially, to laugh, to joke, and tell indelicate stories—and mainly, a yearning to paint pictures. The results of the habit are: Loss of memory, loss of virility, loss of cheerfulness, loss of hopefulness, loss of character, and loss of progeny. Of all the various kinds of sexual intercourse, this has least to recommend it. As an amusement it is too fleeting; as an occupation it is too wearing; as a public exhibition there is no money in it. It is unsuited to the drawing room, and in the most cultured society it has long since been banished from the social board. It has at last, in our day of progress and improvement, been degraded to brotherhood with flatulence—among the best bred these two arts are now indulged only in private—though by consent of the whole company, when only males are present, it is still permissible, in good society, to remove the embargo upon the fundamental sigh.

My illustrious predecessor has taught you that all forms of the "social evil" are bad. I would teach you that some of those forms are more to be avoided than others; so, in concluding, I say, "If you *must* gamble away your lives sexually, don't play a Lone Hand too much." When you feel a revolutionary uprising in your system, get your Vendome Column down some other way—don't jerk it down.

Spring 1879

A Presidential Candidate

I have pretty much made up my mind to run for President. What the country wants is a candidate who cannot be injured by investigation of his past history, so that the enemies of the party will be unable to rake up anything against him that nobody ever heard of before. If you know the worst about a candidate, to begin with, every attempt to spring things on him will be checkmated. Now I am going to enter the field with an open record. I am going to own up in advance to all the wickedness I have done, and if any Congressional committee is disposed to prowl around my biography in the hope of discovering any dark and deadly deed that I have secreted, why — let it prowl.

In the first place, I admit that I treed a rheumatic grandfather of mine in the winter of 1850. He was old and inexpert in climbing trees, but with the heartless brutality that is characteristic of me I ran him out of the front door in his nightshirt at the point of a shotgun, and caused him to bowl up a maple tree, where he remained all night, while I emptied shot into his legs. I did this because he snored. I will do it again if I ever have another grandfather. I am as inhuman now as I was in 1850. I candidly acknowledge that I ran away at the battle of Gettysburg. My friends have tried to smooth over this fact by asserting that I did so for the purpose of imitating Washington, who went into the woods at Valley Forge for the purpose of saying his prayers. It was a miserable subterfuge. I struck out in a straight line for the Tropic of Cancer because I was scared. I wanted my country saved, but I preferred to have somebody else save it. I entertain that preference yet. If the bubble reputation can be obtained only at the cannon's mouth, I am willing to go there for it, provided the cannon is empty. If it is loaded my immortal and inflexible purpose is to get over the fence and go home. My invariable practice in war has been to bring out of every fight two-thirds more men than when I went in. This seems to me to be Napoleonic in its grandeur.

My financial views are of the most decided character, but they are not likely, perhaps, to increase my popularity with the advocates of inflation. I do not insist upon the special supremacy of rag money or hard money. The great fundamental principle of my life is to take any kind I can get.

The rumor that I buried a dead aunt under my grapevine was correct. The vine needed fertilizing, my aunt had to be buried, and I dedicated her to this high purpose. Does that unfit me for the Presidency? The Constitution of our country does not say so. No other citizen was ever considered unworthy of this office because he enriched his grapevines with his dead relatives. Why should I be selected as the first victim of an absurd prejudice?

I admit also that I am not a friend of the poor man. I regard the poor man, in his present condition, as so much wasted raw material. Cut up and properly canned, he might be made useful to fatten the natives of the cannibal islands and to improve our export trade with that region. I shall recommend legislation upon the subject in my first message. My campaign cry will be: "Desiccate the poor workingman; stuff him into sausages."

These are about the worst parts of my record. On them I come before the country. If my country don't want me, I will go back again. But I recommend myself as a safe man—a man who starts from the basis of total depravity and proposes to be fiendish to the last.

June 9, 1879

The Babies. As They Comfort Us in Our Sorrows, Let Us Not Forget Them in Our Festivities

Thirteenth Reunion Banquet, Army of the Tennessee, Chicago

I like that. We haven't all had the good fortune to be ladies; we haven't all been generals, or poets, or statesmen; but when the toast works down to the babies, we stand on common ground, for we've all been babies. It is a shame that for a thousand years the world's banquets have utterly ignored the baby—as if *he* didn't amount to anything! If you gentlemen will stop and think a minute—if you will go back fifty or a hundred years, to your early married life, and recontemplate your first baby, you will remember that he amounted to a good deal, and even something over. You soldiers all know that when that little fellow arrived at family headquarters, you had to hand in your resignation. He took entire command. You became his lackey—his mere body servant, and you had to stand around, too. He was not a commander who made allowances for time, distance, weather, or anything else—you had to execute his order whether it was possible or not. And there was only one form of marching in his manual of tactics, and that was the double-quick. He treated you with every sort of insolence and disrespect, and the bravest of you didn't dare to say a word.

You could face the death storm at Donelson and Vicksburg, and give back blow for blow; but when he clawed your whiskers, and pulled your hair, and twisted your nose, you had to take it. When the thunders of war were sounding in your ears, you set your face toward the batteries, and advanced with steady tread; but, when he turned on the terrors of his war whoop, you advanced in the other direction—and mighty glad of the chance, too. When he called for soothing syrup, did you venture to throw out any side remarks about certain services being unbecoming an officer and a gentleman? No. You got up and *got* it. When he ordered his pap bottle, and it wasn't warm, did you talk back? Not you. You went to work and *warmed* it. You even descended so far in your menial office as to take a suck at that warm, insipid stuff your-self, just to see if it was right—three parts water to one of milk, a touch of sugar to modify the colic, and a drop of peppermint to kill those infernal hiccups. I can taste that stuff yet.

And how many things you learned, as you went along! Sentimental young folks still take stock in that beautiful old saying that when the baby smiles in his sleep, it is because the angels are whispering to him. Very pretty, but too thin— simply wind on the stomach, my friends! If the baby pro-posed to take a walk at the usual hour—half-past two in the morning—didn't you rise up promptly and remark—with a mental addition which wouldn't improve a Sunday school book *much*—that that was the very thing you were about to propose yourself? Oh, you were under good discipline. And as you went fluttering up and down the room in your undress uniform, you not only prattled undignified baby talk, but even turned up your martial voices and tried to *sing*!— "Rock-a-by baby in the tree top," for instance. And what an affliction for the neighbors, too—for it isn't everybody within a mile around that likes military music at three in the morning. And when you had been keeping this sort of thing up two or three hours, and your little velvet-head intimated that nothing suited him like exercise and noise, and proposed to fight it out on that line if it took all night—what did you do? [When Mark Twain paused, voices shouted: "Go on!"] You simply *went* on till you dropped in the last ditch.

The idea that a *baby* doesn't amount to anything! Why, *one* baby is just a house and front yard full by itself. *One* baby can furnish more business than you and your whole Interior De-partment can attend to. He is enterprising, irrepressible, brim full of lawless activities. Do what you please, you can't make him stay on the reservation. Sufficient unto the day is one baby—as long as you are in your right mind don't you ever pray for twins. Twins amount to a permanent riot; and there ain't any real difference between triplets and an insurrection.

Yes, it was high time for a toastmaster to recognize the im-portance of the babies. Think what is in store for the present crop! Fifty years from now we shall all be dead—I trust— and then this flag, if it still survive—and let us hope it may— will be floating over a Republic numbering 200,000,000 souls, according to the settled laws of our increase; our present schooner of State will have grown into a political leviathan—a *Great Eastern*—and the cradled babies of today will be on deck. Let them be well trained, for we are going to leave a big contract on their hands. Among the three or four million cradles now rocking in the land are some which this nation would preserve for ages as sacred things, if we could know which ones they are. In one of these cradles the unconscious Farragut of the future is at this moment *teething*—think of it!—and putting in a world of dead earnest, unarticulated and perfectly justifiable profanity over it, too; in another, the future renowned astronomer is blinking at the shining Milky Way, with but a languid interest—poor little chap!—and wondering what has become of that other one they call the wet nurse; in another the future great historian is lying—and doubtless he will continue to lie until his earthly mission is ended; in another the future President is busying himself with no profounder problem of state than what the mischief has become of his hair so early, and in a mighty array of other cradles there are now some sixty thousand future office-seekers getting ready to furnish him occasion to grapple with that same old problem a second time.

And in still one more cradle, somewhere under the flag, the future illustrious Commander in Chief of the American armies is so little burdened with his approaching grandeurs and responsibilities as to be giving his whole strategic mind, at this moment, to trying to find out some way to get his own big toe into his mouth—an achievement which, meaning no disrespect, the illustrious guest of this evening turned *his* whole attention to some fifty-six years ago. And if the child is but a prophecy of the man, there are mighty few who will doubt that he *succeeded*.

November 13, 1879

The New Postal Barbarism

Hartford, November 22d.

To the EDITOR of THE COURANT: —

SIR: The new postal regulation adds quite perceptibly to my daily burden of work. Needlessly, too—as I think. A day or two ago, I made a note of the addresses which I had put upon letters that day, and then ciphered up to see how many words the additional particularities of the new ruling had cost me. It was *seventy-two*. That amounts to just a page of my manuscript, exactly. If it were stuff that a magazine would enjoy, I could sell it and gradually get rich as time rolled on—as it isn't, I lose the time and the ink. I don't get a cent for it, the government grows no wealthier, I grow poorer, nobody in the world is benefited. Seventy-two words utterly wasted—and mind you, when a man is paid by the word, (at least by the page, which is the same thing) this sort of thing hurts. Here are one or two specimens from those addresses —with the unnecessary additions in italics:

> Editor "Atlantic Monthly,"
> *Care Messrs. Houghton, Osgood & Co.,*
> *Winthrop Square,*
> Boston,
> *Mass.*

Nine words wasted—I used to use only the first line and the word "Boston"—and until the letter-carriers lose their minds the additional nine words can never become necessary.

> Messrs. Arnold, Constable & Co.,
> *Cor. 19th & B'way,*
> New York,
> *N. Y.*

Six unnecessary words.

> Gilsey House,
> *Cor. 29th & B'way,*
> New York,
> *N. Y.*

Six unnecessary words.

Even the dead people in Boston and New York could tell a letter-carrier how to find these prominent houses. That same day I wrote a letter to a friend at the Windsor hotel, New York—surely that house is prominent enough, ain't it? But I could not precisely name the side streets, neither did I know the name of the back street, nor the head cook's name. So that letter would have gone to the dead-letter office sure, if I hadn't covered it all over with an appeal to Mr. James to take it under his personal official protection and let it go to that man at the Windsor just this once and I would not offend any more.

Now you know, yourself, that there is no need of an official decree to compel a man to make a letter-address full and elaborate where it is at all necessary—for the writer is more anxious that his letter shall go through than the Postmaster General can be. And when the writer can *not* supply those minute details from lack of knowledge, the decree cannot help him in the least. So what is the use of the decree? As for those common mistakes, the mis-directing of letters, the leaving off the county, the state, etc.,—do you think an official decree can do away with that? You know yourself that heedless, absent-minded people are bound to make those mistakes, and that no decree can knock the disposition out of them.

Observe this—I have been ciphering, and I know that the following facts are correct. The new law will compel 18,000 great mercantile houses to employ three extra correspondents at $1,000 a year—$54,000—smaller establishments in proportion. It will compel 30,000,000 of our people to write a daily average of ten extra words apiece—300,000,000 unnecessary words; most of these people are slow—the average will be half a minute consumed on each ten words—15,000,000 minutes of this nation's time fooled away every day—say 247,400 hours—which amounts to about 25,000 working days of ten hours each; this makes eighty-two years of 300 working days each, counting out Sundays and sickness—eighty-two years of this nation's time wholly thrown away every day! Value of the average man's time, say $1,000 a year—now do you see?—$82,000 thrown away daily; in round numbers $25,000,000 yearly; in ten years, $250,000,000; in a hundred years, $2,500,000,000; in a million years—but I have not the nerve to go on; you can see, yourself, what we are coming to. If this law continues in force, there will not be money enough in this country, by and by, to pay for its obituary—and you mark my words, it will need one.

Now we come to the ink. No, let us forbear—in fancy I already see the fleets of the world sailing in it.

Isn't it odd that we should take a spasm, every now and then, and go spinning back into the dark ages once more, after having put in a world of time and money and work toiling up into the high lights of modern progress?

For many years it has been England's boast that her postal system is so admirable that you *can't* so cripple the direction of a letter that the post office department won't manage some way to find the person the missive is intended for. We could say that too, once. But we have retired a hundred years, within the last two months, and now it is our boast that only the brightest, and thoughtfulest, and knowingest men's letters will ever be permitted to reach their destinations, and that those of the mighty majority of the American people,—the heedless, the unthinking, the illiterate,—will be rudely shot by the shortest route to the dead-letter office and destruction. It seems to me that this new decree is very decidedly un-American.

MARK TWAIN.

November 25, 1879

Postal Matters

To the EDITOR *of* THE COURANT: —

SIR: A day or two ago I received a formidable envelop from Washington enclosing a letter and some printed matter. This envelop had certain peculiarities about it. For instance, in its right hand upper corner an oval black stamp was printed, bearing the words, "United States Postal service;" in the upper left hand corner the following words were printed, in large, bold type, in three separate lines—thus:

Post Office Department.
Office of the Postmaster General.
OFFICIAL BUSINESS.

In the lower left-hand corner was printed the following words, in two separate lines—thus:

A penalty of $300 *is fixed by law, for using this Envelop for other than* OFFICIAL *Business.*

In this majestic envelop I found the following among other things:

POST OFFICE DEPARTMENT, }
WASHINGTON, D. C., Nov. 30th, 1879. }

S. M. Clements, Esq.
Hartford, Conn.

Dear Sir:

Noticing your letter to THE HARTFORD COURANT upon the recent order of the Postmaster General, I take the liberty of enclosing a few copies of a tract which the Department has prepared in order to meet such hardened cases as yours. After reading the tract and the enclosed clipping (from the Cincinnati *Enquirer*), which latter I wish you would return to me as it is the only copy I have, you will see that the "unnecessary labor" of which you complain was really as unnecessary as the complaint, the only utility of which was to add to the already surplus stock of misinformation in the world, and to enable some needy compositors to increase their strings by several thousand, which latter end might have been just as well attained by the use of bogus.

I send you by this mail a copy of the Postal Laws and Regulations to explain the allusions in the tract, and hope you
will take the trouble to look into the matter thoroughly. The
Department is a unit in regarding the order as the greatest
step towards perfecting the postal service that has been taken
for years, and its officers are confident that when the public
understand it they will sustain it.

Yours Truly,

THOS. B. KIRBY

(Private Secretary to the Postmaster General.)

MY CALLOW FRIEND—When you shall have outgrown the
effervescences of youth, and acquired a bit of worldly experience, you will cease to make mistakes like that. That is to say,
you will refrain from meddling in matters which do not concern you, you will recognize the simple wisdom of confining
yourself strictly to your own business.

There are persons who would resent this innocent piece of
impertinence of yours, and say harsh things to you about it;
but fortunately for you, I am not that sort of person. Whatever else I may lack, I have a good heart. Therefore, in a
humane and gentle spirit, I will try to set you right upon
certain small points,—not to hurt you, but to do you good.

You seem to think you have been called to account. This is
a grave error. It is the Post Office Department of the United
States of America which has been called to account. There is a
difference here, which you have over-looked—I will point
it out. You are not the post office department, but only an
irresponsible, inexpensive, and unnecessary appendage to it.
Grave, elderly men, public instructors, like me, do not call
private secretaries to account. Bear this in mind, it will be a
help to you. The mistake you have made is simple—you have
imagined yourself the dog, whereas you are only the tail. You
have endeavored to wag the dog; this was not judicious; you
should have hung quiescent until the dog wagged *you*. If I
stepped on this tail—and we will grant, for the sake of argument, that I did—it was not to call the tail's attention to
anything, but only to direct the attention of the main body of
the animal to a certain matter. You perceive, it was simply in

the nature of ringing a bell, that is all; my business was not
with the bell itself, but with the owner of it. A bell is a useful
thing, in a measure, but it should not keep on ringing when
one is done with it.

Do I make myself partially understood? Lest there be any
doubt, let me illustrate farther—by parable; for the parable is
the simplest and surest vehicle for conveying information to
the immature mind. You seem to have gathered the impression, somehow, that you are a member of the cabinet. This is
an error. You are only extraneous matter connected *with* a
member of the cabinet. Your chief is one of the guns of that
battery, but you are not. You are not the gun, or the lead, or
even the ramrod; neither do you supply the ammunition. You
only do up the cartridge and serve as a fire-stick to touch it
off. You are not the barrel of molasses, you are only the faucet
through which the molasses is discharged. You are not the
boot, but the bootjack; that is to say, you do not furnish the
idea, you only pull it off. You are not the lightning, but only
the lightning-rod.

Do you perceive? The thing I am trying to convey to you
is, that it does not become you to assume functions which do
not belong to you. You may think it strange that I am closing
this note without saying anything upon the matter which you
have broached. Overlook that, drop it out of your mind—we
do not disturb the repose of private secretaries with affairs
with which they have nothing to do.

The newspaper slip which you have enclosed to me will be
returned to you by one of my private secretaries. I keep eleven
of these things—not for use, but display.

Although I cannot consent to talk public business with
you, a benevolent impulse moves me to call your attention to
a matter which is of quite serious importance to you as an
individual. You, an unofficial private citizen, have written me
an entirely personal and unofficial letter, which you have had
the temerity to enclose to me in a Department envelop bearing upon its surface in clear print this plain and unmistakable
warning: *"A penalty of $300 is fixed by law, for using this envelop
for other than* OFFICIAL *business."* The servants of the government's officers ought to be, for simple decency's sake, among
the last to break its laws. You have committed a serious

offense—an offense which has none of the elements of a joke
about it—and only plain and simple treachery to his duty, on
the part of your superior, can save you from the penalty involved. The kindly and almost affectionate spirit which I have
shown you is sufficient evidence that I do not wish you any
harm, but indeed the reverse. So, if that treachery shall in-
tervene to shield you, I shall not be sorry—as far as you individually are concerned—but I should be unfaithful to my
citizenship if I did not at the same time feel something of a
pang to see a law of the land coolly ignored and degraded by
one of the very highest officers of the government. As far as I
am concerned, you are safe—unless you intrude upon me
again; in which case I may be tempted to bring you before
the courts myself for the violation of that law.

There, now—receive my blessing. Go, and do not mix into
other people's affairs any more. Otherwise you may pick up
somebody who will feed disagreeable words to you instead of
sugar.

MARK TWAIN.

To the EDITOR *of* THE COURANT:—

SIR: If you will allow me a brief word, I can furnish some
information which, for excellent reasons, not two Americans
in twelve hundred are acquainted with. It is this. The issuing
of the wild postal edict of last September raised such a tempest of protestations in every quarter of the country, that the
department, after enduring the siege for a few days, succumbed—partially. It did not retire from the fortress openly,
however. That is to say, it surrendered part of its armament,
but nobody knew about it, for the reason that the fact was
not made public. The fact was printed in the Postal Guide
—that is to say, it was secreted there. If it had got into
the newspapers we should have heard of it, and our complaints would have assumed a diminished form. Here is the
modification:—

"56. When postmasters and employes of the railway mail service
know that matter deposited in their offices for mailing, addressed to a
city without the name of the state being given, is intended for the
principal city of that name, being for instance, addressed to a well-

known citizen, firm, newspaper or institution of such principal city, or to a street and number which could only be found therein, it should be forwarded as directed in section 467. Otherwise the provisions of sections 437, 438 and 740, P. L. & R., 1879, are to be observed."

If that had accompanied the original edict, there would not have been such a storm.

MARK TWAIN.

December 9, 1879

A Telephonic Conversation

I consider that a conversation by telephone—when you are simply sitting by and not taking any part in that conversation—is one of the solemnest curiosities of this modern life. Yesterday I was writing a deep article on a sublime philosophical subject while such a conversation was going on in the room. I notice that one can always write best when somebody is talking through a telephone close by. Well, the thing began in this way. A member of our household came in and asked me to have our house put into communication with Mr. Bagley's, down town. I have observed, in many cities, that the sex always shrink from calling up the central office themselves. I don't know why, but they do. So I touched the bell, and this talk ensued:—

Central Office. [Gruffly.] Hello!

I. Is it the Central Office?

C. O. Of course it is. What do you want?

I. Will you switch me on to the Bagleys, please?

C. O. All right. Just keep your ear to the telephone.

Then I heard, *k-look, k-look, k'look—klook-klook-klook-look-look!* then a horrible "gritting" of teeth, and finally a piping female voice: Y-e-s? [Rising inflection.] Did you wish to speak to me?

Without answering, I handed the telephone to the applicant, and sat down. Then followed that queerest of all the queer things in this world,—a conversation with only one end to it. You hear questions asked; you don't hear the answer. You hear invitations given; you hear no thanks in return. You have listening pauses of dead silence, followed by apparently irrelevant and unjustifiable exclamations of glad surprise, or sorrow, or dismay. You can't make head or tail of the talk, because you never hear anything that the person at the other end of the wire says. Well, I heard the following remarkable series of observations, all from the one tongue, and all shouted,—for you can't ever persuade the sex to speak gently into a telephone:—

Yes? Why, how did *that* happen?

Pause.

What did you say?

Pause.

Oh, no, I don't think it was.

Pause.

No! Oh, no, I didn't mean *that*. I meant, put it in while it is still boiling,—or just before it *comes* to a boil.

Pause.

WHAT?

Pause.

I turned it over with a back stitch on the selvage edge.

Pause.

Yes, I like that way, too; but I think it's better to baste it on with Valenciennes or bombazine, or something of that sort. It gives it such an air,—and attracts so much notice.

Pause.

It's forty-ninth Deuteronomy, sixty-fourth to ninety-seventh inclusive. I think we ought all to read it often.

Pause.

Perhaps so; I generally use a hair-pin.

Pause.

What did you say? [*Aside*] Children, do be quiet!

Pause.

Oh! B *flat!* Dear me, I thought you said it was the cat!

Pause.

Since *when?*

Pause.

Why, *I* never heard of it.

Pause.

You astound me! It seems utterly impossible!

Pause.

Who did?

Pause.

Good-ness gracious!

Pause.

Well, what *is* this world coming to? Was it right in *church?*

Pause.

And was her *mother* there?

Pause.

Why, Mrs. Bagley, I should have died of humiliation! What did they *do?*

Long pause.

I can't be perfectly sure, because I have n't the notes by me; but I think it goes something like this: te-rolly-loll-loll, loll lolly-loll-loll, O tolly-loll-loll-*lee-ly-li-i*-do! And then *repeat*, you know.

Pause.

Yes, I think it *is* very sweet,—and very solemn and impressive, if you get the andantino and the pianissimo right.

Pause.

Oh, gum-drops, gum-drops! But I never allow them to eat striped candy. And of course they *can't*, till they get their teeth, any way.

Pause.

What?

Pause.

Oh, not in the least,—go right on. He's here writing,—it does n't bother *him*.

Pause.

Very well, I'll come if I can. [*Aside.*] Dear me, how it does tire a person's arm to hold this thing up so long! I wish she'd—

Pause.

Oh, no, not at all; I *like* to talk,—but I'm afraid I'm keeping you from your affairs.

Pause.

Visitors?

Pause.

No, we never use butter on them.

Pause.

Yes, that is a very good way; but all the cook-books say they are very unhealthy when they are out of season. And *he* does n't like them, any way,—especially canned.

Pause.

Oh, I think that is too high for them; we have never paid over fifty cents a bunch.

Pause.

Must you go? Well, *good*-by.

Pause.

Yes, I think so. *Good*-by.

Pause.

Four o'clock, then—I'll be ready. *Good*-by.

Pause.

Thank you ever so much. *Good*-by.

Pause.

Oh, not at all!—just as fresh—*Which?* Oh, I'm glad to hear you say that. *Good*-by.

[Hangs up the telephone and says, "Oh, it *does* tire a person's arm so!"]

A man delivers a single brutal "Good-by," and that is the end of it. Not so with the gentle sex,—I say it in their praise; they cannot abide abruptness.

June 1880

Reply to a Boston Girl

This note comes to me from the home of culture:—

DEAR MR ——: Your writings interest me very much; but I cannot help wishing you would not place adverbs between the particle and verb in the Infinitive. For example: "to *even* realize," "to *mysteriously* disappear" "to *wholly* do away." You should say, *even* to realize; to disappear mysteriously, etc. "rose up" is another mistake—tautology, you know. Yours truly

A BOSTON GIRL.

I print the note just as it was written, for one or two reasons: (1.) It flatters a superstition of mine that a person may learn to excel in only such details of an art as take a particularly strong hold upon his native predilections or instincts. (2.) It flatters another superstition of mine that whilst all the details of that art may be of equal importance *he* cannot be made to feel that it is so. Possibly he may be made to *see* it, through argument and illustration; but that will be of small value to him except he *feel* it, also. Culture would be able to make him feel it by and by, no doubt, but never very sharply, I think. Now I have certain instincts, and I wholly lack certain others. (Is that "wholly" in the right place?) For instance, I am dead to adverbs; they cannot excite me. To misplace an adverb is a thing which I am able to do with frozen indifference; it can never give me a pang. But when my young lady puts no point after "Mr.;" when she begins "adverb," "verb," and "particle" with the small letter, and aggrandizes "Infinitive" with a capital; and when she puts no comma after "to mysteriously disappear," etc., I am troubled; and when she begins a sentence with a small letter I even *suffer*. Or I suffer, *even*,—I do not know which it is; but she will, because the adverb is in her line, whereas only those minor matters are in mine. Mark these prophetic words: though this young lady's grammar be as the drifted snow for purity, she will never, never, never learn to punctuate while she lives; this is her demon, the adverb is mine. I thank her, honestly and kindly, for her lesson, but I know thoroughly well that I shall never be able to get it into my head. Mind, I do not say I shall not be able to make it *stay* there; I say and mean that I am not capable of *getting it into* my head. There are subtleties which I cannot master at all,—they confuse me, they mean absolutely nothing to me,—and this adverb plague is one of them.

We all have our limitations in the matter of grammar, I suppose. I have never seen a book which had no grammatical defects in it. This leads me to believe that all people have my infirmity, and are afflicted with an inborn inability to feel or mind certain sorts of grammatical particularities. There are people who were not born to spell; these can never be taught to spell correctly. The enviable ones among them are those who do not take the trouble to care whether they spell well or not,—though in truth these latter are absurdly scarce. I have been a correct speller, always; but it is a low accomplishment, and not a thing to be vain of. Why should one take pride in spelling a word rightly when he knows he is spelling it wrongly? *Though* is the right way to spell "though," but it is not *the* right way to spell it. Do I make myself understood?

Some people were not born to punctuate; these cannot learn the art. They can learn only a rude fashion of it; they cannot attain to its niceties, for these must be *felt*; they cannot be reasoned out. Cast-iron rules will not answer, here, any way; what is one man's comma is another man's colon. One man can't punctuate another man's manuscript any more than one person can make the gestures for another person's speech.

What is known as "dialect" writing looks simple and easy, but it is not. It is exceedingly difficult; it has rarely been done well. A man not born to write dialect cannot learn how to write it correctly. It is a gift. Mr. Harte can write a delightful story; he can *reproduce* Californian scenery so that you see it before you, and hear the sounds and smell the fragrances and feel the influences that go with it and belong to it; he can describe the miner and the gambler perfectly,—as to gait and look and garb; but no human being, living or dead, ever had experience of the dialect which he puts into his people's mouths. Mr. Harte's originality is not questioned; but if it ever shall be, the caviler will have to keep his hands off that dialect, for that *is* original. Mind, I am not objecting to its use; I am not saying its inaccuracy is a fatal blemish. No, it is Mr. Harte's adverb; let him do as he pleases with it; he can no more mend it than I can mine; neither will any but Boston Girls ever be likely to find us out.

Yes, there are things which we cannot learn, and there is no use in fretting about it. I cannot learn adverbs; and what is more I won't. If I try to seat a person at my right hand, I have no trouble, provided I am facing north at the time; but if I am facing south, I get him on my left, sure. As this thing was born in me, and cannot be educated out of me, I do not worry over it or care about it. A gentleman picked me up, last week, and brought me home in his buggy; he drove past the door, and as he approached the circular turn I saw he meant to go around to the left; I was on his left,—that is, I *think* I was, but I have got it all mixed up again in my head; at any rate, I halted him, and asked him to go round the circle the other way. He backed his horse a length or two, put his helm down and "slewed" him to the right, then "came ahead on him," and made the trip. As I got out at the door, he looked puzzled, and asked why I had particularly wanted to pass to the right around the circle. I said, "Because that would bring me next the door coming back, and I wouldn't have to crowd past your knees." He came near laughing his store teeth out, and said it was all the same whether we drove to the right or to the left in going around the circle; either would bring me back to the house on the side the door was on, since I was on the opposite side when I first approached the circle. I regarded this as false. He was willing to illustrate: so he drove me down to the gate and into the street, turned and drove back past the house, moved leftward around the circle, and brought me back to the door; and as sure as I am sitting here I *was* on the side next the door. I did not believe he could do it again, but he did. He did it eleven times hand running. Was I convinced? No. I was not *capable* of being convinced—*all through*. My sight and intellect (to call it by that name) were convinced, but not my *feeling*. It is simply another case of adverb. It is a piece of dead-corpsy knowledge, which is of no use to me, because I merely *know* it, but do not *understand* it.

The fact is, as the poet has said, we are all fools. The difference is simply in the degree. The mercury in some of the fool-thermometers stands at ten, fifteen, twenty, thirty, and so on; in some it gets up to seventy-five; in some it soars to ninety-nine. I never examine mine,—take no interest in it.

Now as to "rose up." That strikes me as quite a good form; I will use it some more,—that is, when I speak of a person, and wish to signify the full upright position. If I mean less, I will qualify, by saying he rose partly up. It is a form that will answer for the moon sometimes, too. I think it is Bingen on the Rhine who says—

> "The pale moon rose up slowly, and calmly she
>   looked down,
>   On the red sands," etc.

But tautology cannot scare me, any way. Conversation would be intolerably stiff and formal without it; and a mild form of it can limber up even printed matter without doing it serious damage. Some folks are so afraid of a little repetition that they make their meaning vague, when they could just as well make it clear, if only their ogre were out of the way.

Talking of Unlearnable Things, would it be genteel, would it be polite, to ask members of this Club to confess what freightage of this sort they carry? Some of the revelations would be curious and instructive, I think. I am acquainted with one member of it who has never been able to learn nine times eight; he always says, "Nine times seven are sixty-three,"—then counts the rest on his fingers. He is at home in the balance of the multiplication-table. I am acquainted with another member, who, although he has known for many years that when Monday is the first of the month the following Monday will be the eighth, has never been able to *feel* the fact; so he cannot trust it, but always counts on his fingers, to make sure. I have known people who could spell all words correctly but one. They never could get the upper hand of that one; yet as a rule it was some simple, common affair, such as a cat could spell, if a cat could spell at all. I have a friend who has kept his razors in the top drawer and his strop in the bottom drawer for years; when he wants his razors, he always pulls out the bottom drawer—and swears. Change? Could one imagine he never thought of that? He did change;

he has changed a dozen times. It did n't do any good; his afflicted mind was able to keep up with the changes and make the proper mistake every time. I knew a man—

June 1880

Edward Mills and George Benton: A Tale

These two were distantly related to each other,—seventh
cousins, or something of that sort. While still babies they
became orphans, and were adopted by the Brants, a childless
couple, who quickly grew very fond of them. The Brants were
always saying, "Be pure, honest, sober, industrious, and considerate of others, and success in life is assured." The children
heard this repeated some thousands of times before they understood it; they could repeat it themselves long before they
could say the Lord's Prayer; it was painted over the nursery
door, and was about the first thing they learned to read. It
was destined to become the unswerving rule of Edward
Mills's life. Sometimes the Brants changed the wording a little, and said, "Be pure, honest, sober, industrious, considerate, and you will never lack friends."

Baby Mills was a comfort to everybody about him. When
he wanted candy and could not have it, he listened to reason,
and contented himself without it. When Baby Benton wanted
candy, he cried for it until he got it. Baby Mills took care of
his toys; Baby Benton always destroyed his in a very brief
time, and then made himself so insistently disagreeable that,
in order to have peace in the house, little Edward was persuaded to yield up his playthings to him.

When the children were a little older, Georgie became a
heavy expense in one respect: he took no care of his clothes;
consequently, he shone frequently in new ones, which was
not the case with Eddie. The boys grew apace. Eddie was an
increasing comfort, Georgie an increasing solicitude. It was
always sufficient to say, in answer to Eddie's petitions, "I
would rather you would not do it,"—meaning swimming,
skating, picnicking, berrying, circusing, and all sorts of things
which boys delight in. But *no* answer was sufficient for
Georgie; he had to be humored in his desires, or he would
carry them with a high hand. Naturally, no boy got more
swimming, skating, berrying, and so forth than he; no boy
ever had a better time. The good Brants did not allow the
boys to play out after nine in summer evenings; they were
sent to bed at that hour; Eddie honorably remained, but

Georgie usually slipped out of the window toward ten, and enjoyed himself till midnight. It seemed impossible to break Georgie of this bad habit, but the Brants managed it at last by hiring him, with apples and marbles, to stay in. The good Brants gave all their time and attention to vain endeavors to regulate Georgie; they said, with grateful tears in their eyes, that Eddie needed no efforts of theirs, he was so good, so considerate, and in all ways so perfect.

By and by the boys were big enough to work, so they were apprenticed to a trade: Edward went voluntarily; George was coaxed and bribed. Edward worked hard and faithfully, and ceased to be an expense to the good Brants; they praised him, so did his master; but George ran away, and it cost Mr. Brant both money and trouble to hunt him up and get him back. By and by he ran away again,—more money and more trouble. He ran away a third time,—and stole a few little things to carry with him. Trouble and expense for Mr. Brant once more; and, besides, it was with the greatest difficulty that he succeeded in persuading the master to let the youth go unprosecuted for the theft.

Edward worked steadily along, and in time became a full partner in his master's business. George did not improve; he kept the loving hearts of his aged benefactors full of trouble, and their hands full of inventive activities to protect him from ruin. Edward, as a boy, had interested himself in Sunday-schools, debating societies, penny missionary affairs, anti-tobacco organizations, anti-profanity associations, and all such things; as a man, he was a quiet but steady and reliable helper in the church, the temperance societies, and in all movements looking to the aiding and uplifting of men. This excited no remark, attracted no attention,—for it was his "natural bent."

Finally, the old people died. The will testified their loving pride in Edward, and left their little property to George,—because he "needed it;" whereas, "owing to a bountiful Providence," such was not the case with Edward. The property was left to George conditionally: he must buy out Edward's partner with it; else it must go to a benevolent organization called the Prisoner's Friend Society. The old people left a letter, in which they begged their dear son Edward to take their place and watch over George, and help and shield him as they had done.

Edward dutifully acquiesced, and George became his partner in the business. He was not a valuable partner: he had been meddling with drink before; he soon developed into a constant tippler, now, and his flesh and eyes showed the fact unpleasantly. Edward had been courting a sweet and kindly spirited girl for some time. They loved each other dearly, and— But about this period George began to haunt her tearfully and imploringly, and at last she went crying to Edward, and said her high and holy duty was plain before her,—she must not let her own selfish desires interfere with it: she must marry "poor George" and "reform him." It would break her heart, she knew it would, and so on; but duty was duty. So she married George, and Edward's heart came very near breaking, as well as her own. However, Edward recovered, and married another girl,—a very excellent one she was, too.

Children came, to both families. Mary did her honest best to reform her husband, but the contract was too large. George went on drinking, and by and by he fell to misusing her and the little ones sadly. A great many good people strove with George,—they were always at it, in fact,—but he calmly took such efforts as his due and their duty, and did not mend his ways. He added a vice, presently,—that of secret gambling. He got deeply in debt; he borrowed money on the firm's credit, as quietly as he could, and carried this system so far and so successfully that one morning the sheriff took possession of the establishment, and the two cousins found themselves penniless.

Times were hard, now, and they grew worse. Edward moved his family into a garret, and walked the streets day and night, seeking work. He begged for it, but it was really not to be had. He was astonished to see how soon his face became unwelcome; he was astonished and hurt to see how quickly the ancient interest which people had had in him faded out and disappeared. Still, he *must* get work; so he swallowed his chagrin, and toiled on in search of it. At last he got a job of carrying bricks up a ladder in a hod, and was a grateful man in consequence; but after that *nobody* knew him or cared anything about him. He was not able to keep up his dues in the various moral organizations to which he belonged, and had to endure the sharp pain of seeing himself brought under the disgrace of suspension.

But the faster Edward died out of public knowledge and interest, the faster George rose in them. He was found lying, ragged and drunk, in the gutter, one morning. A member of the Ladies' Temperance Refuge fished him out, took him in hand, got up a subscription for him, kept him sober a whole week, then got a situation for him. An account of it was published.

General attention was thus drawn to the poor fellow, and a great many people came forward, and helped him toward reform with their countenance and encouragement. He did not drink a drop for two months, and meantime was the pet of the good. Then he fell,—in the gutter; and there was general sorrow and lamentation. But the noble sisterhood rescued him again. They cleaned him up, they fed him, they listened to the mournful music of his repentances, they got him his situation again. An account of this, also, was published, and the town was drowned in happy tears over the re-restoration of the poor beset and struggling victim of the fatal bowl. A grand temperance revival was got up, and after some rousing speeches had been made the chairman said, impressively, "We are now about to call for signers; and I think there is a spectacle in store for you which not many in this house will be able to view with dry eyes." There was an eloquent pause, and then George Benton, escorted by a red-sashed detachment of the Ladies of the Refuge, stepped forward upon the platform and signed the pledge. The air was rent with applause, and everybody cried for joy. Everybody wrung the hand of the new convert when the meeting was over; his salary was enlarged next day; he was the talk of the town, and its hero. An account of it was published.

George Benton fell, regularly, every three months, but was faithfully rescued and wrought with, every time, and good situations were found for him. Finally, he was taken around the country lecturing, as a reformed drunkard, and he had great houses and did an immense amount of good.

He was so popular at home, and so trusted,—during his sober intervals,—that he was enabled to use the name of a

principal citizen, and get a large sum of money at the bank. A
mighty pressure was brought to bear to save him from the
consequences of his forgery, and it was partially successful,—he was "sent up" for only two years. When, at the end
of a year, the tireless efforts of the benevolent were crowned
with success, and he emerged from the penitentiary with a
pardon in his pocket, the Prisoner's Friend Society met him
at the door with a situation and a comfortable salary, and all
the other benevolent people came forward and gave him advice, encouragement, and help. Edward Mills had once applied to the Prisoner's Friend Society for a situation, when in
dire need, but the question, "Have you been a prisoner?"
made brief work of his case.

While all these things were going on, Edward Mills had
been quietly making head against adversity. He was still poor,
but was in receipt of a steady and sufficient salary, as the respected and trusted cashier of a bank. George Benton never
came near him, and was never heard to inquire about him.
George got to indulging in long absences from the town;
there were ill reports about him, but nothing definite.

One winter's night some masked burglars forced their way
into the bank, and found Edward Mills there alone. They
commanded him to reveal the "combination," so that they
could get into the safe. He refused. They threatened his life.
He said his employers trusted him, and he could not be traitor to that trust. He could die, if he must, but while he lived
he would be faithful; he would not yield up the "combination." The burglars killed him.

The detectives hunted down the criminals; the chief one
proved to be George Benton. A wide sympathy was felt for
the widow and orphans of the dead man, and all the newspapers in the land begged that all the banks in the land would
testify their appreciation of the fidelity and heroism of the
murdered cashier by coming forward with a generous contribution of money in aid of his family, now bereft of support.
The result was a mass of solid cash amounting to upwards of
five hundred dollars,—an average of nearly three eighths of a
cent for each bank in the Union. The cashier's own bank testified its gratitude by endeavoring to show (but humiliatingly
failed in it) that the peerless servant's accounts were not

square, and that he himself had knocked his brains out with a bludgeon to escape detection and punishment.

George Benton was arraigned for trial. Then everybody seemed to forget the widow and orphans in their solicitude for poor George. Everything that money and influence could do was done to save him, but it all failed; he was sentenced to death. Straightway the governor was besieged with petitions for commutation or pardon: they were brought by tearful young girls; by sorrowful old maids; by deputations of pathetic widows; by shoals of impressive orphans. But no, the governor—for once—would not yield.

Now George Benton experienced religion. The glad news flew all around. From that time forth his cell was always full of girls and women and fresh flowers; all the day long there was prayer, and hymn-singing, and thanksgivings, and homilies, and tears, with never an interruption, except an occasional five-minute intermission for refreshments.

This sort of thing continued up to the very gallows, and George Benton went proudly home, in the black cap, before a wailing audience of the sweetest and best that the region could produce. His grave had fresh flowers on it every day, for a while, and the head-stone bore these words, under a hand pointing aloft: "He has fought the good fight."

The brave cashier's head-stone has this inscription: "Be pure, honest, sober, industrious, considerate, and you will never—"

Nobody knows who gave the order to leave it that way, but it was so given.

The cashier's family are in stringent circumstances, now, it is said; but no matter; a lot of appreciative people, who were not willing that an act so brave and true as his should go unrewarded, have collected forty-two thousand dollars—and built a Memorial Church with it.

August 1880

Mrs. McWilliams and the Lightning

Well, sir,—continued Mr. McWilliams, for this was not the beginning of his talk,—the fear of lightning is one of the most distressing infirmities a human being can be afflicted with. It is mostly confined to women; but now and then you find it in a little dog, and sometimes in a man. It is a particularly distressing infirmity, for the reason that it takes the sand out of a person to an extent which no other fear can, and it can't be *reasoned* with, and neither can it be shamed out of a person. A woman who could face the very devil himself—or a mouse—loses her grip and goes all to pieces in front of a flash of lightning. Her fright is something pitiful to see.

Well, as I was telling you, I woke up, with that smothered and unlocatable cry of "Mortimer! Mortimer!" wailing in my ears; and as soon as I could scrape my faculties together I reached over in the dark and then said,—

"Evangeline, is that you calling? What is the matter? Where are you?"

"Shut up in the boot-closet. You ought to be ashamed to lie there and sleep so, and such an awful storm going on."

"Why, how *can* one be ashamed when he is asleep? It is unreasonable; a man *can't* be ashamed when he is asleep, Evangeline."

"You never try, Mortimer,—you know very well you never try."

I caught the sound of muffled sobs.

That sound smote dead the sharp speech that was on my lips, and I changed it to—

"I'm sorry, dear,—I'm truly sorry. I never meant to act so. Come back and"—

"MORTIMER!"

"Heavens! what is the matter, my love?"

"Do you mean to say you are in that bed yet?"

"Why, of course."

"Come out of it instantly. I should think you would take some *little* care of your life, for *my* sake and the children's, if you will not for your own."

"But my love"—

"Don't talk to me, Mortimer. You *know* there is no place so dangerous as a bed, in such a thunder-storm as this,—all the books say that; yet there you would lie, and deliberately throw away your life,—for goodness knows what, unless for the sake of arguing and arguing, and"—

"But, confound it, Evangeline, I'm *not* in the bed, *now*. I'm"—

[Sentence interrupted by a sudden glare of lightning, followed by a terrified little scream from Mrs. McWilliams and a tremendous blast of thunder.]

"There! You see the result. Oh, Mortimer, how *can* you be so profligate as to swear at such a time as this?"

"I *didn't* swear. And that *wasn't* a result of it, any way. It would have come, just the same, if I hadn't said a word; and you know very well, Evangeline,—at least you ought to know,—that when the atmosphere is charged with electricity"—

"Oh, yes, now argue it, and argue it, and argue it!—I don't see how you can act so, when you *know* there is not a lightning-rod on the place, and your poor wife and children are absolutely at the mercy of Providence. What *are* you doing?—lighting a match at such a time as this! Are you stark mad?"

"Hang it, woman, where's the harm? The place is as dark as the inside of an infidel, and"—

"Put it out! put it out instantly! Are you determined to sacrifice us all? You *know* there is nothing attracts lightning like a light. [*Fzt!—crash! boom—boloom-boom-boom!*] Oh, just hear it! Now you see what you've done!"

"No, I *don't* see what I've done. A match may attract lightning, for all I know, but it don't *cause* lightning,—I'll go odds on that. And it didn't attract it worth a cent this time; for if that shot was leveled at my match, it was blessed poor marksmanship,—about an average of none out of a possible million, I should say. Why, at Dollymount, such marksmanship as that"—

"For shame, Mortimer! Here we are standing right in the very presence of death, and yet in so solemn a moment you

are capable of using such language as that. If you have no
desire to— Mortimer!"

"Well?"

"Did you say your prayers to-night?"

"I—I—meant to, but I got to trying to cipher out how
much twelve times thirteen is, and"—

[*Fzt!*—*boom-berroom-boom! bumble-umble bang*-SMASH!]

"Oh, we are lost, beyond all help! How *could* you neglect
such a thing at such a time as this?"

"But it *was n't* 'such a time as this.' There was n't a cloud in
the sky. How could *I* know there was going to be all this
rumpus and pow-wow about a little slip like that? And I don't
think it's just fair for you to make so much out of it, any way,
seeing it happens so seldom; I have n't missed before since I
brought on that earthquake, four years ago."

"MORTIMER! How you talk! Have you forgotten the yellow fever?"

"My dear, you are always throwing up the yellow fever to
me, and I think it is perfectly unreasonable. You can't even
send a telegraphic message as far as Memphis without relays,
so how is a little devotional slip of mine going to carry so far?
I'll *stand* the earthquake, because it was in the neighborhood;
but I'll be hanged if I'm going to be responsible for every
blamed"—

[*Fzt!*—BOOM *beroom*-boom! boom!—BANG!]

"Oh, dear, dear, dear! I *know* it struck something, Mortimer. We never shall see the light of another day; and if it
will do you any good to remember, when we are gone, that
your dreadful language— *Mortimer!*"

"WELL! What now?"

"Your voice sounds as if— Mortimer, are you actually
standing in front of that open fire-place?"

"That is the very crime I am committing."

"Get away from it, this moment. You do seem determined
to bring destruction on us all. Don't you *know* that there is no
better conductor for lightning than an open chimney? *Now*
where have you got to?"

"I'm here by the window."

"Oh, for pity's sake, have you lost your mind? Clear out

from there, this moment. The very children in arms know it is fatal to stand near a window in a thunder-storm. Dear, dear, I know I shall never see the light of another day. Mortimer?"

"Yes?"

"What is that rustling?"

"It's me."

"What are you doing?"

"Trying to find the upper end of my pantaloons."

"Quick! throw those things away! I do believe you would deliberately put on those clothes at such a time as this; yet you know perfectly well that *all* authorities agree that woolen stuffs attract lightning. Oh, dear, dear, it isn't sufficient that one's life must be in peril from natural causes, but you must do everything you can possibly think of to augment the danger. Oh, *don't* sing! What *can* you be thinking of?"

"Now where's the harm in it?"

"Mortimer, if I have told you once, I have told you a hundred times, that singing causes vibrations in the atmosphere which interrupt the flow of the electric fluid, and— What on *earth* are you opening that door for?"

"Goodness gracious, woman, is there any harm in *that*?"

"*Harm?* There's *death* in it. Anybody that has given this subject any attention knows that to create a draught is to invite the lightning. You haven't half shut it; shut it *tight*,— and do hurry, or we are all destroyed. Oh, it is an awful thing to be shut up with a lunatic at such a time as this. Mortimer, what *are* you doing?"

"Nothing. Just turning on the water. This room is smothering hot and close. I want to bathe my face and hands."

"You have certainly parted with the remnant of your mind! Where lightning strikes any other substance once, it strikes water fifty times. Do turn it off. Oh, dear, I am sure that nothing in this world can save us. It does seem to me that— Mortimer, what was that?"

"It was a da— it was a picture. Knocked it down."

"Then you are close to the wall! I never heard of such imprudence! Don't you *know* that there's no better conductor for lightning than a wall? Come away from there! And you came as near as anything to swearing, too. Oh, how can you be so desperately wicked, and your family in such peril? Mortimer, did you order a feather bed, as I asked you to do?"

"No. Forgot it."

"Forgot it! It may cost you your life. If you had a feather bed, now, and could spread it in the middle of the room and lie on it, you would be perfectly safe. Come in here,—come quick, before you have a chance to commit any more frantic indiscretions."

I tried, but the little closet would not hold us both with the door shut, unless we could be content to smother. I gasped a while, then forced my way out. My wife called out,—

"Mortimer, something *must* be done for your preservation. Give me that German book that is on the end of the mantel-piece, and a candle; but don't light it; give me a match; I will light it in here. That book has some directions in it."

I got the book,—at cost of a vase and some other brittle things; and the madam shut herself up with her candle. I had a moment's peace; then she called out,—

"Mortimer, what was that?"

"Nothing but the cat."

"The cat! Oh, destruction! Catch her, and shut her up in the wash-stand. Do be quick, love, cats are *full* of electricity. I just know my hair will turn white with this night's awful perils."

I heard the muffled sobbings again. But for that, I should not have moved hand or foot in such a wild enterprise in the dark.

However, I went at my task,—over chairs, and against all sorts of obstructions, all of them hard ones, too, and most of them with sharp edges,—and at last I got kitty cooped up in the commode, at an expense of over four hundred dollars in broken furniture and shins. Then these muffled words came from the closet:—

"It says the safest thing is to stand on a chair in the middle of the room, Mortimer; and the legs of the chair must be insulated, with non-conductors. That is, you must set the legs of the chair in glass tumblers. [*Fzt!—boom—bang!—smash!*] Oh, hear that! Do hurry, Mortimer, before you are struck."

I managed to find and secure the tumblers. I got the last four,—broke all the rest. I insulated the chair legs, and called for further instructions.

"Mortimer, it says, 'Während eines Gewitters entferne man Metalle, wie z. B., Ringe, Uhren, Schlüssel, etc., von sich und halte sich auch nicht an solchen Stellen auf, wo viele Metalle bei einander liegen, oder mit andern Körpern verbunden sind, wie an Herden, Oefen, Eisengittern u. dgl.' What does that mean, Mortimer? Does it mean that you must keep metals *about* you, or keep them *away* from you?"

"Well, I hardly know. It appears to be a little mixed. All German advice is more or less mixed. However, I think that that sentence is mostly in the dative case, with a little genitive and accusative sifted in, here and there, for luck; so I reckon it means that you must keep some metals *about* you."

"Yes, that must be it. It stands to reason that it is. They are in the nature of lightning-rods, you know. Put on your fireman's helmet, Mortimer; that is mostly metal."

I got it and put it on,—a very heavy and clumsy and uncomfortable thing on a hot night in a close room. Even my night-dress seemed to be more clothing than I strictly needed.

"Mortimer, I think your middle ought to be protected. Won't you buckle on your militia sabre, please?"

I complied.

"Now, Mortimer, you ought to have some way to protect your feet. Do please put on your spurs."

I did it,—in silence,—and kept my temper as well as I could.

"Mortimer, it says, 'Das Gewitter läuten ist sehr gefährlich, weil die Glocke selbst, sowie der durch das Läuten veranlasste Luftzug und die Höhe des Thurmes den Blitz anziehen könnten.' Mortimer, does that mean that it is dangerous not to ring the church bells during a thunder-storm?"

"Yes, it seems to mean that,—if that is the past participle of the nominative case singular, and I reckon it is. Yes, I think it means that on account of the height of the church tower and the absence of *Luftzug* it would be very dangerous (*sehr gefährlich*) not to ring the bells in time of a storm; and moreover, don't you see, the very wording"—

"Never mind that, Mortimer; don't waste the precious time

in talk. Get the large dinner-bell; it is right there in the hall. Quick, Mortimer dear; we are almost safe. Oh, dear, I do believe we are going to be saved, at last!"

Our little summer establishment stands on top of a high range of hills, overlooking a valley. Several farm-houses are in our neighborhood,—the nearest some three or four hundred yards away.

When I, mounted on the chair, had been clanging that dreadful bell a matter of seven or eight minutes, our shutters were suddenly torn open from without, and a brilliant bull's-eye lantern was thrust in at the window, followed by a hoarse inquiry:—

"What in the nation is the matter here?"

The window was full of men's heads, and the heads were full of eyes that stared wildly at my night-dress and my war-like accoutrements.

I dropped the bell, skipped down from the chair in confusion, and said,—

"There is nothing the matter, friends,—only a little discomfort on account of the thunder-storm. I was trying to keep off the lightning."

"Thunder-storm? Lightning? Why, Mr. McWilliams, have you lost your mind? It is a beautiful starlight night; there has been no storm."

I looked out, and I was so astonished I could hardly speak for a while. Then I said,—

"I do not understand this. We distinctly saw the glow of the flashes through the curtains and shutters, and heard the thunder."

One after another those people lay down on the ground to laugh,—and two of them died. One of the survivors remarked,—

"Pity you didn't think to open your blinds and look over to the top of the high hill yonder. What you heard was cannon; what you saw was the flash. You see, the telegraph brought some news, just at midnight: Garfield's nominated,—and that's what's the matter!"

Yes, Mr. Twain, as I was saying in the beginning (said Mr. McWilliams), the rules for preserving people against lightning are so excellent and so innumerable that the most incomprehensible thing in the world to me is how anybody ever manages to get struck.

So saying, he gathered up his satchel and umbrella, and departed; for the train had reached his town.

September 1880

"Millions In It"

Hartford, Conn., September 14, 1880.
To the Editors of the Evening Post:

I have just seen your despatch from San Francisco, in Saturday's EVENING POST, about "Gold in Solution" in the Calistoga Springs, and about the proprietor's having "extracted $1,060 in gold of the utmost fineness from ten barrels of the water" during the past fortnight, by a process known only to himself. This will surprise many of your readers, but it does not surprise me, for I once owned those springs myself. What does surprise me, however, is the falling off in the richness of the water. In my time the yield was a dollar a dipperful. I am not saying this to injure the property, in case a sale is contemplated; I am only saying it in the interest of history. It may be that this hotel proprietor's process is an inferior one—yes, that may be the fault. Mine was to take my uncle—I had an extra uncle at that time, on account of his parents dying and leaving him on my hands—and fill him up, and let him stand fifteen minutes to give the water a chance to settle well, then insert him in an exhausted receiver, which had the effect of sucking the gold out through his pores. I have taken more than eleven thousand dollars out of that old man in a day and a half. I should have held on to those springs but for the badness of the roads and the difficulty of getting the gold to market.

I consider that gold-yielding water in many respects remarkable; and yet not more remarkable than the gold bearing air of Catgut Cañon, up there toward the head of the auriferous range. This air—or this wind—for it is a kind of a trade wind which blows steadily down through six hundred miles of rich quartz croppings during an hour and a quarter every day except Sundays, is heavily charged with exquisitely fine and impalpable gold. Nothing precipitates and solidifies this gold so readily as contact with human flesh heated by passion. The time that William Abrahams was disappointed in love, he used to step out doors when that wind was blowing, and come in again and begin to sigh, and his brother Andover J. would extract over a dollar and a half out of every sigh he sighed, right along. And the time that John Harbison and Aleck Norton quarrelled about Harbison's dog, they stood there swearing at each other all they knew how—and what they didn't know about swearing they couldn't learn from you and me, not by a good deal—and at the end of every three or four minutes they had to stop and make a dividend—if they didn't their jaws would clog up so that they couldn't get the big nine syllabled ones out at all—and when the wind was done blowing they cleaned up just a little over sixteen hundred dollars apiece. I know these facts to be absolutely true, because I got them from a man whose mother I knew personally. I do not suppose a person could buy a water privilege at Calistoga now at any price; but several good locations along the course of the Catgut Cañon Gold-Bearing Trade-Wind are for sale. They are going to be stocked for the New York market. They will sell, too; the people will swarm for them as thick as Hancock veterans—in the South.

MARK TWAIN.

September 16, 1880

A Cat Tale

My little girls—Susie, aged eight, and Clara, six and a half—often require me to help them go to sleep, nights, by telling them original tales. They think my tales are better than paregoric, and quicker. While I talk, they make comments and ask questions, and we have a pretty good time. I thought maybe other little people might like to try one of my narcotics—so I offer this one.

M.T.

Once there was a noble big cat, whose Christian name was Catasauqua—because she lived in that region—but she did not have any surname, because she was a short-tailed cat— being a Manx—and did not need one. It is very just and becoming in a long-tailed cat to have a surname, but it would be very ostentatious, and even dishonorable, in a Manx. Well, Catasauqua had a beautiful family of catlings; and they were of different colors, to harmonize with their characters. Catta-raugus, the eldest, was white, and he had high impulses and a pure heart; Catiline, the youngest, was black, and he had a self-seeking nature, his motives were nearly always base, he was truculent and insincere. He was vain and foolish, and often said he would rather be what he was, and live like a bandit, yet have none above him, than be a cat-o-nine-tails and eat with the King. He hated his harmless and un-offending little catercousins, and frequently drove them from his presence with imprecations, and at times even resorted to violence.

Susie—What are catercousins, papa?

Quarter-cousins—it is so set down in the big dictionary. You observe I refer to it every now and then. This is because I do not wish to make any mistakes, my purpose being to instruct as well as entertain. Whenever I use a word which you do not understand, speak up and I will look and find out what it means. But do not interrupt me except for cause, for I am always excited when I am erecting history, and want to get on. Well, one day Catasauqua met with a misfortune; her house burned down. It was the very day after it had been insured for double its value, too—how sin-gular! Yes, and how lucky! This often happens. It teaches

763

us that mere loading a house down with insurance isn't going to save it. Very well, Catasauqua took the insurance money and built a new house; and a much better one, too; and what is more, she had money left to add a gaudy concatenation of extra improvements with. O, I tell you! what she didn't know about catalactics no other cat need ever try to acquire.

Clara—What is catalactics, papa?

The dictionary intimates, in a nebulous way, that it is a sort of demi-synonym for the science commonly called political economy.

Clara—Thank you, papa.

Yes, behind the house she constructed a splendid large catadrome, and enclosed it with a caterwaul about nine feet high, and in the center was a spacious grass-plot where—

Clara—What is a catadrome, papa?

I will look. Ah, it is a race-course; I thought it was a ten-pin alley.—But no matter; in fact it is all the better; for cats do not play ten-pins, when they are feeling well, but they *do* run races, you know; and the spacious grass-plot was for cat-fights, and other free exhibitions; and for ball-games—three-cornered cat, and all that sort of thing; a lovely spot, lovely. Yes, indeed; it had a hedge of dainty little catkins around it, and right in the centre was a splendid great categorematic in full leaf, and—

Susie—What is a categorematic, papa?

I think it's a kind of a shade-tree, but I'll look. No—I was mistaken; it is a *word*; "a word which is capable of being employed by itself as a term."

Susie—Thank you, papa.

Don't mention it. Yes, you see, it wasn't a shade tree; the good Catasauqua didn't know that, else she wouldn't have planted it right there in the way; you can't run over a word like that, you know, and not cripple yourself more or less. Now don't forget that definition, it may come handy to you some day—there is no telling—life is full of vicissitudes.—Always remember, a categorematic is a word which a cat can use by herself as a term; but she mustn't try to use it along with another cat, for that is not the idea.—Far from it. We have authority for it, you see—Mr. Webster; and he is dead,

too, besides. It would be a noble good thing if his dictionary
was, too. But that is too much to expect. Yes; well, Catasauqua filled her house with internal improvements—cat-calls in
every room, and they are O ever so much handier than bells;
and catamounts to mount the stairs with, instead of those
troublesome elevators which are always getting out of order;
and civet-cats in the kitchen, in place of the ordinary sieves,
which you can't ever sift anything with, in a satisfactory way;
and a couple of tidy ash-cats to clean out the stove and keep it
in order; and—catenated on the roof—an alert and cultivated pole-cat to watch the flag-pole and keep the banner
a-flying. Ah yes—such was Catasauqua's country residence;
and she named it Kamscatka—after her dear native land far
away.

Clara—What is catenated, papa?

Chained, my child. The pole-cat was attached by a chain to
some object upon the roof contiguous to the flag-pole. This
was to retain him in his position.

Clara—Thank you, papa.

The front garden was a spectacle of sublime and bewildering magnificence.—A stately row of flowering catalpas
stretched from the front door clear to the gate, wreathed
from stem to stern with the delicate tendrils and shining
scales of the cat's foot ivy, whilst ever and anon the en-
chanted eye wandered from congeries of lordly cat-tails and
kindred catapetalous blooms too deep for utterance, only to
encounter the still more entrancing vision of catnip without
number and without price, and swoon away in ecstasy unutterable, under the blissful intoxication of its too too fragrant breath!

Both Children—O, how lovely!

You may well say it. Few there be that shall look upon the
like again. Yet was not this all; for hither to the north boiled
the majestic cataract in unimaginable grandiloquence, and
thither to the south sparkled the gentle catadupe in serene
and incandescent tranquillity, whilst far and near the halcyon
brooklet flowed between!

Both Children—O, how sweet! What is a catadupe, papa?

Small waterfall, my darlings. Such is Webster's belief. All
things being in readiness for the house-warming, the widow

sent out her invitations, and then proceeded with her usual avocations. For Catasauqua was a widow—sorrow cometh to us all. The husband-cat—Catullus was his name—was no more. He was of a lofty character, brave to rashness, and almost incredibly unselfish. He gave eight of his lives for his country, reserving only one for himself. Yes—the banquet having been ordered, the good Catasauqua tuned up for the customary morning-song, accompanying herself on the catarrh, and her little ones joined in.

These were the words:

> *There was a little cat,*
> *And she caught a little rat,*
> *Which she dutifully rendered to her mother,*
> *Who said "Bake him in a pie,*
> *For his flavor's rather high—*
> *Or confer him on the poor, if you'd druther."*

Catasauqua sang soprano, Catiline sang tenor, Cattaraugus sang bass. It was exquisite melody; it would make your hair stand right up.

Susie—Why, papa, I didn't know cats could sing.

O, can't they, though! Well, these could. Cats are packed full of music—just as full as they can hold; and when they die, people remove it from them and sell it to the fiddle-makers. O yes indeed. Such is life.

Susie—O, here is a picture! Is it a picture of the music, papa?

Only the eye of prejudice could doubt it, my child.

Susie—Did you draw it, papa?

I am indeed the author of it.

Susie—How wonderful! What is a picture like this called, papa?

A work of art, my child.—There—do not hold it so close; prop it up on the chair, *three steps away*; now then—that is right; you see how much better and stronger the expression is than when it is close by. It is because some of this picture is drawn in perspective.

Clara—Did you always know how to draw, papa?

Yes. I was born so. But of course I could not draw at first as well as I can now. These things require study—and practice.

Morning-Song

Mere talent is not sufficient. It takes a person a long time to get so he can draw a picture like this.

Clara—How long did it take you, papa?

Many years—thirty years, I reckon. Off and on—for I did not devote myself exclusively to art. Still, I have had a great deal of practice. Ah, practice is the great thing!—it accomplishes wonders. Before I was twenty-five, I had got so I could draw a cork as well as anybody that ever was. And many a time I have drawn a blank in a lottery. Once I drew a check that wouldn't go; and after the war I tried to draw a pension—but this was too ambitious. However, the most gifted must fail sometimes. Do you observe those things that are sticking up in this picture? They are not bones, they are paws; it is very hard to express the difference between bones and paws, in a picture.

Susie—Which is Cattaraugus, papa?

The little pale one that almost has the end of his mother's tail in his mouth.

Susie—But papa, that tail is not right. You know Catasauqua was a Manx, and had a short one.

It is a just remark, my child; but a long tail was necessary, here, to express a certain passion—the passion of joy. Therefore the insertion of a long tail is permissible; it is called a poetic licence. You cannot express the passion of joy with a short tail. Nor even ordinary excitement. You notice that Cattaraugus is brilliantly excited; now nearly all of that verve, spirit, *elan*, is owing to his tail; yet if I had been false to Art to be true to Nature, you would see there nothing but a poor little stiff and emotionless stump on that cat that would have cast a coldness over the whole scene; yet Cattaraugus was a Manx, like his mother, and had hardly any more tail than a rabbit. Yes, in art, the office of the tail is to express feeling; so, if you wish to portray a cat in repose, you will always succeed better by leaving out the tail. Now here is a striking illustration of the very truth which I am trying to impress upon you. I proposed to draw a cat recumbent and in repose; but just as I had finished the front end of her, she got up and began to gaze passionately at a bird and wriggle her tail in a most expressively wistful way. I had to finish her with that end standing, and the other end lying. It greatly injures the picture. For, you see, it confuses two passions together—the passion of standing up, and the passion of lying down. These are incompatible; and they convey a bad effect to the picture by rendering it unrestful to the eye. In my opinion a cat in a picture ought to be doing one thing or the other—lying down, or standing up; but not both. I ought to have laid this

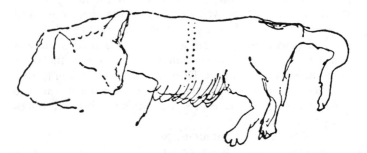

Effects Married but not Mated.

one down again, and put a brick or something on her; but I did not think of it at the time. Let us now separate these conflicting passions in this cat, so that you can see each by itself, and the more easily study it. Lay your hand on the picture, to where I have made those dots, and cover the rear half of it from sight—now you observe how reposeful the front end is. Very well; now lay your hand on the front end and cover *it* from sight—do you observe the eager wriggle in that tail?—it is a wriggle which only the presence of a bird can inspire.

Susie—You must know a wonderful deal, papa.

I have that reputation—in Europe; but here the best minds think I am superficial. However, I am content; I make no defense; my pictures show what I am.

Susie—Papa, I should think you would take pupils.

No, I have no desire for riches. Honest poverty and a conscience torpid through virtuous inaction are more to me than corner lots and praise.

But to resume. The morning-song being over, Catasauqua told Catiline and Cattaraugus to fetch their little books, and she would teach them how to spell.

Both Children—Why, papa! do cats have books?

Yes—catechisms.—Just so. Facts are stubborn things. After lesson, Catasauqua gave Catiline and Cattaraugus some rushes, so that they could earn a little circus-money by building cat's-cradles, and at the same time amuse themselves and not miss her; then she went to the kitchen and dining-room to inspect the preparations for the banquet.

The moment her back was turned, Catiline put down his work and got out his cat-pipe for a smoke.

Susie—Why, how naughty!

Thou hast well spoken. It was disobedience; and disobedience is the flag-ship of the fleet of sin. The gentle Cattaraugus sighed and said—

"For shame, Catiline! How often has our dear mother told you not to do that! Ah, how can you thus disregard the commandments of the author of your being?"

Susie—Why, what beautiful language, for such a little thing—*wasn't* it, papa?

Ah, yes indeed. That was the kind of cat he was—culti-

vated, you see. He had sat at the feet of Rollo's mother; and
in the able "Franconia Series" he had not failed to observe
how harmoniously gigantic language and a microscopic topic
go together. Catiline heard his brother through, and then replied with the contemptuous ejaculation—

"S'cat!"

It means the same that Shakespeare means when he says—
"Go to." Nevertheless, Catiline's conscience was not at rest.
He murmured something about where was the harm, since
his mother would never know? But Cattaraugus said, sweetly
but sadly—

"Alas, if we but do the right under restraint of authoritative
observance, where then is the merit?"

Susie—How *good* he was!

Monumentally so. The more we contemplate his character
the more sublime it appears. But Catiline, who was coarse
and worldly, hated all lofty sentiments, and especially such as
were stated in choice and lofty terms; he wished to resent this
one, yet compelled himself to hold his peace; but when Cattaraugus said it *over* again, partly to enjoy the sound of it, but
mainly for his brother's good, Catiline lost his patience, and
said—

"O, take a walk!"

Yet he still felt badly; for he knew he was doing wrong. He
began to pretend he did not know it was against the rule to
smoke his cat-pipe; but Cattaraugus, without an utterance,
lifted an accusing paw toward the wall, where, among the
illuminated mottoes, hung this one—

"NO SMOKING   STRICTLY PROHIBITED."

Catiline turned pale; and, murmuring in a broken voice, "I
am undone—forgive me, brother," laid the fatal cat-pipe
aside and burst into tears.

Clara—Poor thing! It was cruel—*wasn't* it, papa?

Susie—Well but he oughtn't to done so, in the first place.
Cattaraugus wasn't to blame.

Clara—Why, *Susie!* If Catiline didn't *know* he wasn't allowed—

Susie—Catiline did know it—Cattaraugus told him so; and
besides, Catiline—

Clara—Cattaraugus only told Catiline that if—

Susie—Why *Clara!* Catiline didn't *need* for Cattaraugus to say one single—

O, hold on!—it's all a mistake! Come to look in the dictionary, we are proceeding from false premises. The Unabridged says a cat-pipe is "a squeaking instrument used in play-houses to condemn plays." So you see it wasn't a pipe to smoke, after all; Catiline *couldn't* smoke it; therefore it follows that he was simply pretending to smoke it, to stir up his brother, that's all.

Susie—But papa, Catiline might as well smoke as stir up his brother.

Clara—Susie, you don't like Catiline, and so whatever he does, it don't suit you—it ain't right; and he is only a little fellow, anyway.

Susie—I don't *approve* of Catiline, but I *like* him well enough; I only say—

Clara—What is approve?

Susie—Why it's as if you did something, and I said it was all right. So *I* think he might as well smoke as stir up his brother. Isn't it so, papa?

Looked at from a strictly mathematical point of view, I don't know but it *is* a case of six-in-one-and-half-a-dozen-in-the-other. Still, *our* business is mainly with the historical facts; if we only get *them* right, we can leave posterity to take care of the moral aspects of the matter. To resume the thread of the narrative—when Cattaraugus saw that Catiline had not been smoking at all, but had only been making believe, and this too with the avowed object of fraternal aggravation he was deeply hurt; and by his heat was beguiled into recourse to that bitter weapon, sarcasm; saying—

"The Roman Catiline would have betrayed his foe; it was left to the Catasauquian to refine upon the model and betray his friend."

"O, a gaudy speech!—and very erudite and swell!" retorted Catiline, derisively, "but just a *little* catachrestic."

Susie—What is catachrestic, papa?

"Far-fetched," the dictionary says. The remark stung Cattaraugus to the quick, and he called Catiline a Catapult; this infuriated Catiline beyond endurance, and he threw down the gauntlet and called Cattaraugus a catso. No cat will stand that; so at it they went. They spat and clawed and fought until they dimmed away and finally disappeared in a flying fog of cat-fur.

Clara—What is a catso, papa?

"A base fellow, a rogue, a cheat," says the dictionary. When the weather cleared, Cattaraugus, ever ready to acknowledge a fault, whether committed by himself or another, said—

"I was wrong, brother—forgive me. A cat may err—to err is cattish; but toward even a foreigner, even a wildcat, a catacaustic remark is in ill taste; how much more so then, when a brother is the target! Yes, Catiline, I was wrong; I deeply regret the circumstance. Here is my hand—let us forget the dark o'erclouded past in the bright welkin of the present, consecrating ourselves anew to its nobler lessons, and sacrificing ourselves yet again, and forever if need be, to the thrice-armed beacon that binds them in one!"

Susie—He was a splendid talker, *wasn't* he, papa? Papa, what is catacaustic?

Well, a catacaustic remark is a bitter, malicious remark—a sort of a—sort of—or a kind of a—well, let's look in the dictionary; that is cheaper. O, yes, here it is: "*Catacaustic, n;* a caustic curve formed by reflection of light." O, yes, that's it.

Susie—Well, papa, what does *that* mean?

c. 1880

The Benefit of Judicious Training

Twelfth Annual Reunion Banquet, Army of the Potomac, Hartford

"Let but the thoughtful civilian instruct the soldier in his duties, and the victory is sure." *Martin Farquhar Tupper on the Art of War.*

Mr. Chairman: I gladly join with my fellow townsmen in extending a hearty welcome to these illustrious generals and these war-scarred soldiers of the Republic. This is a proud day for us, and, if the sincere desire of our hearts has been fulfilled, it has not been an unpleasant day for them. I am in full accord, sir, with the sentiment of the toast—for I have always maintained, with enthusiasm, that the only wise and true way is for the soldier to fight the battle and the unprejudiced civilian to tell him how to do it. Yet when I was invited to respond to this toast and furnish this advice and instruction, I was almost as embarrassed as I was gratified; for I could bring to this great service but the one virtue of absence of prejudice and set opinion.

Still, but one other qualification was needed, and it was of only minor importance—I mean, knowledge of the subject— therefore, I was not disheartened, for I could acquire that, there being two weeks to spare. A general of high rank in this Army of the Potomac said two weeks was really more than I would need for the purpose—he had known people of my style who had learned enough in forty-eight hours to enable them to advise an army. Aside from the compliment, this was gratifying, because it confirmed an impression I had had before. He told me to go to the United States Military Academy at West Point, and said in his flowery, professional way that the cadets would "load me up." I went there and stayed two days, and his prediction proved correct. I make no boast on my own account—none; all I know about military matters I got from the gentlemen at West Point, and to them belongs the credit. They treated me with courtesy from the first; but when my mission was revealed, this mere courtesy blossomed into the warmest zeal. Everybody, officers and all, put down their work and turned their whole attention to giving me military information. Every question I asked was promptly and exhaustively answered. Therefore I feel proud to state that in the advice which I am about to give you, as soldiers, I am backed by the highest military authority in the land—yes, in the world, if an American does say it—West Point!

To begin, gentlemen. When an engagement is meditated, it is best to feel the enemy first. That is, if it is night; for, as one of the cadets explained to me, you do not need to feel him in the daytime, because you can see him then. I never should have thought of that, but it is true—perfectly true. In the daytime, the methods of procedure are various, but the best, it seems to me, is one which was introduced by General Grant. General Grant always sent an active young redoubt to reconnoiter and get the enemy's bearings. I got this from a high officer at the Point, who told me that he used to be a redoubt on General Grant's staff, and had done it often.

When the hour for the battle is come, move to the field with celerity—fool away no time. Under this head I was told of a favorite maxim of General Sheridan's. General Sheridan always said, "If the siege train isn't ready, don't wait—go by any train that's handy—to get there is the main thing." Now that is the correct idea. As you approach the field it is best to get out and walk. This gives you a better chance to dispose your forces judiciously for the assault. Get your artillery in position, and throw out stragglers to right and left to hold your lines of communication against surprise. See that every hod-carrier connected with a mortar battery is at his post. They told me at the Point that Napoleon despised mortar batteries, and never would use them; he said for real efficiency he wouldn't give a hatful of brickbats for a ton of mortar. However, that is all *he* knew about it.

Everything being ready for the assault, you want to enter the field with your baggage to the front. This idea was invented by our renowned guest, General Sherman. They told me General Sherman said the trunks and steamer chairs make a good protection for the wreck and rubbish and tidy up the place. However, in the case of a drawn battle, it is neither party's business to tidy up anything—you can leave the field looking as if the city government of New York had bossed the fight.

When you are traversing the enemy's country in order to

destroy his supplies and cripple his resources, you want to take along plenty of camp followers—the more the better. They are a tremendously effective arm of the service, and they inspire in the foe the liveliest dread. A West Point professor told me that the wisdom of this was recognized as far back as Scripture times. He quoted the verse. He said it was from the new revision, and was a little different from the way it reads in the old one. I do not recollect the exact wording of it now, but I remember that it wound up with something about such-and-such a devastating agent being as "terrible as an army with bummers."

I believe I have nothing further to add but this: The West Pointers said a private should preserve a respectful attitude toward his superiors, and should seldom or never proceed so far as to offer suggestions to his general in the field. If the battle is not being conducted to suit him, it is better for him to resign. By the etiquette of war, it is permitted to none below the rank of newspaper correspondent to dictate to the general in the field.

June 8, 1881

Dinner Speech in Montreal

Dinner for Mark Twain, Windsor Hotel, Montreal

That a banquet should be given to me in this ostensibly foreign land and in this great city, and that my ears should be greeted by such complimentary words from such distinguished lips, are eminent surprises to me; and I will not conceal the fact that they are also deeply gratifying. I thank you, one and all, gentlemen, for these marks of favor and friendliness; and even if I have not really or sufficiently deserved them, I assure you that I do not any the less keenly enjoy and esteem them on that account.

When a stranger appears abruptly in a country, without any apparent business there, and at an unusual season of the year, the judicious thing for him to do is to explain. This seems peculiarly necessary in my case, on account of a series of unfortunate happenings here, which followed my arrival, and which I suppose the public have felt compelled to connect with that circumstance. I would most gladly explain if I could; but I have nothing for my defense but my bare word; so I simply declare, in all sincerity, and with my hand on my heart, that I never heard of that diamond robbery till I saw it in the morning paper; and I can say with perfect truth that I never saw that box of dynamite till the police came to inquire of me if I had any more of it. These are mere assertions, I grant you, but they come from the lips of one who was never known to utter an untruth, except for practice, and who certainly would not so stultify the traditions of an upright life as to utter one now, in a strange land, and in such a presence as this, when there is nothing to be gained by it and he does not need any practice. I brought with me to this city a friend—a Boston publisher—but, alas, even this does not sufficiently explain these sinister mysteries; if I had brought a Toronto publisher along the case would have been different. But no, possibly not; the burglar took the diamond studs, but left the shirt; only a *reformed* Toronto publisher would have left the shirt.

To continue my explanation, I did not come to Canada to commit crime—this time—but to prevent it. I came here to place myself under the protection of the Canadian law and secure a copyright. I have complied with the requirements of the law; I have followed the instructions of some of the best legal minds in the city, including my own, and so my errand is accomplished, at least so far as any exertions of mine can aid that accomplishment. This is rather a cumbersome way to fence and fortify one's property against the literary buccaneer, it is true; still, if it is effective, it is a great advance upon past conditions, and one to be correspondingly welcomed.

It makes one hope and believe that a day will come when, in the eye of the law, literary property will be as sacred as whiskey, or any other of the necessaries of life. In this age of ours, if you steal another man's label to advertise your own brand of whiskey with, you will be heavily fined and otherwise punished for violating that trademark; if you steal the whiskey without the trademark, you go to jail; but if you could prove that the whiskey was literature, you can steal them both, and the law wouldn't say a word. It grieves me to think how far more profound and reverent a respect the law would have for literature if a body could only get drunk on it. Still the world moves; the interests of literature upon our continent are improving; let us be content and wait.

We have with us here a fellow craftsman, born on our own side of the Atlantic, who has created an epoch in this continent's literary history—an author who has earned and worthily earned and received the vast distinction of being crowned by the Academy of France. This is honor and achievement enough for the cause and the craft for one decade, assuredly.

If one may have the privilege of throwing in a personal impression or two, I may remark that my stay in Montreal and Quebec has been exceedingly pleasant, but the weather has been a good deal of a disappointment. Canada has a reputation for magnificent winter weather, and has a prophet who is bound by every sentiment of honor and duty to furnish it; but the result this time has been a mess of characterless weather, which all right-feeling Canadians are probably ashamed of. Still, only the country is to blame; nobody has a right to blame the prophet, for this wasn't the kind of weather he promised.

Well, never mind, what you lack in weather you make up in the means of grace. This is the first time I was ever in a city where you couldn't throw a brick without breaking a church window. Yet I was told that you were going to build one more. I said the scheme is good, but where are you going to find room? They said, we will build it on top of another church and use an elevator. This shows that the gift of lying is not yet dead in the land.

I suppose one must come in the summer to get the advantages of the Canadian scenery. A cabman drove me two miles up a perpendicular hill in a sleigh and showed me an admirable snowstorm from the heights of Quebec. The man was an ass; I could have seen the snowstorm as well from the hotel window and saved my money. Still, I may have been the ass myself; there is no telling; the thing is all mixed up in my mind; but anyway there was an ass in the party; and I do suppose that wherever a mercenary cabman and a gifted literary character are gathered together for business, there is bound to be an ass in the combination somewhere. It has always been so in my experience; and I have usually been elected, too. But it is no matter; I would rather be an ass than a cabman, any time, except in summer-time; then, with my advantages, I could be both.

I saw the Plains of Abraham, and the spot where the lamented Wolfe stood when he made the memorable remark that he would rather be the author of Gray's "Elegy" than take Quebec. But why did he say so rash a thing? It was because he supposed there was going to be international copyright. Otherwise there would be no money in it. I was also shown the spot where Sir William Phipps stood when he said he would rather take a walk than take two Quebecs. And he took the walk. I have looked with emotion, here in your city, upon the monument which makes forever memorable the spot where Horatio Nelson did not stand when he fell. I have seen the cab which Champlain employed when he arrived overland at Quebec; I have seen the horse which Jacques Cartier rode when he discovered Montreal. I have used them both; I will never do it again. Yes, I have seen all the historical places; the localities have been pointed out to me where the scenery is warehoused for the season. My sojourn has been to my moral and intellectual profit; I have behaved with propriety and discretion; I have meddled nowhere but in the election. But I am used to voting, for I live in a town where, if you may judge by local prints, there are only two conspicuous industries—committing burglaries and holding elections—and I like to keep my hand in, so I voted a good deal here.

Where so many of the guests are French, the propriety will be recognized of my making a portion of my speech in the beautiful language in order that I may be partly understood. I speak French with timidity, and not flowingly—except when excited. When using that language I have often noticed that I have hardly ever been mistaken for a Frenchman, except, perhaps, by horses; never, I believe, by people. I had hoped that mere French construction—with English words—would answer, but this is not the case. I tried it at a gentleman's house in Quebec, and it would not work. The maid servant asked, "What would Monsieur?" I said, "Monsieur So-and-So, is he with himself?" She did not understand that either. I said, "He will desolate himself when he learns that his friend American was arrived, and he not with himself to shake him at the hand." She did not even understand that; I don't know why, but she didn't and she lost her temper besides. Somebody in the rear called out, "Qui est donc la?" or words to that effect. She said, "C'est un fou," and shut the door on me. Perhaps she was right; but how did she ever find that out? for she had never seen me before till that moment.

But, as I have already intimated, I will close this oration with a few sentiments in the French language. I have not ornamented them, I have not burdened them with flowers or rhetoric, for, to my mind, that literature is best and most enduring which is characterized by a noble simplicity: J'ai belle bouton d'or de mon oncle, mais je n'ai pas celui du charpentier. Si vous avez le fromage du brave menuisier, c'est bon; mais si vous ne l'avez pas, ne se desole pas, prenez le chapeau de drap noir de son beau frere malade. Tout a l'heure! Savoir faire! Qu'est ce que vous dit! Pate de fois gras! Revenons a nos moutons! Pardon, messieurs, pardonnez moi; essayant a parler la belle langue d'Ollendorf strains me more than you can possibly imagine. But I mean well, and I've done the best I could.

December 8, 1881

Plymouth Rock and the Pilgrims

First Annual Dinner, New England Society of Philadelphia

I rise to protest. I have kept still for years, but really I think there is no sufficient justification for this sort of thing. What do you want to celebrate those people for?—those ancestors of yours, of 1620—the *Mayflower* tribe, I mean. What do you want to celebrate *them* for? Your pardon; the gentleman at my left assures me that you are not celebrating the Pilgrims themselves, but the landing of the Pilgrims at Plymouth Rock on the 22d of December. So you are celebrating their landing. Why, the other pretext was thin enough, but this is thinner than ever; the other was tissue, tinfoil, fish bladder, but this is gold leaf.

Celebrating their landing! What was there remarkable about it, I would like to know? What can you be thinking of? Why, those Pilgrims had been at sea three or four months. It was the very middle of winter; it was as cold as death off Cape Cod, there. Why shouldn't they come ashore? If they hadn't landed there would be some reason in celebrating the fact. It would have been a case of monumental leatherheadedness which the world would not willingly let die. If it had been *you*, gentlemen, you probably wouldn't have landed, but you have no shadow of right to be celebrating, in your ancestors, gifts which they did not exercise, but only transmitted. Why, to be celebrating the mere landing of the Pilgrims—to be trying to make out that this most natural, and simple, and customary procedure was an extraordinary circumstance—a circumstance to be amazed at and admired, aggrandized and glorified, at orgies like this for two hundred and sixty years—hang it, a horse would have known enough to land; a horse—pardon again; the gentleman on my right assures me that it was not merely the landing of the Pilgrims that we are celebrating, but the Pilgrims themselves. So we have struck an inconsistency here—one says it was the landing, the other says it was the Pilgrims. It is an inconsistency characteristic of your intractable and disputatious tribe, for you never agree about anything but Boston.

Well, then, what do you want to celebrate those Pilgrims

for? They were a mighty hard lot—you know it. I grant you,
without the slightest unwillingness, that they were a deal
more gentle and merciful and just than were the peoples of
Europe of that day; I grant you that they were better than
their predecessors. But what of that?—that is nothing. People
always progress. You are better than your fathers and grandfathers were (this is the first time I have ever aimed a measureless slander at the departed, for I consider such things
improper). Yes, those among you who have not been in the
penitentiary, if such there be, are better than your fathers and
grandfathers were, but is that any sufficient reason for getting
up annual dinners and celebrating you? No, by no means—
by no means. Well, I repeat, those Pilgrims were a hard lot.
They took good care of themselves, but they abolished everybody else's ancestors. I am a border ruffian from the state of
Missouri. I am a Connecticut Yankee by adoption. I have the
morals of Missouri and the culture of Connecticut, and that's
the combination that makes the perfect man.

But where are my ancestors? Whom shall I celebrate?
Where shall I find the raw material? My first American ancestor, gentleman, was an Indian—an early Indian. Your ancestors skinned him alive, and I am an orphan. Not one drop of
my blood flows in that Indian's veins today. I stand here, lone
and forlorn, without an ancestor. They skinned him! I do not
object to that, if they needed his fur; but alive, gentlemen—
alive! They skinned him alive—and before company! That is
what rankles. Think how he must have felt; for he was a sensitive Indian and easily embarrassed. If he had been a bird, it
would have been all right, and no violence done to his feelings, because he would have been considered "dressed." But
he was not a bird, gentlemen, he was a man, and probably
one of the most undressed men that ever was. I ask you to put
yourselves in his place. I ask it as a favor; I ask it as a tardy act
of justice; I ask it in the interest of fidelity to the traditions of
your ancestors; I ask it that the world may contemplate, with
vision unobstructed by disguising swallowtails and white cra-
vats, the spectacle which the true New England Society ought
to present. Cease to come to these annual orgies in this
hollow modern mockery—the surplusage of raiment. Come in
character; come in the summer grace, come in the unadorned

simplicity, come in the free and joyous costume which your sainted ancestors provided for mine.

Later ancestors of mine were the Quakers, William Robinson, Marmaduke Stephenson, *et al.* Your tribe chased them out of the country for their religion's sake; promised them death if they came back, for your ancestors had forsaken the homes they loved, and braved the perils of the sea, the implacable climate, and the savage wilderness, to acquire that highest and most precious of boons, freedom for every man on this broad continent to worship according to the dictates of his own conscience—and they were not going to allow a lot of pestiferous Quakers to interfere with it. Your ancestors broke forever the chains of political slavery, and gave the vote to every man in this wide land, excluding none!—none except those who did not belong to the orthodox church. Your ancestors—yes, they were a hard lot; but, nevertheless, they gave us religious liberty to worship as they required us to worship, and political liberty to vote as the church required; and so I, the bereft one, I, the forlorn one, am here to do my best to help you celebrate them right.

The Quaker woman, Elizabeth Hooton, was an ancestress of mine. Your people were pretty severe with her—you will confess that. But, poor thing! I believe they changed her opinions before she died, and took her into their fold; and so we have every reason to presume that when she died she went to the same place which your ancestors went to. It is a great pity, for she was a good woman. Roger Williams was an ancestor of mine. I don't really remember what your people did with him. But they banished him to Rhode Island, anyway. And then, I believe, recognizing that this was really carrying harshness to an unjustifiable extreme, they took pity on him and burned him. They were a hard lot! All those Salem witches were ancestors of mine. Your people made it tropical for them. Yes, they did; by pressure and the gallows they made such a clean deal with them that there hasn't been a witch and hardly a halter in our family from that day to this, and that is 189 years. The first slave brought into New England out of Africa by your progenitors was an ancestor of mine—for I am of a mixed breed, an infinitely shaded and exquisite mongrel. I'm not one of your sham meerschaums that you can color in a week. No, my complexion is the patient art of eight generations. Well, in my own time, I had acquired a lot of my kin—by purchase, and swapping around, and one way and another—and was getting along very well. Then, with the inborn perversity of your lineage, you got up a war and took them all away from me. And so, again am I bereft, again am I forlorn; no drop of my blood flows in the veins of any living being who is marketable.

Oh my friends, hear me and reform! I seek your good, not mine. You have heard the speeches. Disband these New England societies—nurseries of a system of steadily augmenting laudation and hosannahing, which, if persisted in uncurbed, may some day in the remote future beguile you into prevaricating and bragging. Oh, stop, stop while you are still temperate in your appreciation of your ancestors! Hear me, I beseech you; get up an auction and sell Plymouth Rock! The Pilgrims were a simple and ignorant race. They had never seen any good rocks before, or at least any that were not watched, and so they were excusable for hopping ashore in frantic delight and clapping an iron fence around this one. But you, gentlemen, are educated; you are enlightened; you know that in the rich land of your nativity, opulent New England, overflowing with rocks, this one isn't worth, at the outside, more than thirty-five cents. Therefore, sell it, before it is injured by exposure, or at least throw it open to the patent medicine advertisements, and let it earn its taxes.

Yes, hear your true friend—your only true friend—list to his voice. Disband these societies, hotbeds of vice, of moral decay—perpetuators of ancestral superstition. Here on this board I see water, I see milk, I see the wild and deadly lemonade. These are but steps upon the downward path. Next we shall see tea, then chocolate, then coffee—hotel coffee. A few more years—all too few, I fear—mark my words, we shall have cider! Gentlemen, pause ere it be too late. You are on the broad road which leads to dissipation, physical ruin, moral decay, gory crime and the gallows! I beseech you, I implore you, in the name of your anxious friends, in the name of your suffering families, in the name of your impending widows and orphans, stop ere it be too late. Disband these New England societies, renounce these soul-blistering saturnalia, cease from varnishing the rusty reputations of your long-vanished ancestors—the super-high-moral old ironclads of Cape Cod, the pious buccaneers of Plymouth Rock—go home, and try to learn to behave!

However, chaff and nonsense aside, I think I honor and appreciate your Pilgrim stock as much as you do yourselves, perhaps; and I endorse and adopt a sentiment uttered by a grandfather of mine once—a man of sturdy opinions, of sincere make of mind, and not given to flattery. He said: "People may talk as they like about that Pilgrim stock, but, after all's said and done, it would be pretty hard to improve on those people; and, as for me, I don't mind coming out flat-footed and saying there ain't any way to improve on them—except having them born in Missouri!"

December 22, 1881

Etiquette

I AT THE FUNERAL

Do not criticize the person in whose honor the entertainment is given.

Make no remarks about his equipment. If the handles are plated, it is best to seem to not observe it.

If the odor of the flowers is too oppressive for your comfort, remember that they were not brought there for you, and that the person for whom they were brought suffers no inconvenience from their presence.

Listen, with as intense an expression of attention as you can command, to the official statement of the character and history of the person in whose honor the entertainment is given; and if these statistics should seem to fail to tally with the facts, in places, do not nudge your neighbor, or press your foot upon his toes, or manifest, by any other sign, your awareness that taffy is being distributed.

If the official hopes expressed concerning the person in whose honor the entertainment is given are known by you to be oversized, let it pass—do not interrupt.

At the moving passages, be moved—but only according to the degree of your intimacy with the parties giving the entertainment, or with the party in whose honor the entertainment is given. Where a blood relation sobs, an intimate friend should choke up, a distant acquaintance should sigh, a stranger should merely fumble sympathetically with his handkerchief. Where the occasion is military, the emotions should be graded according to military rank, the highest officer present taking precedence in emotional violence, and the rest modifying their feelings according to their position in the service.

Do not bring your dog.

II AT A FIRE

Form of Tender of Rescue from Strange Young Gentleman to Strange Young Lady at a Fire.

Although through the fiat of a cruel fate, I have been debarred the gracious privilege of your acquaintance, permit me, Miss [here insert name, if known], the inestimable honor of offering you the aid of a true and loyal arm against the fiery doom which now o'ershadows you with its crimson wing. [This form to be memorized, and practiced in private.]

Should she accept, the young gentleman should offer his arm—bowing, and observing "Permit me"—and so escort her to the fire escape and deposit her in it (being extremely careful, if she have no clothes on but her night dress, not to seem to notice the irregularity). No form of leavetaking is permissible, further than a formal bow, accompanied by a barely perceptible smile of deferential gratitude for the favor which the young lady has accorded—this smile to be completed at the moment the fire escape starts to slide down, then the features to be recomposed instantly.

A compulsory introduction at a fire is not binding upon the young lady. The young gentleman cannot require recognition at her hands when he next meets her, but must leave her unembarrassed to decide for herself whether she will continue the acquaintanceship or ignore it.

To return to the fire. If the boarding house is not provided with a fire escape, the young gentleman will use such other means of rescue as circumstances shall afford. But he will not need to change the form of his proffer of assistance; for this speech has been purposely framed in such a way as to apply with equal felicity to all methods of rescue from fire. If egress may be had to the street by the stairway, the young gentleman will offer his arm and escort the young lady down; if retreat in that direction is cut off by the fire, he will escort her to the floor above and lower her to the street by a rope, fastening it by slip-noose under her armpits, with the knot behind (at the same time bowing and saying "Permit me"); or if no rope be procurable, he will drop her from the balcony upon soft substances to be provided by the populace below—always observing "Permit me," and accompanying the remark with a slight inclination of the head. In either ascending or descending the stairs, the young gentleman shall walk beside the young lady, if the stairs are wide enough to allow it; otherwise he must *precede* her. In no case must he follow her. This is *de rigueur*.

MEM. In rescuing a chambermaid, presentation of card is

not necessary, neither should one say "Permit me." The form
of tender of service should also be changed. Example:

*Form of Tender of Rescue from Young Gentleman to Chambermaid
at a Fire.*

> There is no occasion for alarm, Mary [insertion of surname
> not permissible]; keep cool, do everything just as I tell you,
> and, *D.V.*, I will save you.

Anything more elaborate than this, as to diction and sentiment, would be in exceedingly bad taste, in the case of a
chambermaid. Yet at the same time, brusqueries are to be
avoided. Such expressions as "Come, git!" should never fall
from the lips of a true gentleman at a fire. No, not even when
addressed to the humblest domestic. Brevity is well; but even
brevity cannot justify vulgarity.

In assisting at a fire in a boarding house, the true gentleman will always save the young ladies first—making no distinction in favor of personal attractions, or social eminence, or
pecuniary predominance—but taking them as they come, and
firing them out with as much celerity as shall be consistent
with decorum. There are exceptions, of course, to all rules;
the exceptions to this one are:

Partiality, in the matter of rescue, to be shown to:

1. Fiancées.
2. Persons toward whom the operator feels a tender sentiment, but has not yet declared himself.
3. Sisters.
4. Stepsisters.
5. Nieces.
6. First cousins.
7. Cripples.
8. Second cousins.
9. Invalids.
10. Young-lady relations by marriage.
11. Third cousins, and young-lady friends of the family.
12. The Unclassified.

Parties belonging to these twelve divisions should be saved
in the order in which they are named.

The operator must keep himself utterly calm, and his line of
procedure constantly in mind; otherwise the confusion around

him will be almost sure to betray him into very embarrassing breaches of etiquette. Where there is much smoke, it is often quite difficult to distinguish between new Relatives by Marriage and Unclassified young ladies; wherefore it is provided that if the operator, in cases of this sort, shall rescue a No. 12 when he should have rescued a No. 10, it is not requisite that he carry No. 12 back again, but that he leave her where she is without remark, and go and fetch out No. 10. An apology to No. 10 is not imperative; still, it is good form to offer it. It may be deferred, however, one day—but no longer. [In a case of this nature which occurred during the first day of the Chicago fire, where the operator saved a No. 7 when a No. 6 was present but overlooked in the smoke, it was held by competent authorities, that the postponement of the apology for the extraordinary term of three days was justified, it being considered that the one-day term during which the apology must be offered means the day after the fire, and therefore does not begin *until the fire is out.* This decision was sustained by the several Illinois courts through which it was carried; and experts are confident that it will also be sustained, eventually, in the Supreme Court of the United States—where it still lingers.]

To return to the fire.

Observe: 1's, 3's, 4's, and 5's may be *carried* out of the burning house, in the operator's arms—permission being first asked, and granted; 7's and 9's may be carried out without the formality of asking permission; the other grades may *not* be carried out, except they themselves take the initiative, and signify, by word or manner, their desire to partake of this attention.

Form for Requesting Permission to Carry a No. 1, 3, 4, or 5, out of a Boarding House Which Is on Fire.

The bonds of [here insert "tenderness," in the case of No. 1; or "blood," in the other cases] which enfold us in their silken tie, warrant me, my dear [here insert given name, in all cases; and without prefix], in offering to you the refuge of my arms in fleeing the fiery doom which now, with crimson wing, o'ershadows us.

In cases where a member of one of the prohibited grades signifies a desire to be carried out of the fire, response should be made in the following form—accompanied by a peculiarly profound obeisance:

Form of Response to Indication on the part of a 2, 6, 8, 10, 11, or 12 that she Desires to be Carried Out of a Fire in Arms of Young Gentleman.

In view of the circumstance, Madmoselle [insert *name* only in cases where the party is a 6 or an 8—be careful about this], that but fragile and conventional [here—in case of a No. 2—insert "Alas!"] are the bonds which enfold us in their silken tie, it is with deepest sense of the signal distinction which your condescension has conferred upon me, that I convey to you the refuge of my arms in fleeing the fiery doom which now, with crimson wing, o'ershadows us.

Other material in boarding house is to be rescued in the following order:

13. Babies.
14. Children under 10 years of age.
15. Young widows.
16. Young married females.
17. Elderly married ditto.
18. Elderly widows.
19. Clergymen.
20. Boarders in general.
21. Female domestics.
22. Male ditto.
23. Landlady.
24. Landlord.
25. Firemen.
26. Furniture.
27. Mothers-in-law.

Arbitrary introductions, made under fire, to 12's through the necessity of carrying them out of the conflagration, are not binding. It rests with the young lady to renew the acquaintanceship or let it drop. If she shall desire the renewal, she may so signify by postal card; by intimation conveyed through friend of family; or by simple recognition of operator, by smile and slight inclination of head, the first time she meets him after the fire. In the resulting conversation the young gentleman must strictly refrain from introducing the subject of fire, or indeed of combustibles of any kind, lest he may seem to conceive and remember that he has lately done a heroic action, or at least an action meriting complimentary acknowledgment; whereas, on the contrary, he should studiedly seem to have forgotten the circumstance, until the young lady shall herself—if she so please—refer to it; in which case he will bow repeatedly, smiling continuously, and accompanying each bow with the observation (uttered in a soft, apparently embarrassed, yet gratified voice), " 'm very glad, 'm sure, 'm very glad, 'm sure."

Offers of marriage to parties who are being carried out from a boarding house on fire are considered to be in questionable taste, for the reason that the subject of the proposition is not likely to be mistress of her best judgment at so alarming and confusing a time, and therefore it may chance that she is taken at a disadvantage. Indeed, the most authoritative canons of high breeding limit such offers inflexibly to cases where the respondent is a No. 2. In these instances, the following form should be observed:

Form of Offer of Marriage from Young Gentleman to a No. 2, during Process of Extracting Her from Boarding House on Fire, and Conveying Her out of the Same in His Arms.

Ah, I supplicate, I beseech, I implore thee, dearest [here insert given name of party only], to have compassion upon thy poor kneeling henchman [do not attempt to kneel—this is but a figure of speech] and deign to be his! Deign to engender into bonds of tenderness those bonds of chill conventionality which enfold us in their silken tie, and he will ever bless the day thou didst accept the refuge of his arms in fleeing the fiery doom which now, with crimson wing, o'ershadows us.

Enough has been said, now, as to the conduct which a young gentleman of culture and breeding should observe in the case of a boarding house on fire. The same rules apply, with but slight variations (which will suggest themselves to the operator), to fire in a church, private house, hotel, railway train, or on shipboard—indeed to all fires in the ordinary walks of life.

In the case of a ship on fire, evening dress must be omitted. The true gentleman never wears evening dress at sea, even in case of a fire.

The speeches to be used at a fire may also, with but slight alteration, be wielded with effect upon disastrous occasions of other sorts. For instance, in tendering rescue from destruction by hurricane, or earthquake, or runaway team, or railway collision (where no conflagration ensues), the operator should merely substitute "fatal doom" for "fiery doom"; and in cases of ordinary shipwreck or other methods of drowning, he should say "watery doom." No other alterations are necessary, for the "crimson wing" applies to all calamities of a majestic sort, and is a phrase of exceeding finish and felicity.

Observe, in conclusion: Offers of marriage, during episode of runaway team, are to be avoided. A lady is sufficiently embarrassed at such a time; any act tending to add to this embarrassment is opposed to good taste, and therefore reprehensible.

III VISITING CARDS

One of the ablest of our recent works on Deportment* has this remark:

> To the unrefined or the underbred person, the visiting-card is but a trifling and insignificant bit of paper; but to the cultured disciple of social law it conveys a subtle and unmistakable intelligence.
>
> Its texture, style of engraving, and even the hour of leaving it, combine to place the stranger whose name it bears in a pleasant or a disagreeable attitude, even before his manners, conversation, and face have been able to explain his social position.
>
> The receiver of a visitor's card makes a careful study of its style. If it is in perfect taste, she admires him unconsciously for this evidence of excellent style, refinement, and familiarity with the details of a high social position and delicate breeding.

All this is wisely conceived, and well said. For the cultured, these hints are sufficient; but some elaboration of the matter seems worth while, in the interest of the partly cultured and the ignorant. Now observe, the points noted as concerns the card—and they are exceedingly important—are as follows:

*Social Etiquette of New York: D. Appleton & Co.

1. Its texture.
2. Style of engraving.
3. Hour of leaving it.

If these fall short of the standard established by social law, the visitor is placed in a "disagreeable attitude"; but if, after a careful study of card and hour, the lady finds in them the regulation evidences of the visitor's perfect taste, she "admires him unconsciously." Let us now enter, carefully and orderly, upon particulars.

As to texture. Always use linen cards—never the cheap cotton styles. This is *de rigueur.*

If you are a mere "Mr.," let your name be engraved in a delicate script; your address, in the same script, must be at the bottom of the card, in the left-hand corner; that is, if you are a bachelor; but if you are married, it must be placed in the right-hand corner.

If you bear a title, you should use a German text of a somewhat bold and pronounced character. In America (but in America only), your wife may be referred to by your title—and she may also put it on her card. Examples:

Mrs. Superintendent-of-Public-Instruction Jones
The Rocks, Hogback-on-the-Hudson

Mrs. Clerk-of-the-Board-of-Aldermen Hooligan
The Tombs, 2d Floor, New York

Mrs. 2d-Lieut.-Co.-B.,-42d-Regt.-N.Y.-
Mounted-Militia Baggs
64 Thompson St., New York
Thursdays

"Thursdays" means that that is her reception day—a reminder that formal calls are not received there on any other day of the week.

The *placing* of the name is a matter of moment. It should be engraved on the *back* of the court cards; and on the *front* of the spot-cards and the joker. For obvious reasons the ace of spades is an exception to this rule—the name goes on the back of it.

A single remark, here, may not be out of place: Never use a second-hand deck, when making a ceremonious call. And never use what in vulgar parlance is called an old greasy deck, except in the case of social inferiors and poor kin.

Now as to the *hour*. Never pay a morning call (of ceremony) before breakfast. Figuratively speaking, this law, like the laws of the Medes and Persians, is written in blood. To call before breakfast would in many cases subject the stranger to the suspicion of desiring to compel an invitation to that meal; and would as often subject the host to the necessity of withholding such invitation—for the reason that the European breakfast (now the only correct thing in our higher circles) bars all sudden additions, there not being enough of it for the family. Now inasmuch as the stranger cannot know everybody's breakfast hour, and therefore is liable to infringe the rule innocently, the canons of fashion have provided for him a simple and at the same time sufficient protection: when he has the slightest reason to fear that he has called too early, he must write "B.T.B." in the upper left-hand corner of his card—which signifies *Been to breakfast*.

Do not make an evening visit of ceremony after bedtime. One is liable to be shot. This is on account of the prevalence of burglars. But aside from this consideration, a visit at so late an hour would amount to a familiarity, and would therefore place the stranger in a disagreeable attitude.

Between the limits above defined, visits may be paid at any hour you may choose; though of course one must not wittingly intrude at luncheon or dinner.

Signification, etc., of the Cards

Diamonds—Independent means, and no occupation.
Hearts—Love.
Clubs—Ultra fashion.
Spades—Neutral.

In houses of the best fashion, at the present day, you will find an ornamental table in the hall, near the front door. Deposit your card upon this.

A word just here: Make no unnecessary remarks to the servant. Do not ask him How's the family; nor How's things; nor What's up—nor any such matter. It is but a transparent artifice, whose intent is to move such as are within hearing to admire how easy, and unembarrassed, and veteran to the ways of society the visitor is. All exhibitions of this sort are low. And do not shake hands with the servant, either coming or going; it is an excess of familiarity, and hence is in bad taste. If you know the servant, you may speak his Christian name, if you so desire, but you must not abbreviate it. You may address him as Thomas or William; but never as Tom or Tommy, or as Bill, Buck, or Billy. In the best society one goes even further, and studiedly *miscalls* the name, substituting William for Thomas, and Thomas for William. This is quite good form, since it gives one the appearance of not charging his mind with things of trifling importance. When one moves in the supremest rank of fashion, and has an assured place there, it is his right, sanctioned by old custom, to call *all* servants Thomas, impartially. When the Thomas is a female, the designation stands for her surname.

Now as to a discriminating use of the visiting card—a very important matter since this utensil—so to call it—is capable of expressing quite nice shades of sentiment or purpose.

On a first visit, the person of independent means will indicate this fact by depositing a diamond on the table above referred to. If he is worth only about $200,000, he will deposit a deuce; if he is worth more than this sum, he will indicate it by depositing the proper card, guiding himself by the following table of values.

Denomination	*Value*
Trey	$ 300,000
Four	400,000
Five	500,000
Six	600,000
Seven	700,000
Eight	800,000
Nine	900,000
Ten	1,000,000
Jack	3,000,000
Queen	8,000,000
King	20,000,000
Ace	

The Ace has no limit. It means that the visitor owns a bonanza, or a railway system, or a telegraph system, or a Standard Oil monopoly.

Having once indicated, by your diamond lead, your financial standing, you will not lead from that suit any more, upon subsequent visits. In cases, later, of great enlargement of capital, one *may* play another diamond to indicate it, but it is not good form, except where the tender passion is concerned. It is permissible, then, if the tenderness has not been mutual, but has been mainly concentered in the male; for if a suitor who has led a trey or a four of diamonds in the beginning, and the tenderness, after due assiduity, has not been mutual, he will often find that the acquired ability to play a jack, by and by, has a tendency to mutualize it. Indeed, it is held by some authorities that no unmutualness is so unmutual that it cannot be mutualized by an ace.

Since the club is the symbol of the highest heaven of fashion and style, it necessarily stands at the top of the deck. By virtue of this precedence the club is *always trump*. It not only holds over the other suits, but one may play it *whenever he chooses*. Remember these things. And also this: one should not *lead* a club, except upon the occasion of a first visit. It is necessary then—for these reasons: it indicates that the visitor is of high fashion; and it also indicates, by the denomination of the card, how high up, or how low down, in the fashionable system he belongs. If you are of new date in high circles, and not conspicuous, lead a small spot-card; if new but conspicuous, play a five or a seven, or along there somewhere; if you are of a fine old fashionable family, and personally distinguished, lead a high spot-card gauged to the size of the circumstances; if you are not distinguished, but had a distinguished grandfather, lead the jack; for distinguished great-great-great grandfather, lead the queen; for distinguished ancestor ("ancestor" means foreign and away back) propagated by titled personage, lead the king; for ancestor derived from Lady Portsmouth or other friend of royalty, lead the ace. If your sister, or other lady relative, has elevated you to connection with nobility by marrying a foreign person of title, *this* is the grandest of all distinctions, and takes easy precedence of each and every other claim in our upper society, and gives you right and privilege to lead the "Joker." N.B.—Since clubs are trumps always, it follows that the "Joker" always stands for a club.

The spade being neutral and noncommittal, we always use that suit when our visit is not one of a deep or peculiar significance. Hence we play the spade very much oftener than any other card. Naturally, therefore, it is called our *long suit.*

Now we come to the hearts. Of course this is a most important card, since its peculiar province is to lead us along the primrose path whose sweet goal is matrimony.

In opening the delicate game of love, you should lead a low card—your lowest, indeed—the deuce. How exquisitely this expresses a budding affection! You should say but little, on this first love-visit; on the contrary you should appear pensive and distraught, and seem to suffer. Do not forget to seem to suffer—this is important. Observe the effect of your card upon the lady. If she blushes, though ever so faintly, it is an elegant sign.

Be wary, be watchful, upon subsequent visits. Confine yourself strictly to the deuce; venture no farther while things seem to go well and pleasure mantles in her eye upon reception of card. Meanwhile, continue to seem to suffer, as before. But the moment you detect indifference in her face, the time has come for you to change your lead. Keep your own counsel; but the next time you come, play a low *spade*—an ultra neutral card. You will discover in a moment whether the lady's indifference was assumed or real. If the former, she will blench a little, and perhaps falter in her greeting. [Follow up this advantage; use first opportunity to press hand; if pressure returned, sigh; if sigh returned, appear transfigured; if cannot appear transfigured, approximate it. If pressure not returned, sigh anyhow, as above; take opportunity to speak of shortness of life—brevity of existence is better; refer to morning of life overshadowed, cold world, blighted young hopes, etc., and do the early grave business and "soon be at rest," and that sort of thing. Note effect. If evidently touched, lay into this line pretty strong; keep right along, spread it on thick. Introduce topic of sick mother (sick mother admirable material);

get her to sympathize. Work in other sick relatives, as opportunity offers—but not too many; better leave three out than
have one left over. Keep sharp lookout, and at right time,
draw on your dead. Early dead most pathetic, perhaps, and
therefore preferable. But be careful; do not overdo this feature; the first sample that palls on her, close the cemetery, and
shade off onto suicide. MEM.—Leave her in tears, if it takes
till breakfast.]

Next time you come, play the *trey* of hearts. Play it confidently—there is no occasion for fear.

You are fairly launched now, on the sweet voyage, and with
a fair wind. But be ever wary; do not go too fast. Do not lead
your four spot till you are sure you have gotten far enough
along to warrant it. By and by, venture your five—and so on.
If ever you discover that you have added a spot too soon,
show instant repentance and deep humility by receding a spot
or two—set yourself back a whole month, even—it will have
a good effect.

Meantime, keep always prepared for rivals. For instance, if
you are at the five-spot stage, and you perceive that a rival has
deposited the six on the hall table, don't hesitate—play the
seven and take it. Your boldness will please the lady and win
your forgiveness. If your rival's heart is the biggest one in the
deck, trump it—never weaken. From time to time, cases of
doubt will turn up, but let them not confuse you, for there is
one general law which covers these emergencies: When you
are in doubt, take the trick.

By and by—let us suppose—you have at last climbed
through all the stages, and the blissful moment has come for
the playing your last and highest heart. You should agree upon
a day and hour, with the lady, beforehand, because proposal
of marriage must follow immediately upon this final play.

Let us consider that everything has been done and that the
proposal is the next thing on the docket. Always propose in
evening dress, if you are a civilian; in uniform, if you are in
the army or navy—with sword or saber, but without revolver
or spurs. The Masonic or Odd Fellows' regalia should be
superadded, in both cases, if you hold the privilege. [The
lady should wear orange buds which are still green and have
not begun to open. And other clothing, of course.]

You should make your proposal kneeling upon one knee—using hassock or handkerchief.

Form of Proposal to Spinster—and Responses.

HE: Oh, dearest [insert given name only], will thou join thy sweet destiny to mine, and, hand in hand, journey with me adown life's tranquil stream, sharing its storms and calms, its labor and pain, its joy and sorrow, its poverty and wealth, its sickness and health, its beauteous paths, its arid wastes, and all that the inscrutable hand of fate shall pour out upon us, of sweet and bitter, till death do us part? [Weep, here.]

SHE: Oh, darling [insert given name, if handsome one—otherwise say *Reginald*], truly will thy [insert own given name] journey with thee, hand in hand, adown life's tranquil stream, sharing its storms and calms, its labor and pain, its joy and sorrow, its poverty and wealth, its sickness and health, its beauteous paths, its arid wastes, and all that the inscrutable hand of fate shall pour upon us, of sweet and bitter, till death do us part. [Weep, here.]

HE: Oh, mine own!

SHE: Ah, mine own! [Rise and embrace—but carefully, being regardful of her toilet.]

In case of a widow, proposer will use same form, merely inserting word or two of kindly reference to deceased. Widow will use same form, merely acknowledging kindly notice of deceased with sob, if affliction recent; simple sigh, if more remote.

If proposer is defeated, he may throw up his hand or call a new deal, just as he shall prefer, or as circumstances may dictate.

But if he is elected, he must now drop into the beautiful French custom of fetching a bouquet every day. His first bouquet must be entirely white; after that, a faint shade of color (red) must be added daily. Let the tint deepen gradually day by day, and with such careful precision that there shall still remain a perceptible trace of white down to the very day before the wedding. On that day the last bouquet is delivered—and it must be *absolutely* red—no suggestion of other color in it anywhere.

It is an admirable custom, because it is stylish, and troublesome, and instinct with delicate sentiment, if one ignores the significance which the French people attach to it. But it is going out—at least in some sections of America. In some of our best circles a new custom has already taken its place—and yet it is substantially the French one in a new guise. It is as follows. As a starter, the bridegroom-elect fetches a handkerchief; then a napkin; then a towel—and so on, gradually enlarging, by degrees; and the day before the wedding he winds up with a blanket. The sentiment is the same, and the things keep better.

We do not need to say anything about marriage settlements. Among the French and Comanches, where a bride is a mere thing of barter, worth so much cash, or so many yellow dogs or wildcat skins, the marriage settlement is necessarily a very important matter; but this is not the case with us, so we will not discuss the subject.

c. 1881

Advice to Youth

Saturday Morning Club, Boston

Being told I would be expected to talk here, I inquired what sort of a talk I ought to make. They said it should be something suitable to youth—something didactic, instructive; or something in the nature of good advice. Very well; I have a few things in my mind which I have often longed to say for the instruction of the young; for it is in one's tender early years that such things will best take root and be most enduring and most valuable. First, then, I will say to you, my young friends—and say it beseechingly, urgingly—.

Always obey your parents, when they are present. This is the best policy in the long run; because if you don't, they will make you. Most parents think they know better than you do; and you can generally make more by humoring that superstition than you can by acting on your own better judgment.

Be respectful to your superiors, if you have any; also to strangers, and sometimes to others. If a person offend you, and you are in doubt as to whether it was intentional or not, do not resort to extreme measures; simply watch your chance and hit him with a brick. That will be sufficient. If you shall find that he had not intended any offense, come out frankly and confess yourself in the wrong when you struck him; acknowledge it like a man, and say you didn't mean to. Yes, always avoid violence; in this age of charity and kindliness, the time has gone by for such things. Leave dynamite to the low and unrefined.

Go to bed early, get up early—this is wise. Some authorities say get up with one thing, some with another. But a lark is really the best thing to get up with. It gives you a splendid reputation with everybody to know that you get up with the lark; and if you get the right kind of a lark, and work at him right, you can easily train him to get up at half-past nine, every time—it is no trick at all.

Now as to the matter of lying. You want to be very careful about lying; otherwise you are nearly sure to get caught. Once caught, you can never again be, in the eyes of the good and the pure, what you were before. Many a young person has injured himself permanently through a single clumsy and ill-finished lie, the result of carelessness born of incomplete training. Some authorities hold that the young ought not to lie at all. That, of course, is putting it rather stronger than necessary; still, while I cannot go quite so far as that, I do maintain, and I believe I am right, that the young ought to be temperate in the use of this great art until practice and experience shall give them that confidence, elegance and precision which alone can make the accomplishment graceful and profitable. Patience, diligence, painstaking attention to detail—these are the requirements; these, in time, will make the student perfect; upon these, and upon these only, may he rely as the sure foundation for future eminence. Think what tedious years of study, thought, practice, experience, went to the equipment of that peerless old master who was able to impose upon the whole world the lofty and sounding maxim that "Truth is mighty and will prevail"—the most majestic compound fracture of fact which any of woman born has yet achieved. For the history of our race, and each individual's experience, are sown thick with evidences that a truth is not hard to kill, and that a lie well told is immortal. There in Boston is a monument to the man who discovered anesthesia; many people are aware, in these latter days, that that man didn't discover it at all, but stole the discovery from another man. Is this truth mighty, and will it prevail? Ah, no, my hearers, the monument is made of hardy material, but the lie it tells will outlast it a million years. An awkward, feeble, leaky lie is a thing which you ought to make it your unceasing study to avoid; such a lie as that has no more real permanence than an average truth. Why, you might as well tell the truth at once and be done with it. A feeble, stupid, preposterous lie will not live two years—except it be a slander upon somebody. It is indestructible, then, of course, but that is no merit of yours. A final word: begin your practice of this gracious and beautiful art early—begin now. If I had begun earlier, I could have learned how.

Never handle firearms carelessly. The sorrow and suffering that have been caused through the innocent but heedless handling of firearms by the young! Only four days ago, right in the next farmhouse to the one where I am spending the summer, a mother, old and gray and sweet, one of the loveliest spirits in the land, was sitting at her work, when her young son crept in and got down an old, battered, rusty gun which had not been touched for many years, and was supposed not to be loaded, and pointed it at her, laughing and threatening to shoot. In her fright she ran screaming and pleading toward the door on the other side of the room; but as she passed him he placed the gun almost against her very breast and pulled the trigger! He had supposed it was not loaded. And he was right: it wasn't. So there wasn't any harm done. It is the only case of the kind I ever heard of. Therefore, just the same, don't you meddle with old unloaded firearms; they are the most deadly and unerring things that have ever been created by man. You don't have to take any pains at all, with them; you don't have to have a rest, you don't have to have any sights on the gun, you don't have to take aim, even. No, you just pick out a relative and bang away, and you are sure to get him. A youth who can't hit a cathedral at thirty yards with a Gatling gun in three-quarters of an hour, can take up an old empty musket and bag his mother every time, at a hundred. Think what Waterloo would have been if one of the armies had been boys armed with old rusty muskets supposed not to be loaded, and the other army had been composed of their female relations. The very thought of it makes me shudder.

There are many sorts of books; but good ones are the sort for the young to read. Remember that. They are a great, an inestimable, an unspeakable means of improvement. Therefore be careful in your selection, my young friends; be very careful; confine yourself exclusively to Robertson's *Sermons*, Baxter's *Saint's Rest*, *The Innocents Abroad*, and works of that kind.

But I have said enough. I hope you will treasure up the instructions which I have given you, and make them a guide to your feet and a light to your understanding. Build your character thoughtfully and painstakingly upon these precepts; and by and by, when you have got it built, you will be surprised and gratified to see how nicely and sharply it resembles everybody else's.

April 15, 1882

The Stolen White Elephant*

I.

The following curious history was related to me by a
chance railway acquaintance. He was a gentleman more than
seventy years of age, and his thoroughly good and gentle face
and earnest and sincere manner imprinted the unmistakable
stamp of truth upon every statement which fell from his lips.
He said:—

You know in what reverence the royal white elephant of
Siam is held by the people of that country. You know it is
sacred to kings, only kings may possess it, and that it is indeed in a measure even superior to kings, since it receives not
merely honor but worship. Very well; five years ago, when the
troubles concerning the frontier line arose between Great
Britain and Siam, it was presently manifest that Siam had
been in the wrong. Therefore every reparation was quickly
made, and the British representative stated that he was satisfied and the past should be forgotten. This greatly relieved the
King of Siam, and partly as a token of gratitude, but partly
also, perhaps, to wipe out any little remaining vestige of
unpleasantness which England might feel toward him, he
wished to send the Queen a present,—the sole sure way of
propitiating an enemy, according to Oriental ideas. This
present ought not only to be a royal one, but transcendently
royal. Wherefore, what offering could be so meet as that of a
white elephant? My position in the Indian civil service was
such that I was deemed peculiarly worthy of the honor of
conveying the present to her Majesty. A ship was fitted out
for me and my servants and the officers and attendants of the
elephant, and in due time I arrived in New York harbor and
placed my royal charge in admirable quarters in Jersey City. It
was necessary to remain awhile in order to recruit the animal's
health before resuming the voyage.

All went well during a fortnight,—then my calamities be-

*Left out of "A Tramp Abroad," because it was feared that some of the
particulars had been exaggerated, and that others were not true. Before these
suspicions had been proven groundless, the book had gone to press.—M. T.

gan. The white elephant was stolen! I was called up at dead of night and informed of this fearful misfortune. For some moments I was beside myself with terror and anxiety; I was helpless. Then I grew calmer and collected my faculties. I soon saw my course,—for indeed there was but the one course for an intelligent man to pursue. Late as it was, I flew to New York and got a policeman to conduct me to the headquarters of the detective force. Fortunately I arrived in time, though the chief of the force, the celebrated Inspector Blunt, was just on the point of leaving for his home. He was a man of middle size and compact frame, and when he was thinking deeply he had a way of knitting his brows and tapping his forehead reflectively with his finger, which impressed you at once with the conviction that you stood in the presence of a person of no common order. The very sight of him gave me confidence and made me hopeful. I stated my errand. It did not flurry him in the least; it had no more visible effect upon his iron self-possession than if I had told him somebody had stolen my dog. He motioned me to a seat, and said calmly,—

"Allow me to think a moment, please."

So saying, he sat down at his office table and leaned his head upon his hand. Several clerks were at work at the other end of the room; the scratching of their pens was all the sound I heard during the next six or seven minutes. Meantime the inspector sat there, buried in thought. Finally he raised his head, and there was that in the firm lines of his face which showed me that his brain had done its work and his plan was made. Said he,—and his voice was low and impressive,—

"This is no ordinary case. Every step must be warily taken; each step must be made sure before the next is ventured. And secrecy must be observed,—secrecy profound and absolute. Speak to no one about the matter, not even the reporters. I will take care of *them*; I will see that they get only what it may suit my ends to let them know." He touched a bell; a youth appeared. "Alaric, tell the reporters to remain for the present." The boy retired. "Now let us proceed to business,—and systematically. Nothing can be accomplished in this trade of mine without strict and minute method."

He took a pen and some paper. "Now—name of the elephant?"

"Hassan Ben Ali Ben Selim Abdallah Mohammed Moisé Alhammal Jamsetjejeebhoy Dhuleep Sultan Ebu Bhudpoor."

"Very well. Given name?"

"Jumbo."

"Very well. Place of birth?"

"The capital city of Siam."

"Parents living?"

"No,—dead."

"Had they any other issue besides this one?"

"None. He was an only child."

"Very well. These matters are sufficient under that head. Now please describe the elephant, and leave out no particular, however insignificant,—that is, insignificant from *your* point of view. To men in my profession there *are* no insignificant particulars; they do not exist."

I described,—he wrote. When I was done, he said,—

"Now listen. If I have made any mistakes, correct me."

He read as follows:—

"Height, 19 feet; length from apex of forehead to insertion of tail, 26 feet; length of trunk, 16 feet; length of tail, 6 feet; total length, including trunk and tail, 48 feet; length of tusks, 9½ feet; ears in keeping with these dimensions; footprint resembles the mark left when one up-ends a barrel in the snow; color of the elephant, a dull white; has a hole the size of a plate in each ear for the insertion of jewelry, and possesses the habit in a remarkable degree of squirting water upon spectators and of maltreating with his trunk not only such persons as he is acquainted with, but even entire strangers; limps slightly with his right hind leg, and has a small scar in his left armpit caused by a former boil; had on, when stolen, a castle containing seats for fifteen persons, and a gold-cloth saddle-blanket the size of an ordinary carpet."

There were no mistakes. The inspector touched the bell, handed the description to Alaric, and said,—

"Have fifty thousand copies of this printed at once and mailed to every detective office and pawnbroker's shop on the continent." Alaric retired. "There,—so far, so good. Next, I must have a photograph of the property."

I gave him one. He examined it critically, and said,—

"It must do, since we can do no better; but he has his trunk curled up and tucked into his mouth. That is unfortunate, and is calculated to mislead, for of course he does not usually have it in that position." He touched his bell.

"Alaric, have fifty thousand copies of this photograph made, the first thing in the morning, and mail them with the descriptive circulars."

Alaric retired to execute his orders. The inspector said,—

"It will be necessary to offer a reward, of course. Now as to the amount?"

"What sum would you suggest?"

"To *begin* with, I should say,—well, twenty-five thousand dollars. It is an intricate and difficult business; there are a thousand avenues of escape and opportunities of conceal-ment. These thieves have friends and pals everywhere—"

"Bless me, do you know who they are?"

The wary face, practised in concealing the thoughts and feelings within, gave me no token, nor yet the replying words, so quietly uttered:—

"Never mind about that. I may, and I may not. We gener-ally gather a pretty shrewd inkling of who our man is by the manner of his work and the size of the game he goes after. We are not dealing with a pickpocket or a hall thief, now, make up your mind to that. This property was not 'lifted' by a nov-ice. But, as I was saying, considering the amount of travel which will have to be done, and the diligence with which the thieves will cover up their traces as they move along, twenty-five thousand may be too small a sum to offer, yet I think it worth while to start with that."

So we determined upon that figure, as a beginning. Then this man, whom nothing escaped which could by any possi-bility be made to serve as a clew, said:—

"There are cases in detective history to show that criminals have been detected through peculiarities in their appetites. Now, what does this elephant eat, and how much?"

"Well, as to *what* he eats,—he will eat *anything*. He will eat a man, he will eat a Bible,—he will eat anything *between* a man and a Bible."

"Good,—very good indeed, but too general. Details are

necessary,—details are the only valuable things in our trade. Very well,—as to men. At one meal,—or, if you prefer, during one day,—how many men will he eat, if fresh?"

"He would not care whether they were fresh or not; at a single meal he would eat five ordinary men."

"Very good; five men; we will put that down. What nationalities would he prefer?"

"He is indifferent about nationalities. He prefers acquaintances, but is not prejudiced against strangers."

"Very good. Now, as to Bibles. How many Bibles would he eat at a meal?"

"He would eat an entire edition."

"It is hardly succinct enough. Do you mean the ordinary octavo, or the family illustrated?"

"I think he would be indifferent to illustrations; that is, I think he would not value illustrations above simple letter-press."

"No, you do not get my idea. I refer to bulk. The ordinary octavo Bible weighs about two pounds and a half, while the great quarto with the illustrations weighs ten or twelve. How many Doré Bibles would he eat at a meal?"

"If you knew this elephant, you could not ask. He would take what they had."

"Well, put it in dollars and cents, then. We must get at it somehow. The Doré costs a hundred dollars a copy, Russia leather, bevelled."

"He would require about fifty thousand dollars' worth,— say an edition of five hundred copies."

"Now that is more exact. I will put that down. Very well; he likes men and Bibles; so far, so good. What else will he eat? I want particulars."

"He will leave Bibles to eat bricks, he will leave bricks to eat bottles, he will leave bottles to eat clothing, he will leave clothing to eat cats, he will leave cats to eat oysters, he will leave oysters to eat ham, he will leave ham to eat sugar, he will leave sugar to eat pie, he will leave pie to eat potatoes, he will leave potatoes to eat bran, he will leave bran to eat hay, he will leave hay to eat oats, he will leave oats to eat rice, for he was mainly raised on it. There is nothing whatever that he will not eat but European butter, and he would eat that if he could taste it."

"Very good. General quantity at a meal,—say about—"

"Well, anywhere from a quarter to half a ton."

"And he drinks—"

"Everything that is fluid. Milk, water, whiskey, molasses, castor oil, camphene, carbolic acid,—it is no use to go into particulars; whatever fluid occurs to you set it down. He will drink anything that is fluid, except European coffee."

"Very good. As to quantity?"

"Put it down five to fifteen barrels,—his thirst varies; his other appetites do not."

"These things are unusual. They ought to furnish quite good clews toward tracing him."

He touched the bell.

"Alaric, summon Captain Burns."

Burns appeared. Inspector Blunt unfolded the whole matter to him, detail by detail. Then he said in the clear, decisive tones of a man whose plans are clearly defined in his head, and who is accustomed to command,—

"Captain Burns, detail Detectives Jones, Davis, Halsey, Bates, and Hackett to shadow the elephant."

"Yes, sir."

"Detail Detectives Moses, Dakin, Murphy, Rogers, Tupper, Higgins, and Bartholomew to shadow the thieves."

"Yes, sir."

"Place a strong guard—a guard of thirty picked men, with a relief of thirty—over the place from whence the elephant was stolen, to keep strict watch there night and day, and allow none to approach—except reporters—without written authority from me."

"Yes, sir."

"Place detectives in plain clothes in the railway, steamship, and ferry depots, and upon all roadways leading out of Jersey City, with orders to search all suspicious persons."

"Yes, sir."

"Furnish all these men with photograph and accompanying description of the elephant, and instruct them to search all trains and outgoing ferry-boats and other vessels."

"Yes, sir."

"If the elephant should be found, let him be seized, and the information forwarded to me by telegraph."

"Yes, sir."

"Let me be informed at once if any clews should be found,—footprints of the animal, or anything of that kind."

"Yes, sir."

"Get an order commanding the harbor police to patrol the frontages vigilantly."

"Yes, sir."

"Despatch detectives in plain clothes over all the railways, north as far as Canada, west as far as Ohio, south as far as Washington."

"Yes, sir."

"Place experts in all the telegraph offices to listen to all messages; and let them require that all cipher despatches be interpreted to them."

"Yes, sir."

"Let all these things be done with the utmost secrecy,— mind, the most impenetrable secrecy."

"Yes, sir."

"Report to me promptly at the usual hour."

"Yes, sir."

"Go!"

"Yes, sir."

He was gone.

Inspector Blunt was silent and thoughtful a moment, while the fire in his eye cooled down and faded out. Then he turned to me and said in a placid voice,—

"I am not given to boasting, it is not my habit; but—we shall find the elephant."

I shook him warmly by the hand and thanked him; and I *felt* my thanks, too. The more I had seen of the man the more I liked him, and the more I admired him and marvelled over the mysterious wonders of his profession. Then we parted for the night, and I went home with a far happier heart than I had carried with me to his office.

II.

Next morning it was all in the newspapers, in the minutest detail. It even had additions,—consisting of Detective This, Detective That, and Detective The Other's "Theory" as to how the robbery was done, who the robbers were, and whither they had flown with their booty. There were eleven of these theories, and they covered all the possibilities; and this single fact shows what independent thinkers detectives are. No two theories were alike, or even much resembled each other, save in one striking particular, and in that one all the eleven theories were absolutely agreed. That was, that although the rear of my building was torn out and the only door remained locked, the elephant had not been removed through the rent, but by some other (undiscovered) outlet. All agreed that the robbers had made that rent only to mislead the detectives. That never would have occurred to me or to any other layman, perhaps, but it had not deceived the detectives for a moment. Thus, what I had supposed was the only thing that had no mystery about it was in fact the very thing I had gone furthest astray in. The eleven theories all named the supposed robbers, but no two named the same robbers; the total number of suspected persons was thirty-seven. The various newspaper accounts all closed with the most important opinion of all,—that of Chief Inspector Blunt. A portion of this statement read as follows:—

"The chief knows who the two principals are, namely, 'Brick' Duffy and 'Red' McFadden. Ten days before the robbery was achieved he was already aware that it was to be attempted, and had quietly proceeded to shadow these two noted villains; but unfortunately on the night in question their track was lost, and before it could be found again the bird was flown,—that is, the elephant.

"Duffy and McFadden are the boldest scoundrels in the profession; the chief has reasons for believing that they are the men who stole the stove out of the detective headquarters on a bitter night last winter,—in consequence of which the chief and every detective present were in the hands of the physicians before morning, some with frozen feet, others with frozen fingers, ears, and other members."

When I read the first half of that I was more astonished than ever at the wonderful sagacity of this strange man. He not only saw everything in the present with a clear eye, but even the future could not be hidden from him. I was soon at his office, and said I could not help wishing he had had those men arrested, and so prevented the trouble and loss; but his reply was simple and unanswerable: —

"It is not our province to prevent crime, but to punish it. We cannot punish it until it is committed."

I remarked that the secrecy with which we had begun had been marred by the newspapers; not only all our facts but all our plans and purposes had been revealed; even all the suspected persons had been named; these would doubtless disguise themselves now, or go into hiding.

"Let them. They will find that when I am ready for them my hand will descend upon them, in their secret places, as unerringly as the hand of fate. As to the newspapers, we *must* keep in with them. Fame, reputation, constant public mention,—these are the detective's bread and butter. He must publish his facts, else he will be supposed to have none; he must publish his theory, for nothing is so strange or striking as a detective's theory, or brings him so much wondering respect; we must publish our plans, for these the journals insist upon having, and we could not deny them without offending. We must constantly show the public what we are doing, or they will believe we are doing nothing. It is much pleasanter to have a newspaper say, 'Inspector Blunt's ingenious and extraordinary theory is as follows,' than to have it say some harsh thing, or, worse still, some sarcastic one."

"I see the force of what you say. But I noticed that in one part of your remarks in the papers this morning you refused to reveal your opinion upon a certain minor point."

"Yes, we always do that; it has a good effect. Besides, I had not formed any opinion on that point, any way."

I deposited a considerable sum of money with the inspector, to meet current expenses, and sat down to wait for news. We were expecting the telegrams to begin to arrive at any moment now. Meantime I reread the newspapers and also our descriptive circular, and observed that our $25,000 reward seemed to be offered only to detectives. I said I thought it ought to be offered to anybody who would catch the elephant. The inspector said: —

"It is the detectives who will find the elephant, hence the reward will go to the right place. If other people found the animal, it would only be by watching the detectives and taking advantage of clews and indications stolen from them, and that would entitle the detectives to the reward, after all. The proper office of a reward is to stimulate the men who deliver up their time and their trained sagacities to this sort of work, and not to confer benefits upon chance citizens who stumble upon a capture without having earned the benefits by their own merits and labors."

This was reasonable enough, certainly. Now the telegraphic machine in the corner began to click, and the following despatch was the result: —

FLOWER STATION, N. Y., 7.30 A. M.

Have got a clew. Found a succession of deep tracks across a farm near here. Followed them two miles east without result; think elephant went west. Shall now shadow him in that direction.

DARLEY, *Detective.*

"Darley's one of the best men on the force," said the inspector. "We shall hear from him again before long."

Telegram No. 2 came: —

BARKER'S, N. J., 7.40 A. M.

Just arrived. Glass factory broken open here during night, and eight hundred bottles taken. Only water in large quantity near here is five miles distant. Shall strike for there. Elephant will be thirsty. Bottles were empty.

BAKER, *Detective.*

"That promises well, too," said the inspector. "I told you the creature's appetites would not be bad clews."

Telegram No. 3: —

TAYLORVILLE, L. I., 8.15 A. M.

A haystack near here disappeared during night. Probably eaten. Have got a clew, and am off.

HUBBARD, *Detective.*

"How he does move around!" said the inspector. "I knew we had a difficult job on hand, but we shall catch him yet."

FLOWER STATION, N. Y., 9 A. M.

Shadowed the tracks three miles westward. Large, deep, and ragged. Have just met a farmer who says they are not elephant tracks. Says they are holes where he dug up saplings for shade-trees when ground was frozen last winter. Give me orders how to proceed.

DARLEY, *Detective*.

"Aha! a confederate of the thieves! The thing grows warm," said the inspector.

He dictated the following telegram to Darley:—

Arrest the man and force him to name his pals. Continue to follow the tracks,—to the Pacific, if necessary.

Chief BLUNT.

Next telegram:—

CONEY POINT, PA., 8.45 A. M.

Gas office broken open here during night and three months' unpaid gas bills taken. Have got a clew and am away.

MURPHY, *Detective*.

"Heavens!" said the inspector; "would he eat gas bills?"

"Through ignorance,—yes; but they cannot support life. At least, unassisted."

Now came this exciting telegram:—

IRONVILLE, N. Y., 9.30 A. M.

Just arrived. This village in consternation. Elephant passed through here at five this morning. Some say he went east, some say west, some north, some south,—but all say they did not wait to notice particularly. He killed a horse; have secured a piece of it for a clew. Killed it with his trunk; from style of blow, think he struck it left-handed. From position in which horse lies, think elephant travelled northward along line of Berkley railway. Has four and a half hours' start, but I move on his track at once.

HAWES, *Detective*.

I uttered exclamations of joy. The inspector was as self-contained as a graven image. He calmly touched his bell.

"Alaric, send Captain Burns here."

Burns appeared.

"How many men are ready for instant orders?"

"Ninety-six, sir."

"Send them north at once. Let them concentrate along the line of the Berkley road north of Ironville."

"Yes, sir."

"Let them conduct their movements with the utmost secrecy. As fast as others are at liberty, hold them for orders."

"Yes, sir."

"Go!"

"Yes, sir."

Presently came another telegram:—

> SAGE CORNERS, N. Y., 10.30.
>
> Just arrived. Elephant passed through here at 8.15. All escaped from the town but a policeman. Apparently elephant did not strike at policeman, but at the lamp-post, Got both. I have secured a portion of the policeman as clew.
>
> STUMM, *Detective*.

"So the elephant has turned westward," said the inspector. "However, he will not escape, for my men are scattered all over that region."

The next telegram said:—

> GLOVER'S, 11.15.
>
> Just arrived. Village deserted, except sick and aged. Elephant passed through three quarters of an hour ago. The anti-temperance mass meeting was in session; he put his trunk in at a window and washed it out with water from cistern. Some swallowed it—since dead; several drowned. Detectives Cross and O'Shaughnessy were passing through town, but going south,—so missed elephant. Whole region for many miles around in terror,—people flying from their homes. Wherever they turn they meet elephant, and many are killed.
>
> BRANT, *Detective*.

I could have shed tears, this havoc so distressed me. But the inspector only said,—

"You see,—we are closing in on him. He feels our presence; he has turned eastward again."

Yet further troublous news was in store for us. The telegraph brought this:—

HOGANPORT, 12.19.

Just arrived. Elephant passed through half an hour ago, creating wildest fright and excitement. Elephant raged around streets; two plumbers going by, killed one—other escaped. Regret general.

O'FLAHERTY, *Detective.*

"Now he is right in the midst of my men," said the inspector. "Nothing can save him."

A succession of telegrams came from detectives who were scattered through New Jersey and Pennsylvania, and who were following clews consisting of ravaged barns, factories, and Sunday school libraries, with high hopes,—hopes amounting to certainties, indeed. The inspector said,—

"I wish I could communicate with them and order them north, but that is impossible. A detective only visits a telegraph office to send his report; then he is off again, and you don't know where to put your hand on him."

Now came this despatch:—

BRIDGEPORT, CT., 12.15.

Barnum offers rate of $4,000 a year for exclusive privilege of using elephant as travelling advertising medium from now till detectives find him. Wants to paste circus-posters on him. Desires immediate answer.

BOGGS, *Detective.*

"That is perfectly absurd!" I exclaimed.

"Of course it is," said the inspector. "Evidently Mr. Barnum, who thinks he is so sharp, does not know me,—but I know him."

Then he dictated this answer to the despatch:—

Mr. Barnum's offer declined. Make it $7,000 or nothing.

Chief BLUNT.

"There. We shall not have to wait long for an answer. Mr. Barnum is not at home; he is in the telegraph office,—it is his way when he has business on hand. Inside of three—"

DONE.—P. T. BARNUM.

So interrupted the clicking telegraphic instrument. Before I could make a comment upon this extraordinary episode, the following despatch carried my thoughts into another and very distressing channel:—

BOLIVIA, N. Y., 12.50.

Elephant arrived here from the south and passed through toward the forest at 11.50, dispersing a funeral on the way, and diminishing the mourners by two. Citizens fired some small cannon-balls into him, and then fled. Detective Burke and I arrived ten minutes later, from the north, but mistook some excavations for footprints, and so lost a good deal of time; but at last we struck the right trail and followed it to the woods. We then got down on our hands and knees and continued to keep a sharp eye on the track, and so shadowed it into the brush. Burke was in advance. Unfortunately the animal had stopped to rest; therefore, Burke having his head down, intent upon the track, butted up against the elephant's hind legs before he was aware of his vicinity. Burke instantly rose to his feet, seized the tail, and exclaimed joyfully, "I claim the re——" but got no further, for a single blow of the huge trunk laid the brave fellow's fragments low in death. I fled rearward, and the elephant turned and shadowed me to the edge of the wood, making tremendous speed, and I should inevitably have been lost, but that the remains of the funeral providentially intervened again and diverted his attention. I have just learned that nothing of that funeral is now left; but this is no loss, for there is an abundance of material for another. Meantime, the elephant has disappeared again.

MULROONEY, *Detective.*

We heard no news except from the diligent and confident detectives scattered about New Jersey, Pennsylvania, Delaware, and Virginia,—who were all following fresh and encouraging clews,—until shortly after 2 P.M., when this telegram came:—

BAXTER CENTRE, 2.15.

Elephant been here, plastered over with circus-bills, and broke up a revival, striking down and damaging many who were on the point of entering upon a better life. Citizens penned him up, and established a guard. When Detective Brown and I arrived, some time after, we entered enclosure and proceeded to identify elephant by photograph and description. All marks tallied exactly except one, which we could not see,—the boil-scar under armpit. To make sure, Brown crept under to look, and was immediately brained,—that is, head crushed and destroyed, though nothing issued from debris. All fled; so did elephant, striking right and left with much effect. Has escaped, but left bold blood-track from cannon-wounds. Rediscovery certain. He broke southward, through a dense forest.

BRENT, *Detective.*

That was the last telegram. At nightfall a fog shut down which was so dense that objects but three feet away could not be discerned. This lasted all night. The ferry-boats and even the omnibuses had to stop running.

III.

Next morning the papers were as full of detective theories as before; they had all our tragic facts in detail also, and a great many more which they had received from their telegraphic correspondents. Column after column was occupied, a third of its way down, with glaring head-lines, which it made my heart sick to read. Their general tone was like this: —

"THE WHITE ELEPHANT AT LARGE! HE MOVES UPON HIS FATAL MARCH! WHOLE VILLAGES DESERTED BY THEIR FRIGHT-STRICKEN OCCUPANTS! PALE TERROR GOES BEFORE HIM, DEATH AND DEVASTATION FOLLOW AFTER! AFTER THESE, THE DETECTIVES. BARNS DESTROYED, FACTORIES GUTTED, HARVESTS DE-VOURED, PUBLIC ASSEMBLAGES DISPERSED, ACCOMPANIED BY SCENES OF CARNAGE IMPOSSIBLE TO DESCRIBE! THEORIES OF THIRTY-FOUR OF THE MOST DISTINGUISHED DETECTIVES ON THE FORCE! THEORY OF CHIEF BLUNT!"

"There!" said Inspector Blunt, almost betrayed into excitement, "this is magnificent! This is the greatest windfall that any detective organization ever had. The fame of it will travel to the ends of the earth, and endure to the end of time, and my name with it."

But there was no joy for me. I felt as if I had committed all those red crimes, and that the elephant was only my irresponsible agent. And how the list had grown! In one place he had "interfered with an election and killed five repeaters." He had followed this act with the destruction of two poor fellows, named O'Donohue and McFlannigan, who had "found a refuge in the home of the oppressed of all lands only the day before, and were in the act of exercising for the first time the noble right of American citizens at the polls, when stricken down by the relentless hand of the Scourge of Siam." In another, he had "found a crazy sensation-preacher preparing his next season's heroic attacks on the dance, the theatre, and other things which can't strike back, and had stepped on him." And in still another place he had "killed a lightning-rod agent." And so the list went on, growing redder and redder, and more and more heart-breaking. Sixty persons had been killed, and two hundred and forty wounded. All the accounts bore just testimony to the activity and devotion of the detectives, and all closed with the remark that "three hundred thousand citizens and four detectives saw the dread creature, and two of the latter he destroyed."

I dreaded to hear the telegraphic instrument begin to click again. By and by the messages began to pour in, but I was happily disappointed in their nature. It was soon apparent that all trace of the elephant was lost. The fog had enabled him to search out a good hiding-place unobserved. Telegrams from the most absurdly distant points reported that a dim vast mass had been glimpsed there through the fog at such and such an hour, and was "undoubtedly the elephant." This dim vast mass had been glimpsed in New Haven, in New Jersey, in Pennsylvania, in interior New York, in Brooklyn, and even in the city of New York itself! But in all cases the dim vast mass had vanished quickly and left no trace. Every detective of the large force scattered over this huge extent of country sent his hourly report, and each and every one of them had a clew, and was shadowing something, and was hot upon the heels of it.

But the day passed without other result.

The next day the same.

The next just the same.

The newspaper reports began to grow monotonous with facts that amounted to nothing, clews which led to nothing, and theories which had nearly exhausted the elements which surprise and delight and dazzle.

By advice of the inspector I doubled the reward.

Four more dull days followed. Then came a bitter blow to the poor, hard-working detectives, — the journalists declined to print their theories, and coldly said, "Give us a rest."

Two weeks after the elephant's disappearance I raised the reward to $75,000 by the inspector's advice. It was a great sum, but I felt that I would rather sacrifice my whole private fortune than lose my credit with my government. Now that the detectives were in adversity, the newspapers turned upon them, and began to fling the most stinging sarcasms at them. This gave the minstrels an idea, and they dressed themselves as detectives and hunted the elephant on the stage in the most extravagant way. The caricaturists made pictures of detectives scanning the country with spy-glasses, while the elephant, at their backs, stole apples out of their pockets. And they made all sorts of ridiculous pictures of the detective badge,—you have seen that badge printed in gold on the back of detective novels, no doubt,—it is a wide-staring eye, with the legend, "WE NEVER SLEEP." When detectives called for a drink, the would-be facetious bar-keeper resurrected an obsolete form of expression and said, "Will you have an eye-opener?" All the air was thick with sarcasms.

But there was one man who moved calm, untouched, un-affected, through it all. It was that heart of oak, the Chief Inspector. His brave eye never drooped, his serene confidence never wavered. He always said,—

"Let them rail on; he laughs best who laughs last."

My admiration for the man grew into a species of worship. I was at his side always. His office had become an unpleasant place to me, and now became daily more and more so. Yet if he could endure it I meant to do so also; at least, as long as I could. So I came regularly, and stayed,—the only outsider who seemed to be capable of it. Everybody wondered how I could; and often it seemed to me that I must desert, but at such times I looked into that calm and apparently uncon-scious face, and held my ground.

About three weeks after the elephant's disappearance I was about to say, one morning, that I should *have* to strike my colors and retire, when the great detective arrested the thought by proposing one more superb and masterly move.

This was to compromise with the robbers. The fertility of this man's invention exceeded anything I have ever seen, and I have had a wide intercourse with the world's finest minds. He said he was confident he could compromise for $100,000 and recover the elephant. I said I believed I could scrape the amount together, but what would become of the poor detec-tives who had worked so faithfully? He said,—

"In compromises they always get half."

This removed my only objection. So the inspector wrote two notes, in this form: —

DEAR MADAM, — Your husband can make a large sum of money (and be entirely protected from the law) by making an immediate appointment with me.

Chief BLUNT.

He sent one of these by his confidential messenger to the "reputed wife" of Brick Duffy, and the other to the reputed wife of Red McFadden.

Within the hour these offensive answers came: —

YE OWLD FOOL: brick McDuffys bin ded 2 yere.

BRIDGET MAHONEY.

CHIEF BAT, — Red McFadden is hung and in heving 18 month. Any Ass but a detective knose that.

MARY O'HOOLIGAN.

"I had long suspected these facts," said the inspector; "this testimony proves the unerring accuracy of my instinct."

The moment one resource failed him he was ready with another. He immediately wrote an advertisement for the morning papers, and I kept a copy of it: —

A. — xwblv. 242 N. Tjnd — fz328wmlg. Ozpo, — ; 2 m! ogw. Mum.

He said that if the thief was alive this would bring him to the usual rendezvous. He further explained that the usual rendezvous was a place where all business affairs between detectives and criminals were conducted. This meeting would take place at twelve the next night.

We could do nothing till then, and I lost no time in getting out of the office, and was grateful indeed for the privilege.

At 11 the next night I brought $100,000 in bank-notes and put them into the chief's hands, and shortly afterward he took his leave, with the brave old undimmed confidence in his eye. An almost intolerable hour dragged to a close; then I heard his welcome tread, and rose gasping and tottered to meet him. How his fine eyes flamed with triumph! He said, —

"We 've compromised! The jokers will sing a different tune to-morrow! Follow me!"

He took a lighted candle and strode down into the vast vaulted basement where sixty detectives always slept, and where a score were now playing cards to while the time. I followed close after him. He walked swiftly down to the dim remote end of the place, and just as I succumbed to the pangs of suffocation and was swooning away he stumbled and fell over the outlying members of a mighty object, and I heard him exclaim as he went down, —

"Our noble profession is vindicated. Here is your elephant!"

I was carried to the office above and restored with carbolic acid. The whole detective force swarmed in, and such another season of triumphant rejoicing ensued as I had never witnessed before. The reporters were called, baskets of champagne were opened, toasts were drunk, the handshakings and congratulations were continuous and enthusiastic. Naturally the chief was the hero of the hour, and his happiness was so complete and had been so patiently and worthily and bravely won that it made me happy to see it, though I stood there a homeless beggar, my priceless charge dead, and my position in my country's service lost to me through what would always seem my fatally careless execution of a great trust. Many an eloquent eye testified its deep admiration for the chief, and many a detective's voice murmured, "Look at him, — just the king of the profession, — only give him a clew, it's all he wants, and there ain't anything hid that he can't find." The dividing of the $50,000 made great pleasure; when it was finished the chief made a little speech while he put his share in his pocket, in which he said, "Enjoy it, boys, for you've earned it; and more than that you've earned for the detective profession undying fame."

A telegram arrived, which read: —

MONROE, MICH., 10 P. M.
First time I've struck a telegraph office in over three weeks. Have followed those footprints, horseback, through the woods, a thousand miles to here, and they get stronger and bigger and fresher every day. Don't worry—inside of another week I'll have the elephant. This is dead sure.

DARLEY, *Detective*.

The chief ordered three cheers for "Darley, one of the finest minds on the force," and then commanded that he be telegraphed to come home and receive his share of the reward.

So ended that marvellous episode of the stolen elephant. The newspapers were pleasant with praises once more, the next day, with one contemptible exception. This sheet said, "Great is the detective! He may be a little slow in finding a little thing like a mislaid elephant,—he may hunt him all day and sleep with his rotting carcass all night for three weeks, but he will find him at last—if he can get the man who mislaid him to show him the place!"

Poor Hassan was lost to me forever. The cannon-shots had wounded him fatally, he had crept to that unfriendly place in the fog, and there, surrounded by his enemies and in constant danger of detection, he had wasted away with hunger and suffering till death gave him peace.

The compromise cost me $100,000; my detective expenses were $42,000 more; I never applied for a place again under my government; I am a ruined man and a wanderer in the earth,—but my admiration for that man, whom I believe to be the greatest detective the world has ever produced, remains undimmed to this day, and will so remain unto the end.

1882

On the Decay of the Art of Lying

ESSAY, FOR DISCUSSION, READ AT A MEETING OF THE
HISTORICAL AND ANTIQUARIAN CLUB OF HARTFORD,
AND OFFERED FOR THE THIRTY-DOLLAR PRIZE. NOW
FIRST PUBLISHED.*

Observe, I do not mean to suggest that the *custom* of lying
has suffered any decay or interruption,—no, for the Lie, as a
Virtue, a Principle, is eternal; the Lie, as a recreation, a solace,
a refuge in time of need, the fourth Grace, the tenth Muse,
man's best and surest friend, is immortal, and cannot perish
from the earth while this Club remains. My complaint simply
concerns the decay of the *art* of lying. No high-minded man,
no man of right feeling, can contemplate the lumbering and
slovenly lying of the present day without grieving to see a
noble art so prostituted. In this veteran presence I naturally
enter upon this theme with diffidence; it is like an old maid
trying to teach nursery matters to the mothers in Israel. It
would not become me to criticise you, gentlemen, who are
nearly all my elders—and my superiors, in this thing—and
so, if I should here and there *seem* to do it, I trust it will in
most cases be more in a spirit of admiration than of fault-
finding; indeed if this finest of the fine arts had everywhere
received the attention, encouragement, and conscientious
practice and development which this Club has devoted to it, I
should not need to utter this lament, or shed a single tear. I
do not say this to flatter: I say it in a spirit of just and appreciative recognition. [It had been my intention, at this point,
to mention names and give illustrative specimens, but indications observable about me admonished me to beware of particulars and confine myself to generalities.]

No fact is more firmly established than that lying is a necessity of our circumstances,—the deduction that it is then a
Virtue goes without saying. No virtue can reach its highest
usefulness without careful and diligent cultivation,—therefore, it goes without saying, that this one ought to be taught

*Did not take the prize.

in the public schools—at the fireside—even in the news-papers. What chance has the ignorant, uncultivated liar against the educated expert? What chance have I against Mr. Per— against a lawyer? *Judicious* lying is what the world needs. I sometimes think it were even better and safer not to lie at all than to lie injudiciously. An awkward, unscientific lie is often as ineffectual as the truth.

Now let us see what the philosophers say. Note that vener-able proverb: Children and fools *always* speak the truth. The deduction is plain,—adults and wise persons *never* speak it. Parkman, the historian, says, "The principle of truth may it-self be carried into an absurdity." In another place in the same chapter he says, "The saying is old that truth should not be spoken at all times; and those whom a sick conscience worries into habitual violation of the maxim are imbeciles and nui-sances." It is strong language, but true. None of us could *live* with an habitual truth-teller; but thank goodness none of us has to. An habitual truth-teller is simply an impossible crea-ture; he does not exist; he never has existed. Of course there are people who *think* they never lie, but it is not so,—and this ignorance is one of the very things that shame our so-called civilization. Everybody lies—every day; every hour; awake; asleep; in his dreams; in his joy; in his mourning; if he keeps his tongue still, his hands, his feet, his eyes, his attitude, will convey deception—and purposely. Even in sermons— but that is a platitude.

In a far country where I once lived the ladies used to go around paying calls, under the humane and kindly pretence of wanting to see each other; and when they returned home, they would cry out with a glad voice, saying, "We made six-teen calls and found fourteen of them out,"—not meaning that they found out anything against the fourteen,—no, that was only a colloquial phrase to signify that they were not at home,—and their manner of saying it expressed their lively satisfaction in that fact. Now their pretence of wanting to see the fourteen—and the other two whom they had been less lucky with—was that commonest and mildest form of lying which is sufficiently described as a deflection from the truth. Is it justifiable? Most certainly. It is beautiful, it is noble; for its object is, *not* to reap profit, but to convey a pleasure to the

sixteen. The iron-souled truth-monger would plainly manifest, or even utter the fact that he did n't want to see those
people,—and he would be an ass, and inflict a totally unnecessary pain. And next, those ladies in that far country—but
never mind, they had a thousand pleasant ways of lying, that
grew out of gentle impulses, and were a credit to their intelligence and an honor to their hearts. Let the particulars go.

The men in that far country were liars, every one. Their
mere howdy-do was a lie, because *they* did n't care how you
did, except they were undertakers. To the ordinary inquirer
you lied in return; for you made no conscientious diagnosis
of your case, but answered at random, and usually missed it
considerably. You lied to the undertaker, and said your health
was failing—a wholly commendable lie, since it cost you
nothing and pleased the other man. If a stranger called and
interrupted you, you said with your hearty tongue, "I 'm glad
to see you," and said with your heartier soul, "I wish you
were with the cannibals and it was dinner time." When he
went, you said regretfully, "*Must* you go?" and followed it
with a "Call again;" but you did no harm, for you did not
deceive anybody nor inflict any hurt, whereas the truth would
have made you both unhappy.

I think that all this courteous lying is a sweet and loving
art, and should be cultivated. The highest perfection of politeness is only a beautiful edifice, built, from the base to the
dome, of graceful and gilded forms of charitable and unselfish
lying.

What I bemoan is the growing prevalence of the brutal
truth. Let us do what we can to eradicate it. An injurious
truth has no merit over an injurious lie. Neither should ever
be uttered. The man who speaks an injurious truth lest his
soul be not saved if he do otherwise, should reflect that that
sort of a soul is not strictly worth saving. The man who tells a
lie to help a poor devil out of trouble, is one of whom the
angels doubtless say, "Lo, here is an heroic soul who casts his
own welfare into jeopardy to succor his neighbor's; let us
exalt this magnanimous liar."

An injurious lie is an uncommendable thing; and so, also,
and in the same degree, is an injurious truth,—a fact which is
recognized by the law of libel.

Among other common lies, we have the *silent* lie,—the deception which one conveys by simply keeping still and concealing the truth. Many obstinate truth-mongers indulge in this dissipation, imagining that if they *speak* no lie, they lie not at all. In that far country where I once lived, there was a lovely spirit, a lady whose impulses were always high and pure, and whose character answered to them. One day I was there at dinner, and remarked, in a general way, that we are all liars. She was amazed, and said, "Not *all*?" It was before Pinafore's time, so I did not make the response which would naturally follow in our day, but frankly said, "Yes, *all*—we are all liars; there are no exceptions." She looked almost offended, and said, "Why, do you include *me*?" "Certainly," I said, "I think you even rank as an expert." She said, "Sh—sh! the children!" So the subject was changed in deference to the children's presence, and we went on talking about other things. But as soon as the young people were out of the way, the lady came warmly back to the matter and said, "I have made it the rule of my life to never tell a lie; and I have never departed from it in a single instance." I said, "I don't mean the least harm or disrespect, but really you have been lying like smoke ever since I've been sitting here. It has caused me a good deal of pain, because I am not used to it." She required of me an instance—just a single instance. So I said,—

"Well, here is the unfilled duplicate of the blank which the Oakland hospital people sent to you by the hand of the sick-nurse when she came here to nurse your little nephew through his dangerous illness. This blank asks all manner of questions as to the conduct of that sick-nurse: 'Did she ever sleep on her watch? Did she ever forget to give the medicine?' and so forth and so on. You are warned to be very careful and explicit in your answers, for the welfare of the service requires that the nurses be promptly fined or otherwise punished for derelictions. You told me you were perfectly delighted with that nurse—that she had a thousand perfections and only one fault: you found you never could depend on her wrapping Johnny up half sufficiently while he waited in a chilly chair for her to rearrange the warm bed. You filled up the duplicate of this paper, and sent it back to the hospital by the hand of the nurse. How did you answer this question,—'Was the nurse at

any time guilty of a negligence which was likely to result in
the patient's taking cold?' Come—everything is decided by a
bet here in California: ten dollars to ten cents you lied when
you answered that question." She said, "I did n't; *I left it
blank!*" "Just so—you have told a *silent* lie; you have left it to
be inferred that you had no fault to find in that matter." She
said, "Oh, was that a lie? And how *could* I mention her one
single fault, and she so good?—it would have been cruel." I
said, "One ought always to lie, when one can do good by it;
your impulse was right, but your judgment was crude; this
comes of unintelligent practice. Now observe the result of this
inexpert deflection of yours. You know Mr. Jones's Willie is
lying very low with scarlet fever; well, your recommendation
was so enthusiastic that that girl is there nursing him, and the
worn-out family have all been trustingly sound asleep for the
last fourteen hours, leaving their darling with full confidence
in those fatal hands, because you, like young George Washington, have a reputa— However, if you are not going to
have anything to do, I will come around to-morrow and we'll
attend the funeral together, for of course you'll naturally feel
a peculiar interest in Willie's case,—as personal a one, in fact,
as the undertaker."

But that was all lost. Before I was half-way through she was
in a carriage and making thirty miles an hour toward the
Jones mansion to save what was left of Willie and tell all she
knew about the deadly nurse. All of which was unnecessary,
as Willie was n't sick; I had been lying myself. But that same
day, all the same, she sent a line to the hospital which filled up
the neglected blank, and stated the *facts*, too, in the squarest
possible manner.

Now, you see, this lady's fault was *not* in lying, but only in
lying injudiciously. She should have told the truth, *there*, and
made it up to the nurse with a fraudulent compliment further
along in the paper. She could have said, "In one respect this
sick-nurse is perfection,—when she is on watch, she never
snores." Almost any little pleasant lie would have taken the
sting out of that troublesome but necessary expression of the
truth.

Lying is universal—we *all* do it; we all *must* do it. Therefore, the wise thing is for us diligently to train ourselves to lie

thoughtfully, judiciously; to lie with a good object, and not an evil one; to lie for others' advantage, and not our own; to lie healingly, charitably, humanely, not cruelly, hurtfully, maliciously; to lie gracefully and graciously, not awkwardly and clumsily; to lie firmly, frankly, squarely, with head erect, not haltingly, tortuously, with pusillanimous mien, as being ashamed of our high calling. Then shall we be rid of the rank and pestilent truth that is rotting the land; then shall we be great and good and beautiful, and worthy dwellers in a world where even benign Nature habitually lies, except when she promises execrable weather. Then— But I am but a new and feeble student in this gracious art; I cannot instruct *this* Club.

Joking aside, I think there is much need of wise examination into what sorts of lies are best and wholesomest to be indulged, seeing we *must* all lie and *do* all lie, and what sorts it may be best to avoid,—and this is a thing which I feel I can confidently put into the hands of this experienced Club,—a ripe body, who may be termed, in this regard, and without undue flattery, Old Masters.

1882

Concerning the American Language*

There was an Englishman in our compartment, and he complimented me on—on what? But you would never guess. He complimented me on my English. He said Americans in general did not speak the English language as correctly as I did. I said I was obliged to him for his compliment, since I knew he meant it for one, but that I was not fairly entitled to it, for I did n't speak English at all,—I only spoke American.

He laughed, and said it was a distinction without a difference. I said no, the difference was not prodigious, but still it was considerable. We fell into a friendly dispute over the matter. I put my case as well as I could, and said,—

"The languages were identical several generations ago, but our changed conditions and the spread of our people far to the south and far to the west have made many alterations in our pronunciation, and have introduced new words among us and changed the meanings of many old ones. English people talk through their noses; we do not. We say *know*, English people say *näo*; we say *cow*, the Briton says *käow*; we—"

"Oh, come! that is pure Yankee; everybody knows that."

"Yes, it is pure Yankee; that is true. One cannot hear it in America outside of the little corner called New England, which is Yankee land. The English themselves planted it there, two hundred and fifty years ago, and there it remains; it has never spread. But England talks through her nose yet; the Londoner and the backwoods New-Englander pronounce 'know' and 'cow' alike, and then the Briton unconsciously satirizes himself by making fun of the Yankee's pronunciation."

We argued this point at some length; nobody won; but no matter, the fact remains,—Englishmen say *näo* and *käow* for "know" and "cow," and that is what the rustic inhabitant of a very small section of America does.

"You conferred your *a* upon New England, too, and there it remains; it has not travelled out of the narrow limits of

*Being part of a chapter which was crowded out of "A Tramp Abroad."
—M.T.

those six little States in all these two hundred and fifty years. All England uses it, New England's small population—say four millions—use it, but we have forty-five millions who do not use it. You say 'glahs of wawtah,' so does New England; at least, New England says *glahs*. America at large flattens the *a*, and says 'glass of water.' These sounds are pleasanter than yours; you may think they are not right,—well, in English they are *not* right, but in 'American' they are. You say *flahsk*, and *bahsket*, and *jackahss*; we say 'flask,' 'basket,' 'jackass,'—sounding the *a* as it is in 'tallow,' 'fallow,' and so on. Up to as late as 1847 Mr. Webster's Dictionary had the impudence to still pronounce 'basket' *bahsket*, when he knew that outside of his little New England all America shortened the *a* and paid no attention to his English broadening of it. However, it called itself an English Dictionary, so it was proper enough that it should stick to English forms, perhaps. It still calls itself an English Dictionary to-day, but it has quietly ceased to pronounce 'basket' as if it were spelt *bahsket*. In the American language the *h* is respected; the *h* is not dropped or added improperly."

"The same is the case in England,—I mean among the educated classes, of course."

"Yes, that is true; but a nation's language is a very large matter. It is not simply a manner of speech obtaining among the educated handful; the manner obtaining among the vast uneducated multitude must be considered also. Your uneducated masses speak English, you will not deny that; our uneducated masses speak American,—it won't be fair for you to deny that, for you can see, yourself, that when your stable-boy says, 'It is n't the 'unting that 'urts the 'orse, but the 'ammer, 'ammer, 'ammer on the 'ard 'ighway,' and our stable-boy makes the same remark without suffocating a single *h*, these two people are manifestly talking two different languages. But if the signs are to be trusted, even your educated classes used to drop the *h*. They say *humble*, now, and *heroic*, and *historic*, etc., but I judge that they used to drop those *h*'s because your writers still keep up the fashion of putting *an* before those words, instead of *a*. This is what Mr. Darwin might call a 'rudimentary' sign that that *an* was justifiable once, and useful,—when your educated classes used to say

'*umble*, and '*eroic*, and '*istorical*. Correct writers of the American language do not put *an* before those words."

The English gentleman had something to say upon this
matter, but never mind what he said,—I'm not arguing his
case. I have him at a disadvantage, now. I proceeded:—

"In England you encourage an orator by exclaiming
'H'yaah! h'yaah!' We pronounce it *heer* in some sections,
'h'*yer*' in others, and so on; but our whites do not say 'h'yaah,'
pronouncing the *a*'s like the *a* in *ah*. I have heard English
ladies say 'don't you'—making two separate and distinct
words of it; your Mr. Bernand has satirized it. But we always
say 'dontchu.' This is much better. Your ladies say, 'Oh, it's
*o*ful nice!' Ours say, 'Oh, it's *aw*ful nice!' We say, '*Four* hundred,' you say '*For*'—as in the word *or*. Your clergymen speak
of 'the Lawd,' ours of 'the Lord'; yours speak of 'the gawds of
the heathen,' ours of 'the gods of the heathen.' When you are
exhausted, you say you are 'knocked up.' We don't. When you
say you will do a thing 'directly,' you mean 'immediately'; in
the American language—generally speaking—the word signifies 'after a little.' When you say 'clever,' you mean 'capable';
with us the word used to mean 'accommodating,' but I don't
know what it means now. Your word 'stout' means 'fleshy';
our word 'stout' usually means 'strong.' Your words 'gentleman' and 'lady' have a very restricted meaning; with us they
include the bar-maid, butcher, burglar, harlot, and horse-
thief. You say, 'I have n't *got* any stockings on,' 'I have n't *got*
any memory,' 'I have n't *got* any money in my purse'; we usually say, 'I have n't any stockings on,' 'I have n't any memory,'
'I have n't any money in my purse.' You say 'out of window';
we always put in a *the*. If one asks 'How old is that man?' the
Briton answers, 'He will be about forty;' in the American language, we should say, 'He *is* about forty.' However, I won't
tire you, sir; but if I wanted to, I could pile up differences
here until I not only convinced you that English and American are separate languages, but that when I speak my native
tongue in its utmost purity an Englishman can't understand
me at all."

"I don't wish to flatter you, but it is about all I can do to
understand you *now*."

That was a very pretty compliment, and it put us on the

pleasantest terms directly,—I use the word in the English sense.

[*Later*—1882. Æsthetes in many of our schools are now beginning to teach the pupils to broaden the *a*, and to say "don't you," in the elegant foreign way.]

Woman — God Bless Her

Seventy-seventh Annual Dinner, New England Society of New York

The toast includes the sex, universally: it is to Woman, comprehensively, wheresoever she may be found. Let us consider her ways. First comes the matter of dress. This is a most important consideration, in a subject of this nature, and must be disposed of before we can intelligently proceed to examine the profounder depths of the theme. For text, let us take the dress of two antipodal types—the savage woman of Central Africa, and the cultivated daughter of our high modern civilization. Among the Fans, a great Negro tribe, a woman, when dressed for home, or to go to market, or go out calling, does not wear anything at all but just her complexion. That is all; that is her entire outfit. It is the lightest costume in the world, but is made of the darkest material. It has often been mistaken for mourning. It is the trimmest, and neatest, and gracefulest costume that is now in fashion; it wears well, is fast colors, doesn't show dirt; you don't have to send it downtown to wash, and have some of it come back scorched with the flat-iron, and some of it with the buttons ironed off, and some of it petrified with starch, and some of it chewed by the calf, and some of it rotted with acids, and some of it exchanged for other customers' things that haven't any virtue but holiness, and ten-twelfths of the pieces overcharged for, and the rest of the dozen "mislaid." And it always fits; it is the perfection of a fit. And it is the handiest dress in the whole realm of fashion. It is always ready, always "done up." When you call on a Fan lady and send up your card, the hired girl never says, "Please take a seat, madam is dressing—she will be down in three-quarters of an hour." No, madam is always dressed, always ready to receive; and before you can get the doormat before your eyes, she is in your midst. Then again, the Fan ladies don't go to church to see what each other has got on; and they don't go back home and describe it and slander it.

Such is the dark child of savagery, as to everyday toilette; and thus, curiously enough, she finds a point of contact with the fair daughter of civilization and high fashion—who often has "nothing to wear"; and thus these widely separated types of the sex meet upon common ground. Yes, such is the Fan woman, as she appears in her simple, unostentatious, every-day toilette. But on state occasions she is more dressy. At a banquet she wears bracelets; at a lecture she wears earrings and a belt; at a ball she wears stockings—and with the true feminine fondness for display, she wears them on her arms; at a funeral she wears a jacket of tar and ashes; at a wedding the bride who can afford it puts on pantaloons. Thus the dark child of savagery and the fair daughter of civilization meet once more upon common ground; and these two touches of nature make their whole world kin.

Now we will consider the dress of our other type. A large part of the daughter of civilization is her dress—as it should be. Some civilized women would lose half their charm without dress; and some would lose all of it. The daughter of modern civilization, dressed at her utmost best, is a marvel of exquisite and beautiful art, and expense. All the lands, all the climes, and all the arts are laid under tribute to furnish her forth. Her linen is from Belfast, her robe is from Paris, her lace is from Venice, or Spain, or France; her feathers are from the remote regions of southern Africa, her furs from the re-moter home of the iceberg and the aurora; her fan from Ja-pan, her diamonds from Brazil, her bracelets from California, her pearls from Ceylon, her cameos from Rome; she has gems and trinkets from buried Pompeii; and others that graced comely Egyptian forms that have been dust and ashes, now, for forty centuries; her watch is from Geneva, her card case is from China, her hair is from—from—I don't know where her hair is from; I never could find out. That is, her other hair—her public hair, her Sunday hair; I don't mean the hair she goes to bed with. Why, you ought to know the hair I mean; it's that thing which she calls a switch, and which re-sembles a switch as much as it resembles a brickbat, or a shot-gun, or any other thing which you correct people with. It's that thing which she twists, and then coils round and round her head, beehive fashion, and then tucks the end in under the hive and harpoons it with a hairpin. And that reminds me of a trifle: any time you want to, you can glance around the carpet of a Pullman car and go and pick up a hairpin; but not to save your life can you get any woman in that car to acknowledge that hairpin. Now isn't that strange? But it's true. The woman who has never swerved from cast iron veracity and fidelity in her whole life, will, when confronted with this crucial test, deny her hairpin. She will deny that hairpin before a hundred witnesses. I have stupidly got into more trouble, and more hot water trying to hunt up the owner of a hairpin in a Pullman car than by any other indiscretion of my life.

Well, you see what the daughter of civilization is, when she is dressed; and you have seen what the daughter of savagery is when she isn't. Such is Woman, as to costume. I come, now, to consider her in her higher and nobler aspects—as mother, wife, widow, grass widow, mother-in-law, hired girl, telephone operator, telephone helloer, queen, book agent, wet nurse, stepmother, boss, professional fat woman, professional double-headed woman, professional beauty, and so forth and so on.

We will simply discuss these few—let the rest of the sex tarry in Jericho till we come again. First in the list, of right, and first in our gratitude, comes a woman who—why, dear me, I've been talking three-quarters of an hour! I beg a thousand pardons. But you see, yourselves, that I had a large contract. I have accomplished something, anyway: I have introduced my subject; and if I had till next Forefathers' Day, I am satisfied that I could discuss it as adequately and appreciatively as so gracious and noble a theme deserves. But as the matter stands, now, let us finish as we began—and say, without jesting, but with all sincerity, "Woman—God Bless Her!"

December 22, 1882

The McWilliamses and the Burglar Alarm

The conversation drifted smoothly and pleasantly along from weather to crops, from crops to literature, from literature to scandal, from scandal to religion; then took a random jump, and landed on the subject of burglar alarms. And now for the first time Mr. McWilliams showed feeling. Whenever I perceive this sign on this man's dial, I comprehend it, and lapse into silence, and give him opportunity to unload his heart. Said he, with but ill-controlled emotion:

"I do not go one single cent on burglar alarms, Mr. Twain—not a single cent—and I will tell you why. When we were finishing our house, we found we had a little cash left over, on account of the plumber not knowing it. I was for enlightening the heathen with it, for I was always unaccountably down on the heathen somehow; but Mrs. McWilliams said no, let's have a burglar alarm. I agreed to this compromise. I will explain that whenever I want a thing, and Mrs. McWilliams wants another thing, and we decide upon the thing that Mrs. McWilliams wants—as we always do—she calls that a compromise. Very well: the man came up from New York and put in the alarm, and charged three hundred and twenty-five dollars for it, and said we could sleep without uneasiness now. So we did for a while—say a month. Then one night we smelled smoke, and I was advised to get up and see what the matter was. I lit a candle, and started toward the stairs, and met a burglar coming out of a room with a basket of tinware, which he had mistaken for solid silver in the dark. He was smoking a pipe. I said, 'My friend, we do not allow smoking in this room.' He said he was a stranger, and could not be expected to know the rules of the house; said he had been in many houses just as good as this one, and it had never been objected to before. He added that as far as his experience went, such rules had never been considered to apply to burglars, anyway.

"I said: 'Smoke along, then, if it is the custom, though I think that the conceding of a privilege to a burglar which is denied to a bishop is a conspicuous sign of the looseness of the times. But waiving all that, what business have you to be entering this house in this furtive and clandestine way, without ringing the burglar alarm?'

"He looked confused and ashamed, and said, with embarrassment: 'I beg a thousand pardons. I did not know you had a burglar alarm, else I would have rung it. I beg you will not mention it where my parents may hear of it, for they are old and feeble, and such a seemingly wanton breach of the hallowed conventionalities of our Christian civilization might all too rudely sunder the frail bridge which hangs darkling between the pale and evanescent present and the solemn great deeps of the eternities. May I trouble you for a match?'

"I said: 'Your sentiments do you honor, but if you will allow me to say it, metaphor is not your best hold. Spare your thigh; this kind light only on the box, and seldom there, in fact, if my experience may be trusted. But to return to business; how did you get in here?'

" 'Through a second-story window.'

"It was even so. I redeemed the tinware at pawnbroker's rates, less cost of advertising, bade the burglar good-night, closed the window after him, and retired to headquarters to report. Next morning we sent for the burglar-alarm man, and he came up and explained that the reason the alarm did not 'go off' was that no part of the house but the first floor was attached to the alarm. This was simply idiotic: one might as well have no armor at all in battle as to have it only on his legs. The expert now put the whole second story on the alarm, charged three hundred dollars for it, and went his way. By-and-by, one night, I found a burglar in the third story, about to start down a ladder with a lot of miscellaneous property. My first impulse was to crack his head with a billiard cue; but my second was to refrain from this attention, because he was between me and the cue rack. The second impulse was plainly the soundest, so I refrained, and proceeded to compromise. I redeemed the property at former rates, after deducting ten per cent. for use of ladder, it being my ladder, and next day we sent down for the expert once more, and had the third story attached to the alarm, for three hundred dollars.

"By this time the 'annunciator' had grown to formidable dimensions. It had forty-seven tags on it, marked with the names of the various rooms and chimneys, and it occupied the space of an ordinary wardrobe. The gong was the size of a wash-bowl, and was placed above the head of our bed. There was a wire from the house to the coachman's quarters in the stable, and a noble gong alongside his pillow.

"We should have been comfortable now but for one defect. Every morning at five the cook opened the kitchen door, in the way of business, and rip went that gong! The first time this happened I thought the last day was come sure. I didn't think it *in* bed—no, but out of it—for the first effect of that frightful gong is to hurl you across the house, and slam you against the wall, and then curl you up, and squirm you like a spider on a stove lid, till somebody shuts that kitchen door. In solid fact, there is no clamor that is even remotely comparable to the dire clamor which that gong makes. Well, this catastrophe happened every morning regularly at five o'clock, and lost us three hours' sleep; for, mind you, when that thing wakes you, it doesn't merely wake you in spots; it wakes you all over, conscience and all, and you are good for eighteen hours of wide-awakedness subsequently—eighteen hours of the very most inconceivable wide-awakedness that you ever experienced in your life. A stranger died on our hands one time, and we vacated and left him in our room overnight. Did that stranger wait for the general judgment? *No*, sir; he got up at five the next morning in the most prompt and unostentatious way. I knew he would; I knew it mighty well. He collected his life-insurance, and lived happy ever after, for there was plenty of proof as to the perfect squareness of his death.

"Well, we were gradually fading away toward a better land, on account of our daily loss of sleep; so we finally had the expert up again, and he ran a wire to the outside of our door, and placed a switch there, whereby Thomas, the butler, could take off and put on the alarm; but Thomas always made one little mistake—he switched the alarm off at night when he went to bed, and switched it on again at daybreak in the morning, just in time for the cook to open the kitchen door, and enable that gong to slam us across the house, sometimes breaking a window with one or the other of us. At the end of a week we recognized that this switch business was a delusion and a snare. We also discovered that a band of burglars had been lodging in the house the whole time—not exactly to steal, for there wasn't much left now, but to hide from the police, for they were hot pressed, and they shrewdly judged that the detectives would never think of a tribe of burglars taking sanctuary in a house notoriously protected by the most imposing and elaborate burglar alarm in America.

"Sent down for the expert again, and this time he struck a most dazzling idea—he fixed the thing so that opening the kitchen door would take off the alarm. It was a noble idea, and he charged accordingly. But you already foresee the result. I switched on the alarm every night at bed-time, no longer trusting to Thomas's frail memory; and as soon as the lights were out the burglars walked in at the kitchen door, thus taking the alarm off without waiting for the cook to do it in the morning. You see how aggravatingly we were situated. For months we couldn't have any company. Not a spare bed in the house; all occupied by burglars.

"Finally, I got up a cure of my own. The expert answered the call, and ran another under-ground wire to the stable, and established a switch there, so that the coachman could put on and take off the alarm. That worked first-rate, and a season of peace ensued, during which we got to inviting company once more and enjoying life.

"But by-and-by the irrepressible alarm invented a new kink. One winter's night we were flung out of bed by the sudden music of that awful gong, and when we hobbled to the annunciator, turned up the gas, and saw the word 'Nursery' exposed, Mrs. McWilliams fainted dead away, and I came precious near doing the same thing myself. I seized my shot-gun, and stood timing the coachman whilst that appalling buzzing went on. I knew that his gong had flung him out too, and that he would be along with his gun as soon as he could jump into his clothes. When I judged that the time was ripe, I crept to the room next the nursery, glanced through the window, and saw the dim outline of the coachman in the yard below, standing at a present-arms and waiting for a chance. Then I hopped into the nursery and fired, and in the same instant the coachman fired at the red flash of my gun. Both of us were successful: I crippled a nurse, and he shot off all my back hair. We turned up the gas, and telephoned for a surgeon. There was not a sign of a burglar, and no window had been raised. One glass was absent, but that was where the coachman's charge had come through. Here was a fine mystery—a burglar alarm 'going off' at midnight of its own accord, and not a burglar in the neighborhood!

"The expert answered the usual call, and explained that it was a 'false alarm.' Said it was easily fixed. So he overhauled the nursery window, charged a remunerative figure for it, and departed.

"What we suffered from false alarms for the next three years no stylographic pen can describe. During the first few months I always flew with my gun to the room indicated, and the coachman always sallied forth with his battery to support me. But there was never anything to shoot at—windows all tight and secure. We always sent down for the expert next day, and he fixed those particular windows so they would keep quiet a week or so, and always remembered to send us a bill about like this:

Wire	$ 2 15
Nipple	75
Two hours' labor	1 50
Wax	47
Tape	34
Screws	15
Recharging battery	98
Three hours' labor	2 25
String	02
Lard	66
Pond's Extract	1 25
Springs, 4 @ 50	2 00
Railroad fares	7 25
	$19 77

"At length a perfectly natural thing came about—after we had answered three or four hundred false alarms—to wit, we stopped answering them. Yes, I simply rose up calmly, when slammed across the house by the alarm, calmly inspected the annunciator, took note of the room indicated, and then calmly disconnected that room from the alarm, and went back to bed as if nothing had happened. Moreover, I left that room off permanently, and did not send for the expert. Well, it goes without saying that in the course of time *all* the rooms were taken off, and the entire machine was out of service.

"It was at this unprotected time that the heaviest calamity of all happened. The burglars walked in one night and carried off the burglar alarm! yes, sir, every hide and hair of it; ripped it out, tooth and toe-nail; springs, bells, gongs, battery, and all; they took a hundred and fifty miles of copper wire; they just cleaned her out, bag and baggage, and never left us a vestige of her to swear at—swear by, I mean.

"We had a time of it to get her back; but we accomplished it finally, for money. Then the alarm firm said that what we needed now was to have her put in right—with their new patent springs in the windows to make false alarms impossible, and their new patent clock attachment to take off and put on the alarm morning and night without human assistance. That seemed a good scheme. They promised to have the whole thing finished in ten days. They began work, and we left for the summer. They worked a couple of days; then *they* left for the summer. After which the burglars moved in, and began *their* summer vacation. When we returned in the fall, the house was as empty as a beer closet in premises where painters have been at work. We refurnished, and then sent down to hurry up the expert. He came up and finished the job, and said: 'Now this clock is set to put on the alarm every night at 10, and take it off every morning at 5.45. All you've got to do is to wind her up every week, and then leave her alone—she will take care of the alarm herself.'

"After that we had a most tranquil season during three months. The bill was prodigious, of course, and I had said I would not pay it until the new machinery had proved itself to be flawless. The time stipulated was three months. So I paid the bill, and the very next day the alarm went to buzzing like ten thousand bee swarms at ten o'clock in the morning. I turned the hands around twelve hours, according to instructions, and this took off the alarm; but there was another hitch at night, and I had to set her ahead twelve hours once more to get her to put the alarm on again. That sort of nonsense went on a week or two; then the expert came up and put in a new clock. He came up every three months during the next three years, and put in a new clock. But it was always a failure. His clocks all had the same perverse defect: they *would* put the alarm on in the daytime, and they would *not* put it on at night; and if you forced it on yourself, they would take it off again the minute your back was turned.

"Now there is the history of that burglar alarm—everything just as it happened; nothing extenuated, and naught set down in malice. Yes, sir; and when I had slept nine years with burglars, and maintained an expensive burglar alarm the whole time, for their protection, not mine, and at my sole cost—for not a d——d cent could I ever get *them* to contribute—I just said to Mrs. McWilliams that I had had enough of that kind of pie; so with her full consent I took the whole thing out and traded it off for a dog, and shot the dog. I don't know what *you* think about it, Mr. Twain; but *I* think those things are made solely in the interest of the burglars. Yes, sir, a burglar alarm combines in its person all that is objectionable about a fire, a riot, and a harem, and at the same time has none of the compensating advantages, of one sort or another, that customarily belong with that combination. Good-by; I get off here."

So saying, Mr. McWilliams gathered up his satchel and umbrella, and bowed himself out of the train.

December 1882

On Adam

Royal Literary and Scientific Society Dinner, Ottawa

I never feel wholly at home and equal to the occasion except when I am to respond for the royal family or the President of the United States. But I am full of serenity, courage and confidence then, because I know by experience that I can drink standing and "in silence" just as long as anybody wants me to. Sometimes I have gone on responding to those toasts with mute and diligent enthusiasm until I have become an embarrassment, and people have requested me to sit down and rest myself. But responding by speech is a sore trial to me. The list of toasts being always the same, one is always so apt to forget and say something that has already been said at some other banquet some time or other. For instance, you take the toast to—well, take any toast in the regulation lot, and you won't get far in your speech before you notice that everything you are saying is old; not only old, but stale; and not only stale, but rancid. At any rate, that is my experience. There are gifted men who have the faculty of saying an old thing in a new and happy way—they rub the old Aladdin lamp and bring forth the smoke and thunder, the giants and genii, the pomp and pageantry of all the wide and secret realms of enchantment—and these men are the saviors of the banquet; but for them it must have gone silent, as Carlyle would say, generations ago, and ceased from among the world's occasions and industries. But I cannot borrow their trick; I do not know the mystery of how to rub the old lamp the right way.

And so it has seemed to me that for the behoof of my sort and kind, the toast list ought to be reconstructed. We ought to have some of the old themes knocked out of it and a new one or two inserted in their places. There are plenty of new subjects, if we would only look around. And plenty of old ones, too, that have not been touched. There is Adam, for instance. Who ever talks about Adam at a banquet? All sorts of recent and ephemeral celebrities are held up and glorified on such occasions, but who ever says a good word for Adam? Yet why is he neglected, why is he ignored in this offensive

way—can you tell me that? What has he done, that we let
banquet after banquet go on, and never give him a lift? Considering what we and the whole world owe him, he ought to
be in the list—yes, and he ought to be away up high in the
list, too. He ought to take precedence of the Press; yes, and
the Army and Navy; and Literature; and the Day we Celebrate; and pretty much everything else. In the United States
he ought to be at the very top—he ought to take precedence
of the President; and even in the loyalest monarchy he ought
at least to come right after the royal family. And be "drunk in
silence and standing," too. It is his right; and for one, I propose to stick here and *drink* him in silence and standing till I
can't tell a ministering angel from a tax collector. This neglect
has been going on too long. You always place Woman at the
bottom of the toast list; it is but simple justice to place Adam
at the top of it—for if it had not been for the help of these
two, where would you and your banquets be?—answer me
that. You must excuse me for losing my temper and carrying
on in this way; and in truth I would not do it if it were
almost anybody but Adam; but I am of a narrow and clannish
disposition, and I never can see a relative of mine misused
without going into a passion. It is no trick for people with
plenty of celebrated kin to keep cool when their folk are misused; but Adam is the only solitary celebrity in our family,
and the man that misuses him has got to walk over my dead
body—or go around, that is all there is to that. That is the
way I feel about Adam. Years ago when I went around trying
to collect subscriptions to build a monument to him, there
wasn't a man that would give a cent; and generally they lost
their temper because I interrupted their business; and they
drove me away, and said they didn't care Adam for Adam—
and in ninety-nine cases out of a hundred they got the emphasis on the wrong end of the word. Such is the influence of
passion on a man's pronunciation. I tried Congress. Congress
wouldn't build the monument. They wouldn't sell me the
Washington monument, they wouldn't lend it to me temporarily while I could look around for another. I am negotiating
for that Bastile yonder by the public square in Montreal, but
they say they want to finish it first. Of course that ends the
project, because there couldn't be any use of a monument

after the man was forgotten. It is a pity, because I thought Adam might have pleasant associations with that building —he must have seen it in his time. But he shall have a monument yet, even if it be only a grateful place in the list of toasts; for to him we owe the two things which are most precious— life, and death. Life, which the young, the hopeful, the undefeated hold above all wealth and all honors; and death, the refuge, the solace, the best and kindliest and most prized friend and benefactor of the erring, the forsaken, the old, and weary, and broken of heart, whose burdens be heavy upon them, and who would lie down and be at rest.

I would like to see the toast list reconstructed, for it seems to me a needed reform; and as a beginning in this direction, if I can meet with a second, I beg to nominate Adam. I am not actuated by family considerations. It is a thing which I would do for any other member of our family, or anybody else's, if I could honestly feel that he deserved it. But I do not. If I seem to be always trying to shove Adam into prominence, I can say sincerely that it is solely because of my admiration of him as a man who was a good citizen at a time when it was difficult to be a good citizen; a good husband at a time when he was not married; a good father at a time when he had to guess his way, having never been young himself; and would have been a good son if he had had the chance. He could have been governor if he had wanted to; he could have been postmaster general, speaker of the House, he could have been anything he chose, if he had been willing to put himself up and stand a canvass. Yet he lived and died a private citizen, without a handle to his name, and he comes down to us as plain simple Adam, and nothing more—a man who could have elected himself Major General Adam or anything else as easy as rolling off a log. I stand up for him on account of his sterling private virtues, as a man and a citizen—as an inventor—inventor of life, and death, and sin, and the fashions—and not because he simply happens to be kin to me.

May 23, 1883

Why a Statue of Liberty
When We Have Adam!

Mark Twain was asked to contribute to the album of artists' sketches and autograph letters, to be raffled for at the Bartholdi Pedestal Fund Art Loan Exhibition, and this is his response, which accompanied his contribution:

You know my weakness for Adam, and you know how I have struggled to get him a monument and failed. Now, it seems to me, here is my chance. What do we care for a statue of liberty when we've got the thing itself in its wildest sublimity? What you want of a monument is to keep you in mind of something you haven't got—something you've lost. Very well; we haven't lost liberty; we've lost Adam.

Another thing: What has liberty done for us? Nothing in particular that I know of. What have we done for her? Everything. We've given her a home, and a good home, too. And if she knows anything, she knows it's the first time she ever struck that novelty. She knows that when we took her in she had been a mere tramp for 6,000 years, Biblical measure. Yes, and we not only ended her troubles and made things soft for her permanently, but we made her respectable—and that she hadn't ever been before. And now, after we've poured out these Atlantics of benefits upon this aged outcast, lo! and behold you, we are asked to come forward and set up a monument to her! Go to. Let her set up a monument to us if she wants to do the clean thing.

But suppose your statue represented her old, bent, clothed in rags, downcast, shame-faced, with the insults and humiliation of 6,000 years, imploring a crust and an hour's rest for God's sake at our back door?—come, now you're shouting! That's the aspect of her which we need to be reminded of, lest we forget it—not this proposed one, where she's hearty and well-fed, and holds up her head and flourishes her hospitable schooner of flame, and appears to be inviting all the rest of the tramps to come over. O, go to—this is the very insolence of prosperity.

But, on the other hand—look at Adam. What have we done for Adam? Nothing. What has Adam done for us? Everything. He gave us life, he gave us death, he gave us heaven, he gave us hell. These are inestimable privileges—and remember, not one of them should we have had without Adam. Well, then, he ought to have a monument—for Evolution is steadily and surely abolishing him; and we must get up a monument, and be quick about it, or our children's children will grow up ignorant that there ever was an Adam. With trifling alterations, this present statue will answer very well for Adam. You can turn that blanket into an ulster without any trouble; part the hair on one side, or conceal the sex of his head with a fire helmet, and at once he's a man; put a harp and a halo and a palm branch in the left hand to symbolize a part of what Adam did for us, and leave the fire-basket just where it is, to symbolize the rest. My friend, the father of life and death and taxes, has been neglected long enough. Shall this infamy be allowed to go on or shall it stop right here?

Is it but a question of finance? Behold the inclosed (paid bank) checks. Use them as freely as they are freely contributed. Heaven knows I would there were a ton of them; I would send them all to you, for my heart is in this sublime work!

S. L. C.

December 4, 1883

Turncoats

Political Meeting, Hartford

It seems to me that there are things about this campaign which almost amount to inconsistencies. This language may sound violent; if it does, it is traitor to my mood. The Mugwumps are contemptuously called turncoats by the Republican speakers and journals. The charge is true: we have turned our coats; we have no denials to make, as to that. But does a man become of a necessity base because he turns his coat? And are there no Republican turncoats except the Mugwumps? Please look at the facts in the case candidly and fairly before sending us to political perdition without company.

Why are we called turncoats? Because we have changed our opinion. Changed it about what? About the greatness and righteousness of the principles of the Republican party? No, that is not changed. We believe in those principles yet; no one doubts this. What, then, is it that we have changed our opinions about? Why, about Mr. Blaine. That is the whole change. There is no other. Decidedly, we have done that, and do by no means wish to deny it. But when did we change it? Yesterday?—last week?—last summer? No—we changed it years and years ago, as far back as 1876. The vast bulk of the Republican party changed its opinion of him at the same time and in the same way. Will anybody be hardy enough to deny this? Was there more than a handful of really respectable and respectworthy Republicans on the north Atlantic seaboard who did not change their opinion of Mr. Blaine at that time? Was not the Republican atmosphere—both private and journalistic—so charged with this fact that none could fail to perceive it?

Very well. Was this multitude called turncoats at that time? Of course not. That would have been an absurdity. Was any of this multitude held in contempt at that time, and derided and execrated, for turning his Blaine coat? No one thought of such a thing. Now then, we who are called the Mugwumps, turned our coats at that time, and they have remained so turned to this day. If it is shameful to turn one's coat once, what measure of scorn can adequately describe the man who

turns it twice? If to turn one's coat once makes one a dude, a
Pharisee, a Mugwump and fool, where shall you find language rancid enough to describe a double turncoat? If to turn
your coat at a time when no one can impeach either the sincerity of the act or the cleanliness of your motives in doing it,
is held to be a pathetic spectacle, what sort of spectacle is it
when such a coat-turner turns his coat again, and this time
under quite suggestively different circumstances?—that is to
say, *after a nomination.* Do these double turncoats exist? And
who are they? They are the bulk of the Republican party; and
it is hardly venturing too far to say that neither you nor I can
put his finger upon a respectable member of that great multitude who can put a denial of it instantly into words and without blush or stammer. Here in Hartford they do not deny;
they confess that they are double turncoats. They say they are
convinced that when they formerly changed their opinion
about Mr. Blaine they were wrong, and so they have changed
back again. Which would seem to be an admission that to
change one's opinion and turn one's coat is not necessarily a
base thing to do, after all. Yet they call my tribe the customary
hard names in their next campaign speeches just the same,
without seeming to see any inconsistency or impropriety in it.
Well, it is all a muddle to me. I cannot make out how it is or
why it is that a single turncoat is a reptile and a double turncoat a bird of Paradise.

I easily perceive that the Republican party has deserted us,
and deserted itself; but I am not able to see that *we* have
deserted anything or anybody. As for me, I have not deserted
the Republican code of principles, for I propose to vote its
ticket, with the presidential exception; and I have not deserted Mr. Blaine, for as regards him I got my free papers
before he bought the property.

Personally I know that two of the best known of the Hartford campaigners for Blaine did six months ago hold as uncomplimentary opinions about him as I did then and as I do
today. I am told, upon what I conceive to be good authority,
that the two or three other Connecticut campaigners of
prominence of that ilk held opinions concerning him of that
same uncomplimentary breed up to the day of the nomination. These gentlemen have turned their coats; and they now

admire Blaine; and not calmly, temperately, but with a sort of ferocious rapture. In a speech the other night, one of them spoke of the author of the Mulligan letters—those strange Vassar-like exhibitions of eagerness, gushingness, timidity, secretiveness, frankness, naiveté, unsagacity, and almost incredible and impossible indiscretion—as the "first statesman of the age." Another of them spoke of "the three great statesmen of the age, Gladstone, Bismarck and Blaine." Doubtless this profound remark was received with applause. But suppose the gentleman had had the daring to read some of those letters first, appending the names of Bismarck and Gladstone to them; do not you candidly believe that the applause would have been missing, and that in its place there would have been a smile which you could have heard to Springfield? For no one has ever seen a Republican mass meeting that was devoid of the perception of the ludicrous.

October 1884

Mock Oration on the Dead Partisan

Mr. Chairman: That is a noble and beautiful ancient sentiment which admonishes us to speak well of the dead. Therefore let us try to do this for our late friend who is mentioned in the text. How full of life, and strength, and confidence and pride he was, but a few short months ago; and alas, how dead he is today! We that are gathered at these obsequies, we that are here to bury this dust, and sing the parting hymn, and say the comforting word to the widow and the orphan now left destitute and sorrowing by him, their support and stay in the post office, the consulship, the navy yard and the Indian reservation—we knew him, right well and familiarly we knew him; and so it is meet that we, and not strangers, should take upon ourselves these last offices, lest his reputation suffer through explanations of him which might not explain him happily, and justifications of him which might not justify him conclusively. First, it is right and well that we censure him, in those few minor details wherein some slight censure may seem to be demanded; to the end that when we come to speak his praises, the good he did may shine with all the more intolerable a brightness by the contrast.

To begin, then, with the twilight side of his character: he was a slave; not a turbulent and troublesome, but a meek and docile, cringing and fawning, dirt-eating and dirt-preferring slave; and Party was his lord and master. He had no mind of his own, no will of his own, no opinion of his own; body and soul he was the property and chattel of that master, to be bought and sold, bartered, traded, *given* away, at his nod and beck—branded, mutilated, boiled in oil, if need were. And the desire of his heart was to make of a nation of freemen a nation of slaves like to himself; to bring to pass a time when it might be said that "All are for the Party, and none are for the State"; and the labors of his diligent hand and brain did finally compass his desire. For he fooled the people with plausible new readings of familiar old principles, and beguiled them to the degradation of their manhood and the destruction of their liberties. He taught them that the only true freedom of thought is to think as the party thinks; that the only true freedom of speech is to speak as the party dictates; that the only righteous toleration is toleration of what the party approves; that patriotism, duty, citizenship, devotion to country, loyalty to the flag, are all summed up in loyalty to the party. Save the party, uphold the party, make the party victorious, though all things else go to ruin and the grave.

In these few little things, he who lies here cold in death was faulty. Say we no more concerning them, but over them draw the veil of a charitable oblivion; for the good which he did far overpasses this little evil. With grateful hearts we may unite in praises and thanksgivings to him for one majestic fact of his life: that in his zeal for the cause, he finally overdid it. The precious result was that a change came; and that change remains, and will endure; and on its banner is written—

"Not all are for the Party—*now* some are for the State."

November 1884

The Character of Man

Concerning Man—he is too large a subject to be treated as a whole; so I will merely discuss a detail or two of him at this time. I desire to contemplate him from this point of view—this premiss: that he was not made for any useful purpose, for the reason that he hasn't served any; that he was most likely not even made *intentionally*; and that his working himself up out of the oyster bed to his present position was probably matter of surprise and regret to the Creator. . . . For his history, in all climes, all ages and all circumstances, furnishes oceans and continents of proof that of all the creatures that were made he is the most detestable. Of the entire brood he is the only one—the solitary one—that possesses malice. That is the basest of all instincts, passions, vices—the most hateful. That one thing puts him below the rats, the grubs, the trichinæ. He is the only creature that inflicts pain for sport, knowing it to *be* pain. But if the cat knows she is inflicting pain when she plays with the frightened mouse, then we must make an exception here; we must grant that in one detail man is the moral peer of the cat. *All* creatures kill—there seems to be no exception; but of the whole list, man is the only one that kills for fun; he is the only one that kills in malice, the only one that kills for revenge. Also—in all the list he is the only creature that has a nasty mind.

Shall he be extolled for his noble qualities, for his gentleness, his sweetness, his amiability, his lovingness, his courage, his devotion, his patience, his fortitude, his prudence, the various charms and graces of his spirit? The other animals share *all* these with him, yet are free from the blacknesses and rottennesses of his character.

. . . . There are certain sweet-smelling sugar-coated lies current in the world which all politic men have apparently tacitly conspired together to support and perpetuate. One of these is, that there is such a thing in the world as independence: independence of thought, independence of opinion, independence of action. Another is, that the world loves to *see* independence—admires it, applauds it. Another is, that there is such a thing in the world as toleration—in religion, in politics, and such matters; and with it trains that already mentioned auxiliary lie that toleration is admired, and applauded. Out of these trunk-lies spring many branch ones: to-wit, the lie that not all men are slaves; the lie that men are glad when other men succeed; glad when they prosper; glad to see them reach lofty heights; sorry to see them fall again. And yet other branch-lies: to-wit, that there is heroism in man; that he is not mainly made up of malice and treachery; that he is sometimes not a coward; that there is something about him that ought to be perpetuated—in heaven, or hell, or somewhere. And these other branch-lies, to-wit: that conscience, man's moral medicine chest, is not only created by the Creator, but is put into man ready-charged with the right and only true and authentic correctives of conduct—and the duplicate chest, with the self-same correctives, unchanged, unmodified, distributed to all nations and all epochs. And yet one other branch-lie, to-wit, that I am I, and you are you; that we are units, individuals, and have natures of our own, instead of being the tail-end of a tape-worm eternity of ancestors extending in linked procession back—and back—and back—to our source in the monkeys, with this so-called individuality of ours a decayed and rancid mush of inherited instincts and teachings derived, atom by atom, stench by stench, from the entire line of that sorry column, and not so much new and original matter in it as you could balance on a needle point and examine under a microscope. This makes well nigh fantastic the suggestion that there can be such a thing as a personal, original and responsible nature in a man, separable from that in him which is not original, and findable in such quantity as to enable the observer to say, This is a man, not a procession.

. . . . Consider that first mentioned lie: that there is such a thing in the world as independence; that it exists in individuals, that it exists in bodies of men. Surely if anything *is* proven, by whole oceans and continents of evidence, it is that the quality of independence was almost wholly left out of the human race. The scattering exceptions to the rule only emphasize it, light it up, make it glare. The whole population of New England meekly took their turns, for years, in standing up in the railway trains, without so much as a complaint

above their breath, till at last these uncounted millions were
able to produce exactly one single independent man, who
stood to his rights and made the railroad give him a seat.
Statistics and the law of probabilities warrant the assumption
that it will take New England forty years to breed his fellow.
There is a law, with a penalty attached, forbidding trains to
occupy the Asylum street crossing more than five minutes at a
time. For years people and carriages used to wait there
nightly as much as twenty minutes on a stretch while New
England trains monopolized that crossing. I used to hear men
use vigorous language about that insolent wrong—but they
waited, just the same.

We are discreet sheep; we wait to see how the drove is
going, and then go with the drove. We have two opinions:
one private, which we are afraid to express; and another
one—the one we use—which we force ourselves to wear to
please Mrs. Grundy, until habit makes us comfortable in it,
and the custom of defending it presently makes us love it,
adore it, and forget how pitifully we came by it. Look at it in
politics. Look at the candidates whom we loathe, one year,
and are afraid to vote against the next; whom we cover with
unimaginable filth, one year, and fall down on the public platform and worship, the next—and keep on doing it until the
habitual shutting of our eyes to last year's evidences brings us
presently to a sincere and stupid belief in this year's.* Look at
the tyranny of party—at what is called party allegiance, party
loyalty—a snare invented by designing men for selfish
purposes—and which turns voters into chattels, slaves, rabbits; and all the while, their masters, and they themselves are
shouting rubbish about liberty, independence, freedom of
opinion, freedom of speech, honestly unconscious of the
fantastic contradiction; and forgetting or ignoring that their
fathers and the churches shouted the same blasphemies a
generation earlier when they were closing their doors against
the hunted slave, beating his handful of humane defenders
with Bible-texts and billies, and pocketing the insults and licking the shoes of his Southern master.

If we would learn what the human race really *is*, at bottom,

*Jan. 11/06. It is long ago, but it plainly means Blaine. M.T.

we need only observe it in election times. A Hartford clergy-man met me in the street, and spoke of a new nominee—denounced the nomination, in strong, earnest words—words that were refreshing for their independence, their manliness.*
He said, "I ought to be proud, perhaps, for this nominee is a relative of mine; on the contrary I am humiliated and dis-gusted; for I know him intimately—familiarly—and I know that he is an unscrupulous scoundrel, and always has been." You should have seen this clergyman preside at a political meeting forty days later; and urge, and plead, and gush—and you should have heard him paint the character of this same nominee. You would have supposed he was describing the Cid, and Great-heart, and Sir Galahad, and Bayard the Spot-less all rolled into one. Was he sincere? Yes—by that time; and therein lies the pathos of it all, the hopelessness of it all. It shows at what trivial cost of effort a man can teach himself a lie, and learn to believe it, when he perceives, by the general drift, that that is the popular thing to do. Does he believe his lie *yet*? Oh, probably not; he has no further use for it. It was but a passing incident; he spared to it the moment that was its due, then hastened back to the serious business of his life.

And what a paltry poor lie is that one which teaches that independence of action and opinion is prized in men, ad-mired, honored, rewarded. When a man leaves a political party, he is treated as if the party owned him—as if he were its bond slave, as most party men plainly are—and had stolen himself, gone off with what was not his own. And he is traduced, derided, despised, held up to public obloquy and loathing. His character is remorselessly assassinated; no means, however vile, are spared to injure his property and his business.

The preacher who casts a vote for conscience' sake, runs the risk of starving. And is rightly served; for he has been teach-ing a falsity—that men respect and honor independence of thought and action.

Mr. Beecher may be charged with a *crime*, and his whole following will rise as one man, and stand by him to the bitter

---

*Jan. 11, '06. I can't remember his name. It began with K, I think. He was one of the American revisers of the New Testament, and was nearly as great a scholar as Hammond Trumbull.

end; but who so poor to be his friend when he is charged with casting a vote for conscience' sake? Take the editor so charged—take—take anybody.

All the talk about tolerance, in anything or anywhere, is plainly a gentle lie. It does not exist. It is in no man's heart; but it unconsciously and by moss-grown inherited habit, drivels and slabbers from all men's lips. Intolerance is everything for one's self, and nothing for the other person. The mainspring of man's nature is just that—selfishness.

Let us skip the other lies, for brevity's sake. To consider them would prove nothing, except that man is what he is—loving, toward his own, lovable, to his own,—his family, his friends—and otherwise the buzzing, busy, trivial, enemy of his race—who tarries his little day, does his little dirt, commends himself to God, and then goes out into the darkness, to return no more, and send no messages back—selfish even in death.

1885

On Speech-Making Reform

Tile Club Dinner for Laurence Hutton, New York

Like many another well-intentioned man, I have made too
many speeches. And like other transgressors of this sort, I
have from time to time reformed; binding myself, by oath, on
New Year's Days, to never make another speech. I found that
a new oath holds pretty well; but that when it is become old,
and frayed out, and damaged by a dozen annual retyings of its
remains, it ceases to be serviceable; any little strain will snap
it. So, last New Year's Day I strengthened my reform with a
money penalty; and made that penalty so heavy that it has
enabled me to remain pure from that day to this. Although I
am falling once more now, I think I can behave myself from
this out, because the penalty is going to be doubled ten days
hence. I see before me and about me the familiar faces of
many poor sorrowing fellow sufferers, victims of the passion
for speech-making—poor sad-eyed brothers in affliction,
who, fast in the grip of this fell, degrading, demoralizing vice,
have grown weak with struggling, as the years drifted by, and
at last have all but given up hope. To them I say, in this last
final obituary of mine, don't give up—don't do it; there is
still hope for you. I beseech you, swear one more oath, and
back it up with cash. I do not say this to all, of course; for
there are some among you who are past reform; some who,
being long accustomed to success, and to the delicious intoxication of the applause which follows it, are too wedded to
their dissipation to be capable now or hereafter of abandon-
ing it. They have thoroughly learned the deep art of speech-
making, and they suffer no longer from those misgivings and
embarrassments and apprehension which are really the only
things which ever make a speech-maker want to reform. They
have learned their art by long observation and slowly compacted experience; so now they know, what they did not
know at first, that the best and most telling speech is not the
actual impromptu one, but the counterfeit of it; they know
that that speech is most worth listening to which has been
carefully prepared in private and tried on a plaster cast, or an
empty chair, or any other appreciative object that will keep

quiet, until the speaker has got his matter and his delivery
limbered up so that they will seem impromptu to an audience. The expert knows that. A touch of indifferent grammar
flung in here and there, apparently at random, has a good
effect—often restores the confidence of a suspicious audience.
He arranges these errors in private; for a really random error
wouldn't do any good; it would be sure to fall in the wrong
place. He also leaves blanks here and there—leaves them
where genuine impromptu remarks can be dropped in, of a
sort that will add to the natural aspect of the speech without
breaking its line of march. At the banquet, he listens to the
other speakers, invents happy turns upon remarks of theirs,
and sticks these happy turns into his blanks for impromptu
use by and by when he shall be called up. When this expert
rises to his feet, he looks around over the house with the air
of a man who has just been strongly impressed by something.
The uninitiated cannot interpret his aspect, but the initiated
can.

They know what is coming. When the noise of the clapping
and stamping has subsided, this veteran says: "Aware that the
hour is late, Mr. Chairman, it was my intention to abide by a
purpose which I framed in the beginning of the evening—to
simply rise and return my duty and thanks, in case I should be
called upon, and then make way for men more able, and who
have come with something to say. But, sir, I was so struck by
General Smith's remark concerning the proneness of evil to
fly upward, that"—etc., etc., etc.; and before you know it he
has slidden smoothly along on his compliment to the general,
and out of it and into his set speech, and you can't tell, to save
you, where it was nor when it was that he made the connection. And that man will soar along, in the most beautiful way,
on the wings of a practiced memory; heaving in a little decayed grammar here, and a little wise tautology there, and a
little neatly counterfeited embarrassment yonder, and a little
finely acted stumbling and stammering for a word—rejecting
this word and that, and finally getting the right one, and
fetching it out with ripping effect, and with the glad look of a
man who has got out of a bad hobble entirely by accident,
and wouldn't take a hundred dollars for that accident; and
every now and then he will sprinkle you in one of those

happy turns on something that has previously been said; and at last, with supreme art, he will catch himself, when in the very act of sitting down, and lean over the table and fire a parting rocket, in the way of an afterthought, which makes everybody stretch his mouth as it goes up, and dims the very stars in heaven when it explodes. And yet that man has been practicing that afterthought and that attitude for about a week.

Well, you can't reform that kind of a man. It's a case of Eli joined to his idols—let him alone. But there is one sort that can be reformed. That is the genuinely impromptu speaker. I mean the man who "didn't expect to be called upon, and isn't prepared"; and yet goes waddling and warbling along, just as if he thought it wasn't any harm to commit a crime so long as it wasn't premeditated. Now and then he says, "but I must not detain you longer"; every little while he says, "Just one word more and I am done"—but at these times he always happens to think of two or three more unnecessary things and so he stops to say them. Now that man has no way of finding out how long his windmill is going. He likes to hear it creak; and so he goes on creaking, and listening to it, and enjoying it, never thinking of the flight of time; and when he comes to sit down at last, and look under his hopper, he is the most surprised person in the house to see what a little bit of a grist he has ground, and how unconscionably long he has been grinding it. As a rule, he finds that he hasn't said anything—a discovery which the unprepared man ought usually to make, and does usually make—and has the added grief of making it at second hand, too.

This is a man who can be reformed. And so can his near relative, who now rises out of my reconstructed past—the man who provisions himself with a single prepared bite, of a sentence or two, and trusts to luck to catch quails and manna as he goes along. This person frequently gets left. You can easily tell when he has finished his prepared bit and begun on the impromptu part. Often the prepared portion has been built during the banquet; it may consist of ten sentences, but it oftener consists of two—oftenest of all, it is but a single sentence; and it has seemed so happy and pat and bright and good that the creator of it, the person that laid it, has been sitting there cackling privately over it and admiring it and petting it and shining it up, and imagining how fine it is going to "go," when, of course, he ought to have been laying another one, and still another one; and maybe a dozen or basketful if it's a fruitful day; yes, and he is thinking that when he comes to hurl that egg at the house there is going to be such an electric explosion of applause that the inspiration of it will fill him instantly with ideas and clothe the ideas in brilliant language, and that an impromptu speech will result which will be infinitely finer than anything he could have deliberately prepared. But there are two damaging things which he is leaving out of the calculation: one is, the historical fact that a man is never called up as soon as he thinks he is going to be called up, and that every speech that is injected into the proceedings ahead of him gives his fires an added chance to cool; and the other thing which he is forgetting is that he can't sit there and keep saying that fine sentence of his over and over to himself, for three-quarters of an hour without by and by getting a trifle tired of it and losing somewhat of confidence in it.

When at last his chance comes and he touches off his pet sentence, it makes him sick to see how shamefacedly and apologetically he has done it; and how compassionate the applause is; and how sorry everybody feels; and then he bitterly thinks what a lie it is to call this a free country where none but the unworthy and the undeserving may swear. And at this point, naked and blind and empty, he wallows off into his *real* impromptu speech; stammers out three or four incredibly flat things, then collapses into his seat, murmuring, "I wish I was in"—he doesn't say where, because he doesn't. The stranger at his left says, "Your opening was very good"; stranger at his right says, "I liked your opening"; man opposite says, "Opening very good indeed—very good"; two or three other people mumble something about his opening. People always feel obliged to pour some healing thing on a crippled man, that way. They mean it for oil; they think it *is* oil; but the sufferer recognizes it for aquafortis.

March 31, 1885

The Private History of a Campaign that Failed

You have heard from a great many people who did something in the war; is it not fair and right that you listen a little moment to one who started out to do something in it, but didn't? Thousands entered the war, got just a taste of it, and then stepped out again, permanently. These, by their very numbers, are respectable, and are therefore entitled to a sort of voice,—not a loud one, but a modest one; not a boastful one, but an apologetic one. They ought not to be allowed much space among better people—people who did something—I grant that; but they ought at least to be allowed to state why they didn't do anything, and also to explain the process by which they didn't do anything. Surely this kind of light must have a sort of value.

Out West there was a good deal of confusion in men's minds during the first months of the great trouble—a good deal of unsettledness, of leaning first this way, then that, then the other way. It was hard for us to get our bearings. I call to mind an instance of this. I was piloting on the Mississippi when the news came that South Carolina had gone out of the Union on the 20th of December, 1860. My pilot-mate was a New Yorker. He was strong for the Union; so was I. But he would not listen to me with any patience; my loyalty was smirched, to his eye, because my father had owned slaves. I said, in palliation of this dark fact, that I had heard my father say, some years before he died, that slavery was a great wrong, and that he would free the solitary negro he then owned if he could think it right to give away the property of the family when he was so straitened in means. My mate retorted that a mere impulse was nothing—anybody could pretend to a good impulse; and went on decrying my Unionism and libeling my ancestry. A month later the secession atmosphere had considerably thickened on the Lower Mississippi, and I became a rebel; so did he. We were together in New Orleans, the 26th of January, when Louisiana went out of the Union. He did his full share of the rebel shouting, but was bitterly opposed to letting me do mine. He said that I came of bad stock—of a father who had been willing to set slaves free. In the following summer he was piloting a Federal gunboat and shouting for the Union again, and I was in the Confederate army. I held his note for some borrowed money. He was one of the most upright men I ever knew; but he repudiated that note without hesitation, because I was a rebel, and the son of a man who owned slaves.

In that summer—of 1861—the first wash of the wave of war broke upon the shores of Missouri. Our State was invaded by the Union forces. They took possession of St. Louis, Jefferson Barracks, and some other points. The Governor, Claib Jackson, issued his proclamation calling out fifty thousand militia to repel the invader.

I was visiting in the small town where my boyhood had been spent—Hannibal, Marion County. Several of us got together in a secret place by night and formed ourselves into a military company. One Tom Lyman, a young fellow of a good deal of spirit but of no military experience, was made captain; I was made second lieutenant. We had no first lieutenant; I do not know why; it was long ago. There were

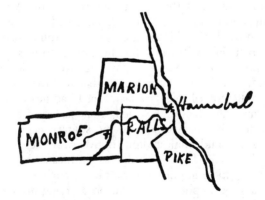

The Seat of War.

fifteen of us. By the advice of an innocent connected with the organization, we called ourselves the Marion Rangers. I do not remember that any one found fault with the name. I did not; I thought it sounded quite well. The young fellow who proposed this title was perhaps a fair sample of the kind of stuff we were made of. He was young, ignorant, good-natured, well-meaning, trivial, full of romance, and given to reading chivalric novels and singing forlorn love-ditties. He had some pathetic little nickel-plated aristocratic instincts, and detested his name, which was Dunlap; detested it, partly because it was nearly as common in that region as Smith, but mainly because it had a plebeian sound to his ear. So he tried to ennoble it by writing it in this way: *d'Unlap*. That contented his eye, but left his ear unsatisfied, for people gave the new name the same old pronunciation—emphasis on the front end of it. He then did the bravest thing that can be imagined,—a thing to make one shiver when one remembers how the world is given to resenting shams and affectations; he began to write his name so: *d'Un Lap*. And he waited patiently through the long storm of mud that was flung at this work of art, and he had his reward at last; for he lived to see that name accepted, and the emphasis put where he wanted it, by people who had known him all his life, and to whom the tribe of Dunlaps had been as familiar as the rain and the sunshine for forty years. So sure of victory at last is the courage that can wait. He said he had found, by consulting some ancient French chronicles, that the name was rightly and originally written d'Un Lap; and said that if it were translated into English it would mean Peterson: *Lap*, Latin or Greek, he said, for stone or rock, same as the French *pierre*, that is to say, Peter; *d'*, of or from; *un*, a or one; hence, d'Un Lap, of or from a stone or a Peter; that is to say, one who is the son of a stone, the son of a Peter—Peterson. Our militia company were not learned, and the explanation confused them; so they called him Peterson Dunlap. He proved useful to us in his way; he named our camps for us, and he generally struck a name that was "no slouch," as the boys said.

That is one sample of us. Another was Ed Stevens, son of the town jeweler,—trim-built, handsome, graceful, neat as a cat; bright, educated, but given over entirely to fun. There was nothing serious in life to him. As far as he was concerned, this military expedition of ours was simply a holiday. I should say that about half of us looked upon it in the same way; not consciously, perhaps, but unconsciously. We did not think; we were not capable of it. As for myself, I was full of unreasoning joy to be done with turning out of bed at midnight and four in the morning, for a while; grateful to have a change, new scenes, new occupations, a new interest. In my thoughts that was as far as I went; I did not go into the details; as a rule one doesn't at twenty-four.

Another sample was Smith, the blacksmith's apprentice. This vast donkey had some pluck, of a slow and sluggish nature, but a soft heart; at one time he would knock a horse down for some impropriety, and at another he would get homesick and cry. However, he had one ultimate credit to his account which some of us hadn't: he stuck to the war, and was killed in battle at last.

Jo Bowers, another sample, was a huge, good-natured, flax-headed lubber; lazy, sentimental, full of harmless brag, a grumbler by nature; an experienced, industrious, ambitious, and often quite picturesque liar, and yet not a successful one, for he had had no intelligent training, but was allowed to come up just any way. This life was serious enough to him, and seldom satisfactory. But he was a good fellow anyway, and the boys all liked him. He was made orderly sergeant; Stevens was made corporal.

These samples will answer—and they are quite fair ones. Well, this herd of cattle started for the war. What could you expect of them? They did as well as they knew how, but really what was justly to be expected of them? Nothing, I should say. That is what they did.

We waited for a dark night, for caution and secrecy were necessary; then, toward midnight, we stole in couples and from various directions to the Griffith place, beyond the town; from that point we set out together on foot. Hannibal lies at the extreme southeastern corner of Marion County, on the Mississippi River; our objective point was the hamlet of New London, ten miles away, in Ralls County.

The first hour was all fun, all idle nonsense and laughter. But that could not be kept up. The steady trudging came to be like work; the play had somehow oozed out of it; the still-ness of the woods and the somberness of the night began to throw a depressing influence over the spirits of the boys, and presently the talking died out and each person shut himself up in his own thoughts. During the last half of the second hour nobody said a word.

Now we approached a log farm-house where, according to report, there was a guard of five Union soldiers. Lyman called a halt; and there, in the deep gloom of the overhanging branches, he began to whisper a plan of assault upon that house, which made the gloom more depressing than it was before. It was a crucial moment; we realized, with a cold sud-denness, that here was no jest—we were standing face to face with actual war. We were equal to the occasion. In our re-sponse there was no hesitation, no indecision: we said that if Lyman wanted to meddle with those soldiers, he could go ahead and do it; but if he waited for us to follow him, he would wait a long time.

Lyman urged, pleaded, tried to shame us, but it had no effect. Our course was plain, our minds were made up: we would flank the farm-house—go out around. And that is what we did.

We struck into the woods and entered upon a rough time, stumbling over roots, getting tangled in vines, and torn by briers. At last we reached an open place in a safe region, and sat down, blown and hot, to cool off and nurse our scratches and bruises. Lyman was annoyed, but the rest of us were cheerful; we had flanked the farm-house, we had made our first military movement, and it was a success; we had nothing to fret about, we were feeling just the other way. Horse-play and laughing began again; the expedition was become a holi-day frolic once more.

Then we had two more hours of dull trudging and ultimate silence and depression; then, about dawn, we straggled into New London, soiled, heel-blistered, fagged with our little march, and all of us except Stevens in a sour and raspy humor and privately down on the war. We stacked our shabby old shot-guns in Colonel Ralls's barn, and then went in a body and breakfasted with that veteran of the Mexican war. After-wards he took us to a distant meadow, and there in the shade

of a tree we listened to an old-fashioned speech from him, full
of gunpowder and glory, full of that adjective-piling, mixed
metaphor, and windy declamation which was regarded as eloquence in that ancient time and that remote region; and then
he swore us on the Bible to be faithful to the State of Missouri and drive all invaders from her soil, no matter whence
they might come or under what flag they might march. This
mixed us considerably, and we could not make out just what
service we were embarked in; but Colonel Ralls, the practiced
politician and phrase-juggler, was not similarly in doubt; he
knew quite clearly that he had invested us in the cause of the
Southern Confederacy. He closed the solemnities by belting
around me the sword which his neighbor, Colonel Brown,
had worn at Buena Vista and Molino del Rey; and he accompanied this act with another impressive blast.

Then we formed in line of battle and marched four miles to
a shady and pleasant piece of woods on the border of the
far-reaching expanses of a flowery prairie. It was an enchanting region for war—our kind of war.

We pierced the forest about half a mile, and took up a
strong position, with some low, rocky, and wooded hills behind us, and a purling, limpid creek in front. Straightway half
the command were in swimming, and the other half fishing.
The ass with the French name gave this position a romantic
title, but it was too long, so the boys shortened and simplified
it to Camp Ralls.

We occupied an old maple-sugar camp, whose half-rotted
troughs were still propped against the trees. A long corn-crib
served for sleeping quarters for the battalion. On our left, half
a mile away, was Mason's farm and house; and he was a
friend to the cause. Shortly after noon the farmers began to
arrive from several directions, with mules and horses for our
use, and these they lent us for as long as the war might last,
which they judged would be about three months. The animals
were of all sizes, all colors, and all breeds. They were mainly
young and frisky, and nobody in the command could stay on
them long at a time; for we were town boys, and ignorant of
horsemanship. The creature that fell to my share was a very
small mule, and yet so quick and active that it could throw me
without difficulty; and it did this whenever I got on it. Then

it would bray—stretching its neck out, laying its ears back, and spreading its jaws till you could see down to its works. It was a disagreeable animal, in every way. If I took it by the bridle and tried to lead it off the grounds, it would sit down and brace back, and no one could budge it. However, I was not entirely destitute of military resources, and I did presently manage to spoil this game; for I had seen many a steamboat aground in my time, and knew a trick or two which even a grounded mule would be obliged to respect. There was a well by the corn-crib; so I substituted thirty fathom of rope for the bridle, and fetched him home with the windlass.

I will anticipate here sufficiently to say that we did learn to ride, after some days' practice, but never well. We could not learn to like our animals; they were not choice ones, and most of them had annoying peculiarities of one kind or another. Stevens's horse would carry him, when he was not noticing, under the huge excrescences which form on the trunks of oak-trees, and wipe him out of the saddle; in this way Stevens got several bad hurts. Sergeant Bowers's horse was very large and tall, with slim, long legs, and looked like a railroad bridge. His size enabled him to reach all about, and as far as he wanted to, with his head; so he was always biting Bowers's legs. On the march, in the sun, Bowers slept a good deal; and as soon as the horse recognized that he was asleep he would reach around and bite him on the leg. His legs were black and blue with bites. This was the only thing that could ever make him swear, but this always did; whenever the horse bit him he always swore, and of course Stevens, who laughed at every-thing, laughed at this, and would even get into such convul-sions over it as to lose his balance and fall off his horse; and then Bowers, already irritated by the pain of the horse-bite, would resent the laughter with hard language, and there would be a quarrel; so that horse made no end of trouble and bad blood in the command.

However, I will get back to where I was—our first after-noon in the sugar-camp. The sugar-troughs came very handy as horse-troughs, and we had plenty of corn to fill them with. I ordered Sergeant Bowers to feed my mule; but he said that if I reckoned he went to war to be dry-nurse to a mule, it wouldn't take me very long to find out my mistake. I believed that this was insubordination, but I was full of uncertainties about everything military, and so I let the thing pass, and went and ordered Smith, the blacksmith's apprentice, to feed the mule; but he merely gave me a large, cold, sarcastic grin, such as an ostensibly seven-year-old horse gives you when you lift his lip and find he is fourteen, and turned his back on me. I then went to the captain, and asked if it was not right and proper and military for me to have an orderly. He said it was, but as there was only one orderly in the corps, it was but right that he himself should have Bowers on his staff. Bowers said he wouldn't serve on anybody's staff; and if anybody thought he could make him, let him try it. So, of course, the thing had to be dropped; there was no other way.

Next, nobody would cook; it was considered a degradation; so we had no dinner. We lazied the rest of the pleasant afternoon away, some dozing under the trees, some smoking cob-pipes and talking sweethearts and war, some playing games. By late supper-time all hands were famished; and to meet the difficulty all hands turned to, on an equal footing, and gathered wood, built fires, and cooked the meal. Afterward everything was smooth for a while; then trouble broke out between the corporal and the sergeant, each claiming to rank the other. Nobody knew which was the higher office; so Lyman had to settle the matter by making the rank of both officers equal. The commander of an ignorant crew like that has many troubles and vexations which probably do not occur in the regular army at all. However, with the song-singing and yarn-spinning around the camp-fire, everything presently became serene again; and by and by we raked the corn down level in one end of the crib, and all went to bed on it, tying a horse to the door, so that he would neigh if any one tried to get in.*

We had some horsemanship drill every forenoon; then,

*It was always my impression that that was what the horse was there for, and I know that it was also the impression of at least one other of the command, for we talked about it at the time, and admired the military ingenuity of the device; but when I was out West three years ago I was told by Mr. A. G. Fuqua, a member of our company, that the horse was his, that the leaving him tied at the door was a matter of mere forgetfulness, and that to attribute it to intelligent invention was to give him quite too much credit. In support of his position, he called my attention to the suggestive fact that the artifice was not employed again. I had not thought of that before.

afternoons, we rode off here and there in squads a few miles, and visited the farmers' girls, and had a youthful good time, and got an honest good dinner or supper, and then home again to camp, happy and content.

For a time, life was idly delicious, it was perfect; there was nothing to mar it. Then came some farmers with an alarm one day. They said it was rumored that the enemy were advancing in our direction, from over Hyde's prairie. The result was a sharp stir among us, and general consternation. It was a rude awakening from our pleasant trance. The rumor was but a rumor—nothing definite about it; so, in the confusion, we did not know which way to retreat. Lyman was for not retreating at all, in these uncertain circumstances; but he found that if he tried to maintain that attitude he would fare badly, for the command were in no humor to put up with insubordination. So he yielded the point and called a council of war—to consist of himself and the three other officers; but the privates made such a fuss about being left out, that we had to allow them to be present. I mean we had to allow them to remain, for they were already present, and doing the most of the talking too. The question was, which way to retreat; but all were so flurried that nobody seemed to have even a guess to offer. Except Lyman. He explained in a few calm words, that inasmuch as the enemy were approaching from over Hyde's prairie, our course was simple: all we had to do was not to retreat *toward* him; any other direction would answer our needs perfectly. Everybody saw in a moment how true this was, and how wise; so Lyman got a great many compliments. It was now decided that we should fall back on Mason's farm.

It was after dark by this time, and as we could not know how soon the enemy might arrive, it did not seem best to try to take the horses and things with us; so we only took the guns and ammunition, and started at once. The route was very rough and hilly and rocky, and presently the night grew very black and rain began to fall; so we had a troublesome time of it, struggling and stumbling along in the dark; and soon some person slipped and fell, and then the next person behind stumbled over him and fell, and so did the rest, one after the other; and then Bowers came with the keg of

powder in his arms, whilst the command were all mixed together, arms and legs, on the muddy slope; and so he fell, of
course, with the keg, and this started the whole detachment
down the hill in a body, and they landed in the brook at the
bottom in a pile, and each that was undermost pulling the
hair and scratching and biting those that were on top of him;
and those that were being scratched and bitten scratching and
biting the rest in their turn, and all saying they would die
before they would ever go to war again if they ever got out of
this brook this time, and the invader might rot for all they
cared, and the country along with him—and all such talk as
that, which was dismal to hear and take part in, in such
smothered, low voices, and such a grisly dark place and so
wet, and the enemy may be coming any moment.

The keg of powder was lost, and the guns too; so the
growling and complaining continued straight along whilst the
brigade pawed around the pasty hillside and slopped around
in the brook hunting for these things; consequently we lost
considerable time at this; and then we heard a sound, and
held our breath and listened, and it seemed to be the enemy
coming, though it could have been a cow, for it had a cough
like a cow; but we did not wait, but left a couple of guns
behind and struck out for Mason's again as briskly as we
could scramble along in the dark. But we got lost presently
among the rugged little ravines, and wasted a deal of time
finding the way again, so it was after nine when we reached
Mason's stile at last; and then before we could open our
mouths to give the countersign, several dogs came bounding
over the fence, with great riot and noise, and each of them
took a soldier by the slack of his trousers and began to back
away with him. We could not shoot the dogs without endan-
gering the persons they were attached to; so we had to look
on, helpless, at what was perhaps the most mortifying spectacle of the civil war. There was light enough, and to spare, for
the Masons had now run out on the porch with candles in
their hands. The old man and his son came and undid the
dogs without difficulty, all but Bowers's; but they couldn't
undo his dog, they didn't know his combination; he was of
the bull kind, and seemed to be set with a Yale time-lock; but
they got him loose at last with some scalding water, of which

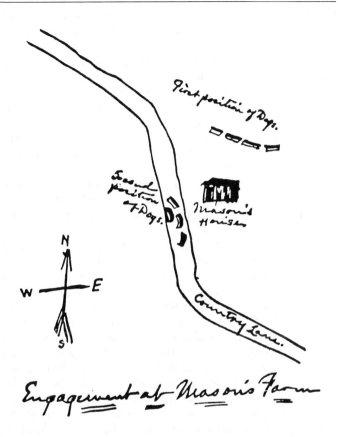

First position of Dogs.

Second position of Dogs.

Mason's House.

N
W — E
S

Country Lane.

Engagement at Mason's Farm

Bowers got his share and returned thanks. Peterson Dunlap afterwards made up a fine name for this engagement, and also for the night march which preceded it, but both have long ago faded out of my memory.

We now went into the house, and they began to ask us a world of questions, whereby it presently came out that we did not know anything concerning who or what we were running from; so the old gentleman made himself very frank, and said we were a curious breed of soldiers, and guessed we could be depended on to end up the war in time, because no government could stand the expense of the shoe-leather we should cost it trying to follow us around. "Marion *Rangers*! good

name, b'gosh!" said he. And wanted to know why we hadn't
had a picket-guard at the place where the road entered the
prairie, and why we hadn't sent out a scouting party to spy
out the enemy and bring us an account of his strength, and so
on, before jumping up and stampeding out of a strong position upon a mere vague rumor—and so on and so forth, till
he made us all feel shabbier than the dogs had done, not half
so enthusiastically welcome. So we went to bed shamed and
low-spirited; except Stevens. Soon Stevens began to devise
a garment for Bowers which could be made to automati-
cally display his battle-scars to the grateful, or conceal them
from the envious, according to his occasions; but Bowers
was in no humor for this, so there was a fight, and when it
was over Stevens had some battle-scars of his own to think
about.

Then we got a little sleep. But after all we had gone
through, our activities were not over for the night; for about
two o'clock in the morning we heard a shout of warning from
down the lane, accompanied by a chorus from all the dogs,
and in a moment everybody was up and flying around to find
out what the alarm was about. The alarmist was a horseman
who gave notice that a detachment of Union soldiers was on
its way from Hannibal with orders to capture and hang any
bands like ours which it could find, and said we had no time
to lose. Farmer Mason was in a flurry this time, himself. He
hurried us out of the house with all haste, and sent one of his
negroes with us to show us where to hide ourselves and our
tell-tale guns among the ravines half a mile away. It was raining heavily.

We struck down the lane, then across some rocky pasture-
land which offered good advantages for stumbling; consequently we were down in the mud most of the time, and
every time a man went down he blackguarded the war, and
the people that started it, and everybody connected with it,
and gave himself the master dose of all for being so foolish as
to go into it. At last we reached the wooded mouth of a
ravine, and there we huddled ourselves under the streaming
trees, and sent the negro back home. It was a dismal and
heart-breaking time. We were like to be drowned with the
rain, deafened with the howling wind and the booming thun-

der, and blinded by the lightning. It was indeed a wild night.
The drenching we were getting was misery enough, but a
deeper misery still was the reflection that the halter might end
us before we were a day older. A death of this shameful sort
had not occurred to us as being among the possibilities of
war. It took the romance all out of the campaign, and turned
our dreams of glory into a repulsive nightmare. As for doubt-
ing that so barbarous an order had been given, not one of us
did that.

The long night wore itself out at last, and then the negro
came to us with the news that the alarm had manifestly been a
false one, and that breakfast would soon be ready. Straightway we were light-hearted again, and the world was bright,
and life as full of hope and promise as ever—for we were
young then. How long ago that was! Twenty-four years.

The mongrel child of philology named the night's refuge
Camp Devastation, and no soul objected. The Masons gave
us a Missouri country breakfast, in Missourian abundance,
and we needed it: hot biscuits; hot "wheat bread" prettily
criss-crossed in a lattice pattern on top; hot corn pone; fried
chicken; bacon, coffee, eggs, milk, buttermilk, etc.;—and the
world may be confidently challenged to furnish the equal to
such a breakfast, as it is cooked in the South.

We staid several days at Mason's; and after all these years
the memory of the dullness, the stillness and lifelessness of
that slumberous farm-house still oppresses my spirit as with a
sense of the presence of death and mourning. There was
nothing to do, nothing to think about; there was no interest
in life. The male part of the household were away in the fields
all day, the women were busy and out of our sight; there was
no sound but the plaintive wailing of a spinning-wheel, forever moaning out from some distant room,—the most lonesome sound in nature, a sound steeped and sodden with
homesickness and the emptiness of life. The family went to
bed about dark every night, and as we were not invited to
intrude any new customs, we naturally followed theirs. Those
nights were a hundred years long to youths accustomed to
being up till twelve. We lay awake and miserable till that hour
every time, and grew old and decrepit waiting through the
still eternities for the clock-strikes. This was no place for town

boys. So at last it was with something very like joy that we received news that the enemy were on our track again. With a new birth of the old warrior spirit, we sprang to our places in line of battle and fell back on Camp Ralls.

Captain Lyman had taken a hint from Mason's talk, and he now gave orders that our camp should be guarded against surprise by the posting of pickets. I was ordered to place a picket at the forks of the road in Hyde's prairie. Night shut down black and threatening. I told Sergeant Bowers to go out to that place and stay till midnight; and, just as I was expecting, he said he wouldn't do it. I tried to get others to go, but all refused. Some excused themselves on account of the weather; but the rest were frank enough to say they wouldn't go in any kind of weather. This kind of thing sounds odd now, and impossible, but there was no surprise in it at the time. On the contrary, it seemed a perfectly natural thing to do. There were scores of little camps scattered over Missouri where the same thing was happening. These camps were composed of young men who had been born and reared to a sturdy independence, and who did not know what it meant to be ordered around by Tom, Dick, and Harry, whom they had known familiarly all their lives, in the village or on the farm. It is quite within the probabilities that this same thing was happening all over the South. James Redpath recognized the justice of this assumption, and furnished the following instance in support of it. During a short stay in East Tennessee he was in a citizen colonel's tent one day, talking, when a big private appeared at the door, and without salute or other circumlocution said to the colonel:

"Say, Jim, I'm a-goin' home for a few days."

"What for?"

"Well, I hain't b'en there for a right smart while, and I'd like to see how things is comin' on."

"How long are you going to be gone?"

" 'Bout two weeks."

"Well, don't be gone longer than that; and get back sooner if you can."

That was all, and the citizen officer resumed his conversation where the private had broken it off. This was in the first months of the war, of course. The camps in our part of

Missouri were under Brigadier-General Thomas H. Harris. He was a townsman of ours, a first-rate fellow, and well liked; but we had all familiarly known him as the sole and modest-salaried operator in our telegraph office, where he had to send about one dispatch a week in ordinary times, and two when there was a rush of business; consequently, when he appeared in our midst one day, on the wing, and delivered a military command of some sort, in a large military fashion, nobody was surprised at the response which he got from the assembled soldiery:

"Oh, now, what'll you take to *don't*, Tom Harris!"

It was quite the natural thing. One might justly imagine that we were hopeless material for war. And so we seemed, in our ignorant state; but there were those among us who afterward learned the grim trade; learned to obey like machines; became valuable soldiers; fought all through the war, and came out at the end with excellent records. One of the very boys who refused to go out on picket duty that night, and called me an ass for thinking he would expose himself to danger in such a foolhardy way, had become distinguished for intrepidity before he was a year older.

I did secure my picket that night—not by authority, but by diplomacy. I got Bowers to go, by agreeing to exchange ranks with him for the time being, and go along and stand the watch with him as his subordinate. We staid out there a couple of dreary hours in the pitchy darkness and the rain, with nothing to modify the dreariness but Bowers's monotonous growlings at the war and the weather; then we began to nod, and presently found it next to impossible to stay in the saddle; so we gave up the tedious job, and went back to the camp without waiting for the relief guard. We rode into camp without interruption or objection from anybody, and the enemy could have done the same, for there were no sentries. Everybody was asleep; at midnight there was nobody to send out another picket, so none was sent. We never tried to establish a watch at night again, as far as I remember, but we generally kept a picket out in the daytime.

In that camp the whole command slept on the corn in the big corn-crib; and there was usually a general row before morning, for the place was full of rats, and they would scramble over the boys' bodies and faces, annoying and irritating everybody; and now and then they would bite some one's toe, and the person who owned the toe would start up and magnify his English and begin to throw corn in the dark. The ears were half as heavy as bricks, and when they struck they hurt. The persons struck would respond, and inside of five minutes every man would be locked in a death-grip with his neighbor. There was a grievous deal of blood shed in the corn-crib, but this was all that was spilt while I was in the war. No, that is not quite true. But for one circumstance it would have been all. I will come to that now.

Our scares were frequent. Every few days rumors would come that the enemy were approaching. In these cases we always fell back on some other camp of ours; we never staid where we were. But the rumors always turned out to be false; so at last even we began to grow indifferent to them. One night a negro was sent to our corn-crib with the same old warning: the enemy was hovering in our neighborhood. We all said let him hover. We resolved to stay still and be comfortable. It was a fine warlike resolution, and no doubt we all felt the stir of it in our veins—for a moment. We had been having a very jolly time, that was full of horse-play and school-boy hilarity; but that cooled down now, and presently the fast-waning fire of forced jokes and forced laughs died out altogether, and the company became silent. Silent and nervous. And soon uneasy—worried—apprehensive. We had said we would stay, and we were committed. We could have been persuaded to go, but there was nobody brave enough to suggest it. An almost noiseless movement presently began in the dark, by a general but unvoiced impulse. When the movement was completed, each man knew that he was not the only person who had crept to the front wall and had his eye at a crack between the logs. No, we were all there; all there with our hearts in our throats, and staring out toward the sugar-troughs where the forest foot-path came through. It was late, and there was a deep woodsy stillness everywhere. There was a veiled moonlight, which was only just strong enough to enable us to mark the general shape of objects. Presently a muffled sound caught our ears, and we recognized it as the hoof-beats of a horse or horses. And right away a figure appeared in the forest path; it could have been made of smoke, its mass had so little sharpness of outline. It was a man on horseback; and it seemed to me that there were others behind him. I got hold of a gun in the dark, and pushed it through a crack between the logs, hardly knowing what I was doing, I was so dazed with fright. Somebody said "Fire!" I pulled the trigger. I seemed to see a hundred flashes and hear a hundred reports, then I saw the man fall down out of the saddle. My first feeling was of surprised gratification; my first impulse was an apprentice-sportsman's impulse to run and pick up his game. Somebody said, hardly audibly, "Good—we've got him!—wait for the rest." But the rest did not come. We waited—listened—still no more came. There was not a sound, not the whisper of a leaf; just perfect stillness; an un-canny kind of stillness, which was all the more uncanny on account of the damp, earthy, late-night smells now rising and pervading it. Then, wondering, we crept stealthily out, and approached the man. When we got to him the moon revealed him distinctly. He was lying on his back, with his arms abroad; his mouth was open and his chest heaving with long gasps, and his white shirt-front was all splashed with blood. The thought shot through me that I was a murderer; that I had killed a man—a man who had never done me any harm. That was the coldest sensation that ever went through my marrow. I was down by him in a moment, helplessly stroking his forehead; and I would have given anything then—my own life freely—to make him again what he had been five minutes before. And all the boys seemed to be feeling in the same way; they hung over him, full of pitying interest, and tried all they could to help him, and said all sorts of regretful things. They had forgotten all about the enemy; they thought only of this one forlorn unit of the foe. Once my imagination persuaded me that the dying man gave me a reproachful look out of his shadowy eyes, and it seemed to me that I could rather he had stabbed me than done that. He muttered and mumbled like a dreamer in his sleep, about his wife and his child; and I thought with a new despair, "This thing that I have done does not end with him; it falls upon *them* too, and they never did me any harm, any more than he."

In a little while the man was dead. He was killed in war;

killed in fair and legitimate war; killed in battle, as you may say; and yet he was as sincerely mourned by the opposing force as if he had been their brother. The boys stood there a half hour sorrowing over him, and recalling the details of the tragedy, and wondering who he might be, and if he were a spy, and saying that if it were to do over again they would not hurt him unless he attacked them first. It soon came out that mine was not the only shot fired; there were five others,—a division of the guilt which was a grateful relief to me, since it in some degree lightened and diminished the burden I was carrying. There were six shots fired at once; but I was not in my right mind at the time, and my heated imagination had magnified my one shot into a volley.

The man was not in uniform, and was not armed. He was a stranger in the country; that was all we ever found out about him. The thought of him got to preying upon me every night; I could not get rid of it. I could not drive it away, the taking of that unoffending life seemed such a wanton thing. And it seemed an epitome of war; that all war must be just that—the killing of strangers against whom you feel no personal animosity; strangers whom, in other circumstances, you would help if you found them in trouble, and who would help you if you needed it. My campaign was spoiled. It seemed to me that I was not rightly equipped for this awful business; that war was intended for men, and I for a child's nurse. I resolved to retire from this avocation of sham soldiership while I could save some remnant of my self-respect. These morbid thoughts clung to me against reason; for at bottom I did not believe I had touched that man. The law of probabilities decreed me guiltless of his blood; for in all my small experience with guns I had never hit anything I had tried to hit, and I knew I had done my best to hit him. Yet there was no solace in the thought. Against a diseased imagination, demonstration goes for nothing.

The rest of my war experience was of a piece with what I have already told of it. We kept monotonously falling back upon one camp or another, and eating up the country. I marvel now at the patience of the farmers and their families. They ought to have shot us; on the contrary, they were as hospitably kind and courteous to us as if we had deserved it. In one of these camps we found Ab Grimes, an Upper Mississippi pilot, who afterwards became famous as a dare-devil rebel spy, whose career bristled with desperate adventures. The look and style of his comrades suggested that they had not come into the war to play, and their deeds made good the conjecture later. They were fine horsemen and good revolver-shots; but their favorite arm was the lasso. Each had one at his pommel, and could snatch a man out of the saddle with it every time, on a full gallop, at any reasonable distance.

In another camp the chief was a fierce and profane old blacksmith of sixty, and he had furnished his twenty recruits with gigantic home-made bowie-knives, to be swung with the two hands, like the *machetes* of the Isthmus. It was a grisly spectacle to see that earnest band practicing their murderous cuts and slashes under the eye of that remorseless old fanatic.

The last camp which we fell back upon was in a hollow near the village of Florida, where I was born—in Monroe County. Here we were warned, one day, that a Union colonel was sweeping down on us with a whole regiment at his heels. This looked decidedly serious. Our boys went apart and consulted; then we went back and told the other companies present that the war was a disappointment to us and we were going to disband. They were getting ready, themselves, to fall back on some place or other, and were only waiting for General Tom Harris, who was expected to arrive at any moment; so they tried to persuade us to wait a little while, but the majority of us said no, we were accustomed to falling back, and didn't need any of Tom Harris's help; we could get along perfectly well without him—and save time too. So about half of our fifteen, including myself, mounted and left on the instant; the others yielded to persuasion and staid—staid through the war.

An hour later we met General Harris on the road, with two or three people in his company—his staff, probably, but we could not tell; none of them were in uniform; uniforms had not come into vogue among us yet. Harris ordered us back; but we told him there was a Union colonel coming with a whole regiment in his wake, and it looked as if there was going to be a disturbance; so we had concluded to go home. He raged a little, but it was of no use; our minds were made up. We had done our share; had killed one man, exterminated one army, such as it was; let him go and kill the rest, and that would end the war. I did not see that brisk young general again until last year; then he was wearing white hair and whiskers.

In time I came to know that Union colonel whose coming frightened me out of the war and crippled the Southern cause to that extent—General Grant. I came within a few hours of seeing him when he was as unknown as I was myself; at a time when anybody could have said, "Grant?—Ulysses S. Grant? I do not remember hearing the name before." It seems difficult to realize that there was once a time when such a remark could be rationally made; but there *was*, and I was within a few miles of the place and the occasion too, though proceeding in the other direction.

The thoughtful will not throw this war-paper of mine lightly aside as being valueless. It has this value: it is a not unfair picture of what went on in many and many a militia camp in the first months of the rebellion, when the green recruits were without discipline, without the steadying and heartening influence of trained leaders; when all their circumstances were new and strange, and charged with exaggerated terrors, and before the invaluable experience of actual collision in the field had turned them from rabbits into soldiers. If this side of the picture of that early day has not before been put into history, then history has been to that degree incomplete, for it had and has its rightful place there. There was more Bull Run material scattered through the early camps of this country than exhibited itself at Bull Run. And yet it learned its trade presently, and helped to fight the great battles later. I could have become a soldier myself, if I had waited. I had got part of it learned; I knew more about retreating than the man that invented retreating.

December 1885

The New Dynasty

Hartford Monday Evening Club

Power, when lodged in the hands of man, means oppression—*insures* oppression: it means oppression *always*: not always consciously, deliberately, purposely; not always severely, or heavily, or cruelly, or sweepingly; but *oppression*, anyway, and *always*, in one shape or another. One may say it cannot even lift its hand in kindness but it hurts somebody by the same act whereby it delivers a benevolence to his neighbor. Power cannot be so righteously placed that it will neglect to exercise its great specialty, Oppression. Give it to the King of Dahomey, and he will try his new repeating rifle on the passers-by in the courtyard; and as they fall, one after another, it hardly occurs to him or to his courtiers that he is committing an impropriety; give it to the high priest of the Christian Church in Russia, the Emperor, and with a wave of his hand he will brush a multitude of young men, nursing mothers, gray headed patriarchs, gentle young girls, like so many unconsidered flies, into the unimaginable hells of his Siberia, and go blandly to his breakfast, unconscious that he has committed a barbarity; give it to Constantine, or Edward IV, or Peter the Great, or Richard III, or a hundred other monarchs that might be mentioned, and they slaughter members of their own family, and need no opiates to help them sleep afterward; give it to Richard II, and he will win the grateful tears of a multitude of slaves by setting them free—to gain a vital point—and then laugh in their faces and tear up their emancipation papers, and promise them a bitterer and crueler slavery than ever they imagined before, the moment his point has been gained; give it to the noblesse of the Middle Ages, and they will claim and seize wandering freedmen as their serfs; and with a totally unconscious irony will put upon THEM the burden of proving that they are freedmen and not serfs; give it to the Church, and she will burn, flay, slay, torture, massacre, ruthlessly—and neither she nor her friends will doubt that she is doing the best she can for man and God; give it suddenly to the ignorant masses of the French monarchy, maddened by a thousand years of unspeakable

883

tyranny, and they will drench the whole land with blood and make massacre a pastime; give power to whomsoever you please, and it will oppress; even the horse-car company will work its men eighteen hours, in Arctic cold or Equatorial heat, and pay them with starvation; and in expanded or in otherwise modified form, let the horse-car company stand for a thousand other corporations and companies and industries which might be named. Yes, you may follow it straight down, step by step, from the Emperor to the horse-car company, and wherever power resides it is used to oppress.

Now so far as we know or may guess, this has been going on for a million years. Who are the oppressors? The few: the king, the capitalist, and a handful of other overseers and superintendents. Who the oppressed? The many: The nations of the earth; the valuable personages; the workers; they that MAKE the bread that the soft-handed and the idle eat. Why is it right that there is not a fairer division of the spoil all around? BECAUSE LAWS AND CONSTITUTIONS HAVE ORDERED OTHERWISE. Then it follows that if the laws and constitutions should change around and say there SHALL be a more nearly equal division, THAT would have to be recognized as right. That is to confess, then, that in POLITICAL SOCIETIES, IT IS THE PREROGATIVE OF Might TO DETERMINE WHAT IS Right; that it is the prerogative of Might to create Right—and uncreate it, at will. It is to confess that if the banded voters among a laboring kinship of 45,000,000 of persons shall speak out to the other 12,000,000 or 15,000,000 of a nation and command that an existing system of rights and laws be reversed, that existing system has in that moment, in an absolutely clear and clean and legal way, become an obsolete and vanished thing—has utterly ceased to exist, and no creature in all the 15,000,000 is in the least degree privileged to find fault with the act.

We will grant, if you please, that for uncounted ages, the king and the scattering few have oppressed the nations—and have held in their hands the power to say what is right and what is not. Now was that power real, or was it a fiction? Until to-day it was real; but FROM to-day, in THIS country, I take heart of grace to believe, it is forevermore dust and ashes. For a greater than any king has arisen upon this the only soil in this world that is truly sacred to liberty; and you that have eyes to see and ears to hear may catch the sheen of his banners and the tramp of his marching hosts; and men may cavil, and sneer, and make wordy argument—but please God he will mount his throne; and he will stretch out his sceptre, and there will be bread for the hungry, clothing for the naked, and hope in eyes unused to hoping; and the sham nobilities will pass away, and the rightful lord will come to his own.

There was a time for sneering. In all the ages of the world and in all its lands, the huge inert mass of humbler mankind,—compacted crush of poor dull dumb animals,—equipped from its centre to its circumference with unimaginable might, and never suspecting it, has made bread in bitter toil and sweat, all its days for the feeble few to eat, and has impotently raged and wept by turns over its despised households of sore-hearted women and smileless children—and that was a time for sneering. And once in a generation, in all ages and all lands, a little block of this inert mass has stirred, and risen with noise, and said it could no longer endure its oppressions, its degradation, its misery—and then after a few days it has sunk back, vanquished, mute again, and laughed at—and that also was a time for sneers. And in these later decades, single mechanical trades have banded themselves together, and risen hopefully and demanded a better chance in this world's fight; and when it was the bricklayers, the other trades looked on with indifferent eye—it was not their fight; and when this or that or the other trade revolted, the ten millions in the other trades went uninterested about their own affairs—it was not their quarrel;—and that also was a time to sneer—and men did sneer. But when ALL the bricklayers, and all the bookbinders, and all the cooks, and all the barbers, and all the machinists, and all the miners, and blacksmiths, and printers, and hod-carriers, and stevedores, and house-painters, and brakemen, and engineers, and conductors, and factory hands, and horse-car drivers, and all the shop-girls, and all the sewing-women, and all the telegraph operators: in a word, all the myriad of toilers in whom is slumbering the reality of that thing which you call Power, not its age-worn sham and substanceless spectre,—when these rise, call the vast spectacle by any deluding name that will please your ear, but the fact remains, a NATION has risen! And by certain signs you may recognize it. When James Russell Lowell makes his courteous appeal for the little company of American authors before a Committee of the United States Senate—who listen as their predecessors have for sixty years listened to authors' appeals, with something of the indifference due a matter of small weight intruded by a faction inconsequent and few—and sits down and his place is taken by a foreman of a printing office, clad in unpretending gray, who says "I am not here as a printer; I am not here as a brick-layer, or a mason, or a carpenter, or as any other peculiar or particular handicrafts man; but I stand here to represent ALL the trades, ALL the industries, all brethren of ANY calling that labor with their hands for their daily bread and the bread of their wives and their little children, from Maine to the Gulf, and from the Atlantic to the Pacific; and when I speak, out of my mouth issues the voice of five millions of men!"—when THAT thunderpeal falls, it is time for the Senatorial lethargy to show sign of life, to show interest, respect—yes, reverence, supple and eager recognition of the master, and to know what might be the King's messenger's commands. And the Senators realize that indeed such time has come.

The authors had with slender hopefulness indicated what they would like the Congress to do; in the other case, without any insolence of speech or bearing, but reposeful with the clear consciousness of unassailable authority, the five-million-voiced printer DICTATED to the Congress—not anything which it MUST do, but certain things which it must NOT do. And that command will be heeded.

This was the first time in this world, perhaps, that ever a nation did actually and in its own person, not by proxy, speak. And by grace of fortune I was there to hear and see. It seemed to me that all the gauds and shows and spectacles of history somehow lost their splendor in this presence; their tinsel and lacquer and feathers seemed confessed and poor, contrasted with this real blood and flesh of majesty and greatness. And I thought then, and still think, that our country, so wastefully rich in things for her people to be proud of, had here added a thing which transcended all that went before. Here was the nation in person speaking; and its servants, *real*—not masters *called* servants by canting trick of speech—listening. The like could not be seen in any other country, or in any other age.

They whom that printer represented are in truth the nation: and they are still speaking. Have you read their Manifesto of demands? It has a curiously worn and old and threadbare sound. And it IS old. It is older than the Scriptures. It is as old as Tyranny—old as Poverty—old as Despair. It is the oldest thing in this world—being as old as the human voice. In one form or another it has wearied the ears of the fortunate and the powerful in all the years of all the ages. And always it seemed the fretful cry of children—the fretful cry of a stranger's children, not one's own—and was not listened to; and did not need to be listened to, since as a matter of course they were crying for the moon, crying for the impossible. So one thought, without listening—without examining. But when *all* the children in a little world cry, one is roused out of his indifference by the mere magnitude of the fact—and he realizes that perhaps something IS the matter; and he opens his ears. And what does he hear? Just what he has heard countless times before, as a mere dead formula of words; but now that his attention is awake, he perceives that these words have meaning. And so he—that is, you—do at last listen, do at last con the details of this rag of immemorial antiquity, this Manifesto of Wrongs and Demands, with alert senses. And straightway the thing that springs to your surprised lips when you are confronted by one or two of the things in that list, is the ejaculation, "Is it possible that so plain and manifest a piece of justice as this, is actually lacking to these men, and must be asked for?—has been lacking to them for ages, and the world's fortunate ones did not know it; or, knowing it could be indifferent to it, could endure the shame of it, the inhumanity of it?" And the thought follows in your mind, "Why this is as strange as that a famishing child should want its common right, the breast, and the mother-heart not divine it; or, divining it, turn away indifferent."

Read their Manifesto; read it in a judicial spirit, and ponder it. It impeaches certain of us of high treason against the rightful sovereign of this world; the indictment is found by a competent jury, and in no long time we must stand before the bar of the Republic and answer it. And you will assuredly find counts in it which not any logic of ours can controvert.

Many a time, when I have seen a man abusing a horse, I have wished I knew that horse's language, so that I could whisper in his ear, "Fool, you are master here, if you but knew it. Launch out with your heels!" The working millions, in all the ages, have been horses—were horses; all they needed was a capable leader to organize their strength and tell them how to use it, and they would in that moment be master. They have FOUND that leader somewhere, to-day, and they ARE master—the only time in this world that ever the true king wore the purple; the only time in this world that "By the grace of God, King" was ever uttered when it was not a lie.

And we need not fear this king. All the kings that have ruled the world heretofore were born the protectors and sympathizing friends and supporters of cliques and classes and clans of gilded idlers, selfish pap-hunters, restless schemers, troublers of the State in the interest of their private advantage. But this king is born the enemy of them that scheme and talk and do not work. He will be our permanent shield and defence against the Socialist, the Communist, the Anarchist, the tramp, and the selfish agitator for "reforms" that will beget bread and notoriety for him at cleaner men's expense; he will be our refuge and defence against these, and against all like forms of political disease, pollution, and death.

How will he use his power? *To oppress*—at first. For he is not better than the masters that went before; nor pretends to be. The only difference is, he will oppress the few, they oppressed the many; he will oppress the thousands, they oppressed the millions; but he will imprison nobody, he will massacre, burn, flay, torture, exile nobody, nor work any subject eighteen hours a day, nor starve his family. He will see to it that there is fair play, fair working hours, fair wages: and further than that, when his might has become securely massed and his authority recognized, he will not go, let us hope, and determine also to believe. He will be strenuous, firm, sometimes hard—he *must* be—for a while, till all his craftsmen be gathered into his citadel and his throne established. Until then let us be patient.

It is not long to wait; his day is close at hand: his clans are gathering, they are on their way; his bugles are sounding the call, they are answering; every week that comes and goes, sees ten thousand new crusaders swing into line and add their pulsing footfalls to the thunder-tread of his mighty battalions.

He is the most stupendous product of the highest civilization the world has even seen—and the worthiest and the best; and in no age but this, no land but this, and no lower civilization than this, could he ever have been brought forth. The average of his genuine, practical, valuable knowledge—and knowledge is the truest right divine to power—is an education contrasted with which the education possessed by the kings and nobles who ruled him for a hundred centuries is the untaught twaddle of a nursery, and beneath contempt. The *sum* of his education, as represented in the ten thousand utterly new and delicate and exact handicrafts, and divisions and subdivisions of handicrafts, exercised by his infinite brain and multitudinous members, is a sum of knowledge compared to which the sum of human knowledge in any and all ages of the world previous to the birth-year of the eldest person here present in this room, was as a lake compared to the ocean, the foot-hills compared to the Alps; a sum of knowledge which makes the knowledge of the elder ages seem but ignorance and darkness; even suggests the figure of a landscape lying dim and blurred under the stars, and the same landscape revealed in its infinitude of bloom, color, variety, detail, under the noontide sun. Without his education, he had continued what he was, a slave; with it, he is what he is, a sovereign. His was a weary journey, and long: the constellations have drifted far from the anchorages which they knew in the skies when it began; but at last he is here. He is here,—and he will remain. He is the greatest birth of the greatest age the nations of this world have known. You cannot sneer at him—that time has gone by. He has before him the most righteous work that was ever given into the hand of man to do: and he will do it. Yes, he is here; and the question is not—as it has been heretofore during a thousand ages—What shall we do with him? For the first time in history we are relieved of the necessity of managing his affair for him. He is not a broken dam this time—he is the Flood!

March 22, 1886

Our Children

Authors Club Dinner, New York

Our children—yours—and—mine. They seem like little things to talk about—our children, but little things often make up the sum of human life—that's a good sentence. I repeat it, little things often produce great things. Now, to illustrate, take Sir Isaac Newton—I presume some of you have heard of Mr. Newton. Well, once when Sir Isaac Newton—a mere lad—got over into the man's apple orchard—I don't know what he was doing there—I didn't come all the way from Hartford to q-u-e-s-t-i-o-n Mr. Newton's honesty—but when he was there—in the man's orchard—he saw an apple fall and he was a-t-t-racted toward it, and that led to the discovery—not of Mr. Newton—but of the great law of *attraction* and gravitation.

And there was once another great discoverer—I've forgotten his name, and I don't remember what he discovered, but I know it was something very important, and I hope you will all tell your children about it, when you get home. Well, when the great discoverer was once loafin' around down in Virginia, and a-puttin' in his time flirting with Pocahontas—Oh, Captain John Smith, that was the man's name!—and while he and Poca were sitting in Mr. Powhatan's garden, he accidentally put his arm around her and picked something—a simple weed, which proved to be tobacco—and now we find it in every Christian family, shedding its civilizing influence broadcast throughout the whole religious community.

Now there was another great man, I can't think of *his* name either, who used to loaf around, and watch the great chandelier in the cathedral at Pisa, which set him to thinking about the great law of gunpowder, and eventually led to the discovery of the cotton gin.

Now, I don't say this as an inducement for our young men to loaf around like Mr. Newton, and Mr. Galileo, and Captain Smith, but they were once little babies, two days old, and they show what little things have sometimes accomplished.

April 22, 1886

Taming the Bicycle

I

I thought the matter over, and concluded I could do it. So I went down and bought a barrel of Pond's Extract and a bicycle. The Expert came home with me to instruct me. We chose the back yard, for the sake of privacy, and went to work.

Mine was not a full-grown bicycle, but only a colt—a fifty-inch, with the pedals shortened up to forty-eight—and skittish, like any other colt. The Expert explained the thing's points briefly, then he got on its back and rode around a little, to show me how easy it was to do. He said that the dismounting was perhaps the hardest thing to learn, and so we would leave that to the last. But he was in error there. He found, to his surprise and joy, that all that he needed to do was to get me on to the machine and stand out of the way; I could get off, myself. Although I was wholly inexperienced, I dismounted in the best time on record. He was on that side, shoving up the machine; we all came down with a crash, he at the bottom, I next, and the machine on top.

We examined the machine, but it was not in the least injured. This was hardly believable. Yet the Expert assured me that it was true; in fact, the examination proved it. I was partly to realize, then, how admirably these things are constructed. We applied some Pond's Extract, and resumed. The Expert got on the *other* side to shove up this time, but I dismounted on that side; so the result was as before.

The machine was not hurt. We oiled ourselves up again, and resumed. This time the Expert took up a sheltered position behind, but somehow or other we landed on him again.

He was full of surprised admiration; said it was abnormal. She was all right, not a scratch on her, not a timber started anywhere. I said it was wonderful, while we were greasing up, but he said that when I came to know these steel spider-webs I would realize that nothing but dynamite could cripple them. Then he limped out to position, and we resumed once more. This time the Expert took up the position of short-

stop, and got a man to shove up behind. We got up a handsome speed, and presently traversed a brick, and I went out
over the top of the tiller and landed, head down, on the instructor's back, and saw the machine fluttering in the air between me and the sun. It was well it came down on us, for
that broke the fall, and it was not injured.

Five days later I got out and was carried down to the hospital, and found the Expert doing pretty fairly. In a few more
days I was quite sound. I attribute this to my prudence in
always dismounting on something soft. Some recommend a
feather bed, but I think an Expert is better.

The Expert got out at last, brought four assistants with
him. It was a good idea. These four held the graceful cobweb
upright while I climbed into the saddle; then they formed in
column and marched on either side of me while the Expert
pushed behind; all hands assisted at the dismount.

The bicycle had what is called the "wabbles," and had
them very badly. In order to keep my position, a good many
things were required of me, and in every instance the thing
required was against nature. Against nature, but not against
the *laws* of nature. That is to say, that whatever the needed
thing might be, my nature, habit, and breeding moved me to
attempt it in one way, while some immutable and unsuspected law of physics required that it be done in just the
other way. I perceived by this how radically and grotesquely
wrong had been the life-long education of my body and members. They were steeped in ignorance; they knew nothing—
nothing which it could profit them to know. For instance,
if I found myself falling to the right, I put the tiller hard
down the other way, by a quite natural impulse, and so violated a law, and kept on going down. The law required the
opposite thing—the big wheel must be turned in the direction in which you are falling. It is hard to believe this,
when you are told it. And not merely hard to believe it, but
impossible; it is opposed to all your notions. And it is just
as hard to do it, after you do come to believe it. Believing it,
and knowing by the most convincing proof that it is true,
does not help it: you can't any more *do* it than you could
before; you can neither force nor persuade yourself to do it at
first. The intellect has to come to the front, now. It has to

teach the limbs to discard their old education and adopt the new.

The steps of one's progress are distinctly marked. At the end of each lesson he knows he has acquired something, and he also knows what that something is, and likewise that it will stay with him. It is not like studying German, where you mull along, in a groping, uncertain way, for thirty years; and at last, just as you think you've got it, they spring the subjunctive on you, and there you are. No—and I see now, plainly enough, that the great pity about the German language is, that you can't fall off it and hurt yourself. There is nothing like that feature to make you attend strictly to business. But I also see, by what I have learned of bicycling, that the right and only sure way to learn German is by the bicycling method. That is to say, take a grip on one villainy of it at a time, and learn it—not ease up and shirk to the next, leaving that one half learned.

When you have reached the point in bicycling where you can balance the machine tolerably fairly and propel it and steer it, then comes your next task—how to mount it. You do it in this way: you hop along behind it on your right foot, resting the other on the mounting-peg, and grasping the tiller with your hands. At the word, you rise on the peg, stiffen your left leg, hang your other one around in the air in a general and indefinite way, lean your stomach against the rear of the saddle, and then fall off, maybe on one side, maybe on the other; but you fall off. You get up and do it again; and once more; and then several times.

By this time you have learned to keep your balance; and also to steer without wrenching the tiller out by the roots (I say tiller because it *is* a tiller; "handle-bar" is a lamely descriptive phrase). So you steer along, straight ahead, a little while, then you rise forward, with a steady strain, bringing your right leg, and then your body, into the saddle, catch your breath, fetch a violent hitch this way and then that, and down you go again.

But you have ceased to mind the going down by this time; you are getting to light on one foot or the other with considerable certainty. Six more attempts and six more falls make you perfect. You land in the saddle comfortably, next time,

and stay there—that is, if you can be content to let your legs
dangle, and leave the pedals alone a while; but if you grab at
once for the pedals, you are gone again. You soon learn to
wait a little and perfect your balance before reaching for the
pedals; then the mounting-art is acquired, is complete, and a
little practice will make it simple and easy to you, though
spectators ought to keep off a rod or two to one side, along at
first, if you have nothing against them.

And now you come to the voluntary dismount; you learned
the other kind first of all. It is quite easy to tell one how to do
the voluntary dismount; the words are few, the requirement
simple, and apparently undifficult; let your left pedal go down
till your left leg is nearly straight, turn your wheel to the left,
and get off as you would from a horse. It certainly does sound
exceedingly easy; but it isn't. I don't know why it isn't, but it
isn't. Try as you may, you don't get down as you would from
a horse, you get down as you would from a house afire. You
make a spectacle of yourself every time.

II

During eight days I took a daily lesson of an hour and a
half. At the end of this twelve working-hours' apprenticeship
I was graduated—in the rough. I was pronounced competent
to paddle my own bicycle without outside help. It seems incredible, this celerity of acquirement. It takes considerably
longer than that to learn horseback-riding in the rough.

Now it is true that I could have learned without a teacher,
but it would have been risky for me, because of my natural
clumsiness. The self-taught man seldom knows anything accurately, and he does not know a tenth as much as he could
have known if he had worked under teachers; and, besides, he
brags, and is the means of fooling other thoughtless people
into going and doing as he himself has done. There are those
who imagine that the unlucky accidents of life—life's "experiences"—are in some way useful to us. I wish I could find out
how. I never knew one of them to happen twice. They always
change off and swap around and catch you on your inexperienced side. If personal experience can be worth anything
as an education, it wouldn't seem likely that you could trip

Methuselah; and yet if that old person could come back here it is more than likely that one of the first things he would do would be to take hold of one of these electric wires and tie himself all up in a knot. Now the surer thing and the wiser thing would be for him to ask somebody whether it was a good thing to take hold of. But that would not suit him; he would be one of the self-taught kind that go by experience; he would want to examine for himself. And he would find, for his instruction, that the coiled patriarch shuns the electric wire; and it would be useful to him, too, and would leave his education in quite a complete and rounded-out condition, till he should come again, some day, and go to bouncing a dynamite-can around to find out what was in it.

But we wander from the point. However, get a teacher; it saves much time and Pond's Extract.

Before taking final leave of me, my instructor inquired concerning my physical strength, and I was able to inform him that I hadn't any. He said that that was a defect which would make up-hill wheeling pretty difficult for me at first; but he also said the bicycle would soon remove it. The contrast between his muscles and mine was quite marked. He wanted to test mine, so I offered my biceps—which was my best. It almost made him smile. He said, "It is pulpy, and soft, and yielding, and rounded; it evades pressure, and glides from under the fingers; in the dark a body might think it was an oyster in a rag." Perhaps this made me look grieved, for he added, briskly: "Oh, that's all right; you needn't worry about that; in a little while you can't tell it from a petrified kidney. Just go right along with your practice; you're all right."

Then he left me, and I started out alone to seek adventures. You don't really have to seek them—that is nothing but a phrase—they come to you.

I chose a reposeful Sabbath-day sort of a back street which was about thirty yards wide between the curbstones. I knew it was not wide enough; still, I thought that by keeping strict watch and wasting no space unnecessarily I could crowd through.

Of course I had trouble mounting the machine, entirely on my own responsibility, with no encouraging moral support from the outside, no sympathetic instructor to say, "Good!

now you're doing well—good again—don't hurry—there,
now, you're all right—brace up, go ahead." In place of this I
had some other support. This was a boy, who was perched on
a gate-post munching a hunk of maple sugar.

He was full of interest and comment. The first time I failed
and went down he said that if he was me he would dress up
in pillows, that's what he would do. The next time I went
down he advised me to go and learn to ride a tricycle first.
The third time I collapsed he said he didn't believe I could
stay on a horse-car. But next time I succeeded, and got clumsily under way in a weaving, tottering, uncertain fashion, and
occupying pretty much all of the street. My slow and lumbering gait filled the boy to the chin with scorn, and he sung out,
"My, but don't he rip along!" Then he got down from his
post and loafed along the sidewalk, still observing and occasionally commenting. Presently he dropped into my wake and
followed along behind. A little girl passed by, balancing a
wash-board on her head, and giggled, and seemed about to
make a remark, but the boy said, rebukingly, "Let him alone,
he's going to a funeral."

I had been familiar with that street for years, and had always supposed it was a dead level; but it was not, as the bicycle now informed me, to my surprise. The bicycle, in the
hands of a novice, is as alert and acute as a spirit-level in the
detecting of delicate and vanishing shades of difference in
these matters. It notices a rise where your untrained eye
would not observe that one existed; it notices any decline
which water will run down. I was toiling up a slight rise, but
was not aware of it. It made me tug and pant and perspire;
and still, labor as I might, the machine came almost to a
standstill every little while. At such times the boy would say:
"That's it! take a rest—there ain't no hurry. They can't hold
the funeral without *you*."

Stones were a bother to me. Even the smallest ones gave
me a panic when I went over them. I could hit any kind of a
stone, no matter how small, if I tried to miss it; and of course
at first I couldn't help trying to do that. It is but natural. It
is part of the ass that is put in us all, for some inscrutable
reason.

I was at the end of my course, at last, and it was necessary for me to round to. This is not a pleasant thing, when you undertake it for the first time on your own responsibility, and neither is it likely to succeed. Your confidence oozes away, you fill steadily up with nameless apprehensions, every fiber of you is tense with a watchful strain, you start a cautious and gradual curve, but your squirmy nerves are all full of electric anxieties, so the curve is quickly demoralized into a jerky and perilous zigzag; then suddenly the nickel-clad horse takes the bit in its mouth and goes slanting for the curbstone, defying all prayers and all your powers to change its mind—your heart stands still, your breath hangs fire, your legs forget to work, straight on you go, and there are but a couple of feet between you and the curb now. And now is the desperate moment, the last chance to save yourself; of course all your instructions fly out of your head, and you whirl your wheel *away* from the curb instead of *toward* it, and so you go sprawling on that granite-bound inhospitable shore. That was my luck; that was my experience. I dragged myself out from under the indestructible bicycle and sat down on the curb to examine.

I started on the return trip. It was now that I saw a farmer's wagon poking along down toward me, loaded with cabbages. If I needed anything to perfect the precariousness of my steering, it was just that. The farmer was occupying the middle of the road with his wagon, leaving barely fourteen or fifteen yards of space on either side. I couldn't shout at him—a beginner can't shout; if he opens his mouth he is gone; he must keep all his attention on his business. But in this grisly emergency, the boy came to the rescue, and for once I had to be grateful to him. He kept a sharp lookout on the swiftly varying impulses and inspirations of my bicycle, and shouted to the man accordingly:

"To the left! Turn to the left, or this jackass 'll run over you!" The man started to do it. "No, to the right, to the right! Hold on! *that* won't do!—to the left!—to the right! —to the *left*!—right! left—ri— Stay where you *are*, or you're a goner!"

And just then I caught the off horse in the starboard and went down in a pile. I said, "Hang it! Couldn't you *see* I was coming?"

"Yes, I see you was coming, but I couldn't tell which *way* you was coming. Nobody could—now, *could* they? You couldn't yourself—now, *could* you? So what could *I* do?"

There was something in that, and so I had the magnanimity to say so. I said I was no doubt as much to blame as he was.

Within the next five days I achieved so much progress that the boy couldn't keep up with me. He had to go back to his gate-post, and content himself with watching me fall at long range.

There was a row of low stepping-stones across one end of the street, a measured yard apart. Even after I got so I could steer pretty fairly I was so afraid of those stones that I always hit them. They gave me the worst falls I ever got in that street, except those which I got from dogs. I have seen it stated that no expert is quick enough to run over a dog; that a dog is always able to skip out of his way. I think that that may be true; but I think that the reason he couldn't run over the dog was because he was trying to. I did not try to run over any dog. But I ran over every dog that came along. I think it makes a great deal of difference. If you try to run over the dog he knows how to calculate, but if you are trying to miss him he does not know how to calculate, and is liable to jump the wrong way every time. It was always so in my experience. Even when I could not hit a wagon I could hit a dog that came to see me practise. They all liked to see me practise, and they all came, for there was very little going on in our neighborhood to entertain a dog. It took time to learn to miss a dog, but I achieved even that.

I can steer as well as I want to, now, and I will catch that boy out one of these days and run over *him* if he doesn't reform.

Get a bicycle. You will not regret it, if you live.

c. 1886

Letter from the Recording Angel

Office of the Recording Angel,
Dept. of Petitions, Jan. 20.

Andrew Langdon,
Coal Dealer, Buffalo, N. Y.

I have the honor, as per command, to inform you that your recent act of benevolence and self-sacrifice has been recorded upon a page by itself of the Book called Golden Deeds of Men; a distinction, I am permitted to remark, which is not merely extraordinary, it is unique.

As regards your prayers, for the week ending the 19th, I have the honor to report as follows:

1. For weather to advance hard coal 15 cents per ton. Granted.

2. For influx of laborers to reduce wages 10 per cent. Granted.

3. For a break in rival soft-coal prices. Granted.

4. For a visitation upon the man, or upon the family of the man, who has set up a competing retail coal-yard in Rochester. Granted, as follows: diphtheria, 2, 1 fatal; scarlet fever, 1, to result in deafness and imbecility. NOTE. This prayer should have been directed against this subordinate's principals, the N. Y. Central RR Co.

5. For deportation to Sheol, of annoying swarms of persons who apply daily for work, or for favors of one sort or another. Taken under advisement for later decision and compromise, this petition appearing to conflict with another one of same date, which will be cited further along.

6. For application of some form of violent death to neighbor who threw brick at family cat, whilst the which was serenading. Reserved for consideration and compromise, because of conflict with a prayer of even date to be cited further along.

7. To "damn the missionary cause." Reserved also—as above.

8. To increase December profits of $22,230 to $45,000 for January, and perpetuate a proportionate monthly increase

thereafter—"which will satisfy you." The prayer granted; the added remark accepted with reservations.

9. For cyclone, to destroy the works and fill up the mine of the North Pennsylvania Co. NOTE: Cyclones are not kept in stock in the winter season. A reliable article of fire-damp can be furnished upon application.

Especial note is made of the above list, they being of particular moment. The 298 remaining supplications classifiable under the head of Special Providences, Schedule A, for week ending 19th, are granted in a body, except that 3 of the 32 cases requiring immediate death have been modified to incurable disease.

This completes the week's invoice of petitions known to this office under the technical designation of Secret Supplications of the Heart, and which for a reason which may suggest itself, always receive our first and especial attention.

The remainder of the week's invoice falls under the head of what we term Public Prayers, in which classification we place prayers uttered in Prayer Meeting, Sunday School, Class Meeting, Family Worship, etc. These kinds of prayers have value according to classification of Christian uttering them. By rule of this office, Christians are divided into two grand classes, to-wit: 1, Professing Christians; 2, Professional Christians. These, in turn, are minutely subdivided and classified by Size, Species, and Family; and finally, Standing is determined by carats, the minimum being 1, the maximum 1,000.

As per balance-sheet for quarter ending Dec. 31st, 1847, you stood classified as follows:

Grand Classification, Professing Christian.

Size, one-fourth of maximum.

Species, Human-Spiritual.

Family, A of the Elect, Division 16.

Standing, 322 carats fine.

As per balance-sheet for quarter just ended,—that is to say, forty years later,—you stand classified as follows:

Grand Classification, Professional Christian.

Size, six one-hundredths of maximum.

Species, Human-Animal.

Family, W of the Elect, Division 1547.

Standing, 3 carats fine.

I have the honor to call your attention to the fact that you seem to have deteriorated.

To resume report upon your Public Prayers—with the side remark that in order to encourage Christians of your grade and of approximate grades, it is the custom of this office to grant many things to them which would not be granted to Christians of a higher grade—partly because they would not be asked for:

Prayer for weather mercifully tempered to the needs of the poor and the naked. Denied. This was a Prayer-Meeting prayer. It conflicts with Item 1 of this Report, which was a Secret Supplication of the Heart. By a rigid rule of this office, certain sorts of Public Prayers of Professional Christians are forbidden to take precedence of Secret Supplications of the Heart.

Prayer for better times and plentier food "for the hard handed son of toil whose patient and exhausting labors make comfortable the homes, and pleasant the ways, of the more fortunate, and entitle him to our vigilant and effective protection from the wrongs and injustices which grasping avarice would do him, and to the tenderest offices of our grateful hearts." Prayer-Meeting Prayer. Refused. Conflicts with Secret Supplication of the Heart No. 2.

Prayer "that such as in any way obstruct our preferences may be generously blessed, both themselves and their families, we here calling our hearts to witness that in their worldly prosperity we are spiritually blessed, and our joys made perfect." Prayer-Meeting Prayer. Refused. Conflicts with Secret Supplications of the Heart Nos. 3 and 4.

"Oh, let none fall heir to the pains of perdition through words or acts of ours." Family Worship. Received fifteen minutes in advance of Secret Supplication of the Heart No. 5, with which it distinctly conflicts. It is suggested that one or the other of these prayers be withdrawn, or both of them modified.

"Be mercifully inclined toward all who would do us offence in our persons or our property." Includes man who threw brick at cat. Family Prayer. Received some minutes in advance of No. 6, Secret Supplications of the Heart. Modification suggested, to reconcile discrepancy.

"Grant that the noble missionary cause, the most precious labor entrusted to the hands of men, may spread and prosper without let or limit in all heathen lands that do as yet reproach us with their spiritual darkness." Uninvited prayer shoved in at meeting of American Board. Received nearly half a day in advance of No. 7, Secret Supplications of the Heart. This office takes no stock in missionaries, and is not connected in any way with the American Board. We should like to grant one of these prayers, but cannot grant both. It is suggested that the American Board one be withdrawn.

This office desires for the twentieth time to call urgent attention to your remark appended to No. 8. It is a chestnut.

Of the 464 specifications contained in your Public Prayers for the week, and not previously noted in this report, we grant 2, and deny the rest. To-wit: Granted, (1), "that the clouds may continue to perform their office; (2), and the sun his." It was the divine purpose anyhow; it will gratify you to know that you have not disturbed it. Of the 462 details refused, 61 were uttered in Sunday School. In this connection I must once more remind you that we grant no Sunday School Prayers of Professional Christians of the classification technically known in this office as the John Wanamaker grade. We merely enter them as "words," and they count to his credit according to number uttered within certain limits of time, 3,000 per quarter-minute required, or no score; 4,200 in a possible 5,000 is a quite common Sunday School score, among experts, and counts the same as two hymns and a bouquet furnished by young ladies in the assassin's cell, execution-morning. Your remaining 401 details count for wind only. We bunch them and use them for head-winds in retarding the ships of improper people, but it takes so many of them to make an impression that we cannot allow anything for their use.

I desire to add a word of my own to this report. When certain sorts of people do a sizeable good deed, we credit them up a thousand-fold more for it than we would in the case of a better man—on account of the strain. You stand far away above your classification-record here, because of certain self-sacrifices of yours which greatly exceed what could have been expected of you. Years ago, when you were worth only

$100,000, and sent $2 to your impoverished cousin the widow, when she appealed to you for help, there were many in heaven who were not able to believe it, and many more who believed that the money was counterfeit. Your character went up many degrees when it was shown that these suspicions were unfounded. A year or two later, when you sent the poor girl $4 in answer to another appeal, everybody believed it, and you were all the talk here for days together. Two years later you sent $6, upon supplication, when the widow's youngest child died, and that act made perfect your good fame. Everybody in heaven said, "Have you heard about Andrew?"—for you are now affectionately called Andrew here. Your increasing donation, every two or three years, has kept your name on all lips, and warm in all hearts. All heaven watches you Sundays, as you drive to church in your handsome carriage; and when your hand retires from the contribution plate, the glad shout is heard even to the ruddy walls of remote Sheol, "Another nickel from Andrew!" But the climax came a few days ago, when the widow wrote and said she could get a school in a far village to teach if she had $50 to get herself and her two surviving children over the long journey; and you counted up last month's clear profit from your three coal mines—$22,230—and added to it the certain profit for the current month—$45,000 and a possible fifty—and then got down your pen and your check-book and mailed her *fifteen whole dollars*! Ah, Heaven bless and keep you forever and ever, generous heart! There was not a dry eye in the realms of bliss; and amidst the hand-shakings, and embracings, and praisings, the decree was thundered forth from the shining mount, that this deed should out-honor all the historic self-sacrifices of men and angels, and be recorded by itself upon a page of its own, for that the strain of it upon you had been heavier and bitterer than the strain it costs ten thousand martyrs to yield up their lives at the fiery stake; and all said, "What is the giving up of life, to a noble soul, or to ten thousand noble souls, compared with the giving up of fifteen dollars out of the greedy grip of the meanest white man that ever lived on the face of the earth?"

And it was a true word. And Abraham, weeping, shook out the contents of his bosom and pasted the eloquent label there,

"RESERVED;" and Peter, weeping, said, "He shall be received with a torchlight procession when he comes;" and then all heaven boomed, and was glad you were going there. And so was hell.

[Signed]
THE RECORDING ANGEL. [seal.]

By command.

c. January 1887

Dinner Speech: General Grant's Grammar

Ninth Annual Reunion Banquet, Army and Navy Club
of Connecticut, Hartford

I will detain you with only just a few words—just a few thousand words; and then give place to a better man—if he has been created. Lately a great and honored author, Matthew Arnold, has been finding fault with General Grant's English. That would be fair enough, maybe, if the examples of imperfect English averaged more instances to the page in General Grant's book than they do in Mr. Arnold's criticism upon the book—but they don't. It would be fair enough, maybe, if such instances were commoner in General Grant's book than they are in the works of the average standard author—but they aren't. In truth, General Grant's derelictions in the matter of grammar and construction are not more frequent than are such derelictions in the works of a majority of the professional authors of our time and of all previous times—authors as exclusively and painstakingly trained to the literary trade as was General Grant to the trade of war. This is not a random statement; it is a fact, and easily demonstrable. I have at home a book called *Modern English Literature: Its Blemishes and Defects*, by Henry H. Breen, F.S.A., a countryman of Mr. Arnold. In it I find examples of bad grammar and slovenly English from the pens of Sydney Smith, Sheridan, Hallam, Whately, Carlyle, both Disraelis, Allison, Junius, Blair, Macaulay, Shakespeare, Milton, Gibbon, Southey, Bulwer, Cobbett, Dr. Samuel Johnson, Trench, Lamb, Landor, Smollett, Walpole, Walker (of the dictionary), Christopher North, Kirke White, Mrs. Sigourney, Benjamin Franklin, Sir Walter Scott, and Mr. Lindley Murray, who made the grammar.

In Mr. Arnold's paper on General Grant's book we find a couple of grammatical crimes and more than several examples of very crude and slovenly English—enough of them to easily entitle him to a *lofty* place in that illustrious list of delinquents just named.

The following passage, all by itself, ought to elect him: "Meade suggested to Grant that he might wish to have immediately under him, Sherman, who had been serving with Grant in the West. *He* begged *him* not to hesitate if *he* thought it for the good of the service. Grant assured *him* that *he* had no thought of moving *him*, and in *his* memoirs, after relating what had passed, *he* adds," etc. To read that passage a couple of times would make a man dizzy; to read it four times would make him drunk. General Grant's grammar is as good as anybody's; but if this were not so, Mr. Breen would brush that inconsequential fact aside and hunt his great book for higher game.

Mr. Breen makes this discriminating remark: "To suppose that because a man is a poet or a historian, he must be correct in his grammar, is to suppose that an architect must be a joiner, or a physician a compounder of medicines." Mr. Breen's point is well taken. If you should climb the mighty Matterhorn to look out over the kingdoms of the earth, it might be a pleasant incident to find strawberries up there. But, great Scott! you don't climb the Matterhorn for strawberries!

I don't think Mr. Arnold was quite wise; for he well knew that that Briton or American was never yet born who could safely assault another man's English; he knew as well as he knows anything, that the man never lived whose English was flawless. Can you believe that Mr. Arnold was immodest enough to imagine himself an exception to this cast iron rule—the sole exception discoverable within the three or four centuries during which the English language proper has been in existence? No, Mr. Arnold did not imagine that; he merely forgot that for a moment he was moving into a glass house, and he had hardly got fairly in before General Fry was shivering the panes over his head.

People may hunt out what microscopic motes they please, but, after all, the fact remains and cannot be dislodged, that General Grant's book is a great, and in its peculiar department unique and unapproachable literary masterpiece. In their line, there is no higher literature than those modest, simple memoirs. Their *style* is at least flawless, and no man can improve upon it; and great books are weighed and measured by their style and matter, not by the trimmings and shadings of their grammar.

There is that about the sun which makes us forget his spots; and when we think of General Grant our pulses quicken and his grammar vanishes; we only remember that this is the simple soldier, who, all untaught of the silken phrase makers, linked words together with an art surpassing the art of the schools, and put into them a something which will still bring to American ears, as long as America shall last, the roll of his vanished drums and the tread of the marching hosts. What do we care for grammar when we think of the man that put together that thunderous phrase: "Unconditional and immediate surrender!" And those others: "I propose to move immediately upon your works!" "I propose to fight it out on this line if it takes all summer!" Mr. Arnold would doubtless claim that that last sentence is not strictly grammatical; and yet it did certainly wake up this nation as a hundred million tons of A No. 1, fourth-proof, hardboiled, hidebound grammar from another mouth couldn't have done. And finally we have that gentler phrase; that one which shows you another true side of the man; shows that in his soldier heart there was room for other than gory war mottoes, and in his tongue the gift to fitly phrase them—"Let us have peace."

April 27, 1887

Consistency

We are continually warned to be consistent—by the pulpit, by the newspaper, by our associates. When we depart from consistency, we are reproached for it by these censors. When a man who has been born and brought up a Jew becomes a Christian, the Jews sorrow over it and reproach him for his inconstancy; all his life he has denied the divinity of Christ, but now he makes a lie of all his past; upon him rests the stigma of inconsistency; we can never be sure of him again. We put *in the deadly parallel columns* what he said *formerly* and what he says *now*, and his credit is *gone*. We say, Trust him *not*; we *know* him now; he will change *again*; and possibly *again* and yet *again*; he has no stability.

There are men called life-long Democrats, life-long Republicans. If one of these departs from his allegiance and votes the other ticket, the same thing happens as in the *Jew's* case. The man loses character. He is inconsistent. He is a traitor. His *past* utterances will be double columned with his *present* ones, and he is damned; also despised—even by his *new* political associates, for in theirs, as in *all* men's eyes, inconsistency is a treason and matter for scorn.

These are facts—common, every-day facts; and I have chosen them for that reason; facts known to everybody, facts which no one denies.

What is the most rigorous law of our being? *Growth.* No smallest atom of our moral, mental, or physical structure can stand still a *year*. It grows—it *must* grow; nothing can *prevent* it. It must grow downward *or* upward; it must grow smaller or larger, better or worse—it cannot stand still. In other words, we *change*—and *must* change, constantly, and keep on changing as long as we live. What, then, is the *true* gospel of consistency? *Change.* Who is the *really* consistent man? The man who changes. Since change is the law of his *being*, he cannot *be* consistent if he stick in a rut.

Yet, as the quoted facts show, there are those who would misteach us that to stick in a rut *is* consistency—and a *virtue*; and that to climb *out* of the rut is inconsistency—and a *vice*.

They will grant you certain things, without murmur or dissent—as things which go without saying; truisms. They will grant that in time the crawling baby *walks* and must not be required to go *on crawling*; that in time the *youth* has *outgrown* the *child's jacket* and must not be required to crowd himself *into* it; they grant you that a child's *knowledge* is becoming and proper to the *child only* so they grant him a school and *teach* him, so that he may *change* and *grow*; they grant you that he must keep *on* learning—through youth and manhood and straight *on*—he must not be allowed to suppose that the knowledge of *thirty* can be any proper equipment for his *fiftieth* year; they will grant you that a young man's opinions about mankind and the universe are *crude*, and sometimes *foolish*, and they would not dream of requiring him to stick to them the rest of his life, lest by changing them he bring down upon himself the reproach of *inconsistency*. They will grant you *these*, and everything *else* you can think of, in the line of progress and change, until you get down to politics and religion; there they draw the *line*. These must suffer no change. Once a Presbyterian, *always* a Presbyterian, or you are inconsistent and a *traitor*; once a Democrat, *always* a Democrat, or you are inconsistent and a *traitor*—a turncoat.

It is curious logic. Is there but *one* kind of treason? No man *remains* the same sort of Presbyterian he was at *first*—the thing is *impossible*; time and various *influences modify* his Presbyterianism; it *narrows* or it *broadens*, grows *deeper* or *shallower*, but does not stand *still*. In some cases it grows so far beyond itself, upward *or* downward, that nothing is really *left of it* but the *name*, and perhaps an inconsequential *rag* of the original substance, the *bulk* being now Baptist or Buddhist or something. Well, if he go over to the Buddhists, he is a traitor. To whom? To what? No man can answer *those* questions rationally. Now if he does *not* go over what is he? Plainly a traitor to *himself*, a traitor to the best and the highest and the honestest that is *in* him. Which of these treasons is the blackest one—and the shamefulest? Which is the real and right consistency? To be consistent to a sham and an empty name, or consistent to the law of one's *being*, which is *change*, and in this case requires him to move forward and keep abreast of his best mental and moral progress, his highest convictions of the right and the true? Suppose this treason to the name of a church should carry him clear outside of *all* churches? Is that a blacker treason than to *remain*? So long as he is loyal to his best *self*, what should he care for *other* loyalties? It seems to me that a man should secure the *Well done, faithful servant*, of his own conscience *first* and foremost, and let all other loyalties go.

I have referred to the fact that when a man retires from his political party he is a *traitor*—that he is so *pronounced* in plain language. *That* is *bold*; so bold as to deceive many into the fancy that it is *true*. Desertion, treason—these are the terms applied. Their *military form* reveals the thought in the man's mind who uses them; to *him* a political party is an *army*. Well, *is* it? Are the two things identical? Do they even *resemble* each other? Necessarily a political party is not an army of conscripts, for *they* are in the ranks by *compulsion*. Then it must be a *regular* army, or an army of volunteers. *Is* it a *regular* army? No, for *these* enlist for a specified and well-understood *term* and can retire without reproach when the term is up. Is it an army of *volunteers* who have *enlisted for the war*, and may righteously be shot if they leave before the war is finished? No, it is not even an army in *that* sense. Those fine military terms are high-sounding, empty *lies*—and are no more rationally applicable to a political party than they would be to an oyster bed. The volunteer soldier comes to the recruiting office and strips himself, and proves that he is so many feet high, and has sufficiently good teeth, and no fingers gone, and is sufficiently sound in body *generally*; he is accepted, but *not* until he has sworn a deep *oath*, or made other solemn form of *promise*, to march under that flag until that war is done or his term of enlistment completed. What is the process when a *voter* joins a *party*? Must he prove that he is sound in *any* way, mind *or* body? Must he prove that *he knows* anything—whatever—is capable *of* anything? Does he take an oath or make a *promise* of any sort?—or doesn't he leave himself entirely *free*? If he were informed by the political boss that if he join it must be forever; that he must be that party's chattel and wear its brass collar the rest of his days, would not that *insult* him? It goes without saying. He would say some rude, unprintable thing and turn his back on that preposterous organization.

But the political boss puts *no* conditions upon him at *all*; and his volunteer makes no promises, enlists for no stated *term*. He has in *no sense* become a part of an *army*, he is in no way restrained of his *freedom*. Yet he will presently find that his bosses and his newspapers have assumed just the reverse of that; that they have blandly arrogated to themselves an iron-clad military *authority* over him; and within twelve months, if he is an average man, he will have *surrendered* his liberty, and will actually be silly enough to believe that he cannot leave that party, for any cause whatever, without being a shameful *traitor*, a deserter, a legitimately dishonored *man*.

There you have the just measure of that freedom of conscience, freedom of opinion, freedom of speech and action, which we hear so much inflated foolishness about, as being the precious possession of the Republic. Whereas, in *truth*, the surest way for a man to make of himself a target for almost universal scorn, obloquy, slander, and insult is to stop twaddling about these priceless independencies, and attempt to *exercise* one of them. If he is a preacher, half his congregation will clamor for his expulsion, and *will* expel him, except they find it will injure real estate in the neighborhood; if he is a mechanic, he will be discharged, promptly; if he is a lawyer, his clients will take their business elsewhere; if he is a doctor, his own dead will turn against him.

I repeat that the new party member who supposed himself independent will presently find that the party has somehow got a mortgage on his soul, and that within a year he will *recognize* the mortgage, deliver up his liberty, and actually believe he cannot retire from that party from *any* motive, howsoever high and right, in his *own* eyes, without shame and dishonor.

Is it possible for human wickedness to invent a doctrine more infernal and poisonous than this? Is there *imaginable* a baser servitude than it imposes? What slave is so degraded as the slave who is *proud* that he *is* a slave? What is the *essential difference* between a life-long *Democrat* and any other kind of life-long *slave*? Is it less humiliating to dance to the lash of *one* master than *another*?

This atrocious doctrine of allegiance to *party* plays directly into the hands of politicians of the *baser* sort—and doubtless for *that* it was borrowed—or stolen—from the monarchical system. It enables them to foist upon the country officials whom no self-respecting man would *vote* for, if he could but come to understand that loyalty to *himself* is his first and *highest* duty, not loyalty to any *party name*. The wire workers, convention packers, know they are not obliged to put up the *fittest* man for the office, for they know that the docile party will vote for any forked thing they *put up*, even though it do not even strictly *resemble a man*.

I am persuaded—convinced—that this idea of *consistency*—unchanging allegiance to *party*—has lowered the manhood of the whole *nation*—pulled it down and dragged it in the mud. When Mr. Blaine was nominated for the Presidency, I *knew* the man; no, I *judged* I knew him; I don't know him *now*, but at *that* time I *judged* I *knew* him; for my daily paper had been painting him black, and blacker, and blacker *still*, for a series of *years*, during which it had no call to speak anything but the *truth* about him, no call to be *malicious* toward him, no call to be otherwise than just simply and honestly *candid* about him, since he belonged to its *own party* and was not before the nation as a detectable candidate for anything. But within thirty days after the nomination that paper had him all painted up *white* again. *That* is not allegiance to one's best *self*, one's straitest *convictions*; it is allegiance to *party*. Nobody likes to eat a ton of black *paint*, and none but the *master* can make the slave *do* it. Was this paper *alone* at this singular feast? *No*; ten thousand *other* Republican newspapers sat down at the same table and worried down *their* ton apiece; and not any fewer than *100,000* more-or-less-prominent *politicians* sat down all over this country and worried down *their* ton apiece; and after long, long and bitter gagging, some *millions* of the *common* serfdom of the party sat down and worried down *their* ton apiece. *Paint?* It was *dirt*. Enough of it was eaten by the meek Republican party to build a railroad embankment from here to *Japan*; and it pains me to think that a year from now they will probably have to eat it all *over* again.

Well, there was a *lot* of queer feasting done in those days. One *learned in the law* pondered the Mulligan letters and other *frightful* literature, and rendered this impressive verdict: he said the evidence would not *convict* Mr. Blaine in a *court of law*, and so he would *vote* for him. He did not *say* whether the evidences would prove him *innocent* or not. *That* wasn't important.

Now, he knew that this verdict was absolutely inconclusive. He knew that it settled nothing, established nothing whatever, and was wholly valueless as a guide for his action, an answer to his questionings.

He knew that the merciful and righteous barriers raised up by the laws of our humane age for the shelter and protection of the possibly innocent, have often and over again protected and rescued the certainly *guilty*. He knew that in this way many and many a prisoner has gone unchastised from the court when judge and jury and the whole public believed with all their hearts that he was guilty. He knew—all credit not discredit to our age that it is so—that this result is so frequent, so almost commonplace, that the mere failure to satisfy the exacting forms of law and prove a man guilty in a *court*, is a hundred thousand miles from proving him innocent. You see a hiccoughing man wallowing in the gutter at two o'clock in the morning; you think the thing all over and weigh the details of it in your mind as you walk home, and with immeasurable wisdom arrive at the verdict that *you don't know he wasn't a Prohibitionist*. Of course you don't, and if you stop and think a minute you would realize that you don't know he *was*, either.

Well, a good clergyman who read the Mulligan and other published evidences was not able to *make* up *his* mind, but concluded to take refuge in the verdict rendered by the citizen learned in the *law*; take his intellectual and moral food at second-hand, though he doesn't *rank* as an intellectual infant, unable to chew his own moral and mental nourishment; he decided that an *apparently colored* person who couldn't be proven to be black *in the baffling crosslights of a court of law* was white enough for *him*, he being a little color blind, *anyway*, in matters where the *party* is concerned, and so *he* came reluctantly to the polls, with his redeeming blush on his countenance, and put in his vote.

I met a certain *other* clergyman on the *corner* the day after the nomination. He was very uncompromising. He said: "I *know* Blaine to the *core*; I have known him from boyhood *up*;

and I know him to be utterly unprincipled and unscrupulous." Within six weeks after that, this clergyman was at a Republican *mass* meeting in the Opera House, and I think he presided. At *any* rate, he made a speech. If you did not know that the character depicted in it meant Mr. Blaine, you would suppose it meant—well, there isn't anybody down here on the *earth* that you can use as a comparison. It is praise, praise, praise; laudation, laudation, laudation; glorification, glorification, canonization. Conceive of the general crash and upheaval and ripping and tearing and readjustment of things that must have been going on in that man's moral and mental chaos for six weeks! What is any combination of inflammatory rheumatism and St. Vitus's dance to *this*? When the doctrine of allegiance to party can utterly up-end a man's moral constitution and make a temporary *fool* of him *besides*, what excuse are you going to offer for preaching it, teaching it, extending it, perpetuating it? Shall you say, the best good of the country demands allegiance to party? Shall you also say it demands that a man kick his truth and his conscience into the gutter, and become a mouthing lunatic, *besides*? Oh, no! you say; it does not demand *that*. But what if it *produce* that, in *spite* of you? There is no obligation upon a man to do things which he ought *not* to do, when *drunk*, but most men *will* do them, just the same, and so we hear no arguments about obligations in the matter; we only hear men warned to *avoid* the habit of *drinking*; get *rid* of the thing that can betray men into such things.

This is a funny business, all round. The same men who enthusiastically preach loyal consistency to church and party are always ready and willing and anxious to persuade a Chinaman or an Indian or a Kanaka to desert *his* Church, or a fellow-American to desert *his* party. The man who deserts to them is all that is high and pure and beautiful—apparently; the man who deserts from them is all that is foul and despicable. This is Consistency with a capital C.

With the daintiest and self-complacentest sarcasm the lifelong loyalist scoffs at the Independent—or, as he calls him, with cutting irony, the Mugwump; makes himself too killingly funny for anything in this world about him. But—the Mugwump can stand it, for there is a great history at his back, stretching down the centuries, and he comes of a mighty ancestry. *He* knows that in the whole history of the race of men no single great and high and beneficent thing was ever done for the souls and bodies, the hearts and the brains, of the children of this world, but a Mugwump started it and Mugwumps carried it to victory. And their names are the stateliest in history: Washington, Garrison, Galileo, Luther, Christ. Loyalty to petrified opinions never yet broke a chain or freed a human soul in *this* world—and never *will*.

To return to the starting point: I am persuaded that the world has been tricked into adopting some false and most pernicious notions about *consistency*—and to such a degree that the average man has turned the rights and *wrongs* of things entirely *around*, and is *proud* to be "consistent," unchanging, immovable, fossilized, where it should be his humiliation that he is so.

December 2, 1887

Post-Prandial Oratory

Forefathers Day Dinner, Congregational Club, Boston

In treating of this subject of post-prandial oratory, a subject which I have long been familiar with and may be called an expert in observing it in others, I wish to say that a public dinner is the most delightful thing in the whole world, to a guest. That is one fact. And here is another one: a public dinner is the most unutterable suffering in the whole world, to a guest. These two facts don't seem to jibe—but I will explain. Now at a public dinner when a man knows he is going to be called upon to speak, and is thoroughly well prepared—got it all by heart, and the pauses all marked in his head where the applause is going to come in—a public dinner is just heaven to that man. He won't care to be anywhere else than just where he is. But when at a public dinner it is getting way along toward the end of things, and a man is sitting over his glass of wine, or his glass of milk, according to the kind of banquet it is, in ever-augmenting danger of being called up, and isn't prepared, and knows he can never prepare with the thoughtless gander at his elbow bothering him all the time with exasperating talky-talk about nothing, that man is just as nearly in the other place as ever he wants to be. Why, it is a cruel situation. That man is to be pitied; and the very worst of it is that the minute he gets on his feet he *is* pitied.

Now he could stand the pity of ten people or a dozen, but there is no misery in the world that is comparable to the massed and solidified compassion of five hundred. Why, that wide Sahara of sympathizing faces completely takes the tuck out of him, makes a coward of him. He stands there in his misery, and stammers out the usual rubbish about not being prepared, and not expecting, and all that kind of folly, and he is wandering and stumbling and getting further and further in, and all the time unhappy, and at last he fetches out a poor, miserable, crippled joke, and in his grief and confusion he laughs at it himself and the others look sick; and then he slumps into his chair and wishes he was dead. He knows he is a defeated man, and so do the others.

Now to a humane person that is a heartrending spectacle. It is indeed. That sort of sacrifice ought to be stopped, and there is only one way to accomplish it that I can think of, and that is for a man to go always prepared, always loaded, always ready, whether he is likely to be called upon or not. You can't defeat that man, you can't pity him at all. My scheme is this, that he shall carry in his head a cut-and-dried and thoroughly and glibly memorized speech that will fit every conceivable public occasion in this life, fit it to a dot, and win success and applause every time. Now I have completed a speech of that kind, and I have brought it along to exhibit here as a sample.

Now, then, supposing a man with his cut-and-dried speech, this patent adjustable speech, as you may call it, finds himself at a granger gathering, or a wedding breakfast, or a theological disturbance or a political blowout, an inquest, or funeral anywhere in the world you choose to mention, and be suddenly called up, all he has got to do is to change three or four words in that speech, and make his delivery anguishing and tearful, or chippy and facetious, or luridly and thunderously eloquent just as the occasion happens to call for, and just turn himself loose, and he is all right, but I will illustrate, and instead of explanations I will deliver that speech itself just enough times to make you see the possibilities.

We suppose that it is a granger gathering, and this man is suddenly called on; he comes up with some artful hesitancies and diffidences and repetitions, so as to give the idea that the speech is impromptu. Here, of course, after he has got used to delivering it, he can venture outside and make a genuine impromptu remark to start off with. For instance, if a distinguished person is present, he can make a complimentary reference to him, say to Mr. Depew. He could speak about his great talent or his clothes. Such a thing gives him a sort of opening, and about the time that audience is getting to pity that man, he opens his throttle valve and goes for those grangers. That person wants to be gorgeously eloquent; you want to fire the farmer's heart and start him from his mansard down to his cellar.

Now this man is called up, and he says: "I am called up suddenly, sir, and am indeed not, not prepared to—to—I was not expecting to be called up, sir, but I will, with what effect I may, add my shout to the jubilations of this spirit-stirring occasion. Agriculture, sir, is, after all, the palladium of our economic liberties. By it—approximately speaking—we may be said to live, and move, and have our being. All that we have been, all that we are, all that we hope to be, was, is, and must continue to be, profoundly influenced by that sublimest of the mighty interests of man, thrice glorious agriculture! While we have life, while we have soul, and in that soul the sweet and hallowed sentiment of gratitude, let us with generous accord attune our voices to songs of praise, perennial outpourings of thanksgiving, for that most precious boon, whereby we physically thrive, whereby our otherwise sterile existence is made rich and strong, and grand and aspiring, and is adorned with a mighty and far-reaching and all-embracing grace, and beauty, and purity and loveliness! The least of us knows—the least of us feels—the humblest among us will confess that, whereas—but the hour is late, sir, and I will not detain you."

Now then, supposing it is not a granger gathering at all, but is a wedding breakfast; now, of course, that speech has got to be delivered in an airy, light fashion, but it must terminate seriously. It is a mistake to make it any other way. This person is called up by the minister of the feast and he says: "I am called up suddenly, sir, and am, indeed, not prepared to—to—I was not expecting to be called up, sir, but I will, with what effect I may, add my shout to the jubilations of this spirit-stirring occasion. Matrimony, sir, is, after all, the palladium of our domestic liberties. By it—approximately speaking—we may be said to live, and move, and acquire our being. All that we have been, all that we are, all that we hope to be, was, is, and must continue to be profoundly influenced by that sublimest of the mighty interests of man, thrice glorious matrimony! While we have life, while we have soul, and in that soul the sweet and hallowed sentiment of gratitude, let us with generous accord attune our voices to songs of praise, perennial outpourings of thanksgiving, for that most precious boon whereby we numerically thrive, whereby our otherwise sterile existence is made rich, and strong, and grand, and aspiring, and is adorned with a mighty and far-reaching and all-embracing grace, and beauty, and purity and loveliness!

The least of us knows—the least of us feels—the humblest
among us will confess, that whereas—but the hour is late, sir,
and I will not detain you."

Now, then, supposing that the occasion—I make one more
illustration, so that you will always be perfectly safe, here or
anywhere—supposing that this is an occasion of an inquest.
This is a most elastic speech in a matter of that kind. Where
there are grades of men you must observe them. At a private
funeral of some friend you want to be just as mournful as you
can, but in the case where you don't know the person, grade
it accordingly. You want simply to be impressive. That is all.
Now take a case halfway between, about No. 4½, somewhere
about there, that is, an inquest on a second cousin, a wealthy
second cousin. He has remembered you in the will. Of course
all these things count. They all raise the grade a little, and—
well, perhaps he hasn't remembered you. Perhaps he has left
you a horse, an ordinary horse, a good enough horse, one
that can go about three minutes, or perhaps a pair of horses.
It may have been one pair of horses at hand, not two pair or
two pair and a jack. I don't know whether you understand
that, but there are people here—. Well, now then, this is a
second cousin, and he knows all the circumstances. We will
say that he has lost his life trying to save somebody from
drowning. Well, he saved the mind-cure physician from
drowning, he tried to save him, but he didn't succeed. Of
course he wouldn't succeed; of course you wouldn't want him
to succeed in that way and plan. A person must have some
experience and aplomb and all that before he can save anybody from drowning of the mind-cure. I am just making
these explanations here. A person can get so glib in a delivery
of this speech, why by the time he has delivered it fifteen or
twenty times he could go to any intellectual gathering in Boston even, and he would draw like a prizefight. Well, at the
inquest of a second cousin under these circumstances, a man
gets up with graded emotion and he says:

"I am called up suddenly, sir, and am, indeed, not prepared
to—to—I was not expecting to be called up, sir, but I will,
with what effect I may, add my shout—voice to the lamen-
tations of this spirit-crushing occasion. Death, death, sir, is,
after all, the palladium of our spiritual liberties. By it—

approximately speaking—we may be said to live, and move and have our ending. All that we have been, all that we may be here, all that we hope to be, was, is, and must continue to be profoundly influenced by that sublimest of the mighty interests of man, thrice-sorrowful dissolution. While we have life, while we have soul, and in that soul the sweet and hallowed sentiment of gratitude, let us with generous accord attune our voices to songs of praise, perennial outpourings of thanksgiving, for that most precious boon by which we spiritually thrive, whereby our otherwise sterile existence is made rich, and strong, and grand, and aspiring, and is adorned with a mighty and far-reaching and all-embracing grace, and beauty and purity, and loveliness. The least of us knows—the least of us feels—the humblest among us will confess, that whereas—but the hour is late, sir, and I will not detain you."

The speech as used at a funeral may be used to prop up prohibition, and also anti-prohibition, without change, except to change the terms of sorrow to terms of rejoicing.

The speech as used at a granger meeting may be used in Boston at the sacred feast of baked beans without any alteration except to change agriculture—where it occurs in the second sentence—to "the baked bean," and to "bean culture" where it occurs in the fourth.

The agricultural speech becomes a prohibition speech by putting in that word and changing "economic" to moral, and "physically" to morally. It becomes a Democratic, Republican, Mugwump or other political speech by shoving in the party name and changing "economic" to political, and "physically" to politically.

Any of these forms can be used at a New England Forefathers dinner. *They* don't care what you talk about, so long as it ain't so.

December 20, 1887

A Petition to the Queen of England

HARTFORD, *Nov.* 6, 1887.

MADAM: You will remember that last May Mr. Edward Bright, the clerk of the Inland Revenue Office, wrote me about a tax which he said was due from me to the Government on books of mine published in London—that is to say, an income tax on the royalties. I do not know Mr. Bright, and it is embarrassing to me to correspond with strangers; for I was raised in the country and have always lived there, the early part in Marion county Missouri before the war, and this part in Hartford county Connecticut, near Bloomfield and about 8 miles this side of Farmington, though some call it 9, which it is impossible to be, for I have walked it many and many a time in considerably under three hours, and General Hawley says he has done it in two and a quarter, which is not likely; so it has seemed best that I write your Majesty. It is true that I do not know your Majesty personally, but I have met the Lord Mayor, and if the rest of the family are like him, it is but just that it should be named royal; and likewise plain that in a family matter like this, I cannot better forward my case than to frankly carry it to the head of the family itself. I have also met the Prince of Wales once in the fall of 1873, but it was not in any familiar way, but in a quite informal way, being casual, and was of course a surprise to us both. It was in Oxford street, just where you come out of Oxford into Regent Circus, and just as he turned up one side of the circle at the head of a procession, I went down the other side on the top of an omnibus. He will remember me on account of a gray coat with flap pockets that I wore, as I was the only person on the omnibus that had on that kind of a coat; I remember him of course as easy as I would a comet. He looked quite proud and satisfied, but that is not to be wondered at, he has a good situation. And once I called on your Majesty, but you were out.

But that is no matter, it happens with everybody. However, I have wandered a little, away from what I started about. It was this way. Young Bright wrote my London publishers Chatto and Windus—their place is the one on the left as you

come down Piccadilly, about a block and a half above where
the minstrel show is—he wrote them that he wanted them to
pay income tax on the royalties of some foreign authors,
namely, "Miss De La Ramé (Ouida), Dr. Oliver Wendell
Holmes, Mr. Francis Bret Harte, and Mr. Mark Twain." Well,
Mr. Chatto diverted him from the others, and tried to divert
him from me, but in this case he failed. So then, young Bright
wrote me. And not only that, but he sent me a printed document the size of a news paper, for me to sign, all over in
different places. Well, it was that kind of a document that the
more you study it the more it undermines you and makes
everything seem uncertain to you; and so, while in that condition, and really not responsible for my acts, I wrote Mr.
Chatto to pay the tax and charge to me. Of course my idea
was, that it was for only one year, and that the tax would be
only about one per cent or along there somewhere, but last
night I met Professor Sloane of Princeton—you may not
know him, but you have probably seen him every now and
then, for he goes to England a good deal, a large man and
very handsome and absorbed in thought, and if you have noticed such a man on platforms after the train is gone, that is
the one, he generally gets left, like all those specialists and
other scholars who know everything but how to apply it—
and he said it was a back tax for *three* years, and no one per
cent, but two and a half!

That gave what had seemed a little matter, a new aspect. I
then began to study the printed document again, to see if
I could find anything in it that might modify my case, and I
had what seems to be a quite promising success. For instance,
it opens thus—polite and courteous, the way those English
government documents always are—I do not say that to hear
myself talk, it is just the fact, and it is a credit:

"To MR. MARK TWAIN: IN PURSUANCE of the Acts of
Parliament for granting to Her Majesty Duties and Profits,"
etc.

I had not noticed that before. My idea had been that it was
for the Government, and so I wrote *to* the Government; but
now I saw that it was a private matter, a family matter, and
that the proceeds went to yourself, not the Government. I
would always rather treat with principals, and I am glad I

noticed that clause. With a principal, one can always get at a fair and right understanding, whether it is about potatoes, or continents, or any of those things, or something entirely different; for the size or nature of the thing does not affect the fact; whereas, as a rule, a subordinate is more or less troublesome to satisfy. And yet this is not against them, but the other way. They have their duties to do, and must be harnessed to rules, and not allowed any discretion. Why if your Majesty should equip young Bright with discretion—I mean his own discretion—it is an even guess that he would discretion you out of house and home in 2 or 3 years. He would not *mean* to get the family into straits, but that would be the upshot, just the same. Now then, with Bright out of the way, this is not going to be any Irish question; it is going to be settled pleasantly and satisfactorily for all of us, and when it is finished your Majesty is going to stand with the American people just as you have stood for fifty years, and surely no monarch can require better than that of an alien nation. They do not all pay a British income tax, but the most of them will in time, for we have shoals of new authors coming along every year; and of the population of your Canada, upwards of four-fifths are wealthy Americans, and more going there all the time.

Well, another thing which I noticed in the Document, was an item about "Deductions." I will come to that presently, your Majesty. And another thing was this: that Authors are not mentioned in the Document at all. No, we have "Quarries, Mines, Iron Works, Salt Springs, Alum Mines, Water Works, Canals, Docks, Drains, Levels, Fishings, Fairs, Tolls, Bridges, Ferries," and so-forth and so-forth and so-on—well, as much as a yard or a yard and a half of them, I should think—anyway a very large quantity or number. I read along—down, and down, and down the list, further, and further, and further, and as I approached the bottom my hopes began to rise higher and higher, because I saw that everything in England, *that* far, was taxed by name and in detail, except perhaps the family, and maybe Parliament, and yet still no mention of Authors. Apparently they were going to be overlooked. And sure enough, they were! My heart gave a great bound. But I was too soon. There was a foot note, in Mr.

Bright's hand, which said: "You are taxed under Schedule D, section 14." I turned to that place, and found these three things: "Trades, Offices, Gas Works."

Of course, after a moment's reflection, hope came up again, and then certainty: Mr. Bright was in error, and clear off the track; for Authorship is not a Trade, it is an inspiration; Authorship does not keep an Office, its habitation is all out under the sky, and everywhere where the winds are blowing and the sun is shining and the creatures of God are free. Now then, since I have no Trade and keep no Office, I am not taxable under Schedule D, section 14. Your Majesty sees that; so I will go on to that other thing that I spoke of, the "deductions"—deductions from my tax which I may get allowed, under conditions. Mr. Bright says all deductions to be claimed by me must be restricted to the provisions made in Paragraph No. 8, entitled "Wear and Tear of Machinery, or Plant." This is curious, and shows how far he has gotten away on his wrong course after once he has got started wrong: for Offices and Trades do not have Plant, they do not have Machinery, such a thing was never heard of; and moreover they do not wear and tear. You see that, your Majesty, and that it is true. Here is the Paragraph No. 8:

Amount claimed as a deduction for diminished value by reason of Wear and Tear, where the Machinery or Plant belongs to the Person or Company carrying on the Concern, or is let to such Person or Company so that the Lessee is bound to maintain and deliver over the same in good condition:—
    *Amount £*_____

There it is—the very words.

I could answer Mr. Bright thus:

It is my pride to say that my Brain is my Plant; and I do not claim any deduction for diminished value by reason of Wear and Tear, for the reason that it does not wear and tear, but stays sound and whole all the time. Yes, I could say to him, my Brain is my Plant, my Skull is my Workshop, my Hand is my Machinery, and I am the Person carrying on the Concern; it is not leased to anybody, and so there is no

Lessee bound to maintain and deliver over the same in good condition. There. I do not wish to any way overrate this argument and answer, dashed off just so, and not a word of it altered from the way I first wrote it, your Majesty, but indeed it does seem to pulverize that young fellow, you can see that yourself. But that is all I say; I stop there; I never pursue a person after I have got him down.

Having thus shown your Majesty that I am not taxable, but am the victim of the error of a clerk who mistakes the nature of my commerce, it only remains for me to beg that you will of your justice annul my letter that I spoke of, so that my publisher can keep back that tax-money which, in the confusion and aberration caused by the Document, I ordered him to pay. You will not miss the sum, but this is a hard year for authors; and as for lectures, I do not suppose your Majesty ever saw such a dull season.

With always great, and ever increasing respect, I beg to sign myself your Majesty's servant to command,

MARK TWAIN.

HER MAJESTY THE QUEEN, LONDON.

December 1887

American Authors and British Pirates

A PRIVATE LETTER AND A PUBLIC POSTSCRIPT.

MY DEAR MATTHEWS:

Come, now, what your cause needs is, that some apparent sufferer shall say a fair word for the other side. That complaint which cannot hunt up a dissenting voice anywhere is out of luck. A thing which is all good or all bad is properly an object of suspicion in this world; we get a sort of impression that it is off its beat; that it belongs in the next world, above or below—climate not suited to it here.

English pirates have hurt me somewhat; how much, I do not know. But, on the other hand, English *law* has helped me vastly. Can any foreign author of books say that about American law? You know he can't.

Look at the matter calmly, reasonably. As I infer, from what you say about your article, your complaint is, that American authors are pirated in England. Well, whose fault is that? It is nobody's but the author's. England furnishes him a perfect remedy; if he does not choose to take advantage of it, let him have self-respect enough to retire to the privacy of his cradle, not sit out on the public curbstone and cry. To-day the American author can go to Canada, spend three days there, and come home with an English and Canadian copyright which is as strong as if it had been built out of railroad iron. If he does not make this trip and do this thing, it is a confession that he does not think his foreign market valuable enough to justify the expense of securing it by the above process. Now it may turn out that that book is presently pirated in London. What then? Why, simply this: the pirate has paid that man a compliment; he has thought more of the book than the man thought of it himself. And doubtless the man is not pecuniarily injured, since the pirate would probably not have offered anything for the book if it had been copyrighted, but would merely have left it in oblivion and unpublished.

I believe, and it stands to reason, that all the American books that are pirated in these latter days in England are of the complimentary sort, and that the piracies work no computable injury to the author's pocket; and I also believe that if this class of books should be copyrighted henceforth, their publication over there would cease, and then all the loss would fall upon the authors, since they wouldn't be any better off, as regards money, than they were before, and would lose their compliment besides.

I think we are not in a good position to throw bricks at the English pirate. We haven't any to spare. We need them to throw at the American Congress; and at the American author, who neglects his great privileges and then tries to hunt up some way to throw the blame upon the only nation in the world that is magnanimous enough to say to him: "While you are the guest of our laws and our flag, you shall not be robbed."

All the books which I have published in the last fifteen years are protected by English copyright. In that time I have suffered pretty heavily in temper and pocket from imperfect copyright laws; but they were American, not English. I have no quarrel over there.

Yours sincerely,

MARK TWAIN.

P. S. (of the feminine sort). I wrote the above (but have concluded not to mail it directly to you) in answer to your letter asking me for facts and statistics concerning English piracies of my books. I had to guess at the probable nature of your NEW PRINCETON article from what you said of it. But I sent out for it this morning, and have read it through. Why, dear, dear distorted mind, I am amazed at you. You stand recorded in the directory, "Brander Matthews, lawyer, 71 Broadway." By your article I half suspected that you were a lawyer, and so I went to the directory to see. It seemed to me that only a lawyer—an old lawyer—a callous, leathery, tough old lawyer—could have the superb pluck to venture into court with such a ragged case as yours is. Why, dear soul, you haven't a leg to stand on, anywhere. I have known you long, and loved you always; but you must let me be frank and say, you haven't a fact that cannot be amply offset by the other side, you haven't an argument that cannot be promptly turned against you.

To start with, you wander a little off to one side of your real case, to tell the world that a couple of reverend British reprobates have been plagiarizing—stealing—from American books. That is a telling fact—if American preachers never steal. But, dear sir, they do. Take this case. E. H. House spends twelve or thirteen years in Japan; becomes exhaustively versed in Japanese affairs; coins these riches into an admirable article, and prints it in the *Atlantic* six years ago, under the title, "The Martyrdom of an Empire." This present year, Rev. James King Newton, A. M., "Professor of Modern Languages, Oberlin College," confers upon the literary museum of the *Bibliotheca Sacra* a crazy-quilt which he wordily names, "Obligations of the United States to Initiate a Revision of Treaties between the Western Powers and Japan." This queer work is made up of rags and scraps of sense and nonsense, sham and sincerity, theft and butter-mouthed piousness, modesty and egotism, facts and lies, knowledge and ignorance, first-rate English and fortieth-rate English, wind and substance, dignity and paltriness, and all through the air about it you seem to catch the soft clear note of flutes and birds, mingled with the wild weird whoopjamboreehoo of the embattled jackass. Now, part of that strange article is original. The rest of it was "smouched" from House's *Atlantic* paper. Will you have a sample?

Atlantic Monthly, May, 1881.	*Bibliotheca Sacra, January,* 1887.
The first effective commercial treaty with Japan was draughted by him in 1858, upon terms which, in general, were not disadvantageous to the unsophisticated people with whom he was dealing.	Mr. Harris made our first commercial treaty in 1858, upon terms which, in general, were reasonable, in an experimental treaty, and not disadvantageous to the unsophisticated people with whom he was dealing.
If he had taken the precaution to insure the absolute expiration of the treaty and its appendages at a proper date, all would have resulted as he desired.	If he had taken the precaution to insure the absolute expiration of the treaty and its appendages at some definite time, all would have resulted according to his honest intention.

| The working of the treaty has proved flagrantly injurious to Japan and proportionately favorable to the foreign powers—exceptionally favorable to England, that country having the most extensive trade connection. | The working of the treaties has proved most disastrous to Japan, and proportionately favorable to the western powers; exceptionally so to England, as she has the largest trade connections. |
| Precisely what this country intended to accomplish by that imposing deed it would be difficult to say. What it did accomplish, etc. | Precisely what our government intended to accomplish by the imposing deed of opening Japan, it would be difficult to say. What it did accomplish, etc. |

There you have four samples. I could give you twenty-four more, if they were needed, to show how exactly Mr. Newton can repeat slathers and slathers of another man's literature without ever missing a trick, when the police ain't around. You can get that thing if you would like to look at it. Brer Newton has issued it in pamphlet form, at a Boston admirer's expense; and has printed up in the corner of the cover, "With the Author's Compliments"—meaning House, per'aps.

But then, we are all thieves, and it wasn't worth your while to go out of your way to call particular attention to a couple of reverend British ones.

However, right away you come down to business, and open up your real case. You say: "In 1876, Longfellow" complained that he had been pirated by twenty-two publishers. Did he mean, *after* England had offered him and the rest of us protection, and was standing always ready to make her offer good?

Next, "in 1856, Hawthorne"—some more ancient history. You follow it with more and more and more examples—of ancient history; ancient history, and, properly and righteously, out of court. By no fairness can they be cited in this modern time; by no legitimate pretext can they be summoned to testify in this case of yours. What you are complaining about, what you are making all this trouble about, is a bitter grievance which passed out of this world and into its eternal grave more than fifteen years ago. When I say eternal, I mean,

of course, if you will let it alone. Matthews, it is a dead issue
—utterly dead, and legally forgotten—and I don't believe
that even you can aggravate Parliament into resurrecting it,
though you certainly do seem to be doing your level best in
that direction.

Now, honestly, as between friend and friend, what could
ever have put it into your head to hunt out such a grotesquely
barren text for a magazine article? *We* are doing all the pirat-
ing in these days; the English used to be in the business, but
they dropped out of it long ago. Just look at yourself and
your fantastic complaint by the light of allegory. Suppose one
of those big Mohammedan slave-dealers in the interior of Africa, lashing his yoked caravan of poor naked creatures
through jungle and forest, should turn his grieved attention
to us, and between his lashings and thrashings passionately
upbraid us with the reminder that "in 1856," and other years
and seasons of a hoary and odious antiquity, we used to own
our brother human beings, and used to buy them and sell
them, lash them, thrash them, break their piteous hearts—
and we ought to be ashamed of ourselves, so we ought! What
should we answer? What should we say to him? What would
you say to him concerning so particularly dead an issue as
that?—as a lawyer, that is, strictly as a lawyer. I do not know
what you would say, but I know what you *could* say. You
could say: "Let me take that obsolete case of yours into court;
my hand is in, I have been handling one that is just like it—
the twin to it, in fact."

In your dozen pages you mention a great many injured
American authors, and a great many pirated American books.
Now here is a thing which is the exact truth about all of those
books and all of those authors: such of the books as were
issued before England allowed us copyright, suffered piracy
without help; and at the very same time, *five times as many*
English books suffered piracy without help on our side of the
water. The one fact offsets the other; and the honors are
easy—the rascalities, I mean. But, such of those American
books as were issued *after* England allowed us copyright, and
yet suffered piracy, suffered it by their authors' own fault, not
England's nor anybody else's. Their injuries are of their own
creation, and they have no shadow of right to set up a single

whimper. Why, I used to furnish a sick child in West Hartford with gratis milk; do you know, that cub's mother wasn't satisfied, but wanted me to come over there and warm it? I may be out in my calculations, but I don't believe England is going to warm the milk for this nursery over here.

Great Scott, what arguments you do set up! John Habberton writes *Helen's Babies*; could have English-copyrighted it; didn't; it was pirated, and he thinks he has something to complain about. What, for instance?—that they didn't warm the milk? He issued other books; took out no foreign copyrights, same as before; is pirated from Canada to Australia, and thinks he has something to complain about, once more. Oh, good land! However, "warned by his early experience, he"— does what? Attempts an evasion of the English law, and gets left. Pardon the slang, it does seem to fit in so handy there. With that attempted evasion in one's mind, the neat bit of sarcasm which Habberton fillips at the morals of "the average British publisher" loses some trifle of its bloom, don't you think?

Consider! Right in the midst of all your and Habberton's discontent and animadversion, you placidly give your cause a deadly stab under the fifth rib, and you don't seem to notice that you have done it at all; you meander right along, fretting the same as before. I refer to this remark of yours—and where you forgot to italicize, I have supplied the defect: "The English courts have held that under certain circumstances prior publication in Great Britain *will give an author copyright in England, whatever his nationality may be*." How could you set down this great, big, generous fact, this fact which offers its fine and gracious hospitalities, without equivalent or even thank-you, to the swindled scribe of all the climes the sun in his course shines upon—even to you yourself—how could you set it down, and not uncover in its magnificent presence? How could you set it down, and not be smitten with a large and sudden realization of the contrast between its open broad palm and the stingy clinched fist of your own country? How could you look it in the face—that friendly, fresh, wholesome, hearty, welcoming, modern countenance—and go on throwing stale mud over its head at its predecessor, an old kiln-dried, moss-backed, bug-eaten, antediluvian mummy that wasn't doing anything to you, and couldn't if it had wanted to? How could you? You are the very wrong-headedest person in America. I tell it you for your own solace. Why, man, you—well, you are geometrically color-blind; you can't see the proportions of things. And you are injudicious. Don't you know that as long as you've got a goitre that you have to trundle around on a wheelbarrow you can't divert attention from it by throwing bricks at a man that's got a wart on the back of his ear? Those blacklegs in Congress keep us furnished with the prize goitre of the moral and intellectual world, and the thing for you to do is to let the wart-wearers strictly alone.

Well, next you cite another case like Habberton's. "Under certain circumstances," as you have said, the protection of the English law was free to both of these authors. You well know that it was their plain duty to find out what those "circumstances" were. They didn't do it, they exploited some smart ostensibilities instead, and their copyright failed. Those "circumstances" are quite simple and explicit, and quite easy to inform one's self about. It follows, and is a fact, that those sufferers had just themselves to blame, and nobody else.

I wonder what *would* satisfy some people. You are an American, I believe; in fact, I know you are. If you want to copyright a book, here at home, what must you do? This: you must get your title-page printed on a piece of paper; enclose it to the Librarian of Congress; apply to him, in writing, for a copyright; and send him a cash fee. That is what you, personally, have to do; the rest is with your publisher. What do you have to do in order to get the same book copyrighted in England? You are hampered by no bothers, no details of any kind whatever. When you send your manuscript to your English publisher, you tell him the date appointed for the book to issue here, and trust him to bring it out there a day ahead. Isn't that simple enough? No letter to any official; no title-page to any official; no fee to anybody; and yet that book has a copyright on it which the Charleston earthquake couldn't unsettle. "Previous publication" in Great Britain of an American book secures perfect copyright; to "previously publish" all but the tail-end of a book in America, and then "previously publish" that mere tail-end in Great Britain, has what effect?

Why, it copyrights that tail-end, of course. Would any person in his right mind imagine that it would copyright any more than that? Mr. Habberton seems to have imagined that it would. Mr. Habberton knows better now.

Let the rest of your instances pass. They are but repetitions. There isn't an instance among your antiquities that has any bearing upon your case, or shadow of right to be cited in it—unless you propose to try a corpse, for crimes committed upon other corpses. Living issue you have none, nor even any spectral semblance of any. Your modern instances convict your clients of not knowing enough to come in when it rains. From your first page to your last one, you do not chance to get your hands on a single argument that isn't a boomerang. And finally, to make your curious work symmetrical and complete, you rest from your pitiless lathering of the bad English publisher, and fall to apologizing to him—and, apparently, to the good one, too, I don't know why: "At bottom, the publishers, good or bad, *are not to blame.*" You are right, for once, perfectly right; they are not to blame—to-day; if they commit a piracy in these days, nine-tenths of the sin belongs with the American author. And since you perceive that they are not to blame, what did you blame them for? If you were going to take it all back, why didn't you take it back earlier, and not write it at all? Hang it, you are not logical. Do you think that to lather a man all through eleven pages and then tell him he isn't to blame after all, is treating yourself right? Why no, it puts you in such a rickety position. I read it to the cat—well, I never saw a cat carry on so before.

But, of course, somebody or something was to blame. You were in honor bound to make that fact clear, or you couldn't possibly excuse yourself for raising all this dust. Now, I will give any rational man 400,000 guesses, and go bail that he will run short before he has the luck to put his finger on the place where you locate that blame. Now listen—and try to rise to the size of this inspired verdict of yours: *"It is the condition of* THE LAW *which is at fault."* (*!*) Upon my life, I have never heard anything to begin with the gigantic impudence of that. The cat—but never mind the cat; the cat is dead; a cat can't stand everything. *"The remedy is to* CHANGE THE LAW"—and then you go owling along, just as if there was never anything more serious in this world than the stupe-fying nonsense you are talking. Change the law? Change it? In what way, pray? A law which gives us absolutely unassail-able and indestructible copyright at cost of not a single penny, not a moment of time, not an iota of trouble, not even the bother of *asking* for it! Change it? How are you going to change it? Matthews, I am your friend, and you know it; and that is what makes me say what I do say: you want a change of air, or you'll be in the asylum the first thing you know.

January 1888

Yale College Speech

Yale Alumni Association Banquet, Hartford

I was sincerely proud and grateful to be made a Master of Arts by this great and venerable university, and I would have come last June to testify this feeling, as I do now testify it, but that the sudden and unexpected notice of the honor done me found me at a distance from home and unable to discharge that duty and enjoy that privilege.

Along at first, say for the first month or so, I did not quite know how to proceed, because of my not knowing just what authorities and privileges belonged to the title which had been granted me, but after that I consulted some students of Trinity, in Hartford, and they made everything clear to me. It was through them that I found out that my title made me head of the governing body of the university, and lodged in me very broad and severely responsible powers. It is through trying to work these powers up to their maximum of efficiency that I have had such a checkered career this year. I was told that it would be necessary for me to report to you at this time, and of course I comply, though I would have preferred to put it off till I could make a better showing: for indeed I have been so pertinaciously hindered and obstructed at every turn by the faculty that it would be difficult to prove that the university is really in any better shape now than it was when I first took charge. In submitting my report, I am sorry to have to begin with the remark that respect for authority seems to be at a quite low ebb in the college. It is true that this has caused me pain, but it has not discouraged me. By advice, I turned my earliest attention to the Greek department. I told the Greek professor I had concluded to drop the use of the Greek written character, because it was so hard to spell with, and so impossible to read after you get it spelled. Let us draw the curtain there. I saw by what followed that nothing but early neglect saved him from being a very profane man.

I ordered the professor of mathematics to simplify the whole system, because the way it was, I couldn't understand it, and I didn't want things going on in the college in what was practically a clandestine fashion. I told him to drop the conundrum system; it was not suited to the dignity of a college, which should deal in facts, not guesses and suppositions; we didn't want any more cases of *if* A and B stand at opposite poles of the earth's surface and C at the equator of Jupiter, at what variations of angle will the left limb of the moon appear to these different parties? I said you just let that thing alone; it's plenty time to get in a sweat about it when it happens; as like as not it ain't going to do any harm anyway. His reception of these instructions bordered on insubordination; insomuch that I felt obliged to take his number, and report him.

I found the astronomer of the university gadding around after comets and other such odds and ends — tramps and derelicts of the skies. I told him pretty plainly that we couldn't have that. I told him it was no economy to go on piling up and piling up raw material in the way of new stars and comets and asteroids that we couldn't ever have any use for till we had worked off the old stock. I said if I caught him strawberrying around after any more asteroids, especially, I should have to fire him out. Privately, prejudice got the best of me there, I ought to confess it. At bottom I don't really mind comets so much, but somehow I have always been down on asteroids. There is nothing mature about them; I wouldn't sit up nights, the way that man does, if I could get a basketful of them. He said it was the best line of goods he had; he said he could trade them to Rochester for comets, and trade the comets to Harvard for nebulae, and trade the nebulae to the Smithsonian for flint hatchets. I felt obliged to stop this thing on the spot; I said we couldn't have the university turned into an astronomical junk shop.

And while I was at it I thought I might as well make the reform complete; the astronomer is extraordinarily mutinous; and so with your approval I will transfer him to the law department and put one of the law students in his place. A boy will be more biddable, more tractable, also cheaper. It is true he cannot be entrusted with important work at first, but he can comb the skies for nebulae till he gets his hand in. I have other changes in mind, but as they are in the nature of surprises, I judge it politic to leave them unspecified at this time.

February 6, 1889

The Christening Yarn

Hartford Saturday Morning Club

Ah, my friends, he is but a little fellow. A very little fellow. Yes—a v-e-r-y little fellow. *But!* [With a severe glance around.] What of that! I ask you what of *that!* [From this point, gradually begin to rise—and soar—and be pathetic, and impassioned, and all that.] Is it a crime to be little? Is it a *crime*, that you cast upon him these cold looks of disparagement? Oh, reflect, my friends—reflect! Oh, if you but had the eye of poesy, which is the eye of prophecy, you would fling your gaze afar down the stately march of his possible future, and *then* what might ye not see! *What?* ye disparage him because he is *little?* Oh, consider the mighty ocean! ye may spread upon its shoreless bosom the white-winged fleets of all the nations, and lo they are but as a flock of insects lost in the awful vacancies of interstellar space! Yet the mightiest ocean is made of *little* things; *drops*—tiny little drops—each no bigger than the tear that rests upon the cheek of this poor child! And oh, my friends, consider the mountain ranges, the giant ribs that girdle the great globe and hold its frame together—and what are they? Compacted grains of sand—*little* grains of sand, each no more than a freight for a gnat! And oh, consider the constellations!—the flashing suns, countless for multitude, that swim the stupendous deeps of space, glorifying the midnight skies with their golden splendors—what are *they?* Compacted motes! specks! impalpable atoms of wandering stardust arrested in their vagrant flight and welded into solid worlds! *Little* things; yes, they are made of *little* things. And he—oh, look at him! *Little*, is he?—and ye would disparage him for it! Oh, I beseech you, cast the eye of poesy, which is the eye of prophecy, into his future! Why, he may become a poet!—the grandest the world has ever seen—Homer, Shakespeare, Dante, compacted into one!—and send down the procession of the ages songs that shall contest immortality with human speech itself! Or, he may become a great soldier!—the most illustrious in the annals of his race—Napoleon, Caesar, Alexander compacted into one!—and carry the victorious banner of his country from sea to sea, and

938

from land to land, until it shall float at last unvexed over the final stronghold of a conquered world!—oh, heir of imperishable renown! Or, he may become a—a—he—he—[struggle desperately, here, to think of something else that he may become, but without success—the audience getting more and more distressed and worried about you all the time]—he may become—he—[suddenly] *but what is his name?*

Papa [with impatience and exasperation]. His *name*, is it? Well, his name's *Mary Ann!*

May 11, 1889

To Walt Whitman

Hartford, Conn., May 24, 1889.

You have lived just the seventy years which are greatest in the world's history, and richest in benefit and advancement to its peoples. These seventy years have done much more to widen the interval between man and the other animals than was accomplished by any five centuries which preceded them.

What great births you have witnessed! The steam-press, the steamship, the steel-ship, the railroad, the perfected cotton-gin, the telegraph, the telephone, the phonograph, the photograph, the photogravure, the electrotype, the gaslight, the electric light, the sewing-machine, and the amazing, infinitely varied and innumerable products of coal-tar, those latest and strangest marvels of a marvelous age. And you have seen even greater births than these; for you have seen the application of anæsthesia to surgery-practice, whereby the ancient dominion of pain, which began with the first created life, came to an end in this earth forever; you have seen the slave set free; you have seen monarchy banished from France, and reduced in England to a machine which makes an imposing show of diligence and attention to business, but isn't connected with the works. Yes, you have indeed seen much; but tarry yet awhile, for the greatest is yet to come. Wait thirty years, and *then* look out over the earth! You shall see marvels upon marvels added to these whose nativity you have witnessed; and conspicuous above them you shall see their formidable Result—Man at almost his full stature at last!—and still growing, visibly growing, while you look. In that day, who that hath a throne, or a gilded privilege not attainable by his neighbor, let him procure him slippers and get ready to dance, for there is going to be music. Abide, and see these things! Thirty of us who honor and love you, offer the opportunity. We have among us six hundred years, good and sound, left in the bank of life. Take thirty of them—the richest birthday gift ever offered to poet in this world—and sit down and wait. Wait till you see that great figure appear, and catch the far glint of the sun upon his banner; then you may depart satisfied, as knowing you have seen him for whom the world was made, and that he will proclaim that human wheat is worth more than human tares, and proceed to reorganize human value on that basis.

With best wishes for a happy issue to a grateful undertaking.

1889

On Foreign Critics

Dinner for Max O'Rell, Boston

If I look harried and worn, it is not from an ill conscience. It is from sitting up nights to worry about the foreign critic. He won't concede that we have a civilization—a "real" civilization. Five years ago, he said we had never contributed anything to the betterment of the world. And now comes Sir Lepel Griffin, whom I had not suspected of being in the world at all, and says "there is no country calling itself civilized where one would not rather live than in America, except Russia." That settles it. That is, it settles it for Europe; but it doesn't make me any more comfortable than I was before.

What is a "real" civilization? Nobody can answer that conundrum. They have all tried. Then suppose we try to get at what it is not; and then subtract the what it is not from the general sum, and call the remainder "real" civilization—so as to have a place to stand on while we throw bricks at these people. Let us say, then, in broad terms, that any system which has in it any one of these things, to wit, human slavery, despotic government, inequality, numerous and brutal punishments for crimes, superstition almost universal, ignorance almost universal, and dirt and poverty almost universal—is not a real civilization, and any system which has none of them, is.

If you grant these terms, one may then consider this conundrum: How old is real civilization? The answer is easy and unassailable. A century ago it had not appeared anywhere in the world during a single instant since the world was made. If you grant these terms—and I don't see why it shouldn't be fair, since civilization must surely mean the humanizing of a people, not a class—there is today but one real civilization in the world, and it is not yet thirty years old. We made the trip and hoisted its flag when we disposed of our slavery.

However, there are some partial civilizations scattered around over Europe—pretty lofty civilizations they are, too—but who begot them? What is the seed from which they sprang? Liberty and intelligence. What planted that seed? There are dates and statistics which suggest that it was the

American Revolution that planted it. When that revolution began, monarchy had been on trial some thousands of years, over there, and was a distinct and convicted failure, every time. It had never produced anything but a vast, a nearly universal savagery, with a thin skim of civilization on top, and the main part of that was nickel plate and tinsel. The French, imbruted and impoverished by centuries of oppression and official robbery, were a starving nation clothed in rags, slaves of an aristocracy of smirking dandies clad in unearned silks and velvet. It makes one's cheek burn to read of the laws of the time and realize that they were for human beings; realize that they originated in this world, and not in hell. Germany was unspeakable. In the Scottish lowlands the people lived in styes, and were human swine; in the highlands drunkenness was general, and it hardly smirched a young girl to have a family of her own. In England there was a sham liberty, and not much of that; crime was general; ignorance the same; poverty and misery were widespread; London fed a tenth of her population by charity; the law awarded the death penalty to almost every conceivable offense; what was called medical science by courtesy stood where it had stood for two thousand years; Tom Jones and Squire Western were gentlemen.

The printer's art had been known in Germany and France three and a quarter centuries, and in England three. In all that time there had not been a newspaper in Europe that was worthy the name. Monarchies had no use for that sort of dynamite. When we hoisted the banner of revolution and raised the first genuine shout for human liberty that had ever been heard, this was a newspaperless globe. Eight years later, there were six daily journals in London to proclaim to all the nations the greatest birth this world had ever seen. Who woke that printing press out of its trance of three hundred years? Let us be permitted to consider that we did it. Who summoned the French slaves to rise and set the nation free? We did it. What resulted in England and on the Continent? Crippled liberty took up its bed and walked. From that day to this its march has not halted, and please God it never will. We are called the nation of inventors. And we are. We could still claim that title and wear its loftiest honors, if we had stopped with the first thing we ever invented—which was human liberty. Out of that invention has come the Christian world's great civilization. Without it it was impossible—as the history of all the centuries has proved. Well, then, who invented civilization? Even Sir Lepel Griffin ought to be able to answer that question. It looks easy enough. *We* have contributed nothing! Nothing hurts me like ingratitude.

Yes, the coveted verdict has been persistently withheld from us. Mr. Arnold granted that our whole people—including by especial mention "that immense class, the great bulk of the community," the wage and salary-earners—have liberty, equality, plenty to eat, plenty to wear, comfortable shelter, high pay, abundance of churches, newspapers, libraries, charities, and a good education for everybody's child for nothing. He added, "society seems organized there for their benefit" —benefit of the bulk and mass of the people. Yes, it is conceded that we furnish the greatest good to the greatest number; and so all we lack is a civilization.

Mr. Arnold's indicated civilization would seem to be restricted, by its narrow lines and difficult requirements, to a class—the top class—as in tropical countries snow is restricted to the mountain summits. And from what one may gather from his rather vague and unsure analysis of it, the snow metaphor would seem to fit it in more ways than one. The impression you get of it is, that it is peculiarly hard, and glittering, and bloodless, and unattainable. Now if our bastard were a civilization, it could fairly be figured—by Mr. Arnold's own concessions—by the circulation of the blood, which nourishes and refreshes the whole body alike, delivering its rich streams of life and health impartially to the imperial brain and the meanest extremity.

April 27, 1890

Reply to the Editor of
"The Art of Authorship"

Your inquiry has set me thinking, but, so far, my thought
fails to materialise. I mean that, upon consideration, I am not
sure that I have methods in composition. I do suppose I
have—I suppose I must have—but they somehow refuse to
take shape in my mind; their details refuse to separate and
submit to classification and description; they remain a jumble
—visible, like the fragments of glass when you look in at the
wrong end of a kaleidoscope, but still a jumble. If I could
turn the whole thing around and look in at the other end,
why then the figures would flash into form out of the chaos,
and I shouldn't have any more trouble. But my head isn't
right for that to-day, apparently. It might have been, maybe,
if I had slept last night.

However, let us try guessing. Let us guess that whenever
we read a sentence and like it, we unconsciously store it away
in our model-chamber; and it goes with the myriad of its
fellows to the building, brick by brick, of the eventual edifice which we call our style. And let us guess that whenever
we run across other forms—bricks—whose colour, or some
other defect, offends us, we unconsciously reject these, and so
one never finds them in our edifice. If I have subjected myself
to any training processes, and no doubt I have, it must have
been in this unconscious or half-conscious fashion. I think it
unlikely that deliberate and consciously methodical training
is usual with the craft. I think it likely that the training most
in use is of this unconscious sort, and is guided and governed and made by-and-by unconsciously systematic, by an
automatically-working taste—a taste which selects and rejects
without asking you for any help, and patiently and steadily
improves itself without troubling you to approve or applaud.
Yes, and likely enough when the structure is at last pretty well
up, and attracts attention, *you* feel complimented, whereas
you didn't build it, and didn't even consciously superintend.
Yes; one notices, for instance, that long, involved sentences
confuse him, and that he is obliged to re-read them to get
the sense. Unconsciously, then, he rejects that brick. Uncon-

sciously he accustoms himself to writing short sentences as a rule. At times he may indulge himself with a long one, but he will make sure that there are no folds in it, no vaguenesses, no parenthetical interruptions of its view as a whole; when he is done with it, it won't be a sea-serpent, with half of its arches under the water, it will be a torchlight procession.

Well, also he will notice in the course of time, as his reading goes on, that the difference between the *almost right* word and the *right* word is really a large matter—'tis the difference between the lightning-bug and the lightning. After that, of course, that exceedingly important brick, the *exact* word— however, this is running into an essay, and I beg pardon. So I seem to have arrived at this: doubtless I have methods, but they begot themselves, in which case I am only their proprietor, not their father.

1890

An Appeal Against Injudicious Swearing

SATURDAY, NOV. 8.

TO THE EDITOR OF THE SUN—*Sir:* Doubtless you city
people do not mind having your feelings hurt and your self-
love blistered, for your horse car and elevated road service
train you to patience and humble-mindedness, but with us
hayseed folk from the back settlements the case is different.
We are so delicate, so sensitive—well, you would never be
able to imagine what it is like. An unkind speech shrivels us
all up and often makes us cry. Now, the thing which happened to-day a New Yorker would not mind in the least; but I
give you my word it almost made me want to go away and be
at rest in the cold grave.

I stepped aboard a red Sixth avenue horse car—No.
106—at Sixth avenue and Forty-second street at 11:45 this
morning, bound down town. Of course there was no seat—
there never is: New Yorkers do not require a seat, but only
permission to stand up and look meek, and be thankful for
such little rags of privilege as the good horse-car company
may choose to allow them. I stood in the door, behind three
ladies. After a moment, the conductor, desiring to pass
through and see the passengers, took me by the lappel and
said to me with that winning courtesy and politeness which
New Yorkers are so accustomed to: "Jesus Christ! what you
want to load up the door for? Git back here out of the way!"
Those ladies shrank together under the shock, just the same as
I did; so I judged they were country people. This conductor
was a person about 30 years old, I should say, five feet nine,
with blue eyes, a small, dim, unsuccessful moustache, and the
general expression of a chicken thief—you may probably have
seen him.

I urged him to modify his language, I being from the country and sensitive. He looked upon me with cold and heartless
scorn, thus hurting me still more. I said I would report him,
and asked him for his number. He said, in a tone which
wounded me more than I can tell, "I'll give you a chew of
tobacco."

Why, dear sir, if conductors were to talk to us like that out in the country we could never, never bear to ride with them, we are so sensitive. I went up to Sixth avenue and Forty-third street to report him, but there was nobody in the superintendent's office who seemed to want to converse with me. A man with "conductor" on his cap said it wouldn't be any use to try to see the President at that time of day, and intimated, by his manner, not his words, that people with complaints were not popular there, any way.

So I have been obliged to come to you, you see. What I wanted to say to the President of the road was this—and through him say it to the President of the elevated roads—that the conductors ought to be instructed never to swear at country people except when there are no city ones to swear at, and not even then except for practice. Because the country people are sensitive. Conductors need not make any mistakes; they can easily tell us from the city people. Could you use your influence to get this small and harmless distinction made in our favor?

MARK TWAIN.

November 9, 1890

Chronology

Samuel Langhorne Clemens born prematurely on November 30 in Florida, Missouri, fifth surviving child of John Marshall Clemens (b. 1798) and Jane Lampton Clemens (b. 1803). Siblings are brother Orion (b. 1825), sisters Pamela (b. 1827) and Margaret (b. 1830), and brother Benjamin (b. 1832). At time of birth Halley's Comet is still visible in the sky (Clemens will often mention this later in life). Family lives in rented house on South Mill Street and father runs store in partnership with John Adams Quarles, husband of Jane Lampton Clemens' sister, Martha Ann "Patsy" Quarles. (Grandparents Samuel and Pamelia Clemens were slave-owning farmers in Campbell County, Virginia, before moving family to southern bank of Ohio River in Mason County, Virginia—now West Virginia—in 1803 or 1804. Grandmother, widowed in 1805, moved with her five children to Adair County, Kentucky, to live with her brother; she married Simon Hancock in 1809. By 1812 father was supporting himself in a Lynchburg, Virginia, ironworks. After paying debts owed to stepfather Hancock, father and siblings settled their father's estate in 1821; John Clemens' share included three slaves. He then read law with Cyrus Walker in Columbia, Kentucky, received his license to practice in 1822, and in 1823 married Jane Lampton, a cousin of Walker's wife; the daughter of Benjamin and Margaret Casey Lampton, she was born in Columbia and was descended from early English and Irish settlers of Kentucky. They moved to Gainesboro, Tennessee, then Jamestown, Tennessee, where John Clemens built a large house, practiced law, opened a store, and bought 75,000 acres of uncleared land before moving in 1831 to nearby Three Forks of Wolf River, where he bought 200 acres of farmland and built a log house. In 1835 the family moved with their remaining slave, a woman named Jenny, to Florida, Missouri, on the Salt River, where John and Martha Ann Quarles were already established and where grandfather Benjamin Lampton and other members of mother's family also lived. After their arrival in June father quickly acquired 120 acres of government land, and then bought a 2¾-acre homesite for $300.)

1836   Clemens is frequently sick and mother is unsure if he will live. Family buys house in town from grandfather Lampton.

1837   Grandfather dies. Father dissolves partnership with Quarles and sets up his own store; heads committees to improve Salt River navigation, develop railroads, and start an academy. Father becomes Monroe County judge.

1838   Family moves into new house built by father. Brother Henry born July 13.

1839   Clemens walks in his sleep (will often do so for several years). Sister Margaret dies of "bilious fever" August 17. Father earns $5,000 from land sales and then purchases $7,000 worth of property in Hannibal, Missouri, a rapidly growing port village of a thousand inhabitants on the Mississippi, 30 miles from Florida and about 130 miles north of St. Louis by water. Family moves to Hannibal in November; other Florida residents move as well, including family friends Dr. Hugh Meredith and schoolteacher Mary Ann Newcomb. Father opens store and family lives in the Virginia House, former hotel that is part of purchased property.

1840   Clemens enters school taught by Elizabeth Horr and Mary Ann Newcomb (will attend three other schools in Hannibal).

1841   Mother and sister Pamela join Presbyterian church in February. Newcomb, who often eats as a paying guest with the Clemenses, opens her own school in basement of Presbyterian church. Father sells house in Florida to uncle John Quarles in August and transfers title to Virginia House to creditor in October.

1842   Brother Benjamin dies on May 12 after a few days of illness. Orion moves to St. Louis to work as printer. Clemens continues to be sickly, and is doctored with castor oil, calomel, rhubarb, and jalap, as well as poultices, socks full of hot ashes, and various water treatments. Has nightmares and continues to walk in his sleep. Family sells Jenny.

1843   Mother moves children from Methodist to Presbyterian
        Sunday school. Clemens enjoys visits to the Quarles' fam-
        ily farm in Florida (will spend two or three months a year
        with them for several years). Takes with him his own
        trained cat (will have lifelong love of cats). Attends coun-
        try summer school with cousins once or twice a week and
        enjoys playing with the slaves on the farm. Becomes espe-
        cially appreciative of the friendship and counsel of Dann, a
        slave in his late thirties (emancipated by Quarles in 1855).
        Father auctions off much of his Hannibal property to pay
        debts. James C. Clemens, a distant cousin, buys one lot on
        Hill Street and leases it to father to build house.

1844   During epidemic in spring, Clemens deliberately catches
        measles from Will Bowen, his closest friend, and nearly
        dies as a result. Father helps found Hannibal Library In-
        stitute (will later head civic committees promoting rail-
        road construction and higher education) and is elected
        justice of the peace. Clemens is horrified when he finds a
        corpse in his father's office (body is of an emigrant to
        California stabbed in a quarrel while in town).

1845   Watches man die in the street after being shot by Hannibal
        merchant William Owsley (who is later acquitted). Group
        of friends includes Will Bowen and his brother Sam, John
        Briggs, Ed Stevens, John Garth, Anna Laura Hawkins,
        and Tom Blankenship. Health improves, and enjoys swim-
        ming, fishing, playing Robin Hood, pirates, and Cru-
        saders. Attends school taught by Samuel Cross.

1846   Mother takes in paying guests for meals. Family sells fur-
        niture to help pay debts and moves in with pharmacist
        Orville Grant; mother supplies him with meals in ex-
        change for rent. In November, father announces candi-
        dacy for clerk of the circuit court (becomes favored to win
        election, held in August 1847). Clemens and friends enjoy
        watching local volunteer infantry drill for service in Mexi-
        can War.

1847   Father dies of pneumonia on March 24. Clemens watches
        through keyhole as Dr. Meredith performs postmortem
        examination. Family moves back to frame house at 206
        Hill Street. Orion, working as printer in St. Louis, pro-

vides main family support, while Pamela gives guitar and piano lessons, mother continues to take in paying guests for meals, and Clemens works at odd jobs, including helping a blacksmith and clerking in a grocery store, a pharmacy, and a bookstore. Begins attending John D. Dawson's school. Witnesses drowning of friend Clint Levering while swimming with a group of friends in the Mississippi in August. While fishing on Sny Island a few days later, Clemens and several friends discover the body of a drowned fugitive slave, whom Bence Blankenship (Tom's older brother) had been secretly supplying with food. Gets job in fall as errand boy and delivers papers for printer Henry La Cossitt at the Hannibal *Gazette*.

1848   Still attending Dawson's school, begins working in late spring in the office of Joseph P. Ament's *Missouri Courier* as chore boy and printer's devil. Lives meagerly in Ament's house as an apprentice. Goes skating late in the year on the Mississippi with friend Tom Nash; when the ice breaks, Clemens manages to get to shore safely, but Nash falls through (illnesses suffered as a result eventually make Nash deaf).

1849   Gold rush emigrants pass through Hannibal en route to California, and 80 Hannibal residents join them, including Dawson, head of the last school Clemens attends, and Samuel Cross. Enjoys company of fellow apprentices Wales McCormick and T. P. "Pet" McMurry. Clemens reads Cooper, Marryat, Dickens, Byron, Scott, and anything else he can find that features knights, pirates, or Crusaders (Henry is considered to be the serious reader in the family).

1850   Joins Cadets of Temperance, briefly gives up smoking and chewing tobacco, and marches in parades with friends. In May, witnesses a poor widow shoot and kill the leader of a group of strangers from Illinois who are trying to force their way into her house. Orion returns to Hannibal from St. Louis and begins publishing weekly newspaper, the *Western Union*.

1851   Clemens leaves *Missouri Courier* and, with Henry, goes to work for Orion as a typesetter and editorial assistant;

although Orion promises Clemens $3.50 a week in wages, no money is ever available. Likes apprentice Jim Wolf, who boards with Clemens family. Publishes first known sketch, "A Gallant Fireman," in the *Western Union* January 16. Cholera epidemic in June kills 24 people in Hannibal. Orion buys Hannibal *Journal* in September. Sister Pamela marries William A. Moffett on September 20 and moves to St. Louis.

1852   Fire destroys *Journal* office, and Orion rents new space. Clemens occasionally writes humorous sketches for the Hannibal *Journal*. "The Dandy Frightening the Squatter" appears in the Boston *Carpet-Bag* and "Hannibal, Missouri" in the Philadelphia *American Courier* in May. Niece Annie Moffett born in July. During Orion's absence on business trips, Clemens becomes responsible for getting paper out. On September 9 signs a sketch "W. Epaminondas Adrastus Perkins," his first known use of a pseudonym.

1853   In January Clemens and Will Bowen give matches to a drunk in the town jail, who later that night sets fire to his cell and burns to death. (Clemens will often recall this incident.) Leaves Hannibal in early June and works as a typesetter in St. Louis for Thomas Watt Ustick, who does the printing for the *Evening News* and other publications. Goes to New York City by steamer and rail in late August. Visits Crystal Palace, center of New York World's Fair. Works for low pay in John A. Gray's large print shop on Cliff Street and boards on Duane Street. Takes pride in his typesetting skill, attends theater, and spends evenings reading in the printers' free library. Has two of his letters from New York printed in Hannibal *Journal* before Orion sells paper in September and moves with mother and brother Henry to Muscatine, Iowa, where Orion buys share in, and becomes co-editor of, the Muscatine *Journal*. Clemens moves to Philadelphia in late October. Works as typesetter, writes letters for the Muscatine *Journal*, and enjoys visiting sites connected with Benjamin Franklin and the Revolution.

1854   Briefly visits Washington, D.C., in February and records his impressions in letter for the Muscatine *Journal*. Returns to Philadelphia for a few weeks, then goes to New York, where he finds high unemployment among printers due to fires that had destroyed Harpers and another publishing house. Goes to Muscatine in spring and works for the *Journal*. Moves to St. Louis in summer and resumes work at the *Evening News*, boarding and lodging with the Paveys from Hannibal at the corner of 4th and Wash streets. Mother moves in with Pamela and William Moffett on Pine Street in St. Louis. Orion marries Mary Eleanor (Mollie) Stotts of Keokuk, Iowa, on December 19.

1855   Writes four letters for the Muscatine *Journal* before Orion sells paper in June and moves to Keokuk, where he sets up the Ben Franklin Book and Job Office, a printing shop. Clemens joins him in mid-June, working for $5 a week and board before becoming a partner in the business (mother remains in St. Louis with the Moffetts). Travels to Hannibal and Palymra in July to collect belongings and arrange for sale of Hill Street house, then goes on to Paris and Florida, Missouri, to settle mother's inheritance from grandfather Benjamin Lampton and great-aunt Diana Lampton. Visits with uncle John Quarles.

1856   Sees mother and Pamela in St. Louis in October, and writes his first "Thomas Jefferson Snodgrass" letter for the Keokuk *Post*. Moves to Cincinnati, where he works as a typesetter and writes two more Snodgrass letters for the *Post*.

1857   Leaves Cincinnati in April by steamboat for New Orleans, intending to seek his fortune in South America, but instead becomes cub riverboat pilot under Horace Bixby for an apprentice fee of $500 (borrows the first $100 from William Moffett, then pays more in installments, though Bixby will not charge him the full amount). Works on several boats and learns Mississippi River between New Orleans and St. Louis. Orion sells Keokuk print shop and goes to Jamestown, Tennessee, where family owns land, to study law and try to survey and sell the property (is unsuccessful in selling land and returns to Keokuk in July 1858 to practice law).

1858   Clemens serves as cub on the *Pennsylvania* under pilot William Brown, whom he considers a tyrant. Arranges job as "mud clerk" (purser's assistant) for brother Henry aboard the boat. Meets and falls in love with Laura M. Wright, the 14-year-old daughter of a Missouri judge (her family does not approve and intercepts letters). Hits Brown after the pilot strikes Henry, then leaves the *Pennsylvania* when no replacement can be found for Brown. Henry remains with crew and is badly injured in a boiler explosion below Memphis on June 13. Clemens arrives in Memphis June 15, and is with Henry when he dies on June 21 (Brown is also among the dead). Feels crazed with grief and guilt. Henry is buried in Hannibal June 25. Clemens resumes apprenticeship and steers for two pilot friends from Hannibal, Bart and Sam Bowen.

1859–60   Receives his pilot's license on April 9, 1859. Becomes steadily employed and well paid for his work. Feels at home in New Orleans and St. Louis, where he sees Pamela and her family. Continues his self-education and studies French. In May 1859 publishes a lampoon of senior pilot Isaiah Sellers (from whom Clemens later claimed he appropriated the pen name "Mark Twain") and writes several other sketches. Orion moves to Memphis to practice law in May 1860.

1861   Clemens becomes member of the Polar Star Lodge 79, a St. Louis Masonic lodge (maintains contact with the lodge until formally resigning in October 1869). Takes mother on a private steamboat excursion from St. Louis to New Orleans and back. In letter to Orion, describes Goldsmith's *The Citizen of the World* and Cervantes' *Don Quixote* as his "*beau ideals* of fine writing." Is much impressed by Frederick Edwin Church's painting *Heart of the Andes*, on exhibit in St. Louis. Through the influence of St. Louis lawyer Edward Bates, attorney general in the new Lincoln administration, Orion is appointed secretary of Nevada Territory in March. By May outbreak of the Civil War has severely disrupted river traffic. After spending some time with family in St. Louis, fearful of being impressed as gunboat pilot by Union forces, Clemens goes to Hannibal in mid-June and helps form the Marion Rangers, group of Confederate volunteers composed of old Hannibal schoolmates, including Sam Bowen, John L. Robards, Perry Smith, and Ed Stevens. After two weeks of camping and retreating across countryside, half the group decides to disband (Absalom Grimes later carried mail for the Confederacy, John Meredith, son of the Clemenses' doctor, became chief of a guerrilla band, and Perry Smith was killed in battle). Clemens returns to St. Louis in early July and leaves with Orion for Nevada on July 18. Travels on steamer *Sioux City* up the Missouri to St. Joseph, Missouri, then goes by stagecoach through Fort Kearny, Scotts Bluff, South Pass, Fort Bridger, and Salt Lake City, arriving in Carson City, Nevada, on August 14. Meets and becomes friendly with Horatio G. Phillips, Robert Howland, and John D. Kinney. Travels to Aurora, Nevada, in the Esmeralda mining district in early September, where he shares claims with Phillips. Takes trips with Kinney to establish timber claims near Lake Bigler (later Tahoe), and accidentally starts forest fire. Speculates in silver- and gold-mining stocks and serves for $8 a day as Orion's secretary during the fall session of the territorial legislature. Meets Clement T. Rice, who will become close friend and journalistic collaborator. Goes on prospecting trip to Humboldt County, Nevada, with Keokuk friend William H. Clagett in December. Reads and quotes from Dickens' *Dombey and Son*.

1862   Returns to Carson City in late January, then to Aurora in April. Continues prospecting with Phillips without much success and writes occasional letters for the Keokuk *Gate City* and Carson City *Silver Age*; begins sending letters to the Virginia City, Nevada, *Territorial Enterprise* in late April, using pen name "Josh." Clemens and Phillips learn advanced techniques of reducing silver ore from Joshua Eliot Clayton. Has falling-out with Phillips. In July begins to feel restless and wants to move on. Becomes partner in potentially lucrative mining claim and shares cabin for a short time with Calvin H. Higbie (will later dedicate *Roughing It* to him). Nurses Captain John Nye, brother of governor of the Nevada Territory, James Warren Nye, for nine days when he is sick with "inflammatory rheumatism." "Josh" letters to the *Territorial Enterprise* attract the attention of business manager William H. Barstow and editor Joseph T. Goodman, and they offer Clemens a salaried job as reporter ($25 per week) in late July. Takes two-week walking trip through the White Mountains along the Nevada-California border, for pleasure and to look for legendary lost gold "cement" mine. Moves to Virginia

City and begins work as local reporter for the *Territorial Enterprise* in late September; duties include covering fall legislative session in Carson City. Writes "The Petrified Man," a hoax made up to "worry" Judge G. T. Sewall of Humboldt County. Begins lasting friendships with Joseph T. Goodman and Dan De Quille (William Wright), fellow reporter and humorist. Becomes responsible for local reporting when De Quille leaves at end of year on extended visit home to Iowa.

1863   Continues to trade in mining stocks, sometimes receiving free shares in return for favorable mention in the *Enterprise*. Orion serves as acting governor of Nevada during Governor Nye's absence from the territory (Nye returns in July). Clemens goes to Carson City for a week and sends three letters to the *Enterprise*, published February 3, 5, and 8, signing them "Mark Twain," his first known use of the name. Continues his mock feud in print with "the Unreliable," the name he has given to his friend and fellow reporter Clement T. Rice. Leaves Virginia City with Rice early in May to visit San Francisco, where he sees Neil Moss, former classmate and son of the wealthiest man in Hannibal, who has been prospecting without success, and Bill Briggs (brother of his close Hannibal friend John Briggs), who is now running a successful gambling establishment. Enjoys San Francisco, staying at the Occidental Hotel and the Lick House. Makes money selling and trading stocks. Arranges to become Nevada correspondent for the San Francisco *Morning Call*. Returns to Virginia City in July and moves into the new White House hotel; it burns down on July 26 and Clemens loses all his possessions, including his mine stocks. Sick with a severe cold and bronchitis, goes to Lake Bigler with young journalist friend Adair Wilson, and then to Steamboat Springs, nine miles northwest of Virginia City, to try its hot mineral water. When Dan De Quille returns to Virginia City and resumes duties as local editor for the *Enterprise*, Clemens goes to San Francisco for a month. Writes "How to Cure a Cold," his first piece for the *Golden Era*, a San Francisco literary weekly. Returns to Nevada in time to serve as recording secretary of the Washoe Agricultural, Mining, and Mechanical Society Fair, held in Carson City in mid-October. Writes a hoax about a man killing his family, "A Bloody Massacre Near Carson"; when it is uncovered,

other papers that had reported it as a true story are furious
and refuse to reprint news stories from the *Enterprise*.
Clemens offers to resign, but Goodman and De Quille
assure him that the anger will diminish and the story will
be remembered. Rents suite of rooms with De Quille at 25
North B Street in Virginia City. Goes to Carson City to
cover convention drafting first state constitution, then returns to Virginia City in time to meet humorist Artemus
Ward (Charles Farrar Browne), who encourages him to
write for the New York *Mercury*. Enjoys spirited Christmas
Eve dinner with Ward, De Quille, Goodman, and others,
which ends with Ward and Clemens walking across the
rooftops in Virginia City.

1864   Reports on rejection by the voters on January 19 of the
proposed state constitution (clause proposing tax on undeveloped mines is unpopular). Publishes two articles in
the New York *Mercury*, "Doings in Nevada" (February 7)
and "Those Blasted Children" (February 21). Sees Reuel
Gridley, friend from Hannibal, in May when Gridley
tours Nevada raising funds for the Sanitary Commission
Fair in St. Louis (Commission aids sick and wounded
Union soldiers). Joins Gridley in repeatedly auctioning off
flour sack, with different towns and groups in Storey
County competing to outbid one another (county eventually contributes $22,000 to the fair). Writes two contro-
versial pieces for the *Enterprise* in late May; one repeats
rumor that Carson City women were diverting funds intended for the Sanitary Commission to a freedman's society, and the other alleges that the Virginia City *Union* has
not fulfilled its bid in the flour-sack auction. When reply
in the *Union* calls him "an unmitigated *liar, a poltroon and
a puppy*," Clemens challenges its editor, James L. Laird, to
a duel, while publicly and privately apologizing to the
Carson City women. After exchanging several letters with
Laird, Clemens publishes the correspondence on May 24,
then becomes concerned about Nevada law outlawing
dueling challenges. Leaves with Stephen E. Gillis, close
friend and news editor at the *Enterprise*, and Goodman for
San Francisco on May 29 (will become ashamed of this
"dueling" episode in later years). Rooms with Gillis in
several hotels, rooming houses, and private homes. Becomes reporter for the San Francisco *Morning Call* for
$40 a week and continues to contribute pieces to the

Golden Era. Meets the Reverend Henry Whitney Bellows, founder and president of the United States Sanitary Commission, and enjoys his sense of humor. Finds long hours at the *Call* tedious and makes new arrangement to work only during daylight hours for $25 a week. Contracts to write four articles for $50 a month (same amount he had received from the *Golden Era*) for newly established literary magazine, the *Californian*, owned by Charles Henry Webb and edited by Bret Harte. Bored with the *Call*, becomes lax about work; resigns on October 10 at the suggestion of one of the proprietors. Writes several articles for the *Enterprise* criticizing San Francisco police for corruption, incompetence, and mistreatment of Chinese immigrants. When Gillis is charged for his part in a barroom brawl, they decide in early December to go to Jackass Hill in Tuolumne County, California, where Jim and William Gillis, Stephen's brothers, and Dick Stoker have pocket-mine claims. Remains in camp after Stephen Gillis returns to Virginia City.

1865   In January goes with Jim Gillis to Angel's Camp in Calaveras County and stays there four weeks (soon joined by Stoker), spending most of the time indoors because of bad weather. Listens to stories told by prospectors, one of which is about a jumping frog, and writes notes in journal. Returns briefly to Jackass Hill and then goes to San Francisco in late February. Moves into the Gillis family rooming house at 44 Minna Street. Writes articles for the *Californian*, and pieces for the *Golden Era*, other California journals, and the *Enterprise*. Befriends Charles Warren Stoddard, another contributor to the *Californian*. Begins writing more often for the *Enterprise* and soon contracts to write a letter a day for $100 a month. Takes on another job with the San Francisco *Dramatic Chronicle* for $40 a week, writing Orion that he is determined to get out of debt. Articles reprinted in New York begin to bring recognition (New York *Round Table* calls him "the foremost among the merry gentlemen of the California press"). Experiences strong earthquake on October 8 that causes significant damage in San Francisco, San Jose, and Santa Cruz. After repeated requests from Artemus Ward for a sketch to include in a book of humorous works, sends "Jim Smiley and His Jumping Frog" to him, but the text arrives too late for inclusion in the book and is published in Henry

Clapp's *Saturday Press*. The story is widely reprinted all over the country.

1866   Stops writing for the *Californian* (both it and the *Golden Era* will reprint articles published in the *Enterprise*). Begins to think of writing a book about the Mississippi, and also reviews his articles, saving some and destroying others. Sails on the *Ajax* on March 7 for the Sandwich Islands (Hawaii) as roving correspondent for the Sacramento *Union*. Arrives in Honolulu on March 18. Explores Oahu on horseback (will also ride on Maui and Hawaii), meets King Kamehameha V, and discovers that he is also a Mason. Goes to Maui by small schooner in mid-April; returns to Honolulu May 22, then sails on May 26 to the island of Hawaii, where he sees the volcano Kilauea erupting. Returns to Oahu June 16. Reads Oliver Wendell Holmes' *Songs in Many Keys* while recovering from saddle boils. Meets Anson Burlingame, American minister to China, in Honolulu and spends time with him and his son Edward. Takes notes while Burlingame interviews survivors of the shipwrecked *Hornet* and writes report for the *Union* that scoops all other papers. Sails for San Francisco July 19 on the *Smyrniote*. Fellow passengers include three *Hornet* survivors; Clemens reads and copies parts of their diaries for article "Forty-three Days in an Open Boat" (published in *Harper's Magazine* in December). Arrives in San Francisco on August 13. Sees Orion and his wife, Mollie, who are in city before sailing for the East Coast. Goes to Sacramento and collects $20 for each week of his trip and $100 for each column of the *Hornet* story. Writes articles for the *Union* and the New York *Weekly Review*, and covers California State Agricultural Society Fair in Sacramento. Delivers first lecture on October 2, speaking on the Sandwich Islands to a large, appreciative audience at Maguire's Academy of Music in San Francisco. Goes on tour, lecturing in Sacramento, Marysville, Grass Valley, Nevada City, Red Dog, and You Bet in California, and then in Virginia City, Carson City, Dayton, Silver City, Washoe City, and Gold City in Nevada. Returns to California and appears in San Francisco, San Jose, Petaluma, and Oakland, concluding tour with a special appearance in San Francisco on December 10 at the request of Frederick F. Low, governor of California, and Henry G. Blasdel, governor of Nevada. Becomes traveling correspondent for the San Francisco *Alta California* and leaves San Francisco December 15 aboard the *America*, captained by Edgar Wakeman. Enjoys company of Wakeman and writes down some of his stories. Crosses Central America by way of Nicaragua.

1867   Arrives in Greytown, Nicaragua, and sails on *San Francisco* to New York. Cholera breaks out and seven passengers die; when ship stops at Key West, a number of fearful passengers disembark. Clemens arrives in New York January 12 and takes rooms at the Metropolitan Hotel (establishment frequented by westerners). Sees old California friends Frank Fuller (who will later manage a series of lectures for Clemens) and Charles Henry Webb, who offers to help him put together a book of sketches (Webb will publish it himself after other publishers turn it down). Through Webb, meets Edward H. House of the New York *Tribune*, Henry Clapp, and John Hay. Sends letters to the *Alta* and makes arrangements to contribute articles to the New York *Sunday Mercury*, the *Evening Express* and the New York *Weekly*. Has no success finding a publisher for the Sandwich Islands letters. Reserves cabin on the *Quaker City* for the first American transatlantic excursion, organized by Henry Ward Beecher's congregation (Beecher and General Sherman are expected to be passengers), then goes to St. Louis to visit family (Pamela's husband had died in August 1865). Publishes three satirical articles on women's suffrage in *Missouri Democrat*. Lectures successfully in St. Louis, Hannibal, Keokuk, and Quincy, Illinois, and sees old friends. Returns to New York on April 15 and soon moves into the Westminster Hotel. *The Celebrated Jumping Frog of Calaveras County, and Other Sketches* published by Webb on April 30 (Clemens is unhappy with Webb's editing and sales are poor). Gives three successful lectures in New York and Brooklyn in May. Accepts assignments to write for the New York *Tribune*, the New York *Herald* (unsigned articles), and the *Alta*. Boards *Quaker City* on June 8. After two days anchored off Brooklyn because of bad weather, the ship sails on June 10 for Europe and the Holy Land. Disappointed by absence of Beecher and Sherman and finds most of the passengers too pious and staid, but makes friends with some, including Daniel Slote, his cabin mate, Moses Sperry Beach, editor of the New York *Sun*, and his daughter Emma, John A. Van Nostrand, Julius Moulton, Dr. Abraham Reeves Jackson, Julia Newell, Solon Long Severance and his wife, Emily, Mary Mason Fairbanks ("Mother Fairbanks"), who becomes one of his closest friends and advisers, and 18-year-old Charles Jervis Langdon, from Elmira, New York, who shows Clemens a picture of his sister, Olivia. Travels to North Africa, Spain, France, Italy, Greece, Russia (where members of the excursion meet with Czar Alexander II at Yalta in the Crimea on August 26), Turkey, the Holy Land, and Egypt. Returns to New York on November 19, and goes to Washington, D.C., where he serves for a few weeks as private secretary to William M. Stewart, Republican senator from Nevada. Acts as Washington correspondent for the *Territorial Enterprise*, *Alta California*, and the New York *Tribune*. Receives several offers from book publishers; prefers one from the American Publishing Company, a subscription firm in Hartford, Connecticut. Returns to New York on Christmas Day and moves in with Dan Slote's family. Invited by Charles Langdon to dine with his family at the St. Nicholas Hotel, meets Olivia Louise (Livy) Langdon (b. Nov. 27, 1845). Goes with the Langdons to hear Charles Dickens read.

1868   Spends New Year's Day visiting with Livy and her friend Alice Hooker. Attends services given by Henry Ward Beecher as guest of *Quaker City* friends, Moses and Emma Beach. Has dinner at Beecher's home and meets his sister, Harriet Beecher Stowe. Returns to Washington on January 8. Delivers lecture "The Frozen Truth," an account of the cruise, and gives a successful toast to "Woman" at the Washington Newspaper Correspondents' Club. Lodges at several addresses, often rooming with John Henry Riley, *Alta* correspondent in Washington. Tries unsuccessfully to obtain Patent Office clerkship for Orion. Stops in New York in late January and arranges to write articles for the *Herald*. Makes agreement in Hartford with Elisha Bliss to have his book on the excursion published by the American Publishing Company. Stays with John Hooker (father of Alice Hooker) and his family in the "Nook Farm" area of Hartford, but is uncomfortable because he cannot smoke openly. Returns to Washington and works on book. Sails for California on March 11 to arrange republication rights for his *Alta* letters from the excursion, which the newspaper had copyrighted. Leaves from New York aboard the *Henry Chauncey*, crosses Panama, boards the *Sacramento*, and arrives in San Francisco on April 2. Sees Anson Burlingame at the Occidental Hotel, where they are both staying. Lectures in San Francisco and interior towns, then travels by train and stagecoach from Sacramento to Virginia City, arriving on April 24. Lectures there and in Carson City. Returns to San Francisco May 5. Reaches agreement with the *Alta* regarding *Quaker City* material. Works intensively on book, revising, arranging, and cutting letters and adding new passages. In June asks Bret Harte to read the manuscript and make suggestions (will remember his help with appreciation). Gives another lecture in San Francisco (reviewed more favorably than the earlier ones). Sails for New York on the *Montana* July 6 and arrives in New York on the *Henry Chauncey* July 29. Stays at the Westminster Hotel, where he again sees Burlingame; writes, with his help, "The Treaty with China," article that is published on the front page of the New York *Tribune*. Goes to Hartford and stays with the Blisses while he works on the book. After brief return to New York City goes to visit the Langdon family in Elmira, New York. (Jervis, b. 1809, and Olivia Lewis Langdon, b. 1810, both natives of New York State, were married in 1832 and lived in a succession of towns in upstate New York, where Jervis worked as a storekeeper. They were ardent abolitionists and "conductors" on the Underground Railroad, and had sheltered Frederick Douglass in Millport in 1842 while he was still a fugitive slave. After settling in Elmira in 1845 the Langdons soon prospered in the lumber business and then became wealthy in the coal trade. Their friends included abolitionists Gerritt Smith, William Lloyd Garrison, Wendell Phillips, and Frederick Douglass, and women's rights advocate Anna E. Dickinson. When Livy was 16 years old, a fall on the ice invalided her for two years. She regained her mobility after being treated by Dr. Newton, a faith healer, although for the remainder of her life she is unable to walk very far.) Clemens falls in love with Livy and proposes to her early in September, but is refused. Leaves on September 8 with Charles Langdon to visit Mary Fairbanks and her husband, Abel, at their home in Cleveland. Goes on alone to see family in

St. Louis. Courts Livy with letters. Visits her again in late September, and then goes to Hartford to work on book. Meets the Reverend Joseph H. Twichell, a Congregational minister who will become one of his closest lifetime friends. Returns to New York in late October and gives lecture, "The American Vandal Abroad," in Cleveland, Pittsburgh, and Elmira in November. Proposes to Livy again and she confesses that she loves him. Promises to reform himself, to become religious, and to stop drinking. Jervis Langdon has a former employee make inquiries in San Francisco about Clemens' past. Resumes lectures in December, appearing in New Jersey, New York (where he again stops in Elmira), Pennsylvania, Michigan, Indiana, and Illinois.

1869   Spends New Year's Day with the Fairbanks in Cleveland. Continues lecture tour through Ohio, Illinois, Michigan, Iowa, Wisconsin, Pennsylvania, and New Jersey. Writes long letters to Livy, and marks up books for her to read, in particular Oliver Wendell Holmes' *The Autocrat of the Breakfast Table* (they call it their "courting-book"); she sends him marked copies of Henry Ward Beecher's sermons. Clemens learns that some Californians have responded unfavorably to Jervis Langdon's inquiries about his character; he tells Langdon that though many people were acquainted with him, only five were close, and that he is no longer the same person he was then. Returns to Elmira; engagement is formally announced February 4. Concerned about earning steady income, investigates buying share in either the Cleveland *Herald*, partly owned by Abel Fairbanks, or the Hartford *Courant*, published in a city where he and Livy have many friends. While working on his book in Hartford in early March, rereads *Gulliver's Travels* and finds that though he had enjoyed it as a boy, he had no idea then how wonderful it was. Writes to Livy about it (and *Don Quixote*, which she is reading) that he "will mark it & tear it until it is fit for your eyes. . . .You are as pure as snow, & I would have you always so— untainted, untouched even by the impure thoughts of others. . . ." Hears Petroleum V. Nasby (David Ross Locke) lecture in Hartford and they become friends. Goes to Boston, where Nasby introduces him to Holmes. Returns to Elmira to read proofs, with Livy's assistance (she will continue to help edit his work). Meets Wendell Phillips in March and Anna E. Dickinson in April when they come to visit the Langdons. Leaves Elmira with Charles Langdon on May 5 and goes to New York and Hartford, where he continues work on book. Engages James Redpath as his lecture agent and begins planning fall tour. Writes articles, including "Personal Habits of the Siamese Twins." Returns to Elmira at the end of May. Finishes reading proofs and goes with Langdon family to the St. Nicholas Hotel in New York, then to Hartford, where they attend the June 17 wedding of Alice Hooker to John Day. Meets Charles Dudley Warner, part-owner of the Hartford *Courant*, at the wedding; he will become a lifelong close friend. After a short visit to New York, returns with Livy to Elmira. Unable to buy a share in the Hartford *Courant*, and feeling the price of investing in the Cleveland *Herald* is too high, on the advice of Jervis Langdon buys a one-third interest in the Buffalo *Express* for $25,000 in August (Clemens puts in $2,500, Langdon lends him $12,500, and the remainder is to be paid in installments). Moves to Buffalo and takes lodgings in rooming house at 39 Swan Street, close to the *Express* office. Makes friends with young newlywed couple living there, John James and Esther (Essie) Keeler Norton McWilliams. Changes the typographical look of the *Express*, using smaller type for headlines and saving larger type for important news. Works closely with part-owner and editor-in-chief Josephus Nelson Larned, who becomes lifelong friend. *The Innocents Abroad*, account of *Quaker City* excursion, is published by American Publishing Company on August 15; it receives good reviews and sells well. Visits Elmira whenever possible. Prepares lecture "Our Fellow Savages of the Sandwich Islands" in Elmira and begins tour in Pittsburgh on November 1. Continues lecturing in Massachusetts, Rhode Island, Connecticut, New York, Washington, D.C., and Maine, using Young's Hotel in Boston as his base. Meets other lyceum lecturers, including humorist Josh Billings (Henry Wheeler Shaw). Begins long, close friendship with William Dean Howells, who had enthusiastically reviewed *The Innocents Abroad*. Returns briefly to Hartford to pick up first-quarter royalty check and finds that the Hartford *Courant* is now eager to have him, but is unable to accept because of his commitment to the *Express*. Sees Langdons in New York in early December. Meets Frederick Douglass in Boston and is impressed by him.

1870   Sends out wedding invitations to old friends, including Dan De Quille, Charles Warren Stoddard, Horace Bixby, and informal invitations to California mining friends Jim Gillis and Dick Stoker. Sees Joseph Goodman when he comes to New York before sailing for Europe. Elated by sales of book. No longer drinks, and cuts down on his smoking. Continues lecturing in New York until January 21. Marries Livy in Elmira on February 2, with Thomas Beecher (half-brother of Henry Ward Beecher and uncle of Alice Hooker) and Twichell performing the service. Sister Pamela and niece Annie Moffett attend. Goes by private train to Buffalo with Livy and a small party of guests on February 3. Clemens expects to be moving into a boarding house and is surprised by gift from Jervis Langdon of furnished house at 472 Delaware Street, with three servants, stable, and horse and carriage (worth more than $40,000). House guests include Pamela and Annie, the Twichells, friends from Elmira, and Petroleum V. Nasby. Clemens goes to the *Express* offices only twice a week. Signs contract in March with *Galaxy* to supply a monthly humorous column, "Memoranda," for $2,000 a year, reserving all republication rights to himself (first column appears in May). Continues writing for the *Express*, but feels that *Galaxy* allows him more freedom. Livy begins to address him as "Youth" (will do so for the rest of her life). Becomes close friends with poet and essayist David Gray, part-owner and associate editor of the Buffalo *Courier*, and his wife, Martha. Mother comes to visit in April (her first meeting with Livy), while sister prepares to move to Fredonia, New York, 60 miles from Buffalo. Jervis Langdon's health deteriorates, and Clemenses go to Elmira for two weeks (will continue to help nurse Langdon; Clemens often sits at his bedside for four hours a night). Goes to Washington, D.C., in early July to lobby for passage of bill to divide Tennessee into two judicial districts (measure would potentially benefit both Jervis Langdon's lumber business and Orion's plans to sell family land near Jamestown). Sees old friends Senator William M. Stewart, Vice-President Schuyler Colfax, and Thomas Fitch (now congressman from Nevada), and meets President Ulysses S. Grant. Sees old friend John Henry Riley. Returns to Elmira and signs new contract with Bliss for book on the West for 7½ percent royalty. Jervis Langdon dies August 6 of stomach cancer. Livy is grief-stricken; Clemens gives her opiates to help her sleep. Livy's mother and Emma Nye, Livy's old classmate, come to visit in Buffalo late in August. Nye immediately falls ill with typhoid; Livy cares for her with help of hired nurse. Clemens continues to write *Galaxy* articles and works on western book. Writes Orion expressing his exasperation over Orion's schemes for selling Tennessee land. Delights in making burlesque woodcut, "Fortifications of Paris," for paper. Visits mother, sister, nephew, and niece in Fredonia. Susan Langdon Crane (Livy's foster sister, b. 1836, who was orphaned in 1840 and then adopted by the Langdons) comes to take care of Livy, who is pregnant and exhausted. Clemens gets Orion a job in Hartford as editor of Bliss's new magazine, *American Publisher*, for $100 a month (first issue comes out in April 1871). Son Langdon born, one month prematurely, on November 7 and at first is not expected to live. Mary Fairbanks comes to help nurse Livy. Clemens goes to New York to meet Webb about obtaining rights to *Celebrated Jumping Frog of Calaveras County*, forgoes $600 due in royalties, and pays Webb an additional $800 for rights and plates (will destroy them). Arranges for Riley to go to South Africa and research book on its diamond fields, which Clemens will write; pays Riley's passage and salary ($100 a month). Contracts with Bliss for South African book and *Mark Twain's Sketches, New & Old*. Son's health continues to be poor.

1871   Attends wedding in Cleveland of Mary Fairbanks' step-daughter, Alice, to William Henry Gaylord (Livy, still unwell, is unable to attend). Hires a wet nurse to care for baby. Livy falls dangerously ill with typhoid in February. Clemens hires nurses and doctors, including Dr. Rachel Brooks Gleason, to care for her and stays up nights watching over her. Susan Crane and Livy's close friend Clara Spaulding assist in nursing. Decides to stop writing for the *Galaxy* in order to work more on books (last "Memoranda" column appears in April). Has come to "loathe Buffalo" and puts house and interest in the *Express* up for sale, hoping to move to Hartford. When Livy's health improves slightly, takes her to Elmira on March 18, intending never to return to Buffalo. Chagrined by unfavorable reception of pamphlet *Mark Twain's (Burlesque) Autobiography and First Romance*, published by Isaac E. Sheldon, the same firm that published *Galaxy*. Works hard on *Roughing It*, his western book, writing at Quarry Farm, located on a hill outside Elmira and owned by Susan and Theodore Crane. Pleased when Goodman visits in April and works with him on the manuscript. Sells interest in *Express* for $15,000, taking a loss of $10,000. Pamela and her son Samuel Erasmus Moffett stay at Quarry Farm in June to take Elmira Water Cure. Livy's and baby's health improve. Writes lecture on "boys' rights." Arranges another lecture tour with Redpath, but asks that he be paid at least as much as his friend Nasby receives. Has Bliss arrange for George Routledge and Sons to publish and copyright *Roughing It* in England. Clemens writes two more lectures and decides that the third, "Reminiscences of Some Un-Commonplace Characters I Have Chanced to Meet," is the one he wants to deliver. Goes to Hartford in August to complete *Roughing It*. Sees mother and Annie, who have come to visit Orion and Mollie in Hartford, and brings them with him to visit Elmira. Baby is very sick again, and Livy discovers that during her illness he has been given laudanum and other sleeping medicines. Clemens goes to Washington in September to secure patent on "elastic strap" (granted patent for "Improvement in Adjustable and Detachable Straps for Garments"). Leases John and Isabella Beecher Hooker's house in "Nook Farm" area of Hartford. Returns to Buffalo to pack, and moves to Hartford in October. Lectures in Pennsylvania, Washington, D.C., Massachusetts, Vermont, New Hampshire, Maine, and New York. Uses Boston as base when delivering New England lectures, meets Thomas Bailey Aldrich, sees Howells and Bret Harte, and is occasionally accompanied by Ralph Keeler, young writer friend from California. Dislikes his prepared lectures and writes one about Artemus Ward, then writes another one based on *Roughing It*. Goes on to Chicago and is struck by the extent of damage caused by the great fire of October 8–9 ("literally no Chicago *here*"). Stays with *Quaker City* friends Dr. Abraham Reeves Jackson and his second wife, Julia Newell, then continues lecturing in Illinois.

1872 Lectures in Indiana, Ohio, West Virginia, Pennsylvania, and New York, where he sees his friend John Hay. Attends birthday celebration for Horace Greeley, editor of the New York *Tribune*, in New York on February 3; other guests include Hay, Bret Harte, Whitelaw Reid, and P. T. Barnum. *Roughing It* is published in February and sells well. Orion quits as editor of Bliss's *American Publisher* and tells Clemens that Bliss is cheating him on production costs of *Roughing It*. Clemens questions figures, but does not break with Bliss. Returns to Elmira in early March. Daughter Olivia Susan (Susy) born March 19. Visits Fairbanks in Cleveland with Livy and mother in early May. Returns to Elmira, then goes to Hartford. South African book is abandoned when Riley develops fatal cancer of the mouth (he will die in September). Son Langdon dies June 2 of diptheria. In July family goes to stay at Fenwick Hall in New Saybrook, Connecticut, to escape summer heat. Prepares prefaces and makes revisions for English edition of *The Innocents Abroad*, published by Routledge. Devises idea for "Mark Twain's Self-Pasting Scrap-Book" (patented June 24, 1873, it is successfully marketed by his friend Dan Slote). Sails for Liverpool on August 21 on the *Scotia*, intending to write a book on England. Speaks at the Whitefriars, a London literary club, and is made honorary member. Tours Warwickshire in open barouche with American publisher James R. Osgood. Meets humorist Tom Hood, son of the poet, actor Henry Irving, clergyman Moncure Conway, and sees Henry Morton Stanley, whom he had met in St. Louis in 1867. Writes letter to the *Spectator* protesting John Camden Hotten's printing of books attributed to him that include articles he did not write. Speaks at the Savage Club, a literary and artistic club. Overwhelmed by social activities, invitations to private houses, and ceremonial functions, is amazed and flattered by his fame in England. Sails for America on board the *Batavia*, on November 12; impressed when Captain John E. Mouland and crew rescue shipwreck survivors in heavy seas and writes letter to the Royal Humane Society recommending that they be rewarded (among fellow passengers signing letter is Edward Emerson, son of Ralph Waldo Emerson). Arrives in New York on November 25. Begins work on novel *The Gilded Age* with friend and neighbor, Charles Dudley Warner.

1873   Buys large lot in "Nook Farm" area of Hartford, planning to build house on it. Lectures in Hartford to raise money for charity, and in New York and Brooklyn in February on the Sandwich Islands. Made a member of the Lotos Club in New York City. Becomes a director of the American Publishing Company (owns $5,000 stock in it). Livy goes to Elmira late in April and Clemens follows after he and Warner finish *The Gilded Age*. Family, accompanied by Clara Spaulding and recently hired shorthand secretary Samuel Chalmers Thompson, sails for England on the *Batavia* on May 17. They initially stay at Edwards' Hotel in London, but after a few weeks move to the Langham because Clemens misses the billiard room there. Intrigued by trial for perjury of claimant to the Tichborne title (claimant is eventually proved to have committed perjury). Sees Henry Lee, naturalist at Brighton Aquarium, and poet Joaquin Miller, whom he had met in California. Arranges for Routledge to bring out *The Gilded Age* in England. Begins writing letters for the *Herald* on the activities of Nasr-Ed-Din, shah of Persia, during his visit to England and Europe (eventually sends five). Meets Thomas Hughes, Herbert Spencer, Charles Godfrey Leland ("Hans Breitmann"), Anthony Trollope, Robert Browning, and Wilkie Collins, among others. Moncure Conway takes Clemens and Livy to Stratford-on-Avon, where they are guests of the mayor. Meets Scottish writer George MacDonald and his wife, Louise, in July. Discharges Thompson as secretary, goes to Edinburgh, Scotland, and meets Dr. John Brown, who is called in to treat Livy, who is exhausted after the hectic London season; the doctor becomes a lifelong friend. Buys the Abbotsford Edition of Sir Walter Scott's works. Clara Spaulding rejoins them after traveling in France. Visits Belfast, becoming friends there with *Northern Whig* proprietor Francis Dalzell Finlay, goes to Dublin, then returns to London. Sees old friend Charles Warren Stoddard, who is in London as newspaper correspondent. Clemenses go to Paris in late September to buy household items. Having spent more money than expected, Clemens has George Dolby, Dickens' agent, arrange for him to lecture in London in mid-October. Accompanies family home to America, sailing on the *Batavia* October 21 and arriving in New York November 2, where Orion is trying to get work as an editor, proofreader, or typesetter on a newspaper. Clemens leaves for England on November 8 to obtain copyright for *The Gilded Age* and to give further lectures. Arrives in London November 20. Moves into the Langham Hotel but feels lonely and asks Stoddard to join him there as secretary and companion. Lectures in December on the Sandwich Islands for a week, then changes to "Roughing It on the Silver Frontier" for the next two weeks. Writes out after-dinner speeches because he is often called on to give them. Feels oppressed by continuous, unusually heavy fog and coal smoke. Elected honorary member of the Temple Club. Finlay visits for a week. *The Gilded Age* published simultaneously in England and America on December 23. Spends Christmas holiday at Salisbury and visits Stonehenge.

1874   Lectures in Leicester and Liverpool. Sails for Boston on the *Parthia* January 13 and arrives on January 26. Introduces lecture by English clergyman and writer Charles Kingsley at the Essex Institute in Salem, Massachusetts. Works on two plays. Lectures in Boston in March. Mary Fairbanks and her children visit Hartford. Sales of *The Gilded Age* are very good. Buys Orion a small chicken farm outside Keokuk (will begin sending regular payments to Orion, who considers them loans, though he will be unable to repay more than nominal amounts of interest). Goes to Elmira in late April and stays in the Langdon house, then moves to Quarry Farm on May 5, where Susan Crane has built a free-standing octagonal study for him. Daughter Clara Langdon born June 8. Works on five-act play *Colonel Sellers*, dramatization of *The Gilded Age*, and *Tom Sawyer*. Pleased when "A True Story" is accepted by Howells for the *Atlantic* (published November 1874), his first piece to appear there. Stops in New York en route from Elmira to Hartford to help with rehearsals for *Colonel Sellers*; play opens September 16, starring John T. Raymond, at the Park Theatre. Returns to Hartford September 19 and moves into still unfinished house designed by architect Edward T. Potter. With Howells' encouragement, begins writing articles about the Mississippi ("Old Times on the Mississippi," first in series, appears in January 1875 *Atlantic*). Decides in November to walk with Twichell from Hartford to Boston; they cover 28 miles the first day and six miles the next before taking the train the rest of the way. Buys a typewriter and writes to Howells on it (later boasts to friends that he was the first writer to use one). Attends *Atlantic* contributors' dinner in Boston on December 15.

1875   Enjoys new home, spending hours playing billiards in room at top of house; close neighbors are the Warners and Stowes. Describes his taste in reading: "I like history, biography, travels, curious facts & strange happenings, & science. And I detest novels, poetry & theology." Continues writing reminiscences of life as a pilot on the Mississippi (installments appear in the *Atlantic* until August). Pleased with royalties received from *Colonel Sellers*, which is successfully touring the country. Goes to New York to attend Henry Ward Beecher's trial for adultery (it results in a hung jury). Decides not to go to Quarry Farm for the summer. Resumes work on *Tom Sawyer*. Invites Dan De Quille to come to Hartford and helps him get his book *The Big Bonanza* published by Bliss (appears fall 1876). Clemens and Howells frequently visit each other in Hartford and Cambridge. Hires George Griffin as butler; he becomes a family favorite (household includes about seven servants, among them nurses for the children). Receives many visitors, including Joaquin Miller and Bret Harte. Finishes *Tom Sawyer* in July. Goes to Bateman's Point, Newport, Rhode Island, at the end of month and stays through August. *Mark Twain's Sketches, New and Old* published September 25 by Bliss. Moncure Conway visits the Clemenses in Hartford.

1876   Engages Conway as agent for English publication of *Tom Sawyer* (Conway is paid 5 percent of royalty). Clemens is ill for several weeks. Employs private secretary to take dictation and answer letters. Makes revisions in *Tom Sawyer* based on Howells' suggestions. Gives talk, "The Facts Concerning the Recent Carnival of Crime in Connecticut," to the Monday Evening Club, Hartford literary group. Mother and sister visit. Clemens goes to Quarry Farm on June 15 for the summer. *The Adventures of Tom Sawyer* published in England by Chatto & Windus. Begins work on *Huckleberry Finn*. Attends centennial celebration in Philadelphia with other authors and reads eulogy to

Francis Lightfoot Lee. Angered by widespread sales in the United States of pirated Canadian editions of *Tom Sawyer*. Works on scatological tale [*Date, 1601.*] *Conversation, as it Was by the Social Fireside, in the Time of the Tudors* (published privately 1880), and reads it to close friends Twichell, David Gray, Howells, and John Hay. Returns to Hartford September 11. In November gives a series of readings arranged by Redpath. Collaborates with Harte on play, *Ah Sin*, Harte staying at the Clemenses' house for two weeks. Becomes friends with Frank Millet when he comes to Hartford to paint Clemens' portrait. American edition of *Tom Sawyer*, published December 8 by the American Publishing Company, sells moderately well. Tauchnitz firm publishes continental edition of *Tom Sawyer* with his approval (Tauchnitz will continue as his European publisher).

1877   Continues work on play with Harte until late February. Relations with Harte become strained over their financial and publishing ties, and then break off completely when Clemens receives an angry letter from him. Oversees rehearsals of *Ah Sin* in Baltimore in April, then returns home on May 1 (play opens in Washington on May 7). Travels with Twichell to Bermuda for short holiday, then goes with family to Elmira in June. Writes "Some Rambling Notes of an Idle Excursion" about Bermuda trip for the *Atlantic*. Begins work on another play, "Cap'n Simon Wheeler, the Amateur Detective" (never produced or published). Attends New York rehearsals for *Ah Sin* in July (produced by Augustin Daly, the play opens July 31 and runs for five weeks). Reads English and French histories and French novels; likes the elder Dumas' novels of the Revolution, and describes Carlyle's *History of the French Revolution* as "one of the greatest creations that ever flowed from a pen." Tries to persuade cartoonist Thomas Nast to go on a lecture tour with him. At banquet in Boston on December 17 delivers the "Whittier Birthday Speech," a burlesque of three tramps who pass themselves off as Longfellow, Emerson, and Holmes. Many listeners, including Howells, are shocked, and some newspapers are severely critical. Chagrined, sends letters of apology to the three writers, all of whom had attended dinner (will eventually become less embarrassed by this incident).

1878   Works on *The Prince and the Pauper*. Signs contract on March 8 with Elisha Bliss for book about Europe, accepting half of the profits in lieu of royalties (Clemens considers separate agreement with Bliss expedient because Bliss is threatening to leave the American Publishing Company). Visits Elmira and Fredonia (niece Annie is now married to Charles Webster). Sails for Europe April 11 on the *Holsatia* with family, Clara Spaulding, and German nursemaid Rosina (Rosa) Hay. Passengers include Bayard Taylor, on his way to become minister to Germany, and journalist Murat Halstead. Family stops in Hamburg for a week and then travels slowly through Germany to Heidelberg, arriving May 6. Clemens takes excursions into the countryside before they leave on July 23 for Baden-Baden. Twichell arrives August 1 (Clemens is paying for his trip). Clemens and Twichell take "walking tour," traveling by rail, carriage, boat, and foot through the Black Forest and the Swiss Alps to Lausanne and Geneva, from where Twichell returns home in September. Family travels through Italy, staying in Venice, Florence, and Rome until November, then settles in Munich for three months, where they study German. Saddened by news of death of Bayard Taylor in Berlin on December 19.

1879   Family goes to Paris at the end of February. Clemens is very ill with rheumatism and dysentery. Feels better in April and works on *A Tramp Abroad*. Dislikes Paris, but enjoys friends who are also there, including Moncure Conway and the Aldriches. Meets artists and literary men who belong to the Stomach Club, including Edwin Austin Abbey and Augustus Saint-Gaudens, and attends wedding of friend Frank Millet. Has two meetings with Ivan Turgenev, a writer he admires. Family leaves Paris in late July and travels through Belgium and Holland, then spends a month in England. Renews old acquaintances there and meets Charles Darwin at Grasmere in the Lake District. Family sails on the *Gallia* August 23 and arrives in New York on September 3, then goes to Quarry Farm. Clemens visits his family in Fredonia. Returns to Hartford in late October. Installs telephone in his home. Attends reunion banquet of Army of the Tennessee, held in Chicago on November 13 with Ulysses S. Grant as the guest of honor (generals Sherman, Sheridan, Pope, Schofield, and Logan are also present). Responds to toast with speech "The Babies." Becomes friends with orator Robert G. Ingersoll. Attends *Atlantic* breakfast in honor of Oliver Wendell Holmes and gives well-received speech.

1880   Goes to Elmira with Livy, who is exhausted from redecorating house and installing furniture bought in Europe. Works for a short time on *Huckleberry Finn*, then sets it aside. Visits mother, who is not well, in Fredonia. Buys four-fifths interest in Dan Slote's patent in Kaolatype, a chalk-plate process for engraving illustrations, and forms company with himself as president, Charles Perkins (his Hartford lawyer and friend) as secretary, and Slote as treasurer. Agrees to finance company with his own money as needed for three months. *A Tramp Abroad* published in March by the American Publishing Company. It sells well, and Clemens earns more money on each book sold than under previous contracts. Increases payments to Orion, telling him that the money is for his role in making him more aware of the need to obtain better terms from publishers. Works happily on *The Prince and the Pauper* and encourages Orion to write autobiography (Orion will write several chapters, but never finishes manuscript). Daughter Jane Lampton (Jean) born July 26. Elisha Bliss dies on September 28 (death will cause Clemens to seek new publisher). Clemens accompanies Grant to Hartford and delivers welcoming speech. Actively supports James A. Garfield, the Republican presidential nominee.

1881   Writes letter to president-elect Garfield, describing Frederick Douglass as a personal friend and asking that he be retained in the office of marshal of the District of Columbia (Garfield makes Douglass recorder of deeds for the District). Pays support for Paris stay of young Hartford machinist Karl Gerhardt and wife, Hattie, so that Gerhardt can study sculpture. Buys additional land next to house to keep neighbor from building and begins renovations of house and grounds. Disillusioned with Slote, hires Charles Webster, niece Annie's husband, to supervise Slote and the Kaolatype concern, and to be his business agent in other matters. Enjoys reading out loud works of Joel Chandler Harris. Spends June and July at Montowese House, in Branford, Connecticut, before going to Elmira. Makes Webster his legal representative in business aspects of the publication of his books by the American Publishing Company. Upset by the shooting of President Garfield on July 2 and his death on September 19. By now has made numerous investments in various speculative ventures, including the Paige typesetter (will eventually invest at least $190,000 trying to get the machine perfected). Howells reads proofs and suggests revisions of *The Prince and the Pauper*. Clemens and James R. Osgood travel to Canada to issue an edition of the book there (their presence in the country is needed to secure Canadian copyright). Clemens reads Francis Parkman's histories of the Anglo-French conflict in North America. *The Prince and the Pauper* is published by James R. Osgood & Co. in the United States in late December (Clemens pays production costs and Osgood produces and markets the book in return for a 7½ percent royalty).

1882 Dan Slote dies. Old friend Edward House visits in February with his adopted daughter Koto, and House is ill for weeks. Clemens and Howells ask Grant to intercede with President Arthur to keep Howells' father as consul in Toronto (Arthur retains him). Visits the aged Emerson with Howells, and is pleased when Emerson eventually recognizes him. In preparation for expanding 1875 *Atlantic* articles about the Mississippi into a book, Clemens travels with Osgood and shorthand secretary Roswell Phelps to St. Louis, then goes by steamboat to New Orleans, where he meets Joel Chandler Harris, George Washington Cable, and old friend Horace Bixby. Travels up the Mississippi with Bixby in pilothouse, stopping off in Hannibal and Quincy, Illinois. *The Stolen White Elephant*, collection of short pieces, published by Osgood. Trip to Quarry Farm delayed when Jean, Susy, and Clemens get scarlet fever and their house is quarantined. Struggles over writing *Life on the Mississippi*. Beginning to have doubts about Osgood's ability to sell books by subscription, makes Webster his subscription agent for the New York area. Remains in Elmira until September 29. Cable visits.

1883 Finishes book. Livy is sick with diphtheria and other ailments for over a month. Goes again to Canada to safeguard copyright. *Life on the Mississippi* published in May by Osgood (contractual terms are the same as for *The*

Prince and the Pauper). Resumes work on *Huckleberry Finn* and enjoys the writing. Collaborates with Howells on play *Colonel Sellers as Scientist*. Begins work on dramatizations of *Tom Sawyer* and *The Prince and the Pauper*. Family entertains many house guests. Becomes very dissatisfied with sales of books under Osgood's direction. Meets Matthew Arnold in Hartford during his American lecture tour.

1884   Cable visits in January and comes down with mumps; nurse is hired to take care of him. Clemens invests in Howells' father's invention, one-handed grape shears. Tries unsuccessfully to get plays produced. Howells reads typescript of *Huckleberry Finn* and suggests revisions. Clemens has attack of gout. Founds his own publishing company, Charles L. Webster & Co., and signs contract in May with Webster, who acts as publisher. Learns to ride a bicycle. Reads proofs of *Huckleberry Finn* from June through August, with help from Howells. Gerhardt makes bust of Clemens. Needing more money, contracts with Major J. B. Pond to do four-month lecture tour with Cable (Pond receives 10 percent commission, Cable $450 a week and expenses, and Clemens the remainder). Joins other Republican "mugwumps," who consider Republican presidential candidate James G. Blaine to be dishonest, in voting for Democrat Grover Cleveland. Lecture tour begins November 5 in New Haven. Learns from Richard Watson Gilder, editor of *Century Magazine*, that General Grant is writing his memoirs. Visits Grant in New York, tells him that terms offered by Century Company are inadequate, and urges him not to sign any contract until Webster & Co. can make an offer; Grant makes no commitments. On recommendation of Cable, Clemens reads Malory's *Le Morte d'Arthur*. In December, visits president-elect Cleveland in Albany at his invitation. *Century* publishes first of three excerpts from *Huckleberry Finn*. Charles Webster offers Grant $50,000 advance for his memoirs.

1885   Continues lecture tour, which includes Hannibal and Keokuk, where mother is now living with Orion. Charles Webster offers Grant choice of 20 percent royalty or 70 percent of net profits. *Adventures of Huckleberry Finn* published in the United States by Webster & Co. on February

16 (sells 39,000 copies by March 14); Clemens again goes to Canada to protect copyright. Webster & Co. buys rights to books published by Osgood for $3,000. Clemens visits Grant in New York on February 21 and learns that he is dying from throat cancer, but again urges him to accept the Webster offer. Grant signs contract on February 27, choosing to receive 70 percent of the profits. Canvassing for the books begins immediately. Lecture tour ends February 28; is very successful financially, and Clemens likes Cable, but is irritated by his strict observance of the Sabbath. Clemens signs new contract that makes Charles Webster a partner in Webster & Co. and gives him more money. When Concord, Massachusetts, library bans *Huckleberry Finn*, tells Webster that they will sell an extra 20,000 books as a result. Arranges for Gerhardt to make bust of Grant. Concerned about Grant's well-being and worried that he may not live to complete the memoirs, Clemens helps in any way he can, reading proofs as pages are set and praising the writing. By May more than 60,000 two-volume sets have been ordered, and production arrangements become costly and complex. Clemens is pleased when Susy begins writing biography of his life. Learns of Osgood's business failure. Writes account of the Marion Rangers, "The Private History of a Campaign that Failed," and shows it to Grant, who enjoys it immensely (published in *Century Magazine* in December as part of its series on the Civil War). Works on sequel to *Huckleberry Finn*, "Tom and Huck among the Indians" (never finished). Family goes to Elmira. Clemens visits Grant at Mount McGregor, New York, June 29–July 2, working with him on the completion of the second volume. Grant dies July 23, only a few days after finishing his memoirs. Clemens is involved in many ventures, including patents for a historical game, a perpetual calendar, and a "bed-clasp" for keeping babies' blankets in place; his major investment, now costing $3,000 a month, is the Paige typesetter. Reads manuscripts for possible publication by Webster & Co. Touched when Oliver Wendell Holmes, Charles Dudley Warner, and others write tributes in the *Critic* for his fiftieth birthday. In December 325,000 copies of first volume of *Personal Memoirs of U. S. Grant* are bound and shipped (second volume appears in March 1886). Clemens begins paying board of Warner T.

McGuinn, one of the first black students at the Yale Law
School, whom he had met during a speaking engagement
at Yale in the fall. (Will also support study of Charles
Ethan Porter, a black sculptor, and pay tuition of a black
undergraduate at Lincoln University. McGuinn graduates
from Yale in 1887 and becomes an attorney in Baltimore,
where he later serves as local director of the NAACP and
wins lawsuit challenging mandated segregation of Baltimore city housing.)

1886   Family continues to entertain lavishly. Howells comes
with his daughter Mildred to see staging of *The Prince and
the Pauper* dramatized by Livy and performed by the
Clemens children and their friends. Clemens frequently
goes to New York on publishing business. Charles Webster gives Julia Grant check for $200,000 on February 27
(Grant family eventually receives between $420,000 and
$450,000 from sales of *Personal Memoirs*). Clemens makes
Frederick J. Hall third partner in Webster & Co. on April
28. Learns in May that after prolonged negotiations, Webster & Co. has signed contract with Bernard O'Reilly,
authorized biographer of Pope Leo XIII; Clemens expects
that the papal biography will be more successful than
Grant's memoirs (is disappointed by sales when book is
published in 1887). Reads from his works at U.S. Military
Academy at West Point. Resumes work with Howells on
play *Colonel Sellers as Scientist* and makes arrangements to
have it produced, but at the last moment Howells asks
that it be withdrawn. In July, takes family to visit mother,
Orion, and Mollie in Keokuk. Hires Frank G. Whitmore
as business agent in August, primarily to supervise construction of the Paige typesetting machine at the Pratt &
Whitney works in Hartford. Begins work on *A Connecticut Yankee in King Arthur's Court*. Reads Robert Browning steadily ("It takes me much longer to learn how to
read a page of Browning than a page of Shakespeare") and
enjoys reading his poetry aloud to the "Browning class," a
group of Livy's friends who meet in his billiard room
once a week. Entertains Henry Morton Stanley in Hartford and gives introduction at Stanley's lecture in Boston.

1887   Attends benefit on March 31 for the Longfellow Memorial
Fund in Boston and reads from "English as She Is

Taught," after being introduced by Charles Eliot Norton, who tells anecdote about Darwin keeping Clemens' works on his bedside table (other readers include Howells, Julia Ward Howe, Edward Everett Hale, Oliver Wendell Holmes, Thomas W. Higginson, George W. Curtis, Thomas B. Aldrich, and James R. Lowell). Defends General Grant's grammar against criticism by Matthew Arnold in speech in Hartford on April 27. Clemens financially backs production of *Colonel Sellers as Scientist*, retitled *The American Claimant* and credited solely to Mark Twain, that has a brief run starring A. P. Burbank. With Livy and several Hartford friends, visits artist Frederick Edwin Church and his wife at Olana, New York (Clemens had long admired him). At Quarry Farm, continues to work with pleasure on *A Connecticut Yankee in King Arthur's Court*. *Mark Twain's Library of Humor* (collaboration among Howells, Clemens, and Charles H. Clark, finished a number of years earlier; introduction written by Howells, signed "The Associate Editors") published in late December by Webster & Co.

1888   Signs agreement stating that Webster (who has been suffering increasingly from painful neuralgia) is to withdraw "from business, from all authority, and from the city, till April 1, 1889, & try to get back his health." Frederick Hall takes over his responsibilities. In April Clemens spends afternoon with Robert Louis Stevenson in New York's Washington Square Park. Visits Thomas Edison at his laboratory in West Orange, New Jersey, in June. Awarded honorary Master of Arts degree by Yale. Theodore Crane has partially paralyzing stroke in Elmira on September 6. Writer Grace King stays with the Clemenses at Hartford, October–November. Crane's condition worsens and he is nursed by Susan and Livy in Hartford in December. Hall buys Webster's interest in firm for $12,000.

1889   Success of prototype Paige typesetter thrills Clemens, although technical problems again develop. Writes letter of tribute to Whitman for publication in *Camden's Compliment to Walt Whitman*, edited by Horace Traubel (Clemens had joined others in financially assisting Whitman in 1885 and 1887). Theodore Crane dies at Quarry Farm on July 3. Clemens is charmed by Rudyard Kipling, who visits him in Elmira (will later read and reread Kipling's works with pleasure). Goes to Hartford to work on revisions of *A Connecticut Yankee in King Arthur's Court*. Hoping to live on profits from Paige machine, calls the novel his "swan-song" and his "retirement from literature" in letter to Howells. Unable to read manuscript because of eye trouble, Livy asks Clemens to have Howells read proofs because she trusts Howells to keep Clemens from offending good taste. Certain that the Paige machine will soon be ready for production, Clemens writes Howells that "after patiently & contentedly spending more than $3,000 a month on it for 44 consecutive months" it is "done at last. . . . Come & see this sublime magician of iron & steel work his enchantments." Invites Joseph Goodman to come east and help find investors for machine. Reads and is deeply impressed with Edward Bellamy's *Looking Backward: 2000–1887*. Anticipating that Chatto, his English publisher, will make changes in *A Connecticut Yankee* to avoid offending English sensibilities, writes letter to them refusing to alter text and saying that the book was "written for England." *A Connecticut Yankee in King Arthur's Court*, published in America December 10 by Webster & Co., with illustrations by Daniel Carter Beard, sells moderately well. Dramatization of *The Prince and the Pauper* by Abby Sage Richardson, produced by Belasco and Frohman, opens on Christmas Day in Philadelphia and is fairly successful.

1890   January, Edward Bellamy visits Clemens in Hartford. Financial problems become acute from continued cost of Paige machine and lack of profits from Webster & Co. (unsold books, subscription costs, and expense of producing and distributing 11-volume *Library of American Literature*, an anthology edited by Edmund C. Stedman, create constant cash-flow problems that drain away his book royalties). Edward House brings suit against dramatization of *The Prince and the Pauper* by Richardson, claiming he had been given the rights long ago. Litigation prevents Clemens from receiving royalties from play and ends their friendship. Family goes for the summer to Onteora Park, artists' and writers' colony in the Catskills near Tannersville, New York. With Goodman's help, Clemens travels frequently in search of investors for the Paige machine. Goes to Keokuk in August when mother has stroke. Susy

enters Bryn Mawr in October. Clara takes piano lessons in
New York twice a week. Mother dies in Keokuk October
27, and Clemens attends funeral in Hannibal on October
30. Goes to Elmira in November, where Livy's mother
dies November 28. Clemens rushes back to Hartford because Jean is ill.

1891   Webster & Co. goes deeper into debt. Attempts at raising
capital for Paige machine are unsuccessful, and Clemens
stops his monthly $3,000 payments in support of project.
Writes articles for magazines. Suffering from rheumatism
in right arm, finds writing difficult. Works on novel *The
American Claimant*. Experiments with dictating into phonograph, but soon gives up. Susy leaves Bryn Mawr in
April, too homesick to continue. Charles Webster dies
April 26. Clemens signs contract with *McClure's Magazine*
to serialize *The American Claimant* in America and Europe
for $12,000 and to write six letters from Europe for $1,000
each. No longer able to afford the maintenance of the
Hartford home, decides to go to Europe, hoping that
baths will help Livy's health (she is developing heart trouble) and relieve rheumatism in his arm, which makes writing almost impossible. They close the house, sell the
horses, and find new positions for their servants. Family
sails with Susan Crane on June 6 aboard the *Gascogne* and
arrives in Le Havre June 14. Stops in Paris before going to
take baths at Aix-les-Bains. Susy and Clara attend boarding school in Geneva. Clemens hears Wagner operas at
Bayreuth in August. Tries other baths at Marienbad.
Settles family in Ouchy, Switzerland, in September, then
hires courier, boatman, and flatboat for ten-day trip down
the Rhône. Family goes to Berlin for the winter and
moves into Körnerstrasse Hotel. Still suffers from pain in
arm and continues to find writing difficult. Moves family
to better rooms in Hotel Royal on December 31.

1892   Clemens develops pneumonia. Doctors recommend that
as soon as he is well enough to travel, Livy and he should
go south. Has private dinner with Kaiser William II on
February 20. Leaves daughters at school in Berlin and
goes with Livy in March to Mentone, France, for three
weeks and then to Italy, spending several weeks in Rome
and Venice before returning to Berlin. Collection *Merry*

Tales published in April in cheaply bound edition, and *The American Claimant* published in May, both by Webster & Co.; sales are poor. Many Germans and Americans visit, including Sarah Orne Jewett and Annie Fields. Family moves to Bad Nauheim for the summer. Clemens goes to New York in mid-June to check on publishing business and makes quick trip to Chicago, where factory has been established to manufacture the Paige typesetter. Returns to Europe in mid-July. Works on "Those Extraordinary Twins" and then turns to *Tom Sawyer Abroad* (published serially in *St. Nicholas*, November 1893–January 1894, and as a book by Webster & Co. in 1894). Twichells visit in August, and Clemens and Twichell go to Bad Homburg, where they meet Edward, Prince of Wales. Susan Crane returns to America. In September the family goes to Florence, traveling slowly because of Livy's health and stopping in Frankfurt am Main and Lucerne, Switzerland, on the way. Moves into the Villa Viviani, Settignano, Florence, in late September. Family enjoys living there, and Clemens concentrates on writing. Clara returns to Berlin to study music. Livy's health continues to be poor. Clemens reworks "Those Extraordinary Twins" into *Pudd'nhead Wilson*. Meets William James.

1893   Works on *Personal Recollections of Joan of Arc* and articles for magazines. Sails to New York for business reasons, leaving on *Kaiser Wilhelm II* March 22 and arriving in New York April 3. Sees Howells and Kipling and goes with Hall to Chicago, where he checks progress of Paige machine and attends the World's Columbian Exposition. Financial panic in America makes problems at Webster & Co. more severe. Feeling disheartened, leaves for Europe aboard *Kaiser Wilhelm II* May 13. Tries to find buyer for his interest in Webster & Co., then suggests selling *Library of American Literature* to another publisher. In June family goes to Munich and to spas, where Livy continues to take baths. Clemens resumes work on *Pudd'nhead Wilson*. Feels depressed and distraught about financial circumstances. Borrows money and seeks financial advice from Charles Langdon. Sails with Clara from Bremen on the *Spree* August 29, arriving in New York on September 7. Sells "The Esquimau Maiden's Romance" to *Cosmopolitan* for $800, and *Pudd'nhead Wilson* to *Century* for $6,500 (appears December 1893–June 1894). After Clara leaves to visit family in Elmira, Clemens rooms with friend Dr. Clarence C. Rice, then takes a cheap room in the Players' Club on September 29. Tries to borrow money to meet pressing debts of Webster & Co. from friends in Hartford and Wall Street brokers and bankers, but panic has made money tight. Through Rice, meets Henry Huttleston Rogers, vice-president and director of the Standard Oil Company (had briefly met him two years earlier), who immediately takes care of an $8,000 debt owed by Webster & Co., and begins examining the problems of the Paige typesetter company. Rogers arranges for his son-in-law, William E. Benjamin, to buy the *Library of American Literature* from Webster & Co. for $50,000 in October. Clemens sees old friends, dines out constantly, is often called upon for after-dinner speeches, and is touched by warmth of his reception in New York. Richard Watson Gilder and Howells pay tribute to him at dinner given in his honor by the Lotos Club on November 11. Clara returns to Europe to study music. Clemens travels with Rogers on December 21 to Chicago in private railroad car to inspect Paige machine.

1894 Goes to Boston to participate in "Author's Reading and Music for the Poor," and has dinner with Annie Fields, Sarah Orne Jewett, and Oliver Wendell Holmes (Holmes will die in October). Sees Mary Fairbanks in New York in February. Gives two readings with James Whitcomb Riley. Becomes closer to Rogers and his family, and enjoys watching Rogers conduct business in his office in the Standard Oil building at 26 Broadway. Gives Rogers power of attorney over all his affairs on March 6. Sails March 7 and arrives in Paris, where family is now living, on March 15. Rogers assigns Clemens' property, including his copyrights and share in the Paige machine, to Livy. Clemens sails for New York on April 7 and arrives April 14. On advice from Rogers, declares the failure of Webster & Co. on April 18 and assumes his share of its debts, causing his personal bankruptcy, which is widely and sympathetically reported in newspapers. Returns to Paris in May. Howells spends a week with him in June. For sake of Susy's health, family goes to La Bourboule-les-Bains in central France. Clemens plans to return to America at Rogers' request, but his departure is delayed by rioting caused by the assassination of French President Carnot on

June 24. Arrives in New York in early July and remains until mid-August, then rejoins family at Étretat in Normandy. Spends October with family in Rouen; Susy is still ill, with persistent high fever. *The Tragedy of Pudd'nhead Wilson and the Comedy of Those Extraordinary Twins* published in November as subscription book by the American Publishing Company (publisher includes earlier version of story as a separate work). Family returns to Paris, where Clemens is confined to bed with attack of gout. Devastated by news in December that Paige typesetter has failed a test in the offices of the Chicago *Herald* because of broken type. Resolves to reimburse his friends, actor Henry Irving and writer Bram Stoker (Irving's manager), for their investment in the machine (they are repaid in spring 1895).

1895   Works on several short pieces for journals, and writes *Tom Sawyer, Detective* (published by Harper & Brothers in November 1896). Finishes *Personal Recollections of Joan of Arc* and sails from Southampton on February 23 on the *New York*. Arrives in New York in early March and arranges serial publication of *Personal Recollections of Joan of Arc* in *Harper's Magazine* (begins in April). In hopes of having the work taken more seriously, asks that installments appear anonymously (his authorship soon becomes known, and book edition, published by Harper & Brothers in 1896, is credited to Mark Twain). Moved by visit to family home in Hartford, now leased to friends John and Alice Hooker Day. Arranges with Major Pond for cross-country lecture tour (Pond receives 25 percent of fee for lectures between New York and San Francisco, and 20 percent for lectures in San Francisco). Clemens returns to France in late March; also aboard ship is Andrew Carnegie, an old acquaintance. Brings family to New York on May 18, then goes to Quarry Farm. Agrees to contract, signed on May 23, with Harpers that gives them rights to Mark Twain books published by Webster & Co. (negotiations with the American Publishing Company for similar agreement continue; Clemens hopes that Harpers will bring out a uniform edition of his works). Prepares lectures, suffers painful carbuncle on leg, and is forced to stay in bed for over six weeks, unable to stand or put on clothes. Leaving Susy and Jean to stay with Susan Crane at Quarry Farm, Clemens, Livy, and Clara leave on July 14 for first lecture

in Cleveland. Travels across country, accompanied by
Pond and his wife. Tells reporters in Vancouver that he
intends to eventually repay every creditor in full. Sails for
Australia aboard the *Warrimoo* on August 23 with Livy and
Clara, beginning around-the-world lecture tour arranged
by firm of R. S. Smythe, who had earlier managed a similar tour for Henry Morton Stanley. Hopes to stop in
Honolulu, but is prevented from landing by outbreak of
cholera. Visits Suva in Fiji Islands and arrives in Sydney
on September 16. Met by Carlyle Smythe, who will serve
as their guide on the tour. Continues to suffer from car-
buncles. Appears in Sydney, Melbourne, Adelaide, and
other Australian towns before large, responsive audiences,
reading from his books and telling stories. Visits gold
fields in Victoria. Sails for New Zealand on October 30
and stops in Tasmania before landing at Bluff. Lectures
throughout South and North Islands, visiting Dunedin,
Christchurch, Wellington, Auckland, and other towns.
Leaves Wellington on December 13 and lands in Sydney
December 17.

1896   Sails for India with Livy, Clara, and Carlyle Smythe from
Albany, Western Australia, on January 4. Enjoys emptiness
and calm of Indian Ocean. Stops briefly in Colombo,
Ceylon, and arrives in Bombay on January 18. Suffers
from persistent bronchial cough. Visits Towers of Silence,
where Parsis expose their dead. Lectures in great hall of
palace at Baroda on January 31. Finds India fascinating and
is warmly received by Indian princes and British officials.
Reads reports of Major William Sleeman, the suppressor
of the Thugs in the late 1830s, and accounts of the 1857
Sepoy Mutiny. Takes train from Bombay to Allahabad and
Benares. Lectures to packed audiences in Calcutta, February 10–13, then goes to Darjeeling in the foothills of the
Himalayas. Exhilarated by first stage of descent from Dar-
jeeling, made for 35 miles in open railway handcar. Re-
turns to Calcutta and then visits Lucknow, Kanpur, Agra,
Delhi, Lahore, Rawalpindi, and Jaipur. Sails from Cal-
cutta for South Africa at the end of March. Stops in Ma-
dras and Ceylon, visits Mauritius April 15–28, and lands on
May 6 at Durban in British colony of Natal. Livy and
Clara stay in Durban while Clemens gives readings across
South Africa. Goes to Pietermaritzburg, Natal capital,
Johannesburg, and Pretoria, capital of the Boer Transvaal

republic. Visits John Hayes Hammond and other "Reformers" imprisoned for their alleged complicity in 1895 Jameson Raid, an aborted invasion intended to bring the Transvaal under British rule (Mrs. Hammond is a Missourian whom Clemens had met previously). After leaving prison, Clemens makes humorous remark to reporter that is misinterpreted as implying that prisoners are being treated leniently. When their confinement is made harsher, Clemens goes to see President Kruger on May 26 to explain the joke (prisoners are soon released). Goes to Bloemfontein, capital of Orange Free State, and Queenstown and East London, in the British Cape Colony. Visits Kimberly diamond mine on July 1. Sails for England from Cape Town with Livy and Clara July 15 and arrives in Southampton on July 31. Takes a house in Guildford, Surrey, for a month. Rogers arranges contract with American Publishing Company and Harper & Brothers, allowing American Publishing to issue subscription volumes, as well as a uniform subscription edition of the complete works, while Harpers will sell individual books and a less-inclusive uniform edition to the trade. Learns that Susy is ill. Livy and Clara leave for America August 15, Clemens remains in England. Susy dies on August 18 of spinal meningitis. Clemens learns of her death by telegram. Livy returns to England on September 9 with Clara and Jean, whose health problems have recently been diagnosed as epilepsy. Rents house at 23 Tedworth Square, Chelsea, London, where they seclude themselves (family will not celebrate birthdays, Thanksgiving, Christmas, or other holidays for several years afterward). Begins writing travel book, *Following the Equator*. Clemens learns that Helen Keller (whom he had met with Rogers two years earlier at the home of Clemens' good friend Laurence Hutton) has lost financial support for her education, and asks Rogers to help her attend Radcliffe College (Rogers does so).

1897   Livy is deeply depressed. Clemens works long hours on book. In February writes Howells, who has published review praising the first five volumes in Harpers' "Uniform Edition," that his "words stir the dead heart of me" and that he feels "indifferent to nearly everything but work." Finishes *Following the Equator* in May. Made an honorary life member of the Savage Club (only Henry Morton Stanley, Arctic explorer Fridtjof Nansen, and the Prince of

Wales had been given honor since club's founding in 1857).
In July family goes to the Villa Bühlegg, Weggis, on Lake
Lucerne in Switzerland. Hears the Fisk Jubilee Singers
perform in village in August and entertains them at home
after their concert; deeply moved, writes Twichell that
"their music made all other vocal music cheap." On anniversary of Susy's death, writes poem "In Memoriam,
Olivia Susan Clemens" (published in November *Harper's
Magazine*). Family moves to the Metropole Hotel in Vienna in late September. Clemens suffers from gout. Inter-
viewers from many newspapers come to the hotel.
Fascinated by current political unrest caused by rivalry
among nationalities of the Austro-Hungarian Empire.
Works for many hours a day, but does not intend to publish much of what he writes. Receives $10,000 advance
from Frank Bliss for *Following the Equator*, published in
November. Clemens and Clara go out in society and attend operas. Family receives daily callers from 5:00 P.M.
on. Clara is accepted as student of famed piano teacher
Theodor Leschetizky. Begins work on "The Man That
Corrupted Hadleyburg" (published in *Harper's Magazine*,
December 1899). Orion dies in Keokuk on December 11.

1898   Meets student of Leschetizky's, Ossip Gabrilowitsch, who
comes to dinner. Works for eight or nine hours at a time.
Tries writing for the stage again, and translates German
plays. Continues to follow Dreyfus case in France and admires Zola for his championing of Dreyfus's cause. Credi-
tors are paid in full, and newspapers compare him to Sir
Walter Scott (who had also redeemed himself from bankruptcy). Because of Clara's study of music, meets many
prominent musicians and attends operas and concerts. Becomes interested in new investments, including a textile
design machine that uses a photographic process and a
patent for producing a peat-wool fiber cloth. Rogers' advice dampens his enthusiasm. Sends articles directly to
magazine editors; if they reject them, has Rogers try to
place them with other publications. Commands high
prices for his work. When Spanish-American War begins
in late April, believes that freeing Cuba from Spanish
domination is a worthy cause. Family goes in late May to
Kaltenleutgeben, small hydrotherapy resort outside Vienna. Livy's health does not improve. Writes article about
the assassination on September 10 of Elizabeth, Empress

of Austria, and watches her funeral. Begins work on early version of *The Mysterious Stranger*. Returns to Vienna in mid-October, moving into the new, luxurious Krantz Hotel (hotels are eager to have Clemens in residence and lower their rates for him). Writes autobiographical passages in November and begins considering publishing an autobiography. Feels more relaxed about financial matters, and is delighted with Rogers' investment of his money. Mary Fairbanks dies on December 8.

1899 Takes family to Budapest for a week when he delivers lecture there. Tells Howells in a letter that "it is a luxury! an intellectual drunk" to write material not intended for publication. Goes with family to London in late May, then to Sanna, Sweden, in July, where they are treated at sanitarium run by Henrik Kellgren (Clemens hopes that Kellgren's methods will be especially beneficial to Jean, who has been having frequent seizures). Writes "Christian Science and the Book of Mrs. Eddy," published October in *Cosmopolitan*. Returns to London in October and moves into apartment at 30, Wellington Court, Knightsbridge, near Dr. Kellgren's London institute, where Jean is treated three times a week (therapy seems to be helpful). Blames outbreak of Boer War in October on Cecil Rhodes and British colonial secretary Joseph Chamberlain. Becomes friends with T. Douglas Murray, who asks him to write introduction to *Jeanne d'Arc: Maid of Orleans*, English translation of the official trial records.

1900 Becomes disillusioned with American policy in the Philippines, and writes to Howells about his divided sympathies concerning the Boer War. Dines out frequently at private dinner parties, including ones given by historian W.E.H. Lecky, whom Clemens greatly admires, and Lady Augusta Gregory. Sees much of Stanley and his wife, Dorothy. Has portrait painted by James McNeill Whistler. In March invests $12,500 in Plasmon, food supplement made from milk by-products, and becomes director of English Plasmon syndicate on April 19 (enthusiastically uses product, and will later invest another $12,500 in venture). Spends summer at Dollis Hill House on northwest outskirts of London. Sympathizes with the Chinese in the Boxer Rebellion. Angry with Murray's "school-girl attempts at 'editing,'" withdraws manuscript of introduction to *Jeanne d'Arc* (it appears as article in *Harper's Magazine*, December 1904). Decides to return to America, having learned that osteopathy, now widely practiced in the United States, is very similar to Kellgren's methods. Family sails October 6 on the *Minnehaha* and arrives in New York on October 15. Receives warm welcome from public, press, and friends. Goes to Hartford to attend funeral of old friend Charles Dudley Warner. Rents house at 14 West 10th Street, New York City. Journalists constantly seek interviews and telephone rings incessantly. Rogers negotiates contract in November with Harpers, giving them first serial rights to Clemens' works for a year at rate of 20 cents per word. Introduces Winston S. Churchill to large New York audience on December 12. Writes "To the Person Sitting in Darkness," denunciation of imperialism, and is encouraged to publish it by Livy and Howells (article appears in *North American Review*, February 1901).

1901   Enjoys company of Howells, who now lives in New York and shares his anti-imperialist views. Clemens attacks missionary propaganda in China, and Tammany machine politics. Frequently invited to make speeches, presides over the Lincoln birthday celebration in Carnegie Hall, February 11. Troubled by attacks of gout. Family leaves on June 21 for summer at Ampersand on Lower Saranac Lake, New York, in the Adirondacks. Visited by Howells' son, John, now an architect. Sails for two weeks with Rogers on his yacht, *Kanawha*, to New Brunswick and Nova Scotia; fellow passengers include Clemens' friends Dr. Clarence Rice and Thomas B. Reed, former Speaker of the House of Representatives. Goes to Elmira for a week. Family finds sad memories make it impossible to live in Hartford. Decides to sell the house there and rents the Appleton mansion overlooking the Hudson in Riverdale, New York. Clemens and Howells receive honorary Doctor of Letters degrees from Yale University on October 23. Livy's health deteriorates. Rogers expresses concern in letter to Clemens about fairness of Ida Tarbell's forthcoming investigative series in *McClure's Magazine* on Standard Oil, saying that she has not approached anyone at the company for comment.

1902   Clemens tells friend at *McClure's* that they should have Tarbell speak with Rogers before running articles (when approached, Rogers agrees to interview; Tarbell will describe him as "candid" in her series). Jean has seizures. Clemens goes on yachting excursions with Rogers, taking an extended cruise to Nassau, Cuba, and Florida. Livy buys a house near Tarrytown, New York, for $45,000, hoping to settle family there. Clara leaves for Paris on April 22 to continue her studies. Clemens receives honorary Doctor of Laws from University of Missouri in Columbia on June 4. Visits Hannibal and St. Louis for the last time. Takes trip on Mississippi with pilot Horace Bixby. Family goes to York Harbor, Maine, for the summer. Because of Livy's fragile health, Rogers puts his yacht at their disposal. Clemens is upset as he witnesses more of Jean's epileptic seizures (had previously seen only three of her attacks, though Livy had been present for many more). Howells' family vacations at nearby Kittery Point. Clemens works on "Was It Heaven? Or Hell?" (published in *Harper's Magazine*, December 1902) and "Tom Sawyer's Conspiracy" (never completed). On August 12 Livy is violently ill, can barely breathe, and has severe heart palpitations; family fears she is dying. She is treated by an osteopath, who comes several times a day, and a regular doctor of medicine, who stays nights. Clara comes from Europe and Susan Crane joins them. Jean's health improves. Clemens hires professional nurse for Livy, but she continues to suffer from attacks and on October 16 returns by private invalid train to Riverdale. Clemens is not allowed to go into her room. Attends large dinner in honor of his 67th birthday, given on November 28 by George Harvey of Harper & Brothers at the Metropolitan Club in New York. Visits Elmira. Jean falls ill with pneumonia on December 23. Clara and nurses keep news from Livy, and Clara takes charge of house. Isabel Lyon, hired as Livy's secretary, now acts as Clemens' secretary. On December 30 Clemens is allowed to see Livy for five minutes. Jean improves.

1903   Sees Livy for five minutes on days when she is feeling better. Rarely goes into city. Livy's health improves during the spring months, and he is allowed to see her for twenty minutes twice a day, and to send her two letters each day. Clemens is forced to stay in bed for a month by attacks of bronchitis, gout, and rheumatism. Sells Hartford house and rents the Tarrytown house (sold December

1904). Visits Rogers, who is recovering from appendec-
tomy, at his Fairhaven, Massachusetts, summer home.
Doctors tell Livy she should go to Europe to recover.
Family leaves Riverdale on July 1, going down the Hudson
on Rogers' yacht to Hoboken, where they take train to
Elmira. At Quarry Farm Livy takes rides in carriage, goes
out in wheelchair, sits on porch, and resumes household
responsibilities. Clemens works in octagonal study on the
hill. Goes to New York on October 3 to see publishers.
Harper & Brothers buys out the American Publishing
Company, and on October 22 Clemens signs contract giving Harpers rights to all his books, receiving guaranteed
payments of $25,000 a year for five years, plus royalties
above that amount. Family sails for Italy on October 24
aboard the *Princess Irene*, accompanied by Isabel Lyon,
their servant Kate Leary, who had been with the family
since 1880, and a trained nurse. Goes to Florence, where
Livy has chosen to settle, and rents the Villa di Quarto, a
large house near the city. Trip is tiring for Livy, but she
improves and thinks she no longer needs nurse, who
leaves on December 7.

1904   Livy's condition worsens and she is confined to bed.
Clemens quickly writes several magazine articles, then
turns to autobiography, dictating to Lyon every day.
Learns that sister-in-law Mollie Clemens died in Keokuk
on January 15 (does not tell Livy, and will also keep from
her news of Stanley's death on May 10). Livy has severe
attacks on February 22 and April 9. Family dislikes landlady and searches for another villa (search proves beneficial
to family's spirits because it encourages them to hope that
Livy will live long enough for them to move). Clemens
declines to invest money in American Plasmon syndicate,
but retains confidence in English branch. Clara sings on
concert stage and Clemens is impressed by her profession-
alism. Livy dies on June 5. Clara breaks down. Jean has
first seizure in 13 months, but she soon recovers and plans
family's return to America. Forced to wait for a ship, they
sail June 28 on the *Prince Oscar*. Charles Langdon, his
daughter Julia Langdon Loomis, and her husband meet
them at the pier and accompany them to Elmira in
Loomis's private railway car. Private funeral services are
held in Langdon house, conducted by Twichell. Clemens
takes cottage in July at Richard Watson Gilder's summer

home in the Berkshires near Lee, Massachusetts (daughters are fond of Gilder). Clara, still suffering from shock, enters a rest-cure establishment in New York City. Jean is hit by a trolley on July 30 while horseback riding; horse is killed, and she is knocked unconscious and suffers torn ankle tendon. Clemens goes to New York on August 10, finds Clara still ill, and is not allowed to see her. Searches for house to live in. Signs three-year lease for house at 21 Fifth Avenue. Stays in the Grosvenor Hotel while furnishings for new house are brought from Hartford. Jean remains in the Berkshires with Isabel Lyon. Spends a few days in late August as guest of George Harvey at Deal Beach, New Jersey, where he sees Henry James, who is also visiting Harvey. Sister Pamela dies in Greenwich, Connecticut, on September 1. Visits Elmira with Jean. Moves in December into Fifth Avenue house, where Jean joins him. Seldom goes out, but is visited by Rogers, Andrew Carnegie, and other old friends.

1905   Troubled by chronic bronchitis. Plays cards with Lyon and listens to music on player organ. Goes with Rogers to Fairhaven in May, then takes house for summer in Dublin, New Hampshire, with Jean. Writes "Eve's Diary" (published in *Harper's Magazine* in December), revises "Adam's Diary," and works on other manuscripts, including "3,000 Years Among the Microbes," and a new version of *The Mysterious Stranger*. Clara goes to Norfolk, Connecticut, to continue rest cure. Jean enjoys summer and visits Clara. Clemens is troubled by gout, dyspepsia, bronchitis, and the summer heat. Visits Clara in August (their first meeting in a year) and finds her well. Returns to Dublin and is forced by gout to stay in bed. Goes to New York in November after visit to Boston. Clara comes to live with him. Sees much of Rogers and his extended family. Attends gala 70th birthday party given in his honor by Harvey at Delmonico's on December 5 (172 guests attend). Relies on Lyon to manage household, financial, and literary matters (Lyon refers to him as "the King").

1906   In January Albert Bigelow Paine, 44-year-old midwestern writer and editor, asks permission to write Clemens' biography. Clemens gives Paine a room in his house to work in, and allows him to go through manuscripts and some

994 CHRONOLOGY

letters and to listen as he dictates sections of autobiography to stenographer and typist Josephine Hobby. At request of Booker T. Washington, gives talk at Carnegie Hall on the 25th anniversary of the founding of Tuskegee Institute. Continues to give speeches and readings, but no longer accepts money for them. Encouraged when Howells is "full of praises" after spending an afternoon reading autobiographical writings. Meets H. G. Wells at dinner at Howells' house. Reluctantly withdraws support for Maxim Gorky, who is raising funds for the Russian Social Democratic party, after Gorky is discovered to be traveling with his mistress. Writes essay "William Dean Howells," praising his "perfect English" (appears in July *Harper's Magazine*). Goes to Dublin in May to again spend summer. Continues autobiographical dictations, intending to have some of them published in his lifetime. Returns to New York in late June on publishing business. Spends month in New York and Fairhaven, often sleeping aboard Rogers' yacht. Returns to Dublin in time for Jean's birthday on July 26. Harvey comes to Dublin to edit autobiography for publication (25 installments appear in *North American Review*, September 1906–December 1907). Takes yachting trip in August with Rogers, his son Harry, and Harry's wife, Mary, niece of William E. Benjamin. Commissions John Howells to design and supervise building of house in Redding, Connecticut. *What Is Man?* published anonymously in limited private edition by DeVinne Press in August. Goes yachting again in October, and is charmed by Mary Rogers. Delighted with gift of billiard table from Rogers' wife, Emilie, on October 30. Plays billiards with Paine, Harvey, and Finley Peter Dunne ("Mr. Dooley"), and feels health improves as a result. Jean, who had suffered a number of seizures during the summer, is sent to a sanitarium in Katonah, New York. Clara takes rest cure before beginning concert tour. Clemens goes with Paine to Washington in December to lobby, along with Howells and others, for new copyright bill; wears white suit to Capitol Hill. Speaker Joseph Cannon, an old friend, gives him unusual privilege of his private room to use as office.

1907   Often feels lonely and dislikes Fifth Avenue house. Attends club dinners frequently. Spends week in Bermuda with Twichell. *Christian Science*, critical treatment of Mary

Baker Eddy, published by Harpers in February. Summers in Tuxedo Park, New York, where Harry and Mary Rogers have home. Goes to England to receive honorary Litt.D. from Oxford University. Sails from New York June 8 aboard the *Minneapolis*, accompanied by Ralph W. Ashcroft, former secretary and treasurer of the Plasmon Company of America. At Brown's Hotel in London, makes friends with Frances Nunnally, 16-year-old schoolgirl from Atlanta, taking her with him on social calls. Plunges into social life in London, going to royal garden party at Windsor Castle, Lord Mayor's Banquet, the Savage Club, and a party given in his honor by the proprietors of *Punch*. Lunches with George Bernard Shaw, who has called him the greatest American author and one of the great masters of the English language. Sees old friends, including the Rogers, who are touring Europe. Attends Oxford ceremony on June 26; others honored include Rodin, Saint-Saëns, Kipling, and Prime Minister Henry Campbell-Bannerman. Clemens receives the most attention of those present. While returning to New York on the *Minnetonka*, makes friends with 11-year-old Dorothy Quick (she later visits him in Tuxedo Park). Arrives in New York July 22 and goes to Tuxedo Park. Hires Ashcroft to attend to business affairs. Falls ill with bronchitis. Clara studies music in Boston. Visits Fairhaven (Rogers had suffered a stroke on July 22). Returns to New York in late October. Sees Howells often, attends dinners, but feels lonely. "Extract from Captain Stormfield's Visit to Heaven" appears in *Harper's Magazine* December 1907–January 1908.

1908   Goes to Bermuda with Ashcroft for two weeks, then returns there in late February with Rogers, who is in poor health, and Lyon (Emilie Rogers joins them in mid-March). Clemens makes friends with several schoolgirls, all between 10 and 16 years old and the daughters of friends and acquaintances. Calls them "angelfish," and conceives idea of forming a club called the "Aquarium." Returns to New York on April 11. Has Tiffany & Co. make enamel angelfish, sends each girl one, and keeps up frequent correspondence with them. Clara goes to England in May on concert tour. Rents house for Jean and her two companions in Gloucester, Massachusetts. House at Redding is completed; Clemens sees it for the first time on June 18, is very pleased, and moves in immediately. Names it "Innocence at Home" (at Clara's insistence, changes name to "Stormfield" in October) and calls his billiard room "The Aquarium," decorating it with pictures of his young friends. Praises house as the ideal home in letter to John Howells. Attends the dedication of the Aldrich Memorial at Portsmouth, New Hampshire, with Howells. Enjoys receiving guests, including "angelfish," who stay two to eight days. Establishes free library in Redding, donating books from his collection, and starts fund to construct new library building. Taxes male house guests $1 for the fund. Goes to New York in August to attend funeral of nephew Samuel Moffett, who had drowned, and suffers from heatstroke and fatigue. Clara returns from Europe in September. House is burglarized on September 18. Although thieves are chased and caught after a brief gunfight, household staff quits and new servants must be hired. Installs burglar alarm. Clemens accompanies Jean from Gloucester to New York, where she sails for Europe on September 26 to consult specialist in Berlin. Clara moves to New York, making frequent visits to Redding. Actress Billie Burke visits several times. Forms The Mark Twain Company, corporation designed to keep royalties within the family even after copyrights expire, with himself as president, Ashcroft as secretary and treasurer, and Clara, Jean, and Lyon as directors (later replaces Lyon and Ashcroft with Paine).

1909   Enjoys listening to pianists Ossip Gabrilowitsch and Ethel Newcomb, who visit as Clara's guests. Gratified to learn that Congress has passed new copyright bill, extending holders' ownership for an additional 14 years. Attends celebration in New York of Rogers' 69th birthday (continues to see Rogers in the city, but turns down most invitations to New York events). Still entertains in Redding, but no longer has many visits from "angelfish." Howells visits for the first time in late March. Clara begins to arouse his suspicions that Lyon and Ashcroft, who marry on March 18, are mishandling his business affairs. Attends Clara's vocal recital in Mendelssohn Hall in New York on April 13. Dismisses Lyon and Ashcroft in mid-April and writes lengthy, bitter denunciation of them. Jean comes to live at Stormfield on April 26 and takes over household management, including secretarial duties for Clemens, who is impressed by the quality of her mind. *Is Shakespeare Dead?*, supporting Francis Bacon's authorship of the plays, published by Harpers. Goes to New York on May 19 to visit Rogers, but is met at the train by Clara, who tells him that Rogers has died that day. Attends funeral services on May 20. Travels to Baltimore to give promised talk at graduation from St. Timothy's School of "angelfish" Frances Nunnally. Finds trip tiring and develops symptoms of heart disease, diagnosed as angina pectoris in July. Clara marries Ossip Gabrilowitsch at Stormfield on October 6. Twichell performs ceremony and Clemens wears Oxford gown for the occasion. Troubled by chest pains, goes with Paine to Bermuda in November for several weeks. Clara and Ossip leave for Europe in early December. Writes little for publication, but continues to work on "Letters from the Earth." Writes "The Turning Point of My Life" (published in *Harper's Bazar* February 1910). Returns to Stormfield for the Christmas holidays. Jean dies on the morning of December 24, apparently having suffered heart failure during a seizure in her bathtub. Clemens is too distraught to attend services or to go to Elmira for her burial. Writes "The Death of Jean." Tells Paine: "It is the end of my autobiography. I shall never write any more." Paine and his family move into Stormfield.

1910   Goes to Bermuda on January 5, accompanied by his butler, Claude Benchotte. Stays at Bay House, Hamilton, home of the American vice-consul, William H. Allen, whose daughter Helen is an "angelfish" and who takes dictation for him at times. Plays golf with Woodrow Wilson, then president of Princeton University. Howells' daughter Mildred is also in Bermuda for her health and visits him often. Sees Dorothy Quick. Chest pains grow more frequent and severe. Paine comes to help care for him. Clemens notices that Halley's Comet is again visible in the sky. Leaves Bermuda on April 12 in great pain. Dies at Stormfield at approximately 6:30 P.M. on April 21. Funeral service is held at the Brick Presbyterian Church in New York. Henry Van Dyke gives short sermon and Twichell delivers an emotional prayer. Buried in Elmira, April 24, in family plot with Langdon, Susy, Livy, and Jean.

Note on the Texts

This volume contains 191 tales, sketches, essays, and speeches by Mark Twain written or delivered between 1852 and 1890. The texts of the works presented here are drawn from *The Works of Mark Twain* edition being published by the University of California Press, from *Mark Twain Speaking* (1976), edited by Paul Fatout, and from initial printed appearances.

Many of these works first appeared in newspapers or periodicals, and some of them were subsequently included in collections of stories and sketches published between 1867 and 1906. Mark Twain kept several scrapbooks of clippings, which were sometimes used as the basis for the book collections. He occasionally revised the sketches and stories for these collections long after the pieces had appeared in newspapers or magazines, but some of the authorized collections were prepared with no involvement by Twain other than the selection of the contents. Many of Twain's revisions were intended to soften or eliminate passages that might have been considered coarse, objectionable, or offensive by his later, larger literary audience. In general, the initial periodical printings of Twain's stories and sketches represent the freshest and most biting versions of his works.

The most authoritative texts of Mark Twain's early stories, sketches, and essays are provided by the *Early Tales & Sketches* volumes of *The Works of Mark Twain* edition published by the University of California Press. Volumes published to date are *Early Tales & Sketches: Volume 1 1851–1864* (Berkeley: University of California Press, 1979) and *Early Tales & Sketches: Volume 2 1864–1865* (Berkeley: University of California Press, 1981), both edited by Edgar Marquess Branch and Robert H. Hirst with the assistance of Harriet Elinor Smith. Three further volumes of the *Early Tales & Sketches* are now in preparation and will include works through 1871. The editors of *Early Tales & Sketches* have collated all known printings of each of the works and, in general, have taken their texts from the initial printings or, when those printings are not known to survive, from the earliest reprintings. They have corrected typographical errors, and in some cases they have made emendations on the basis of Twain's markings on the clippings in his scrapbooks or comparison with sources of quotations included in the texts. Whenever possible, the texts in this volume are those published in *Early Tales & Sketches* or those established by its editors for publication in their forthcoming volumes.

For the works other than speeches that were published during Twain's life and are not included in *Early Tales & Sketches*, the texts printed in this volume are those of the initial printed appearances whether they are in newspapers, magazines, or collections by Twain or by others. For the tales, sketches, or essays that were first published after Twain's death and are not included in *Early Tales & Sketches*, the texts are those of the editions published by The Iowa Center for Textual Studies and the University of California Press, specifically *Mark Twain's Satires and Burlesques* (Berkeley: University of California Press, 1967), edited by Franklin R. Rogers; *Mark Twain's Fables of Man* (Berkeley: University of California Press, 1972), edited by John S. Tuckey; and *What Is Man? and Other Philosophical Writings* (Berkeley: University of California Press, 1973), edited by Paul Baender. For items other than speeches not published during Twain's life and not found in any of the above editions, the texts are those found in *What Is Man? and Other Essays* (New York: Harper & Brothers, 1917), edited by Albert Bigelow Paine, or *Letters from the Earth* (New York: Harper & Row, 1962), edited by Bernard DeVoto. The early editors of works first published after Twain's death often made changes to the texts in an attempt to improve or regularize them; texts in this volume are taken from such editions only in cases where no more authoritative versions of those works have yet been published.

Whenever possible, the texts of the speeches are from *Mark Twain Speaking* (Iowa City: University of Iowa Press, 1976), edited by Paul Fatout. Fatout has examined the surviving manuscripts, typescripts, printed newspaper accounts, reports of proceedings, and reprintings in collections by Twain and others, and has prepared composite versions of the speeches that reflect Twain's style and intentions, as well as his departures from prepared material and interplay with the audience. Two of the speeches in this volume are not included in Fatout's collection and so the texts presented here are those of their initial printed appearances: the text of "License of the Press" is from the posthumous collection *Mark Twain's Speeches* (New York: Harper & Brothers, 1923), edited by Albert Bigelow Paine; the text of "The New Dynasty" is from the *New England Quarterly* of 1957 and was edited by Bernard DeVoto.

The following notes provide a brief printing history of each selection in this volume and indicate the source of each text.

"The Dandy Frightening the Squatter" (pp. 1–2 in this volume) appeared in the Boston *Carpet-Bag* for May 1, 1852, over the signature "S.L.C." The evidence in favor of Mark Twain's authorship of the sketch consists of the signature, its style, and Twain's references to the *Carpet-Bag* in other writings from this period. The text in this volume is from *Early Tales & Sketches: Volume 1*, pp. 64–65.

"Historical Exhibition—A No. 1 Ruse" (pp. 3–6) appeared in the Hannibal *Journal* of September 16, 1852, an issue that Mark Twain edited in his brother Orion Clemens' absence. The text in this volume is from *Early Tales & Sketches: Volume 1*, pp. 79–82.

"Editorial Agility" (pp. 7–8) also appeared in the Hannibal *Journal* for September 16, 1852. This item is not included in the *Early Tales & Sketches*, and so the text in this volume is taken from the Hannibal *Journal* of September 16, 1852.

"Blabbing Government Secrets!" (pp. 9–10) also appeared in the same issue of the Hannibal *Journal* of September 16, 1852, and is also not included in the *Early Tales & Sketches*. The text in this volume is that of the Hannibal *Journal* of September 16, 1852.

"River Intelligence" (pp. 11–13) appeared without a title in the New Orleans *Crescent* of May 17, 1859, in a regular column headed "River Intelligence." Twain was at that time serving on the steamer *A. T. Lacey*, which left New Orleans on May 14. The text in this volume is from *Early Tales & Sketches: Volume 1*, pp. 131–33.

"Ghost Life on the Mississippi" (pp. 14–18) was probably written in early 1861, but remained unpublished until 1948. The untitled manuscript survives in the Jean Webster McKinney Family Papers at Vassar College. The title of the piece was supplied by Samuel C. Webster in 1948 for its first publication in the *Pacific Spectator*. The text in this volume is the one printed in *Early Tales & Sketches: Volume 1*, pp. 147–51, which is based on the manuscript.

"Petrified Man" (p. 19) first appeared in the Virginia City *Territorial Enterprise* of October 4, 1862, an issue not known to be extant. The article was reprinted soon after in the Sacramento *Union* of October 9, the Nevada City (California) *Nevada Democrat* of October 11, the San Francisco *Evening Bulletin* of October 15, and the Auburn (California) *Placer Herald* of October 18, all of which appear to be derived independently from the *Territorial Enterprise* article. Eight additional printings of the article have been found that appear to derive from the four reprintings rather than from the original appearance in the *Territorial Enterprise*. The text in this volume is the one printed in *Early Tales & Sketches: Volume 1*, page 159, which is a reconstruction based on the four independently derived texts.

"Letter from Carson City" (pp. 20–24) first appeared in the Virginia City *Territorial Enterprise*, probably on February 3, 1863. No copies of that issue are known to be extant, but a clipping of the article survives in Twain's scrapbook, now in the Mark Twain Papers. The text in this volume is from *Early Tales & Sketches: Volume 1*, pp. 194–98.

"Ye Sentimental Law Student" (pp. 25–27) appeared in the Virginia City *Territorial Enterprise* for February 19, 1863. A single copy of the page containing this article is known to survive, but was not available to the editors of the *Early Tales & Sketches*. The only known reprinting is in *The Wit and Humor of America* (Indianapolis: Bobbs-Merrill Company, 1907), edited by Kate Milnor Rabb, volume 5, pp. 1818–20. The text in this volume is the one printed in *Early Tales & Sketches: Volume 1*, pp. 217–19, which is based on the Rabb reprinting.

"All About the Fashions" (pp. 28–31) first appeared in the Virginia City *Territorial Enterprise*, between June 21 and June 24, 1863. A clipping of this version survives in Twain's scrapbook now in the Mark Twain Papers. The article was reprinted with added prefatory material by Mark Twain in the San Francisco *Golden Era* of September 27, 1863, under the title "Mark Twain—More of Him." The title in this volume is the subtitle that appeared in the *Golden Era*. The text in this volume is the one printed in *Early Tales & Sketches: Volume 1*, pp. 308–12, where it appears under the title "Mark Twain— More of Him."

"Letter from Steamboat Springs" (pp. 32–36) first appeared in the Virginia City *Territorial Enterprise* of August 25, 1863, under the title "Letter from Mark Twain." The text in this volume is the one printed in *Early Tales & Sketches: Volume 1*, pp. 272–76, where it appears under the title "Letter from Mark Twain."

"How to Cure a Cold" (pp. 37–42) first appeared in the San Francisco *Golden Era* of September 20, 1863. It was reprinted several times in revised form in later collections, sometimes under the title "Curing a Cold." The text in this volume is the one printed in *Early Tales & Sketches: Volume 1*, pp. 298–303, which is based on the first printing.

"The Lick House Ball" (pp. 43–48) first appeared in the San Francisco *Golden Era* of September 27, 1863, in the same issue as the reprinting (with added prefatory material) of "All About the Fashions." The text in this volume is from *Early Tales & Sketches: Volume 1*, pp. 314–19.

"The Great Prize Fight" (pp. 49–56) first appeared in the San Francisco *Golden Era* of October 11, 1863, which is the source of the text printed in this volume.

"A Bloody Massacre Near Carson" (pp. 57–58) first appeared in the Virginia City *Territorial Enterprise* for October 28, 1863, which is not known to be extant. Three contemporary reprintings (in the Gold Hill *News* of October 28, the Sacramento *Union* of October 30, and the San Francisco *Evening Bulletin* of October 31) appear to be derived directly from the *Territorial Enterprise*. Three additional printings derive from the Sacramento and San Francisco appearances. The text in this volume is the one printed in *Early Tales & Sketches: Volume 1*, pp. 324–26, which is based on the three independent reprintings.

"'Ingomar' Over the Mountains" (pp. 59–61) first appeared in the San Francisco *Golden Era* of November 29, 1863, which is the source of the text printed in this volume.

"Miss Clapp's School" (pp. 62–66) first appeared as "Letter from Mark Twain" in the Virginia City *Territorial Enterprise* for January 19 or 20, 1864. The only known extant copies are clippings in Twain's scrapbook in the Mark Twain Papers. The title in this volume is the subtitle from the original appearance. The text in this volume is the one printed in *Early Tales & Sketches: Volume 1*, pp. 334–38, where it appears under the title "Letter from Mark Twain."

"Doings in Nevada" (pp. 67–71) first appeared in the New York *Sunday Mercury* of February 7, 1864, which is the source of the text printed in this volume.

"Those Blasted Children" (pp. 72–77) first appeared in the New York *Sunday Mercury* of February 21, 1864. The text in this volume is from *Early Tales & Sketches: Volume 1*, pp. 351–56.

"Washoe.—'Information Wanted'" (pp. 78–82) first appeared in the Virginia City *Territorial Enterprise* between May 1 and May 15, 1864, in an issue that is not known to survive. It was reprinted in the San Francisco *Golden Era* of May 22, 1864. The text in this volume is the one printed in *Early Tales & Sketches: Volume 1*, pp. 367–71, which is based on the *Golden Era* reprinting.

"The Evidence in the Case of Smith vs. Jones" (pp. 83–90) first appeared in the San Francisco *Golden Era* of June 26, 1864. The text in this volume is from *Early Tales & Sketches: Volume 2*, pp. 14–21.

"Whereas" (pp. 91–96) first appeared in the *Californian* of October 22, 1864. The article was reprinted in several later collections under the title "Aurelia's Unfortunate Young Man." The text in this volume is the one printed in *Early Tales & Sketches: Volume 2*, pp. 88–93, which is based on the first printing.

"A Touching Story of George Washington's Boyhood" (pp. 97–101) first appeared in the *Californian* of October 29, 1864, and was reprinted in several collections. The text in this volume is the one printed in *Early Tales & Sketches: Volume 2*, pp. 95–99, which is based on the first printing.

"The Killing of Julius Cæsar 'Localized'" (pp. 102–07) first appeared in the *Californian* for November 12, 1864, and was reprinted in several collections. The text in this volume is the one printed in *Early Tales & Sketches: Volume 2*, pp. 110–15, which is based on the first printing.

"Lucretia Smith's Soldier" (pp. 108–12) first appeared in the *Californian* for December 3, 1864, and was reprinted in several collections. The text in this volume is the one printed in *Early Tales & Sketches: Volume 2*, pp. 128–33, which is based on the first printing.

"Important Correspondence" (pp. 113–20) first appeared in the *Californian* for May 6, 1865. Twain indicated revisions on a clipping in a scrapbook now at Yale University, but the article was not reprinted. The text in this volume is the one printed in *Early Tales & Sketches: Volume 2*, pp. 149–56, which is based on the first printing and incorporates some emendations from the revised clipping.

"Answers to Correspondents" (pp. 121–62) first appeared in the *Californian* for June 3, June 10, June 17, June 24, July 1, and July 8, 1865. Some portions were reprinted in later collections. The text in this volume is the one printed in *Early Tales & Sketches: Volume 2*, pp. 177–232, which is based on the first printings and incorporates some emendations made in clippings in Twain's scrapbook and some corrections based on original versions of items from other newspapers quoted in the text.

"Advice for Good Little Boys" (p. 163) had its first known appearance in the *California Youth's Companion* of June 3, 1865. The article appeared unsigned and was not included in later collections. This version was discovered subsequent to the publication of the *Early Tales & Sketches*, which takes its text from a later version in the Yreka City (California) *Weekly Union*. The text in this volume is from the *California Youth's Companion* of June 3, 1865.

"Advice for Good Little Girls" (pp. 164–65) had its first known appearance in the *California Youth's Companion* of June 24, 1865. This version was discovered subsequent to the publication of the *Early Tales & Sketches*, which takes its text from the version in *The Celebrated Jumping Frog of Calaveras County, And Other Sketches* (New York: C. H. Webb, 1867), the first of several reprintings in collections. The text in this volume is from the *California Youth's Companion* of June 24, 1865.

"Just 'One More Unfortunate'" (pp. 166–67) first appeared in the Virginia City *Territorial Enterprise* between June 27 and June 30, 1865. No issues or clippings of this version are known to be extant. The text in this volume is the one printed in *Early Tales & Sketches: Volume 2*, pp. 238–39, which is based on the only known reprinting of the article in the Downieville (California) *Mountain Messenger* of July 1, 1865.

"Real Estate versus Imaginary Possessions, Poetically Considered" (pp. 168–70) first appeared in the *Californian* for October 28, 1865, which is the source of the text printed in this volume.

"Jim Smiley and His Jumping Frog" (pp. 171–77) first appeared in the New York *Saturday Press* of November 18, 1865. Manuscripts of two earlier versions survive in the Jean Webster McKinney Family Papers at Vassar. The story was later reprinted in many collections. The text in this volume is the one printed in *Early Tales & Sketches: Volume 2*, pp. 282–88, which is based on the first printing.

" 'Mark Twain' on the Launch of the Steamer 'Capital' " (pp. 178–83) first appeared in the *Californian* of November 18, 1865. The sketch was reprinted in several collections, sometimes under the title "The Entertaining History of the Scriptural Panoramist" or "A Travelling Show." The text in this volume is the one printed in *Early Tales & Sketches: Volume 2*, pp. 361–66, which is based on the first printing.

"The Pioneers' Ball" (pp. 184–85) first appeared in the Virginia City *Territorial Enterprise* of November 19 or 21, 1865. No copies of this printing are known to be extant, but the sketch was reprinted in the *Californian* of November 25 and the San Francisco *Golden Era* of November 26, 1865. Versions of the sketch, under the title " 'After' Jenkins," were reprinted in several collections. The text in this volume is the one printed in *Early Tales & Sketches: Volume 2*, pp. 369–70, which is based on the two contemporary reprintings.

"Uncle Lige" (pp. 186–87) first appeared in the Virginia City *Territorial Enterprise* between November 28 and November 30, 1865. No copies of this printing are known to be extant, but the sketch was reprinted in the *Californian* of December 2, 1865. The text in this volume is the one printed in *Early Tales & Sketches: Volume 2*, pp. 378–79, which is based on the *Californian* reprinting.

"A Rich Epigram" (p. 188) first appeared in the Virginia City *Territorial Enterprise* between December 8 and December

10, 1865. No copies of this printing are known to be extant, but the poem was reprinted in the San Francisco *Daily American Flag* for December 20, 1865. The text in this volume is the one printed in *Early Tales & Sketches: Volume 2*, page 387, which is based on the *Daily American Flag* reprinting.

"Macdougall vs. Maguire" (pp. 189–90) first appeared in the Virginia City *Territorial Enterprise* between December 19 and December 21, 1865. The only known copy is a clipping in Twain's scrapbook now at Yale University. The text in this volume is the one printed in *Early Tales & Sketches: Volume 2*, pp. 403–04, which is based on the first printing.

"The Christmas Fireside" (pp. 191–94) first appeared in the *Californian* for December 23, 1865. The sketch was reprinted under the title "The Story of the Bad Little Boy Who Didn't Come to Grief" in several later collections. The text in this volume is the one printed in *Early Tales & Sketches: Volume 2*, pp. 407–10, which is based on the first printing.

"Policemen's Presents" (p. 195) appeared in the San Francisco *Golden Era* for January 7, 1866, which is the source of the text printed in this volume.

"What Have the Police Been Doing?" (pp. 196–98) appeared in the San Francisco *Golden Era* for January 21, 1866, which is the source of the text printed in this volume.

"The Spiritual Séance" (pp. 199–204) first appeared in the Virginia City *Territorial Enterprise* of February 4, 1866, and was later revised by Twain for inclusion in *The Celebrated Jumping Frog of Calaveras County, And Other Sketches* (1867). The text in this volume is that of *Early Tales & Sketches*, volume 3 (forthcoming), item #202, which reflects revisions made by Twain for the book publication.

"A New Biography of Washington" (pp. 205–07) first appeared in the Virginia City *Territorial Enterprise* between February 25 and February 28, 1866. The text in this volume is from *Early Tales & Sketches*, volume 3 (forthcoming), item #183.

"Reflections on the Sabbath" (pp. 208–09) first appeared in the San Francisco *Golden Era* of March 18, 1866, which is the source of the text printed in this volume.

"Barnum's First Speech in Congress" (pp. 210–13) first appeared in the New York *Saturday Evening Express* of March 5, 1867, which is the source of the text printed in this volume.

"Female Suffrage: Views of Mark Twain" (pp. 214–23) first appeared in the St. Louis *Missouri Democrat* of March 12, 13, and 15, 1867, which is the source of the text printed in this volume.

"Female Suffrage" (pp. 224–27) first appeared in the New York *Sunday Mercury* of April 7, 1867, which is the source of the text printed in this volume.

"Official Physic" (pp. 228–30) first appeared in the New York *Sunday Mercury* of April 21, 1867, which is the source of the text printed in this volume.

"A Reminiscence of Artemus Ward" (pp. 231–34) first appeared in the New York *Sunday Mercury* of July 7, 1867. The text in this volume is that of *Early Tales & Sketches*, volume 3 (forthcoming), item #211, which is based on the first printing.

"Jim Wolf and the Tom-Cats" (pp. 235–37) first appeared in the New York *Sunday Mercury* of July 14, 1867. The text in this volume is that of *Early Tales & Sketches*, volume 3 (forthcoming), item #212, which is based on the first printing.

"Information Wanted" (pp. 238–39) first appeared in the New York *Tribune* of December 18, 1867. The text in this volume is that of *Early Tales & Sketches*, volume 3 (forthcoming), item #216, which is based on the first printing.

"The Facts Concerning the Recent Resignation" (pp. 240–46) first appeared in the New York *Tribune* of December 27, 1867. The text in this volume is that of *Early Tales & Sketches*, volume 3 (forthcoming), item #217, which is based on the first printing.

"Woman—an Opinion" (pp. 247–48) was delivered as a speech to the Newspaper Correspondents' Club Banquet in Washington, D.C., on January 11, 1868. The text in this volume is that of *Early Tales & Sketches*, volume 3 (forthcoming), item #218.

"General Washington's Negro Body-Servant" (pp. 249–52) first appeared in the *Galaxy* for February 1868. The text in this volume is that of *Early Tales & Sketches*, volume 3 (forthcoming), item #220, which is based on the first printing.

"Colloquy Between a Slum Child and a Moral Mentor" (pp. 253–56) was written between January and March of 1868, but not published during Twain's life. The text in this volume is the one printed in *Mark Twain's Fables of Man*, edited by

John S. Tuckey, pp. 106–09, which is based on the surviving manuscript.

"My Late Senatorial Secretaryship" (pp. 257–61) first appeared in the *Galaxy* for May 1868. The text in this volume is that of *Early Tales & Sketches*, volume 3 (forthcoming), item #226, which is based on the first printing.

"The Story of Mamie Grant, the Child-Missionary" (pp. 262–68) was written in July 1868, but not published during Twain's life. The text in this volume is the one printed in *Mark Twain's Satires and Burlesques*, edited by Franklin R. Rogers, pp. 33–39, which is based on the surviving manuscript.

"Cannibalism in the Cars" (pp. 269–77) first appeared in *The Broadway* for November 1868, and was reprinted in several later collections. The text in this volume is that of *Early Tales & Sketches*, volume 3 (forthcoming), item #232, which is based on the first printing.

"Private Habits of Horace Greeley" (pp. 278–81) first appeared in the *Spirit of the Times* of November 7, 1868, which is the source of the text printed in this volume.

"Concerning Gen. Grant's Intentions" (pp. 282–84) first appeared in the New York *Tribune* of December 12, 1868, which is the source of the text printed in this volume.

"Open Letter to Com. Vanderbilt" (pp. 285–90) first appeared in *Packard's Monthly* for March 1869, pp. 89–91, which is the source of the text printed in this volume.

"Mr. Beecher and the Clergy" (pp. 291–95) first appeared in the Elmira *Advertiser* of April 10, 1869, which is the source of the text printed in this volume.

"Personal Habits of the Siamese Twins" (pp. 296–99) first appeared in *Packard's Monthly* for August 1869 and was often included in later collections. The text in this volume is that of *Early Tales & Sketches*, volume 3 (forthcoming), item #237, which is based on the first printing.

"A Day at Niagara" (pp. 300–06) first appeared in the Buffalo *Express* of August 21, 1869. The text in this volume is that of *Early Tales & Sketches*, volume 4 (forthcoming), item #241, which is based on the first printing.

"A Fine Old Man" (p. 307) first appeared in the Buffalo *Express* of August 25, 1869. The text in this volume is that of

Early Tales & Sketches, volume 4 (forthcoming), item #245, which is based on the first printing.

"Journalism in Tennessee" (pp. 308–14) first appeared in the Buffalo *Express* of September 4, 1869. The text in this volume is that of *Early Tales & Sketches*, volume 4 (forthcoming), item #252, which is based on the first printing.

"The Last Words of Great Men" (pp. 315–18) first appeared in the Buffalo *Express* of September 11, 1869. The text in this volume is that of *Early Tales & Sketches*, volume 4 (forthcoming), item #257, which is based on the first printing.

"The Legend of the Capitoline Venus" (pp. 319–24) first appeared in the Buffalo *Express* of October 23, 1869. The text in this volume is that of *Early Tales & Sketches*, volume 4 (forthcoming), item #272, which is based on the first printing.

"Getting My Fortune Told" (pp. 325–28) first appeared in the Buffalo *Express* of November 27, 1869, and was included in later collections under the title "Lionizing Murderers." The text in this volume is that of *Early Tales & Sketches*, volume 4 (forthcoming), item #274, which is based on the first printing.

"Back from 'Yurrup'" (pp. 329–31) first appeared in the Buffalo *Express* of December 4, 1869. The text in this volume is that of *Early Tales & Sketches*, volume 4 (forthcoming), item #275, which is based on the first printing.

"An Awful----Terrible Medieval Romance" (pp. 332–39) first appeared in the Buffalo *Express* of January 1, 1870. The text in this volume is that of *Early Tales & Sketches*, volume 4 (forthcoming), item #276, which is based on the first printing.

"A Mysterious Visit" (pp. 340–44) first appeared in the Buffalo *Express* of March 19, 1870. The text in this volume is that of *Early Tales & Sketches*, volume 4 (forthcoming), item #285, which is based on the first printing.

"The Facts in the Great Land-Slide Case" (pp. 345–49) first appeared in the Buffalo *Express* of April 2, 1870. The text in this volume is that of *Early Tales & Sketches*, volume 4 (forthcoming), item #286, which is based on the first printing.

"The New Crime" (pp. 350–55) first appeared in the Buffalo *Express* of April 16, 1870. The text in this volume is that of *Early Tales & Sketches*, volume 4 (forthcoming), item #288, which is based on the first printing.

"Curious Dream" (pp. 356–64) first appeared in the Buffalo *Express* of April 30 and May 7, 1870. The text in this volume is that of *Early Tales & Sketches*, volume 4 (forthcoming), item #289, which is based on the first printing.

"About Smells" (pp. 365–66) first appeared in the *Galaxy* for May 1870, pp. 48–50, which is the source of the text printed in this volume.

"The Facts in the Case of the Great Beef Contract" (pp. 367–73) first appeared in the *Galaxy* for May 1870. The text in this volume is that of *Early Tales & Sketches*, volume 4 (forthcoming), item #291, which is based on the first printing.

"The Story of the Good Little Boy Who Did Not Prosper" (pp. 374–78) first appeared in the *Galaxy* for May 1870. The text in this volume is that of *Early Tales & Sketches*, volume 4 (forthcoming), item #294, which is based on the first printing.

"Disgraceful Persecution of a Boy" (pp. 379–82) first appeared in the *Galaxy* for May 1870. The text in this volume is that of *Early Tales & Sketches*, volume 4 (forthcoming), item #293, which is based on the first printing.

"Misplaced Confidence" (p. 383) first appeared without a title in the *Galaxy* for May 1870. It was reprinted in later collections under the title "City of Hartford." The text in this volume is that of *Early Tales & Sketches*, volume 4 (forthcoming), item #296, which is based on the first printing.

"Our Precious Lunatic" (pp. 384–87) first appeared in the Buffalo *Express* of May 14, 1870, which is the source of the text printed in this volume.

"A Couple of Sad Experiences" (pp. 388–95) first appeared in the *Galaxy* for June 1870. The text in this volume is that of *Early Tales & Sketches*, volume 4 (forthcoming), item #299, which is based on the first printing.

"The Judge's 'Spirited Woman'" (pp. 396–97) first appeared in the *Galaxy* for June 1870. The text in this volume is that of *Early Tales & Sketches*, volume 4 (forthcoming), item #300, which is based on the first printing.

"Breaking It Gently" (p. 398) first appeared without a title in the *Galaxy* for June 1870. The text in this volume is that of

Early Tales & Sketches, volume 4 (forthcoming), item #301, which is based on the first printing.

"Post-Mortem Poetry" (pp. 399–402) first appeared in the *Galaxy* for June 1870, pp. 864–65, which is the source of the text printed in this volume.

"Wit-Inspirations of the 'Two-Year-Olds'" (pp. 403–06) first appeared in the *Galaxy* for June 1870. The text in this volume is that of *Early Tales & Sketches*, volume 4 (forthcoming), item #303, which is based on the first printing.

"The Widow's Protest" (p. 407) first appeared without a title in the *Galaxy* for June 1870. The text in this volume is that of *Early Tales & Sketches*, volume 4 (forthcoming), item #304, which is based on the first printing.

"Report to the Buffalo Female Academy" (pp. 408–11) first appeared as part of a longer article on the commencement exercises in the Buffalo *Express* of June 24, 1870, which is the source of the text printed in this volume.

"How I Edited an Agricultural Paper Once" (pp. 412–17) first appeared in the *Galaxy* for July 1870. The text in this volume is that of *Early Tales & Sketches*, volume 4 (forthcoming), item #308, which is based on the first printing.

"The 'Tournament' in A.D. 1870" (pp. 418–20) first appeared in the *Galaxy* for July 1870, pp. 135–36, which is the source of the text printed in this volume.

"Unburlesquable Things" (pp. 421–24) first appeared in the *Galaxy* for July 1870. The text in this volume is that of *Early Tales & Sketches*, volume 5 (forthcoming), item #310, which is based on the first printing.

"The Late Benjamin Franklin" (pp. 425–27) first appeared in the *Galaxy* for July 1870. The text in this volume is that of *Early Tales & Sketches*, volume 5 (forthcoming), item #311, which is based on the first printing.

"A Memory" (pp. 428–31) first appeared in the *Galaxy* for August 1870. The text in this volume is that of *Early Tales & Sketches*, volume 5 (forthcoming), item #317, which is based on the first printing.

"Domestic Missionaries Wanted" (pp. 432–33) first appeared in the Buffalo *Express* of August 25, 1870, which is the source of the text printed in this volume.

"Political Economy" (pp. 434–39) first appeared in the *Galaxy* for September 1870. The text in this volume is that of *Early Tales & Sketches*, volume 5 (forthcoming), item #318, which is based on the first printing.

"John Chinaman in New York" (pp. 440–41) first appeared in the *Galaxy* for September 1870. The text in this volume is that of *Early Tales & Sketches*, volume 5 (forthcoming), item #319, which is based on the first printing.

"The Noble Red Man" (pp. 442–46) first appeared in the *Galaxy* for September 1870. The text in this volume is that of *Early Tales & Sketches*, volume 5 (forthcoming), item #320, which is based on the first printing.

"The Approaching Epidemic" (pp. 447–48) first appeared in the *Galaxy* for September 1870. The text in this volume is that of *Early Tales & Sketches*, volume 5 (forthcoming), item #321, which is based on the first printing.

"A Royal Compliment" (pp. 449–51) first appeared in the *Galaxy* for September 1870, pp. 429–30, which is the source of the text printed in this volume.

"Science vs. Luck" (pp. 452–54) first appeared in the *Galaxy* for October 1870. The text in this volume is that of *Early Tales & Sketches*, volume 5 (forthcoming), item #328, which is based on the first printing.

"Goldsmith's Friend Abroad Again" (pp. 455–70) first appeared in three installments in the *Galaxy* for October and November 1870 and January 1871. The text in this volume is that of *Early Tales & Sketches*, volume 5 (forthcoming), item #326, which is based on the first printing.

"Map of Paris" (pp. 471–76) initially appeared in the Buffalo *Express* of September 17, 1870. It was reprinted, with additional prefatory material, in the *Galaxy* for November 1870. The text in this volume is from *Early Tales & Sketches*, volume 5 (forthcoming), item #324, where it appears under the title "Mark Twain's Map of Paris."

"Riley—Newspaper Correspondent" (pp. 477–80) first appeared in the *Galaxy* for November 1870. The text in this volume is that of *Early Tales & Sketches*, volume 5 (forthcoming), item #330, which is based on the first printing.

"A Reminiscence of the Back Settlements" (pp. 481–83) first appeared in the *Galaxy* for November 1870, and was reprinted in later collections under the title "The Undertaker's Chat." The text in this volume is that of *Early Tales & Sketches*, volume 5 (forthcoming), item #331, which is based on the first printing.

"A General Reply" (pp. 484–89) first appeared in the *Galaxy* for November 1870. The text in this volume is that of *Early Tales & Sketches*, volume 5 (forthcoming), item #332, which is based on the first printing.

"Running for Governor" (pp. 490–94) first appeared in the *Galaxy* for December 1870. The text in this volume is that of *Early Tales & Sketches*, volume 5 (forthcoming), item #338, which is based on the first printing.

"Dogberry in Washington" (pp. 495–96) first appeared in the *Galaxy* for December 1870, pp. 881–82, which is the source of the text printed in this volume.

"My Watch—An Instructive Little Tale" (pp. 497–99) first appeared in the *Galaxy* for December 1870. The text in this volume is that of *Early Tales & Sketches*, volume 5 (forthcoming), item #340, which is based on the first printing.

"The Facts in the Case of George Fisher, Deceased" (pp. 500–06) first appeared in the *Galaxy* for January 1871. The text in this volume is that of *Early Tales & Sketches*, volume 5 (forthcoming), item #345, which is based on the first printing.

"The Tone-Imparting Committee" (pp. 507–09) first appeared in the *Galaxy* for February 1871. The text in this volume is that of *Early Tales & Sketches*, volume 5 (forthcoming), item #352, which is based on the first printing.

"The Danger of Lying in Bed" (pp. 510–13) first appeared in the *Galaxy* for February 1871. The text in this volume is that of *Early Tales & Sketches*, volume 5 (forthcoming), item #353, which is based on the first printing.

"One of Mankind's Bores" (pp. 514–16) first appeared in the *Galaxy* for February 1871. The text in this volume is that of *Early Tales & Sketches*, volume 5 (forthcoming), item #354, which is based on the first printing.

"The Indignity Put upon the Remains of George Holland by the Rev. Mr. Sabine" (pp. 517–21) first appeared in the *Galaxy* for February 1871, pp. 320–21, which is the source of the text printed in this volume.

"A Substitute for Rulloff" (pp. 522–23) first appeared in the New York *Tribune* of May 3, 1871, which is the source of the text printed in this volume.

"About Barbers" (pp. 524–27) first appeared in the *Galaxy* for August 1871. The text in this volume is that of *Early Tales & Sketches*, volume 5 (forthcoming), item #361, which is based on the first printing.

"A Brace of Brief Lectures on Science" (pp. 528–38) first appeared in two installments in *American Publisher* (edited by Orion Clemens) for September and October of 1871. The text in this volume is that of *Early Tales & Sketches*, volume 5 (forthcoming), item #362, which is based on the first printing.

"The Revised Catechism" (pp. 539–40) first appeared in the New York *Tribune* of September 27, 1871, page 6, which is the source of the text printed in this volume.

"The Secret of Dr. Livingstone's Continued Voluntary Exile" (pp. 541–42) first appeared in the Hartford *Courant* of July 20, 1872, which is the source of the text printed in this volume.

"How I Escaped Being Killed in a Duel" (pp. 543–46) appeared in *Every Saturday* of December 21, 1872, and in *Tom Hood's Comic Annual for 1873*. The text in this volume is from *Every Saturday*.

"Poor Little Stephen Girard" (pp. 547–48) first appeared in the *Alta California* of March 8, 1873, which is the source of the text printed in this volume. This sketch has sometimes been reprinted under the title "Life As I Find It."

"Foster's Case" (pp. 549–50) first appeared in the New York *Tribune* of March 10, 1873, which is the source of the text printed in this volume.

"License of the Press" (pp. 551–55) was delivered as an address to the Hartford Monday Evening Club on March 31, 1873. The text in this volume is the one printed in *Mark Twain's Speeches*, edited by Albert Bigelow Paine (New York: Harper & Brothers, 1923), pp. 46–52, which was based on the surviving manuscript, the first leaf of which is missing.

"Fourth of July Speech in London" (pp. 556–58) was delivered to a meeting of Americans in London on July 4, 1873.

The text in this volume is from *Mark Twain Speaking*, edited by Paul Fatout, pp. 74–76.

"The Ladies" (pp. 559–61) was delivered before a meeting of the Scottish Corporation of London in November 1873. The text in this volume is from *Mark Twain Speaking*, edited by Paul Fatout, pp. 78–80.

"Those Annual Bills" (p. 562) was included in a letter from Mark Twain to James M. Fields, dated January 7, 1874, and was first published in the collection *Mark Twain's Sketches, New and Old* (Hartford: The American Publishing Company, 1875). The text in this volume is from *Mark Twain's Sketches, New and Old*, page 62, where it appears under the title "Two Poems by Moore and Twain."

"The Temperance Insurrection" (pp. 563–67) first appeared in the London *Standard* of March 26, 1874, which is the source of the text printed in this volume. This article was included in *Europe and Elsewhere* (1923) under the title "The Temperance Crusade and Women's Rights."

"Rogers" (pp. 568–72) first appeared in the collection *Number One. Mark Twain's Sketches* (New York: American News Company, 1874), pp. 13–16, which is the source of the text printed in this volume.

"A Curious Pleasure Excursion" (pp. 573–77) first appeared in the New York *Herald* of July 6, 1874, which is the source of the text printed in this volume.

"A True Story, Repeated Word for Word as I Heard It" (pp. 578–82) first appeared in *Atlantic Monthly* for November 1874, pp. 591–94, which is the source of the text printed in this volume.

"An Encounter with an Interviewer" (pp. 583–87) first appeared in the volume *Lotos Leaves*, edited by John Brougham and John Elderkin (Boston: William F. Gill and Company, 1875), issued in November 1874, pp. 27–32, which is the source of the text printed in this volume.

"The 'Jumping Frog.' In English. Then in French. Then clawed back into a civilized language once more, by patient, unremunerated toil" (pp. 588–603) first appeared in *Mark Twain's Sketches, New and Old* (Hartford: The American Publishing Company, 1875), pp. 28–43. The text in this volume is that of *Early Tales & Sketches*, volume 5 (forthcoming), item #364, which is based on Twain's manuscript, the first printing, and the French-language portions printed in the *Revue des Deux Mondes* of July 15, 1872.

"Experience of the McWilliamses with Membranous Croup" (pp. 604–10) first appeared in *Mark Twain's Sketches, New and Old* (Hartford, 1875), pp. 85–92, which is the source of the text printed in this volume.

"Some Learned Fables for Good Old Boys and Girls" (pp. 611–31) first appeared in *Mark Twain's Sketches, New and Old* (Hartford, 1875), pp. 126–48, which is the source of the text printed in this volume.

"Petition Concerning Copyright" (p. 632) first appeared in *Mark Twain's Sketches, New and Old* (Hartford, 1875), page 175, which is the source of the text printed in this volume.

"'Party Cries' in Ireland" (p. 633) first appeared in *Mark Twain's Sketches, New and Old* (Hartford, 1875), pp. 262–63, which is the source of the text printed in this volume.

"The Curious Republic of Gondour" (pp. 634–38) first appeared anonymously in *Atlantic Monthly* for October 1875, pp. 461–63, which is the source of the text printed in this volume.

"A Literary Nightmare" (pp. 639–43) first appeared in *Atlantic Monthly* for February 1876, pp. 167–69, which is the source of the text printed in this volume. This sketch was often reprinted in later collections under the title "Punch, Brothers, Punch."

"The Facts Concerning the Recent Carnival of Crime in Connecticut" (pp. 644–60) was read before the Hartford Monday Evening Club on January 24, 1876. It first appeared in print in *Atlantic Monthly* for June 1876, pp. 641–50, which is the source of the text printed in this volume.

"[Date, 1601.] Conversation, as it Was by the Social Fireside, in the Time of the Tudors" (pp. 661–66) was written by the summer of 1876, when Twain first showed it to his friend the Rev. Joseph Twichell. The manuscript circulated among various individuals, including William Dean Howells and John Hay, and an unauthorized edition of six copies (according to Hay, who instigated the production) was set from the manuscript and printed in Cleveland, Ohio, around July of

1880. Mark Twain later helped revise and prepare a private edition printed at West Point in 1882. The manuscript is not known to survive. The text in this volume is from the first edition, printed in Cleveland in 1880.

"The Canvasser's Tale" (pp. 667–72) first appeared in *Atlantic Monthly* for December 1876, pp. 673–76, which is the source of the text printed in this volume.

"The Oldest Inhabitant—The Weather of New England" (pp. 673–76) was delivered at the annual dinner of the New England Society of New York at Delmonico's on Forefathers Day, December 22, 1876. The text in this volume is from *Mark Twain Speaking*, edited by Paul Fatout, pp. 100–03.

"Francis Lightfoot Lee" (pp. 677–78) was prepared for the Congress of Authors held July 1, 1876, in connection with the Philadelphia Centennial. It first appeared in print in the *Pennsylvania Magazine*, I (1877), no. 3, pp. 343–47, which is the source of the text printed in this volume.

"My Military History" (pp. 679–82) was delivered at the Putnam Phalanx Dinner for the Ancient and Honorable Artillery Company of Massachusetts at Allyn House in Hartford, Connecticut, on October 2, 1877. The text in this volume is the one printed in *Mark Twain Speaking*, edited by Paul Fatout, pp. 106–09, where it appears under the title "Dinner Speech."

"The Captain's Story" (pp. 683–87) first appeared in *Atlantic Monthly* for November 1877, pp. 589–91, as part of "Some Rambling Notes of an Idle Excursion." The story was later printed separately in several collections. The text in this volume is from *Atlantic Monthly* for November 1877.

"The Invalid's Story" (pp. 688–94) was originally intended as part of the series "Some Rambling Notes of an Idle Excursion" that appeared in *Atlantic Monthly* in 1877, but editor William Dean Howells thought the story too offensive to publish in the magazine. The story first appeared in the collection *The Stolen White Elephant* (1882), pp. 94–104, which is the source of the text printed in this volume.

"Whittier Birthday Speech" (pp. 695–99) was delivered at the *Atlantic Monthly* dinner in honor of the seventieth birthday of John Greenleaf Whittier at the Hotel Brunswick in Boston on December 17, 1877. The text in this volume is the one printed in *Mark Twain Speaking*, edited by Paul Fatout, pp. 110–14, where it appears under the title "Dinner Speech."

"Farewell Banquet for Bayard Taylor" (pp. 700–02) was delivered at a dinner at Delmonico's in New York on April 4, 1878. The text in this volume is the one printed in *Mark Twain Speaking*, edited by Paul Fatout, pp. 116–18, where it appears under the title "Dinner Speech."

"About Magnanimous-Incident Literature" (pp. 703–09) first appeared in *Atlantic Monthly* for May 1878, pp. 615–19, which is the source of the text printed in this volume.

"The Great Revolution in Pitcairn" (pp. 710–21) first appeared in *Atlantic Monthly* for March 1879, pp. 295–302, which is the source of the text printed in this volume.

"Some Thoughts on the Science of Onanism" (pp. 722–24) was delivered at a Stomach Club dinner in Paris in the spring of 1879. The text in this volume is from *Mark Twain Speaking*, edited by Paul Fatout, pp. 125–27.

"A Presidential Candidate" (pp. 725–26) appeared under the title "Mark Twain as a Presidential Candidate" in the New York *Evening Post* of June 9, 1879, which is the source of the text printed in this volume.

"The Babies. As They Comfort Us in Our Sorrows, Let Us Not Forget Them in Our Festivities" (pp. 727–29) was delivered at the Thirteenth Reunion Banquet of the Army of the Tennessee at the Palmer House in Chicago on November 13, 1879. The text in this volume is from *Mark Twain Speaking*, edited by Paul Fatout, pp. 131–33.

"The New Postal Barbarism" (pp. 730–32) first appeared under the headline "Mark Twain on the New Postal Barbarism" in the Hartford *Courant* of November 25, 1879, which is the source of the text printed in this volume.

"Postal Matters" (pp. 733–37) first appeared under the headline "Mark Twain and Postal Matters" in the Hartford *Courant* of December 9, 1879, which is the source of the text printed in this volume.

"A Telephonic Conversation" (pp. 738–41) first appeared in *Atlantic Monthly* for June 1880, pp. 841–43, which is the source of the text printed in this volume.

"Reply to a Boston Girl" (pp. 742–46) first appeared without a title in "The Contributors' Club" section of *Atlantic Monthly* for June 1880, pp. 849–60, which is the source of the text printed in this volume.

"Edward Mills and George Benton: A Tale" (pp. 747–52) first appeared in *Atlantic Monthly* for August 1880, pp. 226–29, which is the source of the text printed in this volume.

"Mrs. McWilliams and the Lightning" (pp. 753–60) first appeared in *Atlantic Monthly* for September 1880, pp. 380–84, which is the source of the text printed in this volume.

"'Millions In It'" (pp. 761–62) first appeared in the New York *Evening Post* of September 16, 1880, which is the source of the text printed in this volume.

"A Cat Tale" (pp. 763–72) was written around 1880, and not published during Twain's life. It first appeared in *Concerning Cats: Two Tales by Mark Twain* (San Francisco: The Book Club of California, 1959), edited by Frederick Anderson, pp. 1–19, which is the source of the text printed in this volume. Anderson's edition is based on the manuscript in the Mark Twain Papers. Twain's characteristic ampersand is rendered as "and"; the early spelling of "Susy" as "Susie" has been preserved. A version of the story was published in 1962 in *Letters from the Earth*, edited by Bernard DeVoto.

"The Benefit of Judicious Training" (pp. 773–75) was delivered at the Twelfth Annual Reunion Banquet of the Army of the Potomac at Allyn House in Hartford on June 8, 1881. The text in this volume is from *Mark Twain Speaking*, edited by Paul Fatout, pp. 151–54.

"Dinner Speech in Montreal" (pp. 776–80) was delivered at a dinner honoring Mark Twain at the Windsor Hotel in Montreal on December 8, 1881. The text in this volume is the one printed in *Mark Twain Speaking*, edited by Paul Fatout, pp. 157–60, where it appears under the title "Dinner Speech."

"Plymouth Rock and the Pilgrims" (pp. 781–85) was delivered at the first annual dinner of the New England Society of Philadelphia on December 22, 1881. The text in this volume is from *Mark Twain Speaking*, edited by Paul Fatout, pp. 162–65.

"Etiquette" (pp. 786–800) was written sometime around 1881, but was not published during Twain's life. It first appeared in 1962, under the title "From an Unfinished Burlesque

of Books on Etiquette," in *Letters from the Earth*, edited by
Bernard DeVoto, pp. 191–208, which is the source of the text
printed in this volume.

"Advice to Youth" (pp. 801–03) was delivered at the Saturday Morning Club in Boston on April 15, 1882. The text in this
volume is from *Mark Twain Speaking*, edited by Paul Fatout,
pp. 169–71.

"The Stolen White Elephant" (pp. 804–23) first appeared
in the collection *The Stolen White Elephant Etc.* (Boston:
James R. Osgood and Company, 1882), pp. 1–35, which is the
source of the text printed in this volume.

"On the Decay of the Art of Lying" (pp. 824–29) was delivered at the Hartford Monday Evening Club on April 5,
1880. It was first published in *The Stolen White Elephant Etc.*
(1882), pp. 217–25, which is the source of the text printed in
this volume.

"Concerning the American Language" (pp. 830–33) first appeared in *The Stolen White Elephant Etc.* (1882), pp. 265–69,
which is the source of the text printed in this volume.

"Woman—God Bless Her" (pp. 834–36) was delivered at
the annual dinner of the New England Society of New York
at Delmonico's on December 22, 1882. The text in this volume is from *Mark Twain Speaking*, edited by Paul Fatout, pp.
173–75.

"The McWilliamses and the Burglar Alarm" (pp. 837–43)
first appeared in *Harper's Christmas* (1882), a special illustrated
32-page large-folio supplement to *Harper's Monthly Magazine*
edited by members of the Tile Club, pp. 28–29, which is the
source of the text printed in this volume.

"On Adam" (pp. 844–46) was delivered at the Royal
Literary and Scientific Society Dinner in Ottawa, Ontario, on
May 23, 1883. The text in this volume is from *Mark Twain
Speaking*, edited by Paul Fatout, pp. 178–80.

"Why a Statue of Liberty When We Have Adam!" (pp.
847–48) first appeared under the headline "Mark Twain
Aggrieved" in *The New York Times* of December 4, 1883, page
2, which is the source of the text printed in this volume.
The title in this volume is the subtitle from the original
appearance.

"Turncoats" (pp. 849–51) was delivered at a political meeting in Hartford in late October 1884. The text in this volume is from *Mark Twain Speaking*, edited by Paul Fatout, pp. 182–84.

"Mock Oration on the Dead Partisan" (pp. 852–53) was written after the election of Grover Cleveland in early November 1884, but may never have been delivered. The text in this volume is from *Mark Twain Speaking*, edited by Paul Fatout, pp. 188–89.

"The Character of Man" (pp. 854–58) was composed early in 1885, but was not published during Twain's life. The text in this volume is the one printed in *What Is Man? and Other Philosophical Writings*, edited by Paul Baender, pp. 60–64, which is based on the revised manuscript.

"On Speech-Making Reform" (pp. 859–62) was probably delivered at the Tile Club dinner for Laurence Hutton in New York on March 31, 1885. The text in this volume is from *Mark Twain Speaking*, edited by Paul Fatout, pp. 190–93.

"The Private History of a Campaign that Failed" (pp. 863–82) first appeared in *Century Magazine* for December 1885, pp. 193–204, which is the source of the text printed in this volume.

"The New Dynasty" (pp. 883–90) was delivered at the Monday Evening Club in Hartford on March 22, 1886. It was not published during Twain's life and was not included in any of the posthumous collections of speeches. It was first published, edited by Bernard DeVoto, in *New England Quarterly*, XXX (1957), pp. 383–88, which is the source of the text printed in this volume.

"Our Children" (p. 891) was delivered at the Authors Club Dinner at Gilsey House in New York on April 22, 1886. The text in this volume is from *Mark Twain Speaking*, edited by Paul Fatout, pp. 210–11.

"Taming the Bicycle" (pp. 892–99) was written around 1886 and was not published during Twain's life. It first appeared in 1917 in *What Is Man? and Other Essays*, edited by Albert Bigelow Paine, pp. 285–96, which is the source of the text printed in this volume.

"Letter from the Recording Angel" (pp. 900–05) was written before September 1887, probably in January 1887, and was not published during Twain's life. It first appeared in

1962, under the title "Letter to the Earth," in *Letters from the Earth*, edited by Bernard DeVoto. The text in this volume is from *What Is Man? and Other Philosophical Writings*, edited by Paul Baender, pp. 65–70.

"Dinner Speech: General Grant's Grammar" (pp. 906–08) was delivered at the annual reunion banquet of the Army and Navy Club of Connecticut at Central Hall in Hartford on April 27, 1887. The text in this volume is from *Mark Twain Speaking*, edited by Paul Fatout, pp. 225–27.

"Consistency" (pp. 909–16) was delivered at the Monday Evening Club in Hartford on December 2, 1887. The text in this volume is from its first printed appearance in *Mark Twain's Speeches* (New York: Harper & Brothers, 1923), edited by Albert Bigelow Paine, pp. 120–30. Italics in the text generally indicate words that Twain had underscored in the manuscript for emphasis.

"Post-Prandial Oratory" (pp. 917–21) was delivered at the Forefathers Day Dinner of the Congregational Club at the Music Hall in Boston on December 20, 1887. The text in this volume is from *Mark Twain Speaking*, edited by Paul Fatout, pp. 230–34.

"A Petition to the Queen of England" (pp. 922–26) first appeared in *Harper's Monthly Magazine* for December 1887, pp. 157–58, which is the source of the text printed in this volume.

"American Authors and British Pirates" (pp. 927–35) first appeared in *The New Princeton Review* for January 1888, pp. 47–54, which is the source of the text printed in this volume.

"Yale College Speech" (pp. 936–37) was delivered at the Yale Alumni Association Banquet at Foot Guard Hall in Hartford, Connecticut, on February 6, 1889. The text in this volume is from *Mark Twain Speaking*, edited by Paul Fatout, pp. 235–37.

"The Christening Yarn" (pp. 938–39) was delivered at the Saturday Morning Club in Hartford, Connecticut, on May 11, 1889, and was also used on other occasions. The text in this volume is from *Mark Twain Speaking*, edited by Paul Fatout, pp. 254–55.

"To Walt Whitman" (pp. 940–41) first appeared in *Camden's Compliment to Walt Whitman* (Philadelphia: David Mc-

Kay, 1889), edited by Horace Traubel, pp. 64–65, which is the source of the text printed in this volume.

"On Foreign Critics" (pp. 942–44) was delivered at a dinner for Max O'Rell at Everett House in Boston on April 27, 1890. The text in this volume is from *Mark Twain Speaking*, edited by Paul Fatout, pp. 257–60.

"Reply to the Editor of 'The Art of Authorship'" (pp. 945–46) first appeared in the collection published in June of 1890 titled *The Art of Authorship* (New York: D. Appleton, 1890), edited by George Bainton, pp. 85–88, which is the source of the text printed in this volume. A brief introductory sentence by the editor has been omitted.

"An Appeal Against Injudicious Swearing" (pp. 947–48) appeared in the New York *Sun* of November 9, 1890, which is the source of the text printed in this volume.

The running heads of left-hand pages are intended to reflect the place of residence of Mark Twain or the Clemens family at the time the selection was published (or for an unpublished item, at the time it was written). A date of publication, of course, does not necessarily represent the date of composition.

This volume presents the texts of the printings chosen for inclusion here, but it does not attempt to reproduce features of their typographic design, such as the display capitalization of chapter openings. New titles have been supplied for a few pieces in cases where the title from the original printing was not composed by Mark Twain and would not serve to distinguish the item from other selections included here; all such instances are noted in the printing history for each item. Otherwise, the texts are reproduced without change, except for the correction of typographical errors. Spelling, punctuation, and capitalization often are expressive features, and they are not altered, even when inconsistent or irregular. The following is a list of typographical errors corrected, cited by page and line number: 7.3, Beaton; 53.3, adversary s; 53.35, opponents; 59.16, accomplished; 60.8, *Scene* 4; 67.30–31, Willing; 70.9, a l; 70.27, CONSTITTTION; 196.12, out out; 197.4, mighn't; 208.32, Arevet; 210.22, hsy; 211.15, uation; 211.38, Libeerty; 215.36, "Yes?."; 228.32, though; 386.1, Galeu; 409.19, possessef; 432.28, villiany; 433.12, missionaris; 522.1, *Substitue*; 523.18, Ruloff; 609.5, "As; 609.25, the the; 610.2, do?; 622.37, in-inscriptions; 626.14, "no; 626.15, anyway."; 626.35, To; 630.2, *Twins*"; 642.13, bluff; 662.9, further."; 666.2, it; 675.25, of; 698.33, "Hold; 698.34, *them?*"; 711.17, flannnel; 732.11, pro-gres?; 735.9, a a member; 738.23, me?"; 774.35, the the wreck; 791.25, henchmen; 832.13, nice!"; 875.13, lighted-hearted; 912.13, freedon. Corrections in second printing: 492.24, physcian; 665.13, Sr W.

Notes

In the notes that follow, the reference numbers denote page and line of this volume (the line count includes chapter headings). No note is made for material included in standard desk-reference books, such as *Webster's Ninth New Collegiate Dictionary* or *Webster's Biographical Dictionary*. Footnotes within the text are Mark Twain's own. Quotations from Shakespeare are keyed to *The Riverside Shakespeare*, edited by G. Blakemore Evans (Boston: Houghton Mifflin, 1974). Quotations from the Bible are keyed to the King James Version. For more detailed notes and references to other studies, see the explanatory notes in the two volumes of *Early Tales & Sketches* (Berkeley: University of California Press, 1979 & 1981), edited by Edgar Marquess Branch and Robert H. Hirst, *What Is Man? and Other Philosophical Essays* (Berkeley: University of California Press, 1973), edited by Paul Baender, and *Mark Twain Speaking* (Iowa City: University of Iowa Press, 1976), edited by Paul Fatout.

For further biographical background, see *Mark Twain's Autobiography*, 2 volumes (New York: Harper & Brothers, 1924), edited by Albert Bigelow Paine; *Mark Twain in Eruption* (New York: Harper & Brothers, 1940), edited by Bernard DeVoto; *The Autobiography of Mark Twain* (New York: Harper & Row, 1959), edited by Charles Neider; *Mark Twain's Own Autobiography* (Madison: University of Wisconsin Press, 1990), edited by Michael J. Kiskis; *Mark Twain's Letters*, 2 volumes (New York: Harper & Brothers, 1917), edited by Albert Bigelow Paine; *The Love Letters of Mark Twain* (New York: Harper & Brothers, 1949), edited by Dixon Wecter; *Mark Twain to Mrs. Fairbanks* (San Marino: Huntington Library, 1949), edited by Dixon Wecter; *Mark Twain–Howells Letters*, 2 volumes (Cambridge: Harvard University Press, 1960), edited by Henry Nash Smith and William M. Gibson; *Mark Twain's Letters to His Publishers 1867–1894* (Berkeley: University of California Press, 1967), edited by Hamlin Hill; *Mark Twain's Correspondence with Henry Huttleston Rogers 1893–1909* (Berkeley: University of California Press, 1969), edited by Lewis Leary; *Mark Twain's Letters: Volume 1 1853–1866* (Berkeley: University of California Press, 1988), edited by Edgar Marquess Branch, Michael B. Frank, and Kenneth M. Sanderson; *Mark Twain's Letters: Volume 2 1867–1868* (Berkeley: University of California Press, 1990), edited by Harriet Elinor Smith and Richard Bucci; *Mark Twain's Letters: Volume 3 1869* (Berkeley: University of California Press, 1991), edited by Victor Fischer, Michael B. Frank, and Dahlia Armon; *Mark Twain's Notebook* (New York: Harper & Brothers, 1935), edited by Albert Bigelow Paine; *Mark Twain's Notebooks & Journals: Volume I (1855–1873)* (Berkeley: University of California Press, 1975), edited by Frederick Anderson, Michael B. Frank, and Kenneth M. Sanderson; *Mark Twain's Notebooks & Journals: Volume II (1877–1883)* (Berkeley: University of California Press, 1975), edited by Frederick Anderson, Lin Salamo, and Bernard L. Stein; *Mark Twain's Notebooks & Journals: Volume III (1883–1891)* (Berkeley: University of California Press, 1979), edited by Robert Pack Browning, Michael B. Frank, and Lin Salamo; *Mark Twain: A Biography* (New York: Harper & Brothers, 1912), by Albert Bigelow Paine; *My Father Mark Twain* (New York: Harper & Brothers, 1931), by Clara Clemens; *Mark Twain, Business Man* (Boston: Little, Brown and Company, 1946), edited by Samuel Charles Webster; *The Literary Apprenticeship of Mark Twain* (Urbana: University of Illinois Press, 1950), by Edgar Marquess Branch; *Sam Clemens of Hannibal* (Boston: Houghton Mifflin Company, 1952), by Dixon Wecter; *Mark Twain's Hannibal, Huck, & Tom* (Berkeley: University of California Press, 1969), edited by Walter Blair; *Clemens of the "Call": Mark Twain in San Francisco* (Berkeley: University of California Press, 1969), edited by Edgar M. Branch; and *Huck Finn and Tom Sawyer among the Indians, and Other Unfinished Stories* (Berkeley: University of California Press, 1989), edited by Dahlia Armon, Walter Blair, Paul Baender, William M. Gibson, and Franklin R. Rogers.

1.3–4   "wood-yard"] A place where cut wood for steamboat fuel was sold.

1.21   guards] The part of the main deck of a steamboat that extends beyond the line of the hull and curves out over the paddle wheels to protect against collisions.

3.7–8   Curts & Lockwood] A dry goods and grocery store in Hannibal, Missouri.

3.14   "saw the elephant,"] "To see the elephant" meant to gain worldly experience usually at some personal cost or pain.

5.35   "seeker . . . difficulties."] Cf. chapter 33 of Charles Dickens' *Posthumous Papers of the Pickwick Club* for "pursuit of knowledge under difficulties." *The Pursuit of Knowledge under Difficulties* (1830) was a book by George Lillie Craik (1798–1866).

7.8   editor of the ——] Joseph P. Ament was editor of the *Missouri Courier*, where Mark Twain had been apprenticed before going to work for his brother Orion Clemens' Hannibal *Journal* in January 1851.

7.10   Pierce and King] In the campaign of 1852, Ament's *Courier* supported the Democratic presidential candidate, Franklin Pierce, and vice-presidential candidate, William King, while Orion Clemens' *Journal* supported Winfield Scott and William Graham, the Whig party nominees. On September 9, 1852, the date in question, an animated meeting about railroad matters was held in Benton Hall, although there is no record of a fire having occurred.

9.8–9   my surname] The previous week's Hannibal *Journal* (September 9, 1852) contained an article ("Family Muss") by Mark Twain signed "W. Epaminondas Adrastus Perkins."

9.13   Gov. King] Austin A. King (1802–70), a Democrat, was governor of Missouri from 1848 to 1853.

9.26   Lord Derby] Prime minister of Great Britain in 1852.

10.15–16   Ensign Jehiel Stebbings] A satirical "war hero" and candidate for president in 1852, created by the *Carpet-Bag*, a humorous literary journal published weekly in Boston from 1851 to 1853.

11.2   Sergeant Fathom] Based on Isaiah Sellers, famous pilot and captain on the Mississippi River from 1825 to 1864, who often contributed "river intelligence" to the newspapers. Twain later recalled the circumstances of this episode in *Life on the Mississippi*, chapter 50.

11.11   'close,'] Skillful in navigating without allowing over-large distances for safety.

11.19   bank full] When the water was at the top of the riverbank, there would be more than enough draft for steamboats in all normal channels, and landmarks along the river would not be hidden underwater, as in a flood.

11.24   "Old Hen,"] To go up to the right of Old Hen Island in the lower Mississippi was to follow the safe channel.

14.23   "Texas,"] A structure that provided cabins for the captain and some of the passengers of a steamboat.

15.15   Egyptian darkness] Cf. Exodus 10:21–22.

19.1   ***Petrified Man***] See also pages 389–92 in this volume.

19.16   Justice Sewell or Sowell] G. T. Sewall had been judge of Humboldt County in the Territory of Nevada since December 1861. He had been a partner in the Silver City *Washoe Times* and had quarreled with Orion Clemens in November 1861 over their contract to print the journals and laws of the first territorial legislature.

20.10   Joseph T. Goodman] Goodman (1838–1917) had been owner and editor of the Virginia City *Territorial Enterprise* since March 1861.

20.33–34   Governor . . . Johnson's] John Neely Johnson (1825–72) was fourth governor of California from 1856 to 1858. He had moved to Nevada in

1860, practiced law in Carson City, and later served on the Nevada supreme court from 1867 to 1871.

21.8   Horace Smith]   Former mayor of Sacramento, California, Smith was a successful lawyer in Carson City. He died in December 1863 of gunshot wounds received in a quarrel over payment for the sale of shares in the Yellow Jacket mine.

21.17   the Unreliable]   Clement T. Rice, reporter for the Virginia City *Union*, with whom Twain carried on a mock-feud in his columns.

21.22   Col. Musser]   John J. Musser had settled in Carson City in 1858, and took part in early efforts to organize the Nevada Territory.

21.27   repeater]   Watch that strikes the hours or briefer intervals.

21.40   "half-a-man-left,"]   That is, "allemande left," a step in the quadrille or square dance in which the man turns his partner on the left.

22.30–31   five thousand . . . Scriptural]   Cf. Matthew 14:15–21.

22.39–40   "I'm sitting . . . Mary,"]   First line of "Irish Emigrant's Lament," music by William R. Dempster and words by Helen S. Sheridan (Helen Selina Sheridan Blackwood, 4th baroness of Duffrin and Ava, 1807–67); this is also the first line of a humorous song titled "Yankee Sarah-nade" by "Samuel Slocum of Goslin Run" that is pasted in one of Twain's scrapbooks.

23.2   "From . . . Mountains"]   Missionary hymn, with music by Lowell Mason (1792–1872) and words by Reginald Heber (1783–1826).

23.5   "Meet . . . alone"]   Song (1826) by Joseph Augustine Wade.

23.5   Judge Dixson]   E. C. Dixson was at various times justice of the peace and probate judge in Carson City, commissioner of Ormsby County, and a representative in the territorial legislature.

23.7   Joe . . . Clayton]   Joseph Winters had migrated from Illinois to California in 1848 and made a fortune in mining and freight. P. H. Clayton was an early settler in Carson City who became prosecuting attorney there in 1860 and helped organize the Democratic party in Nevada.

23.7   the Marseilles Hymn]   The French national anthem, composed in 1792 by Captain Claude Joseph Rouget de Lisle.

23.8   Mr. Wasson]   Warren H. Wasson had settled in Nevada in 1857 and was a rancher, miner, organizer of the provisional territorial government,

United States marshal, Indian agent, and delegate to the Nevada constitutional convention of 1863.

23.8–9   "Call . . . names"]   Music by Charles Jarvis (1837–95) and words by Frances Mary Osgood.

23.10   Judge Brumfield]   W. H. Brumfield was a prominent attorney in Carson City and assemblyman in the territorial legislature.

23.14   "Rock . . mother;"]   A poem by Florence Percy (Elizabeth Akers, later Allen, 1832–1911) that appeared in the *Saturday Evening Post*, June 9, 1860, dated from Rome, May 1860. It was set to music by Ernest Leslie and became a popular song.

23.14   Wm. M. Gillespie]   William Martin Gillespie (1838–85) came to Virginia City from New York in 1861 and was clerk of the territorial legislature, deputy clerk of Storey County, and secretary of the constitutional conventions of 1863 and 1864.

23.14–15   "Thou . . . thee,"]   By Mrs. David Porter (fl. 1860).

23.19–20   my prophetic soul]   Cf. *Hamlet*, I.v.40.

23.25–31   "would not . . . us here."]   "I would not live alway" is from Job 7:16. "I Would Not Live Always" (1834) is a song with music by George Kingsley (1811–84) and words by the Rev. William Augustus Muhlenberg (1796–1877), the last line of which reads "the few lurid mornings that dawn on us here."

23.38–39   graceful . . . horse opera]   "I Had an Old Horse Whose Name Was Methusalem" was a piano routine that Twain was fond of singing and eventually used to open some of his lectures.

24.8   MARK TWAIN]   This is the earliest surviving article with this signature.

25.5   cap]   Foolscap.

28.2–37   A LADY . . . is!]   This introductory letter was written (by Mark Twain) for the *Golden Era* of September 27, 1863, three months after the following sketch first appeared in the *Territorial Enterprise*.

28.2   LICK HOUSE]   Fashionable San Francisco hotel, built in 1863.

28.4   Mr. Barron's]   William E. Barron was a wealthy stockholder in the Gould and Curry Mine.

28.5   Washoe widow]   A woman whose husband was away prospecting. Florence Fane (see note 28.16–17) had invented the "Washoe and Reese River

Widows' Association" in her *Golden Era* weekly columns "to provide for the entertainment of widows during desertion."

28.5–6   Sarah Smith]   By-line of the fashion correspondent for the *California Magazine and Mountaineer*, published by the proprietors of the *Golden Era*.

28.7   Brigham & Co.]   Store in San Francisco that housed the branch office of Madame Demorest's Emporium of Fashion of New York City.

28.8   'Robergh']   A fashionable local couturier.

28.9   Reese River]   Mining district in Lander County, Nevada, scene of a mining rush in 1862.

28.16–17   Florence Fane]   Pseudonym of Mrs. Frances Fuller Victor (1826–1902), novelist, poet, travel writer, and contributor to the San Francisco *Evening Herald* and the *Golden Era*.

28.21   special . . . him.]   This party in honor of Mark Twain is described in "The Lick House Ball," pages 43–48 in this volume.

28.22–23   how . . . cold.]   See pages 37–42 in this volume.

30.21   Mrs. J. B. W.]   Mrs. John B. Winters and her husband were friends of Twain's. Winters, brother of Joseph Winters (see note 23.7), was a Nevada businessman active in mining and milling. Winters also figures in Appendix C of *Roughing It*.

31.28–31   Mr. Lawlor's . . . McDonald's]   William B. Lawlor was a Carson City schoolteacher. Mr. Ridgeway has not been identified. Herman Camp was a Nevada businessman active in mining and stocks. John A. Paxton, from Marysville, California, had opened a bank in Virginia City in 1863. Jerry Long was the Carson County surveyor. S. F. Gilchrist was a Carson City attorney. Mark L. McDonald built and operated a road between Carson City and Virginia City.

35.16–17   "the servants of the lamp,"]   In Henry Wadsworth Longfellow's poem "Santa Filomena," Florence Nightingale is referred to as "the servant of the lamp."

36.5   Palmer]   W. A. Palmer was a Wells Fargo agent in Folsom, California, in 1862 and 1863.

36.17   young Wilson]   Adair Wilson (b. 1841), junior local editor of the Virginia City *Union*.

36.31   the Reverend Jack Holmes]   John Holmes was co-manager (with A. W. Stowe) of the Steamboat Springs Hotel.

37.21   White House . . . Virginia] On July 26, 1863, a fire in the White House, a recently completed boardinghouse where Mark Twain lived in Virginia City, consumed most of his belongings.

37.34   Gould and Curry] Stock certificates in the valuable Gould and Curry mine.

40.6   Lake Bigler] Now Lake Tahoe; originally named in 1852 for California governor John Bigler, a Democrat whose Southern sympathies during the Civil War led Union supporters to suggest another name: "Tahoe," from the Washoe Indian dialect, means "big water."

40.27–28   Columbiad] A large cannon developed for coastal defense.

43.31–32   Messrs. . . . Pease] Jerome Rice, who lived at the Lick House, was a San Francisco real-estate dealer and auctioneer. For John B. Winters, see note 30.21. Thaddeus R. Brooks was a resident of the Lick House and secretary to the San Francisco board of engineers. Frederick Mason was a resident of the Lick House and a San Francisco real-estate agent. Charley Creed may have been the brother of Mollie Creed Low, wife of California governor F. F. Low. E. T. Pease was a resident of the Lick House and a San Francisco broker of stocks and real estate.

44.11–12   Benicia] Settlement on the northern shore of Carquinez Strait; it had been the capital of California in 1853–54.

44.15   Emperor Norton] Joshua A. Norton (1818–80), a San Francisco merchant and real-estate speculator since 1849, lost his fortune in 1853, disappeared, and returned in 1857 in uniform, calling himself "Norton I, Emperor of the United States and Protector of Mexico"; he was supported for the remainder of his life by sympathetic townspeople.

44.27   Messrs. Barron] See note 28.4.

44.37   Goat Island] Now known as Yerba Buena Island, in San Francisco Bay.

45.15   Billy Birch's] William Birch ("Brudder Bones") was a member of the famous San Francisco Minstrel Troupe. He had performed in California and Nevada since 1851.

45.22   Mrs. F. F. L.] Wife of Governor F. F. Low (see note 49.6).

45.40   Mrs. Wm. M. S.] Wife of William M. Stewart (1827–1909), former attorney general of California, member of the Nevada territorial legislature, and later United States senator (1864–75 and 1887–1905) from Nevada.

46.8   arrastras] An "arrastra" was a mechanism for grinding quartz ore.

46.15   Mrs. A. W. B.] Wife of Alexander W. (Sandy) Baldwin (1840–69) of Virginia City, an attorney and law partner of William M. Stewart.

46.27   Mrs. J. B. W.] See note 30.21.

48.18–27   U. S. Grant . . . works!"]   Grant's message to Brigadier General Simon Bolivar Buckner, the Confederate commander of Fort Donelson, Tennessee, sent on February 16, 1862, read, in part: "No terms except an unconditional and immediate surrender can be accepted. I propose to move immediately upon your works." Buckner quickly accepted Grant's terms.

49.6   F. F. LOW]   Governor-elect Frederick Ferdinand Low (1828–94), banker, congressman 1862–63, and collector of the port of San Francisco, had defeated incumbent governor Leland Stanford (1824–93) for the Union (Republican) party nomination.

49.19   Judge Field]   Stephen Johnson Field (1816–99), California state supreme court judge 1857–63, had been named to the U.S. Supreme Court on March 10, 1863.

49.31   Mission]   The mission of San Francisco de Asís, founded in 1776, had been secularized in 1834, and its buildings were eventually taken over for hotels and taverns. Its church is located near the intersection of Sixteenth and Dolores streets in San Francisco.

51.8   Barry and Patten's]   Theodore Augustus Barry and B. A. Patten kept a well-known saloon on Montgomery Street in San Francisco.

51.33   J. Belvidere Jackson]   Captain A. Jones Jackson was provost marshal of the Southern District of California during the Civil War.

52.4   the Greek Slave]   Hiram Powers' marble sculpture (1843) of a nude Greek girl captured by the Turks, one of the most admired and controversial works of the mid-nineteenth century.

52.7   Cliff House]   Local resort near Point Lobos and Seal Rocks, built in 1863.

52.12   Brigadier General Wright]   George Wright (1801–65) was commander of the U.S. Army's Military Department of the Pacific.

52.22–23   "Bell's . . . London"]   *Bell's Life in London and Sporting Chronicle*, a popular British sporting weekly.

52.29   Marysville Infant]   F. F. Low had settled in Marysville, California, in the early 1850s.

55.6   Frank Lawler]   In 1863, Frank Lawlor was bookkeeper at the Lick House and perhaps later its manager; he also had a career as an actor.

55.40   John B. Winters]   Winters (see note 30.21) was a candidate for Congress during Nevada's first attempt at statehood, but the proposed state constitution was rejected in a January 1864 referendum.

57.1   *A Bloody . . . Carson*]   See the later explanation of this hoax in "A Couple of Sad Experiences," pages 392–95 in this volume.

57.26   Sheriff Gasherie]   D. J. Gasherie, Ormsby County sheriff 1862–64.

58.21   Spring Valley Water Company] Main supplier of water to San Francisco. It had recently failed to supply adequate water to some districts and its stock had fallen in value following criticism in the press.

58.25   Daney Mining Company] Operators of a gold and silver mine located on the Comstock Lode in Nevada. The San Francisco *Evening Bulletin* had criticized the company for "dividend cooking"—borrowing money to pay shareholder dividends and inflate the price of the stock.

59.1   *"Ingomar"*] *Ingomar the Barbarian* was a romantic play adapted by Maria Anne Lovell from the German drama *Der Sohn der Wildnis* (1843) by Friedrich Halm (1806–71), who wrote under the name Eligius von Münch-Bellinghausen. It was first produced in 1851 and frequently revived.

59.3   Mr. Maguire's] Thomas Maguire, leading impresario of the San Francisco theater, opened the Opera House in Virginia City in 1863.

59.31–32   Gift Entertainment] A benefit performance, usually for an actor.

60.6   Benkert boots] Mining boots manufactured by L. and C. Benkert Company of Philadelphia and widely advertised and used in California and Washoe mining camps.

61.2   American Flat] Mining camp near Virginia City, Nevada Territory; there was another by the same name in El Dorado County, California.

61.8–10   "Two souls . . . one."] The play *Ingomar* was famous for this couplet, which closed the second act.

62.1   *Miss Clapp's School*] A private school in Carson City, Nevada.

63.11–14   "The boy . . . dead."] Cf. "Casabianca" by Felicia Dorothea Hemans (1793–1835).

63.30–31   Gov. Nye's] James W. Nye (1814–76), district attorney in 1839 and judge from 1844 to 1851 in New York State and first president of the New York City Metropolitan Police Board from 1857 to 1860, was appointed by Lincoln in 1861 to be the first governor of the Nevada Territory. He left the governorship in 1864 to become a senator from Nevada and served from 1864 to 1873.

67.4   *Editor T. T.*] Twain's letter was published in the "Table-Talk" column of the New York *Sunday Mercury*.

72.6   Charley Creed] See note 43.31–32.

72.15   the "Willows"] Popular resort at Mission and Eighteenth streets in San Francisco, featuring a hotel, restaurants, gardens, aquarium, zoo, bowling, dancing, and theater. It was badly damaged by fire in January 1864.

74.3   Flora Low] The only child of California governor Frederick F. Low.

74.5   Florence Hillyer] Daughter of Mitchell C. Hillyer of Virginia City and San Francisco, president of the Choller Gold and Silver Mining Company.

75.30   Solferino] Purplish-red color, named after a dye discovered in 1859, the year of the French victory over the Austrians at the Italian village of Solferino.

76.11–13   "Time was . . . boy!"] Cf. *Macbeth*, III.iv.78–82.

76.25–26   Zeb. Leavenworth] Zebulon Leavenworth (1830–77) was a pilot on the Mississippi River and a friend of Twain's.

80.17   Mr. Rising] The Reverend Franklin S. Rising (c. 1833–68) had been rector of St. Paul's Episcopal Church in Virginia City since April 1862.

80.40–81.1   Scriptures . . . paper] Some local newspapers ran a daily text from the Bible.

84.7   Kanakas] A derogatory term for South Sea Islanders.

88.20   slung-shot] Blackjack.

89.31–32   noblest . . . God] Alexander Pope's "Essay on Man" (line 237) and Robert Burns's "The Cotter's Saturday Night" (stanza 19) both contain the line: "An honest man's the noblest work of God."

91.2   Love's Bakery] William Love operated a bakery in San Francisco in 1864.

93.18   Heuston & Hastings'] A men's clothing store.

97.17   "Old Dan Tucker,"] Song by Daniel Decatur Emmett (1815–1904), written by 1831 and performed in minstrel shows since the 1840s.

97.23   "Sweet Home"] "Home Sweet Home" by Sir Henry Rowley Bishop (1786–1855), words by John Howard Payne (1791–1852), from their operetta *Clari: or, The Maid of Milan* (1823).

98.30   "Auld Lang Syne"] Traditional Scottish melody, words adapted from Robert Burns, first published in 1711.

104.27–28   hinted . . . Shakspeare] Cf. *Julius Caesar*, act III.

108.11   Roman . . . Bancroft] Two leading West Coast publishers that maintained bookstores.

108.12   *Jomini's . . . War*] Baron Antoine Henri Jomini's *Précis de l'art de la guerre* (1836). A translation was published in New York in 1854 as *Summary of the Art of War*.

188.2–4   Tom Maguire . . . Macdougall] A highly publicized brawl had recently occurred between Maguire (see note to 59.3) and W. J. Macdougall, composer and pianist.

188.16   Vestvali] Maguire, a few months earlier, had threatened bodily harm to actress Felicita Vestvali (1839–80) during a dispute over a contract.

196.32   Dr. Rowell] Dr. Isaac Rowell, prominent San Francisco physician and professor of chemistry, was a member of the city's Board of Supervisors and president of the City Railroad Company.

196.32   Ziele] Robert Ziele owned the Pacific Street Flour Mills.

197.33   Captain Lees] Isaiah W. Lees, captain of detectives of the San Francisco police.

208.11–12   Michael Reese] Reese (1815–78) was a real-estate broker and capitalist in San Francisco.

208.25   Dr. Wadsworth's] The Reverend Dr. Charles Wadsworth (1814–82) was pastor of the Calvary Presbyterian Church in San Francisco from 1862 to 1869. He was later known for his friendship with Emily Dickinson, which began with their meeting in Philadelphia in 1855 as she was returning to Amherst from Washington, D.C.

210.1   *Barnum's . . . Congress*] Phineas T. Barnum was running as the Republican candidate for Congress in the Fourth District of Connecticut. He was defeated by Democrat William H. Barnum (no relation) on April 1, 1867. (The election was held in the spring of 1867 in the expectation that the new Congress would meet for the first time in December; in fact, the Fortieth Congress convened on March 4, 1867, in order to enact Reconstruction legislation.)

211.8   Gordon Cumming] Rowaleyn Gordon Cumming (c. 1820–66), hunter in South Africa whose trophies were being exhibited by Barnum. He is mentioned in chapter 47 of *Following the Equator* (1897).

211.16   Miller's] Probably a reference to Ferdinand von Miller (or Müller) of Munich, who cast many celebrated bronzes for American clients. Barnum advertised "entertaining brass portraits of all the celebrated Union generals."

212.6   Amendment] The Southern states were resisting ratification of the Fourteenth Amendment, which had been proposed to the states by Congress on June 13, 1866. It granted national and state citizenship to all persons born or naturalized in the United States and prohibited states from making or enforcing laws that abridged their privileges or immunities as national citizens, deprived them of life, liberty, or property, without due process of law, or denied them the equal protection of the laws. The amendment also stated that the congressional representation of states that denied any of their male citizens the right to vote would be reduced, specified the conditions under

108.12–13   *Message . . . Documents*] President Lincoln's fourth annual message was sent to Congress three days after this piece was published.

112.35   Such . . . serpent] The novels *Such Is Life* and *The Trail of the Serpent*, by British writer Pierce Egan, Jr. (1814–80), had been serialized recently in the *Golden Era*.

113.3–5   HAWKS . . . CUMMINS] Francis Lister Hawks (1798–1866), Phillips Brooks (1835–93), and George David Cummins (1822–76) were eminent Episcopal clergymen.

116.21   laborers . . . vineyard] Cf. Matthew 20:1–16.

116.37   young ravens] Cf. Psalm 147:9.

117.23–24   sparrows . . . unnoted] Cf. Matthew 10:29.

122.33–34   "Yes, . . . thee."] First line of the song "Missionary's Farewell," words by the Rev. Samuel F. Smith (1808–95).

123.13   "Quarter-less twain,"] Leadsman's call meaning one and three-quarters fathoms.

123.18–25   Dan Setchell . . . Phillips] Setchell (1831–66) was a comedian and monologuist whom Twain admired; Louis Moreau Gottschalk (1829–69) was a concert pianist and composer; Adelaide Phillips (1833–82) was an internationally known contralto. All were then performing in the area.

123.37   *votre . . . porte-il?"*] "How is your dog?"

124.12   Signorina Sconcia] Olivia Sconcia was the prima donna soprano of the local opera company.

124.13   "The Last . . . Summer,"] Thomas Moore set his poem "Tis the Last Rose of Summer" (1813) to a traditional Irish melody.

125.16   "Lilly Dale"] Sentimental ballad (1852) by H. S. Thompson.

127.4–5   "What . . . fair"—] From a poem "For the Ladies," in the *Dramatic Chronicle* of June 3, 1865.

128.9   *Sic semper tyrannis,'*] "Thus ever to tyrants." The state motto of Virginia, shouted by John Wilkes Booth from the stage of Ford's Theatre after his assassination of President Lincoln on April 14, 1865.

128.19   5-scent shop] A saloon selling cheap whiskey—at five cents.

128.23–26   "The Assyrian . . . Galilee."] Lord Byron, "The Destruction of Sennacherib" (1815).

128.31   "Johnny . . . home."] "When Johnny Comes Marching Home" (originally published as "Johnny Fill Up the Bowl" in 1863), words and music by Patrick Sarsfield Gilmore (Louis Lambert).

131.2   "kings-*and*,"] The player at draw-poker evidently hoped to convert his hand into a full house.

132.13   "old soldiers"] Cigar or cigarette butts.

133.9–10   "Love's Bakery,"] See "Whereas," pages 91–96 in this volume.

133.35   Stockton] The state insane asylum was in Stockton, California.

134.9–10   Dutch Nix] A "nix" is a hoax; see "A Bloody Massacre Near Carson," pages 57–58 in this volume.

134.31   *Flag*] The San Francisco *American Flag*.

134.37–38   'Let dogs . . . so!'"] Isaac Watts, "Against Quarrelling and Fighting" (1720).

135.10   Tupper] Martin Farquhar Tupper (1810–89); see page 118 in this volume.

135.29–30   just before . . . Root] "Just Before the Battle, Mother" (1863) was George F. Root's popular Civil War ballad.

135.32–33   graveyard . . . Wolfe] Probably Irish poet Charles Wolfe, known to Twain for his "The Burial of Sir John Moore," but see also page 778 and note in this volume.

136.24   extract . . . dailies] The letter had appeared in the San Francisco *Morning Call*, June 18, 1865.

139.20   Academy] The Academy of Music, where the local opera company was performing.

143.1   "O, wad . . . us."] "O wad some Pow'r the giftie gie us, / To see oursels as others see us!" Robert Burns, "To a Louse."

143.17–22   DISCOURAGING . . . *Chronicle*.] This comment appeared in the San Francisco *Dramatic Chronicle* on June 20, 1865.

147.21   Jacob Little] New York financier and stockbroker who died March 28, 1865.

149.5–10   "The horse . . . *Mazeppa*.] Twain's example from "Mazeppa" is spurious.

149.11–19   Sir Hilary . . . *Praed*.] From "Good-Night to the Season."

149.28–30   Copperheads . . . BROWN] Beriah Brown was a leader of the California Democratic party and a critic of Lincoln; he expressed his views through his pro-slavery San Francisco *Democratic Press*.

150.1   General Halleck] Major General Henry W. Halleck (1815– recently been appointed commander of the Military Division of the

150.34–35   misquote . . . *italic*] See page 143.1 and note. The firs tion in the *Golden Era* had italicized the word *wad*.

153.35   coat-of-arms of California] The Great Seal of California b goddess Minerva; at her feet a crouching bear feeds on a cluster of g

155.34   the *Alta*] The San Francisco daily *Alta California*.

166.1   *"One More Unfortunate"*] Cf. Thomas Hood, "The Br Sighs" (1844), line 1.

166.22   Industrial School] A city reformatory for juveniles.

166.26   O, . . . humbug!] Cf. *Hamlet*, I.ii.146.

168.3   MY KINGDOM.] This poem ran in the San Francisco *Evenin tin* on October 20, 1865.

171.2   A. WARD] Artemus Ward (Charles Farrar Browne) had Twain to write a sketch for Ward's book of travels in the Nevada Te Twain sent the following tale, but it arrived in New York too late included in Ward's book and was given to the New York *Saturday* where it was first published.

178.3   MUFF NICKERSON] Mulford Nickerson was a prominen bon vivant.

181.26–27   "Oh, . . . home!"] See note 128.31.

182.5–6   "Oh, . . . deep!"] From the popular song "A Life on the Wave" (1838), music by Henry Russell (1812–1900) and words by Epes S (1813–80).

182.29–30   "Come . . . me!"] From "Willie Reilly," an Irish folks

184.7   Colfax party] A farewell banquet and ball held the precedin gust in honor of Schuyler Colfax, congressman from Indiana from 1869 and Speaker of the House from 1863 to 1869, when he toured the

184.30–31   sozodont-sweetened] "Sozodont" was the brand name widely advertised red dental liquid.

186.4   Dan] Dan De Quille, pen name of William Wright (1829–98

186.8   "bit house"] A saloon selling beer at twelve and a half cents bit").

186.20–21   Diggers] Indians of southwestern Utah and California dug roots for food.

187.6   Reeseriv'] See note 28.9.

which former Confederates could be barred from holding office, guaranteed the repayment of Union Civil War debts, repudiated Confederate war debts, and invalidated claims against the government for the loss or emancipation of slaves. A final section gave Congress the power to enforce the amendment by appropriate legislation.

212.26   fires] Barnum's museums had suffered a series of devastating fires, most recently on July 13, 1865, and March 2, 1868.

214.4   list . . . petitioners] The St. Louis *Missouri Democrat* of March 11, 1867, carried the names of more than 300 signers of a petition to the Missouri legislature asking that the word "male" be struck from the state constitution. Twain had recently arrived in St. Louis to visit his sister and mother.

214.11   Dorcas society] Women's group that carried both charity and religious teachings to the sick and poor; the societies took their name from Acts 9:36.

214.34   waterfalls] Ladies' hairpieces worn at the back of the head.

218.3   MRS. ZEB. LEAVENWORTH] See note 76.25–26.

219.31   COUSIN JENNIE] The *Missouri Democrat* of March 14, 1867, carried two replies to Twain's initial column, one signed "COUSIN JENNIE" and the other signed "A.L."

220.6   Poland . . . ago] In January 1863, Napoleon III of France had unsuccessfully sought the support of Great Britain and the United States in assisting Poles rebelling against Russian rule.

221.27–28   election tickets] In many instances, parties distributed a ballot that the voter could present at the polls.

222.1   new fashion] Detailed registration of voters, especially in cities, had begun as a remedy for fraud and turmoil at the polls.

224.2   ED. T. T.] See note 67.4.

224.38   slimpsey] Frail or weak, primarily referring to cloth.

228.26–27   "good in everything"] Cf. *As You Like It*, II.i.17.

228.27   whatever . . . right] Alexander Pope, "An Essay on Man," Epistle 1, line 294.

228.31   highest . . . State] In 1866, the New York State Assembly created the Metropolitan Board of Health for New York City and empowered the governor to appoint its four members. Governor Reuben E. Fenton appointed three allopathists.

231.8   Hingston] Theatrical agent Edward Peron Hingston (c. 1823–76) had managed Artemus Ward's lecture tour of 1863–65.

232.31   drifts] Galleries opened along the course of the main vein of ore.

232.32–33   sulphurets]   Sulphuret is one kind of silver-bearing ore.

235.22   hoss-bills]   Handbills advertising the qualities of a horse or stallion available for breeding.

236.22   Washn'ton Bower vines]   Or matrimony vine: *Lycium halimifolium*, formerly known as *L. vulgare*.

237.3   gormed]   Also "gaumed": smeared with a sticky substance.

238.4   Government . . . purchase]   A treaty for the purchase of the Danish West Indies (now the U.S. Virgin Islands, including St. Thomas) was concluded by Secretary of State William H. Seward in October 1867, but in 1870 the Senate refused to ratify it. The islands were eventually sold to the United States in 1916. Seward was said to be interested in acquiring naval and coaling stations in the Caribbean.

238.10   attaché]   In "Washington Letter to the *Alta California*," December 14, 1867, Twain referred to an episode in which, allegedly, Seward's son "was sent down to pay" for the islands, and "the sailors stole all the money while he was ashore."

238.27   great storm]   In November and early December 1867, St. Thomas suffered from a hurricane, earthquake, tidal wave, and tornado.

239.23–24   Walrussia]   Derisive term for Alaska among opponents of the treaty of purchase that Seward had arranged with Russia. The treaty was ratified by the Senate in October 1867, but the House of Representatives did not appropriate the purchase money until July 1868.

240.23–24   Admiral Farragut . . . Europe]   David G. Farragut, appointed in 1867 to command the European squadron of the U.S. Navy, was making official calls on heads of state.

241.11   Secretary of War]   Ulysses S. Grant was *ad interim* secretary of war at the time. Edwin M. Stanton had been suspended from the office by President Andrew Johnson on August 2, 1867, for supporting Congressional Reconstruction policy. Stanton was restored to office by the Senate on January 13, 1868.

245.1   I had . . . service]   Cf. *Othello*, V.ii.338.

245.4   Dr.]   Standard abbreviation for "debit."

245.18   Repudiation]   Term used by hard-money advocates opposed to paying off Union war bonds in greenbacks instead of gold. Many Republicans also feared that the Civil War debt incurred by the Union would be repudiated by a future Democratic Congress; section IV of the Fourteenth Amendment (ratified in 1868) prevented this.

245.24–25   Alabama claims]   The United States was demanding that Great Britain pay claims covering losses to Union shipping caused by several Confederate commerce raiders built and fitted out in British territory, of which the *Alabama* was the most famous. The claims were finally arbitrated in 1872.

247.27   Desdemona]   Of *Othello*.

247.30   Joyce Heth]   Joice Heth was a Negro slave who attracted public attention in 1835 when her owners claimed she was the 160-year-old nurse of George Washington. She was purchased and exhibited by P. T. Barnum until her death in 1836.

247.33–34   Widow Machree]   Song (1842), words and music by Samuel Lover, first published in his novel *Handy Andy: A Tale of Irish Life*.

253.24   shining]   Shoe-shining.

253.25   lush]   Cash, money.

258.5   James W. Nye]   Nye (1815–76), senator from Nevada, was known to Mark Twain since 1862 (see note 63.30–31). Twain worked briefly in November and December 1867 as a private secretary for the other senator from Nevada, William M. Stewart (see note 45.40).

258.22   *John Halifax*]   Cf. *John Halifax, Gentleman* (1856), by Mrs. Craik (Dinah Maria Mulock), a British novel that was a best-seller in the United States in 1856.

259.7   water-lots]   A tangle of land claims was enveloping the San Francisco waterfront, because the standard of an "ordinary high water mark" was disputable and because federal and local rights conflicted.

262.1–2   **Mamie . . . Child-Missionary**]   Loosely based on the popular novel *The Gates Ajar* (1868), by Elizabeth Stuart Phelps, later Ward, (1844–1911).

262.36   Knock . . . you.]   Matthew 7:7.

265.27–28   Lay up . . . steal.]   Matthew 6:19–20.

267.17–18   junk bottle]   Type of bottle used for porter or rum.

267.22   Gough]   John B. Gough (1817–86), Anglo-American orator and prominent temperance lecturer.

270.2   Weldon]   Halfway between St. Louis and Chicago, though not on a major railroad line.

270.4   Jubilee Settlements]   Jubilee College, founded in 1839 by the Protestant Episcopal Church.

272.13–17   Daniel . . . Van Nostrand]   Friends of Mark Twain's: Daniel Slote (c. 1828–82) of New York, a stationery manufacturer and companion on the *Quaker City*; Charles J. Langdon, Twain's future brother-in-law; Samuel Adams Bowen (c. 1838–78), a Hannibal playmate and a steamboat pilot; and

John A. Van Nostrand (c. 1847–79), of Greenville, New Jersey, also from the *Quaker City* tour.

273.12   R. M. Howland]   Robert Muir Howland (1838–90) of Aurora, Nevada, a friend of Twain's since 1861. He was a mine superintendent, local marshal, warden of the territorial prison at Carson City, and later United States deputy marshal for California.

278.13–14   their voices . . . Henry]   Joseph Addison, *Cato*, II, i: "My voice is still for war." Patrick Henry, speech in the Virginia Convention, March 23, 1775 (used in the McGuffey readers): "The war is inevitable; and let it come!"

278.14   peace . . . Greeley]   Greeley had proposed foreign mediation of the Civil War in 1863, and in 1864 tried to persuade Lincoln to negotiate a compromise peace with the South. In 1867, he called for a general amnesty for ex-Confederates and signed the bond for releasing Jefferson Davis from prison.

278. 25–26   "Early . . . wise,"]   Benjamin Franklin, *Poor Richard's Almanack* (1735), October.

279.3   Old Hundred]   A favorite hymn tune dating back to the sixteenth century; it was early associated with Psalm 100; in Protestant services it is now best known as the musical setting for the Doxology.

279.10   model garden]   Greeley's interest in improving American agriculture was well known; in 1853 he had moved to a farm.

279.25–26   Young . . . myself]   John Russell Young (1840–99) had become managing editor of the *Tribune* in 1866. Clarence Cook (1828–1900) was art critic, and John Rose Greene Hassard (1836–88) was music and literary critic for the *Tribune*. Twain's occasional sketches for the *Tribune* carried his own by-line.

279.34   penmanship]   Greeley's handwriting was notoriously bad; *Roughing It*, chapter 70, would print a supposed facsimile of a Greeley letter about raising turnips.

280.7   spar off]   Here the term means to push a steamboat through shallow water with poles.

280.12–13   Mr. Chapin's church]   The Universalist congregation of the Reverend Edwin Hubble Chapin (1814–80).

280.34   Toodles]   Title character in a popular one-act farce (1848) by William E. Burton.

282.1   ***Concerning . . . Intentions***]   Ulysses S. Grant was elected president in November 1868 and had not yet assumed office.

282.15   Associated Press]   At this time a working coalition of seven New York City newspapers.

282.31–32   specie basis]   Debates continued over retiring the legal tender notes ("greenbacks"), irredeemable in gold, that were issued during the Civil War and resuming specie payments upon demand.

282.33   whisky frauds]   Various schemes for evading the excise taxes on whiskey had been exposed recently.

283.3   "Let . . . peace."]   The conclusion of Grant's letter of May 29, 1868, accepting the Republican nomination for the presidency; it became the party's main slogan during the ensuing campaign.

283.4–5   bloodshed . . . South.]   During the election campaign of 1868, the Republicans had emphasized continuing Southern violence against Republicans and freedmen.

283.16–17   'Interviews . . . *World*,]   President Andrew Johnson had been criticized for presenting his opinions through exclusive interviews with Joseph B. McCullagh (1842–96), "Mack" of the Cincinnati *Enquirer*, and with Jerome Bonaparte Stillson (1841–80), "J.B.S." of the New York *World*.

283.25   spike down]   A Congressional committee inspection of the Pacific Railroad had reported that, in order to collect the subsidies on completed track and to get as far west as possible, construction was often shoddy.

283.30   Blairs]   Francis P. Blair, Jr. (1821–75), of Missouri, elected to Congress as a Free-Soiler in 1856, supported Abraham Lincoln in 1860 and was a Republican during the Civil War, serving as a division commander under Grant during the 1863 Vicksburg campaign. Blair returned to the Democratic party after the war and was its nominee for vice-president in 1868, when he toured the country bitterly attacking Republican Reconstruction policy. His brother, Montgomery Blair (1813–88), postmaster general under Lincoln from 1861 to 1864, and their father, Francis Preston Blair, Sr. (1791–1876), were also prominent Andrew Johnson supporters who had returned to the Democratic party.

283.35   Nasby's Post-Office]   "Petroleum Vesuvius Nasby" was a character created by David R. Locke (1833–88) as a parody of Southern sympathizers; he was was purportedly postmaster at "Confederate x roads, kentucky."

283.38   Fitch]   Late on Sunday, November 29, 1868, in the midst of legal battles with Cornelius Vanderbilt and others over control of the Erie Railroad, financier James Fisk was served with legal papers upon leaving the company offices. Followed by detectives, he took a carriage and ferry to the Jersey City railroad terminal, from where an engine with a single director's car was seen to speed away into the night. The following day, New York newspapers announced that Fisk and Gould had fled to Canada with millions of dollars in company funds. Fisk immediately issued a denial, explained his departure as a visit to Binghamton, New York, on business connected with the Erie Railroad rolling-mill, and commenced lawsuits for defamation against the newspapers.

286.4   Erie dodge]   Vanderbilt was several times involved in brazen manipulation of the stock of the Erie Railroad.

286.34   Isthmus]   The Isthmus of Panama, where steamer passengers between New York City and San Francisco often crossed Central America.

291.1   *Mr. Beecher*]   The Reverend Thomas Kinnicut Beecher (1824–1900), pastor since 1854 of the Park Congregational Church in Elmira, New York, son of Lyman Beecher, half-brother of Henry Ward Beecher, Catharine Beecher, and Harriet Beecher Stowe, and friend of the Langdon family, Twain's future in-laws. For over a year, he had been conducting Sunday evening services at the Elmira Opera House, drawing crowds of 1300 or more. Twain had attended on February 21, 1869.

292.6–7   "Go . . . creature."]   Mark 16:15.

297.3   Seven Oaks]   The Civil War battle at Seven Pines and Fair Oaks, Virginia, on May 31 and June 1, 1862, proved indecisive.

298.35   Good Templars]   The Independent Order of Good Templars organized fraternal temperance lodges.

301.29   Forty per cent.]   A sweeping set of protective tariffs was enacted after the Reciprocity Treaty with Canada ended in 1866.

302.17–18   "All signs . . . time."]   Common British and American proverb, recorded as early as Ames' *Almanack* for 1729.

303.21   Terrapin Tower]   Modern guidebooks name a Terrapin Point and Terrapin Rocks.

304.20   forty-rod whisky]   Folk term describing whiskey so potent that one could not walk more than forty rods after drinking it.

304.26   Uncas! . . . Red Jacket!]   Uncas was a chief of the Mohegans who sided with the English during the Pequot War; he was the subject of a biography (1842) by W. L. Stone. Uncas was also the name of a noble Indian warrior in James Fenimore Cooper's *The Last of the Mohicans* (1826) and *The Wept of Wish-ton-Wish* (1829). Red Jacket (c. 1756–1830) was a celebrated Seneca chief.

304.27   Hole-in-the-Day]   Ben Holladay (1819–87), who organized mail and freight lines in the West, was reputed to have staged Indian attacks on rival stagecoaches.

307.15   Rhode Island veteran]   The last surviving pensioner from the Revolutionary War, Daniel F. Bakeman, had died in April 1869 at the age of 109 years and 6 months.

308.2   Memphis *Avalanche*]   The name of an actual newspaper.

308.7   *Exchange*]   Postal laws permitted newspapers to send copies to one another free of charge, and it was common for columnists to quote passages from "Exchange," meaning from another newspaper.

308.16–17   "old soldiers,"]   See note 132.13.

309.11–13   Nicholson . . . pay for it.]   Samuel Nicholson (1791–1868), of Boston, author and inventor, devised a new type of pavement—wood blocks on a base of asphalt or hard-packed sand. In the summer of 1869, Twain tried to help his future father-in-law, Jervis Langdon, collect a bill for this pavement due from the city of Memphis.

311.12   forty-rod whisky]   See note at 304.20.

315.2   Marshal Neil's]   Adolphe Niel (1802–69), marshal of France under Napoleon III and later minister of war.

317.15   "Virtue . . . reward;"]   Matthew Prior (1662–1721), *Imitations of Horace*, Book III, ode 2. Originally a Latin proverb, recorded in Plautus, Cicero, Ovid, Diogenes Laertius, Silius Italicus, and Claudius Claudianus; various English forms are recorded in, among others, Sir Thomas Browne's *Religio Medici*, Izaak Walton's *The Compleat Angler*, Barclay's *Ship of Fools*, Dryden's *Tyrannic Love*, and Emerson's "Friendship."

317.15–16   "Procrastination . . . time;"]   Edward Young, *Night Thoughts* (1742), line 393.

317.16   "Time . . . man,"]   Versions of this proverb are found in Geoffrey Chaucer's "Prologue to The Clerk's Tale" (c. 1386), *Everyman* (1520), and John Heywood's *Proverbs* (1546).

317.17   "Necessity . . . invention;"]   Originally a Latin proverb, recorded in English in Horman's *Vulgaria* (1519); George Farquhar (1678–1707), *The Twin Rivals*, I; Richard Franck, *Northern Memoirs* (1694); Wycherly, *Love in a Wood* (1672), III.iii; and Jonathan Swift, *Gulliver's Travels* (1726), iv, among others.

317.18   Josh Billings]   Pseudonym of Henry Wheeler Shaw (1818–85), humorist, lecturer, publisher of the annual *Farmer's Allminax* (1869–80), and a friend of Twain's.

317.23   "None . . . fair,"]   Cf. John Dryden, "Alexander's Feast, or, The Power of Music; An Ode in Honour of St. Cecelia's Day" (1697), line 15.

317.28   Stowe]   Harriet Beecher Stowe's article "The True Story of Lady Byron's Life" (*Atlantic Monthly* and *Macmillan's Magazine*, London, September 1869) charged that Lord Byron (1788–1824) had had incestuous relations with his half-sister, Augusta. It was immediately criticized in American,

English, French, and German periodicals, and in a number of biographies and recollections written in defense of the poet.

317.29–30   "England . . . duty!"]   Message composed by Vice-Admiral Horatio Nelson and sent by flag signal to his fleet at the battle of Trafalgar, October 21, 1805.

317.33–34   "Tramp, . . . marching."]   Civil War song, words and music by George Frederick Root (1820–95).

317.39–40   "The Old . . . surrenders!"]   Comte Pierre Jacques Étienne Cambronne (1770–1842) at Waterloo, June 18, 1815, according to tradition.

318.3   "Alas . . . race!"]   J. C. F. Schiller, *Wilhelm Tell* (1804), act II.

318.17   Garret Davis]   Garrett Davis (1801–72) was congressman (1839–47) and senator (1861–72) from Kentucky. Elected to the Senate as a Unionist Whig in 1861, he joined the Democratic party in 1867, and his enemies complained that only his fluent oratory saved his career and his person.

318.19   H. G.]   Horace Greeley.

318.21   Bergh]   Henry Bergh (1811–88) of New York City had founded the American Society for the Prevention of Cruelty to Animals in 1866. He was a familiar figure in the streets of New York, frequently interfering with streetcar drivers and others who abused their horses.

324.7–8   Petrified . . . Syracuse]   This hoax, also called the Cardiff giant after a small town near Syracuse, had brief fame in October 1869. A buried piece of sculptured gypsum was claimed to be the petrified body of a giant.

326.21–22   Brown . . . Pike]   On May 7, 1868, Thomas Brown and his wife, of Hampton Falls, New Hampshire, were killed with an axe during a robbery by their former hired hand, Josiah L. Pike. Pike's plea of insanity owing to dipsomania was rejected, and he was hanged in November 1869, but he attracted increasing sympathy as his execution approached.

330.18   Canova]   Though best known as a sculptor, Antonio Canova (1757–1822) also did about a hundred paintings.

330.26   Beaumarchais]   Bon Marché in Paris was one of the first modern department stores.

340.4–5   Internal Revenue Department]   Federal income tax was levied as a war measure in 1862 and survived until 1872. Taxpayers were required to "hand in" a return, and assessors had the legal right to call on individuals and inspect their accounting. Twain had been assessed for income tax at least as early as 1864.

341.27–28 ninety-five thousand copies] Around 55,000 copies of *The Innocents Abroad* had been sold by March 15, 1870.

341.30 half] Twain received five percent of the retail or subscription price.

343.2 most modest] Probably a reference to the fourteenth, catch-all item: "From all sources not above enumerated."

343.20 revenue returns] Until April 1870, lists of actual returns were published to prevent fraud.

345.14 General Buncombe] Benjamin B. Bunker (b. 1815) was appointed United States Attorney General for the Nevada Territory by President Lincoln in 1861 and removed from office in June 1863.

345.24 Dick Sides] Richard D. Sides was a pioneer and leading landholder in Carson City, Nevada.

347.2 Hal Brayton] P. H. (Hal) Clayton was a prominent attorney in Carson City; see note 23.7. William Brayton was Humbolt County recorder in 1862.

347.4 Roop] Isaac Roop (1822–69), early settler, former head of the provisional territorial government, and prominent political figure in Nevada and northeastern California, was the acknowledged expert in land claims in the Washoe Valley.

353.17 Lady Mordaunt] Sir Charles Mordaunt (1836–1906) petitioned in February 1870 for divorce on grounds of adultery from his 21-year-old wife of four years, the former Harriet Sarah Moncreiffe. He testified that, following the recent birth of their first child and distraught over its possible blindness, his wife had confessed to him that Viscount Cole was the baby's father and that she had been "very wicked" with Cole, Sir Frederick Johnstone, the Prince of Wales, and "others." A series of witnesses provided circumstantial evidence corroborating his accusation. Sir Thomas Moncrieffe filed a counter-petition, declaring that his daughter had been hopelessly insane since giving birth, and several doctors testified that she was suffering from "puerperal mania." Although not named as a corespondent, Edward, the Prince of Wales, was called as a witness; he denied any impropriety. The petition was dismissed on the grounds of Lady Mordaunt's insanity, but Sir Charles was granted a divorce in 1875, when he successfully named Viscount Cole as corespondent.

354.19–20 Gen. Coleses . . . McFarlands] On June 4, 1867, in Albany, New York, General George Washington Cole (d. 1875) shot and killed his longtime neighbor and friend, L. Harris Hiscock, a Syracuse lawyer and politician, whom he suspected of adultery with his wife. Cole's first trial ended in a hung jury on May 7, 1868, and his second trial resulted in acquittal on December 7, 1868, when the jury professed to be in doubt as to his sanity at the instant of the homicide. In 1859, Daniel E. Sickles (1819–1914), then a member of Congress from New York, shot and killed Philip Barton Key, U.S. Attorney for Washington, D.C., and son of Francis Scott Key, because Key was having an affair with Mrs. Sickles; he was acquitted on grounds of temporary mental aberration. Sickles later served in the U.S. Army (1861–67), lost a leg at Gettysburg, and achieved the rank of major general; he was Grant's appointee as minister to Spain, where he served 1869–75. On November 25, 1869, Daniel McFarland, a Fenian and a Tammany supporter, shot and fatally wounded Albert D. Richardson, a journalist and author and acquaintance of Twain's, in the offices of the New York *Tribune* following a dispute concerning McFarland's divorced wife, Abby Sage McFarland, who was at that time engaged to marry Richardson. The former Mrs. McFarland married Richardson on his deathbed (in a service performed by Henry Ward Beecher and O. B. Frothingham). McFarland was charged with murder and pled temporary insanity. After a highly publicized trial that lasted from April 8 to May 11, 1870, the jury rendered a verdict of not guilty.

357.1–2   os frontis . . . maxillary]   Frontal bone or forehead, and jaw-bone.

360.17   'gallus']   A slang term for "fine" or even "gallant."

360.19   queensware]   Wedgewood china of a distinctive cream color, or any earthenware of such a color, especially if glazed.

365.2   "Independent,"]   Weekly religious magazine published in New York City.

365.2–3   Rev. T. De Witt Talmage]   The Reverend Thomas De Witt Talmage (1832–1902) was the popular minister of the Central Presbyterian Church in Brooklyn.

366.27–28   "Son . . . mine?"]   First two lines of the Charles Wesley hymn "To Be Sung at Work" (1739).

367.11   Chemung county]   Elmira, the home of Olivia Langdon's family, was in Chemung County, New York.

373.17–18   Circumlocution Office]   Government bureau in Charles Dickens' *Little Dorrit* (1855–57).

374.8   EDITOR MEMORANDA]   "Memoranda" was Mark Twain's monthly column in the *Galaxy*.

379.2   the other day,]   The incident was reported in the San Francisco *Bulletin* on March 7, 1870.

379.19   mining tax] From the mid-1850s California levied a foreign miners' tax, usually $4.00 monthly, which in practice bore most heavily on the Chinese.

379.37–38   "Let . . . fall,"] Latin proverb.

380.32   *vaccinated*] The city of San Francisco adopted such an ordinance in 1870 because epidemics of smallpox were allegedly traced to newly arrived Chinese immigrants.

381.38–39   employ . . . journal] Twain worked for the San Francisco *Call* from June to October 1864.

384.3   Richardson-McFarland jury] See note 354.19–20.

384.15   foreman . . . said:] In fact, the foreman of the jury simply reported "Not guilty."

384.26   great-grandfather's step-father] McFarland's defense had cited a deranged male first cousin on the side of McFarland's father.

386.1   John W. Galen, M. D.] A former surgeon general of the U.S. Army issued a long statement favorable to the defense; the name Galen, however, is that of a Greek physician of second-century Rome.

386.4   Charles A. Dana] Editor of the New York *Sun*, which supported McFarland's defense out of loyalty to Tammany Hall and rivalry with the New York *Tribune*, where Richardson had worked and had many friends.

388.2–3   squib . . . Agricultural Department] In the Buffalo *Express* of April 12, 1870, Twain had published his letter to the editor of the *Galaxy*, accepting a contract to conduct a monthly "department" of his choice for that magazine.

389.25   THE PETRIFIED MAN] See page 19 in this volume.

391.36   "London Lancet"] Prestigious medical weekly, where no mention of Twain's hoax has been found.

392.11   MY FAMOUS "BLOODY MASSACRE."] See pages 57–58 in this volume.

393.38   the Truckee] The Truckee River area in western Nevada and eastern California, where farming was practicable.

396.2–3   Pierre Bonaparte trial] In 1870, Pierre Bonaparte (1815–81), nephew of Napoleon I, was acquitted of the murder of French journalist Victor Noir, whom he had killed in a quarrel.

396.9   Jouvins] "In Paris you pay twelve dollars a dozen for Jouvin's best kid gloves." *The Innocents Abroad*, chapter 30.

397.28   'navy'] A Model 1851 Colt revolver, originally produced for the U.S. Navy.

405.30 With . . . called him.] Cf. I Samuel 3:1–10.

408.1 **Report . . . Academy**] Delivered at commencement exercises in June 1870.

418.4–5 telegraph . . . Eden.] Kurna, where the Tigris and Euphrates rivers join to form the Shatt-al-Arab channel, was often identified as the site of Eden. In 1864 the British laid a series of submarine cables westward from Karachi to Fao, where the Shatt-al-Arab flows into the Persian Gulf. By early 1865 the Fao cable had been connected to a land line that ran through Basra and Kurna to Baghdad, where it joined an existing Turkish system linked to Europe, creating the first England-to-India telegraph connection.

418.8 Brooklyn . . . tournament] Two afternoon sessions of a "tournament" were held at a park on the outskirts of Brooklyn in May 1870. The tournament was both a fund-raiser and a gesture of North-South amity; many of the riders came from southern states.

418.19 "tournament" in Lynchburg] A tournament had been held in Lynchburg, Virginia, in October 1869.

419.3–4 Disinherited . . . Maryland] The first four "knights" appeared in newspaper accounts.

419.21–22 suffering . . . blood] Though one "knight" fell ill during the tournament, newspaper accounts did not describe him as wounded.

419.37 Ashby de la Zouch] Site of a tournament in Walter Scott's *Ivanhoe* (1819).

420.1–2 Bois-Guilbert . . . Front-de-Bœuf] Villains in *Ivanhoe*.

421.5 "Byron Scandal"] See note 317.28. Stowe upheld her views, and claimed that Byron was the father of Augusta's child (born 1814) in *Lady Byron Vindicated: a History of the Byron Controversy from its Beginning in 1816 to the Present Time (1869–70)*. Twain wrote, but did not publish, a relevant burlesque.

421.16–17 "Peace . . . Boston] A music festival celebrating the end of the Civil War, held in June 1869.

421.22 Cruikshank] George Cruikshank (1792–1878), eminent British illustrator and caricaturist, did a number of satirical drawings about the "Jubilee" of August 1, 1814, which was held to celebrate the general peace and the 100th anniversary of the accession of the Brunswick family.

421.27 Train] George Francis Train (1829–1904), Fenian (see note 423.10), flamboyant shipping and railroad promoter, world traveler, pamphleteer, lecturer, and political agitator.

421.27 Henri Rochefort] Victor Henri, Marquis de Rochefort-Lucay (1830–1913), radical editor of *Le Figaro*, *La Lanterne*, *La Marseillaise*, and *Le*

Mot d'ordre, supported the Commune of Paris and was arrested and imprisoned in 1873. He was arrested by a squad rather than a single policeman.

421.33   McFarland trial] See pages 384–87 and notes.

422.1   Recorder] The presiding judge at the trial.

422.18   Graham] John Graham (1821–94) was a well-known attorney who directed McFarland's defense. He had earlier defended Daniel Sickles (see note 354.19–20) in 1859, and he later represented William Tweed in 1873.

423.10   Fenian "invasion."] In April 1866 members of the Irish Republican Brotherhood, also known as Fenians, had attempted to seize Campo Bello, New Brunswick, for Ireland, but were prevented by British and U.S. forces. On June 1, 1866, dissident members of the Fenians crossed the Canadian border at Fort Erie, defeated Canadian troops, and returned to Buffalo, New York, where they were arrested and later released. Later invasions of Canada from Frankfort, Vermont, and Malone, New York, were halted by U.S. and Canadian troops May 25–27, 1870.

423.22–23   get by the ears] Quarrel.

423.28   "World"] The New York *World* warmly supported the Fenians.

423.29   "Ridgway,"] Also known as "Limeridge," Ontario, where the Fenians had scored a small victory in 1866.

425.5–6   two different houses] Franklin's family moved soon after his birth, and so two houses in Boston could claim to have cradled his infancy.

426.6–7   Early . . . wise.] See note 278.25–26.

428.25–26   my father's . . . "Hiawatha."] Longfellow's *Song of Hiawatha* was first published in 1855; John Marshall Clemens died in 1847.

432.8   Cohocton] About one hundred miles from Buffalo, in Steuben County, New York.

432.10   letter . . . Bath correspondent] Bath was the county seat of Steuben County. Twain took his detail from this letter, quoting it correctly except for the surname of Judge G. H. McMaster, who had in fact already started to conduct the trial.

436.9   dephlogistic] Phlogiston was thought by early chemists to be the material substance of inflammability.

441.14   find meself;] The opposite of "and found," which meant food and lodging in addition to wages.

443.36   "gallusly"] See note 360.17.

445.4–6   Fenians . . . Canada] See note 423.10.

445.36   Dr. Keim's excellent book] De B. Randolph Keim's *Sheridan's Troopers on the Borders: A Winter Campaign on the Plains* (1870).

446.8   Pi-Ute war]   The Piute War in eastern Oregon and western Idaho during 1866–68.

450.2   Don Cæsar de Bazan]   In Victor Hugo's *Ruy Blas* (1838), drama set in seventeenth-century Spain.

450.19–20   North Adams Chinaman]   In 1870 a group of Chinese were brought to a North Adams, Massachusetts, shoe factory to replace strikers.

451.7   Marshal Serrano]   Francisco Serrano y Domínguez (1810–85), Spanish general and statesman, participated in the overthrow of Isabella II in 1868 and was named regent. He was premier under King Amadeo 1870–71.

452.2–3   Hon. Mr. Knott, M. C.]   James Proctor Knott (1830–1911) of Kentucky served as a Democrat in the House of Representatives from 1867 to 1871 and from 1875 to 1883.

455.1   *Goldsmith's*]   Cf. Oliver Goldsmith's *The Citizen of the World* ("Chinese Letters," 1762). In 1861, Twain had written his brother Orion that he considered this and *Don Quixote* his *"beau ideals* of fine writing."

462.31   Mother Leonard's]   Twain mentioned a Haidee Leonard as well known for her drunkenness and her stays in jail in the San Francisco *Call* in 1864.

467.10–11   the law . . . *Irishman.*]   A California statute of 1850 prohibiting testimony from Negroes and Indians in court cases involving whites was interpreted in 1854 to apply to Chinese as well. This law remained in force until 1873.

468.30   Chinese-speaking Spaniard]   The interpreter was Charles T. Carvalho, a native of Batavia, Java.

470.22   Stiggers]   Pen name of Albert S. Evans, a rival reporter in San Francisco.

471.14   siege of Paris]   During the Franco-Prussian War, Paris was besieged by the German army from September 15, 1870, until its capitulation on January 28, 1871.

471.18   King William's]   William I was king of Prussia from 1861 until his death in 1888; he was proclaimed emperor of Germany at Versailles on January 18, 1871.

471.19   Napoleon's]   Napoleon III (Louis Napoleon Bonaparte), the emperor of France, with 80,000 troops, surrendered to the German army at Sedan on September 2, 1870; he was deposed by a revolution in Paris on September 4.

473.33   BAZAINE.] Since mid-August 1870, a French army of about 130,000 troops commanded by Marshal Achille François Bazaine had been surrounded at Metz, where they surrendered on October 27.

476.3   TROCHU.] General Louis Jules Trochu, appointed military governor of Paris on August 18, 1870, accepted the presidency of the provisional government of national defense formed September 4, 1870, after news reached Paris of the defeat at Sedan and the surrender of Napoleon III.

476.10   WILLIAM III.] William I of Prussia; see note 471.18. Twain referred to him as "William III, King of Prussia" in a burlesque portrait published in the January 1871 issue of the *Galaxy*. His son was the crown-prince, Frederick William.

477.3–4   RILEY . . . dailies.] John Henry Riley (1823–72), a friend and associate of Twain's from San Francisco days until his death. Riley's leading western outlet had been the *Alta California*.

480.22   'Well . . . servant!'] Cf. Matthew 25:21.

480.24   printed . . . before] Twain had published a version of the story in the Chicago *Republican* in April 1868.

486.39   Sylvanus Cobb] Prolific author (1823–87) of pulp fiction.

487.4–5   "Marble Faun"] Novel (1860) by Nathaniel Hawthorne.

490.3–4   Woodford . . . Hoffman] Stewart Lyndon Woodford (1835–1913) was lieutenant governor 1867–69. A former brigadier general, he was the unsuccessful Republican candidate for governor in 1870. John T. Hoffman (1828–88), the Democratic incumbent candidate, was former mayor of New York City and an ally of Tweed's Tammany Hall political machine.

491.31   the Five Points] A slum district surrounding the intersection of three streets (corresponding to present-day Baxter, Park, and Worth streets) and two alleys in the center of the most densely populated part of Manhattan; it was a Tammany stronghold.

491.32   Water street] On the waterfront of Manhattan's Lower East Side.

493.28   BEHOLD THE MAN!] Cf. John 19:5.

495.1   *Dogberry*] Loquacious, self-satisfied constable in Shakespeare's *Much Ado About Nothing*.

495.34   the law itself] Twain was protesting against the regulations that proof-sheets containing material other than typographical corrections could not pass as third-class matter, which cost one-twelfth of letter postage. The crux lay in sections 159 and 166 of *The Statutes Relating to the Postal Service* (1869) and in the difference between a "book" and "author's manuscript."

Twain's direct quotation near the end of his opening paragraph may come from oral restatement by a local postmaster.

501.30 Attorney-General Toucey] Isaac Toucey (1792–1869), U.S. attorney general in 1848–49.

502.14 "right . . . place"] Attributed to Thomas Jefferson.

505.35 Garrett Davis] See note 318.17.

517.2 *George Holland*] Respected comic actor (1791–1870).

517.2 *Rev. Mr. Sabine*] William Tufnell Sabine (1838–1913) was rector of the Episcopal Church of the Atonement in New York City.

517.6–7 Cardiff giant] See note 324.7–8.

518.23–24 five hundred . . . stages] James Sheridan Knowles's *William Tell* had been a favorite on the American stage for 45 years.

519.39 Black Crooks] *The Black Crook*, a popular but controversial musical extravaganza with libretto by Charles Barras (1820–73), featuring dancing girls in tights and introducing the French can-can to American audiences, opened at Niblo's Garden in New York on September 12, 1866. It ran for 475 performances through 1868, and was successfully revived in 1871.

520.1 Cooks, and Kallochs] Horace Cook (fl. 1870), a former pastor of the Seventh Street Methodist Episcopal Church in Manhattan, had recently lost his church because he seduced a parishioner's daughter. Isaac Smith Kalloch (1831–87), a former Baptist pastor at Tremont Temple in Boston, had been tried for adultery in 1857.

522.1 *Rulloff*] Edward H. Rulloff (c. 1820–71) was convicted of murdering a clerk during the August 17, 1870, burglary of a general store in Binghamton, New York, and was sentenced to death. Rulloff had a long record as a burglar and confidence-man, had been in prison, and at various times had posed as a doctor, lawyer, or teacher of languages. Several appeals for clemency addressed to Governor Hoffman were denied, and Rulloff was hanged May 18, 1871. In a private letter to the managing editor of the New York *Tribune*, Twain stated that he hoped to arouse public interest in the idea of commuting Rulloff's death sentence.

522.2 SYDNEY CARTON] Character in Dickens's *A Tale of Two Cities*, who is guillotined in place of Charles Darnay.

522.27–28 Mather, . . . Richmond] Rulloff claimed to be a genius and an expert in philology. He had developed a new comprehensive theory of ancient languages set forth in a manuscript, "Method in the Formation of Language," left unfinished at his death. Richard Henry Mather, professor of Greek and German at Amherst College, visited Rulloff in prison and reported on Rulloff's knowledge of the Greek classics in a published account of his interview in late April 1871. William Lawton Richmond, a prominent attorney, former medical student, and trustee of Allegheny College, was also impressed by Rulloff's knowledge of scientific terms.

528.5 the Nathan murder] Benjamin Nathan, a wealthy stockbroker, was brutally murdered in his mansion at 12 West 23rd Street on the night of July 28, 1870, evidently during a burglary. A large reward was offered, but no one was ever charged with the crime.

528.9 "dog"] The murder weapon was a carpenter's "dog"—an iron bar about 18 inches long turned down and sharpened at each end.

530.10–11 I quote . . . authorities.] The essay quotes intermittently from an anonymous article, "Our Earliest Ancestors," in *Chambers's Journal of Popular Literature, Science, and Arts*, 4th Series, number 7 (August 13, 1870).

534.33–34 Byron-scandal case] See notes 317.28 and 421.5.

535.32 "cave of Aurignac"] In 1860 relics of prehistoric men were found in caves near Aurignac, a village in southern France.

539.10–11 William Tweed] William Marcy Tweed (1823–78) controlled the Democratic political machine of New York, through which he held a variety of state and city offices. Cartoonist Thomas Nast had attacked the "Tweed Ring" for corruption in 1869 and *The New York Times* had begun its crusade in 1870. Evidence provided by county bookkeeper Matthew J. O'Rourke in July 1871 led to sensational disclosures of corruption and Tweed's eventual arrest and conviction.

539.13 St. Ass's Colt Hall] Abraham Oakey Hall (1826–98), mayor of New York 1868–72. For "ass's colt" see Matthew 21:1–7.

539.14 St. Connolly] Richard B. ("Slippery Dick") Connolly (1810–80) was New York City controller; on September 18, 1871, he had deserted Tweed and resigned his office. He later fled the country.

539.14–15 St. Matthew Carnochan] Dr. John Murray Carnochan (1817–87) was quarantine health officer of New York City; he was accused of amassing a fortune through illegal charges.

539.15 sitteth . . . customs] Cf. Matthew 9:9.

539.15–16 St. Peter Fisk] James Fisk, Jr. (1834–72), financier and a director of the Erie Railroad, along with Gould, Daniel Drew, and Tweed.

539.16 St. Paul Gould] Jay Gould (1836–92), partner of James Fisk.

539.16–17 suffereth . . . them;] Cf. II Corinthians 11:23–25.

539.17 St. Iscariot Winans] Orange S. Winans, Republican assemblyman from Chautauqua County, had been accused of accepting a large bribe to betray his party and vote in favor of the Democratic tax bill.

539.18 St. Jacob Vanderbilt] Captain Jacob Hand Vanderbilt (1807–93), younger brother of Cornelius Vanderbilt, was president of the steamship company that operated the Staten Island ferryboat *Westfield*, which exploded on July 30, 1871, killing over 100 people. He was indicted September 7, 1871, for homicide in connection with the deaths, but the case was never prosecuted.

539.18   St. Garvey] Andrew J. Garvey was the city contractor for plastering.

539.19   St. Ingersoll] James H. Ingersoll supplied carpets and furniture to the city.

539.19–20   N. Y. Printing Co.] Supplier of stationery and printing to the city; its controlling interest was held by Tweed.

539.20–21   letteth . . . taketh] Cf. Matthew 6:3.

539.21   St. Peter Hoffman] Governor John T. Hoffman (see note 490.3–4) had been mayor of New York 1865–68.

539.22–23   denied . . . times;] Cf. Mark 14:30 and 66–72.

539.23   St. Barnard] George G. Barnard (c. 1824–79) was elected judge of the New York State supreme court on the Tammany ticket in 1861. He had issued many injunctions favorable to the Tweed Ring, but on September 15, 1871, he granted an injunction stopping any further payments from the city treasury. He was removed from office by a committee of the legislature August 19, 1872.

541.4   *Herald Expedition*] The New York *Herald* had sent Henry M. Stanley (1840–1904) to find the Scottish missionary and explorer David Livingstone (1813–73), who had last been heard from in 1867; Stanley found him in November 1871, but Livingstone chose to stay in Central Africa.

542.18   Ujijiji Unyembembe] Stanley's account in the New York *Herald* reported he had found Livingstone at the settlement of Ujiji on Lake Tanganyika, in an area known as Unyanyembe.

543.17   a Mr. Lord] James L. Laird, owner of the Virginia City *Union*.

549.3   Foster petitions] On April 27, 1871, William D. Foster (1838–73), a former streetcar conductor, was riding on the front platform of the Broadway streetcar while intoxicated and became involved in a dispute with Avery D. Putnam, a New York City merchant, when he repeatedly opened the car door to direct insulting looks and remarks at a young lady passenger. When Putnam, the young lady, and her mother got off the streetcar at 46th Street and Seventh Avenue, Foster struck Putnam over the head with an iron car-hook, killing him. Foster was tried and convicted of murder on May 24, 1871. He was sentenced to death, but a series of stays and appeals prolonged his case until 1873. The delays led to charges that Foster, son of a minor New York politician, was being shielded by city authorities. The petitions on Foster's behalf, which filled more than a page of the New York *Tribune* for March 6,

1873, asked the governor to reduce Foster's sentence to life imprisonment; some former members of the jury were among the signers. Foster was hanged March 21, 1873.

551.10   additional wages]   The U.S. Congress had recently passed a bill (signed by President Grant March 3, 1873) granting its members a salary increase (from $5,000 to $7,500 annually) that was made retroactive for two years. It became widely known as the "salary grab" act.

551.24–25   Charles Reade . . . verdicts]   The popular British novelist was often censured for his "immoral" plots; in early 1873 he won £200 in damages from the London *Morning Advertiser*.

552.20   Mr. Colfax]   Schuyler Colfax (1823–85), congressman from Indiana from 1855 to 1869, Speaker of the House of Representatives from 1863 to 1869, and vice-president from 1869 to 1873, was implicated in the growing scandal involving the favorable sale of stock to senators and congressmen in 1867 by Crédit Mobilier, the finance company organized to pay for the construction of the Union Pacific Railroad. The New York *Sun* made accusations in late 1872, and a House and Senate investigation in 1873 injured the reputations of Colfax and others.

552.24   the "Black Crook"]   See note 519.39.

552.26   *Days Doings*]   *The Day's Doings* (1868–76) was an illustrated periodical that featured sensational scandal stories. It was bought by Frank Leslie in 1873 and made into a family paper.

552.34   Rozensweigs]   Jacob Rosenzweig, a Polish immigrant and abortionist in New York City, was convicted of manslaughter October 28, 1871, in the death of Alice Bowlsby, whose body was found in a trunk at the Hudson River Railroad Depot. Rosenzweig was sentenced to seven years' imprisonment, but was released on a technicality November 13, 1873.

552.37   Foster murder case]   See note 549.3.

554.6   heathen Chinee]   Bret Harte's ballad "Plain Language from Truthful James," which became popularly known as "The Heathen Chinee," was first published in the September 1870 issue of *Overland Monthly*, and without authorization was immediately reprinted in newspapers and broadsides throughout the country.

554.15   ruined]   Although Harte drew some small audiences, he had enough success to justify further lecture tours.

554.19–20   starving . . . guild]   The episode involved W. A. Kendall (d. 1876), a minor San Francisco poet and journalist who had contributed to the *Californian* and the *Golden Era* in the 1860s. Kendall used the pseudonym "Comet Quirls" and was author of *The Voice My Soul Heard* (San Francisco, 1868). In January 1872, Twain, Harte, and Howells had helped pay for his passage from New York to San Francisco. In an article in the San Francisco

Chronicle of December 15, 1872, Kendall made allegations concerning Harte's defalcations and bad behavior.

556.13–14   misunderstandings . . . arbitration] The Treaty of Washington between Great Britain and the United States was concluded May 8, 1871. It provided for resolution of the *Alabama* claims (see note 245.24–25), the disputed water boundary between Washington Territory and British Columbia, and the Canadian fisheries question.

556.29   Motley] John Lothrop Motley (1814–77), historian and diplomat who served as U.S. Minister to Austria and later (1869–70) to Great Britain. He had been removed following a dispute with the Grant administration over the handling of the *Alabama* claims (see note 245.24–25).

556.29   Samuel C. Pomeroy] Pomeroy (1816–91), U.S. senator from Kansas from 1861 to 1873, was charged with bribing state legislators in pursuit of a third term; he is considered the model for Senator Dilworthy in *The Gilded Age* (1873).

557.33   General Schenck] Robert Cumming Schenck (1809–90), former Union general in the Civil War and a participant in the Treaty of Washington negotiations, was U.S. Minister to Great Britain from 1871 to 1876.

559.19   Princess of Wales] Alexandra (1844–1925), daughter of King Christian IX of Denmark, became Princess of Wales in 1863 when she married Victoria's son Albert Edward, Prince of Wales.

560.31–32   Let dogs . . . so.] See note 134.37–38.

560.35–36   Ben Nevis] Mountain in western Scotland and the highest peak in Great Britain.

560.36   Ben Lomond] Mountain on the east side of Loch Lomond.

560.37   Ben Disraeli] Benjamin Disraeli had recently become lord rector of Glasgow University.

561.2   Sairey Gamp] Sarah (Sairey) Gamp, a comic character in Charles Dickens' *Martin Chuzzlewit* (1843–44), is a disreputable old Cockney midwife, rotund, red-nosed, and very fond of liquor.

561.8   Grace Darling] The daughter of a lighthouse keeper, Grace Darling (1815–42) helped her father rescue five survivors from the wreck of the *Forfarshire* off the coast of England on September 6, 1838.

562.1   *Those Annual Bills*] A parody of Thomas Moore's poem "Those Evening Bells."

563.5   Ohio village] The Woman's Temperance Crusade (1873–74) began in Hillsboro, Ohio, following an address there in December 1873 by health advocate Dr. Dio Lewis.

566.38   15 honest . . . kind]   Fifteen members of the 42nd Congress at various times identified themselves with the Liberal Republicans, who accused the Grant administration of tolerating widespread corruption.

572.31–32   "Earl of Ramsgate."]   Ramsgate was a popular resort on the Kent coast of England.

573.9   the comet]   In the spring and summer of 1874 a comet was visible in the northern skies over New York.

573.17   looking glass]   In seventeenth-century British slang, the term also meant a chamber pot.

573.25–26   the 20th inst.]   Astronomers predicted July 20, 1874, to be the date on which the comet would pass closest to the earth and begin to "leave."

573.30–32   No dogs . . . animals]   In the summer of 1874, New York City newspapers were debating the merits of a dog-muzzling law because of many cases of rabies.

574.8   Mr. Hale]   Eugene Hale (1836–1918), congressman from Maine from 1869 to 1879, had declined the position postmaster general in Grant's Cabinet in 1874.

574.40   District of Columbia]   During the spring of 1874 a committee of the House of Representatives investigated corruption in public expenditures in the District of Columbia.

576.17   Mr. Shepherd, Mr. Richardson]   Alexander Robey ("Boss") Shepherd (1835–1902), territorial governor of the District of Columbia, was accused of extravagant spending on public improvements for the city of Washington. Although he was found innocent of personal dishonesty, Congress abolished his office June 20, 1874. William A. Richardson (1821–96) was replaced by Grant as secretary of the treasury in early June 1874, after a House committee issued a "severe condemnation" of his arrangement with John D. Sanborn, an associate of Benjamin Butler's, for the recovery of unpaid taxes.

576.24   back pay members]   Congress had made its last pay raise retroactive. See note 551.10

576.31   Mr. Coggia]   Jerome Coggia of the Marseilles Observatory had first discovered the comet visible in 1874.

578.1–2   *A True . . . It*]   Twain had heard a similar account from a cook with the Crane family at Quarry Farm, where he and his family usually spent the summer.

579.7–8   Blue Hen's Chickens]   Nickname of the Delaware 1st Regiment in the Revolutionary War, who carried with them gamecocks renowned for their fighting qualities bred from a famous blue hen of Kent County. It was later applied to all natives of Delaware.

588.11   the writer] The essay was signed "Th. Bentzon," the pen name of Marie-Thérèse Blanc (1840–1908), who had recently begun a long, prolific career as a literary critic.

615.31   transit of Venus] The transit of Venus across the face of the sun, last seen in 1769, was due to occur in 1882. Plans by astronomers to observe the event were already making news in 1873–74.

623.14   BRANDRETHS PILLS] Benjamin Brandreth's (1808–80) popular purgative Vegetable Universal Pills and Life Addition Pills.

624.3   "S. T.—1860—X;"] A common advertisement, meant to be intriguingly cryptic, for P. H. Drake's Plantation Bitters, a patent medicine.

627.7–8   scientists . . . inscription] Around this time, translations were being attempted of 34 lines of Phoenician-Hebraic characters on the Moabite Stone, erected in 850 B.C. to celebrate a victory in King Mesha of Moab's revolt against Israel. The stone, discovered in 1868 at Dibon, Jordan, by German clergyman F. A. Klein, is now in the Louvre.

633.8   Catholics . . . Armagh] In August 1873, when Twain was touring Ireland, newspapers reported the incident described here.

639.4–12   "Conductor, . . . passenjare!"] Isaac Bromley of the New York *Herald* and Noah Brooks of the *Times* began a craze for doggerel verse with their jingle based on a notice in a horsecar of the Fourth Avenue line, which read "The conductor, when he receives a fare, will immediately punch in the presence of the passenger."

640.6   Talcott Tower] Talcott's Tower was a wooden structure about five miles from Hartford, Connecticut.

663.37–38   boke . . . Montaine] Cf. Michel de Montaigne, "On Some Verses of Virgil."

665.2   bollocks] Testicles.

665.36   Nicholas Throgmorton] Sir Nicholas Throgmorton (1515–71, also spelled Throckmorton) was acquitted in 1554 of complicity in the rebellion of Sir Thomas Wyatt.

665.40–666.1   Sr. Walter . . . wince] In 1592, Raleigh secretly married Throgmorton's daughter Elizabeth, maid of honor to Queen Elizabeth, after making her pregnant. When the queen learned of the marriage, she imprisoned Raleigh in the Tower of London.

666.17–20   Lille . . . Euphuists] Elizabethan author and dramatist John Lyly (c. 1554–1606) wrote *Euphues, The Anatomy of Wit* (1578) and *Euphues and his England* (1580). The style and diction he developed in these works became fashionable in the literature and conversation of cultured society in the late 1500s; later "euphuism" came to mean affectedly refined, high-flown, periphrastic language. Historian John Richard Green, in his *Short History of the*

English People (1874), called Elizabeth I "the most affected and detestable of euphuists."

666.32   Margrette of Navarre] Marguerite of Navarre (1492–1549), author of 72 tales mixing erotica and the code of courtly love; they were collected and published after her death as the *Heptameron*.

669.38   Koh-i-noor] A large diamond that became part of the British crown jewels after the British annexation of the Punjab in 1849. It weighed 108 carats after its 1852 resetting in England.

673.4–6   Who . . . *Twain*] Cf. *Merchant of Venice*, III.ii.327.

674.9   Probabilities] Common heading for weather forecasts in newspapers.

674.17   how many Presidents] Both Republican Rutherford B. Hayes and Democrat Samuel Tilden claimed victory in the 1876 presidential election. Disputed returns from South Carolina, Florida, and Louisiana, and the controversy over the eligibility of an Oregon elector were referred in January 1877 to a 15-man electoral commission; in a series of 8–7 votes, it ruled in Hayes's favor, leading to his election by a single electoral vote.

676.7   go . . . more] Cf. John 5:14.

678.7   four years] Lee served in the Virginia House of Burgesses from 1758 to 1775, except for a short period in 1769.

679.28   General Tom Harris's army] Harris, a prominent resident and political figure in Hannibal, was commissioned as a brigadier general in the Missouri State Guard in 1861.

679.30   Colonel Ralls] John Ralls served as colonel of a volunteer regiment he organized for service against Mexico in 1847.

683.2–3   Captain "Hurricane" Jones,] Based on the eccentric Captain Edgar (Ned) Wakeman (1818–75), who commanded the steamer *America* when Twain sailed on it from San Francisco to Nicaragua in December 1866.

684.27   business . . . Baal] In I Kings 18.

685.1   Isaac*] Properly, Elijah.

689.18–19 "Sweet By and By,"] Hymn (1868) by Joseph P. Webster (1819–75), with words by Sanford Fillmore Bennett (1836–98).

690.35–36 Man . . . between,] Cf. Job 14:1.

691.3–5   "and next . . . forever,] Cf. Psalm 103:15–16.

696.7–10   Through . . . Soul!] From Holmes's "The Chambered Nautilus."

696.16–19 Give . . . latitudes.] From Emerson's "Mithridates."

696.25–26   Honor . . . Pau-Puk-Kee-wis—]   From Cantos II and XI of Longfellow's "The Song of Hiawatha."

696.33–34   Flash . . . days.]   From Holmes's "Mare Rubrum."

697.12   This . . . primeval.]   From the opening of Longfellow's "Evangeline."

697.14–15   Here . . . world.]   From Emerson's "Concord Hymn."

697.22   I am . . . doubt—]   From Emerson's "Brahma."

697.25–27   They . . . *again!*]   Combines lines from different stanzas of "Brahma"; the original reads "I keep, and pass, and turn again."

697.34–35   I tire . . . played!]   From Emerson's "Song of Nature," which reads "I tire of globes and races, . . ."

698.1   right bower]   The jack of trumps and the highest card in the game of euchre.

698.3–4   Thanks, . . . taught.]   From "The Village Blacksmith."

698.8–9   God . . . palm!]   From "A Voice of the Loyal North."

698.16   All quiet . . . Potomac]   "All quiet along the Potomac tonight" — from the Civil War poem "The Picket Guard," by Ethel Lynn Beers (1827–79).

698.19–20   "Barbara Frietchie" . . . "Thanatopsis"]   "Barbara Frietchie," by Whittier, the guest of honor; "Biglow Papers," by James Russell Lowell; "Thanatopsis," by William Cullen Bryant.

698.24–25   Is . . . breed?]   From Emerson's "Monadnoc."

698.36–699.2   Lives . . . Time.]   From Longfellow's "A Psalm of Life."

703.4   Fabulist]   George T. Lanigan (1845–86) had recently collected his *Fables by G. Washington Aesop* (1878), written originally for the New York *World*.

708.16–17   Noah Brooks . . . Monthly:—]   "Personal Recollections of Lincoln" appeared in the February and March 1878 numbers of *Scribner's Monthly*.

711.20–22   de Horsey . . . report]   The London *Times* of December 4, 1878, announced the publication of the report of a recent visit to Pitcairn Island by Admiral Algernon Frederick Rous de Horsey (1874–1922), commander-in-chief of the Royal Navy in the Pacific 1876–79.

712.24–25   "One . . . *acquisition*."]   This sentence appears, without the dash and italics, in de Horsey's report. One American had arrived in 1864,

and had established a respected family, but de Horsey may have referred to a shipwrecked sailor who settled briefly on Pitcairn Island in 1875.

720.9–13   Social Democrat . . . unprecision]   Two socialist organizations, the General German Workers' Union and the League of Workers' Club, united in 1875 to form the German Social Democratic party. In 1878 Chancellor Bismarck sought to link the Social Democrats with two recent unsuccessful attempts to assassinate Emperor William I, although no evidence connected the party with either attack.

722.2   *Stomach Club*]   An informal group of artists and writers that left no written record.

722.30–33   Mr. Brown . . . praise."]   Cf. Fitz-Greene Halleck, "On the Death of Joseph Rodman Drake": "None knew thee but to love thee, / Nor named thee but to praise."

724.8   Vendome Column]   Bronze column at the center of the Place Vendôme in Paris, 143 feet high and roughly 12 feet in diameter, surmounted by a statue of Napoleon; it was reconstructed in 1873 after being toppled by a group of Communards in 1871.

725.30–31   bubble . . . mouth.]   *As You Like It*, II.ii.152–53: "Seeking the bubble reputation / Even in the cannon's mouth."

728.25   fight . . . night]   In a May 11, 1864, dispatch to his superiors during the battle of Spotsylvania, Lieutenant General Ulysses S. Grant wrote: "I . . . propose to fight it out on this line, if it takes all summer."

729.3   *Great Eastern*]   From 1860 to 1899, the largest steamship of its day, at 18,914 tons.

729.29   illustrious guest]   Ulysses S. Grant (1822–85) was the guest of honor.

730.4   new postal regulation]   A clarifying order of September 1879 declared unmailable, under the revised Postal Laws and Regulations, all matter that did not use the officially recognized names of post-offices.

731.8   Mr. James]   Thomas Lemuel James (1831–1916), postmaster of New York City 1873–81, and postmaster general of the U.S. 1881–82, was noted for his efficiency.

736.36   *know*]   Italicized in the original document, the U.S. Official Postal Guide.

745.7–11   Bingen . . . etc.]   Caroline Elizabeth Sarah Norton's (1808–77) poem "Bingen on the Rhine" reads "a soft moon," and "On the red sands of the battlefield."

745.20 this Club] The Contributors' Club of the *Atlantic Monthly* was a department that printed unsigned commentary or brief essays.

748.26 penny missionary affairs] Meetings at which children were encouraged to contribute pennies toward the support of foreign religious missions.

752.23 "He has . . . fight."] Cf. II Timothy 4:7.

754.36 Dollymount] The Dollymount Long Range Challenge Cup, for which Irish and American rifle marksmen eventually competed at Dollymount, near Dublin.

758.4–8 'Während . . . u. dgl.'] Twain quotes a serious warning that during a thunderstorm one should remove metals such as rings, watches, keys, etc. from oneself and not stay in such places where many metals are lying together or are connected to bodies such as a hearth, stove, iron fences, and similar things.

758.29–32 'Das . . . könnten.'] Twain quotes a serious warning that ringing (the alarm) for a thunderstorm is very dangerous, since the clock itself as well as the draft created by the ringing and the height of the tower can attract lightning.

758.37 *Luftzug*] Draft.

761.5 EVENING POST] Twain was citing a news story from the New York *Evening Post* of September 11, 1880.

762.13 Calistoga] Calistoga Springs, north of San Francisco, had become a resort area.

762.17 Hancock veterans] Major General Winfield Scott Hancock (1824–86), who had been a Union corps commander in the Civil War, was Democratic candidate for president in 1880, running against James Garfield.

765.31–32 Few . . . again.] Cf. *Hamlet*, I.ii.188.

770.1–2 Rollo's . . . "Franconia Series"] Jacob Abbott (1803–79) wrote the *Rollo* series for children (28 volumes beginning 1835) and the *Franconia Stories* (10 volumes); Olivia read Abbott's works with the Clemens daughters.

775.10–11 "terrible . . . bummers."] Cf. Song of Solomon 6:4—"terrible as an army with banners." General Sherman's "bummers" foraged for food and supplies for his army during its marches through Georgia and the Carolinas.

776.30–31 a Boston publisher] James R. Osgood, to whose firm Twain was transferring his books.

777.25 a fellow craftsman] Louis Honoré Fréchette (1839–1908), Canadian poet and husband of William Dean Howells' sister.

778.26   Plains of Abraham]   Field adjoining the upper part of the city of Quebec, site of a decisive British victory over the French in 1759 during the Seven Years' War (1756–63).

778.26–27   spot . . . Wolfe stood]   General James Wolfe was the British commander who was killed in the battle. Most accounts relate that he was in a boat crossing the river when he made this famous remark.

779.26   "Qui est donc la?"]   "Who's there?"

779.27   "C'est un fou,"]   "Some fool."

780.1   langue d'Ollendorf]   Heinrich Gottfried Ollendorf (1803–65) developed a method of learning languages without a teacher.

783.3–4   William Robinson, Marmaduke Stephenson]   William Robinson and Marmaduke Stephenson were Quakers who came to Boston in June 1659 to preach in defiance of a Massachusetts Bay Colony law passed in October 1658 that made such actions punishable by death. They were imprisoned, Robinson was whipped, and they were banished from the colony. Ignoring the order, they preached in Salem and Piscattaway, and then returned to Boston and were arrested. They were condemned by the General Court and hanged in Boston September 27, 1659. Two other Quakers were executed in the colony in 1660 and 1661 under the 1658 law.

783.21   Elizabeth Hooton]   Elizabeth Hooton (c. 1600–71), a Quaker and follower of George Fox, began preaching in 1650 in England. She came to Massachusetts in 1661, and twice was imprisoned at Boston and expelled from the colony. She returned a third time in 1662, with a license from the king permitting her to settle. She was imprisoned at Hampton, Dover, and Cambridge for preaching, whipped, and expelled from Massachusetts. She returned a fourth time from Rhode Island and was arrested, whipped, and expelled again. She returned to Massachusetts at least seven more times, and was imprisoned, punished, and expelled on each occasion.

792.38   *Social . . . New York*]   By Mrs. Abby Buchanan Longstreet, first published in 1879.

793.24   𝕿𝖍𝖊 𝕿𝖔𝖒𝖇𝖘]   Common name for the New York City jail.

794.7   laws . . . Persians]   Meaning that a decree issued under such a law could not be revoked; cf. Daniel 6:10 and Esther 1:18 and 8:8.

796.36   Lady Portsmouth]   Louise de Kéroulle, Duchess of Portsmouth (1649–1734), was a mistress of Charles II; her son was the ancestor of the dukes of Richmond.

802.17   "Truth . . . prevail"]   First recorded in John Gower, *Confessio Amantis* (c. 1390).

802.22   monument . . . anesthesia]   The Ether Monument by John Quincy Adams Ward honored Dr. William Thomas Green Morton (1819–68), who demonstrated the use of ether anesthesia during an operation in 1846. Williamson Crawford Long (1815–78) of Georgia had used the method as early as 1842, but his work was not made public until after Morton's demonstration.

803.30–31 Robertson's . . . *Rest*] Several series of sermons by the English divine Frederick William Robertson (1816–53) were published between 1855 and 1870. Richard Baxter (1615–91), an English Nonconformist, wrote *The Saint's Everlasting Rest* (1650).

804.1 **The Stolen White Elephant**] Many details of this story are borrowed from newspaper accounts of the search for the body of wealthy New York merchant Alexander T. Stewart, which was buried April 13, 1878, and stolen from a vault in Weehawken Cemetery on November 7, 1878. Efforts by police and private detectives failed to recover the body, and the family attempted to stop further publicity by issuing a false statement in January 1879 that a ransom of $50,000 had been paid and the body returned. In July 1880, an undisclosed sum was paid and Stewart's body was recovered.

806.6 Jumbo] Name of the African male elephant acquired by P. T. Barnum from the London Zoological Society in 1882.

808.21 Doré Bibles] Gustave Doré (1832–83) lavishly illustrated many books, including the Bible (1866).

818.30 repeaters] Persons voting more than once at the same election.

820.9–11 badge . . . SLEEP."] The Pinkerton Dectective Agency had adopted the "staring, unblinking eye" as its logo for constant vigilance. The motto commonly appeared beneath a large eye on the cover of Allan Pinkerton's books.

825.3 Mr. Per—] Charles E. Perkins was a Hartford attorney, who often acted as Twain's business agent, and a member of the Monday Evening Club, where Twain read this essay.

827.10 Pinafore's time] Gilbert and Sullivan's *H.M.S. Pinafore* was first produced in the United States in 1878; it contains the famed "What, *never*? / Hardly ever!" refrain.

832.11 Mr. Bernand] Probably British playwright William Bayle Bernard (1807–75).

835.10–11 touches . . . kin.] Cf. Shakespeare, *Troilus and Cressida*, III..iii.175.

841.29 Pond's Extract] Pond's "Universal Pain Extractor" or liniment had been sold widely since 1848.

845.27–28 Years . . . him,] Twain had instigated a petition for erecting a monument to Adam in 1879, but political allies suspected a hoax or feared the ridicule of newspaper wits.

847.4–5   Bartholdi Pedestal Fund]   "The Statue of Liberty Enlightening the World" by French sculptor Frédéric-Auguste Bartholdi (1834–1904) was formally presented to the American people on July 4, 1884; it was erected on Bedloe's Island in New York Harbor on a pedestal paid for by public contributions, and was unveiled on October 28, 1886.

847.29   6,000 years]   Some editions of the King James Version of the Bible used a biblical chronology developed by Irish bishop James Ussher (1581–1656) that set the year of creation at 4004 B.C. The chronology underwent various refinements over time.

849.5–6   Mugwumps]   A derisive term, defiantly embraced by the reform faction of the Republican party that in 1884 abandoned presidential candidate James G. Blaine and supported the Democratic nominee, Grover Cleveland.

849.22   1876]   The Republican nominating convention in June 1876 had swung away from Blaine, previously considered the front-runner and the leader after the initial ballot, because of charges of corruption.

851.3   Mulligan letters]   James Mulligan, a bookkeeper for Warren Fisher, Jr., of Boston, had acquired letters written by James G. Blaine to Fisher between 1864 and 1876. The letters suggested that Blaine, as Speaker of the House of Representatives, had accepted favors for legislation aiding the Little Rock and Fort Smith Railroad. Blaine read the letters on the floor of the House and defended himself against the allegations in June 1876.

856.2   one . . . man]   Henry Leavitt Goodwin (1821–99), of Hartford, for many years protested against irregularities in the Hartford transit system and the New York, New Haven, and Hartford Railroad Company.

856.7   Asylum street]   A major downtown street in Hartford.

856.17   Mrs. Grundy]   Self-conscious embodiment of respectability in the comedy *Speed the Plough* (1798), by British dramatist Thomas Morton (1764–1838).

857.1–2   Hartford clergyman]   Probably Matthew Brown Riddle (1836–1916), minister of the Dutch Reformed Church and professor at Hartford Theological Seminary.

857.13   Great-heart]   In John Bunyan's *Pilgrim's Progress*, Part II (1684), Great-heart is the servant of Christian's wise Interpreter who overcomes monsters and escorts Christiana and her children to their destination.

857.36   Beecher . . . *crime*,]   Theodore Tilton, a former member of Plymouth Church, sued Henry Ward Beecher (1813–87) for $100,000 damages on August 20, 1874, charging that Beecher had committed adultery with his wife. Most of the members of Plymouth Church supported Beecher; the widely publicized trial ended in a hung jury, and hearings conducted by a council of Congregational churches later concluded that Beecher was innocent of the charges. After endorsing Grover Cleveland in 1884, however, Beecher suffered ridicule in the press, heckling at his speeches, and threats from church members.

857.40   Hammond Trumbull] James Hammond Trumbull (1821–97), noted historian, bibliographer, and philologist, was a member of Twain's circle in Hartford.

859.2   *Tile Club*] An informal group of artists in New York City who conducted meetings and dinners in their studios on Wednesday evenings from 1877 to 1884.

861.9–10   Eli . . . idols] Ephraim was joined to his idols in Hosea 4:17.

867.38   Colonel Ralls's] See note 679.30.

868.13   Colonel Brown] Hanceford Brown, an early settler in Ralls County, served as county treasurer from 1844 until 1862.

868.14   Buena Vista and Molina del Rey] In the Mexican War, General Zachary Taylor and his army defeated Santa Anna and a larger Mexican force at Buena Vista, February 22–23, 1847. At Molino del Rey, outside Mexico City, U.S. troops under General William J. Worth suffered heavy casualties while capturing Mexican fortifications on September 8, 1847.

870.36   out West . . . ago] Referring to his visit to Hannibal in 1882.

876.27   citizen colonel's] An officer without a regular army background, sometimes elected by a local militia or volunteer regiment.

881.1   Ab Grimes] Grimes left a memoir, published as *Absalom Grimes, Confederate Mail Runner* (1926).

882.28   Bull Run] Unseasoned Union volunteers had fled after their defeat at the first battle of Bull Run on July 21, 1861.

883.11–12   King of Dahomey] Dahomey in West Africa was ruled by King Gelele from 1858 to 1889; his reign was marked by aggression toward his neighbors, vigorous encouragement of the slave trade, and persecution of Dahomian Christians.

883.15–16   high priest . . . Emperor,] Peter the Great had replaced the patriarchate of the Russian Orthodox Church with a synod headed by a procurator, or lay official, under control of the czar in 1721. Alexander III, czar 1881–94, instituted many repressive measures including the persecution of religious nonconformists and minorities, especially Jews.

883.25–26   Richard II . . . slaves] During the Peasants' Revolt of 1381 in England, King Richard II (1367–1400) met with the insurgents and made major concessions that were immediately revoked after the slaying of their leader, Wat Tyler.

886.3–5   Lowell . . . Senate] In January 1886, Lowell (and Twain) had testified before a committee of the U.S. Senate.

886.5   sixty years] In 1826–27, James Fenimore Cooper and others had worked unsuccessfully to revise the copyright law.

886.9   foreman . . . office] Speaking for the Typographical Union, he testified in favor of a bill prohibiting the sale of books not printed in the United States; but Twain invented the speech given here.

886.28   NOT do] The foreman insisted that no books copyrighted elsewhere should be sold in the United States.

887.5–6   Manifesto of demands] The Knights of Labor adopted a Manifesto of Wrongs and Demands in 1878.

892.4   Pond's Extract] See note 841.29.

897.24   spirit-level] A "level," or device (with a bubble in non-freezing liquid) for determining a horizontal plane.

900.4   Andrew Langdon] Andrew Langdon (1835–1919) was Olivia Langdon Clemens' first cousin, but he had little contact with the Clemens family. His businesses included coal, banking, and metals.

903.22   John Wanamaker] In August 1886, Twain had lost a suit to enjoin Wanamaker's department store in Philadelphia from selling copies of *Personal Memoirs of U. S. Grant* (2 vols., 1885–86) below the subscription price. Grant's *Memoirs* was published by Mark Twain's publishing firm, Charles L. Webster & Co.

906.6–8   Matthew Arnold . . . English.] In a review of Grant's *Memoirs* published in *Murray's Magazine* for January–February 1887, Arnold had criticized Grant's improper use of "shall," "will," "should," and "would."

907.30   General Fry] Former Union general James Barnet Fry (1827–94) had been involved in publishing *Battles and Leaders of the Civil War*, in which excerpts from Grant's *Memoirs* had appeared. He immediately responded in the *North American Review* by criticizing Arnold's own prose.

908.21   "Let . . . peace."] See note 283.3.

911.5   *Well . . . servant.*] Cf. Matthew 25:21.

913.15   my daily paper] The Hartford *Courant*.

913.38   Mulligan letters] See note 851.3.

915.31   Kanaka] See note 84.7.

918.31   Mr. Depew] Chauncy Mitchell Depew (1834–1928), politician, attorney for Cornelius Vanderbilt, and popular after-dinner speaker, was considered one of Twain's leading competitors as a wit and raconteur; they often sparred at banquets.

922.14–15   General Hawley]   Joseph Roswell Hawley (1826–1905) of Hartford, a general in the Civil War, was governor of Connecticut in 1866, and then served in the House of Representatives (1872–75, 1879–81) and the Senate (1881–1905).

922.22   Prince of Wales]   Albert Edward (1841–1910), later Edward VII, was well-known for his high standards of dress.

923.17   Sloane of Princeton]   William Milligan Sloane (1850–1928) had been professor of history and political science at Princeton University since 1883.

927.3   MATTHEWS]   Brander Matthews (1852–1929), a literary and dramatic critic, author, and playwright, was active in literary circles, a founder of the Authors' Club in New York, and prominently associated with its offshoot organization, the American Copyright League (founded 1883 and later called the Authors' League). Twain's essay followed Matthews' article in the September 1887 issue of the *New Princeton Review*.

928.29   "Brander Matthews, lawyer,]   Matthews had received a bachelor of law degree from Columbia in 1873, but had devoted himself to literary pursuits since the mid-70s.

929.5   E. H. House]   Edward Howard House (1836–1901) was a journalist, Civil War correspondent, musician, and editor and publisher in Japan; Twain had known him since 1867.

932.6–7   John Habberton]   Author and editor for the New York *Herald*, Habberton (1842–1921) had written the popular *Helen's Babies* (1876), a humorous sentimental novel, and fifteen other books by 1888.

933.36   Charleston earthquake]   The earthquake in Charleston, South Carolina, on August 31, 1886, destroyed many homes and took sixty lives.

934.1–4   Why, . . . now.]   Habberton had published most of his work serially in a magazine before arranging first publication as a book in England.

937.25   Rochester]   Presumably Rochester, New York, home of the Institute of Technology and a university and a center for the manufacture of precision instruments.

942.2   *Max O'Rell*]   Pen name of French humorist and author Leon Paul Blouet (1848–1903).

942.7–11   Sir Lepel Griffin . . . Russia."]   Sir Lepel Henry Griffin (1840–1908) was a British colonial official and the author of several books on India. He wrote about the United States in *The Great Republic* (1884), from which Twain's quotation is taken.

943.22   Tom . . . Western]   Characters in Henry Fielding's *History of Tom Jones, A Foundling* (1749).

944.8   Mr. Arnold]   Referring to Matthew Arnold's recent essay "Civilisation in the United States" (April 1888).

945.3   Your inquiry]   Twain had responded to an inquiry that would result in George Bainton's compilation *The Art of Authorship: Literary Reminiscences, Methods of Work, and Advice to Young Beginners* (1890).

947.3   THE SUN]   A New York daily newspaper.

Index of Titles

1073

Cataloging Information

Twain, Mark (1835–1910).
  Collected tales, sketches, speeches, & essays 1852–1890.
  Edited by Louis J. Budd.

  (The Library of America ; 60)
I. Title. II. Twain, Mark. III. Series.
PS1303   1992b   92–52657
818′409—dc20
ISBN 0–940450–36–4 (alk. paper)

This book is set in 10 point Linotron Galliard,
a face designed for photocomposition by Matthew Carter
and based on the sixteenth-century face Granjon. The paper
is acid-free Domtar Literary Opaque and meets the requirements
for permanence of the American National Standards Institute. The
binding material is Brillianta, a woven rayon cloth made by
Van Heek-Scholco Textielfabrieken, Holland. The compo-
sition is by The Clarinda Company. Printing and
binding by R.R.Donnelley & Sons Company.
Designed by Bruce Campbell.

THE LIBRARY OF AMERICA SERIES

The Library of America fosters appreciation and pride in America's literary heritage by publishing, and keeping permanently in print, authoritative editions of America's best and most significant writing. An independent nonprofit organization, it was founded in 1979 with seed money from the National Endowment for the Humanities and the Ford Foundation.